A gift has been made by:

Jack & Roselyn Stanley

In memory of

Brit Palmer

Lives *of the* Novelists

Lives *of the* Novelists

A History of Fiction in 294 Lives

John Sutherland

Yale UNIVERSITY PRESS

New Haven & London

First published in the United States in 2012 by Yale University Press.
First published in Great Britain in 2011 by Profile Books Ltd.

Yale University Press books may be purchased in quantity for
educational, business, or promotional use. For information, please
e-mail sales.press@yale.edu (U.S. office) or sales@yaleup.co.uk (U.K.
office).

Designed by Sue Lamble.
Typeset by MacGuru Ltd (info@macguru.org.uk).

Printed in the United States of America.

A catalogue record for this book is available from the British Library.
Library of Congress Control Number: 2011938846
ISBN 978-0-300-17947-7 (cloth: alk. paper)

This paper meets the requirements of ANSI/NISO Z39.48-1992
(Permanence of Paper).

10 9 8 7 6 5 4 3 2 1

Contents

There's a huge popular appetite for secrets. As for the biographical 'explanation' generally it makes matters worse by adding components that aren't there and would make no aesthetic difference if they were.

Nathan Zuckerman, *Exit Ghost*, Philip Roth

The personality of a writer does become important after we have read his book and begin to study it.

E. M. Forster, *Anonymity: An Inquiry*

A shilling life will give you all the facts.

W. H. Auden (who instructed his friends to burn all his letters, after his death)

My sole wish is to frustrate as utterly as possible the postmortem exploiter.

Henry James (before touching the light to a bonfire of his personal papers)

Authors are just fictional people about whom we have a few biographical elements, never enough to make them truly real people.

Jacques Bonnet

It does not follow that because a particular work of art succeeds in charming us, its creator also deserves our admiration.

Plutarch (in his *Life of Pericles*), translated by Peter Jones

Preface
A history of fiction in 294 lives

Once upon a time it would have been possible to write a comprehensive 'Lives of the Novelists' – around the time, I would hazard, that Walter Scott wrote his *Lives of the Novelists*. The 1825 field that Scott surveyed was more or less coverable by a single reader poring diligently over the 'greats', skimming the less than great, and sniffing at the waste-of-time majority before tossing it aside. In our time, an army of Scotts would be defeated by the two million or so eligible works in the vaults of the Scottish National Library, successor to the Advocates Library which served Sir Walter's needs.

All modern histories of the novel are wormholes through the cheese (the novelist William Gibson's neat analogy). The story of fiction that follows is almost as idiosyncratic as the subject itself, it being in the nature of worms to burrow less directly than crows fly – both, like literary critics, are scavengers. What I've written has been sustained by the belief that literary life and work are inseparable and mutually illuminating. This is not, as the epigraphs in the prelims suggest, a thesis universally accepted by the novelists themselves, but do worms care what the cheese thinks?

The reader may be shocked by encounters with a number of writers not normally granted entry to the sacred grove. I confess that I do value a range of fiction that literary history has often, in my view, wrongly undervalued. And the writers who have produced it often have the more interesting lives. By the same token, some names – including some great names – are missing from this book. I offer two excuses: first, quarts and pint pots; and second, isn't this book big enough? A single book and one person's reading career (however obsessive) cannot contain or cover this richest of literary fields. What I have aimed to achieve in breadth will, I hope, to some extent make up for these absences. All the novel's varied genres are displayed in what follows, including (though the main focus is on adult literature) one or two writers best known for their books for children whom I could not bring myself to exclude.

It will be easy to see why most of those writers who did get in got in. What they have in common is that they are all novelists who have meant something to me, or who have come my way over a long reading career and stayed with me, for whatever reason.

John Sutherland
London, August 2011

Acknowledgements

I would like to thank John Davey, Jane Robertson, Peter Carson and Penny Daniel for their support, encouragement, assistance and (all too often) correction. The mistakes which remain are, alas, all mine.

Abbreviations

The following abbreviations will be found appended to the entries:

ANB *The American National Biography*
Biog a biography which is a useful starting point
DCB *Dictionary of Canadian Biography*
FN the author's full name(s)
MRT Must Read Text
ODNB *The Oxford Dictionary of National Biography*

The cited biographies and must-reads are my own wholly personal choices. Where biographical sources are not specifically cited they are taken from the biography which is appended at the end of the entry.

1. John Bunyan 1628–1688

I have ... used Similitudes.

John Bunyan was born in Bedford in 1628, in the lowest stratum of that middle England town. His father was an illiterate brazier and tinker, a wandering tradesman. Bunyan later allegorised life's wanderings into a pilgrimage, heavy pack on back.

Largely self-educated, Bunyan had steeped himself in the English gospels. The most familiar portrait shows him with one book under his arm – the Geneva Bible. This is the volume which, at the outset of his *Progress*, Christian claps to his bosom, fingers in his ears, as he runs away from his amazed wife and family, shouting 'Life, life, eternal life' (and to hell with child support). It struck even Mark Twain's Huck Finn as odd. He recalls (among the little he has read) a book 'about a man that left his family, it didn't say why. I read considerable in it now and then. The statements was interesting, but tough.'

Like others of his station in life, the pulpit was Bunyan's university and preachers his teachers. Religion, in Bunyan's view of life, was battle; and the pilgrim's staff was a weapon with which to crack heretical skulls:

> *No Lion can him fright,*
> *He'll with a Giant fight,*
> *But he will have a right*
> *To be a Pilgrim.*

The other cheek was never turned.

He was a Christian soldier, forever marching as to war – literally. Before the age of sixteen John Bunyan enlisted in Cromwell's 'Roundhead' parliamentary army. He recalls that service and the epic victories over the long-haired foe and – not least – his sinful self in the spiritual journal, *Grace Abounding*. There he chronicles his heroic struggle with such vices as bell-ringing (and worse) and his life-and-soul discovery that he was, after all, one of the elect. Election was confirmed when a comrade took his place on guard duty only to be 'shot into the head with a musket bullet'. Could a sign be clearer?

He married around 1650 and had four children by this first marriage. His wife's names are unknown – but it is deduced she strengthened his religious sense of mission. She died in 1658 and he remarried the following year. From 1655 he addressed congregations as a militant Baptist preacher. He despised Quakers almost as much as Royalists. The schisms of this period defy description: they would have split the atom, if it had been theology. In 1660, with the return of the new King Charles (one of the elite, not the elect) from France and the downfall of the Commonweal, Bunyan was imprisoned for obstinately preaching without a licence and 'devilishly and fiendishly' not attending lawful church service.

He would spend, with brief intervals of freedom, some twelve years in Bedford prison – as what we would call a prisoner of conscience. It was there, suffering for his faith, that he conceived and wrote *The Pilgrim's Progress*, as well as a flood of other books, verse and pamphlets. He expected to die in prison and was prone to crippling bouts of what he called 'despond'.

The Bedford jail was, in the late seventeenth century, rather more humane than the human sty which appalled the great prison reformer, John Howard, a hundred years later. It was situated in Silver Street, in the bustling centre of the town. It was in the prison day-room that Bunyan wrote. Inmates, even in a relatively humane penitentiary could not expect candles – leave those to the sinful playhouse.

It was more a kind of house arrest than incarceration, if not actually a 'club penitentiary', as Americans call their open prisons. Solzhenitsyn, who compiled the *Gulag Archipelago* in Stalin's vile camps, was obliged to consign his great narrative to memory, while the incarcerated Bunyan evidently had access to writing materials – and printers. It wasn't quite Proust's cork-lined bedroom, but adequate. Victorians, such as the artist Frederick Walker, liked to picture Bunyan in durance vile, but the truth was less melodramatic. Something more like Virginia Woolf's room of one's own might be more appropriate – but with the lock on the outside.

The full title of Bunyan's great work is:

The Pilgrim's Progress FROM THIS WORLD TO That which is to come. Delivered under the Similitude of a DREAM. Wherein is Discovered, 1. The manner of his setting out.— 2. His Dangerous Journey; and — 3. His safe Arrival at the Desired Countrey.

Bunyan justified the imaginative aspect of his allegorical work (Puritans have always been suspicious of fiction) with an epigraphic quotation from the Book of Hosea 12:10: 'I have ... used Similitudes.' Similitudes, or 'Fiction' was licit: the Bible said so. But it was slippery. Clearly the gospel story was historical truth – not 'similitudinous'. Like every novelist after him, Bunyan was a conceptual fence-straddler: 'Real, but not real.' One leg on either side.

The Pilgrim's Progress's influence on the subsequent history of fiction is clear enough. The pulpit is always there, for a certain kind of novelist. Before embarking on *Vanity Fair* (the title, of course, flagrantly lifted from Bunyan) Thackeray informed the editor of *Punch* – the wonderfully named Mark Lemon – that he regarded his mission as a novelist as 'serious as the parson's own'. D. H. Lawrence went a step further: the novel was, he declared, 'the one bright book of life' – the Bible for modern man. At least, as written by Lawrence it was.

The Pilgrim's Progress is the all-time fiction bestseller. There have been more editions than anyone has counted. It is still widely read by the multitude (particularly in residually puritan America) for the same reason that it was read in the seventeenth century – it is a novel which can be read by those who distrust novels. But Bunyan's achievement is greater than moving tons of copies out of the Amazon warehouse, year-in, year-out. His allegorical narrative made room for the novel to be morally serious. It was the necessary first step for the book of life.

He died as he would have wanted. Having been drenched in a rainstorm and subsequently contracting a chill, he insisted on preaching, precipitating a fatal fever which stopped his voice forever.

FN   John Bunyan
MRT   *The Pilgrim's Progress*
Biog   R. Sharrock, *John Bunyan* (1954)

2. Aphra Behn 1640–1689

She is not so much a woman to be unmasked as an unending combination of masks.
Janet Todd

The novel (or 'new thing') happened in the late seventeenth or early eighteenth century. It coincided with, and arguably depended upon, an array of preconditional factors: for example, mass literacy, urbanisation, mercantilism, the Protestant Ethic, the rise of the bourgeoisie, female emancipation, new technologies, parliamentary democracy and individual authorial genius. Scholars have tried, but a juggling octopus could not keep all those balls in the air. Enough to say – it happened.

'Eaffrey' Johnson was born in 1640 near Canterbury. What scant evidence there is suggests her father was a 'barber'. Among other things, these intimate attenders to the male person were the first ports of call for those with venereal problems. Eaffrey's mother was a wet nurse – a woman, that is, who put her breasts out to hire to mothers of higher station than herself.

In return for services rendered the Johnsons received favours from powerful local families. It was thus, one assumes, that Eaffrey's father, the barber, was appointed in 1663/4 Lieutenant General of Surinam, a British colonial possession. It has a touch of Caligula's horse about it. But the Civil War had (temporarily) disturbed the usual power, patronage and privilege circuits, and Surinam was hardly a plum posting – even for a governor with a royal commission in one hand, and a shaving bowl in the other. Everything about Aphra's early life has a question mark hanging over it.

The colony was located where Guyana now is, between the Orinoco and Amazon rivers (a stream which, as Behn charmingly notes, is 'almost as large as the Thames'). It was not far from where Robinson Crusoe is shipwrecked at exactly the same period of time that Miss Eaffrey was there – if, indeed, she were.

Three colonial powers – France, Holland and England – competed for this far-off patch of colonial dirt, but currently the English flag flew. Surinam was put to the cultivation of sugar: the appetite for the sweetener was ravenous in Europe – as ravenous as that in the US today for the other white powder which South America supplies.

Slaves from Africa worked the plantations for whomever the current overseer was – English or Dutch whips were all the same. Black cattle were notoriously ill treated. It was a black man's hell and a white man's grave. Thus it proved for Aphra's father who evidently died there. Did his daughter accompany him to Surinam? The question vexes readers of Behn's primal novel *Oroonoko*. It seems, from the ostentatious accuracy of her local description and the introduction of actual historical figures, that she indeed knew the place at first-hand. But sceptics argue that she was no more there than the adult Defoe was eyewitness to the Plague Year.

It seems (again, the details are hazy) that in her mid-twenties Aphra Johnson married a trader – possibly in slaves – called Hans Behn. He was Dutch or German and apparently died (in the plague?) or absconded, shortly after the wedding ceremony. Aphra may even have invented him to render herself a 'respectable' widow. Whether or not the shady European spouse existed, Mrs Behn (as she hereafter inscribed herself) knew Europe very well. In 1666 war broke out between England and Holland. Now in her late twenties, Aphra (codename 'Aphora') served as a spy for the newly returned Charles II, in Antwerp. The 'she spy' did good work. Legend, apocryphal alas, has it she warned her country of the Dutch Navy's incursion up the Thames in 1667. But Aphra did not profit from her service to the nation: 1668 found her in debtors' prison. From seventeenth-century 007 to Moll Flanders.

She came in from the cold, with her first play, *The Forced Marriage*, in 1670. Actresses ('Mrs Bracegirdle', et al.) had broken the old 'boys only' convention – so why not go a step higher and write the things? Particularly if you could do it as wittily – and king-pleasingly – as Mrs Behn. One of her comedies, *The Feign'd Courtezans*, is dedicated to Nell Gwyn. Behn would market more profitable fare than oranges to her monarch and his retinue. The wicked Earl of Rochester, she claimed, 'helped' her. He liked helping handsome young ladies.

From her earliest years, she took lovers whom, in the libertine spirit of the age, she evidently preferred to husbands. Two partners figure prominently in what has come down to us. William Scot she may have met in Surinam, and he may have been her 'control' during her career as a spy. A 'regicide', he was later executed. The other partner was a bisexual lawyer, 'Jack' Hoyle. As Janet Todd describes him, Jack was 'a learned, bullying man who would, a few years on, be tried for sodomy and killed after a tavern brawl' – an everyday career in Restoration London.

Late in what would be a short life, Aphra Behn turned to fiction of which *Oroonoko*, published in 1688, is judged her masterpiece. The London theatre, with the monarchy again in bloody dispute, was in recession. And Behn, it is known, was again hard up: in her forties, 'friends' may have been harder to come by.

Whatever the motive for writing it, as with her male counterpart Defoe, fiction was late-life fruit. She died months after the publication of *Oroonoko* and is buried in the cloisters of Westminster Abbey, the first woman author, and the least cloistered, to be so honoured. On her tomb, instructs Virginia Woolf, 'All women together ought to let flowers fall ... for it was she who earned them the right to speak their minds.' One suspects Aphra would have tossed the flowers back.

The 'True Story' as the title proclaims itself (the term 'novel' was yet to be invented) is the manifestly untrue story of a 'Royal Slave'. The oxymoron is piquant in the context of the 1680s. An African prince, Oroonoko, along with his wife Imoinda, has been transported to Surinam, from West Africa, to labour in the plantations. His history is 'set down' by this anonymous young English woman, the daughter of the newly appointed deputy governor, who has just died.

The narrator befriends the luckless African pair. He, being a Prince in Exile (as was Charles II in France), can speak both French and English elegantly. Even in remote West Africa, he has heard of the execution of Charles I and found it – as did all right thinking people – 'deplorable'. The narrator is struck by the couple's native dignity, though their beauty is anything but native. Oroonoko (renamed 'Caesar' by his captors) has straight hair and 'Roman', not negroid, features. He is less a noble savage, a hundred years *avant la lettre*, than a noble, *tout court*. A black blue-blood. We recall that the nickname for the notoriously swarthy Charles II was 'the black boy' (it survives as a common pub name in England).

But Oroonoko is no common slave. He kills two tigers and has a vividly described battle with an electric ('benumbing') eel. When Imoinda becomes pregnant, Oroonoko is determined that his son shall not be born into slavery. He organises an uprising, and is cheated into surrendering on the point of victory. Realising it is the end, Oroonoko cuts off Imoinda's face, after he has cut her throat, so that no one will gaze on her beauty again. He disembowels himself, but is sewn up by surgeons to be executed, sadistically, for the delectation of a white rabble. Behn's Royal Slave is even more stoic, at the moment of regicide, than the Royal Captive, Charles I, calmly puffing away at his pipe as his genitals are cut off.

Oroonoko is short (at 28,000 words it might have problems qualifying for the 1689 Man Booker Prize) and it lacks *Crusoe*'s narrative machinery and masterful suspense (whose *was* that footprint on the foreshore?). But no one can deny Behn's inventiveness and intuitive feel for the as yet undefined elements of fiction. They are well worthy of Woolf's bouquet.

FN   Aphra Behn ('Aphora', née Eaffrey Johnson)
MRT *Oroonoko*
Biog J. Todd, *The Secret Life of Aphra Behn* (1996)

3. Daniel Defoe 1660–1731

It happened one day, about noon, going towards my boat, I was exceedingly surprised with the print of a man's naked foot on the shore, which was very plain to be seen in the sand. Along with Oliver's gruel, the best-known moment in English fiction

If Daniel Defoe had died in 1718 he would be remembered, if at all, as a fertile pamphleteer and pioneering English journalist with an adhesively memorable name. Living as he did, until 1731, he ranks as a founding father of the English novel – as significant a figure in the evolution of the national fiction as Cervantes in Spain or Rabelais in France.

Tantalisingly little is known of Defoe's life. 'Did he in fact exist at all?' asks one recent study. Even more tantalisingly, it is not known why a man close on sixty years of age (Methuselean in the early eighteenth century) should suddenly change his literary modus operandi so drastically and creatively. In the absence of intimate information, one is thrown back on the skeletal public records. The first fifteen years of Defoe's life occupy barely that number of pages in Paula Backscheider's 700-page biography. 'Lives' of Defoe, like hers, dissolve into lifeless catalogues raisonnés of his tracts, articles and occasional writings (whose precise authorship is much disputed) – with a running commentary on the big historical picture in whose foreground any image of 'Daniel Defoe', infuriatingly, refuses to materialise. The curriculum vitae, as we know it, is easily summarised. If there are interesting times in English history, Defoe lived through the most interesting. Something that fascinated him throughout his life, judging by his choice of subject matter, is that he *had* actually contrived to survive an infancy surrounded by such an array of danger. Robinson Crusoe wonders the same thing.

'Daniel Foe' (the French prefix was a later affectation) was born (quite likely, the date is hopelessly insecure) a Londoner in the year of the Restoration 1660. His first conscious observations, as an embryonic historian of his country, would have begun in what Dryden called the *annus mirabilis*, 1666. It was less 'wonderful' than downright terrifying to Londoners. The population of the capital was visited by the worst ever outbreak of bubonic plague; some 100,000 citizens died, it is estimated. Given the population of the metropolis, it was a holocaust – triggered by the black rat's fleas, exploding population and pre-Victorian sanitation. The city burned to the ground in this same 'wonderful' year – a disaster, but one which at least cleansed the city of the plague bacillus. The Great Fire of London supplies vivid entries in Samuel Pepys's Diary: not even the 1941 Blitz did more damage – Old London ceased, almost overnight, to exist. The Foes' house survived, however, something for which they would have offered heartfelt thanks to their stern Presbyterian deity. God had not always been good to them. The adults around young Daniel as he grew up could remember the Civil War – actually a Revolution – of the 1640s in which the monarch was beheaded. In the year of Daniel's birth, monarchy was restored and Oliver Cromwell's corpse (he, alas, being beyond live decapitation) was shredded by jubilant Royalists.

All this happens, oddly, while Robinson Crusoe is on his island. He is unaware of it and doesn't advert to the epochal events of the 1660s on his return, some decades after the wonderful year. Defoe may – part of him – have yearned for a refuge from the dangerous historical excitements of his youth and created that refuge in his most famous fiction about an Englishman outside England. During those years he was, in fact, brought up in the St Giles quarter of central London – an area notorious for its criminality. The Foes were, however, eminently uncriminal. Daniel's father was a tallow chandler, a trade which would have conduced to the boy's precocious literacy. The Foe house would, unlike most in St Giles, have been decently lighted (but smelly – tallow was made of mutton fat, the upper classes had more expensive wax).

The Foe family became Dissenters in 1662 with the passing of the Act of Uniformity. As a sect, it believed in education but, being banned from the seats of higher education and higher professions, they were thrown back on their own resources – which meant books and a premium on reading (Bunyan's Christian, it will be remembered, hies off to the Celestial City, book in hand). A 'persecuted minority', the Dissenters refused sacraments and allegiance to, among other things, newly restored kings. They suffered discrimination, physical abuse and, quite often, jail – with the consoling sense that such mistreatment was proof of Christian worth. Had not the Saviour himself been reviled?

Daniel Foe grew up something of an outsider in his own country – a righteous rebel. What little is known of his school education suggests that he might have been destined for the Presbyterian ministry – 'sacred employ', as he calls it. Instead, he followed his father (now widowed and an increasingly eminent figure in the City) into trade. He was apprenticed in the retail business, with a line in hosiery. Men, as well as women, wore stockings at this period and there was good business to be done (close attention, one recalls, is given to Robinson's goatskin leggings). From his earliest years in business, Defoe was an eager speculator. He had married, prudently enough, in 1684, and his wife, a carpenter's daughter, brought a tidy fortune. We know little else about the marriage.

There were apparently six surviving children – who were lucky to grow up with a father. Restless and rebellious by nature, Defoe rashly threw in his lot with the Monmouth rebellion in 1685, whose aim was to forestall a Catholic takeover. He was taken prisoner at Sedgemoor, a battle in which the rebels were routed, but was fortunate to be spared hanging in the punitive carnage of the Bloody Assizes and Judge Jeffreys. Hereafter Defoe would mount his resistance by the pen, not the sword. He returned to his London trade, prospered and became within a few years a well-regarded man in the City. Details of what he was doing in this period are, as everywhere, scarce. But from his writings it is clear he was fascinated by 'projects' – the subject of one of his early substantial publications in 1697. Man was, as Defoe saw the species, a mechanic animal, *homo faber*. His survey began with Noah's Ark ('the first project I read of') and came down to the latest French fire-fighting equipment; it covered other such instances of human resourcefulness as diving bells.

His own projects were inventive but unlucky. A scheme to harvest musk (from the anuses of cats) was unproductive and he was arrested for debts in 1692, of the huge sum of £17,000. He may also at this period have been speculating in wine and spirits from the Iberian peninsula. There was a brick and tile factory at Tilbury he was connected with, and a printing works in London. Defoe was, one may confidently assert, an energetic and resourceful entrepreneur or, as he would have put it, 'the complete English tradesman'. But he was either unlucky or too reckless.

There was also an element of recklessness in his publications. His first major success as an author was with the long 1703 poem, a satirical polemic, 'The True-born Englishman'. Written in sinewy couplets it contains such provocative lines as:

WHEREVER *God erects a house of prayer,*
The Devil always builds a chapel there:
And 'twill be found, upon examination,
The latter has the largest congregation,

The poem ends with the Dissenters' proud motto: ''Tis pers'nal virtue only makes us great'. It was not a good period to be of that disliked party and raise your voice: in 1702 persecution rose to the level of mob violence. Defoe, ever pugnacious, hit back with the mock ironic 'The Shortest-Way with the Dissenters'. It is another pamphlet, delivered in the spoof voice of a man of (Anglican) reason (that is to say, arrant prejudice), driven to such final solutions as:

> Alas, the Church of England! What with Popery on one hand, and Schismatics on the other, how has She been crucified between two thieves. NOW, LET US CRUCIFY THE THIEVES!

It is very funny – but the authorities did not find it so. Defoe was prosecuted for his 'diabolical and seditious libel', which led to his being fined, jailed and pilloried in 1703. As legend has it, he was pelted not with rotten fruit or stones but flowers by a sympathetic crowd and was released early from the six-month sentence in Newgate (an incarceration which supplied, years later, the opening chapters to *Moll Flanders*).

It was at this time that Defoe formed a relationship with the politician Robert Harley, for whom he became, effectively, a secret agent, or cat's paw. Harley, an arch-Machiavellian, used Defoe's pamphleteering skills in the interests of the government. Secret commissions were passed on in coffee houses and Defoe, often anonymously, would fire off the necessary articles the next day. Both men – the politician and the journalist – took a delight in 'secrecy'. Defoe's hectic stream of publication over the next fifteen years is difficult to follow – scholars are still in dispute about what he wrote and did not write. One thing is certain: he was the most influential journalist in the country, and was routinely accused of being the most mercenary. He lent the power of his pen to both Whigs (with whom his heart was) and Tories, as served his interest best at that particular juncture.

How then did Daniel Defoe graduate into writing fiction, in his sixtieth year? After the publication of his first effort in the field, *Robinson Crusoe*, the reason for continuing in this new line is simple enough. He had – as unexpectedly to him as to his publisher – hit a vein of literary gold. Nothing wonderful was expected of the first edition, for which he received a modest £10. But *Crusoe* went through edition after edition in its first year, 1719. As a contemporary, Charles Gideon, grumbled, 'Not an old Woman that can go the Price of it, but buys the Life and Adventures.' One of Defoe's favourite slogans was that God gave him brains that he might have bread – and that he might fall back on those brains in any emergency. A principal event turning Defoe the pamphleteer into Defoe the novelist was, one may surmise, the downfall of Robert Harley, in 1714. Once England's Cardinal Richelieu he found himself committed to the Tower on charges of high crimes and misdemeanours – politically he was finished.

Defoe had, at this point in his life, turned his coat and written so many lies that fiction ('lies like truth', as Leslie Stephen described *Crusoe*) was second nature to him. Many of his squibs, such as the immensely popular 'A True Relation of the Apparition of One Mrs. Veal' (1706), read like short stories. Mrs V., we are told (Defoe, we are to understand has researched the matter thoroughly), 'was a maiden gentlewoman of about thirty years of age, and for some years past had been troubled with fits'. On the eighth of September, one thousand seven hundred and five (Defoe is owlishly pedantic about the details): 'she was sitting alone in the forenoon, thinking over her unfortunate life, and arguing herself into a due resignation to Providence,' when she was visited by an old friend who wasn't there. It presents itself as a believe-it-or-not piece of journalism and works as a still very readable spine-chiller.

In embarking on the new field of fiction, Defoe was able to draw on a rich trove of precursors: romances, tales of roguery, picaresque tales, spiritual autobiography, whore's memoirs, and travel writing. Spurred on by the success of *Crusoe*, he rush-wrote a mass of fiction in his last decade of life: *Captain Singleton* (1720), *Colonel Jack* (1722), *Moll Flanders* (1722), *Roxana* (1724). Each is related to one of the above precursor categories, but takes narrative well beyond it. There has been much academic dispute about Defoe and the 'Rise of the Novel'. One thing seems indisputable – that there is a link between the fiction he wrote and the Rise of Capitalism – specifically the commercial activity Defoe was engaged in during the first twenty years of his adult life – 'the business of the shop', he called it. What is most striking as an innovation in Defoe's fiction is, however, something much less grand – what the critic John Richetti calls his 'peculiar realism'.

Another term for it is supplied by Henry James, in 1884, referring to his own work: 'One can speak best from one's own taste, and I may therefore venture to say that the air of reality (solidity of specification) seems to me to be the supreme virtue of a novel – the merit on which all its other merits ... helplessly and submissively depend.' Consider, as an example of this Jamesian solidity, the following very incidental episode from *Robinson Crusoe*. The hero has been miraculously (or, as he later comes to believe, for some inscrutable divine purpose) shipwrecked on an island off the coast of South America. Of his former shipmates, presumed drowned, he says: 'I never saw them afterwards, or any sign of them, except three of their hats, one cap, and two shoes that were not fellows.' It is an incidental detail of no significance – but every reader recalls those irritatingly mismatched shoes. But why does Defoe have Robinson mention them? They never come up again in the story.

The most solid, and most specific, of Defoe's fictions masquerading as fact is *A Journal of the Plague Year* (1722). The narrative pivots on the conventional prefatory lie purporting to be 'observations or memorials, of the most remarkable occurrences, as well publick as private, which happened in London during the last great visitation in 1665. Written by a Citizen who continued all the while in London. Never made public before.' The narrator (an actual relative, but in this instance Defoe's glove puppet) is 'HF' – his uncle, Henry Foe. HF, we understand, is no writer but a saddler who deals in leather with America. He is unmarried and has remained in London to witness the 1665–6 cataclysm, because, he believes, it is the 'will of heaven' that he should do so. He has written down his observations because, during the time of plague, newspapers ceased to exist. HF chronicles the gradual rise of the epidemic from sporadic cases, to larger outbreaks, to epidemic, the quarantining of whole quarters of the city and, finally, mass evacuation and flight. The playhouses and bear-baiting pits and places of public eating, 'tippling houses and coffee shops', suffer first curfew, then closure. The dumping of refuse (nightsoil) is prohibited, along with the slaughter of dogs and cats. HF's musing on this ordinance is typical of his laconic, keen-eyed style:

> Wherefore were we ordered to kill all the dogs and cats, but because as they were domestic animals, and are apt to run from house to house, and from street to street, so they are capable of carrying the effluvia or infectious streams of bodies infected even in their furs and hair? And therefore it was that, in the beginning of the infection, an order was published by the Lord Mayor, and by the magistrates, according to the advice of the physicians, that all the dogs and cats should be immediately killed, and an officer was appointed for the execution.
>
> It is incredible, if their account is to be depended upon, what a prodigious number of those creatures were destroyed. I think they talked of forty thousand dogs, and five times as many cats; few houses being without a cat, some having several, sometimes five or six in a house.

Ironically, since rats were principal vectors of the disease (as the carriers of the fleas which spread it), this was fuel on the epidemic fire. It is the detail (down, even, to statistical precision, of the great caninocide and felinocide) which leaves a more powerful effect than the generally restrained description of the corpse carts and charnel pits.

In his last years, he had one more great non-fiction work in him. This was his *Tour thro' the Whole Island of Great Britain* (1724–7). Never let it be thought Daniel Defoe did not think big. He died, it is assumed, in hiding from his creditors, in the aptly named Ropemakers' Alley, in London (Judge Jeffreys would have approved). The wholly inapt cause of death recorded is 'lethargy'.

FN　Daniel Defoe (born Foe)
MRT　*A Journal of the Plague Year*
Biog　P. R. Backscheider, *Daniel Defoe: His Life* (1989)

4. Samuel Richardson 1689–1761

His mind is so very vile a mind, so oozy, so hypocritical, praise-mad, canting, envious, concupiscent. Samuel Taylor Coleridge's verdict on Samuel Richardson

Even in an age when lives are usually invisible to posterity, the little we know about Samuel Richardson is scant – and what is unknown to us is almost certainly unexciting. 'Few writers have led less interesting lives' his biographers glumly conclude, having expended 800 pages and the best part of two academic careers cataloguing Richardson's uninterestingness. Dull as the life may have been, one great question will tantalise those who contemplate it. How did a dropsical, late-middle-aged tradesman, of no previous literary distinction come to write a first novel as momentous as *Pamela*? What little we know of Richardson's first half-century of existence comes from bleak inscriptions in registers, scraps of gossip and a handful of letters which, late in life, he wrote to a Dutch clergyman, Johannes Stinstra.

The Richardsons (among whom Samuel was a recurrent primal name) had been farmers in a small way in Surrey for a hundred years or more. Samuel, however, was born in Derbyshire. His father, Samuel Richardson Sr, had broken with family tradition to work as a skilled 'joiner' or carpenter. He was based principally in London – still in a process of reconstruction after the great fire, and expanding every year with waves of urban migration, among which were the Richardsons. The family got by reasonably well. Samuel Senior inherited some property on his father's death, in the same year as Samuel Junior's birth. But his connection with a rich customer who participated in the Monmouth rebellion entailed losses and temporary rustication. There was some thought that Samuel Jr might go into the church but 'Fortune was not propitious'. There was no money and nine children.

Little is known of Samuel's schooldays and nothing of interest other than the recollection that 'my Schoolfellows used to call me *Serious* and *Gravity*'. As the twig was bent, so the tree was shaped. He may have attended Christ's Hospital Grammar School in London but, if so, received only a basic education; he lamented in later life his inability to read French. This was compounded by a remarkably static life, in which he rarely ventured beyond the sound of Bow Bells. 'Few men were less travelled,' his biographers drily note. From the first, Samuel was a precocious penman. As a youth he acted as a scribe to girls of his acquaintance, wanting to write the right kind of love letter. He enjoyed 'secretaryship' and it led in 1706 to his being apprenticed for seven years as a printer. He was proud of his 'assiduity' in this chosen trade, although the shop he was apprenticed to produced a very minor sort of book and Samuel was aiming higher. He set up his first shop, with his own apprentices, in 1720. Over the following decades his operations would flourish in ever-larger establishments around Salisbury Square, near Fleet Street – the heart of the London book trade.

Following the moral script laid down by Hogarth for industrious apprentices, he married his former master's daughter, Martha. The match was, as he put it, 'prudential' – although he claimed, on her death ten years later, that the marriage had been 'a happy one'. It cannot, unless the young Richardson had a heart of stone, have been entirely happy: the couple had six children (no less than three named 'Samuel'), none of whom survived beyond the 'pratler' stage of life. Martha Richardson's death was doubtless accelerated by grief and physical exhaustion.

Politically Richardson had, by the early 1730s, begun to construct a public character for himself. He was a Tory, with a leaning towards Jacobitism. He printed nothing that could be construed as immoral. His 'list' was mixed, ranging from journals to works of such distinction as Defoe's *Tour thro' the Whole Island of Great Britain*, and there was a literary flavour to his imprint. 'James Thomson,' his biographers recall, 'is the most eminent author for whom he printed' and whom he befriended. The link between author and printer was, typically, intimate at the period. One picks up a silhouette of the man from his catalogues – it is practically all one has.

On the death of Martha in 1731, and that of the last of their surviving children, Richardson remarried in 1733. His second wife, Elizabeth, bore him five daughters and a son (who died in infancy). Like the first, it was a prudent match: she is described as 'a plain and pleasant woman, with no pretensions to intellect or elegance'. In the same year as his second marriage, the first work Richardson is known to have written was published – *The Apprentice's Vade Mecum* (1733). Richardson had, at the time, five apprentices living in his house – some of whom he was emotionally close to. His advice is sensible, informed, and expectedly severe on such delinquencies as drinking, theatres and wenching.

As the decade progressed, Richardson was an increasingly respected figure in the London book trade. His business received a boost with the commission to print the multi-volume *Journals of the House of Commons*. His personal health, however, deteriorated as his fortunes rose. There was a dangerous tendency to 'Rotundity and Liquor' and the early onset of what is now assumed to be Parkinson's disease. By the age of fifty, Richardson is described by his biographers as 'a comfortable family man who from very small beginnings had worked his way up in the world until he was one of the leading printers in London'. How, though, did he manage to become a leading novelist? How, even more surprisingly, did he inject himself into the psychology of a fifteen-year-old girl?

It may be that health was a factor. Writing in his closet was less arduous than being in the workshop, whose smooth running he could delegate to an 'overseer'. Sedentary work had its attractions for a corpulent inactive man with a tireless writing hand. Richardson himself offered two plausible explanations for *Pamela*. Some twenty years before, he had been told 'about a virtuous serving maid who had married her master'. As Defoe's *Moll Flanders* records, it was more usual for servant girls to be sexually abused by their masters. In this case, the girl had, unlike Moll, evaded 'the snares laid for her virtue' – and gone so far as to threaten drowning herself rather than part with her virginity.

It was, Richardson conceded, a 'slight foundation', but it was vivified, coincidentally, by something else. He had been 'importuned' by two fellow publishers ('particular friends') to write a 'little book' advising 'young folks circumstanced as Pamela was' (i.e. country servants) how to 'indite' well-mannered letters. He had in mind 'handsome girls' for whom the traditional 'snares' would be laid. An epistolary conduct book was what was intended. 'Prudence' was stressed on the title page. For his own amusement, initially, he began to write a novel, in letters, on the subject of a 'handsome' young servant girl. In a reminiscence to a friend he offered one of the few domestic glimpses posterity has of him. He had dashed off the first two volumes of what would become *Pamela* in the long dark evenings between November 1739 and January 1740, and 'While I was writing the two volumes, my worthy-hearted wife, and the young lady who is with us, when I had read them some part of the story, which I had begun without their knowing it, used to come in to my little closet every night, with – "Have you any more of Pamela, Mr R.? We are come to hear a little more of Pamela," &tc. This encouraged me to prosecute it.'

The plot of *Pamela* is somewhat sarcastically summarised by his biographers: 'A virtuous servant girl rejects her master's lewd advances and is kidnapped by him and confined in a lonely country house where she continues to fight him off until he is overcome by her virtue to the extent of proposing matrimony, which is instantly accepted.' Improbable and banal as the plot was, the novel had genre-enlarging innovations – epistolary narration was one. The technique created immediacy – sometimes, however, with awkwardness. Just as Byron said that no man shaves himself during an earthquake so no young girl carries on writing a letter (even, nowadays, an email) as some ravishing Tarquin lunges at her breasts. Such unlikelihood jars in a postscript to Pamela's opening letter to her parents:

> I have been scared out of my senses; for just now, as I was folding up this letter in my late lady's dressing-room, in comes my young master! Good sirs! how was I frightened! I went to hide the letter in my bosom; and he, seeing me tremble, said, smiling, To whom have you been writing, Pamela? – I said, in my confusion, Pray your honour forgive me! –

'Just now' strikes a false note. None the less there is a freshness and spontaneity in the narrative which still effervesces. It is heightened by a new kind of realism. Richardson presented himself anonymously as merely the 'editor' of actual letters, which are to be taken as 'true'. The other revolutionary feature is inscribed on the novel's title page:

Pamela; Or, Virtue Rewarded.
In A Series Of Familiar Letters From A Beautiful Young Damsel,
To Her Parents

Virtue is a word with Roman associations which is, historically, the exclusive property of the aristocrat. Damsels in distress in romance are not, before 1740, fifteen-year-old skivvies who empty the chamber pots and do the housework for their betters. *Pamela* is a revolutionary act of social redefinition.

Richardson published the work anonymously in 1740, intending that only six of his friends, at most, should be let in on the secret of his authorship. But it soon leaked out and enlarged his sphere of social contacts: he became acquainted with Hogarth (who went on to illustrate for him) and friendly with Dr Johnson. The latter admired him extravagantly as the antidote to Fielding. 'Sir,' he instructed a not entirely convinced Boswell, 'there is more knowledge of the heart in one letter of Richardson's than in all *Tom Jones*.'

Pamela was hugely successful. Two moralistic sequels flopped, however, and for his next major novel Richardson struck out on new ground. At this point in his career he began, he believed, truly to understand the mind of woman. *Clarissa* was circulated in manuscript among friends. Among the more eminent was the poet Edward Young, who concurred with Johnson in believing that 'this romance will probably do more good than a body of Divinity'. He approved the unhappy ending – others of Richardson's confidential friends were less sure. There was a general uneasiness about length – he should 'sweat' or prune the work into something more manageable. This advice Richardson strenuously ignored – the seven volumes, published serially over 1747–8, come out at a million words.

Clarissa Harlowe is of higher social station than Pamela Andrews. The plot is, however, similar. The heroine's virtue is under prolonged assault from Lovelace (a rake who seems to have wandered into fiction from the Restoration comedy of Wycherley). He, driven to an extremity of lechery, imprisons, drugs and rapes her. The violated Clarissa rejects his compensatory offer of marriage and dies – neglected, as she has been throughout, by her heartless family. Lovelace is killed in a duel by her cousin. Is this, the novel asks, a harlot's progress (as her surname hints) or virtue indomitable? *Clarissa* is, as Dr Johnson proclaimed it, 'a prodigious work – formed on the stalest of all empty stories'. It had none of the 'perverse and crooked Nature' to be found in Fielding – who had formed his career in opposition to Richardson, first with *Shamela*, then *Joseph Andrews* and finally his masterpiece, *Tom Jones*. The Fielding objection sets up one of the principal dialectics in English fiction of the period. Is virtue something learned through experience and error, or an innate 'innocence', something to be 'preserved'? Put another way, do you have to be bad before you can be good? And, if so, is bad bad?

Richardson wrote one more epistolary novel, *Sir Charles Grandison*, in which he took on the challenge of making a 'good man' – rather than a virtuous woman – his hero. The novel has its admirers: Jane Austen liked the consistency of the characterisation; John Ruskin testified that the novel had 'a greater practical effect on me for good than anything I ever read in my life'. But these are minority views: *Sir Charles Grandison* is generally thought to confirm that Richardson's greatest work is its immediate predecessor.

In his last years Richardson prospered as an author (he was hugely admired and translated on the Continent), as a popular moralist, and as a printer-publisher. His last years were passed among four daughters, with whom he had a dutiful if distant relationship, in a fine townhouse and a finer country villa at Parsons Green. Despite chronic infirmity he made his three score and ten, dying of a stroke.

FN   Samuel Richardson
MRT *Clarissa*
Biog T. C. D. Eaves and B. D. Kimpel, *Samuel Richardson: A Biography* (1971)

5. Henry Fielding 1707–1754

Incest! With a mother! Tom Jones

Over the centuries, accounts of Fielding's life seemed as immutable as the inscription chiselled on his tombstone. Biographer after biographer came and (as one of them ruefully lamented) left the author of *Tom Jones* exactly where they found the author of *Tom Jones*. He was born, the eldest of seven children, in Somerset (young Tom Jones's stamping ground). His father, Edmund Feilding (as, for snobbish reasons, he misspelled it) was a senior army officer, of incorrigibly wayward habits. His mother died when Henry was ten, and in his formative years he and his siblings were cared for by a doting aunt. On his wife's death, Edmund promptly remarried a Catholic – to the fury of his rich and titled former in-laws. Legal disputes over property and child custody ensued. Fielding qualifies as the first tug-of-love novelist in English literature. Edmund would eventually die in debtors' prison. As with Dickens and the Marshalsea, it inspired some vivid scenes in the son's later fiction. The maternal, and wholly respectable, grandmother, Lady Sarah Gould, eventually got charge of the children.

Now a child of privilege, Henry was sent to Eton, aged twelve. There he made friends who would later serve him as patrons. The school also gave him a grounding in classical literature. On leaving school in 1724, Fielding drifted to London, where he received instruction in lower forms of literature – notably that spawned around Drury Lane. Headstrong by nature, in 1725 Henry attempted the abduction of a cousin, Sarah Andrews (who had recently come into a fortune). It led to trouble with the local constabulary and – more profitably – the core episode in *Tom Jones*. He was encouraged to write by, among others, his distant cousin, Lady Wortley Montagu (he satirised many things in British society – but never bluestockings). His first attempt at a stage play, in 1728, flopped. The same year he went to study at the University of Leiden where he immersed himself in books and ran up debts – the pattern of his life. He returned after a year and threw himself again into writing for the theatre. His great success was the burlesque, *The Tragedy of Tragedies; or, The Life and Death of Tom Thumb the Great*. Witty mockery was to be Fielding's stock-in-trade.

In 1734 Fielding married well and set up with his wife Charlotte as a retired gentleman in Dorset. But he ran through her money in a year and then, inevitably, it was back to London where he became the manager and chief playwright at the New Theatre in the Haymarket. One of his satires on Walpole's government provoked the 1737 Licensing Act (effectively state censorship – of Henry Fielding, principally). He had satirised himself out of his job.

Aged thirty, he enrolled at Middle Temple to read for the bar, writing all the while savagely anti-Jacobite pieces for the nearby Fleet Street paper, *The Champion*. Fielding qualified as a barrister in 1740 but years of drinking had caught up with him and he was physically disabled by gout. But he could still read and write. He read Richardson's 1740 bestseller, *Pamela*, and wrote the burlesque *Shamela Andrews* (anonymously published in 1741). It evolved into his first proper novel, *Joseph Andrews* (1742). Anti-Richardsonism was the foundation of all his later work: Fielding always needed something to kick against.

Fielding's mood was darkened, and his writing halted, by the premature death of his wife in 1744. Three years later, to his friends' dismay, he married his wife's former maid – six months pregnant as she lumbered up the aisle. Thanks to one of his Etonian patrons, he was appointed JP for Westminster in 1748. Gouty he might be, but he could still sit on a bench. He was a vigorous, commonsensical and notably unvenal jurist. He brought in important reforms in London policing and, had he never published a line of fiction, would be remembered for this side of his career. There were, however, areas in which common sense (as he saw it) was in short supply. In 1749 he published his vast anti-Richardsoniad, *Tom Jones*. In it, he expressed his moral conviction that virtue was earned through experience of life, not something clamped between a maiden's thighs. He would write one other novel – *Amelia* – a more sentimental work, named after his favourite daughter and, supposedly, a memorial (in the portrayal of the heroine) of his dead wife. In 1752, crippled with multiple ailments, Fielding sailed to Portugal in search of health. He died in Lisbon, leaving a typically jaundiced journal of the trip behind him. He was a man who could even make comedy out of his own terminal decay.

Such was the outline of the standard biographies until 1989, when Martin and Ruth Battestin published their massive *Henry Fielding: A Life*. In addition to new circumstantial material (Ruth was a trained historical archivist), the Battestins adopted the more daring techniques of psychobiography. Twelve-year-old Henry's recorded act of spitting in servants' faces, for example, was mulled over as 'a clue to the deepest sources of both his personality and his wilful behaviour'. Deepest? Even deeper clues, however, were detected in the sleeping arrangements Henry and his sister Sarah shared in the Gould establishment. The children slept in the same bed; there were accusations of unspecified 'indecent actions'. Building on this, and such anthropological evidence as Lawrence Stone's that incest was common in the eighteenth century, the Battestins levelled the explosive charge against the two children. Moreover, they suggest, the 'Dreadful Sin' had a formative effect on the later imaginative writing they both produced. Incest, of course, is a subplot in *Joseph Andrews* and in *Tom Jones* – where, for a longish section of the novel, the reader is given to believe that the hero has committed the sin of Nero with his mother. We shall never know. And, for a certainty, Fielding would mock us unmercifully for wanting to know.

FN   Henry Fielding
MRT   *Tom Jones*
Biog M. C. Battestin and R. R. Battestin, *Henry Fielding: A Life* (1989)

6. Samuel Johnson 1709–1784

Fielding being mentioned, Johnson exclaimed, 'he was a blockhead ... What I mean by his being a blockhead is that he was a barren rascal.' BOSWELL. 'Will you not allow, Sir, that he draws very natural pictures of human life?' JOHNSON. 'Why, Sir, it is of very low life.'

Johnson believed, as he instructed Boswell, that 'nobody could furnish the life of a man but those who had eat and drank and lived in social intercourse about him'. Here, therefore, is Boswell describing his subject at table:

> His looks seemed riveted to his plate; nor would he, unless when in very high company, say one word, or even pay the least attention to what was said by others, till he had satisfied his appetite, which was so fierce, and indulged with such intenseness, that while in the act of eating, the veins of his forehead swelled, and generally a strong perspiration was visible.

On the matter of 'social intercourse' (or the other kind), his first biographers (Boswell, Hawkins, Thrale) were privy to things which even Johnson would have wanted to keep hidden. Nor were they averse to pulling the curtain for a discreet peek at his dark side. Mrs Thrale, for example, disclosed to posterity a 'secret far dearer to him than his life': namely Johnson's attachment to 'fetters and handcuffs'. It may have been a penchant for BDSM (modern critics have had a fine time with that hypothesis).

Many biographies of Johnson have been written since Boswell's. The narrative grips from the opening scenes: an ungainly, half-blind, nine-year-old lad – born into a dull town of dull parents – randomly takes up a volume of *Hamlet* while sitting in the basement kitchen. The words on the page induce a hallucinatory vision of Elsinore and ghosts. He throws down the book, and rushes into the street outside, 'that he might see people about him'. An author is born. The dull town was Lichfield. Dr Johnson is still the biggest thing to happen there. He lived his early life over the bookshop his father ran (hence access to *Hamlet*). Books were, however, not selling well and the family struggled. A late-in-life, unwanted child (his mother was forty at the time of his birth) did not help the Johnson finances. Infant Sam contracted scrofula, a disfiguring condition, as ugly as its name. He is also suspected of having suffered from Tourette's syndrome. Throughout life he twitched and was prone to blurt out in conversation – typically (as above) with the aggressive prefix 'Sir!' His eyesight was so defective that he was at risk of setting his wig on fire from leaning too close to the candle, as he read by night. And he was probably alcoholic.

There was, however, nothing wrong with the Johnson brain. Prodigiously precocious (he was reciting the New Testament at three, translating from the classics at six), he had a sound grammar-school education. It seemed he might be destined – despite his manifest gifts – to follow his father into the book trade. But an unexpected legacy enabled him to go to Oxford. The money ran out, however, and he was obliged to leave without a degree (a doctorate would come, *honoris causa*, fifty years later). His subsequent career is legendary: marriage (probably sexless) to a widow, 'Tetty', twenty-one years his senior with money and three children; a spectacularly failed attempt to set up a school (with Tetty's money) which recruited all of three pupils. Finally, with one of those three pupils – David Garrick, no less – Johnson set out on the road to London. Ahead, after years of struggle and authorial humiliation, lay the *Dictionary*, *The Lives of the Poets*, the greatest moral poem in the language (*The Vanity of Human Wishes*), and installation as the 'Great Cham' – the country's (some would say English literature's) presiding man of letters and arbiter of literary taste.

Johnson was also, in one of his minor parts, a novelist. In 1759 his ninety-year-old mother was dying; his father had gone to his reward in 1731. To cover the expense of his mother's last days, Johnson wrote, in the evenings of one week, *The History of Rasselas, Prince of Abissinia*. It is a mixture of thinly applied oriental setting (drawn from travel books) and heavy moral dogmatising, as English as suet pudding (drawn from the fifty-year-old author's life experiences). The *ingénu* hero leaves the comfort of his palace in Ethiopia to range the world, seeking the secret of a happy life. He is accompanied by his sister and a philosopher, Imlac (alias Samuel Johnson). There is, Rasselas discovers, no happiness to be found. Life is, as Johnson said elsewhere, a condition in which much is to be endured and little enjoyed. 'Patience is all' – Christian patience, that is (not for Johnson Voltaire's objectionably Gallic heathen quietism, with that stuff about cultivating your garden). Few novelists, one imagines, could produce the statutory happy-ever-after with the 'Dead March' from *Saul* droning, incessantly, in their ears and their mother's corpse genteelly decomposing at the undertaker's.

Rasselas is no page-turner – sermons on the human condition seldom are. But it brought Johnson £100 and £25 for a prompt second edition. In terms of hourly rate, for a week's scribbling it was the best money of his writing career. None but a blockhead, Johnson said, writes for anything but money. Fifty such princely tales a year (giving himself a fortnight's annual holiday) would have yielded the sum of £6,250: a princely sum. But having no more parents to inter, he wrote no more fiction. The fact was, Johnson regarded such work as unworthy. The novel, as a form, was merely words written on the passing waves of public fancy. He rejoiced to concur with the common reader, but was disinclined to pander to that reader's taste for 'delight'. He registered the existence and popularity of the genre in his 1750 *Rambler* essay on the novel (in which he patented the compound 'modern fiction'), but his personal view is summed up in his uncompromising dismissal of Sterne's great novel: 'Nothing odd will do long – *Tristram Shandy* did not last.' The Johnsonian stricture is heard throughout the genre's history. In James Fitzjames Stephen's verdict on *Oliver Twist*, for example: 'All very well, but damned low.' And, of course, ephemeral, unlasting – unlike dictionaries.

It would be a century and a half before Henry James would, with the help of his advanced coadjutors in the genre, make the English novel 'discutable'. The author of *The Lives of the Poets* would have scorned the worthwhileness of any such project for novelists.

FN   Samuel Johnson
MRT   *Rasselas*
Biog P. Martin, *Samuel Johnson: A Biography* (2008)

7. John Cleland 1709–1789

A Book I disdain to defend, and wish, from my Soul, buried and forgot. Cleland's description of *Fanny Hill*, his story of a 'Woman of Pleasure'

Cleland was, for a novelist (not to say, a writer of dirty books), exceptionally well born. His father, a former army officer of distinguished Scottish lineage, later a civil servant, was a friend of Alexander Pope's. His mother's family were wealthy Anglicized Dutch Jewish merchants who moved in high literary and political circles. Had Cleland done nothing in life he would probably have been passingly footnoted in biographies of the worthies of his time. Had he been himself luckier, or less indecent, he might even have been numbered among those worthies.

Young John spent two years at Westminster School before being expelled. The offence is unknown; delinquency most likely. Over the years of his adolescence one surmises that he was no stranger to London's 'women of pleasure', about whom he was later to write so knowingly. But there may well have been some serious disgrace. Aged twenty-one he was packed off to India, to serve for twelve years as a soldier, and later an administrator, in the East India Company. He returned to London in 1741, as his father was dying. The Clelands had once been well off, but during the 1740s, John Cleland's fortunes waned. He had no luck in trade. In 1748, he was arrested for debts of almost £1,000, and spent a year in the Fleet prison.

Debt drives the pen, and in jail he wrote *Fanny Hill*. The first volume of the 'memoirs of a woman of pleasure' was published in November 1748, the second in February 1749. The author was paid £20 for the copyright. Legend has it that the publishers gained as much as £10,000 by the bargain. Who sprung Cleland from clink is not known. The composition of *Fanny Hill* behind bars, as a kind of extended masturbation fantasy (a 'Wanker's Opera'), by a man denied his doxies, is a pretty anecdote. It may be prettier than true. Twenty years later, Cleland boasted to James Boswell that he had actually written the work in Bombay, in his twenties, as a wager to prove that one could write erotica without ever using a single item of foul language. It seems likely that he revised a pre-existing manuscript in the boring hours of his monastic incarceration.

In late 1749, Cleland was arrested, along with his publisher, and charged with 'corrupting the King's subjects' with his scandalous novel. In court, Cleland 'from my soul' wished the work 'buried and forgot'. He got off. An authorised, 'expurgated' *Fanny Hill* came out in 1750; a pirate edition, in 1751, featured an interpolated homosexual scene (probably not from Cleland's pen) which alarmed the authorities further. According to his obituary in the *Gentleman's Magazine*, Cleland was awarded a pension of £100 a year from the public purse, on condition that he wrote no more corrupting works. This is unlikely – although he may well have received financial assistance from his friends in high places, and some sage warning to mind his step. It was no longer a libertine age.

Cleland was, for the remainder of his life, a productive, unpornographic and consistently unsuccessful Grub Street author. Riding on *Fanny Hill*'s notoriety, he published the novels *Memoirs of a Coxcomb* in 1751 and *The Woman of Honour* in 1768. They neither offended, nor amused, nor sold. He wrote plays (David Garrick was a friend), none of which made him a penny. The promisingly titled *Tombo-Chiqui, or, The American Savage* (1758) did not even make it to the stage. His verse satires failed, as did his eccentric treatises on medicine, language (he discerned a lexical connection between Welsh and Hebrew), and politics. He grew peevish in later life, falling out with friends. He accused Laurence Sterne of trading in pornography; which is rather like Larry Flynt taking a high moral tone with Hugh Hefner. All the while he could never shake off the unwanted fame of being the author of the infamous *Memoirs*. He lived by himself, never married, and had the reputation of being a 'Sodomite'.

Fanny Hill; or, Memoirs of a Woman of Pleasure, as published in 1748–9, takes the form of a confessional letter, describing the heroine's 'progress', and was clearly designed to contradict the joyless moralism of Hogarth's *A Harlot's Progress* (1732) and to mock the timidly parsimonious reference to sex in Defoe's 'whore's autobiography', *Moll Flanders* (1722), both of which aims *Fanny Hill* achieves triumphantly. The name is a somewhat laboured pun on 'Veneris mons' – Venus's hill. It is not clear whether 'fanny' was, then as now, street slang for quim. Fanny is born in a small village in Lancashire, 'of parents extremely poor, and, I piously believe, extremely honest'. When they die of smallpox, the pubescent Fanny makes her way to London. Here she is taken under the wing of the procuress, Mrs Brown. She is introduced into the sensual pleasures of her body (which never fail to delight her more than her clients) by a fellow inmate of the house, Phoebe. Mrs Brown tries to sell Fanny's maidenhead to an ill-favoured customer, but the girl declines to cooperate. Eventually (after a number of exciting voyeuristic episodes) she loses her virginity to a 'young Adonis' called Charles (a gentleman – well endowed financially and physically). Her ecstasies of pain and pleasure are recalled with a barrage of florid but 'modest' euphemism.

Fanny becomes the mistress of a rich merchant, Mr H—. But, bored by the condition of kept woman, she seduces a manservant (even better endowed than Charles) and is cast out with fifty guineas. So ends the first volume. The second opens with Fanny now the occupant of a brothel run by the good-natured Mrs Cole. Finally she is enriched by connection with an old and grateful benefactor. Now prosperous, and just nineteen, she is united with the deviginating Charles and becomes a respectable wife and mother. As she informs her correspondent on the last page: 'If I have painted Vice in all its gayest colours ... it has been solely in order to make the worthier, the solemner Sacrifice of it to Virtue.' Hypocritical minx.

Fanny Hill sold steadily and clandestinely over the following centuries. The fact that the novel contains no four-letter words and is elaborately 'polite' in its descriptions of sex gave it a perverse underground respectability. As a schoolboy, I read a much thumbed copy, printed abysmally in Tangier. ('I wanked over it four times last night,' said the white-faced friend who passed it on to me.) The novel was successfully prosecuted in London in 1963 (following the *Lady Chatterley* acquittal in 1960), but subsequently slipped back into print where it now enjoys the respectability of a place in the World's Classics and Penguin Classics lists. A BBC-TV version, adapted by Andrew Davies in 2007, attracted an audience of seven million.

FN   John Cleland
MRT   *Fanny Hill*
Biog   W. H. Epstein, *John Cleland, Images of a Life* (1974)

8. Laurence Sterne 1713–1768

I wrote not to be fed but to be famous. Sterne, in a letter

The two most playful novelists in English literature, Charles Lutwidge Dodgson and Laurence Sterne (i.e. Lewis Carroll and Parson Yorick) were clergymen of the national church. As a doctrine, Anglicanism has generally – unlike more severe theologies – been tolerant of secular literature, even novels. Sterne embarked on them late in life, as the easy-going holder of three livings. It might be said he was bounced into novel-writing, impelled by his desires to be both famous and mischievous. Sterne's life was, in shape, one long ricochet – and, at the same time, a desperate race with the tubercular bacillus, that occupational hazard (and, arguably, occupational stimulus) of great writers from Keats to Orwell. In *Tristram Shandy*, Sterne will occasionally interrupt his gamesomeness to inform the reader how many dozen drops of blood his lungs have just expelled.

Sterne's father was a junior officer in the British army. His rank did not reflect his ability; senior commissions at this period had to be purchased, not earned. He saw action with Marlborough in that most pointless of conflicts, the War of the Spanish Succession. Roger Sterne ('a smart little man,' Laurence called him) was chronically impecunious but well connected, with family roots in the Yorkshire gentry and the Church of England. The grandest connection – one to be of great assistance to Laurence – was a grandfather who had been Archbishop of York in the late seventeenth century. Ensign Sterne married the widow of a fellow officer, Agnes Sterne ('debt' was involved, according to Sterne) and there were subsequently seven children. Sterne's family life – natal and married – would be emotionally cold and his mother, a chronically improvident woman, the source of lifelong embarrassment. For a while in Dublin she ran a school for seamstresses. In later life (before her death, in 1759) she harassed her son – on one occasion, in 1751, from a debtors' jail.

Despite the end of the war in 1714, it was a lively time for the British Army. Sterne was born in Clonmel, Co. Tipperary, and his first ten years were largely passed in temporary quarters in Ireland, wherever his father was next posted. Stability and direction entered Sterne's life at the age of ten when he was sent to live with his wealthy uncle Richard, in Yorkshire. Here he received eight years of excellent school education. His father, whom he had never really known, died in 1731, as his schooldays ended. He had served gallantly in the defence of Gibraltar but engaged himself on a foolish duel with a fellow officer (the argument, bizarrely, was over a goose, according to Laurence), sustaining a serious sword wound which led to his death.

The tender depiction of Tristram Shandy's father (by far the most described character in the novel) and Uncle Toby's 'obscure hurt' may be filial memorials. Laurence's principal bequest from his father – other than a useful surname – was a lifelong nostalgia for a military career he would never have. As Thackeray (a half-admirer) elegantly put it:

> Trim's montero cap, and Le Fevre's sword, and dear Uncle Toby's roquelaure, are doubtless reminiscences of the boy, who had lived with the followers of William and Marlborough, and had beat time with his little feet to the fifes of Ramillies in Dublin barrack-yard, or played with the torn flags and halberds of Malplaquet on the parade-ground at Clonmel.

As an adolescent Sterne already had those feet on the rungs of patronage – a tricky means of ascension at the period, but necessary for those without other advantages than 'friends'. Physically frail, the army was out of the question. The Church was the only gentlemanly alternative – as a career, never a vocation (leave that to religious 'enthusiasts'). In 1733, family connection secured him a place at Jesus College Cambridge as a sizar (a student whose charges were remitted in return for 'fagging' for more advantaged undergraduates). He was supported by the Archbishop Sterne scholarship, endowed in the name of his ancestor who had been Master of the College. At Cambridge he met the fellow Yorkshireman who would be his bosom friend through life, John Hall-Stevenson, 'Eugenius' in *Tristram Shandy*. In later life, Hall-Stevenson's Skelton Hall ('Crazy Castle') would be a second home for Sterne. It was at Cambridge that he suffered his first forecast of early death. He woke one morning to find that a blood vessel had burst in his lungs. 'I bled the bed full,' he observed laconically.

At university, in addition to steeping himself in the philosophy of Locke (the key, to perpetrate a feeble pun, to his novel), Sterne methodically absorbed the ency-clopaedic store of miscellaneous learning which ornaments his later writing. On graduation and ordination family connections with another friendly uncle (Jacques Sterne, a high church dignitary at York) got him, in his mid-twenties, a living at Sutton-on-the-Forest, a village eight miles north of York. He would occasionally preach at the Minster, although his fame in that line was twenty years in the future.

His first public writing was as a pamphleteer, writing in the Whig interest. It got him both liked and disliked (something that never troubled him). He married well in 1741, choosing as his wife Elizabeth Lumley, whose family, like his, was well con-nected with the Yorkshire gentry. The couple had one surviving daughter, Lydia, of whom Sterne was fond, but the marriage, after an idyllic few years, was brought to the point of breakdown (nervous breakdown, that is, on Elizabeth's part) when he was discovered in bed with one of his wife's maids.

Why, in his late forties, Sterne should have embarked on his novel has never been entirely clear. What is clear is that it was a difficult time in his life. The first two books of *Tristram Shandy* were composed in Yorkshire the same year 'under greatest heaviness of heart'. Sterne was pressed for money; his wife, maddened by his sexual delinquencies, had been temporarily committed to an asylum. His own health was poor, as was that of Lydia. The London publisher, Dodsley, to whom he submitted a sample of this speculative work, suggested fairly radical rewriting and something different from the initial Rabelaisian fantasia on encyclopaedism and more 'Cervantick'.

The first two volumes with no great expectation of continuation, were co-published at York and in London in 1759. Sterne himself picked up some of the expense. As sometimes happens, and is usually hard to explain, *The Life and Opinions of Tristram Shandy, Gentleman* took off like a rocket. Sterne helped manipulate its word-of-mouth appeal, but the more likely explanation for its success is that the world, more specifically London, was ready for such a book. The reading public was bored and wanted novelty. If so, *Tristram* fitted the bill. As reprint followed reprint, Dodsley promptly quintupled his offer for two sequel volumes to £250. William Pitt, no less, was recruited as the dedicatee for the third volume – that which sees, at long last, the birth of the hero and the start (it is forlornly predicted) of the narrative.

A literary lion now, Sterne was painted by Sir Joshua Reynolds and enriched his private life with a glamorous London mistress, the young French singer Catherine Fourmantelle ('Jenny' in the books). It was more wormwood for the maddened Mrs Sterne, who can have taken no pleasure in her husband's overnight fame. On the strength of its earnings he was able to live in higher style in his new living at Coxwold, nicknamed 'Shandy Hall'.

Technically what *Tristram Shandy* bequeathed to English fiction was immediacy – 'writing to the moment'. His sign manual is the 'dash' – typically a '5 em' thing which lubricates the frictionless pace of narrative (speeding up one's reading in the process). *Tristram Shandy*, with its expressive typography (super large capitals, different fonts, the creative use of white space and blocked pages) is a tribute to the growing skill of the mid-eighteenth century London printing trade. The fluidity Sterne aimed at was that of speech. 'Writing,' he wrote, 'when properly managed (as you may be sure I think mine is) is but a different name for conversation.'

He did not have long left to converse with the world. While seeing the fifth and sixth volume of *Tristram Shandy* through the press, in 1761, he suffered his worst ever haemorrhage of the lungs. Recuperation in the warm climates of France and Italy was prescribed. Over the next few years these sunny excursions to nowhere in particular would solidify as Sterne's second great book, *A Sentimental Journey through France and Italy, by Mr. Yorick.* Half-travel book, half-egotising, it codified the period's cult of sentimentality – a vein even more lucratively exploited by Oliver Goldsmith in *The Vicar of Wakefield* (1766). Sentimentalism was one of the ways in which Sterne changed the psychology of his age. Whether his sermons (sell-out occasions when he delivered them in fashionable London pulpits) were as efficacious on the morality of his time is doubtful. But they proved another source of income.

And he needed income. A life of grand touring was expensive, and Sterne's style of life at home was now lavish. *Tristram Shandy* was in its ninth volume as his life drew to a close. His last months were consumed by consumption and a passionate late-life love affair with a married woman, Eliza Draper. *The Journal to Eliza* (modelled on Swift's *Journal to Stella*) is his last work, an exercise in stylised 'spiritual adultery'. He was unfaithful to Eliza, though, as to all the women in his life. He died after a trip to London on publishing business in the company of Hall-Stevenson. In a macabre postlude, Sterne's corpse was stolen from its resting place and recognised – just before dismemberment – on a medical school dissection table at Cambridge: the body was reinterred. The skull was then disinterred in the 1960s from the mass grave in which Sterne's remains had been buried and reinterred, yet again in Coxwold. As was observed, it could be seen as payback for all the Yorick jokes Sterne had perpetrated.

Critical opinion about Sterne will forever be divided. A novel which begins with coitus interruptus and features characters called 'Kysarcius' was not designed to please moralists. Samuel Richardson found the work 'gross' – although he granted it was not sexually 'inflaming'. No maidenheads were put at risk by young bucks reading Sterne. F. R. Leavis, while banishing *Tristram Shandy* from the Great Tradition of English fiction, summed up a pervasive line of objection with his stern verdict: 'irresponsible (and nasty) trifling'.

The Victorians in general disliked him. Thackeray (who none the less learned some useful narrative tricks from Tristram) was harsh in his judgement on the unmanliness of Sterne the man: 'he used to blubber perpetually in his study, and finding his tears infectious, and that they brought him a great popularity, he exercised the lucrative gift of weeping; he utilised it, and cried on every occasion. I own that I don't value or respect much the cheap dribble of those fountains.' Critics of a traditional mind find Sterne irritatingly eccentric. Hence Dr Johnson's strikingly wrong prediction to Boswell: 'Nothing odd will do long. *Tristram Shandy* did not last.' In his authoritative study, *The Rise of the Novel*, Ian Watt excludes Sterne on the grounds of his inherent 'negativity'. He is always demonstrating what fiction *can't* do. This negativity is hilariously bemoaned by Tristram in his famous rumination on progression and digression, in Book IV:

> I am this month one whole year older than I was this time twelve-month; and having got, as you perceive, almost into the middle of my third volume [i.e. according to the original editions] – and no farther than to my first day's life –'tis demonstrative that I have three hundred and sixty-four days more life to write just now, than when I first set out.

He is living 364 times faster than he can write. The novel, any novel, is epistemologically impossible. It's like putting a number on eternity.

Negative as his fictional boundary-marking may be, Sterne has become in the twentieth century the darling of theorists. Like Charlie Chaplin in *Modern Times*, his failure defines the strangeness and essential wrongness of machines; even the machines we call novels – and, in so doing, creates not merely comedy (any clown can do that) but English literature's greatest comic novel. Out of its impossibility, perversely.

FN   Laurence Sterne
MRT *Tristram Shandy*
Biog A. H. Cash, *Laurence Sterne*, 2 vols (1975, 1984)

9. Oliver Goldsmith 1728–1774

We read the Vicar of Wakefield in youth and in age – we return to it again and again, and bless the memory of an author who contrives so well to reconcile us to human nature.
Walter Scott

Goldsmith is the despair of biographers. Little of his life is recorded, and that little is largely anecdotal and rendered dubious by his own incorrigible propensity to gilding the lily. 'He was', says his most authoritative biographer 'an inveterate liar.' He published only one novel. Why he even did that is not clear since, despite chronic penury, he did not, apparently, feel inclined to publish it. In fact he proclaimed a scorn for fiction. None the less *The Vicar of Wakefield* has diffused into the mainstream of English fiction. No work was more influential on the novels of the succeeding century.

Goldsmith was the fifth child of an impecunious Anglican clergyman in Co. Longford, Ireland. His father Charles Goldsmith is recorded as being amiable but feckless and is popularly supposed to have had much of the Revd Primrose about him. The family supplemented his curate's stipend with a small farm. Goldsmith offers a nostalgic picture of his childhood environment in the idyllic passages of his poem, 'The Deserted Village' – but it was not all idyll. Aged eight, Oliver contracted smallpox. It 'ravaged the roses off his cheeks' disfiguring him for life. He would grow up stumpy, ill-favoured and awkward in society, with a thick accent. 'Monkey face' was a hurtful insult thrown at him. As Johnson portentously put it: 'Goldsmith was a plant that flowered late. There appeared nothing remarkable about him when he was young.' His first schoolteacher declared him 'impenetrably stupid'. It soon became apparent, however, that he had a remarkably absorptive mind. From priests (the Goldsmiths were relaxed on matters of faith) he picked in his schooldays a command of French which was the admiration of all who knew him. He similarly picked up his virtuosity with the flute – the inseparable partner on his nomadic path through life.

It was his mother, Ann, who insisted he go to Trinity College, Dublin, which he did in 1745. The entrance examination – translation from the classics – caused him no difficulty. But he was obliged to enrol, to his disgust, as a 'sizar' – a student whose fees were remitted in return for acting as a servant to better-off fellows. Goldsmith was a desultory student. He roistered, gambled (a lifelong weakness), and attended the theatre more readily than the classroom. But he also read phenomenally. His father died during his time at Trinity College and his financial support dried up. He sold ballads for money in the streets and cadged – something at which he was adept. He took his degree in 1750.

There were clergymen in the Goldsmith family going back generations and it was logical for him to go into the Church. But at the initial interview he chose to wear scarlet trousers and intimated that the dark clothes of the profession were not to his taste. The story may be apocryphal but his fondness for clothes was not. He spent money he did not have on finery all his life. The tailors of London wept at his death.

Over the next few years Goldsmith was supported by the bounty of a well-off, and well-disposed, uncle, the Revd Thomas Contarine. The young man's first idea was to emigrate to America but, with all his belongings already on board, he missed the boat, having been delayed by 'a jaunt in the country'. His uncle gave him £50 to return to Dublin and study law but he lost 'every shilling' gambling. In 1752 the family, in some desperation, packed him off to study medicine in Edinburgh – Uncle Contarine again footing the bill. At his new university Goldsmith pigged it in lodgings with only his skeleton, his folios and his cat for company – or so he told his family. Ostensibly in pursuit of his medical studies he spent some time in Leyden. Europe, he found, was much to his taste, and over the next year, 1775 ('the lost year'), he undertook a rambling tour which took in France, Switzerland and Italy. He supported himself, it is assumed, by gambling, borrowing and busking.

After this interlude, he took up what would hereafter be lifelong residence in London. He never completed his medical studies, although he practised for a while, awarding himself, if Edinburgh begrudged it, the title 'doctor'. It was a low point in which he contemplated suicide. Instead he drifted to Grub Street, which, some would say, was scarcely preferable. Goldsmith's wide reading, quick wit and ready pen meant that he was in demand. The metropolitan book world was expanding explosively with increased literacy, peace and new copyright regulation.

Goldsmith had a remarkable skill for digesting, summarising and rendering readably attractive the work of heavier writers – particularly the French. His favoured metaphor was that of the bee which sucks up honey from wherever it lands in its random flights. One of the engaging features of Goldsmith is his self-deprecation. He wrote, at this period, a spoof CV: 'Oliver Goldsmith flourished in the eighteenth and nineteenth centuries. He lived to be an hundred and three years old and in that age may justly be styled the sun of literature and the Confucius of Europe.' The Confucius reference is a joke within a joke. Goldsmith's first substantial publication was the papers gathered as *The Citizen of the World* (1761), a supercilious view of British and European society through Chinese eyes. It still reads well.

The book was a hit and Goldsmith was on his way. He became the friend, fellow conversationalist and 'bosom friend' of Dr Johnson, Edmund Burke and Reynolds at their weekly club meetings at the Turk's Head Tavern, in Soho. They (particularly Reynolds) loved 'Noll'; Boswell less so and declared him an 'impudent puppy' after some ineffably rash comments about Shakespeare's lack of 'merit'. On what evidence we have, Goldsmith had little time for fiction. How, one wonders, could the author of a life of Voltaire (whom he may have met and certainly admired) produce a work as ingenuously sentimental as *The Vicar of Wakefield*? How could a man who never troubled to marry (his sexual life is entirely obscure) put his name to this extended eulogy on 'monogamy'?

His biographer, A. Lytton Sells, plausibly sees Goldsmith's fictional Yorkshire vicar as a dart thrown at an actual Yorkshire vicar's current bestseller. Goldsmith pronounced *Tristram Shandy* 'obscene' and its author Sterne (whose sexual delinquencies were common knowledge) a degenerate disgrace to his cloth. The noble Primrose outlines his un-Sterneian philosophy of life in the novel's opening sentences:

> I was ever of opinion that the honest man, who married and brought up a large family, did more service than he who continued single, and only talked of population. From this motive, I had scarce taken orders a year, before I began to think seriously of matrimony, and chose my wife as she did her wedding-gown, not for a fine glossy surface, but such qualities as would wear well.

Mrs Primrose not only wears, but bears well. They have six children ('the off-spring of temperance', Dr Primrose is in haste to assure us). The family lives comfortably off the father's invested wealth; his £35 a year stipend he gives to the poor. Disaster strikes when Primrose's fortune is lost through the malfeasance of a city speculator, who leaves not 'a shilling in the pound' for his investors. Job-like tribulation ensues. Adversity, however, does not destroy but further ennobles the hero and his family. All ends providentially.

The novel's route into print is mysterious. When, in 1862, Goldsmith found himself in more than usual financial distress with his landlady – arrest was in prospect – Johnson dispatched a guinea. When, a little later he called by, he found the guinea had been expended on a bottle of Madeira. Johnson stuck the cork back in the bottle and 'talked to him on the means by which he might be extricated': 'He then told me he had a novel ready for the press, which he produced to me. I looked into it and saw its merit: told the landlady I should soon return; and, having gone to a bookseller, sold it for sixty pounds. I brought Goldsmith the money, and he discharged his rent, not without rating his landlady in a high tone for having used him so ill.' Johnson was a friend in need if not the astutest of literary agents. The sale ranks with Milton's £10 for *Paradise Lost* as one of the worst in literary history. And, oddly, *The Vicar of Wakefield* was not published for a further four years: the delay has never been satisfactorily explained.

Since 1866, Goldsmith's novel has never been out of print. It never brought him a fair reward but his long poem *The Deserted Village* (reprinted five times in its first year, 1770) and the comedy *She Stoops to Conquer* (1772) earned huge sums. He spent even more hugely on himself (he never troubled to relieve the poverty of his mother), and his taste for purple silk underwear raised eyebrows in the Johnson circle, whose famed mascot by the mid-1760s he was. In 1769, the King appointed Goldsmith Professor of Ancient History in the Royal Academy. Luckily it entailed no lectures or any other work. By now, however, years of deadlines and keeping one hop ahead of creditors was catching up with him, and he died of a fever. His last words – in response to his physician's lugubrious enquiry, 'Is your mind at ease?' – were 'No, it is not.'

Goldsmith's funeral was a sorry affair. He left the vast debt of £2,000. Mary Horneck – the girl who, from her fourteenth year, seems to have loved him – requested that his coffin be unnailed so that she could have a lock of his hair. Johnson's verdict was generous: 'Let not his failings be remembered; he was a very great man.'

FN   Oliver Goldsmith
MRT *The Vicar of Wakefield*
Biog A. Lytton Sells, *Oliver Goldsmith: His Life and Works* (1974)

10. Robert Bage 1730–1801

A strong mind, playful fancy, and extensive knowledge are everywhere apparent.
Walter Scott

Two things are routinely said of Bage by those (few) who ever get around to reading him: one is that more people should read him and the other that *Hermsprong* qualifies as the most bizarre title in English literature. Bage, a child of non-conformity, the Industrial Revolution, and provincial self-improvement, was born (the exact date is uncertain) near Derby, the son of a paper maker 'remarkable only for having had four wives', as Walter Scott (a staunch admirer of *Hermsprong*) laconically put it. Robert was the offspring of the first Mrs Bage, who died shortly after her son's birth, making way for the second.

The family may have been Quaker, although the point is disputed. A friend records that by the age of seven Bage made 'such progress in letters, that he was the wonder of the neighbourhood'. Wondrous clever as he might be, his life's course lay in making paper, not writing on it, and he was apprenticed to the family trade. Paper, at the time, was made out of rags. The process was filthy, but required considerable skill. The finished material was subject to complicated excise demands; one of the many taxes on knowledge which Bage – like other self-improved men – loathed.

Aged twenty-one he married – and it was a good match. His wife is recorded as sweet-tempered and well-dowered. Her money enabled him to set up in the paper and cardboard business independently. The couple would have three sons, two of whom survived to go, like their father, into 'trade'. Bage himself was a shrewd tradesman. In his mid-twenties he set up an arrangement with his fellow businessman and lifelong friend, William Hutton, to wholesale paper for distribution via his (Hutton's) Birmingham warehouse. This supplied 'an ample fortune' (£500) for both entrepreneurs. Bage expanded his commercial activity by going into the ironworks business in 1765. One of his new partners was the formidable Enlightenment thinker, Erasmus Darwin. Darwin thought highly of Bage – as did everyone who met him (including, at the end of his life, the even more formidable William Godwin). As his biographer records (working from the scant records): 'Bage continued his self-education, setting aside three hours each afternoon for reading. In his thirties he taught himself French and Italian and travelled to Birmingham once a week to learn mathematics, which he picked up so quickly that within a month he was teaching his teacher.'

He never went to France, but devoured the doctrines of the *philosophes* who were revolutionising the other country. He was, it is recorded, 'of spare habit' and temperate. Everyone had nice things to say about Robert Bage. Even his horses, 'whom he kept till old age' loved him, Hutton recorded. 'Mild' as his temper was, there were radical influences around him from his childhood. In all his surviving writing Bage strenuously opposes the established Church and Britain's unreformed Parliament. His ideas were sharpened by the 'societies' that flourished in this period of the late Enlightenment in provincial towns and cities. A rationalist, he belonged to the Derby Philosophical Society (founded in 1784, by Darwin). He was more loosely connected with the Lunar Society of Birmingham. That, for him, was far afield. He rarely travelled more than a horse-ride from his Derby home and could never bring himself to spend more than a week in London before hurrying away from the hateful place.

Bage would never have written fiction had his business not run into difficulty. In the early 1780s, a slitting mill failed, resulting in a loss of some £1,500. As Hutton records, with the pleasing stiltedness of eighteenth-century essayistic style: 'Fearing the distress of mind would overcome him, he took up the pen to turn the stream of sorrow into that of amusement; a scheme worthy a philosopher.' Money came into it. But novels were not easy money, then or now, and Bage got between £30 and £50 apiece for the six he wrote. He began writing in his early fifties and his fiction-writing career coincided with that historical moment – with revolutions in France and America – when, as Wordsworth said, it was 'bliss' to be alive.

It was not always comfortable, however. Dissenters and supporters of what was happening in France (particularly) came under state suspicion and occasional mob violence. Bage wrote to Hutton (who had been forced to flee his home by supporters of 'King and Church') that 'Since the riots ... my ears have been insulted with the bigotry of 50 years.' His biographer records that in the early 1790s (a low point, with the premature death of one of his sons) Bage may himself have experienced 'harassment', from local 'bigots' and, of course, the ever-rapacious 'Excise'. In these last years he became a 'hermit', although he continued to run his paper-making business virtually until his death.

Bage's first novel, *Mount Henneth*, 'A Practical Utopia' (1782), tells the tale of a select group of like-minded radicals who, little by little, establish a successful community at Henneth Castle in Wales. Like the three novels that followed (*Barham Downs*, 1784; *The Fair Syrian*, 1787; *James Wallace*, 1788) it was epistolary in form. The novels are amateurish but richly quirky. *James Wallace*, for example, contains the first cricket match described in English fiction. *The Fair Syrian* is written against slavery, and may also claim to be something of a first in that line of protest fiction.

It was with his fifth novel, *Man as he is* (1792) that Bage hit his stride. An aristocratic rake's progress, it coheres better than any of its predecessors and tells a better story. Its titular sequel, *Hermsprong; or, Man as he is not* (1796), is by general agreement Bage's masterwork. The narrative opens in sprightly fashion. The narrator, Gregory Glen, is a by-blow of the local squire and proclaims the fact with satirical glee: 'Alas! I am the son of nobody. I was, indeed, begotten by my valiant father, Gregory Grooby, Esq. upon the body of my chaste mother, Ellen Glen.' Like other radicals Bage regarded the bastardy laws of England as barbaric. Glen's main business is to introduce the hero, Hermsprong. He has been brought up, Rousseauistically, by American Indians and lives, comfortably, in France. He is thus the child of two revolutions. He causes consternation in the hidebound circles of English high society (none the less winning himself a noble bride), to whom his ideas are as outlandish as his name – which is universally and comically mispronounced (e.g. 'Hermsprog').

Jacobins loved the novel and it was still possible, if increasingly unpopular, to be starry-eyed about revolutions. William Godwin went out of his way to meet Bage and reported finding the sixty-seven-year-old author of *Hermsprong* 'delightful' and 'youthful in all his carriage'. As the century closed, however, with war against France, idealism faded. Bage's last pronouncement on world affairs, in June 1799, is terminally gloomy:

> Everything looks black and malignant upon me. Men clamouring for wages which I cannot give – women threatening to pull down my mill – rags raised by freight and insurance – excise-officers depriving me of paper! Say, if thou can'st, whether these gentlemen of the excise-office can seize paper after it has left the maker's possession? – after it has been marked? – stamped? – signed with the officer's name? – excise duty paid? – Do they these things? – Am I to hang myself?

There was no need. He died a year later.

FN   Robert Bage
MRT *Hermsprong; or, Man as he is not*
Biog *ODNB* (Gary Kelly)

11. Olaudah Equiano 1745–1797

*I believe it is difficult for those who publish their own memoirs to escape the imputation
of vanity ... it is also their misfortune, that what is uncommon is rarely, if ever, believed.*
Equiano

Equiano, later known as Gustavus Vassa, was born around 1745 in what is now
the Igbo ('Essaka', as he calls it) region of Nigeria. It was then a part of the Abys-
sinian Empire. Equiano's father was, he records, a village elder. He was also a slave-
owner but, his son hastens to add, a very *humane* slave-owner. By his own account,
Equiano was brought up in a condition of rural simplicity, with numerous siblings.
The environment was Edenic: a world away from the invasions, wars and revolutions which were upheaving Europe, the Indian subcontinent, and North America
during the second half of the eighteenth century. Equiano's childhood environment
was a place, as he describes (in his stilted high Augustan prose):

> where nature is prodigal of her favours, our wants are few and easily supplied;
> of course we have few manufactures. They consist for the most part of calicoes,
> earthern ware, ornaments, and instruments of war and husbandry. But these
> make no part of our commerce, the principal articles of which, as I have observed,
> are provisions. In such a state money is of little use.

He stresses the village's high standards of virtue, cleanliness, abstemiousness
and moral decency, contradicting the image of savagery that one finds, for example,
in *Robinson Crusoe*. There is nothing in Equiano's account of his Igbo/Essaka
upbringing to contradict the slogan on the abolitionist medal: 'Am I not a man and
a brother?' Equiano's account in fact makes the Igbo even nobler than the whites
who presume to ask that question.

Aged around eleven years, Equiano lost his African paradise. He was kidnapped
while playing innocently with his sister, and carried off to slavery. Initially, like his
father's slaves, his masters were African, but then he was sold on to the traders at
the coast. Here he first came into contact with white people. It inspires one of the
more vivid sections in the narrative. They strike him as monsters, as he is thrown
into the cargo vessel which will carry him away to the New World. These pale devils,
with their 'red faces and loose hair' must be cannibals, he assumes: they will eat
him. He faints with shock, horror, fear and despair – and, as he disgustedly recalls,
the stench ('the salutation to my nostrils').

The description of the middle passage is the most affecting, and horrifying (and
the most 'interesting') in Equiano's later published *Interesting Narrative*. His later
career, vivid as it is on the page, can be briefly summarised. Sold on a number of

times, he was transported to Barbados, where he was judged too physically slight for field labour in the sugar plantations. He eventually found himself in the colony of Virginia, where he was bought by a Royal Navy officer, renamed Gustavus Vassa, and – as a personal valet – humanely treated.

Equiano endeared himself by loyal service both to his master and, as a sailor on board ship, to the Crown – in acknowledgement of which, in England, he was, while still a teenager, sent to school to learn how to read and write. Equiano also became a devout Christian, persuading his master to let him be baptised, in 1759 – so that he might go to heaven with the white folk. He might be free up there, but not, for a few years yet, down here. Poor 'Gustavus' was sold on again. He was now a valuable property – a literate, numerate, well-spoken slave. As such he was eventually bought by a Quaker merchant in Philadelphia and put to work as an inventory clerk, on a tiny salary. Equiano eventually saved up the £40 required to buy his freedom.

After manumission, he prudently took up residence in England and went into trade himself for a few years (including 'black gold', or slaves) before allying himself with the British abolitionist movement, whose figurehead he became. He gave heart-rending speeches, preached, and married an Englishwoman. In 1789, with the help of noble patrons, he published *The Interesting Narrative of the Life of Olaudah Equiano, or Gustavus Vassa, the African.* The last phase of Equiano's life was, evidently, happy, but is largely unrecorded. There were two daughters from his marriage; his wife died in 1796 and he followed her a year later, aged (probably) fifty-two. It is not known where he was buried – although he left a sizeable amount to his daughters.

Equiano's interesting narrative was widely circulated in the abolition movement, as eyewitness evidence of the realities of slavery. It was everywhere taken to be autobiography: gospel truth. Equiano was 'the black Ben Franklin'. And so it was accepted for centuries. But a few years ago, scholars – notably Vincent Carretta – found convincing evidence (specifically a baptismal certificate and a ship's muster roll) that Equiano had been born in South Carolina. He was American.

This, if true (and it seems, currently, incontrovertible), means that the most vivid African and slave ship sections of the book – its heart – must be invention, fictional. It does not mean, of course, that the narrative is any less interesting, any more than Lord Jim's experiences in the Indian Ocean are less interesting than Joseph Conrad's in the same waters. But it does mean that what we have is not a memoir but a novel. One can compromise, and label it the first docunovel in English literature – or (given the South Carolina birthplace), American literature.

FN   Olaudah Equiano (renamed Gustavus Vassa)
MRT *The Interesting Narrative of the Life of Olaudah Equiano*
Biog V. Carretta, *Equiano the African: Biography of a Self-Made Man* (2005)

12. Fanny Burney 1752–1840

*'And what are you reading, Miss—?' 'Oh! It is only a novel!' replies the young lady;
while she lays down her book with affected indifference, or momentary shame. 'It is
only Cecilia, or Camilla, or Belinda'; or, in short, only some work in which the greatest
powers of the mind are displayed, in which the most thorough knowledge of human
nature, the happiest delineation of its varieties, the liveliest effusions of wit and humour,
are conveyed to the world in the best chosen language.'* Jane Austen's defence of her craft,
via Fanny Burney, in *Northanger Abbey*

Frances (Fanny) Burney was born in King's Lynn, the third of six children of the
parish organist. Of humble Scottish extraction, her father dropped the shameful
prefix to his birth name, MacBurney. Her mother had French blood, and could
claim slightly higher breeding, if, with it, a taint of Catholic incense. Fanny's father,
Charles, was – as his later career proved – much more than a provincial instrumentalist. He could claim at the time of his death to be the country's major musicologist
(although the term would have struck him as barbarous). His career was crowned
with the award of an honorary doctorate from Oxford in 1769.

Her father was by far the most important figure in his daughter's long life. Her
first published novel, *Evelina*, opens with a filial ode of devotion to 'Dr Burney':

> *Oh Author of my being! – far more dear*
> *To me than light, than nourishment, or rest,*
> *Hygeia's blessings, Rapture's burning tear,*
> *Or the life blood that mantles in my breast!*

In the decades after her popularity as a novelist had passed, she dedicated
herself to her father's biography. *Memoirs of Dr Burney* was released to a world that
had forgotten both of them in 1832. To him, to herself, and to her contemporaries
(including, even Dr Johnson) she was 'Fanny' ('Fannikin' to close family friends).
Under protest from feminist critics 'Frances' is nowadays preferred. She joins Elizabeth Gaskell and Mary Arnold Ward as one of the posthumously rechristened.

In 1760 the family moved to Soho, London, the bustling artistic heart of London
where Burney made his way as a music teacher. His skill, learning and ingratiating
manner made him welcome in drawing rooms as a guest and performer. There was
never much money, but – given the age's Hanoverian passion for *Hausmusik* – his
genius fostered an unusual social mobility. The Burneys' rise in the world is marked
by progressively more fashionable London addresses. A summit in the family fortunes was reached with membership of Samuel Johnson and Hester Thrale's circle,

in the Great Cham's last years. Burney's 'Streatham Journal' (1779–83), containing what Virginia Woolf calls her 'gnat-eyed' observations of the Thrale household, offers a snapshot of Johnson's domestic character – much less 'Johnsonian' than the Boswellian portraiture. He had a particular tenderness for his little 'Evelina', as he was pleased, jokingly, to call her.

Exhausted by child-bearing, Frances's mother had died in 1762. The sisters in the family were largely self-educated and after the loss of their mother they were drawn into a close-knit nucleus, exchanging letters, sharing journals, keeping diaries. We know more about Burney's milieu than about any other writer of the period. Frances began 'scribbling' for her own and her sisters' entertainment very early. She did not inherit (as did her sisters Hetty and Susanna) her father's musical ability and was slightly the less favoured for it. They were sent to Paris to be finished and her brother went to Cambridge, while she was kept at home. But by way of compensation there was plenty of raw material for a future novelist. As Burney's biographer Kate Chisholm notes: 'The novels that Fanny was later to write are sometimes accused of being too full of dramatic incident to be credible, but within the family there were three elopements, innumerable affairs, disappearing children, and a possibly incestuous relationship.' Her brother Charles was one of the most successful bibliophile-kleptomaniacs in English literary history (his memorial is the magnificent Burney collection of early newspapers, now in the British Library) and he advised her on literary matters.

On her father's remarrying, in 1767, a woman whom the girls considered unsuitably crass (the widow of a prosperous King's Lynn wine merchant) Fanny burned her already sizeable *oeuvre* in a 'grand firework of destruction'. At the same time she began keeping a journal which survives as one of her most interesting compositions. It opens with an apostrophe to 'Miss Nobody', in which she promises to record 'my every thought'. One thinks more than one writes and Burney's private memorials, some twenty printed volumes, massively outweigh her four novels (long as they are) and eight surviving plays. Only one of the latter was ever performed, *Edwy and Elgiva*, and it closed after one night. Her most interesting drama, *The Witlings*, a satire on bluestockings, was suppressed by order of her father and her other 'daddy', the man of letters and friend of the family, Samuel Crisp.

Fanny's sisters married and mis-married at the appropriate young age; Frances did not. In Jane Austen's cruelly complected universe, an unmarried maiden's 'bloom' is passed by the age of twenty-five (Anne Elliot is on the very brink of fading). Bloomless she might be but by her mid-twenties Fanny Burney was flourishing as a writer. In 1778, aged twenty-six, she published her first voluminous novel, *Evelina*. Epistolary in form and sub-Richardsonian in tone, it was subtitled 'A Young Lady's

Entrance into the World' – that 'world' being the *monde*, not the Hogarthian street scenes she must have seen from her Soho windows as a child.

Despite the poem at its head, *Evelina* was published without her father's knowledge or permission. The author's own susceptibility as a 'Young Lady' in a man's world is confirmed by her parting with the manuscript of what would be her most popular work for a measly £20. Evelina made a fortune for everyone but her creator. The novel opens with a fighting Preface, in which Burney masquerades as a male author, defending 'the humble Novelist'. Like all her fiction, *Evelina* is a courtship novel which assumes, as its starting point, that women have just one area of freedom in their lives – the right to decide, by acceptance or rejection, who they will marry.

The success of her first novel inspired a successor, *Cecilia: Or the Memoirs of an Heiress* (1782). The plot pivots on the plight of an orphaned heiress whose marriage chances are complicated by the requirement that her husband, whoever he may be, must sacrifice his manly privileges by taking on her surname. Although no heiress by this time Frances had herself turned down at least one offer of marriage. Her wilful spinsterdom was becoming something of an embarrassment. In 1786 family connections acquired for her a position at the royal court as Second Keeper of the Robes to Queen Charlotte (wife to the mad George III). She loathed the work and wilted in it. She contrived to retire, on health grounds, in 1791, with a lifelong £100 pension.

Burney saw her literary future, at this point, as a dramatist. Her guardians disapproved of women being associated with the delinquencies of Drury Lane and it was a generally unsettled period of her life. It was not made any more settled when, at the age of forty-one, in 1793, she married irregularly, after a secret courtship. Her husband was a penniless French aristocrat, Alexandre d'Arblay, a 'constitutionalist' – a radical conservative in a complicated relationship with the Revolution but ultimately obliged to flee for his life. The marriage was serially solemnised by both Protestant and Catholic ritual. Neither ceremony had the Burney family's approval. One child, Alexander, was born in 1794. D'Arblay, an artillery officer, was unable to pursue his profession in England (an Aliens Act was passed in January 1794, prohibiting refugees like him from joining the British army), so Frances buckled to with another novel, with which to make a home for them.

She began serious work on her *grand ouvrage* in August 1794, while still the newest of mothers. The book which emerged was *Camilla, or A Picture of Youth*, published in 1796. Burney was resolved that this time she would not be cheated by publishers and *Camilla* went on to be the occasion of the most successful literary marketing operation in fiction of the decade. At a period when the routine payment to author for a circulating library romance could be as low as £10, Burney would make from this one work the fabulous sum of £2,000. It helped that it was dedicated, by royal permission, to Queen Charlotte. That was not the only big name helping the novel on its way. Together with her husband, Fanny set up a public 'subscription' for the new work. Jane Austen and Edmund Burke were listed among the signatories. Her brother, the light-fingered Charles, sold the copyright (women and Frenchmen had no legal standing) after tendering for bids in March 1796 to a syndicate of publishers, headed by Thomas Payne and Cadell and Davies. They paid an upfront £1,000.

The five-volume, duodecimo sets were marketed (principally for circulating libraries) at a guinea apiece. After only three months, Burney reported to a friend that 'The sale has been one of the most rapid ever known for a Guinea book ... Of the First edition containing the immense quantity of 4000, 500 only remain.' She built a home, Camilla Cottage, on the earnings. A fictionalised biography of the Burney family, *Camilla* chronicles the group story of the Tyrolds, covering twenty years during which the children grow to moral maturity, exhibiting their latent qualities and the effect of the moral instruction of their excellent parent, the Revd Augustus Tyrold. The family resides in Hampshire and there is a charming opening section in which the Tyrolds are taken up by their eccentric and wealthy uncle, Sir Hugh. Playing high-spirited games with little Eugenia Tyrold, this gentleman accidentally lames his niece for life. In an agony of remorse, Sir Hugh makes Eugenia his principal heiress, thus blighting Camilla's marriage prospects. The plot gets very complicated thereafter.

So did life get complicated. With Napoleon's accession, the d'Arblays returned to France, but the family were then stranded on the outbreak of war with England. In September 1811, still stranded in Paris, Frances, aged fifty-nine, underwent a mastectomy without anaesthetic. She recorded the operation in a letter to her sister Esther. It has become (thanks to circulation on the web) her best-known piece of writing for modern readers and has a violent accuracy found nowhere in her fiction.

> I then felt the Knife tackling against the breast bone – scraping it! – This performed, while I yet remained in utterly speechless torture, I heard the Voice of Mr Larry, – (all others guarded a dead silence) in a tone nearly tragic, desire everyone present to pronounce if anything more remained to be done; The general voice was Yes, – but the finger of Mr Dubois – which I literally felt elevated over the wound, though I saw nothing, & though he touched nothing, so indescribably sensitive was the spot – pointed to some further requisition – & again began the scraping! – and, after this, Dr Moreau thought he discerned a peccant attom – and still, & still, M. Dubois demanded attom after attom.

The d'Arblays finally managed to return to England in 1812. The next few years were a time of upheaval with the never-ending war, and the constant fear that their son Alexander would be conscripted into it – on which side was not entirely clear. Prudently he was shuttled into the Anglican Church.

Burney's career as a novelist effectively ended with the all too aptly entitled *The Wanderer; or, Female Difficulties* in 1814. The taste was now for the national tales of Scott, Edgeworth and Maturin. Her last years were passed in Bath in retirement, supported by a queen who was long dead. Her last serious publication was the life of her father, who had died in 1814. Her husband died in 1818 and their son (now a clergyman) predeceased her, from influenza, in 1837. She, now a forgotten and lonely author, lived on until her eighty-eighth year, her old age a testament to the skilled surgeons of Paris.

FN   Frances Burney ('Fanny'; later d'Arblay)
MRT *Camilla, or A Picture of Youth*
Biog C. Harman, *Fanny Burney: A Biography* (2000)

13. Susanna Haswell (Rowson) 1762–1824

Instructress to the young and thoughtless of the fair sex.

The woman bearing the title of America's first novelist was born in Portsmouth, England, where her father worked for the British Navy. Her mother died on Susanna's birth, and her father promptly remarried. In 1767 Lieutenant Haswell was assigned to custom duties in Massachusetts. It was a hot time on the Eastern Seaboard for those with any connection with the hated British 'taxes'. During the American Revolution Haswell was taken prisoner, but allowed to return with his family, on grounds of ill-health, to London in 1778. In all this upheaval Susanna received little schooling – but read widely and saw more of the world than most young women. She showed early talent for singing, and performed publicly from her teenage years. She also earned an honest penny as a governess in her late teens – writing all the while.

Susanna's first novel, *Victoria*, was published in 1786. The heroine of the title is the daughter of a deceased naval officer who is tricked into a sham marriage only to die mad, pregnant and abandoned. Like her later fiction it shows the strong influence of Richardson's *Clarissa*. The bitter theme of abused womanhood recurs through Haswell's fiction. There followed *The Inquisitor* (1788), a bundle of tales displaying the Laurence Sterne-like 'sentimentalism' which was to be her later stock-in-trade. In the same year Miss Haswell married William Rowson. One knows nothing about him other than that he ran a hardware shop (unsuccessfully), played the trumpet (well – thanks to having being trained in the Horse Guards military band), and drank (excessively). Rowson proved to be dissolute and improvident and the responsibility for earning bread for the family table was thrown on his novelist wife. Her career was helped by the fact that the Rowsons had no children to burden her.

Mary,or, The Test of Honour (1789) features a Crusoeish heroine who is cast adrift with her lover en route to Jamaica. They conduct themselves with impeccable virtue on the desert island where they are cast up. *Mentoria, or, The Young Ladies' Friend* was published in 1791 and, in the same year, there took place the unspectacular first publication of *Charlotte [Temple]: A Tale of Truth*, in London. *Rebecca, or, The Fille de Chambre* came out a year later in 1792. In 1793 William's hardware business failed and the Rowsons, man and wife, took to the stage – she as an actress and singer; he as an instrumentalist. While on the boards, Susanna wrote plays with provocative titles, such as: *Americans in England* (1796). Their company toured in America in the early 1790s and the couple stayed on in the country. Susanna, despite her girl-hood persecutions, became an enthusiastic 'Patriot'. It was in Philadelphia that she arranged, momentously, for the republication of *Charlotte Temple: A Tale of Truth* in 1794. The novel was taken on by Matthew Carey, laying the first foundations of what would be one of America's dominant publishing houses, Carey & Lea.

The subsequent 'Charlotte cult' was slow in taking off. The novel had been still-born in England and made no immediate impression in America. There were only three editions by Carey before 1800. But, at the turn of the century the novel had established itself as a year-in year-out seller, particularly when cheap editions became available. By 1815, the publisher had cleared some 50,000 copies and in its first hundred years, under various imprints, *Charlotte Temple* went through 200 editions. Charlotte's popularity with American readers was unchallenged until Uncle Tom swept her out of the way in 1852.

The novel's 'true tale' subtitle persuaded many readers that there was an original 'Charlotte'. A grave in New York was fancifully located and became a place of feminine pilgrimage. There were innumerable stage dramatisations and, later, silent film versions. Tens of thousands of baby girls were named 'Charlotte', in honour of Rowson's saintly heroine. What was it about the novel that made it so manically popular in America? Its suitability for women readers – the new, post-Revolution, mass audience for fiction – was partly responsible. The opening sentence roundly declares that the book is intended 'for the perusal of the young and thoughtless of the fair sex'. You must, of course, buy before you can peruse. Dollars for Mr Carey, cents for Mrs Rowson.

The heroine (the granddaughter of a nobleman) is first encountered as a fifteen-year-old at boarding school in England. Young Charlotte is led astray by her French teacher, Mlle La Rue – a Catholic and (largely for that reason) a loose woman. At La Rue's corrupt persuasion, Charlotte allows herself to fall in love with an English army lieutenant, Montraville. She elopes with him (he promises her, falsely, that 'Hymen shall sanctify our love'). They take up residence in New York. There, misled by a brother officer, Belcour, who secretly wants to make Charlotte his mistress – Montraville redirects his affections to a wealthy heiress, Julia Franklin. Pregnant, unmarried, abandoned, crazed and wandering the snowy streets of New York, Charlotte is spurned by the former Mlle La Rue who, fortuitously, is also in America, and now the wealthy and haughty Mrs Crayton. Charlotte is found, dying, by her father, who arrives just in time to give her his forgiveness on her deathbed. Mr Temple adopts the surviving baby (the 'innocent witness to her guilt'), but resolutely declines to forgive Montraville, who makes amends by killing Belcour in a duel. La Rue/Crayton dies in richly-deserved destitution. Montraville is left to the ceaseless torments of his own guilty conscience.

In 1796, buoyed up by Susanna's literary earnings, the Rowsons settled in Boston. She retired from the stage and opened her 'Young Ladies' Academy' in 1797, writing instructive books for the juvenile female reader until her death. Those later years were rendered wretched by William's incorrigible drinking, wastefulness and infidelities (nobly, the childless Susanna took on maternal care of her husband's bastard child). She wrote a sequel to her great hit, *Charlotte's Daughter, or, The Three Orphans*, usually known by the heroine's name, *Lucy Temple* (in the narrative Charlotte's illegitimate daughter is actually named 'Lucy Blakeney'). A tale of incest narrowly avoided, it was published, posthumously, in 1828. In a remarkably active lifetime Susanna wrote ten novels, six works for the theatre, two volumes of poetry and six instructional books for young ladies. And, of course, America's first best-seller, a hundred years before the term was invented.

FN   Susanna Rowson (née Haswell)
MRT *Charlotte Temple: A Tale of Truth*
Biog P. L. Parker, *Susanna Rowson* (1986)

14. Mrs (Ann) Radcliffe 1764–1823

Ah, woe is me that the glory of novels should ever decay; that dust should gather round them on the shelves; that the annual cheques from Messieurs the publishers should dwinde, dwindle! Inquire at Mudie's, or the London Library, who asks for the Mysteries of Udolpho *now?* Thackeray, writing in 1862

Thackeray was both right and wrong. For most modern readers, the author of *The Mysteries of Udolpho* has been laughed into extinction by the author of a much better novel. If they have ever met at E. M. Forster's imagined round table of novelists in the sky, Mrs Radcliffe could, at least, have pointed out that her novel got £500, whereas *Northanger Abbey* yielded smart Miss Austen a mere tenner. Radcliffe's initial payment (royalties followed) pro-rates as hundreds of thousands nowadays. So much for satire. Moreover Radcliffe, unlike the parson's daughter (who had to use her brother), had a husband to sign her contracts (women had no legal identity at the period).

Whatever the mysteries of Udolpho, those swirling around Ann Ward Radcliffe are quite as impenetrable. What posterity knows about her is dependent on one not very reliable obituary. Her life, writes a contemporary biographer, resembles one of those torn, barely decipherable manuscripts beloved by her and her Gothic disciples. No portrait of Radcliffe survives, although a few personal recollections rhapsodise on her daintiness and prettiness. She was the daughter and only child of a London haberdasher, based in Holborn, who subsequently, in 1770, set up a prosperous emporium for Wedgwood ceramics in Bath (a town which, unlike Austen, Radcliffe never mentions and, it is plausibly supposed, did not like). Ann's parents were well on in years at the time of her birth. Nominally Anglican, they may have had leanings towards Unitarianism. Her family, on both sides, had roots in the north-west and – despite the connection with 'trade' – boasted high literary connections (as, indeed, did the Wedgwoods). As a young girl, shy, mute, unnoticed, 'Nancy' (as she was nicknamed) found herself in the presence of 'several persons of distinction, particularly in literature'. They included Mrs Piozzi (Johnson's domestic biographer) and the formidably evangelical Hannah More.

The Wards also had 'superior relatives' in the Church and in medicine (one, very superior, was a physician to George III). Ann stayed with them during her childhood and picked up necessary social cultivation. Largely home-educated, she had no foreign or classical languages, but an excellent written command of English. In 1788, aged twenty-three, she married a lawyer turned journalist, William Radcliffe. He eventually made himself proprietor-editor of the *English Chronicle* in Bath, a successful paper. It, like its editor, was 'democratically inclined', but not radical. The Radcliffes would have a long, fond, but childless, marriage and it is assumed William encouraged her writing (particularly her poetry).

Radcliffe's fiction took its primal inspiration from *The Old English Baron* (1778), a proto-Gothic novel, by Clara Reeve. Reeve saw the future of English fiction as 'romance' not 'realism'. She was wrong, but for a few decades 'Gothic' (the 'domestic' variety, headed by Radcliffe, and the 'terrible' variety, led by 'Monk' Lewis) flourished. The war with the French put a cramp on tourism, whether 'grand' or humble, and created a compensatory vogue for novels with foreign or otherwise interesting settings. The English reader's mind could travel, if one's feet could not. Radcliffe's first published fiction, *The Castles of Athlin and Dunbayne* (1789) is touristic, and has a male hero, Osbert. Radcliffe's later novels would centre on heroines and go further afield. Her first work, unlike its successors, was published anonymously.

The Castles of Athlin and Dunbayne has features to be found in all the author's novels. She was fascinated by the disruption of the Reformation, the sinister persistence of Catholicism, the threats of secular European rationalism and, above all, by canons of beauty as epitomised in Burke's advocacy of the Longinian sublime and James Thomson's meditative poetry. One object, above all, crystallised this melange for her – the ruined English abbey or castle. Ann and her husband made tireless excursions to such sombre relics of past historical upheaval: history lessons in stone.

From the first, and increasingly, her fiction appealed to young women readers – a growing and powerful market at this period. The name 'Ann Radcliffe' featured on the title-page as a powerful selling point. Her multi-volume novels were, of course, circulating library wares (they were too expensive to be bought by individual readers). Radcliffe's pace and lightness of touch in narration was accompanied by an unashamed indifference to historical and topographical 'fact'. The depictions of Italy, which feature in *A Sicilian Romance* (1790), her second novel, are as fanciful as Ray Bradbury's Mars. Readers of the period were indulgent about such laxities: as Walter Scott said, when challenged that he had never seen the Alps that feature majestically in *Anne of Geierstein*, 'I have seen the paintings of Salvator Rosa.'

Radcliffe's fourth novel, and her best, *The Mysteries of Udolpho* – 'A Romance, Interspersed with some Pieces of Poetry' – earned her a whopping advance of £500: equivalent to roughly £300,000 in modern currency. It cost £1 as a new four-volume set in 1794. *Udolpho* went through three editions in its first year. Its runaway sales warranted an increase in the advance to £800 for *The Italian*, three years later. These sums are put in perspective by the £10 which the Minerva Press, catering to the young female market, customarily paid its luckless hacks. In the 1790s, William Radcliffe was earning under £300 p.a. – a very respectable salary.

Although it laid the ground for the 'horrid' excesses of later Gothic fiction (as superheated by 'Monk' Lewis), *Udolpho* is an unswervingly moralistic novel advocating 'fortitude' and disparaging, by tragic example, 'indulgence'. The story is set in Gascony in 1584. Monsieur St Aubert, an impoverished and widowed nobleman, has retired to his estate where he consoles himself with philosophy. He has a beautiful daughter Emily, whose upbringing he has personally taken in hand. 'All excess is vicious,' he sagely instructs her. St Aubert falls ill and is advised to recover his health by the sea. On their journey, father and daughter fall in with Valancourt, an ardent young chevalier who nobly forgives being accidentally shot by Emily's trigger-happy father. When she is orphaned, she is consigned to the care of a worldly aunt, Madame Cheron, at Toulouse. The aunt turns away the worthy Valancourt, and tries unsuccessfully to marry off Emily to mercenary suitors.

For her part, Mme Cheron is flattered into marriage by a sinister Italian, Signor Montoni. He transports the two ladies off to his sinister lair in the Apennines, the *castillo di Udolpho*, whose rocky setting is thrillingly described. Having discovered, to his rage, that his wife has brought him no fortune, Montoni kills her. Emily, meanwhile, has been subjected to a barrage of apparently supernatural phenomena and is dumbstruck by the discovery of some utterly horrid *thing* that is hidden behind a veil of black silk in a locked room in the castle. The plot gets convoluted beyond the power of summary and ends with virtue rewarded, vice punished, and the thing behind the veil revealed (rather anti-climactically) as a wax dummy.

The Italian (1797) opens, elegantly, with a group of English tourists in Naples in 1764, who accidentally come across the tale of lurid events that took place six years earlier. Vincentio di Vivaldi, the only son of a proud Marchesa, falls in love with Ellena Rosalba, whose origins are unknown. The Marchesa, aided by her confessor, Schedoni, sets out to foil the match. 'His', we are told, 'was not the melancholy of a sensible and wounded heart, but apparently that of a gloomy and ferocious disposition.' Things thereafter get very gloomy and ferocious. It culminates with Schedoni about to murder Ellena, only to discover, from a nearby portrait, that she is his own daughter. He goes on to poison himself.

'The great enchantress', as De Quincey called her, published five novels. Then, having recruited the largest readership in the history of English fiction, and vast sums, she stopped, with twenty-six years of life left. Why the long silence? No one knows. Some surmised that 'she chose to retire from the stage in the very blaze of her fame' – at the top of her game. Others assumed that she was confined in a lunatic asylum, her mind shattered by the Gothic intoxication of her own fiction. All things considered, a stifling excess of gentility and natural reticence seems to have been the real reason for her giving up fiction. As her memorialist, Thomas Noon

Talfourd recalls that 'personal character' meant more to her than 'literary fame ... the very thought of appearing in person as the author of her romances shocked the delicacy of her mind'. Her husband, it is supposed, may have 'restrained' her. She died, it is known, of asthma which had probably disabled her last decades.

Radcliffe enjoyed a revival in the second half of the twentieth century. Her oppressed heroines were read as victims, *avant la lettre*, of the 'feminine mystique'. Trapped in their castles, abbeys and towers by villainous men they were precursors of the middle-class housewife trapped in her suburban kitchen. Jane Austen, her deadliest critic, merely found her fun – and fun to make fun of.

FN   Ann Radcliffe (née Ward)
MRT   *The Mysteries of Udolpho*
Biog   R. Norton, *Mistress of Udolpho: The Life of Ann Radcliffe* (1999)

15. James Hogg 1770–1835

He was a man of contradictions. Karl Miller

He was undoubtedly a man of original genius, but of coarse manners and low and offensive opinions. William Wordsworth

James Hogg was a novelist who wrote a novel so extraordinary that, as with Emily Brontë, it has stretched credulity that James Hogg wrote it. He was born a peasant. In his last years he nursed the not unreasonable hope that George IV (a lover of all things Scottish, after his bekilted 1822 state 'jaunt' to Edinburgh) might knight him. He wasn't, alas, ennobled and died in poverty with a modest reputation, already fading. He had been born in poverty in Selkirkshire, the second son of a sheep-farmer who was plunged into bankruptcy when Jamie was six years old. Ettrick was, at that period, an inaccessible region, although not that far, as the crow flew, from Edinburgh. Crows, however, had it easier than people, who had to lumber along rutted drovers' paths.

'Jamie the Poeter', as his rustic neighbours nicknamed him, spent only two three-month periods at school. He graduated, as he touchingly records, into the class that read the Bible. Paradoxically this deprivation was – in later life – a career asset. The Romantics glorified 'unspoiled' peasants. Hogg, as pictured by his contemporaries, was *Lyrical Ballads* incarnate, Rousseauism in muddy breeches. His head was stuffed with folklore and balladry and, like Robert Burns, his adult tongue handled dialect as fluently as King's English. Following the example of other untutored geniuses, he taught himself to read from odd books that came his way in intervals of cattle-herding. He learned to play the fiddle the same way. Edinburgh – the Athens of the North – was the European home of reason. But the devil (as evident, most famously, in Burns's 'Tam o' Shanter') still roamed the Borders wilderness – or, more properly, belief in the devil did. The Prince of Darkness appears in Hogg's later fiction as a convincingly actual personage.

As a child, Jamie was often, as he recalled, ill-treated, always hungry and ill-clothed. He had, as he reckoned, fifteen masters, none kind to him, before the age of eighteen. In 1790 Hogg, now a man, had the good luck to be employed as a shepherd by a cousin of his aged mother, Margaret. It was this family, the Laidlaws, persons of higher than normal rural cultivation, who improved Hogg's mind. They it was who introduced him to Allan Ramsay's kitsch Scots pastoral, *The Gentle Shepherd*. It was formative and Hogg went on to publish his *Scottish Pastorals* in 1801. The book came and went unregarded. If the Ettrick Shepherd were to make his way in literary Edinburgh, he needed patrons willing to promote him. In the meantime, helped on by the Laidlaws, he graduated to managing small border farms. He was always regarded by fellow farmers as a skilled shepherd (he wrote a manual late in life on the subject, a much more difficult craft than the Romantic poets and literary pastoralists liked to fantasise).

Long convinced of his genius, Hogg had been impatiently awaiting discovery for some years before his first patron, Walter Scott (six years his junior), took an interest in him. Scott was, as the century turned, not yet the author of *Waverley* but a Writer to the Signet (i.e. lawyer) with a life sinecure as Sheriff-Depute at Selkirk. He was, more avidly, a collector of border ballads. The ancient folk-art was dying out and urgently needed memorials. Antiquarians like Scott, Joseph Ritson and Bishop Percy set themselves to the task – typically quarrelling between themselves bitterly. In summer 1802 Scott had learned through his land agent, William Laidlaw, a relative of Hogg's employers, that there was an aged balladeer in the Borders, who had, in her head, a complete version of a piece Scott particularly lusted after, 'Auld Maitland'. This source was Hogg's mother, Margaret.

According to Hogg's version (his most recent biographer offers a much duller scenario), Scott duly galloped, neck and crop, to 'Ettrick's bleakest, loneliest sheil' to hear Mrs Hogg sing (she despised recitation). She crooned out a suspiciously word-perfect version of the 65-stanza 'Auld Maitland', hitherto known to Scott only in tantalising fragments. As with everything surrounding Hogg's life (he confessed to being an incorrigible falsifier), there is the likelihood of stage-management. Hogg, not to mince words, primed his mother and wrote her script. Scott had his doubts but he wanted the ballad so much for the third volume of his *Minstrelsy of the Scottish Border* that he swallowed Hogg's bait, hook line and sinker.

More significantly, Scott recruited Hogg into his Edinburgh circle as a 'brother poet', introducing him 'under the garb, aspect, and bearing of a rude peasant'. The Ettrick Shepherd was a role Jamie was happy to play and it gave lustre to his 1807 verse collection, *The Mountain Bard*. It was a fortuitous change of profession. His farming ventures had failed and he was bankrupt. He had at least one, perhaps two, illegitimate children and had been hailed up for 'uncleanness' by his local church. His native hills were becoming rather too hot for comfort. He moved to Edinburgh to make his way as a 'literary man' – and was taken up by the literary men of the Blackwood's coterie and (after its launch in 1817) by their lively monthly magazine (nicknamed '*Maga*'). In the long-running, often scurrilous, tavern-conversation series, 'Noctes Ambrosianae', Hogg ('the shepherd') figures as a kind of Wamba, or jester figure to J. G. Lockhart (Scott's son-in-law) and Christopher North (a university professor). Hogg's interjections are in salty dialect.

Over these years, Hogg was best known to his contemporaries as a poet, an anthologist and a local curiosity. His material wants were helped when Scott's patron, the Duke of Buccleuch, gave him the freehold of a lakeside cottage, by Altrive at Yarrow, where he would live until the end of his life. With the runaway triumph of the *Waverley* novels, and the less spectacular but substantial success of John Galt, prose fiction was now a respectable line of writing in Edinburgh. Hogg's first significant venture into the field, *The Brownie of Bodsbeck*, was published in 1818. It is set in the seventeenth century, shortly after one of the uprisings which would unsettle Scotland for a century. The Covenanters – religious reformers whose enthusiasm took on revolutionary fervour – had been savagely put down at the Battle of Bothwell Bridge, in 1679. There ensued the purge called 'the killing times'.

Hogg's hero, Walter, exonerated after much distress from his association with the insurgents, returns to his rural home. This is where most novels would wrap things up. But peeking through a window, Walter sees his true love, Katharine, in bed with a reanimated corpse. The denouement becomes increasingly gothic. Hogg's fairies ('brownies') have nothing in common with Peter Pan. One of them castrates a foiled rapist in the narrative: his publishers rather balked at the scene.

In 1820 Hogg married. Hitherto, his friends said, he would do anything for a woman except propose to her. His bride, Margaret Phillips, was more religiously devout than him, considerably younger, and the daughter of a prosperous Dunfermline farmer. The Hoggs would have five children and the marriage is recorded as happy. His finances, however, continued to be rocky; if, as Carlyle said of Scott, that he wrote novels to buy farms, Hogg did the same: fewer novels and smaller farms but just as unluckily. Worse still, Margaret's dowry did not materialise when her father fell on hard times and came, with his wife, to live with (and on) the Hoggs in their cottage at Altrive. In a desperate attempt to raise money for family dependants now as numerous as a small clan, Hogg dashed off *The Private Memoirs and Confessions of a Justified Sinner*. It was published in 1824, anonymously, by Longman in London.

Months before the publication Hogg had published a letter in *Maga*, recounting the exhumation of a suicide's grave, in the Borders, which had generated some mystery, hinting at supernatural phenomena. Was this 'germ' of the forthcoming novel authentic, or sly bait for prospective readers? The first half of the *Confessions* comprises an 'editor's narrative'. The editor is complacent, slightly dull and very unHoggish. The historical setting is the 1680s, an unsettled moment in Scottish history (but when isn't?): the Laird of Dalcastle, an old-school rascal who loves life, takes a much younger, religiously hidebound wife. Her true mate, whom she brings in her entourage, is her spiritual adviser, Robert Wringhim. The Revd Wringhim is an 'ultra-Calvinist', one of the antinomian sect whose creed presumes that the elect have been preordained for salvation – whatever sins they commit. 'Works' are irrelevant. Historically the antinomians did not conceive this as a licence to do whatever they wanted, but as a Caledonian version of kismet. Hogg probes the doctrine, sceptically.

Rabina Orde, the newlywed bride, is violated in the marriage bed and, before making her escape to live by herself, bears two sons. The elder, George, the Laird acknowledges as his. The younger, Robert, he believes (very plausibly) to be the off-spring of Wringhim. The boys are brought up in their parents' now separate establishments. George grows up a lusty young heir, the apple of his father's eye. The hated Robert, who takes on the surname 'Wringhim', grows up a neurotic bigot, suffused with religious malignity. He justifies all his selfishness and malice by his confidence, instilled by his putative 'father', that he is one of the elect. As he enters manhood, Robert is egged on to ever more malicious acts by a mysterious companion, 'Gil-Martin' (the name means 'fox' in Gaelic). Gil has the strange capacity to morph into anyone. He manipulates Robert into assassinating his brother in a midnight brawl which he, Gil, has orchestrated. The Laird dies of grief and Robert inherits the estate. His crime is suspected, and finally detected, by two resourceful ladies of easy virtue, the Laird's mistress, Miss Logan, and a branded prostitute (narrowly escaped from the gallows), Bell Calvert.

The editor's narrative has its unusual aspects but is not entirely unconventional. What sets the reader back is the second half of the novel, Robert's own printed and manuscript 'private memoir and confessions'. He is mad, but not deluded as to the fact that Gil (who is witnessed in both accounts by third parties) actually exists. But he takes his mentor to be Czar Peter of Russia, in disguise. It leads to such deliciously malapropos exchanges as:

> I asked, with great simplicity: 'Are all your subjects Christians, prince?' 'All my European subjects are, or deem themselves so,' returned he; 'and they are the most faithful and true subjects I have.'
> Who could doubt, after this, that he was the Czar of Russia?

By now the reader has apprehended – although Robert has not – that Gil is Satan incarnate. Strangely, and ambiguously, Robert confesses to more murders than we know him to have committed (including matricide). Indeed, at one point it seems that Gil has persuaded him that they should unite to slaughter the whole human race. Even Robert is rather daunted by that prospect. As the new Laird, he suffers months' long blackouts after drinking bouts, then coming round to discover he has done ever more terrible things. His conviction that God will never punish him eventually dissolves into terror. He runs away but is pursued wherever he goes by his erstwhile 'friend', now his 'tormentor'. Finally he descends to labouring as a rural shepherd and hangs himself with a hay rope. This, too, is mysterious to those investigating his death:

> Now the fact is, that, if you try all the ropes that are thrown over all the outfield hay-ricks in Scotland, there is not one among a thousand of them will hang a colley dog; so that the manner of this wretch's death was rather a singular circumstance.

A documentary epilogue, picking up Hogg's letter the year before to *Blackwood's Magazine*, and introducing such real-life figures as Lockhart, describes the exhumation of Robert's body, still pristine even after forty years in the soil.

The *Confessions* failed spectacularly to hit the public taste of the time. It earned the author £2 in 'profits' (miscalled) in the two years Longman kept the book in print. There were moves on their part to recover the £100 advance. The few reviews the novel received concurred in finding it 'trash' – and indecent. It was certainly rawer meat than most fiction offered the circulating libraries. One strains, for example, to imagine Isabella Thorpe and Catherine Morland reading it together before going off to their morning session at the Bath Pump Room.

In the last decade of his life, it was, as always, up and down with Hogg – down predominating. He found himself increasingly cold-shouldered by the Blackwood's coterie. His major achievement in his late years was the founding of the St Ronan's Border Games, the 'Scottish Olympics', as they would later be called. Hogg was, throughout life, a keen sportsman himself. In fact it precipitated his death: in 1832, while curling, he fell through the ice on Duddingston Loch, below Arthur's Seat, and never fully recovered. Another late-life disaster was the publication of his wildly indiscreet 'anecdotes' of Scott, in 1834, capitalising on the excitement of the other writer's death (among other things he reported Lady Scott's addiction to opium). Hogg died, as he had begun life, in poverty.

FN   James Hogg
MRT *The Private Memoirs and Confessions of a Justified Sinner*
Biog Gillian Hughes, *James Hogg: A Life* (2007)

16. Charles Brockden Brown 1771–1810

America has opened new views to the naturalist and politician, but has seldom furnished themes to the moral painter. From the Preface to *Edgar Huntly*

Brown ranks as the first American novelist to have supported himself exclusively by his pen. He was born, one of many children, into a Philadelphia family of Quaker background. The Browns were prosperous import-export merchants. The home environment was liberal, upright, cultivated and open to Enlightenment thinking. And, like other of the community of friends, no enemy to Mammon. Brown's first juvenile literary effort was an epic (unfinished), 'The Rising Glory of America'. Arriving in the world when he did, Brown was born British, though it was no source of pride to him whatsoever. His family, exiles by origin, were pro-Republic – but by religion pacifist at a historical moment when non-violence was conceived as treachery. The family business premises were sacked during the War of Independence by 'patriots'.

Before turning to literature, Brown was, until 1792, a lawyer: it was his family's sensible choice of occupation for him, there being no room in the family business for all its male progeny. He hated the office drudgery, meditated ambitious epic poems, and excitedly followed events in revolutionary Paris. He moved to New York in the mid-1790s – then, as now, where liberated thought was to be found. His principal literary influences were the Jacobin novelist, William Godwin (particularly *Caleb Williams*), Rousseau, Robert Bage and Coleridge – radicals all. A close friend at this period was the theatrical pioneer William Dunlap, who introduced Brown to the heady brew of German *Schauerromantik*, a genre addicted to ruined castles, flamboyant suicide, brigandry, Byronic despair and spectral phenomena.

On the modest success of his first tale of terror, *Wieland* (1798, subtitled 'An

American Tale'), Brown tumbled out another three 'Gothics' over the next eighteen months: *Ormond* (1799); *Arthur Mervyn* (1800), subtitled 'Memoirs of the Year 1793', it deals with the yellow fever of that year in Philadelphia, which, it has been surmised, had life-changing effects on the author himself; and *Edgar Huntly; or, Memoirs of a Sleepwalker* (1799), the first novel to introduce American Indians ('Red-men') into popular fiction – and, for that reason, perhaps nowadays regarded as his best work. The depiction of these 'tom-hawk'-wielding 'savages' is, it should be noted, less than sympathetic.

Brown published seven romances in all, conducted various New York-based literary journals, and enjoyed the reputation of a man of letters of progressive views. His fiction was admired overseas by Shelley and Scott (like his father, the venerable Elijah Brown, Charles was in the export business). His novels are marred, however, to modern eyes, by clunky narrative devices: *Wieland*, for example, pivots on the voice-throwing ('biloquism') of a maleficent ventriloquist, Carwin; and *Ormond* on a heroine who cross-dresses to participate in the French Revolution. But, despite the improbabilities, Brown had an extraordinary vitality of imagination. He plausibly influenced Poe, Hawthorne and Melville.

For unascertained reasons, Brown turned away from fiction after 1800. He may have regarded it as unworthy of a philosopher like himself. He seems to have been afflicted with nagging religious doubt at the same period. He married in 1804 and had four children in six years. Everything in his life, including death, came in a rush. Brown died prematurely of tuberculosis, aged thirty-nine, having left a primal mark on his national fiction. At the time of his death, he had embarked on a 'Complete System of Geography'. He had worlds to conquer: but fiction would not be one of them.

FN   Charles Brockden Brown
MRT   *Wieland; or, the Transformation, an American Tale*
Biog   P. Kafer, *Charles Brockden Brown's Revolution and the Birth of American Gothic* (2004)

17. Walter Scott 1771–1832

He desired to plant a lasting root, and dreamt not of present fame, but of long distant generations rejoicing in the name of Scott of Abbotsford. Scott's biographer and son-in-law, J. G. Lockhart

The only novelist to have a railway station named after one of his novels, 'the Author of *Waverley*' was born the ninth child of a Scottish Writer to the Signet (i.e. solicitor) in Edinburgh's Old Town – the 'Heart of Midlothian' – whose wynds and towering tenements were famous for their 'Gardy Loo!' insanitariness. The most beautiful city in Europe, Edinburgh was always liable to drop an unexpected bucket of filth on your head. He was never sure of the month, or even the year, of his birth. Two little 'Walters' had been born before him and promptly died and Walter III barely made it through the dangerous years of babyhood. At eighteen months old he was lamed for life by infantile paralysis. Scott died, never knowing, any more than did the eminent doctors in his family, what disease it was that had cruelly robbed him of half his manhood. There are accounts of him in his adolescence, hanging crucified from his bedroom rafters, with heavy weights attached to his withered leg, to make it whole again.

Too delicate for the polluted airs of 'Auld Reekie', his early childhood was spent with grandparents on a farm in the Borders, an experience which steeped him in regional folklore and balladry. After education at the High School and Edinburgh University (which he entered at twelve and left at fourteen), Scott was put to work in his father's law firm. Had he not been disabled he would, he said, have entered the army. There were some exciting wars going on. Scott eventually qualified as an advocate, after a second spell at the university, then the centre of European Enlightenment. He married Charlotte Charpentier in 1797. Allegedly the daughter of a French refugee from the 'Terror', she was more probably the by-blow of an English aristocrat. No novelist has been better at keeping his family skeletons in the closet than Walter Scott. The couple were to have four children, including the required son and heir, 'Walter'.

Scott began in authorship with some gentlemanly collecting of Border ballads. His first narrative poem, *The Lay of the Last Minstrel*, came out in 1805. It sold amazingly and was followed by *Marmion* (1808), for which the author received a mighty advance of £1,000 from Archibald Constable, the enterprising publisher with whom Scott's career was to be intertwined. By now, a favourite among the Tory oligarchy who ran Scotland, he had consolidated his professional position with well-paying legal sinecures. His run of bestselling narrative poems continued with *The Lady of the Lake* (1810), a poem whose florid Highlandery – swirling kilts, heather and claymores everywhere – is plausibly credited with founding the Scottish tourist industry. But for all his success, and the money, he was astute enough to realise his thunder was comprehensively stolen by the runaway success of *Childe Harold* in 1812: 'Byron beat me', he confessed candidly. Literary history agrees.

In 1814, Scott diversified into a field where there was no Byron, with *Waverley*, a prose romance centred on the 1745 uprising. Scott's head, as he liked to say, was with the Hanoverians; his heart was with the Jacobites and the Pretender. His hero, Edward, similarly wavers, afflicted with an ideological bipolar disorder, between Scotland's romantic past and her progressive future. *Waverley* took the British and European reading publics by storm. There had been no such success since Samuel Richardson's *Pamela*. Scott had entered the ranks of the novelists, aged forty-three, and shot to the top. But bestselling fiction was not an entirely respectable sideline for the august Clerk to the Court of Session and the novel was published anonymously. The identity of 'The Author of *Waverley*' was a closely guarded secret until 1826. Under his mask, Scott went on to publish a string of historical romances with Scottish settings, of which the best is *The Heart of Midlothian*, with its heroic dairy-maid heroine, Jeanie Deans, and a 1715 Jacobite uprising setting.

Even at Constable's price of a pound-or-more for a multi-volume set, the *Waverley* novels sold prodigiously, enabling Scott to build himself a Scottish baronial mansion, Abbotsford, in the Borders. A favourite of the Prince Regent and of the English Tories, he was created a baronet in 1820. At the same period he embarked on a series of chauvinistic historical romances with an English setting, which were immensely popular and influential. *Ivanhoe* (1819), a romantic tale of knighthood in the time of the Lionheart king, was instrumental in popularising the 'Norman Yoke thesis' – the notion that there was a primal Saxon heritage in Britain which could be recovered and with it national greatness. (Scott, incidentally, regarded himself racially as Saxon, not Celt.) The NYT became dogma among novelists in the Victorian period: Disraeli's 'Young England' and 'One Nation' conservatism is founded on it.

In 1825, at the height of his fame, Scott's business affairs deteriorated catastrophically. He was heavily involved with his printer James Ballantyne and Archibald Constable, both of whom were ruined by the epidemic bank failures of 1825–6. Scott found himself liable for debts of over £100,000. Disdaining the unheroic option of bankruptcy, he contrived to pay off the bulk of this debt through his pen over the succeeding years. It was quixotic, but magnificent. 'We two against the world,' he would say, raising his right hand defiantly against fate.

In his last years, that right hand continued to write ceaselessly but much less brilliantly, and at the expense of his health. 'I shall never see three score and ten,' he wrote in his journal. In this last phase of his career, his main income came from a cheap reprint series of his collected works, undertaken by the publisher Robert Cadell (a former partner of Constable's). The *magnum opus* series, whose volumes were sold at 5s apiece, had a profound influence on the publishing of 'fiction for the people'.

Scott undertook a gruelling trip to Malta and Europe in 1831–2. He had already sustained three devastating strokes and he returned to Abbotsford a dying man. His death in 1832 plunged Scotland into significantly more gloom than that of the unlamented George IV. Scott, for his part, had always been loyal to his liege. It was for his fat royal friend's visit to Edinburgh, in 1822, which he stage-managed, that Scott invented the mythic flimflammery about the 'clan tartan' (for Highlanders, a blanket was a blanket: weave meant nothing).

Scott demonstrated that a novelist could earn massively without losing literary caste. He dignified the historical romance as a major genre – something that took root not just in Britain, but in France and Russia with writers like Hugo, Dumas and Tolstoy. He stretched historical facts outrageously for narrative effect, but as Carlyle observed, he got across the truth that history was made by living people, not dates, wars and Acts of Parliament. He pioneered the three-volume, 31/ 6d novel, a mode of publication that survived until the 1890s as the standard form for the British circulating library. Innumerable genres (the regional novel, the nautical novel, the gipsy novel, the 'Newgate' novel, the sequence novel, the 'kailyard' novel – to name but a few) sprang from his root. He did not merely create fiction, he procreated it.

He was hugely popular in America. The 'Sir Walter disease', as Mark Twain maintained (it was not one of his jokes), bore a primary responsibility for the American Civil War, creating as it did so much false consciousness about 'glory'. The Ku Klux Klan took over much of its ritual paraphernalia (e.g. the ominous burning cross) from Scott. Not just railroad stations but whole towns and thousands of streets were called 'Waverley' in his honour. When Scott died in 1832, the American *Richmond Enquirer* carried the news in a black-bordered issue, normally only used for American presidents.

The social historian Mark Girouard has convincingly traced how the pseudo-medieval cult of 'chivalry', embodied in the ideal of the Victorian 'gentleman', originates with Scott's novels. Scott also invented a romanticised 'Brigadoon and Braveheart' view of 'wild' Celtic Scotland which persists, erroneously, to the present day. No novelist has done so much, yet – perversely – has been so reluctantly read by posterity for his pains.

FN   (Sir) Walter Scott
MRT   *Waverley*
Biog   J. Sutherland, *Sir Walter Scott: A Critical Biography* (1995)

18. Jane Austen 1775–1817

3 or 4 families in a Country Village is the very thing to work on.

One of the many books about the author in 2009 – certainly the bestselling of them – was *Jane's Fame: How Jane Austen Conquered the World*, by Claire Harman. If Harman's unstuffy chronicle of Jane Austen's reputation told the reader anything it was that the 'Lady', as she titled herself, who wrote *Pride and Prejudice*, had come a long way since 1813, when that novel barely cleared a few hundred copies of its first edition. In the last twenty years, Harman plausibly suggested, Jane Austen has 'conquered the world'. She was no longer a writer but a phenomenon, a 'brand', a celebrity author. Jane Austen is to fiction what Coca-Cola is to fizzy drinks.

Thirty years ago, when that world-domination was still a year or two in the future, an American professor, Warren Roberts, published a monograph entitled *Jane Austen and the French Revolution*. It was met with uproarious mirth. If a person knew anything about Austen it was that she never mentions the French Revolution. The *New Statesman* ran a competition inviting similarly ludicrous combinations: 'E. M. Forster and Bodybuilding' and, famously, 'Martin Amis: My Struggle'. Professor Roberts was, however, making a serious point. We repress things which are so important to us that we dare not be conscious of them: the French Revolution was Jane Austen's elephant in the room. Nowadays, we are much more interested in a different pachyderm in the Austen parlour. What, in June 2009, when Harman's book was published, was the most looked-at item of Austeniana? With A-levels coming up, you might guess the Penguin Classics *Pride and Prejudice*, or possibly the DVD of the delightful skit, *Lost in Austen*. Wrong. It was a video, *Porn and Penetration*: a 'knockoff', as the porn and penetration trade calls them.

By the blood-curdling standards of contemporary pornography, *P&P* was harmless burlesque. A troupe of actors in high Regency dress did a series of scenes which, at first sight, looked exactly like those of any Andrew Davies screen adaptation. But then they go a tiny step further. Only one scene, involving Elizabeth Bennet and a billiard table, veered into the mildly distasteful. One did not expect a learned monograph entitled 'Jane Austen and Copulation', even from the dry highlands of American academia. But the point being made by the saucy makers of *Porn and Penetration* was the same as that made by unsaucy Prof. Roberts. Namely, that it is the missing bits which fascinate us most in Austen.

All six novels are about the rocky road to a young woman's happy marriage. Seducers lie everywhere in ambush: Frederick Tilney, George Wickham, John Willoughby, Frank Churchill, William Elliot – predators all. But the novels are, on the face of it, wholly uncarnal. The nearest we get to a sex scene is when Willoughby (sly devil) fingers Marianne Dashwood's sprained ankle with rather more interest than the injured joint might be thought to require by any other than the Barton Park physician. In the background of the narratives, of course, the prurient ear can usually detect some suspicious rustling. 'Coltish' Lydia Bennet, we surmise, is bonking everything in a red coat in the garrison town of Meryton (apt name). But Miss Austen primly averts her eyes from such goings on and keeps the narrative attention firmly focused on the teacups at Longbourn.

It infuriates some readers. 'Narrow gutted spinster,' D. H. Lawrence snarled. A novelist whose thighs were so firmly clamped could never open herself to life.

But was she little Miss Prim? There was controversy in the *Times Literary Supplement* recently (those damned professors) about the passage in *Mansfield Park* in which Mary Crawford recalls: 'Certainly, my home at my uncle's brought me acquainted with a circle of admirals. Of Rears and Vices I saw enough. Now do not be suspecting me of a pun, I entreat.' It is hard to think that a woman as smart as Jane Austen, with brothers serving in the rum-bum-and-lash eighteenth-century navy, with a father who, despite his dog collar, was broad-minded enough to let his daughters read *Tom Jones*, would perpetrate such a double entendre, unknowingly.

Indulge, too, a thought about the names which Austen gives her seducers. In an age when nights were candle-lit, 'wick' was male slang for the male member. Regency bucks would surely have had a quiet snigger at the name 'Wickham' (i.e. 'wick 'em'). 'Willoughby' has an echo of 'willie' – although, one concedes, this is probably a pun too far. But, if one wants to go super-smut, consider that enigmatic comment at the beginning of *Northanger Abbey* in which the reader is told that Catherine's father of ten children 'was a very respectable man, though his name was Richard'. It's always baffled critics. It needn't if you consider the traditional abbreviation of Richard.

Andrew Davies, Ang Lee – and most graphically, Patricia Rozema in the film of *Mansfield Park* – insert the explicit sex they believe Austen left coyly implicit. In Lee's *Sense and Sensibility*, it is made crystal clear that Marianne has surrendered her pearl without price to lustful Willoughby. Did Frank Churchill seduce Jane Fairfax at Weymouth? Is that why she is so strangely pale and withdrawn? Modern readers may well think so. The twenty-one-year-old Emma inquires of the thirty-eight-year-old Mr Knightley, her future husband, how long he has been in love with her. 'Since you were thirteen at least,' he replies. An American (female) student in a class I taught recently uttered the single word 'creeeeepy!' by way of comment. And are we to assume that Mr Knightley has kept himself pure all these years? The leading Austen scholar, Deirdre Le Faye, offers a more down to earth theory: 'It is not excessively far-fetched (if rather un-Austenish) to suspect that Mr Knightley has a respectable lower-class mistress tucked away somewhere. Maybe some innkeeper's wife whom he visits when he goes to Richmond or Kingston markets.'

Austen is to fiction what Elizabeth I was to the throne of England: a virgin queen. But did she not have sexual longings? The film *Becoming Jane* pondered that question with much heaving of the bosom. Why did Jane, after a sleepless night, refuse the one offer of marriage we know her to have received? Did Jane remain single to preserve herself for fiction? Did she die *virgo intacta*? Was she, perish the thought, Sapphic by preference? Why, after her sister's death, did Cassandra burn all their private papers? 'Was Jane Austen Gay?' the *London Review of Books* (those damn professors again) asked, in a 1995 headline. Jane and Cassandra shared a double bed. And what else? The facts about Austen's life were ruthlessly sanitised, *post mortem*, by surviving relatives. Her brother Henry wrote the skeletal mini-biography on which every maxi-biography has since depended. The facts that we do have are readily summarised.

Jane Austen was born in rural Hampshire, the sixth of seven children of a well-off, cultivated clergyman with a good library: strong, it would seem, in fiction (some volumes, like Sterne and Fielding, not always thought suitable for a young lady). The Revd George Austen's relationship with his daughter is, biographers have presumed, evoked in that of Mr Bennet with Elizabeth. She was educated at home, other than a year (1785–6) at boarding school in Reading. She wrote in the small recesses of privacy she was able to create in a crowded home – but shared her work in progress with her family, who were her earliest critics and encouragers. Austen visited friends and relatives in London, Bath, and Lyme Regis – places which later served as locations for her stories. In 1801, the family moved to Bath and, after the Revd Austen's death in 1806, to Southampton; and finally in 1809 they settled in Chawton, Hants, where she wrote her last three novels, the actual composition of which has always been uncertain chronologically. She died, tragically early, of what used to be thought to be Addison's disease, but recently medical experts are less sure and surmise that it may have been TB, or lymphoma. Another thing we shall never know.

Throw it all into the pot and the conclusion is that we know little more about Austen than about Shakespeare. With both writers, the biographical vacuum around their work has done no harm whatsoever. Arguably, with the very greatest writers (to paraphrase Walter Bagehot on monarchy): 'We must not let daylight in upon the magic.'

FN   Jane Austen ('A Lady')
MRT   *Emma*
Biog   C. Tomalin, *Jane Austen: A Life* (1997)

19. M. G. Lewis 1775–1818

The offspring of no common genius. Coleridge on *The Monk*

The naughty novelist of his age, he was universally nicknamed 'Monk Lewis' after his naughtiest novel, *The Monk*. It was the Marquis de Sade's favourite English work of fiction, tellingly an endorsement which perhaps rings more attractively in 2010 than it did in 1810. Lewis was, like William Beckford (author of the similarly notorious *Vathek*), thoroughly homosexual. Unofficial awareness of the fact added to his contemporary allure. His family had been enriched by sugar plantations in the West Indies and his father was Deputy Secretary for War at the time of *The Monk*'s publication. Lewis's mother was a famous society beauty; she was only nineteen when Matthew (her first child) was born. Lewis was between Westminster School and Oxford when his parents' marriage broke up, furiously, in 1790: she ran away with a music master. Emotionally close to his errant mother (with whom he later lived), he enjoyed generous financial and career patronage from his father. For him, it was the ideal domestic arrangement.

Lewis was writing precocious plays at fifteen. He travelled widely in Europe (currently shaken by the French Terror) in preparation for a diplomatic career. He resided in Paris in 1791 (where he imbibed anti-clerical pornography, later exploited in his novel) and in Weimar 1792–3, where he learned German and immersed himself in that country's vogue for *Schauerromantik*. In 1793 he returned to England where his mother actively urged him towards a literary career. Well born and rich, he none the less cut an unimpressive figure in society. A young lady in 1808 described him, witheringly, 'as a slim, skinny, finical fop, of modish address, with a very neatly rounded pair of legs and a very ugly face', the last further disfigured by 'jagged and slovenly teeth'.

In May 1794 he travelled to The Hague, on diplomatic business, having just devoured Ann Radcliffe's *The Mysteries of Udolpho*, which came out that month. While in Holland he wrote sections of *The Monk*, which was duly published the following March. The period 1795–6 was to be a highpoint of florid, post-Radcliffean Gothic. In addition to *The Monk*, it saw John Palmer Jr's *The Haunted Tower* (1795) and *The Mystery of the Black Tower* (1796); and Regina Maria Roche's *The Children of the Abbey* (1796).

In 1796 Lewis was introduced as a Whig MP into the House by Charles James Fox. But following the huge success of his play, *The Castle Spectre* (the title says everything), in 1797 he gave up his planned career in public life. Between 1798 and 1812 he published verse and translations and had a number of melodramas staged. He was, however, cautious never to offend as extremely as he had with his first (and only) novel. In consequence he never enjoyed great fame again, either in print or on the stage.

Lewis was, reportedly, deeply involved in the amoral life of the London theatre set. He became loosely attached to the remarkable party at Geneva, which produced in 1816 John Polidori's *The Vampyre* and Mary Shelley's *Frankenstein*. In later life he inherited his father's estates in Jamaica: he was inclined towards abolition but prudently decided that any unilateral gesture on his part would be pointless (and expensive). It's nice to fantasise that he met Jane Austen's Sir Thomas Bertram as those two *bien pensants* tended to their affairs in the Caribbean. Like Sir Thomas, Lewis visited Jamaica where his attention to the welfare of 'his' blacks was commented on. He died of yellow fever on a return voyage from his plantations in 1818.

The Monk, published anonymously in three volumes in 1796, was still tingling English spines at the time of his death and long thereafter. The British Library contains 'mutilated' copies of the novel which was, at various times, suppressed or furtively merchandised as a 'prohibited' book. The narrative contains gloating descriptions of sexual deviance (a French translation, for example, did not mince words in its title – *Le Moine Incestueux*). The novel also draws on traditionally scabrous 'Nunnery Tales', as spiced up by Jacobin anti-clerical pornographic satire. It was a dangerous book.

The monk of the title is Ambrosio, Abbot of the Capuchins in Madrid. Behind a saintly disguise, he debauches penitents, murders his mother and rapes his sister. In one of the most sensual scenes in the novel, the beautiful Matilda comes to Ambrosio's monastic cell and lovingly sucks the venom from a 'centipiedra' bite in the monk's arm, after which the couple surrender themselves to three days of sexual madness before she reveals herself to be a vengeful sorceress and an agent of the devil. Nemesis finally comes at the hands of the Inquisition. Facing death at the stake, Matilda appears to him again and offers him escape if he will sign over his soul entirely to the devil. This he does, only to be cheated by the Evil One who hurls him down a ravine to suffer unimaginable torment for six days. Insects drink Ambrosio's warm blood and eagles tear out his eyeballs 'with their crooked beaks'.

Lewis's own death was as gothic as anything in his fiction. On board the ship he wrote his will on his servant's hat. With a macabre gothic touch, his body was put in an improvised coffin which was wrapped in a sheet with weights and dropped overboard; but the weights fell out and the coffin bobbed up on the surface – the sheet acting as a sail in the wind – and floated across the waves back to Jamaica.

FN   Matthew Gregory 'Monk' Lewis
MRT *The Monk*
Biog D. L. MacDonald, *Monk Lewis: A Critical Biography* (2000)

20. Mrs Frances Trollope 1779–1863

If Fanny is remembered at all today, it is as an admittedly courageous and hard-working woman who nevertheless neglected her talented son, and was herself a second-rate writer, a political dilettante and a bit of a snob. Biographer Pamela Neville-Sington, who disagrees with the depiction

Most male novelists have learned to read at their mothers' knees. Only one comes to mind who learned to write novels from observing his mother. The essence of what we think of as the Trollopian method – early rising, tradesmanlike application to the task, and indomitable 'cheerfulness' – can be traced directly to Anthony Trollope's mother. There is a description in *An Autobiography* of Mrs Trollope heroically penning her light fiction to keep the wolf from the door, while her children die, one by one, from consumption:

> She was at her table at four in the morning, and had finished her work before the world had begun to be aroused … There were two sick men in the house, and hers were the hands that tended them. The novels went on, of course. We had already learned to know that they would be forthcoming at stated intervals – and they were always forthcoming. The doctor's vials and the ink-bottle held equal place in my mother's rooms. I have written many novels under many circumstances; but I doubt much whether I could write one when my whole heart was by the bedside of a dying son.

The main lines of Fanny Trollope's life are laid down in the second chapter of *An Autobiography* – 'My Mother'. There is no corresponding chapter on 'My Father'. The sprightly daughter of a West Country clergyman, Frances Milton waited until she was thirty before making a good match with a London barrister. Thomas Anthony Trollope had professional prospects and 'expectations' from a rich, unmarried and conveniently antique uncle. The dutiful Mrs Trollope had seven children in ten years (only two were to survive into mature age), while her husband contrived to ruin the family finances buying land, losing briefs and antagonising patrons. The uncle married at the age of sixty-plus and produced heirs as lustily as his nephew. In the crisis of their affairs, in November 1827, Mrs Trollope, aged forty-eight, went off to America for three and a half years. She had in tow her favourite son Henry, two small daughters, a couple of servants, and a young French artist who was devoted to her, Auguste Hervieu. Mr Trollope was not in attendance. Nor was twelve-year-old Anthony.

Mrs Trollope's first destination in America was an Owenite community, Nashoba, in backwoods Tennessee, founded by her friend, Fanny Wright. What

Wright had in mind was a commune in which black and white children would be educated together in a Temple of Science. The Nashoba community also advocated the practice of free or 'rational' love, and, less publicly stated, lesbian freedoms. Mrs Trollope's views on this and other aspects of the Nashoba programme, the degree of her commitment to Owenite ideals, and her precise relationship with Fanny Wright and Hervieu, have been carefully excised from the official record.

Inevitably, the community was a squalid shambles. After ten days and the inevitable rupture with Wright, Mrs Trollope and her brood moved on to Cincinnati. Here she put on dramatic shows and erected a 'bazaar' – 'Trollope's folly,' as it came to be called – a kind of proto-shopping mall (the Paris arcades evidently gave her the idea for it). Ironically, the bazaar came close to succeeding. A key factor in its eventual failure was Mrs Trollope's having affronted her potential clientele, the bourgeois ladies of the town, by living with a French artist away from her husband. She could have been the Donald Trump of her day.

After more than three years in America, Fanny Trollope was fifty-one and broke. She returned to England and published a book – 'blowing up the Merrikins', as Tony Weller would say. The gloriously spiteful *Domestic Manners of the Americans* (they have none) was an 1832 bestseller – in England. Just as profitably, she turned from travel book to fiction, promptly entering the select ranks of the £1,000-a-book authors. Her novels included *Tremordyn Cliff* (1835), the study of a dominant woman (a character type which was to become Trollope's trademark); the anti-slavery novel *Jonathan Jefferson Whitlaw* (1836) – a likely influence on Stowe's *Uncle Tom's Cabin*; the 'social problem' novel *The Life and Adventures of Michael Armstrong the Factory Boy* (1840); and her fictional attack on the country's bastardy laws, *Jessie Phillips* (1843). The work of this ten years is the high point of her career in fiction. It was also the high point in her earning. It was, her son Tom said, as if a fairy godmother had waved her wand over the Trollope household.

With her husband's death in 1835, Mrs Trollope's life became easier – though no less industrious. Latching, with cynical speed, on to every fictional fashion that came along and allying herself with huckster publishers (like Henry Colburn), she continued to delight circulating library readers while infuriating the stuffier kind of male critic with her 'unwomanly' smartness. Mrs Trollope, wrote the young fogey Thackeray on reading her maliciously anti-evangelical novel, *The Vicar of Wrexhill*, 'had much better have remained at home, pudding-making or stocking-making, than have meddled with matters which she understands so ill'.

Having married off her daughter Cecilia (the unfortunate young woman soon died, leaving behind a novel), and launched Anthony into a Civil Service and novel-writing career, finding him his first publisher, Mrs Trollope left in 1844 for villa life in Florence with her older son, Thomas, another part-time novelist. She was sixty-five. Her retirement years were characteristically active. Thomas, his father's son in more than name, needed the cash. As Anthony recalls, 'she continued writing up to 1856 when she was 76 years old; – and had at that time produced 114 volumes of which the first was not written till she was 50. Her career offers great encouragement to those who have not begun early in life but are still ambitious to do something before they depart hence.'

FN   Frances Trollope ('Fanny', née Milton)
MRT *The Vicar of Wrexhill*
Biog Pamela Neville-Sington, *Fanny Trollope: The Life and Adventures of a Clever Woman* (2003)

21. Thomas De Quincey 1785–1859

Oh, just, subtle, and mighty opium! that to the hearts of poor and rich alike, for the wounds that will never heal, and for 'the pangs that tempt the spirit to rebel', bringest an assuaging balm.

What kind of career, in fantasy-literature-land, would Thomas De Quincey have had if he'd been subjected to a twenty-first-century legal system? As a juvenile runaway, living rough on the streets of London, he would have been put into what is laughably called 'care'. As a grown man with a predilection for underage girls ('nympholepsy' he termed it), he might have found himself in prison. As a lifelong abuser of Class A drugs he would have been in and out of court and – in his more raving spells with imaginary crocodiles chasing him through endless Piranesi architecture – he might well have been sectioned. In our enlightened regime, would Thomas De Quincey have left to posterity his acknowledged masterpieces – *Confessions of an English Opium-Eater* or 'On Murder Considered as one of the Fine Arts'? Probably not. He would have been too preoccupied keeping ahead of the long arm of the law and the crossed arms of a straitjacket.

Thomas Quincey (the 'De' was a snobbish affectation) was born in Manchester, the son of a prosperous linen merchant who died early, leaving the care of the family to a terrifyingly evangelical mother. Young Thomas was set up for life by the wise provisions of his father's will. One of his missions in life was to waste that money so deliberately that his last decades would be passed in destitute literary hackery. Sent to a good boarding school, he ran away to shack up in Soho with a fifteen-year-old prostitute. He later spent some time at the University of Oxford – but walked out when he discovered that the oral examination was not, as promised, in Greek but English. He learned early that drugs and drop-out alliterate in life, as well as on the page.

While debauching his constitution with opium tablets, washed down with copious draughts of wine, he was stocking his mind. He wrote nothing of significance until he was in his mid-thirties and his mind full to overflowing and boiling with toxins. One toxin in particular has never been so lovingly described: 'eloquent opium! that with thy potent rhetoric stealest away the purposes of wrath; and to the guilty man for one night givest back the hopes of his youth, and hands washed pure from blood; and to the proud man a brief oblivion for Wrongs undress'd and insults unavenged.' Even more than opium, he was addicted to Wordsworth. When he was able, he migrated to the Lake District, to be near his literary god. He helped Coleridge with money and Wordsworth himself with child-minding, proof-reading and points of punctuation. He was renowned for his conversation – although after 4 p.m., as J. G. Lockhart observed, it did get rather slurred.

After a decade living among the 'Lakers', and having married his young housekeeper, De Quincey drifted back to London. By now he had run through his patrimony and was getting by with grudging handouts from his mother and what he could earn by his pen. It was at this period (around 1822) that he produced the *Confessions of an English Opium-Eater*. It caused a sensation. 'Better, a thousand times better, *die* than have anything to do with such a Devil's own drug!' expostulated Thomas Carlyle, whose notion of angelic medication was something to ease his chronic constipation. Doctors reported an epidemic of deaths from copy-cat overdoses (murder De Quincey-style), in the same way that Goethe's Werther had inspired mass suicide among susceptibly adolescent readers.

Writers from Edgar Allan Poe, through Aleister Crowley (the 'Great Beast' and author of a *hommage*, *Diary of a Drug Fiend*) to W. S. Burroughs and Timothy Leary, have taken their inspiration from De Quincey and his contention that the devil's own drugs give the imagination wings. The *Confessions* made him notorious but not, alas, rich. Despite wretched health, and his own poisonous self-medications, he lived to a great age, latterly in Edinburgh, writing all the time, flitting from one lodging to another – filthy 'even by Scottish standards', as one visitor tartly recorded.

Is that slippery masterpiece a memoir, an extended 'essay' or a novel? It is, whatever the Dewey Decimal system says, the last. If we categorise *CEOE* properly, it is a *Bildungsroman* (a self-portrait novel); indeed, a pioneer text in the genre. The point can be made by isolating one of the central episodes in the *Confessions*.

When, as a seventeen-year-old, Thomas washes up in Oxford Street, 'squatting' (as later teenagers would say), he finds companionship with an even younger street-walker, 'Ann'. They cuddle at night for warmth and, we apprehend, sex. It is a powerful element in the narrative: but is it 'chronicle' or 'plot'? Just prior to his return to decent society, the hero loses contact with her:

> Meantime, what had become of poor Ann? For her I have reserved my concluding words. According to our agreement, I sought her daily, and waited for her every night, so long as I stayed in London, at the corner of Titchfield Street ... The street where she had lodged I knew, but not the house ... If she lived, doubtless we must have been some time in search of each other, at the very same moment, through the mighty labyrinths of London; perhaps even within a few feet of each other – a barrier no wider than a London street often amounting in the end to a separation for eternity!

If she lived, indeed. De Quincey's most recent biographer is inclined to think Ann as fictional as Keats's *Belle Dame*. To think so, of course, is to transmute the fabric of De Quincey's narrative: De Quincey should be reshelved as one of our great novelists.

FN   Thomas Penson De Quincey
MRT *Confessions of an English Opium-Eater*
Biog R. Morrison, *The English Opium-Eater: A Biography of Thomas De Quincey* (2009)

22. James Fenimore Cooper 1789–1851

One day America will be as beautiful in actuality as it is in Cooper. Not yet, however. When the factories have fallen down again. D. H. Lawrence

James Cooper was born in Burlington, New Jersey. His father was a Federalist congressman, the family background Quaker. Soon after James's birth the Coopers (along with their thirteen children) moved to Cooperstown, New York, a village owned, founded and – given the size of his brood – largely populated by Cooper Sr. The family home was surrounded by a vast estate whose wilderness was, by this date (1790), cleared of Indians. But the memory of them remained – not least in the name of Cooperstown's neighbouring Lake Otsego.

James went to Yale aged thirteen (normal at the time) and was dismissed for some innocuous horseplay in 1805. His most serious offence is recorded to have been training a donkey to sit in a professor's chair. Donkeyplay. In 1806, the wild student was sent to sea by his father, with a view to making a man of him. A long career in the US Navy was foreseen. He rose to the rank of midshipman before resigning in 1811. He married in the same year. The couple would have seven children and for the rest of his life Cooper would be a landlubber.

For several years, Cooper was able to live as a gentleman farmer with the $50,000 he inherited from his father on his death in 1809. He allegedly began his career in bestselling fiction in disgust after reading one of Mrs Amelia Opie's homiletic tales aloud to his wife in 1820. Maintaining that he could do better himself, he turned out the Opie-ish *Precaution* (1820), a moral tale instructing parents how to take better care of their offspring. The work was put out as supposedly by an English author, with an English setting. It flopped. However, it is more likely that Cooper was persuaded to turn his hand to fiction by financial need. He had, by 1820, run through his considerable patrimony.

Cooper hit his stride with his second work, *The Spy* (1821), a story with an ultra-American theme. It sold 10,000 copies within the year and was hailed in some quarters as the most successful American novel hitherto produced in the young Republic. There was a general feeling that America needed its Walter Scott. *The Spy* was the first of nine novels dealing with the American past in the crucial years before, during and after the Revolution. Cooper was creating a popular history for the nation – as Scott had done for his nation. *The Spy* drew on American chauvinism following the 1812 naval victory over Britain. Set in the period of Revolution, it is played out on the so-called 'neutral ground' between the British and American forces in New York state. The debt to *Waverley* is manifest.

The Pilot (1824) was initially devised as an old salt's yarn, to correct landlubberly errors in Scott's *The Pirate* (1822) – errors which Scott candidly confessed. Cooper was a great corrector of other novelists' work. He was also a great innovator and *The Pilot* was the progenitor of the line of nautical fiction subsequently exploited by 'Captain' Marryat in England and by Herman Melville in the US – neither of whom needed any correction from James Fenimore Cooper on maritime matters. The novel's titular hero was the country's greatest sailor (and victor over the British at sea), John Paul Jones.

Cooper's most influential 'national tales' were the sequence novels which began with *The Pioneers* (1823). This tale introduces the series hero, Leatherstocking, and chronicles the nation-building forces that drive him, as a 'pioneer', ever westward with the receding 'frontier', bringing destruction and civilisation in his wake. The name is taken from the deerskin leggings worn by the frontiersman hero – variously (and confusingly) called Leatherstocking, Natty Bumppo, Pathfinder, Trapper and Deerslayer. A 'scout', he has the skills of the redskin and the superior intellect of the paleface. He can merge with both peoples – even when they are at war.

In 1826, Cooper published the second of the Leatherstocking novels, *The Last of the Mohicans*. Subtitled 'A Narrative of 1757', it was designed to cash in on the 50th anniversary of the Revolution. The novel is a lament for the indigenous inhabitants of New York State and publication coincided with the decisive phase of the Indian Removal Policy. Rarely has racial extinction been portrayed more beautifully than in the *Liebestod* of Uncas and Cora. The popularity of the Leatherstocking romances triggered a 'Coopermania' in Europe and Britain. The novelist crossed the Atlantic to exploit his popularity, settling there with his family from July 1826 to September 1833. On his return, Cooper produced numerous volumes of travel, historical writing and novels, prominent among which was *The Prairie* (1827), the third Leatherstocking instalment. The frontier has now reached the Western Plains, and the early nineteenth century.

In 1837 Cooper, always quarrelsome, embarked on a 'war' with the local Whig press, firing off a barrage of libel suits and raising some useful money for himself in the process. *The Pathfinder* (1840) was the fourth in the now epic Leatherstocking series. *Mercedes of Castile*, produced in the same year, a story of Columbus's epic voyage of discovery, is generally regarded as Cooper's worst effort in fiction – although there are other candidates for that title. *The Deerslayer* (1841) brought the Leatherstocking saga to a conclusion. However, the series was not chronologically sequential and it is in *The Prairie* that Natty, now eighty (but still a dead-shot with his fearsome long carbine, Killdeer) finally exits. It is not the least of Cooper's achievements that he inspired the funniest critique in American literature, Mark Twain's 'Fenimore Cooper's Literary Offenses'.

> Another stage-property that [Cooper] pulled out of his box pretty frequently was the broken twig. He prized his broken twig above all the rest of his effects, and worked it the hardest. It is a restful chapter in any book of his when somebody doesn't step on a dry twig and alarm all the reds and whites for two hundred yards around. Every time a Cooper person is in peril, and absolute silence is worth four dollars a minute, he is sure to step on a dry twig. There may be a hundred other handier things to step on, but that wouldn't satisfy Cooper. Cooper requires him to turn out and find a dry twig; and if he can't do it, go and borrow one. In fact, the Leatherstocking Series ought to have been called the Broken Twig Series.

True critical words are often spoken in jest. Cooper's fiction is homespun, but it created the underlay for some of the richest themes in American life and literature. It is not fanciful – to take two extreme examples – to see Clint Eastwood and Neil Armstrong ('one small step for man') as progeny of Natty. Cooper spent his last years and died where he had been brought up, alongside Lake Otsego.

FN   James Fenimore Cooper
MRT *The Last of the Mohicans*
Biog George Dekker, *James Fenimore Cooper: The Novelist* (1967)

23. John Polidori 1795–1821

As soon as he reached his room, Lord Byron fell like a thunderbolt upon the chambermaid. From Polidori's diary, 1816

The wet summer of 1816 and the inconvenience it caused a party of distinguished literary tourists (Lord Byron, Percy Shelley, Mary Godwin, Claire Clairmont and John Polidori) is well known. Novels have been written and films made about it. The bad weather began, far away, in Indonesia, with the eruption of Mount Tambora. It hit seven on the Volcanic Explosivity Index, making it the largest such event in a thousand years. The result, worldwide, was the 'year without a summer' and a less deadly eruption of Gothicism in Villa Diodati, alongside Lake Geneva, where the English tourists were staying. Pent up by the foul weather, they beguiled the rainy days and nights with light reading and a competition to write the most spine-chilling ghost story which their bored minds could come up with.

Mary Godwin (soon to be Mary Shelley) was evidently struck by the fact that Milton had once resided in Villa Diodati. She elected to rewrite *Paradise Lost* as *Frankenstein*. Shelley and Byron rather fizzled out: literature was, in the final analysis, more than a parlour game for them. None the less, as a striking entry in Polidori's diary, for 18 June, testifies, they remained receptive listeners: 'L[ord] B[yron] repeated some verses of Coleridge's *Christabel*, of the witch's breast; when silence ensued, and Shelley, suddenly shrieking and putting his hands to his head, ran out of the room with a candle. Threw water on his face, and after gave him ether. He was looking at Mrs. S[helley], and suddenly thought of a woman he had heard of who had eyes instead of nipples, which, taking hold of his mind, horrified him.'

The author of 'The Vampyre', 'Dr' Polidori was, like the eighteen-year-old Mary, young – barely twenty. The two got on well. A graduate of Edinburgh medical school (the youngest ever to qualify, supposedly), Polidori had learned his sawbone trade (which he despised) on cadavers supplied by Edinburgh's famous 'resurrectionists'. Medical science needed corpses: the gallows and the stillborn (the only legitimate supply) were inadequate. Neither would rotting cadavers do. Anatomists needed 'fresh' meat – still warm, ideally – and, in a world without refrigeration, a constant supply of such bodies. Burke and Hare, the most notorious of the resurrectionists, solved the demand-and-supply problem by murder. Their colleagues in the resurrection trade, like Victor Frankenstein, dug up what the gravediggers had buried, only a few hours earlier.

Polidori had written his thesis on 'somnambulism'. He was fascinated by the paranormal. A second generation Italo-Englishman, he was handsome, politically radical and a vibrant conversationalist. He had found himself at the Villa Diodati by a once-in-a-lifetime stroke of luck. Byron, immersed in sexual scandal, had decided that England was too hot for him. He would decamp and he needed a travelling companion – preferably a physician. Byron was taken with Polidori, whom he had met socially. The young man was recruited for the duration of the tour abroad, on a handsome stipend of £500.

Polidori was flattered to the point of intoxication. Byron's closest friend, John Cam Hobhouse, loathed 'Polly-Wolly' and sowed as much distrust as he could. It was unnecessary. The young doctor soon got on Byron's nerves and things were not helped by 'The Vampyre'. Clearly the hero of that short tale, Lord Ruthven *is* Byron. 'Ruthven' was one of the titles of the noble villain-hero in Lady Caroline Lamb's revenge novel *Glenarvon*, which came out in May 1816. It too may well have been light reading at the Villa. It was Lamb, a discarded mistress, who described Byron as 'mad, bad, and dangerous to know'. He, with studied insouciance, dismissed *Glenarvon* as so much 'fuck and tell'. Whether he wanted to pay £500 p.a. for more fuck (or 'suck') and tell was something else. Intended as flattery, Polidori's story was tactless. The plot of 'The Vampyre' is simple. The sinister Lord Ruthven takes the handsome young Aubrey on a continental tour with him. On his travels, Ruthven cold-bloodedly destroys every young person who comes his way. Finally, having sucked Aubrey dry, he turns his dead, grey, irresistible eye on Aubrey's sister:

> Aubrey's weakness increased; the effusion of blood produced symptoms of the near approach of death. He desired his sister's guardians might be called, and when the midnight hour had struck, he related composedly what the reader has perused – he died immediately after.
>
> The guardians hastened to protect Miss Aubrey; but when they arrived, it was too late. Lord Ruthven had disappeared, and Aubrey's sister had glutted the thirst of a VAMPYRE!

No need to call for the ether. One's spine is obstinately unchilled. Byron had soon had more of the young man than he could stand and sent him on his way to cross the Alps, alone, friendless and penniless. On his return to England, Polidori drifted, gambled wildly, and suffered a disastrous head injury in a coach accident in 1818, which exacerbated a temperamental disposition towards melancholy.

'The Vampyre' – that failed compliment – was long forgotten until it rose from the grave in suspicious circumstances. Henry Colburn, the most unscrupulous publisher in London, published it in 1819 as 'by Lord Byron'. Polidori protested bitterly. How Colburn (nicknamed the 'prince of puffers' for his advertising stunts) came by the text has never been explained. He had earlier published *Glenarvon*. With Byron's name attached to it, 'the trashy tale' was sensationally popular. There was nothing new about vampires as such, but what 'The Vampyre' did was to remodel the image, to 'Byronise' it. Polidori profited not at all from the runaway success of his story. He died aged twenty-five, suicidally depressed, and probably by a self-administered dose of prussic acid.

FN   John William Polidori
MRT *The Vampyre*
Biog D. L. Macdonald, *Poor Polidori: A Critical Biography of the Author of 'The vampyre'* (1991)

24. Mary Shelley 1797–1851

The workshop of filthy creation.

'The author of *Frankenstein*' enjoys a bigger reputation with posterity than the vampirophiliac Polidori. Both concepts proved eminently filmable but the new maps of literature introduced by the feminist movement of the 1960s have firmly lodged 'Mary *Wollstonecraft* Shelley' (the double barrelling is significant) into a canon which has no place for 'Polly'. She was born in north London, daughter of William Godwin and Mary Wollstonecraft. He was the author of *An Enquiry Concerning Political Justice* (1793); she was the author of *A Vindication of the Rights of Woman* (1792). Mary never knew her mother, who died of puerperal fever a week after her daughter's birth. Natal trauma scenarios haunted Mary through life and are central to her most famous novel. She grew up with a stepsister, Fanny (the illegitimate daughter of her mother). Godwin then remarried and brought another illegitimate stepsister, Claire Clairmont, into the family.

Whatever their rights, there was a plurality of women at 29 The Polygon, Somers Town. It was an educational advantage for Mary that the family's penury meant most of her learning happened there. Books and radical ideas were as everyday items as breakfast – and more plentiful. Godwin never made money from his writings. As his only legitimate daughter, Mary was her father's favourite (but not her stepmother's) and he took unusual pains to cultivate her mind. Among a range of other subjects, he had her tutored in Latin and Greek. Orthodox educational opinion of the time would have likened it to teaching dogs trigonometry. In her 1831 Preface to *Frankenstein*, Mary recalls 'writing stories' from her earliest years. Godwin too wrote stories – for example, what is plausibly claimed as the first detective story in English literature, *Caleb Williams* (1793). Mary was a published author at the age of twelve, and she was (her father recorded) as pretty as she was intellectually precocious.

Prominent thinkers and leaders of the Romantic movement made it a point to visit Godwin. The most important date in Mary's young life was 11 November 1812 when she met Percy Bysshe Shelley and his wife Harriet, who were making the de rigueur visit. Shelley, who was rich, was a financial benefactor to the ever hard-up philosopher. Over the next months he and Mary fell in love – during clandestine meetings at Wollstonecraft's gravestone, it is romantically recorded. She was not yet sixteen, he was in his early twenties. Godwin found the relationship rather too radical, so the couple duly eloped, without permission, in July 1814 and left for Europe – currently in its pre-Waterloo lull. Shelley's pregnant wife and child were not wanted on the trip. Shelley was no novice at this kind of escapade: Harriet Westbrook had only been sixteen when he had eloped with her to Scotland.

The product of this free-love honeymoon, the poem 'Mont Blanc' – and connection with Mary – marks a palpable growth in Shelley's poetry. But they ran out of money and returned to public obloquy in September, by which time Mary was now pregnant. The child (born in February 1815) died soon after birth. Shelley had, for love, lost not merely public respect but his private wealth. However, things looked up with a handsome bequest from his grandfather and the couple retired to a comfortable house in Windsor (lyricised in Mary's later novel, *The Last Man*). Their second child, William, was born in 1816 – still some months before his parents married. It was not a happy event: their marriage was only made legal by virtue of the heavily pregnant Harriet drowning herself in the Serpentine lake in Hyde Park. It was a month before her decomposed body was discovered, allowing Percy and Mary to legitimise their union.

The Shelleys then took flight again. There ensued the momentous creative cauldron at Villa Diodati – the 'league of incest', as moralists of the time called it. Unlike her husband, who kept urging her towards rational adultery, Mary was neither a believer in free love nor Byronic recklessness. There were good examples not to be. On the way to Switzerland they were accompanied by Mary's stepsister Claire Clairmont, pregnant and abandoned by Byron. Mary was still nursing her four-month-old son. Alongside Lake Geneva, during this 'wet ungenial summer', the company of writers enlivened their confinement in the villa with ghost stories. Mary –momentously – contributed *Frankenstein* as part of the fun.

Over the next few years, the Shelleys were largely nomads in Italy where Mary, not yet twenty, gave birth to a third child, Clara. Ostensibly the Mediterranean climate was kinder to Percy's chronically weak lungs. Italy was unkinder to little Clara's bowels, and she died in infancy of dysentery. Mary was again pregnant while watching her daughter die and sank into profound depression. Novels were, amidst all this domestic catastrophe (Shelley was never a faithful husband), taking form in her mind and in notebooks, including the Italian set *Valperga* (published in 1823) and the remarkable study of father–daughter incest *Mathilda*. Mary's fourth child, Percy, would, mercifully, survive. His father did not. Shelley was drowned in a squall, sailing in the Gulf of Spezia.

The young widow devoted the remainder of her life to the two Percys (her second child, William, had also died of malaria in 1819). She installed herself as the custodian of her husband's literary legacy and, having partly reconciled herself with his family, her son's education. Percy was destined to be the inheritor of a title and a fortune. The family insisted, using the lever of a £250 p.a. allowance, on Mary and her son returning to England, where she was unhappy and chronically lonely and he was turned into exactly the kind of Englishman his father detested. Nor were Mary's relations with her father always good. Mary's financial situation eased when young Percy succeeded to the family title in 1844. She was not, however, to enjoy any happy years, dying of a brain tumour, still in her early fifties. Her radiant beauty had been wiped out by smallpox, some while before. Everything, even death and decay, happened to Mary Shelley too young.

She published novels in the 1820s and 1830s – most of them with the 'Prince of Puffers', Henry Colburn, for cash down and not much of it. Fiction was no longer a parlour game for her. The most interesting of Shelley's later novels is *The Last Man*. The action is set in the last years of the twenty-first century. England has become a republic. The abdicated royal family figure centrally around the person of the anchorite philosopher-narrator Lionel Verney. Shelley and Byron appear under thinnest disguise. The third volume (the climax is tediously late in coming) features a worldwide plague which provokes first anarchy (the Irish make a spirited assault on Albion), then universal death to the human race. Lionel is left – a Robinson Crusoe of the future, the sole survivor of the 'merciless sickle'. Conceptually *The Last Man* is, like *Frankenstein*, strikingly original. And, clearly enough, it allegorises Mary's late-life loneliness. But, as a story, it is sawdust – and unimaginative. Nautical transport two centuries hence is still by sail and wars are fought with the sword. Nor, it would seem, has medicine made great progress.

A stronger case can be mounted for *Mathilda*. The dying heroine narrates her father's incestuous advances on her and her love for the young poet, Woodville, who is later drowned. Is the novel (written during her deepest depression in 1818) a veiled indictment of her father? The blunt fact is that nothing Shelley wrote after *Frankenstein* is anywhere as good as *Frankenstein*. Why? The male chauvinist reply is that her husband helped her out. Without Percy she was only half a writer. So, perhaps, would he have been without her.

The feminist movement which has championed the elevation of Mary to canonical rank takes a different line. It was an enterprising woman scholar who brought *Mathilda* to light in 1959 – and with it the raging controversy over whether Mary was an incest survivor or not. It was the critic Ellen Moers, in 1974, who argued – persuasively – that *Frankenstein* should be read as the 'trauma of the afterbirth'. Such moments as those in Chapter 5, when Victor looks down on what he has given birth to, do not, Moers suggest, strike one as the responses of a father:

> It was on a dreary night of November that I beheld the accomplishment of my toils ... It was already one in the morning; the rain pattered dismally against the panes, and my candle was nearly burnt out, when, by the glimmer of the half-extinguished light, I saw the dull yellow eye of the creature open; it breathed hard, and a convulsive motion agitated its limbs.
>
> How can I describe my emotions at this catastrophe, or how delineate the wretch whom with such infinite pains and care I had endeavoured to form?

Inventor's remorse or post-natal depression?

FN   Mary Shelley (née Mary Wollstonecraft Godwin)
MRT *Frankenstein*
Biog Anne K. Mellor, *Mary Shelley: Her Life, Her Fiction, Her Monsters* (1990)

25. Mrs Catherine Gore 1799–1861

Mrs Gore is a Woman of the World.

The undisputed queen of the 'silver fork' school, Gore fed the fantasies of the middle class about the depravities and sophistications of the upper class with more novels than anyone has been able to count. 'Anonymity' – with the thrilling implication that she was actually 'inside' the world she wrote about – was essential to her enterprise. It also allowed her to over-produce, shamelessly (as many as two novels in a week – under allegedly different hands – in her heyday).

Catherine Moody was born into a respectable bourgeois background. Her father was a Nottinghamshire wine merchant:'trade' – that shameful word – was her background, not 'society'. Charles Moody died around the time of her birth; her mother then remarried and moved to London as the wife of a prosperous physician: a small step upwards in the social scale. The family circumstances were comfortable and – as Catherine's later writing confirms – she was well educated by expensive governesses and tutors. At an early age she showed literary ability and was fondly nicknamed in her family 'the Poetess'.

In 1823 she married Captain Charles Arthur Gore of the Life Guards. Another step up. The Gores were connected with the Earls of Arran. Captain Gore left the service in the same year he married. Spared foreign postings Catherine evidently saw at first hand some of the high Regency London life she describes so intimately in her fiction. As the *Athenaeum* put it, in 1837, 'Mrs Gore writes for the world and she is herself a woman of the world.' For 'world', read *monde*. Richard Hengist Horne, in his pen-portrait of her in *A New Spirit of the Age*, astutely noted that 'Mrs Gore excels in the portraiture of the upper section of the middle class just at that point of contact with the aristocracy.' She herself in the Preface to *Pin Money* (1831) – picking up Mrs Bennet's crass comments in the opening paragraph of *Pride and Prejudice* – claimed that she was transferring 'the familiar narrative of Miss Austen to a higher sphere of society'. Pemberton, not Longbourn, was Gore's territory.

Gore's writing career began, however, with florid historical romances, such as *Theresa Marchmont, or, The Maid of Honour* (1824). She was 'puffed' outrageously by her publisher (the aforementioned 'Prince of Puffers') Henry Colburn, an enterprising rogue. It was under Colburn's imprint that she had her first hit, *Women as They Are, or, The Manners of the Day* (1830). George IV, no less, pronounced it 'the best and most amusing novel published within my remembrance'. Poor Sir Walter. She then embarked on a series of novels illustrative of English society, of which the finest are *The Hamiltons, or the New Era* (1834), a depiction of the social consequences of the 1832 Reform Bill; *Mrs Armytage, or, Female Domination* (1836); *Cecil, or, The Adventures of a Coxcomb* (1841); and *The Banker's Wife, or, Court and City* (1843).

In 1832, for reasons which are unclear (they may involve scandal or, more probably, debt), Gore moved to France and thereafter lived a life of seclusion. Domestically that life was full to overflowing. She had ten surviving children in these years and, doubtless, more pregnancies than that. Although she never managed, or wanted, to break out of the constricting frames of silver-forkery, Gore's is a considerable literary talent. She has, at her best, as easy a narrative manner as Thackeray – a novelist who good-naturedly parodied her while admitting to admiration (*Vanity Fair* owes something to her). She writes a vigorous, slangy prose embedded with sharp epigrams. As a social novelist, Gore handles the theme of money and social mobility ('rising' in the world) more cleverly than any writer, of either sex, of her vintage. She was an able sociologist. Her *Sketches of English Character* (1846) bears comparison with Thackeray's *The Snobs of England* (1846). Her fiction, in line with the changing mood of the time, became more 'domestic' in later years and lost something of its sparkle.

There was little in those later years to sparkle about. The 'hungry forties' were not conducive to Mrs Gore's 'tuft-hunting' (i.e. snobbish) fiction. Of her ten children, only two survived their mother, and she was widowed in 1846. After a heroically long writing career, she inherited a substantial property in 1850, but was impoverished (again) five years later when her former guardian, Sir John Dean Paul, defrauded her of £20,000. He was subsequently sentenced to four years' imprisonment for this and other offences against his clients. Gore died, prematurely, aged sixty-one. She had been blind for several years, but wrote, manfully, to the end. By the time of her death she had yet again written herself into prosperity, leaving £14,000.

FN   (Mrs) Catherine Grace Frances Gore (née Moody)
MRT *Mrs Armytage*
Biog *ODNB* (Winifred Hughes)

26. Harriet Martineau 1802–1876

For my own part, I had rather suffer any inconvenience from having to work occasionally in chambers and kitchen ... than witness the subservience in which the menial class is held in Europe. Martineau, on housework

Harriet Martineau was born in Norwich, the sixth of eight children of a textile manufacturer of Huguenot origin. One of her younger brothers was the later theologian (and in later life, her 'oracle'), James Martineau, and the family was Unitarian, a doctrine which approved of female education. The Martineau circumstances – during Harriet's childhood, at least – were prosperous and Harriet herself was fearsomely precocious. 'My first political interest', she blandly recalls, 'was the death of Nelson. I was then four years old.' Her literary interests were even more advanced: she was reading Milton at the age of seven. It says much about the intellectual earnestness of the Martineau household that she was allowed to do so. The earnestness verged at times on morbidity. She recalls, as a little girl, digging two 'graves' in the garden with her brother James, lying in them, then discussing, afterwards, their impressions of 'death'.

'Life' was to be hard. At the age of twelve there appeared symptoms of the deafness which was to blight her life. She ascribed the ailment to a dishonest wet nurse, during infancy, whose milk had dried up and virtually starved her. Lifelong she was prey to bowel complaints (described with disarming frankness in her autobiography). In her early teens, her hearing was largely gone and with it most of her marriage prospects. Her fiancé, John Hugh Worthington, a young minister, went mad and died shortly after they became engaged. In her autobiography, Martineau stoically records the tragedy as a lucky escape.

In 1829 the Martineau family was utterly ruined when her father's business failed. Thereafter Harriet supported herself by her pen, claiming to find the loss of gentility intellectually liberating. Her material needs were simple and, as a political economist (from the age of fourteen!), she invested her eventually substantial earnings shrewdly. Ideologically Martineau moved from theism to Comtean rationalism and what she called 'Necessarianism' (although, famously, she was to dabble with the mystical cult of mesmerism in her later years, claiming a miraculous cure of her deafness in 1845). In 1852 she moved to London, a liberation that came with a 'room of her own', which she describes charmingly:

> It was a dark foggy November morning when I arrived in London. My lodgings were up two pair of stairs ... A respectable sitting room to the front, and a clean, small bedroom behind seemed to me all that could possibly be desired, – seeing that I was to have them all to myself. To be sure, they did look very dark, that first morning of yellow fog: but it was seldom so dark again; and when the spring came on, and I moved down into the handsomer rooms on the first floor, I thought my lodgings really pleasant. In the summer mornings, when I made my coffee at seven o'clock, and sat down to my work, with the large windows open, the sun-blinds down, the street fresh watered, and the flower-girls' baskets visible from my seat, I wished for nothing better.

She enjoyed her first success with the didactic stories, *Illustrations of Political Economy*, serialised in monthly parts, 1832–5 (the form of publication used by Chapman and Hall, publishers of Dickens's *The Pickwick Papers*, a year later). Up to 10,000 copies of these exemplary fables were sold monthly. By means of crude fictional narratives, the *Illustrations* introduced many of the themes picked up by later Victorian 'social problem' novels. Fiction, she demonstrated, could conduct a dialogue with the higher economics. Martineau thus found herself famous and £600 richer, though other series of the *Illustrations* were less popular. A little of her didacticism went a long way. Her *Forest and Game-Law Tales* (1845), based on spectacularly unsexy research supplied by a parliamentary committee, were over-shadowed by the Corn Law repeal, and flopped.

Martineau's major full-length fiction is *Deerbrook* (1839), a novel which Carlyle, no less, pronounced 'very ligneous' – not the kind of term which would do much for a dustjacket shout-line. This 'study of provincial life' follows the career of two orphaned sisters, Margaret and Hester Ibbotson, who come from Birmingham to the 'rather pretty' village of Deerbrook, to lodge with their cousins, the Greys. The narrative climaxes on a vividly described cholera epidemic. Aptly, if unkindly, called a 'poor novel with a few good pages', *Deerbrook* anticipates some plot complications in *Middlemarch* (George Eliot, as her notes indicate, was also thinking of a cholera episode for her story) and was influential on the so-called 'novel of community'.

In 1834, Martineau travelled to America (not an easy trip at this date for a handicapped single woman) and wrote her impressions up in *Society in America* (1837). Unsurprisingly she was strongly abolitionist. In 1846 she travelled even further afield, to Egypt. As a non-fiction writer Martineau is admired for her candid autobiography (published posthumously), her forthright views on the woman question, her enlightened views on medicine – notably her 1844 essay on 'Life in the Sick-room' – and for her popularisation, and translation, of the inventor of 'sociology', Auguste Comte.

Fiction, however, still played a part in her life's work. In addition to the above, she published: *Five Years of Youth* (1831), *The Playfellow* (1841) and – most interestingly – *The Hour and the Man* (1841), a romance on the career of the Haitian revolutionary, Toussaint L'Ouverture. In her later life Martineau was wealthy enough to construct not just a room, but a whole house of her own, in the Lake District, near her idol William Wordsworth's Grasmere.

FN   Harriet Martineau
MRT   *Deerbrook*
Biog R. K. Webb, *Harriet Martineau: A Radical Victorian* (1960)

27. The Bulwer-Lyttons: Edward and Rosina
1803–1873/1802–1882

Bulwer must be counted among the eminent authors who have not made and not deserved success in married life. Leslie Stephen

What to call him has always been a bibliographer's nightmare. His full name in his peacock prime was Edward George Earle Lytton Bulwer-Lytton. The multiply bar-relled name proclaimed a distinguished pedigree: on the paternal side, his ancestors had been ennobled soldiers since the Conquest and his mother's family (the Lytton line) were distinguished scholars. Novelists, until him, did not figure.

After one of the chronically awful marriages that ran in the Lytton family, his father died when Edward was four. The youngest of three sons, he was brought up, smotheringly, by his mother, which had an indelibly feminising effect on his person-ality. As Harriet Martineau put it, spitefully, he 'dressed a woman's spirit in man's clothing'. Menswear would, in fact, be one of his more lasting legacies. His mother judged her Edward too delicate for Eton. Educated at home or in less gruelling estab-lishments, given the run of one of the best private libraries in England, he emerged a prodigy of learning, precocious authorship and dandyism. At sixteen, he claimed, he had his first and only perfect love affair. Elders broke it off and he carried a frac-tured heart to his grave. At seventeen, he published his first book, *Ismael; an Oriental Tale*. He was judged strong enough to handle Cambridge and, in 1825, he won the Chancellor's Gold Medal for poetry. Now a young 'pseudo-Byron', he burnished his image with an affair with the wicked Lord's cast-off mistress, Lady Caroline Lamb.

In August 1827, Bulwer (as he was called in early life) took a fatal misstep by marrying for love. Rosina Wheeler (1802–82) was Irish by birth – not a recommen-dation. When her mother fled her brutal husband, ten-year-old Rosina had been taken under the wing of an uncle, John Doyle, the Governor of Guernsey. She grew up a beauty, witty but (by the standards of Bulwer's circle) penniless. The courtship was ominously stormy and the match was implacably opposed by Bulwer's mother. In the most drastic of parental rebukes, she cut her disobedient son off without a penny.

It forced him into writing fashionable novels – not in the 1820s a profession for the fashionable. But he had a remarkably adaptive mind. What were people reading? He identified the popular appetite and hit the mark in 1828 with *Pelham*, a mystery story with murder, madness and seduction in high-life as its mainspring. Marketed by the notorious Henry Colburn, *Pelham* was a bestseller and promoted its author to the top of that elite league of novelists who could command £1,000 a title. It was read everywhere and had a lasting effect not merely on genre ('silver fork') fiction but on gentlemen's dress. In one of his digressions the hero lays down twenty-two 'Maxims' as to how the gentleman should array himself. The most momentous was Maxim 17: 'Avoid many colours; and seek, by some one prevalent and quiet tint, to sober down the others. Apelles used only four colours, and always subdued those which were more florid, by a darkening varnish.'

Pelham's maxims drove the Scottish sage, Thomas Carlyle, into paroxysmic satire on the 'philosophy of clothes', in *Sartor Resartus*. The tailors and leaders of fashion fell into line, however. The Bennet girls, in Jane Austen's novel, are thrown into a collective flutter when Mr Bingley calls at Longbourn in a vivid blue coat. Thirty years later, the eligible young man would have been dressed as for a funeral. Bulwer was not merely the new Byron but the new Brummel.

Between 1827 and 1834 Bulwer published eight full-length novels. He won a seat in Parliament and threw himself into the cause of political reform. He was marked as a rising man. Success on the literary and political fronts was, however, marred by spectacular domestic failure. On a trip to Italy in 1834 to research *The Last Days of Pompeii*, relations between him and Rosina broke down. It did not help that, as gossip reported, Bulwer was accompanied by his mistress. There were, by now, two children. A legal separation was enacted in April 1836 and two years later Rosina's children were forcibly removed from her on the grounds of maternal neglect. It was untrue, but Edward wanted custody of his son, the eventual heir to Knebworth. The law was firmly biased towards the father in cases where wealth and titles were at stake. Rosina felt he could quite well make do with his three illegitimate children.

In the same year, Lytton became a baronet, a title of which he was inordinately proud. In the rage of losing her children, Rosina wrote a furious *roman-à-clef*, *Cheveley; or, The Man of Honour* (1839). It regaled the world with Bulwer's brutalities, his meanness (he kept her on a meagre allowance of £400 p.a.) and his gross, bastard-spawning adulteries. Over the subsequent years, Rosina bombarded the press with 'revelations' of Edward's infamy and confected innumerable lawsuits. She wrote as many as twenty letters a day to his clubs, with obscenities scrawled on the envelopes. Although his lawyers frightened off the better class of publisher, she turned out a stream of frantic revenge novels. Her cause was taken up by the satirists of the time, notably Thackeray, who launched his early career with hilarious squibs against the 'Knebworth Apollo'.

Lytton bore it all stoically, taking consolation in his mistresses, his opium pipe (there is a fine picture of him sucking one the size of an Alpine horn), his catamites (as gossip fantasised), and his increasing stature as a novelist. What had shaped up as a promising political career ended when in 1841 he resigned his seat in Parliament and effectively withdrew from public life. But he inherited the Knebworth Estate in 1843 and with it a huge fortune. He needed no longer to write for money and entered on the most interesting phase of his authorial career. His writing is preposterously high-flown (Thackeray was right about that), but he has a remarkable list of innovations to his credit. With *Pelham* he founded the fashionable genre. With *Paul Clifford* (1830) and *Eugene Aram* (1832) he pioneered novels which dealt intelligently with crime. *Quo Vadis*, *Ben-Hur* and, more distantly, the toga melodramas of Cecil B. DeMille can be seen as the progeny of *The Last Days of Pompeii*. *Zanoni* (1842), a 'mystical mystery', inaugurated several works on the paranormal (most readably, the long short story, 'The Haunted and the Haunters', 1859). *The Caxtons, A Family Picture* (1849) and its sequels made fashionable 'domestic' fiction of the Barchester kind. *The Coming Race* (1871), his last substantial work, is a hollow-earth fantasy, introducing subterranean aliens with new, electric technologies who will one day invade the surface of the planet, so fulfilling 'the Darwinian proposition'. H. G. Wells, one suspects, could have recited *The Coming Race* by heart.

By mid-century, Lytton (as he now was) had put his public life back together again. His private life was something else. He had callously abandoned his daughter Emily to die of typhus fever in a London lodging house. Her body was brought back to the magnificent family house at Knebworth and it was given out to the world that she had expired there, by her loving father's side. It is the most despicable of Lytton's actions – unless one credits Rosina's allegation that he once hired an assassin to poison her. She had not even been informed her daughter was ill, a fact she furiously publicised. As always, he rose above her 'calumnies' and, with the help of powerful friends, suppressed any mention of them in the press.

In the early 1850s, Lytton, now a land-owning Whig, decided to return to politics. This second parliamentary career began well with his appointment as Colonial Secretary in Lord Derby's ministry. But Rosina haunted him, like a witch's curse. When he and Dickens (a firm friend) put on a charity dramatic performance at the Duke of Devonshire's house in 1851, Rosina threatened to turn up as Nell Gwyn, the orange girl. A nervous Dickens consulted his Scotland Yard friend, Inspector Charles Field ('Bucket' in Bleak House) and posted private detectives at the door. She could make such occasions very awkward.

Her harassments climaxed at Hertford, in June 1858, where Edward was publicly canvassing. She heckled and was cheered on by the crowd who found the row more interesting than government policy. Lytton, driven to desperate remedies, had her abducted and incarcerated for a month in a private lunatic asylum. Tame doctors provided the necessary certification. The *Telegraph*, as part of its campaign against Derby, took up her cause and she was released. But the episode gave Wilkie Collins his *donnée* for the plot of *The Woman in White* and the wicked baronet, Sir Percival Glyde. Rosina wrote to thank him. An eventual accommodation was reached between the warring couple. She was given a handsomely increased stipend and access to her son Robert, in return for keeping quiet. She fired off one last work of furious fiction in 1858 – the interestingly named *The World and his Wife, or a Person of Consequence: A Photographic Novel* – and otherwise did as instructed. But it was the end of Bulwer's public career. He faded into political obscurity with the fall of the Derby ministry. At least he had his opium pipe.

What is his legacy? Dark clothes (*Reservoir Dogs* would not have been *Reservoir Dogs* without *Pelham*) is one. Another is the annual, widely publicised, competition sponsored by the English Department of San Jose University for the worst opening sentence to a novel, something, that is, as hilariously bad as *Paul Clifford*'s:

> It was a dark and stormy night; the rain fell in torrents – except at occasional intervals, when it was checked by a violent gust of wind which swept up the streets (for it is in London that our scene lies), rattling along the housetops, and fiercely agitating the scanty flame of the lamps that struggled against the darkness.

A third is Knebworth House which, as horrifically 'restored' by Bulwer, will be familiar as the ultra-gothic setting to films such as *The Omen* and *Eyes Wide Open*, while Knebworth's rolling grounds have hosted England's biggest open air pop concerts. Lytton's ghost, those who have slept in his house testify, 'walks'. It is nice to think how annoyed he would be by the Rolling Stones strutting around his estate.

FN   Edward George Earle Lytton Bulwer-Lytton (later Lord Lytton); Rosina Bulwer-Lytton (Anne Doyle, née Wheeler)

MRT *Pelham, Cheveley*

Biog *ODNB* (Andrew Brown)

28. Benjamin Disraeli 1804–1881

When I want to read a novel, I write one.

There is a sense in which Benjamin Disraeli was always young, just as his great opposite, William Ewart Gladstone (who formed his last Cabinet at the age of eighty-three), was always old. Between them, these colossi of Victorian Westminster epitomise a perennial contradiction in British and American politics: we want our leaders to have the energy of youth, but we also want them to have the gravitas of age.

Among his minor achievements, Disraeli was the first politician to introduce hairstyle into politics – something which Byron and Bulwer-Lytton had done for literature a few years earlier. His mop of oiled, jet-black ringlets remained the delight of cartoonists throughout his long career. His hair proclaimed his youth, even in age.

Disraeli's is a wonderful career. The grandson of a humble Jewish immigrant, he clambered up the slippery pole (his term) of politics to the very top. It is a tribute not merely to him but to the openness of what seems at first glance the most closed of political institutions – the British Conservative Party. He had, it must be said, assistance. Benjamin's father, the reclusive scholar Isaac D'Israeli, a non-practising Jew, had his newborn son circumcised according to Jewish rites. But, prudently, he also had the boy baptised in the Church of England at the age of thirteen.

This dual allegiance inspired in Disraeli what one of his biographers, Jane Ridley, terms the 'Marrano mentalité' of the covert Jew. That mental facility aided him in the fluidly strategic shifts of his early party affiliations. In the course of eight years, the young Disraeli was by turns radical, Tory, loyal supporter of his party leader, rebel, and – arguably – back-stabbing traitor. Did Disraeli actually believe in the protectionist arguments he used to bring down his leader in 1846, thus clearing a necessary space for himself at the top? One doesn't know, but tactical treachery would have been quite in character.

As with party, so with sex. The young Disraeli was a gigolo, prepared to sacrifice any woman to the needs of his career (or any man – he may, it is speculated, have had homosexual moments in his youth). He discarded his first mistress, Henrietta Sykes, when she became an embarrassment. He proposed to the widow of his patron Wyndham Lewis, a less than dazzlingly beautiful woman twelve years older than he was – allegedly, according to his opponents, while the coroner was still clumping around in the house. It was Mary Anne's jointure he needed. His debts were such that, were it not for the immunity from arrest for debt given to Members of Parliament, Disraeli would surely have found himself in the clink. By the early 1840s, he owed thousands.

His debut in fiction, the 'silver fork' novel of high life, *Vivian Grey*, was published in 1827 to pay off some earlier vexatious debts. There was uproar when the anonymous novelist – presumed to be someone of importance – was revealed to be a nobody 'and a Jew!' Similarly flashy-trashy-but-very-clever works followed: *The Young Duke* (1831), *Contarini Fleming* (1832) and *Alroy* (1833). These extravaganzas

brought in welcome cash for the author and even more for his unscrupulous publisher, Henry Colburn. They established Disraeli as a leader of the 'fashnabble' novelists (as a contemptuous, but not yet so successful, Thackeray labelled them).

This first career in fiction ended in 1837 when, after three attempts, Disraeli
finally made it into Parliament as Tory member for Maidstone. His second career
was launched in the early 1840s. He had by now put himself at the head of the
reformist 'Young England' clique which was at odds with the party leader, Robert
Peel. To promote his Conservative cause Disraeli published (with Colburn again)
a trilogy of powerful political novels: *Coningsby* (1844), *Sybil* (1845) and *Tancred*
(1847). In them he outlined his creed: an amalgam of neo-feudalist nostalgia, a
disdain for the bourgeois ('Dutch') so-called 'revolution' of 1688, high Anglicanism, and 'one nation' utopianism. *Tancred* asserts his favourite religious proposition,
that Christianity is merely the 'completion' of Judaism and as dependent upon it as
a house on its foundations. But no words from any novel have reverberated so much
through the discourse of British politics as the famous remark of the working-class
aristocrat Stephen Morley in *Sybil* to the blue-blood friend of the people, Egremont,
in the ruins of an abbey, symbolising old England:

> 'Well, society may be in its infancy,' said Egremont slightly smiling; 'but, say what
> you like, our Queen reigns over the greatest nation that ever existed.'
>
> 'Which nation?' asked the younger stranger, 'for she reigns over two.'
>
> The stranger paused; Egremont was silent, but looked inquiringly.
>
> 'Yes,' resumed the younger stranger after a moment's interval. 'Two nations;
> between whom there is no intercourse and no sympathy; who are as ignorant of
> each other's habits, thoughts, and feelings, as if they were dwellers in different
> zones, or inhabitants of different planets; who are formed by a different breeding,
> are fed by a different food, are ordered by different manners, and are not governed
> by the same laws.'
>
> 'You speak of –' said Egremont, hesitatingly.
>
> 'THE RICH AND THE POOR.'

'Young England' was, as its slogan-name asserts, an intellectually youthful
creed (although Disraeli was well into his forties when he expounded it). All three
novels express the optimistic belief that 'the Youth of the Nation are the trustees
of Posterity' and that the world is their oyster, which they with sword will open.
Romantic as the novels are, *Sybil* contains the most graphic depictions of working-
class wretchedness to be found in Victorian fiction. Disraeli had, by the 1840s,
come a long way from silver-forkery. The Young England trilogy represents the
most effective use of fiction by a politician on record in English politics.

For the next two decades Disraeli was preoccupied either with high office, or achieving it. His resignation from the premiership in 1868 (having got the second Reform Bill enacted) allowed him time to embark on a third career in fiction. Now a Longmans, Green author, he wrote the political *Bildungsroman*, *Lothair* (1870) and, at the end of his phenomenally full life (and yet another term as Prime Minister) the narcissistic autobiographical romance, *Endymion* (1880). For this last work Disraeli received the then record sum of £10,000 from Longman. He had ascended to the top of yet another slippery pole. England remains two nations.

FN   Benjamin Disraeli (born D'Israeli, later Earl of Beaconsfield)
MRT   *Sybil, or, The Two Nations*
Biog J. Ridley, *The Young Disraeli* (1995)

29. Nathaniel Hawthorne 1804–1864

That blue-eyed darling Nathaniel knew disagreeable things in his inner soul. He was careful to send them out in disguise. D. H. Lawrence

Nathaniel Hawthorne was four years old when his mariner father died of fever in the Dutch colony of Surinam (the same fever-pit where, one recalls, Aphra Behn sets *Oroonoko*, and where *her* father died). It meant that Nathaniel grew up emotionally close to his sister, Elizabeth ('Ebe'). The two children learned to read together and shared their thoughts. Closeness was further fostered by an obscure injury to his foot which Nathaniel incurred at the age of thirteen playing cricket – this may have been psychosomatic but none the less kept him mooning about at home for a year.

Elizabeth was a strong-minded, highly literate child – she herself had pretensions to authorship – who grew up into a fine-looking, dark-haired, fiercely independent woman. The Hawthornes were the product of two distinguished family lines: the 'Hathornes', who could trace their pedigree back to the original Puritan settlers, and the Mannings on his mother's side – more commercially minded than the Hathornes, who were governors by nature. Nathaniel added the 'w' in young manhood to distance himself, it is presumed, from the Salem witch-trials, in which his ancestor, John Hathorne, had been a judge. He was never easy with that heritage.

On being widowed, Nathaniel's mother moved to her parents' house only a few streets away in Salem, the children's birthplace. The Hathornes later moved to family property in Raymond, Maine, where Nathaniel and Ebe would spend their childhood years – he returning to Salem more often than she.

On Nathaniel's leaving school, their adult paths necessarily separated. He enrolled at Bowdoin College and on graduation, with high, but not class-topping, honours in 1824, he embarked, for over a decade, on his 'attic years'. The Hathornes were now living in Salem again, his mother having returned from Raymond and taken up her abode in her deceased father's house, 'a tall, ugly, old grayish building'. Here Nathaniel secluded himself in his 'haunted chamber'. As he recalled in a memoir twenty years later, 'I scarcely held intercourse outside of my own family; seldom going out except at twilight, or only to take the nearest way to the most convenient solitude.' Ebe was to him, over this period, more than a sister, but less than a wife. It was she, it is recorded, who fetched the books he needed from the Salem public library.

What was going through Hawthorne's mind and soul at this period will never be fully known. He was writing the stories – typically dark in tone – later collected as *Twice-Told Tales*, which brought him some reputation. Full recognition of his genius would await the publication of his major novels, ten years later. It was during these attic years that he wrote one of his darkest meditations on human sin. But what sin? In 'The Minister's Black Veil', a nameless 'secret sin' leads the hero, as a young clergyman, to appear everywhere with his face covered. He obstinately refuses to have it removed, even on his deathbed. In his stories of this period, Hawthorne is given to such resonantly ominous, but vague, statements as that in 'The Haunted Mind': 'In the depths of every heart, there is a tomb and a dungeon.' What is Hawthorne alluding to?

Of specific interest, it is suggested, is an early work called 'Alice Doane's Appeal'. It is, by Hawthorne's standards, poorly constructed, which might explain why he was reluctant to have it reprinted after first publication, anonymously, in 1835. It was Ebe, interestingly enough, after Nathaniel's death, who arranged for 'Alice Doane's Appeal' to be brought back to print. The Doane children, we learn, were orphaned in infancy by a savage Indian attack on their homestead. Leonard and his sister Alice have been brought up together, in Salem. Their 'tie' is of the 'closest' and marked by a 'concentrated fervour of affection'. Enter a stranger, Walter Brome, from the 'Old World' – the snake in the Doanes' garden. 'Evil' by nature, Walter seduces Alice. Strangely, he has strong physical resemblances to Leonard, who senses a horrible 'sympathy' with someone whom he hates. Walter is, it finally emerges, Leonard's twin and – more horribly – brother to Alice. Was he aware of the incestuous implications? The story is maddeningly vague on the matter, as it is on why it was that Walter's existence is unknown, and how he happened to be raised – with a different identity – three thousand miles away.

Leonard kills Walter, and half-buries his body in the winter ice, though it will, of course, rise again. There is a bizarre *Walpurgisnacht* episode in which the dead rise from the Salem graveyard. All those once thought respectable citizens proclaim their secret sins. All are guilty. The story ends with suggestive, but imprecise, phraseology, hinting at things not clearly said:

> We build the memorial column on the height which our fathers made sacred with their blood, poured out in a holy cause. And here, in dark, funereal stone, should rise another monument, sadly commemorative of the errors of an earlier race, and not to be cast down, while the human heart has one infirmity that may result in crime.

What crime? There is other grist in Hawthorne's life for the psychobiographer's mill. Why did he emerge from his 'haunted chamber' in 1835, enter the world of books, become a minor Massachusetts 'Custom House' functionary, and marry in 1841? Why, on his mother's death in 1849, did he embark on that astonishing burst of creativity which, in three years, produced *The Scarlet Letter* (1850), *The House of the Seven Gables* (1851) and *The Blithedale Romance* (1852)? The most sensational investigations focus on Hawthorne's relationship with Ebe. She never married and loathed her brother's blameless wife, Sophia, whom he had married, on the verge of middle age, after a sibling relationship of thirty-eight years. Ebe did everything she could to frustrate the match and never formed a civil relationship with her sister-in-law.

The outright allegation of incest between Nathaniel and Ebe was delivered by two books, published within months of each other, in 1984: Philip Young's *Hawthorne's Secret: An Untold Tale* and, less aggressively, Gloria C. Erlich's *Family Themes and Hawthorne's Fiction: The Tenacious Web*. The incest hypothesis was fanned to the pitch of critical furore, following a review of Young's book in the *New York Review of Books* by Leo Marx. A venerable critic of American literature, Marx seemed to give some provisional assent to the idea that there may have been something of the like between Nathaniel and Ebe, and it could indeed explain things.

The incest hypothesis depends on thematic deductions from texts of the fiction, bolstered by dark hints by friends such as Herman Melville, who detected 'a blackness, ten times black' shrouding Hawthorne's soul. He believed, said Melville, that all his life Hawthorne had 'concealed some great secret, which would, were it known, explain all the mysteries in his career'. Young and Erlich presumed to have found the source of that 'great secret' buried in distant Manning family history. The documentary source (a 'smoking gun') was Joseph B. Felt's *Annals of Salem*, a volume which Hawthorne is known to have borrowed from the Salem Library and which Ebe almost certainly also read (she may even have taken it out for her brother). In 1681, the *Annals* record that Nicholas Manning was, at his enraged wife's complaint, found guilty of incest with his two sisters. This skeleton in the Manning-Hathorne closet had escaped critical notice for 150 years because the *Annals* recorded the event anonymously. As was usual, it was the women who bore the brunt of the public humiliation and punishment in 1681. They were sentenced to a night in prison, to be whipped publicly on their naked bodies (or pay a fine) and to sit on a high stool in the aisle of the Salem meeting house with a paper on their heads inscribed: 'This is for whorish carriage with my naturall Brother.'

The connection with the opening scenes of *The Scarlet Letter* are manifest. Hester Prynne emerges into the marketplace at Salem, with the letter of her sin inscribed on her breast:

> Her attire, which indeed, she had wrought for the occasion in prison, and had modelled much after her own fancy, seemed to express the attitude of her spirit, the desperate recklessness of her mood, by its wild and picturesque peculiarity. But the point which drew all eyes, and, as it were, transfigured the wearer – so that both men and women who had been familiarly acquainted with Hester Prynne were now impressed as if they beheld her for the first time – was that SCARLET LETTER, so fantastically embroidered and illuminated upon her bosom. It had the effect of a spell, taking her out of the ordinary relations with humanity, and enclosing her in a sphere by herself.

Hester's physical appearance, notably her 'dark and abundant hair, so glossy that it threw off the sunshine with a gleam' plausibly recalls Ebe's crowning glory. And, arguably (very arguably), Hawthorne is recalling 'whorish carriage' between himself and his sister. It's exciting stuff. But Philip Roth – abhorrer of biographers – pours cold water on it by noting, with much sarcasm, in *Exit Ghost*, that novelists do not use novels to confess their sins. It would be like inscribing love letters on lavatory walls.

FN   Nathaniel Hawthorne (born Hathorne)
MRT   *The Scarlet Letter*
Biog   P. Young, *Hawthorne's Secret: An Untold Tale* (1984); G. C. Erlich, *Family Themes and Hawthorne's Fiction: The Tenacious Web* (1984)

30. Harrison Ainsworth 1805–1882

I consider myself very like Lord Byron. Harrison Ainsworth in a letter to the Edinburgh Review, aged sixteen

For Victorian novelists, historical romance was the bow of Ulysses. The greatest practitioners (Dickens, Eliot, Thackeray, Hardy, Charlotte Brontë, Bulwer-Lytton) wrote at least one – and of none of them can it be said it was their best work. For every disappointed modern reader of *Romola*, there are ten thousand satisfied readers of *Middlemarch*. No one, it seemed, could emulate the author of *Waverley*. Harrison Ainsworth qualifies as the most consistently successful. He was born in Manchester, the son of a solicitor with a distinguished Lancashire pedigree. He enjoyed the benefit of a grammar-school education: then, as now, Manchester's was the best in the country. At sixteen, having penned some appalling 'Lines on Leaving Manchester School', he was articled to his father's profession (just as Scott had been). No pettifogger, he affected Byronic airs and a taste for antiquarianism from his youth onwards. He was indoctrinated with Jacobite and Tory beliefs which would remain with him throughout his writing career.

When his father died in 1824, aged only forty-six, Ainsworth, freed from the scrivener's pen, travelled south to London – ostensibly to read law at the Inner Temple. He promptly threw himself into the literary world. Shrewdly he married Fanny Ebers, the daughter of his first publisher, in 1826. Dashing as he was, Ainsworth was unlucky in love and both his marriages would end unhappily.

In 1831, inspired by a visit to Chesterfield, he began writing *Rookwood*. Following the French – principally Hugo's – model, he introduced into his gothic tale, which features the highwayman exploits of Dick Turpin (notably the legendary ride from London to York on Black Bess, which Ainsworth invented), *chansons d'argot* and 'flash' or low slang. Dickens would borrow Ainsworthian feathers for the low-life scenes of *Oliver Twist*. Richard Bentley brought *Rookwood* out to huge sales success in 1834 and Ainsworth was hailed as the new Scott. The novel was illustrated, sumptuously, by George Cruikshank. The two men would forge a useful partnership over a series of novels. Later in life, Cruikshank would claim to be the 'inventor' of the narratives. He was certainly the more gifted of the two.

For a couple of years, Ainsworth's star rose higher even than Dickens's. 'The sword', his biographer melodramatically declares, 'was drawn between them.' In addition to aspiring to Scott's mantle, Ainsworth also cultivated a Byronic dandyism with, as one ironist put it, the 'chest of Apollo and the waist of a gnat'. So much for that cockney, Boz. *Jack Sheppard* (1839), the Fieldingesque tale of an eighteenth-century cracksman, again with Cruikshank's Hogarthian illustrations, enjoyed another immense success, at the height of which there were eight pirated dramatic versions running on the London stage. On the strength of it, Ainsworth set himself up in a fine house, Kensal Lodge, and held reign there over a literary salon of other 'fashionables'.

Despite this welcome celebrity, Ainsworth was alarmed by the moral fury stirred up by *Jack Sheppard*. The novel was accused of being a formula for murder when a man-servant, Francis Courvoisier, claimed he was inspired to slit his master's throat after reading Ainsworth's incendiary text. He was, none the less, hanged – fiction not being a strong defence in those days. Ainsworth, pusillanimous by nature, subsequently gave up 'Newgate' (i.e. crime) fiction and followed Scott's example (*Kenilworth*) and Victor Hugo's (*Notre-Dame de Paris*) by making famous historical places rather than notorious criminals the centre of his work. There followed such topographic best-sellers as *The Tower of London* (1840); *Old St Paul's* (1841), his best novel, set amidst the Plague and Great Fire of London, with plentiful borrowing from Defoe; and the floridly illustrated *Windsor Castle* (1843). Although he churned out a flood of other historical romances over the next forty years, Ainsworth's star fell inexorably. Bentley gave him £2,000 for *The Tower of London*. For wretched effusions such as *Beau Nash, or, Bath in the Eighteenth Century*, almost forty years later, he scraped a measly £100 from fifth-rate publishers.

Ainsworth was lucky, or unlucky, however you look at it, to live almost twice as long as his father. His decline from stardom to author's garret is the subject of one of the most poignant literary anecdotes of the period, retold probably more than once by Percy Fitzgerald, one of Dickens's smart young Bohemian set. 'I recall', said Fitzgerald, 'a dinner at Teddington, in the sixties, given by Frederic Chapman, the publisher, at which were Forster and Browning. The latter said humorously, "a sad forlorn-looking being stopped me today, and reminded me of old times. He presently resolved himself into – whom do you think? – Harrison Ainsworth!" "Good Heavens!" cried Forster, "is he still alive?"' Not just alive, but alive for another two decades. If the sword was ever drawn between Ainsworth and Boz, it drooped sadly in later life. But then, Scott himself had also died bankrupt and broken.

FN   William Harrison Ainsworth
MRT *Jack Sheppard*
Biog S. M. Ellis, *William Harrison Ainsworth and his friends* (1911)

31. Charles (James) Lever 1806–1872

From hand to mouth. Lever's description of his artistic method

There are novelists whose sole function in literary life is to inspire greater novelists. Charles Lever ranks high in this minor inspirational league. He was born in Dublin, in 1806, the son of a building contractor from Lancashire, and brought up with the social advantages, and social ambiguities, of his Anglo-Irish class. After Trinity College Dublin, he bounced around Europe and North America, gaining the reputation of a good fellow and a wastrel in the making. He studied medicine in a desultory way, earning himself the sobriquet Dr Quicksilver.

Young Mercury settled down after marrying his childhood sweetheart, Kate, in 1836. Now well on in years, he was encouraged to apply himself to literature by the novelist William Hamilton Maxwell and duly took over the editorship of the *Dublin University Magazine*. Fifteen years older, Maxwell was, like Lever, the son of a prosperous merchant with little inclination to honest labour. He too had attended Trinity College 'in a somewhat desultory manner' and claimed to have seen action at Waterloo where he served as a captain of infantry. Maxwell subsequently married an heiress, took orders, and settled down to the comfortable existence of a hunting parson. His most popular work was the semi-autobiographical *Stories of Waterloo* (1829). Captain Maxwell would have a formative influence on his protégé's later career. The Revd Maxwell less so.

The year 1836–7, when Lever turned to literature, was the high point of Bozmania. The proprietor of the *Dublin University Magazine*, William Curry, persuaded Lever to write a serial, *Harry Lorrequer*, in monthly 'Dickensian' parts. 'Phiz' (Richard Hablôt Knight Browne), *Pickwick*'s illustrator, was recruited to do the full plate etchings for *Lorrequer*'s monthly numbers. He and Lever would eventually work together on fourteen novels – one of the great partnerships in Victorian fiction. 'You ask me how I write,' Lever was once asked: 'my reply is, just as I live – from hand to mouth.' *Harry Lorrequer* began as a single anecdote and its ad hoc continuation is a narrativeless sequence of Pickwickian picaresque episodes that take the military hero from Cork all over peacetime Europe. It hit the public taste, massively. Curry went on to suggest a variation on the theme. As Lever recalled, thirty years later: 'my publishers asked me could I write a story in the Lorrequer vein, in which active service and military adventure could figure more prominently than mere civilian life, and where the achievements of a British army might form the staple of the narrative, – when this question was propounded me, I was ready to reply: Not one, but fifty.'

The first of the fifty was *Charles O'Malley* (1841). The hero is a bravo from Galway who duels and dissipates himself at Trinity before enlisting to fight in the Peninsula, rising to the rank of captain. By a series of unlikely adventures, Charley finds himself at the shoulder of Napoleon at the beginning of Waterloo and by the side of Wellington (to whom he gives battle-winning instruction) at the climax. Thereafter it is peace, prosperity and the obligatory heiress. It was logical for Lever to choose Waterloo. He was in Brussels while writing and O'Malley is a heroic version of his literary patron, Maxwell. Phiz's father had also fought at Waterloo (the illustrations are wildly dramatic). It was a period when the Napoleonic Wars were being triumphantly crowed over in Britain: Nelson's column was erected in 1843 and subscriptions were being gathered for the triumphal arch to Wellington, at the entrance to Hyde Park.

Thackeray, unlike Dickens and Lever, had still to make his mark as anything other than a penny-a-liner. He was hungry for fame and proposed to Chapman and Hall a volume of 'Cockney Sketches of Ireland' (clearly aiming at the success of the firm's *Sketches by Boz*). Thackeray procured letters of introduction to Lever, currently residing in high style in his country house, Templeogue, outside Dublin. A convivial visit ensued in early June 1842 and the Waterloo chapters of *Charles O'Malley*, still fresh on the printed page, were an inevitable topic of conversation. 'Thackeray seemed much inclined to laugh at martial might,' it was later recalled, 'although he still held to the idea that something might be made of Waterloo, even without the smoke and din of the action being introduced.'

Thackeray's 'Waterloo novel', *Vanity Fair*, did not start serialising until January 1847. In the interim, Lever and Thackeray had fallen out catastrophically and descended to flinging satirical mud at each other. His new novel, Thackeray resolved, would be 'a novel without a hero', but also a Waterloo novel without Waterloo – an anti-Leveriad. It would mock war-glorifying romances like that damned *O'Malley* thing. The essence of *Vanity Fair* was the new gravity it brought to fictional depictions of war. It is expressed in the famous narrative defection in the ninth number: 'We do not claim to rank among the military novelists. Our place is with the non-combatants. When the decks are cleared for action we go below and wait meekly. We should only be in the way of the manœuvres that the gallant fellows are performing overhead.' *Vanity Fair* created new parameters as to what was legitimate in the novel of war.

Eight years after the publication of *Vanity Fair*, the young artillery officer Leo Tolstoy was in besieged Sevastopol. He was meditating his first works of fiction – war stories, of course. His diary for 8–9 June 1855 records: 'Laziness, laziness. Health bad. Reading *Vanity Fair* all day.' The 'Waterloo novel' manifestly affected him. In the story he was writing up, 'Sevastopol in May' (1855), we find the following blatant echo of *Vanity Fair*'s last paragraph ('Ah *Vanitas Vanitatum*! Which of us is happy in this world?') and *The Book of Snobs*:

> Vanity! Vanity! Vanity! Everywhere, even on the brink of the grave and among men ready to die for a noble cause. Vanity! It seems to be the characteristic feature and special malady of our time. How is it that among our predecessors no mention was made of this passion, as of smallpox and cholera? How is it that in our time there are only three kinds of people: those who, considering vanity an inevitably existing fact and therefore justifiable, freely submit to it; those who regard it as a sad but unavoidable condition; and those who act unconsciously and slavishly under its influence? Why did the Homers and Shakespeares speak of love, glory, and suffering, while the literature of today is an endless story of snobbery and vanity?

It was not merely the Thackerayan rhetoric, but the Thackerayan tactic, the 'sidestep', which Tolstoy would absorb into his own narrative. The influence of Stendhal on the battle scenes in *War and Peace* has been commented on: that of *Vanity Fair* less so, and that of Charles Lever never. But Tolstoy's constant deflection, or retreat, from the battlefield to what is going on with 'the girl I left behind me' (chapter 30, *Vanity Fair*) cannot but recall Thackeray and, by opposition, Lever. So too do the strategically brief, ironic and calculatedly unLeverian irruptions of Napoleon, as in his encounter (in Book III, Part 2, Chapter 7) with the drunken Cossack, Lavrushka:

> Finding himself in the company of Napoleon, whose identity he had easily and surely recognized, Lavrushka was not in the least abashed but merely did his utmost to gain his new master's favour.
>
> He knew very well that this was Napoleon, but Napoleon's presence could no more intimidate him than Rostov's, or a sergeant major's with the rods, would have done, for he had nothing that either the sergeant major or Napoleon could deprive him of.

No heroes in this novel. It is distinctly Thackerayan. And, for those whose ears are attuned to the sounds of very minor fiction, anti-Leverian. The Irishman had served his literary purpose. He had helped in the creation of two masterpieces: *Vanity Fair* and *War and Peace*. They also serve.

FN   Charles James Lever
MRT   *Charles O'Malley*
Biog L. Stevenson, *Dr Quicksilver, the Life of Charles Lever* (1939)

32. J. H. Ingraham 1809–1860

He is one of our most popular novelists, if not one of our best. Edgar Allan Poe

Ingraham was born in Portland, Maine, into a shipbuilding family. In his teens he went off to sea and, if his own account is to believed, smelled gunpowder in South American revolutions. On his return, he studied at Yale – but there is doubt (as with other areas of his life) as to whether he graduated or whether, indeed, he was ever there. In 1830, he moved to Natchez, Mississippi, where he married the cousin of the episcopalian dignitary and author, Phillips Brooks. After a failed attempt at law, he settled down as a teacher of languages. His wife, Mary, was of planter stock, and brought money to the marriage.

Ingraham began his literary career with travel sketches, for which there was a lively market. His first novel, *Laffite: The Pirate of the Gulf* (1836), was an unexpected hit with the reading public, earning the novice novelist $1,000 from New York's leading publisher, Harper Bros. It may be that readers associated him with his namesake, but unrelated, Joseph Ingraham, the national naval hero, lost at sea in 1800. In a characteristically witty hatchet job, Edgar Allan Poe observed: 'The novelist is too minutely, and by far too frequently *descriptive*. We are surfeited with unnecessary detail ... Not a dog yelps, unsung. Not a shovel-footed negro waddles across the stage ... without eliciting from the author a *vos plaudite*, with an extended explanation of the character of his personal appearance – of his length, depth and breadth, – and, more particularly, of the length, depth and breadth of his shirt-collar, shoe-buckles and hat-band.' Elsewhere, and later, Poe concluded: 'He is one of our most *popular* novelists, if not one of our best. He appeals always to the taste of the *ultraromanticists*.'

His Harper windfall induced 'Professor Ingraham' (as the publisher mendaciously titled him – without authorial protest) to follow up with similar nautical adventure yarns, such as *Captain Kyd; or, The Wizard of the Sea* (1839), which circulated for decades as a dime novel and was, plausibly, a remote influence on Stevenson's *Treasure Island*. Ingraham was sarcastic about what he called 'rigidists' – those who disapproved of fiction as a source of innocent fun. He himself was very flexible on the matter. In 1842 Ingraham was declared bankrupt and set out to remedy his finances with a flood of fiction for magazines, papers and 'yellowback' 10 cent library series – whoever would buy his wares at $100 (his normal price) apiece. In 1845 alone he claimed to have published twenty titles. It is estimated that in the early 1840s, 10 per cent of all the new novels produced in the US were 'Ingrahams'. The sea and piracy remained staple subject matter, although there were more salacious items, such as *The Beautiful Cigar Girl, or, The Mysteries of Broadway*. The ephemerality of these works, perversely, has made them high-value collectors' items in modern times. Little other literary value has been found in this superheated second phase of Ingraham's career.

Under the influence of a pious brother, Ingraham was increasingly drawn to the church. In 1852 he was ordained as an Episcopalian priest and went on to serve in a number of ministries in the South. His fiction changed drastically with this change of life. He became, to use his own term, a 'rigidist'. No more jolly-rogering. In 1855 he published what was to be a perennial bestseller among religious readers, *The Prince of the House of David*. It was followed in 1859 by *The Pillar of Fire, or Israel in Bondage*. Ingraham's third biblical romance, *The Throne of David*, was published in 1860, completing a trilogy on the Holy Land. The novels were epistolary (like the gospels), enabling them to be more easily broken up for Sunday school. In 1859 Ingraham received an honorary LL.D. from the University of Mississippi. Never a professor, he was now, legitimately, a doctor.

By the end of the 1850s, Ingraham had perceptively seen the oncoming war. The most interesting novel of his third, holy, phase is *The Sunny South* (1859), a narrative written from the South by a governess born and brought up in the north. Conceived as a response to *Uncle Tom's Cabin*, the novel pleads for mutual understanding. Ingraham was himself, of course, a Northerner transplanted to the South. But Ingraham did not live to suffer the war. He shot himself in December 1860. He always kept a loaded pistol in the vestibule of his church at Holly Springs, Mississippi (this was, after all, the American South). It seems to have been an accident, although the details are unclear. More twentieth-century readers know Ingraham than think they do. His book *The Pillar of Fire* is the credited source of Cecil B. DeMille's movie starring Charlton Heston, *The Ten Commandments* (1956).

FN Joseph Holt Ingraham
MRT *The Pillar of Fire* (or watch the movie)
Biog R. W. Weathersby II, *J. H. Ingraham* (1980)

POSTSCRIPT

33. Prentiss Ingraham 1843–1904

The extraordinary side of his work is of a nature that appeals to the statistician rather than to the literary critic. The American Bookman's verdict

The only son of J. H. Ingraham, Prentiss went on to become even more prolific with his pen (and handier with his six-gun) than his father. He is credited with the authorship of some 600 novels and 400 novellas under as many as fifteen pen-names – written, it should be added, in his retirement, and, unable to use the type-writer, written in longhand. Prentiss left medical school to fight in the Confederate cause in the Civil War. He was wounded, reached the rank of Colonel, survived, and in love with soldiering went off to fight for Juárez against the French in Mexico. A soldier of fortune, he also fought for the Greeks against the Turks and for the Cubans against the Spanish. As a Colonel with the Cuban army (and a captain in their navy) he was captured and narrowly escaped execution.

In the 1870s, Ingraham settled down in New York, marrying and starting a family. Having lived adventure, he now resolved to write about it and became a lead author in Beadle and Adams's bestselling 'dime novel' series (also giving them many of his father's copyrights, some of whose novels he rewrote). He had a strong line in 'Buffalo Bill' stories – and was, for a while, the buckskin-clad showman's press agent – as well as material drawn from his own military past. Like his father, he was fond of piracy as a subject. Title pages proclaimed him 'Col. Prentiss Ingraham'. Given his speed of production, he could as well have been called 'Machine Gun Prentiss' – the Beadle and Adams steam presses could barely keep up with his production.

He died of Bright's disease, supposedly originating in one of his Civil War wounds, aged only sixty, in the Beauvoir Confederate Soldiers Home, Biloxi.

FN Prentiss Ingraham
MRT anything with 'Buffalo Bill' or 'Pirate' in the title
Biog *ANB* (Randall C. Davis)

34. Edgar Allan Poe 1809–1849

To take Poe with more than a certain degree of seriousness is to lack seriousness oneself.
Henry James

No writing life has been lived at such speed as was Poe's. Like the hero of 'The Premature Burial' he was morbidly aware of death hurtling towards him. In a short life he wrote – other than one chronically bitty novel – short stories and short poems. A long poem, he liked to assert, was a 'contradiction in terms'. Why? Because 'all excitements are, through a psychal [sic] necessity, transient'. Life is too short for *Paradise Lost*. The poem on the Underground, snatched between stations, is quintessentially Poevian. Some of Poe's stories – 'The Masque of the Red Death' or 'The Tell-Tale Heart', for example – are, indeed, sufficiently terse to qualify as the 'condensed novels' (or fictional haikus) that J. G. Ballard, a distant literary offspring, toyed with. No poem or narrative, Poe estimated, could excite 'for more than an hour'. Most of his finest stories can be read in Andy Warhol's talismanic fifteen minutes. It was a fortunate coincidence that Poe's career coincided with the rise of the popular magazine, marketed for an ever-hurrying American population with no hours to waste.

All paths, however, not merely those of glory, led – for Poe – to the grave, and his path was faster than most. It is a challenge to find a story where untimely death is not central – whether premature 'inhumation', the 'red' plague (an allegory, it is suggested, of his child-mother's, child-wife's and his own incipient, blood-spitting, tuberculosis) or murder. In his one so-called novel, *The Narrative of Arthur Gordon Pym of Nantucket* (in fact a bundle of disconnected narratives), there is a veritable holocaust of some twenty-five mariners disposed of (one consumed cannibalistically by the survivors, none granted easeful deaths) before the yarn proper even gets underway. Death, inevitably, awaits Pym, still not twenty years old. The skull on the desk, that standard Ignatian aid to meditation, is common enough in literature. With Poe, the warm flesh is still slithering off the shining bone. Another of his early tales, 'Berenice', has a hero prone – as are many of Poe's heroes – to cataleptic trance. Berenice, the love of his life, wastes away from consumption. On the morning after her funeral he comes round after a long amnesia sitting in his library. His clothes are 'muddy and clotted with gore'. A servant rushes in and points to a spade in the corner:

> With a shriek I bounded to the table, and grasped the box that lay upon it. But I could not force it open; and, in my tremor, it slipped from my hands, and fell heavily, and burst into pieces; and from it, with a rattling sound, there rolled out some instruments of dental surgery, intermingled with thirty-two small, white, and ivory-looking substances that were scattered to and fro about the floor.

He has torn out her teeth. As a superfluous *frisson* Berenice was, it transpires, buried alive, and screamed under the dental operation. She is now, however, well dead and perfectly toothless.

Poe's mother was an actress born in England who made her debut on the American stage, aged nine – a prematurity not even Edgar could match. Eliza Arnold was a veteran trouper before she was out of her teens. She was married at fifteen and widowed at eighteen. She promptly made a second marriage with fellow actor, David Poe, by whom she had three children – while touring the length and breadth of America. Edgar, the second child, was born in Boston. It pleased him in later life to proclaim himself on title-pages 'a Bostonian'. The truth is no writer was more rootless – he could as well have called himself a New Yorker, or a Philadelphian, or a Flying Dutchman.

David Poe abandoned his wife and children two years after Edgar's birth to be heard of no more. He leaves no echo in his son's later fiction, where fathers are wholly invisible. Eliza then succumbed to consumption in 1811, aged twenty-three. Her husband did not stay to watch her die. Edgar, of necessity, did, barely weaned when she left him. The dying (and not-dying) woman would be a central element in his early work, notably in his majestic fantasia about witches, castles and corpses, 'Ligeia'. The three orphaned Poe children were taken on, but not wholly adopted, by well-wishers in Richmond, Virginia, where Eliza had gone to die. Edgar was taken into the Allan family, whose name was inserted into his own. There ensued a textbook Oedipal relationship with his wealthy, alternately generous and skin-flint, 'father', John Allan, a prosperous merchant (among the other wares he dealt in were tombstones). The Allan family spent five years in Britain where Allan had attempted, unsuccessfully, to set up a branch of his business. It was here that Edgar got his early school education, and with it a lifelong penchant for English settings in his stories and poems – drawn (he was the most light-fingered of writers) from the Waverley novels of Sir Walter Scott, then all the rage.

Edgar embarked on his adolescence as a child of privilege. But gambling debts – and a disinclination to own up to them – led to his being kicked out of the University of Virginia and having his allowance withdrawn. He was already exhibiting early signs of dipsomania – something which, like all mind-transforming conditions, fascinated him. He was, as his French admirer Baudelaire insisted, an explorer not an addict –and no territory was more interesting than the darker places of the human mind.

Aged eighteen, lying about his age, and under a fake name, Poe enlisted in the US Army, on a salary of $5 a month. In the same year, 1827, he published at his own expense his first volume: *Tamerlane and Other Poems*. It was universally ignored

– despite the clear evidence of talent which hindsight can detect. A brief reconciliation with John Allan enabled Poe (who had risen in the ranks) to buy himself out, and buy himself into the US military academy, West Point. Here again he excelled before, in his last year, engineering his own court-martial and dismissal. It was the last straw for John Allan and Edgar was disinherited. All he had by way of legacy from his now obscenely rich guardian was his middle name (routinely misspelled). He was not, when one weighs everything up, that bad a foster-son. Despite Baudelaire's admiration, no writer is less the *flâneur* or congenital wastrel than Edgar Allan Poe. It was the pattern of his life to succeed brilliantly, then move on before getting bogged down in the consequences of his own brilliance. If necessary he would drink himself out of the sinecures friends were willing to set up for him.

So, too, with his career as an author. He went from journal to journal, dashing off poems, savage reviews, and stories like a writing Gatling gun. He routinely broke contracts, confecting grievances to do so. His heyday as a writer-editor was with *Graham's Lady's and Gentleman's Magazine*, which he joined in 1841. His pieces raised the circulation fourfold to an astonishing 40,000 copies per issue. Aged twenty-six, he married a thirteen-year-old cousin, Virginia Clemm. True to her name, she probably remained virginal. There is little evidence that Poe had interest (or time) for carnal relationships – although he liked women. His closest bond was with his widowed mother-in-law, 'Muddy' Clemm. Scurrilous accusations of incest were, inevitably, circulated after his death.

Poe was phenomenally successful, but never well off – particularly in the last phase of his life. It was a good year when he earned over $1,000. Regular use of alcohol and occasional indulgence in opium played a part. It is tempting to link this intoxication to the point of blackout with Poe's fascination with epilepsy, catatonia and mesmeric trance. It features as a plot mechanism in many of his stories, most brilliantly in the late (1845) 'The Facts in the Case of M. Valdemar', a horrific voyage into the afterlife, which ends (as does M. Valdemar's stay on this earth): 'Upon the bed, before that whole company, there lay a nearly liquid mass of loathsome – of detestable putridity.'

Despite the notoriety which attached to America's *poète maudit*, surprisingly little is known about the details of Poe's life. Myth has washed in to fill the vacuum and encourages such cultish bizarreries (a favourite Poe word) as the deranged spiritualist, Lizzie Doten, channelling a Poe poem, 'Resurrexi', from beyond the veil. The posthumous lies about Poe put into circulation by his self-appointed, venomously vindictive, 'executor' ('executioner' would be the more appropriate term), Rufus Griswold, have further tainted Poe's image. Griswold's Poe is less the *poète maudit* than a drug-crazed, sex-mad lunatic.

Typically clouded by enigma are the accounts of Poe's death. On 3 October 1849, the forty-year-old was found wandering the streets of Baltimore, ranting deliriously, wearing someone else's clothes. He seemed to be calling out 'Reynolds' (unidentified). One of his distant relatives who had been summoned took one look and refused to take charge of him. Poe was taken to the local hospital's ward for drunks, where he died four days later. Since the death of Virginia a couple of years earlier, he had been chaotic in his personal life, proposing marriage to a series of women and embarking on pointless literary feuds – notably with Longfellow. His genius was, apparently, extinguished. His income, in his last year, had sunk to barely more than $150, largely raised from slurred public recitations of his signature poem, 'The Raven'. 'Nevermore', rather than Longfellow's 'Excelsior', would seem to have been his motto.

Newspapers, concerned that such a great man of American letters should be so destitute, raised subscriptions; friends intervened, without success. What destroyed Poe? Intoxication? Syphilis? Was it, as Baudelaire suggested, his chosen form of suicide? What happened in the missing days of that last week? Had he been drugged and robbed of his clothes in some squalid harbour bar? Had he been beaten up (as some suspected) by West Point cadets out on the razzle? Had he gone into the underworld, like M. Valdemar? Had he, like the hero of 'Berenice', committed some awful crime he could no longer remember? His medical records were lost, or were destroyed. Posterity will never for certain know what killed Edgar Allan Poe. Yet his work lives on. As a grateful Arthur Conan Doyle noted, each of Poe's stories is a root 'from which whole literatures develop'. It still grows.

FN   Edgar Allan Poe (born Edgar Poe)
MRT 'Berenice'
Biog K. Silverman, *Edgar A. Poe: Mournful and Never-ending Remembrance* (1991)

35. Mrs Gaskell 1810–1865

My heart burnt within me with indignation and grief.

Despite enlightened attempts to rebrand her as 'Elizabeth Gaskell', she remains, obdurately, 'Mrs'. To call her anything else jars as painfully on the ear attuned to the Victorian world as would 'the eminent author of *Jane Eyre*, Mrs Arthur Bell Nicholls'. There is a good reason for the title: wifeliness burns at the heart of Gaskell's creativity. To console herself in the mourning period when her only son Willie died of scarlet fever in 1845, she wrote a story of industrial life, strife, suffering and death (no Victorian novelist, incidentally, introduces more deathbeds into her fiction), *Mary Barton: A Tale of Manchester Life* (1848). Her art was forged in the furnace of maternal grief.

Elizabeth Stevenson was born in Chelsea, London, of Unitarian parents. After quitting the Unitarian ministry her father took up the comfortable official position of Keeper of Records to the Treasury. Mr Stevenson's 'doubts', and their impact on the females in his family, form the initial plot of *North and South* (1855). Her mother came from Cheshire, thus setting up from birth the cultural clash between North and South which was to preoccupy the future novelist. Mrs Stevenson died when her daughter was just over a year old, and the very young Elizabeth was effectively adopted by her aunt, Hannah Lumb, in Knutsford, Cheshire – the original of 'Cranford'. She grew up in the small country town, with its outlying farms, whose life she was later to chronicle. It was, however, only sixteen miles from Manchester, the most advanced industrial city in the world. Polarities were everywhere: factory chimneys and tea-cosies.

Like other Unitarian girls, Elizabeth was well educated at school, leaving at the age of seventeen with a working knowledge of modern and classical languages. In 1828 her brother, John Stevenson, a lieutenant in the merchant marine, disappeared at sea. His loss affected her strongly and the brother thought dead who returns to life appears as a motif frequently in her subsequent fiction. Around the same period her father married a woman whom Elizabeth – insofar as she was capable of ungenerous feelings – did not much like, a situation which is recalled as the central plot element in her last novel, *Wives and Daughters*. She nevertheless lived with her father until his death in 1829, after which she returned to Knutsford.

In 1832 Elizabeth married the Revd William Gaskell, a Unitarian assistant minister – and scholar – at the Cross Street Chapel in Manchester. The union was to be very happy. The first dozen years of her life were occupied in family and parochial matters, but she found time to write the odd piece of prose and verse. In 1837, for example, she embarked on a descriptive poem, in the style of Crabbe, called *Sketches Among the Poor*. But her first successful venture in authorship was *Mary Barton*. Initially it was to be called 'John Barton', with the intention of focusing on the miseries of textile mill workers in the trade depression of 'the hungry forties', and the near-revolutionary protest mobilised as Chartism, which demanded a total reform of England's parliamentary system. It was an uncomfortable subject and Gaskell had difficulty finding a publisher for it. She was induced to sweeten the pill with a more romantic central plot and title and the revised novel was accepted in 1848 by Chapman and Hall, Dickens's publishers, who paid her £100.

It was a canny purchase: *Mary Barton* was a hit. Carlyle (prominently quoted on the novel's title-page – and not usually an admirer of the 'novelwright') approved and only the mill owners objected to the anonymous author's depiction of the Lancashire working man's hardships and superior nobility to those who exploited their labour and seduced their daughters. Gaskell's identity was soon known and overnight she became a celebrity. Dickens, another admirer, invited her to contribute to his new weekly magazine, *Household Words*, and it was in its pages that *Cranford* – the saga of the genteel spinster 'Amazons' of Knutsford – first appeared. Gaskell's second full-length novel, *Ruth* (1853), renewed her assault on the middle-class conscience by exposing another 'social problem' of the Victorian era – bastardy and the persecution of the 'fallen woman'. Dickens, it may be noted, paid her considerably less than his star male serialists.

North and South (1855) marked a new level of maturity in Gaskell's art. The story of the complicated love affair of a well-bred Home Counties girl and a northern mill owner reflected many of the tensions of the author's own life and her double cultural inheritance. Following hard on the Preston cotton strike – which Dickens was dealing with, simultaneously, in *Hard Times* – the novel was highly topical, if sentimental in its social recommendations (essentially that masters and men should behave in a more Christian way to each other – foregoing the capitalistic doctrines of 'Political Economy'). Dickens's analysis was sharper.

In the same year, 1855, Gaskell's friend, Charlotte Brontë died. Charlotte's father and her husband invited Gaskell to undertake a biography, so as to put down the wild rumours circulating about the Haworth sisters. The resulting *Life of Charlotte Brontë* is the best of Victorian literary biographies, although it aggrieved living acquaintances of the novelist and a retraction of parts of the book had to be published in *The Times*.

By the late 1850s Gaskell was earning up to £1,000 for her novels. Her next major work, *Sylvia's Lovers*, was begun in 1859, with extensive research into eighteenth-century Whitby. But domestic worries distracted her from this historical tale of love, smuggling and press-gangs which eventually came out in 1863. It was followed by *Cousin Phillis* (1864), a gentler, idyllic (and shorter) work which is Gaskell's masterpiece. *Wives and Daughters* was being serialised at the time of the author's death, and is unfinished. An 'everyday story', it recapitulates in the experiences of its heroine Molly Gibson much of the author's own early life. A mother to the end Mrs Gaskell died of a sudden heart attack while visiting the house she had just bought at Holybourne with the £1,600 proceeds from *Wives and Daughters*, surrounded by three of her daughters. She is buried at Knutsford.

FN Elizabeth Cleghorn Gaskell (née Stevenson)
MRT *Mary Barton*
Biog J. Uglow, *Elizabeth Gaskell: A Habit of Stories* (1993)

36. Fanny Fern 1811–1872

I am convinced that there are times in everybody's experience when there is so much to be done, that the only way to do it is to sit down and do nothing.

'Fanny Fern' was a bestselling novelist, serial wife and newspaper columnist (some accounts say the first columnist in the country, others merely the highest paid). Born Sarah Payson Willis in Portland, Maine, she was the fifth of nine children of a minister who himself doubled as a journalist. Pert from birth, her family nickname was 'Sal Volatile' – no fainting when Fanny was around. New England, with its advanced views on female education, was a lucky place for her to have been brought up. Like her better known brother, N. P. Willis, with whom her subsequent relations were to be vexed, Sarah learned about journalism early, helping her father edit his periodical *The Youth's Companion*.

In 1837 Sarah Willis married the dashing young banker (some accounts demote him to 'bank cashier'), Charles Eldredge. The happy couple had three daughters, but in 1846 Charles died of typhoid fever, leaving his wife and two surviving children destitute. The Willises proved unhelpful. Sarah went on to make a hasty second marriage with a widowed Boston merchant, Samuel Farrington, but they separated within two years. Sarah found herself once more without support and lost custody of her children. She turned to teaching and, in 1851, to her pen.

Under the pseudonym 'Fanny Fern' she began to publish 'fun' sketches in the papers, which proved hugely successful. Her first book, *Fern Leaves from Fanny's Portfolio*, came out in 1853, when the author was a mature forty-two. She went on to write two novels, notably the autobiographical *Ruth Hall* (1856), which reportedly earned her the then massive sum of $8,000. 'A domestic tale of the present time,' the novel ponders the intertwining pressures of wifehood and female authorship in the form of Ruth Ellet's happy marriage (evoking the author's years with Eldredge), her early widowing, and her struggle for fame in the cut-throat, wholly masculine, world of New York journalism. It ends, inevitably, on the happiest and most pious of notes:

> As the carriage rolled from under the old stone gate-way, a little bird, startled from out its leafy nest, trilled forth a song as sweet and clear as the lark's at heaven's own blessed gate.
>
> 'Accept the omen, dear Ruth,' said Mr. Walter. 'Life has much of harmony yet in store for you.'

Ruth Hall is *Jane Eyre* Americanised, modernised and smartened up. As with Brontë's novel, the fact that living figures (not least Sarah's infuriated brother,

Nathaniel) could identify themselves portrayed in its pages led to furore, which led to higher sales.

In 1856 Sarah married the biographer James Parton, a husband eleven years her junior. Now experienced in the matter of such vows, a pre-nuptial agreement ensured that she would keep her substantial earnings. In the same year as her marriage she made a contract with the editor Robert Bonner to write her 'Fanny Fern' columns exclusively for his *New York Ledger*. He paid her a huge salary of $100 a week – an expenditure which he shrewdly made common knowledge. However, it was not all wispy fern leaves, blowing airily in the prints. A 'Whitmanite' (when affiliation with the 'deviant' poet was risky), Willis was also a feminist – if a passive one. The best strategy for women, she believed, was to play possum. Not all her co-ideologues agreed. A daughter born to Willis's last marriage died and she herself died, prematurely, of cancer.

FN Sarah Payson Willis ('Fanny Fern', later Eldredge, Farrington, Parton)
MRT *Ruth Hall*
Biog J. W. Warren, *Fanny Fern: An Independent Woman* (1992)

37. William Makepeace Thackeray 1811–1863

Ah! Vanitas Vanitatum! Which of us is happy in this world?

He was, said the historian G. M. Young, a man travelling through life in a first-class carriage, fearing that he was carrying a second-class ticket. The great 'snobographer' ('snob', incidentally, was a word Thackeray invented in its current sense) was himself, if not quite one of the *genus snobiensis*, unsure of his social status, and constitutionally irritable. His background was upper enough. The Thackerays were Yorkshire gentry, going back generations. William was born in India, where his father was a senior colonial administrator, before dying, prematurely, in 1816 – leaving, in addition to his only legitimate child, a by-blow sibling by his Indian concubine. Thackeray was never stable on the subject of race; nor did he ever acknowledge the existence of his half-sister.

His mother remarried. Her second husband, Major Carmichael Smyth, was a man she had loved as a girl, but whom, she had been told, was dead – to forestall what her guardians saw as an imprudent match. It was a common ruse in that class, at that time. Thackeray loved his stepfather, and immortalised him as his Quixote *de nos jours*, Colonel Newcome, in *The Newcomes*. His mother – sternly evangelical

– he had a much harder time with. Psycho-biographers, who have been attracted to Thackeray like bees to a honeypot, see strains running through all his subsequent emotional life. His mother is depicted in the person of 'virtuous' characters such as Amelia Sedley, or Mrs Arthur Pendennis (to whom, mischievously, Thackeray gave as maiden name that of the most famous courtesan of the time, Laura Bell: both Mrs Pendennis and Mrs Carmichael Smyth were very severe on sexual immorality).

Young William was returned to England, aged seven, to receive the education of a gentleman at Charterhouse and Trinity College, Cambridge. On the way back, the ship touched at St Helena, where he caught a glimpse of the Corsican monster – sowing the seed of a lifetime fascination with the Napoleonic Wars. He went on to let his family down – an idler at school, he left the university 'plucked' (without a degree), having lost most of his sizeable patrimony gambling. And, it is likely, having picked up the gonorrhea which would curtail his life and cause him lifelong urethral difficulties. On being introduced to a Mr Peawell in later years, he sighed 'I wish I could'. On the plus side, his early errors supplied the raw material for his fine *Bildungsroman*, *The History of Pendennis* (1850). Novelists waste nothing – even their own wastefulness.

After false starts in law in England, and drawing and journalism in Paris, the prodigiously gifted – but still wayward – young man embarked on a ten-year-long stint, 'writing for his life' with anonymous or pseudonymous 'magazinery'. It was an apprenticeship but, at a penny-a-line, a tough one. By 1836 he had squandered what remained of his personal fortune and had married, improvidently, an Irish girl with no dowry. Having borne him two surviving daughters, Isabella developed incurable insanity. After 1840 they lived apart and by the time of the publication of *Jane Eyre* in 1847, his situation was exactly that of Mr Rochester – although Thackeray did not keep his wife in the attic, but in a comfortable asylum in Camberwell. It cost him three guineas a week.

By the early 1840s, Thackeray had made a reputation for himself as a savage and incorrigibly 'cynical' satirist, with works like the Hibernophobic *Barry Lyndon* (1844), the autobiography of an Irish bully and braggart (thanks to Stanley Kubrick's film, now among the author's best-known works). He had his first unequivocal success as a writer with *The Snobs of England* (1846–7), published in the congenial columns of the newly launched magazine *Punch*. At the same time he was having difficulty placing a more ambitious narrative, what he then called 'A Novel without a Hero'. Eventually *Vanity Fair*, as it was brilliantly renamed, came out in Dickensian monthly parts, with *Punch*'s publisher, illustrated by the novelist himself. He was thirty-five, had published millions of words, but this was the first work to proclaim his name to the world. He was a scribbler no more.

After a slow start, the 'Waterloo novel' – following the intertwining careers of two young women, one wicked, one virtuous – was a huge hit. Thackeray only managed a fraction of Dickens's sales but, at his zenith, his critical reputation stood higher. Success mellows a man and his worldview was markedly less cynical after *Vanity Fair*. It also accompanied changes in his domestic arrangements: he set up home in Kensington with his daughters and – while remaining a clubman – was also a paterfamilias and less the bohemian. Now at the 'top of the tree', as he crowed to his mother, and regarded as the literary heir to Fielding, he wrote a Victorian *Tom Jones* with his next monthly serial, *Pendennis* (1848–50). As in *Vanity Fair*, one of Thackeray's projects (with characters like Dobbin and Warrington) was to 'redefine the ideal of the gentleman' for his age and for England's dominant middle classes. Another was to raise 'the dignity of literature': to make it a gentlemanly occupation. Dickens, by contrast, was 'low'.

Thackeray's development as a novelist was impeded by his falling victim to the 1849 cholera epidemic, which swept its deadly way through London until put down by the redoubtable Dr John Snow, who realised the capital's water supply was to blame. He survived – thanks to Dickens, who dispatched his personal physician – but Thackeray's energies were never quite up to the literary tasks he set himself thereafter. None the less, he followed up with his most 'careful' novel, *The History of Henry Esmond* (1852). Published in the traditional 'three-decker' form, there was none of the earlier month-to-month helter-skelter with deadlines. The narrative – loosely modelled on Scott's *Waverley* – is set in Thackeray's favourite Queen Anne period. Like Macaulay, and other proponents of the Whig thesis, Thackeray saw the early eighteenth century as the moment when British parliamentary democracy, and its middle-class hegemony, came into being. The mood of *Esmond*, brilliant as its plot structure, political thematising and prose are, was darkened by the novelist's falling in love, desperately and hopelessly, with his best friend's wife. This imbroglio explains a famously unsatisfactory ending. As George Eliot sharply put it: 'the hero is in love with the daughter all the way through and then marries the mother'.

Thackeray's career, thereafter, was glorious but its products less good. None of his subsequent full-length fictions (*The Newcomes*, *The Virginians*, *The Adventures of Philip*) equals what went before. But as editor of the newly launched *Cornhill Magazine*, with the highest-ever stipend for such work, he could, in *The Roundabout Papers*, lay claim to being the best essayist in the language since Addison. No Victorian 'prosed' better. In his last three years, Thackeray was wealthy enough – thanks, in large part, to remunerative lecture tours in America – to design and build himself a Queen Anne-style mansion in Palace Green (it is now the Israeli Embassy in London, something that the casually anti-Semitic novelist would have found suitably ironic).

There were recurrent bust-ups with Dickens and his bohemian proxies – notably the 'Garrick Club Affair' in 1856. He always played the 'gentleman' card, which more often than not trumped his opponents. He died, prematurely, in 1863, before being able fully to relax into his fame, or his earning power, or to become what he always wanted to be – another Macaulay, or, failing that, an MP. The post-mortem revealed that his brain was preternaturally large: something that surprises no one who reads his fiction.

FN   William Makepeace Thackeray
MRT   *Vanity Fair*
Biog   D. J. Taylor, *Thackeray* (1999)

38. Charles Dickens 1812–1870

Annual income twenty pounds, annual expenditure nineteen nineteen six, result happiness. Annual income twenty pounds, annual expenditure twenty pounds ought and six, result misery. Mr Micawber's economics

There have been some eighty 'lives' of Dickens. Yet posterity knows little more of that life, or at least, its inner compartments, than his intimate friend John Forster grudgingly divulged in the biography published while Dickens's body was practically still warm. Dickens was born at Portsea, the son of an £80-a-year clerk in the Naval Pay Office. His mother was the daughter of another clerk who had been disgraced as an embezzler. There were ten Dickens children, five of whom survived, leaving Charles the eldest son. His early childhood was massively unsettled. The family moved to London in 1816, back to Chatham in 1817, and back yet again to London in 1822 to settle in a seedy quarter of Camden Town (immortalised in the Staggs's Gardens chapters in *Dombey and Son*).

John Dickens's salary of £350 a year should have been more than adequate but, like Mr Micawber, he lived beyond his means. The home atmosphere was friendly but lacked the intense love that young 'Boz' (a corruption of his family nickname, 'Moses') craved. By 1824 the family finances were in ruins, and at the age of twelve, Charles was sent off to work in a shoe-blacking factory on the bank of the Thames for a measly few shillings a week. Although this menial labour lasted only a few months, the 'secret agony of my soul' scarred him for the rest of his days. His parents, he bitterly recalled, could not have been happier than if he'd gone off to Cambridge University. The relevant chapters in *David Copperfield* are poignant. But

John Dickens, imprisoned for debt in the Marshalsea, may be thought to have had it harder, if more deservedly. Dickens is unforgiving in his depiction of his father as 'the father of the Marshalsea' in his 1857 novel *Little Dorrit*. Time softened neither his hurt nor his resentment. Fathers have a hard time of it in his novels.

A windfall legacy helped the Dickenses out of their plight, as it does the Dorrits, and afforded Charles some belated schooling. Cambridge, however, was never in prospect. In 1827 the family finances were again rocky and he articled himself as a solicitor's clerk in Gray's Inn, at a pound a week. He hated law, he decided, and drifted to nearby Fleet Street, where he found journalism very much to his taste. He taught himself shorthand and, at the age of seventeen, was an in-demand parliamentary reporter for the London press. He was also beginning to write the newspaper pieces which would eventually be gathered as *Sketches by Boz* – vivid snapshots of London (all but one of his later novels would be set in the city: he never stopped sketching it).

He was now on £5 a week and had hopes of marrying a banker's daughter – but her family frustrated the match. In 1835, work for the *Evening Chronicle* led to his engagement to Catherine Hogarth, daughter of the co-editor of the paper. This time he was not obstructed and they married and set up home with Kate's younger sister, Mary. Dickens had the tenderest feelings for his sister-in-law and her sudden death, in May 1837, was another lasting wound. He kept articles of her clothing, as treasured relics, until his death. There is considerable speculation as to what, precisely, his inner feelings were towards Mary Hogarth – as, indeed, there were scurrilous allegations of an incestuous interest in his other sister-in-law, Georgina Hogarth, twenty years later. The speculation leads to no worthwhile conclusion. Forster knew; we never shall.

Another death proved useful to him in the mid-1830s – that of his senior partner on the new monthly serial for which he was contracted by Chapman and Hall. The illustrator Robert Seymour's suicide (arguably partly inspired by the aggressive energy of his young collaborator) left Dickens in charge of the project. *The Pickwick Papers*, which began publishing in April 1836, started poorly but by the end of its run, in November 1837, it was selling an unprecedented 40,000 an instalment and was the talk of England. Dickens was at the top of the tree. A rival publisher, Richard Bentley, offered the young star editorship of his new *Miscellany*. Dickens accepted and contributed *Oliver Twist* (brilliantly illustrated by George Cruikshank) to its pages. The story of the parish boy who asked for more was gloomier by far than the gallivantings of Mr Pickwick and established a new genre of 'social problem' fiction.

In 1837 the first of Dickens's ten children was born – he was a fond but continuously distracted father. The distractions were gratifying in the extreme, however: well before his thirtieth birthday, he was the country's favourite and best-paid author. Novels such as *Nicholas Nickleby* earned him thousands and sold by the tens of thousands. He rashly took on so many contracts at this stage of his life that there was fear of his 'busting the boiler'. And he was increasingly vexed at the 'brigandage' of publishers – specifically Bentley. He hated other people's hands on his work.

In 1842, a first trip to America – where his novels were all the rage – produced the sharply observed *American Notes* and supplied the American chapters in *Martin Chuzzlewit*. The failure of that novel to maintain his sky-high sales led to a break with Chapman and Hall. Dickens transferred his fiction to Bradbury and Evans, who were printers. Publishers interfered too much: he did not need them. As innovative as he was energetic, he invented the seasonal gift book market with *A Christmas Carol* (1843). At the same period he took time out to travel in Europe and rethink the whole basis of his narrative art. The result was *Dombey and Son*, a palpably darker work, organised by his new narrative planning systems (the famous 'worksheets'). Dickens experimented with autobiographical narration (and some discreet introspection) in *David Copperfield* (1850). His attack on the iniquities of the English legal system, *Bleak House* (1852), continued the experiment and contained his most pointed social criticism to date. Among all else, Dickens was enlarging the sphere and seriousness of English fiction. It could now be a weapon in the novelist's hand.

He drew on his fame to enter public life. With the bank heiress, Angela Burdett-Coutts, he set up a rehabilitation home for London prostitutes called, rather unhappily, Urania Cottage. With Edward Bulwer-Lytton he established the Guild of Literature and Art for indigent writers and artists. In 1850 he started a 2d weekly magazine of his own, *Household Words*, which became the vehicle for his ruminations on current events. His hard-hitting novel on the great Preston strike of mill workers, *Hard Times* (1854), was published in the paper, alongside his journalistic articles on the topic.

In one major respect, Forster does not supply the information for which one must turn to later biographers – namely Dickens's 'Invisible Woman'. The shilling-life facts about Ellen Ternan are well known – but little else is. She was born twenty-eight years later than Dickens, into an acting family. An 'infant phenomenon', she was appearing on the stage almost as soon as she could walk, aged three. Ellen's subsequent career was anything but phenomenal. Fifteen years later, she was a for-hire actress, available to add some professional class to the amateur theatricals which were all the rage at the time. In the late 1850s, Dickens had embarked on a series of such performances to raise money for authors unluckier than himself.

The eighteen-year-old Nelly was contracted to appear in *The Frozen Deep*, a melodrama written by Dickens himself and Wilkie Collins, and the forty-five-year-old novelist fell in love with her. He promptly removed his wife, Kate, the mother of his many children, with the (wholly Dickensian) explanation that she was 'dull'. After 1859 Charles was a bachelor again. As for his love life – not dull, we may deduce. But we can deduce little more. It is a matter of record that Dickens gave substantial sums of money to the Ternan family and left 'Nelly' £1,000 in his will. She gave up the stage in 1860, shortly after the couple's first encounter and must have been supported by someone. She may have lived in France, in a 'mistress's villa' he paid for. In June 1865, in the terrible Staplehurst train crash, Dickens, Nelly and her mother were travelling together on the 'boat train' from Calais. Dickens went to furious lengths to keep the identity of his companions out of the press reports of the accident and himself out of the coroner's court looking into the disaster.

Was Mrs Ternan a chaperone, protecting her daughter's virtue? Or a genteel bawd, profiting from her daughter's being the kept woman of the most famous man in England? A child, still-born in France, has been fantasised about. At a later period Nelly was placed, under a false name, in houses at Slough and at Nunhead, where one of the few surviving Dickens diaries logs visits to her. Nelly took the secrets of her relationship with Dickens to the grave. She shares that grave with the clergyman she later married; most of her later life was given over to ostentatiously good works. In short, the Dickens relationship with Nelly is a black hole. It sucks in speculation, and returns not the slightest glimmer of light.

In his later years, Dickens quarrelled with Thackeray and with Bradbury and Evans, breaking with them to edit a new weekly paper, *All the Year Round*, which he got off the ground with *A Tale of Two Cities* and *Great Expectations* (whose Estella may be viewed as a pen-portrait of Ellen). After the Staplehurst crash, his creative energies notably waned and in his last nine years he completed only two more full-length novels. They continued the journey into the dark begun by *Dombey*. At this stage of his life Dickens was afflicted with gout and, his doctors perceived, early signs of an impending stroke.

Despite their dire warnings, Dickens committed himself to gruelling lecture tours, reading his own work to large audiences. The most exhausting was to America in 1867–8. It netted him £19,000 but more important than the money was the emotional thrill of the readings. He never felt closer to his readers. He collapsed in the dining room of his house at Gad's Hill in 1870 with a fatal cerebral aneurysm, the ink barely dry on his morning session on *The Mystery of Edwin Drood*. A mystery indeed, no one has ever been able to work out how it would end. Dickens left a very un-Micawberish £80,000 on his death.

FN Charles John Huffam Dickens ('Boz')
MRT *Great Expectations*
Biog M. Slater, *Charles Dickens* (2009)

39. Mrs Henry Wood 1814–1887

Dead! Dead! and never called me Mother!

Ellen Price was born in Worcester where her father, a cultivated and musical man, manufactured gloves: the locality and the industry are reflected in the 'Helstonleigh' sections of the author's later fiction. The Price household was strongly Anglican and pillars of the town's cathedral congregation. Ellen spent much of her childhood with her grandmother and while still a girl developed severe curvature of the spine. The disorder, partially remedied by the cruel 'backboards' loved by Victorians with round-shouldered offspring, rendered her a total invalid for four years, and a semi-invalid for the rest of her life. Tiny, she was under five feet tall, fully grown, and the most she could lift throughout life was 'a small book or a parasol'. Her own books (three-deckers, most of them) were anything but small.

In 1836 Ellen Price married a banker, shipping merchant and former consular official, Henry Wood, whose name she always subsequently adopted in her writing. He himself was wholly unliterary and, according to his son, never so much as read a novel – not even his wife's. The couple lived abroad, mainly in France, until 1856, when they returned to Norwood, south London, to live in a rented house. France was the favoured residence of those English people unable to meet their debts and one can presume financial difficulties. Norwood, then as now, was not Mayfair.

There were several children, although the exact number is unclear, some of whom died in childhood. For someone of her physical frame and infirmity, mother-hood must have been onerous. Henry Wood, never a steady provider, seems to have lost the family fortune, obliging his wife to earn money to keep bread on the family table. Her first novel, *Danesbury House* (1860) was written in twenty-eight days for the prize offered by the Scottish Temperance League. A wild tract, it chronicles the downfall of the Danesburys who cut their throats, fatally crash their barouches, expire horribly with delirium tremens, and bankrupt themselves all in consequence of their incurable love of the bottle. The Temperance League loved it, and awarded the tyro novelist the £100 prize. Some of the more vivid descriptions suggest that Henry may have had a certain weakness of the Danesbury sort – but family accounts are loyally discreet.

Wood had become known as a good prospect to the editor Harrison Ainsworth and to the publisher Richard Bentley. The latter, on the recommendation of the former, published *East Lynne* in 1861, giving the still novice author the unusually high price of £600 for the copyright. Melodrama was the taste of the day, and none is more full-blooded than *East Lynne*. The heroine, Isabel Carlyle, elopes from her noble husband ('a blind leap in a moment of passion') with a heartless cad. Divorce follows. Isabel is thought killed in a train crash, but has in fact survived, disfigured. Now white-haired and disguised with green glasses, she returns, unrecognised, to serve as governess to her own children, one of whom dies in her arms, not knowing her as his mother (in the dramatic version of *East Lynne*, she screams the much mocked 'Dead! Dead! And never called me mother!'). The novel embodies Wood's stern belief that for a married woman, adultery is 'far worse than death'. Death, none the less, is what Isabel gets.

Bentley's £600 proved as shrewd as it was generous. Wood's ripe melodrama was a hit with the public – particularly those who patronised the circulating libraries where such three-volume novels were the staple fare. By 1876 Bentley had printed 65,000 copies of the work. Mrs Wood followed up with the equally melodramatic *Mrs Halliburton's Troubles* (1862), the story of a widow who brings up her young brood successfully, despite poverty and in contrast to the wealthy Dare family, whose lawyer head has cheated her out of her inheritance. Given the paucity of biographical evidence, one again suspects elements of the writer's own life are embedded in the plot.

Now a bestselling novelist, Wood rang the changes on all the varieties of melodramatic fiction: family sagas, bigamy and moral dilemmas. There were fifteen novels in seven years after *East Lynne*: she made a lot of money. Henry Wood died in 1866 and the following year his widow, now living in style in St John's Wood, took over editorship of the *Argosy*, the journal in which most of her later fiction appeared, including her 'Johnny Ludlow' papers which recall her childhood in rural Worcester.

Mrs Henry Wood lived her later years in Hampstead. Her son took over editorship of the *Argosy* from his formidable mother in 1887, and wrote a memorial, published in 1894. She died of heart failure, leaving an estate of over £36,000, not having started in serious authorship until her fifties.

FN   Ellen Wood (née Price)
MRT   *East Lynne*
Biog C. W. Wood, *Memorials of Mrs. Henry Wood* (1894)

40. Anthony Trollope 1815–1882

But this I protest: – that nothing that I say shall be untrue. Trollope, *An Autobiography*

Born in London, Anthony was the youngest son of the novelist Frances, a woman of legendary resourcefulness, and a lawyer father, Thomas, a man given to fits of suicidal melancholy and financial recklessness. In the year of his birth the family moved to Harrow, where Thomas tried his hand, unsuccessfully, at farming. The farm, which was leased, proved the grave of the Trollopes' prosperity and the family's misfortunes translated into a grossly inadequate and disturbed schooling for Anthony. From 1823 to 1825 he was a day boy at Harrow School; from 1825 to 1827 a pupil at a private school at Sunbury. Thereafter, until 1830, he was at Winchester College (his father's school), but was forced to leave when his fees were not paid. In 1831 he returned to Harrow as a day boy. During this period he was 'always in disgrace' and exquisitely miserable. He never lost his wounding sense of resentment at not going to university, as did his elder brothers and schoolmates, despite being no cleverer than him. Recent scholarship suggests that in the *Autobiography* Anthony exaggerated his schoolboy miseries; but he did not, one may be sure, exaggerate the hurt he felt at the time and later.

Meanwhile the family fortunes went from bad to worse. In 1827 his mother made her ill-fated attempt to set up a bazaar (a proto-mall) in the United States. Three years later she returned penniless with the older children in the family who had accompanied her. Trollope's father was by now eccentric to the point of mania. Anthony's elder brothers, Tom and Henry, had managed to make some decent start in life but his own future seemed irreparably blighted. The family finances improved temporarily with the runaway success of Mrs Trollope's first book, *Domestic Manners of the Americans* (1832). Nevertheless the Trollopes were obliged to flee from their creditors to Bruges – the last refuge of English middle-class indigence – in 1834. In this domestic exile Henry, the beloved older son, died of consumption. In the same year Trollope's by now unbeloved father died. Meanwhile Anthony tried his hand, without great success, as classical usher at a private school in Brussels. It may have worked for the Brontë sisters, but it did not work for him. The asthma, which would afflict him throughout life, came near to killing him, and in November 1834, through family influence, a place was procured for him in the General Post Office in London, at £90 a year.

During Trollope's seven formative years in the GPO, much happened that posterity will never know about. What we are allowed to know is narrated in one of the jolliest of his early novels, *The Three Clerks* (1857) and its 'hobbledehoy' hero,

Charley Tudor. Over these years the young clerk was mired in what he calls 'the lowest pits'. He alludes, darkly, to 'dirt' and 'looseness'. What coded information do these words contain? Trollope's most sympathetic biographer, N. John Hall, chances his arm with some plausible speculation:

> All the talk in the *Autobiography* about 'dirt' and 'debauchery' and the temptations of a 'loose' life surely meant more than smoking cigars and drinking gin and bitters. Trollope would have thought it unbecoming to go into further details, but gives obvious hints that he was involved with loose women; perhaps when he could afford it he went with prostitutes.

One can probe Hall's 'perhaps' a little more closely. Trollopians will be familiar with the description in Chapter 3 of the *Autobiography* of the novelist's 'worst moment':

> I was always in trouble. A young woman down in the country had taken it into her head that she would like to marry me ... the mother appeared at the Post Office. My hair almost stands on my head now as I remember the figure of the woman walking into the big room in which I sat with six or seven other clerks, having a large basket on her arm and an immense bonnet on her head. The messenger had vainly endeavoured to persuade her to remain in the ante-room. She followed the man in, and walking up the centre of the room, addressed me in a loud voice: "*Anthony Trollope, when are you going to marry my daughter?*" We have all had our worst moments, and that was one of my worst. [my italics]

A strikingly similar scene recurs in a number of the novels – in *An Eye for an Eye*, for example, when the enraged mother, uttering the same question as to marital intentions, has a pregnant daughter. Did Trollope misconduct himself that badly? The standard remedy for young men who got young girls into trouble, and could not marry them (on £90 p.a.?) was to send them abroad. Whether this was the reason he was packed off to Ireland in 1841 to take up the post of surveyor's clerk in that country's postal service we shall never know. All he says is that he left 'twenty-six years of suffering, disgrace, and inward remorse' behind him. Whether he left a bastard behind him is, perhaps, unworthy speculation. He would spend seventeen years in Ireland – where he found a wife, Rose Heseltine, a lifelong devotion to hunting, and his vocation as a novelist. Meanwhile, in the background, some four million Irish were perishing or taking to the coffin boats – a detail Trollope does not mention in *An Autobiography*, concentrating rather on the excellent fox-hunting.

He began writing his first novel, *The Macdermots of Ballycloran* (1847), in 1843. Despite help from his mother – whose name could not but help him – his first efforts foundered, largely because he fell into the toils of some of the most unscrupulous publishers in literary London. He tried his hand at the Irish novel (but who wanted to read those during the starving mid-1840s?) and historical romance. Plays and a strange anatomy of Britain, *The New Zealander* (1856), similarly failed to hit the mark. Meanwhile his Post Office career was going from strength to strength. Over the period 1851–2 he was dispatched to the west of England. He rode a bracing forty miles a day, helping to lay down a postal system which was the envy of the civilised world. Among his many achievements was the introduction of the pillar box into England.

His career as a novelist finally took off with his first Barsetshire novel, *The Warden* (1855), a quiet comedy of ecclesiastical infighting. He had, at last, found his groove. Now based in England, he was travelling widely around the Empire – anywhere letters went he went – and writing travel books. A family man, he set up home with his wife and two growing sons in a fine house at Waltham Cross, Hertfordshire, where he could enjoy some of the best hunting in England. His novel-writing career took a great leap forward when – Thackeray not being able to come up to the mark – he was offered lead position in George Smith's magnificent new monthly magazine, *Cornhill*. *Framley Parsonage* (1861), illustrated by Millais, established Anthony Trollope as a leading literary figure and it also brought him a four-figure payment – a level which he would not fall below for the next twenty years and thirty novels.

His energy at this stage of his life was fabulous. Visiting his brother in Florence in October 1860, he began what was to be a lifelong (and probably platonic) relationship with a young American girl, Kate Field, twenty-five years his junior, a feminist and an actress. She was very different from Mrs Rose Trollope of whom posterity knows little more than her two surnames and that she married who she did. Judging by his pungent travel book, *North America* (1862), Kate was one of the few things to come out of that country that he had time for. She was the inspiration for many of his later fragrant heroines and the occasional feminist.

Trollope was elected to the Athenaeum Club in 1864. He was instrumental in founding the politically influential *Fortnightly Review* and edited *St Paul's Magazine*, which he used as the vehicle for his finest short stories. Fiction cascaded from his pen, written in the everyday before-breakfast sessions which he describes in the *Autobiography*. The Barchester sequence came to an end in 1867 with *The Last Chronicle of Barset*, a powerful study of monomania which critics have seen as ushering in a 'dark phase' in his fiction. It coincided with changes in his life. Trollope had for some time felt stalled in his Post Office career. As a wealthy man of letters, with parliamentary ambitions, he resigned, effective October 1867. At the same time he kicked off his 'Palliser' sequence of parliamentary novels with *Can You Forgive Her?* (1864), followed by *Phineas Finn* (1867). Like the amiable Phineas, Trollope intended to go far in politics. During the course of the novel's serialisation in *St Paul's* (pulling in a cool £3,000 for its author-editor), Trollope took the plunge and stood as Liberal candidate at the Beverley election of November 1868. He was defeated in an egregiously dirty contest immortalised in *Ralph The Heir* (1871).

At this stage in his life, Trollope's fortunes began to wane somewhat. *St Paul's* never did as well as expected and Trollope was obliged to give up the remunerative editorship in 1870. He had produced too many novels too quickly for the public's appetite. Sales and payments fell – not catastrophically but palpably. The Palliser sequence continued ever more darkly towards its conclusion, *The Duke's Children* (1880). Trollope's gloom found magnificent expression in his mordant satire on the morals of his age, and the decay of Englishness, *The Way We Live Now* (1875). The title points to a salient feature of Trollopian art. Thackeray, Dickens and George Eliot consistently antedated the action of their novels by decades; Trollope invariably writes about 'now'. *Sic vivitur*, as his favourite Latin proverb put it – thus we live. His fiction, as *The Times* observed in their obituary, would offer a 'photogravure' of the times he lived in for posterity.

During the 1870s the Trollopes undertook two trips to Australia and New Zealand, where their son Fred was a sheep-farmer. Travel enriched the settings of his later fiction and it was on one of these steamship voyages, from New York to London in 1875, that Henry James, a fellow passenger, jotted down a pen portrait of his indomitably productive friend (of whose fiction, none the less, he had few good things to say):

> The season was unpropitious, the vessel overcrowded, the voyage detestable; but Trollope shut himself up in his cabin every morning for a purpose which, on the part of a distinguished writer who was also an invulnerable sailor, could only be communion with the muse. He drove his pen as steadily on the tumbling ocean as in Montagu Square [his home after 1875].

The thing he feared more than death, Trollope once told his son Henry, was idleness. Anthony never had that gift, his lazy brother Tom observed. He wrote more novels than his readers could swallow and stuffed the manuscripts in his desk drawers for posterity. Following a trip to Ireland in September 1882, he suffered a stroke and died in a London nursing home. Bulletins were issued and the nation mourned a loved figure. He left some £26,000 ('commendable but not magnificent' by his reckoning of such things). The publication of his frank *Autobiography* was held back until after his death. It took the best part of a century before his reputation as a novelist recovered from its damaging revelations about the 'mechanical' way he wrote his novels. A commemorative stone to his memory was laid in Westminster Abbey, disgracefully belatedly, in 1993.

FN   Anthony Trollope
MRT *The Last Chronicle of Barset*
Biog N. J. Hall, *Trollope: A Biography* (1991)

41. Grace Aguilar 1816–1847

Sympathy is the charm of human life.

Well known in her lifetime as a pioneering writer on Judaism – still consulted, if not much read – Aguilar was the author of seven works of popular fiction, the bulk of them published posthumously by her mother. The Aguilars were a Jewish family, emigrating from Portugal in the eighteenth century to England. Grace was born in Hackney, where her father was in business. After a crippling attack of measles when she was twenty-one, Grace, never strong, passed the remainder of her short life as an invalid. Morbillivirus and maternal love made her a novelist, in the same way that a badly set broken ankle, and another estimable Victorian mother, made Anna Sewell the author of *Black Beauty*.

Aguilar was, through her improving novels for girls, an arbiter of what should be the young woman's 'proper behaviour'. It boils down to a first commandment – 'Honour thy Mother'. Especially effective as a conduct-manual, with a sweet coating of fiction, was *Home Influence* (1847), which went through thirty editions in Britain in twenty years, and had a formative influence on the burgeoning American market for improving domestic fiction for teenage girls. The home was their university, and the matriarch its dean. The word 'Mamma' occurs in *Home Influence*, I would guess, ten times as often as in any other novel of the period. Described in its subtitle as 'A Tale for Mothers and Daughters', *Home Influence* was the only one of Aguilar's novels to see print during her lifetime. It was accompanied by a reassuring Preface from the Jewish mother to allay the suspicions of Christian mothers.

Aguilar was better at action within the home than outside it. One of the least convincing scenes in Victorian fiction is that in *Home Influence* where the heroine's father, a General, falls victim to a native's assegai – dying, none the less, in a condition of extreme and voluble piety. The Devon setting of *Home Influence* reflects the fact that Aguilar was, after 1828 (when her consumptive father, was forced to retire), brought up there. Her landscape descriptions are a strength and her seascapes particularly strong. However, she died in Frankfurt, where she had been taken in the vain hope of recovering her health. Exactly why the bulk of her innocuous fiction (but not her writing on Judaism) was held back from publication during her lifetime is mysterious. *A Mother's Recompense*, the sequel to *Home Influence*, was published posthumously in 1851, and *Woman's Friendship* in 1850. Both are stories of domestic life which centre on mother and daughter relationships. In a century plagued with 'surplus women' (i.e. more eligible females than there were male partners for them – a fact revealed by the decennial censuses) there was, for many young Victorian women, nothing else than women's friendship on offer. And, of course, uplifting reading.

FN   Grace Aguilar
MRT *Home Influence: A Tale for Mothers and Daughters*
Biog *ODNB* (Nadia Valman)

42. The Brontës: (Patrick 1777–1861); Charlotte 1816–1855; (Branwell 1817–1848); Emily 1818–1848; Anne 1820–1849

The children did not want society. To small infantine gaieties they were unaccustomed. They were all in all to each other. Mrs Gaskell

The most resonant name in women's fiction of the mid nineteenth century is also the strangest. It originates with a remarkable father. One of ten children of a poor farming family, he had been born Patrick Prunty (sometimes spelled 'Brunty'). The name is common to this day in Co. Down, Northern Ireland. Patrick was born in the region, on St Patrick's Day in 1777, of mixed Protestant and Catholic parentage. He gave early evidence of a quick mind. It led, by the hardest of educational routes, to the young Irishman's registering in 1802 at Cambridge University, with a view to ordination in the Church of England. 'Pruntys' were not common in that exalted place, particularly those with the bog still sticking to their trotters.

There were problems with the name 'Patrick Prunty' – a name which had the same sinister resonances with English congregations as, say, 'Gerry Adams', or 'Martin McGuinness' would have 200 years later. In 1798 there had been bloody uprising in Ireland led by the 'Society of United Irishmen', egged on by France (currently at war with England). Ireland and the Irish were not trusted – or liked – by the

English middle classes in 1802. At this period Patrick, prudently (given his future career in the Church of England) renamed himself 'Brontë'. He distanced himself further from his Ulster origins with a diaeresis, or umlaut – a mark associated with Germany, not Ireland, a country where umlauts are as rare as the venomous snakes which St Patrick banished from the island.

There are two suggested reasons for the Revd Brontë's choice of a new name. The word is an anglicisation of the ancient Greek for 'thunder', which, with his newly acquired classical learning, may have tickled the young Cantab's scholarly *amour-propre*. The more plausibly suggested reason is patriotism – to England, that is. Admiral Lord Nelson had been appointed Duke of Brontë in 1799 by Ferdinand, King of the Two Sicilies and Infante of Spain, grateful for the nautical hero's exploits against Napoleon. Short of renaming himself 'the Revd John Bull', Patrick could not have decontaminated himself more effectively of any disloyal Hibernian affiliation.

By his own formidable efforts – publishing pious verse and two morally improving short novels on the way – he rose in the world into the middle ranks of the Anglican Church, holding a string of curacies until by 1812 he was eligible enough to marry well. His bride, Maria Branwell, was the daughter of a Cornish parson. After nine years of marriage, in which she bore six children, Mrs Brontë would die of an obscure cancer in 1821, aged thirty-seven. Hers was the first Brontë death in the parsonage at Haworth to which Patrick had been appointed perpetual curate. The church served a small mill town in the West Riding of Yorkshire. It was a hugely spread-out parish, involving much walking up steep hills and down dales for the minister and, when they grew up, for his district-visiting daughters. Emily particularly loved the Yorkshire 'wilderness' (Mr Earnshaw, it will be recalled, walks sixty miles back from Liverpool bringing baby Heathcliff to Wuthering Heights).

In the confines of the Haworth parsonage, the Revd Brontë and his children – five daughters and one son, Patrick Branwell (1817–48), the great hope of the family – lived, wrote and died. It was a handsome building from the outside but inside it was a happy hunting ground for the tubercular bacillus. If ever anyone wanted to establish the connection between consumption and literary genius, wind-whipped Haworth is prime evidence. The widowed Patrick made clumsy and unsuccessful attempts at remarriage, and eventually the running of the house was taken over by his sister-in-law, Miss Elizabeth Branwell. A woman in her mid-forties and of evangelical disposition, she was not liked by the elder girls. She seems, however, to have had a soft spot for Anne, the youngest girl, who was less wild than her siblings.

Charlotte and Emily, and their two elder sisters, Maria and Elizabeth, suffered a wretched spell at the Cowan Bridge Clergy Daughters' School, which inspired the hellish, typhoid-ridden Lowood. In *Jane Eyre* it is pictured as sadism institutionalised:

we had no boots, the snow got into our shoes and melted there; our ungloved hands became numbed and covered with chilblains, as were our feet: I remember well the distracting irritation I endured from this cause every evening, when my feet inflamed; and the torture of thrusting the swelled, raw and stiff toes into my shoes in the morning. Then the scanty supply of food was distressing ... From this deficiency of nourishment resulted an abuse, which pressed hardly on the younger pupils: whenever the famished great girls had an opportunity, they would coax or menace the little ones out of their portion.

Anne, the baby of the family, and asthmatic, was spared Cowan Bridge. 'Gentle' is one of the few defining epithets applied to her as a girl. In one of her brief spells of formal education, Anne won a 'good conduct' medal – an award which one strains to imagine decorating the juvenile breasts of Emily, Branwell or Charlotte.

In 1825, the two elder sisters died of consumption, the disease which was to rage through the family. The Revd Brontë decided, wisely, to educate the surviving daughters himself with the aid of tutors. For the next five years they were free to range at will in the well-stocked parsonage library. They were stimulated by the books they found – Scott's romances and Byron's poems notably. Around 1826, the three sisters, together with the brilliant but wayward Branwell, began secretively to write long serials about imaginary worlds. This 'web of childhood' was initially inspired by games with Branwell's toy soldiers. The narratives ranged as far abroad as Africa, featuring Napoleonic and Wellingtonian heroes. At least one of the serials, that involving the fantastic kingdom of Gondal, was kept going by Anne and Emily until as late as 1845. Charlotte, always the most worldly of the sisters, gave up her parallel Angria saga in 1839.

In 1831 Charlotte went for eighteen months to a more congenial school at Roe Head. Emily and Anne followed. Charlotte went on to teach there for a while. At puberty, Anne is recorded as undergoing a religious crisis. Whether these were denominational 'doubts' is unrecorded – but they subsided. She was always the least troubled of the sisters. Charlotte seems to have been more steadfastly devout: everyone remembers the first words in *Jane Eyre* – 'there was no possibility of taking a walk that day'; many fewer the last words – 'Amen; even so come, Lord Jesus!' Emily, on the evidence of *Wuthering Heights*, seemed happy to live her life without Lord Jesus coming into it overmuch. The last lines of her novel could be read as doubting the existence of any afterlife whatsoever:

I sought, and soon discovered, the three headstones on the slope next the moor: the middle one grey, and half buried in heath; Edgar Linton's only harmonized by the turf and moss creeping up its foot; Heathcliff's still bare.
I lingered round them, under that benign sky: watched the moths fluttering

among the heath and harebells, listened to the soft wind breathing through the grass, and wondered how anyone could ever imagine unquiet slumbers for the sleepers in that quiet earth.

No last day trumpet, it seems, will come to wake them. There was now the necessity for the sisters to *do* something with their lives. In the absence of some other man, they could expect no financial support after the death of their curate father (ironically, though, he was destined to outlive them). Oddly, none of the Brontë girls – although handsome, as Branwell's portraits attest, and gifted, as their writing attests – seemed able, or willing, to enter marriage, despite what must have been an ample supply of eligible young clergymen in their circle.

In 1838 Emily became a teacher governess at a school near Halifax, Law Hill, and in 1839 Anne and Charlotte went as governesses to private families. Charlotte's first two positions were short and unhappy. Docile Anne was the least unhappy. She also left in fiction the most realistic account of how humiliating the work was for a well-bred, highly intelligent young woman, superior in every way to her employers. Anne's first employment, aged eighteen, was with the Ingham family at Blake Hall, near Mirfield. The children were spoilt and malicious and she was dismissed after a year. It's nice to think that the Inghams lived to read their nasty selves portrayed as the odious Bloomfields, in *Agnes Grey*. 'Gentle' and 'dutiful' as she may have been, Anne does not gild the governess's life with Jane Eyreish romanticism. She is more of Jane Fairfax's party (in *Emma*) that it is the domestic English slave trade. Particularly stomach-turning is the depiction of young Tom Bloomfield torturing ('fettling') birds. When Agnes remonstrates, she is blandly informed that she is a servant and should mind her own business – 'by gum!'

The sisters did not intend to governess for the rest of their lives. They made various unsuccessful attempts to publish their writing and had a plan, with the financial assistance of an aunt, to establish a school of their own (a dream which finds recurrent expression in Charlotte's later fiction). With a view to preparing themselves, Charlotte and Emily went to Brussels in 1842 to study and teach at a boarding school. Charlotte, then twenty-six, fell hopelessly in love with the proprietor and head of the school, M. Constantin Héger, whom she later portrayed as the exemplarily correct, and morally admirable, Paul Emanuel in *Villette*. Her depiction of Mme Héger is less warm. The sisters returned to Haworth in 1842 and only Charlotte went back to Brussels for a second year at the Pensionnat Héger. Emily, the more poetically inclined sister, was most rooted to Haworth and Yorkshire and seems to have hated leaving it. For Charlotte, the Belgian experience was extraordinarily stimulating emotionally and intellectually, although clearly (as refracted through *Villette*'s Lucy Snowe) she disliked Brussels, despised Catholics, and suffered

horribly from her unrequited passion for her incorruptible professor – suffering distilled into Rochester's cat and mouse game with his governess Jane.

In 1844 the school project fell through. It survives only as a forlorn fiction in
the last paragraphs of *Villette*. At Charlotte's initiative, *Poems* by 'Currer, Ellis and
Acton Bell' (the androgynous names are significant) was published in 1846. It sold
two copies, as legend has it. But it got worse. In 1847, Emily's *Wuthering Heights*
and Anne's *Agnes Grey* were accepted by the notoriously dubious London publisher,
Thomas Cautley Newby, who brought them out lumped together as an abysmally
ugly three-volume set. The world took no notice. Charlotte's *The Professor* (based on
her Brussels experience, but with a stiltedly male hero) was turned down by the eminently respectable house of Smith, Elder and Co., but *Jane Eyre* was eagerly accepted
and published in October 1847 to terrific success. The rogue Newby now published
Anne's *The Tenant of Wildfell Hall* (1848) with the implication that it was actually
the work of 'Currer Bell' – i.e. Charlotte, who in point of fact disliked her sister's
book for its graphic depiction of Branwell's dipsomania. She suppressed its republication after Anne's death.

Anne and Charlotte authenticated themselves by going to London to meet
George Smith and other members of the literary world. Thackeray on this occasion
met Charlotte whom he admired. She dedicated the second edition of *Jane Eyre* to
him, sparking wild rumours that he was the original of Rochester (the only connection was that he, too, had an insane wife). This would be Anne's only trip outside
Yorkshire. Her life had been consistently drearier than those of her sisters who had,
at least, seen foreign parts. After the horrors of the Inghams she had found a slightly
more congenial governess post with the family of the Revd Edmund Robinson, near
York.

At this point, in 1843, Anne's career crossed, fatefully, with that of her brother.
Branwell, having failed to get the hoped for place at university, went on to fail as
a portrait painter. Even more catastrophic was his being dismissed from a clerical
job with the local railway firm under the suspicion of embezzlement. Despite his
known dissipations, Anne secured him a tutor's position with her own employers,
the Robinsons. Branwell was dismissed from that post for 'proceedings ... bad beyond
expression' – namely misconduct (vaguely specified) with Mrs Robinson. Mr Robinson threatened to shoot him. On his dismissal in 1845 he fell into a 'spiral of
despair', which he medicated with opium and alcohol.

Branwell died, of drink, drugs and galloping consumption, in 1848, aged just
thirty-one. The hopes of the family – and some incomplete works of fiction, alas –
went to the grave with him in the family vault at Haworth. As his legacy, Branwell
left, in his sisters' writing, two of the most vivid depictions of chronic alcoholism

in Victorian literature. One is Hindley in *Wuthering Heights*; the other Arthur Huntingdon, in Anne's *The Tenant of Wildfell Hall*. Wildfell's mysterious tenant, 'Mrs Graham', is, it emerges, a refugee from the alcoholic hell her husband Arthur has created. Descriptions of drunkenness are common enough in literature. What is most powerful in *The Tenant* is the close description of the alcoholic death. Helen, the abused wife, and Arthur are brought together in his final hours. Quite aware it will kill him, Arthur demands strong drink. The consequence is delirious terror:

> 'Death is so terrible,' he cried, 'I cannot bear it! You don't know, Helen – you can't imagine what it is, because you haven't it before you! and when I'm buried, you'll return to your old ways and be as happy as ever, and all the world will go on just as busy and merry as if I had never been; while I –' He burst into tears.

The novel was published three months before Branwell's death. Anne may have hoped that plain-speaking, even through one of her characters, would effect a cure. It rarely does – as legions of wives of alcoholics testify. Anne survived her brother by only a few months, dying decently, but tragically early, of the family complaint. One imagines she met her end more dutifully. A few months earlier, consumption had also claimed Emily – who had resolutely refused medical attention. Charlotte noted the fact bitterly: 'It is useless to question her; you get no answers. It is still more useless to recommend remedies; they are never adopted.' Emily is the most enigmatic of the writing sisters. No clear image of her remarkable personality can be formed. Branwell sneered at her as 'lean and scant' aged sixteen. She, famously, counselled that he should be 'whipped' for his malefactions. She evidently thought well of the whip and used it, as Mrs Gaskell records, on her faithful hound, Keeper, when he dared to lie on her bed. A tawny beast with a 'roar like a lion', Keeper followed his mistress's coffin to the grave and, for nights thereafter, moaned outside her bedroom door. A second novel, substantially written by Emily, has not survived, but the solitary achievement of *Wuthering Heights* adds to her mystique.

At thirty-five, Charlotte was the only child of the original six left alive. In 1849 she published *Shirley*, her 'social problem' novel, about the upheavals of the early Industrial Revolution, and the only one of her major works to be set in her native Yorkshire. This was followed, in 1853, by her most introspective work, *Villette*. The following year she married the Revd Arthur Bell Nicholls, her father's curate since 1845. Though not loveless, how passionate the marriage was will never be known. She died of complications arising from pregnancy.

FN   Charlotte Brontë (later Nicholls); Emily Brontë (Jane); Anne Brontë
MRT   *Jane Eyre*; *Wuthering Heights*; *The Tenant of Wildfell Hall*
Biog J. R. V. Barker, *The Brontës* (1994)

43. Maria Monk 1816–1849

I must be informed that one of my great duties was to obey the priests in all things; and this I soon learnt, to my utter astonishment and horror, was to live in the practice of criminal intercourse with them.

There has been a successful campaign over the last half-century to identify, celebrate, and institutionalise an authentic 'Canadian fiction'. One author – arguably the unluckiest novelist ever to write a bestseller – is signally absent from the roll of Maple Leaf honour. In 1836, the year that another young unknown, 'Boz', exploded on the scene with *The Pickwick Papers*, the North American reading public was entranced by *The Awful Disclosures of Maria Monk as Exhibited in a Narrative of Her Sufferings During a Residence of Five Years as a Novice, and Two Years as a Black Nun, in the Hôtel Dieu Nunnery of Montreal*. First published in New York under the respectable Harper imprint, 'Maria Monk' went on to sell 300,000 in five years in pirate, 'underground' editions.

Purporting to be 'true confessions', the *Awful Disclosures* was as much a work of unalloyed fiction as anything Boz wrote. The nuns of Hôtel Dieu, it supposedly revealed, served as concubines for lecherous priests in a neighbouring seminary. These robed rogues indulged a Sadeian taste for flagellation and bondage (passages from the divine Marquis's *Justine* are irresistibly evoked). Tunnels from neighbouring monasteries facilitated the priests' nocturnal ravishing and the resulting bastards of Mother Church were murdered at birth, the little corpses being thrown in a lime pit, after being baptised, of course. Sex Vobiscum. Sex is everywhere under the veil, the robe, under the cardinal's hat and even, it is hinted, under the papal vestments. Pope Gregory XVI, it was implied, had made anal rape a specific priestly duty. His Canadian clergy undertook the task with holy relish.

As the *Awful Disclosures* narrates it, Maria was a good little Canadian girl who – with the purest religious motives – took the veil, having converted in her teens from Protestantism to Catholicism. A horrible mistake. Only a couple of hours after taking her vows, Maria discovers the true nature of conventual devotions at Hôtel Dieu.

> when, as I was sitting in the community-room, Father Dufresne called me out, saying, he wished to speak to me. I feared what was his intention; but I dared not disobey. In a private apartment, he treated me in a brutal manner; and, from two other priests, I afterwards received similar usage that evening. Father Dufresne afterwards appeared again; and I was compelled to remain in company with him until morning.

According to Monk, she was immured in this papal brothel for seven years, at which point, unable to face the idea of her newborn babe (engendered by the Abbé himself) going into the lime pit, she resourcefully made her escape. (It is, incidentally, impossible not to be reminded at such moments of Margaret Atwood's *Handmaid's Tale*.) The first edition of *The Awful Disclosures* finishes here but subsequent editions narrate Maria's initial inclination to drown herself, having dutifully ensured the safety of her babe, and her later resolution to live and expose the evils of popery.

What little truth of Maria Monk's life can be recovered is sad. Born Catholic in Montreal, she was, reportedly, brain-damaged at the age of seven when a pencil was jabbed deep into her ear. From earliest childhood, she was sexually wayward and turned, in her teens, to prostitution. She never set foot in Hôtel Dieu, a wholly respectable institution. Aged eighteen, Maria's mother had her incarcerated in Montreal's Charitable Institution for Female Penitents. Spectacularly impenitent, she got herself pregnant and was expelled, then made her way down to the United States.

In Boston, she witnessed virulent anti-Catholic riots and the burning of a convent. Riding this prejudice, she invented her fables about the Hôtel Dieu to explain her bastard child. It came to the notice of the press and she was written about in the New York newspapers in October 1835. By now she had embellished her fictions, claiming that, just before her lucky escape, she had been instructed to poison a fellow nun who had dared to resist the beastly sexual demands made on her. Overnight, Maria Monk (a happy name in the circumstances) was a Protestant 'cause', and living proof of Catholic licentiousness. The articles were followed up, a few months later, by *The Awful Disclosures of Maria Monk*. The narrative was actually ghosted by George Bourne and John Jay Slocum, two virulently anti-Catholic Presbyterian ministers. They profited handsomely from the book, quarrelling with each other furiously over their spoils, but Monk got not a cent – or what pittance she got she squandered.

The narrative was quickly identified as a squalid sham, a confection put together from Gothic anti-conventual tales, pornography and doctrinal hatred. It was, in short, a novel – and not a very wonderful one (although the same could be said of another bestseller with a not dissimilar anti-Catholic animus, *The Da Vinci Code*). What was wonderful was its perennial appeal. For much of the nineteenth century *The Awful Disclosures* were circulated, hand to hand, as religious pornography, among the sectarian faithful. Like the similarly faked *Protocols of the Elders of Zion*, it was indestructible. Where there was anti-Catholicism, there – sure as night follows day – would be Maria Monk. Where there was anti-Semitism, there would be the *Protocols*.

Monk's later years were short and wretched. In summer 1837, she disappeared from public view, surfacing, momentarily, in Philadelphia where she claimed, preposterously, that she had been kidnapped by Catholic priests and had again escaped. *Further disclosures by Maria Monk* were published, but by now her credibility was fatally eroded. In 1838 she had another illegitimate child – father unknown, but certainly no priest. Now habitually drunken, she married, drifted back to prostitution (her husband having abandoned her) and was, finally, arrested in a brothel charged with stealing from a client. She died, raving, in a New York prison in summer 1849 – an institution which was as evil, one imagines, as that which she had invented in Montreal.

FN   Maria Monk
MRT   *The Awful Disclosures of Maria Monk*
Biog   *DCB*

44. George Eliot 1819–1880

Silly Novels by Lady Novelists are a genus with many species, determined by the particular quality of silliness that predominates in them – the frothy, the prosy, the pious, or the pedantic. George Eliot, on the kind of novelist Eliot is not

In 1934, Lord David Cecil, in his belletrist monograph *Early Victorian Novelists*, observed, with a donnish sigh, that the dust lay heavier on George Eliot than on her great contemporaries: Dickens and Thackeray. That dust has been blown off (though quite a lot has landed on the luckless author of *Vanity Fair*) in the last eighty years. Two mighty winds are responsible for the de-dusting of George Eliot: 1. feminism, and its energetic search for female Shakespeares; 2. the rise of Ph.D.-sponsored 'research'. What once looked like 'dull' is now Arnoldian 'high seriousness'.

Mary Anne (the name is spelt various ways) Evans was born the daughter of a land agent in the service of a member of the Warwickshire aristocracy. Mary Anne's mother was her father's second wife and, like him, of respectable working-class stock (Mary Garth's father, Caleb, in *Middlemarch* is a fond representation of Robert Evans). She grew up devoted to her brother Isaac (unfondly recalled as Tom Tulliver in *The Mill on the Floss*). Her upbringing was evangelical, dutiful, rural and allowed ample access to books. Scott, whom she first read aged eight, would be a major influence. On her mother's death in 1836, she left school to take over running the house for her father and brother. A critical moment in her late adolescence was her principled refusal to accompany her father to church – an act of doctrinal, not filial, rebellion.

She was already steeping herself in works of theology and in Wordsworth, with whom she had a lifelong congeniality. In Coventry, a city intellectually fizzing with literary coteries, she had what was, effectively, the best higher education a woman could get in 1840s England. She was invited, aged twenty-three, to translate D. F. Strauss's work of biblical 'Higher Criticism', *Das Leben Jesu*, into English. The translation, for which she received £20, came out in 1846. In 1848, she met Emerson, which left a profound impression on her already formidable mind. On her father's death in 1849, she received a small legacy of some £90 p.a., which allowed her to travel abroad. She had, at this point, renamed herself 'Marian', a name unassociated with the motherhood of Jesus.

On the strength of her private income, she took up what was virtually unpaid work on John Chapman's *Westminster Review*, the leading journal of ideas of the day (with, inevitably, a tiny circulation – most of us, Eliot once pungently observed, 'walk about well wadded with stupidity'). She was probably romantically involved with Chapman and certainly was so with the philosopher Herbert Spencer, who at the last moment, was supposedly put off by Marian's superficial lack of physical beauty. The third man in her life, George Henry Lewes – himself spectacularly ugly – was a philosopher, scientist, journalist and occasional novelist. He would become her lifelong consort, but never her husband. A practising free-thinker, Lewes had surrendered his wife to a journalist colleague. Having condoned adultery, legal separation was, at the time, impossible. Nevertheless, Marian defiantly called herself 'Mrs Lewes'. The couple suffered ostracism, and much mockery behind their backs. There were no children: rationalists that they were, contraception is the likely explanation.

Over the early 1850s Marian worked at her translation of Spinoza's *Ethics* while Lewes worked on his life of Goethe: high minds in harness. On the side, Marian had begun dabbling in fiction, with the short stories which eventually became *Scenes of Clerical Life* in 1858. They were published under the pen-name 'George Eliot'. This second identity was devised so as not to contaminate Marian's serious writing, not to advertise her questionable (non-)marital status, and – most importantly – to draw a line between herself and 'silly lady novelists', about whose effusions she was scathing. The *Scenes*, which drew on her early life in Warwickshire, were well received, despite their unremitting realism (one, 'Janet's Repentance', is the first study of female alcoholism in literature). Eliot was persuaded by Lewes, and by their sympathetic publisher, John Blackwood, to progress to a full-sized, three-decker novel, *Adam Bede* (1859). Set in the rural Midlands at the period of the Methodist revival, the novel was sensationally popular with library readers. It was no longer possible to keep her identity secret (more so with impostors – all male – pretending to be her). But she retained the masculine pen-name for her fiction.

At the same period, Eliot took charge of Lewes's three sons. The Leweses were now secure financially. In 1860, Blackwood published *The Mill on the Floss*, the most autobiographical of Eliot's novels. Despite some objection to the near seduction of Maggie Tulliver in the third volume, the work confirmed Eliot's standing as one of the leading novelists of the day – and, without question, the leading woman novelist. After some shorter efforts, including the crystalline moral fable, *Silas Marner* (1861), Eliot's next novel – her great work as she projected it – was a tale of fifteenth-century Florence, *Romola* (1862–3). She was offered the highest-ever payment for a novel until then, £10,000. Her historical research was exhaustive: she went into the novel, she said, a young woman and emerged the other end an old woman. But despite the fortune it earned her, and the labour she put into it, *Romola* remains her least read work.

In the early 1860s the Leweses were rich enough to move into a luxurious house, the Priory, in St John's Wood. George Eliot was now a 'Victorian Sage', and in the furious debate over the second Reform Bill she intervened (on the Conservative side) with her 'social problem' novel, *Felix Holt, The Radical* (1866). Reform stuck in her mind, and she returned to the earlier 1832 Bill in the novel that is regarded as her masterpiece, *Middlemarch*. In it, she wove into one design two originally separate stories: that of an idealistic young woman, Dorothea Brooke and that of a scientifically adventurous doctor, Tertius Lydgate. The completed novel ponders many of the issues that had preoccupied Eliot throughout her life: above all, what constitutes the life well lived? Our final view of Dorothea Brooke (as of Dinah Morris, in *Adam Bede*) is ambiguous.

In 1876 Eliot published her last novel, *Daniel Deronda*. Despite its preoccupation with Judaism (typically, Eliot learned Hebrew by way of preparation), the work was immensely successful. In the same year the Leweses purchased a large country house, the Heights, near Haslemere. But Lewes, whose health was chronically poor, died in November 1878. An inconsolable Eliot devoted the remainder of her shattered intellectual energies to editing his *Problems of Life and Mind* – a book which posterity would gladly exchange for another ten pages of *Middlemarch*, describing in clearer detail Dorothea's later life after marrying Ladislaw. Finally, in 1880, she married John Walter Cross, twenty years her junior. In unclear circumstances, Cross appears to have attempted suicide by jumping into a canal in Venice during the wedding trip. A few months later, on 22 December 1880, Marian died of a kidney disorder. She left a little under £43,000.

Cross's pious *George Eliot's Life, as Related in Her Letters and Journals* (1885) is a prime example of the Victorian whitewash biography. It did not, however, whiten the reputation of the adulteress novelist in unforgiving eyes. It was not until 1980 that Westminster Abbey finally relented and allowed a commemorative stone to be laid alongside such exemplars of moral virtue as Edward Bulwer-Lytton.

FN George Eliot (née Mary Anne Evans, later 'Marian')
MRT *Middlemarch*
Biog R. Ashton, *George Eliot: A Life* (1996)

POSTSCRIPT

45. G. H. Lewes 1817–1878

Mr Eliot.

George Eliot lived the years of her great creativity under the shadow of her consort (she called him 'husband'), G. H. Lewes. Posterity has cast Lewes, with ever-deepening obscurity, in her shadow. But their lives, and achievements, are intertwined. And, little read as he is nowadays, he deserves an honoured niche in the history of fiction – not merely as a helper of genius, but an innovator.

Lewes was born into a theatrical family and went to school haphazardly, leaving at sixteen. Like many Victorians, he was a heroic autodidact and intellectual 'amateur'. It was an exciting century to be curious and none was more so than Lewes. He enrolled as a student of medicine in his teens but gave up the profession because of his sensitivity to others' suffering – not even a mission to mend it could overcome his sensitivity. This was not entirely a moral failing. Like Eliot he believed 'sympathy' to be a mark of civilisation and its extension a gauge of progress; for her, the novel was a principal instrument for the instilling of sympathy – awareness of other people's 'equivalent centre of self'. From his medical training Lewes took 'physiology' – the organic relation of parts – as a prime element of his thought. Other elements were the philosophy of Spinoza and, pre-eminently, the developmental 'sociology' ('positivism') of Auguste Comte, whose 'third state' foresaw a utopia brought about by growing human enlightenment.

Lewes spent two *Lehrjahre* (1838–40) in Germany, at a period of European ferment, and returned, with Carlyle, Britain's main disciple of Goethe, whom he met in Weimar. On his return in 1841, he married Agnes Jervis, whose tutor he was. At the time he was supporting himself as an all-purpose journalist, expounding his sternly free-thinking views. In line with his rational, increasingly bohemian, philosophy he did not resent his wife forming a liaison with Thornton Hunt, the son of Keats's patron, Leigh Hunt, and in 1850 Hunt and Lewes set up the journal *The Leader*, one of the most powerful higher journalistic ventures of the period, though never remunerative.

Lewes separated amicably from Agnes when she bore his co-editor a son (she had borne Lewes three). He complicated his personal life further after Herbert Spencer introduced him to Mary Anne Evans, the young bluestocking whom he would help form into George Eliot. The two lived together in their unconsecrated 'marriage' after 1854. Their life was increasingly comfortable on Eliot's large earnings from the fiction he encouraged her to write, and whose marketing (via Blackwoods principally) he managed. In the stability offered by the union with Eliot, Lewes embarked on his massive *Problems of Life and Mind*. It was published posthumously and was, on delivery, as dead as its author.

In an astonishingly wide-ranging career, the more remarkable given the frailty of his own physiology, Lewes wrote two novels. Neither reveals any great gift for the form, but *Ranthorpe*, published in 1847, opened the way for novelists of greater talent than himself. It ranks as the first *Bildungsroman* – or autobiographical – novel in English. It was a genre of fiction which examined particularly the formative years of childhood, adolescence and early adulthood. The tree was shaped, the *Bildungsroman* asserted, as the twig was bent. Alternative names for the form were *Erziehungsroman* and *Entwicklungsroman*. It was, as those words suggest, not English and Lewes was cosmopolitan enough to import it into his native literature.

The *Bildungsroman* genre drew, originally, on Goethe's *Wilhelm Meister's Apprenticeship*. *Ranthorpe* chronicles, with fictional gloss, Lewes's own rackety upbringing. The key moment – vividly done – finds the hero, disappointed in love life and work. In the depths of despair he is about to throw himself to his death off a London bridge when he is rescued by a sage, who introduces him to the life-saving philosophy of Goethe. A successful career for Ranthorpe as a man of letters follows. Such things are speculative, but without *Ranthorpe* casting the mould, British fiction might not have had such mid-century masterworks of the mid-Victorian *Bildungsroman* as *Pendennis*, *David Copperfield*, or, most directly in Lewes's life, *The Mill on the Floss*.

FN   George Henry Lewes
MRT *Ranthorpe*
Biog R. Ashton, *G. H. Lewes: A Life* (1991)

46. Herman Melville 1819–1891

What then is Moby Dick? He is the deepest blood-being of the white race; he is our deepest blood-nature. D. H. Lawrence

The facts of Melville's life (much is hazy) have been exhaustively chronicled, principally by Hershel Parker's leviathan biography. He was born ('Melvill') in New York, with deeper family roots in Boston. Few families had a nobler American pedigree. Herman (the third child and second son) was the descendant of a paternal grandfather who had led the 'tea party' in 1773. His maternal grandfather, of Dutch extraction, had served as a general in the Revolutionary Wars. Herman belonged, as Parker puts it, to 'the highest aristocracy in the country'. It was a crushingly heavy mantle for a child not initially recognised as in any way exceptional. 'Slow in comprehension' was one damning verdict; the more so since Melville's father, Allan, did not in any way add to the familial distinction. The family business in dry goods was bankrupted and Herman's father died when his son was twelve. Hershel Parker's massive biography begins with a vivid vignette of 'the terrified child and the broken man' packing up household valuables for flight from the advancing creditors.

Herman's later childhood was a thing of irregular – but good – schooling and false starts. Following further financial reverses (his amiable brother Gansevoort was now head of the family, and its business), Herman followed the script written by romantic fiction for adventurous lads like him and went off to sea. He did not, as the same script ordained, 'run away'. Gansevoort secured him a berth as a cabin boy on a voyage from New York to Liverpool and Herman spent a few weeks in England before the return trip. The experience is recalled, wryly, in the later novel *Redburn: His First Voyage* (1849). On his return, Melville tried school teaching and clerking, a drudgery he immortalised in his late short story 'Bartleby, the Scrivener' – in which the pen-pushing hero, an American Pooter, withers away, muttering, to every suggestion that he actually do something, 'I would prefer not to.'

Melville's 'life began', as he preferred to say, when, like Ishmael, he again answered the call of the sea and, now bearded and 'wild-haired', enrolled as a 'common sailor' on the whaler *Acushnet* in January 1841. He was crammed for months into the forecastle – one of the only places in America where different races, even blacks and Indians, mixed on equal terms. There were half a dozen languages and a score of bodies crammed into a space the size of a bedroom. As Parker notes, 'mutual masturbation was commonplace, sodomy much less so'. Communal onanism was called 'claw for claw' – sailors going at each other's privates like fighting cocks. In his later fictional version of life aboard the *Acushnet*, Melville refers darkly to the 'sins of Gomorrah', by which he presumably means more criminal intercourse than jovial clawing.

After six months of the stifling intimacies of the foc'sle, the sailors enjoyed a taste of 'liberty' in the Marquesas, in the South Pacific, having sailed around Cape Horn. The *Acushnet* was welcomed by native girls swimming, naked: 'What a sight for us bachelor sailors! How avoid so dire a temptation?' the hero asks in *Typee: A Peep at Polynesian Life* (1846). Melville, it is presumed, didn't. But a few days' liberty was not enough. With a companion ('Toby' in *Typee*), Melville jumped ship. Had they been apprehended, they would have been clapped in irons. They weren't. For Melville, it was his second great escape in life.

How long Melville – he and Toby being soon separated – spent with the Typee natives is not exactly known. But it was long enough to enjoy a voluptuous relationship with 'the beauteous nymph Fayaway', clad in 'the garb of Eden', and to discover that these 'savages' and reputed 'cannibals' were, in fact, as civilised as any American citizen. Melville's observations, as recorded in *Typee*, are anthropologically sensible and decades ahead of his time. This refusal to adhere to the romantic stereotypes ('heathenish rites and human sacrifices') popularised by other novels, perversely, was one reason that his seafaring novels were regarded as merest invention.

If his life started when he embarked on the *Acushnet*, his life as a novelist began when he deserted the ship. He made no attempt to carry on whaling, signing on to sail home on a short-handed barque, the *Lucy Ann*. It was a poorly disciplined vessel and Melville, somewhat reluctantly it seems, made part of a mutiny against the captain. This led to jail – not entirely uncomfortable – in Tahiti, a phase of Melville's adventures which is chronicled in his second novel, *Omoo: A Narrative of Adventures in the South Seas* (1847). Indirectly, the *Acushnet* mutiny inspired what is Melville's finest novella, 'Benito Cereno', in which he explores the malign reciprocities of racism – the servant holding the razor to the throat of his nominal 'owner'. Every ship, every country, is in the possession of the oppressed, if they choose to take it.

Melville was further delayed in his return to America by a stopover in Hawaii. He had now, for a period, 'gone native', freed of the 'tabus' of his country, class and time. While in Hawaii (then the Sandwich Islands) he agitated against the sexual puritanism imposed by missionaries – a theme pursued, fiercely, in *Omoo*. This freebooting phase of his life ended in August 1843, when Melville signed on, in Honolulu, with the US Navy, as an 'Ordinary Seaman'. This final voyage, in a very orderly frigate, is chronicled in *White-Jacket; or, The World in a Man-of-War*, the third in his great sea-going sequence. In the longer journeys at sea undertaken by US Navy vessels, there was, Melville observed, more sodomy or, as he put it, 'The sins for which the city of the plain were overthrown still linger in some of these wooden-walled Gomorrahs of the deep.' Less viciously, these ships had libraries which were better supplied with good fiction than many towns onshore. Melville read widely over these months. Whether he indulged any of the sins of Gomorrah is not known.

A manly and bronzed Herman returned home in October 1844 to find the Melville family fortunes improved. Gansevoort was making his way in public life as an aide to President James K. Polk. Herman was encouraged by his family to turn his rich trove of Marquesan 'yarns' into print. His sea-faring years were over. Having settled down, he began to write his first novel. But *Typee* was not wanted by America's publishers. Bizarrely, Harpers turned it down on the grounds that 'it was impossible it could be true'. Gansevoort, currently posted to London (and very ill – he would die a few weeks later), got it taken by Murray's, the country's leading publisher of travel books, for a generous £100. *Typee* came out in 1846, and was well received. The sequel, *Omoo*, was snapped up.

A confident Melville, now determined on a career in fiction, married in 1847. His wife, Elizabeth Shaw, was from as distinguished a family as his own. The daughter of a chief justice in Massachusetts, she came with money – which the Melvilles (with Gansevoort gone) were short of. The newlywed couple retired to an estate, Arrowhead, in Berkshire County, Massachusetts, where Herman could mix his writing with some genteel farming. Here they lived for a dozen years, as the family grew by four children. Here, too, Melville wrote *Moby Dick* (initially 'The Whale') and where he had a brief intense friendship with the novelist's dedicatee, Nathaniel Hawthorne, living nearby. Much has been made of their very occasional contacts.

The Melville marriage was difficult, however. Herman was temperamental, disappointed and, reportedly, drunken and mentally unstable. Elizabeth Shaw Melville had a lot to put up with. He was publishing steadily, but without the success he knew he deserved. *Moby Dick* baffled its readers, and continued to do so for decades. Was it even a novel? contemporaries wondered, as they ploughed through chapter after chapter of cetaceous zoology, marine myth and abstruse nautical history. Neither was Melville's angular poetry much to American public taste, which preferred Longfellow.

Melville clinched his downward trajectory with the supremely baffling *Pierre: or, The Ambiguities* (1852), the first, and only, of his land-based novels. The hero, Pierre Glendinning, only son of a rich widow, breaks his engagement with the eminently suitable Lucy when he discovers a half-sister, Isabel, the illegitimate daughter of his revered father. The couple run away to New York where he tries his hand, unsuccessfully, at authorship. It all ends tragically. When they learn of the hidden scandal, Lucy and Pierre's mother both die of grief. Isabel and Pierre, who are in prison, contrive to kill themselves. The last paragraphs, as the dead hero and dying heroine are discovered by a friend, conveys the grotesque quality of the whole:

> 'Yes! Yes! – Dead! Dead! Dead! – without one visible wound – her sweet plumage hides it. – Thou hellish carrion, this is thy hellish work! Thy juggler's rifle brought down this heavenly bird! Oh, my God, my God! Thou scalpest me with this sight!'

Pierre fell flatter than flat, taking Melville's reputation with it. Melville's publication rate thereafter slumped, although he was still writing energetically. He turned to lecturing about the South Seas, which he evidently did well. The family moved to New York during the Civil War, and at its conclusion, in 1866, his in-laws contrived to secure him a sinecure as a customs inspector in New York. His later life was nevertheless unhappy. His two sons died before their father; one, apparently, by suicide. Melville's creative energies were directed to an epic poem, *Clarel: A Poem and Pilgrimage in the Holy Land* (1876), which has the distinction of being the longest published poem in American literature. A narrative work, it chronicles a young theology student's quest for belief. When published, it set the seal on a life of failed literary innovation.

The rehabilitation of Herman Melville started in the 1920s. D. H. Lawrence asserted, in his study of classic American writers, that '*Moby Dick* is a great book'. The first serious biography was published in 1923, which similarly focused on the 'mystic' aspect of Melville's work. His writings (with a stress on the more manageable novellas) were installed on educational curricula; doctoral dissertations were written. The 'Melville Revival' received a further boost in the 1970s. E. M. Forster had been an early enthusiast and had identified Herman Melville as a closet homosexual in one of his notebooks, as early as 1926. Benjamin Britten's opera, *Billy Budd*, with Forster's libretto, drew out the perceived sexual implications of the strange love and death triangle between the 'handsome sailor', Claggart, and Captain Edward Fairfax Vere.

This 'new explanation' of Melville and the greatness of his fiction depended on the supposed 'encrypted sexuality' of the texts. Rich pickings for such cryptanalysts were located in Chapter 11 of *Moby Dick*, in which Ishmael and Queequeg share a double bed, before embarking, and such passages as that in the later section describing the removal of sperm from the 'cassock' of the whale:

> Squeeze! squeeze! squeeze! all the morning long; I squeezed that sperm till I myself almost melted into it; I squeezed that sperm till a strange sort of insanity came over me; and I found myself unwittingly squeezing my co-laborers' hands in it, mistaking their hands for the gentle globules. Such an abounding, affectionate, friendly, loving feeling did this avocation beget; that at last I was continually

squeezing their hands, and looking up into their eyes sentimentally; as much as to say,– Oh! my dear fellow beings, why should we longer cherish any social acerbities, or know the slightest ill-humor or envy! Come; let us squeeze hands all round; nay, let us all squeeze ourselves into each other; let us squeeze ourselves universally into the very milk and sperm of kindness.

'Surely the oldest piece of phallicism in all the world's literature,' D. H. Lawrence comments. Oldest, perhaps; oddest, certainly.

FN   Herman Melville
MRT   *Moby Dick*
Biog H. Parker, *Herman Melville: 1819–1851* (1996); *Herman Melville: 1851–1891* (2002)

47. Mrs E. D. E. N. Southworth 1819–1899

'Villain!' gasped Le Noir, shaking his fist and choking with rage; 'villain! you shall repent this in every vein of your body!' From *Capitola's Peril*, a sequel to *The 'Hidden Hand'*

One of the band of American women novelists who came to prominence during the 1850s, Mrs Southworth's style was more gothic and sensational than others of the 'feminised fifties' group. Emma Nevitte's father was a merchant whose import business was ruined and whose health was shattered by the 1812 war with England. He died when his daughter was four. The religious background to Nevitte's childhood was mixed. Her father was Catholic, her mother Episcopalian. She herself was to be more sceptical and a less propagandistic Christian novelist than her peers – Susan Warner, Harriet Beecher Stowe, or 'Fanny Fern'.

The young Emma was, by her own account, 'not beautiful', and later confessed herself jealous as a growing girl of her sister Charlotte, who was. Emma, on the other hand, was the cleverer of the two and began working life as a teacher, aged fifteen, in 1834. In 1840, barely out of her teens, she married an inventor, Frederick Hamilton Southworth and they had two children. However, the marriage soon failed and the couple separated in 1844. In later life Southworth often referred to herself as a widow – presumably so as not to alienate her stricter readers.

Now lacking marital support, with growing children to care for, she returned to teaching and began, in 1846, writing her first novel, *Retribution*, which was published in 1849. All her novels were serialised and *Retribution* appeared in the pages of the *National Era*, the anti-slavery weekly which later popularised *Uncle Tom's Cabin*.

Southworth later formed an alliance with the *Saturday Evening Post* and the *New York Ledger*, the two market leaders in the field of serialised fiction for adult family members. Subtitled '*or the Vale of Shadows, a Tale of Passion*', the narrative of *Retribution* forecasts Southworth's preference for romance centred on sexual betrayal, with Maryland and Virginia settings (highly coloured for Northern readers), violent storms, and 'providential' interventions. The heroine, Hester Gray, is betrayed by her husband Ernest with her closest friend. It is a typical Southworth plot complication.

She followed up with *The Deserted Wife* (1850), in which, given her own history, it is tempting to see autobiography. Southworth's status as the most popular novelist of the day was clinched with *The Curse of Clifton* (1852), which saw her launched on a career that was to produce some sixty bestselling romances. As a serialist, Southworth's stock-in-trade was the vivid, reader-grabbing, opening. *Lionne; or The Doom of Deville* (1859), for example, opens in the Maryland wilderness, where Lieutenant Orville Deville, a young officer, has a glimpse of a girl of the woods ('Lionne') by the vivid illumination of a shaft of lightning. He falls in love with the 'brilliant brunette' on the spot and is, immediately, felled by a falling branch. Is he dead? All this in a few opening sentences.

The money rolled in, but in the early 1850s Southworth and her children suffered chronic sickness and disability. She grossly overworked herself and precipitated a serious breakdown in 1855. She publicly requested her loyal readers in the *Saturday Evening Post* to bear with her, while she convalesced. By the end of the decade, with the huge success of *The Hidden Hand* (1859), she was earning an estimated $6,000 a year: possibly more than any other woman in America at the time, other than courtesans.

The most popular American novel since *Uncle Tom's Cabin*, Southworth's gothic tale, *The Hidden Hand*, was boosted by the readiness with which it could be adapted for the stage. There were an estimated forty dramatised versions – one of them, appropriately enough, starring John Wilkes Booth as the assassin. The novel opens at Hurricane Hall, set in the romantic scenery of 'the Devil's Hoof' in Virginia. The bachelor proprietor of the Hall, Major Ira Warfield ('Old Hurricane'), is called to the bedside of a dying midwife, Granny Grewell. Twelve years before, she had secretly delivered a pair of twins, a boy and a girl. The boy died, the girl was disposed of somewhere in New York. The motive was to misappropriate their rightful inheritance. This dastardly plot is the work of the villainous Colonel Le Noir and his depraved son Craven. Warfield discovers the urchin, Capitola Black, in Rag Lane, New York, where she is a child of the streets and dressed as a boy (cross-dressing features prominently in her subsequent adventures, an oblique allusion to the 'Bloomerism' – women in trousers – which was all the rage in 1850s America).

After fearful complications, Capitola's true identity emerges and poetic justice is measured out, overbrimmingly.

On the strength of the work's popularity in Britain, where there were three piratically dramatised versions running concurrently, Southworth spent the years 1859–62 in London, fuelling the mania for 'Capitola' hats, suits and coats with her immensely popular public readings. True to her abolitionist affiliations, Southworth supported the Union during the Civil War and did voluntary work in hospitals during hostilities. She adapted well to changes in fictional fashion. Always up with the times, by the 1870s Southworth was using a typewriter and in the early 1880s she became a devotee of Swedenborg and spiritualism as the popularity of her fiction waned. By the time of her death, the mass of her readers had preceded her into the next world. Few remained loyal in this.

FN   Emma Southworth (Dorothy Eliza, née Nevitte)
MRT   *The Hidden Hand*
Biog *ANB* (L. Moody Simms)

48. Eliza Lynn Linton 1822–1898

The Girl of the Period is a creature who dyes her hair and paints her face as the first articles of her personal religion.

Remembered, if at all, as the novelist who sold Dickens his beloved house, Gad's Hill in Rochester, Linton was, in her time, a powerful – if reactionary – force in Victorian fiction. She was born in the Lake District, the twelfth child of a clergyman of hidebound Conservative views, yet a manifestly philoprogenitive disposition. Her mother died five months after Eliza Lynn's birth and her father was thereafter generally indifferent to his many offspring, leaving his youngest child with a residual guilt at being the indirect cause of her mother's death. She was, however, surrounded by books and taught herself comprehensively.

In her early girlhood, Eliza underwent what was evidently a severe religious crisis, from which she emerged largely unreligious. In 1845 she enterprisingly took her future into her own hands and went off to London to live by her pen. There she worked on the *Morning Chronicle* for three years, as the first salaried journalist in England. She also wrote three unsuccessful novels. *Azeth, the Egyptian*, the best of them, was accepted by Emily Brontë's notorious publisher, Thomas Newby, for a fee of £50 – payable by the author. The experience rankled all her life.

In 1851, after quarrelling with her editor, Eliza left the *Morning Chronicle* to work as a freelance foreign correspondent in Paris. By this period she knew and – more importantly – was known by many of the most influential literary figures in London, notably Walter Savage Landor, whom she liked to call her 'beloved father'. Her less beloved biological father died, leaving her £1,500 and the property at Gad's Hill, which she sold on to Charles Dickens in 1856. Two years later she married the artist, William James Linton. The couple shared a love of the Lake District, reflected in their work. That love was not, alas, enough to keep them together. William was ten years her senior, politically radical, and a widower with seven children. He quickly ran through her little fortune. The marriage failed and the couple separated – although they never divorced and Eliza kept on good terms with her husband, who drifted to America, and continued to support her stepchildren.

In the 1860s, Linton started a new career in which fiction was to play a major part. From 1866 she worked on the *Saturday Review* and wrote an extraordinarily powerful sequence of anti-feminist articles, collected as *The Girl of the Period* (1869). Hitherto she had been somewhat in favour of women's rights. However, she made herself a novelist of the first rank with *The True History of Joshua Davidson* (1872), a work which sardonically recasts the gospel in a modern setting. The free-thinker Charles Bradlaugh bought 1,000 copies to distribute for his cause. Her other major achievement, *The Autobiography of Christopher Kirkland* (1885), remains one of the best depictions of a writer's spiritual growth (and the woes of authorship) to be found in Victorian fiction: she called it 'the book of my whole career'. It deserves to be read more than it is.

Linton went on to write a string of powerful novels – many with melodramatic plots and usually focused on some problem of the day. Most interesting, if provocative, are those directed against the loathed 'girl of the period' and the 'shrieking sisterhood' (i.e. feminists). Typical is *The One Too Many* (1894), which excoriates the 'Girton girl' as a smoking, drinking, morally depraved harlot. The novel is dedicated to 'the sweet girls still left among us'.

In later life, Linton is reported to have declared, 'All the reforms we have striven for have been granted. Nothing further is now required.' She died of pneumonia, leaving a lively memoir, published posthumously as *My Literary Life* (1899). It was, particularly for a woman of the period, a rather well-remunerated life: she left £16,000 on her death.

FN   Elizabeth Linton ('Eliza', née Lynn)
MRT *The Autobiography of Christopher Kirkland*
Biog N. F. Anderson, *Woman Against Women in Victorian England: A Life of Eliza Lynn Linton* (1987)

49. Beatrice Harraden 1864–1936

My Little BA. Eliza Lynn Linton's nickname for Harraden

Beatrice Harraden was born in South Hampstead, the daughter of a musical instrument importer. She finished her education in Dresden and at Bedford College, London, where she studied classics and mathematics, graduating with a first-class degree. An early aspiration to be a cellist was given up and she went on to devote her subsequent life to travel, writing and, when the movement was at its height, to activity on behalf of women's suffrage. Personally unassuming, physically small and prettier than she modestly gave herself credit for (she thought she had a 'thin, eager, face') and in later life bespectacled, she was, on her entry into London society, a protégé of Eliza Lynn Linton, who affectionately called her 'my little BA'.

Harraden's first novel, *Ships That Pass in the Night* (1893) was a bestseller. The hero and heroine are invalids who fall in love at an Alpine *Kurhaus* for consumptives. According to gossip of the time, this novel – and others she wrote that were centred on similar doomed brief encounters – 'arose from the tragic experience of her life; she fell deeply in love with a man who falsified his clients' accounts and whose body was found not long after in a crevasse on a Swiss glacier'. The narrative of *Ships That Pass in the Night* is veined with bitter and self-wounding remarks about life, such as that by the heroine, Bernardine: 'I am tired of reading ... I seem to have been reading all my life. My uncle, with whom I live [in London], keeps a second-hand book-shop, and ever since I can remember, I have been surrounded by books. They have not done me much good, nor any one else either.' Read on.

Harraden was afflicted with TB herself, and travelled as far afield as southern California for the sake of her lungs. She evidently inherited money from her family, and in her mid-career was not impoverished. The settings of her fiction are correspondingly far-flung. Her later novels are more pugnaciously feminist (she may have been disinhibited by the death of Linton): *The Fowler* (1899), for example, is so titled after a vicious predator who violates women's minds and bodies. Harraden herself never married.

In the early years of the twentieth century, she worked for the Oxford University Press in their dictionary department. She also became increasingly involved with suffragism, direct action and the Tax Resistance League, formed in 1910 (the novelist Flora Annie Steel was a fellow member of the League). In 1913, Harraden allowed her property to be distrained rather than pay the income tax she owed a government which would not grant women the vote. At the auction where her goods were being sold, she and other protesters were assaulted by anti-suffrage 'roughs' and she later brought a charge against the London police for taking no action to protect her. The magistrates were unsympathetic. Though she and her fellow activists got the vote, her last years were penurious, made a little easier by a Civil List pension in 1930. The *ODNB* records bleakly that she died of delirium tremens.

FN   Beatrice Harraden
MRT   *Ships That Pass in the Night*
Biog *ODNB* (Fred Hunter)

50. Sylvanus Cobb Jr 1823–1887

'Meddling monk,' he cried, 'how dare you drag your detestable form hither! Out, reptile, out!' Ejaculation from *The Gunmaker of Moscow*

What, it will be asked, is Sylvanus Cobb Jr – largely unknown, wholly unregarded by literary history – doing in the company of Virginia Woolf and James Joyce? Cobb is a writer of interest for the worthy reason that he helped lay the foundations of mass readership for American fiction. Millions of readers, particularly young readers, passed through his mass-produced stories to higher things. Or, if they did not, they supplied the financial turnover with which publishers could chance their arm with higher things. Fiction, like armies, marches on its belly. Cobb filled it and more.

He was born in Waterville, Maine, the eldest of nine children of a Universalist minister who believed in spreading his word by the printing press as much as by the pulpit. Among the anecdotes which make up all that posterity will ever know about Sylvanus Cobb, he is said to have been expelled from school for arguing with a teacher over a fine point of grammar – which of them was in the right is not recorded. He was subsequently apprenticed as a printer and worked on his father's newspaper, *The Christian Freeman*. Hungry for unChristian freedoms, in 1841 he enlisted in the US Navy. Over the next four years, voyaging to the four corners of the world, he gathered the raw material and colour that ornaments his later romances.

Cobb returned to the US to take up work again with his father. He married his school sweetheart in 1845 and the following year founded a weekly temperance magazine, the *Rechabite*, with his brother Samuel. In its virtuously dry pages appeared his first published story, 'The Deserter'. At this point Cobb was living in Boston. Much jobbing magazine work followed until, in 1856 – now a well-known tale-spinner – Cobb formed an exclusive arrangement to write fiction for Robert

Bonner's phenomenally successful *New York Ledger*. His first serial for Bonner was *The Gunmaker of Moscow; or, Vladimir the Monk*. The work was typical of what followed and, thanks to multiple reprintings, the best known of Cobb's stories. Set in Russia in the sixteenth century, it features a heroic gunmaker, Ruric Nevel, who loves Rosalind Valdai, a ward of the Duke of Tula. The path to happiness is mysteriously helped by a well-disposed black monk of St Michael. The plot is nonsense, but rattles through its ten instalments in the required way, ending with young Ruric winning Rosalind's hand and a knighthood from a grateful Tsar, whom he has saved.

Over the remaining thirty-one years of his life, Cobb wrote an estimated 130 novels, 834 short stories and 2,304 sketches for Bonner's paper. His stories were overwhelmingly romances. Ruric is the first of hosts of innumerable buccaneers, swashbucklers, Gothic villains, all doing their best and worst against exotic settings where, typically, wild things lurk. On the strength of his connection with Bonner, and his indefatigable pen, Cobb could move up in the world and was able to indulge his love of tourism. In 1857 he moved to a luxurious house in Norway, Maine, where he was a prominent local citizen, an active freemason – his 'religion' in later life – and, as war loomed, a captain in Maine's volunteer militia. He did not, however, serve in the Civil War – other than as an encourager of others to fight. He continued to write furiously, and doubtless many soldiers on both sides went to their death with a 'Cobb' in their knapsack (although, one is told, Victor Hugo's *Les Misérables* was the most popular novel in both sides' armies).

At the end of the 1860s, now seriously wealthy, Cobb and his family (how many children he had is unrecorded) moved to a mansion he had built for himself at Hyde Park, Massachusetts. Here it was he died, enriched and beloved by generations of his country's juvenile readers.

FN   Sylvanus Cobb 'Jr'
MRT *The Gunmaker of Moscow; or, Vladimir the Monk*
Biog *ANB* (Charles Zarobila)

51. Charlotte Yonge 1823–1901

She made goodness attractive.

The Victorians had less leisure time than we do, and the day of rest they did have – the Sabbath – was no friend to popular fiction, hence the dominance of the evangelical novel. Yonge, a Tractarian by doctrine, (i.e. halfway to Rome, but with both feet planted firmly in Oxford), is by far the best of the genre and a formidable woman of letters in her own right, with over 150 titles to her lifetime credit. She was born, and died, in Otterbourne, near Winchester, a few miles, it is pleasant to recall, from Jane Austen's grave. Her family were old Devon gentry; her father was a firm-minded churchman and a local magistrate. There were two children, the other being a brother seven years younger than Charlotte. Precocious and virtuous, she became a Sunday school teacher at the age of seven and stuck to the task until she was seventy-eight. She was largely educated by her father 'who believed in higher education for women but deprecated any liberty for them'.

The formative event in Yonge's girlhood was the arrival of John Keble, thirty years her senior, as vicar of the neighbouring parish. Keble, a disciple of Newman's, had left Oriel College (the burning bush of Tractarianism) to make himself practically useful, and help regenerate, England's Christian ministry. Charlotte was confirmed in 1838 and it seems that receiving the sacrament was one of the momentous experiences of her life – she commemorates it in *The Castle Builders; or, The Deferred Communion* (1854). Keble urged Charlotte to use her literary talent for the propagation of Christian – more specifically Tractarian – instruction. But he warned her against the overt preaching which marred the efforts of other religious novelists. He edited her early work himself, rigorously. Before she committed to print, a conclave of the Yonge family resolved it would be wrong for her to make any profit from fiction, unless that money were turned over to some good cause.

Yonge's first great success came with *The Heir of Redclyffe*, in 1853. It tells the story of Sir Guy Morville. Byronic and an orphan, he is distracted by wild passions which he gradually learns to subdue to Christian duty. After daring acts of heroism at sea (such scenes are not, it must be said, Yonge's forte as a narrator), he marries Amy, the woman who has purified him. The novel does not, however, end there. On honeymoon, Guy catches fever and, in a deathbed chapter which became famous in the annals of Victorian fiction, is comforted in his last moments by an Anglican priest, who hears his confession in appropriately High Church style. The story was found universally moving, even by the intelligentsia. William Morris was impressed by it; Rossetti admired it; thousands of soldiers in the Crimea were consoled by it. True to her family decision, Yonge donated the profits to Bishop George Selwyn to buy a schooner for the Melanesian mission to take the Word to the Pacific savage.

Now 'the Author of *The Heir of Redclyffe*', Yonge went on to produce a constant stream of novels for adults and juveniles. The best regarded were the multi-volume saga of the May family, beginning with *The Daisy Chain, or, Aspirations* (1856). In 1851 Yonge had become editor of the magazine, the *Monthly Packet*, a post she was to hold for thirty-nine years. As her Preface puts it: 'it has been said that everyone forms their own character between the ages of fifteen and five-and-twenty, and this Magazine is meant to be in some degree a help to those who are thus forming it'.

Yonge's life was passed within strictly parochial boundaries and she never married. But her strong maternal instincts found an outlet in the series of stories she wrote for young children in her 'Aunt Charlotte' persona. At the same time she wrote one of the more intelligent novels about the problems of Victorian female adolescence, *The Clever Woman of the Family* (1865). Nor did she shrink from the horrors of old-maidhood in such works as *Hopes and Fears; or, Scenes from the Life of a Spinster* (1860). 'She made goodness attractive,' one critic observed. Yonge herself was in no doubt about the use she made of her talent: 'I have always viewed myself as a sort of instrument for popularising Church views.' She never made the mistake of ruining that popularity by churchiness, although the Anglican Church was the most important thing in her life.

Her father died in 1854 and she lived with her mother until she died in 1868. Her only brother died in 1892, and her last years were somewhat lonely – although she kept up a lively correspondence with literary acquaintances. She only twice in her life left England: for a short trip to Normandy in 1869 and another to Ireland. She left almost £13,000 on her death – to Christian charities, needless to say.

FN   Charlotte Mary Yonge
MRT *The Heir of Redclyffe*
Biog *ODNB* (Elisabeth Jay)

52. Wilkie Collins 1824–1889

Make 'em laugh, make 'em cry, make 'em wait. The serialist's motto, traditionally attributed to Collins

Born in London, he was the eldest son of William Collins, the landscape painter and Royal Academician, and named after his father's friend and fellow artist, Sir David Wilkie. The Collins household was bohemian and as a boy Wilkie spent some years with his father in Italy (where he claimed to have lost his virginity at an alarmingly young age) and was educated privately. In 1841, he was articled to work in the establishment of a London tea merchant. The law, it was felt, offered a profession in which a man could write on the side, and in 1846 he entered Lincoln's Inn, and was called to the Bar in 1851, but never practised. His handwriting, however, benefited from his pupillage – Collins's manuscripts, most of which have survived, are among the most legible of the period; and stylistically the most carefully corrected. He had, in intervals from his scrivening, been writing a romance of ancient Rome, *Antonina: or, The fall of Rome*, which was published in 1850. Although it was successful, not least for its gothic descriptions of torture, Collins never wrote another historical novel. His fiction would be as up-to-the-minute as that week's issue of the *Police Gazette* – which, indeed, supplied some of the details and plot matter of his later 'sensation' stories.

Collins's career took off with 'A Story of Modern Life', the sexually superheated melodrama *Basil* (1852). In the Preface, Collins enunciated his doctrine that 'the Novel and the Play are twin-sisters in the family of Fiction'. This was the essence of his high-impact style – drawn, it is plausibly assumed, from the popular newspapers of the day. To paraphrase Henry James, the imperative guiding his fiction was 'melodramatise it! melodramatise it!' In 1851, Collins became acquainted with Dickens. Both men had a passion for drama and for discreet adventuring in Paris. Their minds ran together happily and they collaborated on amateur theatricals. Among higher things, such as generating proceeds for good causes, the activity sanctioned unchaperoned access to young ladies and 'dressing rooms'. One of the young ladies, Ellen Ternan, would become Dickens's 'invisible' mistress. There may well have been some invisible skeletons of the same kind in Wilkie's closet.

Collins soon began contributing short stories and non-fiction to Dickens's weekly magazine, *Household Words*. His first contribution, the horror story, 'A Terribly Strange Bed' (1852) – the canopy of the strange bed descends, by silent screw mechanism, to smother the sleeper – is widely anthologised, even more widely imitated, and shows the clear influence of Poe. Collins went on to publish the full-length mystery novels *Hide and Seek* (1854) and *The Dead Secret* (1857). Both used physical handicap in their plots (deaf-and-dumbness in the first; blindness in the second).

In 1856, Collins had been struck at a court hearing, dealing with the Rugeley poisoner, William Palmer, by the narrative possibilities of witnesses' testimony in the box. The *reportage* technique was brilliantly employed in the narrative of *The Woman in White* (1860). This novel made Collins's name and largely inspired the 1860s vogue for so-called 'sensation' fiction. He followed up with *No Name* (1862), a work which attacked the British laws of inheritance. The *Cornhill Magazine* paid a whopping £5,000 for Collins's next work, *Armadale* (1866). Only Dickens, he exulted to his mother, had been paid so much.

In 1868, he published *The Moonstone*, which is plausibly regarded as the first detective story proper in English. By this period, Collins's health was poor and he was chronically self-overdosed with laudanum to relieve the pain of his rheumatic gout. His eyes, one acquaintance reported, were like 'bags of blood'. He claimed to have written portions of *The Moonstone* in a condition of authorial somnambulism. Fame brought with it a new sense of public responsibility. *Man and Wife* (1870) heralds an overtly propagandistic phase of Collins's career. Not all his readers welcomed it. 'What brought Wilkie's genius nigh perdition?' asked the poet Swinburne, answering, rhymingly, 'some demon whispered "Wilkie, have a mission".' A 'fiction founded on facts', *Man and Wife* protests against the British marriage laws. *Poor Miss Finch* (1872) has another plot drawing on the author's obsessive interest in blindness. The heroine has her sight restored, but actually desires the loss of it again. An improbable sub-plot, involving her future husband's turning blue, is latched onto this paradox.

Collins continued to propagandise in *The New Magdalen* (1873), whose heroine, Mercy Merrick, is a fallen woman who goes as a nurse to the Franco-Prussian War, where she is shot and left for dead. Mercy recovers and changes identities with another, supposedly dead woman, Grace Roseberry, leading to inevitable complications and final redemption at the hands of an idealistic clergyman. The novel was successfully dramatised, as were many of Collins's later works. His reputation rose extraordinarily high in the 1870s, although the writing showed clear signs of fraying. One looks in vain for anything quite as thrilling as the opening scene of *The Woman in White* in which the woman herself (spectral or actual?) appears to an electrified Walter Hartright:

> I had now arrived at that particular point of my walk where four roads met – the road to Hampstead, along which I had returned, the road to Finchley, the road to West End, and the road back to London. I had mechanically turned in this latter direction, and was strolling along the lonely high-road – idly wondering, I remember, what the Cumberland young ladies would look like – when, in one moment, every drop of blood in my body was brought to a stop by the touch of a hand laid lightly and suddenly on my shoulder from behind me.
>
> I turned on the instant, with my fingers tightening round the handle of my stick.
>
> There, in the middle of the broad bright high-road – there, as if it had that moment sprung out of the earth or dropped from the heaven – stood the figure of a solitary Woman, dressed from head to foot in white garments, her face bent in grave inquiry on mine, her hand pointing to the dark cloud over London, as I faced her.

Dickens, who serialised the story in his magazine, thought this one of the two best scenes in English fiction. He did not specify what the other was. In 1871 Collins's appeal widened with a very successful stage version of *The Woman in White*, and in 1873, he made an applauded reading tour of America. In 1875, Chatto reissued his fiction in cheap half-crown form with great sales success.

Occultism fascinated Collins towards the end of his life and *The Two Destinies* (1876) deals with telepathy between childhood friends. *The Fallen Leaves* (1879), is the story of a reformed prostitute (an heiress, as it emerges) and a socialist, Amelius, who courageously marries her. It is generally regarded as Collins's worst novel – although, like other of his 'failures', it demonstrates the remarkable restlessness of his genius. Among his later fiction, *Heart and Science* (1883) caused some stir with its full-blooded propaganda against vivisection, aided by some powerful descriptions of animal surgery.

Despite appalling health, Collins's writing career of forty years is one of the longest and most productive in Victorian popular fiction. His sexual life was, by Victorian standards, irregular, verging on criminal. In the mid-1850s he took up with Caroline Graves (an original for Anne Catherick in *The Woman in White*). From 1868, he also lived with the lower born Martha Rudd, who bore him three children. His estate was divided between the two women. He decreed, however, that his corpse should lie alongside Caroline.

FN   William Wilkie Collins
MRT   *The Woman in White*
Biog C. Peters, *The King of Inventors: A Life of Wilkie Collins* (1991)

53. R. M. Ballantyne 1825–1894

If there is any boy or man who loves to be melancholy and morose, and who cannot enter with kindly sympathy into the regions of fun, let me seriously advise him to shut my book and put it away. It is not meant for him. Preface to *The Coral Island*

The eighth of nine children, Ballantyne was born in Kelso, near Edinburgh, where his family's fortunes were in the process of being ruined in the fallout of Sir Walter Scott's bankruptcy. His uncle, James, had been the great novelist's printer and his father a lifelong comrade of the 'Great Unknown'. Ballantyne had little education – but, since it was Edinburgh, and he came from a bookish family, that little rendered him as literate, probably, as a modern Ph.D. graduate. Importantly, he could write legibly and figure accurately and thereby earn a living. Aged sixteen, he shipped out as an apprentice clerk in the Hudson's Bay Company, at £20 annual salary. The prospect, if not the salary, filled him with 'ecstatic joy'. Letters home to his mother, printed in the papers as 'Everyday Life in the Wilds of North America', caught the attention of the senior Scottish publisher, William Nelson.

It would, however, be some time before young 'Bob' could devote himself to literature. His father died in 1847 and he returned to Scotland to support the teeming family – including that heaviest of Victorian burdens, five unmarried sisters, and he the only breadwinner. He clerked resourcefully in the newly founded railway companies and – a sharp young man – went on to a senior position in a paper factory. He could have been a captain of industry, but in 1856 Nelson invited him to write a boys' book, based on his experiences in the frozen north. Before doing so, Ballantyne 'asked guidance from God'. The Almighty gave him the go-ahead (his family were not at all keen) and there duly appeared *The Young Fur-Traders*. It was a hit. In 1858, still only thirty-two, he produced three of his finest works, *Ungava, A Tale of Esquimeaux Land; The Coral Island;* and *Martin Rattler, or a Boy's Adventures in the Forests of Brazil*. Some sixty books streamed from his inexhaustible pen over the next decades. One reason for the quantity was that his publisher, the canny Nelson, paid a measly £60 for the entire copyright of each of Ballantyne's novels – even the most popular. And the most popular of all was the adventures of Jack Martin, Ralph Rover and Peterkin Gay, the comic runt of the trio, on their coral island where they discover coconut lemonade (a geographical solecism), fish, make fire by rubbing sticks together, narrowly escape being eaten by sharks and cannibals, and have some close shaves with pirates whom, with the aid of the Royal Navy, they slaughter en masse. All very jolly.

Ballantyne had more creative ability than the formulaic nature of his narratives suggests. He could, for example, illustrate his boys' books to professional standards. But why only boys' books? His biographer discerns hypertrophy of the Presbyterian sensibility. Ballantyne 'was acutely embarrassed by having to mention sex in any form.' His heroes could, as in *The Gorilla Hunters* (1861), blast forty luckless beasts for the sheer fun of blasting – but were jelly in the face of a petticoat.

Ballantyne was a self-publiciser of genius. He specialised in lectures which he would open by stalking on stage in buckskin and shooting a stuffed eagle to get his audience warmed up. Or, if the subject were shipwreck, a rescue rocket would be fired to get things going. He particularly prided himself on his Esquimeaux 'canoe songs', which he would introduce, warblingly, as a musical interlude. 'Research' led him to disguise himself as an Arab in the native quarter of Algiers in order to write *The Pirate City* (1874). He submersed himself with nearly fatal results in a diving suit, *Under the Waves* (1876); and marooned himself in a lighthouse in preparation for other tales. He had as much fun, one suspects, writing his stories as generations of (mainly) schoolboys had reading the things.

He married in 1866. His wife Jane ('Jeanie') Dickson Grant was chosen carefully, with his mother's help, from the respectable class of Edinburgh womanhood. Twenty years his junior, she bore her husband four children. Increasingly religious in later life, Ballantyne allied himself with the period's good causes, notably the Royal National Lifeboat Institution, and laboured tirelessly to foster the cult of Victorian manliness in young men. He despised 'muffs' – the class, alas, from which most novelists are drawn. Like Gladstone, he was prone to cruise the midnight streets, with the pious aim of saving young ladies from sin. He had more success with lifeboats.

His last novel was *The Walrus Hunters* (1893) – one of the few species his fiction had hitherto spared. Kurtz's 'exterminate the brutes' could have been taken as Ballantyne's motto. Indirectly, he was responsible for William Golding's *Lord of the Flies*, an inversion of *The Coral Island* for a later, less optimistic era, with a less hopeful view of children's nature and a more reverent attitude to the animal kingdom. He died in Rome, where he had gone to mend his failing health, having suffered from Menière's disease for some years (his biographer hints that syphilis may have been a contributory factor). Harrow School for boys, in whose vicinity he had lived, raised £600 from their pocket money for a monument to his memory.

FN   Robert Michael Ballantyne
MRT   *The Coral Island*
Biog E. Quayle, *Ballantyne the Brave: A Victorian writer and his family* (1967)

54. Mary J. Holmes 1825–1907

Tempest, sunshine and bestsellers.

Mary Hawes was born in Brookfield, Massachusetts, and brought up in New England, but otherwise little is known of her early life. Under the tutelage of her mother, Fanny Hawes, Mary is recorded as intellectually precocious and was teaching at school at thirteen (the death of her father may have forced this child labour). Her first published short story followed two years later.

In 1844 she married Daniel Holmes, just out of Yale. The couple settled in Brockport, New York. They both taught for a while before he found work as a lawyer. There were no children to the marriage but, over the coming years, considerable wealth. Holmes received up to $6,000 for the serial rights of her stories, allowing her ample time to write and travel extensively. It is estimated that some two million copies of her fiction were sold during her lifetime. Her publisher, the Boston house of Appleton, treated her well, in the manner of employers in the so-called 'gilded age' of the American book trade.

Holmes's career was launched spectacularly on the wave of the so-called 'feminised fifties', a decade in which women writers came into their own and dominated American fiction. Her first novel, *Tempest and Sunshine* (1854), is also her best known. It was never out of print during her lifetime, and for decades after. Subtitled a 'Life in Kentucky', the story opens with a young abolitionist New Yorker, Richard Wilmot, arriving in the South to take up work in a local school. He makes the acquaintance of a rich, good-hearted but rough-mannered plantation owner, Mr John Middleton, who has two daughters, both of whom are possessed of huge dowries ($100,000 apiece) to lure prospective fortune-hunting husbands. The older (seventeen), Julia, is dark and passionate; her nickname is 'Tempest'. The younger (fifteen), Fanny, is golden-haired and sweet-natured; her nickname is 'Sunshine'. Morally the sisters are opposites: 'the angel of innocence spread his wing over the yellow locks of the one, while a serpent lay coiled in the dark tresses of the other.'

Unusually for a writer with a New England (home of abolition) background, Holmes offers an idyllic view of the South and a tolerant, anti-Harriet Beecher Stowe view of slavery. Most of the 'Africans' who appear in the narrative are comic buffoons – wholly happy with their lot. Wilmot proposes to the beautiful Julia, and is accepted. But later, after she has encountered a more dashing Yale-educated doctor, Lacey, she cruelly jilts Wilmot. As he lies dying, she refuses to visit his deathbed with the cruel remark: 'Mr Wilmot is nothing to me.' The plot becomes, if possible, even more melodramatic. Fanny, who secretly loved Wilmot, is virtuously appalled. Dr Lacey falls in love with the less dashing Fanny, who has turned down a millionaire, Frank Cameron, and proposes to her. Julia is furious and forges letters to break the engagement. Julia then entraps Lacey into marriage, but the ceremony is interrupted with evidence of her misdoings (echoes of *Jane Eyre*). 'I am guilty,' she publicly confesses and then disappears; her clothes are discovered by the river and she is presumed drowned. Lacey returns to his faithful 'Sunshine'. In a sensational climax (which Wilkie Collins evidently adapted for *The Woman in White*, five years later), Fanny meets a gaunt veiled woman at the grave of her sister Julia. It is Julia herself, 'a living repentant woman'. The sisters are reconciled.

Tempest and Sunshine was followed by another bestseller with a racial theme, again set on a southern plantation, *Lena Rivers* (1856). A string of other novels followed, all popular, though none as popular as her first hit. The Civil War shrank the large constituency of women readers which she had established early in her career in the South. One can, incidentally, detect clear lines of influence in Mitchell's *Gone with the Wind*. Holmes is recorded as having no hobbies – other than foreign travel (reflected in her later fiction). She was, through life, a devoted Sunday school teacher. She died at the age of eighty-two in Brockport.

FN   Mary Jane Holmes (née Hawes)
MRT *Tempest and Sunshine; or, Life in Kentucky*
Biog *ANB* (JoAnn E. Castagna)

55. Dinah Craik 1826–1887

Oftentimes, living is harder than dying. From *The Ogilvies*

Dinah Mulock was born at Stoke-on-Trent, the eldest child of a nonconformist Irish clergyman father. Precociously clever and literary, she was able to help her mother teach at school at the age of thirteen. An inheritance enabled the Mulocks to move to London in 1839. In 1844, she and her mother separated from Thomas Mulock, but a year later Mrs Mulock died. Thereafter, Dinah took on responsibility for the financial support of her family. This situation is projected on to the early career of her most famous character, John Halifax. She began her authorial career writing stories for children and contrived to scrape a genteel living for herself and her dependants, aided with another small inheritance from her mother's family.

Mulock's fortunes improved with the success of her first novel, *The Ogilvies*, which came out in 1849. The narrative follows the route to marriage and eventual happiness of three girl cousins. It was much to the taste of library readers – a constituency which Mulock identified as hers and which she assiduously cultivated over the years. *Olive* (1850) treads more interesting ground with a physically deformed, less than beautiful heroine who contrives, by sheer goodness, to convert an agnostic lover to Christianity. *The Head of the Family* (1852) is a family chronicle, in the currently fashionable 'domestic' style of Bulwer-Lytton's *The Caxtons*. No novelist was more domestic than Miss Mulock.

Her reputation was enormously boosted by her bestseller, *John Halifax, Gentleman* (1856). A story of exemplary capitalist morality, it chronicles a hero who rises by his own virtuous efforts from poverty to business prosperity. It would become one of the great 'gifts' (improving books, given by well-meaning parents to children) of its era. Now wealthy herself and commanding up to £2,000 a novel, Mulock moved in 1859 to Hampstead, where she entertained on a modest scale, and expanded her range. *A Life for a Life* (1859), her most interesting novel, is written in the form of the intertwining diaries ('His Story', 'Her Story') of two sympathetically regarded 'criminals' who contrive to atone for their crimes and eventually marry.

In 1863, Mulock's brother Ben died wretchedly, trying to escape from a lunatic asylum. Dinah subsequently moved to Glasgow to recuperate from the shock. In 1865, now forty, Mulock married George Lillie Craik, eleven years her junior. The couple initially intended to live in Glasgow, but an offer to George Craik from Alexander Macmillan to become a partner in his publishing house brought the newly-weds in London. Dinah was past childbearing age, and the couple adopted an abandoned baby, Dorothy, in 1869. She proved, unsurprisingly, an exemplary mother. After marriage, Craik continued writing popular novels at a rapid rate. An overwhelmingly philanthropic woman, Mrs Craik seems to have lived by the virtues which her novels advocate. She died of heart failure during preparations for her daughter Dorothy's wedding.

FN   Dinah Maria Craik (née Mulock)
MRT   *A Life for a Life*
Biog S. Mitchell, *Dinah Mulock Craik* (1983)

56. George Meredith 1828–1909

The Sage of Box Hill.

The Victorians took very little pleasure in difficult novels. 'There ought to be no need of sitting down before the thing with tools and dynamite like burglars at a safe,' wrote George Saintsbury: 'It is the first duty of the novelist to let himself be read.' He was clearly thinking of George Meredith. None the less Meredith was the writer who, as the era drew to an end, was the most honoured by discriminating Victorians. There was, they felt, something important inside that safe – if only they could crack the damn thing open.

Meredith was born in Portsmouth where his grandfather, Melchizedek, ran the town's principal tailor and naval outfitters. The business was taken over by George's less enterprising father, Augustus Armstrong Meredith (1797–1876). The Merediths' background ('trade'!) was later to figure centrally in the novelist's most accessible (that is to say, least inaccessible) work, *Evan Harrington* (1861). The hero is the son of a preposterously aspirant provincial tailor, Melchisedec Harrington. Can Evan become a 'gentleman'? Meredith's background led to recurrent jibes against him. His style might be high, but his preoccupations were low – as was his subject matter. The scorn was not entirely unfair. There is, particularly in Meredith's early fiction, an extraordinary interest in the degrading services which the petty bourgeoisie offer the upper classes in the form of barbering and tailoring.

Meredith's first published work of fiction, *The Shaving of Shagpat* (1856), is a pastiche 'Arabian Entertainment', which combined both these obsessions. The hero, Shibli Bagarag, must affront oriental custom by shaving the shaggy-pated tailor-monarch Shagpat ('shaggy pate' – not a very brilliant pun). Thus will Shibli become 'Master of the Event'. It is an indication of the gulf between Victorian and twenty-first-century sensibility that Mary Anne Evans, in a review written in 1856 before she was George Eliot the novelist, declared this dire effusion a 'work of genius, and of a poetical genius'.

Meredith was an only child and his mother died when he was five years old. The family tailoring business had declined with peace, after Waterloo. Augustus was, in later life, to be a constant drain on his son's finances. George left school at four-teen, then spent two formative years in Germany. In 1844 he returned to be articled as a solicitor. A year later, and very hard up, he began to write – initially poetry and higher journalism. In 1849 he married Thomas Peacock's widowed daugh-ter, Mary. The couple lived a semi-bohemian life at Weybridge and Meredith clearly came under the stylistic influence of his novel-writing, and eccentric, father-in-law. The marriage broke up painfully; the pains are recorded in Meredith's fine sonnet sequence, *Modern Love* (1862) – a novel in verse. Having borne a son, Meredith's wife ran off in 1858 and died, deserted by her lover, three years later. It was pure *East Lynne*.

Meredith's first full-length novel, *The Ordeal of Richard Feverel* (1859) was banned by the circulating library 'leviathan', Charles Mudie. The great librarian's Calvinist susceptibilities were affronted by the seduction scene in Chapter 38, in which the married hero succumbs to the wiles of the seductive Bella Mount:

> as he looked down on her haggard loveliness, not divine sorrow but a devouring jealousy sprang like fire in his breast, and set him rocking with horrid pain. He bent closer to her pale beseeching face. Her eyes still drew him down.
>
> 'Bella! No! no! promise me! swear it!'
>
> 'Lost, Richard! lost for ever! give me up!'
>
> He cried: 'I never will!' and strained her in his arms, and kissed her passion-ately on the lips.

Mudie helped kill this novel at whose heart is a still-relevant debate over the education of the young child. Should it be based on 'system' or should the child be left to range freely?

In 1862, Meredith took on the position of literary adviser to Chapman and Hall, a culturally dictatorial post he was to hold for the rest of his life. In his role as 'reader', he was to assist the early careers of, among others, George Gissing, Olive

Schreiner, Ouida and Thomas Hardy. Doubtless there were hopeful talents one has never heard of whose careers were killed in the womb by him. In 1864 his life took a distinct turn for the better. He produced a florid romance, *Sandra Belloni* which hit the public taste; he was elected to the Garrick Club, and he remarried. His wife was Marie Vulliamy, whose family was of Swiss Huguenot extraction. She, unlike her predecessor, did not run away. A son, William Maxse, was born in 1865, named after Meredith's close friend (and original of Beauchamp, in *Beauchamp's Career*), the man of action, Frederick Augustus Maxse.

Meredith's reputation grew as his fiction became more and more idiosyncratic. His *Bildungsroman The Adventures of Harry Richmond* (1871), which centres on a boy's longing for his father's admiration, and *The Egoist* (1879), which embodies the author's theory of comedy, have their modern admirers. But, as with all his fiction, there have been insufficient readers to keep the novels consistently in print. It was an early reading of *Evan Harrington* which inspired Henry James to become a novelist. Thirty-four years later, James slammed shut 'with a final furious bang', *Lord Ormont and His Aminta* (1894) – one of Meredith's many 'eloping wives' novels – which he had been grinding through at the rate of 'ten insufferable and unprofitable' pages a day. 'I doubt', James confided to Edmund Gosse, 'if any quantity of extravagant verbiage, of airs, and graces, of phrases and attitudes, of obscurities and alembications, ever started less their subject, ever contributed less of a statement – told the reader less of what the reader needs to know.' A snippet, describing the exodus of the high-born from the capital (including the hero, Lord Ormont, in search of a wife) after the 'season' will give some idea of what infuriated James:

> There was no counting now on Lord Ormont's presence in the British gathering seasons, when wheatears wing across our fields or swallows return to their eaves. He forsook the hunt to roam the Continent, one of the vulgar band of tourists, honouring town only when Mayflies had flown, and London's indiscriminate people went about without their volatile heads.

In other, and fewer, words: 'It was summer and he left London.' What Meredith does with that narrative fact verges on cruelty to the English novel.

From 1885 he was increasingly disabled by a spinal complaint and was, for the last sixteen years of his life virtually paraplegic – although, to the end, it is recorded, 'conspicuously handsome'. On Tennyson's death he was elected President of the Society of Authors. In 1905 he received the Order of Merit and his last days were passed in the unchallenged glory of being the nation's Grandest Old Man of Letters. Largely unread letters today, alas.

FN George Meredith
MRT *The Ordeal of Richard Feverel*
Biog *ODNB* (Margaret Harris)

57. Mrs Oliphant 1828–1897

Rather a failure. Mrs Oliphant's verdict on herself

One of the most prolific Victorian novelists and, like Trollope (whom she in point of fact outwrote two-to-one), Margaret Wilson was an author who contrived to combine mass production with a commendable degree of artistry. She was born in Musselburgh, near Edinburgh, and, although she lived most of her adult life in London, always retained a pronounced Scottishness in her manner and personality.

Francis Wilson, Margaret's father, was an ineffectual figure employed in the excise service: his work necessitated several unsettling household moves. The domestic atmosphere in the Wilson home was strenuously moral and the dominant influence on the children was the resourceful mother of the family. Margaret, whose subsequent life was dogged by tragedy, was to need her mother's firmness of character in full measure herself. The Wilsons were Presbyterian and strongly affected by the 'Disruption' of 1843 which led to a schism and the subsequent formation of the independent Free Church of Scotland. But Margaret, when she had discretion in the matter, chose to be Anglican – she was her own woman.

Her career in writing began when her brother Willie filched the novel she had written, *Passages in the Life of Mrs. Margaret Maitland* (1849), and sent the manuscript off to the London publisher, Henry Colburn. The story, told by herself, of a God-fearing lowland Scottish spinster ('a quiet woman of discreet years and small riches') earned the author £150 – and the publisher much more when it went into three editions as a three-decker for the library market, propelled on its way by praise from Charlotte Brontë. Aged only twenty-one her career was launched and over 100 books were to follow. Wilson did a couple more novels for Colburn, but the critical professional relationship of her career was formed in 1853 when with *Katie Stewart* (a domestic-historical romance of the 1745 uprising) she became a 'Blackwood's author'.

In the early 1850s she moved to London, and in 1852 (against her mother's wish, evidently) she married her cousin, Francis Wilson Oliphant, and settled in Harrington Square. He was an artist specialising in stained glass who worked with Pugin on the remodelling of the Houses of Parliament. Meanwhile, in between child-bearing, Margaret continued writing a string of successful novels for the library market. 'Mrs Oliphant', as she renamed herself, professionally, was happier at this stage of her life than she would ever be again. There were children. She was earning around £400 for every novel she wrote, and she was a minor celebrity – and fondly regarded – in London literary life. She is one of that corps of Victorian novelists, who, to the despair of modern feminists, chose to be identified by the chattel prefix (Mrs Gore, Mrs Gaskell, Mrs Humphry Ward, Mrs Henry Wood). There were, however, already things to vex Mrs Oliphant. Her husband 'Frank' was talented but a poor provider. Margaret, additionally, was obliged to support her alcoholic brother William. But, as ever, she threw herself into the task.

In 1859 disasters struck which tested even her stoical ability to cope. Her husband contracted galloping consumption and died within a few months after a nightmarish journey to Italy. The young widow had two surviving children, was pregnant with a third, and running short of money. Her suffering at this period is recalled in two representatively lachrymose novels, written five years later. *Agnes* (1865) tells the story of the daughter of a blacksmith who marries the heir to a baronet but is left a penniless widow with three young children. *A Son of the Soil* (1865) tells the similarly gloomy tale of Colin Campbell, born to poor Scottish parents, who wins a scholarship to Balliol. He returns idealistically to take charge of his local kirk but discovers his flock is immune to his brilliance and Christian enthusiasm. And his childhood sweetheart, Alice, whom he nobly marries, is now beneath him in mind and spirit. He reconciles himself to a life of reduced fulfilments and hard unrewarding work. While not exact transcriptions of the author's tribulations, these works, and others like them, convey the bleak wretchedness of her early widowhood.

To make things worse for Oliphant, her fiction, of which she had produced an over-supply, no longer appealed as it once had to the library market. Resourcefully, having returned to England from Italy in 1860 to live with her brother Frank, she fought to win back her place at the top of the tree with the enduringly popular seven-volume 'Chronicles of Carlingford'. The series got off to a successful start with *Salem Chapel* (1863). Her payments from Blackwood, in this second phase of her career, soared to £1,000 a title. 'Carlingford' was clearly influenced by Trollope's 'Barsetshire' sequence, but Oliphant's narratives were less ambitious in their social scope and more theological in their content, with a nagging preoccupation with the problems of religious vocation in the modern world. Trollope's clergymen always tend to be civil servants in dog collars. The church is where they happen to work.

Yet financial crisis and personal tragedy continued to dog Oliphant. In 1864, her daughter died and at the same period she took charge of her widowed brother

Frank's four children. Her own two boys went to Eton: both would be a source of infinite vexation and both predeceased her with the same disease that killed their father. She continued to write – fiction, travel books and an excellent house history of her publishers and lifelong friends, the Blackwoods (1897). A Trollope-inspired 'Autobiography' was, unusually for her, left unfinished. A pioneer of the Scottish 'kailyard' ('cabbage patch') school, she was a major inspiration for J. M. Barrie, whose 'Thrums' tales of village life in Scotland draw on her work. She was, it is recorded, Queen Victoria's favourite novelist. Indomitably modest, she regarded herself as 'rather a failure'. She chose to be buried alongside her sons near Eton.

FN   Margaret Oliphant (née Wilson)
MRT *Salem Chapel*
Biog E. Jay, *Mrs Oliphant: 'A Fiction to Herself.' A Literary Life* (1995)

58. Horatio Alger Jr 1832–1899

Alger is to America what Homer was to the Greeks. Nathanael West, author of the savage satire on Algerism, *A Cool Million*

Horatio Alger was the author of a hundred or more 'rags to riches' tales for boys about boys, celebrating the 'American Dream' – the belief that any kid can 'make it' in God's Own Country with the right mix of virtue, 'spunk', hard work and providential 'lucky breaks'. Typically, the Alger stories are set in late nineteenth-century New York. Huge total circulation figures were claimed for them in their original dime (10c) form – as high as 200 million.

He was born in Massachusetts, the eldest son of a grandee, Horatio Alger Sr, in the Unitarian church. Horatio Jr, a precociously clever lad, was enrolled in Harvard's Divinity School at the age of sixteen. On graduation he toured Europe, broadening his mind, and on his return he was ordained. In 1864, he took up a ministry in the small town of Brewster, on Cape Cod. So far, so good. But hardly had he arrived in his new parish, the brilliant young minister resigned. The reason was pederastic buggery. As his church's confidential report described them, Alger's offences were 'heinous ... of no less magnitude than the abominable and revolting crime of unnatural familiarity with *boys*, which is too revolting to think of in the most brutal of our race'. Alger was, on the face of it, unrepentant. The report roundly recommended the death penalty, but the scandal was hushed up thanks to his father's influence, the Church's terror of bad publicity, and the hubbub over the breaking Civil War.

Alger escaped conscription on medical grounds, and his diminutive, 'boy-like', stature. His 'crimes' did not emerge into the public record until the 1970s.

Denied one pulpit, Alger chose another. His first improving tale, *Helen Ford* (1866), is unusual in having a girl heroine. Boys would thereafter be his sole interest. In the later 1860s, Alger became associated with the New York 'Newsboys' Lodging House', as chaplain, visitor, and benefactor. This institution for homeless boys furnished him with valuable raw material. Was he reformed, as his apologists claim, and embarked on a lifelong act of contrition? Or was he still practising his 'revolting crime' with rather more discretion than earlier?

Alger's most enduring contribution to American folklore are his 'Ragged Dick' and 'Tattered Tom' series. Despite his reputation as 'Holy Horatio', Alger avoids the deadly piety of the tracts purveyed in the UK by the SPCK (Society for Promoting Christian Knowledge) and RTS (Religious Tract Society). A selection of his most successful works, whose contents are summed up in their titles, would include: *Ragged Dick; or Street Life in New York with the Boot-blacks* (1867), *Mark the Match Boy* (1869), *Tattered Tom; or, the Story of a Street Arab* (1871), *Tony the Hero; or, a Brave Boy's Adventures with a Tramp* (1880).

Towards the end of his writing career, having glutted the market with improving tales, Alger turned out equally super-selling popular biographies such as *Abraham Lincoln, the Backwoods Boy; or, How a Young Rail-splitter became President* (1883). Alger spent his last years with his sister Augusta, who, on his instruction, destroyed all his personal papers.

FN   Horatio Alger Jr
MRT   *Ragged Dick; or Street Life in New York with the Boot-blacks*
Biog G. Scharnhorst and J. Bales, *The Lost Life of Horatio Alger, Jr.* (1985)

59. George du Maurier 1834–1896

My head's full of plots! I just wish I had your skill with words to tell 'em. George du Maurier to Henry James, in David Lodge's novel, *Author, Author*

The du Mauriers rank as Britain's most distinguished literary, theatre and artistic dynasty: familial proof that genius is hereditary, although they began somewhat less than grand. The patriarch, George du Maurier (1834–96), was the grandson of a French glass blower, called 'Busson'. He assumed the fine-sounding 'du Maurier' surname, propagating, at the same time, the Cartonesque fiction that the family were refugees from the revolutionary tumbrel. They weren't – although the fact was not known, even to Busson's direct descendants, until 1962. Two generations of du Mauriers lived and died, happily believing the family myth that if Madame Guillotine had had her way they wouldn't exist.

George went on to become the lead cartoonist on *Punch* in the mid-1860s and a distinguished illustrator of English fiction – notably Thackeray. The du Maurier pictorial style was detailed and theatrical in composition, and hit the high-Victorian taste. He had aimed even higher. While a twenty-three-year-old art student on the Continent, George had suddenly lost the sight of his left eye, a shocking experience he was later to use in his novel, *The Martian* (1897). It was this setback which turned him from painting to graphic work. In the early 1880s, du Maurier's remaining eyesight began to fail. He was friendly at this period with Henry James, whose *Washington Square* (1881) he had sumptuously illustrated. It was du Maurier who suggested to James (who turned the idea down, although his career was flagging) the melodramatic 'Svengali' scenario that later became *Trilby* – this irony is central in David Lodge's 2005 novel, *Author, Author*.

On his side, it was James who suggested to du Maurier that, for the sake of his eyes, he should turn to fiction. It was a happy thought. *Trilby* (1894) was popular to the point of mania with the British and American reading publics. A romanticisation of his early days as an English art student in the Latin quarter of Paris, illustrated by du Maurier himself, the novel showcases a cross-dressing bohemian gamine, Trilby O'Ferrall, and her evil genius, Svengali. Du Maurier's heavily sanitised *vie bohème* centres on three British art students: Taffy, Sandy and 'Little Billee'. Trilby models for them, until persuaded – by the Anglo Saxon trio – that it is immoral. She takes up laundressing instead. She and Little Billee fall in love but any such indecent match is foiled by his virtuous mother. He goes on to become a famous artist, while she – although tone-deaf – is hypnotised into virtuosity by Svengali (who is also sexually abusing her, we deduce) and becomes a world-famous opera singer. But she can only perform under his mesmeric influence. In a grand London recital, he dies and she is reduced to tuneless bellowing. She dies, beautifully, and Little Billee soon follows her.

Trilby, as du Maurier's illustrations stress, affects male attire. But nowhere in the actual novel does she wear the famous hat named after her. That took off with the stage version of the novel, written by Paul Potter, which opened at the Haymarket Theatre in October 1895, earning the actor-manager Beerbohm Tree so much that he was able to build a new theatre for himself. Du Maurier, who was an innocent in such things, got a measly £75 for the rights. Tree played Svengali, to great effect, with no restraint on anti-Semitic excess. But the star of the piece was Dorothea Baird. Baird's Trilby is, significantly unlike du Maurier's conception of her in his illustrations. Baird's gamine was barefooted – 'Trilby Feet' would become a catchphrase for the fashionably shoeless – and a chain-smoker of cigarettes. She also sported a wide-brimmed, 'trademark' felt hat. The play triggered a secondary wave of mania. Toulouse Lautrec named his yacht *Trilby*. It became a brand name slapped on innumerable gimcrack products. The music hall stars, Marie Lloyd and Vesta Tilley, warbled out songs such as 'Tricky Little Trilby'. Silent film versions followed. The mania eventually died away, but the play left behind it a permanent vogue for the Trilby hat.

The author of *Trilby* did not live to reap the full success of his novel and its adaptations – dramatic, filmic, and sartorial. He died a year after the novel's publication. His son, Gerald du Maurier (1873–1934), would go on to be one of the most successful actors of his time, making his debut, fittingly, in the Potter-Tree dramatisation of his father's novel. Gerald's on-stage style was famously suave. According to his daughter, Daphne: 'If an actor approached a scene with too much enthusiasm, Gerald would ask, "Must you kiss her as though you were having steak and onions for lunch?"' Gerald was knighted in 1922 for services to the stage. He was, alas, as blasé about paperwork as in his stage image. In 1929, harassed by the income tax people, du Maurier sold his name to be used as a brand for the new tipped cigarette, launched worldwide by Imperial Tobacco Canada. It was popular from the first and is still that country's premier brand. Thus two of the three things which have kept the du Maurier 'brand' alive over the decades and century are a titfer and a gasper. The third thing follows.

FN George Louis Palmella Busson du Maurier
MRT *Trilby*
Biog L. Ormond, *George du Maurier* (1969)

POSTSCRIPT

60. Daphne du Maurier 1907–1989

Last night I dreamt I went to Manderley again. Regular winner of 'best first lines in fiction' contests, often misquoted

Gerald married a rising star of the West End stage, Muriel Beaumont. Longing for a male heir to carry on the du Maurier name, he had three daughters – the second of whom was Daphne. Muriel's bright career was sacrificed to her husband's dynastic ambitions. A good wife, she tolerated his flagrant philandering. Daphne grew up, as she put it, with a 'caged boy' (the offspring her father *really* wanted) inside her. From school onwards – where she had a daring fling with the French mistress – Daphne would be drawn to other women – while, it should be added, enjoying more straight sex than all but the most adventurous of her generation. She saw herself as a sexual 'half breed'. Three things were overridingly important in du Maurier's life. For the first twenty years it was her father, Gerald. For ten years thereafter, it was coastal Cornwall around Fowey, which she discovered in her teens, when the family acquired a second home there. It provided the setting of her early, hugely bestselling, historical romances *Jamaica Inn* and *Frenchman's Creek*. And, for the greater part of her later life, the important thing was her Cornish house, Menabilly, the original of Manderley. Du Maurier went so far as to assert, 'I do believe I love Mena(billy) more than people.'

Gerald loomed over her girlhood. She grew up with his smart metropolitan set of theatrical friends (J. M. Barrie was particularly close). Daphne would retain her paternal name, not her husband's, on her title pages and her gravestone. It was engraved on her heart. One of her first books was a filial memoir of Gerald. Observers of her life, with the prurience of hindsight, have perceived incestuous desires (passionately disputed by the surviving family) and, quite plausibly, acts on Gerald's part. When Daphne announced her marriage, aged twenty-five, he is supposed to have burst into tears with the anguished cry, 'It's not fair.' Du Maurier herself added fuel to the speculations. Her third novel, *The Progress of Julius*, published around the time of her marriage, has as its hero a man who kills his daughter Gabriel to keep her from being sexually possessed by another man. Lust is the motive.

Young Daphne was brought up worldly, literate and a little wild. 'Life's no fun,' she said, 'unless there's a danger in it.' She resolved early on to write fiction – not dangerous, but unorthodox. Edgar Wallace (another friend of the family – Gerald had a huge hit with his dramatised thriller *The Ringer*) imbued her with a sense that if one wrote, one must work hard at it and aim at the largest possible readership – romance, if you were a woman, was the ticket. Her first novel, *The Loving Spirit*

(1931), was a full-blooded romance about Cornish ship-builders. A modern young woman, Jennifer, brought up in London, uncovers her family roots and discovers 'the freedom I desired, long sought for, not yet known. Freedom to write, to walk, to wander. Freedom to climb hills, to pull a boat, to be alone.'

As she worked out her apprenticeship in fiction, du Maurier had flings and one long lasting affair with the future film director, Carol Reed (an illegitimate offspring of her father's early patron, Beerbohm Tree – the West End has its own species of incest). At the eligible age of twenty-five she chose her husband, Frederick 'Boy' Browning, a dashing Major in the Guards, a First World War hero, and an Olympic athlete (bob-sleigh). She first laid eyes on him as he sailed into Fowey on his yacht, *Ygdrasil* (the tree of life). He, for his part, had come to that harbour drawn by a fascination with *The Loving Spirit*. Ruby M. Ayres could not have set things up more romantically. Boy was, Daphne told a friend, 'the most charming man in the world'. Professionally he was a career soldier destined for the top. His most enduring mark on posterity is the role he played as one of the commanders of the Arnhem campaign in 1944. In the 1977 film, Browning is played by Dirk Bogarde, and given the resonant last words, 'I always felt we tried to go a bridge too far.'

All this was far in the future in 1932. Boy – actually ten years older than Daphne – did, however, trail some heavy baggage into the marriage. He had never recovered inwardly from the horrors of the first Great War and his dashing image was fragile. If Daphne had a caged boy inside her, he had a shell-shocked warrior. The woman, Jan Ricardo, he was engaged to before Daphne, committed suicide (Ricardo, it is plausibly assumed, contributed something to Rebecca, the first Mrs de Winter). None the less, the first few years of the Browning marriage went smoothly enough. As an army wife, with children – two girls and a boy – Daphne followed her husband in his postings around the Empire. Du Maurier wrote *Rebecca* in Alexandria in 1937. Nostalgia for Manderley is the author's yearning for Menabilly. The novel is her masterpiece – subtle, teasing (what *is* the second Mrs de Winter's name?) and sinister. Most sinister is the implied 'corrupt' relationship between the housekeeper 'Danny' and the former mistress of Manderley:

> 'Now you are here, let me show you everything,' she said, her voice ingratiating and sweet as honey, horrible, false … 'That was her bed. It's a beautiful bed, isn't it? I keep the golden coverlet on it always, it was her favourite. Here is her nightdress inside the case. You've been touching it, haven't you?'

Daphne hated the 'Colonel's lady' life; nor was she one to devote herself to family duties. 'I am not,' she informed one of her close friends, 'one of those mothers who live for having their brats with them all the time.'

Marketed brilliantly by Victor Gollancz in 1938, *Rebecca* sold hugely as the book of the day, and as the book of the film, directed by Alfred Hitchcock, three years later. Buoyed up by the golden stream of royalties and rights, du Maurier was well enough off to take Menabilly on long lease in 1943, and devote herself over the next quarter of a century to its restoration. It was much more rewarding than brats or King's Birthday parades. Her love affair with the house, and its long history, was consummated in a romance about its Civil War adventures, *The King's General* (1946), when it had been violated by Roundhead intruders. During the war Daphne consoled herself with evangelising for moral rearmament and by taking a lover, in whose handsome house the family was billeted. 'Boy', now a General, in charge of airborne forces, served his country gallantly. She was, by now, out-earning her husband ten to one. In 1942 she paid enough income tax, she reckoned, to buy her own Lancaster bomber.

Du Maurier's stories have always filmed well. A couple of her shorter narratives have supplied two classics of the genre, Hitchcock's *The Birds* (1963), and Nicolas Roeg's *Don't Look Now* (1973). *Jamaica Inn* (1936), a rollicking tale of Cornish wreckers; and *Frenchman's Creek*, a Sabatiniesque 'Pirate and the Lady' romance, were filmed during the war as full-blooded costume drama and packed out cinemas with audiences desperate for a couple of hours of escapism. Insights into du Maurier's complex psychology can be found even in these romps. In *Frenchman's Creek*, the heroine, Dona, Lady St Columb, a married woman with children, dresses as a boy to join the pirate crew. Part of Daphne, it would seem, yearned to be where the fighting was – or, more likely, fantasised about it.

Boy returned from the fighting laden with medals – and a haunting sense of having royally cocked up Arnhem – to a marriage gone very cold. On demobilisation, he landed a senior admin post at Buckingham Palace as comptroller of the Household – a job he held until he drank and philandered his way out of it, five years on. Daphne meanwhile prosecuted her career with icy resolution. In 1951, she published the psychological thriller, *My Cousin Rachel*. It plays with the idea of uxoricide – a wife killing a husband (something going through the author's mind, apparently). The twist is that we never quite know if Rachel did murder Ambrose. Du Maurier claimed not to know herself: 'I just couldn't make up my mind.' Nor could she make up her mind about sexual preferences. On her first visit to America, in 1948, she embarked on a shipboard romance with the wife of her American publisher, Ellen Doubleday. It was not fully reciprocated. But a subsequent relationship with the actress Gertrude Lawrence (seduced in her youth by Gerald) was: which of the du Mauriers 'Gertie' found the more satisfying is not recorded.

After a series of catastrophic alcoholic breakdowns, Boy died in 1965. Daphne became ever grander – an upward progress crowned by damehood in 1969. By now reviews were dismissive. Her readers, vintage *Frenchman's Creek*, were growing old with her, she lamented to Victor Gollancz, himself long in the tooth nowadays. But the old read more than the young and her sales were never less than respectable.

The most interesting of her later novels is *The Scapegoat* (1957), filmed with Alec Guinness in the lead at the author's insistence – because he reminded her of her father. A mild thirty-eight-year-old academic, John, meets his exact double on holiday in France and finds himself tricked into being the malevolent (as it turns out) Jacques De Guè. It's half *Return of Martin Guerre*, half *Prisoner of Zenda*. Du Maurier recorded that she put more into the novel than anything since *Rebecca*: 'It is my story ... Every one of us has his, or her, dark side.'

Du Maurier's last novel of any worth, *The House on the Strand* (1969) – successfully filmed, inevitably – was inspired by having, finally, to return Menabilly to its family owners and remove to the nearby dower house. As she said, bricks and mortar always got her creative juices flowing.

FN   Daphne du Maurier ('Dame', later Browning)
MRT *Rebecca*
Biog M. Forster, *Daphne du Maurier* (1993)

61. Frank R. Stockton 1834–1902

The Lady or the Tiger?

Stockton is memorable as the author of *The Adventures of Captain Horn*, the top American bestseller of 1895 – the first year that any such list existed. Stockton, who is also claimed by some as the first American science fiction novelist (dubious, with Poe in the running) was born in Philadelphia, the son of a strict Methodist and superintendent of a community of almshouses in the city. He disapproved of fiction.

The Stockton family suffered two disasters in 1844. The first occurred when a cousin, Robert Field Stockton, accidentally blew up the American Secretary of State and Secretary of the US Navy, while displaying a lamentably inefficient new cannon. As Wellington would have said, 'I don't know what it does for the enemy, but it damn well frightens me.' The second family disaster occurred when Frank's father was dismissed for alleged mismanagement and suspected embezzlement. He never worked again, dying in 1860. It was a sad comedown for a family who could trace their ancestry back to a signatory on the Declaration of Independence. Frank took over as the family breadwinner – living, as he later claimed, on a dime-a-day to do so.

Frank was frail and disabled, which precluded most professions and, more happily, spared him from service in the Civil War, in which – despite his Northern origins – he favoured the South. In his early twenties he began publishing short pieces for magazines and papers, principally aimed at the juvenile market. He married in 1860 and his career took off when in 1867 he became associated editorially with the children's magazine, *Hearth and Home*. He worked as an editor until 1878, when he retired with permanently impaired eyesight. Thereafter he largely supported himself by his pen.

By the end of his career Stockton had published some twenty-one novels. His famous and much-reprinted fable, 'The Lady, or the Tiger?', was first published in *The Century Magazine* in 1882, and made his name – in his own day and posthumously. It is still widely read and discussed (by philosophers, among others). The story is one of the great teases of literature. A commoner falls in love with a princess and is subjected to trial by ordeal. He must choose one of two doors. Behind the one, lies a ravening tiger. Behind the other, a beautiful lady in waiting (not his Princess), whom he must marry, if that is the door he happens to choose. In the watching crowd is the Princess who, discreetly, nods to the door he must choose. At this tantalising point, the story ends.

Stockton – who was prosperous in his later years (no more dime-a-day meals) – achieved mass popularity with the *Adventures of Captain Horn* in 1895, a 'goldfever' story which coincided historically with the current gold-rush to the Yukon. Captain Horn, an American mariner, discovers the fabulous treasure of the Incas, valued at $200 million. He doggedly persists in his 'reasonable' belief that, as the discoverer of this gold, a precise 20 per cent ($40 million) is due to him, and he will not take a dollar more or less than his fair share. Others are less scrupulous. Horn's second mate, George Burke, is destroyed by man-killing traps in the Inca mound, when he secretly returns to plunder the treasure. Another sailor, Andy McLeish, is slowed down by all the gold he is carrying about him and is staked out by savage Indians to be eaten alive by ants. A corrupt Peruvian government tries to appropriate the booty and shyster lawyers exploit the laws of salvage to steal Horn's portion. The honest hero finally contrives to secure his legitimate $40 million share and forces the Peruvian authorities to use the $160 million balance for the welfare of the descendants of the Incas, building schools and hospitals and doing good work.

In 1899 Stockton was voted fifth place among the 'best living American writers' by the readers of the magazine *Literature*. He died of a stroke in 1902. Mark Twain, among other literary dignitaries, paid their respects at his funeral.

FN   Frank Richard Stockton
MRT   *The Adventures of Captain Horn*
Biog   *ANB* (Henry Golemba)

62. 'Walter' 1834–1900

I have in fact become a connoisseur in cunts. Walter on himself

The longest continuous novel of the Victorian period is also the most aggressively anti-Victorian: *My Secret Life*, by 'Walter'. One says 'novel', although it may be what it purports to be: a sexual athlete's frank memoirs from devirgination to (justified) exhaustion, some 1,200 partners later. But, carefully read, most readers will reckon it a life-history no more factual than those of Baron Munchausen, or James Frey. Fiction, that is, through and through. More specifically, *My Secret Life* is a Victorian *Bildungsroman* of the *Great Expectations* kind. 'Great Ejaculations', perhaps.

The likeliest candidate for 'Walter' is nowadays thought to be Henry Spencer Ashbee (1834–1900). Born in south London, Ashbee was, by profession, a trader in cloths and textiles. His line of work involved travel and encouraged a worldly, not to say underworldly, view of the human condition. Ashbee, as cultivated as he was randy, collected books – notably Cervantes and erotica. He wrote on the latter under the pen-names 'Fraxinus' (Latin for 'Ash'), 'Apis' ('Bee'), and the bawdily punning 'Pisanus Fraxi', under which he wrote his classic three-volume bibliography of 'Prohibited Books'. Ashbee left both his Cervantes and pornographic collections to the British Museum with the provision that neither should be destroyed or sold on. He never confessed, or directly alluded to, his authorship of *My Secret Life* – it remained his secret.

My Secret Life was published between 1888 and 1894 in eleven volumes in Amsterdam, under the imprint of the Belgian publisher Auguste Brancart. Only twenty-five sets were printed, at a cost of £60 apiece. At 2.5 million words, it rivals Proust in length and is longer than any other single-title fictional composition in the British nineteenth-century catalogue of books. The very hugeness of the thing is a measure of what was conventionally left out of the above-ground Victorian novel: namely, sex – or, where in the later decades it made a shy entrance, explicit anatomical description of the act with the vulgar terminology used by the mass of the male population and, specifically, by 'gentlemen' in the smoking room.

My Secret Life is nothing if not explicit and vulgar. Page after page records, in minute detail, couplings and sexual experimentation, with partners from every station in life. Words are not minced: as the word-count facility of the electronic text calculates, the word 'cunt' occurs 5,357 times, 'fuck' 4,032 times, 'prick' 3,756 times. 'Clit(oris)' clocks a measly 434. Walter records, in wearisome anatomical detail, using the unbuttoned terminology of the men's smoking room, the ins and outs (ad nauseam) of Victorian sex. In passing, however, he also offers an unblinkered view of much of what the Victorian novel routinely averts its – and our – eyes from. This filling in of background is its peculiar value to the reader of – say – *Middlemarch*. To choose one example from thousands – lavatories. It was not, for example, until 1884 that the Ladies Lavatory Company opened its first 'convenience' near Oxford Circus. What did a lady – all those ladies in Victorian fiction – do before that? Read Walter.

A still virginal, but testosterone-maddened, lad, he liked to wander, voyeuristically, in the grounds of Hampton Court Palace. In summer the park seethed with sightseers. One day young Walter was there with his pal Fred, and his family:

> Fred's mother, mine, the girls, Fred and I went into the park gardens, one day after luncheon. A very hot day, for we kept on the shady walks, one of which led to the place where women hid themselves to piss. My aunt said, 'Why don't you boys go and play, you don't mind the sun,' so off we went, but when about to leave the walk, turned round and saw the women had turned back. Said Fred; 'I'm sure they are going to piss, that's why they want to get rid of us.' We evaded the gardeners, scrambled through shrubs, on our knees, and at last on our bellies, up a little bank, on the other side of which was the vacant place on which dead leaves and sweepings were shot down. As we got there, pushing aside the leaves, we saw the big backside of a woman, who was half standing, half squatting, a stream of piss falling in front of her, and a big hairy gash, as it seemed, under her arse; but only for a second, she had just finished as we got the peep, let her clothes fall, tucked them between her legs, and half turning round. We saw it was Fred's mother, my aunt. Off aunt went. 'Isn't it a wopper,' said Fred, 'lay still, more of them will come.'

It's distasteful in the extreme – but telling. And it tells what is not told elsewhere. Where, for example, does Tess the dairymaid go when she needs to 'go'? Or, perish the thought, Miss Dorothea Brooke?

FN   (presumed) Henry Spencer Ashbee ('Pisanus Fraxi')
MRT *My Secret Life*
Biog Steven Marcus, *The Other Victorians* (1966)

63. Mrs Mary Braddon 1835–1915

Dead Love has Chains.

Mary Braddon was born in Soho, London, the youngest daughter of a solicitor. Her mother left her husband, who was reportedly feckless and faithless, when Mary was only four. Among all this domestic strife she contrived to get a good education, began to write fiction at the precocious age of eight, and was publishing in the magazines, as the family breadwinner, before she was twenty. With the same worthy aim she took to the stage (only one notch above taking to the streets) in 1857 as 'Mary Seyton', and specialised in playing older women.

She was, however, young and comely when off-stage. In 1860, a Yorkshire 'admirer' gave her money to quit the boards and write an epic on Garibaldi. Safe enough occupation for a respectable mistress, he must have thought – even if the fellow was an Italian revolutionary. Instead, she sensibly wrote a sensation novel, *Three Times Dead*, published in 1861. Through it she became acquainted with the Irish publisher John Maxwell, proprietor of the *Welcome Guest* magazine. Exit Yorkshire admirer: enter London patron.

Braddon's great triumph came with *Lady Audley's Secret* (1862), the serial rights for which were bought by Maxwell. The two became lovers and Braddon's first child by her new 'admirer' was born in 1862. *Lady Audley's Secret* was published in volume form by another publisher, William Tinsley, and set Braddon up for life. It likewise set up Tinsley, who built a villa at Barnes shamelessly called 'Audley Lodge' on the profits. The plot is succinctly summarised by Elaine Showalter: 'Braddon's bigamous heroine deserts her child, pushes husband number-one down a well, thinks about poisoning husband number-two and sets fire to a hotel in which her other male acquaintances happen to be residing.'

Braddon's own marital problems were not as easily managed. Maxwell had five children, and a wife currently residing in an Irish lunatic asylum; he was also deeply in debt. A bestselling author in his bed and in his columns was a godsend. In 1874, when the first Mrs Maxwell died, Braddon was free to marry her publisher, and went on to bear him another six children, while continuing to be his principal commercial asset. Revenue from Braddon's fiction installed their growing family in a fine country house. The couple rode out the inevitable scandal when it was revealed to the world that they had been living, and breeding, in sin for ten years – although their servants resigned en masse.

In the mid-1860s, Braddon's price peaked at a massive £2,000 per novel, with a rapid string of bestsellers such as *Aurora Floyd* (1863), *John Marchmont's Legacy*

(1863), *Henry Dunbar* (1864) and *Birds of Prey* (1867). Her output was prodigious, and in addition to her other labours she edited, or 'conducted' several magazines. Many of her novels were dramatised, and she wrote plays herself. She was a top favourite with the circulating library subscriber; with the railway reader (by 1899, fifty-seven of her novels had appeared in yellowbacks for the traveller); and with the lower-class market for whom she wrote in penny journals. Braddon drove herself too hard, and suffered a stroke in 1907, but none the less kept on writing. Her final life tally is some eighty titles, of which *Lady Audley's Secret* was never out of print during her lifetime and became a bestseller again, with the vogue for Victorian sensation fiction in the 1990s.

FN   Mary Elizabeth Braddon (later Maxwell)
MRT *Lady Audley's Secret*
Biog R. Wolff, *Sensational Victorian: The Life and Fiction of Mary Elizabeth Braddon* (1979)

64. Samuel Butler 1835–1902

Christ: I dislike him very much. Still, I can stand him. What I cannot stand is the wretched band of people whose profession is to hoodwink us about him.

The author of two of the most un-Victorian novels of the Victorian period, Butler was born the son and grandson of Anglican grandees. His childhood, and its patriarchal tyrannies, are recalled in that of Ernest Pontifex, in the *The Way of All Flesh* (1903). Butler went to Shrewsbury School and formed there the two great loves of his life: Handel and Italy. He left Cambridge in 1858 with a first-class degree in Classics and a lifelong distrust of academic institutions. He declined the destiny intended for him – holy orders. To save the family's blushes, Samuel was sent as far away as earth permitted, to raise sheep in New Zealand. In the five years (1859–64) that he was there Butler proved a resourceful emigrant, doubling his capital.

Pastoral leisure allowed Butler to read widely – he was an early convert to Darwin. He returned to London in 1864, rich enough to be free of his family (why, he once wondered, were there not orphanages for those luckless children who actually *had* parents). He took up bachelor rooms near Fleet Street and remained there the rest of his long life. In his mature years Butler dedicated himself to painting, music and writing. It was an enjoyable course of life – and a good vantage point from which to snipe at the hated Victorian establishment. In 1865 he published a typically provocative pamphlet, arguing that Christ had not died on the cross, merely fainted (the idea was later picked up by D. H. Lawrence in *The Man Who Died*, 1929). He and a close friend, Henry Festing Jones, allegedly shared the sexual favours of the same woman by weekly calendar arrangement.

Butler's Swiftian reflections on the hypocrisies and moral contradictions of Victorian England were published, at his own expense, as *Erewhon* (1872). Set in New Zealand, the hero Higgs, accompanied by a native, Chowbok (George Lucas evidently read the novel, in creating Chewbacca), journeys over a mountain range to a country called Erewhon – where everything, like the name, is back to front. Crime is regarded as an ailment, and is humanely treated, while illness is regarded as a crime, and punished. The young are instructed in colleges of Unreason and the presiding deity is the goddess Ydgrun (i.e. Mrs Grundy). Higgs escapes by balloon. The satire also plays with Butler's prescient idea that in the future machine intelligence will outstrip human.

Butler went on to produce a torrent of works of a hyper-rationalist tendency, and one supremely eccentric *Bildungsroman*, *The Way of All Flesh*. Begun in 1873, this work, which flays the age in which Butler found himself, was not published until the year after his death. In the novel, Ernest Pontifex, born in the same year as Butler, is mercilessly tyrannised by his clergyman father and bullied at Roughborough School. He studies at Cambridge with a view of taking orders in a Church in whose religion he does not believe. By a series of misadventures, and total innocence about sex, he is convicted, while serving as a curate in London, of indecent assault. Disastrously, his lusts inflamed by the easy conquests retailed to him by his best friend, he mistakes a girl who won't for a girl who will:

> Then it flashed upon him that if he could not see Miss Snow he could at any rate see Miss Maitland. He knew well enough what he wanted now, and as for the Bible, he pushed it from him to the other end of his table ...
>
> About ten minutes after we last saw Ernest, a scared, insulted girl, flushed and trembling, was seen hurrying from Mrs Jupp's house as fast as her agitated state would let her, and in another ten minutes two policemen were seen also coming out of Mrs Jupp's, between whom there shambled rather than walked our unhappy friend Ernest, with staring eyes, ghastly pale, and with despair branded upon every line of his face.

Six months later after release from prison – and no longer a member of decent society – Ernest is free, at last, to grow up and become a rational, and joyously un-Victorian, human being. He has realised the importance of being un-earnest.

Butler's last years were passed in furious quarrels on evolution and freethinking, in which he attacked the orthodoxies of his time and rode his various hobbyhorses, such as his belief that a woman had written *The Odyssey*.

FN   Samuel Butler
MRT   *The Way of All Flesh*
Biog   P. Raby, *Samuel Butler: A Biography* (1991)

65. Mark Twain 1835–1910

I am not an American. I am the American.

Among all the nation's writers, Mark Twain has the firmest hold on the national epithet. From Theodore Roosevelt onwards, American presidents have routinely salted their oratory with down-home Twainisms. Harry Truman had a framed Twain quotation on his desk – 'Always do Right. It will Please some People and Astonish the Rest' – alongside 'The Buck Stops Here'. On the 2008 election trail, Barack Obama routinely reached out to 'our greatest American satirist' (and, it may be noted, the creator of the only classic American novel with a mixed-race hero, *Pudd'nhead Wilson*). There is, in fact, something presidential about Twain himself. 'The Lincoln of our Literature,' William Dean Howells called him.

Great American writers elbow each other aside to aver Twain's supreme greatness. 'Mark Twain', declared Eugene O'Neill, 'is the true father of all American literature.' 'Mark Twain is all of our grandfather [sic],' concurred William Faulkner. 'All modern American literature', said Ernest Hemingway, 'comes from one book by Mark Twain called *Huckleberry Finn*.' Norman Mailer turned it around neatly by noting that much of what Mark Twain wrote had clearly been lifted from Norman Mailer.

The universal panegyric highlights a strange paradox. How can a writer have achieved such eminence with such a small number of incontrovertibly great works? One of his biographers, Jerome Loving, in an otherwise laudatory account, is surely correct in pointing out that '*The Adventures of Tom Sawyer* is possibly the most overrated work in American literature.' Even Hemingway's 'one book' was dropped, mid-composition, for five years and picked up to be hurried, hugger-mugger into the feeblest of concluding chapters. *The Tragedy of Pudd'nhead Wilson* (1894), the first American novel to deal unsentimentally or unbigotedly with race, was written during the turmoil of one of Twain's insolvencies and is marred by unliterary distractions. As for the rest? *The Prince and the Pauper* (1882) and *A Connecticut Yankee in King Arthur's Court* (1889) are charming *amusettes* (to borrow Henry James's term) but no one suggests they are in the *Moby Dick* or *Scarlet Letter* class. Dickens published twelve novels any one of which can be argued to vindicate his status as Britain's greatest. Where are Twain's dozen? What makes him the 'father' of American fiction? What makes him what H. L. Mencken called 'the archetype of *Homo Americanus*'?

The second question is the easier to answer. Twain's life is a parable of the American belief that anyone can make it in that country – any pauper can end up a prince. Born in Florida, Missouri, the son of an unlucky storekeeper, young Sam L. Clemens was lucky to make it through infancy – most of his siblings didn't. His father's insolvency (they were, at their lowest point, reduced to just one slave) and premature death kicked Sam out of school at eleven, to earn a pittance as a printer's devil. Fortunately for American literature, he was not good enough at that line of work to prosper. In his early teens, he struck out from Hannibal, Missouri (immortalised as 'St Petersburg' in *Huck Finn*), to make his fortune importing coca leaf from South America. He might have become the Pablo Escobar of his day, had he not met the legendary Mississippi pilot, Horace Bixby. The romance of the great river, its raffish steamboat life and its eerie call – 'mark twain!,' i.e. two fathoms of water beneath us – occupied him for four years.

He might have stayed a pilot all his working life but for two things: the Civil War and the fact that he was chronically nervous at the helm. As Bixby later said, 'No sir, Sam Clemens knew the river, but being a coward he was a failure as a pilot.' A school dropout Twain was also a draft dodger. The Civil War was not, he decided, for him. It was less 'cowardice' than rational judgement. Instead he tried silver mining in Nevada. There he struck it rich but – 'a millionaire for two days' – his claim was jumped. Finally he hit pay-dirt in San Francisco as a journalist. Here, in 1865, he had his first great stroke of luck. His comic sketch, 'Jim Smiley and his Jumping Frog' became a nationwide hit. It's a story about 'the curiosest man about always betting' who has a prodigiously athletic frog, 'Dan'l Webster'. Having wagered $40, Jim, to his surprise, loses the bet. His crafty opponent – as a leaden belch reveals – has loaded down poor Dan'l's belly with buckshot.

After the fame of his frog tale, Twain had the Midas touch. 'It seems to me that whatever I touch turns to gold,' he later said. But Twain destroyed money. He built houses the size of castles and he had 'a lifelong losing streak' as an investor. He invented the self-adjusting suspenders (i.e. braces) and an early version of the Post-it – both were costly failures. He also sank the equivalent of $4-million in modern cash into a typesetting process which went nowhere. However, Twain was always able to write his way out of financial misfortune – his life is half a dozen American success stories. None the less the question remains: what makes Mark Twain the greatest *American* writer, the founder of his nation's modern literature?

One can answer with three words: voice, eye and attitude.

First, voice: Twain's art was honed at the lectern and in the saloon. He crafted American literature into something that is heard, as much as read. *Huckleberry Finn* (1884) carries a foreword warning the reader that 'in this book a number of dialects are used'. No less than five versions of the 'Pike County' voice will be detected, he says. The novel demands a well-tuned ear. Huck's own dialect has recently been the subject of controversy. Did Twain, as Shelley Fisher Fishkin has controversially argued, lift it from the African Americans he grew up with? Listen to the following famous sentence and judge for yourself (Huck is abasing himself to Jim, whom he has cruelly tricked):

> It was fifteen minutes before I could work myself up to go and humble myself to a nigger; but I done it, and I warn't ever sorry for it afterwards, neither. I didn't do him no more mean tricks, and I wouldn't done that one if I'd a knowed it would make him feel that way.

Interestingly Richard Pryor, the stand-up comedian, acknowledged Twain as his inspiration. Mark Twain, we may say, made American literature *talk* – unlike, say, Henry James, who merely made it *write*.

Secondly, eye: Twain's first successful book was *The Innocents Abroad* (1869), and it was throughout his life his bestselling title. The account of an American's (un)grand tour, the work's proclaimed purpose 'is to suggest to the reader how he would be likely to see Europe and the East *if he looked at them with his own eyes*'. His own 'innocent' American eyes, that is. As later works, notably *A Tramp Abroad* (1880) testify, it was a jaundiced gaze he cast on the world.

This links to Twain's attitude – 'feisty' is the appropriate word. Note, for example, the warning at the head of *Huckleberry Finn*: 'Persons attempting to find a motive in this narrative will be prosecuted; persons attempting to find a moral in it will be banished; persons attempting to find a plot in it will be shot.' Take these three elements – voice, eye, attitude – and, as Hemingway argued, you have the essence of a national literature. After Twain no one could dismiss it as 'English literature written in America'. It was itself. In his Nobel acceptance speech in 1954, Heming-way mused: 'I cannot but regret that the award was never given to Mark Twain.' Why not? Because Twain was a 'humorist,' what Matthew Arnold (that arch-prig) called a 'Yankee funny man'. No comic writer has ever won the world's major liter-ary prize, nor ever will. Stockholm has a poor sense of humour.

FN   Mark Twain (born Samuel Langhorne Clemens)
MRT *Huckleberry Finn*
Biog J. Loving, *Mark Twain: The Adventures of Samuel L. Clemens* (2010)

66. B. L. Farjeon 1838–1903

His mood (when it wasn't irascible) was overflowingly generous. Eleanor Farjeon

Farjeon's father, Jacob, was a London 'old clothes' merchant, an orthodox Jew newly arrived in Europe from North Africa. Young Benjamin was brought up in poverty, 'almost without education', in Whitechapel, but 'rigorously' in the Jewish faith. At thirteen, restless under his father's domestic discipline and having just read Bulwer-Lytton's *The Caxtons* three times, he added a lofty 'Leopold' to his name and determined on authorship as his career, declaring: 'I should be content to die if I had written such a book.' He began working life as a printer's devil at fourteen on the Christian *Nonconformist* newspaper at four shillings a week. Farjeon broke entirely with his family at the age of seventeen, and went off to make his fortune in the Australian goldfields, travelling steerage to Melbourne. An 'atheist uncle' staked him £50 to do so. He later moved on to New Zealand at the age of twenty-three, where he supported himself by journalism on the *Otago Daily Times*, under the editor and future Prime Minister, Julius Vogel.

About the same period, Farjeon began to write fiction. Everyone who knew him at the time was struck by his dynamism. 'He splashed you with his exuberance,' recalled one friend. From the first, the dominating influence was Dickens, whose disciple he proclaimed himself. In 1866, his story of a Melbourne street arab, *Grif*, enjoyed considerable success. The vagrant hero is closely modelled on Jo, the crossing-sweeper, in Dickens's *Bleak House* (1852), even down to the catchphrase: 'He wos wery good to me, he wos.' Passages such as that below, echoing Jo's response to the oleaginous Chadband, would verge on plagiarism was not the imitation so reverently offered:

> He had attended some meetings of the Moral Bootblacking Boys' Reformatory, and had heard a great deal about morality; and, albeit he would have been considerably perplexed if he had been asked to define the meaning of the word, it could not but be presumed that he had been much edified by the moral essays and exhortations to which he had listened. And yet his mental condition, when he came away from those meetings, was one of perplexity. He could not see the connection between morality and a bellyful of food. 'It's all very well,' he would mutter, 'for them coves who's got lots to eat and drink to talk about morality; but what good does it do me?'

In 1868, Farjeon returned to England, encouraged by a letter from his idol, offering to accept 'any original communication' in *All the Year Round*. Enough said. Over the following ten years, he turned out a stream of novels, mostly with the publisher Tinsley. They show the strong influence of Dickens, Walter Besant and Wilkie Collins. The most interesting of them, *Aaron the Jew* (1894), is a powerful indictment of anti-Semitism in the 1870s. Farjeon wrote other novels on the topic of the Jew in England, for example, *Solomon Isaacs* (1877) and *Pride of Race* (1901).

In 1877 he married Margaret, the daughter of the American actor, Joseph Jefferson. She was a Protestant. Farjeon did not himself convert to Christianity, but neither did he impose Judaism on his children. In later life he gave crowd-pleasing readings of his short pieces (most popularly, extracts from *Grif*) in America, following, again, the example of his mentor Dickens. He died comfortably off in Hampstead.

His daughter, the well-known children's author Eleanor Farjeon (1881–1965), evoked her father's household vividly and his personality fondly in *A Nursery in the Nineties* (1935). Especially poignant is her description of his waning grip on public popularity at the turn of the century as dementia clouded his once lively mind.

FN   Benjamin Leopold Farjeon
MRT   *Aaron the Jew*
Biog   *ODNB* (William Baker)

67. Ouida 1839–1908

Je n'écris pas pour les femmes, j'écris pour les militaries. Ouida's boast

Ouida's French-sounding *nom de plume* – and the social plumage it suggests – derives from a childhood corruption of her Christian name. She might, less happily, have been 'Lulu' or, perish the thought, 'Lou'. She was born, humbly enough, Maria Louise Ramé at Bury St Edmunds, where her Guernsey-born father, Louis Ramé, was a teacher of French. Her mother (née Sutton) was as English as Suffolk mutton. M. Ramé gave his quick-witted, artistic and precocious daughter an unusually good education for a country girl of her background but paternal care he did not give. In the 1860s he went off to Paris and – as Louise liked to think – disappeared during the upheaval of the 1871 Commune. Or he may just have walked out on what had proved an uninteresting entanglement in the English provinces. Ouida could never bring herself to believe that.

In 1859, while staying in Hammersmith, Louise was introduced to Harrison Ainsworth, one of the great men in the London literary world. He was kind to her and she sent him a short story 'Dashwood's Drag: Or the Derby and What Came of

It' for his magazine. Ainsworth liked it immensely and took a score more of fashion-ably 'fast' stories from the young authoress. He also took, in serial form, her first novel – *Held in Bondage* (1863), the story of Granville de Vigne, the heir to £20,000 a year, a superb sportsman, and a general swell. Aided by his 'inseparable', Vivian Sabretasche, Granville sets out to win the reigning beauty, 'the Trefusis'. Complications ensue.

Now 'Ouida', she went on to produce her perennial bestseller, *Under Two Flags* (1867). The Hon. Bertie Cecil of the Life Guards flees England to protect the honour of a lady and enlists in the Chasseurs d'Afrique, where he performs prodigies of valour against Arab rebels and incurs the implacable enmity of the sadistic Colonel Chateauroy. In a tremendous final scene he is saved from execution by Cigarette, the *gamin* camp follower who loves him madly, and who throws herself into the hail of firing-squad bullets meant for his breast (ballistically improbable – romantically beautiful).

Ouida was now the *belle* of literary London. She removed, with her mother, to Italy, residing in the Langham Hotel when in London, where she reserved a whole floor, and styled herself 'de la Ramée'. Self-promotion always came easily for her. She created a fascinating and glamorous image in the minds of her English readers and sensational rumours attached to the mysterious Englishwoman with the French name. There were also absurdly high claims made for her romantic fiction. Even Henry James claimed to admire her 'artistry'.

In 1871 a short-lived affair with a Florentine aristocrat – in which she behaved absurdly – provoked the revenge novel, *Friendship* (1878). She was by now settled with her mother in a villa in Florence. Here, for a few years, she lived very well. She was an idealist of sorts. She loved dogs and campaigned against vivisection. She wrote sympathetically on behalf of the oppressed Italian peasantry, in novels such as *A Village Commune* (1881): Ouida was no friend to Communitarianism, which, she believed, was socialism with another name. But she wrote intelligently about international politics, supporting the Boers' struggle in South Africa. Satires such as *Moths* (1880) showed her to be sharp-eyed about European aristocracy.

By the 1890s, Ouida had outlived her *vogue*. Glamour such as hers did not age well. Nor had she looked after her copyrights. Her last eighteen years were passed in increasing penury and she died in virtual destitution, aided by a tiny Civil List pension. She remained, however, indomitably proud and furiously spurned Marie Corelli's attempt to publicise her plight in the 'gutter press' London papers. She also remained an animal lover: at the time of her death she had, it was said, more dogs than readers. Louise de la Ramée died at Viareggio, Italy, of pneumonia. She is com-memorated by a monument – a watering trough for her four-legged friends – in

Bury St Edmunds, a town she herself never commemorated in her cosmopolitan, high-flown, Ouidaesque fiction.

FN 'Ouida' (Maria Louise de la Ramé(e))
MRT *Under Two Flags*
Biog E. Bigland, *Ouida: The Passionate Victorian* (1951)

68. Thomas Hardy 1840–1928

Hanged Woman

Nineteenth-century novelists were fascinated by hangings. Walter Scott secured a good window place, at some personal cost, to observe, at leisure, the public execution of the grave-robber, William Hare (of Burke and Hare) in 1829. There are plenty of stringings-up and enough drawing-and-quartering to satisfy even *Braveheart*-lovers in the *Waverley* novels. Bulwer-Lytton's most notorious novel is about a hanged man, *Eugene Aram*, which pioneered a school of fiction, the 'Newgate' novel, based on the lives of notorious murderers hanged by the neck at Tyburn.

Thackeray attended one such public execution of François Courvoisier in 1840. Like Scott, he purchased a window view. He was appalled by the merriment of the crowd, but transfixed by the grisly 'second murder'. Courvoisier, a valet who had cut his master's throat, claimed to have been inspired to his crime by reading Ainsworth's novel, *Jack Sheppard*, which climaxes with the hero being publicly hanged where Courvoisier himself would swing. A passing remark in Thackeray's 'On Going to See a Man Hanged' (1840), about how the doxies serving spectators in back-alleys around Courvoisier's execution did not exactly remind him of Dickens's virtuous Nancy, sparked off a furious row with the other novelist. Dickens was also fascinated by hanging (in *Oliver Twist* both Fagin and Sikes are 'stretched') and wrote about the repulsive but irresistible attraction of public execution. He introduces a hangman – who ends up hanged – in *Barnaby Rudge*.

Great Expectations opens with the encounter between Magwitch and Pip, which will determine Pip's life, on the Romney marshes. An image forecasts the future of both the escaped convict (ultimately sentenced to hang) and Pip ('born to hang', as Mrs Joe thinks):

> On the edge of the river I could faintly make out the only two black things in all
> the prospect that seemed to be standing upright; one of these was the beacon by

which the sailors steered, – like an unhooped cask upon a pole, – an ugly thing when you were near it; the other, a gibbet, with some chains hanging to it which had once held a pirate. The man was limping on towards this latter, as if he were the pirate come to life, and come down, and going back to hook himself up again.

George Eliot's first novel, *Adam Bede*, climaxes at the scene of a public hanging. One could go on – and doubtless, in a Ph.D. dissertation, some scholar has. But of all the great novelists of his time, Hardy qualifies as the most thoughtful, and most morbidly sensitive, spectator of hangings. They feature prominently in his fiction. Hanging is central to the short stories 'The Withered Arm' and 'The Three Strangers'. Once read, one will never forget the rabbit ('hanged by the leg') squealing night-long in *Jude the Obscure*, nor Little Father Time and his two siblings hanged by the neck, on the clothes-hook in the lodging-house wardrobe. In *Far from the Madding Crowd*, after shooting Troy, Boldwood rings the bell-pull at vast red-bricked Dorchester Gaol, alongside the gateway where he expects to meet his end. Boldwood is actually reprieved – unusual in Victorian England – perhaps because the young Hardy was prevailed on to sweeten his ending by his editor.

Tess of the d'Urbervilles is the story of a murderess who is hanged at Wintoncester, the ancient capital of Wessex, after preparing herself ('pure woman' that she is) on the sacrificial slab at Stonehenge:

Upon the cornice of the tower a tall staff was fixed. Their eyes were riveted on it. A few minutes after the hour had struck something moved slowly up the staff, and extended itself upon the breeze. It was a black flag.

'Justice' was done, and the President of the Immortals, in Æschylean phrase, had ended his sport with Tess. And the d'Urberville knights and dames slept on in their tombs unknowing. The two speechless gazers bent themselves down to the earth, as if in prayer, and remained thus a long time, absolutely motionless: the flag continued to wave silently. As soon as they had strength they arose, joined hands again, and went on.

This is a long shot – just as memorable are Hardy's close-ups of the hanged body; 'the line the colour of an unripe blackberry' on the corpse's neck, for example. Hardy knew what he was writing about. He had witnessed two hangings in his youth that stayed with him all his life and the more famous of the two inspired Tess Durbeyfield. When he was sixteen, as Hardy recalled, seventy years later: 'I am ashamed to say I saw [Martha Browne] hanged, my only excuse being that I was but a youth and had to be in the town at that time for other reasons ... I remember what a fine figure she showed against the sky as she hung in the misty rain, and how the tight black silk gown set off her shape as she wheeled half-round and back.'

The recollection was inspired by a visit in 1926 to the area where Browne had lived, and some inquiries he made there as to whether ancient locals had information about her. In a letter, at the same time, Hardy's second wife, Florence, recorded that watching Browne's execution gave 'a tinge of bitterness and gloom to his life's work'.

More than a tinge, one ventures. The circumstances of Browne's crime and execution – the last public hanging of a woman in Dorset – were memorable. Her hanging was in Dorchester, where the young Thomas had just begun his apprenticeship as an architect. The structure on which the scaffold was erected was the new archway to the prison, facing the North Square, in whose construction the young man's eye would have taken a professional interest (he describes it in detail in *Far from the Madding Crowd*). There was a long tradition of public hangings in Dorchester. They were the occasion of what were bluntly called 'hang fairs'. As with other fairs, open spaces were required. Eventually the prison gateway was settled on as ideal, to give a better view for the crowd. In mid-Victorian cities, such as Glasgow, the crowds could be vast – as many as 100,000. Martha Browne pulled some 4,000, effectively a full house.

The town had been the scene of an orgy of hangings following the Monmouth uprising in 1685: some seventy-five locals were hanged by Judge Jeffreys on his Bloody Assizes. There were those still living in Hardy's day who retailed the legends of these primeval hangings which took place in the amphitheatre, Maumbury Rings, where Henchard summons Farfrae for a gladiatorial struggle, to the death if necessary. Mary Channing, who had poisoned her husband, was hanged, drawn and quartered in the ring in 1705. The event is recalled in *The Mayor of Casterbridge*:

> in 1705 a woman who had murdered her husband was half-strangled and then burnt there in the presence of ten thousand spectators. Tradition reports that at a certain stage of the burning her heart burst and leapt out of her body, to the terror of them all, and that not one of those ten thousand people ever cared particularly for hot roast after that.

Hardy claimed to have had the story from an 'ancestor'. His father (another Thomas) recalled seeing four rick-burners, convicted after the Swing riots, hanged all together, like apples on the bough. There had, however, been no public hangings between 1833 (a fifteen-year-old, feeble-minded arsonist) and Martha Browne in 1856. The revival of the hanging fair added to the excitement. So too did the fact that she was a local woman, whose story was well known and argued over. Martha had been a housekeeper at a local farm. She had married a fellow servant, John Browne, twenty years her junior. She was forty-four years old, beyond childbearing, but generally agreed to be a handsome woman, with a fine head of hair. She brought £30 to the marriage, on the proceeds of which she and her husband set up a small shop. It was a violent marriage – particularly after she found him in bed with a younger woman. Rows followed in which Martha was quite likely beaten. Finally, she caved in her husband's head with an axe. Like Tess (who used a carving knife to similar effect on Alec), the weapon argued a degree of premeditation rather than self-defence. Fatally, Martha insisted that John had been kicked in the head by one of his horses (he had a sideline as a tranter, or carter), although medical evidence contradicted this.

There was sympathy for Martha in the town. The mid-Victorian mood was less vengeful, and less jubilant, about hanging than in earlier times. When the 'other woman' in the affair, Mary Davies, turned up to view the execution, the crowd hissed the hussy away. After the event, the *Dorset County Chronicle* went so far as to argue for the abolition of the death penalty – something that would not happen for a century, after the not dissimilar execution of Ruth Ellis.

Browne's execution was set for 9 o'clock on 9 August. It turned out a drizzly day. Browne had dressed herself in her best black Sunday gown, and her hair was shown to good effect. Accompanied by two (friendly) wardresses, and her clergyman (an antiquarian, who may have inspired Tringham in *Tess*), she shook hands with the officials and displayed a marble-calm composure. Having ascended the eleven steps of the scaffold, over the gateway, her gown was tied round the ankles, to prevent indecent exposure (of, among other things, the special underwear to soak up involuntary defecation). A white hood was placed over her head. The rain (as Hardy noted) meant that her facial features, as she attempted to suck in breath, were clearly visible through the muslin.

In charge of the spectacle was William Calcraft, the most famous hangman in England since Jack Ketch. Calcraft specialised in 'the short drop', which meant death by strangulation rather than a mercifully snapped spine. The dangling victim could take up to four minutes to stop 'dancing'. For the further delectation of the crowd, the body was left, at the end of the rope, for an hour. Calcraft had the right to the victim's clothes and rope, which he routinely sold on to Madame Tussaud's 'Chamber of Horrors'. This state-appointed sadist also earned a second income as prison flogger, wherever he happened to be passing.

The sixteen-year-old Hardy, with a friend, got an early place, virtually under the gallows. Given the thousands' strong crowd, he presumably arrived hours before. He was, he later said, close enough to hear the 'rustle' of Martha's 'thin black gown'. In conversation, sixty years later, he recalled: 'The hanging itself did not move me at all. But I sat on after the others went away, not thinking, but looking at the figure

... turning slowly round on the rope. And then it began to rain, and then I saw they had put a cloth over the face how as the cloth got wet, her features came through it. That was extraordinary. A boy had climbed up into a tree nearby, and when she dropped he came down in a faint like an apple dropping from a tree. It was curious the two dropping together.'

Was it more than 'curiosity' which anchored him to the spot? Biographers quarrel on the subject. Some, like Robert Gittings and Michael Millgate, deduce that hanging was for Hardy obscurely 'erotic'. Gittings, for example, points to 'Hardy's obvious sense of enjoyment and anticipation, followed by a sensation of calm that seems to give the whole experience a sexual character.' Orgasm, in other words. This perverse 'enjoyment' is connected, it is suggested, with Hardy's supposed 'impotence' (another area of hot dispute). Claire Tomalin protests that there was nothing sexually exciting for Hardy in the hanging of Martha Browne. His comments on her dress (the 'rustling gown', 'fine' figure, writhing, etc.) merely observe that – stoic woman that she was – Martha Browne intended to leave the world head held high and 'respectable'. It was 'touching', not aphrodisiac.

Browne's was the last public execution of a woman in England, and the last but one public execution in Dorchester. Hardy went out of his way to watch that as well. James Seale was hanged on 10 August 1858, for cutting the throat of a young woman, and attempting to disguise the act by arson. It was a squalid crime. On the morning of the execution, Hardy rushed home and picked up his father's telescope. He then took up a position on one of the hills around Dorchester from where he could observe Seale, clad in a white smock, drop and 'dance'. As the body fell, Hardy, in his shock, involuntarily dropped the telescope.

There were no more executions in Dorchester, public or secluded. In 1868 the Capital Punishment Amendment Act ended public hanging altogether. If *Tess* had been set in the historical period of *The Mayor of Casterbridge* (mid-1840s) rather than the 1870s, she – like her progenitor Martha Browne – would have swung, danced and dangled in front of a crowd of thousands. It is odd, and perhaps significant, that Angel does not take up his right, as husband of the condemned woman, to be a witness. As it is, he and Liza-Lu (his deceased wife's sister and future bedmate, we apprehend) attend the execution outside Wintoncester prison's walls. Victorian fiction's love affair with public execution had come to an end.

FN   Thomas Hardy
MRT *Tess of the d'Urbervilles*
Biog C. Tomalin, *Thomas Hardy, The Time-torn Man* (2007)

69. Ambrose Bierce 1842–1915?

Philosophy: A route of many roads leading from nowhere to nothing. One of the definitions from *The Devil's Dictionary*

The eccentricity in Bierce's life and works begins with his name. His father Marcus Aurelius gave all his children (of whom Ambrose was the tenth) names beginning with 'A'. Ambrose was, perhaps, lucky not to get 'Aristodemus'. Bierce Sr could trace his pedigree back to the American Revolution. The family had long-established maverick political views. Ambrose was born in Ohio but brought up in Indiana. He earned his first dollar working on an abolitionist newspaper, *The Northern Indianan*. For a short period in his late youth he attended the Kentucky Military Institution, and on the outbreak of the Civil War, Bierce enlisted, serving as an engineer. He saw action in a number of bloody battles and was wounded; on another occasion he was captured and escaped. This inspired 'An Occurrence at Owl Creek Bridge' (1890), his best-known short story. It opens with Peyton Farquhar, a Confederate spy, being sentenced to death by hanging. The opening is done in Bierce's masterly sketch-stroke fashion:

> A man stood upon a railroad bridge in northern Alabama, looking down into the swift water twenty feet below. The man's hands were behind his back, the wrists bound with a cord. A rope closely encircled his neck. It was attached to a stout cross-timber above his head and the slack fell to the level of his knees. Some loose boards laid upon the ties supporting the rails of the railway supplied a footing for him and his executioners – two private soldiers of the Federal army, directed by a sergeant who in civil life may have been a deputy sheriff.

As Peyton drops, however, the rope breaks. He swims away, bullets pinging into the water around him. He scrambles ashore, evades capture and makes his way south – through an increasingly phantasmagoric landscape. Finally he reaches home – his wife, smiling, is waiting to greet him at the door:

> As he is about to clasp her he feels a stunning blow upon the back of the neck; a blinding white light blazes all about him with a sound like the shock of a cannon – then all is darkness and silence!
>
> Peyton Farquhar was dead; his body, with a broken neck, swung gently from side to side beneath the timbers of the Owl Creek bridge.

Major Ambrose Bierce was honourably discharged from the service, a more bitter man than when he had put on his blue uniform, as an idealistic private, in 1861. He went west, where the war had been least traumatic, working as a journalist in San Francisco.

In 1871, Bierce married and in the same year he published his first story, 'The Haunted Valley', in a journal edited by Bret Harte. It was an auspicious start. Bierce's marriage was a 'good' one, as the world judged such things, and brought him money and status. The couple spent some years in England, where he wrote for British papers, and their first two children were born in the country. Bierce returned to San Francisco in 1875, becoming, over time, a senior figure in that dynamic city's newspaper world. In this capacity he formed what would be the most important relationship of his life, with William Randolph Hearst (whom he cordially loathed), joining the magnate's *San Francisco Examiner*, in 1887.

At this point, personal troubles crowded on Bierce. He separated from his wife and one son committed suicide; another would later die of drink. Bierce was increasingly obsessed by the 'Octopus' – the railroad barons, notably Collis P. Huntington, whose steely tentacles, he believed (along with other San Francisco writers like Frank Norris), were strangling the West. Over the next few years, during his relationship with Hearst, Bierce produced the vivid, and often savagely anti-war, Civil War short stories, on which his posthumous reputation rests. The bulk of them are collected as *Tales of Soldiers and Civilians* (1891). Bierce's majestic exercise in 'cynicism', *The Devil's Dictionary*, was published in 1906. In his seventies, Bierce toured the Civil War battlefields where he had fought and bled as a young man. He then crossed the border into Mexico and was never heard of again – perhaps he went to fight again in that country's then raging civil war, perhaps simply to die as an 'unknown soldier'.

This final act has crowned Bierce's career with romantic legend (see, for example, Carlos Fuentes's fantasy of the unchronicled Mexican years, *The Old Gringo*, subsequently filmed, with Gregory Peck in the title role.) There are less dramatic hypotheses. Glenn Willeford speculates that: 'Since his best fiction writing had been the war stories, the old writer wanted to obtain more war material in order to continue in his profession. The only way to accomplish that was to go and experience another war.' Less Old Gringo than Old Hack.

FN   Ambrose Gwinnett Bierce
MRT   'An Occurrence at Owl Creek Bridge'
Biog Carey McWilliams, *Ambrose Bierce: A Biography* (1929)

70. Lewis Wingfield 1842–1891

I was told by my lamented friend George Eliot that she would never read critiques. One of Wingfield's Prefaces, dated from the Garrick Club

'The Honble. Lewis Wingfield', as he insisted on being credited on his title pages, is living, and travelling, proof that interesting lives can result in interesting – if not necessarily great – fiction. Most great fiction, as a general rule, is created in a condition of cloistered retreat from what Conrad called 'the destructive element'. But, occasionally, a novelist hurls himself in – and none plunged more recklessly into the element than Wingfield.

Lewis Wingfield was born the youngest son of the sixth Viscount Powerscourt and educated at Eton and in Bonn. He gave up the army at the request of his mother, who feared for his health, though his subsequent career was anything but mollycoddled. During 1865, he was for a while an actor – and throughout life he was fascinated by the question of how Shakespeare should best be staged. As his *ODNB* entry notes: 'Wingfield has left many examples of his eccentric behaviour, such as going to the Derby as a "negro minstrel", spending nights in workhouses, and pauper lodgings, and becoming an attendant in a madhouse. He travelled in various parts of the East and was one of the first Englishmen to journey in the interior of China.' This last visit inspired his novel, *The Lovely Wang* (1887).

Wingfield was stationed in Paris during the siege by the Prussians in 1870, communicating with the *Daily Telegraph* and *The Times* by balloon. For a while he was a painter (renting Whistler's studio) and later a theatrical costume designer – a subject on which he wrote a book which is still consulted. However, Wingfield's health never recovered from a tour with the British Army in the Sudan in 1884.

In the course of this extraordinary life, Wingfield found time to write a dozen novels. They manifest the same brio as do his exploits. *The Curse of Koshiu* (1888) is among the best things he did in fiction. 'A Chronicle of Old Japan', based manifestly on personal acquaintance with the new Japan, it recounts the fall of the House of Hojo, in the fourteenth century. They can claim to be the bloodiest clan in the country's bloody history, as the reader is lip-smackingly informed: 'When the first of the line erected a strong fortress – the Castle of Tsu, which will serve as background to many scenes in this our chronicle, he gave to it a bloody baptism, by burying beneath the foundations two hundred living men.'

The plot is simple, and strong. Two half brothers, Sampei and No-Kami, one the son of a concubine, the other a spouse, head the Hojo family – so strong an entity, that it dominates even the imperial Mikado himself. The history of Japan, as Wingfield observes, is constructed around fraternal strife: in this case, the cause is a woman. The more savage of the brothers, No-Kami, sentences a righteously rebellious farmer, Koshiu, to be publicly crucified with his wife – his children being beheaded in front of him as he dies. It takes place during 'a beautiful and still evening in autumn, with the opalescent sky of crystalline clearness, which so often in Japan, gives us a hint of the infinite.' During the execution, described lingeringly over a whole chapter, Koshiu curses the Hojo. So it comes to pass. The narrative ends with battle, hara-kiri and the destruction of the Castle of Tsu by cataclysmic earthquake. The Hojo are no more.

It is made clear, from numerous asides, that Wingfield is among the very few Englishmen of his time who have actually seen Japan. And, by many decades, the first to describe, for example, the 'hibachi' barbecue. He had also read his sensation fiction. The novel, which is replete with sex and violence, rattles along. As action fiction goes, *The Curse of Koshiu* is quite as good as Fleming's *You Only Live Twice*, or James Clavell's *Shogun*.

Supposedly, W.S. Gilbert came by the idea for *The Mikado* in 1884, when a Japanese sword clattered down from his wall. One may suspect that Wingfield is also in the mix somewhere. He did not, alas, write any novel about his minstrel experiences at the Derby.

FN   Lewis Strange Wingfield
MRT *The Curse of Koshiu: A Chronicle of Old Japan*
Biog *ODNB* (Joseph Knight, revised by J. Gilliland)

71. Henry James 1843–1916

I am that queer monster the artist. Henry James writing to Henry Adams

Henry James Jr was born in New York. Henry James Sr was a religious philosopher in the Carlyle-Emerson mould – something he passed on to Henry Jr's gifted elder brother, William, author of *The Varieties of Religious Experience* (1902). Henry was never much taken with religion. On either side, his grandfathers were emigrants to America who had struck it very rich: in dry goods on his father's side, cotton on his mother's. James's heroes, such as Newman in *The American* (whose wealth comes from we know not where) and Strether in *The Ambassadors* (whose wealth comes from the manufacture of 'a small, trivial, rather ridiculous object of the commonest domestic use', mischievously supposed to be the chamber pot) are similarly placed. Money has to be made before culture can happen.

Henry's upbringing was richly nomadic – a succession of American schools and instructors, fruitfully interrupted by years in Europe. European museums made an indelible impression. His father's comment that he was a 'devourer of libraries' is much quoted and is, manifestly, no exaggeration. He is recorded as already writing stories 'mainly of a romantic kind' in his early teens.

James made an abortive start in law at Harvard in 1862. The Civil War had broken out and two of his brothers took up arms, while he was exempted on grounds of disability. He described how that disability happened in his late memoir, *Notes of a Son and Brother* (1914). He was eighteen and serving as a volunteer fireman. Fighting a fire in a stable, he found himself 'Jammed into the acute angle between two high fences, where the rhythmic play of my arms, in tune with that of several other pairs, but at a dire disadvantage of position, induced a rural, a rusty, a quasi-extemporised old engine to work and a saving stream to flow, I had done myself, in face of a shabby conflagration, a horrid even if an obscure hurt.' The horrid obscure hurt has been interpreted as everything from castration to lumbago.

James published his first stories and critical pieces during a war they in no way reflected and by his early twenties was recognised as a rising author. He made literary friends easily throughout the whole of his life. His conversational charm was legendary and he developed table-talk into an art form. It is recalled vividly by Ezra Pound: 'The massive head, the slow uplift of the hand, *gli occhi onesti e tardi*, the long sentences piling themselves up in elaborate phrase after phrase, the lightning incision, the pauses, the slightly shaking admonitory gesture ... I had heard it but seldom, yet it is all unforgettable.' One can only wish that Thomas Edison had come along with his great invention fifty years earlier.

In 1864 the James family moved to Boston, whose literary milieu was, if anything, richer than New York's. The Boston publisher, James T. Fields, and his *Atlantic Monthly*, were particularly supportive. James was all the while immersing himself in English and French literature and developing his own theories as to how the art of fiction might be just that – an 'art'. In 1868 he published six stories and fifteen critical pieces, chewing away at the problem. He went to England the following year and was taken up by London literary society, though it was not an unmitigatedly happy period. Letters to his brother dwell on the private agonies of constipation – acute at this period and chronic throughout his life (ingenious links have been made with the tortured motions of his prose style).

It was while in England in 1870 that he learned of the death of his cousin, Mary ('Minny') Temple, from tuberculosis. Immortalised as Milly Theale in *The Wings of the Dove* (1902), he was plausibly in love with her. It is recorded that in late life, 'Locked in a drawer in Lamb House, wrapped in silver paper, James kept a photograph of a young woman. Once when Violet Hunt came to visit, James unlocked his treasure and carefully unwrapped it. He touched it as though it were sacred.' There are those who believe his love for woman died with Minny. What seems clear, from fictions such as 'The Lesson of the Master' (1888), is that James thought marriage, and what came with it, deflected the artist. It took the mind off art as it would have taken a monk's mind off God.

He returned to America on Minny's death, mournfully informing a friend, 'It's a good deal like dying.' He came back to England two years later for what would be residence rather than an extended visit. Henceforth he would be, as he told his brother William, 'ambiguous' nationally. Fiction was above nation. The English novel was paralysed, as a genre, in high-Victorian provincialism, and sadly needed its Flaubert. James, as much at home in Paris as London, would supply it. At this period, he produced his first novels with his hallmark 'international theme', *Roderick Hudson* (1875), *The American* (1876–7), *The Europeans* (1878). The 'innocent abroad' comedy, *Daisy Miller* (1879) reveals a lighter comic touch but a vein of anti-Americanism which displeased some transatlantic readers.

As the decade ended, he was creating his most ambitious work to date, *The Portrait of a Lady* (1881) – the James novel about whose achievement there is least critical dispute. Whether he ever achieved as satisfactory a portrait of a man remains a matter of dispute. The novel was well received but a fluent stream of journalism and travel writing still supplied his main literary income. The English and American reading publics were not, en masse, ready for his novels, and this irked him. Already, authoritative commentators like William Dean Howells were hailing him as a 'master' – the hope of the Anglo-American novel. Why could he not bring in enough money to carry that mission through? His friend George du Maurier, before writing it himself, offered him the plot of *Trilby*, which James declined. He was not *that* desperate. None the less he looked enviously at the thousands Svengali brought its 'inartistic' creator, and the tens of thousands *Robert Elsmere* brought his humble devotee, Mrs Humphry Ward.

Disastrously, he decided to try the stage where novelists like J. M. Barrie were coining it. This effort culminated in the greatest humiliation of his career at the opening night in London's West End of *Guy Domville* in 1895. He misheard the sarcastic hoots from the auditorium and came on stage to render himself a figure of public ridicule. The exquisite humiliation forms the central episode in David Lodge's 2004 novel, *Author, Author*. The spectacular failure of *Domville* marked what Philip Horne calls 'the return to fiction' and James's 'major phase'. He regrouped energetically. He bought and used a bicycle, employed secretaries (the redoubtably named Mary Weld and Theodora Bosanquet), switched to a more aggressive literary agent, and took up permanent residence at Lamb House, in Rye. When in London, he would stay at the Reform Club (whose politics were close to his own). In 1898 he published what is his most-read work today, *The Turn of the Screw*. A ghost story for the Christmas fireside, it demonstrates James's guiding principle that it is not what is narrated, but how it is narrated which creates effect. This thesis is raised to its highest refinement in *What Maisie Knew* (1897).

As the new century opened, he shaved off his beard – creating an anachronistically youthful look – and set to with his most ambitious fiction: *The Wings of the Dove* (1902), *The Ambassadors* (1903), and *The Golden Bowl* (1904). This last, he told his American publisher, was 'the most *done* of my productions – the most composed and constructed and completed'. Having demonstrated in these novels what fiction should be, he defined the topic in the hugely innovative 'New York Edition' of his works, whose prefaces constitute a critical statement of Johnsonian authority.

This Edwardian era is the highpoint of James's literary career. Thereafter deteriorating health brought him down. His last years were loaded with honours: an honorary doctorate from Oxford in 1912, an Order of Merit in 1916. He was roused into patriotic fury by the Great War and took British citizenship in July 1915, largely as a protest against America's remaining neutral as European civilisation went under. In late 1915 he suffered a stroke, greeting 'the distinguished thing', imminent death, with a typically stylish phrase. He died a few months later and, at his own request, was cremated at Golders Green. The family smuggled his ashes back to America. He left less than £9,000.

Over the last few decades, Henry James's sex life has been a topic of intense academic speculation. The most solidly supported thesis is that drawn by the authoritative (but nowadays much controverted) biographer, Leon Edel. In 1905, a doctor recorded, privately, that James had a 'low amatory coefficient'. This odd locution has been glossed as referring, delicately, to the size of the master's *membrum virile*; or, perhaps, his low, or non-existent, sex drive. That minimal drive, Edel grants, may have been directed to his own sex – but was sternly unconsummated. Whether he was a 'queer monster' or not remains a moot point and probably forever will be.

FN   Henry James
MRT   *The Portrait of a Lady*
Biog   L. Edel, *Henry James: A Life* (1985); Philip Horne, *Henry James: a Life in Letters* (1999)

72. Bram Stoker 1847–1912

I am Dracula, and I bid you welcome ...

Little of interest is to be found in the first thirty years of Stoker's life. He was born the middle child of seven in Dublin. His father was a civil servant at the 'Castle' – the HQ of Irish colonial administration. Bram's birth coincided with the 'Great Hunger' and mass emigration from Ireland – themes which ingenious critics have woven into *Dracula*. The Protestant middle classes, for whom the potato was a side-dish, were insulated from the peasants' suffering. Bram's father was twenty years older than his wife Charlotte, and it was she who sowed the seed of literature in her son. She had ample time to do so. Little 'Bram' (so nicknamed to distinguish him from his namesake father) was bedridden with a mysterious ailment for the first seven years of his life. Put another way, he was longer than most children sucking at the mother's breast. Thereafter, he grew strong, shining at Trinity College, Dublin, in the debating hall, classroom, and on the sports field. On graduation, Bram followed his father into the Castle. His career there was rapid: by 1877 young Stoker had risen to the post of Inspector of Petty Sessions. He could think of no young man, Abraham Stoker Sr complacently noted, who had risen so fast.

Photographs confirm Bram to have been strikingly handsome; the epitome of the manly 'red Irishman'. Two events transformed his life in 1878. He married the wispily beautiful Florence Balcombe in that year, winning her hand from a mortified Oscar Wilde. It may be that Bram had the more winning smile: his rival had what Florence saw as 'curly teeth'. The other event involved the theatre. From childhood, Bram had been stage-struck. Henry Irving's touring company played Dublin regularly in the mid-1870s. Stoker, a confirmed Irvingite, wrote an admiring review of the actor's Hamlet, in 1878. It was well received. The young civil servant was summoned to Irving's suite at the Shelbourne where the two men talked until daybreak. The next evening, Stoker was informed that the Great Man had a 'special gift' for him. It turned out to be a recitation of Thomas Hood's melodramatic poem 'The Dream of Eugene Aram'. At the end of his performance, Irving tore off his necktie and collapsed in a swoon. 'The recitation was different, both in kind and degree, from anything I ever heard,' Stoker recalled. His own response he described as 'hysterical'.

Irving impulsively invited Stoker to be his 'stage manager' (his Renfield, as commentators like to jest – or, perhaps, his Harker?). Bram's father was horrified. Was there, commentators have wondered, physical seduction? Stoker was a confessed Whitmanite. On American theatrical tours, he made a point of throwing himself at the feet of the great poet. Whitman's 'inversion' was an open secret. We may ask but will never know: Stoker's private life is a locked cabinet. One biographer, Daniel Farson, a remote descendant, plausibly deduces that after the birth of one child, Irving Noel, Florence withdrew conjugal access, protecting the Dresden-china looks which, even ten years later, led George du Maurier to rank her as one of the three most beautiful women in London. Farson believes that Stoker resorted to actresses and prostitutes and contracted syphilis; something that speculation can link with the infectious vampiric kiss.

The fact is, there is a tantalising blankness in the twenty years of Stoker's manly (but what kind of manly?) prime. Either the cabinet is empty, or – as a trained keeper of documents – he expertly covered his tracks. What does survive is the record of his efficient factotum service to Irving. The Lyceum would never have dominated the London theatrical world as it did without Stoker behind the scenes. As Irving's particular friend, Stoker dined and hobnobbed with the age's celebrities: Wilde (who forgave him Florence), Ellen Terry, Whistler, Conan Doyle and Hall Caine (the beloved 'Hommy-Beg', to whom *Dracula* would be dedicated). And for six years in the 1890s, he worked and researched a work provisionally entitled 'The Un-Dead'. Eventually he came round to the Wallachian word for 'devil', Dracula.

Stoker boned up on Transylvania in the British Museum. Other sources of the novel were nearer to hand, notably fellow Irishman Joseph Sheridan Le Fanu's *Carmilla* (1872). What Stoker brought to vampirology was the frisson of his 'master' Irving's hypnotic stage presence, most spectacularly displayed in his performance as Mephistopheles in *Faust*. Du Maurier's sinister Svengali is also there somewhere. Stoker himself nodded towards Jack the Ripper as a topical inspiration. The fact is, so opaque are *Dracula*'s symbolisms, that one can read virtually anything into them – and critics have.

Two events combined to alter the course of Stoker's life in 1897. One was the completion of *Dracula*; the other the burning down of the Lyceum warehouse, with all the company's props and wardrobe. Irving refused to stage, or even read, the dramatic adaptation of *Dracula* which Stoker had prepared (for copyright reasons). He affected to think poorly of his protégé's novel. It was wounding. The novel was in the event not an overwhelming sales success and would not take off as an international bestseller until the 1930 screen version, *Nosferatu*, made it a goldmine – though not for Irving, nor for Stoker's widow, Florence, who survived him by twenty-five years, most of them tormented by *Dracula* copyright squabbles.

Stoker was no longer necessary to Irving after the Lyceum closed in 1902. The actor, disabled by a series of strokes, died three years later. Whether it was syphilis or not, Stoker's last ten years were difficult. He too suffered strokes and chronic poor health but, none the less, forced himself to turn out six 'shockers', none of them in the same class as *Dracula*. Everyone, it is said, has one novel inside them. Would they were all as good as Stoker's.

FN   Abraham Stoker ('Bram')
MRT   *Dracula*
Biog   B. Belford, *Bram Stoker: A Biography of the Author of 'Dracula'* (1996)

73. Grant Allen 1848–1899

Don't take to literature if you've capital enough in hand to buy a good broom.

Grant Allen was born in Ontario, Canada, where his father was a clergyman of the Irish Church, who had emigrated in 1840. His mother was Scottish. In 1861, the family moved to Connecticut, in the USA, where the sons were taught by a tutor from Yale. It was in the bitter North American winter that Allen had an experience which, he later claimed, shaped his view of the human condition. Skating on a frozen pond, the ice cracked and he was trapped beneath its translucent shelf: he 'died' and was resuscitated. Thereafter, when the question of death came up, Allen would say, 'I have been there', explaining, bleakly, 'there is nothing there'.

After a year broadening his mind in France, Allen went as a prize scholar to Merton College, Oxford, graduating in 1871. Here he became an 'evolutionist' – Darwin filled the hole where his father's God had once been. Allen then made the mistake of marrying early and for love, which prevented any Oxbridge career. When his wife died prematurely, he turned to school-teaching and in 1873 he took up a chair of philosophy at a newly founded Government College in Jamaica, intended to provide higher education for West Indian blacks. The scheme failed.

On returning to England in 1876, Allen made writing his profession – princi-pally on science, evolution and the teachings of Herbert Spencer. In 1884 he gath-ered into a volume several 'Strange Stories' casually contributed to magazines under the pseudonym 'J. Arbuthnot Wilson'. A preface relates how the author 'by trade a psychologist and scientific journeyman' had strayed into the 'flowery fields of pure fiction'. The flowers pleased. Allen turned to and produced some thirty novels in various genres (science fiction, detective novels, sensation novels) over the next fifteen years, under his own name and using a battery of pseudonyms. The novels were remunerative, but he never thought much of them. His story *What's Bred in the Bone* (1891) won a £1,000 prize from *Tit-Bits*, in 1891, which was the largest windfall of its kind received by any Victorian fiction writer.

Allen, whose brain never stopped fizzing, contributed to the evolution of the detective story and was also among the first writers to create female detectives, with his stories centred on the Girton girl, Miss Cayley, and the nurse-detective, Hilda Wade. But the most spectacularly popular of Allen's titles was the 'New Woman' novel-with-a-purpose, *The Woman Who Did* (1895), whose massive sales helped set up the firm of John Lane, which later evolved into Penguin Books. The 'woman who did' is Herminia Barton, who declines to marry, on ethical principles, and nobly lives in flagrant sin. She comes to a tragic (but 'stainless') end. The novel offended both middle-class readers and, emanating as it did from a male hand, rather confused chauvinistic feminists.

Allen died of malarial complications – perhaps picked up in the Caribbean. On his deathbed, he dictated a last Hilda Wade episode to his friend and physician, Arthur Conan Doyle, creator of Holmes and a firm believer in communication beyond the veil with the somewhere-still-living dead. His death, Allen once said, was of 'utter physical indifference to him'. He had, as he said, already been there and experienced its nothingness. He did not anticipate continuing any relationship with his friend. Mr Doyle would rap on the table in vain as far as Mr Allen was concerned.

FN   Charles Grant Blairfindie Allen
MRT   *The Woman Who Did*
Biog P. Morton, *'The busiest man in England': Grant Allen and the Writing Trade, 1875–1900* (2005)

74. Richard Jefferies 1848–1887

O beautiful human life! Tears come in my eyes as I think of it. So beautiful, so inexpressibly beautiful! From *The Story of My Heart*

The writer destined to be England's greatest naturalist-novelist was born near Swindon, in Wiltshire. His father was a farmer in a small way, with forty acres, but unluckily was bankrupted in 1877, and ended up as a jobbing gardener. James Luckett Jefferies (1816–96, he outlived his novel-writing son by many years) is immortalised as Iden, in *Amaryllis at the Fair* (1887). Jefferies is thought to have had mixed feelings about his mother, a Londoner – borne out by the depiction of the embittered Mrs Iden.

Richard was educated locally and at Sydenham, in Kent, among aunts and uncles. Aged sixteen, he demonstrated his independence of spirit by running away to France with a cousin. They intended to make their way to Moscow, failing that America. Jefferies finally settled down in Swindon, where he began to write for Wiltshire newspapers, journals and magazines – mainly on local historical and natural history topics. His views were strongly Conservative, and conservationist. In 1867 he suffered severe illness and was never again to be in good health – tuberculosis had, in fact, been diagnosed in his early childhood. He married Jessie Baden, a farmer's daughter, in 1874 and published, partly at his own expense, his first novel, *The Scarlet Shawl*. It was followed by three similar products – all conventionally romantic and aimed at the library market. They made little impression and it was some time before Jefferies could find a publisher for his more sensitive and introspective work, *The Dewy Morn* (eventually published in 1884). In it he finally hit on his distinctive mix of ruminative countryman essay and narrative plot. His essays on rural distress in *The Times* in the early 1870s were influential, and publicised his name which in turn boosted his fiction.

In 1876 he moved to London where his reprinted papers *The Gamekeeper at Home* (1878) and *Wild Life in a Southern County* (1879) were put together and published. The two strands of Jefferies' prose – descriptive essay and fiction – merged, triumphantly in *Wood Magic* (1881). It was followed by the childhood autobiographical novel, *Bevis, the Story of a Boy* (1882) and the spiritual autobiography of adolescence, *The Story of My Heart* (1883) – his masterpiece and a work which Jefferies had been meditating for seventeen years. *After London* (1885) is a visionary work which foresees the end of urban civilisation (after a catastrophe enigmatically called 'the Event') and the final victory of nature over man's depredations. The novel has found much favour with the Gaia school of contemporary ecology.

In 1881 Jefferies' health collapsed. Tuberculosis and a painful fistula (more specifically, numerous unsuccessful operations on it) made writing an agony. The remainder of his life was passed as an invalid, in various health resorts, impecuniously. He none the less refused aid from the Royal Literary Fund, on moral principle. His last works were dictated to his wife, from his deathbed. He died of tuberculosis, at Goring-by-Sea, aged only thirty-eight, leaving his wife and three children virtually penniless.

FN John Richard Jefferies
MRT *After London*
Biog E. Thomas, *Richard Jefferies: His Life and Work* (1909)

75. Robert Louis Stevenson 1850–1894

Let them write their damn masterpieces for themselves ... and let me alone... Stevenson to his friend, peg-legged W. E. Henley, the 'original' of Long John Silver

Stevenson – 'Louis' to his friends and family – was no longer a young man when he finally got round to writing what in later life he proclaimed 'my first book' – by which he meant his first full-length work of fiction. It was, he believed, his destiny. 'Sooner or later', he recalled, 'I was bound to write a novel. It seems vain to ask why. Men are born with various manias: from my earliest childhood, it was mine to make a plaything of imaginary series of events.' His life, as the latest offspring of the 'Lighthouse Stevensons', had not followed its familial destiny. He would not, he resolved, be a marine engineer – as were his grandfather, father and uncles, whose own monuments still stand, many of them, around the treacherous coasts of Scotland (lightless houses nowadays, alas, in these days of satellite navigation).

Brilliant, sickly, hypersensitive (every biography on him has the index entry 'nightmares'), it was not clear what Louis *would* do as he entered adulthood. What he seemed best cut out for was wandering: no nineteenth-century novelist was more footloose. But he had good excuse – from childhood his chest and lungs were chronically weak, and in the pre-antibiotic era, for those who could afford it, travel was the prescribed medicine. In his twenties he had traversed the Cévennes (astride a donkey, named Modestine) and had voyaged as far afield as North America. Stevenson was what the Californians of the time called a 'lunger' – forever in search of the clime which would supply the clean air which in turn might defer the death sentence that hung over him.

Stevenson first ventured into print with travel writing. It did not yield a professional income, but it sharpened his eye and was a useful apprenticeship for the bestselling fiction still to come. And it was not merely a new lease of life for his lungs which Stevenson found in foreign parts. In California, aged thirty, he took to wife an American divorcée (decently nominated 'widow' on the May 1880 marriage certificate) a full ten years older than himself. It was not what his guardians and friends would have advised and some told him so frankly. But in the event Louis chose wisely. Fanny Osbourne (née Van de Grift) would be a second mother, nurse and partner – and from time to time, the shrewdest of literary advisers. It is on record that Fanny, having spent some instructive time in Western mining towns, could roll her own cigarettes and was handy with a pistol.

No one has much cared to pry into what were the sexual relations between Louis and Fanny. There were no children from the marriage, but among her personal baggage Fanny brought a ten-year-old son, Lloyd, by her first husband (the scape-grace ex-confederate soldier, Samuel Osbourne). Lloyd and his Scottish stepfather would be lifelong friends: and, in later life, literary collaborators. *Treasure Island* confirms that they were collaborators, in a sense, from the very beginning of Louis' novel-writing.

Louis returned to his birthplace, Edinburgh, in September 1880, shortly after his hole-and-corner wedding in San Francisco. Relations with his stern father (last of the Lighthouse Stevensons – and disappointed that it must be so) had been fraught. Scottish Presbyterian fathers rarely approve of bohemian offspring with a taste for velvet jackets and *belles lettres* – and even less so when those offspring are financially dependent and in their thirties. None the less, Louis' parents were glad to see their son settling down – even if it was with a pistol-packing, cigarette-smoking foreign woman of mature years. The Edinburgh homecoming was, as one biographer puts it, 'the prodigal's return'. Despite Fanny's being embarrassingly close in age to the senior Mrs Stevenson, the two women found that a mutual concern for Louis meant that they could be civil to each other – although clearly there was a maternal tug-of-love: 'I think it must be very sweet to you', Fanny told her mother-in-law, 'to have this grown-up man of thirty still clinging to you with his child love.' There is acid in the sugar, together with the implied gloat that she, Fanny, now has Louis' 'man love'.

Home again, Louis wrote a play in collaboration with his friend, the one-legged W. E. Henley, about Deacon Brodie – the Edinburgh cabinet maker and, by night, housebreaker, who was eventually hanged (as his fictional descendant, Muriel Spark's Miss Jean Brodie boasts) on a gallows of his own manufacture and, perhaps, buried in one of his firm's patent coffins. The play did not set the Royal Mile aflame, but indicated the wryly morbid drift of Stevenson's mind. Edinburgh was a city Louis loved but whose weather, as he liked to say, did not love him. It was never less lovable than in the historically bad years from 1879 to 1882, whose calamitous summers plunged the whole country into agricultural distress and a decade of pervasive, Hardyesque, gloom. The summer months of 1881, when *Treasure Island* came into being, were particularly 'atrocious' – 'worse than March' (Scottish March, one should add). Fanny and Louis did not have the funds to wander far, but Edinburgh – 'auld reekie' – had been pronounced by doctors to be hazardous for the invalid's chest.

The cottage of a recently deceased spinster lady ('the late Miss MacGregor') was leased for them in Braemar from 1 August. The Highland air was smoke-free and the area, thanks to Queen Victoria's nearby Balmoral, had become very fashionable. The Stevensons would see the monarch occasionally, accompanied by 'red nosed ladies in waiting'. Rail communications with Edinburgh, via Aberdeen, were excellent: Louis' parents could drop by regularly, and did. The cottage was spacious enough for thirteen-year-old Lloyd Osbourne to spend his school holidays with them and even have his own room which, aspirant artist that the lad was, he could call his 'studio'.

It could have been idyllic, but it was, Louis confided in a letter, 'hell', largely because the weather was 'absolutely and consistently vile'. Confined to the house, he and Fanny resolved to concoct ghost stories (perhaps they fancied the 'late Miss MacGregor' was reluctant to depart her property and 'walked'). It seems plausible that Poe was to hand and that Stevenson refreshed his acquaintance with 'The Gold Bug' – undigested lumps of which resurface in *Treasure Island*. It is similarly plausible that Lloyd, whom Fanny recalls as being 'difficult', passed rainy days reading Marryat, Ballantyne, Kingston and Henty – children's adventure stories (frequently enough featuring desert islands and pirates) which Stevenson still loved. All these would eventually fuse, seamlessly, into the fabric of *Treasure Island* (1883). As he later recalled, however, Lloyd found drawing as welcome a pastime as reading. With his shilling tin of paints, he whiled away wet afternoons creating pictures to display in his 'gallery'. As Stevenson recorded, in mid to late August, when tired of writing or reading:

> I would sometimes unbend a little, join the artist (so to speak) at the easel, and pass the afternoon with him in a generous emulation, making coloured drawings. On one of these occasions, I made the map of an island; it was elaborately and (I thought) beautifully coloured; the shape of it took my fancy beyond expression; it contained harbours that pleased me like sonnets; and with the unconsciousness of the predestined, I ticketed my performance 'Treasure Island'... as I paused upon my map of 'Treasure Island,' the future character of the book began to appear there visibly among imaginary woods ... The next thing I knew I had some papers before me and was writing out a list of chapters.

The map, Stevenson tells us (once told, we can never see it differently) resembled 'a fat dragon standing up'. The fat dragon unleashed the novelist within. After batting piratical fancies to and fro with Lloyd, a tale sprang, effortlessly, from his pen at the rate of a chapter every morning. Other more serious writing chores were suspended. Louis would, he tells us, read aloud the day's instalment 'after lunch' to the family. Desert island as dessert. Later chapters were read in the evening, after the candles were brought in. His voice, said Fanny, was 'extraordinarily thrilling'. A visiting man of letters, Alexander Hay Japp, was privileged to hear the evening instalment and carried off the manuscript to London and publication.

Thereafter, Stevenson never stopped thrilling readers – most of all with *The Strange Case of Dr Jekyll and Mr Hyde* (1886). Seven years later he, Fanny and Lloyd settled in Samoa, in the South Seas, where the sun shone. It was, however, Scottish rain that made him a novelist.

FN   Robert Louis Stevenson (born 'Lewis Balfour')
MRT *Treasure Island*
Biog J. C. Furnas, *Voyage to Windward: The Life of Robert Louis Stevenson* (1952)

76. Mrs Humphry Ward 1851–1920

If only there were more respectable geniuses. Mrs Ward complaining about ubiquitous literary immorality to her son, Arnold

A quiz:

1. Which novelist stopped British women getting the vote for ten years?
2. Which British novelist pioneered the children's play centre system in Britain?
3. Which British novelist was instrumental in inducing America to enter the war against Germany in 1917?
4. Which novelist was instrumental in bringing down the hegemony of the circulating libraries in 1894?
5. Which woman was the most richly remunerated 'serious' novelist of the nineteenth century?

The answer to all of the above is 'Mrs Humphry Ward' – a 'chattel' name she was proud to bear but which has always made later admirers (alas, few of them) as uneasy as would, for example, 'Mrs Leonard Woolf'.

Mary Arnold was born in Hobart, Tasmania. Her father, Thomas Arnold, was an inspector of schools who had emigrated in the 1840s out of missionary idealism; and her uncle was the poet Matthew Arnold. Her Arnold lineage was among the most powerful yet vexatious elements in Mary's later career. A famous cartoon by Max Beerbohm shows her as a schoolgirl, standing in front of her ironically leering uncle, with the caption: 'Why, oh why, Uncle Mat can you not be always *entirely* serious?' She herself had no trouble whatsoever with seriousness. Mrs Humphry Ward ('Ma Hump' to disrespectful contemporaries) incarnated that 'earnestness' about which Oscar Wilde was so flippant. Reading Mrs Ward, Oscar said, was like a meat tea in a Methodist parlour – no green carnations.

Following Thomas's going over to Rome in 1856 the family came over to England. His wife Julia and their three children were temporarily installed at Fox How, the Arnolds' family home in the Lake District, while Thomas went off to Dublin to take up a tutorship secured for him by J. H. Newman at the Catholic University. Thereafter Mary boarded, unhappily, at a succession of schools. She was afflicted with violent headaches and toothaches – for which her sole remedy was dunking her head in a bucket of icy water. Punitive self-discipline was her guiding principle throughout life. In 1865 Thomas Arnold – a man who raised religious 'doubt' to acrobatic heights – converted back to Anglicanism so that he was able to take up a university teaching post at Oxford. Mary was finally reunited with her family in the city she revered.

In July 1872 Mary married a young fellow of Brasenose College, (Thomas) Humphry Ward. Through her husband she acquired influential friends: 'people who counted', in her phrase. In 1873 she was instrumental in setting up the Lectures for Women Committee, which led to the establishment of Somerville College. The Wards had three children: Dorothy, Arnold (the great hope of the family) and Janet. Humphry Ward left academic life to take up a position on *The Times*, as their art critic, in 1881. The family then moved to London where Mary established herself as a literary hostess, in which capacity she became friendly with Henry James in 1882. A trip with James to the theatre led to her first published novel, *Miss Bretherton* (1884), the story of an actress's tribulations and moral growth. It was well received, praised by the 'Master', but sold poorly. None the less she was encouraged to embark on a more ambitious work – *Robert Elsmere*.

After much revision (like George Eliot and *Romola*, the author could have said she entered the novel a young woman, and left it an old woman), Mrs Humphry Ward's drama of religious faith, doubt, religious settlements in 'darkest London' and 'Oxford's agony' was finally published in 1888. It was favourably reviewed by Gladstone (no less) and sold amazingly in Britain and – piratically – in the United States. On the strength of its sales, Mrs Ward secured a record-breaking £7,000 for the American rights of her third novel, *The History of David Grieve* (1892), a work which was held back until that country's signing up to an international copyright agreement. Now rich, Ward bought a large country house, Stocks, in Aldbury in Hertfordshire. Despite alarming collapses in her health, she produced a series of bestselling novels over the next few years. *Marcella* (1894) was her first attempt at a literary heroine, a line continued with *Helbeck of Bannisdale* (1898), which contains a sensitive evocation of her early, fraught, relationship with her father (still dickering between churches, and hopelessly estranged from his cancer-stricken wife).

Ward's philanthropy was practically expressed in the establishment in 1897 of the Passmore Edwards Settlement (named after its principal donor) on the corner of Tavistock Square in Bloomsbury. 'PES', momentously, pioneered the children's play movement in England. The founder's good works are nowadays carried on by the 'Mary Ward Centre', in nearby Queen's Square.

Ward's output of bestsellers continued unabated, although poor health was taking a heavy toll. As the century turned, she could claim to be the second most famous Englishwoman of the Victorian era – she was the one without a crown. The year 1908 would be her pinnacle: in this year she made a triumphant tour of North America where she formed a friendship with her staunch admirer, President Theodore Roosevelt. He was placed in the trophy cabinet alongside Gladstone, her prime-ministerial admirer.

Thereafter, it was downhill. A main cause of distress was the spectacular life failure of her son, Arnold Ward. After a brilliant career at Eton and Oxford, he was elected Liberal Unionist MP for West Hertfordshire in 1910, a seat he held until 1918. But he failed to make any mark and ran up ruinous gambling debts which (ruinous, principally for her) his mother paid off. Her finances thereafter were precarious, not helped by her husband's unlucky speculations in the art market. Catastrophically for her subsequent reputation, Ward consented to head the Women's Anti-Suffrage Association in 1908. The anti-suffragette fiction which followed – *Daphne* (1909) and *Delia Blanchflower* (1915) – triggered a downturn in her popularity which has never been reversed and which accounts for the present oblivion in which her reputation lies. Members of her own family, friends, Somerville College (which she had helped found), and the bulk of those associated with the Passmore Edwards centre were opposed to her political views on women's rights. Her campaigning, however, was indubitably successful in holding back reform until the war (more particularly the wartime need for female labour) made the franchise unstoppable in 1917.

During the years 1914–18, Mrs Ward's authorial fortunes mended somewhat. At the request of Roosevelt, she wrote a work of propaganda for the American market, *England's Effort* (1916), a book which is plausibly credited with helping to bring the United States into the First World War. The war novel *Missing* (1917) and the evocation of the Oxford of her girlhood, *Lady Connie* (1916), are the best fiction she produced in the last phase of her career. But tax demands and Arnold Ward's incessant gaming losses led to Ward finding herself virtually bankrupt in 1919. It was small consolation that she was made a CBE in 1919. By now she was totally disabled by bronchitis, neuritis and heart disease. She died in London, and was buried near Stocks at the church of St John the Baptist, Aldbury, Hertfordshire. Whatever religious 'doubts' she may have had no longer mattered.

FN   Mary Augusta Ward (née Arnold)
MRT *Robert Elsmere*
Biog J. Sutherland, *Mrs Humphry Ward* (1990)

77. Hall Caine 1853–1931

Of all the bores and thick-headed idiots I ever knew, he took the palm. Caine's American publisher

Hall Caine wrote relatively few novels – under a dozen over a forty-year career which began in 1883. But he made a fortune out of lavish stage productions of his work, and, late in his life, film adaptations. Hall Caine was the only Victorian novelist to stalk through movie sets, giving horse's-mouth advice to the players and director. Virtually the whole of the Isle of Man – whose Prospero he was – served as location sets for films of his books. Alfred Hitchcock's last silent film, *The Manxman* (1929), was shot under the beady eye of the great author. The novel featured, as its proud author proclaimed, 'the clash of passions as bracing as a black thunderstorm'. Hitch thought the narrative 'banal' and literary history has agreed with the movie man, not the Manxman.

Hall Caine is the avatar of Samuel Smilesism. No writer self-helped himself to a higher pitch of public eminence – not even Dickens. The poem that fired Caine's juvenile literary ambition was 'Kubla Khan'. He came across it, aged fifteen, in the 'free' Liverpool Public Library (that, he liked to say, was one of his 'universities'; the other was the 'London streets'). Caine himself would live his last decades in a pleasure dome of his own creating – Greeba Castle, on the Isle of Man, from whence he would sweep down, like royalty, in his yellow Rolls-Royce, as the local population gawped deferentially.

But there had been no limousines for the young Thomas Henry Caine. He was born on a flat-bed cart as his family rumbled along to Runcorn with all their household goods. His father was a displaced Manxman. A blacksmith by trade, John Caine had retrained as a shipwright, eventually settling in Liverpool, where Tom, the eldest child, was brought up. A bright boy, with a huge cranium, he was chronically nervous, and – at five foot on tiptoe – diminutive. In later life he insisted on being photographed seated, or standing on steps. His physique precluded following his father into the shipyard: he could no more have done that than Bert Lawrence could have swung a pick alongside his father down the mines.

Tom Caine had one advantage as he started the great adventure of life: a fanatically devoted mother. Like Lawrence, it was his mother who nurtured his love of books, and it was Sarah Caine's maiden name, 'Hall', that he would adopt, erasing the paternal 'Tom', in the years of his fame. The mark of 'Caine' he could not erase. He left school at fourteen, and went to work in an architect's office, becoming a stalwart of working men's self-help clubs. Powerful people liked him. A formative event was his early friendship with Henry Irving and the great actor's factotum, Bram Stoker, who would later dedicate *Dracula* to him (one of the few occasions readers nowadays come across Caine's name). From Irving's grandiose theatrics, he derived a sense of melodramatic grandeur along with a super-heated reverence for Shakespeare. His later, 'great' work was composed at a desk under a bust of the bard. It was one of Caine's foibles to look like the Droeshout engraving of Shakespeare. The bald pate was supplied by nature, early in life. On one occasion, an ocean liner barber carelessly overtrimmed the Bardic beard. Caine skulked in his cabin for days, until regrowth made it possible for him to again face the world as Shakespeare redux.

Even more formative than the Irving and Stoker connection was his relationship with Dante Gabriel Rossetti. It began with a highly intelligent fan letter in 1879 when Rossetti was in the last years of a spectacularly dissipated life. He was lonely, suffused with guilt over the suicide of his wife, Elizabeth Siddal, and sodden with drugs. Caine was taken into the house as the poet-painter's personal assistant, the previous holder of the post having left in a huff over salary. One of his (unwilling) duties was to administer doses of chloral that would have killed less addicted employers. Caine did his work loyally over the last two years of Rossetti's wretched life.

His career in fiction began with the dark Cumbrian tale, *The Shadow of a Crime* (1885). Set in the post-Civil War period, and larded with a dialect which sounds as if it were devised by Professor Stanley Unwin (e.g. 'I'll toitle him into the beck until he's as wankle as a wet sack'), it reaches its peak in a 'tremendous' episode: the 'peine forte et dure' for the hero who, for excessively noble reasons, refuses to plead in a case of murder and must, himself, be judicially murdered. One can picture Caine's successive million sellers as a forever expanding blimp, which never quite burst: *A Son of Hagar* (1886), *The Deemster* (1887), *The Bondman* (1890), *The Scapegoat* (1891), *The Manxman* (1894), *The Christian* (1897). The Caineman marched on, inexorably, through ever more grandiose scenery. The culminating point was *The Eternal City* (1901), set in Rome. It climaxes, after some superheated melodrama, with a vision of 1950 and a utopian republic whose charter is the Lord's Prayer. As one curmudgeonly reviewer put it, 'to enter Mr Caine's city is rather like plunging into a vast cauldron of primitive hotch potch'.

Beneath the gigantic papier mâché constructions of his fiction lies one radioactive biographical fact. The story begins in 1882, shortly after Rossetti's death. Caine was living in digs in Clement's Inn, London, with a pal, Eric Robertson, who was studying for the law. He was at a loose end. As his biographer records:

> In the evenings the young men had a meal sent in from a coffee shop ... The food was brought by two girls who worked there, one of them called Mary Chandler ... The bomb fell one evening in September [1882]. Instead of the girls with their meal the two fathers, or in the case of Mary Chandler the stepfather arrived. Their daughters, they claimed, had been ruined. When did the young gentlemen intend to make honest women of them? ... Mary Chandler [b. May 1869] was just 13.

According to Caine's biographer, nothing more than 'a bit of flirting' had taken place. And even if more had, the age of consent for girls – until 1885 – was thirteen. Humbert Humbert's heaven. None the less, Caine accepted responsibility. Mary was dispatched to Sevenoaks to be educated. She conceived their first child in August 1883 at just fourteen. Caine registered the child as 'Ralph Hall', lying about his and Mary's ages. He eventually married her, in 1886, in Scotland – again lying about key details on the certificate. They had a second, legitimate child and remained married for the rest of their lives.

Curtains such as that shrouding the private life of Hall Caine rarely part, and then only for the briefest of glimpses. But the rule is, we should always assume there is more, buried in the underlay of fiction, than will ever meet the biographical eye – however piercing.

FN   (Sir) Thomas Henry Hall Caine
MRT   *The Manxman*
Biog V. Allen, *Hall Caine: Portrait of a Victorian Romancer* (1997)

78. Sarah Grand 1854–1943

By Suffering made Strong.

Grand was born Frances Elizabeth Bellenden Clarke in Northern Ireland. Both parents were English by birth, her father being a Royal Navy lieutenant assigned to coastguard duties in the province. She gives a sharply observed picture of her child-hood, and its shabby gentility, in the Castletownrock chapters of her novel, *The Beth Book*. In 1861, on the death of her father (who, if the novel is to be believed, was grossly unfaithful to his wife), the remaining family returned to Scarborough, in England. Sarah attended boarding schools, unhappily, and emerged much less well educated than her two brothers. However, this was to be expected – she was a girl.

A nubile girl, as it happened. Aged just sixteen, she was married to Lt-Colonel David McFall. Her husband was twenty-three years her senior, an army surgeon, and a widower with children. The marriage was not a happy one, as Frances was dragged in her husband's train to various postings across the Empire. There was one child, David, born in 1871 – conceived, as the birth date confirms, very early in the union. Thereafter one assumes contraception or a sexually blank relationship. McFall's tyrannous character and the misogynistic branch of medicine he prac-tised in a Lock hospital, for the forcible treatment of incarcerated prostitutes, are portrayed in the character of the wholly hateful McClure in *The Beth Book*. Dan McClure is also a sadistic vivisectionist (as was McFall, one is led to assume), when not forcibly treating women for diseases given to them by men.

Grand began writing the stridently polemical novel *Ideala: A Study from Life* in 1880, although the work was not published until eight years later, at her own expense. The small profits from this first novel allowed her to leave her husband, whom she evidently loathed, in 1890, and decamp with her young son to London, where she supported herself by writing. The author had by now changed her name to 'Sarah Grand' so that she could write more freely than she could as 'McFall'. The marital owner of that name, none the less, must have writhed if he ever read her fiction.

Her reputation was made by the scandalous *The Heavenly Twins* (1893). One publisher who was shown the manuscript turned it down because of the syphilis theme (the unlucky heroine, thanks to a venereally rotten husband, delivers a baby which resembles 'a speckled toad'). Another publisher, under the advice of George Meredith, turned it down as 'too clogged with ideas'. Ironic, since Meredith himself wrote novels famously clogged with verbiage. When it was eventually published, under the imprint of the *Guardian* newspaper office, very unusually, *The Heavenly Twins* sold 20,000 copies and was reprinted six times in its first year. It made its author close on £20,000. Meredith should have been so lucky.

Four of Grand's polemical 'New Woman' novels: *Ideala* (1888), *A Domestic Exper-iment* (1891), *The Heavenly Twins* (1893) and *The Beth Book* (1897) are influential feminist works to this day. She is credited with inventing the term 'New Woman'. Opponents like Mrs Lynn Linton called them 'the shrieking sisterhood' but Grand's heroines do not merely shriek. They find employment, flee the shackles of marriage, believe in 'rational' dress (no crinolines, bustles or corsets), commit guiltless adultery, or live defiantly, in sin, or with lesbian partners. In a fighting preface to *Ideala*, Grand defended her combativeness with the assertion: 'Doctors spiritual must face the horrors of the dissecting room.' She believed that men – not women – with VD should be imprisoned and injected with arsenic, the sovereign pre-antibiotic treatment. Open discussion about venereal infection, and the protection of women from it, was her lifelong campaign.

Grand in fact lived a very long life but wrote (or chose to publish) relatively little, although she lectured widely on progressive topics dear to her. After her husband's death in 1898, she lived in Tunbridge Wells where she was President of the local branch of the Suffragette Societies. In 1920 she moved to Bath, where she lived with a woman friend, and was subsequently mayoress of the city on six occasions. Born during the Crimean War, she lived long enough to have her house destroyed by a German bomb, during the Blitz. In *Who's Who*, Grand slyly entered her principal recreation as 'sociology'. 'Venereology' would, presumably, not have been printable.

FN   Sarah Grand (Frances Elizabeth Bellenden McFall; née Clarke)
MRT *The Beth Book*
Biog A. Heilmann, *New Woman Strategies: Sarah Grand, Olive Schreiner, Mona Caird* (2004)

79. Marie Corelli 1855–1924

I never married because I have three pets at home that answer the same purpose as a husband. I have a dog that growls every morning, a parrot that swears all afternoon, and a cat that comes home late at night. Corelli's spinster credo

Corelli's is the most spectacular of posthumous nose-dives. Until her death in 1924, she held her place as Britain's best known and most notorious bestselling novelist. Works like *Barabbas* (1893) – with its feisty heroine Judith Iscariot (does the stupid woman think 'Iscariot' is a surname, like 'Fotheringay'? asked reviewers) – clocked up cumulative sales of over a quarter of a million at unprecedented speed. Hot cakes didn't come into it. At her zenith in the late 1890s, publishers were elbowing each other out of the way to offer Corelli advances of £10,000 per book. Sixteen years after her death, her annual royalty cheques amounted to £28.

Marie Corelli's fiction extends to her name ('Madonna of the little heart') and the pedigree behind it. She was born plain Mary Mills, in Bayswater, London, the bastard daughter of Charles Mackay, third-rate novelist and second-rate journalist. Her mother was a servant girl, Mary Ellen Mills. Unrated. Six years after Mary's birth, Mackay made an honest woman of her mother. 'Minnie Mackay', as she was now called (although still by law illegitimate), was ill educated but fearsomely bright. In 1876, her mother died and Bertha Vyver, a childhood friend, joined the Mackay household. Initially a companion, she became Mary's closest friend, and probably her lover. With Vyver's help (she was the daughter of a countess) Minnie devised more exciting names than those her background had bequeathed her – with a view to a career in music. Programmes listed 'Rose Trevor' and the more exotic 'Marie di Corelli'. It was a metamorphosis: from below-stairs bastard to concert-hall butterfly.

Music, alas, proved too hard, and in the mid-1880s, she turned to fiction. In 1886, George Bentley, against the advice of his reader, Hall Caine (who, even at this early stage, may have sniffed a dangerous rival), published *A Romance of Two Worlds*. Marie was thirty-one, and resolutely claimed to be seventeen: no beauty, she hated being photographed, insisting that the public should have an idealised picture of her. The camera was altogether too unidealistic a device. Her first novel was inspired, Corelli mysteriously claimed, by a 'peculiar psychic occurrence' and was designed to expound 'the gospel of electricity'. That too was somewhat mysterious. Christianity, evidently, had lost its voltage. *A Romance of Two Worlds*, like everything Marie went on to write, was a runaway bestseller, and was devoured by all classes of reader. By mid-career she had even recruited Queen Victoria as a fan. For Gladstone, she was a writer in the Martin Tupper class, if less godly – Christian godly – than his particular favourite, Mrs Humphry Ward. The Prince of Wales was an admirer of the spiffing little authoress and Marie returned the compliment by introducing 'HRH' into her fiction more frequently than was strictly tasteful.

Professionally, the move from George Bentley to Methuen with *Barabbas: A Dream of the World's Tragedy* in 1893 was momentous. It was the bestselling of all her bestsellers. Together with Hall Caine's *The Manxman* and Mrs Humphry Ward's *Marcella*, Methuen's 6s single-volume Corelli titles did for the venerable three-decker, opening a new era in the history of British fiction, in which buyer not borrower was king and Miss Corelli his queen.

Posterity has had great fun with Corelli's absurdities: the 'corrected photographs'; the gondola complete with Venetian gondolier in which she would glide down the Avon to the amazement of her fellow Stratfordians; the platform in her living room at Mason Croft – Shakespeare's house, of course – on which (four-foot-nothing in her silk stockings) she would perch to receive visitors. The liver, almost fatally bisected by the corsets needed to preserve a wasp-waist in middle age. The conviction for food hoarding (i.e. sugar to make jam) during the First World War – the prosecution brought by neighbours who hated her and that damned gondola.

But Marie, too, was a good hater. Whether like her creation, Mavis Clare, she trained her dogs to raven the invariably slashing notices of her novels is not clear. After *The Sorrows of Satan* (1895), her books carried an instruction on their fly-leaves that no review copies would be sent out. If the hacks wanted her novels, the swine could buy them full-price from the bookshop like everyone else. The reviewers kept slashing and the novels kept selling by the hundred thousand. She loathed the 'New Woman' ('tomboy tennis-players and giantesses') and nurtured messianic delusions, buoyed up by her phenomenal success. In *The Master Christian* (1900), availing herself of the millenarian moment, Corelli addressed all the churches of the world 'in the name of Christ' and instructed them on how to put their holy houses in order. Alas, the £28 royalty cheque and oblivion were just over the horizon.

FN   Marie Corelli (Mary Mackay)
MRT   *The Sorrows of Satan*
Biog E. Bigland, *Marie Corelli: The Woman and the Legend* (1953)

80. Lady Florence Dixie 1855–1905

She is made of the heroic stuff that knows not what defeat means. Women's Penny Paper on Lady Dixie

Florence Douglas was born in Cummertrees, Dumfriesshire, the youngest daughter of the eighth Marquess of Queensberry. The family history was tragic and incorrigibly dissolute: her father committed suicide (by shotgun) as did her twin brother (by knife) in 1891. Her eldest brother was the brute who accused Oscar Wilde of being a 'somdomite' [sic], provoking the trials that, with the treachery of her nephew 'Bosie', destroyed the writer. Florence's upbringing was disrupted at the age of nine when her widowed mother abruptly converted to Catholicism, imposing the faith on her young children and taking them off to Paris. It was an unhappy episode. Meeting her on the Continent, Bulwer-Lytton wrote a poem for the sad young girl, 'Little Florrie Douglas'. Precocious Florrie could write her own verse, thank you very much, Lord Lytton, and published a volume of childhood effusions, under the pseudonym 'Darling'. She went on to publish a bloody dramatic tragedy, *Abel Avenged*, at the age of twenty.

In 1875, aged nineteen, she married Sir Alexander Beaumont Churchill Dixie, nicknamed 'Beau' for his good looks. An inveterate gambler and a heavy drinker, he was in severe financial distress within the decade. There were two sons, George Douglas and Albert Edward Wolston, godson of the Prince of Wales. As Lady Dixie, Florence, with her husband, three brothers and a friend, explored 'the unknown wastes of Patagonia' from 1878 to 1879. There she shot, and ate, wild animals and composed a travel book, *Across Patagonia* (1881). She was war correspondent for the *Morning Post* during the Boer conflict of 1880–81, and the only female. Among other causes she agitated for the rights of African Zulus and English women. She believed in, and designed, rational dress, hated the sexually restricting side-saddle, and was an early advocate for women's soccer, becoming President of the British Ladies' Football Club. It is not recorded what her position was – probably striker.

In 1883, Dixie became the focus of sensational news coverage when it was alleged that at Windsor, where she and her husband were living, she had been the target of a dastardly Fenian murder attempt. Doubts as to the veracity of the incident were raised, questions were asked in the House, and Queen Victoria dispatched John Brown to look into the matter. Her faithful Highlander caught a chill while investigating and died. Dixie sent a wreath of African immortelles to his funeral, and insisted her kidnap tale was true. The Queen graciously responded with a Landseer print. The actual facts of the case were never ascertained.

Dixie's first published novel was *Redeemed in Blood* (1889). An absurd melodrama of high life, centred on the marital trials of Lord and Lady Wrathness, the novel has some vivid Patagonian scenes. Dixie's other fiction includes *Aniwee, or, the Warrior Queen* (1890), a tale of the Patagonian Araucanian Indians. Her best-known work is *Gloriana, or, the Revolution of 1900* (1890). In this bizarre fable, Gloria of Ravensdale disguises herself as a boy, Hector D'Estrange (based on Oscar Wilde), attends Eton and Oxford, and eventually gets her/himself into Parliament. The narrative ends with a visionary panorama of a regenerated London as seen from a balloon in 1999.

In 1902, Dixie published a drama in verse on the persecution of women entitled *Isola, or the Disinherited*. Although she was a good shot, a horsewoman and a strong swimmer, she loathed blood sports in later life (whether it extended to boxing, as regularised by her brother's Marquess of Queensberry's rules is not clear). She published a tract on the subject, *The Horrors of Sport* (1891), but she did not mention the big game hunting which had been one of her early passions. Not a lover of the male sex, apparently, she claimed that 'horses and dogs were her best friends'. Her fiction is unremembered, but in the wastes of Patagonia the three-star Hotel Lady

Florence Dixie hospitably keeps her name alive, as do various encyclopaedias of soccer.

FN   Lady Florence Caroline Dixie (née Douglas)
MRT *Gloriana, or, the Revolution of 1900*
Biog *ODNB* (Dorothy Middleton)

81. Olive Schreiner 1855–1920

Ralph Iron.

Schreiner was born in Wittebergen, Basutoland, the sixth of ten surviving children of a Methodist missionary of German origin. Her father, Gottlob Schreiner, had come to the Cape in 1837 under the auspices of the London Missionary Society. Her mother, Rebecca (née Lyndall) was English and of respectable working-class background. She was brought up, as one her biographers puts it, 'in a context of parental, certainly maternal, severity and the brooding presence of a wrathful God'. A precocious girl who wanted above all else 'to be clever, to be wise', Schreiner educated herself and later claimed to have become a free-thinker at the age of twelve, after her little sister Ellie died and God did nothing about it. Her childhood was unhappy, unhealthy (she suffered from lifelong asthma) and unsettled. Gottlob was forced to move to another part of the country in 1869, following accusations of financial impropriety. In 1872 a broken engagement (and perhaps seduction) wounded Schreiner emotionally and coincided with more attacks of her chronic illness.

In 1873 she left her parents' home to live with a sister in Fraserburg. She had medical friends and evidently considered becoming a nurse and possibly a doctor. But her health was not up to such demanding vocations and instead, in 1874, she took up employment as a governess. Over the next seven years, working for a succession of families, she contrived, painfully, to save up the £60 she needed for her passage to England. Now a proclaimed 'heretic' she was alienated from her family (irreparably when, after her father's death in 1876, her mother converted to Catholicism). While a governess Schreiner had begun to write fiction, initially the autobiographical *Undine*. The author came to think ill of this work and it was not published until well after her death, in 1929.

In 1879 she began serious work on the composition of *The Story of an African Farm* (1883), whose heroine Lyndall's experiences are also clearly autobiographical. The novel has surreal moments, for example, when Gregory Rose disguises himself as a female nurse to tend, in physical intimacy, the dying Lyndall, whom he loves. It ends pessimistically and enigmatically. George Meredith, her publisher's reader, helped her revise the manuscript which was published as by the male writer 'Ralph Iron'. The novel attracted praise, attention and confusion. African farming, many baffled rural readers must have felt, was sadly neglected. It went through three editions in its first year.

In the two years' interval between arriving in England and the publication of her novel, Schreiner once again considered nursing. But the success of *The Story of an African Farm* established her as an author and brought her into contact with Eleanor Marx, who was to be a close friend and influential fellow feminist. As a literary celebrity, Schreiner also made the acquaintance of the sexologist, Havelock Ellis, in 1884. The couple had an intimate if strained relationship in which Ellis took it on himself to psychoanalyse Schreiner. His liberated sexual doctrines were wholly at variance with her puritanism but he introduced her to the new ideas transforming English intellectual life – including Fabianism, the literary world's favoured brand of socialism.

At this period Schreiner received an offer of marriage from her doctor, Bryan (later Sir Bryan) Donkin and entered into a long correspondence with Karl Pearson the brilliant mathematician, and later eugenicist, at University College London. Their relationship, like others in Schreiner's life, seems to have broken down just at that point where it might have become sexually physical. Despite the intellectual stimulus, she was always unhappy and chronically unwell in England. Nor could she capitalise on her early success as a novelist. Other than *The Story of an African Farm* the only literary publication to emerge from the London years was a collection of ethereal allegories, *Dreams* (1890).

In 1889 Schreiner returned to South Africa. It was a period of extraordinary political ferment in the country, much of it stirred up by Cecil Rhodes. After an initial infatuation (which may have been based on a close personal relationship), Schreiner became violently disillusioned with the 'Colossus'. This antipathy was heightened by the 1896 Jameson Raid, designed to take over the Transvaal republic for Britain. In the aftermath, which led to the downfall of Rhodes as Prime Minister and led the way to the Boer War, Schreiner wrote *Trooper Peter Halket of Mashonaland* (1897), a polemical allegory. Peter is an English soldier engaged in 'pacifying' Rhodesia for the British South Africa Charter Company. Christ appears to Peter in a vision to upbraid him for the atrocities committed by his comrades.

In 1894 Schreiner had married a politician and ostrich farmer, Samuel Cron Cronwright, a man eight years her junior. The couple went to live in Kimberley where a daughter was born in 1895, dying almost immediately. The experience, despite the overwhelming pain, helped formulate some of the ideas which were to appear in Schreiner's feminist polemic, *Women and Labour* (1911). Cronwright devoted himself to promoting Olive's literary and political career, even adding her surname to his own. During the 1890s and early twentieth century Schreiner was influential in the struggle for women's rights. But by the date of her return to England in 1913, she was exhausted and lonely. Her marriage had all but fallen apart. Cronwright remained farming in South Africa until 1920, when he joined her in London. But a month later she left for South Africa alone, dying there a few weeks later in her sleep. She had asked that her body be buried on a karoo at Cradock in the veldt, with the bodies of her daughter and pet dog. Cronwright did as requested.

FN   Olive Emilie Albertina Schreiner ('Ralph Iron')
MRT   *The Story of an African Farm*
Biog R. First and A. Scott, *Olive Schreiner* (1980)

82. William Sharp 1855–1905

William Sharp defies biography. William Sharp's biographer

A London-based man of letters, William Sharp was, as the world saw him, a man's man. The publisher Arthur Waugh (Evelyn's father) recalls that 'With his Olympian stature, bright complexion, full head of hair, and well-kempt beard, he attracted attention at once, and took good care to retain it. His manner was a mixture of suavity and aggression ... He knew all the big men.' Among whom he too was big and manly. This epitome of manliness none the less created the novelist 'Fiona MacLeod' and passed her off as a real person, as different from William Sharp as boiled beef is from haggis. Fiona, the world was told, was a Hebridean maid who lived and roamed among the hills and burns of her native Iona. Miss MacLeod often promised to appear in public, but never quite did. Sharp arranged for her to have a bona fide entry in *Who's Who*, where her 'Recreations' are listed as 'sailing, hill-walks, listening' – to which might be added, 'pulling (English) legs'. Towards the end of their lives, when Sharp was feeling the pinch, there was the possibility that MacLeod might have got a Civil List pension – thus rendering her creator the first welfare cheat in English literature.

Sharp occasionally intimated that Fiona was a cousin, or a loved one, or both. 'She' wrote sixteen 'mythic novels' with titles like *Pharais: a Romance of the Isles* (1894), *Green Fire* (1896), *The Sin-Eater and Other Tales* (1895). The last, incidentally, is the distant inspiration of a dire 2003 movie, starring Heath Ledger. The story's opening paragraph will give some idea of why MacLeod's effusions might appeal to Hollywood:

> A wet wind out of the south mazed and moaned through the sea-mist that hung over the Ross. In all the bays and creeks was a continuous weary lapping of water. There was no other sound anywhere.
>
> Thus was it at daybreak; it was thus at noon; thus was it now in the darkening of the day. A confused thrusting and falling of sounds through the silence betokened the hour of the setting. Curlews wailed in the mist; on the seething limpet-covered rocks the skuas and terns screamed, or uttered hoarse rasping cries. Ever and again the prolonged note of the oyster-catcher shrilled against the air, as an echo flying blindly along a blank wall of cliff. Out of weedy places, wherein the tide sobbed with long gurgling moans, came at intervals the barking of a seal.

The 'big men' of the Celtic revival – W. B. Yeats, Ernest Rhys, George Meredith, 'The Prince of Celtdom' – were all taken in by Fiona and the barking seals. Sharp never offered any convincing explanation for his deceptions.

As his/her biographer despairingly puts it, around him are a series of 'vacua' – an unresounding emptiness. The shilling facts are barely worth that sum, though MacLeod's might be. Sharp was born in 1855, in Paisley, the son of a prosperous businessman. Holidays in the Hebrides left a lifelong mark and by adolescence, he claimed, 'I had sailed up every loch, fjord, and inlet in the Western Highlands and Isles.' At eighteen, he 'took to the heather', joining a band of gypsies for three months. Thereafter, the prison door clanged shut. First Glasgow University, which he dropped out of, then a lawyer's office. He was released by being transported to Australia for a year, ostensibly for his lungs. It was also the standard way of dealing with offspring who had got a servant pregnant, or done some other embarrassing thing.

He returned, aged twenty-three, to work in a London bank, before becoming a full-time man of letters. He wrote poetry, which was politely admired, and a moderately successful sensation novel. In 1884, he married his first cousin, though there would be no children – and, it is delicately hypothesised, there may have been no sex to produce one. 'Don't despise me,' he once said, 'when I say that in some things I am more a woman than a man.' In 1889, Sharp (under his own name) wrote his best work of fiction, *The Children of Tomorrow*. An 'art novel', it climaxes with the sculptor hero and his lover struck by a single bolt of lightning, their blasted bodies remaining 'so tightly knit that they seemed as one'. Symbolic, perhaps – fused and intergendered.

It was in 1891 that he conceived Fiona MacLeod, coinciding with a trip to Italy and his falling in love with the beautiful Edith Wingate Rinder whom he, and the less impressed Mrs Sharp, met on holiday. Rinder was one of the *noli me tangere* beauties who wafted, breaking hearts on the way, through the Celtic literary coterie. She would be Sharp's Maud Gonne. His wife Elizabeth seems to have borne up under these amorous complications better than him. He came to the brink of nervous breakdown in1897, and died in Sicily in 1905, only fifty years old – psychically exhausted, one assumes, from the effort of bottling two selves in one frame.

FN   William Sharp ('Fiona MacLeod')
MRT (WS) *The Children of Tomorrow*; (FM) *Pharais*.
Biog F. Alaya, *William Sharp – 'Fiona MacLeod', 1855–1905* (1970)

83. L. Frank Baum 1856–1919

Imagination has given us the steam engine, the telephone, the talking-machine, and the automobile. Baum's argument in favour of the fairy story

Lyman Frank Baum was born in New York State, one of nine children of a barrel-maker, enriched in the 1860s by the Pennsylvania oil business – a tin-man of a kind. The Baum family circumstances were comfortable, verging on splendid. Young Frank, timid by nature and afflicted with a chronically weak heart, was prohibited boyish rowdiness and physical activity and would never enjoy robust health. His sheltered upbringing may explain the otherwise odd fact that the central figure in his most famous story is 'Dorothy' not 'Don', 'Dick', or 'Dave'. On the subject of names, he disliked 'Lyman' and went by 'Frank' through life. In his early years he loved fairy stories and developed a passion, with the rest of America in the 1870s, for Dickens whose 'Christmas Books' – notably that about Ebenezer Scrooge's imaginary voyages – made a manifest impression. He was less taken with the German gothic school (the Grimms' tales, specifically), which contained 'horrors'. Easily frightened himself, he believed that children should not be terrified with their bedtime entertainment.

Worried that their son was becoming a cissy, his parents, wrong-headedly, sent him off to a military school. This brought on a heart attack which nearly killed him, and he was educated at home thereafter. His first productions as an author were on a printing press his father bought him. By the age of seventeen he was editing, and producing, his own magazine for fellow philatelists: stamp-collecting was one of his passions. The rearing of fancy chickens, oddly, was another. His favoured breed was the 'Hamburg'. Baum's first book, published in 1886, was entitled: *A Book of Hamburgs: A Brief Treatise upon the Mating, Rearing, and Management of the Different Varieties of Hamburgs.*

A third passion was the stage. Benjamin Baum, his father, was an oil-man, with an interest in theatres in New York and Pennsylvania. Frank's first literary efforts were musical plays which he wrote, directed and starred in. It was on tour that Baum met his future wife, Maud Gage. She was a college student at Cornell when he met her, an ardent feminist, beautiful and strong-minded. The couple married in 1882. The union was happy, although Baum was generally believed to be henpecked. After his marriage he ran the family firm, despite suffering another string of heart attacks. It was a troubled few years. Trade depression and embezzlement had brought the business to the verge of bankruptcy. His father now dead, Frank sold off the Castorine oil company and went west to Dakota where, for a year or two, he ran a general store. In 1890, in another spell of hard times, that business collapsed as well.

Baum tried journalism for a year or two. His provincial newspaper, *The Aberdeen Saturday Pioneer*, was notable for the virulence of its editorials (some written by Baum), arguing for the extermination of the local Sioux Indians – something that has embarrassed his admirers. (In 2006, his descendants issued a formal apology to Native Americans.) Again Baum went bankrupt, and in 1893 the family moved on to Chicago where Frank scraped a living as a travelling salesman, selling crockery. It was his mother-in-law – like her daughter a fervent feminist – who, hearing him tell bedtime stories, advised him to put them into print and make some real money. His first *Mother Goose* book for children came out in 1897. This coincided with another collapse in his health – he could no longer handle the arduous salesman's life. Thereafter, writing for the children's market was his principal activity. To this end he teamed up with the illustrator, William W. Denslow. After a successful run with the 'Goose' tales, they collaborated on the even more successful *The Wonderful Wizard of Oz* in 1900.

It had begun as a story told to his own children. Oz (the name was probably taken from Baum's office filing cabinet, containing his papers 'O–Z') would become, along with Neverland, Wonderland, Narnia and Hogwarts, one of juvenile fiction's most visited territories. The fable, and its successors, made the Baums rich again. On finishing the work (originally called 'The Emerald City'), Baum knew instinctively that he had done something special. He had his pencil framed and placed over his desk under the inscription: 'With this pencil I wrote the manuscript of "The Emerald City".'

Two years later, an 'adultized' stage version came out. Both book and play were sensationally popular. Baum spun off a series of numberless 'Oz' sequels over the following years and was one of the first generation of American writers to adapt his work for the screen, moving himself and his family to Hollywood to do so. In 1914, he founded the Oz Film Manufacturing Company, which was later taken over by Universal Studios. (In Southern California where the family settled, Baum made another name for himself as a grower of prize dahlias.) He died, America's most loved story-teller, after a lingering illness in 1919. His last book, *Glinda of Oz*, came out posthumously.

More people, over the years, have 'seen' *The Wizard of Oz* than have read it – and most have seen it in the MGM 1939 movie version (the eighth) starring Judy Garland. The outline is fairly faithful to what Baum wrote and Denslow pictured. The book was conceived and published during one of the recurrent depressions in American commercial life: one of the points that Baum makes in his 1900 preface is that his story is 'modernized' – set in the uncomfortable present. This realism at the heart of the fantasy is something that makes it an innovative 'fairy story'. The narrative opens on an impoverished Kansas farm, in a bleak landscape. An orphan, Dorothy is cared for by her Uncle Henry and Aunt Em. Her guardians are not unkind but their life is hard. Dorothy's bosom friend – her only friend – is her dog Toto. The bleak Kansas sharecropper landscape of the opening scenes in the film was done in black and white, and Dorothy's dream in blazing Technicolor. The film, released in the same year as John Steinbeck's *The Grapes of Wrath*, has the same background of hardship among farming folk on the plains of America.

Over the last half century, in which *The Wizard of Oz* has become one of the best-known fairy stories in the world, 'deep readers' have got to work on it, with some justification. Baum had been very impressed, in 1894, by a hunger march on the White House organised by the political activist, Jacob Coxey. The unemployed, in their thousands, marched across America to the capital. Eventually 'Coxey's Army' was broken up in Washington and the leaders arrested on charges of 'trespassing on the White House lawn'. The phoney Wizard of Oz has been read as representing the President of America – all talk and no action (in 1900 the President was William McKinley, who was assassinated a year after the publication of *The Wizard of Oz*). On their epic march up the yellow brick road (taken to be an allusion to the gold standard, which Coxey and other populists wanted to get rid of), Dorothy, the farm girl, represents the decent working classes, while the Scarecrow represents the rural poor. The Tin Man represents the toiling masses in the factories. Whatever its political subtexts, *Oz*, particularly after Baum's work came out of copyright in 1969, holds its place as one of the richer franchises in American light entertainment.

FN   Lyman Frank Baum

MRT   *The Wonderful Wizard of Oz*

Biog   F. J. Baum, *To Please a Child: A Biography of L. Frank Baum* (1961)

84. H. Rider Haggard 1856–1925

Mr E. M. Forster once spoke of the novelist sending down a bucket into the unconscious; the author of She *installed a suction pump.* V. S. Pritchett

Henry Rider Haggard was born at West Bradenham Hall, Norfolk, the sixth son of William Meybohm Haggard, a local squire. His mother was an heiress, enriched with East India Company money. In the distant family background there were dashes of Jewish and Indian blood – this has interested modern commentators more than it ever did Haggard. His father ran his estate in feudal not to say tyrannic style and Haggard's later fascination with brutal African chiefs – Twala, Chaka, Dingaan – is easily connected with his childhood servitude. Arriving so late in family life, in a culture dominated by primogeniture, he was less important than brothers who were bought commissions. He was judged stupid and unworthy of the expense of public school: his destiny, his father cruelly observed, was to be a 'greengrocer'. Happily the old brute lived long enough (1893) to see his son the richer man.

When Henry was nineteen, his father pulled strings to enable him to go to South Africa as secretary to Sir Henry Bulwer. Around this time he had fallen madly in love, but his father was not having any imprudent matches. The young fool, it was sternly decreed, could not marry until he had made his way in the world. They were exciting times and South Africa was an exciting place to make his mark. Britain was about to annex the Transvaal from the Boers and the Zulu Wars were raging. Haggard, like the whole nation, was entranced by British gallantry at Rorke's Drift in 1879, and the eleven Victoria Crosses the Queen was pleased to award to her soldiers. It pained the young man that he was a mere pen-pusher in this stirring time, but it made him proud to be an Englishman.

Initially he did very well in Africa. At an unprecedentedly young age he was appointed Master of the High Court in the Traansval. He lived well and took down his share of big game, but in other ways things did not go so smoothly. He rashly gave up his civil service position for ostrich farming and failed to get rich. There were injudicious love affairs, an illegitimate child, and dissipation – he is suspected to have taken African mistresses. There are oblique hints in the fiction – in the dusky beauty Foulata, for example, who, having given her all to her 'lord' (i.e. the Saxon Captain John Good), goes meekly to her death with the universal truth: 'the sun may not mate with the darkness, nor the white with the black.' Not quite true. Mating is one thing, marriage another.

On his return to England in 1879, having given up on Africa, Haggard promptly married a Norfolk heiress, Louisa Margitson. But she was not the woman he wanted.

That young woman, Mary Elizabeth 'Lilly' Jackson, who had been the cause of his going to Africa in the first place, had not – to his chagrin – been prepared to wait and had married a banker. Love denied union is a plot situation which would come up frequently in Haggard's subsequent fiction, most poignantly in *Nada the Lily* (1892), where the heroine dies immured in a cave, her tiny hand – pushed through a crevice – held by a wounded Umslopogaas, unable to free her.

The newly married Haggards returned to South Africa and ostrich farming but the reacquisition of the Transvaal by the Boers forced their departure. Haggard had little time for Dutch settlers, although he liked Zulus. He made the point in his first, stillborn, book, *Cetywayo and his White Neighbours* (1882). The couple had a son, who died aged ten, and three daughters. Haggard was still young and could foresee a costly life ahead of him and no legacy coming his way. Subsequently he trained for the Bar and, although he qualified, never practised. The work, he discovered, did not suit him – nor did London. Two pursuits would preoccupy the second half of his life: writing romance and farming the land – in that order.

Spurred by the ambition to emulate Stevenson's *Treasure Island* (1883), he wrote – in six weeks – *King Solomon's Mines* (1885), which was an immediate hit. Adventure was highly saleable in the mid-80s. A vast generation of keen young readers had been released into literacy by the 1870 Universal Education Act. They gobbled up Haggard's rattling tales insatiably. It wasn't just the adventure. As enticing an aspect of the book is indicated by one of the publishers who turned the manuscript down, in disgust: 'Never has it been our fate to wade through such a farrago of obscene witlessness ... Nothing is likely in the hands of the young to do so much injury as this recklessly immoral book.' The nipples on the Breasts of Sheba and the omnipresent topless Zulu maidens decorating the action strike the modern reader as quaint rather than erotic, whereas in the 1880s they were sexual dynamite. Even more so was the voluptuous Ayesha: Haggard was particularly proud of the ageless 'She-who-must-be-obeyed'. He proudly recalled going to his literary agent and slapping down the manuscript of *She: A History of Adventure* (1887) – another six weeks' labour – with the boast: 'There is what I shall be remembered by.'

Facile with his pen, Haggard turned out fiction by the torrent and everything with his name on it sold. His themes and subject matter varied, moving between gothic, mystic and science-fiction subject matter (in the last of the Quatermain series the hero is a time-traveller, having exhausted Africa's possibilities). He explored other colonialisms, as in *Montezuma's Daughter* (1893). His servitude in law produced the highly readable *Mr Meeson's Will* (1888) where a publisher's last will and testament is tattooed on the heroine's back. Will it stand up in court?

In the years of his fame, the jilt Lilly came back into his life. Her 'prudent' marriage had gone horribly wrong: her husband turned out a cad who infected her with venereal disease, before dying of it and leaving her penniless. Haggard took over the care of her and her family. Out of love? He had always been fascinated by women's fading beauty. It prompts an odd footnote by Horace Holly in *She*. The most beautiful of women on the face of the earth (for 2,000 years!) has suddenly decayed into a 'hideous little monkey frame, covered with crinkled yellow parchment'. Holly, jilted in youth by the only woman he has ever loved because he had no money, muses:

> What a terrifying reflection it is, by the way, that nearly all our deep love for women who are not our kindred depends – at any rate, in the first instance – upon their personal appearance. If we lost them, and found them again dreadful to look on, though otherwise they were the very same, should we still love them?

Did Rider still love the syphilitic Lilly?

Enriched by his books, the Haggards left London for comfortable country life in Norfolk. There he made himself an authority on English agriculture, producing a two-volume survey of *Rural England* in 1902. His political aspirations were foiled when he failed to win East Norfolk for the Unionists in 1895 (like all his class he regarded Ireland as a colonial possession). In the twentieth century he undertook various government missions and was knighted for public service in 1912. Always popular in America (George Lucas would make a fortune out of recycled Haggard in his *Indiana Jones* series), his romances were the favourite reading of President Theodore Roosevelt. He was awarded a KBE in 1919 in recognition of his war work.

He continued writing vivid romances up to his death, elaborating the long-running *She* and *Quatermain* sagas interminably. The last spawned no less than fifteen titles (Allan Quatermain, in his mid-fifties in the first of the series must, one suspects, have dipped a toe in Ayesha's immortalizing Pillar of Fire to have made it to 1927). Haggard was an early exponent of the dictation, secretary and typewriter mode of composition. In his later years he became obnoxiously racist and anti-Semitic, a vein of the prejudice can be traced back to rabbi-hating *She*. He died firmly believing that 'great ultimate war ... will be that between the white and coloured races'. Where are Sir Henry Curtis, Captain Jack Good, and Quatermain the Hunter when we need them?

FN   ('Sir') Henry Rider Haggard
MRT *King Solomon's Mines*
Biog D. S. Higgins, *Rider Haggard: The Great Storyteller* (1981)

85. Joseph Conrad 1857–1924

I think every Conrad story is a movie. Orson Welles

Conrad's reputation has passed through three distinct phases since his death. The first – and most vexatious to him (he was easily vexed) was Conrad the bluff nautical yarn spinner. Texts such as *Youth, Typhoon* and *The Shadow Line* were exalted. He was thought good for schoolboys. The second phase came with F. R. Leavis's including him in the 'Great Tradition' of English fiction, between Henry James and D. H. Lawrence. It refocused attention on the densely notated moral complexities of the narratives. Leavis particularly valued *Nostromo* and *Victory*. With postwar global decolonisation, *Heart of Darkness* was widely prescribed in schools and universities as an enlightening text on the iniquities of imperialism. Conrad's posthumous sales soared, as did a sense of pedagogic self-righteousness. This was reversed with Chinua Achebe's denunciation of the novella in 1973 as the bigoted effusion of a 'bloody racist'. Conrad's reputation plunged. It would be a brave professor in the current climate who would set *The Nigger of the 'Narcissus'* for study.

The philosopher closest to Conrad's heart was Schopenhauer. Life, as the grim German philosopher saw it, is a constant struggle between the mind, which perceives life's pointlessness, and the will, which declines to surrender to that perception. This Schopenhauerian strife explains the otherwise baffling tribute by Marlow to the criminally insane Kurtz, the man who has slaughtered, raped and plundered his way across Africa, making it darker than before: 'It was an affirmation, a moral victory paid for by innumerable defeats, by abominable terrors, by abominable satisfactions. But it was a victory!'

The most haunting image of Conrad's heroic type is the 'Professor' in *The Secret Agent*, his hand forever grasped around the rubber bulb in his pocket. If he presses it, he will blow himself, and all around him, to smithereens:

> He was a force. His thoughts caressed the images of ruin and destruction. He walked frail, insignificant, shabby, miserable – and terrible in the simplicity of his idea calling madness and despair to the regeneration of the world. Nobody looked at him. He passed on unsuspected and deadly, like a pest in the street full of men.

So the novel ends. Alongside Conrad, even the arch pessimist Schopenhauer might seem a trifle Panglossian.

The source of Conradian gloom can be plausibly tracked back to his earliest years. He was born in what is now Ukraine. Poland had been sliced into nonentity by imperial neighbours – Prussia, Austro-Hungary, and, most hatedly, Russia. The country survived only as a romantic cause. Teodor was the only child of Polish patriots of noble descent who sacrificed their lives for that hopeless cause. His father Apollo Korzeniowski (1820–69), a member of the Polish resistance, was arrested in 1862 and deported with his family to exile in the bleak hinterland of Russia. It killed Conrad's mother in three years and his father in seven. 'Consumption' was on the death certificates: it should have been 'Russia'. Apollo – aptly named – died a hero but had achieved nothing – heroically. The first words five-year-old Teodor is known to have written are an inscription on the back of a photograph describing his father as 'a Pole, a Catholic, a nobleman'.

Thus began the strange concoction of a patriotic Slav who became a loyal Englishman: a master of the English language who thought most readily in French but in the delirium of fever babbled wildly in his natal Polish (something recorded vividly in his short story, 'Amy Foster'); a writer who changed his name to 'Conrad' for its English resonance – that being the name of Byron's corsair hero – but which had a private resonance. 'Konrad' was his father's favourite name for him. Orphaned at eleven, Conrad was taken under the wing of a wealthy and indulgent uncle, Tadeusz Bobrowski. From his earliest teens he wanted to go to sea and would not be talked out of this 'Quixotic' ambition, as his displeased guardian thought it. Poland had scarcely more naval tradition than Switzerland. The English nautical novelist Frederick Marryat, mixed with a congenital romanticism, seem to have been responsible for the young man's infatuation with salt water.

At sixteen he left for Marseilles, where he would stay four years picking up whatever maritime jobs came his way. He was a lowly steward, a seaman and, by his own account, a gun-runner. The exact details of this formative period are wholly obscure. But it is recorded that he attempted suicide in 1878 after running up gambling losses in Monte Carlo. He fired at his heart; the bullet went 'through and through', but missed. He would never be good with money. If women came into it, posterity will never know.

The French authorities were sticklers about marine qualifications, but Britain was less strict about who sailed under the Red Duster. Conrad, moreover, saw England as the only country in the world whose flag offered 'true liberty'. Over the following sixteen years he worked his way up through the ranks of the British merchant marine until he gained his first command in 1886, at which point he also took British citizenship. Over these adventuring years he saw the world, most of it under canvas, and crossed what he called the 'shadow line' from youthful idealism to maturity. However, he saw less of South America than *Nostromo* suggests, while the Malay Peninsula and Borneo he came to know intimately – *Lord Jim* is soundly based, as is the novel's central event, the desertion of a pilgrim ship by its cowardly officers: something that actually happened. Momentously, he paddled up the Congo River in 1890 as skipper of a decrepit steamer to the inland station of the iniquitous Société Anonyme Belge pour le Commerce du Haut-Congo, run by a dying manager called 'Klein' (renamed, not very obscuringly, 'Kurtz' in *Heart of Darkness*). 'Before the Congo I was a mere animal,' Joseph Conrad later wrote. Like Marlow, it was there he looked over the edge of the abyss into the black nothingness which is human life.

Conrad had fully immersed himself in what he called 'the destructive element' by the last decade of the nineteenth century and had formed his worldview, something summed up in such pungent Conradisms as: 'Droll thing life is – that mysterious arrangement of merciless logic for a futile purpose', 'We live, as we dream, alone', 'All a man can betray is his conscience.' They speckle all his fiction. A bequest from his ever kind uncle inaugurated a second career as a writer, beginning with 'a story of an Eastern river', *Almayer's Folly* (1895) – an auspiciously mature work. Conrad was blessed in his literary friends – men such as the critic Edward Garnett, the publisher William Blackwood, fellow novelists like Ford Madox Hueffer, and, particularly, his literary agent James B. Pinker who ingeniously worked his author's copyrights and patiently put up with his often outrageous demands for money.

Nothing flowed easily from Conrad's pen. The most costive of writers, getting a novel out of him, one friend said, was like a Caesarean birth. His aristocratic background expressed itself not merely in a majestic appearance, dress and haughty bearing (no novelist photographed better), but in an unquestioning expectation for things he could not, in the first half of his writing career, afford: country houses (he preferred Kent, by the sea), servants, limousines, chauffeurs, first-class travel. As Cedric Watts records, by 1909 Conrad's debts totalled £2,250, at a time when the average annual earnings of a doctor were about £400. In 1896 Conrad had confirmed that he was a seafarer no more by marrying. His wife, Jessie George, sixteen years younger than him, had been a typist – a useful skill. There would be two sons, Borys and John – one carrying a Polish name, the other an English one. The next ten years following his marriage comprise what Watts calls 'the major phase' – and three acknowledged masterpieces: *Lord Jim* (1900), *Nostromo* (1904), *Under Western Eyes* (1911).

The First World War (in which Borys was severely shell-shocked, never to recover) and the Russian Revolution paralysed Conrad creatively. His growing popularity made him suspect he must be writing below his best self. None the less it is hard to think he ever wrote anything better than 'The Secret Sharer' (1912) or *The Shadow Line* (1917). This feeling was compounded by a creeping sense of being somehow passé. The novel had moved forward; he, as a novelist, had not. *Victory* (1915) came out in the same year as Lawrence's *The Rainbow; The Rover* (1923) came out within months of Joyce's *Ulysses* (1922). The comparisons are not entirely in Conrad's favour.

He was, in his last years, seen by the public as a giant. He graciously turned down a knighthood offered by Ramsay MacDonald's government. Visits to Poland and, particularly, America, in 1923, confirmed his now worldwide celebrity (the Soviet Union never liked him, nor he them). By this point his health was deteriorating fast. Chain-smoking shortened his life: a 'mountain of ash', as he once said, memorialised each of his great works. The memorial he actually chose for his gravestone was:

> *Sleep after toyle, port after stormie seas,*
> *Ease after warre, death after life, does greatly please.*

As Cedric Watts tersely reminds us, 'these are the words uttered in Spenser's *Faerie Queene* by "a man of hell, that calls himself Despair"'. Not a cheerful passport to eternity.

FN   Joseph Conrad (born Józef Teodor Konrad Korzeniowski)
MRT *Lord Jim*
Biog J. Stape, *The Several Lives of Joseph Conrad* (2007)

86. Ella Hepworth Dixon 1857–1932

Shall we never have done with the New Woman? The Times, reviewing Dixon's one novel

I spent ten years of my academic life compiling a guide to Victorian fiction. It involved the highly pleasurable task of reading some 3,000 novels. 'What masterpieces have you found, overlooked by literary history?' I was asked. 'Only one', I would reply. 'Ella Dixon.' 'Who?' was the inevitable response; followed by, 'What did she write?'

Ella was born in London, the daughter and seventh child of William Hepworth Dixon, long-serving (1853–69) editor of the *Athenaeum*, the most authoritative literary journal of the nineteenth century. Being seventh meant, she jested, that her life would be fortunate: if fairy stories were to be believed. Whatever else, her subsequent life was no fairy story. 'A Knight of the Inkstand', as his daughter called him, W. H. Dixon was the offspring of a Lancashire, puritan family, enriched by trade. In her very early childhood, Ella's father was a thriving man: a JP and a noted traveller (he helped found the Palestine Exploration Fund). The family occupied a large house by the Regent's Park – one of the finer addresses in London. But the good life did not last. Dixon suffered a series of reverses in the 1870s, a formative period for his daughter. In 1874, their home was wrecked by an industrial explosion and Dixon himself was disabled by a fall from a horse in 1878. There were also financial misfortunes. He died, prematurely, when his daughter was in her early twenties.

Her mother was an 'advanced' woman, an Ibsenite and, as Ella recalls 'almost the first woman in London to call in a *woman* doctor when my brother Sydney was born'. Ella was educated expensively in London and Heidelberg, studied painting in Paris, and followed in her father's footsteps by editing *The Englishwoman* during the course of 1895. She never married and, even for a woman of her class in the 1890s, travelled widely and moved freely in the London literary world. A successful journalist by profession, Dixon wrote short stories, collected under the cumbersome, but indicative, title: *One Doubtful Hour and other Side-Lights on the Feminine Temperament* (1904).

Dixon's only published novel is *The Story of a Modern Woman* (1894). Painfully autobiographical, it has as its heroine Mary Erle, the orphaned daughter of a renowned man of letters. As a little girl, she scorns dolls (and the Ibsenite dolls' house, we presume). Mary aims at an independent life in a world as yet unready for female independence. It means struggle. Failing as an artist, she scrapes a living as a journalist, living in poor lodgings all the while. She discards her lover, Vincent (a married man), and is left at the end of the narrative independent, at last, wretchedly alone, but still a fighter. The last scene is of the heroine, at twilight, at Highgate cemetery, a glimmering London at her feet.

Dixon also wrote *My Flirtations* (1892) by 'Margaret Wynman', a 'lively and catty' series of sketches, supposedly written by a coquette. Towards the end of her life, she was militant for the cause of women's rights, and lived to see partial victory for the 'Modern Woman'. She left a memoir of literary London, *As I Knew Them: Sketches of People I Have Met on the Way* (1930), which is extraordinarily unrevealing, confirming the author's intention to remain one of her age's *inconnues* – impenetrably private.

FN   Ella Nora Hepworth Dixon ('Margaret Wynman')
MRT   *The Story of a Modern Woman*
Biog Valerie Fehlbaum (intro), *Ella Hepworth Dixon: The Story of a Modern Woman* (2005)

87. Mary Cholmondeley 1859–1925

With men it is take, take, take until we have nothing left to give. The mother's outburst in Cholmondeley's notorious novel, *Prisoners*

Cholmondeley was born at Hodnet, in Shropshire, the eldest of five daughters of a clergyman and distantly related to the Marquess of Cholmondeley. A lifelong sufferer from asthma, she was educated mainly at home by a family governess and by her father. Her childhood was, she later recorded, heavily 'repressed', although there was no shortage of books for her to broaden her mind with – and they were not all conventional books. Mary's mother, unusually, was interested to the point of obsession with science. From the ages of sixteen to thirty Cholmondeley lived in the country, helping her father with his parochial duties – her mother having been afflicted with creeping paralysis. Mary never married; being convinced from childhood that she did not possess the looks which would attract a man.

In 1896, when the Revd Cholmondeley retired, for health reasons, as Rector of Hodnet (having lost the bulk of his property), the family moved from their country vicarage to live in a London flat. Mary, who had written her first novel aged seventeen, began to circulate her work among publishers as early as 1883. Her first published novel, *The Danvers Jewels* (1887), published anonymously, was an ingenious, sprightly, sub-*Moonstone*, detective story. It was successful enough to warrant a sequel, *Sir Charles Danvers* (1889).

During the late 1880s, her parents' health was failing, as was Mary's – although she was now the family's principal breadwinner. She necessarily lived a retired life, out of the world, although her fiction was smart and Shavian. Her novels, particularly when they satirised established religion, sometimes scandalised and always contained a substratum of barely sublimated female rage. The imprisoned butterfly is one of her favourite images. *Diana Tempest* (1893) displays Cholmondeley's melodramatic tendencies attractively, with a plot centred on murder. The novel was dedicated to the author's sister, Hester, who had died aged twenty-two. The dedication is accompanied by a complaint about God, the tyrannical father, and foe to women: 'He put our lives so far apart we cannot hear each other speak.' The story centres on a hidebound father, Colonel Tempest, who dies in a condition of religious mania. *Diana Tempest* was the first book to appear under Cholmondeley's own name. Her father, one gathers, did not approve of a novel-writing daughter.

Red Pottage (1899) is the novel which has lasted best. It features a duel, a guilty man's self-destruction, and some sharp satire against religious cant. The last aspect of the work provoked denunciation from a London pulpit which delighted the author. *Red Pottage* also has a revealing scene in which the heroine Hester's antipathetic clergyman brother, James, discovers the manuscript of her latest work of fiction (she publishes her novels secretly and anonymously), for which she has received the promise of £1,000. The filthy thing reminds him of the novels of the detestable atheist, George Eliot, and he burns the only copy she has.

Cholmondeley went on to produce five novels in the twentieth century, one of which, *Prisoners* (1906), ran into libel trouble and irritated many of her acquaintance who discovered themselves portrayed in the work. In later life she subsided into silence, living with her sister Victoria in London and Suffolk.

FN　Mary Cholmondeley
MRT　*Red Pottage*
Biog　P. Lubbock, *Mary Cholmondeley: A Sketch from Memory* (1928)

88. Arthur Conan Doyle 1859–1930

Holmes takes my mind from better things.

Doyle was born in Edinburgh, one of nine children of an alcoholic father. An Irish artist turned Scottish civil servant, Charles Doyle was consigned, in later life, to a series of lunatic asylums. In the late 1970s a notebook surfaced whose lucid wit suggested that he may have been the victim of 'wrongous confinement'. It was not an unknown resort of vindictive wives – divorce, Victorian-style. The novelist recorded little of his feelings about his luckless parent. A wealthy 'lodger' in the Doyle household – Dr Bryan Waller – slipped into the paternal (and possibly spousal) role, yet in none of his autobiographical writings does Doyle allude to the mysterious Waller, whose existence was uncovered by twentieth-century detective work.

Arthur Doyle (now additionally named 'Conan', later hyphenated, for a godfather with whom his relationship is obscure) was educated at the fee-paying Jesuit college, Stonyhurst. For the rest of his life he spoke with a pronounced Scottish accent and was ambivalent about religion. At sixteen he spent a year in Austria before enrolling at Edinburgh University's medical school. He loved the Alps and would have been gratified by the modern pilgrimages by Holmes fans to the Reichenbach Falls.

His first story, 'The Mystery of Sasassa Valley', was published in 1879. In 1880 he spent seven months in the Arctic as ship's doctor on a whaler. The following year he graduated, a 'sixty per-cent examinee' with a respectable degree, and made another trip to Africa. After an unsuccessful experiment in partnership, he set up in medical practice at Southsea, near Portsmouth, in July 1882. His income had reached £300 a year by 1885, enabling him to marry the sister of one of his patients. Little is known of Louise Hawkins, other than that she had some money and may have nudged her husband towards spiritualism. A few years after the marriage she contracted tuberculosis which, although he was a trained doctor, Doyle did not diagnose until the disease was fatally advanced. He may have felt corrosive guilt at his oversight.

All through his early years at Southsea, Doyle had kept up his writing on the side and in 1886 played around with stories centred on an 'amateur private detective', called 'J. Sherrinford Holmes'. The outcome was the Sherlock Holmes novella, *A Study in Scarlet* (1887). No top-drawer publisher would take it and it was eventually serialised in a magazine edited by Mrs Beeton's husband. As usual with innovative works, the big-name publishers got it wrong. This mystery of double murder in Utah and London caught the public taste and Doyle followed it up with another Holmes adventure, *The Sign of Four* (1890). Doyle put something of himself into Sherlock Holmes but the sleuth was mainly inspired by a sharp-eyed teacher at Edinburgh, Dr Joseph Bell, a virtuoso at diagnosing illness by symptomatic 'clues', invisible to others. Early in 1891, Doyle submitted two stories to H. Greenhough Smith of the *Strand Magazine*. The editor reportedly realised 'that here was the greatest short story writer since Edgar Allan Poe'. These Sherlock Holmes stories were devised to correct 'the great defect' in current detective fiction – lack of logic. They were illustrated by Sidney Paget, who supplied the detective with his trademark deerstalker and aquiline profile.

Doyle's heart was never really in detective fiction. Holmes, he complained, 'takes my mind from better things'. Nevertheless the stories were phenomenally popular in Britain and America and overshadowed everything else Doyle would ever write. In fact, his writing was extremely diverse. It includes such ambitious historical romances as *Micah Clarke* (1889), a story of the 1685 Rebellion and its defeat at Sedgemoor, told autobiographically by one of Monmouth's humble followers. *The White Company* (1891), another historical romance, was the author's own favourite work. The action is set in the Hundred Years War with France, and follows the exploits of a company of English bowmen. Doyle also invented the series heroes Professor Challenger (see *The Lost World*, 1912) and Brigadier Gerard. But, vary his game as he might, he was doomed to be the creator of Sherlock Holmes however much he chafed under it. In 1893, he killed the detective at the Reichenbach Falls, only to have to bring him back to life in 1901 and again in 1903.

Much as he came to hate him, Holmes made Doyle rich. With the aid of the agent A. P. Watt, the novelist was earning as much as £1,600 a year by his pen in 1891, and by the end of the century was one of the richest of British men of letters. Doyle was a hearty man, loving cricket (he played for the MCC, and on one glorious occasion bowled out W. G. Grace), shooting and motoring – an expensive hobby which Holmes subsidised handsomely, as he did world travel and a country-house lifestyle. No pigging it in Baker Street digs for Arthur Conan-Doyle. *Rodney Stone* (1896) reflects Doyle's enthusiasm for the manly art of pugilism. Set in the early nineteenth century, it introduces Beau Brummel and other historical notables into the action, and earned the author £5,000, a handsome purse. Above all, Doyle loved skiing. He picked up the enthusiasm in Davos (where his wife went for the sake of her lungs) and popularised the sport – enriching Switzerland even more than Holmes had enriched the *Strand*'s proprietor, George Newnes.

Louise Doyle was thirteen years dying. For ten of those years her husband was passionately involved with a woman almost young enough to be his daughter. Free at last, he married Jean Leckie in 1907, a year after the death of Louise. Doyle had children (with both Louise and Jean), but his relationship with them seems to have been remote.

Doyle was a convinced imperialist. During the Boer War he offered his rusty medical services to the armed forces and propagandised for the English cause. One of his anti-Boer 'war pamphlets' sold half a million copies. He was knighted by a grateful government in 1902. Doyle was similarly active as a patriotic front-line reporter in the First World War and made himself England's foremost novelist-propagandist, along with Mrs Humphry Ward (whom he admired) and Hall Caine (whom he despised). He lost a son and a favourite brother to the Great War, which may have predisposed his cranky adherence to spiritualism in his last years.

All his adult life, Doyle was extraordinarily diligent as a writer to the press and attached himself to innumerable causes. Some, such as his defence of wrongly convicted criminals, were noble. His campaign to clear the alleged 'horse slasher', George Edalji, inspired a worthy act of literary *hommage*, Julian Barnes's novel, *Arthur and George* (2005). Other causes – notably his crusade on behalf of the 'Cottingley fairies' – brought ridicule. Few writers have retained their posthumous popularity more bestsellingly. It is nice to think of his spirit (did such things, as Doyle believed, exist) slipping into a Leicester Square cinema to catch a showing of the 2009, Guy Ritchie-directed, Robert Downey Jr-starring movie *Sherlock Holmes*.

FN (Sir) Arthur Ignatius Conan Doyle
MRT *The Adventures of Sherlock Holmes*
Biog Martin Booth, *The Doctor, the Detective, and Arthur Conan Doyle* (1997)

POSTSCRIPT

89. John (Edmund) Gardner 1926–2007

He is a genius, a philosopher, an abstract thinker. Sherlock Holmes on his arch-foe, Moriarty

John Gardner's final novel, the neo-Victorian *Moriarty*, ended a writing career far from where it started. The son of a clergyman, he served 'with no distinction', as he modestly recorded, as a Royal Marine commando, at the end of the Second World War. After the war, and study at Cambridge, he was persuaded by his father to enter the Anglican priesthood – but his career in the Church failed ('Probably the biggest mistake I ever made'). He had been writing since the age of eight (when, as he records, he wrote on the first page of a notebook, 'The Complete Works of John Gardner'), and his name as an author was launched in 1963 with the publication of *Spin the Bottle* – what members of Alcoholics Anonymous call a 'drunkalog'. Of all the fifty-four books he published, it's the one that most deserves to survive.

Gardner recovered from his addiction, and in 1964, created his serial hero, Boysie Oakes. Like Len Deighton's Harry Palmer, Boysie was an anti-Bond: the Flashman of spooks. As Gardner admitted, towards the end of his life: 'though I have denied it many times – he was of course a complete piss-take of J. Bond'. Ironically, in 1981 the piss-taker Gardner was commissioned to continue the 007 series, after Ian Fleming died inconveniently early. He performed the chore competently, although in later life he confessed that, powerful earner though it was, he had 'never been really fond of J. Bond'. He was, however, fond of the two 'Moriarty' novels he published in the mid-1970s. Gardner had intended to write a trilogy, but the third volume (to be called *The Redemption of Moriarty*) was stalled by legal problems. It was finally written, a quarter of a century on, as *Moriarty*. Gardner was then battling with the cancer that would kill him while completing it.

Moriarty is Sherlock Holmes's Blofeld. As the great detective explains in Conan Doyle's 'The Final Problem' to his dim fellow lodger in 221B Baker Street, 'He is the Napoleon of crime, Watson. He is the organiser of half that is evil and of nearly all that is undetected in this great city. He is a genius, a philosopher, an abstract thinker. He has a brain of the first order. He sits motionless, like a spider in the centre of its web, but that web has a thousand radiations, and he knows well every quiver of each of them.' Gardner's *Moriarty* kicks off with a conundrum which has tormented all died-in-the-wool Holmesians. How many Moriartys are there (Doyle indicates at least three: a professor, a Colonel, and a station master). And why are they all called James?

Gardner's solution is witty and supplies the hinge on which his last novel swung merrily along. Of course, spoilsports will argue that Conan Doyle didn't give a damn about such trifling details, thinking Holmes not worthy of it: 'He keeps me from better things,' Doyle famously complained. 'There are no better things,' Holmesians retort. In the final instalment, Moriarty has returned to London from some profitable master-criminality in the US to discover that his empire has been taken over by 'Idle Jack'. Jack's main source of income is supplying the metropolis with virgins from the Third World to sate the lust of English degenerates. Our less beastly crime lord's reconquest of his turf is complicated by a traitor in his 'Praetorian Guard'. Could it be the 'evil Chinee', Lee Chow, who can slice up a foe with his knife faster than you can say 'chop chop'? Or Albert Spear, with the ominous 'lightning scar down his right cheek'? Moriarty will find out. And yes, Moriarty will be redeemed.

FN   John Edmund Gardner
MRT   *Moriarty*
Biog   John-Gardner.com

90. Frank Danby 1859–1916

Who will clean the soil?

The daughter of a Jewish, but religiously lapsed, artist and photographer, Hyman Davis, Julia Davis was educated at home by Mme Laura Lafargue, the eldest daughter of Karl Marx. She had eight siblings: one brother, James Davis ('Owen Hall' – a pun on 'owing all') was also a writer but, as his rueful pen name suggests, not entirely successful. Julia was successful. In 1883 she married a well-off wholesale cigar merchant, and minor poet, Arthur Frankau (d. 1904). It was the grand era of the 'Havana' and the couple lived prosperously on its aromatic fumes.

On their marriage, the Frankaus broke, formally, with Judaism. Julia began writing for the *Saturday Review* and, as 'Frank Danby', produced a novel, *Dr Phillips: A Maida Vale Idyll* in 1887. The work, which was allegedly part written by George Moore, provoked indignation for its savage depiction of British Jewish life as philistine, money-grubbing and devoted entirely to the 'Deity, Gain'. *Dr Phillips*, scandalous as it was found by those it principally wrote about, went through five editions in ten years, and fed the unthinking prejudices of the novel-reading middle classes.

Frankau followed this bestseller with *A Babe in Bohemia* (1889). A Zolaesque tale of seduction, it tells the story of a venereally diseased epileptic girl who finally goes to the bad and cuts her throat with an open razor, in a seizure. 'The blood was bad', concludes the narrator, 'and drains into the soil. But who will clean the soil?' *A Babe in Bohemia* is one of the hardest hitting novels of its time. The chronically cautious *Athenaeum* disgustedly called it 'an excursion into the drains and dustbins of humanity' and the novel was piously banned by the metropolitan circulating libraries. Inevitably, it sold like hot cakes in consequence.

Subsequently Frankau gave up fiction to study engraving – something in which she had long been interested. In 1903 she returned to the novel with *Pigs in Clover*, another anti-Semitic novel dealing with the vulgar comedies, as she maliciously saw them, of Anglo-Jewish domestic life. Her last satire on Judaism, *The Sphinx's Lawyer*, was published in 1906, in the immediate aftermath of the 1905 Aliens Act, which was cruelly obstructing the immigration of Jews fleeing pogroms in Europe and Russia. Modern literary history is perplexed by Frankau, who was gifted, witty and a woman who made a successful career for herself when it was not easy to do so: 'self-hating Jew' is the commonest conclusion. But a clever self-hater.

She moved in high literary society and was an acquaintance of Oscar Wilde, George Moore and Arnold Bennett. In her youth, she was a keen bicyclist and in later life as keen a motorist. Frankau's eldest son, Gilbert, was also a bestselling novelist, as was Gilbert's daughter, Pamela. Another granddaughter, Joan (Frankau) Bennett, was a distinguished Cambridge academic. She examined my MA dissertation in 1964, which contained some sharp comments about 'Frank Danby'. Bennett asked pointed questions at what was a surprisingly tough viva. Unaware of her family connection, I was taken aback by how well she knew these obscure novels. She passed my work, without, however, the distinction I was hoping for.

FN Frank Danby (Julia Frankau; née Davis)
MRT *Dr Phillips: A Maida Vale Idyll*
Biog *ODNB* (Elizabeth Eccleshare)

91. George Egerton 1859–1945

Femme incomprise.

The most influential of the so-called 'New Woman' novelists, Egerton's life is complicated by the official accounts she put out during her lifetime. She was born in Melbourne, Australia. Her father was Irish and an army officer (dishonourably discharged), her mother was Welsh. Mary Chavelita Dunne was brought up as Catholic as her Christian name suggests, but lost her faith in later life. As the family moved around the antipodes she saw something as a child of the New Zealand wars against the Maoris.

The young Mary Dunne entertained hopes of being an artist, 'but family affairs prevented the course of study'. These family affairs were her mother's death and her father's incorrigible gambling. She trained, instead, as a nurse. In 1884 she emigrated briefly to America and in 1888 she eloped with a married man, Henry Higginson (called in one of her official versions 'H. H. W. Melville'). The couple went to live in Norway where Egerton became imbued with the Ibsenism which is prominent in her later work. Higginson was a drunken brute and Egerton left him after a year (the official version has him die in 1889). She moved to England – although she seems to have spent some time in Ireland – and in 1891 married what one commentator calls 'an idle destitute Canadian', George Egerton Clairmonte. Officially he was a respectable minor novelist. But in 1901 they divorced, flagrant adulteries being the grounds (the official version has Clairmonte dying soon after the divorce).

Meanwhile, as 'George Egerton' ('George' was her mother's maiden name) she had huge success with *Keynotes* (1893), a volume she supposedly wrote in two, inspired, weeks. It comprises sketches, or *études*, of the modern woman as she undergoes various crises: alcoholism, sex problems, suicidal *anomie*. The tendency of Egerton's work, epitomised in *Keynotes* (and its resonant title) is away from narrative to snapshots of the woman at a significant 'psychological moment' of her life in which she discovers the 'terra incognita of herself'. Embellished with illustrations by the congenial Aubrey Beardsley, it was a bestseller and inaugurated a series of uniform 'Keynotes' novels by many, mainly female, hands. 'Not since *The Story of an African Farm*', wrote *The Queen*, 'has any woman delivered herself of so forcible a book.'

Egerton apparently became the mistress of her (and Oscar Wilde's) publisher, John Lane. *Keynotes* was followed by similar collections of modish short stories and sketches of the *femme incomprise*: *Discords* (1894), *Symphonies* (1896), *Fantasias* (1897). For all its feminist toughness, Egerton's writing has great delicacy. More than her sister 'New Woman' novelists, she was influenced by the aesthetics of decadence and by the European novel – particularly Knut Hamsun, to whom *Keynotes* is dedicated. In 1901 she made a third marriage to the authors' agent, Reginald Golding Bright, fifteen years younger than her, and became herself a leading dramatic agent for such playwrights as G. B. Shaw and Somerset Maugham. Her only child, George, was killed in the First World War. Her husband died in 1941 and her last years were financially distressed.

FN   George Egerton (Mary Chavelita Golding Bright; née Dunne)
MRT *Keynotes*
Biog *ODNB* (Alison Charlton)

92. Kenneth Grahame 1859–1932

There is nothing – absolutely nothing – half so much worth doing as simply messing about in boats.

The author of *The Wind in the Willows* – that archetypally English idyll – was, in bio-graphical fact, a Scot. Grahame was born into the Edinburgh professional classes, but the solid family framework around him dissolved, almost immediately, as if by witch's curse. His mother died of fever, giving birth to her fourth child, before Kenneth was six and his barrister father fell into alcoholism. For the last twenty years of his life Grahame Sr drank and died alone, in France. He never communi-cated with his children, who were left to the care of an extended family. There are no fathers, no mothers, no wives, no siblings in the animal world of *The Wind in the Willows*. This was Kenneth Grahame's lot in the human world. And there were other handicaps – he was afflicted with a weak chest, and, like Richard Jefferies, the condi-tion of his lungs called for fresh air. Kenneth spent a lot of time in the countryside – ostensibly for his health, but in the long run, in both men's work, the outcome was healthier still for English literature.

After public school at Oxford, a city he adored, there arrived the great sorrow of Grahame's life: he did not 'go up' to the University. His guardian uncle deter-mined the boy must do something useful (and cheaper on the custodial pocket) than lounging around in college for three years. It was, according to his biographer, 'the most crushing blow that Grahame suffered, perhaps in his whole life'. It's a strange notion of catastrophe, but real enough for Grahame. Paradise was now forever lost. Instead, Kenneth was installed, by patronage, into the cogs and wheels of the Bank of England. In this great machine he would work, mechanically, for thirty years. A 'flier', Grahame rose to the top, but it was not something he had chosen for himself. He was imprisoned: Threadneedle Street was his Chateau d'If.

Although Oxford had been denied him, Grahame imbibed the university's 1890s Paterian-Wildean decadence. Gem-like flames licked, decorously, around his ankles. He bought into Great-God-Pan-worshipping 'neo-paganism', a cult which, guardedly, promulgated all those Hellenic practices that Victorian England frowned on – not least after the savage Labouchere Amendment of 1885. He had, like all the golden youth, a secret portrait in his attic. By day a dutiful *fonctionnaire* in the 'Bank', by night Grahame walked around Soho, a bohemian. Literary introductions furnished him an entry into John Lane's *Yellow Book*. His first volume of collected pieces, *Pagan Papers* (1893) carried a frontispiece by Aubrey Beardsley. A green carnation could not have been more emblematic. The papers were well received. Grahame (all the while slaving by day at the Bank) followed up two years later with another series, delicately recapturing childhood experiences: *The Golden Age*. In the same year, 1895, disaster struck with the Wilde trials, bringing with them a traumatic cultural nervousness. The *Yellow Book* gave way to Harmsworth's yellow press – notably the *Daily Mail*, then, as now, the scourge of everything 'abnormal' in British life. 'Paganism' and a preoccupation with childhood experience were high on the list of things abnormal.

In this period of collective recoil Grahame suffered a life-threatening illness, empyema, described as 'a collection of pus within a naturally existing anatomical cavity'. Medicine too has its allegories. It required a risky operation on Grahame's lungs, and the deflation of one of them. And, just as riskily, in 1899 he married. The marriage proved a disaster, although it put to rest any suspicions about his private life. He was forty; his wife, Elspeth, in her late thirties. Sex was discontinued almost as soon as it had begun. It produced one son in 1900 – who would be, eventually, the cause of sadness, but it was for young Alastair, as bedtime entertainment, that *The Wind in the Willows* was conceived and eventually published in 1908.

In the book Grahame pictures an ideal menage: women do not come into it. In their 'digs', like Holmes and Watson, Ratty and Moley are two chaps living together: it's a Darby and Darby situation. No Joans need apply. The story, as the author insisted, was 'clean of the clash of sex'. Other clashes do intrude into the narrative. The oiks – weasels and stoats – who take over Toad Hall, recall those terrifying Trafalgar Square rioters on 'Bloody Sunday', 1887. That event had been, in its different way, as traumatic for the middle classes as the Wilde business. Thank God for the English copper, with his truncheon.

Grahame's later life was a tragedy in slow motion. His wife became cranky and Alastair – disabled from birth – was pushed into an Oxford University where he didn't belong, during a war in which the world was tearing itself apart. On 13 May 1920 he stretched himself on the railway tracks, one night, in the meadows outside Oxford which his father most loved, and let an express train decapitate him. Meanwhile, the marital life of the Grahames became uncosier by the year: 'Elspeth seldom got up before eleven, often went to bed in her clothes ... Much of the time she spent on her divan, sipping hot water. She ate practically nothing and mouse-nests proliferated in the larder; she put Kenneth into special underwear which was only changed once a year. It is perhaps not surprising that he took a long solitary walk every day.' A living bruise, the solitary walker in his soiled underwear wrote nothing of significance after *The Wind in the Willows*. He left his estate to the Bodleian Library.

FN   Kenneth Grahame
MRT *The Wind in the Willows*
Biog P. Green, *Kenneth Grahame: a biography* (1959)

93. J. M. Barrie 1860–1937

May God blast anyone who writes a biography of me. J. M. Barrie's curse

Barrie was born in Kirriemuir, Forfarshire, the ninth child of a handloom weaver and a devoutly Presbyterian mother. He composed an intimate portrait of her in his bio-novel, *Margaret Ogilvy* (1896), published a year after her death – an event whose pain he never outlived. Family death had scarred him earlier, too. Aged seven, he was traumatised by the horrific drowning of his brother David in a skating accident. Seven years older than 'Jimmy', David was his mother's favourite (on one occasion, Jimmy dressed up in his dead brother's clothes, in a hopeless act of emulation) and ranks as the first of Barrie's 'lost boys'. James himself, for reasons which are plausibly seen as psycho-traumatic, stopped growing: as an adult, he was forever boy-sized – under five feet tall. In a literal sense he never grew up.

Yet there was no littleness in his brain. At thirteen, he went to school in Dumfries and from there he progressed to Edinburgh University, graduating in 1882. From early youth (when he was addicted to 'penny dreadfuls'), Barrie resolved on a career in literature and in 1883, a year of deep economic depression in Scotland, he secured a post as leader writer to the *Nottingham Journal.* At around the same period he was trying his hand at semi-fictional sketches set in 'Thrums' (i.e. Kirriemuir). They were popular with English readers and helped found the 'kailyard' (cabbage patch) genre of sentimental ('pawky') Scottish fiction. Scots have had a more equivocal response to the kailyard cult, which, like the tartan-romanticism invented by Walter Scott and the 'wha's like us' machismo of Mel Gibson's *Braveheart*, promotes an artificial image of the country.

Barrie was sucked, by the usual metropolitan magnetism, to London in 1885 where he began writing for the magazines. After the Universal Education Act of 1870 the readership for such wares had enlarged explosively. There were opportunities aplenty for an energetic young Scot with a ready pen and good manners. Editors liked his work, and talked him up. His first efforts in fiction parallel the 'Jack of all Trades' nature of his early magazinery. *Better Dead* (1887), published at the author's own expense, is a sub-Stevensonian 'murder as a fine art' joke. More successful was *Auld Licht Idylls* (1888), a compendium of his Thrums pieces centred around the narrator's austere religious sect. In the same year he produced the more substantial *When a Man's Single*, by 'Gavin Ogilvy' (his mother's maiden name). The Scottish hero, Rob Angus, comes down to London to make his way in journalism. It's so transparently the author's own story as to qualify, like much of Barrie's fiction, as memoir. There followed *A Window in Thrums* (1889) and *My Lady Nicotine*

(1890), a set of smoking club stories (tobacco was Barrie's principal vice – assuming one discounts, as most thoughtful observers do, paedophilia).

Runaway success came with *The Little Minister* (1891). A physically diminutive, but passionate, Presbyterian minister, Gavin Dishart, falls in love with a beautiful 'Egyptian' (i.e. gypsy girl), Babbie, to the indignation of his Thrums congregation – Israelitish to the core. At the highpoint of the narrative, Gavin deserts his pulpit to attend a pagan marriage ceremony in the forest, while a storm of biblical violence rages, as an obbligato to the terrible things happening on earth.

> The rain increased in violence, appalling even those who heard it from under cover. However rain may storm, though it be an army of archers battering roofs and windows, it is only terrifying when the noise swells every instant. In those hours of darkness it again and again grew in force and doubled its fury, and was louder, louder, and louder, until its next attack was to be more than men and women could listen to. They held each other's hands and stood waiting. Then abruptly it abated, and people could speak. I believe a rain that became heavier every second for ten minutes would drive many listeners mad. Gavin was in it on a night that tried us repeatedly for quite half that time.

Thrums meets sex – the encounter is apocalyptic. *The Little Minister* (a dramatic version of which had run successfully on Broadway) was filmed in 1934, with Katharine Hepburn as a ravishing Babbie with an uncertain Scottish accent.

Barrie's mind was now turning to marriage – imprudent marriage by Auld Licht's stern standards. His choice was a young actress, no taller than himself, Mary Ansell. The Barries' marriage proved childless and wretched, and manifestly embittered his later fiction. The couple divorced in 1909. It is suggested he was impotent, although this did not come up in the proceedings, the grounds being her adultery. The balance of biographical opinion is that if there were a sexual relationship between the married couple it was not passionate.

Barrie's maturity as a novelist came with the linked *Bildungsromane Sentimental Tommy* (1896) and *Tommy and Grizel* (1900), which chronicle the progress of a raw Thrums lad, Tommy Sandys. The first volume deals with Tommy's early days in working-class London and his return, tail between his legs, to Scotland. The second volume describes his return to London and a tragic end – defeated by cosmopolitan corruption. He dies on the railings of the house of an aristocrat who has seduced him. 'His last reflection before he passed into unconsciousness was – serves me right!'

As the century turned, Barrie abandoned fiction for the more lucrative prospects offered by the London and New York stage. His dramatic adaptation of *The*

Little Minister would earn him £90,000 in British and American box office receipts – fabulous by the standards of the time. But even this stream of gold was dwarfed by the income from *Peter Pan*, the copyright that never grows old (it is still, thanks to a special act of Parliament, yielding income for Barrie's beloved Great Ormond Street Hospital for children, in London). Conceived in 1904 as a play, the story of the boy who never grew up was extended by Barrie into a novel, *Peter and Wendy*, two years later and further extended, fictionally, as *Peter Pan in Kensington Gardens* in 1911.

His last decades were loaded with public honours. He was created a baronet in 1913, given the Order of Merit in 1922, and elected Chancellor of Edinburgh University in 1930. At his own wish he was buried alongside his mother in Kir-riemuir. The Barries' spirits, one suspects, must have been troubled over the last few years by raging speculation: was he a paedophile? The question is given extra force by Michael Jackson's choosing to name his Southern Californian Edenic play-ground 'Neverland'. Suspicion centres on an ostensibly philanthropic act on Barrie's part. In the 1890s he regularly ran across a clutch of five little boys in Kensington Gardens, where he himself walked his massive St Bernard dog, Porthos (Barrie was tiny enough to have ridden the beast, like the horses in Rotten Row). He formed an avuncular relationship with the children. Their father, Arthur Llewelyn Davies (who had not entirely approved of 'Uncle' Jimmy's attentions to his children) was a lawyer. Their mother, Sylvia (née du Maurier, a daughter of George du Maurier, novelist and artist) was more favourably disposed.

A parent might well be slightly put out by the novel, *The Little White Bird*, which Barrie published in 1902. It transparently allegorises his relationship with the chil-dren. In one dubious scene, 'Captain W', a childless writer, with a dog called Porthos, describes a 'tremendous adventure' – namely that little David (clearly based on Bar-rie's favourite among the children) asks to spend the night with the 'Captain':

> 'Why, David,' said I, sitting up, 'do you want to come into my bed?'
> 'Mother said I wasn't to want it unless you wanted it first,' he squeaked.
> 'It is what I have been wanting all the time,' said I, and then without more ado the little white figure rose and flung itself at me. For the rest of the night he lay on me and across me, and sometimes his feet were at the bottom of the bed and some-times on the pillow, but he always retained possession of my finger, and occasion-ally he woke me to say that he was sleeping with me.

It was out of his increasingly intense relationship with the children that Barrie wrote the play *Peter Pan: or, the Boy Who Wouldn't Grow Up*. It was first put on during the pantomime season, in late December 1904, with a young actress, Nina Bouci-cault, playing Peter and much visual gimmickry (flying children, for example).

The largely adult audience was charmed. The dedication, as later printed in the expanded novel version, *Peter and Wendy*, was 'To Sylvia and Arthur Llewelyn Davies and their boys (my boys)'. As he later told the children, I made Peter by rubbing the five of you violently together, as savages with two sticks produce a flame.'

The boys would soon become even more 'his'. Arthur died in 1907, prematurely, and Sylvia followed him in 1910. Barrie adopted the boys a year later, following their mother's express wish. The future careers of the boys, despite Barrie's now paternal solicitude, was interspersed with tragedy: one died in 1915, in the Great War; another was drowned at Oxford in 1921 (it may have been suicide – and he may have been gay). Peter Llewelyn Davies, who had suffered under the shadow of his namesake, Pan, a creature he hated, threw himself under a train in 1960, having destroyed all Barrie's intimate correspondence with him. One of Peter's publicly expressed resentments was that when he died in 1937, 'Uncle Jim' left his huge wealth not to his surviving boys, but to his secretary, Lady Cynthia Asquith. The copyright of *Peter Pan* had been made over separately to the Great Ormond Street Hospital in 1929.

Was Barrie a paedophile? The longest surviving of the boys, 'Nico', who lived until 1980, recorded: 'I don't believe that Uncle Jim ever experienced what one might call "a stirring in the undergrowth" for anyone – man, woman, or child ... I never heard one word or saw one glimmer of anything approaching homosexuality or paedophilia: had he had either of these leanings in however slight a symptom I would have been aware ... He was an innocent – which is why he could write *Peter Pan.*'

FN   (Sir) James Matthew Barrie
MRT   *The Little Minister*
Biog   A. Birkin, *J. M. Barrie & The Lost Boys* (1979)

94. Charlotte Perkins Gilman 1860–1935

There is no female mind. The brain is not an organ of sex. Might as well speak of a female liver.

Charlotte Perkins was born in Hartford, Connecticut, the daughter of a man of letters, Frederic Beecher Perkins. The Perkinses were a cultivated family, rooted in a cultivated community. Harriet Beecher Stowe was a distant relative. Political energy – fuelled by abolitionism – was instilled into Charlotte at birth, but the family was fractured irredeemably when, shortly after her birth, Frederic Perkins left them. The reasons are not clear, although a doctor's opinion that if his wife Mary ('loyal as a spaniel') had another child she would die, may have been a factor. Thereafter her father played no part in Charlotte's life. She recalled meeting him, aged fifteen, in the Boston Public Library – 'not having seen him for years' – and kissing him. He ignored her thereafter.

Charlotte's mother, severe by nature, forbade the reading of novels. She was physically vital as an adolescent, visiting a gymnasium twice a week and running a mile every day. She disdained corsets and the trivial enthusiasms of American girl-hood. On leaving school she studied at the Rhode School of Design, leaving without any formal qualifications, but with the skills to design greeting cards and tutor young people in art.

Her biographer speculates that she had a quasi-lesbian relationship ('Boston marriages', as they were called) in her early twenties. In 1884, however, she married the artist, Charles Walter Stetson, destined to be an unhappy union. After the birth of their first child, a daughter, Charlotte was plunged into post-natal depression. There was a history of depression in the Beecher family and Harriet Beecher Stowe had also suffered from it. But marriage itself was clearly another factor. In 1887, the advice of S. Weir Mitchell, a specialist in 'women's disorders', was called on. A believer in the 'rest cure' (i.e. solitary confinement and sensory deprivation), he prescribed the regime described, horrifically, in Gilman's most famous story, 'The Yellow Wall-paper', where the cure is portrayed as patriarchal sadism. The unnamed heroine in the story is, for her own good, locked up in the attic of a house, after the birth of her daughter, Mary. Her husband John, and his sister Jennie, have incarcerated her on the advice of 'a physician of high standing'. Personally, the heroine confides, 'I disagree with their ideas ... I believe that congenial work, with excitement and change, would do me good. But what is one to do?' What she does is fixate on the yellow wallpaper and go completely mad.

In a late-life essay, 'Why I wrote "The Yellow Wall-paper"', Gilman described her own, therapy-induced breakdown, and her escape. The story was written to help other women so afflicted by 'treatment'. As she drily noted, 'I sent a copy to the physician who so nearly drove me mad. He never acknowledged it.' With the growth of American feminism in the 1960s her short story was adopted as prescribed reading in schools and colleges. Charlotte escaped the 'rest cure' by fleeing to Pasadena, California, from where she divorced her husband. They remained, none the less, on amicable terms. He married her best friend (for whom, it is speculated, Charlotte's feelings had been overtly erotic) and took over the care of their child. In California Charlotte (still 'Stetson'), and now genuinely 'cured', began to write and lecture on feminist subjects.

She was, by nature and intellectual conviction, utopian, believing in the possibility not merely of equality, but of gynocracy, a theme pursued in her novel, *Herland: A Lost Feminist Utopian Novel* (1915; the subtitle was added later for modern readers), which foresees a woman-dominated world. Androcracy, she firmly believed, could be overset. Her most influential non-fiction work was *Women and Economics: A Study of the Economic Relation Between Men and Women as a Factor in Social Relations* (1898). The major element in her thinking was that circumstances, and with them societies, were eminently changeable – if sufficient pressure were applied. To that end she wrote a body of fiction of which only 'The Yellow Wall-paper' (first published in magazine form in 1892) has 'lasted'. But her books, the magazine she edited (*The Forerunner*) and her hundreds of articles, had a palpable impact on the thinking, and social reforms, of her time – notably women's suffrage.

In 1900 she married a cousin, George Houghton Gilman, an attorney of passive character and seven years younger (her sexual interests, in her early Pasadena years, seem to have been principally lesbian). The Gilmans lived contentedly, by all accounts, in Southern California, until his death, in 1934. Gilman, afflicted with breast cancer and a believer in euthanasia, killed herself with chloroform, which she had methodically stored, a year later, leaving an autobiography, *The Living of Charlotte Perkins Gilman* (1935) and a suicide note of Roman stoicism, stating: 'When all usefulness is over, when one is assured of unavoidable and imminent death, it is the simplest of human rights to choose a quick and easy death in place of a slow and horrible one.' She also believed in 'neatness' in suicide, leaving something easy to clear up (not the 'debris of the battlefield') for the woman who would, inevitably, have to tidy up afterwards.

FN   Charlotte Anna Gilman (née Perkins; first married name 'Stetson')
MRT 'The Yellow Wall-paper'
Biog A. J. Lane, *To "Herland" and Beyond: The Life and Work of Charlotte Perkins Gilman* (1990)

95. S. Weir Mitchell 1828–1914

I sent a copy to the physician who so nearly drove me mad. He never acknowledged it.
Charlotte Perkins Gilman, about her story 'The Yellow Wall-paper'

Mitchell is notorious to fiction readers of the late twentieth century as the physician who invented and popularised the 'rest cure' therapy for neurotic ('neurasthenic', 'hysterical') women. He has been thoroughly demonised by feminist literary criticism since the 1960s. The iniquities of the Mitchell rest cure are immortalised in two classic 'rediscovered' works of feminist fiction, 'The Yellow Wall-paper' and Kate Chopin's *The Awakening* (1899).

Mitchell was born in Philadelphia, the son of a professor of medicine. He had a difficult relationship with his father, a surgeon, and in his youth suffered the chronic depression he later took it on himself to cure. A phobic aversion to blood made it impossible for him to follow his father's line of medical work. None the less he had a brilliant academic career, finishing his studies in Paris – then the centre of neurological research. He returned in the mid-1850s, to take up partnership with his father. On his father's death in 1858 he took over the family practice. In the same year he married. His wife died, four years (and two children) later, of diphtheria. Mitchell served, gallantly, as a surgeon in the Union Army in the Civil War.

During his war years, Mitchell was particularly concerned with the treatment of head wounds and what would later be called 'shell shock' – nervous trauma. He had always been fascinated by the brain and its disorders, and 'paralysis' – stillness ('peace', to draw an obvious analogy) – he believed, was curative for the organ's disorders (he had an utter disdain for sexual explanations of psychic disorder). He considered (something that Charlotte Perkins Gilman fiercely refuted) that men's and women's brains were different. By the mid-1860s he had established himself as the country's leading expert on nervous complaints. He remarried in 1874 and his second wife furnished him an entry to Philadelphia's social elite. It was at this period that Mitchell devised his 'rest cure' as a therapy particularly appropriate for women. Women who underwent it, such as Gilman and Chopin, were less convinced of its efficacy.

Sigmund Freud admired him, but for his part, Mitchell did not admire Freud – on coming across a volume by the 'sex-mad' Viennese psychoanalyst, he threw the 'filthy thing' into the fire. Mitchell had, from youth onwards, tried his hand at poetry and short stories. His first full-length novel, *In War Time*, serialised in the *Atlantic Magazine* in 1884, drew on his own war experiences twenty years before. It was well received, as were its successors. Fame, bestsellerdom and a doctorate of letters from Harvard, came with *Hugh Wynne, Free Quaker* in 1897. Reportedly, Mitchell spent seven years working on *Hugh Wynne*, which was then written in six weeks. Its publication was cannily timed to coincide with the centenary of 1796, whose main celebrations were held in Philadelphia. The war theme of the novel chimed with the recent American victory over the Spanish at Manila Bay and the surge of patriotism which accompanied it. Mitchell's novel runs slightly against this grain by examining the tricky issues of pacifism and 'cowardice'.

Mitchell had Quaker family connections. 'Free Quakers' were those dissidents who believed in the idea of a 'just war' and they were firmly disowned by the main body of the Society of Friends. In the novel *Hugh Wynne*, a born Quaker turned 'free Quaker' tells his story autobiographically. The narrative revolves around a lengthy description of the Revolution and its changing fortunes. Hugh, having escaped captivity and joined the Revolutionary army, rises to the rank of captain in the Pennsylvania Foot, and eventually to Colonel on the staff of the Commander in Chief, Washington. A subplot narrates the dastardly treachery of Benedict Arnold, in whose machinations Hugh is unwittingly and unwillingly caught up. Hugh sees Arnold years later in London, a wasted man: 'There is a God who punishes the traitor,' he complacently observes.

Is there any connection between the diabolic evangelist of the 'rest cure' and the bestselling novelist? There conceivably is. Mitchell's therapy was, manifestly, an extension of the curative tranquillity of the Quaker service, the silence that puts one in connection with God. Anyone asked the question in 1900, 'Who is the more important writer of fiction, S. Weir Mitchell or Charlotte Perkins Gilman?' would probably have replied, 'Who is she?' He, in his heyday, was regarded as the 'new Ben Franklin'. Now that they have both gone to their final rest cure it is he, not her, who is the forgotten author. Is that a peal of woman's laughter one hears?

FN   Silas Weir Mitchell
MRT *Hugh Wynne*
Biog Richard D. Walter, *Weir Mitchell, M.D., Neurologist: A Biography* (1970)

96. Amanda Ros 1860–1939

The Authoress.

On 26 September 2006, one of the smallest literary festivals ever organised was held in the John Hewitt pub, Belfast. Small attendance was in order. The festival's mission was to celebrate 'The World's Worst Novelist'. Amanda Ros has always had a loyal band of what, in other circumstances, might be called 'admirers'. Anna Margaret McKittrick was born in County Down. 'By birth,' she later proclaimed, 'I am an Irishwoman, though a dash of German blood piebalds my veins.' A clever girl, Miss McKittrick trained as a schoolteacher, and, aged seventeen, married Andrew Ross, stationmaster at Larne Harbour. For authorial purposes she later knocked an 's' off her married name and borrowed 'Amanda' from the gothic fiction she loved.

Ros's novels and verse were vanity-published; the first of them with a donation from her husband, on their tenth wedding anniversary. Her vanity, it must be said, was more than adequate to her talent. The Ros *oeuvre* comprises the novels *Irene Iddesleigh* (1897); *Delina Delaney* (1898); *Donald Dudley* (1900); and *Helen Huddleson* (unfinished at the time of her death, in 1936; as was the similarly promising *The Lusty Lawyer*). There were also two volumes of verse: *Poems of Puncture* (1912) and *Fumes of Formation* (1933). In later life, ensconced in a house she called 'Iddesleigh', she was widowed and well enough propertied from small inheritances to concentrate on her writing.

Though Amanda Ros was generally beneath reviewers' notice, the humorist Barry Pain picked up *Irene Iddesleigh* and was humorous at the author's expense. Amanda struck back by describing the London *literateur* as a 'cancerous irritant wart'. She composed a celebratory poem on his death in 1928, rejoicing that there was one less pain in her life. The authoress, as she always termed herself, had the last laugh.

A club of men of letters, including such luminaries of the London literary world as Lord Beveridge, Desmond MacCarthy, and the *Punch*-man, F. Anstey, met regularly to compete with the most ludicrous passages from her work they could come up with. In Oxford, the 'Inklings' – donnish fellows in every sense, such as J. R. R. Tolkien, C. S. Lewis and Charles Williams – would meet in their favourite pub, the 'Bird and Baby' in the dark days of the 1940s, for readings from the Ros *Gesamtwerk*. The victor ludorum was judged to be he who could read longest while keeping the straightest face. Aldous Huxley also ran a Ros-club, which met to savour the lady's stylistic flights and felicities. The author of *Brave New World* was, the deluded lady declared, 'the only critic who understands my writing.' Too true, if she but knew it.

Her most devoted reader, she fondly believed, was King George V, who had, she claimed, no less than twenty-five copies of her work in his library. The reverse fandom has continued, cultishly, to the present day. A contemporary website dedicated to the search for the world's worst writers (www.nickpage.co.uk/worstweb) confidently raises Ros's writing arm, winner and still champion, well ahead of her only serious rival, the laureate of cheese, James McIntyre (1827–1906). McIntyre, a Canadian dairy farmer, unsurprisingly, was the author of such works as 'Ode on the Mammoth Cheese'. It opens: 'We have seen thee, queen of cheese, / Lying quietly at your ease,' and gets cheesily worse. But not worse enough to rival Ros's prose sublimities.

Nick Page, host to the above website, hazards that Ros's *Delina Delaney* 'begins with possibly the most baffling opening sentence in any literature':

> Have you ever visited that portion of Erin's plot that offers its sympathetic soil for the minute survey and scrutinous examination of those in political power, whose decision has wisely been the means before now of converting the stern and prejudiced, and reaching the hand of slight aid to share its strength in augmenting its agricultural richness?

The authoress made a late-life marriage in 1922 after the death of Andy Ross in 1917, and died Mrs Thomas Rodgers.

FN   Amanda Ros (Anna Margaret Ross; née McKittrick; second married name
          Rodgers)
MRT *Irene Iddesleigh*
Biog J. Loudan, *O rare Amanda* (1954)

97. Owen Wister 1860–1938

The great playground of young men. Wister on the West

It is ironic that so many pioneer writers of Westerners were Easterners. Jack Schaefer, author of *Shane*, wrote what is considered by many to be the best example of the genre ever, without having gone any further west than Ohio. Owen Wister was born and bred in Pennsylvania, where his father was a wealthy physician. The Wisters were upper-class Philadelphians and well connected. Owen's mother was a member of the Kemble acting dynasty. He was educated in the best schools in America and Europe before going on to Harvard where he formed the most important friendship in his life, with Theodore Roosevelt. Like the future president, Wister had a mystical reverence for American wilderness.

After shining at university, Wister intended to devote himself to musical composition and studied in European conservatories. His ambitions were frustrated, however, partly by lack of parental support. He returned, disconsolately, to America where he worked for a while in the law. But his health was also failing. On the advice of S. Weir Mitchell (the physician-novelist later demonised by Charlotte Perkins Gilman), he went west. Mitchell's advice worked better than for the author of 'The Yellow Wall-paper'. Wyoming was both therapeutic and inspirational.

A physically revived Wister returned to Harvard and took a degree in law, setting up practice in Philadelphia in 1888. But the West called him, irresistibly. After several trips he began producing cowboy romances, which proved popular in magazine form and were collected in volumes with brand-name titles such as *Red Men and White* (1896). The work of Wister's which had the longest lasting impact, and effectively reformed the dime-novel Western into something resembling a respectable genre was *The Virginian* (1902). The work sold powerfully and the play adapted from it, starring Dustin Farnum, ran for ten years. *The Virginian* was further popularised by the six movie versions, notably the 1929 version starring Gary Cooper.

It is a polite novel, which endorses *politesse*. The most famous words in novel, play and film – 'when you call me that, SMILE' – are rendered forever mysterious by the fact that in none of them is the verbal insult specified. In deference to his patron, Theodore Roosevelt, Wister further toned down a description of a horse sadistically having its eye gouged out. The episode appeared in the magazine version but not in the book version – which is dedicated to Roosevelt, with the note: 'some of these pages you have seen, some you have praised, one stands new-written because you blamed it'. 'Teddy' represented Wister's ideal politician. For both of them the West ('this great playground of young men') was a necessary testing ground for the American race, where those fittest to survive and carry American civilisation forward would 'select' themselves by struggle. The unfit would not survive. Indians (Native Americans) fell into the second category.

As is often noted, Wister's conception of the cow-puncher is a reincarnation of the medieval 'very parfit' knight, with the attendant code of chivalry and honour. The cowboy was 'the last romantic figure upon our soil', Wister claimed. The setting is the plains of Wyoming and the foothills of the Tetons, in the period 1874–90. Even at the time Wister was writing, the pristine West was, as he lamented, 'a vanished world. No journeys, save those which memory can take, will bring you to it now ... Time has flowed faster than my ink.'

The narrator (like the Virginian, unnamed, but evidently Wister himself) comes from New York to Medicine Bow in Wyoming, by train; he is visiting the ranch of a friend, Judge Henry. He is met at the station by the laconic cow-puncher, the 'Virginian', who will conduct him to their destination. The men have various adventures in town before leaving, including the gambling scene, which features the legendary 'smile' instruction. The narrator is impressed by the physical grace and homespun eloquence of his guide, who later becomes his mentor during his 'tenderfoot' stage of apprenticeship into the ways of the Wild West. Insofar as the random episodes have a plot, they revolve around the Virginian's growing love for the easterner schoolmarm, Molly Wood, whose heart he wins when he rescues her from drowning. She in turn educates him, giving him good books to read – Hawthorne, George Eliot ('she talks too much' is his not inapt comment) and above all, Walter Scott, who confirms the Virginian in his sense of what honour is.

That honour is tested in the last scene of the novel when he has to choose between Molly and duty. He has been called out by a bad man. It is the eve of his wedding and the peace-loving Molly tells him if he loves her, he will turn his back and not fight. But the Virginian has to do what he has to do. He goes out and shoots his man. 'New England conscience' – in the form of Molly's anxiety – 'capitulates to love'.

Wister himself had capitulated in 1898, marrying a cousin, Mary Channing. He wrote only one other novel of any interest after *The Virginian* – *My Lady Baltimore* (1906), which was not a Western. His later years seem to have been generally frustrated. He was rabidly patriotic in the First World War. Nothing he wrote had anything like the effect of *The Virginian*, whose narrative is still plundered, time after time, by Hollywood.

FN   Owen Wister
MRT   *The Virginian*
Biog D. Payne, *Owen Wister: Chronicler of the West, Gentleman of the East* (1985)

98. Amy Levy 1861–1889

A Jewish Jane Austen. Lisa Allardice

Levy was born at Clapham into a cultured and orthodox Jewish family, generally relaxed on matters of religion, who actively encouraged their daughter's precocious literary talents. Her father, Lewis Levy, was a stockbroker. She was educated, from fifteen, at school in Brighton and then at Newnham College, Cambridge, where she was the first Jewish woman to matriculate. This pioneer status was, apparently, stressful and she left after her first year, without a degree.

Levy had been publishing verse since her thirteenth year. At university in 1881 her first volume of poetry came out under the distinguished imprint of Grant Richards. Entitled *Xantippe and Other Verse*, after Socrates' fabled shrew of a wife, the work proclaimed the independence of spirit which had been latently evident, even in childhood. The style is markedly Browningesque – the intellectuals' favourite poet at the time. In the title poem, Xantippe ends her melancholy monologue with what looks like imminent defenestration – following her suicidal husband.

The details of Levy's subsequent life are tantalisingly mysterious. She may have taught, or even have worked in a factory from idealistic motives. She was a close friend of novelists Olive Schreiner and Clementina Black; and of socialists such as Eleanor Marx. There was an informal coterie of these progressive women formed around the British Museum Reading Room, in Bloomsbury and in the newly formed University Club for Ladies. She is plausibly claimed by modern admirers, and close readers of her verse, as having been lesbian. In 1884 she published another volume of poetry with the typically self-deprecating title *A Minor Poet and Other Verse*. The minor poet of the title poem commits suicide with the final words – 'Too heavy is the load. I fling it down.'

In 1886, she is known to have travelled to Italy, where she met the poet, feminist and novelist, Vernon Lee. Her first published novel, *Reuben Sachs* (1888) is the story of a sexually unscrupulous would-be politician, and the woman Judith he sacrifices. Its depiction of Jewish life in London as grossly materialistic caused a furore and was widely taken as a race libel, as had been Julia Frankau's similarly anti-Semitic *Dr Phillips* (1887). In an earlier essay, in the *Jewish Chronicle* in 1886 on 'The Jew in Literature', Levy had made crystal clear that she wished to deromanticise the image projected by philo-Zionist works such as *Daniel Deronda*.

Her subsequent novel, *Miss Meredith* (1889) was less tendentious. It is the story in autobiographical form of an English governess, Elsie Meredith, who falls in love with the son of the Italian household, where she is employed as an 'upper servant'. Its lightness of tone suggests it may have been written some time before its actual publication. Levy also wrote the shorter fiction *The Romance of a Shop* (1888), in which four Lorimer sisters (based on Clementina Black and her sisters) set up their photography business in Baker Street.

Prey to depression, Levy committed suicide in her parents' London home, in an upstairs room, by suffocating herself with charcoal fumes, having just corrected her fifth and final volume of poems for press and dedicated it to Clementina Black. Oscar Wilde was an admirer and published Levy in his magazine *Woman's World*, and wrote a gracious obituary for her. She was, he said, 'a girl who has a touch of genius'. Aged twenty-seven at the time of her death, 'girl' is not – as it might otherwise have been – offensive. And recent advocates have detected more than a 'touch' of genius in her work. She is recorded as the first Jewish woman to be cremated in England. Her family burned her private papers, leaving the details of her life as forever inscrutable as her corporeal ashes.

FN   Amy Judith Levy
MRT   *Reuben Sachs*
Biog   L. H. Beckman, *Amy Levy: Her Life and Letters* (2000)

99. Florence L. Barclay 1862–1921

All work was 'spiritual work' to my mother. Florence Barclay's daughter

Florence Charlesworth was born and spent her early years in a country rectory at Limpsfield, Surrey, one of a number of daughters of a well-off clergyman. Florence's family nickname – tender but double-edged – was 'Benny', because her parents 'so wanted a son', a Benjamin. It was a writing family. Her aunt, Maria Louisa Charlesworth, published pious tales for the young, notably the perennially popular *Ministering Children* (1854). A semi-invalid, Miss Charlesworth lived with her brother Samuel's family, and was a permanent fixture in Florence's domestic circle.

A man of a 'reserved, undemonstrative nature', who had married late in life, the Revd Charlesworth was excessively high-minded. When Florence was seven, he gave up his comfortable living in Surrey to take up one in Limehouse, the most deprived area in the East End of London (where, one may recall, Wilde's Dorian Gray goes for his illicit pleasures of the night).

Precocious, even by Victorian standards, 'Benny' taught herself to read by the age of three. The New Testament was among the first things she read. She later underwent a number of religious crises in childhood. Governess-educated, she gave evidence of a remarkable singing voice from her earliest years and was performing publicly at the age of twelve, assured that she would go to the Royal Academy of Music. But it was not to be. 'Florrie' (as Benny now was) married the Revd Charles W. Barclay in 1881; a family friend, he had singled her out as his future wife, when she was just eleven. The couple married in her father's Limehouse church, in front of a crowd of 2,500 loyal parishioners. Florence had always yearned to visit the Holy Land, and tread where 'He' had trod. Before returning to his ministry, her husband indulged his young bride with a four-month wedding trip to Palestine. It was a formative experience in her adult life.

Already pregnant (she would have five children in as many years, eight in all), Florence returned to Hertfordshire to assume the duties of an Anglican clergyman's wife. Her husband was rich – there was a second home in the Isle of Wight and family holidays in Switzerland – but the Revd Barclay was also clerically dutiful to a self-martyrising degree, and imposed the same stern discipline on his wife. Florence (named after the heroine of the Crimea) was willing, and in the intervals that child-bearing allowed, conducted Bible classes, undertook district visiting and trained the choir. But it was too much and in 1891 she suffered a breakdown, brought on by peritonitis, and was an invalid for a year. In this unwonted (and wholly unwanted) leisure she began writing fiction under the male pseudonym 'Brandon Roy'. In 1905 she was again stricken by illness – her heart being strained by an energetic bicycle ride to Cromer (she was a staunch believer in physical exercise for women and the 'Bloomerism' rational dress associated with it). She was confined to bed for nine months and it was during this weary time that she wrote *The Rosary*, although the work was held back for three years, until 1909.

Florence was fascinated, insofar as an orthodox country parson's wife decently could be, by telepathy and believed, like Christ, that she could perform miracles. She was discreet about her powers, but it seeps, thematically, into *The Rosary* – which manifestly contains other elements of Barclay's own life. The narrative opens in the full glory of a summer afternoon at an English country house, seat of the Duchess of Meldrum. She has a niece, Jane Champion, who is twenty-nine, and who has, all her life 'filled second place very contentedly'. Jane is first encountered by the reader playing a bracing round of golf. At the same weekend party is a young aristo-crat, Garth Dalmain ('Dal'), an atheist. At *his* country seat (there is a lot of country sitting), Castle Gleneesh, he overhears Jane singing a song, 'The Rosary', whose theme is that life should be a string of devotional beads, 'each hour a pearl, each pearl a prayer'. On the spot Dal falls in love with Jane and is converted to Christian-ity. When Jane refuses his offer of marriage he rushes off. She regrets her harshness ('Oh my God, send him back!') and the scene shifts to Egypt. What should she do? Jane asks the Sphinx. She returns to Castle Gleneesh, only to find that Dal has been blinded in a shooting accident. All ends well, with (tuneful) marriage in a little Epis-copal chapel in the hills.

The novel was preposterously successful. By 1921, sales of over a million were claimed. *The Rosary* popularised Ethelbert Nevin's song of the same name, which is central in the novel's plot. So profitable was the book that its American publisher, Harpers, named one of its new buildings 'The Rosary'. Barclay donated the proceeds of *The Rosary* and her other dozen or so novels to worthy causes, principally homes for motherless children. She did treat herself to a limousine and a chauffeur – but only in order the better to lecture (i.e. preach) on pious themes to the large audiences she could command. In 1912, an accident in her vehicle caused a cerebral haemorrhage, though this did not prevent her throwing her formidable energies into the fight for women's suffrage. She died of complications incurred by operations to relieve the ailments which had earlier allowed her to become a novelist, exacerbated, her doctors solemnly reported, 'by her long hours of writing'.

FN   Florence Louisa Barclay (née Charlesworth)
MRT *The Rosary*
Biog *The Life of Florence Barclay; a study in personality* (by 'one of her daughters', 1921)

100. O. Henry 1862–1910

Bar-room Maupassant

William Sydney Porter was born in Greensboro, North Carolina, the second son of a doctor. His early years were spent in a 'somnolent' community in the south, in the optimistically named Reconstruction Period following the Civil War. After the death of his mother, when he was three, he was brought up by an aunt and his maternal grandmother. He began his working life in an uncle's drugstore, as an apprentice pharmacist. Once qualified in this useful trade he moved, aged eighteen, to Texas, where he began to cultivate his skills as a quick-draw cartoonist and illustrator and – in his own grandiloquent phrase – 'ran wild on the prairies'. He married in 1887, to his Greensboro sweetheart, and cut back, somewhat, on the running wild. In 1891, rising in the world, he went to work in Austin's First National Bank.

Porter's literary career took off in the mid-1890s when he began turning out short stories for local newspapers. His career as a banker meanwhile crashed when he was charged with embezzling the sizeable sum of $5,000 – filched, apparently, to help launch his own comic paper, *The Rolling Stone*. He was drinking heavily and this has always been an obscure episode. Porter went on the run to central America where he freebooted for two years beyond the long arm of the Texas marshal. He returned to Austin, and arrest, on being informed that his wife, Athol, was dying. After her death in 1897, he was sentenced to five years' imprisonment from 1898. While a prisoner in Ohio, Porter began seriously to write and publish short stories for national magazines and papers, principally to support his now motherless daughter, and took care to have the material dispatched by a middleman, so as to conceal its origin in the penitentiary system. In 1901 he was released, with remission for good conduct, and moved to New York. Under the pseudonym 'O. Henry' (the origin of the pen-name is obscure), he began to turn out a torrent of short fiction which brought him immense celebrity and wealth. New York settings and urban *Weltschmerz* predominate in his narratives.

He specialised in what Vachel Lindsay called 'the triple hinged surprise', and Aristotle called 'peripety'. 'The Cop and the Anthem' is a prime example of what became famous as the 'O. Henry ending', shown at its sharpest in his best-known collection, *Cabbages and Kings*. Soapy, a New York street bum, does everything he can to get arrested – ordering meals in expensive restaurants he can't pay for, committing flagrant acts of petty larceny and minor affray. He wants to be put away in prison for a while – winter is coming on and he needs warm quarters until spring when he can return to the streets. But fate perversely smiles on him. He cannot get anyone to press charges for his deliberate misdemeanours. Disconsolate, he goes into a church, where organ music is playing. It moves him profoundly, and, as he stands outside the church, he finds himself a changed Soapy:

> He would pull himself out of the mire; he would make a man of himself again; he would conquer the evil that had taken possession of him. There was time; he was comparatively young yet; he would resurrect his old eager ambitions and pursue them without faltering. Those solemn but sweet organ notes had set up a revolution in him. To-morrow he would go into the roaring downtown district and find work. A fur importer had once offered him a place as driver. He would find him to-morrow and ask for the position. He would be somebody in the world. He would –
>
> Soapy felt a hand laid on his arm. He looked quickly around into the broad face of a policeman.
>
> 'What are you doin' here?' asked the officer.
>
> 'Nothin',' said Soapy.
>
> 'Then come along,' said the policeman.
>
> 'Three months on the Island,' said the Magistrate in the Police Court the next morning.

O. Henry describes himself in a letter of his early New York years, when his best work was done, as 'living all alone in a great big two rooms on quiet old Irving Place three doors from Wash Irving's old home'. A widower, Porter remarried in 1907, unhappily. He had been a heavy drinker all his life and was now clinically alcoholic.

It was probably as much an occupational hazard as moral delinquency. His tales have a great deal of brass rail, sawdust and spit, bar-room story about them; like Walt Whitman, he fed on the New York street life. Two quarts of whisky a day, although it hastened his death, never slowed his pen.

Between 1907 and 1910, O. Henry published some seven volumes of collected short stories. He died, aged only forty-eight, of alcohol-induced cirrhosis of the liver, in North Carolina where he had gone to recover his health. His posthumous fame (as the 'Yankee Maupassant') grew with constant reprintings of his work and film adapations. In 1919 an annual 'O. Henry Award' was established for the outstanding short story of the year. Few of the winners have been as readable as him.

FN   O. Henry (William Sydney Porter)
MRT *The Voice of the City* (collection)
Biog R. O'Connor, *O. Henry: The Legendary Life of William S. Porter* (1970)

101. Violet Hunt 1862–1942

The sweetest Violet in England. Oscar Wilde's flowery compliment

The daughter of the novelist Margaret Raine Hunt and artist Alfred William Hunt, Violet was born in Durham and – the family moving to London in her childhood – grew up among the Rossetti circle. She sat for a number of painters, notably Edward Burne-Jones and Walter Sickert. In later life she became a sworn enemy of D. G. Rossetti for his treatment of his model, Elizabeth Siddal, whose biography she wrote – tendentiously. From girlhood she was spectacularly beautiful: 'Botticelli by Burne-Jones,' according to the actress Ellen Terry. Hunt was governess-educated, and precociously literary. She was publishing poems, and being paid for them, before she was in her teens. Her father, himself a leading watercolourist, intended her to be a painter and she studied at Kensington Art School until the age of twenty-eight, turning her skills to connoisseurship rather than practice. Thereafter she was, like her mother, a well-known London hostess and woman of letters, admired by, among many others, Oscar Wilde, who is popularly supposed to have proposed to her.

If Oscar did offer to make her his wife (a dangerous thing, it would later prove) she had the sense to refuse. But other choices in her love life were less sensible. A consort of the novelist Ford Madox Ford (i.e. Hueffer, ten years her junior) she was for a while after 1911 known as 'Mrs Hueffer' – illegitimately since the first Mrs Hueffer, from whom Ford separated in 1909, was unwilling to divorce her husband.

Hunt nevertheless defiantly entered 'married 1911' into her *Who's Who* entry – one of her more imaginative works of fiction. 'Who' she married she did not mention.

Her previous lovers included the novelists Oswald Crawfurd, Walter Pollock and Somerset Maugham. She preferred married men, she once said, because they were harder to catch. She was, true to her name, a hunter. Her later lovers included H. G. Wells, who had the distinction of seducing her rather than being seduced by her. 'I rather like her,' said D. H. Lawrence, who met her at one of her London parties, 'she's such a real assassin.' He, evidently, escaped her sexual clutches. She was nicknamed 'Violent Hunt' by her friends who tended to agree with Lawrence about how dangerous she was. Crawfurd was among her longer-lasting paramours. He was married, a notorious philanderer, and infected her with the venereal disease which eventually killed her – although it can hardly be said to have cut short her life (she died in Kensington, during the German Blitz on London – waving her fist, one would like to think). As a director of Chapman and Hall and an influential figure in the London literary world, he was able to assist her career.

Hunt took an active interest in feminist causes and founded the Women Writers' Suffrage League. She was a friend of Henry James and an early patron of D. H. Lawrence. Her own fiction includes *The Maiden's Progress* (1894), a 'novel in dialogue' which follows the career of 'Moderna', a modish heroine of eighteen, first discovered in her bedroom in Queen's Gate, languishing on her bed in a white peignoir; and *The Human Interest* (1899), a story of modern 'sex problems' with a novelist heroine, Egida, who is a 'great Ibsenite'. Hunt's dozen or so novels are cynical in tone and often funny. Her ghost stories, *Tales of the Uneasy* (1911), retain some popularity. Her weird tale, 'The Prayer', displays Hunt's light Jamesian touch. It opens with a wife, kneeling by her just deceased husband's deathbed:

> 'Edward – dear Edward!' she whispered, 'why have you left me? Darling, why have you left me? I can't stay behind – you know I can't. I am too young to be left. It is only a year since you married me. I never thought it was only for a year. "Till death us do part." Yes, I know that's in it, but nobody ever thinks of that! I never thought of living without you! I meant to die with you …
>
> 'No – no – I can't die – I must not – till my baby is born. You will never see it. Don't you want to see it? Don't you? Oh, Edward, speak! Say something, darling, one word – one little word!'

Her prayer is answered. Edward is pulled back with 'reluctant moans … over the threshold of life'. Bad things happen thereafter for Mr and Mrs Arne and their baby.

The last years of Hunt's life ('flurried years,' she dismissively called them in her 1926 memoir) were excessively troubled with money problems (although she left almost £9,000 on her death), illness, lawsuits and the personal disappointments of a beautiful woman who had outlived her beauty, her money, and her time. She is best remembered to posterity as the original of Florence in Ford's masterwork, *The Good Soldier* (1915). Somerset Maugham based Rose Waterford on her in *The Moon and Sixpence*. Novels remember her, even if her own novels are forgotten.

FN   Isobel Violet Hunt
MRT *The Maiden's Progress*
Biog B. Belford, *Violet: The Story of the Irrepressible Violet Hunt and her circle of lovers and friends* (1990)

102. Edith Wharton 1862–1937

The continued cry that I am an echo of Mr James ... makes me feel rather hopeless.
Wharton to her editor at Scribner's, 1904

Wharton's life is fascinating; even more so is the Whartonian lifestyle. What stands out from any examination of it is the extraordinary wealth of the 'leisure class' into which Edith Jones was born (and which, in her later fiction, she anatomises as precisely as did her favourite sociologist Thorstein Veblen, who invented the term). Her immediate family was not quite among the fabled New York '400' upper-crust families. Their riches were not 'embarrassing', but they were well within the privileged enclave of what the future novelist would call the Age of (New York) Innocence – before, that is, Europe poured its racial dregs through Ellis Island.

The young Miss Jones was spared from the need ever to work by a bequest from a distant relative that left her, in modern currency values, a millionairess for life. Edith Wharton, as she became, was raised in a milieu of opulent furniture and emotional frigidity. When she was eleven, she 'timorously' showed her mother the opening of a story she had written in which a Mrs Tompkins says to a Mrs Brown, 'If only I had known you were going to call I would have tidied up the drawing-room.' Mrs Jones's 'icy' rebuke to her daughter was 'Drawing-rooms are always tidy.' Wharton, chronically ill during childhood, was tutored at home, in a series of tidy drawing-rooms. Thereafter, she taught herself in libraries. This education served her well and in her prime she was able to hold her own in salon conversation with Henry James and André Gide – in either French or English, as required.

Bustled into marriage with a philistine mate, Wharton endured twenty-eight years before divorcing him. The union was probably sexless. Wharton's fulfilling relationships were with friends as cultured as she had made herself, and her husband 'Teddy' (Edward Robbins Wharton) did not fall into that category. His congenital dimness was compounded by late-onset congenital madness. He casts a paler shadow in biographies of Wharton than his wife's lap-dogs (there survives a wonderful photograph of Wharton with a couple of pooches draped around her neck like a fox fur).

For the better part of her life, Wharton would be half-rooted in upper-class New York, while physically resident in France, where she died in 1937 and where her now grown-over grave is. However, the grass does not grow over Wharton's literary reputation, and after a posthumous slump it has boomed in recent years. Posterity now knows her much better than did her contemporaries. In the 1960s, private papers were released for the benefit of R.W.B. Lewis's authorised biography. As a result Wharton was no longer encased in the sophisticated corsetry of her public image – 'Henrietta James' – nor the delicately bred lady in front of whom André Gide did not think he could discuss the 'perversions' in his writings, such as *Si le grain ne meurt.*

Wharton had destroyed all her intimate correspondence – even more incineratingly than Henry James – but traces of her private life remained in the archive, recoverable to the 'publishing scoundrel' of Aspernian inclinations. Lewis gleefully spilled exciting details about Wharton's adulterous fling, in middle age, with the 'bounder' Morton Fullerton. 'You are dazzling ... You are beautiful ... But you're not kind,' observed Henry James – whose heart may also have been a little broken by the caddish young man. There were, manifestly, raging fires beneath the Whartonian ice. Looking beneath the surface of novels such as *Ethan Frome* (1911), contemporary readers are privileged to see them in ways their predecessors were not – the work of a writer of passion.

Most exciting of all (until Lewis came along) was Wharton's unpublished sketch 'Beatrice Palmato', with its breathtakingly graphic – and outrageously erotic – description of a father's rape of his half-daughter. Lewis printed it as an appendix: thus assuring that his biography would be everywhere discussed and sell like hot cakes. The fragment had long been available in open files of her papers at Yale and other scholars knew of it, but had refrained doing any more than gossip among themselves out of deference for Wharton's memory. She herself would no more have wanted it published than to be seen riding naked on a white horse down the Champs Elysées.

'Beatrice Palmato' was written around 1917, when the author was in her late fifties. According to surviving notes, the heroine of the tale was to be the half-daughter of a Portuguese banker, living in London. Her mother has committed suicide in a lunatic asylum. She is married – without little physical satisfaction, we assume.

The fragmentary narrative opens with the father's words 'I have been, you see, so perfectly patient.' Patient no longer, under the parlour's 'pink-shaded lamps', he plunges her hand beneath her peignoir into her bosom. She feels 'her two breasts pointing up to them, the nipples hard as coral, but sensitive as lips to his approaching touch'. Having touched, and kneaded the breasts 'like the bread of angels', his tongue twists like a 'soft pink snake' around them, 'till his lips closed hard on the nipples, sucking them with a tender gluttony'. So it goes, to a climax of fellatio and cunnilingus. It's described graphically:

> Suddenly his head bent lower, and with a deeper thrill she felt his lips pressed upon that quivering invisible bud, and then the delicate firm thrust of his tongue, so full and yet so infinitely subtle, pressing apart those close petals, and forcing itself in deeper and deeper through the passage that glowed and seemed to become illuminated at its approach. 'Ah –' she gasped, pressing her hands against her sharp nipples, and flinging her legs apart.

Any printer, publisher or bookseller handling this kind of material could have expected a police raid. What was Wharton doing writing it? She did not, one may surmise, expect to submit it to Scribner's. Its purpose was, as lawyers say, to 'lay a foundation'. Incest would play, allusively and atmospherically (but never graphically) about the published story – were she ever to get round to writing it up.

From another quarter, Wharton has also been a beneficiary of the post-1960s feminist criticism. Her latest 853-page biography – probably the most authoritative which will ever be written – is by her first woman biographer, Hermione Lee, one of whose motives was to rescue Wharton from what she ironically terms 'gallant male biographers' – men like Lewis, that is, who, whatever their 'gallantry', could never know what it was like to be a woman. The third boost to Wharton's current reputation has been Technicolor, notably Martin Scorsese's sumptuous 1993 adaptation of *The Age of Innocence* (1920) exploring what Henry James would call the 'solidity of specification' in Wharton's ornately descriptive fiction (not to say her own formidable expertise in interior decoration and gardening) which works extraordinarily well on the screen. Her melodramatic plotlines – as in Terence Davies's 2000 film adaptation of *The House of Mirth* (1905) – work somewhat less well. None the less Hollywood has done more to put Wharton's fiction on bookshop shelves than all the professors in the English-speaking world.

FN Edith Newbold Wharton (née Jones)
MRT *The Age of Innocence*
Biog H. Lee, *Edith Wharton* (2007)

103. W. J. Locke 1863–1930

Slight, but one of the most delightful and charming essays in fiction of recent years.
Harold Williams, half praising *The Beloved Vagabond* in 1918

One of the comic highlights in *Howards End* is Leonard Bast's recounting to the Schlegel sisters his midnight ramble. What inspired this act of depressing nocturnal vagabondage? What had Len been reading – one knows he's a bookish sort of cove? He drops the names Meredith, Jefferies, and 'RLS', with the aim, patently, of impressing his new friends. But, given the date of *Howards End*'s publication (1910) and of its action (a couple of years earlier), it is likely that a direct inspiration for Bast's taking to the road was W. J. Locke's 1906 bestseller, *The Beloved Vagabond*. It was not, for a certainty, a volume the Schlegels would have had on their coffee table.

Locke was born in Demerara, British Guiana, and went to school in Trinidad. His parents were English, colonial, and well off. He attended St John's College, Cambridge, as a scholar, graduating with a degree in mathematics in 1884. For six years or so, in the early 1890s, he worked as a schoolmaster at, among other places, Clifton College, Bristol. Given the schools that employed him, Locke was evidently good at his job but, as evidently, did not much like it. There may have been some disgrace. Biographical details are scarce – itself sometimes a significant detail. His first novel, *At the Gate of Samaria* (1895), deals with sexual (heterosexual) improprieties. *The Morals of Marcus Ordeyne* (1905) has as its hero a former schoolmaster who gets into a pickle with a married woman. *Derelicts* (1897) has a hero falsely accused of fraud. Locke's health may also have been a problem – he contracted tuberculosis in the early 1890s. Another of his novels, *A Study in Shadows* (1896) is set in Switzerland, where Locke may have gone for his lungs.

For whatever reason, he gave up the classroom. From 1897 to 1907 he served as secretary to the Royal Institute of British Architects and moved to London. The post evidently gave him time to write and his career as a bestselling author took off, meteorically, with *The Beloved Vagabond*. It inspired a 'happy tramp' genre, later exploited by Wells in works such *The History of Mr Polly* (1910) and, pre-eminently, by Jeffery Farnol in *The Broad Highway* (1911). Locke's vagabond is a 'wandering philosopher', Paragot, a wine-loving Gascon. Paragot buys a young cockney boy, Augustus Smith, for half-a-crown, and renames him 'Asticot', on the whimsical grounds that 'it expresses you better'. Asticot becomes a disciple and Paragot's Boswell. A figure with a romantic past, Paragot is initially the manager of a Bohemian London club. Losing this position after a dispute with the owner, he takes to the highway, serenading passers-by with his violin. Thereafter, the novel complicates, peripatetically. *The*

Beloved Vagabond is laced with much high-flown philosophising about life, society and freedom and launches a barrage of cheerful insult against 'the Great British God Respectability'. Respectable British readers duly rewarded Locke with an annual income of £15,000 in his heyday and the novel was filmed four times.

Divorce court records reveal that Locke was cited as co-respondent in the 1910 divorce suit against the woman who became his wife, in 1911. She was an actress, working with him in his capacity as a playwright (twenty-four of his bestsellers were dramatised for the West End stage). The couple had no children and lived quietly at Hemel Hempstead, in a large house – large enough, indeed, to convert into a hospital for the war-wounded, particularly Belgians (the same refugees who, elsewhere, inspired Agatha Christie's Hercule Poirot) in 1914. The Belgian government decorated Locke for his philanthropy after the war. He continued writing novels until his death in Paris, clocking up a lifetime total of thirty-two, though none enjoyed the runaway success of *The Beloved Vagabond*. Leonard Bast should have been so lucky.

FN   William John Locke
MRT *The Beloved Vagabond*
Biog *ODNB* (E. O'Brien, revised by Charlotte Mitchell)

104. Thomas Dixon 1864–1946

Civilisation has been saved!

Dixon was born during the Civil War in North Carolina, one of five children of a Baptist minister. Before the war the Dixon family was rich; after the war they found themselves plunged into abject poverty – down there with the 'darkies' they had always lorded it over. The disgrace had a (de)formative effect on the growing Thomas. During these hard years his father (also 'Thomas Dixon') rode with the Ku Klux Klan and became a senior member, or 'Wizard', as did other disaffected members of his family. The KKK, an underground movement, had been formed by veterans of the Confederate Army to assert white supremacy (by violence if necessary) against reforms imposed by the victorious North and the hated Republican Party. It established a surrogate aristocracy for an unfairly, as they thought, degraded master-class.

A clever boy, Thomas entered Wake Forest university aged fifteen and went on, four years later, to Johns Hopkins on a full scholarship, qualifying, after an unsuccessful stab at a career on the stage (his lifelong love), as a lawyer. One of his contemporaries at Hopkins, and a personal friend, was the future President, Woodrow Wilson. While at law school, his father urged him towards a political career and in 1885 he was elected to the North Carolina legislature – but resigned a year later to enter the Baptist ministry. In the same year, 1886, he married. He was a wildly popular 'lyceum lecturer' and gave dramatic sermons to admiring congregations as far north as New York and Boston. John D. Rockefeller was one of the admirers. By 1895 he had mustered sufficient support to form his own 'People's Church', based in Manhattan, whose doctrines cunningly mixed Christianity and protest politics. He undertook gruelling lecturing tours across the continent, firing up audiences wherever he spoke. His health was not strong, however. In 1903 he and his family (there were three children) retired to a quieter life in Virginia.

Dixon's career in fiction began with his seeing a stage performance of *Uncle Tom's Cabin*, which inflamed his dormant KKK sentiments. He resolved to strike back, with *romans à thèse* asserting the Southern cause. There followed *The Leopard's Spots* (1902), *The Clansman* (1905) and *The Traitor* (1907), which were bestsellers – particularly *The Clansman*, which sold 40,000 copies in its first ten days of publication. *The Clansman* is proudly dedicated to the author's uncle, a 'Grand Titan of the Invisible Empire' (i.e. the KKK). It opens with victory for the Union being shouted through the streets of Washington. Young, beautiful, and 'fair' Elsie Stoneman has nursed back to health a young Rebel officer, Ben Cameron, who will face the firing squad when he recovers for the crime of fighting behind enemy lines as a 'guerrilla'. Elsie goes to Lincoln and successfully pleads in person for Ben's life. The fatherly President gladly grants a pardon. He goes on to explain that his aim for the United States has never been negro emancipation, perish the thought, but repatriation of the former slaves to Africa: 'I can conceive of no greater calamity than the assimilation of the Negro into our social and political life as our equal.' 'Mulatto citizenship' is an abomination to every right-thinking American.

Elsie and Ben duly marry and return to his native South Carolina, only to discover that 'the white man's day is done'. The couple suffer vile humiliations and atrocities. Ben's father, the saintly Dr Cameron, is hauled off to prison in shackles by a jeering band of the South's new negro tyrants. A band of blacks gang-rape Ben's former love, the 'belle' Marion Lenoir, and her mother. Unable to live with the shame the ladies commit suicide. The Klan avenges them – bloodily. The 'Fiery Cross' burns everywhere; the white-sheeted riders restore justice and (for the uppity blacks) condign retribution. The novel's last words are: 'Civilisation has been saved, and the South redeemed from shame.' Hallelujah.

Dixon composed a version of *The Clansman* for touring companies in 1906. Waves of immigration through Ellis Island at the turn of the century had inflamed national xenophobia, so these were also good years for the Klan. Having found his new vocation – and having lost much of his fortune in the financial crash of 1907 – Dixon embarked on a series of race-propaganda novels. They sold in their day, but none, other than *The Clansman*, lasted – nor deserved to. Immortality was bestowed on that garbage-novel when D. W. Griffith took it as the source for his epochal film, *Birth of a Nation*, in 1915. Dixon was the first novelist ever to receive 'subsidiary rights' ($2,000) for a film adaptation of his work. His old classmate, President Wilson, arranged for private showings of the movie for his cabinet, the Supreme Court, and the Houses of Congress. The KKK, unsurprisingly, seized on Griffith's film as a recruiting sergeant.

Dixon realised the huge new 'congregation' that was available through film and set up his own studio in Los Angeles, adapting five of his novels for the screen between 1915 and 1923. His career as a film-maker failed as did later speculations in land: he was totally wiped out in the Great Crash of 1929. His last twenty years were passed in poverty, bereavement and political frustration (particularly with the 'Communist' Roosevelt). He retired to North Carolina and made ineffectual interventions in public life. In 1937 his wife died; and two years later he was crippled by a stroke, lingering on, an invalid, for seven years. He made a bedside second marriage with his personal assistant and died a forgotten man. However, *Birth of a Nation* remains one of the acknowledged founding classics of American film. If there is an afterlife, it is pleasing to think of Dixon on 4 November 2008, seething, even more boilingly, in his racist hell at the presidential (no less) triumph of 'mulatto citizenship'.

FN   Thomas F. Dixon, Jr
MRT   *The Clansman*
Biog R. C. Cook, *Fire from the Flint: The Amazing Careers of Thomas Dixon* (1968)

105. Israel Zangwill 1864–1926

The Dickens of the Ghetto.

Zangwill was born in Whitechapel, London. His father, a businessman in a small way, had fled persecution in Russia, arriving in England in the 'Year of Revolution', 1848. His mother was a Jewish refugee from pogroms in Poland. The family background was impoverished and the Zangwill household was nomadic during Israel's early years. He first went to school in Bristol where his intellectual gifts became apparent, but in 1872 the family returned to London where Israel attended the Jews' Free School in Whitechapel. Aged ten, he was already writing stories of school life. At sixteen he won a short story competition in addition to every educational scholarship going. He eventually graduated from London University in 1884 (having attended night classes) with the highest honours in Languages and Philosophy.

By this point in his life Zangwill had shifted from the religious orthodoxy of his father to something more moderate. He gave up a career in school teaching in 1888 and devoted himself to writing. His first published novel was *The Premier and the Painter* (1888) co-written with Louis Cowen. A fantasy, the work owes something to Mark Twain's *The Prince and the Pauper*. Zangwill was always alert to the popular touch in fiction. In 1890 he founded the comic paper *Ariel*, which he edited until 1892. In its pages he published various short stories, collected as *The Bachelors' Club* (1891) and *The Old Maids' Club* (1892). A gifted practitioner of the detective novel, it was Zangwill who invented the 'locked room' puzzle-plot – murder behind closed doors. But he was already marked out for something higher than popular fiction, and was commissioned by the Jewish Publication Society of Philadelphia (alarmed by American anti-Semitism, triggered by waves of immigrants fleeing Russian persecution) to write something quite different – a novel about his people. What the JPSP had in mind was a '*Robert Elsmere* for Jews' and Zangwill duly produced *Children of the Ghetto* (1892).

It was hugely successful with all classes of reader. Subtitled 'A Study of a Peculiar People', the narrative takes the form of a bundle of interlinked tales, giving the sense of a tight-knit, if often quarrelsome, community. The first half of the narrative is set among the first-generation Jewish ghetto population (the '*Schnorrers*' and shopkeeping petty bourgeois) of London's Stepney and Whitechapel districts, swollen by the recent influx of Polish refugees. The second part, 'The Grandchildren of the Ghetto', deals with the lives of second-generation Jews (much less sympathetic to Zangwill) who have become rich and cultivated. The novel ends with the promise of new lives in the new 'Promised Land', America. 'Assimilation' and 'Emigration' – the two great Jewish themes in fiction – are pondered throughout.

Zangwill followed up the success of this work with *Ghetto Tragedies* (1893) and *Dreamers of the Ghetto* (1898). In 1896 he met Theodor Herzl, then in London from Hungary to proselytise for a Zionist state in Palestine. Zangwill became an eager convert and on Herzl's death in 1904 he took over leadership of the movement and was a proponent of the so-called Uganda plan for an African homeland for Jews. In later life his active pro-Zionism modified its 'territorialism' into a campaign for more general tolerance for diaspora communities.

As a writer, after 1900 Zangwill concentrated on plays for the English and

American stage, of which the most famous was *The Melting Pot* (1908). It was he who put this most equivocal of concepts into general circulation. His last years were clouded by poor health and political frustration: in the depth of his disillusionment he gave a notorious speech in New York, in 1923, declaring Zionism to be dead. In 1903 he married a Gentile, Edith Ayrton (daughter of the physicist William Ayrton) who was also a novelist, and they had three children.

FN   Israel Zangwill
MRT   *Children of the Ghetto*
Biog J. H. Udelson, *Dreamer of the Ghetto: The Life and Works of Israel Zangwill* (1990)

106. M. P. Shiel 1865–1947

Sensible people ought to have a complete set of Shiel. Rebecca West

Matthew Phipps Shiel was born in Montserrat in the West Indies, where his father was a jobbing tailor, merchant and lay Methodist minister. Both his parents were of mixed race and Shiel's grandmothers had been slaves – something he kept from public knowledge during his lifetime. His father was pale enough to pass for white, which enabled a colonist's education for his son and heir. The ninth child, he was preceded by numerous sisters, and at the age of fifteen was 'crowned' by his father 'King Felipe of Redonda' – that being a rocky islet in the Caribbean. One of the Leeward group, Redonda was used by gulls, principally as a convenient place to drop guano or birdshit. The Shiels had no legal claim to it – but then, what historical claim did the English have to Montserrat? Shiel took his kingship seriously – a source of much merriment to that remainder of the human race who happened not to be his subjects.

He came to England in 1885. That same year the Criminal Law Amendment Act was passed, whose 'sexual indecency' provisions would have serious implications for Shiel, as they did for Oscar Wilde. He studied medicine, briefly, at St Bart's before discovering an aversion to blood (although he would spill it by the bucket in his later fiction). He tried school-teaching, but after 1895 supported himself by his pen. His literary idol was Poe; he was also congenial with the *fin-de-siècle* decadents (Arthur Machen was a close friend) and split his time between London and Paris. Doing what has never been precisely recorded.

As a novelist, Shiel specialised in wildly imaginative science fiction ('berserk Poe') with a sideline in detective novels. *Prince Zaleski* (1895), his first published work, appeared in John Lane's Keynotes series. It takes the form of three crime mysteries, all solved by an exotic detective with a taste for marijuana. The book was well received and was followed by *The Rajah's Sapphire* (1896), the story of a gem which haunts its owners. *The Yellow Danger* (1898) fantasises Chinese world domination: somewhat improbably, the oriental potentate Yen How becomes infatuated with Ada Seward, a Fulham nursemaid, and starts a genocidal war to get her. His oriental hordes are foiled by Shiel's Anglo-Saxon hero, John Hardy, in a sea battle which claims the lives of twenty million.

The Purple Cloud (1901) is the work of Shiel's that posterity has come most to admire. The hero, Adam Jeffson ('the second parent of the world'), goes to the North Pole and thus misses the poisoning of the rest of humanity by a cloud of 'cyanogen' gas. He spends seventeen years in solitary, pyromaniac splendour before finding his Eve, cowering in a wood in Constantinople. *The Purple Cloud* earned Shiel the status of an apocalyptic prophet, a role he played with gusto over the following years.

Shiel married twice, the first time in 1898. He abandoned that wife and a daughter after five years. His second marriage lasted from 1919 to 1929. There is, however, considerable mystery about his private life, which was complicated. By the first decade of the twentieth century, Shiel's popularity had waned and in 1914 disaster struck when he was sentenced to sixteen months in Wormwood Scrubs. It used to be thought that he was imprisoned for fraud – his financial situation was desperate at this period. He himself blandly described it in later life as 'work for the government'. In fact, as the critic Kirsten Macleod has discovered from examination of his literary remains, Shiel's 1914 conviction was for 'indecently assaulting and carnally knowing' his twelve-year-old 'stepdaughter', Dorothy Sircar, with whose mother, Elizabeth Price, Shiel had formed a common-law marriage, and by whom he had a child. The 1885 law had raised the age of consent from thirteen to sixteen; plus there was the added offence of incest. In an extraordinary letter to his publisher from prison, Shiel protested: 'I myself am wildly non-English ... I have copulated, *as a matter of course* , from the age of two or three with ladies of a similar age in lands where that is not considered at all extraordinary.' Dorothy, he complacently noted, was two years past puberty. Perfectly eligible for a non-Englishman like himself.

Shiel, who lived to a great age, became preoccupied with racist fantasies of the 'Overman' in his later years. His last work, *Jesus*, was apparently finished but remains unpublished. He seems to have died a religious maniac, having anointed as his successor to the kingship of Redonda the excessively minor poet John Gawsworth, who reverently kept Shiel's royal ashes in a biscuit tin on his mantelpiece, dropping a pinch as condiment into the food of any particularly honoured guest. The comedian and scholar of nineteenth-century decadent literature, Barry Humphries, was (unwillingly) one such diner – 'out of mere politeness'.

FN   Matthew Phipps Shiel
MRT   *The Purple Cloud*
Biog   K. Macleod, 'M. P. Shiel and the Love of Pubescent Girls: The Other "Love That
        Dare Not Speak Its Name"' in the journal *English Literature in Transition*, 2008

107. H. G. Wells 1866–1946

We're in a blessed drain-pipe, and we've got to crawl along it till we die. The draper's assistant, Minton, in *Kipps*

Wells had many enemies to combat through life. One enemy, over whom his victory was at best equivocal, was the English class system. 'Bertie' (he did his best to expunge that ghastly lower-class name in later life) was born, the youngest and frailest of four children, in Bromley, on the outskirts of London. His father was a talented professional cricketer, turned untalented shop-keeper, dealing in crockery and cricket bats. This was a period when cricket was firmly divided between 'players' and 'gentlemen'. Joe Wells was no gentleman but he was a demon bowler. A couple of years before his last son's birth he had taken four wickets in as many balls for Kent against Sussex, but his county career ended in 1877 with a broken thigh – incurred, Bromley gossip had it, in an amorous adventure involving high walls and an angry wife. Joe, his biographers record, 'always seemed poised to flee when things got difficult' but, unlike Mr Polly, never made it himself over the wall.

Wells's mother, Sarah, had been an 'upper' servant before marriage. She and Joe bickered and drifted apart. Sarah Wells kept up her connection with Uppark, the grand country house in Sussex, where she had earlier been in service. The upstairs-downstairs life (with himself firmly below) is described in the early Bladesover chapters of *Tono-Bungay* (1909), as is the ineffable scorn directed at the young hero by the daughter of the house for 'dropping his aitches'. This class disability is raised to an art form in Mr Polly's epic – he would say, 'intrudacious' – combat with the English language. People sneered at Wells's 'squeaky' voice and 'put on' accent all his life. Class will out.

In his years at a private school for the sons of tradesmen, Thomas Morley's Commercial Academy, young Wells was marked as phenomenally clever. But that, in the 1870s, was no passport to better things in life. Meritocracy was a century away. Being cleverer than 'gentleman scholars' at Oxbridge would not help young Wells any more than sporting prowess would have helped his 'player' father to the presidency of the MCC. The inevitable bankruptcy of Joe's shop led to Bertie's being apprenticed in 1880, aged thirteen, first as a chemist's boy at Windsor. But Sarah Wells – now housekeeper at Uppark – could not afford the cost of training him as a pharmacist. He was then indentured as a draper's assistant in a department store in Southsea. What lay before him is anatomised, loathingly, in the description of the hero in *The War in the Air*: 'Bert Smallways was a vulgar little creature, the sort of pert, limited soul that the old civilisation of the early twentieth century produced by the million in every country of the world. He had lived all his life in narrow streets, and between mean houses he could not look over, and in a narrow circle of ideas from which there was no escape.' This fate is immortalised in the mordantly comic histories of Kipps and Mr Polly. Both are rescued from careers as counter-jumpers by unexpected bequests – that standby of the Victorian novel, rarely encountered in life.

Wells's own escape from the Kippsian 'drain-pipe' was more audacious. He wrote no more moving letters than those to his mother in 1883, beseeching her to let him break the indentures she had – at great sacrifice – paid for. He would, he threatened, kill himself if she did not allow him to free himself. He wanted more out of life than forelock-pulling with the prospect of his own modest 'establishment' – if he were lucky. His father's luck in that line did not encourage optimism. Sarah responded by gallantly staking what was left of her life's savings on her son's being indeed worthy of better things.

The British school system was, at this period, recruiting trainee teachers from the lower classes – teachers required to deal with the masses of lower-class pupils enrolled by the 1870 Elementary Education Act. The government programme offered the bookish young Wells (as it would, a little later, D. H. Lawrence) a narrow gateway into higher education and 'the professions'. It was a step up. In 1884, after a couple of years as a pupil teacher, Wells won a scholarship to the Normal School of Science (later Imperial College) at South Kensington. There he was exposed to the culture of the metropolis and the full force of late Victorian scientific discovery, principally from T. H. Huxley, 'Darwin's Bulldog', his freshman teacher. 'The year I spent in Huxley's class,' he later wrote, 'was beyond all question, the most educational year of my life.'

That year, and the years that followed, were hard: his scholarship afforded him a guinea a week – starvation wages – and the damage to his health was lifelong. Lifelong, too, was his conversion to materialism, free-thinking and socialism – all fuelled by a diffused anger. He never finished his degree – London proved too distracting.

In 1887 he accepted a job teaching science at a boarding school in Wales. A few months later, a pupil fouled him on the football pitch, which precipitated a general health breakdown and months of convalescence. Nevertheless, in 1890 he got his B.Sc, did some tutoring in London, wrote a textbook on biology, married a cousin, and promptly abandoned her for one of his students, Amy Robbins, with whom he made a second marriage in 1895. He would philander his way through life.

Newspapers and magazines were by now taking occasional pieces from him. He had been toying, since his time at college, with a 'scientific romance', initially called 'The Chronic Argonauts'. It became *The Time Machine* (1895) and was hugely successful. He followed up with a string of other foundation texts of early science fiction: *The Island of Dr Moreau* (1896), *The Invisible Man* (1897), *The War of the Worlds* (1898), *When the Sleeper Wakes* (1899), *The First Men in the Moon* (1901). He had left the classroom behind, but Wells remained incorrigibly didactic. His redefinitions of socialism – which included state-enforced eugenics – were idiosyncratic. The 'low grade man', he ordained in *A Modern Utopia* (1905), must be 'eliminated'. He himself was no longer low grade.

Wells's fiction changed as Victorian England gave way to the twentieth century. *Love and Mr Lewisham* (1900) began a line of autobiographical novels which reached a highpoint with *Ann Veronica* (1909), a 'New Woman' novel; and *The History of Mr Polly* (1910). His personal life over these years was beyond chaotic. At the time of writing *Mr Polly*, his current mistress, Amber Reeves, had just borne him a daughter. Three years on, his next mistress, Rebecca West, would bear him a son. There were two sons by his second wife, Jane. He called it 'free love', but a price was exacted. Mr Polly contemplates divorce from his awful wife Miriam (an ungrateful depiction of his mother) by cut-throat razor. Wells may sometimes have felt something similar – until the next interesting piece of skirt passed by.

As the 'future' arrived (some of it – such as the war in the air – strikingly as prophesied by him), Wells transcended mere fiction. It was too small a container for his mind. He became what the Victorians called a 'sage', the twenty-first century calls a 'public intellectual', and his Southsea mates in the draper's shop would have called a 'right old gasbag'. He wrote histories of the world and told the world what to do (he was much in favour of the League of Nations). He wrote some interesting fiction, including his war novel, *Mr Britling Sees it Through* (1916), which is courageously unjingoistic about the beastly Hun. His last ambitious effort in fiction, *The World of William Clissold* (1926) is over-inflated to busting with its author.

What gives Wells's best (i.e. early) fiction its distinctive tang is the black vein of gloom running through it. The Invisible Man, like the sighted man in the Country of the Blind, finds himself an alien – doomed, despite his advantage, to be an outsider and a social inferior. The world does not like people better than itself. The work which is regarded as Wells's most optimistic, *The Shape of Things to Come* (1933) is dedicated, subversively, to a social thinker even more pessimistic than himself, Ortega y Gasset. At its most controlled, Wellsian pessimism takes the form of satire, as in *Tono-Bungay*'s scathing comedy on quack medicine and the incorrigible foolishness of the buying public. There's not one born every day but millions. Comedy, however, cannot keep the awfulness at bay. The Time Traveller, as far in the future as his machine will carry him, stands on a bleak seashore, regarding a fading sun, with only a giant crab for company. Is this what it was all for – science, art, progress, novels? Wells lived to see the atom bomb he had foreseen half a century before dropped on the country of the Samurai which, half a century earlier, he had seen as his ideal. He witnessed his well-meaning eugenic theories tested to destruction by the Nazis. His final thoughts, expressed in his testament, *Mind at the End of its Tether* (1945), are as hopeless as Kurtz's: 'Homo Sapiens in his present form is played out ...There is no way through the impasse. It will be the Dark Ages over again, a planetary instead of a European Dark Ages.' 'The horror! the horror!'

Writing to a friend, Rebecca West commemorated him cruelly and kindly: 'Dear H. G., he was a devil, he ruined my life, he starved me, he was an unexhaustible source of love and friendship to me for thirty five years, we should never have met, I was the one person he cared to see to the end, I feel desolate because he is gone.' The finest portrait of Wells in extremis is found not in straight biography but in David Lodge's 2011 docunovel, *A Man of Parts*. The prelude pictures 'H.G.' in his Regent's Park flat. London, blacked out, is under bombardment from the Germans. He is very ill. He does not want to die but must. The end of civilisation and his own end merge. There is one final surge of the energy which has fuelled his remarkable career. To a new Preface to the Penguin reissue of *The War in the Air*, he adds 'the epitaph he wished to have inscribed on his tombstone: "I told you so. You *damned* fools."'

FN   Herbert George Wells
MRT *The History of Mr Polly*
Biog N. and J. Mackenzie, *The Time Traveller: The Life of H. G. Wells* (1973; revised edn 1987)

108. Arnold Bennett 1867–1931

They write of unimportant things. Virginia Woolf on Bennett, Wells and Galsworthy

Arnold Bennett was born in the Staffordshire Potteries, or 'Black Country' – a region his fiction would make as famous as Hardy's Wessex. He was one of six children of a struggling Hanley solicitor. The family was Methodist, high-minded, and unusually close-knit. When away from his mother, in later life, Arnold wrote to her every day; on occasion seven times a day. Arnold excelled at school (particularly in French, prophetically) but with all those Bennett offspring higher education could never be afforded, even for a clever lad, and at sixteen he was put to work in his father's office. By night he studied and penned pieces for local newspapers. A loan from his mother enabled him to go to London in 1889. The transplant from the industrial Midlands to *fin de siècle* London was electrifying and he promptly gave up any interest in law. His first literary contact was with John Lane – in whose *Yellow Book* (alongside Wilde and Beardsley) he published his early efforts. Lane it was, on the advice of John Buchan (another rising star), who published Bennett's first novel, *A Man from the North* (1898). Bennett was meanwhile coining it with reviews for the London prints: Gissing's 'New Grub Street' held no terrors for Arnold.

By the turn of the century he was sufficiently prosperous to move his now indigent family into a farmhouse in Bedfordshire. At this period he wrote his first Black Country novel, *Anna of the Five Towns* (1902) – a work whose mood and plot is influenced by his father's concurrent death. The five towns are the linked centres of pottery production in Staffordshire. It was followed by a very different novel, drawing on the author's currently cosmopolitan lifestyle, *Grand Babylon Hotel* (1902). Grand Hotels and the Five Towns would be motifs throughout Bennett's forty-volume strong fictional *oeuvre*. Bennett had made himself a valuable literary property and his commercial affairs were entrusted to the agent J. B. Pinker – to whom he was introduced by his friend H. G. Wells.

After the death of his father in 1903, Bennett went to live in Paris for what would be ten years. On his trips to London, he would stay in the Savoy, where the waiters were circulated with his photograph and a dish (a fishy omelette) was named after him by the head chef (who was reciprocally honoured as 'Rocco' in *Imperial Palace*). H. G. Wells, who knew all about philandering (and, as J. B. Priestley claimed, had the 'better taste in women'), liked to put it about that Bennett was 'undersexed'. This would seem to be borne out by his not marrying his French mistress, Marie Marguerite Soulié, a woman eight years his junior, until he was forty. But portions of Bennett's journal, suppressed until the 1980s, suggest sexual sophistication – and perhaps more than that. Four years before his marriage, he recorded, from conversation with a Parisian *poule*: 'Concerning sexual perversions. Chichi gave me several of her own experiences. As of the man who always wished to make love on the floor, *more canino*. The man who had his *fesses* beaten until they bled ... I explained to her the philosophy of the passion for pain in the enjoyment of love and how it grew on a man like drink.'

It was during the Paris years that Bennett produced much of his best fiction: *Whom God Hath Joined* (1906), *The Old Wives' Tale* (1908), the first volume in the *Clayhanger* trilogy (1910), and the comic novel, *The Card* (1911). By now the streams of literary, journalistic and stage earnings had made Bennett the richest author in England, and he enjoyed his riches as only the once-poor can. He bought himself a yacht and travelled the world. On the outbreak of war in 1914, he joined the Ministry of Information, where his intimate knowledge of France proved useful. His private misgivings about the conflict are reflected in *The Pretty Lady* (1918).

With one of his literary roots in the 1890s and his French connections, Bennett was a friend to modernism. He was, none the less, set up as a target by Ezra Pound, in 'Hugh Selwyn Mauberley' as the crass, sales-grubbing 'Mr Nixon' and – more argumentatively – by Virginia Woolf, who defined her finely touched impression in contradistinction to Bennett's clumping realism. Sides have been taken by partisans ever since. Woolf is currently well ahead. Somerset Maugham – who liked Bennett and hobnobbed with him in Paris – thought him 'like a managing clerk in a city office'. Vulgar, that is, with poor French. It did not help that Bennett retained his provincial accent, perhaps to cover up a bad stammer from which, like Maugham, he suffered.

After the war, Bennett gave up his country house, his mother having died in 1914, and separated from Marguerite in 1921. He formed a 'marital understanding' with an actress Dorothy Cheston, who was twenty-five years younger (she later changed her surname, by deed-poll, to 'Bennett'). The union was 'open' and fraught. In 1926, when their only child, Victoria, was being born, Bennett wrote to Dorothy on the subject of her two, simultaneously running, lovers. 'No doubt normal husbands', he drily observed, 'would regard it as quite proper for you to have two men at once and to leave our baby in my charge ... But I am abnormal.'

During the 1920s, Bennett produced some of his best fiction: *Riceyman Steps* (1923), *Lord Raingo* (1926), and *Imperial Palace* (1930). And, in the *Evening Standard*, he exercised an authority as a reviewer which has rarely been equalled. The official account of his death is that on holiday in France, with Dorothy, he contracted typhoid from tap-water and died of infection three months later. His last, enigmatic, words are recorded as being 'the bill, the bill': appropriate for one so associated with good living. He left some £40,000, which meant that he had no reason to be frightened of hotel bills. Dorothy lived to the ripe age of eighty-six which meant that the dark suspicions that Bennett's family and friends had about her were suppressed. It was suspected, for example, that she misconducted herself with Bennett's nephew, Richard, while her husband lay dying and that she ripped a valuable ring from his dying hand. Most luridly, H. G. Wells was led to exclaim, hysterically: 'She's a bitch and she *killed* Arnold.' Arnold's sisters concurred, disbelieving, apparently, the official version of his death.

FN   Enoch Arnold Bennett
MRT *The Card*
Biog M. Drabble, *Arnold Bennett: A Biography* (1974)

109. John Oliver Hobbes 1867–1906

If the gods have no sense of humour they must weep a great deal.

Pearl Richards was born in Boston, America. Her family was enriched by patent medicines, notably Carter's Little Liver Pills. Pearl grew up deeply attached to her father, John Morgan Richards (1841–1918): a cultivated magnate, he purchased the *Academy* literary magazine (a precursor of the *TLS*) in 1896. The Richards family moved to London in 1868 and it was in that city the young girl spent her formative years. She was brought up in the style approved for upper-class English girls, attending boarding schools in Berkshire and at Paris. Her literary sensibility was remarkably precocious, her first story being published when she was nine.

Richards was presented at court in 1886 and, aged nineteen, she married an English banker, Reginald Walpole Craigie (1860–1930), whom she had met in America. There was one child, a son, born in 1890, whom she had tried unsuccessfully to abort with a particularly violent bout of horse-riding. In the same year the couple parted. She did not give marriage much of a try but her partisans point out that he was drunken, unfaithful, and infected her with venereal disease. Whatever else, Craigie gave his wife the principal theme of her subsequent fiction – utterly wretched marriage and the rottenness of the male sex. The couple were eventually divorced messily, on the grounds of his adultery, in 1895. Three years earlier Craigie had converted to Catholicism. She took a lifelong vow of celibacy, as a conventual gesture. At the same period she resolved both to educate herself and to pursue a career in literature. She had earlier enrolled to study at University College London, the 'Godless Place in Gower Street', for whose English Department she retained a lifelong affection. In the divorce proceedings she had been accused of misconduct with a UCL professor.

In 1891 she published her first novel, *Some Emotions and a Moral*. The story of an ill-assorted and mutually unfaithful marriage, the work is written with a light, worldly wise touch – and was very successful. Since it first appeared in Fisher Unwin's 'Pseudonym Library', the author was obliged to devise a pen-name, John Oliver Hobbes. 'John' she took from her father, 'Oliver' from Cromwell, and 'Hobbes' from the author of *Leviathan*. No woman qualified. She followed up with other modish studies of sex and bohemian manners, dedicated to her view that 'if the gods have no sense of humour they must weep a great deal'. Representative of this highpoint of her career is *The Herb-Moon* (1896), the story of the courtship between a young clerk, Robsart, and an older woman, Rose, whom he initially supposes to be a widow. In fact, she is married to a husband locked up in a lunatic asylum. After many years (and his winning a VC in the Indian Mutiny) they eventually marry. The odd title is a proverbial reference to long engagements. On the strength of such chronicles of sexual cross-purpose, her striking looks, her wealth, and her father's literary clout, Hobbes became a fashionable London woman of letters. Her most enduring work is the pair of novels with a pronounced Catholic-Disraelian theme, *The School for Saints* (1897) and *Robert Orange* (1900).

George Moore, with whom she was sexually (if chastely) and emotionally involved, represents Hobbes vindictively in his fiction. In later life she was – like Mrs Humphry Ward – a member of the Anti-Suffrage League and president of the Society of Women Journalists, 1895–6. She never enjoyed good health, and died young. A John Oliver Hobbes scholarship was established in her memory at University College London (even winners vaguely presume it is in honour of the author of *Leviathan*). Carter's Little Liver Pills were designated a quack remedy (at least as regards the liver's well-being) by the FDA in 1951 and have since disappeared from the drugstore shelves.

FN   John Oliver Hobbes (Pearl Mary-Teresa Craigie; née Richards)
MRT *The School for Saints*
Biog M. D. Harding, *Air-Bird in the Water: The Life and Works of Pearl Craigie (John Oliver Hobbes)* (1996)

110. Norman Douglas 1868–1952

Caprese.

There was a time when, in smart literary conversations, Norman Douglas was regarded as one of the smartest things going. Part of that smartness was his keeping, for the whole of his long depraved life, one jump ahead of the law. Douglas raised literary escapology to a Houdini level. He was caricatured everywhere in the fiction of his period. The most vivid portrait is the giggling, drunken, wicked, travel writer, with exquisite manners and frayed shirt cuffs, 'James Argyle' in D. H. Lawrence's *Aaron's Rod*. Douglas was actually admired, when not despised, by Lawrence and unequivocally admired by E. M. Forster, Ford Madox Ford, and even Virginia Woolf. Graham Greene – in his Capri visits – reckoned him a 'friend'. Joseph Conrad was a house guest and, on one occasion, helped save Douglas from arrest. Elizabeth David, another long-term Caprese, cooked for him, and picked up recipes from him. Echoes of Douglas's one lastingly important novel, *South Wind* (1917), are thrown back everywhere in Aldous Huxley's earliest work. Nabokov also admired Douglas and 'Sebastian Knight' has a newly published copy of *South Wind* on his shelves. James Joyce used Douglas's non-fiction book on the street games of London children as a quarry for *Finnegans Wake*.

Douglas was born of mixed Scottish and German extraction in Austria. His mother was the daughter of a baron, his father a distinguished archaeologist, who killed himself chamois-hunting when Norman (the third son) was five. There was money as well as breeding in the Douglas family, deriving from cotton mills in Germany. He was educated at English schools although German remained his first language (of many) throughout life. As a prelude to a long career in sexual delinquency he was kicked out of Uppingham School, aged fifteen. He completed his education at a *Gymnasium* in Karlsruhe where, over the following six years, he embarked on a promising career in zoology. He was publishing in learned journals before he was twenty.

Douglas's first, life-changing, visit to the island of Capri, 'Siren Land', was in 1888, ostensibly to capture blue lizards. Reptiles were his special subject. In later life he affectionately called the children he abused 'crocodiles'. Douglas resolved on a career which would enable him to travel and in 1893 he sailed through the necessary examinations and entered the British Foreign Office. His first posting was to St Petersburg. What might have been a promising start in life was dashed by his incorrigible sexual turpitude. He conducted affairs, simultaneously, with three aristocratic Russian women and impregnated one. He was lucky to escape with his life and prudently took early retirement. He had, fortuitously, just come into his patrimony. Now rich, he purchased a villa in Naples. The following year, 1898, he married a cousin, Elsa FitzGibbon – it was an inauspicious register office affair. She was pregnant and he feared he had contracted a dose of syphilis. The couple devoted themselves to travel, had two sons and many quarrels.

The first year of the new century saw Douglas's first literary production, *Unprofessional Tales*. It was written in collaboration with his wife in North Africa and published under the pseudonym 'Normyx'. The dedication was to Ouida, a fellow lover of Italy. However, the Douglases divorced in 1904 on the grounds of her adultery – her protests about his pederasty did not hold up in court. Having disposed of his sons at British boarding school, Douglas then removed to Capri, where he built himself a villa. The publication of his successful travel book, *Old Calabria* (1915), coincided with the total loss of his fortune. For the second forty years of his life he lived by his pen and sponged his way to the comfortable lifestyle that was essential to him. In 1904 he claimed his sexuality had switched: from this point on his interests were exclusively pederastic.

Douglas's Mediterranean travel writing chimed with the public taste. But his career was more conveniently prosecuted in London, where he moved in 1910. From 1912 to 1916 he worked, as assistant editor, on Ford Madox Ford's *English Review*. He was now a figure in literary circles and a sought after diner-out, relished for his naughtiness. The naughtiness went rather too far when, in 1916, he was arrested for indecent assault on a sixteen-year-old boy. The war years were not (as for D. H. Lawrence, whose *Rainbow* was on the censor's bonfire) tolerant years for the sexually heterodox. Douglas, as he would always do, fled, 'burning his bridges behind him', as was his motto. He jumped his bail and escaped jail, later composing a mocking valediction: 'Norman Douglas of Capri, and of Naples and Florence, was formerly of England, which he fled during the war to avoid persecution for kissing a boy and giving him some cakes and a shilling.'

Douglas returned, inevitably, to tolerant Capri. At this point, in 1916, he set to writing *South Wind* – his love letter to the island. What he particularly loved, and celebrated, was its ability to evaporate everything – particularly things like sex, religion and politics that so preoccupied the larger world – into airy unimportance.

South Wind is a conversation novel – Peacock-like if one looks backward, Huxley-like if one looks forward in literary time. It is essentially plotless. There is some faint dribble of narrative towards a crime of violence which has no impact whatsoever. What stays in the mind, and can still delight, is the clever schoolboy flights of satire – as that on the island's patroness of sailors, Saint Eulalia:

She was born in 1712 at a remote village in the Spanish province of Estramadura. Various divine portents accompanied her birth. Her mother dreamed a strange dream about a sea-serpent; her father was cured of a painful gouty affliction; the image of Saint James of Compostella in the local church was observed to smile benignly at the very hour of her entry into the world. At the age of two years and eleven months she took the vow of chastity. Much difficulty was experienced in keeping the infant alive; she tormented her body in so merciless a fashion. She refused to partake of food save once in every five weeks; she remained immovable 'like a statue' for months on end; she wore under her rough clothing iron spikes which were found, after death, to have entered deeply into her flesh. She was never known to use a drop of water for purposes of ablution or to change her underwear more than once a year, and then only at the order of her confessor who was obliged to be in daily contact with her.

South Wind came out in England in 1917, the grimmest, coldest year of the war: an event which, although contemporary in setting, it studiously makes no reference.

After the war, with Capri as his base, Douglas toured the fleshpots of Europe. He had a profitable sideline in collectors' editions of his monographs about Capri finely produced by his Italian publisher, Pino Orioli, famous as the publisher of the first edition of *Lady Chatterley's Lover*. Orioli's editions de luxe helped him get by, along with the odd annuity, legacy, and much cadging. *Lady Chatterley* irritated him intensely. In 1928, the year Orioli published it, Douglas brought out his privately printed booklet, *Some Limericks*, which comprised scabrous poems with mockingly owlish apparatus. When I was in the army, in the late 1950s, national servicemen were still merrily (and unknowingly) bawling out Douglas's limericks. A particular favourite was:

> *There was a young man from Australia*
> *Who painted his bum like a dahlia.*
> *Tuppence a smell was all very well*
> *But thruppence a lick was a failure.*

So much for *Kangaroo*.

In 1937, offences against minors (including, by way of variety, infant girls) forced Douglas out of Italy, with only an hour to spare. More painfully, the Second World War forced him back to London. He was now a much-faded figure on the literary scene and wretched on the short rations allowed even a gentleman like himself. After the war he returned, gratefully, to Capri, where he lived out his long vicious life, crippled in his last years by arteriosclerosis. He died, apparently from a self-administered overdose of drugs: excess had always been his style. According to *Time* magazine, he died 'in penury in a rented villa'. In fact he was still, from various sources, pulling in £1,000 a year – which probably counted as penury to Norman

Douglas. There are two versions of his last words. One has it that they were 'love, love, love'. Another, more plausible, is they were: 'Get these fucking nuns away from me.'

FN   George Norman Douglas(s)
MRT   *South Wind*
Biog   M. Holloway, *Norman Douglas: A Biography* (1976)

111. Booth Tarkington 1869–1946

Boyhood is the longest time in life for a boy.

Tarkington is a famous novelist whose actual name is everywhere forgotten. Echoes of his grandiloquent prose (in Orson Welles's fruity baritone and filmic montage) have kept his work, if not its author, fresh and alive, while contemporaries like Winston Churchill (the other one, the American who wrote novels) – judged greater in their time – have faded utterly. Booth Tarkington was Indiana-born (a 'Hoosier') and a lifelong booster of the region, particularly his native Indianapolis which changed during Tarkington's lifetime from a quiet rural town to an industrial powerhouse – this is the background to George Minafer's 'comeuppance', and his family's decay, in the last scenes of *The Magnificent Ambersons* (1918). Tarkington's first novel – not his best but his most characteristic – was *The Gentleman from Indiana* (1899). His father was a lawyer, later a judge, and his pedigree was locally 'magnificent'. Like the Ambersons, the Tarkingtons were among Indianapolis's 'top 500'. Booth's unused forename, 'Newton', honoured an uncle, currently Governor of California.

Tarkington attended Princeton where he enjoyed king-of-the-campus status: he was voted most popular man in his 1893 class. A fellow student recalled him as 'the only Princeton man who had ever been known to play poker (with his left hand), write a story for the *Nassau Lit* (with his right hand), and lead the singing in a crowded room, performing these three acts simultaneously.' Such ambidexterity rarely makes for academic achievement and Tarkington did not graduate (although in the years of his fame Princeton would award him two honorary degrees). He tried public life, unsuccessfully, and was, for one term in 1902, a State Representative in the Indiana government. He married twice; the only child to his marriages dying early. The vicissitudes of childhood would be a principal theme in his best-known and bestselling fiction.

Tarkington had his first bestseller with *Monsieur Beaucaire* (1900), a 'no man is a hero to his valet' spoof on the current American rage for historical fiction. His hero is an aristocrat who disguises himself as a barber. The novel was made into a successful silent movie, with Rudolph Valentino and later into a 1940s comic vehicle for Bob Hope. Tarkington's stories slipped very easily onto the screen – it was a major source of his large income in later life. But he had even greater success with his comic epics about the trials of youth. Adolescence, the awkward years between childhood and adulthood, was a psycho-genetic category invented in America at this period by G. Stanley Hall. Tarkington popularised it in *Penrod* (1914). Penrod Schofield – invariably accompanied by his dog Duke, and latterly with his gang: Sam Williams, Maurice Levy, Georgie Bassett and Herman (the second Jewish and the last black) – is an eleven-year-old rebel against the middle-class values of his Midwest family and community. His little battles are narrated in arch-ironic style by Tarkington. *Penrod* clearly draws on *Tom Sawyer* and just as clearly inspired Richmal Crompton's *Just William* (1922). Addressed principally to adult readers, both depictions of juvenile machismo exude tolerant adult amusement at the barbarism of the young male child in Western civilization. *Penrod* inspired the sequels *Penrod and Sam* (1916) and *Penrod Jashber* (1929).

Tarkington continued this bestselling vein with *Seventeen* (1916). With eighteen-year-olds (and, after 1917, American boys) dying by the hundred thousand in France in 1914–18, his idylls offered escape to a safer, if imaginary, world. Adolescence *agonistes* of a more tragic kind is portrayed in Georgie Minafer of *The Magnificent Ambersons* (1918). This novel made up a trilogy with *The Turmoil* (1915) and *The Midlander* (1924) and earned Tarkington two prizes and a front page on *Time* magazine in 1925. Like everyone else, the young Orson Welles read them admiringly.

Around this period Tarkington was losing his sight, and his later novels – none of which enjoyed the success of the earlier – were dictated. Royalties and film rights enriched him and allowed him to indulge a taste for English eighteenth-century painting and fine furniture for his mansion in Indianapolis. He was increasingly right-wing in later years, conceiving a violent distaste for FDR, the New Deal, and virtually everything that happened after 1929 – not least to his beloved Indianapolis. It is this lifelong visceral antagonism to change, together with a fatalistic acceptance of it, which gives eloquence to such speeches as Eugene Morgan's – the Henry Ford 'man of the future' – in *The Magnificent Ambersons*. The speech is delivered, verbatim, by Joseph Cotton in the Welles-directed film:

> 'I'm not sure [George] is wrong about automobiles,' [Eugene] said. 'With all their speed forward they may be a step backward in civilization – that is, in spiritual civilization. It may be that they will not add to the beauty of the world, nor to the

life of men's souls. I am not sure. But automobiles have come, and they bring a greater change in our life than most of us suspect. They are here, and almost all outward things are going to be different because of what they bring. They are going to alter war, and they are going to alter peace. I think men's minds are going to be changed in subtle ways because of automobiles; just how, though, I could hardly guess.'

Eugene then leaves, with a smile, as the Ambersons gloomily ponder his prophetic words and their own downfall under the motorised wheels of an unstoppable future.

FN   Newton Booth Tarkington
MRT *The Magnificent Ambersons*
Biog J. Woodress, *Booth Tarkington: Gentleman from Indiana* (1955)

112. Erskine Childers 1870–1922

Take a step forward, lads. It will be easier that way. Childers to the firing squad, about to execute him

Childers' father was Britain's leading authority on Pali (i.e. ancient Indian) culture; he died young – from tuberculosis, reportedly exacerbated by overwork. His son Robert inherited his father's scholarly mind but added to it an indomitable yearning for a life of action, adventure and high personal risk. Although he was born in London, Childers inherited his passionate (and eventually fatal) affiliation to Ireland from his mother, a County Wicklow heiress. (She died, eight years later of the same TB that had killed her husband.) After leaving Cambridge with a law degree, Childers took up a post, from 1895 to 1910, as a clerk in the House of Commons. This was a period when Home Rule was constantly in dispute and under debate.

A passionate yachtsman and, at this period, a true British patriot, he volunteered to fight in the Boer War, writing a memoir of his frustrating experiences which mainly involved looking after horses. It was published in 1903. He came back opposed to the war he had earlier believed in. As a novelist, Childers' principal, and abiding, achievement was the publication of his spy novel, *The Riddle of the Sands*, published, to great sales success, in the same year. Subtitled 'A Record of Secret Service' and written in pseudo-documentary style, the narrative is set against the background of a Germany secretly arming itself ('she grows, and strengthens, and waits'). 'Carruthers of the FO' and his friend, Arthur H. Davies, go yachting on the sand-bar bedevilled Baltic waters where they witness Germany's rehearsal for the invasion of England. The Admiralty is informed. Childers' novel can be plausibly credited with (1) blue-printing a genre – the spy/secret agent novel; (2) whipping up anti-German sentiment, in the long run-up to the First World War; (3) inspiring the establishment of the British secret services (later MI5 and MI6).

On a trip to Boston, the heartland of Irish America, Childers met and married his wife, Mary Osgood, in 1904. They had two sons and the marriage, Childers later declared, was the greatest happiness of his life. His subsequent books were on military history; and his main recreation continued to be yachting – particularly in the Baltic, off the coast of Germany. Meanwhile, over the pre-war years, he was increasingly preoccupied with Irish affairs. He resigned his Westminster clerkship in 1910 and, as early as 1914, was using his yacht, *Asgard*, to run guns to anti-British Irish 'Volunteers' – some of them ended up being used in the 1916 uprising. By this point Childers himself was a convinced nationalist.

On the outbreak of war, Childers was commissioned into the RNVR. His intimate knowledge of the German coastline – from years of yachting along it – was invaluable to his country. Winston Churchill, First Lord of the Admiralty, was an admirer of *The Riddle of the Sands*. Childers received rapid promotions and decorations for gallantry flying reconnaissance aircraft. He was convinced Ireland should be a republic, and enraged by the British government's ferocious oppressions in Ireland after the 1916 uprising, particularly its use of the militarised, and brutal, 'Black and Tan' force to cow the civilian Dublin populace.

Childers settled in Ireland in 1920 to engage directly in the emergent state's confused and bloody politics. Opposed to any form of partition (as agreed in the 1921 treaty with England), he joined the rebel Republican Army and was captured, at his mother's house, by soldiers of the Irish Free State government. After a court martial in Dublin, on trumped-up charges of possessing an illegal weapon, he was shot by a firing party with each member of whom, it is recorded, he cheerfully shook hands before his execution. He was regarded as a traitor by both Irish and English factions, and as a hero by parallel factions in both countries. He remains, as his biographer puts it, a 'riddle' – only his personal bravery is indisputable. Few novelists, with only one novel to their credit, can be said to have trademarked a whole genre. One of his sons became the fourth president of Ireland.

FN   Robert Erskine Childers
MRT   *The Riddle of the Sands*
Biog   A. Boyle, *The Riddle of Erskine Childers* (1977)

113. Saki 1870–1916

My earliest recollection of Hector, my younger brother, was in the nursery at home, where, with my elder brother Charlie, we had been left alone. Hector seized the long-handled hearth brush, plunged it into the fire, and chased Charlie and me round the table, shouting: 'I'm God! I'm going to destroy the world!' Saki's sister, Ethel

No writer more trenchantly diagnosed the deposits of savagery beneath the high sheen of Edwardian society than 'Saki'. Hector Hugh Munro (his birth name) was born in Burma. In an event which rivals the grotesquerie of his later stories, his mother died of shock, after being charged by a runaway cow on a lane in rural Wessex. His father was a serving senior officer in Burma (the family had strong Scottish military traditions), with only six weeks' furlough every four years. In what was effectively an orphan, if not impoverished, condition, the three Munro children – of whom Hector was the youngest – were entrusted to the care of two maiden aunts near Barnstaple, Devon. 'Care' is not the word the Munro offspring would have used. Aunts Charlotte and Augusta hated each other and created a domestic climate that verged on 'mental cruelty', as Ethel Munro recalled. Graham Greene, that connoisseur of lost childhoods, saw Saki's as one of the most creatively lost in literature. He channelled his bitterness into therapeutic dark comedy.

Saki slaughtered his aunts, particularly the more sadistic Augusta, time and again, in his later short stories: most memorably in 'Sredni Vashtar'. In that story Conradin has a tame, but incorrigibly vicious, polecat-ferret. It is his 'most treasured possession'. He keeps Sredni, whom he has invested with divine properties, hidden in the back garden. His guardian, the odious Mrs De Ropp (i.e. Aunt Augusta) goes into the shed to investigate – and, if necessary, undertake some vermin extermination. However, as she peers into the hutch, it is she who is exterminated. Ethel supplies the necessary background.

> There was a most intelligent Houdan cock, who was Hector's shadow; he fed out of his hand and loved being petted. Unhappily he got something wrong with one leg, and had to be destroyed. I believe a 'vet' would have cured him ... No one but myself knew what Hector felt at the loss of the bird. We had early learnt to hide our feelings – to show enthusiasm or warmth was sure to bring an amused smile to Aunt Augusta's face. It was a hateful smile.

Conradin is sickly, but revives amazingly after he realizes his aunt is lying dead with a blood-guzzling ferret at her throat. The story ends: '"Whoever will break it to the poor child? I couldn't for the life of me!" exclaimed a shrill voice. And while they debated the matter among themselves, Conradin made himself another piece of toast.'

Doctors assured the aunts that Hector would not make old bones. On leaving 'home', he, like Conradin, perked up amazingly. At first he resolved to join his father in the Burmese police service, but a bout of malaria ended that career after a year. He returned in 1894 to London, where, rather than waste time at university, he resolved to write. Evidently he was supported by family money. He buried himself in the British Museum stacks and six years later emerged with the wholly unlikely volume, *The Rise of the Russian Empire* (1900). As those who have read it testify, the narrative has a symptomatic interest in the sadistic practices of the Tsarist torture regimes – cooked up in a narrative tone of Gibbonian irony.

These were oppressed years, following the disgrace of Oscar Wilde. It seems certain, as his biographers suggest, that Munro was homosexual and, possibly, pederastic. Support for this is given by the prominence of the naked boy figure in stories such as 'Gabriel-Ernest' *or* the typically surreal, but disturbing, comic episode in another of his stories in which the mischievous 'Reginald' (Saki's recurrent antihero, and alter ego) takes a church boys' choir ('shy, bullet-headed charges') bathing in a woodland stream, hides their clothes, and obliges them to parade 'in Bacchanalian procession through the village'. Singing naked, that is, and, presumably, priapically aroused. 'Reginald's family never forgave him,' the story ends, 'they had no sense of humour.'

Whatever the reason, it is clear that the shadowy life of the *Privatgelehrte* in London (North Soho, preferably) suited Munro. The breakthrough in his literary career came when the editor of the *Westminster Gazette*, J. A. Spender, commissioned a regular series of short squibs for 'the seagreen incorruptible', as the loftily liberal paper was called. Munro did parodies of Lewis Carroll and Kipling, and invented the Oscar-like, witticising 'Reginald' to leaven Spender's heavy pages. It was at this point that he devised 'Saki' – a name derived (although it's hard to make it fit) from FitzGerald's *Rubáiyát of Omar Khayyám* – though 'sarcastic' seems the more obvious origin. The Reginald stories were gathered into book form in 1904, and enjoyed a second success between hard covers.

In 1902 Munro – whose whole career is marked by the oddest turns – was dispatched as a foreign correspondent to the war-torn Balkans, by the *Morning Post*. Like Byron, he probably found more outlets for his private pleasures abroad than even in London's Fitzrovia. He got to know the region as an 'old hand', particularly Macedonia. In 1908 he returned to London, took up residence in Mortimer Street, close to his beloved BM (closer still to the WC1 fleshpots), and embarked on the most productive phase of his fiction-writing career. In addition to his most famous stories, he produced two full-length novels: *The Unbearable Bassington* (1912), a retrospect of his embittering childhood; and *When William Came* (1913), a German invasion fantasy. The novels work less well than the stories. Acid is most effective in droplet form.

On the outbreak of war, Munro, true to his ancient clan blood, joined up. He refused a commission, although one was offered him by a good Highland regiment. He insisted on serving at the Front, although he was over-age and incapacitated by malaria. We know more about his death than most of his life. It was a 'dark winter morning' in November 1916, in the lines alongside the blood-soaked village of Beaumont-Hamel. The troops were standing to. A friend engaged him in conversation: 'A number of fellows sank down on the ground to rest, and Hector sought a shallow crater, with the lip as a back-rest. [His friend] heard him shout "Put that bloody cigarette out!" and heard the snip of a rifle-shot.' A sharp-eyed sniper had got him. To have reached thirty, Saki once wrote, 'is to have failed in life'. He reached forty-five. As Dominic Hibberd notes, 'He is listed on the Thiepval memorial as one of the many soldiers whose bodies were never found.' His sister Ethel methodically destroyed all his personal papers, thus preserving for ever the secrets of his life.

FN   Saki (Hector Hugh Munro)
MRT   'Sredni Vashtar'
Biog   A. J. Langguth, *Saki: A Life of Hector Hugh Munro* (1981)

114. B. M. Bower 1871–1940

She never liked the deception.

Bertha Muzzy (known in her family as 'Bert') was born the ninth of ten children in rural Minnesota. Her mother was a schoolteacher, her father a sometime 'dry' farmer, as they were called, of progressive political views. When Bert was sixteen her family moved to Big Sandy, Montana, where she encountered the range life that was to be her later stock-in-trade. Bower was married three times, first to Clayton J. Bower (1890) from whom she took her strategically initialised and androgynous pen name. She began writing for publication (and money) in 1903. The following year she introduced 'Chip, of the Flying U' in Street and Smith's *The Popular Magazine*. Chip Bennett went on to become one of the cowboy genre's most popular and profitable series heroes. His name was inspired by the author's youngest brother, who loved Saratoga-style potato chips.

Throughout Bower's life, her publishers insisted she disguise her sex. As a result of the deception – which fooled most readers – details of her early life were carefully buried and remain unknown. The narrative of her breakthrough novel, closely read, none the less betrays the woman's hand. Della Whitmore returns to the family ranch, the Flying U (named after its brand), on graduating from medical school in the east. She wins over the hard-bitten cowpoke, Chip, even uncovering a latent artistic talent in him. He and his 'Little Doctor' kiss, and are a team over many subsequent novels. There was no such bliss for the author. In 1905 she divorced Clayton (who had taken to calling his wife 'my little red-headed gold-mine') after what is recorded only as an 'unforgivable act' in the Midwestern cabin where they lived with their two children. In 1912 Bower promptly married Bertrand W. Sinclair, her literary adviser (and, probably, another marital gold-digger), twelve years her senior and himself a writer of less successful Westerns. The couple settled down in Great Falls, where a daughter was born.

The book version of *Chip, of the Flying U* (brought out in 1906 by the New York publisher Dillingham, with fine illustrations by Charles Marion Russell) established Bower as a writer of Westerns second only to Owen Wister, author of *The Virginian*. Bower's favoured state was not Wister's Wyoming but Montana, where some forty of her sixty-eight novels would be set. On the strength of her swelling income, the family moved to a mansion in the clement climate of Santa Cruz, in 1908, but Bower went on to divorce Sinclair also in 1912. Like his predecessor he was a heavy drinker. Bower herself suffered a series of health breakdowns around the age of forty. None the less she signed a contract with Little, Brown to produce two books a year – which she manfully did for the next three decades. In 1920, she married a cowboy and another heavy drinker, Robert E. ('Bud') Cowan. The couple tried, quixotically, to run a silver-mine in Nevada. It proved less successful than the literary gold Bower could spin, effortlessly, with her pen and that third marriage also failed.

Chip, of the Flying U was popularised worldwide, and for many years, by a string of films: Tom Mix, Hoot Gibson, and, after 1939, Johnny Mack Brown all starred in the lead role. In later life – with no one left to call her Bert – she insisted friends (even little girls) call her 'Bower'. She spent her last years in California where she toured in the 'solid cars' she enjoyed – tapping away, all the time, on her typewriter to keep the studios happy.

FN   Bertha Bower (née Muzzy; later Clayton, later Sinclair)
MRT   *Chip, of the Flying U*
Biog   Kate Baird Anderson (granddaughter), http://libraries.ou.edu/locations/docs/
        westhist/bower/introduction.html)

115. Stephen Crane 1871–1900

The idea of falling like heroes on ceremonial battle-fields was gone forever; we knew that we should fall like street-sweepers subsiding ignobly into seas of mud. Ford Madox Hueffer on the corrective effect of *The Red Badge of Courage*

When asked for his curriculum vitae, Crane would begin with the first Stephen Crane who arrived in the colony in 1635 and skip to his third namesake who had narrowly missed being a signatory to the Declaration of Independence. Stephen Crane IV (as he saw himself) was a proud 'son of the American Revolution'. But that ancestral glory had passed. The Cranes had come down in the world when he was born, the youngest of fourteen children, of whom his four immediate predecessors never made it to childhood. He himself was sickly from birth and may not have been expected to survive. His father, Jonathan Townley Crane, was a Methodist minister whose views bordered on pusillanimous fanaticism. He held that dancing was the root of all evil. He died when his youngest son was eight. Stephen's mother, M. Helen Crane, was forty-five at the time of his birth, and not overwhelmingly motherly. Fourteen births, and five funerals, can wear out a woman's tenderness. A crusader against the demon rum, she was a pillar of the Women's Christian Temperance Union (they disliked the acronym WCTU for the irrelevant implication of the two first letters). She died mad in Stephen's late teens.

Raised in New Jersey, in a domestic atmosphere of 'exhortation', young 'Steve' had plenty to rebel against. Undistinguished at school and oddly slow to read or write, in his teens he spent two years at a military academy. These, he claimed, were the happiest years of his life. He left with faux lieutenant's pips on his shoulders and went on to college – where he was welcome for his prowess on the baseball diamond (he was a catcher and shortstop) but was kicked out for spectacularly bad grades. It was baseball, he said, which taught him all he had to know about combat.

In 1891, on the death of his mother and the inheritance of some money, he moved to New York, took up residence in a boarding house, and began serious work on his first novel. He was, lifelong, fascinated by prostitutes and the 'hellish' street life of lower Manhattan. The two were brought together in *Maggie, A Girl of the Streets* (1893). The plot of the novel is hackneyed – a good girl is done wrong by her man, stoops to folly, and drowns herself in the East River. The streets are more interesting than the girl, as the lively opening paragraphs predict:

> A very little boy stood upon a heap of gravel for the honor of Rum Alley. He was throwing stones at howling urchins from Devil's Row who were circling madly about the heap and pelting at him.

His infantile countenance was livid with fury. His small body was writhing in the delivery of great, crimson oaths.

'Run, Jimmie, run! Dey'll get yehs,' screamed a retreating Rum Alley child.

'Naw,' responded Jimmie with a valiant roar, 'dese micks can't make me run.'

New York is war – already evident is the journalist's sharp eye and economy of phrase. Manhattan, said Crane, was where all the 'bad stories' (i.e. the best stories) come from, and he had an unerring eye for them. However, *Maggie* could not find a publisher and was brought out by Crane himself at a cost of $700 under the pseudonym 'Johnston Smith'. It was stillborn. He followed his other gift and drifted into the booming metropolitan newspaper world. Had Stephen Crane never written a line of fiction he would be remembered as a brilliant reporter. Among his classic pieces of this early period is 'An Experiment in Misery', when he lived, for a day and night, as a down-and-out bum. Orwell must have studied it carefully.

He was, meanwhile, keeping his hand in with fiction and poetry ('Lines' as he called them) which, as yet, went nowhere. He had various relationships with the kind of woman his parents would have shuddered to know. Until she died, the woman always closest to him was his sister Agnes, a surrogate mother. *The Red Badge of Courage* was born of a boast that he could write a better battle story than Zola's *La Débâcle*. It came out in book form in 1895 when Crane was twenty-three – still youthful. The story records the war experience of Private Henry Fleming in the Civil War. A farm boy, he volunteers to fight for the North, but has no political conviction or sense of history. It is not a novel about war, so much as about the 'psychology of fear'. Henry runs away from his first fire-fight. A disgusted comrade hits him, savagely, on the head. This is mistaken as an honourable war wound – his 'red badge of courage' – and he returns to the fray and fights: 'He is a man.' The statement hangs, ironically, over the novel's last paragraph.

Crane is a connoisseur of corpses and the physiognomy of death (the result, one suspects, of many visits to the Manhattan morgue). In his flight from the battle, Henry runs through the woods where he comes on:

a dead man who was seated with his back against a columnlike tree. The corpse was dressed in a uniform that once had been blue, but was now faded to a melancholy shade of green. The eyes, staring at the youth, had changed to the dull hue to be seen on the side of a dead fish. The mouth was open. Its red had changed to an appalling yellow. Over the gray skin of the face ran little ants. One was trundling some sort of bundle along the upper lip.

The Red Badge went through fourteen printings in its first year. One veteran, a colonel no less, clearly remembered serving with Crane at Antietam, almost ten years before the novelist was born.

In 1895 Crane travelled to the West and New Mexico. It broadened his horizons well beyond Manhattan ('Damn the East!', he proclaimed on his return) and furnished the setting for some of his finest short stories – 'The Blue Hotel' and 'The Bride Comes to Yellow Sky.' His relationships with women remained obscure and mysterious. In the year of his *Red Badge* triumph he conducted an epistolary romance with a 'pure woman' and wrote a novel, *The Third Violet* (1897), on the strength of it. Derived clearly from du Maurier's *Trilby*, with an artist hero, it is a comedown from *Red Badge* as, the author forlornly predicted, all his fiction must be. Women of the street continued to fascinate him. As a reporter, covering a story, he witnessed a prostitute, Dora Clark, being arrested on a trumped-up charge of soliciting. He took up her case through his newspaper columns and in court. On the witness stand, his reputation was blackened by the admission that he used opium (in a Baudelairian experimental spirit) and had recently been living in sin with a fellow woman reporter.

Thereafter, the New York Police Department was out to get Stephen Crane. Prudently he turned his skills to war reporting, where the foe was less deadly than Manhattan's finest. Now a star reporter, he received assignments from the colossus of American journalism, William Randolph Hearst. Like Hearst, Crane did not wait for stories, he made them happen. Things were happening in the mid-1890s in Cuba, which was in the bloody throes of breaking free from Spain. On a secret gun-running voyage to Cuba, in aid of the insurgents, the boat Crane was sailing in, the *Commodore*, foundered and sank with loss of life. Crane spent three days in an open boat at sea, but survived, and out of the experience came his fine novella, *The Open Boat*. Like *The Red Badge*, the story ponders survival. As the exhausted survivors come ashore, a corpse (the engine room man, Billie) is washed up in the surf: 'In the shallows, face downward, lay the oiler. His forehead touched sand that was periodically, between each wave, clear of the sea.' No writer handles vignette better than Crane.

His interest in impure women was inextinguishable and strangely decent. Over the last years of his life, he formed an unsolemnised union with Cora Taylor, a twice married Florida brothel madam, five years older than him. Possessed of true grit, Cora accompanied her man, as America's first woman war correspondent, she claimed, to the front lines of the Graeco-Turkish conflict. In 1897 the couple moved to the English home counties, of all places, where, in fine style, at Brede Place in Sussex, they lived wildly beyond their means. Crane became intimate with Conrad, Henry James, H. G. Wells, and Ford Madox Hueffer – all of whom loved him and lived more or less nearby. To fill his purse he made forays to cover the Spanish Cuban War and – at its climax – witnessed the American marine landing at Guantanamo and the 'rough riders' heroism at San Juan Hill. His reporting, and related short stories, are brilliant. But he caught a fever which hastened his death. Not exactly a red wound, but proof of his courage.

'I go through the world unexplained,' Crane liked to say. Tantalisingly little is known of his life and that little is polluted by his first biographer, Thomas Beer, whose narrative contains material as fictional as anything in *The Red Badge*. One would give all the acres of biography on Henry James for a hundred pages telling us more about Crane's life. He is recorded as habitually carrying a volume of Poe in his pocket. His last weeks – 'a bloody way of dying', as he described it to Wells – was appropriately gothic. Suffering with terminal consumption, a rectal abscess, and the malaria he brought back as a war wound from Cuba, he was shipped out to a resort in Germany's Black Forest where, after a few days, he died. His body was transported back to England. Cora determined it should be sent on for final burial in his native New Jersey. No rest, even in death. 'He was dying from the start,' observed a laconic Hemingway. It took Stephen Crane less than thirty years to do it.

FN   Stephen Crane
MRT   *The Red Badge of Courage*
Biog   Christopher Benfey, *The Double Life of Stephen Crane* (1992).

116. Theodore Dreiser 1871–1945

I spent the better part of forty years trying to induce him to reform and electrify his manner of writing. H. L. Mencken

Theodore Dreiser was born in Terre Haute, Indiana, a second-generation 'new American'. His sternly Catholic German father, John Paul, had fled Prussia in 1844 and in America had fallen in love and eloped with a seventeen-year-old Mennonite, Sarah. They would have ten surviving children, brought up speaking German. Theodore had a grossly unsettled upbringing. His father enjoyed brief prosperity in the textile trade, rising to the status of mill-owner during the Civil War period, when the demand for uniforms created a short-lived boom. That prosperity evaporated with the end of the war and – quite fortuitously – the arrival of little Theodore into the family circle. The father he knew in his childhood would be an odd-job man, a loser, consoled only by an ever fiercer devotion to his religion.

As Paul's fortunes slumped, the family flitted from one shabby dwelling to another. Among all the hardship Theodore was his mother's favourite. His biographer, Richard Lingeman, sees the child's reciprocal adoration as the reason Dreiser – although sexually promiscuous to the point that sterilisation was once considered –could never make a lasting relationship with any other woman. He would be emotionally misshapen for life. What schooling he picked up was scrappy, although he read voraciously. A key moment was the family's drift to the outskirts of Chicago in 1882. The booming city was, Dreiser later recalled, 'the wonder of his life'. The move was assisted by a relative who had made it big as a brothel-keeper. In 1887 the sixteen-year-old Theodore left home and threw himself into the heart of the city's seething life, sent on his way by his mother with three dollars and a lunch bag.

In Chicago, the young hopeful tramped the streets, looking for work, picking up jobs where he could. With 50,000 new incomers a year, all with similar hopes, you needed luck to survive. Fortune smiled, briefly, on him when a relative financed a year at Indiana University and that single year at Bloomington enabled him in later life to proclaim himself a 'college man'. But in 1890 his mother died – and with her, he said, died any idea of home and family. After his brief spell of higher education he took to the streets again. He was chronically lonely and never well. He confessed in his later memoirs to irrepressible masturbation – the prelude to a life of inveterate Don Juanism: he carried, as it pleased him to say, a lifelong 'cross of passion'. The twenty-year-old Dreiser – lanky, wall-eyed, penniless, bronchitic, virginal – was not a young man to excite interest in the girls he fantasised about, though he would make up for those delayed gratifications in later life when fame and money added a lustre to his unprepossessing appearance.

In 1892 he finally found a niche in journalism as a space-rate (i.e. freelance) reporter and reviewer for the *Chicago Globe*. There was no long-term future in such hackery, but it was an apprenticeship and got his pen moving. He broadened his view of things, more particularly America, with a year's bumming around the country in 1894, gravitating, inevitably, to New York, a city whose dynamism dwarfed even that of Chicago. His ideas were forming. He was now a disciple of Herbert Spencer and the English thinker's Social Darwinism. He had immersed himself in Balzac and would be, for life, a believer in literary realism – 'veritism', as it was called. In New York, he kept body and soul together as a 'magazinist' – a better vehicle for a man of ideas than deadline-pressed newspaper reporting. Weeklies and monthlies were booming. Many of Dreiser's pieces were trite – but some, such as the account of a lynching (later fictionalised as the story 'Nigger Jeff') and the account of a night (one of many over the years) in a flophouse forecast the novelist to come.

His brother Paul (Dresser), meanwhile, had made it earlier in life as a popular song-writer (his greatest hit was 'On the Banks of the Wabash, Far Away') and would be a welcome source of financial handouts to Theodore during the thirty more years of penury – although he had little time for his brother's sentimental warbles. In 1898, after an extended engagement, he married Sara Osborne White, a schoolteacher from Missouri. The couple never really cohabited and soon separated. He denied her the children she craved; she denied him the divorce he wanted. It was, as the term then had it, a MINO – a marriage in name only. He found consolation in innumerable affairs and one-night stands with other women – 'varietism', he called it.

Dreiser had been trying his hand at magazine stories and in 1900 he embarked on his first novel, *Sister Carrie*. He encountered difficulties in finding a publisher which would have deterred authors less dogged than he. His addiction to windy abstractions was one thing which put off potential publishers. That which begins Chapter 8 is typical Dreiserism: 'Among the forces which sweep and play through-out the universe, untutored man is but a wisp in the wind.' To reach what Dreiser offers, readers have to inure themselves to such ubiquitous windbaggery. Even more objectionable at the time was *Sister Carrie*'s explicitness about the sexual act. The age was not ready for it. The manuscript was finally accepted by Doubleday on the recommendation of the congenial novelist (another 'realist') Frank Norris, who proclaimed the work a 'masterpiece'. Then Mrs Doubleday happened to read it, and *Sister Carrie* was firmly rejected. Masterpieces were one thing: references to women's breasts being handled something quite other. Unwisely, Dreiser resolved to hold Doubleday to their initial agreement. They published it, insisting on many cuts of 'offensive material', but delivered the novel effectively still-born into the world. Dreiser's veritism went down badly with the few reviewers who looked at it. The *Chicago Tribune* complained, 'Not once does the name of the Deity appear in the book except as it is implied in the suggestion of profanity.' There was some consolation in that *Sister Carrie* was hailed in Britain – where writers such as Thomas Hardy and George Moore had created a less godly climate for fiction.

Sister Carrie has one of the nineteenth century's more hackneyed plots – that of the fallen woman. Dreiser adds a twentieth-century twist. Caroline Meeber falls, quite as hard as George Eliot's Hetty Sorrell, Hardy's Tess, or Moore's Esther Waters, but goes on to pick herself up with spectacular success. The action opens in 1889 with the heroine on the train to Chicago, casting never a backward look at the farming family she is leaving behind her. Carrie is eighteen years old, endowed with latent beauty, intelligence, innocence and – most importantly – talent. On her journey she is accosted by Chas. H. Drouet. A salesman by profession, Drouet is a seducer by nature. In the big city Carrie finds herself so much urban flotsam. The only work she can find is as a $4.50 per week shop assistant. In the face of this prospect she succumbs to Drouet's charms, encouraged by 'two soft green ten-dollar bills' he gives her. Now 'fallen', she falls in with another admirer, the middle-aged, prosperous saloon manager, George W. Hurstwood – a married man (something Carrie does not at this point know) with children her age. He yearns discontentedly for 'sympathy' and thinks he has found it in Carrie. Drouet lands Carrie, now his mistress, a part in an amateur theatrical in which, to everyone's surprise, she shines brilliantly. Hurstwood gains some advantage over his rival by hinting at marriage – bigamously, as it would have to be.

In the finest scene in the novel, while closing up his saloon he discovers the firm's safe unlocked. It contains $10,000. The physical feel of the money tempts him and 'the imbibation of the evening' has rendered him reckless. He takes the cash out, to fondle it as one might caress a beautiful woman, and 'While the money was in his hand, the lock clicked. It had sprung. Did he do it? He grabbed at the knob and pulled vigorously. It had closed. Heavens! he was in for it now, sure enough. The moment he realized that the safe was locked for a surety, the sweat burst out upon his brow and he trembled. He looked about him and decided instantly. There was no delaying now.' Fate having delivered the money into his hand, he elopes with Carrie. Did he mean to steal the money? Dreiser leaves it enigmatic. Hurstwood and Carrie end up, married but not married, in New York. For him, thereafter, it is the long descent to the flophouse and burial in Potter's Field. His last words are 'what's the use?' Meanwhile Carrie, ignorant of George's fate, becomes a Broadway star, though she is unconvinced by the uses of fame and fortune.

As the century turned, Dreiser found himself blocked artistically, chronically ill, depressed and, for all his promiscuities, alone. There followed what his biographer calls 'the lost decade'. He published no fiction between 1900 and 1911, other than an unexcised text of *Sister Carrie*. The obstacles put in that novel's way he saw as clinching evidence of prejudice against anyone 'who attempted anything even partially serious in America'. He had started writing his second novel, *Jennie Gerhardt*, in 1901. The story of a German-American girl, it developed themes opened in *Sister Carrie* but found the same disfavour with publishers (try another line of work, one good-naturedly advised him) or, when belatedly published in 1911, with reviewers and readers. Dreiser fell back on magazinery. But his fiction, unsuccessful as it was in the marketplace, had attracted the support of opinion-forming friends, notably H. L. Mencken, who devoted himself to promoting the Dreiser cause.

Unabashed, he progressed – in his third foray into fiction – with a massive work on the robber baron, Charles T. Yerkes. This interest in 'capital' marks the embryonic stirrings of overt Marxism in his thinking. The Yerkesiad, he proclaimed, would be 'American in theme, European in method', and, true to his first literary love, Balzacian in length. America, Dreiser believed, was so big that 'you can't write about it in a small peckish way'. Dreiser took three large bites at Yerkes with *The Financier* (1912), *The Titan* (1914) and *The Stoic* (1947) – the last unfinished at the time of his death in 1945. Large as the canvas was, Dreiser failed to capture his subject. Even less successful was the 'art novel' he published *The 'Genius'* (1915), not helped by the observable fact that the genius he had in mind was Theodore Dreiser.

Dreiser's German background tilted him towards his ancestral homeland during the Great War. It helped his career as little as did his anti-Semitism in the run-up to the Second World War and his late life admiration for the USSR (until he actually went there and discovered Communism did not deliver clean sheets and hot running water). His willed opposition to current political orthodoxies was one of the reasons he never got the Nobel his proponents have always maintained he richly deserved. It was during the First World War that he began research on his one indisputably great novel, *An American Tragedy*. And it was as the war ended that he discovered the most enduring of his many mistresses, Helen Richardson. Some twenty-five years his junior, and looking younger than that, Helen was distantly related. She was, as he liked to call her, his 'Golden Girl'. One of his diary entries, in the early days of their relationship, records what she brought into his life: 'From 10 to twelve I work on mss. Two to 4:30 play with Helen. We copulate 3 times. At 5 return to work & at 7 get dinner. 9pm to bed.'

The manuscript he was working on, post-coitally, was *An American Tragedy*. It would be published, after the usual long quarrels with the publishers, in 1925. The idea for the novel was an actual murder. In 1906 Chester Gillette, a junior clerk at a skirt factory, impregnated a working girl, Grace Brown, thus foiling his aim to rise in life by marrying the boss's daughter. He duped the mother of his unborn child with an offer of marriage, took her to an idyllic lake in the Adirondacks, and may or may not have clubbed her with a tennis racket and allowed her to drown. It is possible that at the last moment Gillette lost his nerve and did not intend to do it. But after huge publicity he went to the electric chair. Dreiser moved the action of *An American Tragedy* to the 1920s. 'I call it an American tragedy,' he explained, 'because it could not happen in any other country in the world.' America's pervasive 'tragic error', he argued, was the belief that you could rise in life to fulfil your dream and were justified in whatever means you chose to do it – like clubbing an inconveniently fertile girl to death with a tennis racquet.

At last Dreiser had hit the jackpot: the reviews were ecstatic. *An American Tragedy* sold more copies in a month than all his earlier fiction combined. And it helped rather than hindered that it was banned in Boston. It was, wrote one critic, the 'Mount Everest' of American fiction: at 400,000 words it was certainly mountainous. The publisher, Boni & Liveright, was obliged to bring it out in two volumes, even after Dreiser had shortened the text drastically. 'What's 50,000 words between friends?' he is reported to have quipped.

Mencken, until this point Dreiser's stoutest friend, took exception to the verbosity. It was, he wrote, less a novel than 'a heaping cartload of raw materials for a novel.' The criticism ruptured the friendship between the men for a decade. Poor all his life, Dreiser was now, at the age of fifty-four, flush. He was able to run three or four women simultaneously – Helen was the only one who lasted – and build himself a country mansion in upper New York State. He called the place 'Iroki', Japanese for 'the spirit of beauty'.

In his last decades, Dreiser wrote little fiction and drifted towards socialism, deism and incorrigible pessimism. He wrote memoirs, of which *Dawn: an Autobiography of Early Youth* (1931) stands out, crusaded against literary censorship and stood –sometimes at personal risk – alongside the striking workers of America. During the Second World War he frankly expressed the hope that Germany would crush England, a country he loathed as heartily as Josef Goebbels. His wife died in 1942, but he did not remarry and left no (acknowledged) children. His last illness-racked years were spent in the warmth of southern California. One of his last acts was to join the Communist Party – had he lived, Senator Joe McCarthy and the House Un-American Activities Committee would have had fine sport with him. His fellow 'red', and late-life friend, Charlie Chaplin read one of Dreiser's militantly political poems ('The Road I Came') over the novelist's coffin as it was lowered into the soil of Forest Lawn. It should have been Chicago.

FN Herman Theodore Dreiser
MRT *An American Tragedy*
Biog Richard Lingeman, *Theodore Dreiser: An American Journey* (1993)

117. Zane Grey 1872–1939

I love my work but do not know how I write it.

Zane Grey was born in Zanesville, Ohio, a town named after his maternal grandfather. On his mother's side, he could trace his ancestry further back to Mayflower days. Unsurprisingly it inspired a strong sense of his all-American heritage. Grey's father was, rather less inspiringly, a dentist of undistinguished ancestry. A gifted athlete, as was his brother Romer, the young Zane (he wisely dropped the 'Pearl' his parents had lumbered him with) won a baseball scholarship to the University of Pennsylvania, an Ivy League institution. He graduated in 1896 with a degree in dentistry (having extracted himself from an awkward paternity suit – he had a weakness for women throughout life) and set up in practice in New York where, in 1905, he married seventeen-year-old Lina ('Dolly') Roth, an extraordinarily energetic woman, and an English major from Hunter College. She encouraged her dentist husband to write Westerns in the great tradition of James Fenimore Cooper – there was more gold in them thar hills than in the mouths of New Yorkers. In subsequent years Lina acted as Grey's editor and literary agent. It was a full-time job. At the zenith of his popularity, sales of Grey's Westerns in America were reckoned to be second only to the Bible. He was an unfaithful husband, but she tolerated his waywardness in return for her 50 per cent share of his royalties.

Grey's first novel *Betty Zane* (1903) was an act of homage to his Ohio ancestors. It was hard to write – he was never naturally fluent, and Dolly tidied his prose up – but it put him on the road. Supported by her savings, he gave up his New York surgery and moved to a cottage in rural Pennsylvania to concentrate on fiction. There was a ready market for Westerns in the East Coast's booming story magazines aimed at the unhappily urbanised American male, frustrated men who subscribed longingly to Owen Wister's belief that the West was 'the great playground of young men' and that the cowpuncher was 'the last romantic figure on our soil'. Grey made his first momentous trip to Arizona in 1907, in the company of old-timer Colonel C. J. ('Buffalo') Jones, which blazed the trail for *The Heritage of the Desert* (1910). He went on to hit the jackpot with *Riders of the Purple Sage* (1912). The novel was bought by the top New York publisher Harper, after the proprietor consulted his wife on the matter. Throughout his career Grey's publishers cannily partnered him with gifted illustrators such as N. C. Wyeth and Charles Russell; for this novel it was Douglas Duer.

Riders has one of the best and most imitated openings in Western fiction. The narrative is set in the early 1870s and features a maiden in bondage, Grey's standby scenario. Jane Withersteen is heiress to a vast ranch among the purple sage of the Utah–Arizona border. She is a Mormon (somewhat lukewarm in her faith, as it emerges) and is under siege from the lecherous 'Elder' Tull who wants her for his harem and his property portfolio. The action opens with a young 'rider' (cow-puncher) about to be whipped by Tull for the offence of being liked by Jane – a relatively mild punishment: Mormons, it is hinted, routinely castrate 'Gentiles' who hang round their women. Enter a lone rider, dressed in black, packing two black Colt pistols. His name is 'Lassiter'. The stranger faces down Tull and his men and rescues Bern Venters from the Mormon lash. Lassiter is the archetypal lone wolf: middle aged, world-weary but alert, hard and lean as whipcord, a man of few words who is invincible in gunplay. A line of film stars, notably Tom Mix and Randolph Scott, made their careers playing Lassiter variants. The line can be followed through to Clint Eastwood, the last scene of whose last Western, *Unforgiven* (even down to the whipping), is the first scene of *Riders of the Purple Sage*. Hollywood, which has always been nervous of meddling in religion, habitually transformed Grey's villainous Mormons to Indians.

On the breakthrough success of his novel (the first Western to make the *New York Times* bestseller list) and the scores that followed, Grey went on to live a Hemingwayesque life, basing himself on the West Coast. Other than writing, his main occupations were big-game hunting, ocean fishing and world travel. He loved Santa Catalina, the island off the Southern California coast, handily close to Hollywood. His residence survives on the island as a thriving 'Zane Grey' pueblo hotel where the Western-styled rooms are named after various of his bestsellers. The bison he brought to the island still graze free. He also had a hacienda in Altadena, underneath the San Gabriels, where he could hear the coyotes howl by night; and hunting lodges in Arizona and Oregon, where the grizzly still roamed. His lifestyle required an incessant stream of fiction (and film rights) to support it. In all he turned out some fifty-eight full-length Westerns for which worldwide sales of 250 million are claimed. With 108 film adaptations of his stories, he tops the achievement of any other writer, in any genre.

Although Grey killed wildlife joyously, with bullet, shotgun pellet and barbed hook (in later life he would fish up to 300 days a year – giving the tuna a rest only when scrawling his daily 5,000 words), novels such as *The Thundering Herd* (1925) lament the wanton destruction of the American buffalo and *The Vanishing American* (1925) that of the American Indian. This elegiac mood is more pronounced in his later works, when the 'frontier' had reached the Pacific and was now only a myth – but a myth which his fiction burnished. Phenomenal though his earnings were, Grey ran through them as quickly as they poured in. By the mid-1930s, his popularity waned somewhat. His work did not lend itself to the new 'singing cowboy' style of new stars like Gene Autry. Ignoring his cardiac symptoms, he continued to over-exert himself. The heart, Grey maintained, was only a muscle and thrived on exercise. He was wrong, and died of a heart attack in 1939. His last words were, reportedly, 'Don't ever leave me, Dolly.'

FN Pearl Zane Grey
MRT *Riders of the Purple Sage*
Biog Frank Gruber, *Zane Grey: A Biography* (1970)

118. W. Somerset Maugham 1874–1965

Lizard of Oz.

According to his most recent biographer, Selina Hastings, Maugham was 'for much of his long life … the most famous writer in the world'. The outline of that long and most famous life (but not all its secret chambers) is well enough known from Maugham's own accounts – autobiographical and fictional. He was born in Paris, the belated fourth son of a staid British solicitor, in practice in the French capital. His early years – in which he was brought up as French – were, he always insisted, his happiest. That happiness ended with his mother's death, in childbirth, when he was eight. Two years later, his father died. That loss young Willie could cope with. His mother, he said, not long before his own death, was the only person he had ever loved and her loss left a lasting wound.

It was at this period that his lifelong stammer developed. In his autobiographical novel, *Of Human Bondage*, it is allegorised as a Byronic club foot. The ten-year-old Maugham, to all intents a little French boy, was transplanted to an uncle's uncongenial vicarage in Kent and thence to the King's School in Canterbury. He loved the cathedral – and he chose, at the end of his life, to be buried nearby – but, despite the influence of chapel, choirs and sermons, lost all religion while still at school. He was bullied and reacted by becoming a prize-winning swot. He was no good at team sports, although he was an athletic golfer and swimmer in later life, and at this period discovered he was bisexual. 'I tried to persuade myself,' he later said, 'that I was three quarters normal and that only a quarter of me was queer – whereas really it was the other way round.' His word 'normal' is telling. Throughout his life 'an appearance of conventionality', Hastings notes, was 'all important' to him. Appearance was as far as it had to go.

Unconventionally, he did not go to university, but took a *Lehrjahr*, aged seventeen, in Germany before going to study medicine at St Thomas's in London. Practice in the teeming slums, south of the river, laid the foundation for his first, Zolaesque, novel: *Liza of Lambeth*. The story of a factory girl, exploited, seduced, battered, abandoned, who dies in childbirth, it ends where *Oliver Twist* begins. Published in 1897 (the 'year of jubilee' as Gissing calls it in *his* Lambeth novel), it was well received and gave him an exit route from medicine. By then Maugham had discovered that his 'real' world was that created by his pen – a scalpel-like instrument in his hands. He would, in later work, ruthlessly anatomise friends and acquaintance, often cruelly: Aleister Crowley (the 'Great Beast') in *The Magician* or, most devastatingly, Hugh Walpole – whose reputation never recovered from his depiction as Alroy Kear – in *Cakes and Ale* (1930), a novel whose brilliance has faded for modern readers because Maugham so efficiently annihilated his subject. 'He just looks on,' said Joseph Conrad of *Liza*. The eye that looked on was cold and, in later life, was everywhere seen as reptilian: 'The Lizard of Oz,' Noël Coward called him. The lizard he most resembled, arguably, was the chameleon – Maugham was uncannily adept at changing his literary and theatrical styles to the changing moment and the ever-shifting preferences of his readers and audiences.

After a couple of less successful novels he turned to Maupassant-like short stories and Ibsenesque drama. His first play, *A Man of Honour* (a 'problem play', as they were called, about a toff who marries a barmaid, with gloomy outcomes) was staged in 1903. For three decades thereafter the West End stage was, as Max Beerbohm joked, 'Maughamised'. In 1908, he had no less than four plays running simultaneously. It made him very rich. His wealth was expertly looked after by the shrewdest of London agents, J. B. Pinker and a wise Wall Street admirer, whom he met on his first trip to America, in 1910. Maugham's nomadism was by now established, as was his sexual adventurism. Wilde's fate was still raw and Maugham (never a great drinker or roisterer) was discreet. He used 'safe houses' for casual sex and employed 'secretaries' for longer relationships. His appetite, one partner recalled, was 'voracious'; his sexual demands 'simple'.

He was also cultivating himself as a man of wealth and taste. He could indulge his interests and 'collect' – particularly Impressionists, with whose techniques he felt an affinity. In 1911 he began writing the one work of his fiction which is sure to last, *Of Human Bondage* (1915). It tells the story of Philip Carey, and follows, with some dramatising variation, the course of Maugham's own life from his mother's premature death to his medical training. As a young man, Philip falls in with Mildred, a waitress, later a prostitute. Sex is typically a trap in Maugham's narrative, and invariably finds a man's Achilles heel (most vividly for the clergyman, Davidson, in 'Rain', who sets out to save Sadie's soul, cannot resist her body, and cuts his throat, post coitum). It is plausibly assumed that Mildred was based on one of Maugham's young male lovers. Maugham himself was 'trapped' – as he plausibly claimed – into marriage by an alimony-wealthy divorcée, Syrie Wellcome. The quarter of him that was not gay always enjoyed the occasional brief fling with women. Syrie got pregnant by him twice, declined to have their second child aborted, and demanded marriage. Maugham resentfully acquiesced. Marriage was one thing, Syrie would discover; married life something else.

'Passionately patriotic,' the forty-year-old Maugham volunteered for the Red Cross in 1914, and was then recruited as an agent in Britain's embryonic secret intelligence service, spying for his country in Switzerland and Russia. His cold eye made him good at the great game. He carried a pistol in his pocket and this most exciting phase of his life inspired the post-war 'Ashenden' stories which, in turn, inspired Ian Fleming's James Bond.

At this period, he was making his first exploratory trips to the Pacific and the Malay states, east of Suez. It would be one of his richest territories – for the Paul Gauguin bio-novel, *The Moon and Sixpence* (1919), and his short stories, most famously 'Rain' and 'The Letter' (both multiply filmed). He finished the war with a bad dose of TB, which required a year's sanatorium treatment. He was, by now, living by expensive arrangement apart from his wife and new-born daughter (named after his wretched heroine, Liza), with the first of his 'secretaries', the American Gerald Haxton. Haxton was charming, alcoholic and sexually mischievous – a thorough-going 'cad'. As the film director George Cukor said, 'he kept Maugham in touch with the gutter'. Maugham was merely a visitor to such low places. After the war, he took up residence in a Moorish palace – the Villa Mauresque, on the Riviera, which would be his home for forty years. After Haxton drank and smoked himself into terminal TB, he installed another long-term secretary, Alan Searle – rougher trade, but more serviceable to the now ageing writer: the 'ideal nanny' one visitor called Searle.

Between the wars, film adaptations added to Maugham's fabulous income. He wrote as diligently as he had done when hard up, 'unable to persuade myself,' as he said in his memoir, *The Summing Up* (1938), 'that anything else mattered'. A contingent important thing was his reputation as a writer and it infuriated him in late life when he was 'only' awarded a Companion of Honour, instead of the Order of Merit received by E. M. Forster. That mattered. The Depression, thanks to his American financial adviser, did not affect his prosperity, or the luxurious life that was now necessary to him. It did not, however, put him above world-historical events and he was obliged to decamp to the US during the Second World War.

Afterwards he returned to his Riviera villa, surrounded by one of the world's best private art collections. That world – including Winston Churchill, a leader of it – came to him, nowadays. English morality (his sexual preferences were by now an open secret) kept him in a state of semi-exile from what had never really been his homeland. He visited England regularly until the publication of a late-life memoir, *Looking Back*, in 1962. It was judged ungentlemanly in its attack on the recently dead Syrie, and led to his being ostracised by fellow members of the Garrick. It devastated him. 'Alone with Alan, he wept and wept ... the two of them returned to the Mauresque ... and Maugham never came to England again.' Three years later he died, aged ninety, mad, raving and wretched.

FN William Somerset Maugham
MRT *Of Human Bondage*
Biog Selina Hastings, *The Secret Lives of Somerset Maugham* (2010)

119. John Buchan 1875–1940

He does not like to hear about his own books; he refuses to be classified as a literary man.
Taffy Boulton, an Oxford contemporary

Buchan was born in Perth, the eldest son of a Free Church minister. A 'high-flier', he won a bursary to Glasgow University and three years later a classical scholarship to Brasenose College, Oxford, where he glittered as the most brilliant undergraduate of his year. Among the private documents of this period is a list drawn up by him of 'Things to be Done and Honours to be Gained'. They were indeed done and gained – and early in life. In the 1898 *Who's Who* there is the extraordinarily precocious entry: 'Buchan, John, undergraduate ...' He was just twenty-three and already a 'Who'.

While still an undergraduate, Buchan read manuscripts for Oscar Wilde's publisher, John Lane; was elected President of the Union; and contributed to Lane's *fin de siècle Yellow Book*; and, effortlessly, he took one of the best firsts of his year. He had begun to write fiction – mainly historical romances set in his native Lowland Scotland. Among the 'Things to be Done' was the resolve to make himself the second Walter Scott. On graduation, Buchan read for the Bar – the first rung to any number of top careers in British public life. Along the way he married Susan Charlotte Grosvenor and had four children – Alice, John, William and Alastair.

Those already at the top always took to Buchan. Still in his mid-twenties, he was invited to South Africa by the High Commissioner, Alfred Milner, to assist with postwar reconstruction. The British concentration ('refugee') camps for interned Boers made a deep impression. So, less favourably, did the Jewish entrepreneurs Buchan encountered, leading to a black vein of prejudice which can sometimes embarrass modern admirers. A Haggardian novel, *Prester John* (1910), about the mythic leader of all the Africas, resulted. What is striking is Buchan's prescient thesis that Britain's eventual problems would come not from rival European colonial powers, but from the 'Kaffirs.' 'Supposing a second Tchaka turned up,' the old-hand Wardlaw muses, 'who could get the different tribes to work together ... If they got a leader with prestige enough to organize a crusade against the white man ... Africa for the Africans.' The echo thrown back is 'Mandela'.

Back in England, Buchan wrote legal treatises and joined his friend and contemporary Thomas ('Tommy') Nelson as chief literary adviser to the great Scottish publishing house of Nelson, making monthly trips up to Edinburgh. He would never be poor thereafter. Now happily married, Buchan failed at his first attempt to get into Parliament, as a Unionist, in 1911. He would later serve – dutifully – as member for the Scottish universities. As war drew closer, Buchan suffered the first symptoms of a duodenal ulcer – the trademark illness of the overdriven. In August 1914 he was ordered to bed by his doctors where – restless as ever – he began scribbling his 'shilling shocker', *The Thirty-Nine Steps* (1915). Richard Hannay's single-handed rescue of Britain from the Hun is much read, but few readers pause to look at the dedication to 'My Dear Tommy'. Nelson, like Buchan's younger brother, Alastair, would die at the Battle of Arras. The invalid Buchan ached to join the fray, and did so, as best he could manage, with his immensely arduous twenty-four-volume serial *History of the War* (1915–19) for Nelson. He was recruited into the newly formed military intelligence service, and did sterling work in recruiting fellow-novelists as propagandists.

In adult, post-war life, Buchan was loaded with more honours than even the undergraduate had forecast. His ascent to the truly great of his time climaxed with appointment as Governor-General of Canada in 1935, as Baron Tweedsmuir. He was a good choice: as imperialists go, few were more enlightened. It was his right hand which signed Canada's declaration of war on Germany in 1939.

Buchan's fiction, all dashed down with his left hand, falls into various categories. Most long-lastingly popular are the five Hannay 'shockers'. Sir Edward Leithen, a barrister (and an evident self-portrait), features in a string of quieter thrillers. Thirdly, Buchan wrote a series of comic-adventure yarns centred on the retired Glasgow greengrocer, Dickson McCunn, and his 'Gorbals Diehards' band of street urchins. Buchan never managed a serious novel. The nearest he came was his last, *Sick Heart River*, begun in 1939, as he was dying. In it, Leithen, himself dying of TB, meditates on his life as successful barrister, Cabinet Minister, secret agent and man of the world. His 'inner world is crumbling', his achievements are hollow, his honours meaningless. He devotes his remaining months of life to the search for a French Canadian gone missing in the frozen North who can, it is hoped, preserve the North American federation. Leithen dies for Empire: the one worthwhile thing.

Buchan himself died of a cerebral thrombosis – that other ailment of the over-achiever – aged just sixty-five. He had done a multitude of great things in his career. Had he done fewer of them, he might have written a great novel. But would he have admired himself for so doing? 'Writing is a delightful hobby', he told a friend, 'but it becomes stale and tarnished if adopted as a profession.'

FN John Buchan (later Baron Tweedsmuir)
MRT *The Thirty-Nine Steps*
Biog J. Adam Smith, *John Buchan and His World* (1979)

120. Edgar Rice Burroughs 1875–1950

I write to escape ... to escape poverty.

An acknowledged 'King of the Pulps', Burroughs was born in Chicago where his father, a Civil War veteran, had his own electrical battery business. Aged fifteen, Edgar spent six months on a relative's ranch in Idaho – to shield him from an influenza epidemic raging in his home city. No namby-pamby, it was in Idaho, as he liked to claim, that he acquired a lifelong love of the great outdoors, hobnobbed with cowpokes, and became himself an expert 'trick' horseman and handy with a six-gun. He was always good at tall tales. From 1892 to 1895 he was enrolled in the Michigan Military Academy, but his military career was set back when he failed his entrance examination for West Point. His father, who resolutely termed himself 'Major Burroughs', was very disappointed. In 1896 'Eddie', as he was known, enlisted to fight the Apache in Arizona, in the US Seventh Cavalry. He saw little action, a heart condition was diagnosed and, on his honourable discharge in 1897, Burroughs's military career ended ingloriously. He left, as he had entered, a buck private.

In 1899, he bought a copy Darwin's *Descent of Man*, a work which profoundly influenced the subsequent conception of 'Tarzan of the Apes', a decade later. It would be a troubled decade. Burroughs married a childhood sweetheart, Emma Hulbert, in 1900. For ten years thereafter he tried his hand at a bewildering series of jobs: he was a miner, a railroad policeman, a construction worker, and even – at low points – a door to door pencil-sharpener salesman, before, as his last resort, turning to fiction. Burroughs began writing *A Princess of Mars* (a 'John Carter' story) and *Tarzan of the Apes* around 1911. The apeman tale was sold to the pulp magazine, *All-Story*, and published entire in its pages in October 1912: fame was instantaneous. The John Carter SF romance did equally well and both novels initiated hugely successful series. The Pellucidar series was launched in 1914, marking a third epochal leap forward in pulp SF. Its adventures were located in a subterranean civilisation (the idea was borrowed, transparently, from Verne's *Journey to the Centre of the Earth*). Burroughs published sixteen novels in these three series between 1911 and 1914. His fourth long-running series, the 'Venus' chronicles, was launched, considerably later, in 1932. He would publish some seventy-five novels in all. Thanks to film adaptations, *The Land That Time Forgot* (1918) is the work of his which, along with the interminable Tarzan saga, has lasted best.

An astute curator of his literary property, Burroughs profitably sold subsidiary rights to his stories to Hollywood. The first Tarzan films began to appear in 1918. He disapproved of what film-makers did with his work, but gratefully pocketed the dollars. Seeking what was left of the American frontier, Burroughs left his home town Chicago in 1919 for Southern California, where he was to spend the rest of his life. Now very rich, he bought a vast ranch in the San Fernando Valley which he called, shamelessly, 'Tarzana'. He sold off lots during the 1920s real estate boom. By 1930 there was sufficient population for Tarzana to incorporate itself. In 1923, Burroughs had incorporated himself as Edgar Rice Burroughs, Inc. By this point in his career he was earning up to $100,000 a year. Few novelists have escaped poverty more successfully.

Politically, Burroughs was a hard right-winger; also a hard drinker, he was a vociferous opponent of Prohibition. In 1934 he divorced his first wife, Emma, by whom he had had three children, and in 1935 made a second marriage. He moved to Hawaii in 1940 but in 1941 his second marriage broke up. The following year, despite his advanced age, Burroughs managed to persuade the authorities to accredit him as a war correspondent in the Pacific theatre. Nearly seventy now, he was the oldest correspondent so to serve. One of the last of the Tarzan adventures, *Tarzan and the Foreign Legion* (1947), portrays an apeman similarly immune to the passing years.

Burroughs suffered a serious heart attack in 1949. That pesky defect, which had denied him a military career all those years ago, finally caught up with him and he died in 1950.

FN Edgar Rice Burroughs
MRT *Tarzan of the Apes*
Biog R. A. Lupoff, *Master of Adventure: The Worlds of Edgar Rice Burroughs* (2005)

121. Sabatini 1875–1950

He makes the past live again. Sabatini's publisher, Hutchinson

'Sabatini', as he was universally known to readers, was born in Jesi, Italy. He may well have been illegitimate – a theme which is prominent in his later fiction. His father, Vincenzo Sabatini, was a well-respected Italian singer; his mother, Anna Trafford, a singer from Lancashire – whose musical traditions were as strong if less glorious. After much touring across the world, the Sabatinis settled in Portugal in the 1880s to set up a music school. Rafael Sabatini was educated in Liverpool, Switzerland and Portugal, developing a phenomenal fluency in European languages and a better awareness of European culture and history than he could have got from any university. After a false start in the coffee business he began contributing to magazines in the late 1890s. It was, he liked to quip, always more fun writing romance than reading it. His romance drew on the 'Powder and Wig' historical romances of Stanley Weyman, a genre which Sabatini would significantly enhance. He was also influenced by S. R. Crockett and, more remotely, by Dumas *père*. He himself credited as a major influence Mary Johnston, the American costume romance novelist who had been briefly popular at the turn of the century.

Identified as an upcoming writer, Sabatini was recruited by the Amalgamated Press and Pearson empires, both of whom had a huge appetite for popular fiction for their myriad magazines. Fame came in the early 1920s, when America – and more particularly Hollywood – discovered him. *The Sea Hawk*, a buccaneering romance, was published in the UK in 1915, but made the American bestseller list belatedly in 1923, on the strength of a swashbuckling Douglas Fairbanks film version – after which, he was on his way. Sabatini married Ruth Goad Dixon, the daughter of a prosperous paper merchant, in 1905. They had one son, Rafael-Angelo, who later died tragically aged eighteen, in a motor accident. He then divorced and made a second marriage in 1935 to a relative by marriage. The Sabatinis lived most of their later lives out of the world on the English-Welsh border (Sabatini loved borderlands) where he could indulge his fanatic love of angling.

During the interwar years, he earned fabulously on the strength, mainly, of lavish Hollywood film options. But such wealth was not without its problems, and in the late 1930s he launched a quixotic countersuit against the American tax authorities, which he lost expensively. Thanks to rerun movies on TV, his most famous work is probably *Captain Blood: His Odyssey* (1922). According to George MacDonald Fraser (on whom Sabatini was an influence, and to whom he paid homage in *The Pyrates*) it is 'one of the great unrecognised novels of the twentieth century, and as close as any modern writer has come to a prose epic'. Dr Peter Blood is first discovered as an Irish surgeon, peacefully plying his trade in the West Country. He scornfully declines to ally himself with Monmouth's uprising in 1685, but he tends a wounded rebel officer and is sentenced by a remorseless Jeffreys to be hung, drawn and quartered. He turns the tables by diagnosing the consumption that is slowly throttling the hanging judge. Death is commuted to transportation to Barbados. Here he falls under the lash of the sadistic Colonel Bishop, but is comforted by Bishop's angelic niece, Arabella. Dr Blood escapes, captures a Spanish man-of-war and transforms himself into the buccaneer Captain Blood. The second half of the novel is taken up with Blood's exploits on the Spanish Main (more or less following the historical exploits of Henry Morgan) on his good ship *Arabella*. The action ends with him united with Miss Bishop, avenged on her uncle, and reconciled with the English authorities. The novel was filmed in 1935 with Errol Flynn in the starring role – his first leading part.

A 1952 Technicolor film adaptation of *Scaramouche* (1921), whose narrative is set in pre-Revolutionary France, is famous for the longest sword fight in film history between an athletic Mel Ferrer and slightly less athletic Stewart Granger – who has the better head of hair, but less expertise with the *glissades* and *sixtes*. Sabatini's political views were staunchly republican. *Scaramouche* has as its epigraph a quotation from Michelet: 'sensible people who lament the ills of the Revolution really ought to shed some tears on the ills which led up to that event'. In 1921, this pro-Revolutionary sentiment (given events after 1917 in Russia) was inflammatory. The main plot element has the young Revolutionary swordsman, the harlequin Scaramuccia, turn out to be the bastard son of his duellist-rival, the wicked Marquis. This story was taken over by George Lucas, for the *Star Wars* epic (same romance, different costumes). Presumably the young genius of SF-movies saw the film as a teenager in his native Modesto.

Sabatini is buried in Switzerland, a country he had visited annually, in earlier years, to indulge his love of skiing. Over his grave his wife erected a headstone bearing the opening line from *Scaramouche*: 'He was born with a gift of laughter, and a sense that the world was mad.'

FN   Rafael Sabatini
MRT *Captain Blood: His Odyssey*
Biog http://www.rafaelsabatini.com

122. Edgar Wallace 1875–1932

The good stuff may be all right for posterity. But I'm not writing for posterity.

Edgar Wallace did for English fiction what Henry Ford did for the horseless carriage. His was the Model T of fiction. Ford jested you could have any colour you wanted – so long as it was black. So, too, the Wallace addict could have: *The Ringer*, *The Squeaker*, *The Forger*, *The Joker*, *The Mixer*, *The Cheater*, *The Gunner*, *The Twister*. Wallace's were books for the day – the hour, almost. Oddly, the only work that survives is the one he was working on at his death, in Hollywood, *King Kong*. His fertile brain, apparently, came up with the scenario. Wallace's name is buried, alas, in the credit basement. Few take note of the 'King of the Thrillers' while watching the King of the Gorillas.

In pedigree, Richard Horatio Edgar Wallace is the archetypal Wellsian 'Little

Man' – a cockney sparrer. He was born in 1875, on All Fools Day, spectacularly illegitimate. He was the child of a touring actress, a second-line performer in a third-rate troupe, Mary Jane 'Polly' Richards. A young widow at the time of her son's conception, she surrendered her virtue at a drunken party to the company's romantic lead, Richard Horatio Edgar. Edgar claimed not to remember the encounter and Polly sneaked away to bear her shameful offspring in secret in Greenwich. Barely hours after birth, he was farmed out to the family of an amenable Billingsgate fishmonger, who brought him up as 'Richard Freeman'. Smart as paint, young Dick earned an honest penny as a printer's devil, a newspaper vendor, and – as an early photograph indicates – a villainous-looking milk-van boy. He was dismissed from the last position for lifting a few dishonest pennies from the coin bag – cash was always his great weakness. Aged eighteen, Edgar enrolled in the army, under the name Wallace. He wanted to see the world, before becoming one of its wage slaves. The medical examination records him as being possessed of a chest, expanded, of 33ins. He was stunted, like most children of the slums. The army would, they promised, 'make a man of him'.

Trained in the infantry, he was shipped to South Africa, in 1896, and wangled a transfer into the Medical Corps. It was a cushy berth. This was the high period of Kiplingesque barrack balladry. Wallace turned his own quick wits to profit as the 'Tommy Poet'. In 1899, as the war with the Boers broke out, Wallace – no fool – married a local girl and bought himself out. By this point the Tommy Poet had cultivated contacts in the press. Reuters took him on; the *Daily Mail* ('The Megaphone', as it would be in his thrillers) bought the occasional piece. As a reporter (he despised the term 'journalist'), he shrewdly ingratiated himself – by bribery, if necessary – with clerks, orderlies and others 'in the know'. He knew the lay of the land better than the hacks sent out from Fleet Street with their cleft sticks, topees and Royal Ordnance maps. Young Wallace pulled off a series of scoops – endearing himself to the great mogul, Northcliffe, and infuriating the CiC, Kitchener, who would rather have shot English newspapermen than Johnny Boer.

With peace, Wallace and his wife Ivy (a daughter having died) returned to Britain and the *Daily Mail*. His stipend was a comfortable £750 p.a., but Wallace's life, however much he earned, was always a rollercoaster: lunch at the Savoy, bailiffs in the kitchen. An eye for the ladies and the horses – and a legendary open-handedness – kept him forever on the brink of insolvency. In 1905, he produced his first novel, *The Four Just Men*. The idea was ingenious. Four cosmopolitan vigilantes, of impeccable breeding, set out to overset Britain's xenophobic Aliens Act (Wallace was always a champion of the underdog). The narrative pivots on a locked room mystery. The Home Secretary no less is warned that unless he liberalises the legislation, he will die. The minister ensconces himself in his Portland Place office, surrounded by guards. He is assassinated. But how? Read on.

Wallace, still slaving as a hack and a racing tipster (his preferred occupation), picked a winner in 1911 with his next serious foray into fiction, *Sanders of the River* (the first of eleven books of stories). Before being sacked by Northcliffe (furious at the neverending libel suits his star reporter incited), he had been dispatched to the Belgian Congo – the heart of darkness. He spun out of this experience a series of adventure tales, chronicling Mr Commissioner Sanders' mission to bring 'civilisation' to 'half a million cannibal folk' with his Maxim machine gun and Houssa storm-troopers. Conrad's Kurtz would have approved.

Wallace, now divorced, remarried in 1927 (to one of his secretaries, twenty years his junior) and middle-aged, came into his own as a mass producer of fiction in 1920. His agent, A. P. Watt, negotiated a sweet deal with Hodder and Stoughton for what was, effectively, a fiction assembly line. H&S would pay him £250 advance for any and every title. Wallace rose to the challenge, with 150 novels over the next twenty-five years. All he needed was his Dictaphone (he hated the labour of actually writing), pyjamas, a freshly brewed pot of tea every half hour (heavily sugared), and his cigarette holder, nearly a foot long, to keep the smoke from his eighty-odd cigarettes a day, out of his eyes. He boasted he never walked more than four miles a year (and then only between bookies at the track). He feared draughts and went to extreme measures to protect himself against them. He travelled habitually in a closed yellow Rolls-Royce; his windows were kept shut in all but the warmest weather, and he wore two sets of underwear.

In financial difficulty, despite his vast income (he had a theatrical success with *The Ringer* (1929), starring Gerald du Maurier, and was chairman of the British Lion Film Corporation), Wallace accepted Hollywood's lucre in 1932. RKO loved him. A new career, even more splendid, was in prospect. But the oceans of over-sweetened tea he had swallowed over the years caught up with him. As he waited, impatiently, for the Hollywood starlet who would warm his bed that night, he fell into a terminal diabetic coma. It was a teetotal tragedy, unique in a location where innumerable of his profession had drunk themselves to early death (Wallace was only fifty-eight), but all with stronger brew than Mr Lipton supplied. He left huge debts, and some grieving turf-accountants. The bells tolled and flags in Fleet Street were lowered when his body returned. As his memorial in Ludgate Circus testifies, he had given literature his brain, but his heart was in the daily newspaper – like fish and chips.

How good a writer was he? Orwell, unfairly, labelled him proto-fascist, a 'bully worshipper'. But Orwell would have thought a Belisha beacon fascist. Politically

Wallace was proletarian-liberal – a man of the people. And he knew precisely what fiction the people wanted.

FN   Richard Horatio Edgar Wallace (born Richards, brought up in youth as 'Richard Freeman')

MRT *The Four Just Men*

Biog M. Lane, *Edgar Wallace: The Biography of a Phenomenon* (2nd edn,1964)

123. Jack London 1876–1916

Sailor on horseback

Born into an irregular marriage, the bastard son of a vagabond astrologer and a failed boarding-house keeper, Jack London was the main support of his family at ten years old – a 'work beast' before he was even a man, rising at three in the morning to deliver newspapers in Oakland, California. He left school at fourteen, having derived most of his education from Oakland Public Library, its librarian Ina Coolbrith, and a mutilated copy of Ouida's novel *Signa*. By fifteen he was the 'Prince of the Oyster Pirates', poaching molluscs in the shallow waters off San Mateo. 'Dreadful trade', as Shakespeare's Edgar would say.

Before he was eighteen, Jack had sailed the Siberian waters as a seaman on a seal-hunter. Two years later, a befurred London plodded over the Klondike snows, as a gold-miner. In the interim he was one of the enlisted unemployed in Jacob S. Coxey's 'army' as it marched bravely on Washington, demanding a new deal for the American worker. They were brutally disbanded by the DC police and charged with trespassing on the White House Lawn. He deserted from Coxey's ranks to ride the rods, hop freight cars and generally hobo all over the North American continent. He served time for vagrancy in Erie County Penitentiary (he had been to see the Niagara Falls by moonlight – the true London touch), then returned to enrol in high school. Two years later he entered Berkeley from where, anticipating his hippy successors, he dropped out after a semester. He then worked ten-hour days at 10 cents an hour, shovelling coal, in waterfront jute mills.

But it was not all harpoon, ice-axe and shovel. Before he was thirty, London had made a reputation as an intrepid journalist, reporting to the American people from the 'abyss' of London's East End slums and the trenches of the Russo-Japanese war. Lesser men would have paused their career at any one of these points. But for London it was ever onward on what he called the 'Adventure Path' of life, and he seems always to have anticipated his premature death. Adventurers are not good insurance risks. Since selling his first story ('To the Man on Trail') in 1899, London had written as energetically as he did everything. Those writings are mirror reflections of his life experience – most comprehensively the autobiographical novel *Martin Eden* (1909). *The Road* (1907) records his Coxey experience. *The Call of the Wild* (1903) recalls his expedition to the frozen north and the volume of Darwin he took in his back-pack. *The Sea-Wolf* (1904) recalls his seal-hunting voyage across the Pacific. Everything with Jack London's name on it sold bestsellingly. He could even sell socialism – as in the dystopian *The Iron Heel* (1908). (Jack did, however, make the radically qualifying point that his was 'the socialism of the caveman'.)

In his last years he was earning around $75,000 annually. No author in the annals of American literature had ever made it so big. He married twice; the first marriage broke down in 1903. In 1905 he took to himself a new 'mate woman', Charmian Kittredge. Neither union gave him the Jack London Jr he craved, but the second lasted. In the same year, 1905, he bought a 1,000-acre property in California's Sonoma County, which he would later cultivate as his 'Beauty Ranch' – it is depicted, idyllically, in *The Valley of the Moon* (1913). At its centre he began erecting a mansion to be called 'Wolf House': a fitting habitation for one who had shown himself so indisputably a leader of the human pack. Ominously, it burned down on the day he and Charmian were to move in.

To his millions of admiring contemporaries, Jack London, as he approached his fortieth year – with the prospect of decades ahead of him – embodied the bounding energy of his still young nation. He was Herbert Spencer's social Darwinism incarnate, an overman, a Carlylean hero, a Horatio Alger rags-to-riches story, a champ. Why, then, did he commit suicide – as it seems probable that he did – in 1916? On the night of 22 November, Jack London injected into himself a lethal overdose of morphine. Apologists have claimed that it was accidental: or that it was something organic (kidneys, perhaps) that killed him. The suicide thesis is, however, supported by its omnipresence as a theme in his work. London had, as his 'alcoholic memoir' *John Barleycorn* (1913) records, attempted to drown himself, aged sixteen. The event furnishes the climax of *Martin Eden*, and its last paragraph:

> His wilful hands and feet began to beat and churn about, spasmodically and feebly. But he had fooled them and the will to live that made them beat and churn. He was too deep down ... There was a long rumble of sound, and it seemed to him that he was falling down a vast and interminable stairway. And somewhere at the bottom he fell into darkness. That much he knew. He had fallen into darkness. And at the instant he knew, he ceased to know.

There was a Jack London who was the embodiment of American manhood, a London who joyed in the glory of his body, with as much energy surging in him as a one-man Olympic team: 'I boxed and fenced, walked on my hands, jumped high and broad, put the shot, and tossed the caber, and went swimming.' (The 'caber', like Niagara by moonlight, is another true London touch.) But there was another Jack London who saw, only too clearly, the skull beneath the skin, who was fascinated by easeful death, and could write: 'I am aware that within this disintegrating body which has been dying since I was born I carry a skeleton, that under the rind of flesh which is called my face is a bony, noseless death's head.' It was that Jack London, one suspects, who reached for the hypodermic syringe, not the dumb-bell, in the dark watches of 22 November 1916.

FN   Jack London (John Griffith London; surname 'Chaney' on his birth certificate)
MRT *Martin Eden*
Biog R. Kingman, *A Pictorial Life of Jack London* (1979)

124. Rex Beach 1877–1949

A true pardnership is the sanctifiedest relation that grows. From Beach's novel, *Pardners*

A 'he-man' novelist, sometimes labelled the poor man's Jack London, Beach specialised in tales of the Yukon, celebrating, in all its husky glory, manly comradeship in the frozen North. His forte as a novelist were fight scenes featuring graphically described bone-breaking, eye-gouging and groin-kicking – all rather 'advanced' at the time. Beach was born in Michigan, in a log house as he liked to recall in later life, somewhat exaggeratedly. His father in fact ran a fruit farm – a line of work which Rex took up himself in late life. The family moved to Florida in 1886. After a brief spell at Rollins College, Rex spent a year studying law in Chicago, before throwing it up to play professional football. Athletic, and yearning for the outdoor life, Beach joined the gold rush to the Klondike (like Jack London) in 1900 where (like Jack London) he spectacularly did not make his fortune – failing even to reach the minefields (Jack London did, but never struck it rich).

Denied gold, Rex won silver representing his country in water polo in the 1904 Olympic Games, in St Louis. The next year, he took up writing. His first novel, *The Spoilers* (1905, love and pick-axes in the Yukon) laid the way for a string of bestselling 'Alaskan Adventures'. *The Spoilers* made the bestseller lists in 1906, as did *The Barrier* (1908), a story of half-breeds in Alaska; and *The Silver Horde* (1909), a novel about salmon and the romance of canning them. Beach had married in 1907 and taken up residence in New York state, moving later to Florida with his wife Greta; the couple were childless. Beach committed suicide by shotgun in 1949, having suffered for two years from cancer of the throat and been recently widowed (in a number of ways, Rex Beach anticipates the career and death of Ernest Hemingway).

Beach was notable for the pioneer canniness with which he cultivated and exploited film rights to his literary property. He was the first American author routinely to insert a clause about movie adaptation into his book contracts. This foresight paid off: *The Spoilers* was filmed at least five times, on each occasion earning fresh revenue for its author (the novel was also adapted into a long-running stage play). Beach supervised a six-reel 1916 movie version, in which he himself appears. In 1930 Paramount brought out a version starring Gary Cooper. Most famously, in 1942, John Wayne and Marlene Dietrich starred in a Universal Studios version. It is not fanciful to trace a line from Beach to Duke's tough-guy film persona.

He made a third fortune in later life from flower and vegetable growing and scientific farming, exploiting skills he had inherited from his father. Canny to the end, one of his last acts was to secure a then (1948) record-breaking $100,000 film-rights payment for his last novel, *Woman in Ambush* (published posthumously, in 1951 – never filmed).

FN   Rex Ellingwood Beach
MRT   *The Spoilers*
Biog A. R. Ravitz, *Rex Beach* (1994)

125. Warwick Deeping 1877–1950

Deeping was by no means without talent. The Times obituary

Warwick Deeping was, for a few years, the most read novelist in the English-speaking world. He could also, despite his popularity in America, claim to be among the most tweedily English. Born in Southend, Essex, he was the son and grandson (on both sides) of Southend doctors, successful and highly respected citizens in their line of work. The only boy in his family, on leaving the Merchant Taylors' boarding school in London, Warwick progressed to Cambridge, to read science and medicine, graduating with his MB in 1902. He trained for some time in London hospitals with a view to following the family profession, but the details of his life at this period are hazy, and suggest profound career uncertainties.

Some of his experience may be reflected in that of Kit in *Sorrell and Son* – also an only son and a clever young doctor. Like Kit, Deeping married early, to Maude Phyllis Merrill, in 1904. He could not, one imagines, have done so without financial support from his family (fathers enjoy a notably warm image in Deeping's fiction). The marriage was to be lifelong, happy, but childless. The couple lived after marriage in Battle, near Hastings, where Deeping's father and family had retired in 1900. From 1911 until 1919, they lived in a house they had themselves built. His father's death, in 1909, may have furnished Deeping with sufficient legacy for him to further explore what to do with his life.

He had published his first novel, *Uther and Igraine*, in 1903. The Arthurian historical romance was well received. It, and a couple of similar modishly William Morris efforts, induced the author to give up his medical practice in Hastings altogether and try for literary fame. Later, the Great War introduced grimmer conflict than that of the Round Table: somewhat too old to carry a rifle in 1914 (he was thirty-seven) Deeping served with the Royal Army Medical Corps in France, Belgium, Gallipoli and Egypt. The RAMC typically took heavy casualties and he evidently saw frontline action. On demobilisation in 1919, Warwick and Maude moved to a new house in rural Surrey, where, despite his wealth, they would remain for the rest of their lives.

After the war he returned to fiction – but of a harder kind than earlier. In his new mode, Deeping enjoyed a sensational success with his 'ex-serviceman' novel, *Sorrell and Son* (1925), which went through forty British editions in the next fifty years, topped the American bestseller list and inspired two movies – one silent, one 'talkie'. It is the story of 'Captain Sorrell', a decorated frontline officer and single father (divorced – he is the innocent party), who loses caste after the war and is obliged to work as a hotel porter – but suffers all for the sake of his son Kit. The novel is less bitter than A. S. M. Hutchinson's even better selling ex-serviceman novel, *If Winter Comes* (1921). None the less it insists on old class hierarchies (Kit, for instance, habitually addresses his father as 'pater' – Americans loved that kind of thing). Unlike Hutchinson's bleak chronicle, or Richard Aldington's even bleaker *Death of a Hero* (1929), *Sorrell and Son* ends upliftingly. Sorrell Sr is returned to the gentleman class before dying, gallantly, of cancer: Kit becomes a leading London surgeon.

Deeping's novels lorded it over the American bestseller lists in the 1920s and early 1930s. *Doomsday* (1927) caught on to the rural, 'mud and blood' theme found in Mary Webb's *Precious Bane*. *Old Pybus* (1928) has as its hero a father whose sons show the white feather. *Roper's Row* (1929) is a doctor's tale, of the kind later popularised by A. J. Cronin and Lloyd C. Douglas. *Exiles* (1930) takes as its setting a community of Britons living on private incomes abroad. *The Road* (1931) is a wartime novel, as is *Old Wine and New* (1932). These were Deeping's glory years, and his bestsellers made a mint of money for him. They seem not to have altered materially the quiet life he and his wife chose to lead. His *Who's Who* entry lists his mild recreations as tennis, golf, motoring, gardening and carpentry. Cassell's publicity photos (he was loyal to the one publisher throughout his career) portray a tweedy, pipe-smoking gentleman of the old school. By the mid-1930s, Deeping's massive popularity had begun to wane, but he continued to write fiction up to his death, and posthumous works appeared for seven years after. He left £33,000 – a fortune in 1950. His wife survived him by twenty-one years.

Warwick Deeping, the novelist, is little revisited nowadays. But he gave his name to an anti-submarine vessel (commissioned in 1934) which was sunk by German torpedo boats, in relatively shallow waters, off the Isle of Wight in 1940. It has become a favourite wreck among the recreational diving community and keeps the Deeping name alive.

FN   George Warwick Deeping
MRT   *Sorrell and Son*
Biog   *ODNB* (Jennifer Butler)

126. Jeffery Farnol 1878–1952

Novelist, Landscape Painter, Wood Carver, Boxer, Master of Fence and Athlete. Edward Farnol's description of his brother, Jeffery

Farnol was born in Birmingham, the son of a factory-employed brass-founder. One of the appreciation societies which, to this day, hold him in affection, records Jeffery's seed-time as a romantic novelist:

> His father, Henry, nightly read aloud to his wife as she sat sewing, after the boys had been put to bed. But Jeffery & his younger brother Ewart would creep silently down the stairs in their nightshirts & sit outside their parents' door listening to their father's beautiful, sonorous voice enacting all the characters while reading Alexandre Dumas, James Fenimore Cooper, Robert Louis Stevenson, Charles Dickens or Sir Walter Scott.

When Jeffery was ten, the family moved to London, spending time at Lee in Kent, a county whose laureate he would later be. He left school early. From the first he aspired to be a writer, not a metal worker, and for a number of years sponged off his family, doing nothing. Finally, when his father encountered his layabout son emerging sleepily from his bedroom at noon (as he, the father, returned from his morning shift), there was a blazing row. It 'ended by Jeffery being told that a job would be found for him with an engineering firm in Birmingham where he would be taught the useful craft of tool making'. He duly went off to lodge with an aunt; his brief experiences in the tool-making workshop were later romanticised in *Beltane the Smith* (1915). According to legend, a fracas with a foreman who called him a liar led to the apprentice being fired. A less legendary account has him being sent home for idling on the job. Observers record Farnol as being physically tiny (he wore size 5 in shoes throughout life) but ferociously physical by way of compensation. In later life he worked out with the age's premier body-builder, Eugene Sandow, and mastered the many arts of fencing. His rapier technique was admired.

For a while Farnol lodged again with his long-suffering family in London and studied at Westminster School of Art night classes. From childhood he had loved wood carving, particularly ships and dramatic scenes from history. But art did not pay; nor did model-making; or, at this stage, writing. In 1900 he married Blanche Hawley, the sixteen-year-old daughter of an American artist, over in England to visit relatives. She was, like him, diminutive (a 'Pocket Venus') and probably pregnant before the marriage. Neither family was informed of the event.

Farnol borrowed £12 from his brother Edward, and emigrated to New York in 1902. Through the good offices of his artist father-in-law, the moderately eminent F. Hughson Hawley, he was employed there as a scene painter at the Astor Theatre. Farnol and Hawley, who had wanted better things for his daughter than an impecunious English dwarf with a paintbrush, quarrelled. The marriage broke up, temporarily, and Jeffery went off to slum it by himself in a 'rat infested studio' in New York's 'Hell's Kitchen'; a low period of his life, commemorated in *The Definite Object* (1917). He continued to write, doggedly, and in 1907 finally got a volume published, *My Lady Caprice*. It did not set the East River on fire. But it was over these tough years that he wrote the 200,000 words of his Regency romance, *The Broad Highway: A Romance of Kent*. No American publisher would take the manuscript on the grounds that it was 'too long and too English'. Enterprisingly, Blanche sent it to her mother in England, who submitted it to Sampson Low, who accepted it with a £250 advance.

Published in 1910, *The Broad Highway* went on to be a massive hit in the UK, and a year later in America, where it sold getting on for half-a-million copies. 'Too English' was now a strong selling point. Farnol's narrative opens with a humorous 'Ante Scriptum' in which the author mulls over with a 'companion of the road' what kind of novel he shall write. The action opens in the Regency period with the reading of 'Buck' Vibart's eccentric will. To one nephew, the scholarly Peter, he leaves ten guineas. To another nephew, the 'rake' Maurice, he leaves £20,000. Either nephew will be eligible for a half a million pounds, 'if either shall, within one calendar year, become the husband of Lady Sophia Sefton of Cambourne'. Rollicking complications ensue. Farnol's nimble picaresque, sword-clashing, and rose-tinted vision of the Regency period was much imitated – most profitably by Georgette Heyer and Barbara Cartland. Suddenly windfall-rich, the reunited Farnols returned to Britain and settled in a country house, Sunnyside, in Lee, Kent. Jeffery set to writing a string (eventually forty-strong) of 'Regencies', pirate tales and stories of the road. None achieved the runaway sales of *The Broad Highway*, although the Farnol name assured good sales right up to the time of his death. His theme – the pleasures of exuberant youth, usually in some romanticised past period of English history – never varied.

Farnol was too old and too short-sighted, to serve in the First World War. Like other bestselling novelists, such as Hall Caine and John Buchan, he propagandised and reported from the Front, adding palpably to the pressure to get America into the fight. After the war, as a biographer records, 'his fondness for gangsters and dandies did not always serve him well. He took into his employ a certain cad who robbed him of thousands of pounds over many years.' A chronically quarrelsome man, he fell out with his surviving brother Edward (Ewart had been killed in the war). Persistently unfaithful, he divorced his first wife in 1938, marrying a younger woman, Phyllis, in the same year. They lived in Eastbourne until Farnol's death, with one adopted daughter. His second wife completed his last novel, *Justice by Midnight* (1956), for those old enough to remember the author of *The Broad Highway*.

FN   John Jeffery Farnol
MRT *The Broad Highway: A Romance of Kent*
Biog J. A. Salmonson, 'The life and times of Jeffery Farnol' (http://www. violetbooks.com/farnol-bio.html)

127. E. M. Forster 1879–1970

Works of art, in my opinion, are the only objects in the material universe to possess internal order.

Jane Austen went to the grave a virgin, leaving six full-length novels behind her. Would those novels have been better had Miss Austen had as lively a sex life as, say, slutty Lydia Bennet? E. M. Forster was a virgin until the age of thirty-nine when he had his first 'full' sexual experience (a 'hurried sucking off,' his most recent biographer, Wendy Moffat, informs us) with a passing soldier on a beach in Alexandria. By that point, five of Forster's six novels were written and the last, *A Passage to India*, drafted. Until he was thirty, with his *oeuvre* behind him, he did not, he later confessed, 'know exactly how male and female joined'. 'Muddle and mystery' between the sheets as well as in the Marabar caves.

Does a writer's carnal experience matter? D. H. Lawrence, the most unzipped of British novelists, believed it did. His chauvinist sneer at Austen as a 'narrow gutted spinster' indicates that some rumpy-pumpy would have done wonders for her fiction. Of Forster, Lawrence told Bertrand Russell, 'Morgan sucks his dummy – you know, those child's comforters – long after his age.' He should, one deduces, have graduated to his grown-up sucking earlier, for the good of English literature.

Moffat had first access to Forster's recently (2008) derestricted diaries and plunged up to her armpits in them. Her thesis is that *Maurice* – the *Bildungsroman* in which Forster chronicles his own homosexual ordeal – is 'his only truly honest novel'. The other five avoid the point. For Moffat, the primal moment in Forster's life was when the over-mothered five-year-old discovered that by rubbing his groin against tree trunks, while picturing his tutor's moustache, he could perform the child's 'dirty trick'. It might, one supposes, explain something about the wych-elm and the pigs' teeth in *Howards End*. Forster's progress in self-abuse is tracked by the indefatigable Moffat to its heroic heyday, when he did it 'thrice in one afternoon' in his eighty-second year, when – despite the trauma of two prostate operations (brought on by 'excessive masturbation,' his doctor gravely informed him) – 'the worm that never dies' gave its 'last wriggle'. At prep school, a callous classmate yelled out: 'Have you seen Forster's cock? A beastly little brown thing.' At the same school, Forster was abused by a passing paedophile who afterwards proffered a compensatory shilling, which was politely declined. At his public school, Forster was derided as a 'cissy' – that most hurtful objurgation in the schoolyard lexicon.

King's College Cambridge was, by contrast, a haven. What was 'cissy' at Tonbridge School was 'hellenism' among the more refined spirits where Morgan found lifelong friends, but no sexual fulfilment – impossible, of course, in a world terrorised by the Wilde scandals. Forster was also inhibited by ineradicable delicacy. Unlike Lytton Strachey – who gloried in the word – he would not even spell out 'bugger' in full in the diaries Moffat has pored over. Forster lost his faith at Cambridge (too little 'fun and humour' in the gospels) and found a warm place with the Apostles. Their ethical creed, expounded by G. E. Moore, would sustain him. It was at Cambridge he discovered what 'friendship' – homosexuality without sex – could be.

After graduation, Forster took the Edwardian Grand Tour with his mother, the redoubtable Lily. 'Gide hasn't got a mother!,' he once complained, in reference to the franker author of *Si le grain ne meurt*. But views from *pensione* rooms and longest journeys furnished what he needed for his *annus mirabilis*, 1904, when three of his novels were substantially composed. At twenty-five he found his life 'rather sad and dull'. He had, he felt, passed 'the romantic desirable age' in a condition of lust-racked virginity. He resolved to smoke in public on the grounds 'it gives a reason for you'. Whether it was the cigarettes or not, at this point in his life, partners began to figure. First was Syed Ross Masood, a Muslim Indian – their relationship was 'joyful but inconclusive'.

With the success of *Howards End*, Forster found himself a celebrity, rich but still virginal. There occurred at this point the event he describes (in his preface to *Maurice*) as life-changing. On a visit to the sexual anarchist Edward Carpenter, the sage's partner, George Merrill, tapped him, 'just above the buttocks'. It seemed, he said, 'to go straight through the small of my back into my ideas, without involving my thoughts'.

Forster had a goodish First World War as a 'searcher', tracking down, from the accounts of the wounded, soldiers 'missing in action'. The work took him to Alexandria. Here he came into contact with the poet C. P. Cavafy – a more modern, less inhibited Hellene than had ever come his way at Cambridge. Sexually, Forster's life began at forty. With the young Egyptian, Muhammad al-Adl, he had his first 'anxious but very beautiful affair'. Moffat's description of the breakthrough moment is a good example of her no-nonsense style: 'Mohammed gave Morgan a "sudden hard kiss" and after "a gruff demur" leaned back, untied his linen trousers, and let Morgan masturbate him. This was a milestone. The struggle was over.' And so, alas, were the novels. There followed a second visit to India and a Hindi 'boy', Kanaya, to match the Muslim. (Moffat, who spares us nothing, records that this was an occasion when Forster 'penetrated', deviating from his preferred pattern.)

'The middle age of buggers,' Virginia Woolf confided to her diary (with Forster in mind) 'is not to be contemplated without horror.' But it was Woolf, not Forster, who killed herself. The event, Forster confided to *his* diary, 'turned my shit pale green and almost scentless'. Forster's later years proved anything but horrific. A younger set of gays, led by the *über*-louche Joe Ackerley, created a new network of friends – to whom he was a Gandhiesque icon. He stood fast during the Second World War, articulating the liberal ideals for which Britain was fighting in noble broadcasts and essays. His last years were passed in the comfortable berths of a residential fellowship at his alma mater, King's, and the cosy arrangement he set up, in joyous criminality, with the love of his life, the metropolitan (married) policeman, Bob

Buckingham, twenty-three years his junior. He was, reportedly (although, luckily for him, no one did report him), happy and, at last, a practising homosexual. But no longer a practising novelist. He suffered a stroke and died in Cambridge.

FN   Edwin Morgan Forster
MRT   *A Passage to India*
Biog   P. N. Furbank, *E. M. Forster* (2 vols, 1977, 1978); W. Moffat, *E. M. Forster: A New Life* (2010)

128. Mazo de la Roche 1879–1961

Other women change their names.

A pioneer of the romantic 'saga' for mainly women readers, de la Roche's sixteen-strong Jalna/Whiteoaks sequence is reckoned to have sold over 11 million copies worldwide. Roche was born at Newmarket, Ontario, in rural Canada, the only child of a dry-goods salesman. Aiming higher in life, she added a French prefix and some aristocratic class to her name. 'De la Roche', as she now called herself, was brought up near Toronto, with many moves of childhood residence (the father's business never thrived) and lived most of her adult life in the company of a cousin, Caroline Clement, who had been adopted by Roche's parents. De la Roche and Clement themselves adopted a pair of orphans during their years together. They were also ardent dog lovers – and, possibly, commentators have speculated, lovers. There is some dispute, and fierce refutation, as to whether de la Roche might not have been a 'child molester', Clement being an infant when their relationship began.

De la Roche was for some years a student of art and began writing for the magazines in the early years of the twentieth century. Her first volume, a collection of linked short stories, *Explorers of the Dawn*, was published in 1922. The idea for 'Jalna' (the grand home through many generations of the 'Whiteoaks' family) came to her while spending some time in a summer cottage by a landed estate in Ontario. It was, of course, a fantasised vision of her own non-existent aristocratic background. *Jalna* (1927), a runaway bestseller in America, Canada and England, was the first of sixteen novels in the series, culminating with *Morning at Jalna* (1960). Nine of the series deal with the years after the late 1920s, the remainder range backwards into the family's past. The dominant character is the hundred-year-old matriarch, Adeline.

Aimed principally at the woman reader, the *Jalna* saga was partly inspired by

Galsworthy's *Forsyte Saga* and it bequeathed richly to the later emerging genre of multi-episodic radio and TV soap opera. Following the success of her series, de la Roche and Clement lived in style in Britain until 1938, when the author's bad health, and fears about coming war, returned them to Canada. During their residence in the UK, they were frequent guests at Windsor – someone there evidently liked the novels.

FN   Mazo de la Roche (born Mazo Roche)
MRT   *Jalna*
Biog   J. Givner, *Mazo de la Roche: The Hidden Life* (1989)

129. Daisy Ashford 1881–1972

My own idear is that these things are as piffle before the wind. Mr Salteena, being stoical in the face of disaster

Surveying the large outlines of nineteenth-century fiction, one is struck by a singular gender difference. Women novelists tend to start early in life – often long before they become women – as if somehow born to the job. Men rebound into writing fiction later in life, typically after failing in, or defecting from, other more 'serious' jobs. Women novelists in the nineteenth century are – many of them – spectacularly precocious. Writing is not a last, but a first resort. One thinks of Grace Aguilar penning her first play at the age of twelve. Or Mary Shelley, composing *Frankenstein* at the age of seventeen. Or Jane Austen, reading out first drafts of 'First Impressions' to her family (father prominent, one likes to imagine, nodding appreciatively at the Mr Bennet jokes). And, of course, the sisters in Haworth – pre-pubescent – weaving their magical Angrian and Gondalian webs of narrative. What impels them to do it? To please their fathers, or father-figures, is the answer that the psychobiographers suggest. It's very plausible. If true, the clinching example of girl's fiction as a paternal offering is Daisy Ashford, the youngest novelist ever to achieve worldwide fame.

Daisy was brought up in Lewes, Sussex, into a prosperous and numerous Catholic family. As a nine-year-old girl she wrote novels after tea and before bedtime (a strict 6 o'clock) for the delectation of her father, a Civil Servant in the War Office: a readership of one. He copied the stories out for her, in a more legible adult hand, but retained her turns of phrase and orthography. Given the size of the Ashford brood, Daisy clearly won more than her fair share of paternal attention. Before she could put pen to paper, she dictated her first story to her father, 'The Life of Father

McSwiney', which she composed, aged four. Daisy's mature *oeuvre* includes 'The Hangman's Daughter', 'Where Love Lies Deepest', and the novel on which her fame rests, *The Young Visiters*.

The Young Visiters was published in 1919 by Chatto and Windus, as a curiosity, with an introduction by J. M. Barrie, who – manuscript in hand – vouched for the bona fides of the 'nine-year-old authoress' and that the work was 'unaided'. The Chatto editor in charge of the project, Frank Swinnerton, himself a novelist, interviewed the now fortyish author before giving it the go-ahead. She was, he recalled, 'shy, giggling and tremendously excited at the prospect of being published'. Miss Ashford daringly asked Swinnerton for as much as £10. Chatto came through, voluntarily, with £500 and eventually paid thousands more. As the *Daily Mail* recorded, one half of London was laughing over *The Young Visiters* in 1919. The other half was impatiently waiting for the next edition to be printed, so they could get hold of the work that everyone else was in fits about.

Miss Ashford wrote nothing more after going to board at a convent school aged thirteen, in Haywards Heath. Fiction was put away with other childish things. She married a farmer, ran a hotel, and had children of her own. Doubtless she told a rattling good bedtime story. Her identity as the authentic author of a work, often considered a fake because it was so good, was confirmed, at the end of a long and useful life, in 1972, in a *Times* obituary. The flavour of the romance is given in the first paragraph:

> Mr Salteena was an elderly man of 42 and was fond of asking peaple to stay with him. He had quite a young girl staying with him of 17 named Ethel Monticue. Mr Salteena had dark short hair and mustache and wiskers which were very black and twisty. He was middle sized and he had very pale blue eyes. He had a pale brown suit but on Sundays he had a black one and he had a topper every day as he thorght it more becoming. Ethel Monticue had fair hair done on the top and blue eyes. She had a blue velvit frock which had grown rarther short in the sleeves. She had a black straw hat and kid gloves.

Ethel is also given to 'sneery' looks when things do not go quite her way.

Daisy, one deduces, had come across library copies of the romances of Rhoda Broughton (*Cometh up as a Flower, Red as a Rose is She*, etc). But beneath the precociously fluent – but comically inept – veneer of high romantic rhetoric there is the hawk-eye of the child. The child's view, in any number of ways, registers the surfaces of quotidian life missed by the less innocent, but more penetrative, adult eye. Thirty-seven-year-old ('elderly' indeed) Edward Casaubon's attachment to nineteen-year-old Dorothea Brooke, for example, requires for its full moral analysis the adult seriousness the author of *Middlemarch* brings to the affair. But what are the characters wearing on that important first visit to Lowick when the Casaubon–Brooke match is tentatively formed? We know about the marriage suit he has in mind, but what colour is the suit which the Revd Casaubon is wearing that day? Of what material is Dorothea's visiting dress? The innocent eye sees more, and sees less.

FN   Margaret Mary Julia Ashford ('Daisy', later Devlin)
MRT   *The Young Visiters*
Biog   R. N. Malcolmson, *Daisy Ashford: Her Life* (1984)

130. Mary Webb 1881–1927

Oh, filthy, heavy-handed, blear-eyed world, when will you wash and be clean?

Mary Meredith was born in rural Shropshire – the region in which she set her fiction. She was proud of her 'blood'; it ran pure Celtic on both sides of her family. Her father, George Meredith, was Welsh by origin (and, coincidentally, bore a famous novelist's name); he is described as a 'country gentleman and tutor'. Mary's mother, a distant descendant of Walter Scott, was from Edinburgh by birth. Mary was the first of six Meredith children. She spent her early years in a fine country house in Much Wenlock. Her father took in boarding pupils and did some gentle-manly farming in the extensive grounds. Mary 'adored' him and was, in a sense, his prize pupil. The family was well off and she also had a governess. At fourteen she was sent away to be 'finished' at a school in Southport. Aged twenty, Mary was afflicted with what would be a lifelong thyroid deficiency, Graves' disease. Easily curable now, it was not then and was particularly traumatic for a young woman. She was a lifelong invalid and – crucially – facially disfigured by the condition with goitre, protuberant eyes and chronic lassitude. From birth a reserved girl, she became a reclusive woman.

The Merediths moved home several times during Mary's adolescence and young womanhood – always, however, to rural locations. Then her life was thrown into emotional turmoil by the death of her father in 1909. The following year she met a teacher, Henry Webb (a nephew of the channel swimmer hero, Captain Webb) and they married in 1912. He was, her biographers tactfully agree, a father substitute. There would be no children to the marriage. Webb's work took him and his wife to Weston Super Mare, far from her beloved Shropshire. Uprooted, Mary began writing her first regional novel, *The Golden Arrow*. The central character, John Arden, was clearly based on her father. The Webbs returned to Shropshire in 1914, where she finished the novel which was published in 1916.

It was followed up promptly by another Shropshire saga, *Gone to Earth* (1917), in which Webb hit her grim groove. It was well reviewed. Amazingly, Rebecca West chose it as her book of the year – something one can only ascribe to a critical neurosis triggered by the war (going badly for the Allies in 1917) and her disastrous love affair with H. G. Wells. As the title suggests, *Gone to Earth* is a novel which should be prescribed reading for all members of the House of Commons, when they debate, as they seem likely to do until the crack of doom, the issue of hunting with dogs. The heroine, Hazel Woodus, is one of Webb's hallmark children of nature, a denizen of the woods, hills and streams – with something of the witch (as her mother was) about her. She carries with her a fragrance of 'morning air' and her soulmate is a pet fox, 'Foxy'. Her father makes coffins – ominously. Ominous too is the opening paragraph:

> Small feckless clouds were hurried across the vast untroubled sky – shepherdless, futile, imponderable – and were torn to fragments on the fangs of the mountains, so ending their ephemeral adventures with nothing of their fugitive existence left but a few tears.

The novel is set during the First World War (in which Webb had three serving brothers). Delectable Hazel catches the eye of the local squire, a hunting man, Jack Reddin. One glimpses, as in a distorting mirror, reflections of *Tess of the D'Urbervilles*. To cut a long story short (which Webb doesn't), Hazel has to choose between two legs or four. The novel ends with him leading a hunt (tally ho!) in which, to save Foxy, Hazel scoops the beast in her arms and plunges down a mine-shaft. *Liebestod*.

By the early 1920s the Webbs could afford to buy their own house, Spring Cottage, at Lyth Hill, near Shrewsbury. Henry had taken up a teaching post in London in 1921, so Mary had time to herself to write. The frequent separation put the marriage under strain, but Mary's visits to London, and her increasingly well-regarded fiction, raised her profile in the literary world. Earning well from her fiction, with no family to distract her, Webb had the leisure to be a woman of letters and develop the sub-Brontëan genre of fiction in which she was now a leading light. This eminence was certified by the award of the Prix Femina prize for *Precious Bane*, in 1924. The novel is historical, set in the early nineteenth century and, inevitably, in Shropshire. The heroine is Prue Sarn – another child of nature, beautiful but for a harelip (the link with Webb's own disfigurement is painfully obvious) which renders her, in the eyes of the village, perhaps a witch. Despite this, Prue is chosen as his love by a manly weaver, Kester Woodseaves. The novel ends, unusually for Webb, happily, when Kester – like Lochinvar – scoops Prue up to gallop away with her on his horse. A barrage of erotic dialogue ensues:

'Tabor on, owd nag!' says Kester, and we were going at a canter towards the blue and purple mountains.

'But no!' I said. 'It mun be frommet, Kester. You mun marry a girl like a lily. See, I be hare-shotten!'

But he wouldna listen. He wouldna argufy. Only after I'd pleaded agen myself a long while, he pulled up sharp, and looking down into my eyes, he said –

'No more sad talk! I've chosen my bit of Paradise. 'Tis on your breast, my dear acquaintance!'

And when he'd said those words, he bent his comely head and kissed me full upon the mouth.

Webb was by now extremely ill and her marriage was effectively at an end. She was unable to finish what would have been her sixth novel, the yet more historical medieval romance, *Armour Wherein He Trusted*. She died, aged forty-six, in October 1927, and 'went to earth' in the grounds of Shrewsbury Cathedral.

Precious Bane had been hugely admired on its publication by the Conservative Prime Minister, Stanley Baldwin. He voiced his admiration for her 'neglected genius' in April 1928, in a speech at the annual Royal Literary Fund Dinner. It was written up in the newspapers the following day and, six months after her death, Webb became the novelist of the day. Cape published a collected edition of her novels which sold like hot cakes.

It was not all Baldwinian praise. A smart young London journalist on the *Evening Standard*, Stella Gibbons, was given the task of editing the *The Golden Arrow*, which was being serialised in the newspaper in 1928. The result, four years later, was the witty spoof, *Cold Comfort Farm*. Flora Poste, a metropolitan 'flapper', is orphaned and goes to live in her aunt Judith Starkadder's farm, in 'Howling, Sussex'. 'We are not like other folk, maybe,' she is warned. But they are very like the folk in *Precious Bane*. Gibbons catches the Webbian tone wittily, as in the opening to Chapter 3 of *Cold Comfort Farm* (see the passage from *Gone to Earth*, above): 'Dawn crept over the Downs like a sinister white animal followed by the snarling cries of a wind eating its way between the black boughs of the thorns.' Flora is not daunted by broodingly handsome Seth (whom she packs off to Hollywood), the child of nature Elfina, or old Ada Doom, who saw something nasty in the woodshed and has never got over it. She cheerfully propels all of them into the twentieth century.

FN   Mary Gladys Webb (née Meredith)
MRT *Precious Bane*
Biog G. M. Coles, *Mary Webb* (1990)

131. James Joyce 1882–1941

There is no foulness conceivable to the mind of madman or ape that has not been poured into its imbecile pages ... Ulysses would make a Hottentot sick. Alfred Noyes, author of the perennially popular poem, 'The Highwayman'

Joyce was born in Dublin, middle-class and Catholic. He died neither – nor even a Dubliner, a city he never revisited in the last twenty-one years of his life. Half-iron-ically, it pleased him to claim aristocratic lineage and he sported a heraldic Joycean device in later life but his youthful family circumstances were humbler. He was the eldest surviving son of John Stanislaus Joyce and Mary Joyce (née Murray), a wife ten years younger and many ranks lower, as her husband thought, in social stand-ing. Mary would die prematurely, exhausted by thirteen pregnancies. Her death was traumatic for 'Jim' and echoes, guiltily, through the opening chapter of *Ulysses*. A brood of nine children and a series of reckless mortgages impoverished John Joyce. His son had to adapt to coming down in the world and picked up the tricks of genteel cadging which would serve him in good stead as an author.

Ireland itself was in a period of decline in the late nineteenth century. The opening section of *A Portrait of the Artist as a Young Man* (1916) centres on a raging argument about Parnell, the nationalist hero who was brought down by scandalous sexual misconduct with Kitty O'Shea. Wilde's downfall was not more sensational. 'Dante' (the Joyce family nickname for his aunt Elizabeth) exults at Catholic morali-ty's victory: '– Devil out of hell! We won! We crushed him to death! Fiend!' Stephen's father weeps for Ireland. Stephen (i.e. James Joyce) merely observes.

As he grew up, Joyce, like Stephen Dedalus, came to think little of his father – perhaps because, like his namesake, he was unwilling to fly high. He acknowl-edged the inheritance of a fine tenor voice and musical talent; otherwise, he owed no great filial debt. But fathers, as Joyce's fascination with *Hamlet* testifies, are not easily erased from their sons' lives. John Joyce figures prominently in the *Portrait*, in *Ulysses*, and as Earwicker in *Finnegans Wake*. John had failed many careers. In Joyce's boyhood he was a local government official. The family was well enough off, and at this stage small enough for the six-year-old eldest son to be sent off as a boarder to Clongowes Wood College in co. Kildare. True to the proverb the Jesuits would have him for life – but not quite as the order would have wanted. Joyce pro-fessed to hate Clongowes and distilled his hatred into *A Portrait* where Stephen, true to his martyr's name, is bullied, 'pandied' (corporally punished), misunderstood by teachers and – at the very lowest point – tipped into a cesspit, precipitating a dan-gerous bout of amoebic dysentery. The school records him as a brilliant pupil and, oddly, given his acute myopia, a decent sportsman.

He was withdrawn from Clongowes for non-payment of fees in 1891 – the year of Parnell's death. It was not a comfortable home which welcomed him back to Dublin. His father's improvidence, and drunkenness, and possible financial mis-dealings had brought the family to bankruptcy. Joyce gives a picture of the domes-tic squalor in *A Portrait*: '[Stephen] pushed open the latchless door of the porch and passed through the naked hallway into the kitchen. A group of his brothers and sisters was sitting round the table. Tea was nearly over and only the last of the second watered tea remained in the bottoms of the small glass jars and jampots which did service for teacups.' But there was worse than destitution: John Joyce was violent when drunk and his domestic brutality is vividly depicted in the short story in *Dubliners*, 'Counterparts'.

Joyce finished his primary education at another Jesuit institution, Belvedere College. It was a local day school and did not charge. The teachers liked him and he was seriously inclined towards the priesthood. He responded sensitively to the beauty of ritual and – as Chapter 3 of *A Portrait* records – hypersensitively to the terrors of damnation. Hell, for him, was a gigantic Clongowes cesspit: 'Consider then what must be the foulness of the air of hell. Imagine some foul and putrid corpse that has lain rotting and decomposing in the grave, a jelly-like mass of liquid corruption. Imagine such a corpse a prey to flames, devoured by the fire of burning brimstone and giving off dense choking fumes of nauseous loathsome decomposi-tion.' Terror acted as a moral discipline on Joyce until 1898, when he met a 'gay girl' and ventured to have sex. Thereafter 'He would never swing the thurible before the tabernacle as priest.' When his mother died, he refused her dying wish to kneel by her bed. Where religion was concerned he would be, in his word, 'elusive'. Uncaught. However, the indoctrination of his early years could not be entirely rinsed out. In his last year of life he was asked why he carried stones in his pocket to pelt at local dogs. 'Because they have no souls', he replied. What, very soon, would happen to his?

Joyce went on to university and graduated in 1902 with a lowly pass degree. He was much better educated than that measly award suggests. He left University College Dublin fearsomely well read, a skilled dialectician and intellectually 'soli-tary' – his own man. *Non serviam* was his motto. The principal influence on him in these formative years was Henrik Ibsen, whose spirit, he recorded, blew through him 'like a keen wind'. In his tract, *The Quintessence of Ibsenism*, George Bernard Shaw conceived the Norwegian's principal instruction to be 'repudiation of duty'. James Joyce repudiated church, nationalism and the infatuations of the Irish liter-ary renaissance ('Ancient Ireland is dead just as ancient Egypt is dead'). His first significant publication was an essay on Ibsen for the *Fortnightly Review* (April 1900). It drew praise from William Archer, Ibsen's English disciple and a commendatory letter from the playwright himself. Archer shrewdly nudged the young Irishman away from drama to what he could do best – prose narrative and lyric poetry. It was at this period that Joyce began recording what he called 'epiphanies': moments laden with meaning, crystallised in language.

There were a number of false starts. In 1902 he went to Paris to study medicine. He lacked the necessary qualifications, but the city's bohemian culture captivated him. He returned to less captivating Dublin after a year, to teach. This is the root-less interim commemorated in *Ulysses* – specifically a week or so that he lodged in a Martello tower, in summer 1904. He developed what would be a lifelong addiction to drink, along with his current, even more bibulous, bosom friend, Oliver St John Gogarty ('Buck Mulligan'). He toyed with the idea of a singing career. Meanwhile he was struggling with a long *Bildungsroman*, initially called 'Stephen Hero', even-tually to be given the Rembrandtian title, *A Portrait of the Artist as a Young Man*. He would be a middle-aged man before it was published. He was also working on a set of poems called 'chamber music' – chamber as in chamber-pot, music as in the tinkle of a whore's urine. Joyce's scatological sexual tastes have provided mixed distaste and fascination for the Joyce industry. Cesspits always had their strange fascination for him.

In 1904 he managed to smuggle some of the stories later to be published in *Dubliners* into print, under the loaded *nom de plume* 'Stephen Dedalus'. Another turning point came on 10 June 1904, when he first encountered Nora Barnacle, a hotel chambermaid. She was, to his gratified astonishment, easy-going sexually. He came to regard her as his 'soul' and his 'Ireland'. At exactly the same period he met the man who would inspire Leopold Bloom. In the autumn of this eventful year he resolved to leave Ireland with Nora, soon to be pregnant with their first child, Giorgio. He had jumped the gun but he would not make his father's philoprogenitive error. The method of contraception the couple favoured, initially, was that described in *Ulysses* between Molly and Leopold – sleeping head to toe. They would not marry until 1931.

Why Joyce should have gone into exile remains slightly obscure – although he wore the condition as a badge of integrity, along with 'cunning' and 'silence'. He may have wanted a place more tolerant of a man and a woman 'living in sin'. Self-preservation as an artist may have come into it. Ireland, as Stephen puts it, was the sow that eats her farrow.

A series of mishaps with teaching posts across Europe led to them finally taking up residence in the tiny nowhere state, Trieste, where he found secure employment in the Berlitz school. The Berlitz method was to teach a language by conversation – dialogue – which suited Joyce, as did the morally relaxed atmosphere of the coastal state. Joyce by now had several literary projects on the go – most hopefully his Dublin short stories which the English publisher, Grant Richards, had agreed to take before getting cold feet. It was a bumpy road to eventual publication in 1914. Censorship problems were invariably the problem. The delayed publication of these naturalistic stories skews one's sense of Joyce's extraordinary evolution stylistically and, in a decade, their social relevance had aged. The most important of them is 'The Dead', which he finished in 1907. In the spiritually inert character of the 'West Briton' journalist, Gabriel Conroy, he left a sly self-portrait of himself in his twenties:

> He was a stout tallish young man. The high colour of his cheeks pushed upwards even to his forehead, where it scattered itself in a few formless patches of pale red; and on his hairless face there scintillated restlessly the polished lenses and the bright gilt rims of the glasses which screened his delicate and restless eyes. His glossy black hair was parted in the middle and brushed in a long curve behind his ears where it curled slightly beneath the groove left by his hat.

'The Dead' centres on Conroy's discovery that his wife had had, before he knew her, a young lover who 'died for love of her.' His obsessive investigation into his wife's inner mind, fuelled by his jealousy, led to the finest achievement of *Ulysses*, 'Penelope'. In this final section, as she falls asleep, all of Molly Bloom's life comes crowding in, culminating in a re-enactment of the orgasm that Leopold could never give her:

> I put the rose in my hair like the Andalusian girls used or shall I wear a red yes and how he kissed me under the Moorish wall and I thought well as well him as another and then I asked him with my eyes to ask again yes and then he asked me would I yes to say yes my mountain flower and first I put my arms around him yes and drew him down to me so he could feel my breasts all perfume yes and his heart was going like mad and yes I said yes I will Yes.

Nora claimed to have read none of her husband's books – even those that wrote about her. In 1906 Nora was pregnant again with a daughter, Lucia, born to be doomed. As he approached thirty, Joyce published his first book, a volume of poetry, *Chamber Music* (1907). The poems are charming but – for this writer – strangely antique. For example xxxii, which opens:

> *Rain has fallen all the day.*
> *O come among the laden trees:*
> *The leaves lie thick upon the way*
> *Of memories.*

There was no money in poetry. Joyce then ventured on a madcap scheme to open a cinema in Dublin, managed from Trieste. It came to nothing, as did the most recent attempt to publish *Dubliners*, which ended with a thousand copies destroyed before sale. It was Ezra Pound who at this point took charge of Joyce's career, arranging for the serial publications of *Portrait* (it came out whole in London in 1917) and, later, *Ulysses*. It was Pound, too, who agitated to get Joyce handouts from the Civil List and the Society of Authors. Most importantly, Pound put him in touch with the woman who would be his principal patron, Harriet Shaw Weaver, who took the Irish author (whom she had never met) as her pensioner. *Ulysses* is routinely acclaimed as the greatest novel of the century. It is as much the product of cultural philanthropy (Weaver) and literary agency (Pound) as modernism.

It was at this relatively stable point in his writing career that Joyce began serious work on *Ulysses*. As with everything in his life, it did not go smoothly. World war meant the family moving to Zurich in 1915. What would be chronic, and eventually blinding, eye problems had set in. Joyce's drinking was periodically pathological; he smoked heavily and he was sedentary by nature. Every room, he believed, should have a bed in it. The furore over Lawrence's *The Rainbow* meant that no British publisher would take an unexpurgated text which contained the word 'fuck'. And Joyce would never expurgate. The novel – if one calls it that – was marginally less objectionable in the US and most acceptable in Paris, after the war, where it was put out, in full, by the expatriate American bookseller, Sylvia Beach.

Ulysses, once published, was universally notorious but rarely read throughout, even by its most ferocious opponents and warmest advocates. It was the more difficult for the average reader by virtue of each section of narrative inventing a separate technique. It was an 'encyclopaedia', as Joyce called it, which changed its form as its content changed. The public was not used to such things. Nor were the authorities indulgent. The first volume edition of *Ulysses* published in London was widely confiscated and banned, despite a dauntingly impressive subscription list. It would not be until 1934 that an enlightened court case in the US acquitted *Ulysses*. The Bodley Head edition came out two years later in the UK – but not in Ireland.

By now, the family of four had moved to Paris – the only place for a modernist to live, Pound urged – but Joyce's health was precarious. All his teeth had been extracted, he was virtually blind in one eye, and prone to crippling depression. But he forged ahead with his most ambitious work *Finnegans Wake*. This, and the dire condition of his daughter Lucia, would be his main preoccupations over the years that remained to him. A gifted artist, Lucia conceived a hopeless, and utterly rejected, infatuation for Samuel Beckett – whose only interest was her father. She sank into a state diagnosed as schizophrenic – although the diagnosis has been much debated, as is the possibility of incest within the family. She was eventually institutionalised.

Joyce finished *Finnegans Wake* in 1939 as war, once again, consumed Europe and enforced flight. Once again Switzerland was their refuge. In this last work, in his last years, Joyce had brought fiction 'to the end of English'. The title alludes to a folk ballad about a drunken bricklayer, thought dead, who is resurrected (he wakes at his wake) when whisky is accidentally sprinkled in his coffin. The first line is one of the most famous in literature:

> riverrun, past Eve and Adam's, from swerve of shore to bend of bay, brings us by a commodius vicus of recirculation back to Howth Castle and Environs.

Very few readers make it to the last line:

> A way a lone a last a loved a long the
> PARIS, 1922–1939.

Joyce died in Switzerland of complications arising from stomach ulcers.

FN   James Augustine Aloysius Joyce
MRT   *Ulysses*
Biog   R. Ellmann, *James Joyce* (revd edn, 1983)

132. Virginia Woolf 1882–1941

Virginia Woolf was a sane woman who had an illness. Hermione Lee

Hermione Lee's life of the novelist opens with a shriek of scholarly pain: 'My God how *does* one write a biography?' A principal embarrassment is Woolf's own fragmentary attempts at autobiography. They have had as disturbing an effect for the would-be life writer as the clandestine 'fragment' Dickens slipped into Forster's hand, divulging his hitherto suppressed childhood experiences in the blacking factory. The poison pill in Woolf's life also involves childhood trauma. At the 'Memoir Club' (a Bloomsbury outfit, as self-regardingly exclusive as the Cambridge Apostles), the forty-something Woolf delivered a couple of papers recalling her troubled adolescence. The first, entitled '22 Hyde Park Gate' (the family address in her teens), was given in November 1920. Both of Virginia's parents had passed through earlier marriages. Her mother Julia brought to her second union with Leslie Stephen two sons (he brought a mentally disabled daughter, Laura), George and Gerald, both much older than Virginia, the second youngest of eight children in the house, and her slightly older sister Vanessa.

George Duckworth ('my incestuous brother'), Virginia told the Memoir Club, had molested her, around the time of her puberty. The molestation was related in a mock-gothic style, verging on pastiche of the kind of fiction Woolf habitually mocked: 'Sleep had almost come to me. The room was dark. The house silent. Then, creaking stealthily, the door opened; treading gingerly, someone entered. "Who?" I cried. "Don't be frightened", George whispered. "And don't turn on the light, oh beloved. Beloved –" and he flung himself on my bed, and took me in his arms.' The 'old ladies of Kensington and Belgravia', she added, never knew that George Duckworth was the lover, as well as the brother, to 'those poor Stephen girls'. She repeated a version of the story in a second address to the club, in which George again appears as the ravishing Tarquin.

As Lee reminds us, although Bloomsbury talked daring sex, their performance between the sheets was often less impressive. There is, Lee detects, 'something inconclusive' in Woolf's account: George was still living and the Duckworth Press published her early books. Her relationship with her bumbling half-brother in later life was mildly contemptuous but generally good-natured and she wrote affectionately about him when he died some years before her. If they occurred, his abuses may have been 'more emotional than penetrative', Lee concludes and goes on to declare, with a bluntness of phrase designed to blow away the fogs of feminist mystification which swirl around the Woolf abuse/rape/incest hypotheses, 'There is no way of knowing whether the teenage Virginia Stephen was fucked or forced to have oral sex or buggered.'

Virginia Woolf drowned herself in 1941 (no doubt about that), fearing the onset of another of her horrific attacks of madness and possibly alarmed – as was most of Britain at the time – by the prospect of German invasion. As the wife of a leftist intellectual Jew, she had every right to feel apprehensive. Anxiety is something discernible in her last novel, published at this period, *Between the Acts* (1941). In the period leading up to her last, fatal act, she was also jotting down notes for an autobiography, with an essay provisionally entitled 'A Sketch of the Past' (1939). She was, at the time, much taken with Freud (the Hogarth Press, which she and her husband Leonard ran, was Freud's authorised English publisher – something else Heinrich Himmler would not have liked) and what she called 'autoanalysis'. Childhood sexual experience was, according to Freudian doctrine, formative.

In her autoanalytic explorations she evidently trawled up a traumatic 'recovered memory'. It is not found anywhere else in her voluminous private journals and correspondence. Why, she mused, did she so fear mirrors and reflections of herself in them?

I thus detect another element in the shame which I had in being caught looking at myself in the glass in the hall. I must have been ashamed or afraid of my own body. Another memory, also of the hall, may help to explain this. There was a slab outside the dining room door for standing dishes upon. Once when I was very small Gerald Duckworth lifted me onto this, and as I sat there he began to explore my body. I can remember the feel of his hand going under my clothes; going firmly and steadily lower and lower. I remember how I hoped that he would stop; how I stiffened and wriggled as his hand approached my private parts. But it did not stop. His hand explored my private parts too. I remember resenting, disliking it – what is the word for so dumb and mixed a feeling? It must have been strong, since I still recall it.

She returned to the event in a letter to her friend, Ethel Smyth, a few weeks before her suicide. How could one write an honest autobiography, she asked, unless one came clean about such essentially dirty things?

In the next two decades, along with the whole company of 'Bloomsberries', Woolf's star sank – mainly under the sneering assaults of the new critical puritans (the 'Leavisites') at Cambridge. The first authoritative biography, by Virginia's nephew Quentin Bell, in 1972, glossed over the 'abuse' episodes as part of the rough and tumble of an otherwise extraordinary family life – if anything Bell seemed sympathetic to the Duckworth lads. The emergence in the mid-1960s of the women's and gay liberation movements, and their impact on academic scholarship, elevated Woolf to canonical status. Doctoral dissertations, monographs, learned articles, popular spin-off pieces, and whole journals dedicated themselves to her life, her works and the importance of a 'room of one's own'. The 'abuse' moments were seen as centrally significant to understanding Virginia Woolf and she herself was now a writer of near-Shakespearian importance to English literature.

Tendentious, but typical, was Louise A. DeSalvo's *Virginia Woolf: the Impact of Childhood Sexual Abuse on Her Life and Work* (1989), which opened with the uncompromising declaration: 'Virginia Woolf was a sexually abused child; she was an incest survivor.' Lee, coming rather later into the biographical game in the mid-1990s, handles the abuse material more judiciously. She is disinclined to see the Duckworths as conspiratorial rapists. She opposes the idea that molestation 'can be made to explain all of Virginia Woolf's mental history'. There were other, quite as damaging, psychic injuries. In her 'Sketch', for example, Woolf herself lays heavier stress on the death of her mother, in 1890, when she was thirteen: 'This brought on, naturally, my first "breakdown" ... I was terrified of people ... For two years I never wrote. The desire left me, which I have had all my life, with that two years break.' None the less Lee allows that there are, arguably, traces detectable in the fiction. Why, she asks, is there just one kiss described in all of Woolf's work (in *Mrs Dalloway*)?

Other critics have been more single-minded on the matter. That Virginia was 'incested' is ubiquitous orthodoxy and, like Dickens's blacking factory trauma, the royal road to understanding her tormented genius. A main element in this new orthodoxy is the contention that Woolf's work and life is founded on a principled recoil from the 'male-made mess' of the world (the First World War she saw, in some moments, as a 'preposterous masculine fiction'). It is taken for granted that she was sexually frigid with men, but joyously liberated in her 'sapphic' relationship, in her mature years, with Vita Sackville-West (who, none the less, like Leonard, was 'scared to death of arousing physical feelings in her because of the madness'). A complicating factor is the well-recorded fact that at the time of her marriage to Leonard Woolf, in August 1912, Virginia genuinely wanted children ('brats', as she fondly called them). Leonard, however, feared the 'excitement' of pregnancy would trigger catastrophic mental breakdown. It may be, too, that impregnation would not have been easy. Clive Bell confided to Mary Hutchinson (his mistress) that 'Woolf fucks her once a week but has not yet succeeded in breaking her maidenhead.' As late as 1933, Virginia herself was jesting on the subject, suggesting that she and a friend might have 'the operation' (surgical rupturing of the hymen) done side by side in a Bond Street clinic.

By the early 1920s, the marriage, both partners confided to different friends, was 'chaste'. Neither party was unfaithful to the other. It was merely that sex had been turned off, like some irritatingly dripping tap. Leonard seems to have been the dominant partner in this suspension of full marital intimacy, supported by medical advice. After menopause, Virginia told a friend she regretted not having forced Leonard to take the risk, 'in spite of doctors'. The unborn children made her 'wretched in the early hours'. Whether children actually crying, night after night, would have been fulfilling who can say? Put another way, could Mrs Ramsay, with those 'brats' around her ankles and at her breast, have written *To the Lighthouse*?

FN   Adeline Virginia Woolf (née Stephen)
MRT   *To the Lighthouse*
Biog H. Lee, *Virginia Woolf* (1996)

133. Sax Rohmer 1883–1959

Dr. Fu-Manchu – the yellow peril incarnate in one man.

Sax Rohmer was born 'Arthur Ward' in Birmingham, the only child of Irish immigrants. His father was a clerk; his mother is recorded as alcoholic. The family moved to London when Arthur was an infant and his school education was intermittent, although he picked up an impressive literacy from his father. It is likely, given his later fascination with xenophobia, that he suffered prejudice ('bog-trotter!') in his early years. The lifelong flight from his birth-name suggests this as does his posturing for publicity photographs, in later life, in silk kimono and pigtail, looking sinister, wholly un-Irish and more ridiculous than even Peter Sellers could ever do justice to.

He later took on the surname 'Sarsfield' because, allegedly, his mother misinformed him that they were descended from the seventeenth-century General of that name. 'Sax' was good old-fashioned 'Sax[on]' and 'Rohmer', sometimes with an umlaut, was Nordic enough to pass a *Sturmabteilung* name check.

Little is known about Rohmer's life and he obfuscated what details are known outrageously. He briefly followed his father into clerking before drifting into Grub Street. He was fascinated by ancient Egypt and his first recorded fiction is the short story 'The Mysterious Mummy', for *Pearson's Magazine*, in 1903 (the plot involves a thief hiding in a sarcophagus to steal a priceless vase).

Rohmer loved the Edwardian music hall. He wrote sketches and songs and his first published book was a ghosted autobiography of the famous comedian 'Little Tich' (Harry Relph). In 1909 he married Rose Elizabeth Knox, the daughter of another, less famous, comedian, who was herself a performer in a juggling act. Rose was also a clairvoyant and supposedly the young Sax asked her how he could make his fortune. Her Ouija board responded: C-H-I-N-A-M-A-N. Rohmer would later create the series hero, Morris Klaw, an 'occult detective' who solves crimes by dreams and ESP. And the Chinaman clue proved prescient because Rohmer's breakthrough bestseller was *The Mystery of Dr Fu-Manchu*, published by Methuen in 1913. It draws, rather too obviously, on Guy Boothby's magnificent arch-criminal in *Dr Nikola* (1896) and Rohmer lifts a number of actual scenes from the other novelist. He had clearly also taken on board M. P. Shiel's bestseller *The Yellow Danger* (1898). A perplexed Colin Watson notes, 'The plots of the Fu-Manchu novels, such as they are, would be quite meaningless in paraphrase. They are a jumble of incredible encounters, pursuits, traps and escapes. Who is trying to accomplish what, and why – this is never explained. All that seems certain is that a titanic struggle is being waged by a man called Nayland Smith to thwart the designs of Fu-Manchu.' True enough, but they were read; and as film adaptations, watched by millions for the best part of half a century.

The narrative of the first in the series (of fifteen eventually) opens with Sir Denis Nayland Smith, a British government official in Burma, making a surprise call on his old London friend Dr Petrie (Smith's Dr Watson, as he is to be). Smith is enjoying a spot of leave during which he intends to save the 'White Race' from the fiendish plots of Dr Fu-Manchu. 'He is no ordinary criminal,' Smith informs an appalled Petrie: 'He is the greatest genius which the powers of evil have put on earth for centuries. He has the backing of a political group whose wealth is enormous and his mission in Europe is *to pave the way!* Do you follow me? He is the advance-agent of a movement so epoch-making that not one Britisher, and not one American, in fifty thousand has ever dreamed of it.' Except, that is, Sax Rohmer and his legions of readers.

An opium addict, Fu-Manchu is physically deformed. He is possessed of 'viridescent eyes' with which he hypnotises his victims: he is a 'profound chemist', a white slaver, and 'the genius of the yellow peril'. Like Guy Boothby's arch-fiend Dr Nikola (who has his cat Apollyon), Fu-Manchu has a sinister pet – a trained marmoset. It emerges that his immediate plan is to kill all high-ranking Britons who know anything whatsoever about the East. Nayland Smith is, naturally, top of the list. The yellow devil uses extravagantly ingenious methods to accomplish his goal: 'the Zayat Kiss' (poisonous centipedes), the 'Call of Siva' (thuggee assassins), the 'Green Mist' (gas), and, in the novel's climax, 'Fungi Cellars', in which poisonous mushrooms grow at lethal speed. After a series of encounters, in which Smith finally foils his adversary, the yellow villain escapes from a burning house, taking care, however, to leave a letter promising his return.

In addition to selling millions, Rohmer's novel may have been influential in bringing in the international control of narcotics in 1914 – the measure which W. S. Burroughs thought more catastrophic than the First World War – or the 1882 Chinese Exclusion Act, which kept the yellow peril, as he called it, from swamping the US until 1943. (Another novelist, Pearl S. Buck, was helpful in reversing the obnoxious measure.)

In the First World War, Rohmer fought briefly in the Artists' Rifles before being invalided out. In the postwar period, Fu-Manchu and other lurid tales enriched him, while he as resolutely impoverished himself by his addictive gambling. He built himself a country house, travelled across the world – with disastrous stops at Monte Carlo's green baize tables. He sold his rights to the Fu Manchu franchise for a reputed $4 million shortly before his death, but left only a measly thousand pounds.

FN   Sax Rohmer (Arthur Henry Sarsfield Ward)
MRT *The Mystery of Dr Fu-Manchu*
Biog C. Van Ash and E. S. Rohmer, ed. R. E. Briney, *Master of Villainy: A Biography of Sax Rohmer* (1972)

134. Edna Ferber 1885–1968

Being an old maid is like death by drowning, a really delightful sensation after you cease to struggle. Ferber, on being single

One of the twentieth century's most popular chroniclers of the American Dream, Ferber was born in Kalamazoo, Michigan, into a first-generation Jewish family. Her father was a Hungarian-born shop-owner whose business was to prove chronically unsuccessful in the New World. Her mother was from a well-off Chicago family. The Ferbers moved to several Midwestern towns during Edna's childhood, experiencing anti-Semitism, which partly motivated their moves. She stayed for longish periods with her mother's family in Chicago and graduated from high school in Appleton, Wisconsin. Although she was clearly gifted, family circumstances made college impossible. Her father's sight failed and Edna took over the Ferber store, running it well enough to free the family from debt. The intrepid, 'capable' woman succeeding against the odds was to be the mainstay plot in her subsequent fiction.

In her twenties, Ferber took up work as a journalist in Wisconsin, Milwaukee and Chicago. She suffered a serious breakdown in her health in 1909, at which period she began seriously to write fiction. Her first story, 'The Homely Heroine', was published in *Everybody's Magazine* in May 1910. She wrote her first novel, *Dawn O'Hara, the Girl who Laughed* (1911) while recuperating from her illness. Ferber had her first notable success with her short-story series featuring Emma McChesney, travelling saleswoman, over the years 1913–15, and they were successfully (and remuneratively) adapted for the stage. She served in the American Red Cross during the First World War, following which, her novel *The Girls*, the story of three generations of spinsters (from old maid to flapper), came out in 1921.

In 1924 she hit the big time with the number 1 bestseller, *So Big*. It established a vogue for narratives celebrating American ethnic diversity and American grit – a theme to which Ferber brings interesting sidelights. The action is set in the first two decades of the twentieth century and the central character is the inevitably indomitable Ferber woman, Selina Peake. A school teacher in the 'Dutch district', southwest of Chicago, Selina marries a 'truck farmer' (i.e. smallholder, who takes his produce to market daily), Pervus Dejong. They have one son, Dirk, nicknamed 'So Big' from his favourite childhood phrase. When Pervus dies, Selina takes on the farm and makes a go of it, raising high-quality produce and delicacies for the swank hotels of the city. By the sweat of her brow Selina makes a better life for Dirk who goes to college and becomes a member of Chicago's upper class. He is a wealthy idler, unworthy of the maternal sweat which has made his life so easy. Ferber, one deduces, had profound doubts about the hedonism of the 'jazz age' depicted in F. Scott Fitzgerald's *This Side of Paradise* (1920). *So Big* won a Pulitzer, certifying her as one of the country's distinguished writers.

Ferber then moved to New York, accompanied by her mother, and in Manhattan was recruited into the 'Algonquin Hotel' set (*New Yorker* writers, such as Benchley, Parker and Thurber were its nucleus). Her later bestsellers include *Show Boat* (1926) which enjoyed enduring success as a Jerome Kern and Oscar Hammerstein musical. Her 'oil well', as she called it, was the novel *Cimarron*, which came out in 1930. This 'American Epic' opens with the great 1889 'Run', or 'land grab' in Oklahoma. Sabra Venable, a genteel southerner, migrates with her devil-may-care husband Yancey Cravat to the new territory, with the traditional 'Whoop-ee!' Yancey, an 'enormously vital' man, is nicknamed 'Cimarron' by virtue of an admixture of 'Indian' in his genetic make-up. He and Sabra settle in the (fictional) town of Osage, where he sets up a newspaper, the *Oklahoma Wigwam*, before going off to join Roosevelt's Rough Riders. As usual in Ferber's fiction, the plucky woman has to take charge. Twenty years pass. Oil is discovered and transforms the Oklahoma economy. Sabra becomes Oklahoma's first congresswoman. In the last scene Yancey returns, a dying bum. Sabra 'forgives him everything' and comforts him as he drifts away ('Sleep my boy'). An anthem to American women pioneers, *Cimarron* is dedicated to Ferber's own mother.

Ferber produced a string of bestsellers on similar sprawling themes, including *Giant* (1952), which became the film vehicle for James Dean's final performance. Her twelve novels and nine plays were adapted into no less than twenty film adaptations. She never married and, it is suspected, may not have had a sexual relationship with anyone of either gender.

FN   Edna Ferber
MRT *So Big*
Biog J. G. Gilbert, *Ferber, A Biography* (1978)

135. DuBose Heyward 1885–1940

Oh yo' daddy's rich and yo' ma' is good-lookin', So hush, little baby, don' yo' cry.
Heyward's lyrics for 'Summertime'

DuBose Heyward wrote the slim novel *Porgy* (1925) which was later immortalised by George and Ira Gershwin. The folk opera of the crippled black man and his 'woman'

Bess was first staged on Broadway – on 10 October 1935 – with the black lead singers, Todd Duncan and Anne Brown. It was touch and go until the last minute that it might be whites in black face. Heyward's name would have been known to the audience on that New York evening as the author of 'the first major southern novel to present blacks realistically.' But for every million who listen, nowadays, to Miles Davis's rendition of 'Summertime', for which Heyward wrote the lyrics, less than one reads the fiction which is the ballad's literary source. A great-great-grandson of Thomas Heyward, Jr., a signatory to the Declaration of Independence, the novelist's paternal ancestors were South Carolina planters. One of them, Nathan Heyward, had prosecuted the revolutionary, Denmark Vesey, who in 1822 incited the slaves (a majority of Charleston's population) to take over the city. Vesey's uprising, timed for Bastille Day, failed. He was hanged along with thirty-five other uppity blacks.

Wheels turn. The Heywards lost everything in the Civil War and Dubose's father was reduced to working ('like a black', as the phrase was) in a Charleston rice mill. He fell in the machinery and was killed, when his son was three years old, after which care of the family fell on Heyward's resourceful mother, Jane. The family lived in a succession of shacks, 'too poor to paint, too proud to whitewash', as the local jest put it, but not so poor (no white family was, even after the war) as to have to do all their own household chores. Heyward's biographer records that his first language, picked up from house servants, was Gullah – the dialect used by local blacks of Angolan origin. Jane (Janie) Screven Heyward made herself an authority on Gullah culture, and she supplemented the little money she made by elegant needlework, giving tea party performances of 'darkey songs and stories'. By the time of her death in 1939, she was recognised as one of the most accomplished 'dialect recitalists' of her time – a parlour anthropologist.

Heyward dropped out of school at fourteen. His first employment was collecting 'funeral money' from blacks – who superstitiously believed that by handing over an obol-like dollar they would keep the Grim Reaper at bay. In 1905, he got a position as a cotton checker on the docks, supervising black labourers, and was appalled by waterfront degradation and criminality – the inspiration for his 'Catfish Row'. But he admired the manliness which could effortlessly tote a 500-pound bale. Chronically frail himself – he contracted polio at eighteen – his biographer speculates that 'Heyward's fascination with the brute humanity he observed on the docks was driven by envy.'

In 1908 he went into the real estate business and made a fortune, retiring at the age of forty to devote himself to writing *Porgy*. He was encouraged by his wife, Dorothy, also a writer, whom he had married in 1923. They had met at a writers' workshop, in New Hampshire. Heyward inherited his mother's fascination with

Gullah culture and in 1922, published *Carolina Chansons*, a medley of 'grotesque negro legends ... superstitions ... imagery and music'. As his biographer records, he was – as a result of his research – developing a powerful social conscience. In the same year, 1922, for a world burdened with a less developed social conscience, the wild 'Charleston' dance became the rage across white America. The greatest African American poet of the century, Langston Hughes, praised the black world Heyward had constructed, 'with his white eyes', but for the modern reader of *Porgy*, it is the white ears which pose the greater problem. The hero, for example, has one vice – gambling. When a character holds up the street-corner crap game in which Porgy is a player, to boast about his 'lady', a 'born white folks' nigger', another player breaks in: 'Yo' bes sabe yo' talk for dem damn dice. Dice ain't gots no patience wid 'oman!'

Is this ethnography or racist caricature? When Porgy is described as having 'unadulterated Congo blood', unlike the octoroon, Sporting Life, what point is Heyward making? Is white blood, stretching in a continuous stream back to the Declaration of Independence, a nobler fluid than that originating in the Heart of Darkness? African American readers are uneasy about a writer whom his biographer, unironically, calls 'A Charleston Gentleman', and whose magnum opus gained worldwide fame thanks to two Jewish composers. As Kendra Hamilton complains,'*Porgy and Bess* has been a way for whites, in America and in Europe, to participate vicariously in fantasies of what they imagine African-American life to be.' 'Whites' have generally had no such qualms: the Gershwin opera is regularly revived. The novel, alas, remains obstinately out of print.

Heyward went on to a remunerative career lecturing and screenwriting in Hollywood. He has lead credits on the film of Eugene O'Neill's *The Emperor Jones*, and Pearl S. Buck's *The Good Earth*. Both centre on heroes of colour – his specialty. He continued writing fiction dealing with a 'Color Line' which would not be erased in American society until twenty years after his death. His later novels include *Mamba's Daughters* (1929) and the play *Brass Ankle* (1930); a powerful study of miscegenation.

FN   Edwin DuBose Heyward
MRT *Porgy*
Biog James M. Hutchisson, *DuBose Heyward: A Charleston Gentleman and the World of Porgy and Bess* (2000)

136. D. H. Lawrence 1885–1930

A rotten work of genius. Ford Madox Hueffer's verdict on Lawrence's early novel, *The Trespasser*

Novelists' deaths are quite as interesting as novelists' lives. None more so than that of D. H. Lawrence. His mother is reported to have been told by a friend that her infant son would be riding in his carriage by the time he was forty. She replied, sighing, 'Ay, if he *lives* to be forty!' Better health might have rendered David Herbert Lawrence a sooty collier, or one of the more interesting prostheticians in Nottingham, or an outer-London schoolteacher, or, had he not been certified 'unfit', one of the many mute inglorious authors whose name liveth for evermore not in literature, but on lichen-covered 1914–18 village war memorials. It was a lifelong hearse that carried the author of *Women in Love* past all those destinies to literary greatness.

Lawrence was the fourth child of five, of a miner in a coal-mining village some ten miles from Nottingham. Arthur John Lawrence had married above himself to a woman who had almost become a schoolteacher. Lydia Beardsall had been won over by the sheer force of his animal magnificence, but life in a miner's cottage proved less wonderful. It was a mixed marriage and one whose mixture Lawrence would ponder throughout his short career – most lyrically in the prelude to *The Rainbow*: the men are clogged in the nutritious soil, the women's eyes are fixed on the sky and the church on the horizon. How to be both 'rooted' and yet 'grow towards the light'?

Lawrence's father (whose potent fucking is imaginatively glorified in Mellors' domination of Connie Chatterley) was a collier in the pit-pony-and-butty pre-industrial era, when mining was manual and 'dignified'. He was, as *Sons and Lovers* records, periodically drunken. But eventually his wife Lydia 'broke' him – or, as Lawrence ambivalently puts it, she broke his 'manhood'. The son was never sure whose side he was on in that struggle. John Lawrence was instinctively scornful of those 'stool-arsed jacks', like his younger son. Lawrence grew up with twin heritages, twin dialects, and radically conflicting ideas as to what life was about. He was, it was clear, too frail for the pits – even if his mother had allowed him. He found salvation through that wretchedly tiny aperture allowed the working-class child – 'the scholarship'. His brains got him to Nottingham High School, he was the first boy from his village to go there. He did not, however, shine. He was carrying too much class baggage and even at this age a profound disbelief in 'systems'.

Bert, as he was then called, left school at sixteen with two more years learning than most miners' sons. He got himself a clerical position with a firm in Nottingham which sold surgical appliances; his salary was a little under ten shillings a week. As recorded in *Sons and Lovers*, Bert was not initially his mother's favourite. Lydia Lawrence was uninterested in her sons until they outgrew childhood and could qualify as 'lovers' – adults that is. Her eldest, William Ernest, had arrived at that point in life first. He ('another stool-arsed jack') was doing well in London when he was stricken down by pneumonia and erysipelas and died. Lydia was distraught – widowhood could not have affected her more bitterly. Bert also came down with pulmonary illness a few months later and came close to dying. That attack was, with hindsight, the first touch of the TB that would later kill him. At this point, however, it saved him. As recorded in *Sons and Lovers*, Mrs Lawrence transferred her radioactive affection to her second son. It was reciprocated. Paul's last whispered word in the novel is the Strindbergian ejaculation, 'Mother!'

Lawrence was now writing early drafts of *The White Peacock*. He had grown up handsome but not yet bearded. There were, as he left his teenage years behind him, other women in his life – most importantly Jessie Chambers. A farmer's daughter, well educated, with a fine sensibility, she collaborated with him on his early writing. Late in life Lawrence was asked by a friend why he had not married Jessie. He replied, arrogantly: 'It would have been a fatal step. I should have too easy a life, nearly everything my own way, and my genius would have been destroyed.' Instead, his health and his mother's tenacious grip led to his staying close to home as a pupil-teacher in Eastwood for three years. He performed well enough to go on to Nottingham University and enrol for a teaching certificate, though not a degree course. Would higher education have made him a more confident writer, or would it, like Jessie, have clipped his 'genius'?

In later life, Lawrence had no doubt on the matter: institutional education kills. In *The Rainbow* he is eloquent about the 'marsh stagnancy' of universities. Ursula Brangwen finds in her course at Nottingham that 'the whole thing seemed sham, spurious; spurious Gothic arches, spurious peace, spurious Latinity, spurious dignity of France, spurious naïveté of Chaucer. It was a second-hand dealer's shop, and one bought an equipment for an examination.' The well-equipped Lawrence sailed through his exams. More importantly, at the same period, 1907, he published his first short story, 'A Prelude' – submitted under the name 'Jessie Chambers'.

Now qualified, Lawrence left home to take up a teaching post in far-off Croydon. He was good in the classroom and had affairs with fellow teachers – all stored away for later fictional use. In his spare time he was reading widely in philosophy and religion, forming an idiosyncratic worldview. Faithful Jessie again proved her usefulness by posting some of his work to the country's leading literary magazine, the *English Review*. Ford Madox Hueffer recognised its quality and, having seen the manuscript of *The White Peacock*, helped secure publication for the novel with Heinemann.

The years 1910 to 1911 saw crisis and breakthrough. His mother fell ill with cancer. In *Sons and Lovers*, which he began writing at this time, Gertrude Morel is killed – humanely but graphically – by her son. Lydia Lawrence died naturally, but for her son, traumatically – more so since part of him wanted her death. Shortly afterwards, he became briefly engaged to a woman he had known at college. In winter 1911, his lungs again collapsed – dangerously. In his convalescence he dashed off *The Trespasser* for a new patron, Edward Garnett at Duckworth publishers. School teaching was now no longer an option. His near-death illness had branded him an infectious danger to the young (a charge which would recur, in other guises, throughout his life). He would now be an author, or nothing. As an author he had, one of Duckworth's advisers said, 'every possible fault' and 'genius'. The title pages of his fiction introduced what would be his public name from now on. He hated his birth-names. Baptism, like Resurrection, was, he had decided, something to be Lawrentianised. He would be 'D. H.' to the world and 'Lorenzo' to his intimates.

Lawrence had resolved to travel and consulted a professor he had known at Nottingham for advice and addresses. Ernest Weekley was a Germanist and an etymologist. His wife, Frieda, born von Richthofen, was ten years younger than her husband and six years older than Lawrence. They had three children. At first sight almost, Lawrence and Frieda fell in love, and a few months later eloped. It meant the scandal of divorce and painful separation for Frieda from her children. There was no question who were the guilty parties – except, of course, that Lawrence did not see it as guilt. In Europe, with Frieda now beside him, he wrote 'Paul Morel' (as *Sons and Lovers* was called). Heinemann found the sex too hot for their list but Duckworth accepted the novel and published it in 1913 to strong reviews and modest sales. Lawrence was, at the same time, writing plays, essays and – most successfully – short stories, and forming long-lasting literary friendships: most significantly with Middleton Murry and his partner, Katherine Mansfield.

Lawrence's growth as a creative writer over these years was amazing. He was embarking on the project which would eventually see print as *The Rainbow* and its sequel, *Women in Love* (called conjointly, in their earlier form, 'The Sisters'). He forged a new, hypersensitive 'feminine' technique for the project. Publishers, encouraged by the reception of *Sons and Lovers*, had taken notice of him and new friends and patrons were talking him up. He and Frieda had married four months before the outbreak of war. Lawrence was in no immediate danger of call-up – Kitchener did not need invalids, yet. But they would be confined to England for the duration of hostilities and, given Frieda's nationality (the flying ace, the 'Red Baron', Manfred von Richthofen, was a distant relative), they would also be hard up. Lawrence's response was to withdraw into the shelter of a utopian community: he called his 'commune' by the ancient Hebrew name (borrowed from one of his new literary friends, S.S. Koteliansky) 'Rananim'. Primitive Teutonic elements were mixed in, most spectacularly the blood-mixing *Blutbrüderschaft* immortalised in the wrestling scene between Birkin and Crich in *Women in Love*. Rananim was set up in coastal Cornwall where, in one of the more comical episodes in a very uncomical era, he and Frieda were accused of signalling to U-boats with semaphoric underclothes on their washing line. Persecution as spies coincided with Lawrence's prosecution as a pornographer when *The Rainbow* (1915), his finest novel to date, was confiscated and banned in September 1915. There was no great mobilisation of support from the enlightened – wartime was not propitious for the assertion of literary freedoms. Instead, his publisher, Methuen, meekly took their medicine.

Lawrence was not meek, however, and forged ahead with *Women in Love*, whose manuscript was everywhere turned down. The novel was seen as dangerously unpatriotic. In its published form Lawrence would add, on the last page, what looked like sympathy for the Kaiser and his reported comment: 'Ich habe es nicht gewollt' (I didn't want it). For Lawrence all this was proof that the tree of life, Ygdrassil, was dead in England. Vitality must be found elsewhere. It got worse. Following the Universal Conscription Act in 1917, as the war looked very grim for the allies, Lawrence was called up for a medical. Clearly unfit to serve in any capacity, he suffered the indignity of the digital-anal violation he later described, with undiminished fury, in 'The Nightmare' section of *Kangaroo*.

With the war over, and as soon as their passports arrived, the Lawrences took what would be a permanent farewell from his home country. He left, as a parting present, *Women in Love*: finally publishable, not yet appreciated. The remainder of his life was a pilgrimage in search of sun, elemental contact, or simply motility for the sake of moving ('Comes over one an absolute necessity to move' opens his finest travel book, *Sea and Sardinia*, 1921). Health was another motive force. No word, certainly not 'fuck' or 'cunt', frightened him as much as 'tuberculosis'. Whatever his physicians said, he persisted in calling his chronic, ever worsening condition 'bronchials'. The Lawrences voyaged and journeyed to and through Italy, Mexico, New Mexico, Australasia, Ceylon and the US. Novels, like *Kangaroo*, were hurled off in weeks not months. He was ever alert to the appeal of primitivism. But his 'eye' for small scenic detail is unrivalled among novelists. Botanists, zoologists and ornithologists might envy that eye. As David Ellis notes: 'one critic has worked out that in his first novel, *The White Peacock*, 145 different trees, shrubs or plants are identified and 40 different kinds of birds.'

Lawrence was, as ever, dependent on rich patrons. The kindest, richest and most useful was Mabel Dodge Luhan, who gave the Lawrences the run (and eventually the title deeds) of her Kiowa Ranch, in Taos. Lawrence's ashes now repose there, reportedly. In his last phase, during travels to primitive places, he largely switched from earthy men heroes to airy women heroines (it is *Lady Chatterley's Lover*, not 'The Gamekeeper's Mistress'). In 1925, while reading aloud his long short story about a magnificent stallion and his female rider, *St Mawr*, he spat up a gob of blood. The dreaded word was no longer avoidable, but such was his formidable vitality that he kept death at bay, defying the predictions of his doctors, for five more years.

Lawrence and Frieda returned to Tuscany. His last years saw the completion, after three drafts, of *Lady Chatterley's Lover* – his last English novel. Its plea for new, 'hygienic' sexuality was the more urgent given its author's now years' long impotence. Lawrence's fiction is at its most interesting when he weaves the conflicting elements of religion and sex. Awaiting death, he produced his Gospel of St Lorenzo, 'The Escaped Cock', later retitled 'The Man Who Died'. The first part of the story fantasises Christ (never named, and distinctly Lawrentian) coming back to life in the tomb where his corpse has been laid. No miracle, he has been 'taken down too early'. An Aesopian prelude, which gives the piece its first title, describes a 'dandy' cockerel whose vital energies are tethered by the peasant (clearly Italian) who owns him. It escapes as Christ rolls away the rock from his tomb.

Throughout life, the Eastwood lad in Lawrence had loved jokes about 'cocks'. His first work is called the 'white peacock' because a man's cock is the only part of the body which normally never sees the sun, even when he pees. It is the same naughtiness that led him to call the second draft of *Lady Chatterley's Lover* 'John Thomas and Lady Jane'. He had, all his life, been fascinated by one of the central paradoxes of the New Testament. When Christ is resurrected – not as a spirit but in the *flesh* (as will be all his followers) – what are the carnal implications? In the full version of 'The Man Who Died', the man goes on, after resurrection, to lose his virginity to a prophetess of Osiris. Both partners in the congress are religio-sexually fulfilled by their act. The story concludes with the 'Man' rowing away from the Temple where his flesh has truly 'risen':

> The man who had died rowed slowly on, with the current, and laughed to himself: 'I have sowed the seed of my life and my resurrection, and put my touch forever upon the choice woman of this day, and I carry her perfume in my flesh like essence of roses. She is dear to me in the middle of my being. But the gold and flowing serpent is coiling up again, to sleep at the root of my tree.'
> 'So let the boat carry me. To-morrow is another day.'

As Anthony Burgess notes, *Gone with the Wind* ends with the same truism. There were, alas, very few days remaining for D. H. Lawrence.

FN   David Herbert Lawrence
MRT *Women in Love*
Biog J. Worthen, *D. H. Lawrence: A Literary Life* (1989)

137. H. Bedford-Jones 1887–1949

'King of the Pulps.'

If writing fiction were an Olympic event, the smart money would be on Henry James O'Brien Bedford-Jones. 'Henry James' throws back a peculiarly unhelpful echo in this context. In full flow, in the 1930s, the heyday of the pulp magazines, HBJ had four typewriters rattling away on his desk, a dozen *noms de plume*, a regular annual output of a million words, and he clocked up a lifetime score of some 1,500 magazine stories and close on a hundred novels. No one will ever know precisely because no one can see any good reason for exhuming and counting the stuff.

There were, of course, other production-line factories producing pulp: the Tom Swift franchise in the US, or Sexton Blake in the UK. But HBJ was a one-man factory – hence his kingly title. His name developed brand loyalty over the decades and he was paid well above the hack-rates of literary legend. As his biographer, Peter Ruber records: 'During the height of the Great Depression, when even Bedford-Jones experienced setbacks and declining word rates, the editor of *Liberty* Magazine offered him a salary of $25,000 a year if he would write exclusively for them. He turned it down with a laugh. He was accustomed to earning $60,000 or more per year, which he needed to support his lifestyle, his family, several residences across the country, his book and stamp collecting. Anecdotes gathered around HBJ's writing prowess: for example, 'Henry can't come to the phone,' his wife is reported to have said on one occasion, 'He's working on a novel.' 'I'll hold on until he's finished,' replies the caller. Ironic by nature, HBJ formally ceded his 'royal' title to Erle Stanley Gardner in March 1933, on receiving a complimentary copy of the other author's first Perry Mason adventure, *The Case of the Velvet Claws*. The two men went on to be close friends.

Often dismissed as the poor man's Edgar Rice Burroughs (which is unfair), what HBJ most obviously aspired to be was the Alexandre Dumas of his day. Dumas, of course, favoured the factory system and, much to the chagrin of his 'ghost' Auguste Maquet, he gave no literary credit to his assistant, who had to wait for a 2010 film (*L'Autre Dumas*) to make his case. Dumas once wrote a novel in three days for a bet.

HBJ did likewise, most days of the working week, for his living. Can one admire a writer who performs at this breakneck rate for anything other than his literary athleticism? Those who have read widely in HBJ's pulpy corpus (there is no disgrace in having read only a small portion of it) have a high regard, as do I, for *D'Artagnan* (1928), one of his many Dumas *hommages*. The *faux*-scholarly preface conveys the slyness of HBJ, writing at his best and gently mocking his genre:

> This story augments and incorporates without alteration a fragmentary
> manuscript whose handwriting has been identified as that of Alexandre Dumas,
> and as such authenticated by Victor Lemasle, the well known expert of Paris. So
> far as can be learned, it has remained unpublished hitherto ... The publisher, who
> is the owner of the manuscript in question, is of course fully informed as to what
> portion of this novel is from the pen of Dumas, and what from the typewriter of

H. Bedford-Jones.

Ann Arbor, April 1, 1928

Had he stuck to one line of pulp, Ruber believes, HBJ would be better regarded than he is today – in the Rider Haggard class, perhaps. But he was too versatile for his own good as regards literary reputation. A random selection of his titles will give an idea of his range:

'All Quiet on the Tanker Front' (1943)
'The Amazon Women' (1939)
'The Badman's Brand' (1928)
'The Bishop of Somaliland' (1936)
'The Blind Farmer and the Strip Dancer' (1940)
'Blood of the Scanderoon' (1931)
'Bombs and Olive Oil' (1943)

The more you write, the less you have time to live. None the less, Bedford-Jones's life – what little record of it survives – was eventful. He was born in Napanee, Ontario, Canada. The family was second-generation Irish and Henry's father was a Protestant minister. He dropped out of college after a year and moved to Michigan where he found work as a newsman. He was naturalised as an American in 1908 and moved, a couple of years later, to Chicago. From there he again drifted on, around 1914, to Los Angeles.

Wherever he went, HBJ wrote fluently and copiously for newspapers and magazines. His main outlet for short fiction was the *Blue Book* magazine, for whom he would eventually write some 350 stories and serials under a barrage of pen-names. There were numerous other outlets. The market for magazine fiction was ravenous, stoked by wood-pulp paper, steam presses and America's high level of popular literacy. It was, for someone as good at it as HBJ, a rewarding line of work, if you could stand the heat – and he was pure asbestos. He was recruited into fast-order fiction as his main line of work by a patron, William Wallace Cook. Himself a prolific writer of dime novels and pulp fiction, Cook had written many of the Nick Carter (detective), Buffalo Bill and Klondike Kit stories and dime novels in the first decades of the twentieth century. The occasion of HBJ's becoming Cook's friend is told by Ruber: 'When Cook's first wife took ill and died unexpectedly, one legend recalled, he was too distraught to meet that week's obligation of a 25,000-word novel. After the funeral, Bedford-Jones hastened home and wrote the novel under Cook's name in a single draft, delivering it to the Post Office just before it closed. A week later Cook was surprised to receive an acceptance letter and check for something he knew nothing about. A grateful Cook introduced the young man to all the influential merchandisers of pulp in New York.'

HBJ's middle years, in the 1930s, were tormented by an ugly divorce. Concerned that his youngest son was being maltreated by his first wife, he had the boy abducted. The mother then had him prosecuted for kidnapping – a serious offence following the sensational Lindbergh case. Getting the charges dropped (with the help of Erle Stanley Gardner – a lawyer as well as King of Pulp II) cost a fortune. HBJ wrote through the crisis, at the usual dizzying speed. Only diabetes, in the last five years of his life, slowed him down. In this handicapped state he concentrated on his rare-book collection and, having written so furiously, gently read his way into well-earned rest.

FN   Henry James O'Brien Bedford-Jones
MRT   Take your pick
Biog   Peter Ruber, Darrell C. Richardson and Victor A. Berch, *King of the Pulps: The Life and Writings of H. Bedford-Jones* (2003)

138. Vicki Baum 1888–1960

It was all quite different in America.

A German – later American – popular novelist who ranks in her own language with such bestsellers as Erich Maria Remarque, Hans Fallada, Erich Kästner and Leon

Feuchtwanger, Baum was – unlike them – consistently successful in English translation. Her cosmopolitan melodramas profoundly influenced Hollywood cinema in the
1930s, especially in collaboration with Greta Garbo (another glamorous expatriate)
who starred in *Grand Hotel* in 1932. It was from Baum's book that Garbo took her
famous declaration, 'I want to be alone.' This novel and its follow-up *Shanghai '37*
(1939) established the vogue for sprawling *Narrenschiff* melodrama with modish
settings and vaguely pessimistic mood. Arthur Hailey's *Hotel* is a bastard offspring,
best avoided.

Baum's origins were Austrian bourgeois-Jewish. Her original vocation was
music: while still a teenager she performed as a harpist in Viennese concert halls.
Musical milieux (and unhappy harpists) would recur in her later fiction. Baum
moved to Germany around 1912 on receiving a contract to play with the Darmstadt city orchestra. She had married her first husband, Max Prels in 1906. Prels is
described as 'a Viennese coffee-house habitué and sometime contributor to literary
magazines'. After her marriage, Baum began to write stories, some of which were
published under her name, others under Prels's name. Her first published novel,
Frühe Schatten (a chronicle of adolescent *Weltschmerz*) was published in 1914. It
made no mark.

Baum divorced Prels and married Richard Lert, the conductor of the Darmstadt
orchestra, around 1916. The marriage was happy and Baum abandoned music for
motherhood. The couple, along with the German population as a whole, suffered
financial hardship during the First World War. Baum's first husband, Prels, was
meanwhile working for the Berlin publisher, Ullstein, and amicably furnished an
introduction for his ex-wife. Having given up the harp for good, Baum now resolved
to write full-time. During the war years and early 1920s she duly churned out a
string of undistinguished 'entertainment novels' – romances aimed at the young
adult woman reader.

Proficient as she was at this line of work, Baum was not by nature a hack.
Thomas Mann was her idol. Her technique in her mature fiction derives from the
critical doctrine of *Neue Sachlichkeit* ('New Objectivity', hyper-realism). On the
strength of *Stud. chem. Helene Willfür* (1928), a New Woman novel with a well-
researched scientific background, Baum was awarded an exclusive contract by Ullstein. Her fiction was serialised, and her glamorous image publicised, in Ullstein's
Berliner Illustrierte Zeitung, which, in the 1920s, boasted the largest magazine circulation in the world. It was in the *BIZ* pages that *Menschen im Hotel* (1929), i.e.
Grand Hotel, was first published. Ullstein's publicity made much of Baum's working
in a Berlin hotel to gather material, as had Arnold Bennett at the Savoy for his hotel
novel, *Imperial Palace*. *Grand Hotel*'s success was boosted in the American market by

a Broadway adaptation, which ran for 257 nights. The American publisher, Double-day, subsequently invited Baum to New York to promote their translation of the novel and by July 1931, *Grand Hotel* had sold 31,000 copies and topped *Publishers Weekly* bestseller list.

Once in America, Baum took up remunerative employment in the film industry, despite a total ignorance of the techniques of screenwriting, and still imperfect English. In 1932, with the triumph of the Nazis, she and her family entered permanent exile, settling in Hollywood, where she helped promote the 1932 MGM production of *Grand Hotel*, starring John Barrymore, Greta Garbo and a young Joan Crawford. The film was a box office hit, and made Baum a household name among English-speaking readers. A string of works aimed at that market (and the big screen) ensued: *Men Never Know* (1935), *Career* (1936), *A Tale from Bali* (1937), *Grand Opera* (1942).

After 1933 her books were banned and burned in Germany. By the end of the 1930s she was writing primarily in English, and continued to do so until her death in 1960. It was only after the Second World War that her fiction was translated back into German. Despite the fame of *Grand Hotel*, Baum's better novel is *Shanghai '37*. The story of nine intertwining lives is centred, again, on the grand hotel milieu with an extravagantly international dramatis personae. The novel touches on such topical themes as the rise of Nazism and climaxes with the Japanese invasion of Shanghai and the assault on the international community there. One of the cowering English children in the unnarrated hinterland of the novel – it is pleasant to fantasise – was little James Ballard.

In the 1950s, Baum enjoyed modest book-club successes with novels such as *The Mustard Seed* (1953) and *Written on Water* (1956). But for the English market, she tends to be remembered, if at all, as a one-title author, and a vehicle for Garbo. Baum categorised herself as a 'first-rate second-rate author'. She left a posthumously published autobiography, with the ironic title, *It Was All Quite Different*, in 1964.

FN   Vicki Baum (Hedwig Baum; later Prels, later Lert)

MRT   *Grand Hotel*

Biog   L. J. King, *Best-Sellers by Design: Vicki Baum and the House of Ullstein* (1988)

139. Raymond Chandler 1888–1959

American style has no cadence.

Chandler was born in Chicago. On both sides of his parentage he could claim Irish-Quaker extraction. His father Maurice was a railway engineer at a period when new tracks were creating work all over the continent. Maurice followed the job, was drunken when at home, and soon drifted away from his son and wife. Chandler's mother, Florence Thornton, was resourceful in the face of this breakdown. Chandler would always need such women in his life – older, competent, emasculating. Florence (a newer American than her husband) emigrated, first to Ireland, where she had relatives, then to England where she had better-off relatives. Still beautiful, she had affairs, Chandler recalled much later, but she was not fool enough to remarry.

Raymond's rich English uncle Edward took an interest in the clever little boy. His way was paid through Dulwich College, a minor public school, in south London. He was a day boy, living with his mother in a grand house nearby, but the five years he spent at Dulwich College were formative. Chandler had the old school tie tattooed on his soul for life. He won prizes and took full advantage of the 'classic' education offered him. Uncle Edward, open-handed as he was, would not stump up for university, which, given his ability, Chandler would have walked into. Aged sixteen, he left Dulwich with the expectation that, after a year learning languages in Europe, he would enter the Civil Service.

What he did in Paris is unknown other than that, to his later chagrin, he neglected to lose his virginity. He duly took the Civil Service exams and came out at the top of the list. It was obligatory to naturalise. At what later point he became American is fuzzy. He was appointed as a junior clerk to the Admiralty but only lasted six months before resigning. He could not, he later said, stand the 'suburban nobodies'. Or, one deduces, the banality of the desk-bound career that lay ahead: without a degree, without membership of the best London clubs, he would never get to the top of Whitehall's slippery pole and would be another Pooter trudging to work and back with a briefcase, brolly and bowler.

Not a single letter of Chandler's before 1937 survives or much other documentary record. The only accounts we have of his early life are circumspect and casual recollections in his late years. When, in those years, his publisher suggested an autobiography, it was fended off with a Chandlerism: 'Who cares how a writer got his first bicycle?' There are things one does care to know. Why, for example, did Uncle Edward pull the plug on him? Whatever the reason, the money stopped coming and Raymond and his mother had to move to less salubrious lodgings. For a year or two he scraped a living as a journalist and wrote reams of poetry in his spare time – some of which was published (it's not very good).

In 1912 he returned to America and took a succession of clerking jobs in small towns before ending up in California. 'Why?' he was once asked. 'Everyone does,' he replied. In San Francisco, at a very low point, he worked as a tennis-racquet stringer at a measly $12.50 a week. A clerical position with an ice-cream firm in Los Angeles furnished enough to rent an apartment. Possessed of superb manners, cultivated, interestingly 'foreign', and – at this stage of his life good-looking – Chandler was taken up by well-off friends. He brought his mother over to live with him. Chandler stuck with the creamery for three years and his mother for life.

It was now 1917 and he was twenty-eight. Enthused by the war, in which so many of his 'fellow' Englishmen were dying and, perhaps, unenthused by four years with Mom, he decided to join in the fight. America was not recruiting so he went north to Canada to join up. Chandler saw action in France and sustained a serious head wound. Given his public school background, it is odd that he was not commissioned. He left the service a sergeant. It is plausibly suggested that his later, pathological, drinking and regular blackouts may have originated in the psychophysical trauma of his months in the trenches. Head injury (by 'sap', fist and pistol butt) as his biographer Tom Hiney notes, is prominent in his fiction.

Honourably discharged, Chandler rejoined his mother and went back to work in the creamery. At this period there entered the second woman in his life, Pearl Eugenie Pascal. The wife of a concert pianist (her second marriage), in the throes of a divorce, 'Cissy', as everyone called her, was a woman of the world. Tantalisingly, only one studio photograph of her seems to have survived. It confirms Chandler's repeated compliments as to her 'peach skin' beauty. He also mentioned other snaps of her naked, from her 'modelling' days – which were now far behind her. Cissy was old enough (by eighteen years) to be Chandler's mother. But he had one already, and she disapproved. Any formal union was put on ice for four years. It's strange that a thirty-plus decorated veteran, creator, no less, of the most famous tough guy in detective fiction, should await his mom's consent, or death (Florence was afflicted with a lingering cancer) before marrying the woman he loved. It is curious too that he let himself be duped as to Cissy's proclaimed age (something that a quick look at her sheaves of divorce papers would contradict). Until after they married he believed she was in her pre-menopausal early forties.

The jobs were, as in his novels, easier than the dames. Cissy had raised Chandler's sights beyond the creamery. As the roaring twenties took off, Los Angeles was a city of opportunity: the West was wild again. Chandler went into the oil business and shot to the top. Within a couple of years he was earning a grand a month. In a few years more he was a Vice President earning a whopping (for the mid-1920s) $40,000 p.a. It beat stringing racquets. Other things fell neatly into place. Florence died in 1924 and within days Chandler was able to marry Cissy. There would never until many years later be anything that could be called a home for the couple: just apartments, hotels, and, of course, no children. He loved the patter of little feet, Chandler said – running in the opposite direction.

The early years of the marriage were good. But as he rose up the executive ladder boozing, absenteeism and misconduct with secretaries led to Chandler's being fired in 1932. It coincided with the Depression and what would be decades of semi-invalidism for the fast-ageing Cissy. For reasons that are mysterious, Chandler decided, close on forty-five, to give up drink and become a professional writer. He cocooned himself in cheap lodgings with Cissy, who seems, nobly, to have gone along with a suddenly hard life. For several years Chandler imposed a gruelling writer's apprenticeship on himself. He chose crime writing, he said, because it was 'honest'. Poverty, too, was 'purifying'. The Chandlers scraped by on savings and what was left of her alimony.

He had set his sights on *Black Mask*, the magazine that had launched Dashiell Hammett, pioneering in its pages 'hardboiled' detective fiction and a classier product than was purveyed in the pulps. The hardboiled genre originates in one short story of Hemingway's, 'The Killers'. Nothing happens in the story. A couple of gangsters come into a 'greasy spoon' restaurant, engage in wisecracking, but laconic, badinage with the guy behind the counter. They've come to kill someone. That's it. Chandler realised there was space in this new crime fiction genre (which Hemingway had immediately moved on from) to establish a whole new style, and over the late 1930s created a niche as a regular contributor to *Black Mask*. But he was not prolific; he could never turn stuff out at the speed of, for example, his new friend Erle Stanley Gardner. He cultivated a specialism in the Los Angeles-based 'Private Eye'. By this point he knew LA, the canyons, boulevards, beaches and hills, as well as Hammett had known Baltimore – with the difference that his city was more interesting.

Hammett's Sam Spade is the progenitor of Marlowe, although the Private Eye pedigree can be tracked at least as far back as 221b Baker Street. The name – tempting to literary critics as the supposition is – owes nothing to Conrad. Marlowe was one of the house names at Dulwich College. What Chandler perfected was voice. His favoured narrative mode is autobiographical – the tone is laconic, wise cracking, seen-it-all, reminiscential. His rhetoric can be categorised as a love of litotes, hyperbole, extravagant simile, zeugma. But above all he aimed at what he called 'cadence' – a quality which American literature (unlike English) sadly lacked. An opening paragraph of his finest novel, *Farewell, My Lovely* (1940), will indicate the packed cadenzas (sudden falls) in his prose:

> It was a warm day, almost the end of March, and I stood outside the barber shop looking up at the jutting neon sign of a second floor dine and dice emporium called Florian's. A man was looking up at the sign too. He was looking up at the dusty windows with a sort of ecstatic fixity of expression, like a hunky immigrant catching his first sight of the Statue of Liberty. He was a big man but not more than six feet five inches tall and not wider than a beer truck ... he looked about as inconspicuous as a tarantula on a slice of angel food.

Marlowe is, as usual, a *flâneur*, drawn in, not diving into, events. He is, by the end of *Farewell, My Lovely*, revealed as the only decent thing in LA, a city which, as in Nathanael West's vision of it, is ripe for wrathful destruction. Chandler anatomised Marlovian Man in an essay, 'The Simple Art of Murder' (1944) and its famous imperative: 'Down these mean streets a man must go who is not himself mean, who is neither tarnished nor afraid.' And why 'must'? *Noblesse oblige*. Marlowe, as Chandler put it, is a 'shop-soiled Galahad' (and, like Galahad, sexually pure) in a world beyond salvation and whose filth he can never quite shake off and whose mean streets he can never leave. There is nothing west of the West Coast – no frontier left in which to exercise true American values.

Having perfected his instrument in *Black Mask* and conceived his hero (Philip Marlowe grew out of a PI called John Dalmas), Chandler broke into full-length fiction with *The Big Sleep*. The book was taken by a class publisher, Knopf, and sold reasonably. But the opinion-forming critics ignored it. It was the fate of the first four 'Marlowes' to be critically disregarded. Between *The Big Sleep* in 1939 and *The Little Sister* in 1949 Los Angeles was transformed from a sleepy little Western town to megalopolis: the city of the future. The same period saw also the massive growth of the film-studio system. Chandler and Cissy had been lifted from years of penury by his book (particularly paperback) royalties but re-entered the ranks of the seriously rich when Hollywood discovered Chandler. More particularly, the director Billy Wilder discovered him after reading *The High Window* (1942).

A short, bitter, marriage ensued, which produced a masterpiece. The two men hated each other: Wilder thought Chandler a pansy; Chandler thought the philandering hard-drinking Wilder a degenerate with the manners of an oaf. Moreover, the film Wilder had recruited him for was based on a short story by James M. Cain. If there was anything Raymond hated more than Billy it was the author of *Double Indemnity*: 'James Cain – faugh! Everything he touches smells like a billygoat. He is every kind of writer I detest, a *faux naïf*, a Proust in greasy overalls ... Such people are the offal of literature.' None the less, out of this raging studio feud came the classic film *noir* for which, as scriptwriter, Chandler deserved an Oscar (he was nominated for a later, less worthy script for John Huston's *The Blue Dahlia*, 1945). He went on to collaborate with Hitchcock on another classic in the dark genre, *Strangers on a Train* (1950). He had a higher estimate of Patricia Highsmith, although he thought her work overplotted – never a charge which would be levelled against the author of *The Big Sleep*, a work whose plot even the author himself could not explain to the director Howard Hawks, who adapted it with Chandler's favourite screen Marlowe, Humphrey Bogart.

Hollywood, subsidiary rights, and radio franchise (a medium particularly congenial with Chandler's style) meant that he would never, after 1945, be poor again. But Hollywood – as with Faulkner and Nathanael West – dismantled the carefully constructed defence systems which had allowed him to become a writer. Wilder, particularly, took a Mephistophelean glee in destroying Chandler. 'Chandler was typical of a man who was an alcoholic and was on the wagon and was married to a very old lady, and so he had no sex and no booze ... But the small revenge I had – because at the very end, he hated me – was that he started drinking again.' Once again, as in those lost years in the oil business, it was the bottle in the briefcase, the long morning sessions that used up the whole day, and furtive adulteries – Cissy was closing on her seventies, chronically frail, and often seriously unwell. His own health was increasingly poor.

Chandler would grind out two more Marlowes – *The Little Sister* (1949) and the aptly named *The Long Good-Bye* (1953). Neither ranks with his best early work, although, so exiguous is his *oeuvre*, that one is very glad to have them. His fiction was always better thought of in his other home country, England, and positively revered by the French in its Gallimard *Série noire* livery. American critical opinion remained unimpressed and his work was accused of racist and misogynistic taints.

Cissy died in 1954 – she was eighty-four. Keeping her alive had been Chandler's noblest achievement. With her gone, he fell apart. A few months later he attempted suicide in his shower (to prevent too much posthumous mess), aiming two shots at his head. So drunk was he that he missed. In 1955 he returned to England, enjoyed his fame ('in England,' he said, 'I am an author'). He made a fool of himself – he had a poor head for drink at this stage – with a succession of women. Some of them, Natasha Spender notably, did their best to put him back together again, but all gave up, eventually. As he told Natasha, poignantly, 'I know what you are all doing for me, and I thank you, but the truth is I really want to die.'

A few pieces of writing sputtered out along with a stream of lonely long lovely letters to anyone whose address he happened to have in his address book. They were written in his long insomniac nights when all that comforted him was his type-writer and his extraordinary gift with words. He died exhausted in hospital in La Jolla, California. One knows far too much about the foolish, drink-addled Chandler of the 1950s and far too little about the first fifty years of his life. The big question remains unanswered: why, in the mid-1930s, did he turn to writing crime novels? And how did this man – whose personal life is so pathetic – create such wonderful crime novels?

FN   Raymond Thornton Chandler
MRT   *Farewell, My Lovely*
Biog   T. Hiney, *Raymond Chandler* (1997)

140. Katherine Mansfield 1888–1923

I intensify the so-called small things.

Few authors' lives rival Katherine Mansfield's for chaos. It is as if she were blown into shrapnel reassembled as collections of short stories. She was, she proclaimed, a writer first and a woman second. Ottoline Morrell, the Bloomsbury hostess, said Mansfield was as aware of being a writer as Victoria was of being a queen. She was born Kathleen Mansfield Beauchamp: the variant forenames and surnames she would adopt for herself through life are the bane of biographers. As baneful for those close to her was that with every different name they encountered a differ-ent woman. Multiple personality was not with Mansfield a disorder but a vocation. She had, she boasted, 'hundreds of selves'. Her father Harold had but one and that, by dull colonial standards, admirable. A New Zealand import merchant, he rose to become a magnate and, simultaneously with his daughter's death, Sir Harold. The title would not have impressed her; the irony might have done.

Harold outlived his daughter to read her published satires on him (most scath-ingly in 'Prelude' and 'At the Bay'). None the less he supported her through life with an annual allowance without which she could never have been a 'writer first'. The big event in her childhood, chronicled in 'Prelude', was the family move in 1893 from Wellington to a rural home at Karori. It is only at such moments – between things – that, for Mansfield, the 'real self is found'. In 'Prelude', written twenty years after the move it chronicles, there is no 'event' but central foci on the mother's dream of the horrors of childbirth, the benign impercipience of fathers, and an aloe growing in the new house's garden. It is an infinitely slow plant, associated with bitterness, which flowers every hundred years. It may flower this year – but the bitterness is always present.

In 1903 Beauchamp sent his daughters to be 'finished' at Queen's College, London. Kathleen's three years at the famously progressive establishment in Harley Street were formative. Here she met the bosom friend, Ida Baker (self-renamed, androgynously, 'Lesley Moore') whom she would regard as her 'wife'. Mansfield read Ibsen and – most momentously – the contaminating Oscar Wilde. She travelled to the Continent and felt cosmopolitan. At this point it seemed her musical ability as a cellist would be her career.

She returned, unwillingly, to New Zealand. By the standards of her class she was now indeed 'finished'. She should, following the social script written for her, have settled down, had children, and been content, as she contemptuously saw it, sitting on the veranda shelling peas for supper. She rebelliously published some small pieces in local papers and had a couple of lesbian flings – one with a Maori. The first resolution in her infant diary had been to grow up a Maori missionary. Not, of course, an apostle of interracial free love. New Zealand was too small and – paradoxically – too 'English' to hold her. 'My heart keeps flying off to Oxford Circus – Westminster Bridge at the Whistler hour', she sighed in the privacy of her journal. She finally nagged her father into sending her back to London with an allowance, with the vague expectation that she would pursue a career in music. In her heart she already saw herself as a writer.

She left the colony in July 1908 never to return, other than in her stories. In London, Ida Baker was again her anchor. She needed one. Her life, over the next ten years, was tempestuous. She fell in love with an expatriate New Zealand musician, Arnold Trowell. He did not love her, and she got herself pregnant by his twin brother Garnet. He would not marry her so she persuaded her music teacher, George Bowden (many years her senior) to make an honest woman of her at the Register Office. She wore mourning to the ceremony and spent her wedding night with Ida: the marriage was never consummated. Her mother, on being informed, came over and packed her errant daughter off to a German spa, where she miscarried. On learning that there had also been lesbian entanglements, Mrs Beauchamp disinherited her degenerate daughter. Mansfield put together her first collection, *In a German Pension* (1911), out of the experience. She was now Katherine Mansfield: she disinherited her family.

She went on to have an affair with a worthless Pole, Floryan Sobienowski. He it was who probably infected her with the gonorrhoea (untreated) which precluded any more children and inflicted great pain in later life. Her German stories had brought her to the attention of A. R. Orage, editor of the magazine *New Age*. Mansfield was soon prominent in literary London, evoking starkly different responses – even in the same people. Victoria Woolf opined, in her grand way, 'to no one else can I talk in the same disembodied way about writing'. But the body offended her. Mansfield, she recorded in her diary, 'stank like a civet cat who had taken to street walking'.

She wasn't a streetwalker, but Mansfield had cultivated the useful habit of taking editors as lovers. Orage had been one. The next, and even more important to her career, was John Middleton Murry. An Oxford undergraduate, of working-class origins, Murry had launched a literary journal with the jazzy name, *Rhythm*. A literary submission by Mansfield led to a relationship of furious instability. Both partners were superbly good-looking and totally neurotic. He, as it happened, was also disabled by gonorrhoea when they met (picked up from a genuine streetwalker). He gave up Oxford for Katherine. The couple hobnobbed with the leading modernists of the day. Murry was unfit for military service during the Great War and, for an intense few months, he and Katherine lived with D. H. Lawrence and Frieda von Richthofen in their little utopian community in Cornwall. Murry, however, was disinclined to offer Lawrence the *Blutbrüderschaft* he demanded. Katherine was terrified by Lawrence's battering of Frieda and threatening, with every apparent intention of doing so, 'I'll cut your throat you bitch.' The couple sought utopia elsewhere and were both royally punished as Crich and Gudrun in *Women in Love*. When she was dying of consumption, Lawrence dispatched to Mansfield what one might call a 'get worse' card, 'you are a loathsome reptile I hope you will die'.

Murry and Mansfield had an 'open union', fidelity was an irrelevance. The story she wrote in 1918, 'Je ne parle pas français', plausibly considered her best, reflects this 'openness'. Raoul Duquette – a gigolo by preference, a prostitute and a pimp when he has to be – sits in a Paris bar, regarding the world, in late afternoon, admiring his own image in the mirrors around him. He is, among everything else, the author of self-published, literary *amusettes*. A memorable phrase pops into Raoul's mind. On the writing pad and blotting paper, which such cafés supply their customers, he sees the titular phrase about not speaking French. It brings back the memory of a passionate relationship with an Englishman, Dick, who abandoned him only to return to Paris with an English girl, 'Mouse'. The couple had eloped. Once arrived at the Parisian hotel, arranged by Raoul, Dick promptly abandoned Mouse on the supremely English grounds that his mother would disapprove. Raoul also deserted her on the supremely Parisian grounds that it was none of his business – and might be expensive. But her plight has left him a tender memory. Duquette is the amalgam of two foreign lovers who had exploited Mansfield. Dick is the pussy-footed Murry. Love-rats the lot of them.

Murry and Mansfield married in 1918 in a London Register Office. It was, said

Mansfield, like a 'silly birthday' – meaningless. By now her consumption was galloping and the remainder of her life was a desperate chase for the sun and a cure. The publication of her third collection, *The Garden Party and other Stories* (1922) established her as one of the major writers of her time. But her time was pathetically short. Death was now a prominent theme in her stories (notably 'The Fly' – with its hinted echo, 'as flies to wanton boys are we to the Gods, they kill us for their sport'). The Murrys' financial situation was at last secure with his appointment, at £800p.a., as literary editor of the *Athenaeum*. Mad with terror, Mansfield sought cure and salvation with a series of quacks: her spleen was bombarded with X-rays, her 'soul' was attended to by a Russian guru ('a levantine psychic shark,' Wyndham Lewis called him). The bacillus in her lungs was ignored. She died, not even having reached the Dantean middle age of thirty-five.

FN   Katherine Mansfield (Kathleen Mansfield Beauchamp; later Bowden, later Murry).
MRT   'Prelude'
Biog   C. Tomalin, *Katherine Mansfield: A Secret Life* (1987)

141. Michael Sadleir 1888–1957

Bibliomane.

To his contemporaries Michael Sadleir must have seemed a successful businessman with some strange hobbies. He was, over the four decades of his professional working life, a publisher with the firm of Constable. The making of books was Michael Sadleir's main business in life yet posterity tends to remember him (if at all) as a collector of books (the greatest Victorian bibliomane ever) and a biographer (he did definitive lives of Edward Bulwer Lytton, and of the Trollopes, mother and son). Sadleir is remembered least of all as a writer of period (Victorian/Edwardian) romance – specifically that variety to which today we apply the term 'bodice ripper'. He was the son of the don (erstwhile Vice Chancellor of Leeds University), Michael Sadler (sic). Sadler Sr was also an enlightened collector and critic of modern art – something that brought philistine obloquy down on him from donnish colleagues. It was a happy filial relationship, as the younger Michael records in a tender memoir of his father, published in 1949.

Michael Jr had a gentleman's upbringing: Rugby and Balliol, from which he took a good second in history, and won the Stanhope Prize for an essay on the playwright

Sheridan. In 1912 he joined the venerable firm of Constable & Co. Publishing, like 'wine', was a trade open to gentlemen. He would remain with the firm – as editor and later director – for forty-five years. There was an inevitable interruption for the Great War, during which Sadleir served in the War Trade Intelligence Department. After the war he was seconded, briefly, to the League of Nations before returning to the world of books where he remained happily for the rest of his life.

He began collecting nineteenth-century fiction volumes during the 1920s, building up what would become the best collection in the world. He sold it in 1952 to the University of California at Los Angeles (UCLA), who built a special library for it: they paid the then immense sum of $65,000 – some of Sadleir's prize volumes would, nowadays, attract three times as much apiece. Sadleir married in 1914. His wife, Edith, was the daughter of an Anglican canon. They had one daughter and two sons, the elder of whom was killed serving in the navy in the Second World War. It was in the early 1920s that Sadleir first turned his hand to writing fiction. His taste was for period works, with a strong dash of 'low life' and salacious plot. It was to protect his eminent father's name from the associations of that fiction, and its low-life aroma, that he altered his surname to 'Sadleir'.

It is reported that Sadleir's friends good-naturedly did not refer to his novels – as one might not allude to a recent divorce or some other social disgrace. And it seems that he stopped writing fiction for many years, after being made a director of Constable in 1920: novels being beneath the dignity of his exalted rank – one could be a publisher of these things, but not decently write them oneself. It would be like doing one's own gardening (the Sadleirs had a fine country house in Gloucester-shire). The second phase of Sadleir's fiction writing career is more interesting. It begins with *These Foolish Things* in 1937, a London novel; followed in 1940 by the sensationally popular *Fanny by Gaslight*, another (and better) London novel. During the Second World War there was a public appetite for escapism which Sadleir's story was cannily designed to satisfy. *Fanny by Gaslight* was reprinted four times in its first year (as a publisher, Sadleir could handle the paper rationing problem) and sold 150,000 copies in its full-price, hardback form. It was adapted as a big-budget film in 1944, starring James Mason as the evil Lord Manderstoke and Stewart Granger as virtuous Harry.

The reader is introduced to Fanny Hooper as an apparently respectable English-woman, living on a small pension in France. Miss Hooper is befriended by a young British publisher, Warbeck. She tells him her life story, which he believes to be sale-able. Fanny [Vandra] Hopper [sic] was an illegitimate child, consigned by her servant mother to the care of her ostensible father, William 'Duke' Hopwood, in London in the late 1850s. Duke in fact runs a respectable gin palace, the Happy Warrior, and a less respectable brothel for the aristocracy, in Piccadilly. Despite his trade, Duke is a generous and generally admired man of the world. But he falls foul of a degenerate client, Lord Manderstoke, who revenges himself on Duke by beating a girl-prostitute to death and leaving her corpse to be found by the police in the Happy Warrior. Duke is killed, trying to escape arrest.

The narrative then jumps to 1871 when Fanny (now 'Hooper') goes into service with the aristocratic Seymores. She finds herself attracted to the mysterious head of the house, Mr Clive, who is – in fact – her father. Forced to move on, Fanny declines to become a high-class whore, but serves as a maid in an upmarket brothel, whose business is meticulously described. The story builds to a melodramatic climax in which Lord Manderstoke, malign as ever, provokes Fanny's true love, Harry, into a duel. Harry is mortally wounded. His well-born family – outraged by the connection – forbids Fanny from seeing him, even on his deathbed. Seven months later, their daughter is born. Fanny dies in 1933 as Warbeck is completing the writing up of her story – which he respectfully offers the English reading public, seven years later, to take their minds off the Luftwaffe's falling bombs.

Fanny by Gaslight rattles along with all the vivacity of the 'Anonyma', soft-core Victorian pornography which the bibliophile Sadleir relished and collected. It is the precursor, and arguably progenitor, of such neo-Victorian productions as Jean Rhys's *Wide Sargasso Sea* (1966), John Fowles's *The French Lieutenant's Woman* (1969), A. S. Byatt's *Possession* (1990) and D. T. Taylor's *Derby Day* (2011).

FN   Michael Thomas Harvey Sadleir (born Sadler)
MRT   *Fanny by Gaslight*
Biog *ODNB* (Derek Hudson, revised by Sayoni Basu)

142. Sapper 1888–1937

James Bond is Sapper from the waist up and Mickey Spillane below. Ian Fleming, on the moral physiology of 007

Herman Cyril McNeile was born in the sublimely inaptly named Higher Bore Street, in Bodmin, Cornwall. The one thing he did not do, as a novelist, was bore – nor would anyone claim any 'higher' quality in his fiction. He was the son of a naval captain, later a prison governor (if his disciplinary practices were anything like those endorsed by Sapper the inmates must have had a hard time of it). Young Herman was educated at Cheltenham College and the Royal Military Academy, Woolwich, as training for the army career his family had in mind for him. He duly joined the Royal Engineers (fondly called 'sappers' by the infantry) in 1907. Traditionally the army's cleverest officers are to be found in RE ranks. His Germanic Christian name may have been an embarrassment: in adult life he was known as 'H. C. McNeile'. As expected, he served gallantly in the First World War (trench warfare put engineers in the frontlines and often under them), winning a Military Cross at the Battle of Ypres and receiving the wounds that would lead to his premature death, while still in his forties. Like other men going off to war, he married in 1914. His wife Violet Baird was the daughter of a half colonel of the Cameron Highlanders. He himself would rise to the same rank of Lieutenant-Colonel.

McNeile published several novels (as 'Sapper' – the army discouraged authorship) with a military theme. Supposedly Lord Northcliffe of the *Daily Mail* was so impressed that he pulled strings to get 'Sapper' demobilised to biff the Hun on the pages of his newspaper. After the war McNeile retired from the army, took up residence in Sussex, and in 1920 began publishing his 'Bulldog Drummond' adventure stories. They were, as marketed by Hodder and Stoughton, wildly popular, catching the postwar mood of free-floating resentment, particularly among the middle classes, who felt betrayed by a 'Victory' which had cost so much and returned so little.

As we first encounter him, Captain Hugh Drummond, DSO, MC, has been demobilised after a 'good' war and is bored by peace. He rackets around the Junior Sports Club and at home has a fanatically loyal man-servant, the 'square-jawed ex-batman', James Denny. Bulldog is physically massive and ugly in a handsome sort of way, a heavy smoker, a heroic beer drinker, a fine boxer and – when his fists fail – trained in the eastern arts of Ju Jitsu by a Japanese master 'Olaki'. Bulldog (so nicknamed for his ferocity in trench fighting) needs work, so he puts an advertisement in the papers: 'Demobilised officer, finding peace incredibly tedious, would welcome diversion. Legitimate if possible; but crime, if of a comparatively humorous description, no objection. Excitement essential.' In response to his advertisement, Bulldog is recruited by a smashing young filly, Phyllis Benton. Her father has been imprisoned by the sinister 'Carl Peterson', a stateless master-criminal dedicated, as such swine inevitably are, to the destruction of England. Peterson's accomplice is his 'daughter' (in fact his lover) Irma. As the 'Comte de Guy' Peterson plots to bring about a total stoppage of British industry by manipulating 'Red' trade union organisers and intellectuals. 'A gigantic syndicalist strike' is set in motion. The long-term aim is to 'Bolshevise England'.

'Your little old country', an American tells Drummond, 'is, saving one, the finest on God's earth; but she's in a funny mood. She's sick.' There develops a strange respect between Peterson, Drummond and Irma, who eventually falls in love with the British hero. The action mainly revolves around capture and escape sequences, often enlivened by graphic scenes of torture. There is much cheerful homicide on Drummond's part, whose motto is 'hit first and apologise afterwards'. Peterson and his beautiful henchwoman escape and Bulldog goes on to marry Phyllis.

The novel introduces the chums who are to make up Drummond's 'gang' in subsequent instalments: Peter Darrell (playboy and MCC cricketer), Ted Jerningham (a Casanova), Algy Longworth (a languid fop), and Toby Sinclair (all-purpose good sort). In the 'second round' with Carl Peterson, *The Black Gang* (1922), Bulldog and his Black Gang chums counter-attack the 'Red International' which is undermining Britain via its socialist stooges. There is an opening episode in which two East-End Jewish white slavers ('of the worst type ... they generally drug the girls with cocaine or some dope first') are flogged by the Black Gang 'within an inch of their lives'. Bulldog's mentor, Sir Bryan Johnstone, tells the Home Secretary: 'We can't go on being the cesspit of Europe, sheltering microbes who infect us as soon as they are here. We want disinfecting. We want it badly.'

Carl Peterson returns for *The Third Round* (1924) and, finally, for *The Final Count* (1927), in which he hovers lethally over England in an airship, loaded with deadly liquid gas. Drummond forces his foe to drink his own poison. As he dies, Peterson 'stood revealed for what he was. And of that revelation no man can write.' Just as well, perhaps, that this author doesn't try.

Bulldog Drummond was dramatised for the London stage by McNeile in 1922 with Gerald du Maurier – son of the Victorian novelist (George), father of the twentieth-century novelist (Daphne) – in the lead. The first film based on the character came out in the same year. Eventually Ronald Colman played the part in what became a long-running series. The ten Sapper novels, and the film rights, made McNeile rich as the world spiralled into Depression.

The formula was influential. In one direction, it leads to W. E. Johns's juvenile hero Biggles. In another direction, Bulldog Drummond clearly blueprints James Bond, as Ian Fleming candidly admitted. After McNeile's early death in 1937, the copyright was left to the author's collaborator, Gerard Fairlie (thought to be the 'original' of Bulldog), who continued it with half a dozen posthumous titles. Lt-Col. McNeile was buried at Woking Crematorium with full military honours. He left £26,000.

FN   Sapper (Herman Cyril McNeile)
MRT *Bulldog Drummond*
Biog *ODNB* (Jonathon Green)

143. Hervey Allen 1889–1949

The only time you really live fully is from thirty to sixty.

Born in Pittsburgh, the son of a father described as 'an entrepreneur and inventor', young Hervey Allen is recorded as growing up 'emotionally distant' from his parent, whom he blamed for impoverishing the family with his crackpot schemes. Allen was originally destined for a career at sea, but after injury on the athletic field while training at the US Naval Academy at Annapolis (where he had won a scholarship), he was honourably discharged. He returned to his hometown university, graduating in 1915 with a degree in economics, and a sheaf of as yet unpublished poems.

He had, meanwhile, enrolled in the National Guard, whose lower standards of physical fitness did not disbar him. He signed up for idealistic motives, hoping to be sent to Mexico, in support of the democratic revolution in that country. Woodrow Wilson was tempted to intervene, but in the event didn't. Instead, in 1917, on America's declaration of war, Allen was commissioned into the Pennsylvanian infantry and posted to France. He was badly wounded at the Battle of the Marne – mustard-gassed and shell-shocked – and had the idealism knocked out of him. While recovering in hospital he wrote his hugely successful anti-war poem, *The Blindman: A Ballad of Nogent L'Artaud* (1919). A soldier encounters a villager, blinded a few days earlier in an artillery barrage. He is looking for his daughter, Elenor. The soldier takes the man to the ruins of his house, where the corpse of Elenor lies, gnawed by rats:

> *The Blindman leaned against the door;*
> *'And tell me, sir, about the war,*
> *What is it they are fighting for?'*
> *'Blindman,' I cried, 'can you not see?*
> *It is to set the whole world free!*
> *It is for sweet democracy –*

All the father can 'see' is that 'my little Elenor is dead'. *The Blindman* qualifies, with Dalton Trumbo's *Johnny Got his Gun* and e.e. cummings's *The Enormous Room* as one of the classic American anti-war works about 'the War called Great'.

With peace, Allen studied literature at Harvard, specialising in Edgar Allan Poe, a writer on whom he would eventually write a creditable monograph. On graduation, he taught English at Vassar and published a memoir of his war experiences, *Toward the Flame: A War Diary*, in 1925. He still hoped to make a name for himself as a poet. Injudiciously – given the stern disciplines of the time – he fell in love with, and later, in 1927, married, one of his students, Annette Andrews. The ensuing scandal hounded him out of academia and the couple took up residence in Bermuda, supported by her parents and whatever writing Hervey could pick up.

Allen now began writing fiction and spent five years working away on his first published novel, *Anthony Adverse*. The swashbuckling saga of sex and piracy in the eighteenth-century Caribbean was accepted by Farrar & Rinehart and went on to make both author and publisher rich. At 1,200 printed pages, costing a daunting $3, it was marketed astutely as 'three novels for the price of one'. *Anthony Adverse* topped the American bestseller lists for two successive years, 1933–4 and pioneered the 'blockbuster' work of fiction as a viable ware. That customers in their droves would buy such a big costly thing was a revelation to the book trade. Farrar & Rinehart declared themselves 'stunned' by the novel's sales. The narrative opens with an extended prelude, dated '1775'. Don Luis, a Spanish grandee, has taken a young Scottish girl, Maria, twenty-five years his junior, to wife. While on their honeymoon in France, Maria forms a liaison with a young Irish officer, Denis Moore. The marquis discovers he has been cuckolded and kills his rival in a staged duel. Maria dies giving birth to Denis's child, whom Don Luis leaves as a foundling, to be brought up in a convent in Leghorn. Years pass and the waif grows up as Anthony Adverse – destined for a life as adventurous as his name.

The novel's long-term sales were boosted by Warner Brothers' film, with its million-dollar-budget, cast of thousands, and a fleet of galleons the size of the Armada. The movie starred Fredric March and scooped up all the 1936 Oscars. It also made Allen very rich. He and his wife lived their last decades in Florida, where Allen died happily composing an epic cycle of novels set in colonial America. He loved the state's Everglades, and was an early environmental activist. As a pacifist and hater of war after 1918, he was a patriot again (as he had been in 1916, when he was hot to go to Mexico) after the Japanese attack on Pearl Harbor in 1941.

None of Allen's subsequent novels achieved the popularity of *Anthony Adverse*, which marched on to claim 1.5 million sales worldwide at the time of his death. It was very much a novel for the Depression years – escapist, and a Beach Book (as similar sized blockbusters would later be called) for readers who could not, this year alas, afford to go to the beach. For all the formative impact his novel had on the American fiction trade, Allen is one of the forgotten of American literature. Had he followed his head rather than his heart, and not 'misconducted' himself with a student, he would probably have been remembered as a distinguished Poe scholar.

FN   William Hervey Allen, Jr
MRT   *Anthony Adverse*
Biog   S. E. Knee, *Hervey Allen: (1889–1949): A Literary Historian in America* (1988)

144. Enid Bagnold 1889–1981

I exchanged Sickert for Beaverbrook.

According to her own, autobiographical, account, no life was jollier than Enid's: 'I was born', she recorded, 'with the first motor cars, and I never thought I should die. Death is so unnatural.' Bagnold's father was a senior army officer of peppery disposition. When she sent him the manuscript of her first novel 'He absolutely forbade publication. He said he couldn't go into his club in London ... "I should feel," he said flatly, "as if she'd been raped under a hedge by a sergeant."' A higher class of sexual experience awaited Enid, it would transpire. The formative event in her girlhood was her father being appointed to a governor's position in the West Indies, which meant three years in Jamaica, with horses, mules and donkeys, and coloured servants to wait on her, hand, foot and hoof.

The family returned to England when she was fourteen – a magical age for her throughout life. She was packed off to Julia Huxley's progressive Prior's Field school in Godalming, and was finished, according to the conventions of her class, in Switzerland, and duly 'came out'. She should, of course, have promptly 'gone in' as the wife of some suitable young gent, but against the grain of her class she resolved to study art in Camden, working with and sitting for Walter Sickert (possibly Jack the Ripper, if a fellow lady novelist, Patricia Cornwell, is to be believed).

Eager to be seduced but 'terrified to be touched', she lost her virginity in 1914 – ominous year – to the great cocksman of the age, Frank Harris. She felt, she said, 'like a corporal made sergeant'. She picked up from Harris (now a very old and rather beaten-down dirty dog) tricks of the journalistic trade. During the First World War, Bagnold worked as a nurse and ambulance driver, but criticisms of the hospital service in her book, *A Diary Without Dates* (1918), led to dismissal. She began serious writing after the war and married Sir Roderick Jones, the chairman of Reuters news agency, in 1920. He was twelve years her senior. The couple settled in Sussex in a fine house previously owned by Edward Burne-Jones, their needs attended to by 'two nurses, a nurserymaid, a chauffeur, two gardeners, a groom and a strapper'.

In between children, and social engagements, Bagnold wrote a number of well-received plays and novels, notably the much revived *The Chalk Garden* (1955) and the bestselling *National Velvet* (1935). The last is a Cinderella-in-jodhpurs story of fourteen-year-old Velvet, one of three sisters with 'zulu bodies and golden hair', who masquerades as a male jockey to win the Grand National on a piebald horse she bought at a fair. The first edition was prettily illustrated by Bagnold's thirteen-year-old daughter, Laurina. The tone of the work is illustrated by its first sentence: 'Unearthly lumps of land curved into the darkening sky like the backs of browsing pigs, like the rumps of elephants.' The novel was adapted for the stage and triumphantly filmed, starring Elizabeth Taylor, in 1944. By 1975, the book version had sold some 2 million copies in American paperback.

Bagnold faced death ('a terrible old nuisance') as she had lived – with unforced gaiety and the pluck so valued by her class, writing to the end. The last line in her memoir is: 'This morning the surgeon has replied and made a date. How horrible, and yet it's like being engaged.' Enid's brother Ralph Bagnold founded the Long Range Desert Group during the Second World War. Her great-granddaughter is the wife of David Cameron, British Prime Minister at the time of writing. Enid would have liked that.

FN   Enid Algerine Bagnold (later Lady Jones)
MRT *National Velvet*
Biog A. Sebba, *Enid Bagnold: A Biography* (1986)

145. Erle Stanley Gardner 1889–1970

I know something about what the public wants and a hell of a lot about what the public doesn't want. Erle Stanley Gardner

The creator of Perry Mason (smooth defence attorney) and Bertha Cool (big, foul-mouthed PI), with estimated worldwide sales under a barrage of pen-names of some 400 million, Gardner qualifies as one of the top-selling popular novelists in the English language. He had over 140 novels in print at the time of his death, including some eighty 'Perry Masons', whose titular hallmark was the prefix 'The Case of ... ' There were also twenty-eight 'Bertha Cools' in print. At the highpoint of his career he was publishing five titles a year, feeding the voracious 25-cent Pocketbook market.

Gardner was born in Malden, Massachusetts. His father was a mining engineer whose work took him all over the US, eventually landing the family in California when Erle was thirteen. He remained a Southern Californian for the rest of his life. As a young man he boxed for purse money and – all too ready with his fists – was expelled from college in 1909, in his first month of study, for slugging his professor. Through private study, Gardner went on to qualify as a lawyer in 1911. He was still boxing and, reportedly, sported two black eyes on the day he passed his Bar exams.

For a while, however, he worked as a salesman before setting himself up as an attorney in the Los Angeles area where he practised successfully until 1933.

He contributed his first story to a pulp magazine, aged thirty-four, in 1923. Thereafter, lawyering by day and writing by night, he produced hundreds of such stories, many under pseudonym. His first Perry Mason story, *The Case of the Velvet Claws* appeared in 1933 and his first Bertha Cool story in 1939. He contributed more stories to *Black Mask* (over 130) than any other of that magazine's distinguished stable of hardboiled crime writers (Hammett, Chandler, Cain, etc.). The Mason series was boosted by the *Saturday Evening Post*, which serialised them from the 1930s to the 1950s and, latterly, by the TV series, starring a lugubrious Raymond Burr as Mason, which ran from 1957 to 1966. As a plot-writer, Gardner loved unexpected twists, surprises and ambushes on the reader – typically, in a courtroom climax. The hardboiled quality in his early work gave way to an easier-going, ironic mode of narration, particularly in the aptly named 'Cool' stories, but he always took great professional pains with the legal accuracy of his plots.

Having established himself as a writer, Gardner set up production of his fiction on factory lines, using dictaphones and armies of secretaries. The pulp magazines which flourished between the wars had an insatiable appetite for his wares. In 1938 Gardner, now rich, took up residence at the Temecula Ranch near Riverside, some fifty miles from LA. Although he gave up active legal work in 1933, with the sale of his first full-length novel, he was a founding member of 'The Court of Last Resort' (now more soberly called the Case Review Committee), a legal aid organisation for the wrongly imprisoned.

Gardner was an avid sportsman and – it is reported – spoke fluent Mandarin (many of his early clients were indigent Chinese) and was a keen naturalist, particularly expert on the breeding habits of the grey whale. Although guns figure centrally in many of his stories, his own favoured weapon was the bow and arrow and he was a frequent and expert contributor to *Ye Sylvan Archer* magazine. In 1913 Gardner married Natalie Talbert, a legal secretary, and they had one daughter, Grace. However, they separated and the marriage was dissolved in 1935, although the couple were never formally divorced. When his wife died in 1968, Gardner married another of his many secretaries, Agnes Jean Bethell – the supposed original of Perry Mason's sidekick, Della Street. Unsurprisingly, Gardner lived to win every prize for which an American crime writer is eligible, most more than once.

FN   Erle Stanley Gardner
MRT   *The Case of the Velvet Claws*
Biog   Francis L. and Roberta B. Fugate, *Secrets of the World's Best-Selling Writer: The Story Telling Techniques of Erle Stanley Gardner* (1980)

146. Agatha Christie 1890–1976

It is as complete and shameless a bamboozling of the reader as was ever perpetrated.
Raymond Chandler on *And Then There Were None*

Agatha Miller was born in Torquay, the last of three children of an American father, Frederick, and an English mother, Clarissa (Clara). The Millers were well off and cultivated. Henry James and Rudyard Kipling were on household visiting terms. The years between five and twelve were, she recalled, 'wonderfully happy'. Her father, who 'never did a hand's turn in his life' was 'a very agreeable man' but feckless. He died of a heart attack when Agatha was eleven and life for the Millers thereafter was less *wonderfully* happy. A brother, 'Monty', went to the bad spectacularly after the war, and died, rather disgracefully, in 1929, leaving the Millers, as Agatha's biographer puts it, a 'matriarchy'.

Agatha had been educated among this matriarchy as 'a little lady': she read voraciously – but, as her manuscripts reveal, never quite mastered grammar or spelling. Later she studied music in France with a view to an eventual career as a pianist or singer. In the event neither her nerves nor her voice were strong enough. Aged twenty she spent a season in Cairo, where she 'came out'. On her return to England she joined the country-house party circuit, absorbing the Edwardian gentility which breathes serenely over her subsequent fiction. At this period of her life she wrote poetry and had tried her hand at at least one unpublished novel. She married Archie Christie, a dashing officer in the Royal Flying Corps, at Christmas 1914 – his being the third proposal she had received. 'I love him dreadfully', she told her mother, who opposed the marriage. Almost immediately Lieut. Christie was posted to France and Agatha cried all night.

Christie survived the war – a sinus complaint invalided him out of active service in the air, and relegated him to a desk job. During hostilities Agatha worked at Torquay Hospital and was put in charge of the dispensary. Here she gained her formidable practical expertise about drugs and poisons. In 1916, on leave from hospital, she wrote *The Mysterious Affair at Styles* (1920), a locked-room murder story, introducing the retired Belgian detective, Hercule Poirot, who, as always, solves the mysterious affair by the application of his infallible 'grey cells'. The wax-moustached and slightly comical detective was inspired by the cluster of war refugees from Belgium currently exiled in Torquay – but Poirot would stay on. He reappears in some thirty-three novels and fifty-two short stories, until his demise in *Curtain* (1975), alongside his Dr Watson, the stolid and unimaginative Captain Hastings.

After the war the Christies moved to London. Archie got a job in the city and made money (but not much). Agatha got pregnant, giving birth to a baby girl, Rosalind, in 1919. She was a conscientious mother but not enthusiastic about the role nor, some have suggested, sex. There were no more children. But books there were. Christie had arrived on the literary scene at a period when detective fiction was all the rage. She varied her output with *The Secret Adversary* (1922), a 'romantic' thriller which introduced a light vein of comedy in the form of the detective duo, Tommy and 'Tuppence' Beresford. But her great advance came with *The Murder of Roger Ackroyd* (1926), another 'Poirot'. The novel laid down Christie's main formula over the subsequent decades: a mysterious murder (typically by poisoning), a claustrophobic setting (typically a country house, but sometimes a ship or a train), a shortlist of suspects all equally plausible, trails of false clues and reader deceptions, ending with a startling denouement.

As the 1920s drew on, Agatha was the main earner in the Christie household. Money, not art, was always a main concern for her – and often a murder motive in her fiction. The year 1926 was the critical one in her life: her mother died and her marriage broke down. Archie, she learned, had been unfaithful. On 6 December 1926 British newspapers carried front-page headlines about Mrs Christie's mysterious disappearance. A car with articles of her clothing was found abandoned. A huge woman hunt was mounted. Eleven days later she was discovered in a hotel at Harrogate, registered under the name of Archie's mistress. The unconvincing explanation given out to the world was that she had suffered an attack of 'amnesia'.

After divorce in 1928, with her daughter now at boarding school, Christie consoled herself with travel. A trip by train to the Middle East inspired her most famous novel, *Murder on the Orient Express* (1934), and at the site of the ancient city of Ur she visited a dig in 1928 and met the archaeologist Max Mallowan. They married in 1930: he was fourteen years younger than her and a Roman Catholic. The marriage lasted forty-five years and both partners continued their careers successfully – Mallowan being knighted for his services to archaeology in 1968. Christie would, somewhat later, earn her own title, for services to popular literature. She was now producing two to three novels a year. *The Murder at the Vicarage* (1930) had introduced her other great series hero, Miss Jane Marple, the genteel spinster sleuth from St Mary Mead. In her fiction of this period Christie also introduces a mocking self-portrait, in the form of the muddle-headed writer of mysteries, Ariadne Oliver.

Christie had her greatest pre-war success with the 'locked room times ten' mystery, *Ten Little Niggers* (1939) – *Ten Little Indians* in the US. With the outbreak of war Christie wrote and stored away 'last' cases for Poirot (*Curtain*) and Miss Marple (*Sleeping Murder*): both were published shortly before her death. As she explained in her autobiography, they were written 'in anticipation of my being killed in the raids, which seemed to be in the highest degree likely as I was working in London'. However, she survived to write seventeen books during the war and, as before, she worked in a hospital dispensary. Her husband Max joined the Royal Air Force and spent much of the war serving in North Africa. The author's only grandchild, Matthew, was born in 1943. After the war Christie continued to write voluminously, adapting her settings to the new age of austerity – a planet away from the Edwardian milieux of her youth. Her now global popularity was boosted by theatre dramatisations and film versions of her stories. In 1954 she had three plays of her own composition running simultaneously in London's West End, including the interminable *The Mousetrap* (1948). Christie professed not to like any film versions of her novels, even the immensely popular Margaret Rutherford Marple series.

The novels of the last phase of Christie's life tend to be perfunctory performances. An exception is *The Pale Horse* (1961), in which a mass poisoner uses the exotic toxin, thallium. Allegedly the mass poisoner Graham Young (who also favoured thallium) was caught because the investigating detective had read and remembered the Christie novel. Uncomfortable as such settings as 'swinging London' were for Miss Marple in *At Bertram's Hotel* (1965), her readership continued to grow. She was never out of fashion. Despite long-running tax problems, Christie, 'The Queen of Crime', was a wealthy and honoured woman of letters. She was awarded a CBE in 1956 and was made a Dame of the British Empire in 1971. She died in 1976. Her tombstone at Cholsey in Berkshire is inscribed 'Agatha Christie the Writer'.

FN   Agatha Mary Clarissa Christie (née Miller; later Mallowan)
MRT *The Murder of Roger Ackroyd*
Biog L. Thompson, *Agatha Christie:An English Mystery* (2007)

147. Richmal Crompton 1890–1969

'I'll thcream and thcream and thcream till I'm thick.' Violet Elizabeth Bott

Richmal Lamburn was born in Lancashire, the middle child of a Church of England parson. Her three-years-younger brother Jack (in later life a man of action, and a writer of action novels) evidently inspired a bit of William Brown. Crompton's elder sister, Gwen (nothing like Ethel Brown) was throughout their joint lifelong spinsterdom Richmal's closest friend. The 'Crompton' middle name was in honour of a maternal grandfather who, for no recorded reason, swallowed a lethal dose of prussic acid when Richmal was three.

Her home life was unlike William's cosy, bourgeois, home-counties menage – Mr Brown doing his something in the city, Mrs Brown darning socks, Robert at his dramatic society, the delectable flapper Ethel fending off beaux, the incorrigible maid breaking the crockery ('It came to pieces in me 'and, M'um'), the gardener mysteriously busy in the potting shed – and, of course, Just William, schoolboy, Outlaw, proud owner of Jumble, and sworn rebel against all the above. Aged eleven (William's age, for four decades), Richmal was bundled off to a 'clergy daughters' boarding school in Warrington. A bright pupil, she won a place to read classics at Newnham, but prudently turned it down in favour of the £60 p.a. scholarship Royal Holloway College, London, offered her. She was canny about money. On graduation, with a respectable 'second', she entered the teaching profession and eventually found a long-term post at Bromley High School for Girls. For the fifteen most formative years of her life she lived in wholly boyless institutions. Early 1920s England was also notably manless, thanks to the Kaiser.

Richmal wrote her first William stories for the *Home Magazine* and *Happy Mag.* (sic): they were published in volume form by the magazine magnate, George Newnes. The first book, with its hallmark illustrations by Henry Thomas, was *Just William* (1922). The last, some forty volumes on, was *William the Superman* (1968). Crompton's naughty schoolboy bestrode the twentieth century like a ragamuffin colossus. It changed, he never did. As early as the fifth volume, Crompton called William her 'Frankenstein's monster'. She made fitful attempts (as had Doyle with Sherlock Holmes) to kill him, but 'he insisted on having his own way'. William the Unkillable. Crompton wrote thirty-odd books for adults, some of which, like the early *Bildungsroman, The Innermost Room* (1923) and her collection of ghost stories, *Mist* (1929), stand up well. But no one liked them as much as William's exploits – or reads them nowadays – as they do William.

Crompton's life took an irreversible turn in her early thirties with polio, causing her to lose the use of her right leg, and another in her early forties, when she developed breast cancer. What sexual experiences she had – if any – are unrecorded. Her pen name, 'Richmal', her family name, 'Ray', and her tomboyish girlhood are too slight to build on. She may, like Jane Austen, have died a virgin novelist. 'I am probably,' she said, 'the last surviving example of the Victorian professional aunt.' And, by all accounts, a fond one. Thanks to William, the only man in her life, she could live in a grand house – 'The Glebe', in Bromley – and leave a healthy £60,000 on her death.

The William stories are both formulaic, invariably involving some ingenious act of juvenile rebellion against the adult world, and flexible – adapting, hand in glove, to the historical period in which they were conceived and first published. A prime example is 'William and the Nasties', published in the *Happy Mag.*, June 1934.

William, having caught wind of what's going on in Germany, declares himself by schoolboy putsch 'Him Hitler' ('Her[r] Hitler' is, needless to say, 'girly'). The Outlaws, now stormtroopers, duly hound the Jewish sweetshop owner, Mr Isaacs, but after a while they find the whole business somehow 'wrong', and befriend their victim. The story was later suppressed, but it is noteworthy that it precedes (and foretells) by four years, *Kristallnacht*.

Crompton drew on Tom Brown, *Stalky & Co.*, P. G. Wodehouse and, above all, Tom Sawyer. The stories are saturated with English class prejudice. Hubert Lane and Violet Elizabeth Bott are rich and vulgar: the 'evacuees' with whom William goes to war during the war are ineffably common. But, as Crompton's biographer argues, there is always a subtle Twainian satire against the author's own class in her stories.

In her later years Crompton turned to table-rapping and a belief in reincarnation. Independent to the end, she died of a heart attack, having driven herself home, alone, from a dinner party, in her controls-modified car.

FN   Richmal Crompton (born Richmal Crompton Lamburn)
MRT *Just William*
Biog   M. Cadogan, *Richmal Crompton: The Woman behind William* (1986)

148. Richard Aldington 1892–1962

Nationalism is a silly cock crowing on his own dunghill.

Aldington was born in Portsmouth and brought up in various seaside towns – which he later despised as the epitome of Englishness. The son of a solicitor's clerk and a (not very good) novel-writing mother, he received the school education of his class, which did not much educate him but did enable him to make himself, in later life, a high-achieving autodidact. In 1910, he enrolled at University College London – the 'Godless Place in Gower Street'. It was, he later declared, an institution designed to turn out 'ten thousand pedants for one poet'.

Aldington resolved to be the one among ten thousand and left UCL's 'buttressed respectability' after a year for Soho and 'the freer if frowstier fields of bohemianism'. In those frowsty fields he became intimate, if never quite a leading spirit, with avant-gardistes such as Ezra Pound, T. E. Hulme, Herbert Read, H. D. (Hilda Doolittle). Together they brought in the 'Revolution of 1912' – or imagism, as less impressed literary historians term it. Aldington married the Revolution's star practitioner, H. D., in 1913. It would be a modishly open union: photographs of the period display a goatee-bearded Ezra lookalike – poetic to the core. Three years later, after the outbreak of war, the image is of a smart young infantry officer, with the obligatory 'tache', swagger stick and middle-distance stare.

Unlike fellow poets (Isaac Rosenberg, Wilfred Owen, Charles Sorley), Aldington survived the trenches, gas and shellshock, although the pointlessness of it all imbued him with cosmic despair – he claimed to have attempted suicide twice. For the rest of his life he maintained, 'There are two kinds of men: those who have been to the front and those who haven't.' It was his personal heart of darkness. The relationship with H. D. broke up without animosity, as both followed their wayward lusts. In the 1920s Aldington settled down with his new partner, as a tweedy man of letters, working for the *TLS*. He was increasingly intimate with T. S. Eliot, whom he had met in 1917. He bought a cottage in Berkshire and countryfied himself.

Aldington had begun writing *Death of a Hero* almost the day the war finished but it would not see print until 1929 (the same year as Remarque's *All Quiet on the Western Front*). He called it a 'jazz novel'. It's not clear what he meant by the term. Transparently autobiographical, it tells the story of George Winterbourne, who, in the trenches, discovers the real enemy is not the Hun but England – 'a country where there are so many old fools and so few young ones'. Wholly disillusioned he hurls himself into a hail of machine-gun fire: 'The universe exploded darkly into oblivion.' Chatto (who had just rejected *Lady Chatterley's Lover*) agreed to publish Aldington only with some savage wielding of the blue pencil. Aldington insisted on asterisks to mark the 'mutilation'. It is necessary, said Zola, to 'kill the hero'. Aldington did it twice: with his first novel (and a couple of pallid successors), and his gloriously iconoclastic biography of T. E. Lawrence, published (to screams of patriotic outrage) in 1955.

The belated publication of his novel produced in Aldington what psychiatrists call 'abreaction'. The despair he had felt in 1917 flared up again and he stalked into the Soho restaurant where Herbert Read and T. S. Eliot were dining to announce, 'I'm on my way to Paris … I've done with this country.' He clinched it with a postcard to Eliot 'on which was written a single four-letter word'. What word is not recorded. Perhaps four asterisks. Thereafter, Aldington was, like his friend D. H. Lawrence, a passionate pilgrim living by his pen in Europe, then, during the Second World War, in America. He died in France. On his gravestone, Aldington instructed there be written Wilfred Owen's assertion: 'My subject is War, and the pity of War. The Poetry is in the Pity.' Not the heroism.

FN   Richard Aldington (born Edward Godfree Aldington)
MRT   *Death of a Hero*
Biog   C. Doyle, *Richard Aldington* (1989)

149. Djuna Barnes 1892–1982

Suffering for love is how I have learned practically everything I know.

Barnes was born into a bohemian, free-thinking, sexually liberated family, the daughter of an artist, 'Wald' Barnes, and Elizabeth Chappell, an English-born concert violinist. A convinced advocate of polygamy, Wald moved in his mistress during Djuna's childhood. Barnes was brought up on the family farm in New York state, alongside a tribe of siblings and half siblings. The domestic environment was comfortably off, liberated, but irregular in the extreme – Djuna may, it is suspected, have suffered incestuous rape. Her early education certainly suffered. Aged seventeen, she was coerced into marriage with the fifty-two-year-old brother of her father's mistress. The marriage lasted only a few weeks.

The family broke up when Djuna was twenty, and she left for New York where she worked as a well-paid journalist, based in the city's Latin Quarter, Greenwich Village. She was meanwhile writing on the side in an aggressively avant-gardiste manner. Her first major literary work, *The Book of Repulsive Women* (1915), is a collection of her poems ('rhythms') and her drawings – decadent and frankly, for the time, lesbian. She had affairs with lovers of both sexes, but child-bearing she abominated.

Like other advanced writers, Barnes was drawn to Paris after the First World War, initially as a journalist. She remained there as a creative writer for fifteen years. The city was, in the 1920s, a cauldron of literary modernism: Hemingway, Stein, Durrell, cummings and Miller had all cultivated their talents there, and 'prohibited' authors, such as Joyce (whom Barnes came to know well) and Lawrence, could freely publish work banned in their home countries. Paris was also as tolerant of variant forms of human sexuality as of new forms of literature. Barnes embarked on an intense – and doomed – relationship with the expatriate American artist and sculptor, Thelma Ellen Wood.

Ford Madox Hueffer published Barnes's work in his *Little Review* and her Joycean and semi-autobiographical novel, *Ryder*, came out in 1928. In it, she seems to come to terms, psychologically, with her wayward father. The narrative covers fifty years in the life of a family, in which Djuna Barnes's own family is easily recognisable (notably 'Wendell' for Wald). *Ryder* was, inevitably, seized as obscene in America, by the US Postal Services, who – with the Society for the Suppression of Vice – acted as the country's official censorship board. It took them a few weeks to uncover the 'filth' lurking under the carapace of literary experimentalism. However, the seizure did wonders for the author's reputation.

Barnes's second book, *Ladies Almanack*, a florid exercise in eighteenth-century pastiche, was wholly unpublishable in America on the grounds of its openness about lesbianism. In the late 1920s, and in the wake of her painful separation from the increasingly drunken Thelma Wood, Barnes was working on *Nightwood*, the novel on which her subsequent reputation mainly rests. A narrative of ambitious scope and high modernity, Spenglerian in tone and Joycean in method, *Nightwood* chronicles the decay of Western civilisation alongside the complications of personal sexuality: specifically the author's relationship with Thelma. The book was again judged unpublishable in the US, but was accepted in Britain by Faber and Faber. T. S. Eliot, chief editor, wrote an introduction in which he asserted the novel was 'so good ... that only sensibilities trained on poetry can wholly appreciate it'. The novel appeared, prudently toned down, in 1936 in the UK and a year later in the US.

On the outbreak of war, Barnes returned to New York, and Greenwich Village, in 1940. *Nightwood* had been much acclaimed, but sold poorly. There weren't that many Eliotic sensibilities trained on poetry around unfortunately. She could no longer be trusted with journalistic assignments, was drinking heavily and dependent on handouts from well-wishers, notably Peggy Guggenheim, whom she had come to know in her Parisian glory years. Other friends also remained loyal to her. She managed to control her alcoholism in 1950 and produce her last significant work of literature, the scaldingly autobiographical play *The Antiphon* (1958). Apart from that, her last forty years were reclusive and unhappy – periodically embattled, creatively extinct and little honoured.

FN   Djuna Chappell Barnes
MRT   *Nightwood*
Biog   Phillip Herring, *Djuna: The Life and Work of Djuna Barnes* (1995)

150. Max Brand 1892–1944

There has to be a woman, but not much of a one. A good horse is much more important.
Brand's formula for a good Western

Max Brand (the pen name is now a registered trademark in America – literally a brand name) was variously nicknamed the 'King of the Pulps', 'the Great Faust' and 'the Western Giant'. From 1917 until his death in 1944, Brand hosed out an estimated 30 million words of fiction, some 900 stories, and around 600 full-length novels. He wrote under as many as twenty pseudonyms in all the major popular genres (Westerns, mysteries, hospital stories, melodramas, even science fiction). His formula for success was simple: 'All you have to do is concentrate on a snappy beginning and a smash for the close.' Some 350 of Brand's titles are reckoned to be Westerns, of which the first was *The Untamed* (1919) and the most famous *Destry Rides Again* (1930), as filmed with Marlene Dietrich. In passing, Brand invented the character of Dr Kildare, and can thus claim, along with his pulp kingship, to be the grandfather of the TV soaps and 'hospital melodrama' – see, for instance, *Young Dr Kildare* (1941).

It is one of the unlikely features in an amazing life that he changed his name, for professional reasons, from the ultra-literary 'Frederick Schiller Faust' (Germans being unpopular in America in 1917, when he began to write). He was born in Seattle and spent most of his childhood in Modesto, in the San Joaquin Valley, California. His family – German Jewish on his father's side, Irish on his mother's – was badly off, and Brand remembered all his life the shame of unpaid bills and the hardship of working as a child farm-hand. His father was an unsuccessful lawyer – not that it mattered as Frederick was orphaned in his early teens, his mother dying in 1900, his father in 1905. He would have to make his own way in the world.

Aided by a $50 loan from a friend, Brand got to the University of California at Berkeley in 1911. He left, after four lively years, without a degree, in bad odour for having attacked the university president as pro-Kraut in the student paper. He had already developed the habit of heavy drinking which was to plague him through life. But it was not all bad: at Berkeley he met the sweetheart, Dorothy Schillig, whom he later made his wife in 1917. On leaving college, Brand set off on a trip across the world and made it as far as Hawaii. The war having broken out in Europe, and his country still neutral, he crossed to Canada and enlisted in the armed forces in 1915, hoping to fight in France. No luck.

Returning to the US, he came to the notice of the Frank A. Munsey company – America's major producers of pulp fiction. They were, as it happened, looking for someone to replace their star author, Zane Grey. Faust wanted to be a great poet and was hopefully peddling a 10,000-line epic about Tristram and Isolde. He was given a plot outline by an unimpressed senior editor, sent down the corridor of the Munsey building, where he duly tossed off his first magazine story in six hours at the standard Munsey rate of a penny a word. Brand never stopped typing thereafter and the pennies never stopped coming. He initially covered the whole spectrum of romance: historical swashbucklers, crime stories, gangster stories, romantic melodrama. It was at this period he adopted the 'Max Brand' authorial name.

Faust finally managed to enlist in the US army in 1918. While stationed in Virginia he began writing *The Untamed*, his first full-length Western. It was a success and set 'Max Brand' on what was to be his main line of literary work. For the first time in his life he was making real money. In 1920, the Fausts (there were now three children) settled in New York state, with enough land for him to breed the savage white bull terriers he particularly liked. But in 1921, aged twenty-nine, Faust suffered a heart attack and was informed by his physicians that he was living on borrowed time. But sick as he was, 'Max Brand' continued to write furiously. He had formed what was to be a long association with Street & Smith's *Western Story Magazine* and would eventually produce 306 titles for this firm, at a nickel a word.

Max Brand ('the Jewish cowboy,' as he mockingly called his alter ego) came to dominate the Western category in its glory years, holding a middle ground between Zane Grey and Louis L'Amour, who came a decade later. All three writers have a strong grasp of what might be called innocent clichés of the genre – the saloon brawl, the tomboy cow-girl, the doxy with the heart of gold, the shoot-out, bunkhouse comedy, etc. Brand's zestful tone is evident from such titles as *Flaming Irons*, *The Galloping Broncos*, *Outlaw Breed*, *Singing Guns*.

During his most productive decades, Brand produced on average a novel every three weeks under a score of authorial names and imprints. At his peak he earned up to $100,000 a year. In 1925, disgusted with Prohibition, he and his family moved to Florence, Italy, where he spent most of the interwar years in a palatial villa, living with great extravagance 'like a medieval prince'. By the mid-1930s Brand had graduated from the 'pulps' to the up-market 'slicks', a cross-over which no other writer in his genre managed. He was now cheek by jowl with Hemingway and Fitzgerald. In 1938 Brand moved his family to Hollywood where he wrote scripts for the major studios at a salary of $1,500 a week. Here he made the acquaintance of such distinguished contemporaries as Thomas Mann and Aldous Huxley and worked alongside William Faulkner on the script of *The Charles de Gaulle Story*. In 1944 Brand persuaded *Harper's Magazine* to assign him (aged fifty-two, with a chronically bad heart) as a front-line war reporter. He was terribly wounded by enemy shellfire in May 1944. Gallantly he instructed medics to attend to younger casualties first. He had had his time – and died shortly thereafter.

FN   Max Brand (Frederick Schiller Faust)
MRT *Destry Rides Again*
Biog William F. Nolan, *Max Brand, Western Giant. The Life and Times of Frederick Schiller Faust* (1986)

151. Pearl S. Buck 1892–1973

A man is educated and turned out to work. But a woman is educated and turned out to grass.

When, on 11 November 1938, Pearl S. Buck heard on the radio that she had won the Nobel Prize for Literature, she ejaculated: 'I don't believe it.' A natural enough response – except that, as Hilary Spurling records, she said it in Chinese. Pearl Comfort Buck was raised in two cultures which had 'nothing in common except their subordination of women'. She started writing late – needing first to break out of marital bondage and lose her Christian faith. Once begun, she clocked up thirty-eight novels. If she had published thirty-seven, and the missing one was *The Good Earth*, there would have been no Nobel. Pearl Buck would have been like Edna Ferber (with whom she was often confused) – one of fiction's once-great forgettables.

It is an indication of Buck's unworldliness that her first intention was to call her novel 'Wang Lung', the name of *The Good Earth*'s peasant hero. Wang loses his smallholding, meanwhile China is rent into pieces by famine, revolution, civil disorder – and, not least, unwanted American missionaries. Wang, at his lowest, works as a rickshaw boy and barge-puller. He rises – thanks largely to the efforts of his wife, O-lan – to become a prosperous landowner (and the owner, also, of concubines more to his taste than worn-out O-lan). Buck's publisher, however, discreetly pointed out that 'wang' was urban slang for – well, you know, even if Mrs Buck didn't. The published title was taken from Ecclesiastes.

It is conventional to dismiss Buck's Nobel Prize as a sympathy gesture to China – in the wake of the horrific rape of Nanking (where much of *The Good Earth* (1931) is set). Rape is a recurrent event in Buck's fiction, as it was in her China. It was routine in the regular riots, political uprisings and, less publicly, in marriage. Buck was haunted by the fact that gang-rapists would often not stop, even after the woman was dead. She witnessed the victims of such atrocities; she also witnessed feral dogs devouring the carcasses of unwanted girl babies. Buck recalls, as a primal moment, herself as a five-year-old regarding the three-inch 'golden lily' foot of her 'amah' (nanny): 'a lump of mashed bone and livid discoloured flesh made from heel and toes forced together under the instep, leaving only the big toe intact.' Little Pearl's own feet, the amah thought, were like 'rice flails' and her blonde curls 'inhuman'.

Pearl's father was born dirt-poor in West Virginia. By heroic self-improvement and self-denial, Absalom Sydenstricker qualified as a Presbyterian minister – his faith was fanatical. Two centuries earlier, Pearl laconically remarked, he would have burned witches. Absalom joined the American 'missionary invasion' of China in

1880. It was necessary to have a helpmate, so he chose a wife, Caroline Stulting, as he might have chosen a mule. (What *she* needed was a wife, Pearl would jest in her later, frantically busy, life.) The children Caroline bore either died or lived to be regarded by their father as 'accidents which had befallen him'. Pearl's mother died, worn out, hating her husband, hating Christ and – above all – hating China. On that, and only that, mother and daughter disagreed.

The American attitude to China – with its 'heathen' quarter of the world's souls – was one of grand contempt. They were, declared Theodore Roosevelt, 'an immoral, degraded and worthless race'. The Chinese Exclusion Act was passed in 1882 and not repealed until 1943 (Buck lobbied against it furiously). She became a woman in China. She finished her education at an American college where she was regarded as 'a freak who could speak Chinese'. For her part, she thought white Americans smelled – a 'rank odour, not quite a stink'.

In America, Pearl Sydenstricker found a husband. John Lossing Buck was another missionary and the couple returned to China in 1917, where Lossing laboured to improve peasant farming. They had one child, born mentally retarded in 1921. The birth entailed a hysterectomy, which was devastating, but it meant that, unlike her mother, Pearl escaped the missionary-wife trap. There would be no more children – other than the half-dozen she adopted in the years of her later fame. She took a lover – a poet, nicknamed 'the Chinese Shelley'. Her husband's embraces, she confided to a friend, were a 'violation of all that is best in me'. She took to writing, mainly to pay the expenses of her institutionalised daughter, Carol. She chose fiction because 'that is what most people read.' Buck's first novel, *East Wind: West Wind* (1930) was accepted, after a dozen rejections, by Richard Walsh, who founded his publishing house on her bestsellers. After they had both disposed of their first spouses by divorce, they married. It was a companionable arrangement.

'Chinahand Buck,' William Faulkner called her, but after visiting the location of the movie of *The Good Earth* in 1934, Buck never saw China again. In 1972 she vainly tried to accompany President Nixon on his history-making visit, but was coldly rejected for a visa. During the Second World War – when China was America's ally – Buck's star rose. But it fell again with the victory of the Communists in the 1940s. Hoover opened a file on her, fattened with her active support for the 'Negro' cause in the 1950s. America had 'lost China', and needed scapegoats.

Buck invented the word 'Amerasian' for the children spawned and abandoned by American troops in Korea, Japan and Vietnam. More practically, she founded an agency to settle them in the US. 'We're all half castes,' she said, 'if we go back far enough.' Her good works, in later life, were prodigious. She was, Spurling concludes, a better and more interesting woman than she was a novelist.

FN   Pearl S. Buck (Pearl Sydenstricker; later Buck, later Walsh)
MRT   *The Good Earth*
Biog H. Spurling, *Burying the Bones: Pearl Buck in China* (2010)

152. James M. Cain 1892–1977

James Cain – faugh! Everything he touches smells like a billygoat. He is every kind of writer I detest, a faux naif, a Proust in greasy overalls, a dirty little boy with a piece of chalk and a board fence and nobody looking. Such people are the offal of literature.
Raymond Chandler

Cain was born in Annapolis, the son of a college literature professor. The family was devoutly Irish Catholic but Cain claimed to have lost his faith at thirteen – however, the prominence of confession as a device in his fiction suggests some fragments survived. He was educated at Washington College, Maryland, where his father was currently serving as president. Extraordinarily precocious, he was enrolled into higher education at fourteen and graduated at eighteen. He went on to teach at Washington College, while working for his Master's degree in dramatic arts. At this period Cain contemplated a career as a professional singer, his mother's profession, but it didn't work out. Cain supported himself as an odd-jobbing journalist in Baltimore before joining the American expeditionary force in Europe in 1918, where he edited an army newspaper. On discharge Cain returned to newspaper work in New York, rising to the position of managing editor of the *New Yorker* in 1931. At this period he was strongly influenced – stylistically and ideologically – by H. L. Mencken, with whom he drank, womanised and had a good time during the 'jazz age', while espousing fashionably left-wing views.

Cain married four times (in 1919, 1927, 1944 and 1947) and was three times divorced. He left an economically depressed New York to work as a Hollywood scriptwriter in 1932. Two years later, at forty-two years old, having been fired by Paramount Studios for drunkenness and with a young family to support, he produced his first novel, *The Postman Always Rings Twice* (1934). Its hero, Frank Chambers, is a drifter and a jailbird – no-good. The setting, vividly portrayed, is Depression-era California. It would be unsurprising to see the Joads' wheezing Hudson 6 roll by. Frank finds himself at a small roadside café and gas station, the Twin Oaks Tavern, about twenty miles outside LA. He bums a meal, intending to leave without paying the naive Greek owner, Nick Papadakis. Then he sees Nick's wife, Cora. Steamy sex, murder and treachery follow. The novel is remarkable for the violence of the love-making ('I bit her. I sunk my teeth into her lips so deep I could feel the blood spurt into my mouth'). It was this that so appalled Raymond Chandler – whose Philip Marlowe always has his pants virtuously zipped. Frank's narrative takes the form of a death-row confession and ends, bleakly, 'Here they come.' The gas chamber awaits.

The Postman Always Rings Twice was hailed as a masterpiece of the newly fashionable 'hardboiled' genre and established Cain as the leading rival of his fellow Baltimoreian, Dashiell Hammett. 'I tried to write as people talk,' he said in explanation of his distinctively spare style. The Cain style was much admired, particularly in his so-called 'California novels', and is cited as an influence on writers as far afield as Camus (specifically *L'Étranger – The Outsider*) and David Mamet. *The Postman Always Rings Twice* was twice adapted for the screen, but even more influential on the evolution of the crime *noir* movie was Billy Wilder's adaptation of Cain's novella *Double Indemnity* (1943), on whose script Raymond Chandler collaborated (very queasily). As adapted for the film, Walter Neff, the narrator hero, is an insurance agent who falls for a client, Phyllis Dietrichson, and, like Frank Chambers, conspires with her to murder the luckless Mr Dietrichson. If the crime can be staged so as to look like an accident, they will collect 'double indemnity' – twice the payoff. It ends bloodily, with a dying Walter dictating a confession into his firm's dictaphone. As successful, on both page and screen, was the melodrama about murder, pie-making, incest and unhappy motherhood, *Mildred Pierce* (1941). Joan Crawford won an Oscar for her performance in the 1946 screen adaptation.

These three works represent Cain's major contributions to literature and film. Of his dozen or so other works, only *Serenade* (1937), the story of a homosexual singer, holds up at all well, although the subsequent film made from it is dire. Although he moved away – ill-advisedly, his admirers think – from the hardboiled scenarios and sharp-edged vernacular dialogue of his early stories, Cain remained fascinated with what he called the 'love rack' – tortured romance scenarios and fatal women.

His late-life efforts to write a higher kind of fiction were poorly received. But the camera always loved James M. Cain, and no less than nine of his novels were adapted into film – with the exception of the three above, forgettably. He always resented the millions the studios were making from his work and attempted, unsuccessfully, to mobilise his fellow screenwriters into a guild in the early 1940s. He drank too much, ulcerated his stomach, and got by – very comfortably – on paperback revenues and film rights. He returned to his native Maryland in 1947, living there, comfortably but furiously, until his death at a great age.

FN   James Mallahan Cain
MRT   *The Postman Always Rings Twice*
Biog   R. Hoopes, *Cain: The Biography of James M. Cain* (2nd edn, 1987)

153. Captain W. E. Johns 1893–1968

Gawd 'elp the 'Un as gets in 'is way today.

Johns is one of that elite corps of authors known to readers by their military rank.
'Captain' W. Golding, or 'Captain' E. Waugh would not trip as easily off the tongue
– but, ironically, both of them really were captains. It was a rank Flying Officer
Johns never achieved, but which he bestowed on himself in later life. It would have
been churlish of the Air Ministry to deny him the small promotion. Johns was not
merely the author of 169 books (for boys, mainly) but, on the strength of the 104
Biggles titles, the RAF's most successful recruiting sergeant (to confuse ranks still
further). Generations of young readers grew up wanting to pilot Sopwiths. Their
children yearned for the 'Spits' of 666 Squadron and, in turn, their children for the
jet-propelled Meteor. Biggles, as chronicled by the Captain Marryat of the air, flew
them all – with grace, insouciance and that Anglo-Saxon cold blood, so envied by
lesser races.

William Earl Johns was born in Hertfordshire, the son of a tailor, the grandson
of a butcher. A bright boy, he attended the local grammar school, already burning
with the ambition to be a soldier. Jingoism, in the wake of the Boer War and the
Khaki Election of 1900 was the spirit of the age. Johns left school at sixteen and
took up work as a sanitary inspector in Norfolk. More to his taste was the Territorial
Army, which he joined – as a private soldier – shortly before the outbreak of war in
1914. At the same period, before leaving for the Front, he married the local vicar's
daughter, Maude (a woman twelve years his senior). The wedding bells pealed loudly
in 1914. For many young men it was the only way not to die a virgin. A son William
was duly born, shortly after. As an ironic observer of an earlier war observed, 'now
they ring their bells. Soon they will wring their hands.'

Johns fought in the doomed Gallipoli campaign, rising, if that's the word, to the
rank of Lance Corporal. After a bout of malaria he was commissioned in September
1917 into the Royal Flying Corps and spent some months in a training unit. Given
the unreliability of the aircraft at the time, it was more dangerous than Passchendaele. In July 1918, he was posted to France to fly heavy bombers (the ugly DH4)

and on 16 September his squadron took off for a raid on Mannheim. His plane was hit over Germany by ack-ack and brought down by attacking fighters. Johns' rear gunner was killed and Johns himself was badly wounded and taken prisoner: there was considerable hostility to bomber crews among the civilian population (in the area Johns came down a whole class of Sunday school children had been killed). Such warfare was, even in wartime, regarded as criminal and Johns was sentenced to be shot. This was commuted and he was transferred to a prisoner-of-war camp at Strasbourg and, after an unsuccessful attempt at escape, to a more secure installation at Ingolstadt. Here he served out the remaining weeks of the war, which ended on 11 November 1918.

Johns had been wrongly listed as missing, presumably killed in action, and no correction was made. His return from the dead on Christmas Day 1918 was unexpected by his (still mourning) family. Had Johns actually been shot dead, the twentieth century would have lost a children's writer second only to Enid Blyton in appeal. Interestingly, the event seems to have affected Johns himself. Biggles is always a fighter, never a bomber pilot – and his ace air skills are invariably used for defensive, not offensive, actions. After the war, Johns' biographers drily note that 'he did not want to return to work as a sanitary inspector'. He obtained a short service commission with the newly formed RAF and was entrusted principally with recruiting duties. In this capacity he rejected one 'John Ross' (Lawrence of Arabia). The rejection was subsequently overturned by higher-ups.

In the postwar years the Johnses' marriage broke down. Maude, the vicar's daughter, denied her husband a divorce and his second, lifelong, union was unsolemnised, although 'Doris May Johns' passed as his wife. Her brother, Howard Leigh, would be the long-serving illustrator of the Biggles books. These were not written, however, until Johns was discharged from the RAF and had made a new career in aviation articles, principally for the juvenile market. Biggles took off in 1932, in *Popular Flying*, a magazine which Johns edited. 'James Bigglesworth' was born in India and educated in England. The first collection *The Camels are Coming* (1932) – Sopwiths, that is, not the humped variety – is closest to the author's own war experience. Biggles is a young pilot, under the paternal care of the old hand, Mahoney. In this collection, he has his one love affair – with a woman who turns out to be a German spy. In the last story in the collection ('The Last Show'), as the war is coming to its end, a battle-fatigued Biggles is on the verge of alcoholism.

Biggles was a huge success and Johns turned out up to four full-length titles a year in the 1930s. Many of the stories recall First World War heroism. In those with a contemporary setting, Biggles is demobilised and runs an air company – while doing nation-saving undercover work for the country's intelligence services (there is a lot of Buchan in these yarns). Biggles now, like William Brown, has his 'gang': Lord Bertie Lissie, the Hon. Algy [Montgomery] Lacey and – for proletarian colour – Flight Sergeant Ginger Hebblethwaite. No women are around. There is nowadays a lively web fanfic archive, fantasising sexual relations between Biggles and his pals.

Johns made himself very unpopular with Whitehall by his constant – and shrewd – criticisms of Air Ministry and government policy. Pressure from high places led to his being fired from his editorships in 1939. On the outbreak of war, another Ministry, that of 'Information' (Propaganda was a word that only the Hun used), reinstated him as an advocate for the RAF. Biggles duly joined up, and did his bit to win the Battle of Britain. The Air Ministry humbly requested Johns to boost WAAF recruitment with a series heroine: he responded with 'Worrals' – Biggles in skirts. The War Office subsequently requested their own hero: Johns came through with the Commando 'Gimlet'.

After the war, Biggles rather thrashed around – like many returned heroes. Most of his missions were as a vaguely defined 'air detective'. A low point was *Biggles: Foreign Legionnaire* (1954). Johns himself was increasingly out of key with his time. A 1964 UNESCO survey identified Biggles as still the most popular juvenile hero in the world, but the formula was wearing very thin. In *Biggles and the Deep Blue Sea* (1968), the hero takes on a gang of slimy hashish-running Arabs. It was the summer of love when many teenagers were getting their kicks puffing rather than glorying vicariously in English pluck (the narrative also features a battle with a giant squid, straight out of Jules Verne). Johns died, making a cup of tea, halfway through his last, never to be completed, volume, *Biggles Does Some Homework*. It would have been 105 – an ace total.

FN   William Earl Johns
MRT *The Camels are Coming*
Biog P. B. Ellis and P. Williams, *By Jove, Biggles! The Life of Captain W. E. Johns* (1981)

154. Phyllis Bentley 1894–1977

Their cause was mine.

Born and brought up in Halifax, Phyllis Bentley was the youngest daughter of a master dyer and finisher. Her mother was from another family enriched in the local cloth trade. Phyllis was brought up in a domestic environment which she called 'essentially proper, essentially respectable, essentially middle-class'. Bentley got her school education, well away from Halifax, at Cheltenham Ladies' College. After gaining a degree (external) from London University it was her plan to go into teaching. After some unhappy months teaching and volunteering locally, with wartime emergency, she went to work in the munitions industry in 1918, eventually gravitating to a post of administrative responsibility in the Ministry of Munitions.

During the First World War she wrote her first work of fiction, a collection of short stories, *The World's Bane*, published at her own cost in 1918. It sold wretchedly, as did Bentley's follow-up titles, *Environment* (1922) and *Cat in a Manger* (1923). Depressing as the sales returns were, there were sufficient friendly reviews – and a native obstinacy – to keep her writing. Moreover, her father having died in 1926, it fell to Bentley to keep the family business afloat and care for her mother. Her career as a regional novelist was inaugurated by an invitation from the Bradford Mechanics' Institute to lecture on the subject, and the event inspired her to start a densely local novel set in the West Riding about unhappy marriage. Indomitable pluck in the face of inexorable gloom would be the theme of much of Bentley's subsequent fiction. *The Spinner of the Years* was published, after rejection by a string of publishers, in 1928. It earned words of praise from Arnold Bennett and – most gratifyingly – J. B. Priestley: England's favourite Yorkshireman.

More significantly for her career, Bentley's historical saga, *Inheritance* (1932), was accepted for publication by the newly set-up and dynamic Victor Gollancz imprint. Gollancz – soon to establish the Left Book Club and become a major force in British socialism – was attracted by the *echt* working-class subject matter and he would be Bentley's publisher for the rest of her long career. Meanwhile the family firm, E. J. Bentley & Sons, had been virtually ruined by the worldwide slump. The effect of the 1930s Depression was particularly harsh on the industrial heartlands of the North and its now massively unemployed population. 'Their cause was mine,' Bentley declares in her autobiography. *Inheritance* chronicles three generations of the Oldroyd and Bamforth families – the first of whom rise and fall ('from clog to clog') as their industry booms and busts over a century of existence. The love interest (master's son falls in love with mill girl, the daughter of a radical; should he marry her or the daughter of a fellow Tory and millowner?) intertwines with social history. The early chapters of *Inheritance*, set in the period of the Napoleonic Wars, depict battles between modernisers and Luddites (Bentley is sympathetic to both sides). The Ten Hours Bill, the chilling effect of the American Civil War, the gradual decline of the industry in the face of overseas competition and, climactically, the 1930s nail-in-the-coffin catastrophe are all chronicled.

Inheritance represented a considerable effort of historical research by Bentley, undertaken in local archives and picked up from Halifax lore – so much so that it has often been prescribed as painless history lessons in schools. Bentley initially intended to finish the novel on her characteristic note of gloom, with the fall of the House of Oldroyd, but was persuaded to introduce a gleam of optimism by a friend's forlorn 'Give us some hope!' The novel was a runaway bestseller – particularly among patrons of the 'tuppenny' cornershop libraries which dominated the distribution of popular fiction in the 1930s. Bentley was encouraged to continue with an Oldroyd trilogy (it was televised in 1967, giving the novels a second lease of bestselling life) and, having hit her groove, she never deviated from it. She followed with a string of some twenty works in a similar vein, with her hallmark regional setting and grim, but plucky, world view (e.g. *A Modern Tragedy*, 1934, another Great Depression saga).

During the Second World War, Bentley served her country a second time, working in the American Division of the Ministry of Information. Over these years she wrote and published her critical monograph, *The English Regional Novel* (1941). It makes clear the kinship she felt, as an Englishwoman, a Yorkshirewoman and a woman writer, with the Brontës – particularly Emily. Like her, Bentley never married. She was awarded an OBE in 1970 to add to the honorary doctorate which the University of Leeds gave her in 1949. Halifax regards her as its most distinguished daughter.

FN   Phyllis Eleanor Bentley
MRT *Inheritance*
Biog E. Ford. 'Phyllis Bentley: novelist of Yorkshire Life', *Contemporary Review*, February 1997

155. Dashiell Hammett 1894–1961

Hammett gave murder back to the kind of people that commit it for reasons.
Raymond Chandler

Hammett was born in Maryland, of Catholic parents. 'Dashiell' was a maternal family name, a corruption of 'De Chiel'. His father was by turns a clerk, a salesman, a streetcar conductor and – most continually – a drunk. There were three children. Hammett was educated in Baltimore, a city ('Poisonville' he later called it) he loved not at all. He left high school at fifteen (some accounts claim thirteen) when – his father failing to do so – he was obliged to provide for the family. He worked as a newsboy, railroad messenger and stevedore. He learned to drink heavily and caught the first of many doses of venereal disease.

From 1915 to 1918, Hammett was employed as a Pinkerton detective agent in Baltimore – three years which supplied the raw material for thirty years of writing. In 1918, he joined the US Army. During the remaining months of the war he served in a home posting in the motor ambulance corps. It was at this period that he contracted the TB and early onset emphysema which plagued his later life. He was discharged in May 1919, with the rank of sergeant and a 25 per cent disability pension. In spring 1920 he left for the West Coast (whose climate was kinder to his lungs) where he worked again for Pinkerton. One of his assignments was the notorious Fatty Arbuckle case in 1921. In the same year he married a nurse, Josephine Nolan, who had attended him in hospital and whom he had got pregnant. They went on to have two daughters.

In 1922 Hammett's TB flared up and writing was the only occupation he could handle. His first 'Continental Op' story was published in *Black Mask* in October 1923. The 'Op' is 'fat, fortyish and the Continental Detective Agency's [i.e. Pinkerton's] toughest and shrewdest operator'. Around him, Hammett constructed formulaic stories featuring crime detection, gang-busting, locked room murders, and high order physical violence – all narrated in cool, laconic, disillusioned, waste-no-words style. He had created a dialect for the 'hard-boiled detective novel': a genre at the other end of the spectrum from the cosy English 'Colonel Mustard in the library' crime novel.

In 1926 Hammett separated from his wife and children on medical advice: he was infectious. Although his doctors' prognoses were gloomy Hammett threw himself into a productive burst of writing over the next four years. In 1929 he published his first book, *Red Harvest*. Initially it was called 'The Cleansing of Poisonville' and featured the 'Continental Op'. It was followed by *The Dain Curse* (1929). Both books sold well and on the strength of their success Hammett abandoned his family and moved, with a girlfriend, to New York, where he was fashionable enough to be taken up by the *New Yorker*, Algonquin Hotel, set. The kind of novel he had patented was not just profitable, it was smart. *The Maltese Falcon* was published in 1930, a runaway bestseller which was reprinted seven times in its first year. It introduced the San Francisco PI, Sam Spade – a man who looks 'rather pleasantly like a blond satan'. Hammett followed it in 1931 with an even better novel, *The Glass Key*. Its title comes from *Alice in Wonderland* and the novel portrays a through-the-looking-glass world in which politics and gangsterism are inseparable. The story is told by Ned Beaumont, a cold-eyed gambler on a lifelong losing streak. *The Glass Key* was the author's personal favourite of his works.

Hammett moved on to Hollywood, and even bigger paydays. Here, momentously, he fell in with Lillian Hellman, a writer for MGM and a budding playwright. She was twelve years younger than he. Their relationship lasted until his death, although after 1942 it is recorded as having been asexual. Hired as a writer for Paramount, Hammett set up house in the Sutton Club Hotel, where he wrote *The Thin Man* (1934). He was, in Hellman's words, 'the hottest thing in Hollywood'. He drank deep with Faulkner and Nathanael West and gained a reputation as a philanderer. He had his own limousine and a black chauffeur, 'Jones' – and, of course, Hellman. Nora and Nick Charles (the 'thin man' and his wife) represent a glamorised version of their sophisticated café life: all martinis, silk sheets and wisecracks. Hellman too would become 'hot' after her hugely acclaimed play, *The Little Foxes*, was produced on Broadway in 1939. But Hammett's literary activity effectively finishes at this point. Over the next few years he was still wealthy from film and radio options on his work, but he was often drunk and missed deadlines. He was now manifestly alcoholic and in early 1936 was hospitalised for several weeks. He whiled away the boredom of sobriety reading Karl Marx.

He had belatedly divorced his wife in 1937, but he and Hellman chose not to marry. Both of them were radicalised by the Spanish Civil War. Hammett carried the brand of the 'premature anti-Fascist' for the rest of his life – something that haunted him in the witch-hunting 1950s. Bravely, Hammett helped organise screenwriters and spoke at communist rallies. In 1941, the second film version of *The Maltese Falcon*, starring Humphrey Bogart and directed by John Huston, was released. A highpoint of film *noir*, it is as faithful to the original novel as the moralistic code of Hollywood allowed.

In 1942, after several attempts, Hammett rejoined the army, aged forty-eight, and served as a military journalist. He was discharged in September 1945, as before with the rank of sergeant: he was not officer class. After the war, in New York, his drinking again spiralled out of control until he finally went on the wagon in 1948. Drunk or sober, he was paralysed by writing block and it was his daily habit to spend hours uselessly at his typewriter. He made no progress with his last work, *Tulip*, which was abandoned around 1952–3. In 1951, he was sent to prison for six months for refusing to testify in a communist-hunting trial. He was fifty-seven years old and tubercular. For the rest of his life, he was persecuted, unmercifully, by the Internal Revenue Service (IRS) for unpaid taxes. The TV and radio networks dropped his serials under pressure from right-wing groups, and his income fell drastically. He had a heart attack in 1955 and died six years later of lung cancer, tended faithfully by Hellman who, after negotiation with the IRS, inherited his copyrights. His family got nothing.

Raymond Chandler, in 'The Simple Art of Murder', observes that 'Hammett gave murder back to the kind of people that commit it for reasons, not just to provide a corpse; and with the means at hand, not hand-wrought duelling pistols, curare, and tropical fish.'

FN   Samuel Dashiell Hammett
MRT *The Glass Key*
Biog R. Layman, *Shadow Man: The Life of Dashiell Hammett* (1981)

POSTSCRIPT

156. Lillian Hellman 1905–1984

Old paint on canvas, as it ages, sometimes becomes transparent. When that happens it is possible, in some pictures, to see the original lines: a tree will show through a woman's dress, a child makes way for a dog, a large boat is no longer on an open sea. That is called pentimento because the painter 'repented,' changed his mind.

Lillian Hellman made her name as a dramatist, scriptwriter, helpmeet to Dashiell Hammett and – in her later years – a memoirist. She may also be claimed, if in a very minor and dubious way, for fiction. In the second of Hellman's three autobiographical volumes, evocatively entitled *Pentimento* (1973), she recalls her years of engaged political activism in 1930s when she was a doughty fighter against European fascism. *Pentimento* was a bestseller and film rights were acquired. One chapter – some fifty pages in the book – was adapted into the film *Julia*, three years later and was very well received and garnered Oscar nominations. It was everywhere accepted as fact, not fiction. The narrative, in both versions, chronicles a friendship in adolescence between Lillian (played in the film by Jane Fonda) and 'Julia' (played by Vanessa Redgrave). The relationship is passionate. 'I have had plenty of time to think about the love I had for her,' Hellman muses: 'too strong and too complicated to be defined as only the sexual yearnings of one girl for another. And yet certainly that was there. I don't know, I never cared, and now it is an aimless guessing game.'

They go their separate ways: Julia to study psychoanalysis in Vienna under Freud, Lillian to fame as a dramatist, and partner to Dashiell Hammett (played in the movie by Jason Robards). Their paths cross again in the mid-1930s and the women's early thirties. Julia has been active in the anti-underground in Germany, specifically the imminent Nazi takeover of Austria. Lillian, at great personal risk, undertakes to bring $50,000 to Julia's group in transit via Berlin to a writers' conference in Russia (Hellman was a staunch Stalinist). During their brief meeting, cash and catch-up information are exchanged and Lillian learns that her friend has a daughter. Some time after her return to the US, she discovers that Julia has been murdered – a heroine of the resistance. So, of course, was Lillian Hellman a heroine.

Stephen Spender, the English poet, caught up with the film in America, where he was lecturing. He had actually been in Vienna in 1934–5. It was a dramatic period of his life: he was there with his gay lover, Tony Hyndman ('Jimmy Younger' in Spender's autobiography, *World Within World*), but while in Austria he had met a dazzling young American psychoanalyst, Muriel Gardiner. She had come to Vienna to study under Freud's circle, had a failed marriage behind her and a young daughter, Connie. Spender fell in love with Muriel, to Tony's immense chagrin. She was the first woman he had slept with and the relationship produced love poetry and a letter of apology to his fellow gay, Christopher Isherwood: 'I find actual sex with women more satisfactory, more terrible, more disgusting,' he reported, enigmatically.

Muriel was, when Spender met her, active in the Viennese underground. She was engaged in the dangerous business of smuggling at-risk Austrians out of the country to safety. Spender hoped to marry her, but delayed fatally, and in the interval she fell in love and married a fellow resistance member, Joseph Buttinger. The Buttingers escaped to America in 1938 before the outbreak of war. Spender, and his second wife Natasha, became their close friends after the war. It was apparent to Spender that 'Julia' must be Muriel (whose underground code-name was 'Mary'), although Hellman never identified her heroine, other than by first name, nor did she ever – in the later legal hubbub – offer any documentary evidence as to who Julia actually was. The problem was, Hellman had never met Gardiner. 'Am I Julia?' Muriel asked in a letter which was never replied to. At the Spenders' encouragement, after the 'who is Julia?' controversy was widely aired (putting a big question mark over the movie), Gardiner wrote her own autobiographical account of her activities in pre-war Vienna, *Code-Name Mary: Memoirs of an American Woman in the Austrian Underground*, published in 1983. Hellman died a year later. She never factually contradicted Gardiner's account, although she resolutely denied it in conversation and correspondence until her dying day. But how had she come by it? All was clear when it emerged that the two women had shared a lawyer, Wolf Schwabacher, who had evidently passed on Gardiner's story. It had lodged, like grit, in Hellman's sensibility and resulted in 'Julia'.

One of the great catfights in American literary history was triggered when Mary McCarthy, on the Dick Cavett talk show, alleged that every word Hellman wrote was a 'lie' – including 'the' and 'and'. It was the wisecrack which stung. In the legal confrontation which followed, McCarthy offered as clinching evidence 'the unbe-lievability of Julia'. She was, of course, no more unbelievable than Anna Karenina or Jane Eyre. Knowingly or unknowingly, Hellman had written not memoir, but a little novel. And, like many novels, a beautiful lie.

FN   Lillian Florence Hellman (later Kober)
MRT *Pentimento*
Biog C. Rollyson, *Lillian Hellman: Her Legend and Her Legacy* (1988)

157. Aldous Huxley 1894–1963

A fully fledged, fuzzy-brained California mystic. John Carey on Huxley

Aldous Huxley died on the same day as JFK: bad career move, as Gore Vidal might say. Half a century on, he survives better than his fiction or his 'philosophical writing' warrant. Two books above all have kept his posthumous reputation buoyant. *Brave New World* (1932) is, on the face of it, as clever but ephemeral as most of Huxley's writing. Its targets (Freud, Ford, meritocracy) and its phobias (sex, sex, sex) have dated badly, or else been overtaken by events. But curriculum framers in schools have always liked dystopias (they generate lively classroom discussion) and, along with *Nineteen Eighty-Four* and *The Handmaid's Tale*, Huxley's vision of life in 'World State, A.F. 632' has been grafted, permanently it would seem, into the British education system. The other book of Huxley's to keep his name fresh is *The Doors of Perception* (1953), which has won its author a place alongside Timothy Leary in the pantheon of Class-A substance evangelism. As biographers stress, Huxley's experiments with mescaline, under the influence of which he was vouchsafed a vision of the chair-ness of chairs, were timid. They resemble nothing so much as nervous Victorian dab-blings with Mr Sludge, the Medium. It's a nice question as to whether Leary or Huxley has destroyed more young brain cells. Huxley has certainly sold more copies.

No writer wrote more clearly from his life wounds than Aldous Huxley. The most grievous of those traumas was the suicide of his older brother, Trevenen, who hanged himself when Aldous was twenty. The event resurfaces, symptomatically, everywhere in his fiction and a particularly vivid depiction comes in the last para-graphs of *Brave New World*. After an orgy of sexual riot followed by self-flagellating disgust, John the Savage, who is too good for the new world, strings himself up in a lighthouse: 'Slowly, very slowly, like two unhurried compass needles, the feet turned towards the right; north, north-east, east.'

Trev killed himself in 1914. The background is tangled and obscure. 'Huxley No. 2,' as he called himself, was a rock-climber, blond, outgoing, well liked. He, like Aldous and Julian, was brilliant and from his cradle marked for intellectual greatness. But for all his gifts, he was haunted by a sense of dynastic inadequacy: the genetic confluence of the Arnold and Huxley clans, with, on one side, the great liberal Matthew Arnold; and on the other, the great nay-sayer Thomas Huxley ('Darwin's Bulldog'). Even Aldous had difficulty living up to it. At Eton, Trev 'worked beyond his strength', bringing on that strange Edwardian condition, 'brain fag' and developing a stammer. He went up to Balliol in 1907, following in Julian's footsteps (Julian would be a lecturer at the college by 1910; Aldous would enter as a scholar in 1913). In 1909 he got a First in Maths. Then, as his career track demanded, he switched to Greats, where, to the amazement of his family, he managed only a Second. For a Huxley-Arnold not to excel was to fail utterly. Trev hung on at Oxford as a postgraduate, helping Aldous, who was held back by his bad eyes (he had gone partially blind while at Eton as a result of an untreated eye infection). In 1913, Trev sat the Civil Service exam and did poorly. 'Huxley No. 2' was a certified second-rater – a fate worse than death.

In 1914, afflicted by fits of melancholia, a condition to which the Huxleys were congenitally prone, the young man was removed to the Hermitage, a private nursing home in Surrey. 'Nerves' were diagnosed – but the main cause of his distress was not divulged until Julian Huxley's autobiography, *Memories*, was published in the 1970s. Trev had fallen in love with one of the maids at the family's country house. She was attractive and intelligent, but indelibly common. In true Arnoldian fashion, the young man resolved to 'raise' her, taking her to plays, concerts and lectures. Sarah, the Huxley family's senior maid, threatened to expose the relationship. As one of the family put it, brutally: 'The girl was village educated in a mild way. It couldn't have worked. His friends could never have been hers; nor hers, his ... We sent her off into London somewhere.'

It was a finely calibrated thing. The elder brother Julian (later to become the world's leading zoologist) could marry a Swiss governess, Juliette Baillot, but no Huxley could marry a *housemaid*. They could, of course, use them sexually; that was one of the conveniences of genteel life. Aldous lost his virginity to an upper servant in 1913, when he was nineteen. He had found himself alone in his father's London house in Westbourne Terrace, and 'decided to go out for a stroll during which he picked up a girl who he assumed to be an au pair on her evening off. He took her back to the house and made love to her on the sofa.' Huxley was, in his biographer Sybille Bedford's words, 'extremely susceptible to pretty women', and this event marked the beginning of an athletically active sexual career. In *Time Must Have a*

Stop (1945), the devirginating initiation is painted more darkly. The nineteen-year-old hero, Sebastian, takes a prostitute back to his father's empty house, for a 'shudderingly' awful experience: loss of virginity amid rubber corsets, 'bored perfunctory kisses' and 'breath that stank of beer and caries and onions'.

Trev, by contrast, wanted desperately to do the right thing by his housemaid, and it is probable that he was sent to the Hermitage – as she was sent 'into London somewhere' – to separate them. If so, it failed disastrously. While he was at the Hermitage, he heard that the girl was pregnant, something he seems previously not to have known. On a Saturday morning in August 1914, Trev left the Hermitage for a walk on the Downs. He did not return. Since he had an appointment in London on Monday there was no great alarm. He had perhaps gone up to town early. When no news had been heard of him after a week, a search was mounted. His body was found in a nearby wood. As a mountaineer he knew all about ropes and their breaking strain. He had climbed a tree, tied a rope around a branch fourteen feet up, put the noose around his neck, and jumped. Both the rope and his neck snapped. His broken and soiled body was found on the ground.

Echoes of Trev's suicide, and what led up to it, hover like a moral stink over all Aldous's fiction. Had his brother done the 'right thing' in the face of having done the 'wrong thing' – or merely succumbed to a second-rater's lack of moral ruthlessness? Servants were there to serve – not least the upper class's sexual requirements. Huxley never quite worked the problem out. His last novel, *Island* (1962), is, as Frank Kermode bluntly says, 'one of the worst novels ever written'. Few have bothered to disagree. Inferior as the book is, the informed reader catches a glimpse of Trev for the last time, *in articulo mortis*. The narrative opens with the hero, Will Farnaby, having fallen from a tree, 'lying like a corpse in the dead leaves, his hair matted, his face grotesquely smudged and bruised, his clothes in rags and muddy'. He has thrown himself down from a cliff-face onto the tree (which broke his fall) on being surprised by a snake. Will, however, is not in Surrey but in a South Seas Eden. He survives to endure the barrage of Buddhistic-rationalist preaching that all Huxley's later heroes have to put up with. Weaker men would throw themselves off the cliff again. Was Trev the weaker, or the stronger, or merely the unluckier of the brilliant Huxley brothers? Aldous could never decide.

FN   Aldous Leonard Huxley
MRT   *Brave New World*
Biog N. Murray, *Aldous Huxley* (2002)

158. J. B. Priestley 1894–1984

Priestley became in the months after Dunkirk a leader second only in importance to Mr Churchill. And he gave us what our other leaders have always failed to give us – an ideology. Graham Greene

J. B. Priestley was born in Bradford, the son of a schoolmaster. His mother, an Irishwoman – 'probably a clogs-and-shawl mill girl' – died two years after her son's birth, leaving him to be brought up by a kindly stepmother. His origins in Bradford ('Bruddesford') coloured his subsequent life. Socialism he inherited from his 'puritanical' father; puritanism, signally, he did not. Libido and labour intertwined throughout his adult life. On leaving grammar school, Priestley had his first employment in a wool merchant's office. He read H. G. Wells's *The History of Mr Polly* in 1910 and lost his virginity in 1913. There was some local journalism – nothing to prophesy great things, although it was clear that his future was not in wool. Priestley volunteered ('chump that I was') on the outbreak of war and served in the infantry, rising to the rank of subaltern. He was lucky only to be wounded (multiply but not cripplingly) and gassed. Lieutenant Priestley finished his service for king and country in the Entertainment Unit of the British Army. The experience of Haig's 'sausage machine' sickened and hardened his socialism and class consciousness – and, possibly, his Anglophobia. Orwell, never a friend, suspected him of Soviet sympathies during the Cold War.

On being demobbed in 1919, Priestley took up a place at Trinity Hall, Cambridge. The war's carnage had left places for northern grammar school boys like him. He read history and graduated with a 2:1. He already had a wife and a child (and, quite soon, a pregnant mistress). On graduation he went to London where he freelanced as a journalist. In 1925 his wife Pat died of cancer and Priestley made a second marriage to Jane Wyndham Lewis in 1926. This relationship was strained by his infidelities – notably a steaming affair with the young actress, Peggy Ashcroft. Although his image was that of a plain man's 'Jolly Jack' – and he was facially as ugly as a 'potato' – Priestley's adult life was sexually athletic.

In his early London years Priestley became friendly with the bestselling novelist, Hugh Walpole. The two of them concocted a 'correspondence novel', *Farthing Hall*, in 1929 – it was a useful apprenticeship. Priestley's first novel under his own name, *The Good Companions* (1929) was astonishingly successful, selling thousands of copies every day in its first months of publication. The novel is dedicated to Walpole, 'for a friendship that has even triumphantly survived a collaboration' and is a modern picaresque ('gas-fire Dickens', his publisher called it), dealing with a travelling troupe of players with the unhappy name, the 'Dinky Doos', who specialise in a 'non-stop programme of Clever Comedy and Exquisite Vocalism'. Plot complications follow. It was sneered at by the literary elite. 'If I wrote *Anna Karenina* they'd still say I was turning out twaddle for the mob,' he complained, bitterly. The hauteur of London critics was something that rather disinclined him towards fiction in later years when he aimed at being a sage.

Angel Pavement (1930) did as well with the 'mob', and, unlike its predecessor, made the American bestseller list. The tone is grimmer, reflecting the post 1929 slump. 'Not a glimmer of sentimentality', as Priestley put it. The action centres on the firm of Twigg & Dersingham, eminently stuffy dealers in veneer and inlay, based in 'Angel Pavement', a sleepy cul-de-sac in the City. The business shenanigans of a 'piratical' chancer, James Golspie, drive the plot.

In later life, Priestley referred to these two unashamedly middle-brow works as his 'golden gushers'. He had struck it rich and could move to a mansion in Highgate – where the Hampstead intellectuals lived. In 1934, he published his Cobbett-inspired *English Journey*, whose reportage brought home the working-class realities of the slump to middle-class England. In Hollywood, in the mid-1930s, where his services were in demand, Priestley came across the pseudo-scientific theories of Ouspensky, Jung and – most influentially – J. W. Dunne. The result was his 'time plays', *I Have Been Here Before* (1937), *Time and the Conways* (1937), *An Inspector Calls* (1946), and a work of science fiction and apocalypse, set in Arizona, *The Doomsday Men* (1938). 'Twaddle', indeed.

Just as successful was the romantic comedy of newly-wed complications in Yorkshire, *When We Are Married* (1938) – the first play ever to be televised. By the outbreak of war, in 1939, Priestley was finally the English sage he had always wanted to be. He could easily have gone to America, but stayed to face the music – which would have been very hot, had the Gestapo got hold of him. Priestley was outspokenly patriotic during the Second World War, particularly in his BBC *Postscripts*, after the Sunday 9 o'clock news, in the perilous months after Dunkirk. As Graham Greene said, only Churchill was more efficacious in raising the fighting spirit of the English people. Churchill – or others in authority – did not relish the comparison and, it is alleged, got him off the air. Priestley's left-wing views – and harping on about 'new world orders' after victory – were the given explanation. His attempt, later in the war, to enter active politics with his idiosyncratically conceived 'Common Wealth Party' failed.

Priestley could none the less sting as a political gadfly and was a founder member of the Campaign for Nuclear Disarmament, during the Cold War. He had public, knockabout, quarrels with highbrow adversaries such as F. R. Leavis and toffs like Evelyn Waugh. His trump card was always his sales, his box office receipts, his national fame, the love of the 'mob'. He divorced his wife Jane (who had been heroically complaisant) in 1952 to make a third, lasting, marriage, after years of mutual adultery, in 1953 with the writer and archaeologist Jacquetta Hawkes. The British people liked him the more for his honest, straight-speaking radicalism. He was always the most amiable of dissidents, in his Yorkshire tweed, puffing thought-fully on the inevitable pipe, speaking 'sense' and – as he confessed – constitution-ally 'tactless', convinced that he had 'a hell of a talent', but no genius. Even Mrs Thatcher liked him, although it was in James Callaghan's premiership ('Sunny Jim' was very much a politician in the Priestley mould) that the Queen awarded him his Order of Merit in 1977. He had turned down two peerages on socialist principle.

None of his later novels have lasted, even those, such as the two-volume *The Image Men* (1968), which he thought his best work. Nor has his great literary-philosophical work, *Literature and Western Man* (1960) endured. His principal success, in the last phase of his career, was the partnership in 1963 with Iris Murdoch, on the dramatic adaptation of her novel *The Severed Head*. He was, in his later years, one of England's cultural 'teddy bears', in the mould of John Betjeman and his fellow Yorkshireman, Alan Bennett: the incarnation of English grumpy niceness. And the author of two enduringly readable novels.

FN   John Boynton Priestley
MRT   *Angel Pavement*
Biog   V. Brome, *J. B. Priestley* (1988)

159. Henry Williamson 1895–1977

He offended. Daniel Farson's epitaph on Williamson

Had Hitler won the war, Henry Williamson might well have been installed as Minister of Fiction. But Hitler lost, and Williamson was cast into oblivion. His biographer, Daniel Farson, offers a pathetic vignette of the novelist sitting in his 'writing hut' at the bottom of his garden, waiting for honours and reviews that would never come. The bloody traitor should have stuck to otters was the general verdict. Williamson was born near Lewisham, one of the sons of a city bank clerk with whom his relationship was, at best, cold. After an unhappy few weeks as a city clerk himself, he eagerly signed up aged nineteen ('sixteen' he liked to boast) so as 'not to miss the fun' on the outbreak of war in 1914. He was in the frontline in weeks. Williamson's whole worldview was transformed by an event there, at Christmas 1914, when an unofficial truce led to a friendly meeting between enemy soldiers in no man's land. 'There, on the one side,' he recalled 'were all the Germans in field-grey, together with our chaps, all talking and exchanging photographs.' Chaps together.

As momentous was his experience of his first offensive, a few weeks later. Exhilaration at the opening barrage ('like the end of Wagner's *The Ring*') gave way to horror, terror and despair, as the 'push' slaughtered men by the hundred thousand. Williamson was commissioned in June 1915, fell apart at the Somme, and was invalided back to England, shell-shocked in 1917. His breakdown is chronicled in *The Patriot's Progress* (1930). He wrote no less than seven novels about the war. Men who had gone through what he went through, Williamson believed, became solitary, anti-social and inherently anti-patriotic, for the rest of their lives. His two marriages –both of which ended in separation – were troubled by a chronic inability to form long-lasting relationships, or to stay faithful within them. Relations with his numerous children were similarly troubled.

After an unhappy year at home, in which he bounced about in various menial journalistic jobs, drank too much, and seriously contemplated suicide, he was thrown out by his father and went to live in a cottage in Georgeham, north Devon, on his £40 p.a. army disability pension. Here he began writing seriously. At this period there occurred what he records as the other most important event in his life: his discovery of Richard Jefferies' books. He also married in 1925; there would be six children. Between 1918 and 1928, his energies were directed to the quartet of connected novels published as *The Flax of Dream*. Like all of Williamson's anthropocentric work, it is a version of his own life. The hero, Willie Maddison, he called his 'brother'. The setting is an idyllic Devon, a region for which, although not born there, Williamson's feeling rivalled Hardy's (he made the obligatory pilgrimage to Max Gate, where he talked too much).

Fame came with the publication of a book about one of the few inhabitants of North Devon that Williamson had time for. *Tarka the Otter: His Joyful Water-life and Death in the Country of the Two Rivers* proved hard to write. The manuscript was revised seventeen times, and rejected by various publishers. Once in print, in 1927, it won the Hawthornden Prize, became a bestseller, and a reliable source of income for the rest of his life. His attitude to the animal world, depicted in *Tarka*, was unsentimental. He had nothing against otter- fox- and stag-hunting and his own behaviour to animals could be brutal. 'He is alleged', his biographer writes, 'to have seized a kitten and smashed its brains out on the kitchen floor when he caught it destroying the fish dinner laid out in honour of a titled guest.'

In the 1930s, Williamson – one of whose grandparents was German – became intoxicated by the rise of Nazism and what he saw on a trip to Bavaria in 1935. 'The feeling I had while among the masses of people listening to Adolf Hitler at Nuremberg', he rhapsodised, 'was one of their happiness and goodness.' Provocatively, he wrote a preface to the collective reissue of *The Flax of Dream* series in 1936, enlarging on this Nazi goodness. He fantasises a meeting between himself and a certain corporal, in that momentous Christmas 1914 truce. The preface, less lyrically, describes 'Jews from the ghettoes of Poland ... who become property owners of houses, streets of houses, small businesses and firms, almost overnight'. And it concludes with the sentence that sealed Williamson's fate: 'I salute the great man across the Rhine, whose life symbol is the happy child.'

Hitler was one god; during this period Williamson also hero-worshipped T. E. Lawrence. In a letter of May 1936, he described Hitler as the 'father of his people: a man like T. E. Lawrence'. Lawrence of Arabia, Williamson believed, was the man who could save England. He was, or believed himself to be, on the verge of setting up a meeting between his two heroes, just before T. E. Shaw (i.e. Lawrence) had a fatal accident on his motorcycle in May 1935, having just telegrammed Williamson (did the Zionists do it?).

In the late 1930s, a period in which he was shoulder-to-shoulder with Oswald Mosley's British Union of Fascists, Williamson moved to Norfolk where he bought a smallholding which he farmed, on progressive principles. During the Second World War he was questioned by the authorities, briefly imprisoned, but not, as he later claimed, interned. His mode of life was so hermit-like that ostracism had no great impact. And he was so unimportant politically that any martyrdom was denied him. After the war Williamson returned to Exmoor and cottage life. Here he embarked on a second autobiographical saga, the fifteen-part *A Chronicle of Ancient Sunlight*. It was begun in 1951 and concluded in 1969, with *The Gale of the World* – a novel in which Williamson recklessly blackguarded what few friends he had. The first volumes, which take in the war years, are among the best things he ever did. But he had difficulties finding top-rated publishers and the novels came into the world reviewless. One critic called the *Chronicle* 'the most unfashionable novel of our time'. It went beyond fashion, however, into the question raised by Céline in France: how much political poison does it take to destroy literary genius?

Or how much psychic trauma? Williamson's second marriage broke up as his saga was concluding. Their son remembered him 'beating up my mother, and bruises and screams, and I would come along and I would attack and as soon as I attacked him he would start crying, and say "What am I doing, that my son should have to stop me beating my wife" ... I think it was something to do with the pressure of war.' After his second wife left him, Williamson was what he had always wanted to be, solitary – but not lonely. Well into his seventies, it is recorded, he retained his sexual appeal. He died, bemused and senile, having sweltered through the summer of 1976, looking, as one of his sons put it, 'like a mummified Viking'.

FN   Henry William Williamson
MRT *The Patriot's Progress*
Biog D. Farson, *Henry, An Appreciation of Henry Williamson* (1982)

160. Louis Bromfield 1896–1956

I wanted peace and I wanted roots.

A writer who, in his maturity, occupied the dubious territory between literary respectability and bestsellerdom, Bromfield was born 'Brumfield' in Ohio, of Scottish/American pioneer extraction, into a farming family. He was destined to take over the family farm and duly enrolled at Cornell University to study agriculture but, at the age of nineteen, resolved on a drastically different vocation, switching to courses in journalism at Columbia. As his later career would reveal, his attachment to farming was not extinguished – merely postponed. In the First World War years, 1917–19, Bromfield served with the French army as an ambulance driver, winning a Croix de Guerre for gallantry and the Légion d'honneur. He had broken off his studies to serve and Columbia awarded him an 'honorary war degree'. He returned to his country a hero and settled in New York where he picked up what work he could as a journalist, marrying socialite Mary Appleton Wood in 1921. Despite the ubiquitous delinquencies of Prohibition and the Jazz Age, the marriage proved happy and durable.

Bromfield's first novel, *The Green Bay Tree*, was published in 1924. Like everything he wrote, it evinced stylistic loyalty to the great English and American realists. Bromfield always went for firm storylines, strongly drawn characters and plain prose. His early fiction comprised what he called 'panel novels', or novels written to a blueprint design. *The Green Bay Tree* employs a familiar 'New Woman' scenario; the heroine, Ellen Tolliver, is a pianist who leaves her small American town for cultural freedoms offered by the larger world. Conflicts ensue.

Bromfield followed up with *Possession* (1925), which consolidated his new line of work as a novelist who could live by his pen. In the same year, 1925, he embarked on what was initially intended to be a vacation in France, which turned into a fourteen-year-long sojourn. He settled with his family at Senlis, outside Paris, where two of his three daughters were born. In France, as one of the 'lost generation', Bromfield befriended, among other advanced spirits, Gertrude Stein and Ernest Hemingway (whom he helped get into print). His next novel *Early Autumn* (1926) won a Pulitzer Prize, and showed little trace of the lost generation's experimentalism or daring. Whatever else, Louis Bromfield was not 'lost': few novelists have directed their careers more profitably. *A Good Woman* (1927) marked Bromfield's entry into the bestseller lists – where he would occupy a secure berth for a decade. This story of a mother in the Midwest who sacrifices her prospects in life for the well-being of her child, was to the taste of middle-class, Book of the Month club-subscribing America. So too was *The Strange Case of Miss Annie Spragg* (1928), which recounts the life (told after her death) of an American spinster who has just died in Italy.

In 1932 Bromfield spent four months in India, a country which preoccupies much of his later fiction. At the same period, he returned to the US. 'I wanted peace and I wanted roots for the rest of my life,' he recalls in his autobiography. Those roots, he determined, were in Ohio – not Paris, or New York. The decision to go back is reflected in *The Farm* (1933), an agrarian saga covering 100 years of farming life in Ohio, which is Bromfield's finest effort in fiction. But in 1935 he revisited India. It was the prelude to his greatest popular success in fiction, *The Rains Came* (1937), set in the Indian state of 'Ranchipur', ruled by an enlightened and progressive Maharajah and Maharani. The country is still under British colonial rule, represented in the novel by two doctrinaire tyrants, Lord Esketh and General Agate. Tom Ransome, a rich Anglo-American artist, has come to India to find some meaning in his otherwise empty life. He finds it. The climax is the bursting of a mighty dam, an equivocal symbol of progress and the imposition of Western notions of civilisation on the Orient. The monsoon endures. Bromfield was virulently anti-British in this phase of his life – sentiments reflected in his polemic *England, a Dying Oligarchy* (1939).

The Rains Came rode high in American bestseller lists for two years and was adapted into a wildly melodramatic movie in 1939. It installed Bromfield on Hollywood's celebrity A-list. In 1945, it was he who hosted the wedding of his friends, Humphrey Bogart and Lauren Bacall. Now very rich, Bromfield bought three large tracts of land in Richland County, Ohio, in 1939, renaming them 'Malabar Farm'. He introduced progressive agrarian techniques and made his name as an innovative pioneer of 'sustainable' farming. His estate is now an Ohio State Park. Probably of the millions who visit, relatively few know that he was a novelist. There are worse literary monuments. He continued to churn out novels in the 1940s and 1950s. Always solidly popular with a loyal corps of readers, his fiction was no longer bestselling nor critically fashionable. Thirty years after his death, he was posthumously elected to the Ohio Agricultural Hall of Fame.

FN   Louis Bromfield (né Brumfield)
MRT   *The Farm*
Biog   D. D. Anderson, *Louis Bromfield* (1964)

161. Peter Cheyney 1896–1951

Prince of hokum

If Cheyney is remembered at all, it is as a mass producer of ersatz 'Yank' thrillers for the British market and upmarket gangster *noir* for the French market (more fools them). At his zenith (1936–46), Cheyney was selling up to 5 million a year, with beyond-parody titles such as *Dames Don't Care* (1937), *Dangerous Curves* (1939), *Your Deal, My Lovely* (1941). Cheyney 'out-Wallaced Edgar Wallace' in his best years. The Cheneyesque bouquet may be sampled by the following, where an under-cover G-Man is explaining to a low down dirty rat that he is about to be rubbed out: '"Listen, wop," I tell him, "An' you ought to listen because you ain't goin' to hear any more after this. I'm goin' to make a certainty of you. I'm goin' to finish you like the lousy rat you are."'

Cheyney was born, *echt* cockney, in Whitechapel, the son of an oystermonger. His salvation was a mother who took charge of her five children, kicking out their Billingsgate-and-booze stinking dad, to make herself proprietor of an Oxford Street corsetière emporium. Kate Cheyney was tigerishly ambitious for her sons, particularly 'Reggie'. She contrived to get him into a minor public school and thence a 'respectable' job as a lawyer's clerk. It was a huge step up from the fish barrow, but he had his eye on higher, less Pooterish things than Mum wanted. Cheyney's friend Michael Harrison, whose biography is entitled, uncompromisingly, *Peter Cheyney: Prince of Hokum*, infers that Cheyney's sexuality was deformed by his overpowering mother. He would marry three times, childlessly. 'Reggie' was initially drawn to the West End music hall. He wrote patter and song lyrics, and occasionally trod the boards himself. His brother, Arthur, was a stage performer who routinely warmed up audiences for Chaplin and Karno.

Like all his generation, Cheyney was swept up into the First World War in which he claimed, throughout life, to have been 'severely' wounded as an officer in the Royal Warwickshire, leading his men over the top into battle. In fact, he received a nick on the earlobe barely more serious than that which women endured for their earrings. No wound was blightier: on the strength of it, he wangled a desk-job in his English depot, rising to the lowly rank of lieutenant at the time of his 'demob'. But showbiz still called and Cheyney married a music hall starlet, Dorma Leigh, in 1919. The marriage certificate records the groom as 'Captain Evelyn Cheyney' and the wedding photo has him in uniform with three pips and a suspicious row of medals. He would in later life double-barrel himself as 'Southouse-Cheyney' and affect a gold monocle and the de rigueur tortoise-shell cigarette holder.

The marriage collapsed in a couple of years, on vague 'conjugal' issues. Throughout the jazzy 1920s and bleak 1930s, 'Peter', as he now was, scraped a living in the Soho-based entertainment world. In 1933, his career stabilised, with an editorial post on the *Sunday Graphic*. His politics were now right-wing and he was a supporter and friend of Oswald Mosley. He had been ingrained with casual anti-Semitism from his early years in Whitechapel. Cheyney's personal life further stabilised with remarriage in 1934. Like the first, the union was convenient rather than passionate. The second Mrs Cheyney was the daughter of a colonial DC, divorced, possessed of two children, money and class. Now closing on forty, Cheyney finally found his *métier*. In 1936 he published his first FBI agent 'Lemmy Caution' ('let me caution you') tale, *This Man is Dangerous*. The books were marketed, astutely, by William Collins, with elegantly kitsch jacket illustrations by John Pisani. Over the next fifteen years, Cheyney's output was prolific: 150 full-length novels and short-story collections – the bulk was constructed around series heroes. Partnering Caution was Slim Callaghan, first introduced in 1938, a seedily mackintoshed, 100-fag-a-day smoking Sam Spade, with an office in High Holborn. During the Second World War, Cheyney came up with the 'Dark' series of spy novels, featuring the activities of a secret espionage unit, under the command of spymaster Everard Peter Quayle. These are reckoned the high point of a resolutely low-flying literary career.

Despised by the literary in Britain and unread in America, Lemmy Caution attracted a cultish following among French intellectuals – confirming, one imagines, Anglo-Saxon suspicions about that strange crew. The American émigré actor, Eddie Constantine, first appeared as Caution in *La Môme Vert-de-gris* (*The Gun Moll*) in 1953. With his pocked, Bogartian mannerisms, the former lover of Edith Piaf brought an authentic tough-guy chic to the image. The Parisian *culte Cheyney* reached its apogee in 1965 with Jean-Luc Godard's film *Alphaville*, starring Constantine and subtitled –without exaggeration – 'a strange adventure of Lemmy Caution'. It is sad that Cheyney never lived to chortle at its strangeness.

He made a third marriage in 1948 and died, prematurely, three years later, vastly corpulent and wholly exhausted. Drink, as with his father, may have been a cause. Overwriting was certainly another. He left the huge sum of £52,000, a

Times obituary of amazing mendacity, and a bizarre place in the Parisian literary pantheon.

FN   Reginald Evelyn Peter Southouse Cheyney
MRT *This Man is Dangerous*
Biog M. Harrison, *Peter Cheyney: Prince of Hokum* (1954)

162. Scott Fitzgerald 1896–1940; and Zelda 1900–1948

I think my novel is about the best American novel ever written. Fitzgerald to Maxwell Perkins about *The Great Gatsby*

Francis Scott Key Fitzgerald was born in St Paul, Minnesota, the first surviving child of a wicker-furniture manufacturer. He was named in honour of a distant relative, Francis Scott Key, who wrote the American national anthem, 'The Star-Spangled Banner'. If he did not write the Great American Novel, Fitzgerald had a lifelong connection with the Great American Song. Both Scott's parents were Catholics. His father was from Maryland, old enough to remember the Civil War. Edward Fitzgerald imbued his son with the genteel values, and exquisite manners, of the 'Old South'. His mother Mollie was second-generation Irish, with 'new money' (from the grocery wholesale business) in her family background. In 1898, when Edward's business failed, the family moved to New York State where he took up work as a salesman for the pharmaceutical firm, Procter and Gamble. When Edward was dismissed from that job, in 1908, the family moved back to St Paul, where Mollie Fitzgerald's inherited money saw them through. The sense of having been once wealthy and now 'poor' scarred young Scott indelibly: the glamour of money was the great theme of his life. None the less the Fitzgeralds were well enough off for him to attend a Catholic 'prep' school in New Jersey. He was already writing furiously and intending to make it his career.

In 1913 Fitzgerald entered Princeton University. Here he continued to concentrate on writing and football and neglected his studies. He left Princeton, without graduating, in 1917, when America entered the First World War, to take a commission in the infantry. Expecting to die on the field of battle, Fitzgerald dashed off a novel ('The Romantic Egotist' – a self-revealing title) as his epitaph. He sent it off to the prestigious publisher, Scribner's, who rejected it while expressing interest in this gifted but still unfledged author. In 1918 Lieutenant Fitzgerald was posted to Montgomery, Alabama. Here he fell in love with an eighteen-year-old, golden-haired belle, Zelda Sayre, and she with him. The daughter of an Alabama Supreme Court judge, the Sayres had no high opinion of Zelda's beau. As her biographer, Nancy Milford, puts it: 'Fitzgerald was a charming and attractive but uncertain young man; he had not graduated from Princeton, he was Irish, he had no career to speak of, he drank too much, and he was a Catholic.' Despite this catalogue of faults the couple became engaged, with the understanding that they would marry when he had the means to support her in the (expensive) style to which Miss Sayre was accustomed.

The war ended in November 1918, denying Fitzgerald the opportunity to win his spurs. On demobilisation, he went off to New York, intending to make his fortune with his pen and marry Zelda. She, however, was unwilling to wait for his fame and broke off the engagement. It was altogether a bad time for Fitzgerald. Scribner's again rejected 'The Romantic Egotist' but remained perversely encouraging. Fitzgerald had better luck with short stories for the glossy magazines ('slicks') which boomed in the post-war period. He would, over the course of his career, dash off 160 of them, and they were always a sure source of income. *The Great Gatsby*, which hovers, ambiguously, between novel and novella in length, draws on the author's early mastery of the short fiction form. Finally, with the aid of Scribner's brilliant chief editor, Maxwell Perkins, Fitzgerald came through with something publishable. *This Side of Paradise*, which drew heavily on the author's Princeton experience, was published in March 1920. It was an instant bestseller and Fitzgerald was, at twenty-four, a literary celebrity. A week after the novel's publication he and Zelda married.

The roaring 1920s was a decade made for Scott and Zelda (and, in 1921, their only child, Scottie – cute as her name suggests). He was the laureate of the jazz age and in many ways its icon: the camera loved him. The most admired of all celebrities and buoyed up with his apparently inexhaustible literary earnings, Fitzgerald moved between fashionable resorts in Europe and America (including, significantly for *The Great Gatsby*, a spell in Great Neck in 1922). His second novel, *The Beautiful and Damned* (1922), enjoyed similar success, while confirming the cult of 'beautiful losers' to be found in all his mature work. Fitzgerald was even at this early stage displaying the symptoms of alcoholism and Zelda the early signs of her later dementia. Also evident was a growing artistic tension between the couple. As he went from success to success, Zelda failed – as a would-be ballet dancer and a novelist – to rival her husband's triumphs: her only novel, *Save Me the Waltz* was published in 1936. It provoked behaviour that was increasingly irrational.

In April 1924 the Fitzgeralds departed the hectic world of Prohibition America and settled in the French Riviera, where Scott set to work on his third novel, *The Great Gatsby*. Its composition, and the Fitzgeralds' marriage, were threatened by Zelda's falling in love with the French aviator Edouard Jozan. Despite the distraction,

Fitzgerald, by now a consummate craftsman, laboured on this work in collaboration with his editor Perkins. *The Great Gatsby* was published in April 1925. A few weeks later, in Paris, Fitzgerald met Ernest Hemingway – a novelist still to make his name. Their friendship would be close, complex and brutally competitive. For Fitzgerald it would also be destructive.

The Great Gatsby did not enjoy the unequivocal success of its predecessors. More-over, even with the large sums he was earning from his short stories and film rights, they were always broke. Money problems would afflict Fitzgerald for the remainder of his career. The couple spent the next few years mostly in France (the main setting for his fourth novel, *Tender is the Night*). Like other expatriate Americans, they were hit hard by the 1929 crash; and the long Depression which followed made Fitzgerald seem, along with the jazz age he personified, historically irrelevant. When it was published, belatedly, in 1933, *Tender is the Night* registered a distinct slump in his appeal.

In 1930 Zelda suffered the first of a series of breakdowns. Despite psychiatric treatment (which was cripplingly expensive), her condition worsened until she was permanently under professional care in the mid-1930s. Their daughter, Scottie, was largely looked after by friends, although Fitzgerald remained a solicitous father. But his drinking was now out of control: this was the period which he called 'The Crack Up'. Friends like Hemingway believed he would never write a good novel again unless he ditched his 'nutty' wife, which Fitzgerald – true to his cradle Catholicism – resolutely declined to do. In the last three years of his life, Fitzgerald (a 'forgotten man', as he now thought himself) worked as a well-paid, but undistinguished, scriptwriter in Hollywood. He has no major screen credits and his drinking led to his being regarded as unreliable by the studios. A vivid depiction of Fitzgerald in these last, wretched, years is given in Budd Schulberg's novel *The Disenchanted* (1950). A rueful self-portrait is given in Fitzgerald's 'Pat Hobby' stories, and their Hollywood-hack, drink-sodden, comic hero.

Yet his genius was not quite extinguished. Fitzgerald's hugely promising Hollywood novel, *The Last Tycoon*, was only half finished at the time of his death, in December 1940. He died of a heart attack in the apartment of his mistress, the gossip columnist Sheilah Graham. Zelda survived until 1948, when she died in a fire at the hospital in which she had been confined.

FN   Francis Scott Key Fitzgerald; Zelda Fitzgerald (née Sayre)
MRT   *The Great Gatsby*; *Save Me the Waltz*
Biog Arthur Mizener, *The Far Side of Paradise* (2nd edn, 1965); N. Milford, *Zelda: A Biography* (1970)

163. Scott Fitzgerald 1896–1940;
Ernest Hemingway 1899–1961

I'm not going to get into the ring with Tolstoy. Ernest Hemingway
The victor belongs to the spoils. F. Scott Fitzgerald

According to Scott Donaldson, the idea for an interfused Fitzgerald/Hemingway biography came to him in a dream of the two novelists going at each other hammer and tongs in a boxing ring. It was, even as fantasy-pugilism, a mismatch: 'Ernest simply used Scott as a punchbag.' But Fitzgerald would not fall. The dream gave Donaldson his biographer's key: 'Hemingway needed to strike out at his former friend at least as much as Fitzgerald wanted or needed to be hurt.' Their 'failed friendship' was founded on a reciprocal and destructive neediness – Hemingway vs. Fitzgerald. Donaldson's approach is gimmicky – but points to an observable fact about writing novels. It is, among all else, a competitive, sometimes a gladiatorial, activity. There are winners and losers: and combat – insofar as literature permits it – as much as luck, patronage or merit often determines who wins and who loses. According to Donaldson, the pattern of the Fitzgerald–Hemingway fisticuffs falls into three phases. Fitzgerald, the older man by three years, became famous early with *The Beautiful and Damned* (1922). When the writers first met in the Dingo Bar in Paris in April 1925, Hemingway still had his name to make. They bonded instantly and took off on a boozy trip to Lyons, swilling five bottles of Macon in the car. Fitzgerald was 'as excited as a girl', Hemingway later recalled.

As in love, so in literary friendships, there is always one who admires and one who lets himself be admired. Fitzgerald was the smaller man physically, had never seen war, and had any number of neuroses. 'Sissy' was one of the unfriendly words Hemingway would apply to his admirer; 'pretty', 'coward' and 'butterfly' were others. Fitzgerald introduced his friend to Maxwell Perkins, editor to the great. 'He's the real thing,' he wrote, lapsing as everyone who met Ernest did into Hemingwayese. Fitzgerald loaned Hemingway money and gave crucial advice on changes to *The Sun Also Rises* (1926) – assistance that in later life Hemingway was at pains to deny. For his part, Fitzgerald succumbed somewhat to the 'awful pull' of the Hemingway style. Over the next five years, Hemingway's star rose high; meanwhile Fitzgerald toiled unavailingly to produce a worthy successor to *Gatsby*. He sold his literary soul churning out 'crap' short stories for the 'slicks' – glossy magazines. He and his wife Zelda turned self-destruction into a ruinous lifestyle. Fitzgerald drank himself paralytic; she went crazy.

Unlike Hemingway (who had four wives, all abused), Fitzgerald could never discard his women. Hemingway saw this as a failure: 'Poor old Scott,' he sighed, 'he should have swapped Zelda when she was still saleable five or six years before she was diagnosed as nutty.' As the years rolled on, 'poor Scott' was the invariable epithet. Why was he to be pitied? Because he was too easily intoxicated by cheap glamour. He was too easily intoxicated by expensive liquor. He couldn't 'hold it'. Hemingway, of course, approved of excessive drinking. 'A man does not exist until he is drunk,' he believed. But you had to drink like a man, not a girl on her first date. Above all, Hemingway thought that 'poor Scott' lacked discipline as an artist. He 'cheated too damned much'; there was 'too much bloody flashy writing' in his fiction; his was a 'lovely, golden, wasted talent'. With friends like Hemingway, who needs critics?

In the last phase of their relationship, before Fitzgerald's premature death at the age of forty-four, their relationship was conducted almost entirely through Maxwell Perkins. The pendulum had, in fifteen years, swung all the way. 'Hemingway is the best writer in the USA today,' Fitzgerald wrote at the end of his short life. 'I used to want to be the best damn writer in the USA. I still do.' His last royalty cheque was for an ominous $13.13. 'My God,' he wrote, 'I am a forgotten man.' He, unlike Ernest, would never win the Nobel.

Everyone knows two things about the writers' friendship. One is Hemingway's wisecrack when Fitzgerald observed, 'The very rich are different from you and me.' 'Yes,' Hemingway shot back, 'they have more money.' Donaldson establishes that the putdown is a total Hemingway invention. It still circulates, viciously scathing Fitzgerald's memory – as it was intended to. The other universally known truth is that Fitzgerald consulted Hemingway after Zelda complained that his penis was 'too small'. Was it, Fitzgerald timidly inquired over lunch in Michaud's restaurant? Hemingway summoned him into the 'consulting room' (i.e. the men's lavatory) where he examined the organ. It wasn't all *that* small, he concluded. Hemingway then took Fitzgerald off to the Louvre, where the two greatest American novelists of their time spent an afternoon solemnly measuring the appendages on Greek statues. It is not recorded whether Papa flashed his.

Was there a homoerotic element in this obsessed friendship? 'I'm half feminine,' Fitzgerald once confessed. On his part, Hemingway was brought up as a little girl during the formative years of his childhood. His 'exhumed' novel, *The Garden of Eden*, revealed a surprising fascination with sexual role-play in this manliest of writers. Donaldson examines the homoerotic thesis scrupulously, but finally comes round to a simpler explanation: They were drunks; both of them drank to keep depression at bay. Fitzgerald called his attacks 'stoppies'; for Hemingway they were the 'black ass'. The only difference was that Hemingway had the bigger frame, a healthier lifestyle and a greater tolerance for alcohol. None the less, wet brain got him in the end. Fitzgerald composed his own epitaph: 'I was drunk for many years, and then I died.' Hemingway had twenty years longer – that was the only difference. 'Whoever won the battle between Scott and Ernest for writer of his generation,' Donaldson concludes, 'they both lost the war to alcoholism.'

FN   Francis Scott Key Fitzgerald; Ernest Miller Hemingway
MRT   *The Great Gatsby; The Sun Also Rises*
Biog S. Donaldson, *Hemingway vs. Fitzgerald: The Rise and Fall of a Literary Friendship* (1999)

164. William Faulkner 1897–1962

The War quit on us. Faulkner's observation on having 'missed' the Great War

William Faulkner's war service – more specifically, his versions of it – are a sore point for his admirers (which included, among others, the Nobel Prize committee). What comes to mind is the raving George IV on his deathbed, convinced he had fought gallantly at the Battle of Waterloo. William C. Falkner (sic) was born in America's Deep South. His family moved a few miles when he was five, to nearby Oxford, Mississippi – that 'little patch of native soil' which would become the rich territory of all his major fiction. The first-born son, 'Billy', was named after a great grandfather, 'Colonel' William C. Falkner (né Faulkner – he changed his name for reasons unknown), a Civil War hero.

It was a heavy burden to bear for a boy with an early addiction to Romantic poetry (particularly the 'decadent' Swinburne), who grew up a puny five-foot-five in a family of husky six-footers. Billy's father, Murry, ran a livery stable – at a time when Henry Ford was sending this particular line of business into the knackers' yard of history. Decay was all around the growing lad and the South would not 'rise again' in William Faulkner's time. The ineradicable belief was that it had been driven down by Yankees. Billy was precocious and showed early gifts in drawing, painting and poetry. From his tenth year onwards he devoured classic fiction. Balzac was a particular favourite and he would adopt the French writer's multi-volume sequence format in his own writing. In his adolescence he saw poetry as his main form. He also began on what would be a lifelong career in alcoholism in his teenage years.

A bank clerk by day, young Falkner spent many of his leisure hours on the campus of 'Ole Miss', the University of Mississippi. He and his friends were entranced by the glamour of the epic war being fought in Europe. Falkner saw his first aeroplane in 1915. The romance of conflict in the clouds, of an Arthurian kind – so different from the carnage of the American Civil War – became an obsession. As in Yeats's poem, 'An Irish Airman Foresees His Death' ('I know that I shall meet my fate / Somewhere among the clouds above'), *glorious* death was foreseen.

On 6 April 1917 the US declared war on Germany. Falkner promptly volunteered, hoping to join the army aviation corps. Aware that he was physically unprepossessing, he stuffed himself with bananas and swilled pints of water, to blag his way through the medical. It didn't work. He was turned down for not meeting the height and weight requirements. He was now certified that most inferior of American things, a wimp: a seven-stone weakling. But he wasn't. He resolved to enrol in the British Royal Flying Corps (soon to become the RAF). It had a recruiting office in New York, and training bases in Canada. No bananas were required, but some subterfuge was necessary. With his pal Phil Stone, Falkner cultivated a British accent (traces would remain, in his Southern drawl, throughout life) and purloined forged papers which recorded he was as English as Edward VII and had been born in Finchley. He changed his name to 'Faulkner', reversing what his namesake ancestor had done. He and Phil carried fabricated letters of reference from an English vicar called, improbably, Edward Twimberly-Thorndyke. The scrutiny of those enlisting to join the fight in 1917 was not rigorous. The war was going very badly for England. Despite his 33-inch chest and 'feeble moustache', Faulkner was 'in'.

Cadet Faulkner duly reported for training in a base near Toronto, on 9 July 1918. As the romantic scenario required, he left behind him a girl, Estelle, who he loved madly and who – as the same scenario required – allowed him the *summum bonum* before he went off to death or glory. He went on to marry Estelle in 1929 and they had one daughter. As a cadet, his uniform had white chevrons, and he did not enjoy full officer status – the King's commission would come later and so would the flying. First there was dreary drill and interminable lectures. There were lumbering two-seater biplanes on the base, but none of the frontline Sopwith Camels (made immortal, elsewhere, by Captain W. E. Johns). Nor were cadets allowed near any actual aircraft for months. Men were much more expendable than equipment. Over the four months of his training, Faulkner sent wildly dramatic letters home – some of his most inventive early fiction. They chronicled a series of daring-do exploits, climaxing – as he described it to his amazed family – in a reckless loop-the-loop which led to him crashing, upside down, and having to be cut out of his machine. He had cost the British monarch, he chortled, some £2,000.

Biographers have looked, but there seems to have been no record of this event, and no committee of inquiry – invariably required when an expensive item of military property is destroyed in training. Would a trainee pilot (in a two-seater) have survived dismissal from the course for a manoeuvre which, as Faulkner implied, was carried out in a spirit of sheer devilry? Joseph Blotner, author of the immense biography which has biblical status among Faulknerians, concludes, grimly: 'It seems clear that Cadet Faulkner did not crash. Did he ever fly?' Probably not, Blotner intimates. He was what the cadets contemptuously called a 'kiwi' – a bird that never takes to the air.

Faulkner graduated in November 1918, the same month, as he bitterly said, 'the war quit on us'. For his return home to Oxford, Mississippi, he had bought himself an officer's uniform, complete with pips and swagger stick (he would sport a military-looking trenchcoat for the rest of his life). He was still a cadet, and would not receive an 'honorary' lieutenant's rank for two years. Impersonating an officer is a court martial offence – although in the chaotic demobilisation of millions no one in 1918 checked up on the bona fides of 'Lieut.' Faulkner. He was, however, a fake. He continued to elaborate his 'war' over the following years, developing a 'mythical limp' and alluding, vaguely, to broken legs in his 'crash'. His friend and patron, Sherwood Anderson, was convinced Faulkner had a silver plate in his skull. As the decades passed, the warrior fantasy grew. Faulkner hinted, obliquely, at having seen combat over Germany. In 1943, sending a good-luck charm to a young relative who was training with the RAF, Faulkner said he would have liked to have sent his dog tags: 'but I lost them in Europe in Germany ... I never found them again after my crack-up in '18'. There was no 'crack-up'.

After the war Faulkner drifted aimlessly. He drank heavily, visited brothels, and had a series of jobs, the longest lasting must have been as one of the least efficient employees in the history of the US Mail. He jacked that job in with the jaundiced comment: 'I reckon I'll be at the beck and call of folks with money all my life, but thank God I won't ever again have to be at the beck and call of every son of a bitch who's got two cents to buy a stamp.' During this fallow period, he was writing (mainly poetry) and gathering ideas and creative energy. His first novel was written, he claimed, over a few weeks in 1925 in New Orleans, before departing on a tour of Europe. He was encouraged by Anderson, who was instrumental in getting it into print in 1926, with Boni & Liveright, an imprint which guaranteed influential reviews. *Mayday*, later retitled *Soldiers' Pay*, covers three months (April to May 1919) and is an example of what the Germans termed *Heimkehrliteratur* – return-home fiction. British bestsellers in the genre were *If Winter Comes* by A. S. M. Hutchinson and *Sorrell and Son* by Warwick Deeping. A deeply resentful genre, this variety of fiction depicts the shabby treatment the returned 'hero' receives from those for whom he has risked all. The resentment is graphically evident in *Soldiers' Pay* (for which read 'short-change') in the return of the mortally wounded, DFC-decorated RAF veteran who is at the centre of the narrative:

> Donald Mahon's homecoming, poor fellow, was hardly a nine days' wonder even. Curious, kindly neighbors came in – men who stood or sat jovially respectable, cheerful: solid business men interested now in the Ku Klux Klan more than in war, and interested in war only as a matter of dollars and cents; while their wives chatted about clothes to each other across Mahon's scarred oblivious brow.

The story opens with three discharged veterans returning home by train. One is an air cadet, Julian Lowe (faintly symbolic name) who has never flown; the second, Gilligan, an exuberant doughboy infantry private; the third, Mahon, the horrifically wounded heroic pilot thought dead by his family and unfaithful fiancée in Georgia. Mahon, in his dying days, is taken charge of by Gilligan and a war widow Gilligan falls in with (and later falls in love with, as does the cadet). There is a supremely telling moment, early in the narrative, when Lowe – who has never seen the action he was trained for – regards the shattered body of Mahon and thinks: 'To have been him! ... Just to be him. Let him take this sound body of mine! Let him take it. To have got wings on my breast, to have wings; and to have got his scar, too, I would take death to-morrow.' He speaks, one apprehends, for his author.

One of the fascinations of *Soldiers' Pay* is that Faulkner writes better as the novel progresses. Chapter 8, with its flashbacks to combat, and the dogfight which destroyed Mahon, is particularly impressive. One sees the emergence of the author of *The Sound and the Fury* (1929), three years later. The other fascinating aspect of *Soldiers' Pay* is the light it throws on the schizoid quality of the novelist – all novelists – who can both be themselves and something beyond themselves. 'Lies were important to Faulkner,' Richard Gray observes. You could argue they are important to all novelists. Fiction and falsity are inextricable. Cadet Faulkner had been close enough to the real thing to smell it. It was close enough – if not for his personal military ambitions, then for his writing. And if some of the fiction washed back into his image of himself (a work of fiction for most men) it is a thing of little importance.

FN   William Cuthbert Faulkner (born Falkner)
MRT   *Soldiers' Pay*
Biog   J. Blotner, *Faulkner: A Biography* (2 vols, 1974)

165. Dennis Wheatley 1897–1977

I have never yet met anyone who practised Black, or even Grey, Magic who was not hard up.

Dennis Wheatley was born into one of the few branches of 'trade' traditionally regarded as a career fit for gentlemen. His father was a prosperous West End wine merchant. Dennis was the only son and was brought up in the expectation of his taking over the family business. The Wheatleys lived, comfortably but not ostentatiously, in Streatham. It was not – then or now – an address to boast about and Dennis, who had a broad streak of amiable snobbery in his make-up, aimed from his earliest years to leave the South London *palais de dance*, Lyons Corner House, and picture palace well behind him. But he was unhappy at his public school, Dulwich College (where, it's nice to think, he was a near-contemporary of Raymond Chandler) and left after a year for the more bracing education offered by a naval academy. 'He never shone academically,' records his friendly biographer, which is an understatement. He never even mastered the art of spelling. He read fiction voraciously, however, and three novels shaped him: *The Prisoner of Zenda*, *The Scarlet Pimpernel* and *The Three Musketeers*. His own fiction would ring innumerable changes on their adventure plots.

On leaving school (no question of university) he spent a *Lehrjahr* in Germany, where he learned all about Hock and Moselwein and, it being 1913, witnessed the ominous militarisation of that country. On the outbreak of war, young Wheatley was among the first to sign up. He was also, fortunately for him, among the last to see frontline action. A series of cushy postings, unsought by him, as a junior officer in the Territorials kept him out of the fight until late 1917. After a few weeks in the trenches he was invalided back – it was not wounds, or gas, but his chronic bronchitis.

Wheatley's diary (his 'fornicator's game book' he called it) records engagements with a startlingly large number of *filles de joie* during these years. Clap was always more of a wartime risk for him than the Hun. He was, meanwhile, conducting courtships with respectable girls, often two at a time, of his own – or preferably higher – class. Despite having all his teeth removed at an early age, rotted by his lifelong addiction to sweetmeats and dessert wine, he was dashingly handsome and man-of-the-worldish. During the war Wheatley also fell in with a male companion who would have a profound effect on him. On demobilisation they became inseparable friends. Eric Tombe, a self-professed decadent (an 'intellectual sensualist', Wheatley called him) introduced him to the occult and to interesting delinquencies of the Dorian Gray kind. Tombe was a confidence trickster and led his wine-merchant friend into dangerous places. He was eventually murdered, by an even shiftier rogue than himself. Wheatley immortalised Tombe in the person of the devilishly good-looking, scar-faced vigilante, Gregory Sallust ('Sexlust,' to connoisseurs of Wheatleyism).

Wheatley married in 1922, just after Tombe's disappearance. (His decomposed body was discovered in a cess pit, a year later.) His bride was an heiress and a son, Anthony, was born soon after. It was a troubled period, with social upheaval in the air. Wheatley brandished, and actually fired, his old service handgun against strikers in 1926. To the end of his days he feared Red Revolution. His early novel, *Black August*, foresees Bolshevik takeover by 1960 (the novel clearly inspired Constantine Fitzgibbon's much superior *When the Kissing had to Stop*) and in his best novel, *The Haunting of Toby Jugg*, Satan allies himself with the Kremlin, to bring about a duopolistic world dominion: for ever and ever. Wheatley had an instinctive sympathy with Oswald Mosley, but he was too old-school English, and inherently decent to join the BUF and kow-tow to that German riff-raff in ludicrous black uniforms. The plum-coloured dinner-jacket was Wheatley's uniform. He took over the wine business on his father's death in 1927 and brought flair to the company. Among other things, he takes credit for inventing what he calls the 'Napoleon Brandy racket' – very ancient, usually wholly faked up, liquor, in cobwebbed bottles. It was one of his finer works of fiction.

However resourceful he was, it was a bad time for high-priced luxury goods and the slump bankrupted the firm in 1932. His first marriage had failed (his adultery) and it was his second wife, Joan, who pointed out that people may have stopped drinking expensive plonk but they were still reading Edgar Wallace, the 'King of Thrillers'. Wallace had died in 1932 and Wheatley perceived a vacancy for that throne, methodically setting himself up as 'the Prince of Thrillers'. An astute merchandiser of consumables – whether in bottles, cases or hard covers – in liaison with Hutchinson, his lifelong publisher, he 'pushed' his first novel, *The Forbidden Territory* (1933), by means of 20,000 advertising postcards. In current terminology, Wheatley invented the mail shot. It worked for thrillers as well as it had for Beaujolais nouveau. The novel was reprinted seven times in the first seven weeks.

The Forbidden Territory is a disciple's updating of Wallace's *Four Just Men* (itself an update of Dumas's famous three). It introduced a crime-fighting, Commie-bashing, quartet headed by the aristocratic Duc de Richleau, the drawling embodiment of cosmopolitan and wine-bibbing cool. He has 'devil's eyebrows' and a connoisseur's taste for Imperial Tokay wine and Hoyo de Monterrey cigars – the characteristic whiff of a 'Wheatley'. Richleau's comrades include the subtle Jewish intellectual,

Simon Aron and the supercharged all-American Rex Van Ryn. William Joyce (later 'Lord Haw-Haw', the Nazi radio propagandist) with whom Wheatley had a passing acquaintance, relayed the fact that Goering was a great admirer – alas, given Aron's race, the books were banned for the larger German public. Joyce also told his Nazi superiors that Wheatley would make an excellent *Gauleiter* for London, after the country's takeover.

Once he had found his public, Wheatley varied his game skilfully. *Black August* (1934) introduced Gregory Sallust, and a run of eleven novels over thirty-four years. Other series heroes were Julian Day (suave diplomat) and Roger Brook (Wheatley's Scarlet Pimpernel). In all his novels, Wheatley was at pains to introduce at least one 'hot scene' – typically a fragrant English maiden whose virtue is in peril from some foreign violator. The novel of Wheatley's which endures is *The Devil Rides Out* (1934), in which Richleau et al. take on the Evil One himself. It would be the first of eight such occult romances. In them Wheatley drew on 'research', as he called it, about necromantic rituals, which were in fact picked up, second-hand, from personal acquaintance with Aleister Crowley (the 'Great Beast') and Montague Summers (the 'Evil Priest').

There was a rage for detective fiction at the period, and in 1936 Wheatley pioneered the 'Crime Dossier' detective novel, with *Murder off Miami*. It arrived as a box containing physical 'clues' (cigarette ends, envelopes, etc.) with loose leaves of narrative in pseudo-documentary form. As a novelty, they sold brilliantly. The first cleared 200,000 copies and earned a laudatory third leader in *The Times*. By the time war broke out in 1939, Wheatley had restored his lost vintner's fortune with fourteen bestsellers. Whatever the limitations of the novels, Wheatley had a remarkably fertile imagination. It had been recognised in high places and he was recommissioned, this time into the air force, and recruited to advise the War Cabinet on 'Deception'. His papers, 'for the eyes only' of George VI and the Chiefs of Staff, were wildly fantastic, but not without a certain shrewdness. It was Wheatley who, as the German invasion seemed imminent, suggested turning round all the road signs in southern England. It created much confusion for the uninvaded British people. When the war was won, one of his papers suggested, the whole German male population should be sterilised in the interest of European peace. Joyce was right; he would have made a good *Gauleiter*.

He left with the rank of acting Wing Commander. Now very rich, he retired to a fine country house where he collected fine wine, furniture, stamps and books. He would clock up some seventy-five thrillers by the time of his death. He loathed the Labour government ('half way to communism') – and its 19 shillings in the pound taxes – but was too patriotic to retreat into tax exile. By the 1960s his novels were very old-hat. But New Age obsession with the occult revived interest in him. *The Devil Rides Out* was picked up by Hammer Films in 1968 with Christopher Lee, as a superbly OTT Richleau, and a script by Richard Matheson (author of *I Am Legend*, source-text for the 2007 zombie film). The Hammer adaptations kicked off a Wheatley cult, including, along with the diabolist nonsense, the preposterous *The Lost Continent*. It was made of seaweed, floated in the Sargasso Sea, and was infested with monstrous crustaceans and cannibalistic descendants of marooned pirates. The studio ran out of money halfway through, and had to do desperate things with papier mâché.

Wheatley, a firm believer in reincarnation, had at least one second life. He died, full of age and money, indomitably 'jolly' to the end (he wanted a gigantic champagne party for his 'return', rather than a wake for his departure), leaving a fortune of some £80,000.

FN   Dennis Yates Wheatley
MRT   *The Haunting of Toby Jugg*
Biog P. Baker: *The Devil is a Gentleman: The Life and Times of Dennis Wheatley* (2009)

166. Elizabeth Bowen 1899–1973

I am fully intelligent only when I write.

Stephen Spender and his wife were on visiting terms with Elizabeth Bowen during the war years, when the poet and novelist were both London fire-watchers. Natasha Spender liked to recall a supper party with Bowen in early autumn 1940, during the Blitz. The guests had adjourned to the balcony, overlooking Regent's Park, to smoke their after-dinner cigarettes in the warm night air. As the bombs rained down on the city, Bowen turned to her guests and stammered: 'I really do apo-apologise for the noise.' War, she confided to Virginia Woolf, made her feel 'vulgar'. Few presented loftier defiance to the Hun, even when, as happened two years later, a V-1 landed on the balcony where Bowen and her guests had been standing on that earlier evening.

War was the soundtrack to her life. She was born, Anglo-Irish in southern Ireland, during the Boer War. She was a teenager during the First World War. The Irish Civil War raged around her beloved 'Big House', Bowen's Court, in the early 1920s. It, unlike others, was spared the Republican torch. She worked for the Ministry of Information (Orwell's 'Minitruth') when not an air-raid warden, in the Second World War. Her last novel, *Eva Trout, or, Changing Scenes*, was published in 1968, as the B-Specials ran riot, the Provisional IRA was born, and another Irish war broke out. By now her Big House was rubble.

Her stammer, unlike the stutter, a physiological defect, she plausibly ascribed to 'psychic' causes. The only child of a grossly broken family, she was also a displaced person most of her life: yet, paradoxically, an extraordinarily serene one. If there is a word which describes her (ignoring, for the moment, Virginia Woolf's deadly accurate 'horsefaced'), it is *hauteur*. She was the only child of a prosperous Dublin lawyer. The Bowens traced their line back to the Cromwellian beginnings of the 'Ascendancy'. Their fine country seat had been erected in 1775 and was the enduring love of Elizabeth's life. When, in later life, she decided to write a memoir, she called it *Bowen's Court* (1964). Elizabeth's father suffered a catastrophic mental breakdown when she was six. Elizabeth and her mother moved to poky lodgings in Hythe, on the south coast of England. Here, her mother died of cancer five years later.

A remote committee of aunts then took charge. The distress echoes through her fiction – most incisively in *The Death of the Heart* (1938) in which Portia, the pubescent heroine, finds herself the 'odd', orphaned child, prey to any sexual predator or victim of any negligent guardian. Bowen once said she wrote to 'feel grown up'. Doubtless she smoked her sixty cigarettes a day for the same reason (few pages carry a stronger whiff of nicotine than hers): a bewildered child is always somewhere in the background.

Bowen's father recovered sufficiently to remarry in 1918 – but did not create a home for her. She took refuge in her own marriage in 1923, the event coinciding with the publication of her first volume of short stories. It was the more important event for her. She chose as her spouse a middle-ranking educational bureaucrat, Alan Cameron, six years her senior. He was English, had a third from Oxford, and had distinguished himself as an officer in the war. His eyes were permanently damaged by gas; he was unintellectual, and as devoted as a Basset hound. Bowen did not use his name on her books and the marriage was apparently unconsummated. Cameron would eventually fade out as a drink-sodden, unregarded parenthesis to his wife's brilliant career, conscious of himself as 'Blimpish', fat, red-faced, walrus-moustached, cuckold: a figure of fun to his wife's smart friends (and possibly her as well, as the pathetic Major Brutt in *Death of the Heart* suggests). None the less he supplied what Bowen needed in the formative years of that career – 'fatherhood,' she called it. Sex was as off-limits in the marriage as incest would have been with her other father.

During the early years of the marriage, Cameron ascended the rungs of the Civil Service. Momentously, for his wife, he was appointed Secretary for Education for Oxford, in 1925. They took up residence in Old Headington, close to Lord and Lady Tweedsmuir (i.e. the novelist John Buchan), who became her special friends. Over the next ten years, Bowen's literary personality would bloom. With nothing but a modest boarding-school education behind her, she was cultivated by a coterie of the university's most fashionable dons: Maurice Bowra, Lord David Cecil, Isaiah Berlin, and later the Bayleys, John and Iris Murdoch. She had, enthused Bowra, 'the fine style of a great lady'. Oxford adored her novels and the adoration was crowned with an honorary doctorate in later life.

Oxford was the making of Elizabeth Bowen – but what it did to her fiction was dubious. It pleased her friends – and dedicatees – to believe that she was writing novels for them principally. She was cocooned in a coterie of warmth which gave her strength, but stunted her development. Writing in response to her early copy of *The Heat of the Day* (1949), Rosamond Lehmann gushed about 'the sustained excitement, the almost hyper-penetration, the pity and terror. It is a great tragedy … Oh, and the wild glorious comedy, the pictorial beauty, the unbearable re-creation of war and London and private lives and loves. You do, you really do, write about love. Who else does, today?' This over-pitched praise from a claque of cultural power-brokers encouraged a vein of inane portentousness. Chapter 5 in the novel Lehmann is raving about throws off, in its second sentence, the following: 'The lovers had for two years possessed a hermetic world which, like the ideal book about nothing, stayed itself on itself by its inner force.'

What on earth does that mean? Yet, on the opposite page, is a passage of sublime delicacy, describing the spiritual inertia of wartime London, awaiting nocturnal destruction from the air. What follows is a snatch of Bowen's best: 'The night behind and the night to come met across every noon in an arch of strain. To work or think was to ache. In offices, factories, ministries, shops, kitchens the hot yellow sands of each afternoon ran out slowly; fatigue was the one reality.' How can a writer write so well and so awfully? Coterie caressing encouraged Bowen to neglect the perennial weakness of her narrative, an inability to handle mechanism. At the conclusion of *To the North* (1932), one of the two heroines, who has made a bad choice in love, sets up a *Liebestod* – careening up the Great North Road, her cad lover in the passenger seat, intending to crash and end it all. In an open car, roaring along a busy highway at 70 mph, they converse with the suavity of a couple in a quiet nook in the Savoy Riverside Bar.

On her father's death in 1930, Bowen inherited Bowen's Court. She was the first woman in the line to do so and, it would prove, the last of either sex. For the next thirty years she would move, socially, between metropolitan England and rural Ireland. In 1935 Alan Cameron was appointed secretary to the Central Council for Schools Broadcasting and Bowen established herself as a London literary hostess at 2 Clarence Terrace, the fine property overlooking Regent's Park, acquired on lease from the Crown.

While her marriage was sexless, her life was not. In Oxford she had flings (including, apparently, some lesbian episodes) and a flagrant affair with Humphry House, a pioneer Dickens scholar. She went on to have another steaming affair with Goronwy Rees, 'journalist, Soviet agent, and fellow of All Souls', as Deirdre Toomey sardonically describes him. Both lovers were a decade her junior – she liked her men young ('fatherly' Alan, by contrast, was six years her senior). House was astonished, after they first went to bed in 1934, to discover – after twelve years of marriage and thirty-five years of life, including the roaring twenties – that Bowen was a virgin. Once she got the hang of it she was a harsh mistress. House and Rees found themselves mercilessly punished in her fiction for their defections to other women; in House's case, the scourging continued up to her last novel in 1968 (the poor man had been dead fifteen years). Rees was so enraged by the depiction of himself as the paedophiliac Eddie in *The Death of the Heart* (1938) he had to be talked out of libel action by E. M. Forster.

Bowen's centrepiece is *The Heat of the Day* (1949), her wartime novel, worked on for ten years until its publication in 1949. The plot – mechanically inept, as usual – revolves around a beautiful Regent's Park hostess, in her forties, so irresistible that rather than serve his country's interests, an MI5 agent blackmails her into sex by offering not to betray her lover, Robert, as a Nazi spy. The novel chronicles the great romance of Bowen's life, with Charles Ritchie, a Canadian diplomat (seven years younger) whom she met in 1941. He is the dedicatee of the book in which he is depicted as Robert. Their most rapturous love-making took place at Bowen's Court, in the marital bed presumably. In 1945 she told him that he was 'my real life, my only life'; the relationship lasted thirty years. Alan meanwhile found solace in the whisky bottle. That Ritchie himself was married meant nothing to Bowen: her lovers' wives were never more than tiresome distractions.

Cameron finally succeeded in drinking himself to death in 1952. She described his going as like the death of a 'next of kin' – not, by any means, her 'only life'. As postwar Britain reconstructed itself, Bowen became a public woman. There were honours – doctorates, decorations, committee work. One of her friends nominated her for the Nobel Prize. She earned well but the expense of living in an age of austerity in two expensive houses was crippling. She was obliged to sell Bowen's Court in 1959 to a farmer who, in an act of class revenge, pulled it down. She eventually took up residence in Hythe, where she had been a displaced little girl all those years ago. She died of lung cancer.

FN   Elizabeth Dorothea Cole Bowen (later Cameron)
MRT   *The Heat of the Day*
Biog   *ODNB* (Deirdre Toomey); V. Glendinning, *Elizabeth Bowen* (1977)

167. Vladimir Nabokov 1899–1977

The cradle rocks above an abyss, and common sense tells us that our existence is but a brief crack of light between two eternities of darkness. Opening line of Nabokov's autobiography, *Speak, Memory*

Nabokov was born in St Petersburg, the cosseted eldest child of a rich, prominent and aristocratic family. His father was a politician of liberal convictions and high literary cultivation. Vladimir's early life, as lovingly recalled in *Speak, Memory*, was idyllic: nurses and nannies cared for him; tutors instructed him. St Petersburg's best school gave him the best education available in the country and he was driven to school in a Rolls-Royce. 'I was bilingual as a baby,' he modestly recalled and, of those two languages, English was the first he read, while French was spoken at home. A tutor was recruited to teach him Russian. The family had large properties in town and in the country and Vladimir's passion for butterflies – in which he would become one of the world's experts – was formed in childhood at the family estate. They were, in a sense, *his* butterflies – just as, a few decades earlier, the Nabokovs had owned serfs.

Vladimir Vladimirovich Nabokov was eighteen – a fully formed product of the *ancien régime* with a brilliant future before him – when the Bolshevik Revolution broke. He would never own a home to call his own for the rest of his life. Nor would he have a country he could call his own. The Nabokovs narrowly escaped with their lives, eventually taking up residence in Berlin among a community of similarly expatriated White Russians. Among them, Nabokov's father again rose to prominence. But they were no longer rich and Vladimir's higher education had to be paid for with a string of pearls that his mother, Elena, contrived to smuggle out of Russia in a pot of face powder. He spent three years (1919–22) studying modern languages at Trinity College, Cambridge.

He was a gifted student at Cambridge: the university was hospitable to émigrés, and Nabokov might, like Ludwig Wittgenstein or Paul Dirac, have found a lifetime berth there. He was already writing poetry and criticism. Events, however, forbade a donnish destiny. His father was shot – by a hopelessly incompetent assassin – in Berlin. Vladimir was there at the time, on vacation, and subsequently remained in Germany to embark on his first career in fiction. There was a large enough community of exiles to supply a reading public for Russian novels but not a large enough market to make it profitable. He made ends meet by teaching languages and tennis (at which he was an ace). Nabokov's first effort in fiction, a love story distilling the melancholies of exile, was published in 1926. The sardonic tones of his later work would emerge later.

Handsome, cosmopolitan and debonair, Nabokov had a number of affairs before, in 1925, marrying Véra Evseyevna Slonim, a Russian Jewish émigrée. They had met at a masked ball – the symbolism pleased Nabokov. His literary mask was 'V. Sirin', under which *nom de plume* he wrote seven novels in Russian for Russians. Russia, now the USSR, ignored them. Nabokov also developed his sidelines in lepidoptery and chess (he specialised, unsurprisingly, in 'problems'). By the late 1930s, Berlin was no longer a safe city for a Russian with a Jewish wife and the family (now with a six-year-old son, Dmitri) moved to Paris. It was a period of crisis for Vladimir: his marriage was troubled, he was tormented with psoriasis, and depressed by never-ending exile. He contemplated suicide. However, a number of important things emerged from these mid-life troubles, most important of which was his resolution to write in English. The result was *The Real Life of Sebastian Knight* (1941). The novel is a series of riddles. Is one's own life one's own? The narrator begins to suggest that, like the knight on the board, he is in the hand of an intelligence he does not understand. 'I am very happy that you liked that little book,' Nabokov later told Edmund Wilson, 'I wrote it ... in Paris, on the implement called *bidet* as a writing desk – because we lived in one room and I had to use our small bathroom as a study.'

With the outbreak of war the Nabokovs fled to America. Here, in 1941, *Sebastian Knight* was published. Nabokov was befriended by literary admirers, notably Edmund Wilson, who helped ease him into a succession of posts at American colleges, teaching comparative literature, Russian, and lepidoptery. His tenure case at Cornell inspired a famous wisecrack. When, in support of a permanent position, the committee was reminded that he was a distinguished novelist, one member objected: 'should we then make a rhinoceros professor of zoology?' His failure to secure a permanent place inspired the ironic campus novel, *Pnin* (1957). Along with *Pale Fire* (1962), it reflects Nabokov's mordant belief that American academics are to a man 'mediocrities'.

As he liked to jest, a twelve-year-old 'nymphet' freed him from this campus mediocracy. The birth of *Lolita* was as cosmopolitan as its creator's career. He showed the novel, rewritten from a 1939 sketch, to Edmund Wilson in 1954. Wilson (who had himself written a 'dirty book', *The Memoirs of Hecate County*) passed *Lolita* on to his publishers. They turned it down on sight ('Do you think we're crazy?' one editor asked) – the American public wasn't ready for paedophilia and incest even if packaged in hyper-literary gloss. Eventually *Lolita* was published in 1955 by Maurice Girodias's Olympia Press, a Paris firm that specialised in sophisticated porn written in English. Chauvinistically, the French authorities only concerned themselves with French language products – foreigners were perfectly free to corrupt themselves.

In its green Olympia livery, *Lolita* enjoyed an underground éclat. In the 1955

Christmas round-ups, Graham Greene cited it as one of his 'books of the year' in the (London) *Sunday Times*. It provoked an apocalyptic diatribe against 'filth' from the *Sunday Express*'s John Gordon, a veteran campaigner for British purity. Greene, even more provocatively, founded a 'John Gordon Society', comprising some of London's leading intellectual lights, to oppose book-banning. All this publicity encouraged the American publisher, Putnam, to buy the book's rights and a 'legitimate' *Lolita* duly appeared in 1958. It shot to the top of the *New York Times* bestseller list (contesting the Number 1 spot with another 'Russian' work, *Dr Zhivago*), holding its position for two years.

The hero-narrator of *Lolita* is Humbert Humbert (a pseudonym), born in 1910, 'a Swiss citizen of mixed French and Austrian descent, with a dash of Danube in his veins', an academic and minor poet. He is sexually obsessed with what he calls nymphets, little girls 'between the age limits of nine and fourteen'. Their nature, he believes, 'is not human, but nymphic (that is, demoniac)'. They victimise poor fellows like him. Humbert is left some money by 'mon oncle d'Amerique' and – the Old World incarnate – travels to the New World. Following a nervous breakdown, he goes to recuperate in Ramsdale, New England. It is 1947. He lodges with a widow who has a twelve-year-old daughter, Dolores ('Lolita') the nymphet of his lustful dreams:

> Lolita, light of my life, fire of my loins. My sin, my soul. Lo-lee-ta: the tip of the tongue taking a trip of three steps down the palate to tap, at three, on the teeth. Lo. Lee. Ta.
>
> She was Lo, plain Lo, in the morning, standing four feet ten in one sock. She was Lola in slacks. She was Dolly at school. She was Dolores on the dotted line. But in my arms she was always Lolita.

Following a series of happy accidents, including her seducing him in a motor hotel, he takes off with his little nymphet on an odyssey across the highways of America. It all ends tragically after Lolita dumps Humbert for Clare Quilty, a pornographer of genius. Everyone dies, including Lolita, 'in childbed [sic] giving birth to a stillborn girl'.

The book and Stanley Kubrick's 1962 movie (of which Nabokov approved) enriched him and from 1959 he lived in Switzerland in a four-star hotel – a comfortable nowhere. He continued *Lolita*'s explorations with language in *Ada, or Ardor: A Family Chronicle*, becoming increasingly self-important and given to such haughty utterances as: 'I don't think that an artist should bother about his audience. His best audience is the person he sees in his shaving mirror every morning.'

From 1974 until his death, from mysterious viral infections, Nabokov worked on a final novel, *The Original of Laura (Dying is Fun)*. The novel was never completed and he instructed the manuscript be destroyed. He was not one to leave working materials lying about: 'Rough drafts, false scents, half-explored trails, dead ends of inspiration,' he once wrote, 'are of little intrinsic importance. An artist should ruthlessly destroy his manuscripts after publication, lest they mislead academic mediocrities into thinking that it is possible to unravel the mysteries of genius.' The lordly crack about mediocrities (a category which includes, for Nabokov, many of the reading public, most living authors, and all professors of literature) is hackle-raising, but no genius was more concerned with 'finish'. And if not finished one way the book must be finished the other – destroyed. Nabokov's wife and son, defying (like Max Brod and Kafka) his instruction, preserved and in 2009 published *The Original of Laura (Dying is Fun)*. The scrappy, bewildering, narrative ends with a thesaurus of finalities:

efface
expunge
erase
delete
rub out
wipe out
obliterate

Perhaps it should have been.

FN   Vladimir Vladimirovich Nabokov
MRT *Lolita*
Biog B. Boyd, *Vladimir Nabokov: The Russian Years* and *The American Years* (2 vols, 1990, 1991)

168. Margaret Mitchell 1900–1949

If I were a boy, I would try for West Point, if I could make it, or well I'd be a prize fighter – anything for the thrills. Margaret Mitchell, aged fifteen, in her diary

The author of *Gone with the Wind* ('*GWTW*' to its in-group fans) was born in Atlanta, Georgia, where her father was an attorney with a distinguished southern blood-line. Her mother, 'Maybelle', was Irish by ancestry and fiery by temperament and – one may plausibly suppose – the original of Scarlett O'Hara. As a child, Margaret saturated herself in the history of the South, and specifically of Atlanta during the Civil War and Reconstruction. They were still relatively recent and deeply felt events and there were those living who could remember the burning of their town, which is the centrepiece of both novel and film. 'It's happened before and it will happen again,' Maybelle once told her daughter, 'and when it does happen, everyone loses everything and everyone is equal. They all start again with nothing at all except the cunning of their brain and the strength of their hands.' Personal disasters, and the need to start over again and again, certainly afflicted Mitchell in her young womanhood. Her fiancé was killed fighting in France in 1918. Her mother died in the 1919 influenza epidemic and her father was invalided at the same period. Margaret was obliged to give up her studies at Smith College, Massachusetts, to come home and take charge – all of which can be tied in, allegorically, with the fictional sufferings of the indomitable Scarlett, and her return to Tara after the sack of Atlanta and the ruin of her plantation, with the stoical 'tomorrow is another day'.

It was still the custom for young Southern ladies to 'come out' and Margaret made her debut in 1920. She is reported as being lively – a 'flapper' even – and unafraid of risk. It was in this spirit that she contracted a disastrous marriage with 'Red' K. Upshaw in 1922 (arguably one of the originals of Rhett K. Butler), an ex-football player, a rogue and a bootlegger. He is reported to have raped his wife – not that any such act was criminal at the time. But Mitchell was not prepared to take it and the couple parted, bitterly, after a few months, divorcing in 1924. She went on to make a wiser second marriage with the newspaperman John Marsh in 1925, the best man at her first wedding. This match, unlike the first, worked out. Mitchell retained her birth name for her fiction and used 'Peggy Mitchell' for her journalism.

Peggy was a successful local journalist, doing regular columns and interviews for the Atlanta papers. Legend has it that she began writing her 'Civil War Novel' while recovering in bed with a broken ankle. Her husband brought her the necessary research materials, and she polished off the work in a few months – then, famously, left it to moulder in a cupboard for six years. There it might have remained for ever were it not that in 1935 Mitchell was assigned to show a Macmillan publishing executive, Harold Latham, around her town. He was scouting for new material and persuaded her to let him see the dilapidated manuscript of *Gone with the Wind*. It was accepted instantly and rushed out, with mammoth publicity, on 30 June 1936. By December, Macmillan was advertising the novel with the slogan, 'One million Americans *can't be wrong*. Read GWTW!' It was a runaway bestseller and won a Pulitzer for its literary excellence, in 1937. The director of Macmillan, a gentleman publisher, awarded all the firm's employees an 18 per cent bonus.

The novel headed the bestseller list for two years. Mitchell sold the film rights to MGM for $50,000 and *GWTW* was adapted, using the new process of Technicolor, by David O. Selznick, in 1939. Amid huge publicity, the studio recruited the unknown (in the US) British actress, Vivien Leigh, for Scarlett. Clark Gable (very well known in the US) was chosen for Rhett. Selznick kept the main outlines of Mitchell's plot, although the film softened favourable references to the Ku Klux Klan, with whom, in the novel, Butler proudly rides. The movie was launched in Atlanta in December 1939. It is reckoned in sheer money terms to have been the most successful film of all time and a perennial favourite. Gable's not giving a damn regularly comes up in movie-great-moment polls.

Margaret Mitchell, now her town's most famous living citizen, died in 1949 when she was hit by a car, crossing a street, close to her home. The luckless driver was convicted of manslaughter and imprisoned – not so much for the crime as for the local importance of his victim. He was lucky not to be hanged. Peggy was, friends confirmed, chronically careless about crossing streets. Mitchell was never easy with her fame, and *GWTW* is her only published novel during her lifetime. A much inferior work, *Lost Laysen*, written when the author was sixteen, was discovered among her papers and published in 1996. The house on Peachtree Street, where she lived for most of her life and which is now a museum to her memory, is the target of regular arson attempts by those who resent the 'racism' of her novel.

FN   Margaret Munnerlyn Mitchell (later Upshaw and Marsh)
MRT   *Gone with the Wind*
Biog   A. Edwards, *Road to Tara: The Life of Margaret Mitchell* (1996)

169. Lewis Grassic Gibbon 1901–1935

Mearnsman.

Lewis Grassic Gibbon – the pen-name of James Leslie Mitchell – is put forward as his country's great twentieth-century novelist: the Scottish D. H. Lawrence. Gibbon's reputation substantially rests on *A Scots Quair* ('quire' or 'gathering of sheets'), also called 'The Mearns Trilogy' and published in a single volume in 1946. 'Mearns' was an ancient name for Kincardineshire, now itself an ancient name after the county reorganisation of 1975. This cycle of novels follows the career of a Scotswoman, Chris Guthrie, from childhood on a croft in the north-eastern coastlands, through the disruption of the First World War and two marriages, to middle age in a soulless city, 'Dundon', which combines ugly features of Aberdeen and Dundee into something uglier than either.

'Of peasant rearing and peasant stock,' Gibbon was brought up on a farm near Stonehaven, Aberdeenshire. He left school at sixteen and made a false start as a journalist. It ended with disgrace and attempted suicide when he was discovered fiddling his expense accounts. He then embarked on a ten-year stint in the armed forces, which was largely unprofitable and ruined his digestion for life, but which took him to the Middle East, an experience that profoundly affected the development of his idiosyncratic view of world history. As an RAF clerk, Corporal Mitchell learned methodical writing habits that stood him in good stead when, on discharge in 1929, he became an author. He died of a perforated gastric ulcer – attributable, he always thought, to RAF canteen grub – in 1935 at the age of thirty-four, in the middle of a creative burst that had produced sixteen books (twelve of them novels) in seven years.

Say 'Scotland' and few people (and no travel agents) will think of the bleak, windswept, comparatively featureless north-eastern coastal region that separates St Andrews from Aberdeen. The Mearns is not a beauty spot, even to golfers, and has no glamorous historical associations. But for Gibbon, it is elemental Scotland. Dunnottar Castle is a landmark that recurs in the novels and Gibbon often recalls 'Old Mortality', the crazed Cameronian in Scott's novel who haunted the area's churchyards, devoting his life to the Sisyphean task of keeping legible the mossed-over memorials to the Covenanter martyrs of 1685. Gibbon, in one of his many parts an expert archaeologist, has a similar devotion to old stones. Typically, his narratives open with mistily prehistoric preludes, and his heroes and heroines have mystical attachments to the distinctive red clay and rock of the region, to Stone Age monuments and palaeolithic flints. His extended descriptions of these features of the Mearns landscape constitute his most powerful writing. At the time of his death, Gibbon had not clearly worked out his relationship to Scotland, more particularly to the Scottish tongue. Like the poet Hugh MacDiarmid, he experimented with braid Scots, a literary idiom which – while acknowledging a shared base of Anglo-Saxon – asserts its separateness from English; a dialect which, as the journalist J. L. Mitchell, Gibbon used with the scholarship boy's swanky virtuosity. For the English reader, *A Scots Quair* often requires access to Jamieson's *Dictionary of the Scottish Language*.

As a novelist, Gibbon was lumbered with heavy ideological baggage in the form of diffusionism and Clydeside socialism. Diffusionism, a now unfashionable school of anthropology associated with G. Elliot Smith, proposed that civilisation originated in upper Egypt, around three millennia BC. From this *Kulturkreis* the skills of civilised society were diffused by 'ancient mariners'. (One of Smith's crazier propositions was that the aborigines learned their mummification skills from Egyptian merchants.) The crofting practices of north-east Scotland represented an umbilical link with the fertile mud of ancient Egypt. It was here that the traders first landed with their precious cargo. For Gibbon, the 'independent tenant retainer' or tenant farmer of the Mearns is the 'essential Scot'. In this he differs from Scott and Buchan, who took the essential Scot to be the Border reiver. Similarly, Gibbon's paganism distinguishes him from J. M. Barrie's cosily Presbyterian Thrums, a town based on the neighbouring Kirriemuir. The diffusionist thesis held that modern civilisation represents a falling away from an original Edenic state.

As it diffuses, culture weakens like ripples in a pool; it is also corroded by urbanisation and disrupted by war. Progress, in the optimistic nineteenth-century sense, is an illusion or, as Gibbon put it in a polemical essay, 'barbarism is no half-way house of a progressive people towards full and complete civilisation: on the contrary, it marks a degeneration from an older civilisation'. In Gibbon's diffusionist reading of Scottish prehistory, the agrarian Picts (Gibbon's ain folk) were infinitely superior to the 'stupid' warmongering Celts, possessors of a 'degenerate, bastardised, culture' who swept in from the west and north to harass them. For him the Celts are 'one of the greatest curses of the Scottish scene, quick, avaricious, unintelligent, quarrelsome, cultureless and uncivilisable'.

Superficially this looks like ineradicable lowland prejudice against north-western neighbours – bandits and caterans all. 'Tink' ('Highland bastard') is the ubiquitous racial slur in the mouths of Gibbon's rural characters. One looks in vain in his fiction for the romanticised image of the ancient Gael invented by Scott and popularised by Hollywood. Gibbon has an associated distaste for the nostalgic Kailyard sentimentality associated with Ian Maclaren, J. M. Barrie and S.R. Crockett: his Scottishness is sharp-edged, unapologetically bigoted and hard to come to terms with. It is typical that he reserves the highest flights of his lyricism for the smell ('guff,' 'feuch', 'whiff') of shit – the aromatic midden, fragrant farmyard dung and the rich bouquet of freshly manured fields.

The inherent pessimism of diffusionism – its core vision of a fine old civilisation violated by invading tribes of cultureless savages – made sense of the First World War. It also supplied the ideological framework for the trilogy's progress from croft, through small town, to large industrial city – each step another fall towards darkness. The only remedy held out in the final section, *Grey Granite* (1934), is an angry anglophobic socialism. Gibbon's work holds up least well where it comes closest to MacDiarmid's *Hymns to Lenin*. Here, for instance, is Ewan Tavendale, beaten up in his cell by the Duncairn bobbies for leading a strikers' demonstration:

he lay still with a strange mist boiling, blinding his eyes, not Ewan Tavendale at all any more but lost and be-bloodied in a hundred broken and tortured bodies all over the world, in Scotland, in England, in the torture-dens of the Nazis in Germany, in the torment-pits of the Polish Ukraine, a livid, twisted thing in the prisons where they tortured the Nanking Communists, a Negro boy in an Alabama cell while they thrust the razors into his flesh, castrating with a lingering cruelty and care.

Gibbon's best work, *Sunset Song* (1932), was concerned with his native region in the period before the First World War and with characters that belonged to a still earlier generation. Much of the power of *Sunset Song* resides in John Guthrie, the heroine's appalling father. Guthrie batters his son, forcing him eventually to flee to the other side of the world, and rapes his wife, who finally kills herself and her youngest children rather than face the nightly ordeal of the marital bed. The clever daughter Chris, a scholarship girl, is forced to give up education to skivvy for the widowed Guthrie and to labour in his fields. Gibbon wrote nothing more affecting than the description of Guthrie, mortally wounded by falling against a stone, thrashing in his own farmyard, cursing and calling his daughter 'a white-faced bitch'. Yet at his funeral Chris grieves, reverencing 'the fight unwearying he'd fought with the land and its masters'. In 1925 Gibbon had married Rebecca Middleton and had one son and one daughter; the family lived in Welwyn Garden City where he fought a different fight.

What, then, are Lewis Grassic Gibbon's claims to be considered anything other than a talented provincial – the kind of writer D. H. Lawrence might have been had he devoted his lifelong creative energies to promoting the interests of rural Nottinghamshire? In many ways it is easier to make the case against over-valuing Gibbon. A Modernist by period, he attempted no major technical novelty (beyond his decentred narrative and a disinclination to use inverted commas which infuriated some of his stuffier compatriots). He himself declared in 1930 that Scottish literature would have to wait fifty years before it could produce a Virginia Woolf or a James Joyce. When he made the prophecy, he might reasonably have expected to be around to see MacWoolf and MacJoyce. As it is, a huge 'what if' hangs over his prematurely ended career. He never had a chance to show how good he really was and whether he had another *Sunset Song* in him.

FN   Lewis Grassic Gibbon (born James Leslie Mitchell)
MRT *Sunset Song*
Biog W. K. Malcolm, *A Blasphemer and Reformer: A study of James Leslie Mitchell* (1984)

170. Georgette Heyer 1902–1974

I think myself I ought to be shot for writing such nonsense.

Few novelists have resisted their publishers' publicity departments more doughtily than Georgette Heyer. Over a career of some fifty years, sixty volumes and sales in the countless millions, she gave not a single interview. She never hung out with fellow authors – 'inkies', as she called them (she herself wore white gloves on social occasions) – and not on account of shyness. She had a visceral distaste for the 'nauseating' falsities of book promotion and, as her heroines would have put it, 'trade' – even the book trade that made her so enviably rich. She was the daughter of George Heyer, a Wimbledon school-teacher who wrote poetry and did literary translations. The name – whose pronunciation the family had anglicised to 'hair', not 'higher' – reflects the Russo-Jewish origin of her grandfather, another George Heyer. She began writing stories as a teenager in the company of two friends. Baroness Orczy and Jeffery Farnol were the girls' favoured authors: Scarlet Pimpernels and Regency vagabonds would stay with her for life.

Young Georgette had no ambitions to get into print, however: these early ventures in fiction were for the private entertainment of her ailing, haemophiliac brother, Boris. It was her father who encouraged her to go public with her first historical romance, *The Black Moth*. Written when she was seventeen, it was a hit, and was followed by a dozen more in the same mould over the next ten years. They sold strongly, and had titles which attracted devotees like iron-filings to a magnet: *The Great Roxhythe* (1923), *The Masqueraders* (1928), *Beauvallet* (1929), *Powder and Patch* (1930). As Heyer always insisted, her romances were stiffened by 'research' – those massed ranks of notebooks which raised her work above that of her principal 'plagiarist', Barbara Cartland (a woman she royally despised). Some of her novels she wrote with an eighteenth-century quill pen, authenticating the self-immersion in 'her' period. It is not recorded whether she affixed a beauty spot to her cheek while writing.

In the 1930s, Heyer varied her staple historical romance with detective stories. Jaunty in style, e.g. *Why Shoot a Butler?* (1933), they featured the series heroes made fashionable by Dorothy L. Sayers and the 'cosy' country-house settings which were Agatha Christie's stock-in-trade. But she gave the genre up on the sensible grounds that Regency sold better than murder in the conservatory.

Her father, one of the few people whose opinion of her work she trusted, died prematurely in 1925, playing a hard game of tennis with her fiancé, Ronald Rougier. The couple married a few weeks later. Rougier was a mining engineer and prospecting meant long sojourns in rough areas of Africa and Macedonia. There was one child, a son Richard, born in 1932. On her father's death, Heyer took over financial responsibility for the family. Her brothers were still at school; her mother was 'difficult'. She persuaded her husband to settle in England and, after a few unlucky commercial ventures, to study law, with a view to becoming a barrister: a respectably professional line of work. She, of course, would pay: or, put another way, her bucks, beaux and beauties would pay. Rougier qualified and eventually, in 1959, was made a QC. In later life her husband was the only judge whose opinion of her work she trusted.

In 1937 Heyer produced what is usually thought of as her best work, *An Infamous Army*. Like *Vanity Fair*, it is a Waterloo novel – but, she maintained, better researched than Thackeray. She was wrong about this, but, as editors discovered, she was not the kind of woman to be contradicted on such matters. It was a source of pride to her to learn that *An Infamous Army* came to be prescribed in the war history course at Sandhurst. The other contender for 'best Heyer' is *The Spanish Bride* (1940), a novel of the Peninsular War. Yet it was the Regency romances which sold most reliably, and the best of this genre her loyal readers judge to be works of the early 1940s, such as *Devil's Cub*, *Faro's Daughter* and *Regency Buck*.

There seems to have been a mysterious domestic crisis (a 'bad time', her biographer calls it) which cast a palpable shadow over these wartime works. The Rougiers moved to the select apartment block, the Albany, in Piccadilly (near Regent Street, pleasingly), where they lived elegantly, expensively and very privately. Not even the most addicted admirer of her work would know her married name – under which she went into society – until they read it in the obituaries. And most of those who met Mrs Rougier socially had no idea she wrote novels. In the 1950s Heyer set up her own company, Heron Enterprises, something that never quite, as she intended, put her beyond the grip of the Inland Revenue. She hated modern times: 'Oh Christ!', she ejaculated in one letter of the mid-1950s, 'why did I have to be born into this *filthy* age?' It was a 'disgusting era'. She had no time for contemporary fiction ('kitchen sinks and perverts'). A staunch Jacobite (one of her earliest novels, *The Masqueraders*, glorified the Bonnie Prince), she stamped her foot in rage when the Queen dared to name her son and heir 'Charles'. A Conservative voter, she could not stand their Albany neighbour, Ted Heath: 'the most deplorable Prime Minister that our country has had since Lord North lost the American Colonies'. In fact, she 'loathed' all the current crop of politicians: 'the only one of the bunch who has courage and a great many proper ideas', she believed, 'is Enoch Powell'. Her views on geo-politics were similarly unreconstructed. 'Isn't it FUN,' she wrote to a friend in 1967, 'to see the Israelis beating hell out of the Wogs?'

Heyer lost control of her weight in later years and was disabled by chronic ailments, which she wrote through indomitably, producing her novel-a-year at least. They remained in print – particularly after the paperback revolution of the 1960s – pulling in as much as £70,000 in a good year. Most were good years. She died of lung cancer in 1974 and after her death her husband saw through the publication of an incomplete historical novel , *My Lord John* (1975), set in the Middle Ages which was, he claimed, the period she had really wanted to get to grips with. Rougier died not long after his wife's death. Their son Richard went on to be a famously witty judge.

Heyer's Regency fiction continues to have loyal readers and some eminent supporters – notably A. S. Byatt. Others, like Marghanita Laski, writing in the year of Heyer's death, find the 'universal blandness' numbing and her novels comically sexless: 'if ever Miss Heyer's heroines lifted their worked muslin skirts, if ever her heroic dandies unbuttoned their daytime pantaloons, underneath would be only sewn-up rag dolls'.

FN   Georgette Heyer (later Rougier)
MRT   *An Infamous Army*
Biog J. A. Hodge, *The Private World of Georgette Heyer* (1984)

171. John Steinbeck 1902–1968

A rather cagey cribber. Scott Fitzgerald on Steinbeck

John Steinbeck was born in Salinas, northern California, of mixed Irish and German descent. His father was a local government official, his mother a teacher. Steinbeck recalls the Salinas Valley of his childhood in the opening pages of *East of Eden* (1952) as itself an Edenic place to start life. He also recalls the natal moment at which the writer in him was born, when, aged eleven, he was introduced to Malory's *Morte d'Arthur* by his Aunt Molly. He pictures himself, a little boy sitting under a tree, 'dazzled and swept up' by the tales of knight-errantry. A romantic streak would colour his artistic make-up for the whole of his writing career – a career which can be seen as a long dialogue with other writers and thinkers. Steinbeck is the most creatively absorbent of novelists: fictional blotting paper. Alternatively, he is what Fitzgerald contemptuously terms him – a 'cribber'.

One can follow the track of that cribbing. In late adolescence, Steinbeck came under the spell of Jack London's *Martin Eden*. Following London's rugged lead, he dropped out of college at Stanford and went on the road as a hobo, making a fitful stab at running away to sea. His first novel, *Cup of Gold* (1929), based on the adventures of the Elizabethan buccaneer Sir Henry Morgan, was an acknowledged homage to James Branch Cabell's florid historical romances. In 1929 he was introduced to Hemingway's work by his future wife, Carol Henning, who gave him a copy of 'The Killers'. Romantic Cabell was thrown overboard: modernism had caught up with John Steinbeck. Put another way, he became 'the poor man's Ernest Hemingway'. Henning also introduced him to left-wing politics and he duly became 'the poor man's John Reed' – for a few years. She can be seen as the political force behind Steinbeck's early 'strike novel', *In Dubious Battle* (1936): one of Steinbeck's manifest gifts was in devising sonorous titles; he never needed to crib in that department.

There is only one recorded personal encounter between Steinbeck himself and Hemingway, in New York in the early 1940s. John Hersey, who set it up, records that the occasion was a 'disaster'. Steinbeck had given fellow novelist John O'Hara a blackthorn stick. Hemingway grabbed the stick from O'Hara and broke it over his own head and threw the pieces on the ground, claiming it was a 'fake of some kind'. Drink was probably behind his actions, but one is tempted to allegorise the episode as Hemingway protesting Steinbeck's appropriation of 'his' style. That is how Steinbeck read the event, at least. According to Hersey, 'Steinbeck never liked Hemingway after that – not as a man.'

In 1930, Steinbeck, now resident in the unspoiled Pacific coast around Monterey, met his guru in the form of Ed Ricketts. A maverick marine biologist, Ricketts passed down to his disciple the biological materialism that was to run through all Steinbeck's subsequent writing. Its most memorable expression is Rose of Sharon's suckling the starving stranger at the end of *The Grapes of Wrath*. Ricketts convinced Steinbeck of the necessity of 'non-teleological thinking' – the wisdom of the mollusc. When not instructing, Ricketts was a drinking buddy and – Steinbeck's latest biographer hints – there may have been something homoerotic between the men. Ricketts is portrayed as 'Doc' in *Cannery Row* (1945). With his premature death in 1948 (his car was hit by a train), there is an observable reverberation in Steinbeck's writing – throughout life, he insisted that he was a 'writer' not an 'author'. He was bereft.

There were, however, other gurus to follow. Steinbeck's path crossed in the 1930s with that of the mythographer, Joseph Campbell, who introduced him to Jungian symbolism. In the seigneurial tradition of the West Coast sage, Campbell cuckolded his disciple: Steinbeck lost a wife – his first of three – but gained a literary device. The turtle which crawls across the road at the beginning of *The Grapes of Wrath* should have 'Ricketts' emblazoned on one half of its shell and 'Campbell' on the other. Campbell's thinking rings out from what is the most quoted of Steinbeck's 'philosophical' pronouncements: 'The new eye is being opened here in the west – the new seeing. It is probable that no one will know it for two hundred years. It will be confused, analyzed, analogized, criticized, and none of our fine critics will know what is happening.'

The Pastures of Heaven (1932) followed an immersion in *Winesburg, Ohio*. Sherwood Anderson did for Steinbeck's artfully fragmented narrative structure what Hemingway had done for his literary language. Thus Steinbeck was finally primed for his first great work – and sales success – *Of Mice and Men* (1937). The tragic story of the vagrant farm-workers Lennie and George elicited accusations of downright plagiarism from Scott Fitzgerald, who wrote indignantly to Edmund Wilson:

> I'd like to put you on to something about Steinbeck. He is a rather cagey cribber. Most of us begin as imitators but it is something else for a man of his years and reputation to steal a whole scene as he did in 'Mice and Men'. I'm sending you a marked copy of Norris' 'McTeague' to show you what I mean. His debt to *The Octopus* is also enormous and his balls, when he uses them, are usually clipped from Lawrence's 'Kangaroo'.

On his part, Edmund Wilson thought that Steinbeck's next great work, *The Grapes of Wrath* (1939) owed more than it should to the 'newsreel' sections of John Dos Passos's *U.S.A.* trilogy, which came out the year before. Woundingly, even Steinbeck's former high school teacher, Miss Cupp, gave it as her opinion that *The Grapes of Wrath* was not an 'authentic' book. Whatever the cavils, the epic journey of the Joads in their Hudson truck along Route 66 to the false Eden of southern California had the good luck to coincide with Roosevelt's New Deal. No novel since Upton Sinclair's *The Jungle* was more effective in, temporarily, touching the American social conscience. It headed the bestseller list for two years and earned Steinbeck the 1940 Pulitzer Prize. In England it inspired what an unimpressed Graham Greene called a 'fetish' for Steinbeck – something akin to whips, rubber and bondage: low things of that kind.

During the Second World War, Steinbeck put his pen to his country's service. He proved himself a distinguished war correspondent and wrote a propaganda novel, *The Moon is Down* (1942). It was commissioned by the OSS (forerunner of the CIA) and celebrates heroic civilian resistance against Nazi occupation in Norway. When Steinbeck visited Scandinavia after the war, it was to be greeted with a headline: 'John Steinbeck, all of Denmark is at your feet.' In Sweden he was told that *The Moon is Down* had 'fired the confidence' of Scandinavian freedom-fighters 'during the war's darkest hours'. Gratitude was in order, and would be richly repaid in 1962 with the world's highest literary award.

Steinbeck himself pointed to some odd inspirations with his next major work of fiction, *East of Eden* (1952). He had, he confided, drawn on the Book of Genesis and Henry Fielding. Cain, Abel and murder among the furrows one can see; Tom Jones and Blifil, it must be said, seem planets away from the fratricide of Cal and Aron Trask in the bean-fields of Salinas Valley of the pre-First World War years. He called *East of Eden* 'my first book'; it is certainly his longest. It returned to the bestseller lists in the twenty-first century when Oprah Winfrey endorsed it.

Steinbeck divorced his second wife in the same year Ricketts was killed. His marriage to his third wife, Elaine Scott (herself recently divorced from the film actor Zachary Scott), coincided with a new, and highly remunerative, line of Hollywood work. Steinbeck did the screenplay for Elia Kazan's Brando-starring *Viva Zapata!* (1952). Kazan also did the James Dean-starring adaptation of *East of Eden* (1955). The association with Hollywood's sexiest 'Method' actors kept sales of all Steinbeck's work healthy. So too did the fact that his fiction was being prescribed at high-school level, particularly the novella-fable, *The Pearl* (1947) – one of Steinbeck's most tediously Campbellian efforts.

Scandinavia paid its wartime debt to Steinbeck with the award of the Nobel Prize in 1962. It was the period in which the new Jewish school of New York fiction (Roth, Bellow, Mailer, Malamud) was ascendant. The *New York Times* hailed Steinbeck's achievement with a breathtakingly denunciatory editorial, questioning the mental abilities of the Swedish judges. In the same paper Alfred Kazin did an op-ed entitled 'Does a Moral Vision of the Thirties Deserve a Nobel Prize?' It was less the laureate's wreath than a toilet seat which his country placed on John Steinbeck's brow. Steinbeck duly made his acceptance address a counter-attack on 'an emasculated critical priesthood singing their litanies in empty churches'. Fight back as he might, the Prize was dust in his mouth. He wrote no more fiction – and, once the champion of the Hoovervilles, his politics wavered rightwards. Notoriously he supported Lyndon B. Johnson's Vietnam policy and did some of the frontline reporting he had done in the Second World War. His health was not up to such exertions, however, and he died prematurely of heart failure before witnessing the squalid flight of his country's helicopters from Saigon, wretched Vietnamese hanging on to the landing skids. Unluckier, even, than the Joads.

FN   John Ernst Steinbeck III
MRT   *The Grapes of Wrath*
Biog J. Parini, *John Steinbeck: A Biography* (1995)

172. John Hersey 1914–1993; John O'Hara 1905–1970

Stylish decency. John Clute on John Hersey
Thoroughly obnoxious. Jonathan Yardley on John O'Hara

The two Prufrocks swelling the scene in the epic blackthorn-stick contest between Hemingway and Steinbeck warrant a mention. Between them, the quartet represents four distinct adaptations of the realist traditions of American fiction. John Hersey was born in China, the son of Christian missionaries. He returned with his family to America, aged ten, and went on to study at Yale. Unprivileged, Hersey worked his way through university with menial jobs on the side. He completed his studies at Clare College, Cambridge (on full fellowship).

He worked briefly as a secretary to Sinclair Lewis, the Nobel Prize-winning novelist, after graduation – but disliked the man. His gifts as a journalist were recognised early and in his mid-twenties he was recruited by *Time* magazine. By the end of the 1930s he was running their Chinese bureau (Hersey was fluent in Mandarin from childhood). He made his first, of two, marriages in 1940. He was an intrepid war reporter during the Second World War, covering the Allied invasion of Italy, being downed four times while flying in combat zones and witnessing, from the frontline, the bloody marine invasion of Guadalcanal. Although never uniformed, Hersey saw more battle than most soldiers; and risked his life more than most. Unsurprisingly he came to hate war.

Hersey is sometimes claimed as the father of 'New Journalism'. He can as easily be portrayed as a pioneer of docufiction or, what he called 'the novel of contemporary history'. Fiction, Hersey believed, 'is a clarifying agent [that] makes truth possible'. His first effort in this clarifying genre was *A Bell for Adano*, published while the fighting was still at its height, in 1944. A mixture of war reportage (it began as a factual article in *Life* magazine), propaganda and fiction, *A Bell for Adano* was a bestselling book, a hit Broadway play, and a big-budget film (1945). It opens with the stark declaration: 'Major Victor Joppolo, U.S.A, was a good man.' Joppolo is an officer in 'Amgot', the 'Allied Military Government of Occupied Territory'. His assignment is the Sicilian coastal village of Adano. Joppolo (Italo-American and bilingual) establishes himself as Adano's benign *Duce*. A 'good man' – and a married man – he has an affair with a local girl (something that involved Hersey in a libel suit when the wife of the officer on whom Joppolo was based read the book).

Hersey reserves his greatest savagery not for the Fascists, who are buffoons, but for the American commander in chief, 'General Marvin' (i.e. General George S.

Patton). 'I can tell you perfectly calmly,' the narrator declares, 'that General Marvin showed himself during the invasion to be a bad man, something worse than what our troops were trying to throw out.' The novel is glued together by Joppolo's efforts to acquire a bell for the church of San Angelo, to replace the one taken away for scrap metal during the war. *A Bell for Adano* won a Pulitzer prize. A year later, an assignment from *Life* magazine brought Hersey to occupied Japan. There he came across a document by a Jesuit missionary who had survived the atom bomb and he tried to interest the *New Yorker* in an article. Earlier he had written the story of torpedo boat PT109, and a certain Lt. John F. Kennedy, and was in good standing with the magazine. After much agonising, the editors William Shawn and Harold Ross decided to commission a 31,000-word piece, which would occupy the whole of their cartoonless 31 August 1946 issue.

Ostensibly reportage, Hersey's 'Hiroshima' employed the narrative techniques of fiction. It follows the experiences of six survivors – all intensively interviewed by the author: a clerk, a doctor, a tailor's widow, a German priest, a surgeon and a Japanese Methodist minister. The interviewees were chosen to overturn the monolithic image of the subhuman 'Jap' promulgated during hostilities. The descriptions of the physical effects of the 'Bomb' were horrific: melted eyeballs, bone-rotting radiation sickness, and – the image that went around the world – a victim whose only relic was a shadowy profile on a wall; the rest of him vaporised. The *New Yorker* sold out in hours and reprinted several times to meet demand. In some quarters (notably his former employer, *Time*) Hersey was regarded as perniciously leftist. Undaunted, he followed up his Goyaesque 'Horrors of War' mission with *The Wall* (1950), a novel based on the Nazi destruction of the Warsaw Ghetto, while the world – and Stalin – watched.

Hersey returned in 1950 to his alma mater, Yale, as the master of Pierson College, and later a professor. He opposed the Vietnam War, and marched against it, activism which displeased his Ivy League employers. He continued to write novels, the best of which is *The War Lover* (1959). Set in one of the many 'Mighty Eighth' air force bases in England, the 'war lover' of the title is Buzz Morrow, a B17 (Flying Fortress) pilot, who drops deadly cargoes of high explosive on civilians in Germany with extraordinary skill and daring. He is brave, but borderline psychotic. But is that, Hersey's novel ponders, the whole nature of 'bravery'? *The War Lover* is not quite *Strangelove* but notches better than *Memphis Belle*. It was filmed, starring Steve McQueen as Buzz, in 1962.

Hersey divorced, married again, had five children in all, and died at Key West where he and his wife shared a compound with his friend, the African-American novelist, Ralph Ellison. He was fondly remembered by generations of students at

Yale. Writing his obituary, John Clute discerned a core of 'stylish decency' running through everything Hersey did – one could raise the epithet to 'nobility'.

Stylish decency was never the calling card of John O'Hara. Words like 'oaf', 'lout' and 'brute' attach themselves to him, particularly in his drinking days. 'A strange, unpleasant man,' one critic calls him. Paul Douglas, the Hollywood star, once grabbed O'Hara by his necktie and made a good attempt at throttling him, after an especially obnoxious piece of drunkenness. Many wished Douglas had succeeded.

O'Hara was born an Irish Catholic, the oldest of eight children of a surgeon, in the small Pennsylvania coal-mining town of Pottsville. He recalls his upbringing in the short stories collected as *The Doctor's Son* (1935) – there are particularly vivid descriptions of the 1919 flu epidemic. Intransigent from youth onwards, he was expelled from three schools – the last for drunkenness. His father died when John was twenty, which meant he could not, as planned, go to Yale. It embittered him for life (Ernest Hemingway suggested, sarcastically, that writers should chip in for a 'fund' to send him there to stop the bloody man complaining). Suddenly penniless, another no-good 'Mick', for a couple of years he jogged along with menial work ('soda jerk', gas meter reader, gardener) until, aged twenty-three, he landed a job as a journalist. It was the post-Prohibition era, and the jazz age; there was lots of easy money and easier morality. O'Hara was a facile reporter and got work from top papers in Philadelphia and New York. He also lost many of those jobs for drunkenness – and often nasty drunkenness. He married and divorced soon after, in 1933.

O'Hara had had stories taken by the *New Yorker*, which led him to think he might do something more ambitious in that line. Down to his last three dollars, he holed up in his New York lodging and set to writing a full-length novel to keep the wolf from the door. It was called *Appointment in Samarra* – the title borrowed from an oriental fable popularised by Somerset Maugham: a merchant's servant sees 'Death' in Baghdad looking at him fixedly, and assumes he is soon to die. He tells his master: 'I will ride away from this city and avoid my fate. I will go to Samarra and there Death will not find me.' The merchant subsequently asks Death why he threatened his servant in Baghdad. Death replies: 'That was not a threatening gesture ... I was astonished to see him in Baghdad, for I had an appointment with him tonight in Samarra.' Kismet.

On the strength of his novel's first few thousand words, O'Hara got an advance from his publisher. The story chronicles the last three days of a Cadillac dealership owner, Julian English, in 'Gibbsville' (i.e. the author's hometown). A member of the town's country club set, with a beautiful wife, Julian's life is on the skids. Drunkenly, he throws a highball (ice cubes included) into the face of a man he owes money to,

'Harry Reilly'. O'Hara took no care to mask the originals of his characters. Harry was, as all Pottsville recognised, based on the uncle of Bill O'Reilly, the Fox news commentator at whom many viewers may have wanted to throw things heavier than ice cubes. It is Prohibition and, like all his class, Julian hobnobs with bootleggers and gangsters. How else will the country-club set get their highballs? In return, the mobsters buy their limousines from Julian. Caroline abandons him when he's caught canoodling with a floozy. Julian finally kills himself, on the front seat of one of his finest cars, the garage doors locked, engine poisonously (but silently – it is a Cadillac) running.

The novel was a hit and favourable comparison was made with *The Great Gatsby*. Like that novel, *Appointment in Samarra* has a virtue lacking in O'Hara's late-life fiction – it is short. His follow-up, *BUtterfield 8* (1935) is similarly lean. A *roman-à-clef*, O'Hara's heroine, Gloria Wandrous, is based on Starr Faithfull whose body was found at Long Island in June 1931. The autopsy revealed that she had been drugged, abused and beaten up before drowning. She was twenty-five years old, drank heavily, and was promiscuous. As a schoolgirl she had been debauched by Andrew J. Peters, the wealthy former mayor of Boston. O'Hara's title alludes to the new telephone codes introduced by the New York Telephone Company in December 1930. Gloria is, literally, a call-girl. The narrative follows the last few drink-sodden days of Gloria's life, in which her history of sexual exploitation, beginning with childhood molestation, is graphically described. The film rights to *BUtterfield 8* earned O'Hara a cool $100,000. The movie came out in 1960, starring Elizabeth Taylor, and won her an Oscar. Apart from pocketing the hundred grand, O'Hara had nothing to do with the glossy adaptation, which bore only glancing resemblance to the novel he had written thirty years earlier.

Now a hot property, O'Hara could sell his short stories everywhere (most prominently in the *New Yorker*). His next bestselling novel, *Pal Joey* (1940), takes the form of semi-literate letters (i.e. bundled short stories) to an anonymous 'friend' by a small-time club crooner and hoofer – a cheery, no-good louse. He always signs himself off 'yr pal, Joey'. Ring Lardner's *You Know Me, Al* was the clear inspiration – and a much funnier epistolary effort. *Pal Joey* was made into a Rodgers and Hart Broadway musical (viz the song, 'The Lady is a Tramp', i.e. 'whore'), and a wholly preposterous movie starring Frank Sinatra and Rita Hayworth (1957). The film removed such unappealing features as Joey being an unrepentant gang-rapist.

O'Hara was now riding very high indeed. He had remarried in 1937 and, as Jonathan Yardley tartly puts it, 'set himself up in Princeton, hobnobbed with the rich, lobbied shamelessly for literary awards and club memberships, togged himself out in expensive tweeds, riding boots and other accoutrements of the country squire manqué, insulted just about everybody, including many who thought he liked them, and in general made himself thoroughly obnoxious.' The distance between Irish Catholic and WASP in upstate Pennsylvania was one which he dedicated his life to crossing, and his fiction to anatomising. He was in demand as a journalist-commentator (he was, inevitably, infuriatingly provocative) and short-story writer. Yet he was going nowhere in his work and – resident mainly in New York – drinking pathologically. In the early 1950s O'Hara pulled his life together. Spurred by warnings by his physicians that he was on his way to his own appointment in Samarra, O'Hara kicked alcohol: it was a remarkable act of willpower. His second wife died in 1954, and he promptly remarried. After a row with the *New Yorker*, he resolved to write no more short fiction.

He embarked, instead, on a series of loosely interlinked massive social melodramas, set in 'Gibbsville', beginning with *A Rage to Live* (1949). They got bigger and bigger, selling ever better, culminating in the truly elephantine, near thousand-page, *From the Terrace* (1958). O'Hara thought these corpulent bulks his best work, and fully expected a Nobel Prize for them. Most readers (those he retains) see him as a novelist who peaked – impressively but temporarily – in the 1930s.

FN   John Richard Hersey; John Henry O'Hara
MRT   *A Bell for Adano; Appointment in Samarra*
Biog   JH: *ANB* (Carroll Viera); JO: F. MacShane, *The Life of John O'Hara* (1980)

173. George Orwell 1903–1950

From a very early age, perhaps the age of five or six, I knew that when I grew up I should be a writer.

Orwell's status as a writer of novels is debatable, but Orwell's status as a non-fiction writer is unimpeachable. He made reportage not merely a valid literary form but an instrument of social hygiene and personal therapy. Winston Smith becomes 'the last man in Europe' (Orwell's first title for *Nineteen Eighty-Four*) as opposed to a 'citizen' (i.e. serf) when he clandestinely buys himself pen and paper and finds a corner beyond the watching eye of the telescreen to write down what actually happened at what? – a public hanging. That, as it happened, was the subject of Orwell's first significant published essay, 'A Hanging' (1931). Winston is by profession a *Times* reporter, AD 1984. It is still the 'paper of record' – but its principal activity is destroying or perverting history. 'He who controls the present, controls the past. He who controls the past, controls the future' – so runs the Party slogan. Winston's day job is to consign awkward material (like the truth) down the 'memory hole'.

One notes that Orwell also consigned huge chunks of his own personal record down that same hole. Why, asks his latest biographer forlornly, are there so few photographs, no sound recordings, nothing on film? Why did he insist 'no biography', and marry, on his deathbed, a woman whom he trusted to carry out that prohibition as a sacred duty? One is thrown back on Orwell's own accounts. How reliable are they? Did he really shoot the elephant – or was the beast as allegorical as Moby Dick? The biographical framework is clear. He was born Eric Blair in Bengal, India, the only son of a 'sub-deputy opium agent, 4th grade' close to retirement. Pooter in a solar topee. Richard Blair is remembered by his son as a remote 'elderly man forever saying "don't"'. Orwell calibrated his family's social standing, with contemptuous exactitude, as 'lower-upper middle class'.

Eric was bright and went on scholarship to a good 'prep' school, St Cyprian's. Late in life he wrote a scathing account of those schooldays, 'Such, such were the Joys'. It was not enjoyable. The chronicle begins with eight-year-old 'Blair' being beaten for bedwetting. They would never, he claimed, have caned the bare arse of a boy whose parents earned £2,000. Whether or not he was actually thrashed and humiliated has been questioned. If so, it did not stop him cruising to a full scholarship to Eton, with schoolmate Cyril Connolly, whose recollections of St Cyprian's frankly contradict young Blair's. In his five years at Eton, 1917–21, he resolutely 'slacked'. It was the first of many *non serviams*. But he read voraciously and made friendships which, like Connolly, proved useful in his later literary career. University was not an option: his academic record was now too undistinguished and his family too poor.

In a momentary spasm of loyalty to the Crown he was duly gazetted an officer in the Indian Imperial Police, Burma branch. He would spend five years in the tropics, waited on hand and foot by servants, his sexual needs supplied by concubines, buoyed up by the Empire's indelible sense of racial superiority over the Burmese 'niggers'. He professed to hate the Empire which he saw as a 'racket', but he had as little time for the Burmese – 'evil spirited little beasts' – whom he was paid to beat, hang or shoot if they got out of line. Why he joined the India Service is a mystery: why he stayed there five years is a greater mystery. One's suspicion is that it was the sex.

He resigned and returned to lodge with his retired parents in Southwold while he meditated his next step in life (which would appal them). He resolved to become a tramp. Why? It may have been self-punitive – his forty days in the desert – or it could have been political, inspired by the 1932 Jarrow 'National Hunger March'.

Or it could have been an act of literary homage to Jack London's *The People of the Abyss* and W. H. Davies' *Autobiography of a Super-tramp*. In any case, Orwell spent two years slumming it and his tale of two cities was published in 1933 as *Down and Out in Paris and London*. He 'kipped' in workhouses and shared hostels with cockneys in the summer hop fields of Kent. A writer whom Orwell valued extravagantly was Henry Miller, whose *Tropics* record an unending Parisian sex orgy. For Orwell, if we believe him, it wasn't dipping his wick but his arms, up to the pits, in scummy water as a *plongeur* – dish-washer.

Down and Out was taken by the newly established Victor Gollancz, a socialist publisher. It got good reviews, but its author would have been back in the work-house on the royalties. There followed a year lost to biography. One picks up his trail in 1931 Hampstead, where he was working part-time in a bookshop, doing the odd bit of journalism on the side and working on his first novel. Gollancz and other English publishers (a 'gutless' crew, Orwell always thought) were nervous about the libels in his self-hating *Burmese Days*. It was published, belatedly, in the US in 1934. Meanwhile his second novel, *A Clergyman's Daughter*, was published as his debut work in England in 1935. A dried-up spinster, approaching the horrors of middle age 'on the shelf', Dorothy Hare suffers a bout of amnesia, escapes from her Suffolk parsonage to find emotional fulfilment in the hop fields of Kent and the meaning of life in London's streets. Orwell's later verdict on the novel was pungent: 'bollocks'.

He was prouder of his third novel, *Keep the Aspidistra Flying* (1936). Gordon Comstock's miseries, catering for philistine know-nothings ('do you have the new Ethel M. Dell?') in a Hampstead bookshop, draw on Orwell's own counter-jumper servitude. Gordon dumps the epic poem he is writing, grows up and sells out. He becomes an adman. Winston Smith's 'triumph' is coming to love Big Brother: Gordon comes to love the aspidistra, emblem of the 'lower-upper middle class'. He has an immediate hit with his 'Pedic Perspiration' ('BO of the Feet!') campaign. Oddly enough, Orwell might have been a customer for that product; he was morbid about smells. Who else would have analysed the fourth book of *Gulliver's Travels* in terms of horseshit being sweeter to the nostrils than human shit?

Although he resolutely declined to be a party man, the Socialists saw him as one of theirs. Gollancz advanced him £500 to write about unemployment in the coalmining north. The result was *The Road to Wigan Pier* (1937) – wholly displeasing to Gollancz for its critique of party hacks. Orwell was by now able to move into his own house, in Hertfordshire, and to marry. His wife, Eileen O'Shaughnessy, was an Oxford graduate whom he had met in bookish Hampstead. Virtually nothing is known about the marriage. There would be no children – Orwell claimed to be sterile.

Orwell, whose life never moved in straight lines, resolved – having just married – to fight for the Republic in Spain and joined the anarchist-leaning POUM and saw service on the Aragon front. It was a quiet sector, but a Nationalist sniper got him in the throat. On his return to Barcelona, he found himself at even greater risk of death from the Stalinists, who were 'purging' the city in their usual efficient way. Orwell's disillusion with 'movements' crystallised in *Homage to Catalonia*. Gollancz refused it, on the grounds of apostasy but it was taken by Frederic Warburg, Orwell's most congenial publisher, and sold miserably. If there was one thing the British reading public did not want to know about in 1937 it was war.

The next novel, *Coming Up for Air* (1939), is Orwell's best. In a virtuoso act of ventriloquism, he took on the voice and personality of George Bowling, a shrewd, tubby, middle-aged insurance salesman, recently possessed of a set of gleaming false teeth. Having come into a seventeen-quid windfall, George resolves to visit that foreign country, his childhood past in Lower Binfield – a place where the sun always shone and the fish always bit. It's a disaster. You can't go home again, because history has wiped out home as efficiently as the bombs did Guernica (Picasso's painting was on display in England at the period). The novel signals a deepening pessimism in Orwell, which would reach its climax in O'Brien's forecasting the future to Winston – 'a boot stamping on a human face – forever'. The pigs will always own the farm; innocent boys will always be caned for bedwetting.

When war broke out, Orwell was still primarily a hack journalist. He reviewed over one hundred books in 1940. He was, for the moment, patriotic ('my country, right or left'), but too old and too sick to carry a rifle any more. He eventually landed a job in a sub-section of the BBC's World Service ('half lunatic asylum, half girl's school'). After a couple of years he moved on to a more comfortable berth as literary editor of the socialist paper, *Tribune*, for whom he produced his finest essays, under the proclamation 'As I please'. He and his wife (who was dangerously ill – although Orwell seems not to have noticed how seriously) adopted a child, Richard, in 1944.

As the war drew to a close, he tried every major publisher with his Swiftian satire on totalitarianism, *Animal Farm*. It was initially turned down on the grounds of (a) 'Let's not be beastly to the Russians'; (b) as T. S. Eliot put it, the pigs were, after all, extremely intelligent, and should run the farm. When the Iron Curtain descended, in 1945, Orwell's fable would become a textbook for the 'free world': Martin Secker and Warburg published it in this year in the UK and it was taken by Harcourt Brace in the US in 1946. Everyone now wanted to be beastly to the Russians.

Eileen died as the war ended. Now, at last, in the £1,000-a-year class, Orwell moved to his own animal farm, on the island of Jura, with his younger sister as housekeeper. The western island was one of the few places which might survive the atomic war he confidently expected. In this outpost, and terminally ill with tuberculosis, he worked on his last book, *Nineteen Eighty-Four* (1949). The new antibiotics arrived months too late to save him. He ended his days in University College Hospital in London where he married Sonia Brownell (popularly believed to be depicted as Julia in his last novel) in October 1949. The marriage, one assumes, was unconsummated. He died three months later. A professed atheist, but contrarian to the end, he decreed he should be buried according to the rites of the Church of England. It recalls his best poem:

> *A happy vicar I might have been*
> *Two hundred years ago*

One remembers that Swift was a vicar two hundred years ago. But hardly happy.

FN   Eric Arthur Blair ('George Orwell')
MRT *Coming Up for Air*
Biog D. J. Taylor, *Orwell: The Life* (2003)

174. Evelyn Waugh 1903–1966

We resemble a man going round a castle seeking vainly for an entrance, and sometimes sketching the façades. Arthur Schopenhauer, *The World as Will and Idea*

The country house – emblematically Brideshead – is central in any consideration of Evelyn Arthur St John Waugh. 'Waugh Hall', at least, is implied by that barrage of forenames. There was, as it happened, no such structure, around his birthplace at 11 Hillfield Road. The novelist Dan Jacobson, not a passionate admirer, suggests that on the front wall of that humble bungalow in Golders Green (nowadays nestled alongside a drive-through car wash) there should be no memorial blue plaque but a large exclamation mark. As a young man, Waugh is alleged to have tramped to the Hampstead post office, to get a more distinguished London district stamp on his correspondence. If not true, it ought to be.

'Doubting Hall' is the name of one of the acceptably grand edifices in Waugh's fiction. It alludes to Christian's imprisonment, by Giant Despair, in *The Pilgrim's Progress*. Waugh's principal doubt – and occasional despair – in life was which entrance he should use. If he could not, until his fourth decade, possess such property by right of birth, the attitudes that went with it were easily adopted. He had, noted his first biographer Christopher Sykes, an 'instinctive dislike of the working classes', as if such a thing was irrational, like a fear of heights. In fact it was entirely rational and founded in horror at what was happening to 'his' England.

What was it, in Waugh's view, that had been so fatally lost in the twentieth century? Deference, principally: that quality which, Walter Bagehot argued, held England together and revolution at bay. Carlyle more bluntly called it 'servant-ship'. In one of his startlingly candid remarks about himself, Waugh proclaimed that, in the lower classes, he tolerated 'servility' but abominated 'familiarity'. The only likeable working-class character one recalls in his twenty-novel-strong dramatis personae is Nanny Hawkins at Brideshead. Like the undimmed lamp-light in the chapel (whose walls Charles has dutifully decorated, in his own act of higher servantship), she survives. Like the chapel, her utter servility is a beacon of hope. Is Lord Marchmain's soul more important than Hooper's? asked Conor Cruise O'Brien, alluding to Charles Ryder's jumped-up junior officer. Yes, Waugh would have answered, were he being honest. And Nanny's soul? Yes, too, although unlike Hooper she would get entrance into Heaven on the Marchmain ticket – someone must iron those celestial robes. Whole classes of society and even whole nations come under Waugh's sentence of dismissal. In a novel set entirely in America, *The Loved One* (1948), there is not a single admired American – and lots of Jews (or 'Five-to-twos' as Sir Ambrose vulgarly calls them). Waugh's idea of the 'melting pot' (i.e. miscegenation) is conveyed in the star Baby Aaronson, surgically mutilated first into Juanita del Pablo, 'surly, lustful, and sadistic', then, when the League of Decency steps up its pressure, remutilated into the Irish Colleen – with false teeth to match: 'She never had to smile before and her own set were good enough for a snarl. Now she'll have to laugh roguishly all the time. That means dentures.'

As did his Oxford contemporary, Cyril Connolly, Waugh probably cursed the gods that he was born with no title before his name. But at least he could put 'Esquire' after it. He was raised in the upper middle classes. His father, Arthur Waugh, was a director of Chapman and Hall. A brilliant young publisher he became, in age, like the house itself, stuffy and self-important. Edward Chapman and William Hall had grown fat on their ownership of the Dickens copyright – the author whose career they had inaugurated, when they too were brilliant young publishers, in 1836. Waugh allegorised this stultifying *trade* legacy in *A Handful of Dust* (1934) where Tony Last is imprisoned in the jungle, doomed to read Dickens aloud, until the day he dies. Meanwhile his country house, Hetton, with its 'Carpet and canopy, tapestry and velvet' is modernistically vandalised by Bauhaus glass and chrome. 'Your head aches, does it not?' asks Tony's illiterate Negro captor, solicitously. 'We will not have any Dickens today... but tomorrow, and the day after that, and the day after that. Let us read *Little Dorrit* again. There are passages in that book I can never hear without the temptation to weep.' Arthur Waugh, like any Victorian paterfamilias, read out Dickens to his children and was the President of the Dickens society. It left a lasting bruise.

Arthur Waugh was fixated, to the point of passion on his 'firstborn', Alec (see below), some five years older than Evelyn. Waugh minor felt unwanted (it was rumoured in the family he was an 'accident'), and, if a child *were* wanted, the Waughs preferred it should be a girl: 'I always longed for a daughter,' confessed Arthur. Hence, it is plausibly suggested, the androgynous name. By Tolstoy's cruel law, the Waugh family had their distinctive way of being unhappy. Evelyn was benignly overlooked and arguably it soured something in him – and the satirist was born: cold, domestically exiled, bitter. He came to despise his father – 'decrepit' enough to be his grandfather – a fat Pickwickian figure, with obscurely dubious fetishisms to do with young girls, bicycles and bottoms. Asked why he was so charming to friends and so unkind to his father, Waugh retorted, with the frigidity of Prince Hal, 'I can choose my friends, but I cannot choose my father.'

After day school in Hampstead, Evelyn went as a boarder to Lancing. He describes it, with razor-sharp class analysis, in *Scott-King's Modern Europe* (1947): 'Grantchester [i.e. Lancing] is not the most illustrious of English public schools but it is ... entirely respectable; it plays an annual cricket match at Lord's; it numbers a dozen or so famous men among its old boys, who, in general, declare without apology, "I was at Grantchester."' In short, it was not Eton. He later said he liked none of the boys at Lancing and disliked most of the masters, although he got a sound education there. Waugh won a scholarship to Hertford College, Oxford. It was not Christ Church, just as Lancing was not Eton. A 'subdued little college' he calls it in *Brideshead Revisited*. Like Golders Green, it added to his insecurities. Oxford was, none the less, 'Arcadia' and he fell in with the brilliant set orbiting around Harold Acton. His boyish looks helped. He was 'a prancing faun', Acton thought, if a little unadventurous in his style of dress. Waugh would grow more flamboyant in later years, with a preference for check and houndstooth.

Dandyism and insolence was the Actonian 'criticism of life'. Sex-starved, obscenely privileged, drunken, moneyed, they relieved their *ennui* with surrealistic pranks. Their great bequest to civilisation, other than Waugh's chronicles, were Oxford Bags (the invention of Acton himself) and the cult of the 'party':

> Masked parties, Savage parties, Victorian parties, Greek parties, Wild West parties, Russian parties, Circus parties, parties where one had to dress as somebody else, almost naked parties in St John's Wood, parties in flats and studios and houses and ships and hotels and night clubs, in windmills and swimming-baths, tea parties at school where one ate muffins and meringues and tinned crab, parties at Oxford

where one drank brown sherry and smoked Turkish cigarettes, dull dances in London and comic dances in Scotland and disgusting dances in Paris – all that succession and repetition of massed humanity…Those vile bodies …

The whole point of the party was that – unlike the orgy, the revel, or the carnival – it affronted conventional morality and, like Poe's masque of the red death, signalled the end of a civilisation. At Oxford, Waugh partied with all the rest – with the cold satirical eye which glints maliciously in the passage above, from his 1930 novel *Vile Bodies*. It was published, elegiacally, as the universal party came to an end with the Great Slump.

Waugh had some unsensational homosexual adventures, commemorated in the furtive Latin inscriptions of his late fiction. He wrote diaries all his life but destroyed those of his three Oxford years. He worked not at all: to spare himself even minimal labour he switched from history – a 'heavy reading' subject – to English, losing his scholarship in the process. Daring as his set was, Humphrey Carpenter surmises that Waugh was a heterosexual virgin until he married in his mid-twenties. There may, others surmise, have been a prostitute or two. Like others of Acton's set, Waugh earned a gentleman's third which he did not trouble to collect. The outside world was less insouciant about unqualified young men who felt they were owed a living. The main embarrassment, of course, was the necessity to *earn* a living in the first place; something that Guy Crouchback, Sebastian Flyte or Tony Last need never concern themselves with.

Waugh was a gifted painter and wanted to pursue a career in art in Paris. His father, however, would not fund that nonsense. Nor would Evelyn, like Alec (or his college friend Anthony Powell), go into publishing – his father's trade. For a while he tried carpentry – a craft dignified by Christ's apprenticeship to it and by Waugh's own predilection for William Morris. But, inevitably, he accepted the advice which he puts into the mouth of a college scout in *Decline and Fall* (although, unlike Paul Pennyfeather, Waugh's delinquencies did not lead to his being sent down): 'I expect you'll be becoming a schoolmaster, sir. That's what most of the gentlemen does, sir, that gets sent down for indecent behaviour.' As what would now be called a 'supply teacher' (never, perish the thought, 'permanent'), Waugh was very unhappy. He attempted suicide by drowning but was foiled by an inconvenient shoal of jellyfish. None the less, during these dreary years, he picked up raw material for his first novel.

His aimlessness was compounded by a disastrous marriage in 1928. His bride, Evelyn Gardner, was referred to among friends as She-Evelyn and in Debrett as the Hon. Evelyn. Her mother, Lady Burghclere, was frosty. Waugh records that in her eyes he was of that class which one might *know* socially, but never marry into. Waugh's career dilemmas and social humiliations are given comic expression in

Decline and Fall, published in the same year he married, 1928. Paul Pennyfeather, after being unfairly expelled from Oxford, is robbed of his inheritance, undergoes Candide-like misfortunes as a Gabbitas and Thring temp-teacher, is tricked into marriage 'above' his station in life, and imprisoned (unfairly) for white slavery. He returns, finally, under an alias, to Oxford to study for religious orders.

Two years after marriage the Evelyns divorced: she had brazenly cuckolded him, although his sexual nervousness may have pushed her in that direction. Alec Waugh's first marriage was dissolved about the same time, on grounds of non-con-summation. Waugh's furious hurt is chronicled, just this side of the libel law – a well-trodden patch in his fiction – in *A Handful of Dust*. It was exacerbated by the co-respondent being the Etonian heir to a baronetcy – one of She-Evelyn's own class and not at all like the socially verminous John Beaver in the novel. 'I did not know it was possible to be so miserable and live,' he later wrote. It is to this traumatic misery that one traces the persistent vein of violence against women in Waugh's fiction. In *Black Mischief* (1932), his sardonic *Heart of Darkness* satire, Basil's girl-friend Prudence is cooked in a cannibal pot and eaten with some relish by her unwitting lover. At the end of *The Loved One*, Dennis eats his lunch sandwich while the blameless young girl, Aimee, whom he has driven to suicide, is cremated in the pets' funeral home oven. He had kept both sandwich and corpse in the pet's icebox.

Waugh's bitterest novel, *Vile Bodies*, was published in the same year – 1930 – that he separated from Evelyn and joined the Catholic Church. He was drawn to Rome on historical rather than doctrinal grounds; he needed something 'solid' his friend and fellow convert Graham Greene deduced. His model in going over was Edmund Campion, whose biography he wrote at this time. Campion too had con-verted at a relatively late age. Waugh's biography of Campion is his least read work of non-fiction. His least read work of fiction, *Helena* (1950), was the one he chose to read aloud to his family, more than any other of his works. He regarded *Helena* (per-versely to most minds) as his best novel. Helena, the English daughter of Old King Coel, is memorable in the annals of Roman imperial history for being the mother of Constantine, the Caesar who made Christianity the Empire's official religion. He reigned at that moment that the Empire was declining. Gibbon argues, in his famous fifteenth chapter, that Christianity caused Rome's decline. Waugh disagrees: it was rebirth. And the well-born English lady Helena it was who, as recorded in the annals of Roman Catholic history, went to Jerusalem and discovered the sacred fragments of the true cross on which Christ was crucified.

A dispensation from Rome, annulling his first marriage, allowed Waugh to marry again, in 1937, this time more congenially. His bride, Laura Herbert, was Catholic and the daughter of a Conservative MP with aristocratic connections. She was thirteen years younger than him and unassertive. Her main interest in later life was prize cattle. Again, however, the bride's family disapproved. Waugh, they felt, was 'a common little man' who left a 'bad smell'. There would be children – seven of them – and, thanks to a munificent wedding present, Waugh at last came into possession of the country house he always felt was his due, Piers Court, in Gloucestershire.

Waugh joined the colours, eagerly, in 1939, fired by the Ribbentrop–Molotov pact which put all the hated anti-Christs in the same basket. 'The enemy', he wrote in the first volume of his *Sword of Honour* trilogy, 'at last was plain in view, huge and hateful, all disguise cast off. It was the Modern Age in arms.' The Modern Age in arms proved, alas, to be the Modern Age of Cock-up. A slightly superannuated, diminutive and pudgy 'commando', wholly unlike the popular image of that feared brigade, Waugh saw little action other than in Crete (another royal cock-up) where he efficiently assisted the inglorious evacuation of the British expeditionary force, under the merciless assault of German dive bombers. It was his finest moment. He did not love his 'men', nor they him. One, perhaps apocryphal, anecdote from this wartime period, is that guards were posted at his quarters lest he be assassinated. Even less did he love the jumped-up conscript junior officers whom the war had allowed into the officers' mess – a genus immortalised in Lieutenant Hooper in the prelude and epilogue to *Brideshead Revisited*. Waugh saw the post-war world as Hooperism everywhere.

Waugh hated post-war England under the 'Attlee-Hooper terror' even more than he had hated the licentious 1930s. Literature, along with everything else, had now decayed beyond saving. In *The Loved One* (1948), two British poets, one old, the other young, sit in a shabby Beverly Hills bungalow alongside an empty, decaying swimming pool. Neither troubles to write poetry any more. Somewhere else, in the real world a couple of miles away, Aldous Huxley was prostituting his mind with scripts for Walt Disney's *Alice in Wonderland* and Sam Goldwyn's *Pride and Prejudice*. Disgust and mental breakdown (who could stay sane in such a world?) fuels Waugh's fine memoir-novel, *The Ordeal of Gilbert Pinfold* (1957); the Pinfolds were the ancestral owners of Piers Court – a telling little identity theft. The hero's 'strongest tastes were negative. He abhorred plastics, Picasso, sunbathing, and jazz –everything in fact that had happened in his own lifetime. The tiny kindling of charity, which came to him through his religion, sufficed only to temper his disgust and change it to boredom.'

According to Anthony Powell, Waugh longed for a knighthood but queered his pitch by testily not accepting an interim CBE. 'Irritability', he confessed in a late TV interview (satirically immortalised in *Pinfold*), was his cardinal fault. He had moved, in his last ten years, to another country house, Combe Florey, Somerset. For Waugh 'the country ... is a place where I can be silent'. He died, young in years, old in spirit, and largely silenced. His posthumous reputation received a huge boost from the 1981 TV version of *Brideshead Revisited*. 'How I found God and lived in a big house,' Kingsley Amis, as dyspeptic himself as Waugh, called John Mortimer's adaptation. It pulled in viewing figures of 10 million – most of whom Waugh would have despised, along with their ghastly colour television sets. It would, however, have amused Waugh mightily, had he lived to 2010 (alas impossible given his birth date) to see former members of the Bullingdon Club, vandals whom he had immortalised in the first paragraph of his first novel, lording it in 10 and 11 Downing Street and the London Mayor's Office. Was there no glass left in Oxford to break? he would have asked.

FN   Evelyn Arthur St John Waugh
MRT *Brideshead Revisited*
Biog M. Stannard, *Evelyn Waugh: The Early Years; No Abiding City* (2 vols, 1986, 1992)

POSTSCRIPT

175. Alec Waugh 1898–1981

Alec was their firstling and their darling lamb. Evelyn Waugh on his brother Alec

Alec Waugh is principally interesting to literary history for the dark shadow he cast, in childhood, on his five-and-a-half-year younger brother. Not that he felt himself the brighter of the two. 'If I were to pick up the autobiography of Alec Waugh,' he once said, 'the first name that I should look for in the index would be Evelyn Waugh.' Born when he was, Alec enjoyed an Edwardian childhood while Evelyn (b. 1903) suffered a wartime childhood – shops, cinemas, rations and loneliness. Neither of the boys was tall; at five-feet-five they were, in fact, just this side of titchy. Alec, however, did not let lack of inches handicap him. In his four years at Sherborne School, he was a 'blood' on the rugby field and a match-winning slogger on the cricket pitch. He also won the school prize for poetry. He was clever in the classroom and comradely outside it. 'My brother', wrote Evelyn, dourly, in 1962, 'was a zestful schoolboy ... I was not a zestful schoolboy.'

Arthur Waugh, the paterfamilias, had two great loves in life: his wife 'K' came well down a list topped by Sherborne and his 'firstborn'. Alec, his father dreamed, would be a great Shiburnian – school captain, at least. When the school broke up for the hols, a banner was raised at the gates of their Golders Green bungalow reading 'Welcome Home Heir to Hillfield'. Put out more flags, the sardonic Evelyn may have thought. So besotted with his son Alec was he that Arthur's friends and colleagues seriously feared for his sanity. He fired off daily letters, reproduced in Alexander Waugh's family biography, which are less those of a Victorian parent than of a passionate lover. He awaited his son's dutiful replies, we are told, 'sweatily'. His father's hopes, and quasi-incestuous lusts, were a heavy burden for any son. None the less, Alec made a good fist of it. There was a small hiccup about his pubescent addiction to self-abuse and the suicidal guilt that accompanied it. (Evelyn, by contrast, 'frigged' madly without the slightest juvenile remorse – or, as he reported, pleasure.) Alec, touchingly, brought himself to climax with Marlowe's 'Hero and Leander' – a poem that mixes athleticism with romance. Arthur, in a stream of crazily anxious letters, warned that the vice would lead to 'paralysis and softening of the brain', rot of the moral fibre, loose women and syphilis. Alec did not stop, but wisely stopped confessing it. Neither did he confess to his father that he was falling in love with a string of pretty heartbreakers at the school. Perhaps his moral fibre *was* rotting. He would grow up to be a shameless womaniser – 'the bald lecher' was his nickname on Evelyn's side of the family.

In 1915 Shirburnians were dying in the trenches faster almost than first-form boys were joining the school. Disaster of a more personal nature struck when Alec's nocturnal Don Juanism was discovered by the school authorities. Expulsion was automatic (Oscar Wilde was still a raw memory) but Alec was allowed, on Arthur's tearful pleading, to sit out his last term. But he was proscribed as a 'dirty little beast' and boys were warned to keep away from him. It was expertly hushed up: Evelyn, incredibly, did not learn of his brother's 'disgrace' until 1962, if we believe him.

Alec was old enough to answer Kitchener's call, but at seventeen too young to fight at the Front. During his protracted officer-cadet training at Berkhamsted, he mastered the art of the Vickers machine gun and courted (despite a lingering preference for boys) Barbara Jacobs, the daughter of the famous writer of his father's era, W. W. Jacobs – still remembered for his spine-chiller 'The Monkey's Paw'. Whatever his other moral derelictions, Alec was not, at this period, drunken. He rose every morning two hours before reveille, to write a novel. In seven weeks he had a manuscript of 115,000 words entitled, grandiloquently, *The Loom of Youth*. Privately he called it his 'love letter to Sherborne'. The work in progress was dispatched to his father for correction and censorship. When eventually published the novel was prefaced with a second love letter, to his father, loftily confessing that 'whatever altars I may have raised by the wayside, whatever ephemeral loyalties may have swayed me, my one real lodestar has always been your love'.

The Loom of Youth (1917) is a work of mind-numbing simplicity. It chronicles Gordon Caruthers's triumphs on the footer field, cricket pitch and in the classroom during his four years at 'Fernhurst' and reads like a guide to public school life for those poor swine (most of England, that is) unlucky enough not to attend one. For example: 'Breakfast is always rather a scramble, and nowhere more so than at a Public School. The usual Fernhurst breakfast lasted about ten minutes. Hardly anyone spoke, only the ring of forks on plates was heard and an occasional shout of "Tea" from the Sixth Form table.' When Gordon is himself a sixth-former, the narrative touches delicately on what is going on between him and a lower-form boy when, instead of applying themselves to evening prep, they bathe in 'the feverish waters of pleasure'.

The novel was circulated to a string of publishers, including his pater's Chapman and Hall, who thought it too hot to handle – on libel grounds principally, although the recent burning of Lawrence's *The Rainbow* was also a deterrent. It was eventually taken by Grant Richards, a newly founded house with no reputation to lose. In the intervening months before being old enough for the Front, the newly commissioned Alec continued with his overtures to Barbara, two years younger than he ('a dumpy muskrat of a girl', Alec's biographer calls her). It was her photograph, and his father's, that he took with him when he was finally posted to France. He survived Passchendaele by a fluke (100,000 of his comrades didn't) and soon saw war as the horrible thing it was. Disillusionment inspired the fine poem 'Carrion', a meditation on a corpse being eaten by rats in no man's land. 'I've done with warfare,' Alec wrote after the Somme – but it had not done with him. He surrendered to the Germans in the next big battle. 'My brother was no hero,' Evelyn was at pains to point out in later life and there were persistent allegations of a lack of pluck. When the situation was hopeless officers were expected to die, Webley revolver in hand, shouting 'for King and Country'.

While he saw out the war as a prisoner of war, Alec's novel was enjoying a wholly unanticipated success, running through five editions in as many months. The author was extravagantly praised. 'Your son is an astounding young man,' wrote H. G. Wells to Arthur, who needed no reassurance whatsoever on that score. *The Loom of Youth* was not, however, the source of unalloyed paternal pleasure. Sherborne saw it as 'a poisoned dagger' aimed at the school's heart. Alec's name was ritually removed, like Dreyfus's epaulettes, from the roll of Old Shirburnians, and Arthur was obliged himself to resign the same honour. It was the bitterest moment of his life. But it did not extinguish his love for his first-born – nothing could.

On his return in 1919, Alec married his Barbara. It would be a disaster; he was unable to consummate the union and the marriage was annulled two years later. According to Alec, 'inexperience was entirely to blame'. Girls, he discovered, were rather different from boys when it came to bathing in the feverish waters. He was, however, a quick learner and after this initial setback became a lifelong philanderer. He married twice more. His second wife, an Australian heiress, enabled him to buy his country house, Silchester, shortly before Evelyn acquired Piers Court. Joan Waugh indulged her husband's love of what he called 'hot countries' and hotter women, but the marriage fell apart, having yielded three children. In later life, Alec took American citizenship and a third wife. Engagingly modest, living entirely for sybaritic pleasure, he regarded himself as a 'very minor writer' with a genius for a brother.

His father had persuaded him not to publish two novels on homosexual themes while *The Loom of Youth* was still sensational. A small success with a less dangerous novel in the late 1920s, and his wife's wealth, allowed him to give up the sinecure with Chapman and Hall which Arthur had secured for him. Thereafter, apart from some stints as a creative writing instructor, he never worked again (other than writing). His life subsequently was that of a seedy international playboy. He wrote a lot – publishers were always interested in anything with the name 'Waugh' on the title page – and everyone liked him. In 1956 his melodrama about inter-racial love, *Island in the Sun*, enjoyed an unexpectedly huge success. A month or two earlier he had been considering ending it all with prussic acid. The novel and the movie (starring Harry Belafonte, who sang the title song) coincided with the boom in West Indian reggae music and growing civil rights unrest in the US. After the success of *Island in the Sun* Alec, Evelyn sarcastically observed, 'never drew a sober breath'.

Alec and Evelyn rarely crossed each other's paths over the years. Oddly it was the younger brother who seems to have been the more envious. In 1957 Evelyn brought a lawsuit against the *Daily Express*, a paper which had never forgiven him for the depiction of Beaverbrook as Lord Copper in *Scoop*. The *Express* columnist, Nancy Spain had claimed, gleefully, that *Island in the Sun* had sold more copies than all Evelyn's novels combined – so much for satire. The verdict was swung Evelyn's way by Alec good-naturedly testifying, in person, that Spain's allegation was untrue. The author of *Brideshead* ended up some £7,000 richer, untaxed. An amusingly spiteful portrait of the writer in old age is given by his nephew, Auberon:

> He lived for much of the year in Tangier, Morocco, where an old age pension from the state of New York enabled him to equip a house with cook, butler, and houseboy; at other times, he lived austerely as writer-in-residence at a midwestern university, eating his meals from divided, plastic plates in a room above the

students' canteen, and emerging from time to time to entertain his friends in London at elegant dinner parties, where he wore immaculately tailored but increasingly eccentric suits.

He died in Florida.

FN   Alexander Raban Waugh ('Alec')
MRT   *The Loom of Youth*
Biog A. Waugh, *Fathers and Sons: The Autobiography of a Family* (2004)

176. Nathanael West 1903–1940

West was about the most thoroughly pessimistic person I have ever known.
Robert M. Coates

West was born Nathan Weinstein, the son of first-generation Russian-Jewish immigrants from Lithuania. In the country they left, and that in which they settled, the Weinsteins were prosperous, secular and assimilationist by lifestyle. Nathan's father Max, a builder, had arrived in New York in the late 1890s at a period when Manhattan was exploding skywards. Brought up in an English-speaking household on Manhattan's Upper West Side, the future novelist did not regard himself as a Jew at all, but as an 'American'. Critics like Edmund Wilson (himself snootily WASP) none the less detect in West's work 'a kind of Eastern European suffering in common with Gogol ... and a sad, quick Jewish humour'.

At high school, Nathan (nicknamed 'Pep') was a contemporary of fellow Jew Lionel Trilling, later the most influential literary critic of his age: more influential, indeed, than Edmund Wilson. Unlike the over-achieving Lionel, Pep was defiantly idle – but quite as omnivorous in his private reading as the future King of Columbia University. He also knew his own mind, and from the first developed a distaste for the 'muddle-class' realism of Sinclair Lewis and Theodore Dreiser and a taste for French aesthetes and intellectual dandyism of the Wildean kind.

Nathan enterprisingly falsified his abysmal school transcript to get into Tufts where, after a couple of terms, he again falsified his academic record to transfer to Brown University. He was no model student – arriving, as he did, dripping with a dose of gonorrhoea, the effects of which embarrassed him for life in relations with women. At Brown he formed the most important relationship of his literary life with fellow undergraduate S. J. Perelman – later in life, the Marx Brothers' scriptwriter. Nathan scraped a degree. He always intended to be a writer and to that end in 1926 he 'went West' (as it pleased him to joke) by legally changing his name. It was an act of self-fashioning. At the same period he persuaded his father – who wanted his son to follow him into the family property business – to stump up for a trip to Paris where, for three months, the young would-be writer could lose himself among the Lost Generation.

For years he had been working on his first novel, *The Dream Life of Balso Snell*, a phantasmagorical satire on human delusion. Its concept bit off far more than even an embryonic genius could chew, but the novel's 'play on styles' was a useful apprenticeship. Returning from Paris in January 1927, West went to work as a night manager in a New York residential hotel. This observation post on the passing metropolitan tide suited him, as did the bohemian society of Greenwich Village. He had not the slightest long-term interest in the hotel business, however, and followed his idol, H. L. Mencken, in his maxim 'my sole interest is my writing'. In March 1929, Perelman introduced him, momentously, to a woman who wrote an agony column for a Brooklyn paper, and who showed him a batch of heart-rending letters. Later West would criminally steam open letters at the hotel he managed to examine the suffering they contained. Thus was born *Miss Lonelyhearts*.

West published his first story in 1929. The world collapsed in October that year, taking the Weinsteins' prosperity, which had been dwindling for some years, down with it. The Depression radicalised West politically. He would certainly have been hauled up as a 'Red' before McCarthy had he lived to be fifty-five. The unluckiest of writers, his debut novel, *Balso Snell* (six years in the writing), was delivered to the world in 1931. It was stillborn as the combined result of the financial collapse of its publisher, its printer, the whole US bookshop network and, with the Wall Street crash, the purchasing power of the American citizen. Had it made the shop windows and libraries of the country, *Balso Snell*'s bitter whimsy was anyway out of key with the mood of the moment.

West soldiered on with *Miss Lonelyhearts* (1933). His own description of the novel is succinct: 'A man is hired to give advice to the readers of a newspaper. The job is a circulation stunt and the whole staff considers it a joke. He welcomes the job, for it might lead to a gossip column, and anyway he's tired of being a legman.' Being an agony aunt, he discovers, is worse than doorstepping. It's an open line to the misery of the world. The eponymous, unnamed hero becomes a Christ-figure, tormented by a nihilist editor, Shrike (a bird which West, a knowledgeable ornithologist and avid hunter, particularly loathed). In Delehanty's bar, where hard-bitten newspapermen hole up, he is regarded contemptuously as a 'leper-licker'. He is, ultimately, assassinated by a cripple he tried in vain to help spiritually. The novel, razor-sharp in its writing, is a parable of Marxist alienation. W. H. Auden, one of the novelist's admirers, called it 'West's Disease'. Unfortunately the author's albatross-luck struck again. *Miss Lonelyhearts* was glowingly reviewed but, thanks to a distributor's glitch, no copies reached the bookstores. But even a novel as great as *The Great Gatsby* withered on the vine at this period, with only a couple of thousand sales. Towards the end of his life West calculated that all his novels combined had barely brought him a thousand dollars' income.

For his third novel, *A Cool Million* (1934), he refined his 'comic strip' technique. A Voltairean parody of Horatio Alger, it is ironically subtitled '*The Dismantling of Lemuel Pitkin*' and has the even more ironic epigraph: 'John D. Rockefeller would give a cool million to have a stomach like yours. (Old saying).' Assured that 'the world is an oyster', and buoyed by an Algerist belief in the American Dream, Lemuel sets out on his life's adventure. America defeats him and he ends up a prostheticised clown, dismembered daily on stage for the amusement of burlesque-house audiences. Meanwhile, the American financial system crashes, the 'Leather Shirts' take over the country and adopt the martyred Lemuel Pitkin as their Horst Wessel.

In 1933 West was hired as a screenwriter by Columbia Studios, then under the management of the crassest of moguls, Harry Cohn. Cynic about the movie industry that he was, the work came easily to West and for the last years of his life he was a prisoner of what he called the 'dream dump'. It furnished the material for his last effort in fiction, *The Day of the Locust* (1939). While his friend Scott Fitzgerald, in *The Last Tycoon*, targeted moguls such as Irving Thalberg, West did Hollywood from the bottom, with painter Tod Hackett (i.e. 'Death-Hack'), an artist forced into studio hackery, dreaming all the while of the burning of Los Angeles. The novel ends with a 'premier' outside a thinly disguised Grauman's Chinese Theater, on Hollywood Boulevard, under a huge marquee sign: 'Mr Kahn a Pleasure Dome Decreed'. (He was, luckily for him, no longer working for Cohn who, anyway, would have needed one of his flunkeys to explain the Coleridge allusion.) The rubber-neck crowd explodes into city-destroying rioters, engendered by the sheer *tedium vitae* of LA life. 'Sunshine isn't enough' was West's verdict on the west.

Aged thirty-seven, a few days after Scott Fitzgerald had died of a heart attack, West crashed his car, driving back from a hunting trip. He was a 'murderous' driver and had recklessly shot a crossing. He was killed, as was his newly married wife, Eileen McKenney, who normally, for reasons of self-preservation, refused to drive with him. As Freud maintained, there are no accidents in life. Everything has its motive – particularly self-destruction.

FN   Nathanael West (born Nathan Weinstein)
MRT *Miss Lonelyhearts*
Biog J. Martin, *Nathanael West: The Art of His Life* (1970)

177. Margery Allingham 1904–1966

The whole of life is about escape.

Allingham's parents ('second-generation London Irish') were journalists – her father Herbert specialising in hack adventure stories for the magazines. The line of work paid better than the quality fiction he was capable of writing, and he was not a writer to make sacrifices for art. Born in Ealing, Margery was brought up, until her thirteenth year, in an old rectory in rural Essex which she found idyllic, despite difficulties with her mother 'who never wanted children'. As the family fortunes waned with the decline of her father's energies, the Allinghams returned to London and Margery – a 'nervy, big-boned girl' and a precocious writer of stories – was bundled off to the Perse boarding school in Cambridge. She went on to study speech and drama at Regent Street Polytechnic in London, partly to 'cure her stammering and snobbery' but mainly 'to learn to write under my father'. She actually outwrote him. He was, however, her closest male companion until her twenties – a period of life which, incredibly, she passed ignorant of the 'facts of life', as sex was coyly called. Her speech impediment ('my ingrown hobble') was cured, but her lifelong tendency to thyroid-driven bulimia was not. It put an end to any dreams she might have had of a stage career – what trade paper, she wryly asked, advertised for 'fat actresses'? Her first effort in fiction, *Blackkerchief Dick* (1923), a tale of eighteenth-century smuggling, in her father's derring-do mould, was published when she was nineteen. It signposts two lifelong preoccupations: her love of coastal Essex and her fascination with spiritualism.

For a few years Margery earned an honest penny reviewing films – the new-fangled 'talkies' were all the rage. She took up longer fiction again at the time of her marriage in 1927 to Philip ('Pip') Youngman Carter, an artist who would later specialise as a skilled designer of book jackets, including those covering his wife's novels. She wrote, throughout life, under her father's surname. 'Sex', Youngman Carter ruefully confessed, 'was of minor importance to us.' Margery, in later life, described it as 'petrol' – a fuel which could be usefully diverted to writing ends. There were no children from the marriage, which seems to have had little internal combustion to it, but intermittent fondness.

Allingham's first thriller – which she suppressed in later life – was *The White Cottage Mystery* (1928), followed by the work which made her name and which introduced the amateur detective, Albert Campion, *The Crime at Black Dudley* (1929). The narrative was dictated to Pip, who took it down longhand. The younger son of a duke, and described on his first appearance as a 'silly ass', Campion owed something to Sayers's Lord Peter Wimsey. He would later marry Lady Amanda Fitton, introduced in *Sweet Danger* (1933) and, over the course of thirty years and eighteen novels, would evolve into something much less silly and ass-like. Allingham's finest 'Campion' is *The Tiger in the Smoke* (1952): the 'Smoke' is London and the 'Tiger' is a sadistic killer, Jack Havoc, just out of prison and on the homicidal prowl. The narrative grips from its first sentence ('It may just be blackmail') to its last ('The body was never found'). The novel's composition was preceded by Allingham's discovery of Pip's flagrant adulteries, which led to a three-year separation, and extreme emotional distress – for her, particularly.

Her mature novels take the form of intricate puzzle pieces which cross-hatch sinister crime with light social comedy. 'The thriller,' she believed, 'is a work of art as delicate and precise as a sonnet.' None the less, she voiced from time to time the ambition to write a 'real novel', but never quite got round to it, any more than her father had. Allingham and her husband had moved to Tolleshunt D'Arcy in 1934 (with her money, of course), where they were to spend the remainder of their life. Rural Essex was where Allingham felt safe. As her biographer notes, 'A secret unhappiness with her appearance may have contributed to her decision to move out of London.' She had grown enormously fat.

Youngman Carter, who always chafed at being 'Mr Allingham', had a good war. A would-be squire in the country and a man about town in London, his dash was turned to advantage in the army during the war and he retired with the rank of Lieutenant Colonel, in the Service Corps. In peacetime, as friends observed, he was 'pitied and patronised ... for living out his professional life in the shadow of his undeniably famous wife', whereas in the officers' mess he had been respected.

Allingham wrote more slowly in her later years. Huge sales in Penguin and in America (where she was a cultish favourite) kept her afloat and a step ahead of the ravenous taxman. In *The Beckoning Lady* (1955), she dramatises her epic battles with the Inland Revenue – a foe more tigerish than even Jack Havoc. Like her father, she was a chain smoker and died prematurely of cancer, aged sixty-two. Her terminal illness was preceded by a spell in Colchester's lunatic asylum, to recover from the recurrent breakdowns which had afflicted her through life. Youngman Carter completed her last novel, *Cargo of Eagles* (1968), and, after a vain attempt to keep the Campion novels going, died a couple of years later.

FN   Margery Louise Allingham (later Youngman Carter)
MRT   *The Tiger in the Smoke*
Biog   J. Thorogood, *Margery Allingham: A Biography* (1991)

178. Graham Greene 1904–1991

It is not a good idea to have only one biography of Greene. Biographer Michael Shelden

A quiz. Answer to the following 'yes', 'no' or 'maybe':

1. George Orwell shot an elephant
2. Olaudah Equiano was born in Africa
3. Jeffrey Archer attended Oxford University
4. Oscar Wilde died of syphilis
5. Graham Greene played Russian roulette

The answer to the first four is 'no'; to the fifth – 'yes', 'no', or 'maybe', according to whichever account of Graham Greene's life one selects. 'Maybe', in fact, is the word that attaches itself adhesively to everything posterity has been allowed to know about this most enigmatic of writers. Norman Sherry notes, warily, in the preface to his monumental 'authorised' (but grossly impeded) biography, 'A man who would write two versions of his diary was not a man who would give up his secrets easily.' Nor did he.

Sherry's attitude is properly deferential. Had he not admired Greene, he would not have spent the best (thirty!) years of his scholarly life on the project to be roundly abused at the end of it. The countering devil's advocate case was put by Michael Shelden, perhaps the least authorised biographer in literary history. The opening sentence of Shelden's biography, *The Man Within*, establishes the presiding shriek of denunciation: 'Young Graham Greene acquired a diverse experience of sin. He drank to excess, chased prostitutes, flirted with suicide, investigated whipping establishments, volunteered to spy against his own country.' In other words, a sexual degenerate and a traitor, to which, as the Sheldenian catalogue unrolls, one can add 'rabid anti-Semite', 'insincere convert to Catholicism' and 'practising paedophile'. Greene too, it is alleged, lusted rampantly after nine-year-old Shirley Temple's jiggling 'rump'. It was, implies Shelden, no accident that Greene should be the principal advocate for *Lolita* being published in the UK. No novelist, Shelden argues, has ever more appropriately worn the DOM's gabardine raincoat (in point of biographical fact, the trenchcoat was Greene's favoured dress). Shelden's disgust at Greene's sexuality is encapsulated in an index entry of de Sadeian depravity:

sex 68ff, 110, 192
anal sex 175
flagellation 161
incest theme 201–3

How, one wonders, can these sexual depravities be related to the novels which one used to read with such enjoyment? Shelden's implied answer is that Greene hated women and abused them. Similarly he hates his readers and abuses us. We should realise it.

Shelden's iconoclasm extends to the most famous of Greene's life-episodes – 'The Revolver in the Corner Cupboard'. Greene tells us that in 1923, paralysed with *Weltschmerz*, he took a firearm ('a small ladylike object') owned by his brother, loaded it with one bullet and strolled into the woods alongside his home. He then spun the chamber, put the muzzle 'into my right ear', and pulled the trigger. He lived. It was a cure – or so Greene claimed. The authorised biographer, Sherry, accepts the episode as both iconic and gospel: it happened. Shelden begs to differ: there was no Russian roulette; almost certainly the cartridges were blanks; the 'weapon' was a harmless starting pistol – all Greene risked was a ringing in the ears, if, indeed, the event happened at all. Quite likely it was a literary trope, lifted from Stevenson's short story, 'The Suicide Club' (1882) – RLS was a distant relative of Greene's.

The 'shilling facts' of Greene's life, about which there is less dispute, are as follows. He was the fourth son, of six children, of the headmaster of Berkhamsted School, where he himself went to school. As a schoolboy, Greene lived, ambiguously and unhappily, on both sides of the 'baize door'. At Berkhamsted he was tormented by a classmate (later identified as 'Carter') who was the 'incarnation of evil'. Greene also recalled the influence Marjorie Bowen's now wholly forgotten historical romance, *The Viper of Milan*, had on him, aged fourteen. Bowen's villainous Visconti supplied, he later said, 'the pattern' to which Catholicism would later give theological shape: 'perfect evil walking the world where perfect good can never walk again'. A key date in Greene's personal literary history was 1916. After the death of Henry James, he believed, the novel lost its 'religious sense – the sense of the importance of the human act.' It was a morally lost art form.

Greene's adolescence was troubled. There was a breakdown and psychotherapy, but he survived to go up to Oxford in 1922, where, in later life, none of his brilliant contemporaries (Waugh, Connolly, Henry Green, Betjeman) recalled him as other than a slight chill in the room. Like other unhappy undergraduates, he took solace in poetry. In his final year he vanity-published *Babbling April* (1925), the title alluding to T. S. Eliot's 'cruellest month'. Wastelands would be a lifelong interest. The other poet most admired by Greene was Lord Rochester, the rakehell who, after a life of epic sin and debauchery, converted to eleventh-hour Catholicism on his deathbed. Rochester came to embody, for Greene, that paradox of Charles Péguy's which is the epigraph to *The Heart of the Matter*: 'The sinner is at the very heart of Christianity.' The more sinful, the closer to God.

At Balliol, Greene read history, developed a strong head for drink, took a good 'second', and fell in love with a girl working in the local bookshop (Blackwell's), Vivienne Dayrell-Browning (1905–2003). A Catholic convert, Vivienne encouraged Greene to come across before they married in 1927. There would be two children, born in the 1930s, but not much happiness. *Babbling April* fell stillborn from the press. On leaving Oxford, Greene kept body and soul together by journalism. Had he stuck at it, it pleased him to recall in later life, he might – who knows? – have risen to the dizzy height of Letters' editor on *The Times*. On the side Greene – always a meticulous budgeter of his time – wrote a trio of Rafael Sabatini-style historical romances. *The Man Within* (1929) was accepted by Heinemann (his publisher for life, as they would be) and struck the public fancy, selling a whopping 13,000 in hardback. On the strength of these sales, and the contract that came with them, Greene turned to fiction full-time.

However, the two novels that followed missed the mark. Like John Buchan, Greene resolved to jump-start his career with a 'shocker'. His fourth effort, *Stamboul Train* (1932), chronicles murder, espionage and sexual shenanigans on the Orient Express as the train thunders, first-class, through various Ruritanias. Greene was not, as yet, a widely travelled writer. This 'entertainment', as Greene would classify his thrillers, did the trick. It sold hugely and was optioned by the movie industry. Greene now knew that if ever his 'novels' fell short he could make up his income with coarser fare. He followed up with the even more lurid *This Gun for Sale* (1936). In *Stamboul Train* Greene indulged a vein of malicious mischief, which came to be one of his hallmarks in fiction. His fellow Heinemann author, J. B. Priestley, was recognisably defamed as the sexual pervert, Q. C. Savory, and a libel suit was narrowly avoided. Why did Greene do such things? In 1938, as film reviewer on *Night and Day*, he incurred massive libel damages for his employer (shipwrecking the magazine only six months after its launch) with his review of *Wee Willie Winkie* and the allegation that Shirley Temple's backside figured in middle-aged men's masturbation fantasies. So it may have done, but it was naughty to say so in print.

Now a high-earning man of letters, Greene and his family moved to a large town house by Clapham Common (it is where Sarah and Henry live in *The End of the Affair* – Greene loved such in-jokes). Greene's first Catholic novel (or was it an entertainment? He was never sure) was *Brighton Rock* (1938) a tale of razor gangs, mortal sin and eternal damnation in Brighton – a town, famous for its dirty week-ends, which the author knew considerably better than Stamboul. *The Power and the Glory* (1940), set in a post-revolutionary, Catholic-persecuting Mexico, which he had visited in the late 1930s, took Greene further into daring fictional experiments with theology. Could one be a fornicating 'whisky priest' and still administer the sacraments to God's satisfaction? Greene followed up with the two novels which are routinely judged his best. In *The Heart of the Matter* (1948), set in wartime Sierra Leone, the hero Scobie embraces mortal sin (suicide) to validate his forgivable sin (adultery), also, as it happens, embezzling an insurance company in the process. Is Scobie a good man? In *The End of the Affair* (1951) set in a wartime England, God is conceived as a jealous lover – the great co-respondent in the sky. Is He a good God?

In 1943 Greene had published the first of his espionage novels, *The Ministry of Fear*. He knew the world he was writing about. On the outbreak of war he had been recruited by the Ministry of Information (Orwell's 'Minitruth'). Later in the war, he was transferred to MI6 and posted to Sierra Leone for two years. His unit was charged with counter-espionage and one of his direct superiors was Kim Philby – later unmasked as the leader of the 'Cambridge Spies'. Greene was fascinated by Philby and, after the traitor's flight to Moscow, wrote the fine novel, *The Human Factor* (1978) in which the moral dilemmas of Philbyesque treachery are scrupulously – if ambiguously – anatomised.

Greene separated from his wife in 1946. He had fallen in love with the rich, beautiful wife of a British politician, Catherine Walston (1916–1978), the original for Sarah in *The End of the Affair*. Like Sarah, she proved, finally, elusive. Loyalty to her Labour politician husband and five children, rather than the intrusion of the Almighty, seems to have ended the affair.

No novelist, until John Grisham, has more successfully adapted into film than Greene; and no work of his adapted more successfully than the screenplay-novella *The Third Man* (1949), a movie which – marinated in deepest *noir* – cooks all the Greenian themes to a point just short of parody. Vienna, the ruined imperial city, occupied by four competing armies, in which the only community is via the sewers, is Greeneland's *locus classicus*. In later life, now a literary eminence, Greene travelled widely – finding, as his novels reflect – hearts of darkness and ugly Americans everywhere. *The Quiet American* (1955) eerily foretells the Vietnam debacle; *The Burnt-Out Case* (1961) follows Conrad's Marlow to an upriver Congolese leper colony. *The Comedians* (1966) is set in Papa Doc's Haiti, where the state religion is voodoo, bastardised Catholicism. Meanwhile, in his later years, Greene himself lived luxuriously in his apartments on the French Riviera and Paris, or his villa on Anacapri, or the Ritz, invariably, when passing through London. If the sublunary world was hell, he saw it through the glaze of a five-star hotel window and the stained window of an idiosyncratic – or, as he called it, paradoxical to the end – 'atheistic' Catholicism.

FN   Henry Graham Greene
MRT   *The End of the Affair*
Biog M. Shelden, *Graham Greene: The Man Within* (1994); N. Sherry, *The Life of Graham Greene*, 3 vols (1989, 1994, 2004)

179. Patrick Hamilton 1904–1962

My new best friend. Nick Hornby, on first reading Patrick Hamilton

Hamilton was born into a wretched enclave of the Edwardian middle classes. His father was an unsuccessful author, failed barrister and a drunk, sozzling his way through a £100,000 inheritance. Bernard Hamilton's first marriage had been with a prostitute whom he tried, vainly, to 'save'. His second wife, Patrick's mother, was a painter and writer, but the marriage was unhappy, as were the three children's spectacularly unfulfilled lives. Patrick was born in Sussex, and educated at a series of good schools, including Westminster. He was not one of its prize products. As a child he suffered poor health (aged fifteen, he caught the epidemic Spanish influenza) and grew up neurotic, shy and myopic. His impressionable early years were passed during the First World War – not something to add gaiety to any boy's life. University was not an option – bright as Patrick manifestly was, he simply could not pass the exams – and the family money was running short. His father, whose malign shadow haunted his children throughout their lives, wanted him to go into business, but from the first he was determined to be a writer or actor. His mother and sister supported him financially, but reluctantly.

His stage career failed, although he picked up a shrewd sense of what worked with audiences. Hamilton's first efforts in authorship were poetry in the then fashionable Georgian style, but fiction turned out to be his true *métier*. Aged only twenty, he published his first novel, *Monday Morning* (1925), forming in the process a lifelong friendship with the publisher, bibliophile, and himself an occasional novelist, Michael Sadleir. It was an auspicious start and other novels followed, in the depressive-realistic style of Gissing or the jaunty comic style of W. W. Jacobs (Hamilton heartily loathed modernism): *Craven House* (1926), *Twopence Coloured* (1928), *The*

Midnight Bell (1929), *The Siege of Pleasure* (1932). Hamilton had a gift for the reso-nant title, and the books went down well with library readers.

His breakthrough came not with fiction but with the hit stage play, *Rope* in 1929. It was a long-time earner for him (more so when Alfred Hitchcock adapted it, brilliantly, for the screen in 1948). A bleak melodrama, centred on a psychopathic murderer, the plot hinges on a fine *coup de théâtre* – a corpse secreted throughout the action (unknown to the audience) on stage. Hamilton followed up with another hit, the Victorian psychological thriller, *Gas Light* (1938), revived for the West End theatre in 2009. Its action depends on the vagaries of the gas-mantle. The gimmick, used on stage, is that the brightness, or dimness, of any one light depended on how many people in the house were turning the utility on or off in other rooms.

Hamilton had a disastrously unhappy personal life, exacerbated by chronic alco-holism. In 1927, following his father's example, he fell for a prostitute. The misery fed, creatively, into the trilogy, *Twenty Thousand Streets Under the Sky* (1935), Ham-ilton's 'black history' of London. He married Lois Martin in 1930. With his stage successes and his growing reputation as a novelist it should have been the saving of him, but while walking through Earls Court in January 1932 he was hit by a drunk driver. His face was scarred, he lost the use of an arm and contracted a permanent limp. It coincided with the 'Slump', and ten years of misery for the nation. Patrick Hamilton would be 'walking wounded' for the rest of his life. Many people assumed, embarrassingly, that his disability was a war injury. His marriage also failed.

In the same depressed middle period of his career, Hamilton published his mas-terpiece: *Hangover Square, or, The Man with Two Minds: a Story of Darkest Earl's Court in the Year 1939* (1941). 'The Man' is George Harvey Bone, an amiable dolt, with 'great golfer's wrists', who finds himself in 'the wrong set': upper middle-class idlers and boozers whose days are passed doing nothing in Earls Court. Hamilton catches their in-group slang with devastating accuracy. Bone falls in love with a 'bitch', Netta, who exploits, betrays and humiliates him. Unluckily for her, he is schizo-phrenic. When the 'click' occurs in his brain, a deadly second personality takes over. The 'other' Bone drowns Netta in her bath with the apology, 'I'm sorry, I didn't hurt you did I?' and kills her lover. He then makes his way to Maidenhead – for obscure reasons – where he kills himself. The headline in the gutter press reads: 'Slays Two. Found Gassed. Thinks of Cat'. The novel ends in September, 1939, with Chamber-lain's declaration of war on the radio. *Hangover Square* was given the Hollywood film treatment in 1945. The result regularly, and deservedly, wins awards as the worst film-fiction turkey ever projected on to the silver screen.

Unfit for active service and now rich enough to do nothing but drink and make himself unfit for anything, Hamilton spent the war years watching the odd game of cricket, and hobnobbing with a select group of friends in Fitzrovia (haunt of those other legendary drinkers, Dylan Thomas and J. MacLaren Ross). In his last years, writing was beyond him, though he still had money from the plays (*Gaslight* was also filmed twice, the second time with Greta Garbo in the lead). He completed one other major work of fiction, *Slaves of Solitude* (1947).

His marriage was long wrecked, although the divorce did not come through until 1953. He had lived for years as a bachelor in clubs and at the Albany, the select address in Piccadilly, and in 1954 he remarried (to Lady Ursula ('La') Winifred Stewart). There is some doubt as to whether, even sober, Hamilton was sexually robust. In his last years he was wholly sodden and died of cirrhosis. Everyone agrees nowadays that he is less read than he should be: but posterity, obstinately, declines to read him.

FN   Anthony Walter Patrick Hamilton
MRT *Hangover Square*
Biog S. French, *Patrick Hamilton: A Life* (1993)

180. Christopher Isherwood 1904–1986

I have no sense of myself as a person exactly, just as a lot of reactions to things.

'Xtopher', wrote Stephen Spender in 1931, 'is a cactus.' Prickly, solitary, self-suffi-cient, hard to love, untouchable, Isherwood confirmed Spender's judgement with his everywhere quoted catchphrase, '*I am a camera* with its shutter open, quite passive, recording not thinking.' A narcissistic camera one should add. 'His princi-pal subject', says his biographer, 'was himself.' Selfishness is the source of the dia-mantine clarity of his vision, its hardness and, ultimately, its insensitivity. Magnus Hirschfeld, the Berlin sexologist, diagnosed Isherwood, unpejoratively, in the 1930s as 'infantile ... possessed of the sexuality of a schoolboy'. The artist Keith Vaughan saw him in late middle age as a 'dehydrated schoolboy'. Humphrey Spender, who photographed him sensitively, thought Christopher incapable of loving anyone but Christopher. Not that it inhibited him from physical contact: by the early 1950s, it is calculated, he had had some 400 partners – including Don Bachardy, thirty years younger, who was with Isherwood from the early 1950s until his death. An artist, Bachardy spent Isherwood's last days – he was dying slowly of prostate cancer – sketching his lover's face; creating, on paper, one of the few literary death masks of modern times.

Isherwood was born into what he called the English 'poshocracy', with a double-barrelled name (Christopher William Bradshaw-Isherwood), a family seat in Cheshire, money and a pedigree stretching back to the sixteenth century. His life's work would be a serial severance of everything that connected him to Marple Hall, his family, his king and his country. He was helped when his father, a professional soldier, was killed in the First World War, when Christopher was eleven. His mother, Kathleen, became the focus of his youthful repudiations; something that caused her pain, and him little worry. Like Coriolanus, who banished Rome, Isherwood disowned his family. When in the 1940s he took out American citizenship, he stripped his name down to 'Christopher Isherwood'. He would, one suspects, have been happy with 'Christopher X' or Spender's 'Xtopher'.

At Cambridge, he wilfully failed his exams and later walked out on the medical training into which the aspirations of his mother had forced him. If he couldn't be a squire, Kathleen wanted her son to be at least a Harley Street physician. It was not at all what Isherwood wanted, any more than he wanted to live under England's 'heterosexual dictatorship'. Sexually democratic Berlin, where he expatriated himself in 1930, 'meant boys': *Strassenjunge* and *Puppenjunge* (street kids and rent boys) impoverished by the Depression, desperate to sell their bodies. Not gay but *pleite* – skint. Berlin also supplied the stimulus to become what W. H. Auden, the leader of their 1930s 'gang', dictated Christopher should be, 'The Novelist of the Future'. In Weimar Germany, together with fellow 'gangsters' Auden and Spender, Isherwood embraced Homer Lane's 'doctrine of original virtue', which held that 'there is only one sin: disobedience to the inner law of our own nature'. Or, as the more ironic Rabelais put it, 'vous fay ce que vouldras'. Isherwood always did.

Berlin represents the first, and most creative, phase of his fictional career with *Mr Norris Changes Trains* (1935) and *Goodbye to Berlin* (1939). The sharply etched, comic depictions of Herr Issyvoo, Mr Norris and – most memorably – Sally Bowles capture the comedy of Weimar Berlin at the point of its fall, as effectively, but more wittily, than even Brecht did in his *Threepenny Opera*. Less successful was Isherwood's indulgently autobiographical novel, *Lions and Shadows* (1938), subtitled 'An Education in the Twenties'. Unsurprisingly, Isherwood does England badly. It was, after all, not his kind's country.

Nor was Germany, after the rise of Hitler and his black-uniformed, pathologically homophobic goons. In January 1939, Auden and Isherwood left together for America. On board the boat taking them from England, 'Christopher heard himself say: "You know, it just doesn't mean anything to me any more – the Popular Front, the party line, the anti-Fascist struggle. I suppose they're OK but something's wrong with me. I simply cannot swallow another mouthful." To which Wystan replied:

"Neither can I".' In America, Auden would be 'East Coast', Isherwood – drawn magnetically by Hollywood – 'West Coast'. The cactus thrives in southern California and so did Xtopher. In New York Auden turned to the Western religion of his fathers: in Los Angeles Isherwood went over to the Eastern mysticism of the tinseltown gurus. Vedanta gave him some release from the tyranny of being himself. 'I am so utterly sick of being a person – Christopher Isherwood, or Isherwood, or even Chris,' he had told John Lehmann, a few years earlier.

In America, both Auden and Isherwood outgrew the need for 'boys'. Between purgative bouts of transcendentalism, Isherwood drank too much and never succeeded – beyond making a comfortable income – as a screenwriter. He was consistently misogynistic, sometimes anti-Semitic, always witty, rarely nice. Throughout life, and particularly in America, he was a force for enlightenment in sexual politics – it was where his frontline was. He wrote fiction of which the bundled sketches (the genre perfected in the Berlin stories) of *Down There on a Visit* (1962) shows his light touch to advantage. The best work of fiction from this second phase of Isherwood's writing career – among a ton of tedious writing about Vedanta and some brilliantly bitchy autobiography – is *A Single Man* (1964). A novel about being gay in the 1960s, it is, among its other attractions, a classic Los Angeles story and was filmed to critical acclaim in 2010, directed glossily by Tom Ford.

Isherwood died very rich, leaving some $2 million. It was largely supplied by profitable, and grossly romanticised, adaptations on stage and film (notably *Cabaret*) of his Sally Bowles Berlin story.

FN   Christopher William Bradshaw Isherwood
MRT   *Mr Norris Changes Trains*
Biog P. Parker, *Isherwood: A Life* (2004)

181. Henry Green 1905–1973

It's best they shouldn't know about one.

Henry Yorke sprang from two classes of English life which traditionally have had little interest in reading novels and even less interest in writing the things: aristocrats and plutocratic factory owners. Yorke's father was a wealthy industrialist; his mother came from noble stock. Vincent Yorke's stock, in his Birmingham shop floor, was lavatory furnishings – among other unliterary necessities of life. A younger brother, Henry Yorke was less hearty than his siblings and much less so than his father: a domestic tyrant who survived to a great age rendering his son's later life 'unmitigated hell'. Henry was born in Tewkesbury and serenely progressed from Eton to Oxford, joining there an elite (the 'Brideshead Generation') which would clubbably dominate literary London for decades. The Bridesheads loved university – in a sense they never left it – but despised university education. Swots rated scarcely higher than oiks in their register. Green disdained even the modest efforts required for a gentleman's third, leaving Oxford degreeless. He had, however, finished an accomplished first novel, *Blindness* (1926), an allegory of the writing life for which Blind Man's Buff would always be his favourite analogy. He had already chosen his inscrutable pen-name, 'Henry Green', having rejected the even less chromatic 'Brown'.

Red was the actual colour of the year 1926 – and Green entered the real world at a time of cataclysmic upheaval. The General Strike shook old England – based as its structure was on old blood and old money – and factory owners were also in the firing line. Once the strikers' hash was settled Green went to work on the shop floor of the Yorkes' Farringdon factory in Birmingham. He was apolitical by nature, but the experience honed his uncannily sharp ear for class dialect: no novelist is more virtuosic with the phonemes of English life than Henry Green. One *hears* the texts – it's a distinctive experience. Family destiny soon promoted Henry to senior managerial rank. He moved to London, where he would remain – as his *Who's Who* entry proclaimed – an 'industrialist' until 1959. 'The office routines of Henry Yorke,' his biographer tells us, 'were useful, even essential to the imaginative work of Henry Green': the more so since his routines were highly remunerative, never onerous, and brought a chauffeur, butler and good cook with them. Yorke married Adelaide Biddulph, the well-off daughter of a banker, in 1929. He was thus doubly protected against the oncoming slump and able to nurture his finely crafted prose during the depths of the Depression. In their West End establishment the Yorkes employed five live-in servants. Servants were of great interest to him, as a novelist.

Over the next twenty years, the body of work on which Green's reputation relies emerged. Their titles are highly characteristic and wholly inscrutable: e.g. *Living* (1929), *Loving* (1945), *Caught* (1943), *Back* (1946), *Party Going* (1939). What novel could not call itself '*Living*'? Green's fiction surrenders its purposes grudgingly, and with fewer wasted words than even Elmore Leonard who is on record as saying that eloquence lies in 'not saying anything – if that'. Green is, as John Ashbery aptly put it, 'the Cordelia of modern novelists'. Her terse rejoinder to her father Lear, 'Nothing', could well have been borrowed as one of his titles. As his biographer records, 'Green never wrote under his real name, wouldn't let his publishers distribute biographical information about him, and disliked being photographed' (except, occasionally, from behind). He also disliked travel, which, as he enigmatically informed his closest friend, Anthony Powell, 'interferes with my masturbation'. Or, one might add, his adulteries, which in later life were numerous and, despite his pathological secretiveness, much gossiped about in his circle.

During the war, Green was one of the 'progressive novelists' Waugh was snide about who joined the London Fire Service, brandishing their piddling 'syringes' against the Dornier and Heinkel aircraft. The author of the *Sword of Honour* trilogy was, of course, a commando. During the Blitz, Green – who resolutely remained 'in the ranks' – actually came under more fire than many frontline troops. His views on the service, as reflected in *Caught*, are, however, characteristically jaundiced. In the course of that war (an event he found excessively boring), Green composed what is agreed to be his finest work, *Loving* – a narrative centred on English servants in a large house, the 'Castle', during wartime in neutral Ireland, with its central character a senior footman, who is angling for a vacant butlership. Meanwhile, somewhere else, millions are dying. But what do the Normandy Landings matter, when a butlership is at issue?

In a 1958 *Paris Review* interview, with his unlikely admirer, the pornographer Terry Southern, Green recalled getting the idea for *Loving* from a manservant in the fire service during the war, who had asked an ancient butler 'what the old boy most liked in the world. The reply was: "Lying in bed on a summer morning, with the window open, listening to the church bells, eating buttered toast with cunty fingers." I saw the book in a flash.' That radioactive word was, one suspects, inserted as a little jab at the author of *Candy*.

Green was a confirmed alcoholic by his forties. He effectively stopped writing in the early 1950s and was expensively retired from the family firm at the end of the decade to welter in drink until his death. Green's narrative technique is an acquired taste: but all agree on its uniqueness. He admired modernists like Kafka and Joyce, he informed Southern, but they were 'like cats which have licked the plate clean. You've got to dream up another dish if you're to be a writer.' In life, as in art, indirection was his (mis)guiding principle. 'Most of us walk crabwise to meals and everything else,' he declared. 'The oblique approach in middle age is the safest thing.'

FN   Henry Green (Henry Vincent Yorke)
MRT *Loving*
Biog J. Treglown, *Romancing: The Life and Work of Henry Green* (2000)

182. Arthur Koestler 1905–1983

Often when I wake at night I am homesick for my cell in the death-house in Seville and, strangely enough, I feel that I have never been so free as I was then.

As a general rule, the fuller the life, the less the fiction. It is astonishing that in a career as packed with excitement as Arthur Koestler's, he was able to take time off to write even one novel. Had he chosen, he could have written that novel in any of the five languages which were, at different times, his 'first'. He could also, over the course of his life, have called half a dozen countries home (the fictional setting he preferred was 'Neutralia' – a version of Samuel Butler's Erewhon.) And no novelist has come closer to death in life more often.

Koestler served – or, at least, enrolled – in the French Foreign Legion (P. C. Wren never did) and wielded a shovel with the British Army Pioneer Corps, latrine-digging. He also served time in several jails – once under the threat of imminent execution. He shared a poison potion with Walter Benjamin in readiness for the expected Nazi invasion in France. Benjamin, unfortunately, was obliged to swallow his. Koestler and Camus, the two most filmstar-handsome intellectuals of their time, chased skirt together. One of his innumerable conquests was Simone de Beauvoir, then the consort of J. P. Sartre (not handsome). 'He kept pushing and pushing until I said "yes" to shut him up,' de Beauvoir tartly recalled: 'I really detested him, that arrogant fool.' Like others who prated about ethics, Cyril Connolly recalled, 'you couldn't leave your wife alone with him for a minute'. The list of women who claimed, plausibly, to have been ravished by Koestler is impressive. They included his friend Michael Foot's wife, Jill Craigie. Koestler was living proof of the proverb 'he who has a Hungarian friend needs no enemy'. None the less, this monstrously unstable, incorrigibly selfish man wrote a novel which, arguably, if it did not change history, changed the way the West saw its recent history. He should have won the Nobel Prize – twice at least. He never did.

Koestler's father, Henrik, was a textile importer in Budapest, a self-made, highly intelligent man. His mother was Austrian, of patrician Viennese descent. The family was Jewish by blood, secular in practice, and well off. Arthur was the only child. German was spoken at home; Hungarian outside, in a city rich in its Jewish-European culture. Henrik's business collapsed during the First World War, and the family moved to Vienna – Arthur's life was never to be settled again. He picked up education in various schools, demonstrating himself to be fearsomely precocious and combative. In his teens he studied engineering in Vienna, but never graduated. He could not see the point of exams: they assumed someone who knew more than him.

In 1926 he took off for Palestine, to work on a kibbutz. After a few weeks the kibbutz decided Israel did not need him. Koestler, who took the rejection badly, found his true vocation as a journalist. It was at this period that he espoused the hardline Zionist theory of Vladimir Jabotinsky that Israel (as it was to be) could only establish and maintain itself by strength and, if necessary, violence. It was also Koestler's stern view that Jews should either emigrate to their homeland or assimilate wholly to where they were. He left Palestine in 1929 to live by his pen in Paris and Berlin and then there occurred what he described as the 'explosion' in his brain. By 1931, he was a card-carrying member of the German Communist Party and, when required, a street-fighter. He married a fellow Party member in 1935, and separated from her in 1937. Koestler, as brave as he was reckless, exposed himself to huge personal risks in the Spanish Civil War, which led to his being imprisoned by the Francoists and sentenced to the firing squad. Only intervention at high level from Britain saved him. The experience – months' long – in the death cell was formative.

In the next couple of years he supported himself by writing sex encyclopedias – a field in which he had also undertaken much risky fieldwork. He also wrote *Spanish Testament* (1937) about his experiences, published by Gollancz. In 1938 he finished writing his first novel, *The Gladiators* (in German) – on Spartacus (a favourite Marxist theme, see Howard Fast, page 523) and resigned the Communist Party, which he believed to be in a condition of 'moral degeneration' and no longer worthy of him. In the novel (first called *Slavenkrieg* – slave war), Spartacus is portrayed as a proto-socialist who failed in his revolution because he lacked the necessary Jabotinsky-ian ruthlessness. *The Gladiators* appeared a few months before the outbreak of the Second World War and made no impact.

Undiscouraged, he threw himself into his next novel, *Darkness at Noon*, in Paris. It was translated from German into English by his current consort, sculptress Daphne Hardy. Following the outbreak of war, Koestler had been interned in France and his papers confiscated, so the novel's manuscript had to be smuggled across the Channel by Hardy. As Michael Scammell notes, 'Rarely can a major novel have been written at such breakneck speed or under such conditions of chaos and fear, with arrest and persecution a palpable threat and whole chapters written inside a concentration camp'. Koestler escaped the camp, however, and joined the Foreign Legion. After a few months he deserted and made his way to England in 1941, as an illegal immigrant, intending to commit suicide if apprehended or turned back. Once arrived, he was again put behind bars and remained so when *Darkness at Noon* was published, in 1940.

The novel centres on Rubashov a former party leader in an unidentified state – clearly the USSR. It begins with him being brutally woken from his dreams by the secret police and taken off for a months' long interrogation. The novel was inspired by the 1930s Moscow show trials in which leader after leader appeared in court – apparently not coerced physically – to confess absurd capital crimes against the regime before being shot. Accepting their fate was one thing – but why had they accepted their guilt? In the novel, the interrogator Ivanov, a former friend, relentlessly brings Rubashov (who in point of fact was indomitably loyal to the Party) to a realisation that whatever his 'subjective' illusions, 'objectively' he is a traitor to the cause – specifically to 'No. 1' (i.e. Big Brother, Stalin, Hitler). Ivanov himself is liquidated, to be replaced by the more brutal Gletkin. Rubashov, his brain thoroughly washed, is duly shot. The novel had a powerful impact on thinking in the West – and, clearly, on his friend Orwell's *Nineteen Eighty-Four*.

After a year in the 'Alien Pioneer Corps', and a mental health breakdown (which may have been confected), Koestler was transferred to the Ministry of Information. Not all his information – such as his early publicity about the fact of the Holocaust – went down well. In 1943, he found time to write a third novel, *Arrival and Departure*. A sequel to *Darkness at Noon*, it takes the form of a prolonged psychoanalysis of Peter Slavek ('slave' and 'Slav' are evoked), a former revolutionary in Neutralia. Gradually he comes to terms with his serial betrayals, political compromises and guilt. *Arrival and Departure*, the first novel Koestler wrote in English (the language he came to admire for its having 'no fat, only muscles'), was relatively unsuccessful.

In late 1945 Koestler returned to Palestine – currently in turmoil. The result was his other major work of fiction, the *roman à thése*, *Thieves in the Night* (1946). The Koestlerian hero, Joseph, is rejected by a Gentile woman on seeing that he is circumcised. Joseph embarks on a voyage of discovery into his genetic origins in Palestine. He works on a kibbutz and, after this apprenticeship, throws himself into the Zionist struggle. The novel contains sharp satire of the British officials enforcing the Mandate and tendentious portrayals of the Arabs as – among other bad things – rapists and killers (centrally of Joseph's lover, Dina). Joseph ends the novel a conscientious terrorist.

Koestler became a British citizen in 1948. By now he had a new partner, Mamaine Paget (English despite her name – stunningly beautiful, inevitably) who became his second wife in 1950. They moved to France. Koestler was now not merely a defector from communism, but its most formidable foe. He edited a CIA-sponsored collection by prominent intellectuals similarly disaffected, *The God That Failed* (1949). It seemed at this point he might emigrate to the US, where he was now welcome. Instead he took up semi-permanent residence in London, now a wealthy man. In 1965 (Mamaine having died) he married his long-time secretary, Cynthia Jefferies and published two further novels, *The Age of Longing* (1951) and *The Call*

Girls (1972), which are mere shavings from his workshop floor. The major works of his late period – *The Sleepwalkers*, *The Act of Creation*, *The Ghost in the Machine* – are books which, each of them, would for lesser men have required a lifetime's immersion in different disciplines.

A powerful force in British and world debate, he was the prime example of Sartre's *auteur engagé*. He remained, to the end, astoundingly wide-ranging in the issues and ideas he engaged with. Among other things he was a campaigner against capital punishment, and for the right to suicide. Terminally ill – but writing to the end – he committed suicide, persuading his luckless wife (decades his junior and in good health) to go with him. On the web, the paranoid suggestion that he was murdered by Mossad is rampant. Looking at his extraordinary life it may well be true.

FN   Arthur Koestler
MRT   *Darkness at Noon*
Biog   M. Scammell, *Koestler: The Literary and Political Odyssey of a Twentieth-Century Skeptic* (2009)

183. Anthony Powell 1905–2000

The thing that counts in writing is staying power. It's that, more than anything, that gives you a reputation.

The first paragraph of *A Question of Upbringing* (1951), the first volume of Powell's twelve-volume *Dance to the Music of Time* sequence, opens with a London road-mending in winter. Nothing is happening: 'The men at work at the corner of the street had made a kind of camp for themselves, where, marked out by tripods hung with red hurricane-lamps, an abyss in the road led down to a network of subterranean drain-pipes.' The description meanders on for another 200 words, ending: 'The grey, undecided flakes, continued to come down, though not heavily, while a harsh odour, bitter and gaseous, penetrated the air. The day was drawing in.'

Where, the reader wonders, is all this going? Nowhere very quickly, it's safe to assume, like the hole in the road. But the effect is instantly hypnotic. No writer in English is more the master of the slow tempos of life than Powell. *Afternoon Men*, his first published novel, is the chronicle of city fellows with huge expanses of post-meridian time, and nothing to fill it with – except, of course, cocktails, gossip and another cocktail. It captures, as in a sealed capsule, the feel of the dull leisure of the high inter-war period. What was unstoppably coming, of course – and one feels the imminence gathering through the 'Dance' sequence – was another 'Great War', even more cataclysmic than the last. That *would* be a happening.

Anthony Powell was the only child of a distinguished soldier and a mother, some fifteen years older than her husband. He was officer class; she had her roots in the landowning classes of England. Somewhat perversely, he grew up prouder of his Welshness (his surname, he ordained, should be pronounced to rhyme with 'Noel' and not 'towel'). At Eton he fell in with Henry Green and Cyril Connolly and at Balliol College, Oxford, with Evelyn Waugh, as one of what would later be called the 'Brideshead Generation'. One of Powell's critics wittily retitles his great work 'A Dance to the Eton Boating Song'. Stylish ennui was the approved attitude and Powell, like Connolly, would be a connoisseur of the corrosive 'enemies of promise', his chosen terrain being the 'acceptance world'. The term is derived from city jargon for 'selling short' – i.e. money for jam.

He left Oxford – though in one sense he never did – with the de rigueur 'gentleman's third' in history and drifted to London, as if drawn by a magnet. 'I am a metropolitan man,' he once said of himself. He joined the publisher Duckworth where his father had 'friends'. One of his early signings was Evelyn Waugh, whose *Decline and Fall* would influence his own work. *Afternoon Men* came out under the Duckworth imprint in 1931, to be followed in quick succession by *Venusberg* (1932) and *From a View to a Death* (1933). They are, all of them, wittily dispirited versions of 'the way we live now' – or, more precisely, how Powell's class lived. In December 1934 (always his favourite month – he liked the gloom) Powell married Lady Violet Georgiana Pakenham, an offspring of the English Catholic aristocracy. The couple would have two sons. Was the marriage happy? 'I should like to say more about Powell's marriage, but I can't,' his biographer sighs.

In 1936 Powell left Duckworth for a short spell of scriptwriting in Los Angeles. It did not please, although it was remunerative. On the outbreak of war, he gave up writing for the duration. After a false start in the infantry – for which years of indolence had rather unsuited him – Powell found his niche in 'intelligence', working as a liaison officer with expatriate allies from occupied countries in Europe. He was demobilised in 1945 with the rank of major, a chestful of decorations, and a sense of vague remorse that he had had such a cushy war – and, as he said, a very 'boring' one. One of the allusions which comes up, time and again, in the wartime volumes of *Dance* is from Alfred de Vigny's ironically titled *Servitude et grandeur militaires*. The French poet served in the army for fourteen years without seeing any action whatsoever. Powell's father had seen real action in the earlier war.

In 1948, he fell, as he always did, into a comfortable berth as the *Times Literary Supplement* fiction review editor. In 1950 he inherited a fortune from an uncle he barely knew. Money, too, always seemed to fall his way, and enabled him to move into a fine country house, The Chantry, in Somerset. Another bequest, when his father died, in 1959, insulated him against the inconveniences of post-war austerity. Financial security also enabled him to embark on his grand project, *A Dance to the Music of Time*, and to take his own time doing it. The sequence was launched in 1951 – the year of the 'Festival of Britain' which, in his prelude to his grand project, *The Sword of Honour* trilogy, Waugh portrays as the end of English civilisation. Under his series hero's less jaundiced, but equally gloomy eye, Powell surveys fifty years of England. The viewpoint is conservative, like Waugh's, but less irritably so. Powell rarely put people's backs up. 'Tony is the only Tory I have ever liked,' said George Orwell – someone who elsewhere repudiated everything Powell's class stood for. The design is loose-knit. Characters drift in and drift out with no more purpose than jellyfish in the ocean stream. Nothing is hurried – but time passes and things do happen. The reader is given the task of assembling, rather than being told, what is going on. *The Acceptance World* (1955) opens, typically, with a lavishly slow motion description of a seedily genteel hotel, some fortune-telling, and an uneventful tryst between the unsinkable Uncle Giles and his nephew Nicholas – neither of whom has what Othello calls 'occupation'. This life-drift only makes sense in terms of Jenkins's antagonist, Widmerpool, the 'getter on', a coming man who – inevitably – will die a lord. Should one strive, or let life happen and observe it, ironically, keeping afloat as best one can?

In later life, Powell's closest friend was Malcolm Muggeridge, a former comrade in army intelligence and now the editor of *Punch*. Powell was recruited to the magazine in 1953, as literary editor, on the then huge salary of £1,500 p.a. Alongside *Dance*, which he completed in 1975, Powell kept private journals which, when published in 1982, revealed an increasingly bilious temperament. His last novel, *The Fisher King*, came out in 1986. He turned down a knighthood – even though it was offered by a Conservative administration. It would, probably, have looked paltry alongside his wife's lineage – or perhaps too Widmerpoolian. He left over £1.5 million on his death and a fictional sequence to rival Balzac's.

FN   Anthony Dymoke Powell
MRT   *The Acceptance World*
Biog   M. Barber, *Anthony Powell: A Life* (2004)

184. Ayn Rand 1905–1982

If any civilisation is to survive, it is the morality of altruism that men have to reject.

If there were an award for the most influential bad novelist in literary history, Ayn Rand would be a contender. A woman of ferocious competitive instinct, she would be furious if she did not also win that award. Alisa Zinov'yevna Rosenbaum was born, Russian Jewish, in St Petersburg in 1905. Her father ran a pharmacy business. The Rosenbaums were relaxed about religion but 1905, the year of Alisa's birth, was a bad year to be Jewish as pogroms raged across Russia. The year 1917 was an even worse time to be bourgeois. The Bolsheviks seized their pharmacy and the Rosenbaums were forced to flee to the Crimea. With the success of the Revolution they returned to Leningrad, as it now was, where Alisa studied philosophy at university. She came to loathe Communism and was developing a lifelong interest in Nietzsche – not a favourite of the party.

Granted a lucky visa to visit relatives in the US, she fled the USSR for ever in 1926. An astonishingly enterprising woman, she settled in Hollywood to become a screenwriter – in a language not her own, and a society of which she knew very little, and a medium which had only just discovered 'talkies'. She changed her name to Ayn Rand, married (a pliant young actor, Frank O'Connor, of no talent whatsoever), became a US citizen in 1931, and made a living for herself in films, a business never easy to thrive in. It helped that she was – if not filmstar-beautiful – strikingly handsome and unafraid to use her body in pursuit of higher things. Her career took its definitive turn in 1932 with the anti-Soviet screenplay, *Red Pawn*, for Josef von Sternberg. The film was never produced but got her noticed. Hereafter her writing was ferociously free-enterprise. She was, it was later said, a 'hob-nailed Reagan'. Gordon ('greed is good') Gecko was a Pinko alongside Ayn Rand. She wrote an autobiographical novel about the horrors of the Soviet Union, *We the Living* (1936), and a Huxley-style dystopia, *Anthem* (1938). The dystopia is better, but neither is good. Both are pure Ayn.

She was politically active during the war years and brought out her first bestselling work of fiction, *The Fountainhead*, with its architect hero (based on Frank Lloyd Wright), Howard Roark, in 1943. He embodied her fanatic belief in individual heroism. A film, starring Gary Cooper, was made in 1949. Inevitably she was called as a friendly witness in the House Un-American Activities Committee investigations into 'Red' infiltration into Hollywood. Now well off with the royalties from *The Fountainhead*, Rand was formulating her views into a sub-Nietzschean philosophy she called 'Objectivism', founded on a belief in 'Rational Selfishness'.

She propagated her views in her massive sermon to the world, *Atlas Shrugged*, published in 1957. The novel revolves around the idea of the wealth-creators (i.e. moguls, magnates and millionaires) of the US following the corrupt example of their workers – trade unionising and going on strike. The capitalistic Atlas shrugs off the burden of making himself rich, and the mass of the population ('grabbers') descend into the dystopian chaos they have brought on themselves with their irrational demand that the state look after them. The moral, as one disaffected blogger puts it, is that 'Poor People Are Lazy Assholes.' Close on 1,200 pages long (200 of which were an appended politico-philosophical manifesto), *Atlas Shrugged* was not your ordinary popular novel and reviews were scathing. Robert Kirsch declared in the *Los Angeles Times* that 'It would be hard to find such a display of grotesque eccentricity outside an asylum.' But the charismatic Rand had access to the new medium of TV talk shows and used the exposure to popularise her novel and its message. She lectured indefatigably on its Objectivist themes. The first 100,000 copies, published on 10 October 1957, gradually cleared. Then cleared again and again. American sales of 5 million were clocked up by 1984.

Rand's Objectivism took the philosopher-hero John Galt's oath ('I swear by my life and my love of it that I will never live for the sake of another man, nor ask another man to live for mine') and his iconic 'sign of the dollar' as its prime articles of faith. Rand herself affected personal jewellery emblazoned with the same sacred $. As Rand's ideas percolated into orthodox republicanism, the coherence of her group broke up. Her younger disciple, and designated heir, Nathaniel Branden, had been her lover for many years. He committed the treachery of falling in love with a younger, more beautiful, someone else. His disgrace and public ejection from her inner council was shattering to the movement as a whole.

In later years, Rand became ever more strident in the expression of her Objectivist doctrines and died of a heart attack, having survived lung cancer (she was a chain smoker), aged seventy-seven. She was buried in the Kensico cemetery, Valhalla, New York: alongside the casket was a six-foot-tall floral display in the shape of the sacred dollar.

FN   Ayn Rand (née Alisa Zinov'yevna Rosenbaum; later O'Connor)
MRT   *Atlas Shrugged*
Biog   A. C. Heller, *Ayn Rand and the World She Made* (2009)

185. C. P. Snow 1905–1980

Snow thinks of himself as a novelist. F. R. Leavis

Viewed from one angle C. P. Snow ranks as the most honoured author of his age. The reverse shot sees him as the most overblown. He went to his grave loaded with lifetime awards; a CBE ('a fairly high one'), 1943; a knight, 1957; a life peer, 1964; but, for all the gongs and ermine, any reputation as a novelist worthy of posterity's attention has gone to the grave with him. Two phrases he put into circulation survive him: 'the corridors of power' and 'the two cultures'. Snow was the second of four sons of a clerk in a Leicester shoe factory – a passionate church organist, serial adulterer, and a weak man. Charles's background was, in his phrase, 'petty bourgeois-cum-proletarian'. His subsequent career, he resolved, should be anything but petty. Snow's first twenty years are a parable of Smilesian self-improvement: he was a 'flier'. The clever boy in a backstreet family, he won a grammar school scholarship; he left at sixteen, but studied by night for entrance to university. At London University he got 'a good first' and an MSc in chemistry, followed by a studentship at the Cavendish, Cambridge, a laboratory 'stiff with Nobel Prize winners'.

Among these giants of science, young Snow did research on the 'infra-red spectra of simple diatomic molecules', which led, in 1930, to a college fellowship and a stipend of £750 a year. It was an extraordinary achievement, but – in the final analysis – Snow was at best a 'competent' (his word) scientist among the best in the world. There was, thankfully, the second culture to fall back on. Snow had from his early years aspired to rank with 'the great Russian and French writers': Stendhal, Tolstoy, Balzac. He made his first stabs at fiction with potboilers – detective and SF novels – but 'genre' was for second-raters. Snow always aimed at the peaks. Settling into his groove he began his eleven-strong sequence, *Strangers and Brothers*, in 1935. The long life history of Lewis Eliot is patently autobiographical and has easily identifiable characters from public and university life. Its composition would jog along until 1970, keeping company with its author's rise in the world.

During the early war years, Snow carried a cyanide vial in his pocket. He had two entries on the Gestapo death list, he informed friends, some of whom would have been flattered to have one. He was recruited by 'Intelligence' as a scientific adviser – keeping the Cabinet informed about what the boffins in the backroom were doing and where the Nazis had got to with their nuclear research. 'I think I was pretty effective,' he records. His best novel, *The Masters*, was begun with the leisure of peacetime and published in 1951. It chronicles a battle for high college office which comes to symbolise a clash between old and new learning. The novel was widely read at a period when British universities were struggling to redefine themselves. Curricula were duly revised along Snow's suggested bilateralism: indeed, a whole 'new' university, Keele, was set up in his intellectual image.

Snow, despite some early homosexual experiences (candidly confessed to), had conducted affairs, alluded to in his novels. In 1950 he married the recently divorced novelist, Pamela Hansford Johnson (1912–81), a lover of some years standing. The marriage was socially high-profile and successful, but he was not faithful. Johnson was either unaware or complaisant. The couple's only child Philip was born in 1952.

After the war, Snow was smoothly shoe-horned into the upper echelons of industry, as Director of Personnel at GEC. He stayed in the post for fourteen years. *Strangers and Brothers*, meanwhile, pulsed out, tracking, remorselessly, its author's upward progress. The peaks were in sight, he was now a sage. In 1959 he took the nation to task in his Rede lectures, entitled: *The Two Cultures and the Scientific Revolution* (1959). There were, he argued, 'New Men' and 'Old Men'. The one knew Shakespeare but were stumped by the Second Law of Thermodynamics: the other vice versa. There was, he implied, one man who effortlessly bridged the two – there should be more Snows. The two-culture thesis was influential and adopted as holy writ in the sixth forms of Britain. Congenial as it was with liberal educationists, it provoked ferocious refutation from the leading literary critic of the time, F. R. Leavis. In an answering lecture in 1962, Leavis, much the more effective polemicist, denied any such facile cultural split and mocked the pontifical tone of Snow's argument which, as he bitingly observed, only genius could justify: but, then, who could imagine genius using such a tone? As for Tolstoyan pretension, 'Snow is, of course, a – no, I can't say that; he isn't: Snow thinks of himself as a novelist ... his incapacity as a novelist is ... total ... as a novelist he doesn't exist; he doesn't begin to exist ... not only is he not a genius ... he is intellectually as undistinguished as it is possible to be.' Snow's reputation among the discriminating few, and his *amour propre*, never recovered.

With the public at large his reputation was unaffected, however. A lifelong socialist, Snow was one of the darlings of the 1964 Wilson administration, wedded as it was to the utopian belief that 'the white heat of technology' would make Great Britain great again. It was entirely in line with Baron Snow of Leicester's view of things. It was not, otherwise, a happy decade for the Snows. As the 1960s swung on, they were increasingly preoccupied with the nation's moral decay – principally the growth of the pornography industry and crimes such as the Moors murders. Evil resurgent is dramatised in Snow's tenth novel, *The Sleep of Reason* (1968) and Johnson's *j'accuse*, *On Iniquity* (1967).

Snow looked prematurely ancient and Yoda-like almost from youth. A sceptical

Pamela Hansford Johnson consulted *Who's Who* for confirmation when informed that the bald, fat, wrinkled fellow she was falling in love with was as young as he claimed to be. Not that age mattered. 'I have a certain charm, when I choose to exercise it,' Snow blandly informed his biographer (luckily male). He smoked and drank immoderately, and was disabled in body and fogged in mind towards the end of his life, when his main writing was ponderous reviews for the *Financial Times*. His own financial affairs were in apple-pie order: he left £300,000 on his death. Johnson died shortly after.

FN   Charles Percy Snow (later Baron Snow)
MRT *The Masters*
Biog J. Halperin, *C. P. Snow: An Oral Biography* (1983)

186. Rex Warner 1905–1986

The only modern novelist I like is Kafka

While confessing to arrant Kafkaism, Warner routinely added that his other principal influence was Tobias Smollett – English cheese and Czech chalk. The son of an Anglican parson in Gloucestershire, who encumbered his son with the archetypally Victorian forenames 'Reginald Ernest', and a mother whom he candidly hated, Warner attended a minor public school. He shone on the rugger field and in the classroom, winning a scholarship to Wadham College, Oxford, to read classics. That subject was then presided over by the formidable Maurice Bowra – a man whose genitals, one of his hero-worshippers later recorded, resembled the ruins at Delphi. They were frequently on view at Parson's Pleasure, where dons bathe nude and can exchange donnish pleasantries.

As Anthony Powell recalled, 'Bowra always talked as if homosexuality was the normal condition of an intelligent man.' Warner shared Bowra's philhellenism, but not his sexual proclivities. At Oxford he made a flying start and in the first round of 'final' examinations ('Mods') he racked up a record number of alphas – more, even, than had Bowra. Score one for heterosexuality. A glittering academic career was in prospect – but never materialised. In his third year, Warner suffered a spectacular nervous breakdown. Bowra, never one to let sympathy interfere with a witticism, recalled: 'he was said to see the transcendental deduction of the categories lying in solid blocks across the room.' Warner's first wife, Frances Grove, diagnosed in her husband an irreconcilable clash between 'Hebraism and Hellenism' – Oxford and the real world; hetero and homo. There was also an infection of fashionable Marxism and incipient alcoholism.

Having lost a year of study, Warner transferred from classics to English – a softer option. The change of subject had momentous career consequences. It brought him together with W. H. Auden, Stephen Spender and other founder members of the 'Thirties group'. Like Auden, Warner scraped a 'gentleman's third' (Spender – never one to do things by halves – flunked out with no degree whatsoever). Like his comrades, Warner fell back on school-teaching to keep the wolf from the door. During the slump there were no easy jobs – even for gents. His first serious efforts as a writer reflect the mechanophiliac 'pylon' poetry Spender was writing in the early 1930s and Auden's perverse sentiment that the most beautiful walk in Oxford was along the stinking canal by the gasworks. No dreaming spires for these young men. But the main influence on Warner's writing originated elsewhere: the Muirs, Edwin and Willa, had translated Kafka's *The Castle* in 1930 – it exploded like a bomb on insular British culture.

Warner's first published novel, *The Wild Goose Chase* (1937), is a Kafkaesque allegory of totalitarianism. The novel's best-known episode is a football match in which the pitch elastically reshapes itself to favour the home side. This chapter (which Spender believed the *second* best thing of its kind ever written – the first is unrecorded) was published in the house journal of the Thirties group, John Lehmann's *New Writing*. Like others in that group, Warner was at this period what he called in later life a 'near communist'. But the Ribbentrop–Molotov pact, as with other fellow travellers, extinguished any loyalty he might have had to Moscow. Warner wrote his masterpiece, *The Aerodrome* (1941), in the run-up to the Second World War and published it during the conflict. Fictionally it echoes Orwell's 'As I write, highly civilised human beings are flying overhead, trying to kill me.' *The Aerodrome*'s narrative pivots on the binary opposition of an old English village, presided over by the 'Rector', and the new, nearby aerodrome, presided over by the 'Air Vice Marshal'. One represents totalitarian 'apparat', the other liberal English 'muddle', as E. M. Forster called it. Woven into this design is a complicated love story centred on the orphan hero, Roy (a version of 'Rex', as critics note). To win the war, Old England has to ape its enemy, destroying the principles for which it initially fought the war. Victory merely recreates the enemy in yourself – such is the irony of history. During the war Warner, too old and too crocked to serve, taught and wrote. It was, he said, 'escapism'. At the war's end, he was sent on a BBC mission to Germany and the concentration camps. What he saw, inescapably, precipitated another breakdown. The first, at Oxford, had made him a modern novelist; the second extinguished that career.

As Theodor Adorno famously pronounced, writing, after Auschwitz (Belsen in Warner's case) was pointless. Warner accepted a series of cushy British Council jobs, well beneath his talents, in Greece and Germany, and drank excessively. He changed marriage partners, leaving his loyal wife and three children for Barbara Hutchinson, the wealthy widow of a Rothschild. Later he drifted to America, where he landed even cushier college jobs at Bowdoin and Storrs. Life became one long, sodden, sinecure. Over the years he mainly translated classical texts. His *Thucydides*, in its Penguin Classic (half-crown) livery, sold over a million copies. His desultory efforts in fiction, particularly an unlucky essay in Wodehousian comedy, were less wanted by the reading public.

In his seventies, Warner retired to rural Oxfordshire with Frances (his first wife, who he remarried in 1966), where, despite a heroic intake of alcohol in the neighbouring pub, he survived until his eighties. At his funeral, as his biographer records, 'no figures from the London literary world were present'.

FN Reginald Ernest Warner ('Rex')
MRT *The Aerodrome*
Biog S. E. Tabachnik, *Fiercer than Tigers: the Life and Works of Rex Warner* (2005)

187. Samuel Beckett 1906–1989

Sodom and Begorrah. Dylan Thomas on *Murphy*

Beckett was born in Foxrock, near Dublin, Ireland, to a Protestant family. He records the occasion of his birth with gloom-edged precision: 'I was born on Friday the thirteenth and Good Friday too. My father had been waiting all day for my arrival. At eight p.m. he went out for a walk, and when he returned, I had been born.' Biographers have queried the date, time and paternal absence. Elsewhere Beckett recalls: 'You might say I had a happy childhood.' He does not quite say it himself. His father was a prosperous housing contractor (not *quite* an architect, as Beckett pedantically observed). His mother, musical by nature, had no luck moving her younger son, Sam, towards that 'safe' line of work, but she remained the dominant figure in his life until well into middle age. As a child, he loved games, particularly cricket in which, ever enigmatic, he batted left-handed and bowled right-handed. Ireland, between 1916 and 1922, was in rebellious upheaval but it did not materially affect the Becketts, or him. He attended the same school as had Oscar Wilde (Portora Royal) where, like his elder brother Frank, he was more distinguished as an athlete than as a scholar. Even at this early stage of his life, he was observed to be unusually 'private'. What he later called his 'crescendo of disengagement' had begun.

Beckett went on to read Modern Languages at Trinity College, Dublin, in 1923. He steeped himself in French poetry and Dante (like cricket, a lifelong passion) and drank heavily. On graduation, he took up a two-year teaching assistant post at the École Normale in Paris. Here he was introduced to James Joyce, whose occasional amanuensis he became. There was a complicated relationship with Joyce's disturbed daughter, Lucia, who was infatuated with him. It led to a 'bust up'. He could not bring himself to love Lucia, he said enigmatically, because he was 'dead'. James Joyce he was very much alive to. In Paris, Beckett published his first books, the long poem *Whoroscope* (about Descartes) and a study of Proust.

On his return to Ireland he seemed destined for an academic career. But his habits were increasingly – and rebelliously – bohemian and he eventually gave up the university. After an unsettled few years, much illness, and a frustrating inability to find his *métier* as a writer of fiction, he settled in Paris in 1937. Again he took up the role of Joycean acolyte. 'To the dismay of some of his friends,' his biographer records, 'Beckett began to imitate Joyce's mannerisms.' It extended to imitating the master's distinctive footwear: like Cinderella's sisters (Beckett's feet being the larger) he had to squeeze his feet into the master's shiny, but smaller, shoes.

For some five years Beckett had been working on an autobiographical work, narrated by a 'Mr Beckett', called *Dream of Fair to Middling Women*. Clearly an act of Joycean homage, it mixes dialects, neologisms, parody and jokes (one of the best being the title – a department in which Beckett was always strong). It opens with the hero masturbating and pursues a maze of subsequent mind-centred fantasies. *Dream of Fair to Middling Women* proved unpublishable and Beckett himself later dismissed it as 'immature and unworthy'. He was better pleased with the short stories collected under a title which would make it wilfully difficult to see the light of print in his home country – *More Pricks than Kicks*.

Beckett was getting by at this period of his life with handouts from his parents. He was disturbed emotionally and submitted to their wish that he undergo psychoanalysis in London. He was interested to discover in himself a 'womb fixation' – an unhealthy attachment to his mother. He had not, in Jungian terms, been 'entirely born'. It was an idea which would recur throughout his later writing and drama. His major work of the 1930s was the novel *Murphy*. The narrative again plays out within the hero's mind. A Dubliner and a 'seedy solipsist', Murphy inhabits a condemned building in London where he ruminates, naked, in a rocking chair. There is an intricate denouement via a chess game with revised rules. The hero dies in an explosion detonated by a downstairs jakes. His will instructs that his cremated remains be flushed down the loo of the Abbey Theatre. *Murphy* was the first of his novels to be bilingualised into French by Beckett himself. It was rejected by close on fifty publishers, well reviewed on its eventual publication in 1938 by discriminating critics, and sold abysmally.

In 1938 Beckett was stabbed – nearly fatally – in the Parisian streets by a pimp, having refused the services of a 'lady of the evening'. He was lucky not to die. When he found himself in the courts of justice alongside his assailant, he asked him why he had done it. 'I don't know,' was the reply. The remark had significance for Beckett. He had by now firmly resolved that 'I didn't like living in Ireland' and he chose to remain in France after the outbreak of war in 1939. During the German Occupation, as an Irishman, he was technically neutral but he involved himself, at great peril, with the French Resistance. After being betrayed, he spent two years underground (for a while in the cellar of the novelist, Nathalie Sarraute) and won a post-war Croix de Guerre. He had undertaken this life-threatening work, he said, for personal reasons, not for the French nation: 'I was outraged by the Nazis, particularly by their treatment of the Jews.' It was in the Resistance that Beckett formed what would be a lifelong attachment to Suzanne Deschevaux-Dumesnil (though they did not marry until 1961).

During the war he suffered intolerable nervous stress, something that feeds into the novel he wrote during these years, *Watt* (1953) – the punning title is arch-Beckett. The hero is a servant, embarking on the service of a Mr Knott (another pun). It removes to a lunatic asylum where a character 'Sam' appears. The novel ends with the now familiar mental dissolutions. Beckett, in his mid-life forties, saw himself principally as a novelist – writing in both French and English. Once asked was he English, Beckett replied '*au contraire*'. He would have so replied had he been asked if he was French, and – conceivably – if he was Irish. He was forever contrary. *Watt* was followed by *Mercier et Camier* (1946), *Molloy* (1951), *Malone Dies* (1951) and *The Unnamable* (1953). All ponder cosmic loneliness, all are ruminative in form (there is a famous scene in *Molloy* in which the hero returns to the seaside, with his sixteen 'sucking stones' – can you, the novel ponders, squeeze the past out of a stone?) All his work poses the large question, why live? Typically the hero, like Malone, is stripped as naked as Lear on the heath. Malone's only contact, as he lies, man alone, interminably dying, is an old lady who brings him a daily dish and a clean chamberpot.

By the 1950s Beckett had recognition among advanced literary circles as an experimental, but crotchety, writer. World fame came to him as a dramatist with the absurdist play, *Waiting for Godot* (1953), particularly after its sensational 1956 launch on the London stage. *Godot* ushered in the theatre of the absurd as a dominant style: it revolutionised drama and cinema. His later career saw the award of many prizes, crowned by the Nobel in 1969. He wrote some minimalist fiction in his last years, e.g. *Worstward Ho* (1983), gnawing the same old bones into ever more boniness.

FN   Samuel Barclay Beckett
MRT *Murphy*
Biog J. Knowlson, *Damned to Fame: the Life of Samuel Beckett* (1996)

188. John Dickson Carr 1906–1977

He is the acknowledged master of that classic rarity, the tale of detection in which detection is seen to take place, the clues really are shared with the reader, and crimes of majestic and multifarious impossibility are shown at last to have been possible after all, if not always very plausible. Kingsley Amis on Carr

One of the leading writers of detective fiction in the twentieth century, Carr was unusual in having equal appeal to British and American reading publics and being in himself bi-national. He was born in Uniontown, Pennsylvania, the son of a lawyer, later a congressman. He was educated at Haverford College – then, as now, an exclusive private institution – and in 1928 studied for a year at the Sorbonne. By his own account, Carr rebelled against the script written for him by his father: 'They sent me to a school and university with the idea of turning me into a barrister like my father. But I wanted to write detective stories. I don't mean that I wanted to write great novels, or any nonsense like that! I mean that I simply damn well wanted to write detective stories.'

Carr's first novel, *It Walks by Night,* a Poe-like mystery, strongly reminiscent of 'The Murders in the Rue Morgue', based on the exploits of the Paris detective Henri Bencolin (a character clearly based on Poe's Dupin), was published in 1930. In 1932 Carr married an Englishwoman, Clarice Cleaves (they met, appropriately enough, on a transatlantic liner), and moved to England. Over the next ten years he published an average of four novels a year, many under such easily penetrable pseudonyms as 'Carr Dickson'. Over these years he also worked for the BBC, and established himself as a well-known figure on the cultural landscape. He came to my knowledge when I was a schoolboy, with his BBC radio dramatisations, *Appointment with Fear,* narrated by the creepily voiced 'Valentine Dyall'. The Carrs had three children. He was not, his biographer discloses, a faithful husband.

With America's entry into the Second World War, Carr returned to America to volunteer his services after enduring the Blitz in England. He was reassigned to return to wartime Britain by his new employer, CBS, and assisted with news propaganda. After the war he again briefly resettled in England, only to leave in disgust at the welfare-state reforms brought in by the Labour government in 1948. With the Tory victory of 1951 Carr returned to Britain once more and thereafter shuttled between the two countries, eventually (having always been a heavy drinker and smoker) dying of lung cancer in South Carolina, where he had lived since 1967.

Among the many styles of detective and historical fiction Carr practised himself in his eighty or so books, he was renowned particularly for his mastery of the 'locked room mystery'. Much of what he wrote, from his first book on, can be traced back to the Poevian room in the Rue Morgue. In addition to Bencolin, who was dropped after three appearances, Carr – as 'Carter Dickson' – concentrated on two series heroes: Dr Gideon Fell, introduced in *Hag's Nook* (1933); and Sir Henry Merrivale, introduced in *The Plague Court Murders* (1934). Fell is hugely fat, a historian and works as the unofficial aide of Chief Inspector Hadley of Scotland Yard. He is modelled on G. K. Chesterton (creator of 'Father Brown'). Merrivale is a patrician barrister and a physician: his liaison figure at the Yard is Chief Inspector Humphrey Masters.

Carr constructs his narratives as puzzles – challenges to the reader's ingenuity and acuity. There should be, he believed, not one but a whole 'ladder of clues'. He believed firmly in the 'fair play' principle – no Roger Ackroydian tricks are to be sprung on the reader. Admirers, even passionate admirers such as Kingsley Amis, concede a price is paid in Carr's surrender to formula, pattern and narrative principles. 'At every emotional turn,' says Amis, 'he is likely to plunge into the style of the novelette.' On the plus side, to quote Amis again, Carr can 'grip' like no other crime writer:

> The hero of *The Burning Court* comes across, in the most prosaic way possible, a photograph of a Frenchwoman who according to the caption was guillotined for murder in 1861. 'He was looking at a photograph of his own wife.' End of Chapter One. There must be those who, on reaching that point for the first time, would be able to lay the book aside and go out to a Mahler concert, say, without turning a hair. Not I; I had a hard enough time just now getting my copy back on to its shelf after checking that reference.

As 'Roger Fairbairn', a pseudonym first used for *Devil Kinsmere* (1934), Carr developed a sideline in historical romances and 'historical' crime such as *The Bride of Newgate* (1950), an eighteenth-century detective story; and *The Hungry Goblin* (1972), a Victorian detective story.

Carr received the Grand Master Award from the Mystery Writers of America in 1963 and it is hard to think of any writer more deserving. Not only did he practise, he also wrote astute critical and biographical works which gave shape, historical sequence and hierarchy to the chaotic mass of crime fiction since Poe invented the genre. Carr, for example, wrote what was, for many years, the authoritative study of Arthur Conan Doyle. He was privileged by the estate, unlike his successors, to see the author's 'locked archive'. Locked rooms and the mysteries therein were Carr's speciality.

FN   John Dickson Carr
MRT   *The Burning Court*
Biog   D. G. Greene, *John Dickson Carr: The Man who Explained Miracles* (1995)

189. Catherine Cookson 1906–1998

Bugger them all!

Numbers stack up around her. She published over ninety novels, under her own name and under the pseudonyms Catherine Marchant and Katie McMullen (see below for the origin of this second pen name). In the 1990s she topped the Public Lending Right list, which records borrowings from public libraries, year in, year out – beating even Dick Francis. Her combined sales, at the time of her death, were calculated at over 100 million. She is plausibly reckoned to have been the most-read British novelist of her time. It was, given her lifespan, quite a long time – even though she did not start publishing until her mid-forties.

As remarkable as the statistical bulk of Cookson's achievement are the obstacles she was obliged to overcome to get there. They are chronicled in her autobiography, *Our Kate* (1969) and her novel *Fifteen Streets* (1973). Catherine Cookson was born the illegitimate daughter of Catherine Fawcett and brought up in Tyne Dock, East Jarrow, a slum vividly described in Cookson's various 'fifteen streets' settings. The area was dominated by the ship-building industry. Catherine's mother was, when working, 'in service' and away from home. The name 'McMullen' was that of her grandparents, whose family background was Irish Catholic. Illegitimacy was shameful (as, to some degree, was Irish Catholicism) and as a young child Catherine was kept in ignorance of her parentage and assumed 'Kate' was her elder sister. Cookson romanticises this deception, wildly, in one of her most popular later novels, *The Glass Virgin* (1969). It added to the family shame that Kate 'drank'.

Young Catherine became familiar with the pawn shop, the off-licence and the bailiff's knock.

Catherine was unhappy at the Catholic school she attended. 'God came into my life', she recalled 'and with him came the Devil, and Miss Corfield, the schoolmistress of St Peter and Paul's, Tyne Dock, and with her came mental and physical torture'. She was, none the less, very bright and submitted her first story, 'The Wild Irish Girl' (a telling title) to the local South Shields paper, aged eleven. It was rejected: so, she might well have thought, was she – by the whole world. She left school at thirteen and, as soon as she was allowed, left home, which had become threateningly violent, to work first as a housemaid, at 10 shillings a week plus board, then in a workhouse laundry in South Shields. A skilled laundress and, as it was observed, an able manager, she later moved to Hastings, where she was employed at that town's workhouse in a middle-managerial capacity. Over time she scraped together enough from her wages to buy a large town house, take in lodgers and add even more income to her savings account. Her personal, more specifically her sexual, life in her twenties and early thirties is obscure. It seems likely that she had, if not a lesbian, then a long-running passionate friendship with another, older, woman, Nan Smyth, with whom she ran the boarding house for nine years until her marriage.

What is clear is that Catherine was all the while improving herself and reading widely. In 1940 she was respectable enough to marry a grammar-school teacher, Thomas Cookson, without any sense of his coming down in the world by his choice of bride. There were, to the couple's mortification, repeated miscarriages and no surviving children from the marriage. Cookson, it emerged, suffered from a chronic vascular complaint (which would, in later life, cause her blindness). She recalls this period of her life, the war years, as profoundly depressed and sometimes dangerously so, to the point of nervous breakdown. In 1948, Cookson records losing her faith: 'I dared to make a stand against superstition, against faith, against God ... I sent tearing heavenwards words that made me tremble with fear even as I forced them out. But I was saying them aloud and defiantly. I was answering back my fears for the first time. What the hell does it matter! To blazes and bloody damnation with it all! God, dogma, the Catholic Church, the Devil, Hell, people, opinion, laws, illegitimacy – and fear. *Bugger them all!*'

Writing was then suggested to her as a therapy and she became a founder member of the Hastings Writers Group in 1947. Knowing the value of money, she put her mind to fiction aimed, primarily, at the woman reader which, as she astutely guessed, would sell. In 1950, aged forty-four, she published her first novel, *Kate Hannigan*. The heroine's life mirrors that of Cookson's mother Kate, sympathetically romanticised. Kate Hannigan is the prettiest and smartest girl in the Fifteen

Streets and catches the eye of Dr Rodney Prince, an unhappily married man. Love and scandal ensue.

Kate Hannigan hit the mark and launched Cookson on her bestselling way. A fluent writer (in later life, after her sight failed, as fluent a dictator to the tape recorder), she went on to compose a string of multi-volume sagas and sequence novels. Notable is the 'Tilly Trotter trilogy' – another indomitable working-class girl who braves gossip and scandal – and the more Brontëan 'Mallen trilogy'. Cookson was never afraid of themes more socially controversial than what were usually found in the 'romance' genre. In *Colour Blind* (published in unregenerate 1953), she has a hero, Bridget McQueen, who gets herself pregnant by a 'coloured' seaman. The family is ostracised, Bridget is urged to have an abortion (criminal at this period). None the less, she follows her heart, defies prejudice, and marries her daughter's father. It's a brave novel for the time when boarding houses and pubs all over Britain would advertise 'no coloureds'. Her strongest settings, however, remained the north-east where she had been raised and where, as her fiction won her fame, she and her husband relocated. Cookson enjoyed climactic triumph with Tyne Tees TV's adaptations of her novels. Between 1989 and 2001, eighteen mini-series adapted from her novels were screened, starring actors such as Sean Bean and Catherine Zeta-Jones and a team of dialogue coaches to get the accent right.

A very rich woman in her later years, Cookson was also spectacularly philanthropic. Among many other gifts, she donated £100,000 to St Hilda's College, Oxford, and £50,000 to Girton College, Cambridge (having been a thirteen-year-old school-leaver herself). One million pounds went to research into the blood disorder, telangiectasia, which had blighted her life and denied her children. Her PLR income she donated to a fund for authors less profitable than she (virtually every novelist who ever wrote, as it happened). She regained her Catholic faith in her serener later years and was awarded a DBE in 1993 – not, as it should have been, for her services to literature but for her charitable activities and acts of patronage.

FN   Catherine Ann Cookson (née Davies/ McMullen; later Dame)
MRT   *Kate Hannigan*
Biog   K. Jones, *Catherine Cookson: the Biography* (1999)

190. Robert E. Howard 1906–1936

I rather like Mr Howard's stories. J. R. R. Tolkien

Howard never put his name to anything that could be called a novel. But his narrative fantasies, dribbled out for pulp magazines, have been, and still are, radioactive in the fiction (graphic novel, print novel, film, comic book, cartoon, computer-game) they inspire. His own life was short and very ordinary: the son of an itinerant Texas physician and a mother, Hester Howard, who was chronically tubercular. A saintly woman, Hester had contracted the disease tending the sick. Robert idolised her all his life. In his nomadic childhood he picked up tales and lore in country areas and cow towns where inhabitants could still recall the frontier lawlessness which was already being mythologised in Hollywood. The reading matter available to young Robert was principally comics and the pulp fiction on sale at local drugstores or left around in bus stations. Through them he picked up a third-hand social Darwinism and racism of the Jack London, *übermenschlich* kind. Somewhere, it is speculated, he may have come across a scholarly volume on the Scottish Picts: his 'Celtic' blood was one of his dearest personal possessions and the cult of barbarian purity took early root in his sensibility.

When he was thirteen, the family settled in the small central Texas town, Cross Plains. In early adolescence he developed a passion for boxing – both the sport and stories about the 'ring'. He enrolled in mail order body-building courses and did some fairground fighting. From fifteen years old Howard immersed himself even more enthusiastically in the pulp magazines which flooded the country in the 1920s. A particular favourite was *Adventure* and its lead author Talbot Mundy (1879–1940). whose 'Tros of Samothrace' left a clear mark. While still at school, Howard did a number of menial jobs around town: desk work, interspersed with manual work in the fields and – at one low point – garbage collection. It was a comedown for the son of a professional man – as was the fact that he had no interest in attending college. He had not shone at school and was observed to be chronically shy and melancholy by temperament. He wrote reams of poetry.

He was also writing fiction furiously, though his efforts were everywhere rejected until, aged eighteen, *Weird Tales* magazine accepted his caveman story 'Spear and Fang'. The opening is touchingly reflective of the author's own sense of his unrecognised genius:

A-aea crouched close to the cave mouth, watching Ga-nor with wondering eyes. Ga-nor's occupation interested her, as well as Ga-nor himself. As for Ga-nor, he was too occupied with his work to notice her. A torch stuck in a niche in the cave wall dimly illuminated the roomy cavern, and by its light Ga-nor was laboriously tracing figures on the wall. With a piece of flint he scratched the outline and then with a twig dipped in ocher paint completed the figure. The result was crude, but gave evidence of real artistic genius, struggling for expression.

Battle to the (species) death between *Homo sapiens* and Neanderthal ensues.

Weird Tales became Howard's principal outlet. The magazine, launched in 1923, was chronically underfunded, but it would publish many distinguished writers in its weird genre – notably H. P. Lovecraft. This 'father of fantasy' became a correspondent, literary adviser and patron of Howard's. Collectively, *WT* contributors imagined a mythic universe, with superhuman heroes, and 'pure' violence expressed – principally – through the sword. Howard varied his product with two-fisted series heroes such as Solomon Kane, Sailor Steve Costigan, hitting his destined groove with King Kull, barbarian monarch, and the king of the Picts, Bran Mak Morn. These, however, were mere stepping stones to his monumental creation, Conan the Barbarian.

There is something indelibly juvenile about Howard's fiction, and he himself never outgrew the wish-fulfilment and extravagant lusts of adolescence (naked maidens, stripped of their silks and narrowly evading the ravisher's cruel thrust, feature prominently in his stories). An only child, he lived with his family – close above all to his mother – all his life. To keep his father happy he enrolled for a four-year course in book-keeping which he had no intention of making his career. By the early 1930s he was making good money, and could afford his own car. He had one, unconsummated, love affair, with a Cross Plains schoolteacher, Novalyne Price. Her late-life memoir of the unhappy episode is the basis of the excellent film on Howard, *The Whole Wide World* (1996), starring Vincent D'Onofrio as Howard and Renée Zellweger as Novalyne.

Conan came into the world in December 1932 – a child of Black Monday, 1929. Fantasies of omnipotence compensated, all too obviously, for the collective impotence inflicted on American manhood by Wall Street and rampant unemployment. The eugenic theories popular at the time – later prostituted by the Nazis – are distantly articulated in the mighty Cimmerian. Norman Spinrad, in 1972, published a witty alternative universe novel, *The Iron Dream*, in which Hitler emigrates to America and becomes a Sword and Sorcery author. What kind of German dictator, one wonders, would the author of Conan the Barbarian have been? Conan is first introduced as a stranger in a low-life Zamorian beer hall:

> This person was as much out of place in that den as a gray wolf among mangy rats of the gutters. His cheap tunic could not conceal the hard, rangy lines of his

powerful frame, the broad heavy shoulders, the massive chest, lean waist, and heavy arms. His skin was brown from outland suns, his eyes blue and smoldering; a shock of tousled black hair crowned his broad forehead. From his girdle hung a sword in a worn leather scabbard.

Conan's era is 'the Hyborian Age' before the rise of the so-called 'great' civilisations ('civilisation corrupts' is a theme in Howard's fiction).

Howard's hero was a huge success and he was attracting adulation at the time of his death. His suicide was precipitated by the breakdown of his love affair with Novalyne, the failure of magazines (pre-eminently the forever financially strapped *Weird Tales*) to pay up but – most of all – by his depressive temperament exacerbated by the terminally ill condition of his mother. As Howard's leading critic, Rusty Burke, records:

> On the morning of the 11th [June 1936] , Robert asked the nurse attending Mrs. Howard if she thought his mother would ever regain consciousness, and was told she would not.
>
> Robert Howard got up and walked into his room, where he typed a four-line couplet on the Underwood typewriter that had served him for ten years:
>
> *All fled, all done,*
> *So lift me on the pyre.*
> *The feast is over*
> *And the lamps expire.*

He then walked out of the house and got into his 1935 Chevy. The hired cook stated later that she saw him raise his hands in prayer. Was he praying or preparing the gun? She then heard a shot, and saw Robert slump over the steering wheel. He lingered eight agonising hours before dying from the wound to his head. His mother died the next day, never having regained consciousness. They were buried alongside each other. Since his death, Howard has achieved cult status and his creations – principally Conan the Barbarian and Red Sonya – have become industrial-scale franchises. It seems unfair, somehow, that he would never know.

FN   Robert Ervin Howard
MRT   *Red Nails*
Biog L. Sprague de Camp in collaboration with C. Crook de Camp, and J. Whittington
          Griffin, *Dark Valley Destiny: The Life of Robert E. Howard* (1983)

191. Jim Thompson 1906–1977

All of us that started the game with a crooked cue …

Thompson was born in Anadarko, Oklahoma. He gives a vivid account of his first twenty years in the autobiographical *Bad Boy* (1953). Thompson's father was a feckless legal accountant and erstwhile sheriff. While Jim was growing up, the family led an unsettled existence in Oklahoma, Texas and Nebraska. Thompson was largely self-taught. While still at school, he worked as a cub journalist and – most formatively – as a bellhop in a Fort Worth hotel during Prohibition and the roaring twenties. Here it was he picked up his grittily disillusioned view of life: 'Failure, it seemed, could only be offset by ability. The "sharp" received every consideration, the dull got nothing.' Such 'sharpness' is the most valued commodity in Thompson's grim world. A second formative influence was his encounter with a confidence trickster, Allie Ivers, who inspired the character of Roy Dillon in Thompson's best known novel, *The Grifters* (1963).

At the age of eighteen Thompson came down with 'a complete nervous collapse, pulmonary tuberculosis and delirium tremens'. On his recovery – and hotly pursued by Prohibition Officers – he took to the road. *Bad Boy* ends at this point with Thompson laughing ironically at his fate ('I guess I just don't know of anything else to do'). *Faute de mieux* Thompson went on to work as a journalist, but had continued problems with drink. His novel *The Alcoholics* (1953) ends with the hero, transparently Thompson himself, being checked into a sanatorium with little hope of his emerging a changed man. Nor did he. Thompson spent a short period at the University of Nebraska in 1929 and it was here that he began to write fiction. He married in 1931 and had three children – but he was an egregiously bad husband and father.

From 1936 to 1938 Thompson was involved with the Oklahoma Federal Writers Project. At this stage of his life he was radically left-wing. The Depression, as with James M. Cain, darkened and hardened his view of America. After publishing two straight hardback novels with a political message in the early 1940s – neither of which made the slightest mark – Thompson (now in California) took up work as a journalist with the *San Diego Journal*. He wrote his subsequent fiction principally for Lion Books, a downmarket firm. The relationship was cultivated by Arnold Hano, a senior editor at Lion in the early 1950s, who encouraged Thompson to write his blacker-than-*noir* crime novels.

Thompson's fiction was marketed in paperback (with print runs as high as 200,000) as a short-life drugstore-stand product. Serious interest in Thompson as a genre genius began to generate in the 1980s. The quintessentially Thompsonesque thriller is *The Killer Inside Me* (1952). Lou Ford, the hero-narrator is deputy sheriff in 'Central City', a small town in Texas. On the surface, Ford is a good old hometown boy, but inside he is consumed by what he calls 'the sickness', a need to murder. His doctor father discovered early on that his son was a psychopath, and sterilised him. The novel – narrated autobiographically with a chilling charm – begins with Lou becoming involved with a new whore in town, Joyce Lakeland. She is a masochist and enjoys Lou's violence as foreplay. But he batters her to death (as he thinks), and sets up the son of a local businessman to pay for the crime. A string of other murders ensue: Lou strangles a suspect Greek boy, who thinks Lou is his only friend (making it look like suicide) and beats his fiancée Amy to a pulp, after a particularly satisfying love-making. The novel ends in a bloody shoot-out, and Lou's conclusion that everyone starts the game with a crooked cue.

The Killer Inside Me is, like Jack Finney's *Invasion of the Body Snatchers*, a prime example of 1950s, Cold War paranoia. You can trust no one – not even the small-town lovable sheriff. Thompson's novel also indicates the greater freedoms of pulp fiction at this period where sexual reference is concerned. While middle America was recoiling at the 'frankness', so-called, of novels like *Peyton Place*, Thompson could create scenes such as that in which Lou's fiancée Amy, who has guessed during oral sex (by his 'smell') that he has earlier made love to Joyce, turns on him with: 'You screwed her. You've been doing it all along. You've been putting her dirty insides inside of me, smearing me with her.' Lou responds by beating her to death.

When Hano left Lion in 1954, and the imprint gave up paperback originals with the collapse of the ANC-based wholesaling system, the most creative phase of Thompson's life came to an end. His career then took a new turn with a new patron. Stanley Kubrick was an admirer, and contracted Thompson to do the screenplays for *The Killing* (1956) and *Paths of Glory* (1957), an anti-war film, set in the First World War, which is more savagely radical than anything else the director did. Less gloriously, Thompson did script work for the TV series *Ironside*. His late and posthumous popularity was boosted by films made of his own work, notably the Steve McQueen-starring *The Getaway* and Stephen Frears's Oscar-winning adaptation of *The Grifters* (1989). Women, whisky, and hard living had long done for Thompson who once told his wife Alberta (the woman who cannily managed his posthumous estate) that he would have to wait ten years after his death until he was famous. So it was.

FN   James Myers Thompson ('Jim')
MRT   *The Killer Inside Me*
Biog   R. Polito, *Savage Art: A Biography of Jim Thompson* (1995)

192. Leslie Charteris 1907–1993

Everything I write is designed to be milked to the last drop of revenue.

Charteris was born Leslie Charles Bowyer Yin in Singapore, the son of an English mother and a Chinese surgeon father. Mandarin was his first language. On the break-up of his parents' marriage in 1919, he left Singapore with his mother, to be educated at public school in England. He qualifies – though no one has actually awarded him the title – as his adopted country's first post-colonial novelist, or America's, depending how you look at it.

Yin left King's College, Cambridge, degreeless, in order to write. He had sold his first story while still in his teens. Xenophobia may have played a part in his abandoning university. The word 'half-breed' would haunt him and doubtless play into the ultra-occidental style of his most famous fictional character, Simon Templar. His father disowned him, as a ne'er-do-well. In 1926, Yin disowned his father, in a sense, by changing his name by deed poll to Leslie Charles Bowyer Charteris Ian. It was ostensibly a tribute to the founder of the Hellfire Club, Colonel Francis Charteris. Other accounts suggest the name was plucked from a telephone directory for its overt Englishness. Pseudonymy, masquerade and disguised identity would be central in Charteris's later thrillers.

For a few years, Charteris 'hoboed' in classic thriller-writer apprentice-style. He picked up knowledge of the 'real' world – as a bartender, seaman, gold-prospector and professional bridge player. He lived in Paris for some time, toying with a career in art. The only extant filmed interview with him is conducted in fluent French. His debut novel *X Esquire* was published in 1927 and featured the first of his many 'gentleman avenger' heroes, who saves England from a dastardly plot to flood the country with lethal ciggies. It sold well. Simon Templar, the 'Saint', was introduced in Charteris's third novel, *Meet the Tiger* (1928). A gentleman of means, in his early thirties, Templar is tall, dark, Savile Row-suited, ultra-English and impeccably looked after by his 'man' 'Orace. He was to remain unchangingly young for three decades.

Charteris's career was boosted by his association with the Amalgamated Press's weekly magazine, *The Thriller*, launched in 1929. In 1930, the Saint patented his haloed matchstick man as his calling card. Other stock ingredients, honed over the decades, were Templar's Scotland Yard contact, Chief Inspector Teal, and his female accomplice, Patricia Holm, whom the Saint never quite gets around to marrying. Charteris himself made four marriages and was divorced three times. Encouraged by his American sales, he removed himself (and the Saint) to the US in 1932 and stayed there many years. There was lingering 'yellow peril' phobia (specifically the vicious Chinese Exclusion Act) which denied him citizenship for ten years. He eventually got it – Americans loved him, even if America didn't. *The Saint in New York* (1935) was hugely successful, especially after the 1938 film and its successors, starring the suave expatriate English actor, George Sanders. Were it not for his oriental features, Charteris was good-looking enough to have played the role himself.

Edgar Wallace had died in 1933 and the creator of Simon Templar succeeded him as 'King of the Thrillers'. The Saint was further popularised by a radio series (starring Vincent Price – like Sanders, another career smoothie), which ran from 1945 to 1951 in America. There was also a Saint comic strip, *The Saint Mystery Magazine* and, most long-runningly, a TV series launched in 1961, starring Roger Moore. The fiftieth *Saint* book came out in 1983. A big budget Hollywood film, starring Val Kilmer (no Sanders, he), came out in 1997. The formula was simple and repetitive. A crime is committed requiring redress from a modern Robin Hood. Templar steps in to do what the flat-footed police cannot. Templar's vigilantism, for all its suavity, is fuelled by right-wing political sentiment and snobbery – the persistent failing of British thrillers. Villains (sinners?) are typically lower-class or foreign.

Charteris married the beautiful film star, Audrey Long, fifteen years his junior, in 1952. He was now wealthy – enriched by multi-media subsidiary rights. The couple returned to England, where Charteris lived the good life (he enjoyed five-star restaurants and the sport of kings), and died leaving a fortune. Extraordinarily intelligent (he was a founder member of Mensa) and intellectually curious, Charteris also invented a pictorial sign language called Paleneo.

FN   Leslie Charles Bowyer Charteris Ian (born Yin)
MRT   *The Saint Omnibus* (1939)
Biog   http://www.lesliecharteris.com/

193. James A. Michener 1907–1997

I am a damned good writer.

Although he did not begin writing until he was forty, Michener made a literary form distinctively his own. The 'epic' deals, typically, with the evolution of some great entity – an American state, such as Texas, the birth of a nation, or one of mankind's 'great steps', such as the conquest of space. His choice of subject was always astute. *Centennial* (1974), his biggest bestseller, for example, was timed so that its millions-selling paperback form would appear in the bicentennial year, 1976. The hallmark of the Michener novel is girth. If not the Great American Novel, he certainly wrote the bulkiest. 'I have two pieces of advice,' one critic wrote of Michener's latest effort: 'first, don't buy it. Second, if you do, don't drop it on your foot.' Latterly his books would be prefaced with the names of armies of researchers. Generations of American journalism students must have worked their way through college, subsidised by the Michener hourly rate for leg-work.

James Albert Michener was born (the exact day is unrecorded), probably in Doylestown, Pennsylvania, possibly in New York. His mother, Mabel Michener, was a widow of Quaker descent. When he was nineteen, and a freshman in college, James learned that his 'father' had in fact died some five years before his birth. Michener never knew who his father was or, if he knew, never told. He told many lies on the subject. It was, the novelist recalled, a hard childhood: 'we were evicted six times because my mother couldn't pay the rent.' An industrious schoolboy, Michener won a scholarship to Swarthmore College in 1925. In later life it pleased him to pretend it had been an athletic scholarship. He also liked to claim, with as little plausibility, that he was a 'troublemaker' and had been expelled – 'even though they knew I was probably the brightest kid on the block'. In point of fact, he was a dutiful, weedy undergraduate of middling academic attainment, regarded as wholly inoffensive, if 'moody', by his fellow students. He graduated in the ominous year of 1929, and took up teaching work in Pennsylvania schools. In 1935 he made the first of his three marriages. The couple had little in common, apparently, beyond tennis.

In 1941 Michener accepted a post as editor in Macmillan's textbook division, a post which brought him to New York just as war broke out. Aged thirty-five, he was among the oldest American males to be drafted. He was commissioned into the US Navy in 1943. His country required no great sacrifice from Lieutenant Michener. His duties, as a supplies officer, were those of a 'superclerk', but his service, momentously, took him to the South Pacific. Out of this experience would emerge his first book, *Tales of the South Pacific* (1947). The tales were picked up by the *Saturday Evening Post* and by Rodgers and Hammerstein for the musical, *South Pacific*. The book, to the amazement of intellectual New York, won a Pulitzer.

Michener had drifted apart from his wife (she was, he drily put it, 'a war casualty'), and divorced and remarried in 1948. In 1952, he formed a long connection with *Reader's Digest*, giving him a direct line to middle America. *Sayonara* (1954) dealt, *Madame Butterfly* style, with the interracial love of an American officer and a Japanese woman and was filmed, starring Marlon Brando. A better book, which produced a better film, was *The Bridges at Toko-Ri* (1953), a sensitive study of the stressful last mission of an American fighter-bomber pilot in the Korean War. Out of his association with *Reader's Digest* Michener developed a crossover genre later known as 'faction'. It was to be the foundation of his first 'epic', the massive 'soul of a nation' narrative, *Hawaii* (1959). The story starts with geology and ends with American statehood.

The book's 'melting pot' optimism was to the taste of the American reading public. Politically Michener had been Republican but in the 1960s he campaigned for Kennedy and himself stood unsuccessfully for Congress. His failure to win a seat was, he claimed, one of three great disappointments in his life. The others were never winning the Nobel Prize (like Proust, he would modestly point out) and the childlessness of his marriages. The last was not for want of trying. Michener divorced again in 1955 and again promptly remarried, remaining with his third wife, Mari Toriko Sabusawa until her death in 1994.

He had at last found his groove as a novelist. Blockbuster (literally, in his case, the size of building blocks) followed blockbuster: *The Source* (1965) – Israel, *Chesapeake* (1978) – from first migrating goose to Watergate, *The Covenant* (1980) – South Africa), *Space* (1982). A man of frugal habit, Michener would, it was said, haggle over the price of a newspaper. None the less he made major donations to good causes – including $2 million to his alma mater, Swarthmore. His one recorded vice was overwork. He produced a book (typically a *big* book) every year between 1947 and 1977. After a massive heart attack in 1965, he took better care of himself physically. Well into his sixties he would jog every day. Although he was convinced that malnourishment in his Depression childhood had damaged his constitution, he lived to a great and honoured, if un-Nobelised, age. Courageously, he resolved to end his life by refusing dialysis.

FN   James Albert Michener
MRT *Hawaii*
Biog John P. Hayes, *James A. Michener: A Biography* (1984)

194. John Creasey 1908–1973

When he founded the Crime Writers' Association in 1953, he [Creasey] and his noms de plume outnumbered the total membership. Keith Miles

The most fecund of British crime fiction writers, Creasey has some 560 known titles to his credit, written under scores of pseudonyms. The truth is, no one has ever precisely been able to count his *oeuvre*. He was ruefully proud of his 743 rejection slips – authors tend to be precise about those sad scraps of paper. Creasey was born in Southfields, London, one of nine children of a working-class coach-builder. His family circumstances were straitened and as a child he was afflicted by polio, having to relearn how to walk at the age of six. His school education ended at fourteen and he tried, it is recorded, some twenty-eight different lines of work: none of them turned out well. He was already writing by night and submitting pieces to the two-penny thriller-papers which were popular between the wars. Some were published (the first in 1925), but most were not. Other hopefuls would have conceded defeat in the face of such repeated rejection, but his tenth novel, *Seven Times Seven* (a *Four Just Men* knock-off), was finally accepted, published and well received in 1932. Thereafter, Creasey stepped up his writing to factory pace, averaging 6,000 words a day, a full-length novel in six days, fifteen novels a year. He had found his groove.

His series heroes, especially the 'Toff' series (Charteris knock-offs) were two-penny cornershop library favourites. Creasey had an uncanny knack for framing his thrillers to the sociopolitical nervousness of the day – whether it was the Nazis in the 1930s or the Reds in the 1950s. By the 1940s he was one of the wealthiest writers in England – now a 'toff' himself, living in a country house and chauffeur-driven in a Rolls-Royce with its hallmark 'Toff' insignia proudly emblazoned on its doors. His coach-builder dad would have been proud of young John. He was clearly proud of himself.

Creasey was awarded an MBE in 1946 for contributions to philanthropic causes during the Second World War. He stood for Parliament on a number of occasions, founding his 'All-Party Alliance' to do so. No allies joined up. Had he succeeded, PM Creasey would, he fondly believed, have solved the nation's financial crises with no trouble whatsoever. He labelled his philosophy 'selfism'. No luckier in love than politics, and just as selfish, he made four marriages. With Creasey, everything crystallises into numbers: he was published in twenty-eight languages, sold 80 million copies of his work, and – an inveterate traveller – circumnavigated the world twice. Whether in eighty days, like Phileas Fogg, is not recorded.

He founded the Crime Writers' Association in 1953; *John Creasey Mystery Magazine*, which ran from 1956 to 1965; and his own publishing house, Jays Suspense Books. In their day, the most popular of Creasey's series heroes were the 'Baron' (John Mannering, an art dealer), the 'Toff' (the Hon. Richard Rollison, to all appearances a wealthy playboy, in fact a modern Robin Hood), Patrick Dawlish (a Private Investigator), and George Gideon (a Scotland Yard detective). The twenty-one-title-strong Gideon series of Scotland Yard 'Police Procedurals', which opened with *Gideon's Day* (1955) and finished posthumously with *Gideon's Drive* (1976), was issued under Creasey's pen name 'J. J. Marric'. The pseudonym was derived from his then wife Jean, and their sons Martin and Richard. Gideon is the most deeply characterised and least sentimentalised or glamorised of Creasey's heroes: a hard-working London cop, with a wife and six children, doing a difficult job against the odds. He was based on the author's friend, Commander George Hatherill, the officer who brought the mass-murdering John Christie and John ('acid bath') Haigh to justice, and who led the successful hunt for the Great Train Robbers in the 1960s. 'Show us as we are,' Hatherill had implored his writing friend. Creasey obliged.

Gideon inspired a line of policemen with human faces (e.g. Taggart, Inspector Morse). The series was televised and span off a gritty, but still watchable British film, *Gideon's Day* (1958), starring Jack Hawkins and directed by John Ford. The 'Department Z' series (i.e. a fantasised MI6), particularly *The Enemy Within* (1950), were an acknowledged source for Ian Fleming's Bond novels, which began in 1953 with *Casino Royale*. It is a mark of generational difference that Creasey's counterpart of 'M', Gordon Craigie, keeps a barrel of beer on a trestle, and a row of pewter tankards in his HQ. No stirred not shaken martinis or damn Balkan Sobranies for him.

FN   John Creasey
MRT *Gideon's Day*
Biog Richard A. Robinson (http://www.johncreasey.co.uk/)

195. Ian Fleming 1908–1964

We are the only two writers who write about what people are really interested in: cards, money, gold and things like that. Ian Fleming to Somerset Maugham

Ian Fleming was born in Mayfair, aptly enough, the second of four sons of Valentine Fleming. 'Val' was a banker, a Conservative MP (much liked by Winston Churchill) and during the First World War a dashing and decorated hero. He died in the trenches in 1917. The surviving Flemings were left comfortably off, but the sons, by a clause in their father's will, could not inherit unless their mother remarried (which she never did) or died – which she did not do until a few days before the death of Ian. As a result, the men in the family were always hard up and, in a condition of 'Great Expectations', predisposed to live beyond their means.

Ian's mother, Evelyn, was a dominant influence on his early career. So, too, by being so much more successful than him, was his brilliant older brother, Peter, who – after an effortless first at Oxford – made his name early as an intrepid explorer and travel writer: a man of action. Ian recoiled into a *je m'en fous* playboyism – elegant inaction – aided by charm, aquiline good looks (which he projected onto

James Bond) and winning manners, although, as Cyril Connolly cattily remarked, he routinely made the mistake of going home for breakfast after sleeping with a woman. At Eton he acquired little other than a broken nose in the wall game, as a result of a collision with Henry Douglas-Home, brother of the future PM. Nothing undistinguished, even a bash on the conk, for Ian Fleming. He lost his virginity in the local Windsor Kinema (the film is not recorded). It was a matter of lifelong pride that he was, two years running, Victor Ludorum on the school sports day.

University was judged to be beyond his abilities and he was packed off to Sand-hurst. On a weekend pass he contracted gonorrhea from a 'hostess' at the 43 Club in Soho (even his dose of clap had a superior ring to it), and was withdrawn by his appalled mother, medicated and, aged twenty, shuttled off to what his biographer calls a 'finish-ing school for men in Kitzbühel, Austria'. It suited him. He was good at languages, good at skiing and loved abroad. This was not, alas, sufficient to get him into the Foreign Office, whose exams he failed. Family connections, and his mother's relentless push, got him into Reuters News Agency. The hectic pace and general cynicism of a life at the forefront of breaking headlines suited him, as did the travel involved.

Ever restless and constitutionally prone to crippling boredom, he gave up Reuters for the city, which suited him not at all. One friend described him as the 'world's worst stockbroker' – this at a period when competition on the floor of the exchange was not fierce. Luckily for him, unluckily for the world, war broke out and he was promptly recruited into naval intelligence, as a smart young fellow who knew German and Germans. In the Admiralty's 'Room 39' it was Fleming's job to brainstorm – coming up with stunts to win the war. He saw it as playing at 'Red Indians' (who, of course, invariably lost their wars). One of his brainwaves was to drop a submarine pillbox off the coast of Dieppe to keep a periscopic eye on what the Germans were up to. Few of his ideas were implemented and most were as absurd as the witch doctor in Evelyn Waugh's *Sword of Honour* trilogy, employed by British Military Intelligence to give the Führer horrible nightmares. None the less Fleming was liked and promoted to Commander. Irritatingly, all he actually com-manded was in-trays, out-trays and ashtrays. As someone privy to the genuinely war-winning facts of Ultra and Enigma, he could never go anywhere that the enemy might capture him – not even a submarine pill box off Dieppe. He saw out the war a pen-pusher and a desk warrior. It rankled.

On demobilisation he joined the Kemsley newspaper group, whose flagship was the *Sunday Times*. His job, as manager of the foreign desk, entailed 'a little work, a lot of golf, women and lunch', as Ben Macintyre crisply puts it. Among other unusual privileges, Fleming had three months' holiday a year. It was in these breaks that he established his second home in Jamaica, building himself a house that he called

'Goldeneye'. The name alluded to one of his less madcap wartime operations. While England shivered in bitter winters, fuel cuts, over-darned socks and strikes – locked in the miserable place by currency exchange controls (which, as a foreign correspondent, did not apply to Ian Fleming) – this child of fortune basked in the sun, smoking his limitless cigarettes and drinking his sundowners. In mitigation, he carried it off with style, as a junior colleague at the *Sunday Times* recalled: 'To us young blokes on the paper then, he always seemed to have a mythological quality. We couldn't take him quite seriously, but you had to hand it to him: we envied his whopping salary – £5,000 a year, or some £200,000 in modern money ... We admired the lordly way he roared off in his Ford Thunderbird around lunch time on Friday to get in nine holes of golf before dinner while we soldiered on to the small hours of Sunday morning.'

It was not always the links that he was roaring off to. His love life flourished with numerous affairs, the most durable of which was with Ann Rothermere, wife of the *Daily Mail* proprietor. She and Fleming had a child, which died stillborn, three years before she divorced her husband in 1951, to become Ann Fleming. She was pregnant again (by Ian) at the time of the wedding in 1952. Caspar would be their only child. A woman who hobnobbed with the likes of Cyril Connolly and Evelyn Waugh, Annie imposed a sense of inferiority on her husband which spurred him on to do something spectacular himself.

He began writing his first book at the period of their marriage. *Casino Royale* ('pornography', as a wholly unimpressed Annie called it) was helped into print by Fleming's good turns to a friend. During the war, one of Fleming's junior officers, William Plomer (in peacetime a man of letters), had made the mistake of importuning a guardsman at a railway station who – unlike others of his comrades – was not for sale. Fleming extricated Plomer from what would have been a court martial and certain jail-time. In the early 1950s, Plomer was a senior adviser to Jonathan Cape: the IOU was called in and *Casino Royale* was published by the most exclusive imprint in literary London. It was like OUP publishing *No Orchids for Miss Blandish*. The opening sentence had a peculiar resonance for the reader of 1953:

> The scent and smoke and sweat of a casino are nauseating at three in the morning.

At this period pubs closed at 10 p.m. BBC TV (the only choice) 'closed down' at the same early hour with the 'Queen' and Horlicks. To remember what life was like at three o'clock in the morning most citizens would have had to cast their minds back to wartime and blackouts. James Bond would save them from that ever happening again.

Casino Royale introduced Fleming's 007 at a period when, following the Burgess and Maclean scandal, Britain's secret agents seemed to be all of them homosexuals in the pay of Moscow. Bond – derived, genetically, from Bulldog Drummond – is old-fashioned English derring-do incarnate and a lady-killer. Fleming would go on to write a 'Bond' a year until his premature death. In the above opening scene in the French casino Bond is on his seventieth cigarette of the day and has downed enough drink to have lesser men stomach-pumped. But he still has wit and energy enough to foil the dastardly Le Chiffre – as he will, in subsequent adventures, Dr No, Blofeld and the collective evil designs of SMERSH.

Jonathan Cape's name ensured a certain chic for *Casino Royale*, but it was not seen as anything other than higher-class pulp. Kingsley Amis devoted a considerable effort to arguing otherwise. There is, he said, 'a power and freshness about the book which, in an age less rigidly hierarchical in its attitudes to literature, would have caused it to be hailed as one of the most remarkable first novels to be published in England in the previous thirty years.' The Bond books were consumed massively, if not respected as Amis would have liked. They offered a shop window onto a world denied the mass of the British population. Sweets, to take a small example, only came 'off ration' a couple of months before *Casino Royale*'s publication – and promptly disappeared from the shelves, as the nation gorged its long-frustrated sweet tooth. Getting on for a decade after victory, life was austere and homogenised. Bond's favoured Taittinger Blanc de Blancs Brut and hand-made Sobranie Balkans were the fantasy equivalent of Winston Smith's Victory Gin and Victory Cigarettes in *Nineteen Eighty-Four* (i.e. 1948). In a world of utility clothes and state-manufactured soap, Bond's cakes of *Fleur des Alpes*, and Jermyn Street shirts were another world – and a lusted-after world.

As Fleming's biographer Andrew Lycett notes, the social climate had changed by the end of the 1950s, when it was increasingly possible to credit Harold Macmillan's assertion, 'You've never had it so good.' It was at this period of his career that critics began looking sharply at James Bond and none more so than Paul Johnson, in a famous diatribe in the *New Statesman* in April 1958, entitled 'Sex, snobbery and sadism'. It opened: 'I have just finished what is without a doubt the nastiest book I have ever read. It is a new novel entitled *Dr. No* and the author is Mr. Ian Fleming … There are three basic ingredients in Dr No, all unhealthy, all thoroughly English: the sadism of a school boy bully, the mechanical two-dimensional sex-longings of a frustrated adolescent, and the crude, snob-cravings of a suburban adult.' But, as a perplexed Johnson was obliged to note, whatever else, the author was *not* 'suburban': 'Mr Fleming was educated at Eton and Sandhurst, and is married to a prominent society hostess, the ex-wife of Lord Rothermere …

Fleming belongs to the Turf and Boodle's and lists among his hobbies the collection of first editions.' Baffling.

Baffling too were the sales. Annie Fleming's friends might scoff (they did – Fleming had once overheard them laughing uproariously at the galley proofs of *Casino Royale*) but when did Cyril, or Evelyn, sell a million in paperback? Or Paul Johnson, come to that. A feature which would become more and more interesting to commentators over the years, particularly after Fleming's death, were the whipping scenes in his novels. Le Chiffre, for example, lays into the bare buttocks of 007 with a relish which, presumably, was rare even in the least regulated boarding houses of English public schools. Was Fleming himself a flagellomaniac? There were sensational newspaper 'revelations' on the subject and his own joke to Annie that after a night of love she would be drinking her cocktails 'standing up' for a day or two. His 'tastes' are rendered an in-joke in the 2006 film (the second) of *Casino Royale*:

> BOND (*being tortured*): I've got a little itch, down there. Would you mind? (*Le Chiffre whips him again*)
> BOND: No! No! No! No! To the right! To the right! (*Le Chiffre whips him again*)
> BOND: Aaghh! Yes! Aarrgh! Yes! Yes! Yes. Now the whole world's gonna know that you died scratching my balls!

It was the films, beginning with *Dr No* in 1962, which made Bond into a multimedia franchise which continues to turn over more money per annum than any other literary creation of the twentieth century, with the possible exception of the Harry Potter films. Celluloid converted what little realism the novels had (none at all, anti-Bondists like John le Carré and Len Deighton protest) into fantasia. But, manifestly, fantasy was what audiences wanted and would pay for.

The early films had an easy, 1960s knowingness (the stolen Goya on the stair at Dr No's mansion, for example) which was in tune with a time in which 1950s austerities were being forgotten and critical standards relaxed. No more fuddy-duddy. Even Britain's most eminent, and starchiest, film critic, Dilys Powell, approved of the early film adaptations. Fleming himself never made great claims for anything with the name 'Ian Fleming' on it: his books, he said, were 'adolescent'. Be that as it may, their appeal was hugely enhanced by being, now, 'books of the film'. Supposedly, according to Ben Macintyre, both John F. Kennedy and Lee Harvey Oswald were reading Bond novels the night before the Dallas assassination.

'Fleming,' according to his biographer Andrew Lycett, 'was a complex and often unhappy man.' Physically, he was living proof that hard living was inadvisable for anyone intending to be around to collect their pension. It was not unusual for him to drink a daily bottle of gin during the war and switch to the same intake of bourbon after it. He smoked like a chimney – through a Noël Coward-style holder in later years. He had his first major heart attack in 1961 and would die, aged only fifty-seven, after a series of them. Ill, but not quite extinct, he wrote, in his last year, the charming fable about the kind of exotic car he loved, *Chitty Chitty Bang Bang*. It suggests that he could, had he lived longer, have satisfied readers even younger than adolescents. The story had originally been invented as a bedtime entertainment for Caspar. It was one of the few consolations of Fleming's early death that he did not survive to witness the death of his son, from a self-administered drug overdose, in 1975.

FN   Ian Lancaster Fleming
MRT   *Casino Royale*
Biog   A. Lycett, *Ian Fleming* (1995); B. Macintyre, *For Your Eyes Only: Ian Fleming and James Bond* (2008)

196. Louis L'Amour 1908–1988

That's the way I'd like to be remembered – as a storyteller. A good storyteller.

Louis L'Amour holds the title of bestselling author ever of Westerns. By the time of his death, 105 of his titles were in print and it was estimated some 200 million copies of his novels had been sold – the more surprising since he did not begin writing until his mid-thirties and had no great success until a few years after that. L'Amour was born 'Louis Dearborn LaMoore', the youngest of seven children, in Jamestown, North Dakota, where his father was a 'large animal' (i.e. principally horse) veterinarian. L'Amour claimed French-Irish pioneer ancestry and recorded that 'I am probably the last writer [of Westerns] who will ever have known the people who lived the frontier life.' In 1923, during the post-war Depression, and following the arrival of the automobile, which deprived veterinary surgeons of much of their business – and any lingering tang of the 'frontier life' – the LaMoores sold up and drifted to the southwest. Louis left school at fifteen (in later life he declared himself to be 'self-educated') and embarked on what he called his 'knockabout', or 'yondering' years – which he patently romanticised in later life. He was, as he protested, a 'good storyteller'.

What is clear is that he saw the world. Between 1923 and 1941 he claimed to have been, among other manly things: a cattle-skinner, hay-cutter, circus elephant handler, lumberjack, professional prize-fighter (winning, he claimed, fifty-one out of fifty-nine fights), a rod-riding hobo and an ocean-going seaman. He claimed also to have ridden with Tibetan bandits. He had early ambitions to be a poet, and it was for verse that he devised the pen name 'L'Amour'.

In 1942, after the outbreak of war, L'Amour joined the US Army and saw active service, as a lieutenant, in the European campaign. On demobilisation in 1946, he settled in Los Angeles, where he began seriously writing short stories for pulp magazines. Before the war he had published a few pieces, including hard-boiled crime and historical romance, as well as Westerns. Between 1950 and 1953 he published four 'Hopalong Cassidy' novels (a franchise exploited by many hands, but originated by Clarence E. Mulford in 1904) under the pseudonym 'Tex Burns'. He was writing a story a week, for the standard $100, and living in friends' spare rooms.

His first success as 'Louis L'Amour' was *Hondo* (1953, as it was eventually titled) which was adapted into a big-budget movie starring John Wayne. Wayne, in fact, liked the short story on which the novelisation was based ('The Gift of Cochise') so much he bought it for his own production company. It is the only role in his long career in which Wayne plays a 'half-breed' – part-white, brought up by Indians, and discriminated against by both races. The novel, which routinely features in 'best ever Western' polls, sold an estimated 2 million copies by the time of L'Amour's death. On the strength of this success, he signed a contract with Bantam Books, by which he would supply three titles a year. In 1956 he married a TV actress (she had earlier appeared in *Gunsmoke*), Katherine Adams, twenty-six years his junior and the couple had two children – Beau (1961) and Angelique (1964).

The early 1960s was a period in which Westerns were popular on TV and in film, and L'Amour, financially secure, took up residence with his family in a Beverly Hills mansion. He was now the mogul of Western writers. He had published his first 'Sackett' novel, *The Daybreakers*, in 1960. Initially featuring two brothers, Tyrel and Orrin, it extended into a long saga, comprising seventeen volumes, concluding with *Jubal Sackett* (1985). Bantam claimed to have sold over 30 million copies of the series. The decade marked the highpoint of L'Amour's creativity: in 1960 he produced what many consider his best novel, *Flint* (ageing gunman returns to the West to die in peace, but he can't. John Wayne picked up the theme in his last film role, *The Shootist*, in 1976). In 1963 L'Amour's epic *How the West was Won* was adapted into a five-part mini-series and a big-screen film. Some forty of his titles were filmed in all and his later career was garlanded with awards and decorations: a 'Golden Spur' from the Western Writers of America in 1969, a Congressional (National) Gold Medal in 1983 and the Presidential Medal of Freedom from Ronald Reagan (a great fan) in 1984, a posthumous Ph.D. from Bowling Green University (the home of popular fiction studies) in 1988. He died of lung cancer – a non-smoker, he presumably contracted the disease as a miner in his 'yondering' years.

FN   Louis Dearborn L'Amour (born LaMoore)
MRT   *Hondo*
Biog R. L. Gale, *Louis L'Amour* (1985; revised edition, 1992)

197. Eric Ambler 1909–1998

Our greatest thriller writer. Graham Greene

Eric Ambler was the son of Lancashire parents both of whom had been puppeteers and music-hall performers, under the stage name 'The What Nots'. They specialised in 'living marionettes', i.e. real character dolls (precursors of *Spitting Image*), but didn't make the big time. Eric was born and brought up working-class – but decent – in London. There was, however, a jailbird Uncle Frank in his life. The First World War necessarily meant an austere lifestyle, but pulp fiction was one affordable pastime. As a schoolboy Eric devoured the 'Nelson Lee' Library (a series based on a schoolmaster who is also a private detective, aided by a juvenile Watson, his pupil 'Nipper'). He was also devoted to John Buchan's 'Hannay' and E. W. Hornung's 'Raffles' stories and the sub-Zendaish romances which were then the rage. He lost any religious belief early in life: 'Supernatural Christianity is false,' he determined, 'prayer is useless.'

An unusually clever lad, he won a scholarship at sixteen to attend Northampton Engineering College, Islington, but dropped out to do odd-job work around the time of the 1926 General Strike – an event which he records as politicising him. By the early 1930s, after some desultory attempts at higher education, Ambler was settled in an advertising agency, writing copy: 'a deeply dishonest business – learning how to arrange half-truths so they didn't look like half-truths.' He particularly recalls a jingle for a chocolate laxative, Ex-Lax, and the famous Horlicks bedtime drink 'night starvation' campaign. In 1929 he got a married lady pregnant and had to borrow 16 guineas (doctors never dealt in pounds) from a friendly uncle for a criminal abortion. But he was good at his job, and earned enough to travel in Europe without any avuncular help.

He was constitutionally footloose and dated his inception into writing as 1934 when, on holiday in Marseilles, he lost all his travel money playing poker-dice with a barman. He retreated to his hotel room, with only Joyce's *Portrait of the Artist as a*

Young Man to read and fantasised about murdering barmen. The following year he published his first Ruritanian thriller, *The Dark Frontier*, with Hodder and Stoughton, a firm with a traditional line in thrillers. Crude as the plotwork is, the scenario is strikingly prophetic. A gang of Balkan Fascists develops an atom bomb (this is 1935, remember) and blackmails the free world with it. Ambler had steeped himself in the work of novelists, like Somerset Maugham and Compton Mackenzie, who had first-hand knowledge of MI6 and the result was *Uncommon Danger* (1937), a spy thriller with a Levantine setting. It was filmed in 1943 as *Background to Danger*, directed by Raoul Walsh, starring George Raft. *Epitaph for a Spy* (1938) followed and was serialised in the *Daily Express*, earning Ambler a six-book contract from Hodder. He was, he said, never sure whether he was writing thrillers 'or parodies of thrillers' – he settled for the definition 'good trash'.

In the late 1930s Ambler was often in Paris where he met his first wife, the American fashion correspondent, Louise Crombie. They married in the year everything changed, 1939. In the same year, on the eve of the Second World War, he published *The Mask of Dimitrios*, reckoned to be the best of Ambler's works. It was filmed in 1944 with rather more 'B-movie clichés' than the author liked. Book and film have an elaborate flashback structure – fashionable in the 1940s – reconstructing, as his corpse (is it, though?) lies in the morgue, the elusive character of Dimitrios Makropoulos – murderer, assassin, spy, drug-trafficker – in his murky career from Smyrna to Paris. The narrator, Latimer, concludes:

> But it was useless to try to explain him in terms of Good and Evil. They were
> no more than baroque abstractions. Good Business and Bad Business were
> the elements of the new theology. Dimitrios was not evil. He was logical and
> consistent; as logical and consistent in the European jungle as the poison gas
> called Lewisite and the shattered bodies of children killed in the bombardment of
> an open town.

Ambler had been disillusioned, like other previously left-leaning literary people, by the Ribbentrop–Molotov Pact, and was now less radical and more straightforwardly patriotic in his views (although he would vote for Attlee, not Churchill, in 1945). Given his American connections, not least his wife and the thousands Hollywood was paying him, he could, like Aldous Huxley or Christopher Isherwood, have gone to America. He chose to stay and face the music: 'I don't think I believe in democracy,' he once said, 'except in wartime.'

While awaiting call-up – thirty-year-olds not being in immediate demand – he wrote *Journey into Fear* (1940), a story of international intrigue and arms smuggling, set in Turkey. The novel was filmed in 1942, starring a comically unhappy

Orson Welles. By now Ambler's fiction had fallen into its groove: all his plots used a device lifted from Anthony Hope's *The Prisoner of Zenda* – an essentially apolitical Englishman is caught up in the intrigues of Middle European politics, high finance and espionage; only narrowly escaping with his life before returning to the safety (and moral decencies) of England.

Ambler entered the armed forces as a private soldier. He was commissioned into the Royal Artillery, before being transferred to the army cinematographic unit. Here he worked with a number of the country's leading film-makers, Thorold Dickinson and Carol Reed notably, producing material for the War Department to uplift the morale of the fighting man. Wars are won by lenses, as well as bullets. He later worked alongside US film director John Huston covering the Allies' Italian campaign, ending the war a full colonel and director of the army film unit. He had also earned, from his country's principal ally, an American Bronze Star. Ambler had a good war and one which pointed the way to a decent post-war career, writing for movies. 'The script', he believed, 'is the heart of a film.' And he was one of the greatest scriptwriters around. He worked with David Lean (unhappily), and had an unexpected hit with the Ealing Studios adaptation of Arnold Bennett's Black Country comedy, *The Card*, in 1952, a novel he had loved since childhood. Although he did not much care for what Hollywood did to his own novels – Jean Negulesco's *The Mask of Dimitrios* (1944) made him physically sick – he was internationally known and could write his own ticket in the film world. But, as the 1940s ended, he had not written an original book for some ten years. 'In the army', he realised, 'I had lost the habit of a concentrated and solitary writing routine.'

Ambler returned to authorship under a pseudonym, 'Eliot Reed', and with a collaborator, Charles Rodda. His career as a thriller writer under his own name was relaunched with *Judgement on Deltchev* (1951), a Cold War spy story with an against-the-grain (for the time) pro-Soviet slant. He also wrote screenplays for Nicholas Monsarrat's *The Cruel Sea* (1953) and *A Night To Remember* (1958), the first and better *Titanic* movie – two high-points of British post-war film. Both celebrate English sangfroid in the face of hardship and disaster. The instincts of the wartime propagandist were ineradicable. He adapted his by now venerable international intrigue formula for the Cold War with thrillers such as *The Intercom Conspiracy* (1969); *The Levanter* (1972), a title which doomed the novel's sales prospects; and *The Care of Time* (1981), his seventeenth novel. But by this point his real money came from screenplays – as much as $1,500 a week when he was under contract in Hollywood (roughly what the average British worker was earning a year).

Ambler divorced his first wife in 1958 and moved with his second (Joan Mary Harrison, a film and television producer, and a former assistant to Alfred Hitchcock) to Switzerland, to protect his dollars from the English taxman and enjoy spending them. He had done his bit for his country – and more. He remained domiciled in Switzerland for sixteen years, returning when Mrs Thatcher's reforms made England again hospitable to the super-rich like himself. An OBE in 1981 may have eased his way back. He died in London. Towards the end of his life he wrote an elegant memoir, with the punning gravestone title: *Here Lies Eric Ambler*.

FN   Eric Clifford Ambler
MRT   *The Mask of Dimitrios*
Biog E. Ambler, *Here Lies Eric Ambler* (1985)

198. Chester Himes 1909–1984

I never found a place where I even began to fit.

An African-American writer of crime thrillers, notable for their Harlem setting and crazed comedy, Himes was born in Jefferson City, Missouri, in a middle-class home, the family later settling in Cleveland, Ohio. His father was a college teacher of trade skills – something which followers of Booker T. Washington fondly believed would raise the black race in America. The family broke up during his childhood – largely, as Himes later claimed, on the grounds of his mother being so much lighter-skinned than her husband that she could pass for white 'and believed she should'. Thereafter Chester's adolescence and early adult life was troubled, as he bounced between the race barriers in America. According to his autobiography, while working as a bus boy (i.e. waiter's assistant) in a fashionable hotel in Cleveland, he attempted suicide by throwing himself down a lift shaft, after being snubbed sexually by two white girls. He spent a year or so at Ohio State University, before being expelled for what is vaguely described a 'prank'. He confesses using drugs at this period, and met his first wife at an opium party.

Himes began to write while serving a seven-and-a-half-year sentence in the Ohio State Penitentiary for armed robbery, in 1928. The brutal 'third degree' inflicted on him by white detectives to extract his 'confession', scarred him for life. Some of his early stories appeared in *Esquire* with his prison number as their byline. Himes's start in literature coincided with widespread liberal anger in the US as a result of the 'Scottsboro Boys' case (1931–7) in which nine black men were falsely accused of raping a white woman. It led, after Supreme Court intervention, to the first faltering steps towards civil rights reforms thirty years later.

Himes was paroled in 1936. On his release, the Grand Old Man of black American writing, Langston Hughes, took an interest in him. He married Jean Johnson in 1936, did a couple of years with the Federal Writers Project, and moved on to Los Angeles in the early 1940s. There he picked up work in the film industry and published his first novels, notably the *roman à thèse*, *If He Hollers Let Him Go* (1945). Set in the LA factories (where, with white folks in khaki, immigrant blacks could at last find blue-collar work), the novel's barbed title signals Himes's willingness to confront the 'race theme' head on. He was in LA at the period of the Zoot Suit race riots, in 1943 and politically aligned himself with the NAACP and the American left. He hollered – but to little effect. With the Cold War, Himes had little expectation that 'niggers' like him would ever be let go. There was also, he recalls in his autobiography, an ugly break-up with the white woman he was currently dating, in which he came perilously close to killing her. It would have meant the electric chair.

He made his permanent residence in Paris in 1953, as had Richard Wright, James Baldwin and a number of distinguished black jazz musicians. In France he could sleep with whomever he liked, irrespective of pigmentation (or, in Baldwin's case, sexual preference) and he could use drugs (like the tenor saxophonist, Don Byas). You could also be a communist, like Wright, if you liked and no one like Joe McCarthy would hassle you. Moreover, your talent would be encouraged: it was expatriate liberty hall. In the 1950s, Himes also met Lesley Packard, a journalist at the *Herald Tribune*, and spent the rest of his life with her. She nursed him when he had a stroke in 1959 and they eventually married in 1978.

A friend, Marcel Duhamel of Gallimard's *Série Noire*, who had translated Himes's early fiction, suggested the author might try his hand at detective stories in the mode of Dashiell Hammett – much admired in France at the time. The suggestion, and the $1,000 Duhamel advanced him inspired Himes's 'Harlem domestic stories', as he called them. There is, on the face of it, little 'domestic' in Himes's black Manhattan – a ghettoised world of pimps, drugs, gambling, religious mania, all laced with zany humour. Himes never knew Harlem as intimately as his novels suggest. But there was no market for crime *noir* by a black man about Cleveland (or Los Angeles, come to that, until Walter Mosley, Himes's most eminent disciple, came along). The first of the series, *A Rage in Harlem* (1957) has a typically complicated plot: Slim and his girl Imabelle steal a trunkful of gold in Natchez. She runs off and attempts, unsuccessfully, to fence the loot in Harlem via a numbers racketeer, Easy Money. Imabelle teams up with an incredibly guileless undertaker's assistant, Jackson. Re-enter Slim, looking for his gold – violently. *A Rage in Harlem* introduced the bantering detective team of Coffin Ed Johnson and Grave Digger Jones, whose burly, 'hog-farmer' demeanour and brutal way with suspects (Coffin Ed is paying off a flask of acid thrown in his face) would feature in six subsequent novels.

In Himes's contrarian analysis, it is the black criminal – and policeman – who preys most ruthlessly on black folk. In *Cotton Comes to Harlem* (1965) a preacher milks vast sums from his congregation for a phoney back-to-Africa movement. At the period of the civil rights revolution, when white institutional racism was perceived as the black community's historical problem, Himes's scenarios were regarded as cynical, defeatist and a confirmer of ingrained prejudices about his people. Himes's defenders align him with the European absurdists, as did Himes himself. The Harlem stories made Himes 'the most celebrated writer in France who couldn't speak French'. He won prizes and (in France, at least) critical acclaim. He wrote one work of interracial pornography, *Pinktoes* (1961) for Maurice Girodias's Olympia Press: joining the ranks of Nabokov, Lawrence and Henry Miller in the notorious 'DB' (dirty book) list.

Himes, now very well off, and at last in a stable marriage, moved to Spain in 1969. *Cotton Comes to Harlem* (1965) was filmed in 1970 (directed by Ossie Davis) and inspired a series of so-called 'blaxploitation' films and a new vogue for Himes's work. Himes wrote a two-part autobiography towards the end of his life (*The Quality of Hurt*, 1972, and *My Life of Absurdity*, 1976). His best novel is judged by admirers of his work to be *Blind Man with a Pistol* (1969). I prefer the early 'domestic' stuff.

FN   Chester Bomar Himes
MRT   *Cotton Comes to Harlem*
Biog   J. Sallis, *Chester Himes: A Life* (2001)

199. Malcolm Lowry 1909–1957

Frankly I think I have no gift for writing. Lowry, in a notebook

Gordon Bowker's authoritative biography opens: 'Trying to follow Malcolm Lowry's life is like venturing without a map into a maze inside a labyrinth lost in a wilderness.' There follow 672 pages of 'trying'. Devotional websites record that *Under the Volcano* (1947) once came eleventh in an 'all-time greatest novel' competition. It would certainly come top (or, by a nose, second – see the following postscript) in any such competition for the greatest novel about alcoholism. Lowry's life and fiction goes further than any on record into the mysterious heart of booze. More specifically, he defines the essential paradox: is alcoholism the mark of some inadequacy in the face of life – or a voyage of discovery into the meaning of life?

There are smaller questions. Gordon Bowker, in his 672 pages, lays repeated stress on the 'tiny size of his penis', which at school earned Lowry the nickname 'lobster'. In later life also, comrades mocked his lack of 'endowment'. On the face of it, the size of the novelist's tool should be of no more literary significance than Virginia Woolf's anything but tiny nose, but in Lowry's case it links – or so it is speculated – to his dipsomania. Switch to the alternative theory. There is a striking episode in the second chapter of *Volcano* in which the hero and his recently divorced wife are sitting in a *cantina*, drinking. It is morning. 'Must you', Yvonne asks, 'go on and on for ever into this stupid darkness? ... Oh Geoffrey, why do you do it!' But it's not darkness, Geoffrey replies: 'Look at that sunlight there, ah, then perhaps you'll get the answer, see, look at the way it falls through the window: what beauty can compare to that of a *cantina* in the early morning.' And suddenly, 'uncannily', Yvonne sees that it is beautiful: light, not darkness. Geoffrey is searching, as he thinks, for that moment of drunkenness when he alone in the world is sober. Of course his life is a catalogue of disaster: he has failed as a consul, a husband and a brother. But somehow, when his body is tossed into the ravine (that grotesque womb) at the end of the narrative, along with a dead dog, it is exaltation. 'He had reached the summit.'

Lowry was the youngest of four sons of a prosperous cotton broker in Cheshire. His siblings pursued eminently respectable careers while Malcolm went to the bad – and created literature. He was sent to the best boarding school in Cambridge, and a good college in the same city, St Catharine's College. In between, aged sixteen, he ran away to sea for a brief period as a cabin boy on a Conradian voyage to the Far East. His fellow crew-members hated and humiliated him.

At university, Lowry – already manifestly alcoholic – infuriated his teachers. He apprenticed himself, instead, to an American writer – his Mephistopheles – Conrad Aiken. Aiken was the first to perceive Lowry's genius, and fused it with his own artistic experiments in self-destruction. Drunken, divorced, fired from Harvard for 'moral turpitude', his life forecast that of his protégé. Aiken was a tutor from hell, but his *Blue Voyage* (1927), chronicling a phantasmagoric Atlantic crossing, was influential on Lowry's first published novel *Ultramarine* (1933), based on the sixteen-year-old author's maiden sea voyage. He scraped out of Cambridge with a third (only by virtue of his submitting scraps of his novel-in-progress, one of his examiners said), in 1932. For the next thirty years, he would live on a monthly pension from his father. Like that supplied to William S. Burroughs, part of the deal was that he should stay out of his family's way – and, ideally, out of England. Calamity, as Aiken's wife Clarissa observed, followed Lowry like a shadow. It took him five years to write *Ultramarine*, and two years to get it accepted. The manuscript was promptly lost by the publisher who took it on, Jonathan Cape. Luckily a carbon copy survived from the wastepaper basket into which the author had thrown it.

Lowry married his first wife, Jan Gabrial, in Paris in 1934. She was American, cultured and an actress. Lowry wooed her with the typescript of *Ultramarine* and she fell, as she said, 'totally in love with the writer'. About the man she was never so sure. She confessed herself unimpressed by his lack of (penile) 'inches' and his *ejaculatio praecox*. He learned, however, to control his prematurity by singing 'The Star-Spangled Banner' to himself during sex. The only child Lowry is known to have engendered was terminated by abortion, soon after his marriage.

In New York, in 1935, Lowry spent his first spell of several in a lunatic asylum, New York's Bellevue – this was the raw material for Lowry's incomplete novel, *Lunar Caustic* (1963). The couple moved on to Mexico, it pleased him to observe, on the Day of the Dead, 1936. It was a place where an expatriate could live cheaply on the £150 a month the 'old man' forked out. The Lowrys settled for two years in Cuernavaca ('Quauhnahuac' in *Volcano*) but during this period, as with 'Geoffrey Firmin', Lowry's marriage broke up and, with the expropriation of foreign oil companies, Britain's diplomatic representation in Mexico was withdrawn. The Fascists had won Spain and looked likely to take over the rest of Europe, and, over the same period, Lowry spiralled into drinking excessively, even by his heroic levels of intake: 'Once he consumed a whole bottle of olive oil thinking it was hair tonic with a high alcoholic content. Finally he got the shakes so bad that he improvised a pulley system to hoist the glass to his lips.' Destructive to his liver, it was grist for *Under the Volcano*. Having gathered his material, Lowry went off to the west coast of Canada to live, relatively abstemiously, and write it up. In this monastic exile he was supported by his second wife, Margerie Bonner, another American, former actress, divorcée and herself a novelist.

From 1940 onwards, Lowry wrote and rewrote his great work. It took nine years in all: 'time enough to fight three world wars', he sardonically noted: although he left warfare to others, doing everything he could to avoid conscription. His brothers, meanwhile, kept the Lowry name honourable by fighting for their country. After a huge number of rejections, the novel was published in 1947 and enjoyed immediate success. Lowry sketched out various ambitious sequels, but they came to nothing, leaving only a scatter of brilliant short stories.

Now well off, he and Margerie returned to England in 1955, to live in a cottage in Ripe, East Sussex. After a spectacularly drunken evening, Lowry died – whether it was suicide (he habitually swallowed barbiturates like 'lemon drops') or accidentally inhaled vomit which killed him has never been established. He died, as he lived, leaving questions, and one great novel. The novel's greatness was not much augmented by a John Huston-directed, Albert Finney-starring film in 1984.

FN   Clarence Malcolm Lowry
MRT   *Under the Volcano*
Biog   G. Bowker, *Pursued by Furies: A Life of Malcolm Lowry* (1993)

POSTSCRIPT

200. Charles R. Jackson 1903–1968

There isn't any cure. From *The Lost Weekend*

During the long composition and revision of *Under the Volcano*, Lowry – who had been repeatedly, and plausibly, accused of plagiarism during his career – was appalled by the publication in 1944 of Charles R. Jackson's *The Lost Weekend*. His own novel, complete but still unaccepted, would not be published until 1947. Jackson's account of Don Birnam's terminal, five-day binge in 1936 Manhattan has striking similarities with Geoffrey Firmin's final bender. In both novels there is a trio of principal characters – two brothers and a dithery girlfriend. Sections of the novels, notably the description of hallucinatory DTs, are eerily similar. In *The Lost Weekend*, a tiny mouse emerges from a crack in the wall, opposite the sodden Birnam. A bat swoops, there is a crunch, and a stream of blood streaks down the wall. Birnam screams. In *Under the Volcano* the Consul is sitting 'helpless' in the bathroom, while the wall in front of him is swarming with insects:

> A caterpillar started to wriggle toward him, peering this way and that, with interrogatory antennae. A large cricket, with polished fuselage, clung to the curtain, swaying it slightly and cleaning its face like a cat, its eyes on stalks appearing to revolve in its head ... the very scars and cracks of the wall, had begun to swarm.

When he read the novel in April 1944, Lowry wrote nervously to a friend: 'Have you read a novel *The Lost Weekend* by one Charles Jackson, a radioman from New York? It is perhaps not a very fine novel but admirably written about a drunkard and hangovers and alcoholic wards as they have never been done (save by me of course).' He later wrote to Jackson, who seems not to have been worried (he had, after all, got his boozeiad out first). It compounded Lowry's nervousness that the novel was adapted into an Oscar-winning film in 1945.

Jackson's life was quite as chaotic as Lowry's. He was born in Summit, New Jersey, one of five children. His father walked out when he was ten; a younger sister and brother were killed in an automobile accident a couple of years later. Charles had no education beyond school, leaving Syracuse University shortly after enrolling. Presumably as with his clearly autobiographical hero, Don Birnam, who is kicked out of Dartmouth for homosexual overtures to fraternity brothers, there was some ugly, hushed-up, scandal. Jackson worked in a New York bookstore and contracted TB in 1927. It was four years before he was pronounced cured, after treatment in various sanatoriums, including two years in Switzerland (inspired to go there by Thomas Mann's *The Magic Mountain*). He came through his ordeal with the loss of one lung. It was during these years that he acquired his catastrophic drinking habits. He returned to New York at the depth of the Depression, and in the period of universal alcoholic excess following the repeal of Prohibition. He finally cleaned up in 1936, with the help of the newly founded AA fellowship and the woman who became his wife, Rhoda Booth, a *Fortune* magazine editor (the original of 'Helen' in the novel). He landed a job with CBS, doing drama scripts.

Like Don Birnam, and his novel 'The Bottle', Jackson resolved to write the first novel to describe alcoholism as it really is, rather than as it is demonised in temperance tract fiction such as *Ten Nights in a Bar-Room*, or romanticised as a ladder to the stars in novels such as *Tender is the Night*. Fitzgerald was, none the less, a writer Jackson idolised – there's a comic moment in the novel when Don, smashed, phones up the wearily sober great author. *The Lost Weekend* was a bestseller and its sales, along with the $50,000 he got for the film rights, enriched its author. He bought a large house in New Jersey, and retired there with his wife and two daughters. He wrote three more novels over the next ten years. Only *The Fall of Valor* (1946) enjoyed anything like the éclat of its predecessor. It takes on another 'daring' subject: a married man, with two daughters, falls in love with a young marine officer. By the early 1950s Jackson had fallen off the wagon and was in financial difficulties. His last ten years were painful, and his life fell apart, beyond any hope of being put together again. In addition, his pulmonary problems returned. His final novel, the grim *A Second-Hand Life* (the story of a sexually loose girl, Winifred Grainger) was published in 1967. He committed suicide the following year at the Chelsea Hotel, the favourite resort of bohemian writers in New York.

Billy Wilder's film of *The Lost Weekend*, which is viewed on TV reruns more often than Jackson's novel is read nowadays, makes two substantial alterations to its source text. One change is to the fatalism of the novel as regards alcoholism. Jackson's Don Birnam, a 'periodic' drunk, is not 'cured' as is Ray Milland's Birnam in the last scene of the film. He will, we apprehend, have other lost weekends and bouts, until either the closed ward or the morgue brings him to the Last Weekend. As the homosexual attendant Bim tells him in Bellevue (where his public drunkenness has brought him):

> There isn't any cure, besides just stopping. And how many of them can do that? ... If they do stop, out of fear or whatever, they go at once into such a state of euphoria and well-being that they become over-confident. They're rid of drink, and feel sure enough of themselves to be able to start again, promising they'll take one, or at the most two, and – well, then it becomes the same old story all over again.

The other change is to Birnam's homosexuality, which is glossed over entirely in the film. In the novel it is clear that Birnam's drinking is at least partly driven by sexual confusion and the explosive pressures that build up in the closet. And the drink closet.

FN   Charles Reginald Jackson
MRT   *The Lost Weekend*
Biog   M. Connelly, *Deadly Closets: The Fiction of Charles Jackson* (2001)

201. Nicholas Monsarrat 1910–1979

Who remembers the old fights? Who wants to?

No novelist of his time conveyed more articulately than Nicholas Monsarrat the tepid rage of Britain in the post-war period when the country won a war, mislaid a great Empire, lost its national nerve, but preserved a saving decency. There is an illustrative moment in *The Cruel Sea*, when the captain hero (as sterling a type as ever appeared on a Players' cigarette packet) returns to port from the deadly Western Approaches, leaving in his wake corpses still bobbing on the waves, to find civilian dock-workers on strike for more wages: 'These were ... the people whom sailors fought and died for; at close quarters, they hardly seemed to deserve it.' None the less, Captain Ericson returns to battle.

Monsarrat was the son of an eminent surgeon in Liverpool, the second of three boys, two of whom came to tragically early deaths. At the family's country home in Anglesey, he developed an early love of yachting. He was educated at Winchester, where he was bullied and progressed to Trinity College, Cambridge, to complete his gentleman's education with a third in Law. It would not have disqualified him from a good career. But Monsarrat never bought into the values of his class – nor, however, did he ever quite discard them. For most of the 1930s he chose to be like the black-sheep down-and-outer Orwell describes in the doss-house – his ragged trousers held up with an Etonian tie. In London, with only a typewriter in his luggage, he slept rough and 'saw life'. He wrote novels which were promisingly smart, but never earned back the standard £30 advance. He sold the *Daily Worker* in Piccadilly, marched with the unemployed and proclaimed an 'ardent' pacifism.

By the end of the decade, he was actually getting somewhere with his fiction. His fourth novel, *This is the Schoolroom*, a *Bildungsroman*, was well received by the critics. But, published a week before the outbreak of war, it was swallowed up by history. It was a hectic period. Monsarrat married in the same week (to Eileen Rowland; they had one son). An avowed pacifist, he donned the black uniform of the St John Ambulance Brigade, based (as befitted his background) in Harley Street. The bombs didn't come. Ambulanceman Monsarrat patrolled the streets 'armed with iodine and sal volatile in case any ladies fainted'. Things changed when his father sent him an advertisement from *The Times* ('a paper I would not be seen dead with'), asking whether '*gentlemen* with yachting experience' would be interested in commissions 'as Temporary Probationary Sub-Lieutenants in the Royal Navy Volunteer Reserve'. Was ever an invitation colder? Monsarrat joined up, telling himself that 'pacifism was useless in wartime.' He would spend three years on escort corvettes – unglamorous bathtubs armed with popguns, so unstable on high seas that sailors unlucky enough to sail them jested they 'would roll on wet grass'. Sub-Lt. Monsarrat (former ambulanceman) was given the task of tending to the survivors from sunk ships. It was horrific: 'What did one do for the tortured lascar with the mortal oil seeping down into his gut? ... Often I willed such men to die, even as I tended them; and sometimes they agreed.'

Monsarrat, himself a 'temporary', admired the permanent officer class, while inwardly mocking their incorrigible bone-headedness. He was good at the job and ended up commanding a frigate. After 1945 he could have continued at the Admiralty, commanding a desk. Instead he joined the Colonial Service. What finally induced him to abandon, for the rest of his life, the country he had fought for was an official recipe from the Ministry of Food to senior civil servants, recommending 'a squirrel pie recipe'. For those who qualified, 'free cartridges would be supplied by the local pest officer to shoot the squirrel with'. If gentlemen were reduced to eating rodents it was time to leave. He was appointed to Johannesburg, to open the UK information office. In the boredom of that job, between heavy drinking and reckless adulteries (about which he is engagingly frank) he wrote *The Cruel Sea* (1951).

By now he expected little from publishers, but the British book trade was desperate for the British *The Naked and the Dead* – Norman Mailer's authentically eye-witness, war-is-hell novel. This, Cassells decided, was it. The *Cruel Sea* went on to become an international bestseller and an Eric Ambler-scripted film in 1953. The emblematic scene in both page and screen versions is the depth-charging of ship-wrecked British sailors, hooraying as they mistakenly assume that the corvette is steaming forward to pluck them out of the water, when the Captain, as mistakenly, thinks there is a submarine beneath them and has decided that they are expend-able and must be blown up. Captain Ericson, played throatily by Jack Hawkins, gets drunk and in the film (not the novel) later comes out with his agonised groan: 'it's the war, it's the *bloody* war'.

Monsarrat was now rich, and could indulge himself with the first Jaguar XK120 in South Africa and a second wife, Philippa Crosby (he would, in fact, marry three times and own many fine cars). He stayed on in the service and took a posting to Ottawa, Canada, which was relatively unbloody. Disdaining the war novel sequel his publishers craved, he produced *The Story of Esther Costello* (1953), a satire on Amer-ican hucksterism which, as a novel and a Hollywood adaptation, was a thought-provoking flop. He resigned the Colonial Service in 1956. He could not have stayed on, what with the novel he published that year: *The Tribe That Lost its Head* is far and away Monsarrat's best thing in fiction. Set in an imaginary island, Pharamaul, off the West Coast of Africa, it allegorises the tensions of old, complacent British colonial rule (more benign than that in the nearby Republic of South Africa) in the aftermath of Kenya's Mau Mau insurgency – on which Monsarrat had views which would have made Sanders of the River look namby-pamby.

The black hero, Dinamaula, is the Oxford-educated chief-in-waiting of the U-Maula tribe who returns to take up his position as tribal chief. Like the occiden-talised Seretse Khama (with whom Monsarrat had dealings, and whom he person-ally despised), he has chosen to marry a white woman, which complicates things. The Maulas – a child-like people who have lived quite happily under a regime which has not changed since the rule of their 'Mother across the Sea' (Victoria) – are inflamed by ideas of self-determination fed them by mischievous British newspaper-men and doltishly doctrinaire Socialist politicians. Rebellion ensues. The tribesmen, whose pagan Christianity demands blood sacrifice, ritually crucify and rape some luckless missionaries and white women. Summary executions follow and a press conference, given by a wholly disillusioned young administrator, David Bracken:

> 'You mean that they actually crucified him [Father Schwemmer]?'
> 'Yes,' said David.
> 'A deed of madness!' exclaimed Father Hawthorne. 'Those poor, misguided children.'

David looked at him. 'Yes, indeed. Misguided, *greedy* children.'

'What do you mean by "greedy", Mr Bracken?'

'I should have told you that they ate him as well.'

That had been the end of the Press conference.

It echoes the black-comic ending of Waugh's *Black Mischief* (1932), when Basil asks the chief what was the delicious stew they had last night and is told 'Your girl friend'. But Monsarrat's view was not – like Waugh's – that of the satirical tourist, and the novel emanates radical uncertainty about whether Empire (like the war) was worthwhile. Monsarrat is no Blimp. Nor does he believe, like the senior colonial official Macmillan (mischievously named after the PM who loosed the winds of change over Africa) that, in a couple of centuries or so, the Africans may conceivably be ready for emancipation. It was, he believed, all a mess – but the Englishman's mess.

This novel was, in the context of 1956 (and with the Belgian Congo debacle imminent), explosive. Monsarrat remarried and retired, prosperously, to Malta where, in his last years, he wrote his lively volumes of memoir and worked on an epic-length version of the Flying Dutchman myth. At his wish, his ashes were scattered in the sea he believed cruel, by the Royal Navy.

FN   Nicholas John Turney Monsarrat

MRT   *The Cruel Sea*

Biog N. Monsarrat, *Life is a Four-Letter Word* (1966); N. Monsarrat, *Monsarrat at Sea* (1975)

202. William Golding 1911–1993

Golding is a little too 'nice' for my taste. Artur Lundkvist, the Nobel judge who stood out against Golding getting literature's most eminent prize in 1983

In 1972 William Golding – well on the way to his Nobel Prize – was a guest of the Cecils (Lord Cecil, that is) at Cranbourne Manor. The 'Bloomsbury groupie Frances Partridge' (John Carey's scathing description) was also there. She recorded meeting Golding in her diary: 'a short, squarish, bearded man, smelling rather like an old labourer'. Ah yes, that proletarian *stink*. George Orwell is eloquent on the subject in *The Road to Wigan Pier*: stale urine, old cabbage, *sweat*. It is no coincidence that when Gordon Comstock sells out, in *Keep the Aspidistra Flying*, he goes on to earn his daily bread advertising sock-deodorants. Doubtless when Vita Sackville-West came in from tending the garden at Sissinghurst, she smelled of nothing but attar of rose. Amazing that some of the labouring classes can actually write, but, 'little Latin and less Greek', you know.

Golding, although he never lived to read what Partridge thought of him, glowed, lifelong, with the underdog's radioactive anger. He lived, he once said, *under*, not *in* the British class system – and that system was indestructible. Blast Britain to smithereens with nuclear bombs, dump a bunch of innocent kids on an Edenic desert island, and class reasserts itself like funny putty – Jack Merridew the toff, Piggy the oik – thus it was, and thus it will always be. The obstructions in Golding's way were the familiar ones. He was two generations up from the artisan's cottage. His father, an awesomely polymathic autodidact, made it to the schoolteacher class. The fact that he was never able to rise above the rank of deputy head embittered his later years. William went to Marlborough grammar school. Not far away in distance – but a universe away socially – was Marlborough College. Golding liked to say he would happily blow up every public school in England. But he was no simple anarchist; in later life he lusted after a knighthood and bullied friends in high places to get him one. Inferiority complexes are complex things.

Following the upward trajectory of the clever grammar school boy, and at huge financial sacrifice to his parents, Golding went to Brasenose College, Oxford: it was a 'disaster'. Why? As John Carey records, the public school boys outnumbered the grammar bugs twenty to one. 'Not *quite* a gentleman' was the verdict passed on him by the university authorities in their confidential dossier. But despite his pathological timidity, which he bravely disguised, Golding served gallantly in the Royal Navy in the Second World War when even 'not quites' could join the officer class and get killed for king and country and the preservation of the English class system. He was even given a command. Not a first-rate vessel, of course – those were reserved for those with a public school or Dartmouth pedigree – but a LCT(R) (Landing Craft Tank, Rocket Armed), a kind of floating tea-tray, with what the Russians called a 'Molotov Organ' (multiple rocket barrels) mounted on it. It was not a craft to be proud of. But it had a formidable punch.

Golding's experience in the navy convinced him that 'man produces evil as a bee produces honey'. After the war he followed his father into the classroom where his observations of boys confirmed his beliefs about universal evil. He was not, one of his colleagues cattily recalled, a 'gifted' teacher. His nickname among the boys was 'Scruff'. Over the post-war years he forged an idiosyncratic personal philosophy. Extraordinarily, as John Carey discloses, he never read with any attention 'the three most crashing bores of the Western world' – Marx, Freud and Darwin. According to Carey, he went to his grave not even having read Thomas Hardy. When the two of them were visiting Salisbury Cathedral, the critic, and one of his principal supporters, Frank Kermode, asked Golding how he boned up the medieval construction techniques which are so meticulously described in *The Spire* (1964). 'Oh', Golding replied, 'I just came here and said to myself, "if I were to build a spire how would I go about it?"' He created his novels the same way. In the private journal to which Carey had privileged access, Golding recalls a fumbled juvenile attempted rape. More amusingly, he recalls discovering the joys of masturbation while shinning up a flagpole. He jilted a girl he was engaged to for the woman he married (Ann Brookfield). Guilt, and bad dreams, pursued him through life. Married for over fifty years, it seems there was never a moral lapse – other than, perhaps, too warm a friendship with the American scholar Virginia Tiger (wonderful name), which vexed Ann Golding mightily.

There was, undeniably, an ugly side to Golding, particularly in later life. He was frequently drunken, rude on occasion, arrogant and preoccupied with money. But Carey is at pains to stress how savagely hard Golding was on himself. He could never persuade himself that he was a good man. Those who knew him best thought he was. But regularly through life Golding would announce that had 'Wilhelm Geltinger' been born in Germany, not England, he would have been as happy an SS man as he was an RNVR officer.

The foundation stone of his career was the working partnership Golding forged with his Faber editor, Charles Monteith. It was Monteith who rescued the everywhere rejected *Lord of the Flies* from the slush pile, and crafted it into publishable shape with the author. Monteith would in fact be midwife to all the major works. They were all difficult deliveries. And, over the years, the novels themselves got more difficult. You can keep a dinner party conversation going for hours with *Lord of the Flies* (1954). Mention *Darkness Visible* (1979) and all you will hear is the clatter of cutlery on plates. As the silence grows oppressive, someone will venture how wonderful is the opening scene, where Matty – the burning child – emerges from a Blitz inferno. But thereafter, who can say what the novel is doing, for all the aura of power it exudes.

The social and artistic tensions which tormented Golding were evident at what should have been the most affirming moment of his professional life. Aged seventy-two, he received the first intimation that he was to be 1983 Nobel Laureate by phone, at 10 a.m., on the morning of 6 October. He was so informed by a Swedish journalist who said, tantalisingly, that he had a '50–50 chance'. The award was confirmed by lunchtime. The 50 per cent adverse possibility was, despite the notorious secretiveness of the Stockholm literary committee, made public in the days thereafter. One of the committee, the seventy-seven-year-old poet, Artur Lundkvist, had single-handedly tried to blackball Golding's nomination, in favour of a Senegalese poet, Léopold Senghor. Lundkvist explained, 'I simply didn't consider Golding to possess the international weight needed to win the prize ... I admire Anthony Burgess very much. He is of far greater worth than Golding and is much more controversial.' The author of *Lord of the Flies* was, he concluded, 'too nice'. Lundkvist's spiteful criticisms soured what should have been the crowning moment of Golding's literary career.

FN (Sir) William Gerald Golding
MRT *Lord of the Flies*
Biog John Carey, *William Golding* (2009)

203. John Cheever 1912–1982

Vodka for breakfast.

John Cheever was born in New England, the son of a shoe salesman, an early casualty of the Great Depression. Slump meant a rackety childhood for young John. He grew up around Boston, disliking his mother, who was capable, and despising his father, who was incapably drunken. It was his mother, after her husband's surrender to the bottle, who kept the family together. Contradictory feelings about his parents fed through into the torment of Cheever's later life: why was he so wedded to suburban respectability when he so hated it? He poses the question himself, with rueful wit in the 1978 preface to his collected stories:

> These stories seem at times to be stories of a long-lost world when the city of
> New York was still filled with a river light, when you heard the Benny Goodman
> quartets from a radio in the corner stationery store, and when almost everybody
> wore a hat. Here is the last of that generation of chain smokers who woke the
> world in the morning with their coughing, who used to get stoned at cocktail
> parties and perform obsolete dance steps like 'the Cleveland Chicken.'

Fondly nostalgic, or clinically contemptuous? Even Cheever, one suspects, could not have said.

Like Scott Fitzgerald, Cheever is a connoisseur of the crack-up – but he survived. He is, similarly, a scrupulous topographer of Richard Yates's 'Revolutionary Road', but he survived even that bourgeois hell. The author of ' The Season of Divorce' (if one saw that title running wild in Arabia, one would scream 'Cheever!') – bisexual, anti-social (he never joined the Country Clubs he chronicled) and incorrigibly adulterous – Cheever died with a Mrs John Cheever of forty years by his bedside.

As a boy, he received a bad education at a good school – Thayer Academy. He was expelled in the twelfth grade on grounds (as he variously fictionalised the event in later life) of either sexual delinquency, smoking, or poor classroom performance. Interestingly, he barely scraped a 'C-minus' in English: his 'best' subject. He serenely turned his disgrace into a short story, and submitted it to Malcolm Cowley at the *New Republic*. The magazine published 'Expelled' in October 1930. Cheever had declared his precocious resolve to be a writer when he was eleven years old: he was now in print, in a top-rated national magazine, at eighteen. College was out of the question: times were too hard and his academic achievement too feeble. So young Cheever bummed for a couple of years around Boston. But it was, a friend told him, 'a city without springboards for people who can't dive' (swimming was always Cheever's sport). New York was the only place for writers. Cheever followed the advice. He was lucky, soon after arrival, to land a visiting berth at Yaddo. The writers' colony was located 'in the woods', on 400 acres, at Saratoga Springs and hosted, in its four-star accommodation, the best young writers in the country. Cheever would return, like a migrating bird, throughout life. Yaddo confirmed where his real community was.

It was Cowley, Scott Fitzgerald's literary adviser, who instructed Cheever to cultivate the short story as his *métier* and the *New Yorker* as his principal outlet. Harold Ross's magazine, into which Cheever's fiction slipped as easily as Cinderella's foot, would be what he called his 'lifeboat'. But a price was paid: throughout life, there would be the recurrent criticism, to which the author, in his gloomier moments, subscribed, that beneath the smart surface of his writing there was no more 'substance' than in a Charles Addams cartoon. After a brief spell with the Federal Writers' Project, whose proletarian zeal appalled him (too much 'substance' by far) he married in 1941. Mary Winternitz was of Yale patrician stock. A talented woman, she deserves commemoration as probably the most tolerant spouse in literary history. Like other healthy males of his age Cheever was drafted. Like Richard Yates, he was judged not quite officer material (writers, alas, seldom are) but in his case sufficiently clerical not to be sent, along with his infantryman comrades, into the meat grinder of the Pacific theatre. Private Cheever was transferred into the signal corps and a cushy home posting which allowed him time to write voluminously. His first collection, *The Way Some People Live*, was published in 1943.

Demobilised, the Cheevers could live well on Mary's income as a teacher and his $5,000 stipend from the *New Yorker*. In 1947 he published his everywhere anthologised story, 'The Enormous Radio'. It bears all the author's trademarks. The Westcotts live on the twelfth floor of a Manhattan apartment house, in swish Sutton Place. Their principal leisure activity is classical music on the radio. But a new set which they acquire has the alarming habit of transmitting conversations going on in the other apartments. The Westcott marriage breaks up under the pressure of knowing what's going on around them. The Cheevers (now parents) joined the middle-class, white-flight, migration to the suburbs in the early 1950s. At Scarborough, Westchester County (the 'Shady Hill' of his stories), Cheever would find his richest material. His first novel, *The Wapshot Chronicle* (effectively interknit short stories) was published in 1957. In the high Eisenhower era he was earning $50,000 a year or more: real money. In 1961 the family moved to Ossining, in Westchester. Cheever taught some creative writing classes at the nearby penitentiary, Sing Sing, the hardest of America's hard-time 'joints'. The homosexuality of the jail fascinated him.

In 1964, Cheever published his most famous story, 'The Swimmer' in the *New Yorker*, which opens: 'It was one of those midsummer Sundays when everyone sits around saying, "I *drank* too much last night".' Neddy Merrill, hung over, middle-aged – but still possessed of the slenderness of youth – feels so good that he resolves not to sit around boozing but to swim from the Westerhazys' pool to his own, in Bullet Park, eight miles away. He will dip in the string of neighbourly pools that connect them. Subtly, the story modulates into a version of Ambrose Bierce's 'An Occurrence at Owl Creek Bridge'. Pool by pool, the wreckage of Neddy's life gradually reveals itself: he is alcoholic, bankrupt, deserted by his wife, friendless. The story ends with him, naked and exhausted, pounding on the door of a house, which is no longer his, by an empty pool.

'I want a life of impossible simplicity,' Cheever wrote in his journal for 1966. Alcohol, uncertain sexuality and infidelity did not simplify things. He underwent therapy from the mid 1960s, but was too clever for his analysts to pin down. In 1975 he touched bottom and sobered up, with the help of AA, whose members, inevitably, he despised as freaks and losers. In recovery, he at last allowed himself to become guiltlessly homosexual. He could never, however, quite eradicate the uneasiness that his writing was less important 'than ironing shirts in a Chinese laundry'. But the money and awards which showered on him reconciled him somewhat. In 1977, he even made the front cover of *Newsweek* magazine. It was in recovery, and at the top of the world, that he produced the novel *Falconer* (1977). Its 'germ' (as Henry James would call it) is outlined in a journal entry for 1977: 'A story about a man of forty-six who enters prison. He falls in love with Jody, who escapes; he is visited by his wife; he suffers the agony of drug withdrawal; and he escapes.' *Falconer*'s thinly disguised Sing Sing is a world away from Shady Hill. But both are Cheever's world.

After his death from kidney cancer, Cheever left his journal – an extraordinarily self-searing document – to be published. The last entry reads: 'I have climbed from a bed on the second floor to reach this typewriter. This was an achievement.' He was, his son Benjamin records, 'a writer almost before he was a man'. And it was as a writer he chose to die.

FN John Cheever
MRT *Falconer*
Biog B. Bailey, *Cheever: a Life* (2009)

204. Lawrence Durrell 1912–1990

English life is really like an autopsy. Durrell's verdict on his homeland

Nobody who did not personally suffer post-war austerity will appreciate the intoxication with which my generation devoured Lawrence Durrell's *The Alexandria Quartet* (*Justine*, *Balthazar*, *Mountolive* and *Clea*), when its first volume appeared in 1957. Even now, my saliva glands moisten at the first marvellous words of *Balthazar* (1958):

> Landscape-tones: brown to bronze, steep skyline, low cloud, pearl ground with shadowed oyster and violet reflections. The lion-dust of desert: prophets' tombs turned to zinc and copper at sunset on the ancient lake. Its huge sand-faults like watermarks from the air; green and citron giving to gunmetal, to a single plum-dark sail, moist, palpitant: sticky-winged nymph.

'Do you know what they're saying about me?' Durrell indignantly asked one of his friends, 'that my prose is as sticky as *nougat*.' For those Britons (Durrell, working for the Foreign Office in Egypt at the time, was not one of them) who had endured a dozen years of sweet-rationing, prose-nougat was the next best thing. And for the bulk of the British population cooped up with the measly £10 travel allowance, *The Alexandria Quartet* was the only tourism on offer – and if it was sex tourism (before *Lady Chatterley*, Durrell was considered very adult) so much the better.

For a period in the early 1960s, Durrell's star was ascendant. *Justine* (1957), the *New York Times* declared in 1960, 'demands comparison with the very best books of the century'. Durrell was ranked with Proust, with Borges, with Svevo: the literate young adored him. Durrell's opaque aphorisms ('art, like life, is an open secret') were pondered in every Gaggia-wheezing coffee bar, and the author's postman in the South of France had a nervous collapse from having to carry so many sacks of mail to Durrell's door. Hindsight suggests that Durrell was overrated. He was, as T. S. Eliot put it with his usual precision, 'extraordinarily good. But the scale is small.' Nougat, nougat, nougat. Durrell appears to us now a significant writer, with a secure niche in the early 1960s, but not the giant that he was once taken for. His poetry, however, remains highly regarded.

Durrell was born Anglo-Indian in Jullundur in the Punjab. His father was a civil engineer, one of the practical men who kept India going. His son 'Larry', although he had the standard public school education, never felt he belonged in 'Pudding Island', as he called England. Nor did he willingly spend much of his life there. His was very much an away game. It is not clear that he was ever, properly, a British citizen. Durrell, intellectually brilliant though he clearly was, declined to pass his university exams. There were much more interesting things to do. And his mind was temperamentally undisciplined. It was his 'sluttish Irish' blood, on his mother's side, coming out, he liked to claim. He could never be bothered to learn to spell, but mastered Einstein more thoroughly than any other novelist of the century (*The Alexandria Quartet* is, among much else, a conscious experiment in relativity). Oxbridge would probably have neutered him; although it would have needed a bigger than usual pair of gelding shears to do so.

Travel, especially travel to exotic places, was Durrell's university. After his father's death in 1928, he persuaded his mother (along with that 'family and other animals' about whom his brother Gerald wrote) to move from Bournemouth to Corfu. Bohemian adventures in pre-war Soho and Paris followed. Durrell 'hymned and whored' his way through young manhood, playing jazz in nightclubs, trying everything 'short of selling my bottom to a clergyman'. And, of course, he wrote. Henry Miller and Anais Nin extinguished any lingering vestiges of his English upbringing. Like them, he wrote a novel, *The Black Book* (1938), publishable only in naughty Paris. In nothing was Durrell more bohemian, or athletic, than his sex life. He had four marriages, many affairs and innumerable sexual encounters. Women, particularly in his later years, he regarded as 'poultices' to be slapped on his never-ending sexual itch, for temporary relief. Durrell enjoyed his promiscuity without guilt or personal damage. His near and dear ones were not so lucky. Larry 'destroyed' wives, his brother Gerald observed. The effects on his younger daughter, Sappho-Jane, were particularly catastrophic. Shortly before hanging herself in 1985, she wrote in her journal: 'I feel very threatened by the fact that my father is sleeping with women who are my age or younger. I feel he is committing a kind of mental incest.' With the publication of Sappho's journal in 1991, shortly after Durrell's death, ugly accusations of actual incest surfaced. His biographer discredits them; but there is no doubt that Sappho-Jane was unlucky in her father.

The formative period of Durrell's career, his 'good war', was the four years he spent as a press officer in wartime Egypt, from 1941 to 1945. Out of it (and his second marriage to the original of Justine) came *The Alexandria Quartet*. Contemporary readers now will probably be struck, as his contemporaries were not, by Durrell's pervasive racism. For him, Arabs were 'apes in nightshirts'. Rootless cosmopolitan that he was, he hated Islam and hated all orthodoxy – and, most of all, Pudding Island.

FN   Lawrence George Durrell
MRT *Justine*
Biog I. S. MacNiven, *Lawrence Durrell: A Biography* (1998)

205. Patrick White 1912–1990

Some critics complain that my characters are always farting. Well, we do, don't we?

Patrick White can claim to be Australia's greatest novelist – he was, after all, the first of his countrymen to win the Nobel Prize for Literature. Australians have tended to see him differently – as 'Australia's most Unreadable Novelist'. As the more readable Thomas Keneally notes, White always positioned himself as offensively alien to his country, who return the compliment with only grudging respect – in Australia, but not of it. When he won his Nobel in 1973 White declined to accept it personally. 'I don't want to pretend to be me,' was his reason. Nor did he want to be the literary equivalent of Qantas Airways. He dispatched, in his place, Sidney Nolan, the painter who figures, under thin disguise, as Hurtle Duffield in White's recently published *The Vivisector* (1970). It was a bit like Dickens sending Mr Pickwick. Except that White was making a serious point – if you reward me, know the nature of my art.

The Vivisector is a manifesto novel. White was a passionate lover of animals: he preferred Schnauzers to human beings. For people like him, vivisectors are the devil incarnate. But, White believes, the artist must do just that: cut up the living tissue of the innocent. It is the artist's 'doom'. When Duffield is old enough to work things out, he tells the woman he loves: 'I don't want to be like other people.' He is stirring a vat of animal excrement as he says it. White elsewhere pictures novels as 'resistant growths' within himself which must be 'cut out' of the writer. Stirring shit, excising cancers – these are not the joyous images of creation. Forget nightingales.

White was born in Knightsbridge, London, where his parents, enriched on generations of sheep-farming, were enjoying a luxurious vacation. Victor White was in his forties and emotionally remote; Ruth White, his wife and second cousin, was ten years younger and neurotic. On their return, the family moved to Sydney, principally because Ruth had taken against her rural in-laws. White's vignettes of his parents are unforgiving. There were, however, things he might, were he not so cross-grained, have been proud of. The Whites had made it against formidable odds. Patrick's great-grandfather had emigrated, penniless, to New South Wales in 1826 as a flockmaster, with nothing but his pastoral. Thereafter 'Almost all the Whites remained wedded to the land, and there was something peculiar, even shocking, about any member of the family who left it. To become any kind of artist would have been unthinkable.' Until, that is, 1912.

To break so drastically with 'wool and leather' meant rebellion. It helped that Patrick was chronically asthmatic (most of *Voss* was written flat on his back in bed). Poor health meant long periods by himself while others of his age were at play. Books, 'locked words', were his world. He had his first erection, he recalls, aged seven. It perplexed him, but then most things did. He was writing ambitiously before he was ten. His parents were wholly nonplussed. For his part, he resented 'their capacity for boring me'.

To make a (English) man of him, he was sent, aged thirteen, to public school in England. He loathed his four years at Cheltenham College: he was a 'foreigner', scarcely 'daring to open my mouth for fear of the toads which might tumble out and the curled lips, cold eyes, waiting to receive renewed evidence of what made me unacceptable to the British ruling class.' At Cheltenham he flaunted an Anglophobic interest in Ibsen and Strindberg, 'a taste my English housemaster deplored: "You have a morbid kink I mean to stamp out", he said, and he then proceeded to stamp it deeper in.' Like Ibsen's Brand, White's lifelong motto would be: 'No compromise!' He carried away from Cheltenham nothing that he much valued other than recollections of its smells: 'especially those of crushed ants, smoke rising from twigs and bark kindled in the open, bread and mushrooms frying in biscuit tins on a schoolroom stove, hot darkness and spilled semen.' There are worse educational legacies.

'Till well into my life', White recalls, 'houses, places, landscape meant more to me than people.' After liberation from his 'English prison', he persuaded his parents to let him spend two years as a 'jackaroo' (cowboy) on family sheep and cattle stations in the northern outback. They were 'the bleakest places on earth ... plagued alternately by drought and flood'. It was cosmically lonely. His fellow jackaroos regarded him as a Pom. He would become more pommish when he returned in his early twenties to Kings College, Cambridge, from where, in 1935, he graduated with a degree in Modern Languages. Like the novelist resident at the college, E. M. Forster, he now knew himself to be homosexual. He did not choose it, he said, it chose him.

Most gays, he said, were 'colossal bores'. Whether Forster came into that category is not recorded.

He had steeped himself in European literature, in which his tastes were stark: 'for me', he said, 'Tolstoy is the only literary genius who survives his own hypocrisy.' He continued to detest England outside London, the city which offered discreet freedoms to a young man whose sexual preferences were, until 1967, criminal and nowhere less understood than in Australia. The other attractions of London were its bohemian underworld and its theatre. When in town, he went up to five times a week. He chose to stay on in London after leaving Cambridge. 'At last', he sardonically recalled, fifty years later, 'I felt, I was *into* life, in a green pork-pie hat and a black polo sweater.' By now his parents regarded him as a 'freak'. The hat cannot have helped. The clinching break was his refusal to attend a cricket match at Lords with his father, over on a visit. None the less they afforded him an allowance.

White's first novel, *Happy Valley*, was published in 1939. It was well received and reassured him that 'I had become a writer'. The world remained to be convinced that he was a writer worth buying: 'I left for New York expecting to repeat my success, only to be turned down by almost every publisher in that city.' His mother, whose favourite author was Ruby M. Ayres, disapproved of *Happy Valley* – as did all the family and the relatively few Australians who read it. His father, White believed, had never read anything between hard covers other than a studbook and was damned if he was going to change now. Eventually White placed a second novel in New York, *The Living and the Dead* (1941), set in pre-war London. It led to 'pseudo success'. These 'wretched books', he later believed, are 'best forgotten.'

White returned to England to fight for a country he did not belong to. He was over-age, in poor health, gay, and legally resident in a country not at war. None the less in 1940 he was commissioned as an RAF intelligence officer. He spent a long and formative stint in North Africa. 'My chest got me out of active service and into guilt,' he writes, while conceding that he did at times come under fire. He despised 'frivolous and corrupt Alexandria' (Forster's beloved city) but was fascinated by the desert. He was reading Dostoevsky and 'wrote three of the novels for which I am now [in 1981] acclaimed'. Johann Ulrich Voss was conceived in the Western Desert of Egypt, as Erwin Johannes Rommel did his damnedest to kill Voss's creator. Why, one may wonder, is White's most famous character German? Because he isn't English or Australian.

In Egypt, White fell in love and formed what would be a lifelong union with a young Greek liaison officer, Manoly Lascaris. After demobilisation, White and Lascaris decided to go to Australia where they bought a farm at Castle Hill outside Sydney. Locals thought them 'rich Jews'. Over the next eighteen years they planted trees and raised animals. 'Painfully', White was now writing the novel which ushers in his mature phase, *The Tree of Man* (1955), set in the farming world of Australia at the turn of the century. The novel was well received in England and the United States but 'greeted with cries of scorn and incredulity in Australia: that somebody, at best a dubious Australian, should flout the naturalistic tradition, or worse, that a member of the grazier class should aspire to a calling which was the prerogative of school-teachers!' *Voss* (1957), which followed, 'fared no better'. It was at this point that White was branded 'Australia's most Unreadable Novelist'. In *Riders in the Chariot* (1961) a scene in which the Jewish refugee Himmelfarb 'was subjected to a mock crucifixion by drunken [Australian] workmates … outraged the blokes and the bluestockings alike'. He was now Australia's most unpatriotic novelist as well. Everything combined to make him 'a foreigner in my own country'. But, as his fiction relentlessly enquired, what was that country? Was it the Sydney depicted as 'Sarsparilla' in *Riders*, or was it the vast, empty central desert in which Voss perishes? The couple moved back to Sydney in 1964 where they 'withdrew from circulation'. Over the next quarter century White would, from time to time, make known his liberal sentiments on Aboriginal rights, gay liberation and the environment. He was staunchly anti-royalist.

There is much dispute about White, but little dispute that he wrote one major work of world literature. *Voss* is a novel of exploration: of Australia and of what White calls 'the deep end of the unconscious'. Set in the mid-1840s, the hero is a version of an actual German, Ludwig Leichhardt, who died, it is assumed, in the desert on his third expedition across the island. Voss's motives are uncertain even to himself. He is given to such utterances as: 'If I were not obsessed … I would be purposeless.' Australia cannot be explored, mapped or understood. It can only be imagined. Voss is sustained, on his final journey, by a Platonic relationship with a young girl in Sydney, Laura Trevelyan, whose uncle – a rich, vulgar draper – has financed him. It is Laura who understands his fascination with 'desert places' while the rest of Australia 'huddles in its ports'. His 'legend', she asserts, 'will be written down, eventually, by those who are troubled by it'. 'It's tough being a genius,' concludes Thomas Keneally, 'thus, we Aussie punters could never quite love him. But, by God, his work still richly deserves our respect.' White's blunt verdict on his homeland is the hopeful observation that 'it is possible to recycle shit'.

FN   Patrick Victor Martindale White
MRT *Voss*
Biog D. Marr, *Patrick White: A Life* (1991)

206. Howard Fast 1914–2003

I was born and grew up in the greatest, the noblest achievement of the human race on this planet – which was called the United States of America.

Fast was born in the urban working class, to which he had lifelong allegiance. His father, a Ukrainian-Jewish immigrant (born 'Fastovsky'), was a $40-per-week factory operative in the New York garment industry – a wage slave. Howard's mother died in his early boyhood. He was educated to high-school level, selling newspapers on street corners to help his father support the family during the grim Depression years. He read voraciously and wrote effortlessly. At this early stage of his life, Jack London (particularly *The Iron Heel*) was a formative influence. The year he left school, 1931, he sold his first Wellsian fiction ('Wrath of the Purple') to *Amazing Stories*. It earned him $37. His first novel, *Two Valleys* (1933), an American revolutionary war epic, was written while Fast was an eighteen-year-old page at the New York Public Library. In the early 1930s slump years, he hoboed around America. His opinions were increasingly radical, verging on revolutionary.

Fast married and settled down in 1937. After the outbreak of war he was appointed to a clerical position in the US Office of War Information in 1942 and later worked as a war correspondent. Over this period Fast continued to turn out novels. His fiction, at this stage, had a preachy left-wing flavour, for example *The Last Frontier* (1941), a novel about the extermination of the Cheyenne Indian tribe in 1878, and *Citizen Tom Paine* (1943), a bestseller. The American public always prefer American heroes to American genocide. By 1943, he had formally allied himself with the American Communist movement. The result, in his writing, was protest fiction such as *Freedom Road* (1944), a novel admired by New Dealers and endorsed, as one of her favourites, by Eleanor Roosevelt herself.

After the war, any earlier connection with the Reds was dangerous. This was the period in which Fast wrote his best-known novel, *Spartacus* (1951), a highly embellished story of the slave revolt against Rome in AD 71, while incarcerated in prison, serving a sentence of three months for contempt of Congress during investigation of his so-called Un-American Activities. He declined to name names. Defiantly Fast ran for Congress himself the next year, under the American Labour Party ticket. Now a criminal – and too hot for legitimate publishers to handle – Fast was obliged to publish *Spartacus* himself. The novel was filmed in 1960 by director Stanley Kubrick (Dalton Trumbo, like Fast a politically radical author, wrote the script). It starred Kirk Douglas as the revolutionary leader and was much admired by *cinéastes* but regarded as 'Marxian' in right-wing circles. (Marx himself thought

Spartacus was 'the most splendid fellow in the whole of ancient history'.) Typical of the universal timidity was the *New York Times*'s verdict: '*Spartacus* is a tract in the form of a novel ... proof that polemics and fiction cannot mix.'

Others were more openly approving. Fast's fiction led to his being awarded the Stalin peace prize in 1954, at the height of the Cold War. Two years later, as for other fellow travellers in the West, the Soviet god failed for Fast with the brutal invasion of Hungary. Although never an open critic, he defected from active Communist partisanship and became what might be called a 'fellow floater'. In addition to his many historical novels, Fast wrote a string of detective novels as 'E. V. Cunningham', featuring the Japanese-American detective, Masao Masuto. Fast's most comprehensive effort in fiction is the socialist-realist trilogy comprising *The Immigrants* (1977), *Second Generation* (1978) and *The Establishment* (1979). The multi-volume saga covers the interlocking fortunes of four families (WASP, Irish Catholic, Jewish, Chinese) over the course of a hundred years in San Francisco. The central character, Dan Lavette, who builds a corporate empire, marries a Nob Hill heiress, but remains emotionally attached to his oriental mistress. The six-part sequence did well and supplied Fast with a comfortable last few years to what had been a turbulent life. Those last years were passed in Connecticut. He had never received a penny, he liked to say, which had not been earned by 'the sweat of my brow' – just like, he might have said, his most famous creation:

> This, then, is Spartacus, who does not know the future and has no cause to remember the past, and it has never occurred to him that those who toil shall ever do other than toil, nor has it occurred to him that there will ever be a time when men do not toil with the lash across their backs.

If he knew nothing else, Fast knew the lash.

FN   Howard Melvin Fast
MRT *Spartacus*
Biog A. MacDonald, *Howard Fast: a Critical Companion* (1996)

207. Saul Bellow 1915–2005

Fiction is the higher autobiography.

Born Solomon Belov, near Montreal in Canada, Bellow's family was first-generation immigrant, embarked from St Petersburg. Originating in the Baltic states, his father got to Russia on forged papers. More forged papers (fictions, if one wants to be ingenious) had enabled the Belovs to get to the New World in 1913. Saul was the only one of the four children to be born there, but aged eight, he was hospitalised for six months with breathing problems. He read precociously in English and dated his lifelong love affair with literature from those months of enforced idleness. Relatively well off in Russia, Saul's father, Abram, kept the family afloat in the New World with a variety of menial jobs. At one particularly low point, he was a bootlegger – supplying liquor to the Prohibition-parched US. After the disastrous hijacking of a consignment, which led to Abram being severely beaten up, the family followed the booze to Chicago – Bellow's home town as it was to be – in the early 1920s. They had relatives there. Yiddish was spoken at home; English in the world outside.

Bellow's youth in Chicago – a wild city in those Prohibition and Depression years – is depicted vividly in *The Adventures of Augie March* (1953). The early sections of that novel are dominated by Augie's mother. Bellow's mother Liza (manifestly Mrs March) died when he was seventeen. A devout woman, she had wanted her youngest child to be a violinist or a rabbi. His later relationship with Judaism was always vexed. Music, however, was second only to literature as the love of his life – he was more faithful to it than to any woman. But his father did not encourage his son's musical or literary bents: 'You write and then you erase,' he once said, 'You call that a *profession?*'

At the city's universities (Chicago and Northwestern) Bellow studied literature and anthropology. This was the period of the 'numerus clausus' when Jews were regarded as troublesomely clever outsiders and their entrance was restricted. There were no American-Jewish writers on the American university literary syllabus and the head of his English department, Walter Blair, advised Bellow not to pursue graduate studies in English: 'You've got a very good record, but I wouldn't recommend that you study English. You weren't born to it.' Another version of the story has it that Bellow was coolly informed, 'No Jew could really grasp the tradition of English literature.' Dubious as that was, even then (Lionel Trilling would conclusively disprove the proposition at Columbia), Bellow evidently felt something along the lines of 'Well, then, damn you, I'll create a new literary tradition.' Defiance is the driving force in all his writing, and his life. It is expressed, fists clenched against the world, in the famous opening declaration of *Augie March*:

I am an American, Chicago born – Chicago, that somber city – and go at things as I have taught myself, free-style, and will make the record in my own way: first to knock, first admitted; sometimes an innocent knock, sometimes a not so innocent. But a man's character is his fate, says Heraclitus, and in the end there isn't any way to disguise the nature of the knocks by acoustical work on the door or gloving the knuckles.

In other words, I'll do it my way, to quote another great Canadian (Paul Anka, if you didn't guess).

Bellow graduated from Northwestern in 1937 in the depths of the Depression. It 'helped', he later maintained, in that there was no Lorelei of a profession (a real job) to distract him. His aim, from the first, was to be a writer but he kept body and soul together with short-term teaching jobs. He always felt at home in universities, but never let himself be owned by one – even, in later life, Chicago. Tenure was for hacks. He was at this period moving between Chicago and New York – his next home town. For a year, 1943–4, he worked in the office of the *Encyclopedia Britannica* (richly evoked in *Augie March*) on a 'Great Books' project. An attempt to join the US Navy was turned down on the grounds that he was Canadian. An attempt to join the Canadian Army was also unsuccessful, this time on health grounds (he had a hernia). Eventually Bellow was accepted by the US Merchant Marine. He was still training when the bomb dropped and it was all over.

His first published novel, *Dangling Man* (1944) is set in this war-time limbo (the title evokes Villon's poem, written before he was hanged, 'Ballade des pendus'). *Dangling Man* is a journal novel by 'Joseph' (evoking 'Joseph K.' in Franz Kafka's *The Trial*). Unable to face the agonising freedom of 'dangling', Joseph embraces 'flunkeydom' (what Philip Larkin elsewhere calls 'the toad work') – employment he despises. He does not, he concludes, 'do well alone', but loneliness, he accepts, is the human condition. Already Bellow's 'freewheeling' style and his preference for Chekhovian brevity is evident – as is his preoccupation with self. Saul Bellow was always, in some form, Saul Bellow's subject matter.

After the war, Bellow again took up short-contract teaching positions at various universities across the US. His second published novel, *The Victim* (1947), ponders anti-Semitism and anomie. The central character is Asa Leventhal. A Pooterish figure, working at a menial level in a publishing house, Leventhal is David Riesman's 'Lonely Crowd' personified. 'A small gray masterpiece', V. S. Pritchett called the novel. He might write novels about cosmic loneliness but Bellow was part of a vibrant social network in the 1940s. He was by now prominent in the Greenwich Village scene which was redefining American modern culture. His Chicago youth was celebrated in the first of his novels to draw widespread critical attention, *The*

Adventures of Augie March (1953). '*Bildungsroman*' and 'picaresque' were two terms American reviewers reached for in describing it. The action is set during the Depression years: Augie is born into a Jewish family which is falling apart. His mother is terminally disabled, and he is close to none of his siblings. Augie rejects the 'Russian' past which an older generation would impose on him and takes on the world. Bellow's narrative, as Alfred Kazin noted, is flavoured with burlesque and idioms as sharp as the Yiddish of his childhood home.

By this stage Bellow had formally repudiated Europe, after a spell on a Guggenheim fellowship in post-war Paris, where he wrote the first part of *Augie March* and discovered Jean-Paul Sartre to be a 'con' (the American, not French word – although both might be applicable). Bellow was now the darling of the New York intellectual elite, conscious as they were that the era of the Southern novelists (Faulkner, Penn Warren, Katherine Anne Porter) had passed. As ever, the Great American Novel was in prospect and Saul Bellow was being groomed as the great (Jewish) American novelist. There were those who objected to what they saw as literary politicking. Norman Podhoretz reviewed *Augie March* sceptically in *Commentary*. In his indiscreet memoir, *Making It*, Podhoretz relates being approached at a literary party by a drunk and told: 'We'll get you for that review if it takes ten years.' Bellow himself was mortally affronted.

In 1956 Bellow published *Seize the Day*, a work which has clear resemblances to Arthur Miller's play, *Death of a Salesman*, with the difference that Bellow is unafraid to make his salesman protagonist, Tommy Wilhelm, clearly Jewish; something that Miller was too nervous, or too calculating, to do with Willy Loman. Bellow's fantasia, the strangely Rider Haggard-like *Henderson the Rain King* (1959), about an American millionaire (enriched by pig-farming) who does a burlesque Hemingway in Africa, widened his international readership despite a slashing review in the *New York Times*, which pronounced the novel 'silly' and Henderson 'a bore cursed with the most embarrassing flow of fancy talk in a library of recent fiction. Henderson's ravings are almost enough to make one yearn for Tarzan's subhuman dialogue ("I Tarzan. You Jane.").' None the less it was the comically quixotic Gene Henderson whom Bellow regarded himself as closest to.

Bellow heeded the warning, and reined in his grotesquerie. With *Herzog* (1964), and its protagonist Moses Herzog, he tuned the Bellovian 'voice' which distinctively marks the fiction of the novelist's prime – a kind of eloquent rant against the times, the United States, the human condition and the universe. Cuckolded by his best friend, Moses lets off steam with letters to, among others, President Eisenhower. The result is a blend of the classic epistolary novel and the Marx Brothers. The funniest of his creations, *Herzog* ends, unfunnily, 'At this time he had no messages for anyone. Nothing. Not a single word.'

Humboldt's Gift (1975) is a depiction of the literary life, with all the complexities (principally those to do with sexual relationships) that frustrate creativity. At this point in his career, Bellow's fiction becomes even more autobiographical and the tenor of his thought more radically conservative. *Mr Sammler's Planet* (1970) has a hero who is a Holocaust survivor and a jaundiced eye for young radicals and the decay of American civility. Bellow is estimated to have won more prizes than any other American novelist. The award of the Nobel Prize in 1976 would not, he insisted, sink him under its gravestone weight. Nor did it. But it complicated his writing. The dilemmas of establishment fame are depicted, ironically as ever, in *The Dean's December* (1982).

Bellow recorded himself as being poor until his early forties, and not rich until his later years. Alimony and child support drained those riches. He married five times (James Atlas, his biographer, believes that Bellow needed the crack-up of a good divorce to get his creative juices flowing for the next novel) and was analysed four times (like divorce, an expensive luxury). His later work is, much of it, concerned with the pathos of ageing, in such works as *More Die of Heartbreak* (1987) and *The Actual* (1997). One of the *Partisan Review* circle, Bellow had dabbled with Trotskyism in the wild days of his youth. In age he veered as far to the opposite political position. The older he got the less Bellow seemed to like the world he inhabited. He was often accused of racism and prejudice and seemed at times pugnaciously to invite controversy. In a *New Yorker* interview in 1988, he notoriously asked, apropos of Black and Multicultural Studies, 'Who is the Tolstoy of the Zulus? The Proust of the Papuans?' When, in 1993, he left Chicago to take up a lectureship at Boston University, a delegation went to the *Boston Globe* and asked if they knew that the city was harbouring a racist. 'Banned in Boston,' as they used to say.

He remained unusually vigorous in his old age, becoming a father (with the last and youngest of the mothers of his children) in his mid-eighties. It was at this period that he produced his late, and controversial, masterpiece, *Ravelstein* (2000), a portrait of the artist as a very old man. The Abe Ravelstein of the title was everywhere recognised to be the author's close friend and colleague at Chicago University, Allan Bloom, the author of the bestselling jeremiad, *The Closing of the American Mind* (1987, 1994) – 'woe upon this philistine country!' Equally, the narrator Chick was recognised to be Saul Bellow. Bloom, a homosexual and, according to the novel, an odiously self-indulgent sybarite, had died in 1997 – of Aids, the novel asserted.

Ravelstein provoked indignant protest on two counts. First, that Bellow had 'outed' Bloom, whom he claimed to love, which was disloyal. Secondly, that there was no evidence Bloom had in fact died of Aids (something that after the novel's publication Bellow accepted), or that he bore any resemblance to the *À Rebours*,

Des Esseintes-like hedonist that Bellow had portrayed. On the surface, nothing very much happens in the novel except hospitals, Jewish jokes and talk. A lot of *Ravelstein* is like overhearing two old codgers rabbit on about what it is like to be two old codgers. But major themes gradually emerge. The novel explores, in its attractively rambling way, two dauntingly large and touchy themes: death and American Jewishness. 'What is it to die?' the old men ask each other. 'No more pictures' is the best they can come up with.

FN   Saul Bellow (born Solomon Belov)
MRT *Herzog*
Biog J. Atlas, *Bellow: A Biography* (2000)

208. Herman Wouk 1915–

I felt there's a wealth in Jewish tradition, a great inheritance. I'd be a jerk not to take advantage of it.

Wouk (pronounced 'Woke') was born in New York, the son of first-generation Russian Jewish immigrants. He was raised in the Bronx, and at the precocious age of sixteen went to Columbia University, graduating in 1934. At college Wouk edited Columbia's humour magazine, the *Jester*. An account of his childhood and young manhood during the Depression and New Deal years is given in *The City Boy* (1948) and, in greater detail, in *Inside, Outside* (1985). Wouk's first employment was in radio and from 1936 to 1941 he was a gag writer for the comedian Fred Allen – this furnished the background to his novel, *Aurora Dawn* (1947). Snappy dialogue was to be a strength in his subsequent fiction. After a brief hiatus working for the US Treasury, he joined the US Naval Reserve in 1942, seeing active service (winning four campaign stars) on destroyer minesweepers and rising to the rank of lieutenant. It was on board ship that he began writing his first serious fiction in 1943, advised by his former Columbia teacher, Irwin Edman.

Wouk was discharged in 1946, having married his sweetheart, Betty Brown, the previous year; they were to have three sons. On re-entering civilian life, Wouk became a full-time writer. *Aurora Dawn, or, The true History of Andrew Reale* (1947) is a satire on hucksterism in the radio industry. Written in a sub-Fieldingesque style, it was found 'unbearably arch' by the *New Yorker*. It was followed the next year by *The City Boy: the Adventures of Herbie Bookbinder and his cousin, Cliff* (1948). A story of life in the Bronx in the 1920s, the novel is a *hommage* to Booth Tarkington and *Tom Sawyer*.

Wouk was finding his way. He established himself as a bestselling writer of literary substance with his fourth published novel, *The Caine Mutiny* (1951), subtitled 'a Novel of World War II'. It narrates the story of a regular-service captain, Philip Queeg, who – after sustaining a protracted mental breakdown – is relieved of his command during a typhoon in which his obstinacy threatens to sink the *Caine* minesweeper on which they are sailing. The mutineer is a Princeton graduate who has recently joined the service, Willie Keith. In the subsequent court martial, Keith is successfully defended, and Queeg broken down on the witness stand, by a Jewish lawyer, Lieutenant Barney Greenwald. In a stroke of theatre, Greenwald subsequently denounces Keith and praises the Queegs of the US Navy as the saviours of Western civilisation from fascism. It was people like Queeg, he says, who had saved those like his grandmother from becoming soap with which to wash Goering's fat backside. Contemporary reviewers were slightly suspicious that – coming as soon as it did after the war – *The Caine Mutiny* smacked of something less than patriotism. But the novel made the bestseller list and earned its author a Pulitzer Prize. A successful, and faithful, film was made starring Humphrey Bogart as Queeg, in 1954.

Marjorie Morningstar (1955) is the story of a stunningly beautiful Jewish girl from her late adolescence, through love affairs and a failed stage career, to respectably dull matronhood. It was, in terms of sales, the most popular hardback novel of 1955. Although praised by one critic as a 'modern Jewish *Vanity Fair*', others applied the term 'soap opera' (a recurrent slur on Wouk's fiction) and the *New Yorker*, never a friend, labelled it 'a damp and endless tale'. *Youngblood Hawke* (1961), even longer, is the story of a novelist, transparently based on the life of Thomas Wolfe. It attracted mainly negative reviews, but sold strongly and, like *Marjorie Morningstar*, was made into a successful film. The ease with which Wouk's narratives converted to the screen fattened his wallet but did not raise his stock with the literary critics. His love of large, saga-like novels, his workmanlike, realistic narrative technique, and his adherence (in a world destabilised by existentialism and beatnik rebellion) to old-fashioned moral categories led one commentator to label him 'the only living nineteenth-century novelist'.

In 1971, Wouk returned to the subject which had been calling him since the early 1950s. *The Winds of War* (1971) inaugurated his Tolstoyan narrative of the Second World War, based on the career of Victor 'Pug' Henry, who rises from the rank of Commander to Admiral, and is an eye-witness to many great events and historical figures (including Churchill, Roosevelt and Hitler). *The New York Times* affected to find the work 'long, mildly interesting, moderately informative', but readers devoured it by the million. It was followed in 1978 by the sequel, *War and Remembrance*. Taken together, the 2,000-page narrative was – unironically

– compared by the *Christian Science Monitor* to Thucydides, although the by now familiar 'soap opera' criticisms were levelled by less respectful commentators. The two novels were given vast popular currency by the fifteen-hour TV 'miniseries' made of them in 1983 and 1989. Wouk's subsequent work, *Inside, Outside* (1985), a story of 'being Jewish' in America; *The Hope* (1993) and *The Glory* (1994) – two fictional accounts of the history of post-1947 Israel – reveal his twin interests in using fiction to explore his personal heritage and the vast geopolitical events of the twentieth century. In the 2008 presidential election, John McCain divulged that his favourite author was Herman Wouk. Obama went for Philip Roth. How many votes it swung either way is hard to say.

FN   Herman Wouk
MRT *The Caine Mutiny*
Biog A. Beichman, *Herman Wouk: The Novelist as Social Historian* (2004)

209. Harold Robbins 1916–1997

Hemingway was a jerk.

Despite the date of death inscribed above, and the fact that his ashes rest in a gilt urn 'in the form of one of his bestselling books' in the Palm Springs mortuary, California, 'new' Harold Robbins novels continue to appear. He is not channelling from the next world, however: the estate – unwilling to let a goose that lays such golden eggs honk its last – authorises chosen scribes to write up the scenarios and plot lines which, allegedly, the great teller of tales *would have composed* were he still with us. Robbins would have chortled. He always liked a joke on those suckers, his readers. He was 'beyond cynicism', as one of his friends put it. Enemies said worse things.

Robbins's life was a remarkable one, but nowhere near as remarkable as the version of that life that he publicised. According to the account given in his obituaries and in the source used elsewhere in this book, the *American National Biography*, his early years were a mixture of Horatio Alger rags-to-riches and downright roguery. This is how the Robbins history of Robbins (as confirmed by the *ANB*) goes. He was born in New York of unknown parents and abandoned at birth. A birth certificate named him 'Francis Kane'. Although presumed Jewish, he was placed in a Roman Catholic orphanage, where he learned to use his fists. Aged eleven he was adopted by a Manhattan pharmacist named Rubin, whose surname (along with 'Harold') he took and later adapted.

Harold dropped out of school and ran away from home at fifteen. No ingénu, he had started to smoke grass at the age of eight and had graduated to cocaine at the age of twelve. At the same age he lost his virginity to a prostitute. When pressed for cash, he would jerk street-perverts off for a quarter (he would provide the Kleenex – the tools of the trade). 'I thought that was normal,' he later recalled. 'I didn't think there was anything wrong with it.' Nor, presumably, with his next line of work as a numbers' runner for illegal gambling syndicates in Black Harlem. There he pushed drugs on a more ambitious scale. One of his clients, he claimed, was Cole Porter. True to the Alger model, Harold the dead-end kid eventually saw the light, 'went straight' and, to quote the lucklessly suckered *ANB*: 'On his savings, he took flying lessons and bought an old airplane. With an $800 loan, he flew to Virginia and the Carolinas, bought entire fields of unharvested crops, and sold the produce to New York stores. By age twenty, he was worth $1.5 million. In 1939 he sought to profiteer on sugar, buying shiploads at $4.85 per hundred pounds, but he was wiped out when the Roosevelt administration froze the price of sugar at $4.65 per hundred.' It was Howard Hughes, he claimed on other occasions, who had taught him to fly. He returned the compliment by making the tycoon the hero of *Nevada Smith* (the film of 1966, based on the characters in *The Carpetbaggers*).

Having lost his first millions, he enterprisingly landed a job at the Universal Pictures warehouse, uncovered rampant fraud and was soon the company's youngest Vice President. Dates get rather hard to fit in at this point – but Robbins claimed, while soaring to executive heights at UP, he was also serving as a submariner in the war. The claim, as spun out to a succession of gullible journalists, was clinched with some convincing details about life below the waves: 'I was on a submarine, and if you're on a submarine for 22 days you want sex ... We were either jacking each other off or sucking each other off. Everybody knew that everybody else was doing it. If you were able to handle it, you could get fucked in the ass, but I couldn't handle it that well. We jerked off too, but you get bored with that.' Whatever else, Robbins's CV was never boring. His submarine, he once claimed, had been torpedoed and he was the only survivor.

He came to fiction, he recalled, when challenged by another senior executive to come up with a better story to adapt into film than was currently coming UP's way. The result was *Never Love a Stranger* (1948), the story of Frank Kane, which follows, more or less, the preceding narrative of Harold Robbins's first twenty years. It was published by Knopf (surprisingly, given that firm's literary prestige) and was a bestseller, after fending off some passing prosecutions for obscenity. The rest of the story can be followed in the *Publishers Weekly* bestseller lists. Robbins can claim to be one of the five top-selling novelists ever.

Robbins's biographer, Andrew Wilson, joyously pokes holes in the tallest tales Robbins perpetrated – those about Harold Robbins. He was not a foundling boy; nor was he, as he liked to claim in his wilder moments, an illegitimate offspring of the last Russian Tsar. His first (Chinese!) wife did not die of a diseased parrot bite. He was not an intrepid submariner; in fact young Harold prudently dodged the draft. He did not make a fortune and lose it in the commodities market. He was born, Wilson's digging revealed, Harold Rubin. His mother had died and his father adopted him into the new family he had made. Rubin Sr was a prosperous Brooklyn pharmacist (that much was true) and a generous parent. Harold's upbringing was middle class and unexceptional: there were house servants and holidays in Florida. Harold was educated at the prestigious Manhattan High School. Masturbation was not on the curriculum, nor was coke served in the canteen. He did not make millions in 'futures', flying planes across the continental US to do so.

He met his first wife, Lillian, at school. She was not, as Harold later claimed, a vaginally virtuosic Chinese dancer, nor did she die of a parrot bite. The marriage to Lillian (described as 'plain') lasted twenty-eight years and survived a string of affairs and illegitimate offspring. It was his taste for orgies, later in life, that drove her to divorce him. As for his meteoric business career, Lillian's father was someone at Universal Pictures and got his future son-in-law a lowly job in the firm's accounts department. The bit about writing his first novel to prove he could do better than the stuff being served up at the time seems to have been true.

Whatever lay behind him once he took up the pen, Harold Robbins certainly sold books in amounts which there was no need to exaggerate. Hemingway once asked him why he wrote: 'wealth', replied Robbins. Money wasn't enough; it was 'wealth' that Robbins made. *The Adventurers* (1966), a wildly romanticised roman-à-clef, based on the South American playboy politician, Porfirio Rubirosa, brought Robbins close on $3 million with the film rights. The film, starring Candice Bergen and Alan Badel, regularly scores high in all-time-turkey competitions. In the heady liberated period after the *Lady Chatterley* acquittal of 1960, Robbins's fiction probably produced more 'hard-ons' (as he called them) than Viagra. Robbins was among the first to appreciate that post-Chatterley 'permissiveness' allowed not merely sexual explicitness, but sexual sadism – episodes such as that in *The Carpetbaggers* (1961) in which the hero identifies the man who raped and skinned his mother by his tobacco pouch (it's made from his mother's breast).

Less stomach-turning is the heroine in *The Betsy* (1971), who can only orgasm to the scream of an over-revved car engine. Something like that is found every twelve pages in Robbins, one smut-hound calculated. On the topic of cars, he owned, in his heyday, a fleet of twelve customised Rolls-Royces and a yacht to rival the billionaire

Saudi arms dealer Adnan Khashoggi's (the thinly veiled 'Baydr' in the 1974 roman-à-clef, *The Pirate* (1974)). *A Stone for Danny Fisher* (1952), retitled *King Creole* (1958) for the film version, was produced as a vehicle for Elvis Presley, when James Dean – already cast for it – was killed. Some nine of his novels were adapted for the screen. Presley's performance is not good, but the best of the lot; Dean would have been interesting.

Harold's heyday came and went. He spent his millions and when he died, aged eighty-one, a living witness to the preservative powers of cocaine, gambling and lechery, his debts ran into seven figures. Was it money, sex or sheer chutzpah that drove Robbins? Probably sex. He had an insatiable appetite for wives (five of them) and call-girls (one London agent wryly recalled recruiting doxies by the dozen for his visiting star author). Screwing was, however, off the menu in his last years, after – high on cocaine – he fell in his shower and shattered his pubic bone. No more hard-ons for Mr Robbins. God, one deduces, must be a literary critic. None of his famous friends came to his funeral. It added the necessary Gatsby touch.

FN   Harold Robbins (born Harold Rubin)
MRT   *The Carpetbaggers*
Biog   A. Wilson, *Harold Robbins: The Man who Invented Sex* (2007)

210. Anthony Burgess 1917–1993

MELVYN BRAGG: What must you do to be famous?
ANTHONY BURGESS: Die.

Even those who have read little of his fiction will know certain things about Anthony Burgess. Best known is the fact that he had a death sentence pronounced on him in 1959, when a brain specialist diagnosed a tumour. With a predicted year to live, he wrote five Damoclean novels to support his future widow. Among them is his most famous, *A Clockwork Orange* (1962), for which, to add to the feat, he invented a new language – Nadsat. Perversely he welcomed the death sentence as twelve months of guaranteed immortality: 'I had been granted something I had never had before: a whole year to live. I would not be run over by a bus tomorrow, nor knifed on the Brighton racetrack. I would not choke on a bone. If I fell in the wintry sea I would not drown.' But neither, with his head about to rot off, could he do a proper job of work: he would have to become a professional writer to provide for his wife. He 'sighed and put paper in the typewriter'. The prognosis proved wrong and the terminal year extended into three decades of paper rolling through the typewriter.

Burgess, we should recall, was an inveterate spoofer. One of his more famous spoofs was reviewing his own pseudonymously authored fiction – tepidly. The tumour crisis has been questioned by biographers (most fiercely by Roger Lewis) as Burgess was not always to be trusted in such matters. In 1980, for example, he did an interview with his co-religionist Graham Greene, for the *Observer*. It led to a public quarrel when the older novelist accused Burgess of putting words in his mouth that he (Greene) had to look up in a dictionary.

Unlike Greene, John Burgess Wilson (his birth name) was born Catholic, in Manchester, the son of a lowly accountant father who played the 'old joanna' in pubs and picture houses by night for money. His mother, who had worked the music-halls as 'Beautiful Belle Burgess', died shortly after his birth in the great flu epidemic of 1919, as did his sister. He was brought up by an aunt until his father married one of the licensees he worked for. She did not much care for her stepson. The circumstances of his boyhood were *echt* working class but moderately prosperous and he had a good basic education at various Catholic schools. With music all around in his home he taught himself to play the piano, cultivating a precocious musical gift. His life was thrown into turmoil again, aged nineteen, when his father died of a heart attack, leaving his financial affairs in disorder. Wilson went on to earn himself an undergraduate degree (only an upper second, to his chagrin) in English at Manchester University in 1940. While a student he had met his future wife, Lynne Jones, and they married in 1942. She was a war bride and he was by then a sergeant in the Education Corps, one of the cushier berths in the army.

In his autobiography, *Little Wilson and Big God* (1988), Burgess records the most traumatic episode of the Second World War for him and even more so for his wife. In 1944, Lynne was violently attacked by a gang of American GI deserters during the London blackout. Unlike for Alex and his Droogs in *A Clockwork Orange* the motive was robbery, not sex. Her wedding ring was wrenched from her finger, breaking the bone: it evidently struck Burgess as symbolic as well as horrific. Lynne, who was pregnant, was kicked unconscious and miscarried what would have been their first child. Moreover, the injuries she sustained prevented her ever conceiving again. In later life she drank compulsively to the point of physical violence and collapse, taunting Burgess with her infidelities, precipitating impotence within the marriage, and his tit-for-tat adulteries outside it. The worst of these miserable years lay ahead and were only ended with her alcoholic death in 1968. Divorce was prohibited by the rules of a faith which was ingrained into his being.

Otherwise, not to understate things, Burgess had a peaceful war, spending much of his wartime in Gibraltar. He enjoyed teaching and – more particularly – lecturing. Some might say he never did anything else throughout the whole of his life. On demob in 1946, Burgess taught in a grammar school and a teacher-training college. Restless by nature, he took up work with the colonial teaching service and, in 1954, was posted to Malaya. It was a leisurely life, still offering a few colonial comforts not to be found in austerity Britain. And Burgess always claimed he wrote best with the sun on his back. Phenomenally proficient with words, he learned the local language, Jawi, and began writing fiction in earnest – at the rate of a novel a year (later collected as *The Malayan Trilogy* or *The Long Day Wanes*). The first of his published works, *Time for a Tiger* (1956), is named after the local hooch's advertising slogan and chronicles the break-up of the teacher-hero's marriage – comically. While the British Empire was breaking up, Malaya was, at this time, in the very uncomical grip of the 'Emergency' – the Chinese communist uprising.

Burgess's writing, from the beginning, was marked by a Joycean verbal exuberance, tempered by cosmic melancholy – Burgess's worldview was quintessentially theological. In personal life, and in the great trends of history, he discerned an inevitably recurring swing between Augustinian moral tolerance and Pelagian moral severity. This meshed with his belief in free will – sloganised by Alex's 'What's it going to be then, eh?' which heads every one of *A Clockwork Orange*'s seven sections. Goodness, Burgess believed, could only be achieved by a progress through sin. You cannot be programmed, or educated, into virtue: it is as unnatural as the titular orange. Burgess's grimly post-lapsarian worldview is articulated at its most mechanical in his dystopia, *The Wanting Seed* (1962) in which a future society swings, historically, between Roman orgy (Gusphase) and Puritan tyranny (Pelphase). That, he believes, is the systole and diastole of the universe – its great pendulum. His religious doctrine is given its fullest expression in the best of his novels, *Earthly Powers* (1980), a panorama of the twentieth century, as seen through the saurian eyes of an aged Catholic queer (based, as knowing reviewers apprehended, on Somerset Maugham). Remove established religion from life, *Earthly Powers* asserts, and the vacuum will fill with Jonestown fanaticism and rivers of cyanide-laced Kool-Aid. *Earthly Powers* was pipped at the post for the Booker that year by William Golding. Forewarned and piqued (*Rites of Passage* is not, all agree, Golding's best novel) Burgess unsportingly boycotted the ceremony, claiming, unconvincingly, that he had no dinner jacket.

On his return to England from Malaya, and after his twelve-month brain-cancerous furlough, Burgess's career had taken off in the 1960s. A natural performer, he was always in demand as a bluff reviewer and TV interviewee. His novels, after the 1960 barrage, sold brilliantly. He was regarded as an authority on Joyce, writing good books on the author, and composing an operetta for radio, *Blooms of*

Dublin (1982), based on *Ulysses*. The bible of the 'theorists' who were taking over British literary criticism was Roland Barthes' *S/Z* (1970). Burgess retorted, wittily, with his novel *M/F* (1971). He shied at the Bond mania with an 'eschatological' spy novel, *Tremor of Intent* (1966). There seemed to be nothing he could not turn his hand to, if not better than the competition, then more cleverly. At the same time, there were harrowing complications in his private life. In one of his casual adulteries in 1964 he had made love to a young Italian research student who promptly disappeared from his life. She was married to a black man but bore a white (Burgess's) child, Andrew. This information was withheld from him until after Lynne's death from cirrhosis in 1968, when he was finally free, by the strict doctrines of his church, to do something about it. Liana Macellari (a countess) eventually became Burgess's second wife in 1968 and they went on to set up home, finally, in Monaco (for tax reasons – both partners were rich). 'Am I happy?' Burgess asked himself in his second volume of autobiography *You've Had Your Time* (1990), 'probably not.' But, he granted, nothing on earth could have made him happy and, quite likely, neither would heaven – if he got there. By way of consolation for the unhappiness, there was the money.

In his later years Burgess wrote increasingly experimental fiction, notably *Napoleon Symphony* (1974) and *ABBA ABBA* (1977). His most enduring work will, however, be the minimally experimental 'Enderby', comic-autobiographical quartet. The third volume, *The Clockwork Testament, or Enderby's End* (1974), plays brilliantly with Stanley Kubrick's incorrigibly Jewish revision of the indelibly Catholic *Clockwork Orange* in the 1971 film (for which, to his chagrin, the novelist only got £5,000 in subsidiary rights – but consoling millions in knock-on sales). 'Clockwork Marmalade,' Burgess called the film. He liked it, though.

FN   Anthony Burgess (John Burgess Wilson)
MRT *Earthly Powers*
Biog A. Biswell, *The Real Life of Anthony Burgess* (2005); R. Lewis, *Anthony Burgess: A Life* (2002)

211. Arthur C. Clarke 1917–2008

Any sufficiently advanced technology is indistinguishable from magic.
A. C. Clarke's 'third law'

Four things are universally known about Arthur C. Clarke. The first is that he 'invented' (slightly more plausibly than H. G. Wells invented time travel) the geostationary satellite. The second is that Clarke, as a guru-commentator seen worldwide on live TV during the 1969 moon landing, bequeathed space exploration much of its vocabulary (e.g. 'Houston, we have a problem'). Thirdly, in collaboration with Stanley Kubrick, Clarke wrote the story for the film which trail-blazed the Apollo mission – *2001: A Space Odyssey* (1968). And, running against the grain of that distinguished life achievement, is the radioactive fourth thing. In 1998, on the very eve of receiving a knighthood, the dubbing was postponed when the *Sunday Mirror* 'exposed' Clarke as a pederast, who, having lived in Sri Lanka for thirty years, had preyed on young boys there. The tabloid headline, over an unflattering photograph, ran: 'SMIRK OF A PERVERT AND A LIAR'. Clarke categorically denied the allegations, but never sued. As such mud does, it stuck, adhesively, in the popular mind. Say 'Clarke' and most people will think 'One Giant Step for Man' and 'but wasn't there something about little boys?'

Clarke was born into a farming family in Minehead, Somerset. He retained through life the yokel's West Country burr. He arrived at a bleak time of year (December) and an even bleaker year, 1917, the low point in the Great War. Minehead's streets were full of dark-clothed women, and fathers with black armbands. Clarke's subsequent visions of a millennially distant, conflictless universe, inhabited by glistening star-children can plausibly be traced back to those 1917 casualty lists and weeping widows. His fiction is forever yearning for a future world in which nationhood is transcended and, with it, conflict – or, as his best novel puts it, mankind's childhood ended and with it all the physical mess of humanity: birth, copulation, death. He saw the future, and it was a sterile intensive care unit for the species. Young Arthur's interest in the genre in which he would later star (there is, literally, an asteroid honorifically named after him) began with SF pulp left behind as trash by American doughboys, in the First World War. He did well at his grammar school, but there was no prospect of university. It was the Depression. Clarke, already deft with his pen, was enrolled as a clerical grade civil servant in 1936 – a 'safe' job.

The world was not safe, however, and on the outbreak of war he joined and trained in radar, specifically 'Ground Controlled Approach'. It was an unglamorous theatre of war – but vital. The Allies were losing as many aircraft in landing accidents as from enemy flak. Clarke left the service in 1946 a flight lieutenant. He entered King's College, London, to do maths and physics, graduating with a first. He was, by now, a stalwart of the British Interplanetary Society and it was under its amateur aegis that he published his pioneering article on 'Extra- Terrestrial Relays – Can Rocket Stations Give Worldwide Radio Coverage?' – on telecommunication satellites. Clarke was a firm believer in the benefits science fiction writers like himself could bring to science. 'I'm sure we would not have had men on the moon if it had not been for Wells and Verne,' he told a US Congressional committee in 1975. 'I'm rather proud of the fact that I know several astronauts who became astronauts through reading my books.' His first book, *Prelude to Space* (1951), was dashed off in a couple of weeks in 1947. It was, however, the Dan-Dareish *The Sands of Mars* (1951) which made him well known (Clarke was, as it happened, an adviser to the *Eagle* boys' comic).

Clarke's early visions were technotopian: they celebrated 'the inevitable march of technology to new worlds'. That new world was forecast in Ralph Tubbs's 'Dome of Discovery' at the Festival of Britain. Religion would come later into his doctrinal mix. Clarke was in correspondence with C. S. Lewis in the early 1950s and Lewis's theology fused in Clarke's fictional vision with Olaf Stapledon's billenarian cosmicality and Bernard Shaw's fond forecast, in *Back to Methuselah*, that one happy day (roll on) the human race would outlive sex and, at last, be able to think straight – just like GBS. *2001* is a world without women, in which star-children are engendered by what? The stars.

Clarke's sexuality, despite the tabloid battering at the door, remained a locked cupboard. He made a marriage in 1953 which lasted six months. Michael Moorcock recalls: 'Everyone knew he was gay. In the 1950s I'd go out drinking with his boyfriend.' If so, it was a bad time to be that way. The 'Great Purge', as it was called, was in full flow. Even aristocrats, like Lord Montagu, were not immune. Clarke left England for Ceylon (Sri Lanka) in 1956. Here he could write – networked to the globe, in his later years, by the web. He is the first writer to have thanked a word-processing programme, 'WordStar', as his secretarial aid. In the Sri Lankan years he produced his major work, the *Rama* tetralogy (benign extraterrrestrials leave a ground-control approach beacon in space) and his 2001 tetralogy (benign aliens leave a similar beacon on Jupiter). SF is considered inherently unsexy: defending himself against the 1999 tabloid allegations, Clarke confided that since 1962 he had been impotent, an after-effect of polio. One speculates whether this Abelard-like condition enhanced his genius or simply removed the distraction unluckier writers must labour under.

FN   (Sir) Arthur Charles Clarke
MRT   *2001: A Space Odyssey*
Biog   N. McAleer, *Arthur C. Clarke: The Authorized Biography* (1992)

212. Muriel Spark 1918–2006

There's a lot of people think they can take my books and analyse me from them. On that principle Agatha Christie would be a serial killer.

At dinner parties in the 1970s one would converse with friends who had read Spark's famous novel, who had seen the Vanessa Redgrave stage adaptation and the Maggie Smith film adaptation. If they knew anything, they knew *The Prime of Miss Jean Brodie* (1961). But one could always stop conversation dead by asking – 'What do we know about Sandy's family?' We have virtually no idea about her home life and parents. By contrast we know the whole roll-call of the Marcia Blaine School's teaching staff: Miss Lockhart, the chemistry mistress, who has enough explosive 'to blow up this school'; Miss Gaunt of the bony head and horse-blanket skirt; even the comic *tricoteuses,* the sewing misses Ellen and Alison Kerr. And, of course, the ruthless head teacher, Miss Mackay, dedicated to ridding her school of the seditious Miss Jean Brodie. Although *The Prime of Miss Jean Brodie* is an archetypal Edinburgh novel, the city itself is as faint as tissue paper behind the action. These blanks serve to focus attention on the exquisite machinery of Spark's narrative. The novel brings as little externality into its workings as a Swiss watch brings Alpine scenery. It is this introversion which fascinates critics like Frank Kermode for whom Spark was a 'poet novelist'. Her fiction needed scenery (whether Peckham, Jerusalem, or New York's East River) as little as *Waiting for Godot* needs it. The surname, Sandy Stranger (with its nod to Camus), says a lot. Spark's technique – her whole career – depends on tactical erasure.

She was born Muriel Sarah Camberg in 'the very worst year that the world had ever seen so far' and brought up in a cramped flat in Edinburgh's Morningside, an area often mocked by grittier Edinburgh for its faux gentility. Her background was not, however, genteel. She was the second child of an engineer employed by the North British Rubber Company. Barney Camberg was Scottish-Jewish; his wife Cissy was raised Christian and called herself a 'Gentile Jewess'. Spark investigates the paradox of this 'non-conforming alliance' in the character of Barbara Vaughan in *The Mandelbaum Gate* (1965). Edinburgh in the inter-war years was less anti-Semitic than London. None the less Spark recalled a climate of 'social nervousness'. She was never close to her mother – who comes in for severe treatment in the memoir *Curriculum Vitae* (1992) – her father, or her brother Philip, six years older and very much a 'Jewish Jew'. In later life, communication with her family would break down for years on end, although in the years of her earning prime she was generous with handouts. She was red-haired (hence 'Sandy', in *The Prime of Miss Jean Brodie*) and

541

sharp-witted, winning a bursary to James Gillespie's, a small fee-paying day school in nearby Marchmont.

Muriel matriculated in 1934 which qualified her for university entrance if the Cambergs could have afforded it. Instead she took a course in secretarial skills. In 1937, still not twenty, she became engaged to marry Sydney Oswald ('Solly') Spark, a lapsed Jew and thirteen years her senior. He had accepted a three-year school-teaching post in Southern Rhodesia. It was an escape from Edinburgh and 'take a letter, Miss Camberg' drudgery, but Muriel's decision was disastrous. Solly teetered constantly on the brink of a nervous breakdown; he was violent and in his mania prone to firing off his pistol around the house. By the time their first child, Robin, arrived in 1938 the marriage was over for her. But not for him. This meant divorce had to be confected on the grounds of her desertion, which in turn undercut her claim to custody of Robin. With the outbreak of war, Spark found herself trapped in southern Africa. She kept body and soul together with office jobs, had the occasional affair, and gathered material later used in stories like 'The Go-Away Bird' (an apt description of Muriel Spark, she liked to jest). She managed eventually to get away on a troop ship in 1944, leaving Robin behind. When the boy came back a year later, he was shipped off to Edinburgh to be brought up by her parents. One of her later lovers tartly observed that 'Robin looks upon Muriel as someone who visits him occasionally and gives him presents.'

On her return to England, Spark was recruited to work in wartime intelligence, specifically 'black propaganda'. She lived in the Helena Club in Kensington, immortalised as the 'May of Teck Club' in *Girls of Slender Means* (1963), established 'for the Pecuniary Convenience and Social Protection of Ladies of Slender Means below the age of thirty Years'. Since in that novel the Club sits on a ticking unexploded bomb and there is rampant fornication on the roof-top, 'social protection' might be thought less than perfect. Perhaps the Helena Club arranged things better. Her mood at this period (1945) was jaunty. Feeling depressed about Blitz-ruined London would have been 'like feeling depressed about the Grand Canyon'. After final victory, Spark took up editorship of the Poetry Society's *Poetry Review* (1947–9) and became the society's general secretary. Among much else she learned the important lesson that 'literary men if they like women at all, do not want literary women but girls'. She had a series of affairs with 'literary men', one of which, with Derek Stanford, lasted ten years and she well beyond girlhood with her prime in sight. The couple edited several books together. On being dismissed from the *Poetry Review*, on the issue of payment to poets, she set up another journal. It failed, but she was all the while refining her sensibility. 'Alienation from her family,' notes Martin Stannard, 'was now complete.' They did not, in Brodie's phrase, 'have her for life'.

In her mid-thirties Spark turned out a string of thoughtful works of literary criticism: Mary Shelley and Emily Brontë were of particular interest. So, more momentously, was Cardinal Newman. She had been moving towards Rome for some time and converted in 1954. Her resolve, for some time after, to embrace chastity did not help her current love relationship. But her career in fiction was jump-started in 1951 when, against 7,000 rivals, she won the *Observer* Christmas story competition with 'The Seraph and the Zambesi'. Today's readers recognise it as a mix of post-colonial and magic realism. It is to the credit of the judges, in a period when grim realism ruled, that they recognised its quality. The cash prize was, in the money value of the time, a fortune and she moved to lodgings in Camberwell, under the supervision of a redoubtable Irish Catholic landlady, 'Tiny' Lazzari. Spark kept her Camberwell 'attic', just down the road from Peckham Rye, long after she could afford better.

Her first novel, *The Comforters* (1957) distributed discreetly in manuscript, won golden opinions from co-religionists Graham Greene and Evelyn Waugh. This middle period of her life coincided with a period of florid madness brought on – Stannard surmises – by a gross overdose of the 'pep pills' then freely off prescription as dieting aids. She was as much a junkie as Bill Burroughs. At the height of her derangement, Spark believed T. S. Eliot was sending her coded messages in his plays. He was not, he sagely confirmed. Retreat in a monastery, detox and psychotherapy brought her back to herself. *The Comforters* is a subtle exploration into the poetics of fiction. Is the heroine Caroline the author or the creation of an author she has not yet located? There is a pervading sense of unease. Spark once said that she fondled her characters as a cat fondles birds. Their free will, or lack of it, would be a presiding theme in Spark's fiction, most elegantly posed in *The Driver's Seat* (1970) where Lise composes her murder as a novelist might assemble a plot. Frank Kermode is insistent that Spark is not a religious but a theological novelist. She was not a dutiful Catholic, apparently. What is consistent in all the play with theology in her work is the lightness of touch: the faint, but repeated, allusion to 'strait is the gate' in *Girls of Slender Means* in the lavatory window that only the slenderest girls can squeeze through; those that can't are doomed when the bomb goes off. Jean Brodie's obsession with who betrayed her stresses the necessity of Judas if human redemption is to happen. In *The Ballad of Peckham Rye* (1960) the diabolical Dougal has two bumps on his head – horns are hinted at. Or they could just be bumps on Freud's 'sometimes a cigar is just a cigar' principle. In *Memento Mori* (1959), telephone calls, reminding the recipient of death, come from nowhere it seems. God? It was, Spark believed, 'bad manners' to be heavy-handed – even when dealing with issues like mortality, salvation, guilt or sin. Leave heavy-handedness to Moses and his tablets.

International celebrity came when the *New Yorker* devoted the whole of an issue to *The Prime of Miss Jean Brodie* in 1961. The magazine went further by giving her an office, with the understanding that whatever she chose to write they would print. She was set up in an apartment in Manhattan. Jean Brodie was, she liked to say in later years, her 'milch cow'. Slender means no more. At one reckless moment she bought a racehorse. Spark found she liked the metropolitan lifestyle – *haute couture*, exclusive restaurants, expensive jewellery, jazz dives. She was also possessed of a beauty which she took great care of. Her New York stint established a pattern by which she would get the best of whatever 'exiledom' she found herself in, until the place palled. Irrational quarrels were usually the indication that she was ready for a move. She became increasingly quarrelsome with age. She left Macmillan who had published her for thirty years because of a misprint on a blurb which was not, as she saw it, taken seriously enough. As with places, so with lovers – she wore them out. 'Your sole conception of love is selfish,' complained one. But selfishness was essential to her art.

In what was intended to be her *magnum opus*, *The Mandelbaum Gate* (1965), she came to grips with her gentile Jewishness. But 'magnum' was not her *métier*. Jewish critics in New York made that clear to her. In 1966 she moved to Rome. In Italy she resided in a series of grand residences, complete with a full complement of staff, a PA and a butler. Novels were now pulsing from her pen at a high rate and all sold well. She took on large topics – Watergate in *The Abbess of Crewe* (1974), for example – and experimented with Alain Robbe-Grillet's skeletal *roman nouveau* (*The Driver's Seat*). Her styles were as restless as her physical movements. Her central preoccupation remained theological, particularly the question of the malevolence of God. She had worn it down to the bone in *The Only Problem* (1984). The hero is writing a monograph about the *Book of Job* and 'he could not face that a benevolent Creator, one whose charming and delicious light descended and spread over the world, and being powerful everywhere, could condone the unspeakable sufferings of the world ... "It is the only problem," Harvey had always said.' Sometimes it is impossible to suppress the suspicion that Spark became a Catholic for the raw material it supplied her as a novelist rather than for the welfare of her soul.

Her last years were poisoned by a feud with her son Robin, now an artist. An orthodox Jew, he questioned her 'Gentile Jewish' hybridity. Furiously, she cut him out of her will, leaving everything to her aged personal assistant, Penelope Jardine. He would have to get by with what she hurtfully called his 'lousy paintings'. She was made a Dame in 1993. Her last years were plagued by osteoporosis which she endured stoically. She died in Florence and is buried there.

FN   (Dame) Muriel Sarah Spark (née Camberg)
MRT *The Prime of Miss Jean Brodie*
Biog M. Stannard, *Muriel Spark: The Biography* (2009)

213. Mickey Spillane 1918–2006

Hemingway hated me. I sold 200 million books, and he didn't.

He was christened 'Frank Morrison Spillane', but 'women', he claimed in later life, 'liked the name Mickey'. Young Spillane was brought up in a 'very tough' neighbourhood in New Jersey. His father was a bartender and a Catholic; his mother, a Protestant. He claimed to have read all of Melville and Dumas before he was eleven. After high school, he went to Kansas State College, starred briefly on the football field, and dropped out. In the *de rigueur* way of aspirant writers at the time, he kicked around in the Depression of the 1930s, working for a while as a Long Island lifeguard – 'women', he discovered, liked that too. In 1935 he began submitting work to 'slick' magazines, 'working my way down', as he later recalled, 'to the comic books: Captain Marvel, Captain America, Superman, Batman – you name it, I did them all … a great training ground for writers.' Fast-order work would be Spillane's speciality. *I, the Jury* (1947) was dashed off in nine days. When the car containing his manuscript of *The Body Lovers* (1967) was stolen two decades later, he claimed to be concerned only about the loss of his wheels: 'the missing manuscript just means another three days' work'.

Spillane served in the US Air Force during the Second World War and, by his own account, flew fighter missions. In interviews he claimed two bullet wounds and a civilian knife scar sustained while working undercover with the FBI to break up a narcotics ring – but one may be suspicious. On demobilisation he worked in Barnum & Bailey's circus as a trampoline artist (the setting is used in his 1962 novel, *The Girl Hunters*). More profitably, he bounced back into writing.

Spillane himself acknowledged the influence of only one crime writer on his work, Carroll John Daly, creator of the private eye, Race Williams. He flaunted his lack of authorial polish, claiming, mischievously, never to introduce characters with moustaches or who drank cognac because he could not spell those words. *I, the Jury* introduced the series hero Mike Hammer, whose tough-talking, woman-beating, whisky-swilling machismo answered the needs of the post-war 'male action' market and its nervous uncertainties about masculinity now that there weren't Japs or Krauts to kill. Estimates suggest global sales of around 200 million. By 1980, seven of the top fifteen all-time bestselling fiction titles in America were Hammer novels. 'People like them,' Spillane blandly explained. The climax of a Mike Hammer narrative invariably features sadistic execution. The most hilarious is in *Vengeance is Mine* (1950), which ends with the line (just before she/he gets it in the gut) 'Juno was a Man!'

The link was often made between Spillane and Joe McCarthy, and over the years Hammer's victims were as likely to be 'reds' as 'hoods'. Whatever, they were rubbed out. In *One Lonely Night* (1951), the hero mows down forty communists with a machine-gun. Originally there were eighty, but the publishers 'thought that was too gory'. Spillane regarded himself as a super-patriot, and was so regarded by others. John Wayne gave him a Jaguar XK140 in honour of his anti-communism and Ayn Rand (author of *Atlas Shrugged*) commended his prose style to her neo-con disciples. Spillane's patriotism was, however, always tinged with a pessimistic, quasi-religious sense of doom. In the early 1960s he predicted a race war in America, although he seems not to have been a racist himself. He was old enough to have experienced anti-Irish prejudice against 'Micks'.

The Hammer novels are written as spoken monologue and are stylistically direct. Spillane had great faith in the slam-bang opening, believing that 'the first page sells the book'. He claimed never to read galleys or rewrite. He had, however, an odd compulsiveness about punctuation, and once insisted that 50,000 copies of *Kiss Me, Deadly* (1952) be pulped after the comma was left out of the title. The Hammer novels enjoyed new leases of life and income for the author in film, radio, comic-strip and television adaptation. *I, the Jury* was filmed twice (1953, 1982), as were other Hammer books. The only film that has any distinction is Robert Aldrich's exaggeratedly *noir*, *Kiss Me Deadly* (1955). Spillane disliked it – not least because of the missing comma. Possessed of rugged good looks, he played Hammer himself in the film of *The Girl Hunters* (1963), turning in a commendable performance.

As an author of pulp, Spillane's guiding principle was that 'violence will outsell sex every time', but combined they will outsell everything. As part of the promotion for his novels he adopted a Hammeresque persona, which was transparently an act. He once told a British interviewer, 'I always say never hit a woman when you can kick her.' When asked 'Is that the treatment you give Mrs Spillane?,' he primly replied, 'We're talking about fiction.' There were two long gaps in Spillane's career. The first followed his conversion to the Jehovah's Witnesses in 1952, which led to a ten-year hiatus in novel-writing. He returned to form in 1961 with the best of the Hammer novels, *The Deep*. There was another gap, between 1973 and 1989, during which he again wrote no full-length fiction, though he did try his hand (as a dare with his publisher) at two, well-received, children's books. During this period he was famous to the American television-watching public for his appearance in Miller Lite beer commercials, though he was reported not to be a heavy drinker. Over his last decades, to his disgust, Spillane received increasing critical respect for his contributions to the idiom of crime fiction, and for having played a pioneer's role in the post-war paperback revolution.

FN   Mickey Spillane (born Frank Morrison Spillane)
MRT *I, The Jury*
Biog M. A. Collins and J. L. Taylor, *One Lonely Knight: Mickey Spillane's Mike Hammer* (1984)

214. Carroll John Daly 1889–1958

My conscience is clear; I never shot anybody that didn't need to die.
Daly's PI, Race Williams

Daly is plausibly credited with inventing – or, at least, pioneering – the hard-boiled, PI (Private Investigator/Private Eye) detective genre, rendered classic in the *Black Mask* magazine, with his 1922 story 'The False Burton Combs'. He can also be said, not least by the man himself, to have invented Mickey Spillane. Daly was born in Yonkers, New York, and educated, with a stage career in mind, at the American Academy of Dramatic Arts. He started at the bottom of his chosen profession as an usher and rose to be manager of a theatre in Atlantic City. He was not, it would appear, successful in this line of work – although it was in these years, presumably, that he picked up his facility with vernacular American idiom.

In 1913, he married Margaret G. Blakely. Little else is known of his personal life, other than anecdotal fragments, but he was apparently agoraphobic and dentist phobic. Fear of open places (and, perhaps, predatory orthodontists) led him to isolate himself as an eccentric recluse in White Plains, on the outskirts of New York. Once, it is recorded, he did venture into the metropolitan wilds of Manhattan, only to forget where his house was on his return. A neighbour had to point it out to him. 'Once,' another anecdote goes, 'for the sake of research, Daly decided that maybe he should get to know what it was like to handle a gun. Daly, leaving his temperature-controlled home, went and bought a gun only to be arrested for carrying a concealed weapon. As one friend observed, "That was the end of Carroll John Daly's research."' He had a wealthy uncle who put funds his way with which he could sit at home and spin out his tough-guy fantasies. He finally made it into print in *Black Mask*, aged thirty-three, preceding Dashiell Hammett's first 'Continental Op' story in the magazine's pages by a few months. Daly's most significant literary creation was his thuggish Private Eye, Race Williams, whose 'ethic', as Daly called it, is summed up in boasts such as the following, in *The Snarl of the Beast* (1927):

It's the point of view in life that counts. For an ordinary man to get a bullet through his hat as he walked home at night would be something to talk about for years. Now, with me; just the price of a new hat – nothing more. The only surprise would be for the lad who fired the gun. He and his relatives would come in for a slow ride, with a shovel-ful of dirt at the end of it.

A beastly snarl indeed.

Daly's star sank at *Black Mask* with the appointment of the magazine's influential editor, Joe 'Cap' Shaw, who despised the artless crudity of Daly's literary style. It showed up badly against the felicities of Hammett, or Chandler. Daly's connection with *Black Mask*, having served its purpose by pioneering a genre in which he no longer excelled, ended in 1934. Thereafter he simply fed the country's pulp fiction and comic-book industry with low-grade product. Daly was, however, yanked back into the public eye by Mickey Spillane. In interviews given in the late 1940s, when he was the bestselling novelist in America, the creator of Mike Hammer acknowledged that Daly was the only novelist who had ever influenced him. Spillane dutifully wrote to Daly (whose address he had, with difficulty, discovered) to say: 'Yours was the first and only style of writing that ever influenced me in any way. Race was the model for Mike; and I can't say more in this case than imitation being the most sincere form of flattery. The public in accepting my books were in reality accepting the kind of work you have done.'

It was graciously done. But when Daly's literary agent was shown the letter she promptly set about suing the multi-millionaire Spillane for self-confessed plagiarism. Daly as promptly fired her, with the rueful comment that Spillane's was the only fan letter he had ever received.

FN   Carroll John Daly
MRT   *The Snarl of the Beast*
Biog   W. F. Nolan, *The Black Mask Boys* (1985)

215. Jacqueline Susann 1918–1974

Way back then, they didn't think Shakespeare was a good writer.

Jacqueline Susan (Jackie added the final 'n' to clarify the pronunciation) was born in 1918, the granddaughter of Jewish immigrants from Lithuania. In the complex caste system of their Philadelphia community, the Susans ranked aristocratically high. Jackie's conversion to Catholicism in the late 1950s was less a religious thing than a hankering for 'class'. Her father, Bob Susan, had lots of class. He was a sought-after painter of society portraits and sophisticated nudes. Handsome Bob was also a philanderer. 'I could have had all the women whose portraits I painted,' he boasted, 'plus all their mothers and their daughters.' It was no idle boast. Jackie learned the 'facts of life' when, aged four, she blundered into her father's studio and found him 'humping' (her word) one of his sitters. She remained incurably curious about 'humping' all her life. When she threw away her diaphragm thirty years later to give her husband Irving the child he craved, she set up full-length mirrors in the bedroom so as to observe 'the miracle of conception'.

A bright schoolgirl with a mind of her own, Jackie decided against college (although in later life she would claim an Ivy League background when it suited her). Like Anne Welles in *Valley of the Dolls* (1966), Jackie found freedom in New York: here she could 'breathe'. She arrived there at eighteen years old in 1936 and (like Anne Welles again) gravitated straight to Broadway and café society. The Stork Club, Copacabana, El Morocco, and the 21 club called irresistibly to her. But stardom as an actress and cover fame as a model eluded the young Jackie. She was tall, had wonderful legs, a lion's mane of black hair and good facial bones, but her 'pores' were too big: film close-ups magnified them into craters. Nor could she sing. And, as a fashion model, there was the boobs and waistline problem. Diet pills, which she popped by the bottle-full, handled the weight, but not those little but all-important imperfections of shape. Jackie had lots of bit parts, a few supporting roles, was featured in fashion magazines, but never achieved the celebrity she craved. The star was stubbornly not born. As she said, no one would turn and say, 'Isn't that Jacqueline Susann?' when she walked into 21. Of course, she tried the casting couch – any couch. To use one of her own phrases, she was a love machine. One of her friends suggested she should install a revolving door and a cloakroom checkout service outside her bedroom.

Jackie slept with anyone who might help, even after her marriage in 1939 to the complaisant press agent (and her benign Svengali), Irving Mansfield. Coco Chanel, it is said, had a fling with the young Jackie. If true, the bit about the 'little black dress' never quite got through to her: Jackie always wore clothes that could blind you close-up and deafen you at ten yards. One persistent rumour was that to pay for those clothes (loud, she may have been, cheap never), Jackie did some discreet high-paid call-girl work in the 1940s. However, making love was in itself of no intrinsic interest to her. One of her intimates recorded that she claimed never in her life to have had an orgasm. The most she ever got out of sex physically was 'body warmth'; and she probably took more than she gave of that.

In late 1962 she was diagnosed as having cancer and underwent a radical mastectomy. It was to be one of her two best-kept secrets. The other was that her only child, Guy (born 1946), was institutionalised with irreversible autism. She put away the full-length bedroom mirrors and redirected her maternal feelings to her poodle. Jackie, who firmly believed that 'women own the world only when they are very young' and that '40 is Hiroshima', felt she was on the terrible brink of menopause – if she were to live that long. A year before her mastectomy, aged forty-three, she had undergone her first face-lift ('I'm a realist'). Her 'good years' had gone: what could she do in the bad years to come? In *Valley of the Dolls*, Jennifer North kills herself with an overdose of 'dolls' rather than face a one-breasted middle age. Doubtless the thought crossed Jackie's mind – to go out like Marilyn (one of the inspirations for Jennifer, along with Carole Landis).

Wisely, in *Valley of the Dolls*, she wrote about what she knew best: Manhattan, show business and, above all, pills. She was a long-time unrepentant prescription junkie. She took 'tranks' (Librium by choice) to get through the day; amphetamines (Preludin) to clear the day's hurdles and suppress the appetite; and to get to sleep at night, lots of barbiturates, or 'barbies' (hence 'dolls'). Jackie's first thought was to call her novel 'The Pink Dolls'. The eventual title was a private joke. Although you would never guess it from the book, the author's favoured form of 'doll' was the suppository. It is not difficult to imagine what the 'doll valley' is.

Her views on the art of fiction were refreshingly primitive: 'I don't think any novelist should be concerned with literature. Literature should be left to the essayists.' Essayist Gore Vidal famously remarked on reading *Valley of the Dolls*, 'She doesn't write, she types!' But Jackie was not even much of a typist. The first draft of the novel, as one of the publisher's rewrite team recalled, was 'hardly written in English' and it took a lot of labour to bring it up to a standard of 'readable mediocrity'. Jackie toughed out the snide criticisms as she toughed out everything and by 1967, Susann had made it, at last. People did indeed turn around in 21 and say, 'Look, there's Jackie Susann.' It must have been sweet, but it was as short-lived as her remission from cancer. There were three more novels, written under increasing pressure. They were all bestsellers, but nothing to equal *Valley of the Dolls*, boosted as it was by the 1967 blockbuster film, starring Sharon Tate.

Nobody knew she was ill. The 'dolls' helped, but mainly it was willpower and vanity that kept her secret. She died in 1974. On the urn containing her ashes, Irving gallantly took three years off her age. No need to let everyone know.

FN   Jacqueline Susann (born Jacqueline Susan)
MRT   *Valley of the Dolls*
Biog B. Seaman, *Lovely Me: The Life of Jacqueline Susann* (1987)

216. Iris Murdoch 1919–1999

I knew it was going to be bad getting old ... I didn't know it was going to be this bad.
Kurt Vonnegut, *Slaughterhouse-Five*

Anyone who cares to do the demographic stats on this book will note that as the centuries pass the novelists live longer. And long lives mean late-life novels which, in many cases, meditate just that fact – longevity and what it means. Iris Murdoch, the distinguished philosopher and rather more distinguished Booker Prize-winning novelist, was born in Dublin in 1919. *The Sea, The Sea*, her actual Booker Prize-winning novel, was published in 1978. A literary critic putting those dates together, along with the fact that *The Sea, The Sea* was Murdoch's nineteenth novel and her most widely applauded, will conclude, sagely, that this is to be approached as fruit of the author's maturity – the crest of her creative wave. An actuary would see it differently. In her sixtieth year, Miss Murdoch was facing state-ordained retirement from the national workforce (men, in those unregenerate days, had to labour another five years to earn their gold watch). Fancifully, if one wanted an alternative title for *The Sea, The Sea*, one could call it 'Retirement, Retirement'. Not very catchy, one grants, but apropos. The novelist's life, like drama, has its fifth act.

Retirement – as those who have crossed the actuarial line will attest – is a paradoxical threshold. Viewed from one angle (through the rosy lens of Saga company brochures, for example), retirement is the gateway to a new life. At last the senior citizen will have time to do all those things which have been put off over the years. One is free to enjoy 'the remains of the day', as Kazuo Ishiguro puts it, in *his* Booker Prize-winning novel about retirement (written, the date-conscious will note, when that event was a long way off for him). The sun is at its most lustrously golden before nightfall. But retirement – the last '*vita nuova*' – is also the prelude to death. How much time will one have? When will the reaper strike? This is the theme in Kingsley Amis's (yes, another) Booker Prize-winning novel about retirement. *The Old Devils* (1986) opens, darkly and comically, not with the hero serenely contemplating a glorious sunset, but nervously scrutinising his morning stools in the lavatory pan for the tell-tale flecks of blood, harbingers of cancer. It's an ironic allusion to the white-haired Falstaff, as we encounter the retired hero in *Henry IV Part 2*, anxiously awaiting the medical report on his urine sample. The smart-mouthed little page who took the flask to the dispensary reports that the surgeon thought it was excellent urine – but he would hate to be the man who passed it. Few golden years in prospect for this old devil, one apprehends.

Murdoch invariably answered '*The Tempest*' when asked, as distinguished writers routinely are, which was her 'favourite Shakespeare'. It's an elemental play and its dominant element is water. It opens with a vividly depicted shipwreck. All on board the vessel are drowned five fathoms deep – and subsequently emerge, Venus-like, reborn from the waves. They drown into life. *The Tempest* is conventionally seen as Shakespeare's farewell to the London theatre which he had dominated for twenty years: it was his retirement play. Theatrical lore has it that Prospero's valedictory speech, in which he breaks his staff and departs the island over which he has been sovereign ruler, allegorises the playwright's formal retirement from his own little world – the Globe. It will be a solemn last few years. After Miranda's marriage to Ferdinand, Prospero will:

> *... thence retire me to my Milan, where*
> *Every third thought shall be my grave.*

As the biographers tell us, Shakespeare – still a hale fifty-something – was more of the Saga, live-it-up, party. No hair-shirts and hermit's cave for Will in his retirement. He had left Stratford a humble glove-maker. He would return as a gentleman with a heraldic device over his front door. William Shakespeare *Esquire* had resolved fully to enjoy the remains of his day. Alas, that dreaded contingency intervened – typhoid, it is plausibly assumed, carried him off long 'before his time', aged a mere fifty-one. Legend has it that drink too may have played a part.

In *The Sea, The Sea*, Murdoch's allusion to *The Tempest* is constant but subtle. Charles Arrowby, the bumptious narrator, has an international reputation as director of plays for the London stage. As an actor, his most applauded performance was as Prospero, but Charles has no great fame in the acting department. He is now in his mid-sixties, and still at the top of his profession. But he has determined to retire while he still has life to live and energies to live it. Born in Stratford-upon-Avon, he chooses not to take up retirement there, but in a quiet village, Narrowdean, on the coast (which coast is never quite clear – Murdoch can be frustratingly vague about such details). He will, in the many years of his coastal seclusion, write his memoirs, 'recollected', as he fondly intends, in Wordsworthian 'tranquillity'. 'Wifeless, childless, brotherless', Charles is entirely the captain of his fate. He *manages* his life, he likes to say. 'A theatre director', he tells us, 'is a dictator.' In German, the two terms are the same – *Führer*. Charles, little Hitler that he is (but not, for all that, entirely unlikeable), will direct the fifth act of the Arrowby drama as precisely and authoritatively as he has ruled over the West End theatre. The 'contingent' – those factors which not even dictators can control – intervenes. Serenely contemplating the ocean Charles sees a monster 'rising from the waves':

I can describe this in no other way. Out of a perfectly calm empty sea, at a distance of perhaps a quarter of a mile (or less), I saw an immense creature break the surface and arch itself upward. At first it looked like a black snake, then a long thickening body with a ridgy spiny back followed the elongated neck ... I could also see the head with remarkable clarity, a kind of crested snake's head, green-eyed, the mouth opening to show teeth and a pink interior.

Commentators of the Freudian persuasion have had a fine time with that last detail: opticians, too, might wonder about an OAP who can discern eye-colour and teeth at 500 yards.

Charles is flummoxed. Is it hallucination, a trick of the eyes? A flashback to a bad trip taken, years ago, on LSD? Is he – horrible thought – losing his mind, and with it his 'control' over reality? The novel gives us no answer. Contingency never yields to analysis or explication. The monster returns once more in the narrative, but remains inexplicable. Monstrous contingency continues to invade the carefully blueprinted Arrowby retirement plan. One by one, characters pop up from his old life to plague his new life. They include actress-lovers, Lizzie Scherer and Rosina Vamburgh; theatrical colleagues, such as the servile and gay Gilbert Opian; Peregrine Arbelow, who Charles callously cuckolded; and Charles's cousin, James, mysteriously dismissed from the army in which he had risen to the rank of general and now, apparently, a Buddhist guru. Or, possibly, a pro-Tibetan freedom-fighter. Or, as it finally emerges, Charles's saviour from the hell of himself. Things do not turn out as he plans. This is not a play he is directing – it is life. And life, even those last much-planned, carefully annuitised last years, defies direction.

Alzheimer's, alas, destroyed the fine mind which created *The Sea, The Sea*. As her husband John Bayley records, poignantly, in her last days she gazed not at the sea, wary of monsters that might rise up, but at the Teletubbies.

FN   (Dame) Jean Iris Murdoch (later Bayley)
MRT *The Sea, The Sea*
Biog P. J. Conradi, *Iris Murdoch: A Life* (2001)

217. Frederik Pohl 1919–

The most consistently able writer science fiction, in its modern form, has yet produced.
Kingsley Amis

No author has been so much inside the confines of his genre as Fred Pohl, nor, given his great age, so long inside it. If there is a twentieth-century incarnation of science fiction (SF) – as H. G. Wells was its nineteenth-century incarnation – Pohl is it. His father was a 'plunger', a ne'er-do-well salesman who dragged his family all over the country. There were times in Pohl's childhood 'when we lived in suites in luxury hotels and times when we didn't live anywhere at all'. After the age of seven, Fred was brought up in 'Depression Brooklyn' which, despite 'the money having run out', he recalls as, culturally, a 'warm place'. The moment when 'the irremediable virus entered my veins' was in 1930 when 'I came across a magazine named *Science Wonder Stories Quarterly*, with a picture of a scaly green monster on the cover'.

A clever boy, Fred got a place at Brooklyn Tech, aged twelve. The school was dedicated to the 'revolutionary concept' that the educational system could produce the technologists the twentieth century needed. Financial difficulties meant his dropping out, aged fourteen before he could contribute to that grand vision. His parents had separated the year before, his 'plunging' father having taken 'one short-cut too many and wound up in trouble with the law'. Technology lost out. In his early teens Pohl was involved in the hobbyist world of SF fanzines and was fanatical about movies. It was, he recalls, the era of 'films for everyone'. The silver screen was the only escape on offer from the grey reality of the hardest economic times in history. Two films were formative on young Fred: the afterlife fantasy *Death Takes a Holiday* (1934) and the Wells/Korda collaboration, *Things to Come* (1936) – 'greater than *Metropolis*, more meaningful than *2001*'. These works penetrated into 'the deep-down core of my brain'. At the same period Pohl was what he calls a 'Boy Bolshevik'. Much of the SF of the 1930s was, he maintains, leftist: proto-revolutionary. He proudly carried a Young Communist League card for four years and volunteered to join the Abraham Lincoln Brigade, to fight in Spain, but was rejected as too young and too useless. But his spirit was willing.

SF was, by the late 1930s, mobilised in terms of fiercely competitive 'clubs'. Pohl's club was 'The Futurians'. It brought him into fruitful connection with, among others, Isaac Asimov (about whose more florid imaginings, Pohl – an ironist by temperament – has always had serious misgivings). Another Futurian with whom Pohl had the most collaborative relationship of his career was the gifted Cyril M. Kornbluth (1923–58). Aged eighteen, Pohl was 'sampling the mixed diet of the freelance writer. Your time is your own. But it is the *only* thing that you own that you can sell.' Selling science fiction was easy. This was the 'high autumn of the pulps'. Some 'pulpsters', Pohl recalls, could turn out 10,000 words a day, under a battery of pseudonyms. But the whole payment budget for a magazine could be under $200 an issue. Slowcoaches went hungry; it was a hot-house genre.

Pohl made his first of five marriages in 1940 (the last, his longest, to Elizabeth Anne Hull, an academic and science fiction expert, has lasted since 1984). He was inducted into the US military forces 'on April Fool's Day, 1943' and served until November 1945 as a sergeant in the air corps weather service, looking up at the empty skies, appropriately enough. After the war, and again remarried, he took up work as a literary agent. Asimov was one of his early clients. He achieved, as he ruefully recalls, the quite amazing feat of going broke as a literary agent. A second divorce, and the need to coin some cash (specifically to clear $30,000 in accumulated debts) drove him back to writing and editing SF. Thank God for those hardships. The 1950s represent the highpoint of Pohl's writing: it was over these years, in collaboration with Cyril Kornbluth, that he produced his classic SF satires on Eisenhowerian consumerism and 'mature' capitalism. *The Space Merchants* (1953) began as the short story 'Gravy Planet'. It constructs, wittily, a world in which corporate business has taken over the functions of government and advertising the function of news. It's done, like all Pohl's work, with a strong storyline and a Hemingwayesque economy of phrase. All those years writing fast for the pulps had impressed on him indelibly the need to keep the reader turning pages before going to the drugstore to get another title by the same author. Kingsley Amis pronounced *The Space Merchants* to be the best SF novel ever written. It has my vote as well.

The collaborators' *Gladiator-at-Law* (1955) switched the satire to a world in which law simply existed to further corporate interests. The Pohl–Kornbluth twenty-third century fantasy *Wolfbane* (1959) has not held up so well, but it seems clear that sardonic Kornbluth added something necessary. One of the other writer's works in his own right, the short story 'The Marching Morons' (first published in the magazine *Galaxy* in 1951), is routinely voted one of the best works ever in the genre. The hero, John Barlow, goes into suspended animation and wakes, centuries in the future, to discover that (thanks to the inverse relationship of intelligence to procreation of children) the moronic have inherited the earth: idiocracy rules. After Kornbluth's premature death in 1958, the razor's edge is less apparent in Pohl's work, although *A Plague of Pythons* (1964), which fantasises dictatorship via metempsychosis, is as good as anything he has written. The work, like *Fahrenheit 451*, can be read as an allegory of a world sofa-bound by the miracle of TV and the vicarious pleasures it provides, while the buttocks expand into uncontrolled obesity.

Two factors redirected Pohl's career as the decade came to an end. One was the collapse of the wholesaler and distributor, the American News Company, in 1957, which decimated the pulps and SF magazines. The other was the death of Kornbluth. Pohl had some intellectual sympathy with the so-called 'New Wave' which transformed SF in the 1960s and 1970s, elevating the genre (as its practitioners fondly hoped) to new levels of literariness and cultural respectability. As an adviser to Bantam Books, Pohl actually promoted the careers of experimentalists such as Samuel R. Delany – a writer who has been seriously compared with James Joyce. But it was not Pohl's kind of SF, nor could he love it. His later years were devoted to the 'Heechee' series, whose central concept (reminiscent of Arthur C. Clarke) is of benign aliens, leaving blueprints wherewith humans can themselves progress towards the stars.

Pohl has won every honour his genre has to offer: many more than once. A thoughtful practitioner, he wonders: 'I have committed my life to science fiction. It is fair to ask why. I mean, I'm smart enough. I could have had several quite different careers, and some of them, at least at the time, looked a lot more attractive in terms of dollars and pride. When you come right down to it, is making up lies about things that have never happened really a respectable way for a grown man to spend his days?' 'Why, sure,' he answers. On the basis of the classics he and Kornbluth have given us, one is inclined to agree.

FN   Frederik George Pohl, Jr
MRT *The Space Merchants*
Biog F. Pohl, *The Way the Future Was* (1978)

218. J. D. Salinger 1919–2010

There is a marvelous peace in not publishing.
Salinger, in conversation with the *New York Times*, 3 November 1974

When he died in 2010 Salinger's obituaries had been held in reserve, unchanged, for decades. That written in the *Guardian*, for example, was by someone who had predeceased the novelist by many years. Recluses are not unknown in literature, but few have been as puritanically reclusive as Salinger – a man 'famous for not wanting to be famous'. Jerome David Salinger was born in New York. His father was well off and Jewish, with second-generation roots in Lithuania – a country whose brutal pogroms enriched twentieth-century American fiction with Norman Mailer,

Saul Bellow, Nathanael West and Jacqueline Susann. The American Academy of Literature should raise a monument in Vilnius. Once arrived in the land of the free Sol (Solomon) Salinger ran an imported kosher cheese and ham business. It was a cheap luxury which, with skilful management, weathered the 1930s Depression. The Salingers enjoyed an affluent Manhattan life – not least their pampered only son, 'Sonny'.

Legend (never contradicted by her son) had it that Salinger's mother, Miriam (Marie) Jillich Salinger, was of Scottish/Irish extraction – and that she might even have been disowned by her family for marrying a Jew. In fact Miriam came from a prosperous German American family, who had done well in Iowa. She was a Gentile, but so relaxed were Sol and she about religion that there was no friction. Young Salinger was brought up secular and it was not until much later in life that he found his gods – idiosyncratically. They would not be Jewish gods; he was not one of those who grow back to their roots.

Salinger was strongly attached to his mother (he dedicated *The Catcher in the Rye* to her) and she was indulgent where other parents might have wielded the rod. Young Sonny was expelled from his exclusive private school for lack of industry. He was then enrolled in a military academy in Pennsylvania, which he liked – although he punished it as the original of Pencey in *Catcher*. He graduated in 1936 – at the same age as Holden Caulfield. He then enrolled in New York University but dropped out after a year. This was now his wayward pattern. His father sent him off to Poland, ostensibly to learn about canned picnic ham. If Sonny learned anything from this episode, his biographer laconically observes, it was that 'Pigs' were not for him. His father could forget any fond 'Salinger and Son' fantasies. More to the young man's taste was Vienna, where he spent some months before the outbreak of war, perfecting his German and, it is deduced, falling in love.

What did Sonny (later 'Jerry') want to be? Either an actor (his powers of mimicry and range of voice were much noted) or a writer. With a view to the latter he enrolled in a creative writing class at Columbia where, momentously, he came under the wing of a teacher, Whit Burnett, who edited a literary magazine, *Story*, on the side. Burnett had a remarkable eye. *Story* 'discovered' Mailer, Capote, Tennessee Williams and Salinger. At the age of twenty-one, after Burnett gave him his start, Salinger was precociously publishing in 'slicks' (glossy magazines – not 'pulp') such as *Collier's Weekly* and *Esquire*, and had his eye on the big one, the *New Yorker*. He finally got there in 1941, only to have his smooth upward path interrupted by the Japanese attack on Pearl Harbor.

At this stage of his life Salinger was a handsome, ironic, wisecracking, ladies' man. The lady he fell in love with was Oona O'Neill, daughter of the Nobel

Prize-winning dramatist. She was, like all the women in his life, markedly younger than him (sixteen to his twenty-two), a predilection he shared with Charlie Chaplin, who eventually snatched Oona away. Salinger's fiction is fascinated by the young, a year or so either side of puberty (Holden Caulfield, Seymour Glass, Esmé, Franny) and this fascination inspired Norman Mailer's acrid crack that Salinger's is 'the greatest mind ever to stay in prep school'. He certainly left it in April 1942 when he was drafted and, after some intense lobbying ('I want to be an officer so bad,' he confessed) was commissioned as an infantry counter-intelligence officer. The army needed fluent German speakers. The war did not distract him from what he really wanted to be, however. For some time he had been writing stories based on a character called 'Holden Caulfield', with the sense 'he deserves to be a novel'. In 1944 Lt Salinger was posted to England. His unit, the 12th Infantry Regiment, landed on Utah Beach in the invasion and suffered extensive casualties. It suffered even more in the pointlessly bloody Hürtgen Forest battle and the Battle of the Bulge – more casualties, it is estimated, than any other infantry outfit. His biographer titles the chapter dealing with Salinger's war, 'Hell'. He won five battle stars and a decoration for valour.

Salinger had a bloody war – much bloodier than Mailer's, who hardly saw a shot fired in anger. But unlike Mailer, he never spoke or wrote about his frontline experiences, nor about the effect which the liberation of Dachau concentration camp had on a Jew, all of whose Viennese-Jewish friends, he discovered, had perished in the Holocaust. It was, his daughter later recalled, 'the unspoken', the unwritable, the irremovable. One recalls the last line of *Catcher*, 'don't ever tell anybody anything. If you do, you start missing everybody.'

After the war, Salinger penned two breakthrough stories for the *New Yorker*, 'A Perfect Day for Bananafish' and 'For Esmé – with Love and Squalor'. Both can be read as tinged with something his generation of exhausted warriors had never heard of, PTSD (post-traumatic stress disorder – earlier called 'shellshock'). Both stories expressed longing for childhood/adolescent worlds, a world Kenneth Slawenski calls 'children ice skating and little girls in soft blue dresses'. Three years later, *The Catcher in the Rye* would confirm this psychological retreat into the childhood past. Holden's three-day escape into New York, published in 1951, became wildly popular in the youth-rebellion decade of the 1960s, but is actually rooted in the year 1936–7, when Salinger was sixteen and the nightmare still to come invisibly in the future. These time settings are routinely overlooked by readers.

On demobilisation, Salinger, for reasons which are obscure, chose to stay in Germany as a civilian working for the Defense Department. Even more puzzling, he married a German woman, Sylvia Welter, wangling her French papers ('fraternisation' – marriage with the former enemy – was forbidden). Sylvia is recorded as having been a fanatic anti-Semitic Nazi and the marriage dissolved almost as soon as it formed. Salinger returned to New York in 1946 and took up residence in his former stamping ground, Greenwich Village. For a few years his lifestyle was bohemian – drink, girls, cards and a dedication to the perfection of his stories. 'Bananafish' (published in the *New Yorker*, in January 1948) introduced at length the Glass family, his main subject matter over the next two decades. The saintly Seymour Glass, back from war, disgusted with the human race, commits suicide (his earlier life emerged, collage-like, in later stories). The title alludes to a story within the story, told on the beach to a little girl, Sybil, about the fabulous fish whose piggish gluttony (like the monkey's hand in the peanut jar) is his downfall.

'For Esmé – with Love and Squalor' (published in the *New Yorker* in April 1950) also sets the fallen world of adulthood against the Wordsworthian purity of the child. In Devon, England, two months before the Normandy invasion, 'Sergeant X' meets a young, charmingly precocious girl, Esmé (manifestly upper class). On learning that the American writes, she lodges a request for a story, adding, 'I'm an avid reader':

> I told her I certainly would, if I could. I said that I wasn't terribly prolific.
>
> 'It doesn't have to be terribly prolific! Just so that it isn't childish and silly.' She reflected. 'I prefer stories about squalor.'
>
> 'About what?' I said, leaning forward.
>
> 'Squalor. I'm extremely interested in squalor.'

The story is a perfect example of Salinger's control of idiom infused with tactful symbolism: Esmé's father's broken watch – her later gift to him – is the last object described in the story: time has gone wrong.

Amazingly Salinger had difficulty in getting *The Catcher in the Rye* accepted. One editor thought Holden 'crazy'. Who wanted that? Holden – the 'great phony-slayer' (Mary McCarthy's description) eventually appeared in print in July 1951. Only the children in Holden's world are unphony – his dead brother Allie and his little sister, Phoebe. He has run away from school – but he will never arrive at where he is running towards, any more than Dorothy will get over the rainbow. Holden will never, in his own image, be the catcher, saving children from the 'fall' (the cliff on the edge of the rye field – adulthood, we deduce). What he needs – and will never get – is someone to 'catch' him. On the run in New York, staked by a handout from his grandmother, Holden drops out for three days: he drinks, has an unsuccessful date with an old flame, calls up a prostitute, is mugged by her pimp, and is hit on by a gay teacher (a 'flit'), writing it all up from a hospital in California. Is it what therapists nowadays call 'journaling' – an exercise to facilitate cure? Or is it a memoir?

As the 1950s moved on, Salinger turned away from the literary world ('It's a goddam embarrassment, publishing') into writing as pure meditation, a private, unshared act of 'self realization' in which readers were unwelcome intruders. The gobbets of the Glassiad which he released, grudgingly (to an increasingly disaffected *New Yorker*), perplexed his admirers. He did not seem to care. He found congenial cosmic reassurance in Zen and Buddhism, Taoism and Vedanta. In 1952, he left New York for Waldenesque seclusion in Cornish, New Hampshire, building a workshop in the garden (his 'bunker') of his 90-acre property. In 1955 he had married a woman fifteen years his junior, Claire Douglas.

It was assumed that he was working on the Glass Family saga and its seven offspring that had begun with 'Bananafish'. Particles emerged into print with 'Franny' (1955), 'Raise High the Roof Beam, Carpenters' (1955), 'Zooey' (1957) and 'Seymour: An Introduction' (1959). He made the cover of *Time* in September 1961 and his last foray into print with a new work was 'Hapworth 16, 1924', a novella that took up 80 pages in the *New Yorker*. It takes the form of a letter from summer camp written by seven-year-old Seymour Glass (the suicidal character in 'Bananafish'). 'Hapworth 16' was received badly – and Salinger took the reception badly.

His marriage to Claire Douglas produced two children and lasted twelve years (a very long time by Salinger's standards: his two other longest relationships were with his beloved Schnauzer Benny and his trusty typewriter). His religious prohibition on sex-for-pleasure evidently contributed to the break-up, as did the Thoreauesque life at Cornish. It seems the characters in his fiction were as real to him as any actual humans. When Elia Kazan implored him for permission to dramatise *Catcher* for the Broadway stage, Salinger declined on the grounds that 'I fear Holden wouldn't like it.' As the years passed he buried his tracks (letters, private papers) as methodically as he could, and had a series of relationships with increasingly younger women.

Joyce Maynard, an eighteen-year-old student when he first became involved with her in 1972, published a venomous account of their early-1970s relationship, which caused him chagrin. In 1986, he used every resource of American law successfully to neutralise a biography by Ian Hamilton, who wrote a rueful un-biography instead. It confirmed a widespread suspicion that America's most famous novelist had finally flipped. As his last public act, in 2009, Salinger again successfully used the lawyer to suppress a follow-up to *Catcher in the Rye*, '60 years on'. He married, for the third time, in 1992 – a woman forty years his junior. The bunker protected him for almost half a century. The fearsome literary estate he set up, before his death, may well keep what the bunker contained out of posterity's view for ever.

FN   Jerome David Salinger
MRT *The Catcher in the Rye*
Biog K. Slawenski, *J. D. Salinger: A Life Raised High* (2010)

219. Charles Willeford 1919–1988

*Like, some of these other Tankers I knew used to swap bottles of liquor with infantrymen
in exchange for prisoners, and then just shoot 'em for fun. I used to say, 'Goddamn it,
will you stop shooting those prisoners!' And they would just shrug and say, 'Hell, they'd
shoot us if they caught us!'*
Willeford recalling his war-time experience as a tank commander

Charles Willeford lived more life, and a harder life, than most writers. Born in Little
Rock, Arkansas, his father died of TB in 1922 and his mother of the same disease
shortly after. He was brought by relatives in Los Angeles and ran away, aged thirteen, hoboing through America. In 1939, he joined the army, marrying before
being posted overseas to Europe in 1942. A non-commissioned tank commander,
Willeford fought at the Battle of the Bulge (not too far from J. D. Salinger and Kurt
Vonnegut), won the Silver Star, the Bronze Star, a Purple Heart and the Luxem-
bourg Croix de Guerre. He remained in the army after the war, running a services'
radio station in Japan until 1949. His first publication, a book of poetry, was published in 1948.

Discharged, and divorced, following an unsuccessful attempt to study art in
Peru, Willeford joined up again in 1949 – this time round, the US Air Force. He
would remain in uniform until 1956, remarrying and publishing three novels along
the way. According to his blurbs he was thereafter variously a professional horse
trainer, a boxer, a radio announcer, and an artist in France. He acquired a degree
and taught English from 1967 to 1985, at the Miami-Dade Community College,
in Florida. He divorced for a second time in 1976. For some years Willeford had
reviewed mystery novels for the *Miami Herald* and had himself written a handful
of crime and PI potboilers. They promised nothing wonderful. But in the four last
years of his life, beginning with *Miami Blues* (1984), he produced a cluster of works
which are among the best things ever done in the genre. They feature the series
hero, Detective 'Hoke' Moseley, and are set in a closely observed Florida criminal
underworld, in the aftermath of the huge Cuban ('Mariel') influx of the 1970s,
when a spiteful Castro emptied his jails and asylums onto America's shores.

The Moseley novels are tinged with a wry comedy, summed up in one of his
favourite epigrams from the congenially sardonic Karl Kraus: 'Life is an effort that
deserves a better cause.' An ironic portrait of the hero emerges over the course of
the Moseley sequence. When first encountered, he lives (if that is the word) in a
hotel – the Eldorado – where he has a rent-free room in return for moonlighting as
hotel detective. He is barred promotion by the Homicide Division's affirmative action

policy, which favours Blacks, Latins and women. In pursuit of a psychopathic robber in *Miami Blues*, Hoke is beaten to a pulp, has his dentures destroyed, and his service revolver and badge stolen. The robber goes on a criminal rampage, impersonating Hoke with the stolen ID – the final insult.

One of the unusual aspects of the series is the progression in the hero's life from one novel to another, rendering it a genuine sequence rather than a series. In *New Hope for the Dead* (1985; epigraph: 'Man's unhappiness stems from his inability to sit quietly in his room' – Pascal), Hoke has risen somewhat. He is on active homicide duty, but has an awkward partner, Ellita Sanchez, with whom, such being life on the street, he eventually shacks up. A complication is his ex-wife dumping their two daughters on him after she has taken off with a black baseball player. *Sideswipe* (1987; epigraph: 'There's a lot of bastards out there!' – William Carlos Williams) finds Hoke, a pregnant Ellita and his two teenage daughters living cosily in a suburban rented house. *The Way We Die Now* (1988; epigraph: 'No one owns life. But anyone with a frying pan owns death' – William Burroughs) finds Hoke still working on the 'cold case' file. Domestically his life is happier than it has ever been, and he is thirty-five pounds heavier on Ellita's cooking. He has 'all the advantages of a family man (except for a regular sex life) and few, if any, of the disadvantages.' It cannot, of course, last.

Nor, alas, did its author. Having received a massive $225,000 advance, Willeford died as the glowing reviews were coming in. He was buried, in recognition of his distinguished war service, at Arlington National Cemetery. Epitaph: 'A hell of a lot better writer than you might think'?

FN   Charles Ray Willeford
MRT   *Miami Blues*
Biog   www.dennismcmillan.com/charleswillefo/biograp.htm

220. Isaac Asimov 1920–1992

If my doctor told me I had only six minutes to live, I wouldn't brood. I'd type a little faster.

Asimov was born in Petrovichi in the USSR, the son of a prosperous miller unlucky enough to be a Jew in a savagely anti-Semitic time and place. They were luckier than some. Asimov's family contrived to emigrate to the USA, and the infant Isaac was naturalised in 1928. Asimov Sr went on to run a candy store in Brooklyn. At home Yiddish was Isaac's first language. He grew up a brilliant, over-achieving high school pupil, going on to take degrees in biochemistry at Columbia University, culminating in a Ph.D. in 1948. A year later, Dr Asimov (he relished the title, even more than Jewish mothers proverbially do) was appointed to a teaching post in biochemistry at Boston University. He would lecture in its school of medicine for the remainder of his professional career, with a break for war service, 1942–6. He was proud, to the point of arrogance, of the Asimov brain (and a long-serving Vice President of Mensa to certify its 200+ IQ score).

An early fan of pulp SF (much to his father's disgust – although the Asimov candy stores had a profitable sideline in the product), Isaac came under the wing of the ferociously right-wing John W. Campbell, editor of *Astounding Science Fiction*, a man, it was said, who made Ayn Rand look like a pinko. Asimov published his first story with Campbell in 1939, an ominous year, and his first science fiction novel, *Pebble in the Sky* (Earth becomes radioactive, following nuclear war), was published in 1950 – a period when nuclear war was imminently expected and middle-class America was investing in fallout shelters and guns to defend them against working-class, shelterless, Americans. In that same year – 1950 – there appeared Asimov's most famous volume, *I, Robot*, a collection of short stories published over previous years, expounding the author's 'Three Laws of Robotics'. Those involved in the relevant scientific field have always taken them seriously. The most ambitious – verging on Messianic – of Asimov's fictional projects, the 'Foundation' trilogy (1951–3), followed shortly after. It aimed to emulate, with the blunter tools of science fiction, Gibbon's *Decline and Fall of the Roman Empire*. Nothing small for Isaac Asimov.

The most prolific of writers, Asimov published some sixty works of SF, fifteen crime mysteries (which he began writing in 1956), a hundred or more popularising works of 'science fact', and scholarly treatises on Shakespeare, the Bible and quantum mechanics – 600 titles in all. He retired from full-time academic life to concentrate on writing in 1958, winning all the highest awards in SF with monotonous regularity. *The Gods Themselves* (1973) scooped up both the Hugo and the Nebula Prizes for that year. A Science Fiction Writers of America poll in 1979 voted 'Nightfall' the best SF story of all time (first published in 1941, it portrays a planet in which night comes only once a millennium).

Asimov was married twice and is recorded as being a 'claustrophile', phobic about flying (he took to the air only twice in his life), agnostic ('Humanist' was his term), an admirer of P. G. Wodehouse, and grotesquely malcoordinated physically. Michael White's 'unauthorised' biography (1994) sprinkles some blackwash on the Asimov image. He was promiscuously unfaithful in his first marriage, although uxorious in the second. He underwent bloody tenure and promotion battles at Boston

University – who never, in his view, fully 'respected' his genius. He tried to dodge the draft in 1941 – and, finally, his 'Three Laws' may not have been his original idea. None the less, Asimov's greatness survives the odd black spot on it.

He died of Aids acquired from a bad blood transfusion during a heart bypass operation in 1983. The fact was revealed only ten years after his death, to protect the reputation of his doctors – and, one suspects, *his* posthumous reputation. His collected papers, donated to his Boston University alma mater, occupy 71 metres of shelf-space. Elsewhere in the Library there are printed volumes by him in nine out of the ten Dewey Decimal classification categories: a record.

FN Isaac Asimov (born Isaak Yudovich Ozimov)
MRT *I, Robot*
Biog M. White, *Isaac Asimov: A Life of the Grand Master of Science Fiction* (1994; 2005)

221. Ray Bradbury 1920–

The Louis Armstrong of SF. Kingsley Amis

Ray Bradbury was born in Waukegan, Illinois (the Green Town of his fiction), where his father worked as a telephone lineman. The family, uprooted by the Depression, moved nomadically during Ray's childhood, mainly between Illinois and Arizona, a state whose desert landscapes influenced the author's later depictions of Mars. Bradbury claimed to have picked up his impressive learning from 'Carnegies' (public libraries) and his lifelong dedication to science fiction from coming across copies of Hugo Gernsback's *Amazing Stories* at the age of six. Equally precociously, he was writing his own stories in the genre at eleven. As a child Ray was fascinated by magic and, like others of his generation, was entranced by the 'Century of Progress' exhibit at World's Fair in Chicago, 1933.

Eventually the family settled in southern California in 1934. This was to be Bradbury's home and literary base for the rest of his life. He left school at thirteen; there was no question of college. He haunted public libraries and sold newspapers on street corners. His first SF story was published in 1938 and in 1941 he attended a writing class run by Robert A. Heinlein, already a star of the genre. He would be, however, the least formulaic of writers in an overwhelmingly formulaic genre. Bradbury's philosophy was: 'When writing, just jump off the cliff and build your wings on the way down.' Forrest J. Ackerman was helpful at this stage of Bradbury's career, promoting him on the fanzine and word-of-mouth networks which 'SF's number one fan' (as Ackerman was called) had mobilised in the Los Angeles area – along with the world's greatest collection of genre memorabilia. Bradbury was rejected for military service in the Second World War on grounds of poor eyesight. Literature was the gainer. At the same period – 1942 – he took up writing full-time, turning out a string of short stories for the pulps and slicks which were booming during the war. A favourite outlet was *Weird Tales*, whose title neatly defines the Bradbury style.

He married in 1947, having met his future wife, Marguerite ('Maggie') McClure (1922–2003) in a bookshop where, initially, she mistook him for a shoplifter – shabbily trench-coated as he was in the burning Californian sun. After marriage, Maggie helped support her husband, working in an advertising agency, while he stayed at home to write. 'Had she not,' as one obituary wittily put it, 'the proverbial butterfly would have been squashed and the future of high-imaginative literature would have been altered for all time.' They would eventually have four daughters together and, at their most populous, twenty-two cats – Mrs Bradbury loved the beasts. Judging by the eight-legged, robotically venomous Mechanical Hound in *Fahrenheit 451*, Ray seems to have shared a feline dislike of all things canine. Bradbury admitted infidelities to his biographer, but the marriage, which lasted fifty-six years, manifestly survived them.

Recognition of his talent came early – as it often does in SF, with its highly developed critical and word-of-mouth circuits. He won an O. Henry Award in 1948 and a 'best author' award from the National Fantasy Fan Federation a year later. In 1950 Bradbury broke through into international fame with *The Martian Chronicles*, a collection which was 'made' by an influential review from Christopher Isherwood. The stories in the volume compose a haunting panorama of pioneer life on a Mars which is alternately Edenic and horrific. Bradbury's most famous novel, *Fahrenheit 451* (1953), a fable of book-burning in the future, targeted the current McCarthyite witch-hunting in the United States and satirised the intellectually numbing spread of television, and its destruction, as Bradbury saw it, of print culture. 'I don't try to describe the future. I try to prevent it,' he said. He could also misunderstand it.

At this period Bradbury was recruited to work in film. Among other assignments, he wrote the screenplay for John Huston's *Moby Dick* (1956). When he confessed to the director that he'd never read Melville's novel, he was assured it was OK: the studio paid people to do that kind of thing for you. His own work was also successfully filmed, notably *Fahrenheit 451*, directed by François Truffaut, in 1966. In later life, Bradbury's knees buckled with the honours with which SF loves to load its most admired practitioners. His great achievement, particularly in the shorter fiction was to raise the quality of writing in the genre, opening the way to the literary experimentations of New Wave writers in the 1970s and 1980s. Bradbury liberated SF from the accusation made by Kurt Vonnegut (in the person of his SF hack 'Kilgore Trout') that its writers had great ideas, but couldn't write worth a damn.

In a genre preoccupied with technology and hardware, Bradbury was unusual in never having a driving licence and not flying (and then very reluctantly) on an aeroplane until he was sixty-two. Arthur C. Clarke, an enthusiast for gadgetry, gave him a laptop computer, only to discover, as Bradbury's biographer records, that 'he used it as a drink coaster'. Bradbury suffered a devastating stroke in 1999, which left him able only to communicate by pen and pad. He none the less contrived to write fiction, even in this terminal condition. All he had ever needed was pen, paper, imagination and a mental cliff to fall off.

FN   Raymond Douglas Bradbury
MRT *Fahrenheit 451*
Biog S. Weller, *The Bradbury Chronicles: The Life of Ray Bradbury* (2005)

222. Charles Bukowski 1920–1994

I can't see any other place than L.A.

James Joyce's *Portrait of the Artist as a Young Man* actually opens with the portrait of the artist as a baby. Little Stephen sits alongside the family feet as they argue – passionately – about Ireland and the Parnell scandal. Charles Bukowski's portrait of himself as a young man in *Ham on Rye* (1982), opens, allusively, with much the same scene:

> The first thing I remember is being under something. It was a table, I saw a table leg, I saw the legs of the people, and a portion of the tablecloth hanging down. It was dark under there. I liked being under there. It must have been in Germany ... I felt good under the table. Nobody seemed to know that I was there.

Say 'Hank Bukowski' and most readers will think 'Barfly, Bum, Bohemian' – not a lover of Joyce. *Ham on Rye*, dedicated to the author's early years, is so-called because he's Los Angeles through and through, but German (rye bread) by origin. Bukowski had many gifts, not least for resonant titles such as this: for example, *Crucifix in a Deathhand*; *At Terror Street and Agony Way*; *All the Assholes in the World and Mine*; *Erections, Ejaculations, Exhibitions and General Tales of Ordinary Madness*.

But, many will think, the title which sums up his life work best is that of the column which he wrote for many years in a semi-underground newspaper, 'Notes of a Dirty Old Man'.

The DOM was born Heinrich Karl Bukowski, the son of a German mother and a German-American serviceman serving in Europe after the First World War. He claimed – frequently – to have been 'bastardised' by his 'monster father' but his Catholic parents were in fact decently married and considerably less monstrous than he paints them. The Bukowskis moved to Maryland in 1923, where Heinrich Karl became Henry ('Hank') Charles, although his parents' habit of dressing him as a 'German' led to bullying and a solitary early childhood. It was not helped by disfiguring acne – a lifelong affliction: he was 'so ugly', he said, 'that girls spit on my shadow'. His pimples were the 'size of apples' and left volcanic craters still visible on photographs of his face sixty years later. In 1930 the Bukowskis moved on to Los Angeles. An early chapter in *Ham on Rye* describes his father being humiliated stealing oranges, by a gun-wielding farmer, who did not take kindly to citrus poaching. He claims thereafter to have despised his parent and to have suffered beatings from him – 'a cruel shiny bastard with bad breath', and not that much of a provider. Aged sixteen, as he proudly recalls, he knocked the shiny bastard out and the beatings stopped. At the same time, he discovered his love of alcohol. Like LA, it would be his friend for life.

Dyslexia, a dysfunctional family, and disrespect for all authority made him an awkward child. He recalls bullying and furtive investigations of little schoolmates' panties. Bukowski left Los Angeles High School to study journalism at community college, but he soon dropped out and picked up menial work where he could. These drop-out years are commemorated in Bukoswski's 1975 novel, *Factotum*. Although in free fall socially, he was reading widely and intelligently and it was in the LA Public Library that he came across the author who would be most influential on his mature writing, John Fante – specifically Fante's novel *Ask the Dust* (1939). Fante cultivated a style of fragmented immediacy, with low-life LA settings and a high autobiographical element (there was 93 per cent autobiography in his own fiction, Bukowski later calculated).

Bukowski did not quite dodge the draft, but he more or less evaded it, letting others fight for America. He occasionally voiced a liking for Hitler. 'If he had any politics he was a fucking fascist,' observed one friend. Psychiatrists judged him, eventually, unfit to serve. 'Extreme sensitivity' was the odd reason recorded on the report. Sex may have come into it. He did not, as he liked to confess, get laid until he was twenty-three. His early attempts at writing were everywhere rejected and over the next decade he went into a long debauch – his 'barfly' years, as he called them. He had by now dropped 'Henry' in favour of 'Charles' in his pen name. Henry reminded him too much of his father, he said. He nevertheless kept the family first name in his fictional alter ego (and hero of five of his six novels), 'Henry Chinaski'. Over these years he kept body and soul together with short-term 'shit jobs'. He roomed in crummy lodging houses, bummed around America, and was regularly in and out of the drunk tank. When he had money, he drank it or lost it at the race track – his other addiction.

In these early vagrant years Bukowski came across another work which would contribute to his own distinct style, Dostoevsky's *Notes from Underground*. His experiences in the lower depths of Los Angeles furnished him with the store of material he would recycle, and lavishly exaggerate, in his later writing. It was during this period that he fell in with his first long-time partner, Jane Cooney Baker. Like Bukowski, she was alcoholic, morally dissolute and considerably less of a catch than Faye Dunaway, who plays her in the 1987 film *Barfly*. He regarded her as his muse and used her as his bed-warming room-mate for five years. But Baker lacked Bukowski's canny survival instincts and their dissipation *à deux* broke up and she drank herself to death a couple of years later.

Bukowski lavished Baker's memory with elegies and then went on to marry the poet Barbara Frye in 1957. Physically deformed, acutely shy, Frye had never even had a boyfriend before Bukowski. The marriage lasted two years. In the early 1950s Bukowski had entered the employment of the US Mail, as a postal sorter and carrier. He would toss parcels around by night, and write furiously by day, honing the image of himself as hell-raising, bohemian, barfly *maudit*. This ten-year stint is commemorated in his first novel, *Post Office* (1971). The rise of the Beats (to whom Bukowski owed no literary allegiance, or respect, whatsoever) created a cultural environment favourable to Bukowski's idiosyncratic West Coast bohemianism. Wild men were in. The difference between him and Kerouac was that he was really wild, not a mama's boy.

His poems were at last being picked up by the small magazines which were thriving at the time. His first chapbook, *Flower, Fist and Bestial Wail*, was published in 1959. At around the same time, the death of his father brought him a handsome $15,000 nest egg, which he prudently squirrelled away for a rainy day. Making up for lost time, Bukowski consoled himself with a string of partners by one of whom, Frances Smith, he had a daughter. According to Howard Sounes, the first word the little girl learned to read was 'liquor'. Smith was herself a well-regarded hippy poet and was instrumental in getting the bearishly anti-social Bukowski talked about where it mattered. At this period, encouraged by one of his small-press patrons, he began writing short pieces of autobiographical fiction around the character 'Henry

Chinaski'. They were collected as *Confessions of a Man Insane Enough to Live with Beasts* (1965). His growing profile in avant-garde West Coast circles led to what would go on to be a career-long association with the most distinguished of the 1960s small presses, Black Sparrow. Guaranteed payment allowed Bukowski, at the age of fifty, to leave the Post Office and, at last, write full time.

He promptly began writing novels drawing on Fante and Hemingway, using his distinctive spare, dismembered, ironic and self-centred style. Above all, his fiction was 'real'. 'Writing,' he once said, 'was never work for me ... All I had to do was be there.' New women passed through his life. He used them (cruelly in some cases) in his 1978 novel, *Women*. Throughout the 1970s and 1980s Bukowski's reputation grew – he was becoming a literary cult. The image was carefully promoted by readings in which he would drunkenly rant and turn violently on his audience. They lapped it up. His readings survive in a DVD entitled *There's Gonna be a God Damn Riot in Here*. In point of fact, as Howard Sounes records, the 'God Damn Riot' was all an act. But a good one – and profitable: he could pull in as much as $1,000 a riot.

The tenor of his personal life was less riotous. In the 1970s he embarked on a relationship with the sculptress Linda King. According to his publisher, John Martin, 'she was probably the first real sexual relationship he'd ever had in his life'. He bought a house and a smart BMW. He was still drinking heavily – but he had always been able to handle quantities which would destroy less robust writers. These were the years of what he grandly called his 'final decadence' – but none the less in a comfortable house he owned, with a good car and a well-stocked full refrigerator. And always a new woman. In 1976 Bukowski met Linda Lee Beighle. She was twenty-four years his junior and an aspiring actress. The relationship lasted, in the usual on-and-off way, and they married in 1985. Worldwide fame, and the monumentalisation of the Bukowski image, came with the movie *Barfly*, two years later, in which Mickey Rourke played Chinaski and Faye Dunaway played 'Wanda' (i.e. Baker). Bukowski's mixed feelings about the movie are inscribed in his outrageous 1989 *roman-à-clef*, *Hollywood*. See, for example, his pen portrait of 'Tab Jones', a Welsh singer who has made it big in Las Vegas:

> Here is this Tab Jones. He sings. His shirt is open and the black hairs on his chest show. The hairs are sweating. He wears a big silver cross in these sweating hairs. His mouth is a horrible hole cut into a pancake. He's got on tight pants and he's wearing a dildo. He grabs his balls and sings about all the good things he can do for women. He really sings badly, I mean, he is *terrible*. All about what he can do to women, but he's a fake, he really wants his tongue up some man's anus.
>
> Poor Tom.

In his later years Bukowski became very rich but never admitted to himself that he had sold out. He died, not of the booze he had swilled all his life, but of leukaemia, leaving behind his last novel, *Pulp*. His gravestone (arguably his last poem) reads:

Henry Charles Bukowski Jr.
Hank
('Don't Try')
1920–1994

Between the dates is the image of a professional boxer.

FN   Henry ('Hank') Charles Bukowski Jr (born Heinrich Karl Bukowski)
MRT   *Ham on Rye*
Biog   H. Sounes, *Charles Bukowski: Locked in the Arms of a Crazy Life* (1998)

223. Dick Francis 1920–2010

She's a tremendous help when I'm looking for words.

Francis was born in Pembrokeshire of semi-gentrified stock. His father was a prosperous dealer in horseflesh, and the child grew up surrounded by the beasts which would be the most important thing in his life. Infant Dick won his first race, aged eight, and left school at fifteen, intending to be a jockey. A sudden growth and weight spurt in his teens meant that his chosen line would be 'jump', not 'flat' – the sport of kings and midgets. Francis was an unusual child in wanting to grow up but not to grow.

Of military service age when war broke out, Francis volunteered for the cavalry but was recruited into the RAF – first as a non-commissioned engine-fitter, then, after much pestering on his part, as a pilot. He got his wings, and his pips, in 1944. In his autobiography, he says that he was actively involved in the dam-buster raid. Since that heroic event took place in 1943, he could not have done – unless as a civilian stowaway with the bouncing bombs in the bomb-bay. In fact his war service was disappointingly uneventful, though not, it must be said, from any lack of personal pluck. The career he chose on leaving the service in 1947 meant at least one bone-breaking fall a season and bruises all the way. On his marriage, in the same year, 1947, photographs show the bridegroom's right arm in a sling. Francis would break his collar bone nine times in his riding career – a recurrent injury that eventually drove him out of the sport. His wife Mary was a graduate in modern languages, a teacher and a woman of extraordinary energy (even after a bout of polio in 1949) and of volubly right-wing views. They had two sons, Merrick and Felix. The year 1947 was a good one in every way for Francis, with sixteen wins and marriage to the woman of his life.

Francis was always reckoned in the top ten of his profession, and as champion jockey in 1953–7, he rode for the Queen Mother. But in 1956 Francis's life, as he liked to say, 'ended'. Everything else would be 'afterlife'. It was a dramatic final act: in the Grand National that year, riding for the QM, leading the field by many lengths, Francis's horse, Devon Loch mysteriously collapsed only yards short of the finishing line. Francis had never won the National, the peak of a jump jockey's career, and his disappointment was bitter. Was Devon Loch nobbled? Perhaps; it's a recurrent theme in Francis's thrillers. But the most likely explanation seems to have been a gigantic fart which was so explosive as to prostrate the unluckily flatulent beast. Francis retired, having ridden 2,305 races and 345 winners. In his retirement he began writing insider and tipster columns for the *Sunday Express*, a line of work (pitifully paid) which he continued until 1973. His first racing world thriller, *Dead Cert*, came out in 1962. He would thereafter, until 2001, produce one a year.

According to the novelist himself, he was no Henry James: 'I start at Chapter 1, page 1, and plod on to THE END.' Starting gates and finishing lines made him comfortable. His invariable practice was to begin a new book every 1 January, and deliver the MS to Michael Joseph on 8 May for publication in September. As *Private Eye* put it, with neat sarcasm, in 1992: 'All his novels are narrated by a male hero. Although this hero begins with a handicap, whether physical or psychological (bereavement, divorce, unrequited love, family tragedy, whatever), he always comes out a winner, proving himself brave and honest, honourable and taciturn, heterosexual but horse-loving, one of nature's gents.' What one detects in the above – as with many who profess to be dismissive of Francis – is that the (anonymous) critic clearly *reads* the novels. Once opened, a Francis thriller sticks to the eyes like glue.

Nobbling and criminal betting coups are recurrent plot devices. In racing circles, Francis is routinely accused of bringing his sport into disrepute. The charge is belied by his evident love of it. His series hero Sid Halley, injured former champion jockey, is self-confessedly a version of the author (see, for example, *Odds Against* (1965), *Whip Hand* (1979) – Francis has a knack in racy titles). *Forfeit* (1968) is regarded as Francis's most self-revealing novel. His autobiography, *The Sport of Queens* (1957), is anything but self-revealing. According to Julian Symons (the critic who made crime fiction critically respectable), 'Francis has been overpraised.' One of his more famous overpraisers was Philip Larkin, who declared Francis 'always 20 times more readable than the average Booker entry' (he knew whereof he spoke – Larkin was chair of the panel in 1978. Francis, alas, was not longlisted for *Trial Run*). Francis was also a favourite with Kingsley Amis, Queen Elizabeth II, and, of course, his employer, her 'mum'.

Dick and Mary Francis, both broken in body, retired to Florida in their last years. Graham Lord's flagrantly 'unauthorised' biography, published in 1999, alleged outright that Mary had ghosted every one of the 'Dick Francis' novels. According to Lord, she confirmed his thesis, telling him that her authorship was suppressed in order to preserve the 'taut ... masculine' feel of the works. Two pieces of evidence support Lord. First is the fact that the Francises did not sue him. Second that on Mary's death in 2000 Francis 'retired' from writing. He came back, eight years later, in 'collaboration' with his son Felix. But what does it matter? Horses don't win races by themselves: jockeys don't win races by themselves – they win them in partnership. Why shouldn't it be the same with novels? He was the horse, she was the jockey.

FN   Dick Francis (Richard Stanley Francis)
MRT *Forfeit*
Biog G. Lord, *Dick Francis: A Racing Life* (1999)

224. P. D. James 1920–

Taming our sleeping tigers.

There is a telling moment in *Original Sin* (P. D. James's ninth novel, published 1994) when Adam Dalgliesh, P. D. James's well-read Scotland Yard detective and published poet, with special responsibility for 'sensitive' cases, surveys the study of a deceased and old-fashioned spinster detective novelist. No one likes Esmé Carling's brand of fiction any more. Her bookshelves Dalgliesh notes (with an uneasy sense of his own superannuation), are dominated by 'women writers of the Golden Age':

> Surveying the titles so reminiscent of the 1930s, of village policemen cycling
> to the scene of the murder, tugging their forelocks to the gentry, of autopsies
> undertaken by eccentric general practitioners after evening surgery and unlikely
> denouements in the library, he took them out and glanced at them at random.
> *Death by Dancing*, apparently set in the world of formation ballroom competitions,
> *Cruising to Murder, Death by Drowning, The Mistletoe Murders*. He replaced them
> carefully, feeling no condescension.

James, seventy-four years old when she published *Original Sin*, belongs, in terms of years lived, to Esmé Carling's generation. In terms of the evolution of her genre – the crime novel – she writes very much to the present. Moreover she has taken that genre to levels of literary respectability far beyond those represented by Gladys Mitchell (1901–83), clearly the target of James's mild satire here (Mitchell, oddly, was Philip Larkin's favourite crime novelist; for her cosiness, one suspects). Ruth Rendell, James's coeval in the genre, hails *Original Sin* as 'the *Middlemarch* of crime novels' – in other words, 'Literature'.

Phyllis Dorothy James was born in 1920 in Oxford, into a gas-lit world permeated by the 'distinctive odour of Anglicanism' – to which she remains faithful. Her father, just back from machine-gunning Germans, worked in the Inland Revenue. Her upbringing, as she recalls it in her autobiography, was glum but not cruel. In a *Guardian* interview she recalled that 'My storytelling began very early, certainly well before I was 10. We lived then in Ludlow on the Welsh borders and my younger sister, brother and I slept in one large nursery, a double bed for Monica and myself, and Edward in a single one against the wall. I was expected at night to tell them stories until either I rebelled or they fell asleep. The stories were invariably improbably exciting and mysterious, and the animal hero was called, somewhat unoriginally, Percy Pig.'

She realised, almost as soon as she was capable of realising anything, that she was the child of an unhappy marriage. Her father, an intelligent man, suffered from that post-First World War trauma then called 'neurasthenia' – dead emotions. Her mother, a warm, 'unintelligent' woman, had a total nervous breakdown and was forcibly institutionalised in an asylum when Phyllis was fourteen. Her memory of the event – one of the most damaging of her life – is 'blank', suppressed. The running of the house, and care of Monica and Edward, devolved on her as eldest child. She was, from childhood, eminently capable of taking such things on. Why does this gifted woman choose to write detective stories? Because, she says, she loves 'structure' and 'order'. And – one might impertinently presume – is simultaneously running away from the acute disorder of her childhood. 'Even as a child,' she recalls, 'I had a sense that I was two people; the one who experienced the trauma, the pain, the happiness, and the other who stood aside and watched with a disinterested ironic eye.'

Aged sixteen, she was obliged by the family's financial difficulties to leave school, where she would have done well, to work at various clerking jobs. While helping out with a festival dramatic production in Cambridge she met and fell in love (not 'overwhelmingly') with a medical student, Connor Bantry White. They married in 1941, 'five days after I came of age'. Everyone was marrying – it was the war. But as with her father, the war did not end with peace. Returning from service abroad in the Royal Army Medical Corps, Connor began to show signs of mental illness and alcoholism. James, meanwhile, had risen in her line of work (the wartime absence of male competition helped) to a professional level. She was, in her thirties, a senior administrator in the health service in London.

Like Trollope, she had long been in the habit of getting up before 'work' to write. 'I think,' she recalls, 'I knew that I would be a novelist almost as soon as I was able to read, but for a variety of reasons – including the war, my husband's illness, the need to find and persevere in a safe career which would provide the necessary weekly cheque – I was a late starter.' Her debut novel – and Adam Dalgliesh's – *Cover Her Face* (the Othello allusion hints at her own desperately unhappy marriage, as does the reversion to her maiden name) appeared in 1962. 'P. D. James' was forty-two years old. Her chosen pen name led many readers to assume she was a man. In what D. H. Lawrence called the 'man's world' she was a 'flier'. She had now moved to the Home Office where, following fast-track promotion, she was placed in charge of the Criminal Policy department. In 1964 her husband, after having spent years in various mental institutions, died at home of an overdose of drink and drugs, leaving two children for his wife to look after alone – he was forty-four years old. It was probably suicide. She thinks of him tenderly every day, she records in her autobiography.

As a civil servant, James was obliged to retire in her sixtieth year, which enabled her to turn her full attention to various good works on committees and writing. They were mainly, but not exclusively, Dalgliesh mysteries, a half a dozen of which appeared over the next fifteen years at two to three-year intervals. Their popularity was hugely boosted by TV adaptations, in which Dalgliesh was played by Roy Marsden as a moustached, taciturn, ruminative character. A radically different work was James's dystopia, *The Children of Men* (1992). The point is, there are no children: it is 1994 (not for James a far distant catastrophe) and men's fertility has plummeted, globally, to zero. No child is born after 1995 – sexual intercourse completes the journey it started with the pill in 1960. It is masturbation *à deux*. The world has been contracepted – society collapses. The novel was successfully filmed in 2009.

In 1991 James was made a life peer, sitting on the Conservative benches. In 1999, she published her autobiography, *Time to Be in Earnest*. It divulges relatively little of her private life (Faber wittily chose as its cover illustration half of her youthful portrait), but offers a vivid insight into her mind:

> So tomorrow, on 3rd August, I shall write the first entry in a record which I propose to keep for one year, from my seventy-seventh to my seventy-eighth birthday. Will I persist with this effort? Only time will tell. And will I be here at the end of the year? At seventy-seven that is not an irrational question. But then is

it irrational at any age? In youth we go forward caparisoned in immortality; it is only, I think, in age that we fully realize the transitoriness of life.

There is much that I remember but which is painful to dwell upon. I see no need to write about these things ... Like dangerous and unpredictable beasts they lie curled in the pit of the subconscious... . But then I am a writer ... I, a purveyor of popular genre fiction, and that great genius Jane Austen have the same expedient for taming our sleeping tigers.

The novel-writing cure, but not something available, alas, on the NHS. James suffered life-threatening heart failure in 2007. In hospital she devised what, it was said, would be her last (fourteenth) Dalgliesh novel, *The Private Patient* (2008) – murder in the operating theatre. Dalgliesh would be, by conservative estimate, some ninety years old by this date (still sprightlier than Poirot, who was applying his little grey cells to murders at the age of 130). The critic Peter Kemp identifies the essence of Dalgliesh mysteries as indeterminacy – solutions which remain cloudy: 'Characteristically at the end of one of her novels the mystery has been solved but all sorts of other quandaries remain. In some cases the victim is more repulsive than the murderer and you can see why the murderer has done it.' Often the murderer does it to purge the past – often the very distant past. In James's 1997 bestseller, *A Certain Justice*, there is any number of suspects (seven, as I calculate) for Dalgliesh to ponder on when a rising young woman lawyer is killed. It turns out to be the oldest barrister in her chambers, a man in his mid-seventies, avenging a wrong of some thirty years ago.

Beneath the whodunnit plots, and the long evolution of Adam Dalgliesh's interestingly deviant detective, P. D. James's novels are obsessed (the word is not too strong) with the generational conflict between young and old professional classes and what one might call 'the pathos of modernisation'. Her core readership, one suspects, is substantially composed of middle-aged, professional people, like herself, falling behind their time and none too pleased about it.

FN   (Baroness) Phyllis Dorothy James (later White)
MRT   *Original Sin*
Biog   P. D. James, *Time to Be in Earnest: A Fragment of Autobiography* (1999)

225. Paul Scott 1920–1978

There is a relation between the hours of our life and the centuries of time. Emerson

'India', linguists tell us, originally indicated every far-off country. 'Raj' is a word of Sanskrit origin, whose alternative modern form is the German 'Reich'. Britain's bloody conflict with the Third Reich in the early 1940s, and its scarcely less bloody struggle to preserve the 400-year-old Raj at the same period, supply the background to Paul Scott's *Raj Quartet*. Those few years are, historically, the moment of truth when things fell apart to reveal what had always been at the centre of Empire. Many admirers of Scott will have had a threefold experience of the *Quartet*. They will have read the novels as they came out, fitfully, between 1966 and 1975, and reread them as a single, coherent, entity. And they will have viewed the twelve-part 1984 Granada Television adaptation, *The Jewel in the Crown*. The TV narrative was dominated, as is the *Quartet*, by Ronald Merrick, played by Tim Pigott-Smith. Merrick is a corrupt and brutal police superintendent as we first encounter him; a bemedalled colonel, and ostensibly happily married, as we (and India) take our leave of him in the final instalment.

It is fiendishly difficult to establish any moral line on Merrick. He is no simple villain. It's complicated by the fact that his background is perplexingly parallel to that of his creator. Of lower-class origins (his father was a corner tobacconist) young Ronald was yanked out of school at fourteen. So too was fourteen-year-old Paul when his father's business as a commercial artist went bust. An intelligent lad, Merrick had 'just enough education to scrape into the Indian Police Service'. But not, of course, to hold the King's Commission, until, that is, the Japanese victories of 1942, when the armed forces were only too happy to use men of his calibre. Merrick was later commissioned in the Indian Army Service Corps (an unsmart branch of the military). He could never have aspired to the promotion in peace-time. Merrick is said, behind his back in the 'mess' and the 'club', not to be 'one of us' – white, that is, but not 'pukka'. Merrick's CV is the mirror reflection of the author's life. Scott was conscripted into the army as a private in 1940 and was shipped out to India three years later as an officer cadet with the scratch army mustered to repel an expected Japanese invasion (including, as it happened, Brian Aldiss). He would be an officer – but not *quite* a gentleman. 'Scott', as his biographer, Hilary Spurling, summarises it, 'ended up a captain in the Indian Army Service Corps, organising supply lines for the Fourteenth Army's unexpectedly successful reconquest of Burma'. Grocer to Britain's frontline heroes, that is.

His uneasy social pedigree means Merrick can never give the 'right' answer to that officer-class question 'and where were you at school, Ronnie?'. But the same *déclassé* status in the mess gives him a clarity of vision denied his class-blinkered colleagues. 'Amateurs', as he contemptuously calls them. He sees colonial India for what it really is. So too, one assumes, did Scott. There are, of course, differences. Merrick is a repressed homosexual and lick-lipping sadist. Scott, for all his life-failings, wasn't – at least not a sadist, as far as we know. Unlike Merrick, Scott had married in 1941. His wife Penny was a nurse and in later life a novelist herself. They had two daughters, both born after the war.

Demobbed and back in Civvy Street, Scott picked up his pre-war trade of accountant, before joining the firm of what was to become David Higham Associates as a literary agent in 1950 – in which capacity he was mightily vexing to his client, Muriel Spark (who mistakenly thought he was officer-class born and bred). Scott also had literary ambitions of his own – all deriving from his Indian experiences. *Johnny Sahib* (1952), rejected seventeen times, was the first of half-a-dozen post-colonial fictions. All, as Spurling meaningfully notes, deal with 'complicated' male friendship. In 1960 Scott gave up his day job (no small thing – he was now a director of the firm) to write novels. In 1964 'he flew back alone to India on a journey which he knew would make or break him as a writer'. It came close to breaking him. He was short of money, chronically unwell with amoebic dysentery, undergoing severe marital problems, and drinking like a fish. None the less, he was able, after a few months in the country, to embark on his great chronicle of the decline and fall of the Anglo-Indian Empire. Paul Scott knew that he had a great literary adversary when he conceived his quartet – namely the author of *A Passage to India*. 'Forster', Scott said, 'loomed over literary India like a train terminus beyond which no other novelist could be permitted to travel.' Scott ignored the ban: he was singularly immune to the 'glamour' of India which had so gripped Forster.

Quoted more than once in the *Quartet* is Emerson's observation that 'there is a relation between the hours of our life and the centuries of time'. In awarding the Booker Prize in 1977 to the dying Scott, for his tailpiece novel to the *Quartet*, Philip Larkin paraphrased Emerson: '*Staying On* covers only a few months, but it carries the emotional impact of a lifetime, even a civilisation.' Scott was not present to hear Larkin's praise. He died, a few weeks later, in London's Middlesex Hospital. His wife Penny had begun legal proceedings to end the marriage, but colon cancer got there first.

FN   Paul Mark Scott
MRT   *The Raj Quartet*
Biog   H. Spurling, *Paul Scott: A Life* (1990)

226. Patricia Highsmith 1921–1995

I never think about my 'place' in literature, and perhaps I have none.

Patricia Highsmith's achievement was to produce fiction that contrives to be simultaneously repulsive and irresistibly readable. To paraphrase Thoreau, her characters live lives of quiet psychopathy. *A Suspension of Mercy* (1965) – sometimes the most mysterious things in Highsmith's mysteries are the titles – is a typical invention. A couple, Sydney and Alicia, are living in rural Suffolk in a condition which, to the outside world, looks idyllic. He is a writer, she is an artist. But the picture-postcard appearance is illusion. The 'inner' Sydney and Alicia are ravening beasts:

> Sometimes he plotted the murders, the robbery, the blackmail of people he and Alicia knew, though the people themselves knew nothing about it. Alex [his literary collaborator] had died five times at least in Sydney's imagination. Alicia twenty times. She had died in a burning car, in a wrecked car, in the woods throttled by person or persons unknown, died falling down the stairs at home, drowned in her bath, died falling out the upstairs window while trying to rescue a bird in the eaves drain, died from poisoning that would leave no trace.

Alicia does indeed come to a sticky end.

Homicide is the rational response to the human condition in Highsmith's moral universe. 'Murder,' she believed, 'is a kind of making love, a kind of possessing.' On the face of it, such apophthegms look like the bourgeois-offending small-talk of the existentialists, with whose left-bank doctrines Highsmith was infatuated in the late 1940s. There is, however, a difference. Unlike Meursault (she read *The Outsider* in 1947), Highsmith's killers positively relish their killing. It's as natural as, well, making love. The big difference between the classic Hitchcock movie *Strangers on a Train* (1951) and its source novel is that in Highsmith's version Guy (literally a nice guy) does actually kill Bruno's father, honouring the exchange of murder forged, over highballs, in the private compartment thundering across the Texas plains. Hitchcock's targeted audience was not up for that. At least, not in 1951.

Crime and Punishment was one of Highsmith's favourite novels (she actually read it a couple of months before beginning *Strangers on a Train*), but her Raskolnikovs routinely escape the afflictions of law and conscience – and sometimes even punishment. In *The Glass Cell* (1964) the hero, Philip Carter, is wrongfully convicted and, in prison, strung up by the thumbs by sadistic guards. Mutilated and forcibly addicted to morphine by a homosexual prison doctor, he contrives to kill his torturer and, on his release, kill his faithful/faithless wife's lover, before settling down happily to carry on where he was before he went to prison. The novel ends with an exchange with a detective who knows, but cannot prove, Philip's guilt:

> 'We won't stop watching you, Carter.'
> 'Oh, I know that,' Carter said. 'I know.'

He's in a glass cell – but so are we all.

Highsmith's novel-writing career began with *Strangers on a Train*. Even more out of step with her moralising, Eisenhowerian time is her second published novel, *The Price of Salt* (1952), brought out under the pseudonym 'Claire Morgan'. A lesbian romance, the story originated in Highsmith's own life. Working to keep body and soul together in Bloomingdale's (it was not until late in her career that she made real money writing) she was struck by a rich, sophisticated and, as it emerged, married customer. It was love at first sight – the accidental encounter is always central in her world – and Highsmith, as does her heroine, stalked 'Carol' and won her from a furious, litigious husband. The couple go on a wild drive across America (an inspiration, it is plausibly surmised, for the hit film, *Thelma and Louise*). What makes the novel remarkable for its time is not merely the full-blooded lesbianism, but the fact that the affair ended happily. 'Prior to this book,' Highsmith wrote in a 1989 afterword, 'homosexuals male and female in American novels had had to pay for their deviation by cutting their wrists, drowning themselves in a swimming pool, or by switching to heterosexuality (so it was stated), or by collapsing – alone and miserable and shunned – into a depression equal to hell.'

Mary Patricia Plangman was born in Fort Worth, Texas, on 19 January 1921, sharing a birthday, as she liked to recall, with Edgar Allan Poe. She was an unwanted child: her mother had tried to abort her with a swig of turpentine (the smell of which Highsmith 'adored' in later life – but murder always smelled good to her). She was born some five months after her parents' divorce and, aged three, was named Highsmith after her stepfather. Her early years were passed in New York, interspersed with boarding-house life back in Fort Worth, which she hated. Indeed, she hated her childhood; it was, she later recalled, a 'little hell'. She would never be convinced on the subject of the joys of family life ('No thanks,' was her verdict) and may well have been sexually abused, her biographer suggests, between the ages of five and six. Both Highsmith parents were commercial artists. Unhappy though her early years were, she inherited a love of crafting wood and a gift for painting. Her mother's second marriage was no happier than her first – although it lasted long enough to see Patricia through college (Barnard). On graduation in 1942, she based herself in Greenwich Village, where she turned her hand to comic-book scripts – something which critics have made much of, seeing a crossover from the sharp-edged world of the graphic narrative to her own high-concept scenarios.

Like other intellectuals, she was drawn to communism – not dangerous at this period of military alliance with the Red Army. She gradually made a name for herself with sharply written short stories, for which there was a good market in the early post-war years. In 1948, a turning point in her career, she was invited, at Truman Capote's instigation, to the writers' colony Yaddo, where she roomed alongside Flannery O'Connor and Chester Himes and wrote the first draft of *Strangers on a Train*. Raymond Chandler, who did the original script for Hitchcock, thought the swapping murders McGuffin 'ludicrous'. Hitchcock thought differently: he was probably right. At this period Highsmith tried psychoanalysis and was relieved to discover it could not make her sexually straight – or any other kind of straight. She was, she concluded, a 'bad seed' and resolved to go 'the whole hog' with her 'perversions'. She was not always safe to know: one lover poisoned herself with nitric acid; few parted on good terms with her.

Her later career was spent largely in Europe where – thanks to Gallimard's *Série noire* – the kind of fiction she and Himes wrote was highly regarded. Her later-life homes would be in England, France and finally the nowhere country, Switzerland. In these years she had many relationships, most transitory. In later life, alcoholism made them more so. 'Perhaps it's because I don't like anyone,' she mused, although on other occasions she would justify her instabilities with the thought 'my personal maladies and malaises are only those of my own generation and of my time heightened'. But it was not just her. There was, she diagnosed, a hollowness, or 'vacuum' at the heart of American life in the 1950s – a theme she examined in one of her finest 'human condition' novels, *The Blunderer* (1954), whose hero, Walter Stackhouse, finally resolves that being murdered is preferable to living the life of a successful, happily married lawyer in New York. Not that writing was any solution for Highsmith – it was merely a preferable use of life to all others. 'Sometimes,' she wrote in her journal, 'I think that the artistic life is a long and lovely suicide,' adding, 'and I am not sorry that it is so.'

Whenever – in a spirit of experiment – she tried heterosexuality, she found it was like 'steel wool in the face'. In later life some unpleasant harshness protruded in her always misanthropic views. She had no time for the American civil rights movements and was, in conversation, often anti-Semitic: 'if the Jews are God's chosen people, that's all one needs to know about God,' she wrote. Feminists (always complaining about something) annoyed her intensely. Her long-lived, anything but feminist, mother annoyed her even more. Her warmest feelings were reserved for Siamese cats and snails. Neither, she believed, 'made demands'. In her later career she hit a rich creative vein with her series hero, Tom Ripley – art forger, criminal fence, contract killer, bon viveur. Like much of her work, the Ripliad adapted smoothly to the screen. It constitutes around a quarter of her published fiction and has proved the longest lasting.

She died of leukaemia in Switzerland, a rich woman, leaving some $3 million of her wealth to the Yaddo institution which had put her on the writing path all those years ago.

FN   Mary Patricia Highsmith (born Plangman)
MRT *Strangers on a Train*
Biog A. Wilson, *Beautiful Shadow: A Life of Patricia Highsmith* (2003)

227. Kingsley Amis 1922–1995

Oh fuck the Beatles. I'd like to push my bum into John L's face for forty-eight hours or so, as a protest against all the war and violence in the world.
Amis writing to Philip Larkin, 19 April 1969

Kingsley Amis's last completed novel, *The Biographer's Moustache* (1995), was a sardonic missive to his Boswell. Moustached or not, no novelist of his post-war (once 'Angry', latterly 'hidebound') generation has been more thoroughly 'done' by what are now called – a term he would vituperatively have despised – the 'life writers'. Amis wrote his own, indiscreet, memoirs. Supporting them (and occasionally contradicting them) are three biographies and a voluminous edition of his astonishingly self-revealing correspondence. If, for his closest friend, Philip Larkin, life was 'first boredom, then fear', it was for him – Amis quipped – 'first boredom then more boredom'. The boring facts are easily summarised. He was born middle-class and suburban. He attended the City of London school, an institution perched uneasily between 'public' and 'grammar', and won an Exhibition (not *quite* a scholarship) to St John's College, Oxford, in 1941, where he formed his bond with the congenial Larkin over traditional jazz, traditional literature and Hogarthian quantities of beer. His studies were interrupted when he was called up in 1942. He was commissioned into the Royal Signals (not *exactly* the Household Cavalry) but saw no action. Boredom he got plenty of.

After the war he got a first, did a B.Litt., which he eventually failed, met his first wife, Hilary (Hilly), married her (they having decided not to abort their first child), and landed a job at Swansea University College (not *exactly* Balliol). It was on a visit to Philip Larkin, assistant librarian at Leicester University College – lower in academic esteem than even Swansea – that he got the idea for *Lucky Jim*. The novel, when it came out in 1954, was seen as a manifesto text in the 'Angry Young Men' movement, which was getting up middle England's nostrils. Amis's poetry, into which much of his early creative energy was diverted, was disruptively associated with the 'Movement' movement: a return to Augustan clarities in verse. He was – though uneasy with the role– a rebel writing prose, and a traditionalist in poetry.

His career as a novelist and increasingly acerbic commentator on various aspects of Englishness is exhaustively chronicled, but one aspect of his life invites further investigation for the effect it had on his fiction. 'Boozer' could have been chiselled on Amis's gravestone – not that posterity needed any reminder that he was, above all else, a laureate of the bottle. In 2010, *Everyday Drinking* (1983) was re-released to nostalgically warm reviews. It gathered pieces originally written for the *Telegraph* in 1972, a period when Larkin was writing for the same paper on jazz – subjects they had both applied themselves to at Oxford, while effortlessly scooping up their 'firsts'. Alcohol plays a pivotal role in the opening and closing sections of *Lucky Jim*. In the first comic set-piece, a high cultural weekend at the country house of Professor Welch, Jim – in a welcome break in the carolling and recorder-playing – hies off to the pub to drink at least ('I never count') eight pints and returns to neck half a bottle of sideboard sherry (from which Welch had earlier poured 'the smallest glass Jim had ever been offered'), makes a rebuffed attempt on the virtue of his girlfriend Margaret, whom he's not actually all that keen on, and retires to bed, fag in mouth (soon to burn its way through the bedclothes). There follows the famous hangover description at the opening of Chapter 6:

> Dixon was alive again. Consciousness was upon him before he could get out of the way; not for him the slow, gracious wandering from the halls of sleep, but a summary, forcible ejection. He lay sprawled, too wicked to move, spewed up like a broken spider-crab on the tarry shingle of the morning. The light did him harm, but not as much as looking at things did; he resolved, having done it once, never to move his eyeballs again. A dusty thudding in his head made the scene before him beat like a pulse. His mouth had been used as a latrine by some small creature of the night, and then as its mausoleum. During the night, too, he'd somehow been on a cross-country run and then been expertly beaten up by secret police. He felt bad.

Viewed from one angle, Jim is an oaf: he deserves to feel bad. Viewed from another, he is a rebel – a word much in vogue in the early 1950s. The genius of the Angry Young Man was to realise that you could be both simultaneously.

Jim's malefactions in Welch's house forecast the novel's finale – the funniest episode in the novel and, many maintain, the funniest in all twentieth-century English fiction. The hero has been dragooned into giving a lecture on 'Merrie England'. He is royally pissed – well beyond 'merry'. The inner Jim takes over as he reads his text at the lectern:

> Within quite a short time he was contriving to sound like an unusually fanatical Nazi trooper in charge of a book-burning reading out to the crowd excerpts from a pamphlet written by a pacifist, Jewish, literate Communist.

Finally Jim erupts with what he really thinks about Merrie England, 'without consciously willing any words'. It is, to use a favourite Amisism, a load of 'bum'. Legless, he again collapses. It is total disgrace, but liberation. Jim is unshackled; free at last. He gets the money and the girl and is last seen embarking on a good life and lots of sex. What has liberated Jim? Drink.

Over the years between *Lucky Jim* (1954) and *Jake's Thing* (1978), Amis himself screwed and drank mightily – while writing superb comic fiction. He was the Henry Fielding of his day, just as Jim Dixon was the Tom Jones of post-war fiction. But a penalty was paid. By the time his second marriage to Elizabeth Jane Howard had broken up in 1980 Amis was clinically alcoholic (as Master Jones, we may presume, would have become more Squire Western than Squire Allworthy in his later years). Howard delivered an ultimatum: me or drink. It was no contest: Howard left. As happens with third-stage alcoholics, Amis was, at the time, impotent. His 'thing' was useless. He described his condition in a horrifically candid letter to Larkin (29 September 1979): 'I haven't had a fuck for more than a year and a wank for over a month. Don't tell anyone. Your thing about not reading anything new struck a chord. Nearly all my reading is comfort-reading now, done while I wait for whisky and sleeping-pills to get me torpid enough to go to bed – alone of course.'

This is worse than feeling 'bad'. It's Kurtz's 'The horror! The horror!' It's also a condition painfully familiar to career alcoholics. The cure (drink) has become the disease (drinking). By this stage in his life Amis – once among the handsomest of his novel-writing kind – was decrepit. An old friend, encountering him in a Hampstead pub at this period, observed, 'It was hard to reconcile his figure with the man I remembered. At fifty-seven, he appeared twenty years older.' Amis was acutely aware of his condition, and suffered. In later life he was prone to do a 'Jim Dixon' (saying what he really felt) with disastrous consequences. One notorious example was recalled by the younger novelist, Julian Barnes, in Zachary Leader's biography: 'In 1986 – after the successful publication of Barnes's *Flaubert's Parrot* ... Kingsley invited Barnes and his wife Pat Kavanagh to dinner at the Garrick. Additionally needled by the fact that Barnes had visited South Africa and his wife had grown up there, Kingsley snapped into racist mode, offering opinions such as "You should shoot as many blacks as possible" (at which point Kavanagh left in distress).'

Jake's Thing chronicles, with painful exactitude, the end-point alcoholic liberation lands you in. The hero Jake, like Jim, is an educationally pointless academic, a Reader in Early Mediterranean History at Oxford (Dixon was a junior lecturer in Medieval History at a redbrick university – identifiably Leicester). *Jake's Thing* opens with a disastrous drinking scene and the following narrative revolves around the fact that 'something that used to be a big part of his life isn't there any more': he is impotent. Fascinatingly, Amis goes on to ponder whether freedom from sex is a plus, or a minus. In *The Alteration* (1976) – one of the less appreciated of his novels – an alternate universe is fantasised in which the English Reformation never happened, and Grand Opera still features castrati. The hero, Hubert Anvil, is a child with a wonderful voice. He sings like an angel. Is it worth – for him, and for his art – giving up sex to keep that otherwise unachievable artistry?

Age, of course, also emasculates. The longings of age for the potency – the drunken potency – of youth is pondered in the finest of Amis's late novels (the one for which he rightly got the Booker Prize), *The Old Devils* (1986). The theme is crystallised in one of his late, typically light but ironic, poems, 'Senex' (Latin for 'old man' but also 'sans sex'):

> *To find his sexual drives had ceased*
> *For Sophocles was no disaster;*
> *He said he felt like one released*
> *From service with a cruel master.*
> *I envy him – I miss the lash*
> *At which I used to snort and snivel;*
> *Oh that its unremitted slash*
> *Were still what makes me drone and drivel!*

Droning and drivelling, one should add, some great fiction. Would Kingsley Sobersides have given us *Lucky Jim* or *The Old Devils*?

FN   (Sir) Kingsley William Amis
MRT *Jake's Thing*
Biog Z. Leader, *The Life of Kingsley Amis* (2006)

228. Alistair Maclean 1922–1987

There's no art in what I do.

Alistair Maclean was brought up in the Scottish Highlands, near Inverness, one of four sons of a Free Church minister. Gaelic was his first language. He attended school in Inverness and Glasgow – where a heavily accented English became his tongue. With his leaving certificate in his hand, and after a brief period of clerking, he volunteered for the navy in 1941. As an able seaman, and later a leading torpedo operator, Maclean served on escort duties for Russian convoys and later in the Pacific theatre. Although the heroes of his war-action novels are all officers, Maclean himself never rose higher than non-commissioned rank. Nor, although he saw active service, did Maclean have a bloody war. It evidently rankled. In his alcoholic later years, he would boast that he had killed over 200 of the enemy, been captured by the Japanese, tortured and escaped.

Demobbed, Maclean enrolled at Glasgow University and on graduation, with a middling degree in English, took up school-teaching. He took a German wife in 1953 and started a family – eventually there were three children. His sea-story, 'The Dileas', won a *Glasgow Herald* writing contest in 1954 and encouraged him to submit a full-length manuscript to the Glasgow publisher, Collins. *HMS Ulysses*, like Nicholas Monsarrat's *The Cruel Sea*, was a 'tell it how it really was' novel about the Arctic convoys, and the inhuman pressures the theatre placed on sailors. Ian Chapman, the editor who nursed Maclean's early career, astutely sniffed a bestseller, while other editors at Collins were appalled at the crudity of his writing. The novel gained an extra boost from Admiralty attempts to suppress it as a slander on the Senior Service. But Chapman was right and *HMS Ulysses* sold phenomenally. Maclean gave up the classroom chalk for the bestselling pen.

His later career was nomadic. The rapacious demands of the Inland Revenue drove him to tax exile in Switzerland. Hollywood lured him with dollars to Los Angeles. 'I have no home,' he said at the end of his life. His first marriage ended with divorce in 1972. He remarried (a Frenchwoman this time), but this also ended in expensive divorce five years later. He had come by now to despise himself for what he wrote. It drove him to acts of crazed generosity with money – and to drink. Alcohol destroyed his marriages but not his ability to churn out fiction and his earnings never tapered off. Even at his most sodden, he was pulling in a million a year: the pot never stopped boiling for Alistair Maclean. He had the knack (which coevals such as Desmond Bagley or Jack Higgins lacked) of creating narratives which adapted smoothly to film. He wrote, as Chapman said, 'visually' (verbally, as others said, he was no great shakes). The opening sentence of his first, and best, novel, *HMS Ulysses*, illustrates Chapman's point: 'Slowly, deliberately, Starr crushed out the butt of his cigarette.'

Two of his works, thanks to TV re-runs, have immortalised his name: *The Guns of Navarone* (1957) and *Where Eagles Dare* (1969). The last was proposed to Maclean by the movie producer Elliott Kastner, who put in the order for 'an adventure story that would *sweat* ... set in the Second World War, with five or six guys overcoming enormous obstacles to rescue someone'. Starring in the film was Richard Burton. He and Maclean bonded on the set over vodka and then – as drunks do – came to blows after too much alcohol. The novelist claimed to have floored the actor. The film critic Barry Norman perceived a telling parallel. Burton was an actor of genius, who had sold out to Hollywood. Maclean wanted to be a great writer, but knew he never could be. Both soothed their professional chagrin with drink.

Maclean died in Switzerland. There was a memorial service in his home village in the Scottish Highlands. The local paper memorialised him, unkindly, as 'The Daviot Drunk'.

FN Alistair Stuart Maclean
MRT *HMS Ulysses*
Biog J. Webster, *Alistair Maclean* (1991)

POSTSCRIPT

229. Robert Shaw 1927–1978

Quint's tale of the USS Indianapolis [in the film Jaws*]was conceived by playwright Howard Sackler, lengthened by screenwriter John Milius and rewritten by Robert Shaw following a disagreement between screenwriters Peter Benchley and Carl Gottlieb. Shaw presented his text, and Benchley and Gottlieb agreed that this was exactly what was needed.*

Imprisoned, like a fly in amber, in one of the films adapted from Maclean's fiction, was a much more gifted novelist. Robert Shaw played 'Major Keith Mallory' (his last complete role) in *Force 10 from Navarone* (1978), a feeble sequel to the earlier and much superior Navarone actioner, in which Gregory Peck had played Mallory. It was Shaw's fate to find himself immured in the inventions of lesser writers than himself. He is most famous for having invented, after some creative fisticuffs, Quint's 'Indianapolis' monologue in Steven Spielberg's film adaptation of Peter Benchley's *Jaws*

(1975) – a creation which ranks with Orson Welles's interpolated 'cuckoo clock' riff in *Citizen Kane*. Welles was Graham Greene's equal. Peter Benchley was nowhere near as good a novelist as Robert Shaw.

Shaw was born in Lancashire, the son of an alcoholic doctor who had married one of his nurses and later killed himself with an overdose of opium when his son was twelve. He passed on his drinking disease. Shaw taught for a while, after leaving school in Cornwall (whose regional accent is detectable, even under his assumed American accent) and before coming to study in London at RADA. At school he excelled at sport, and might – had his career gone differently – been a professional rugby player (as was David Storey, for a while). In his acting career he would gravitate towards physical roles. Like Richard Burton, he could not afford to waste his considerable acting talent on the stage, where he had made an early reputation as a Shakespearian actor. Film paid more. His most commendable screen role was as Aston in the 1963 adaptation of Harold Pinter's *The Caretaker*. Notably memorable is the character's extended monologue about the abusive effect of electro-convulsive therapy on his brain. But Shaw's name was made, and his career likewise, by his performance as the psychopathic SPECTRE assassin, Red Grant, in the James Bond film *From Russia with Love*, which also came out in 1963.

Like Burton, Shaw enjoyed (if that's the word) riotous sessions with fellow drunk and screenwriter, Alistair Maclean, on adaptations of that novelist's work. He died on the set of a wholly undistinguished film, aged only fifty-one, leaving a clutch of distinguished novels. 'I would rather', he once said, 'go down as having written one good novel than be acclaimed as a great actor.' The best of his novels, *The Hiding Place* (1959) and *The Man in the Glass Booth* (1967), deal with imprisonment. In the first two, British airmen who have bailed out of their bomber during the Second World War are imprisoned by a German in his cellar, and deluded – for years after the Allies' victory – that Germany has actually won the war. They make their escape into a world of confusion. The man in the glass booth is a Nazi war criminal (inspired by Adolf Eichmann), on trial in Jerusalem.

Shaw died leaving three wives, ten children, five novels and debts of hundreds of thousands to the American Internal Revenue Service (IRS) – with whom he was always in hot water. His novels are now out of print and undeservedly unread, while *Jaws* replays, year in year out, on TV and in revival houses. Wetherspoon's pub has been named after him in his birthplace of Westhoughton, Lancashire, although he always felt his home was Ireland, where he spent the last seven years of his life when not on set – in the Gaeltacht village of Tourmakeady, Co. Mayo. Ireland's enlightened laws had allowed him to live there tax-free. A memorial was raised to him in the village in 2008.

FN   Robert Archibald Shaw
MRT   *The Hiding Place*
Biog K. Carmean and G. Gaston, *Robert Shaw: More Than a Life* (1994)

230. Kurt Vonnegut 1922–2007

Here is a lesson in creative writing. First rule: Do not use semicolons. They are transvestite hermaphrodites representing absolutely nothing. All they do is show you've been to college.

On the night of 13 February 1945, three months before the end of the Second World War, Kurt Vonnegut was a POW sheltering in an underground animal slaughterhouse during the devastating fire-bombing of Dresden. Slaughterhouse Five (*Schlachthof Fünf*) was the shelter from the slaughter. 'We got through it' Vonnegut wryly recalled, 'because we were quartered in the stockyards where it was wide and open and there was a meat locker three stories beneath the surface, the only decent shelter in the city. So we went down into the meat locker, and when we came up again the city was gone and everybody was dead. We walked for miles before we saw anybody else: all organic things were consumed.' Vonnegut and his fellow American POWs, exhumed at dawn from their underground coffin, were set to work 'corpse mining' – excavating blackened bodies for a second cremation on open piles. The live meat took care of the dead meat.

Vonnegut survived the slaughter to write *Slaughterhouse-Five* (1969). Thousands didn't survive. In the novel, Billy Pilgrim, the unheroic hero, is a POW in the same shelter as Vonnegut during the devastating fire-bombing. He too survives – but he goes crazy. Vonnegut published many personal accounts of his Dresden experience – as well as that in *Slaughterhouse-Five*. The following is from an interview in 1974. 'I was present in the greatest massacre in European history, which was the destruction of Dresden by fire-bombing ... The American and British air forces together killed 135,000 people in two hours. This is a world's record. It's never been done faster, not in the Battle of Britain or Hiroshima. (In order to qualify as a massacre you have to kill *real* fast). But I was there, and there was no news about it in the American papers, it was so embarrassing.' RAF estimates later downscaled the civilian casualties to a 'mere' 35,000. But Vonnegut's point stands. Fiction, like history, has been generally silent about Dresden. Victors, as Hitler said, write history. They also forget the embarrassing bits. Vonnegut himself had almost insuperable personal difficulties writing his 'Dresden novel'. He had to forge an entirely new 'schizophrenic' technique, weaving realism, SF schlock (little one-eyed green men from Tralfamadore, resembling toilet plungers), and slapstick social comedy into a startlingly innovative pattern.

The thesis of *Slaughterhouse-Five* is T. S. Eliot's – mankind cannot bear too much reality. Life is so horrible, that only fiction can deal with it – and, crucially, the more horrible the life experience, the more fantastic (unrealistic) the fiction. After Auschwitz, Theodor Adorno famously declared, poetry was impossible. One of the underlying contentions of *Slaughterhouse-Five* is that after Dresden, fiction (specifically 'War and Peace' fiction of the old Tolstoyan kind) is impossible. A way out of the impasse was science fiction. Billy Pilgrim, a time and intergalactic traveller (or, more likely, merely nuts) ends his post-Dresden pilgrimage incarcerated no longer by Nazi Germany but by aliens from the planet Tralfamadore, some 446,120,000,000,000,000 miles from earth, whither he has been transported by flying saucer (widely believed in during the 1960s).

Billy's imprisonment on planet Tralfamadore is in a geodesic dome – a style of architecture much favoured by hippy communes in the 1960s – made tolerable by furniture from Sears, Roebuck (less favoured by hippies), and the even more luxuriously upholstered, but wholly brainless, starlet Montana Wildhack, who is also flying-saucered across the vast tracts of space as Billy's 'mate' (she is also one of Hugh Hefner's playmates). They will be earthling specimens in the Tralfamadorian national zoo, kindly treated and grateful for the dome, the furniture, and each other. 'I was there,' is a constant interruption in the text. In two places in the novel, Vonnegut actually gives himself a Prufrockian speaking part. Walter Scott was not present at Culloden. Tolstoy wasn't at Borodino, Thackeray wasn't at Waterloo, nor was Stendhal. Norman Mailer – though the myth persists – didn't see a lot of action in the Pacific campaign. Interestingly, Vonnegut himself did not call *Slaughterhouse-Five* a 'novel' but, more awkwardly, 'my Dresden book'. Billy Pilgrim is not Vonnegut, but a fellow POW called Joe Crone who did not survive the war. Crone was, like Billy, comically malcoordinated, a soldier doomed always to be the platoon klutz. He let himself starve to death before the firestorm and is 'buried somewhere in Dresden, wearing a white paper suit'. Vonnegut resurrected him.

Vonnegut did not, in the conventional sense, write *Slaughterhouse-Five* – it rose out of his subconscious like a slow bruise. Immediately after the war he found he could not remember the event: 'There was a complete blank where the bombing of Dresden took place ... And I looked up several of my war buddies and they didn't remember either.' In his first, fuzzy, conception of his 'Dresden book', he imagined something like the popular war movies of the period: 'I saw it as starring John

Wayne and Frank Sinatra.' Ironically, these two 'dirty old men', as Mary O'Hare calls them, in Chapter One of *Slaughterhouse-Five*, declined to serve their country in the Second World War, but made millions out of playing war heroes onscreen where the bombs don't hurt.

One problem for Vonnegut, both as a POW and an author, was his ethnicity. He was an American with a name more German than most of the enemy he was sworn to kill. Kurt Vonnegut Jr was born in Indianapolis, into a wealthy German-American family, settled in the New World for two generations. His father, with whom he had a fraught relationship, was a successful architect and painter. His mother, Edith Lieber Vonnegut, was heiress to a brewing family, highly cultivated, a published author, and a lifelong depressive. She would eventually kill herself on Mother's Day, 1944, while her son was serving abroad. Others in the Vonnegut family, including Kurt, would make suicide attempts during the course of their lives.

The Vonneguts, although they kept the family name, followed the 'Americanisation' routine in their ethnic community after the First World War. They studiously immunised their son from any German cultural influences. He might as well, Vonnegut ruefully said, have been brought up Tibetan. If Goethe was Greek to him, he was strongly influenced, growing up, by the stars of radio comedy (Bob Hope, Jack Benny, Jimmy Durante). The more depressing the Great Depression of the 1930s, he observed, the funnier and zanier the jokes. At his father's insistence, he enrolled in 1940 to do biochemistry (a 'useful' subject) at Cornell. In 1943 he enlisted in the US Army. As a serviceman Vonnegut never put himself forward for promotion on the persuasive grounds that all officers were 'shits'. It was as a scout (i.e. in a dangerous forward position) with the 106th Infantry Division that Vonnegut was taken prisoner during the Battle of the Bulge, one of the more ignominious episodes in American military history. On his release and demobilisation, he married. At the same period he enrolled on the GI Bill in the University of Chicago's MA programme in anthropology. He flunked. The examiners failed his thesis on 'simple tales'. Some would flunk his fiction for the same reason.

Work was fairly easy to come by during the post-war boom and Vonnegut got a job in the PR department of the vast multinational, General Electric. On the side he was writing his own stuff. His first short story was published in 1950. Other pieces for the 'slicks' (upmarket magazines) followed. Confident of his powers he left GE to write a satire on the company, *Player Piano* (1952). He was in business. Science fiction was in vogue and he did well with his first Tralfamadorian comic-epic, *The Sirens of Titan* (1959). Fame came with *Cat's Cradle* (1963), another whimsical dystopia centred on a miraculous new chemical compound ('ice nine'). It caught the fancy of the campus market. Other novels followed and his reputation grew. World fame, and critical respect, did not come until *Slaughterhouse-Five*, a novel which he brought into its final shape with the help of a Guggenheim grant to revisit Dresden (described in the novel's non-fiction first section), a stint at the University of Iowa's writers' workshop, and acute personal problems with his family.

Slaughterhouse-Five was a bestseller, as were the novels which followed. None, however, garnered great esteem with pundits. Vonnegut's whimsy, when not fused with Kurtzian 'horror', was not regarded as truly serious. His first marriage was dissolved in 1979 and he remarried the photographer Jill Krementz, whose portraits perfectly catch Vonnegut's sardonic charm. That charm, and his anti-war convictions, wittily purveyed, served him well on talk-shows and as a lecturer in his later years – particularly with campus audiences, who remained faithful to him long after the popularity of *Cat's Cradle* among the larger reading public had waned. His last public words, after a college lecture, were: 'Thank you for your attention, and I'm outta here.'

FN   Kurt Vonnegut, Jr
MRT *Slaughterhouse-Five*
Biog K. Vonnegut, *A Man Without a Country* (2005)

231. Austin M. Wright 1922–2003

Absorbing, terrifying, beautiful and appalling. Ruth Rendell on *Tony and Susan*

Question: What do the following have in common?

1. Dorothy L. Sayers
2. J. I. M. Stewart
3. Austin M. Wright
4. Trevanian
5. Lionel Trilling
6. David Lodge

Answer: they are all university professors of literature who wrote novels 'with their left hand'. 'Hobbyists,' the professionals might sneer. Ambidexters is the more friendly verdict. On the face of it, the conjunction 'professor-novelist' is unsurprising. Marinaded career-long in fiction, lecturing on it omnisciently for a living, who would not try their arm at what they were so good at pontificating about? Creative writing. But what is surprising, on reflection, is that so few professors have done it or, more precisely, done it and got their work published, and the majority of those who have done it (the above are exceptions) seem to have been second-raters or worse.

In philosophy, a discipline which nestles alongside literature in university arts faculties, professors of philosophy (A. J. Ayer, Bertrand Russell, Isaiah Berlin, Wittgenstein) have been great philosophers. Professors of literature ... the canon speaks for itself. For those of a cynical cast of mind, it bears out the Wildean quip that those who can, do. Those who can't, teach: scholarly eunuchs in the harem of literature. Those university teachers who have gone into the real world of fiction have, in general, taken one of a few paths. That most favoured in the early twentieth century was donnish amateurism, and a daring descent from high to low literature, as a country clergyman might daringly visit a brothel. Dorothy L. Sayers's Lord Peter Wimsey detective novels belong to this category as, more worthily, does J. I. M. Stewart's (pen name 'Michael Innes') forty-odd crime novels – of which the most admired remains the first he published, *Death at the President's Lodging* (1937). A fellow of Christ Church College, Oxford, for most of his long career Stewart was entrusted with the last volume of the *Oxford History of English Literature*, covering the modern period. Crime fiction does not get a look in. The right hand of scholarship wilfully does not know what the left hand is doing.

Lionel Trilling is an interesting case, and almost unique among professorial novelists. The first Jewish academic to get tenure at Columbia, a leading member of the leftist 'New York Intellectuals' who clustered around the *Partisan Review*, Trilling wrote one work of fiction, *The Middle of the Journey* (1947). Intelligence, believed Trilling, is a human being's moral duty. *The Middle of the Journey* is an excessively intelligent rumination on the political hysteria which would climax with the outright madness of McCarthyism and the emasculation of American universities for a generation. The book is generally found dull, not helped by the self-aggrandisingly Dantean title.

The other most-favoured mode is setting literary criticism and literature in a relationship analogous to that between theoretical and applied physics. 'Applied fiction' we might call it. The principal exponent of this genre in the UK is David Lodge, currently the country's leading novelist of ideas – principally literary critical ideas. For him the novel is a laboratory, where those ideas can be tested.

In America, more arresting because of its rather different mixture of modes, is the case of Austin M. Wright. According to the terse memorials on his death, aged eighty, Wright's life was uneventful and modestly successful. Born in Yonkers, New York, he graduated from Harvard, with a degree in geology, in 1943. On graduation he was conscripted and then demobilised from the army in 1946. Taking advantage of the GI Bill, Wright switched his intellectual interests, taking an MA and Ph.D. in Literature at the University of Chicago. The departmental 'line' at the time was firmly that of the theorist Kenneth Burke, whose *Philosophy of Literary Form* (1941) was a dominant influence. Chicago, at that period, was fascinated by the mechanics of fiction.

The newly graduated Dr Wright took up an appointment at the University of Cincinnati in 1962, marrying in the same year. He would have three daughters in the course of his fifty-two-year-long marriage. He remained in Ohio until his retirement in 1993, and beyond, rising through the ranks to an endowed chair. In his last ten years he enjoyed the status of an admired emeritus member of his department. Wright was the regular winner of awards for teaching excellence, but published only two monographs: *The Formal Principle in the Novel* (1982) – a work whose contents are as Burkean as its title – and *Recalcitrance, Faulkner, and the Professors: A Critical Fiction* (1990). Neither book created much stir in a subject currently intoxicated with French theory from the pens of younger trendier professors.

Wright also wrote seven crime thrillers, all of which play with the idea of narration. One of Wright's novels, *Tony and Susan* (1993) stands out: not merely for its thrill (testified to by every reader) but its cunning play with the aesthetics of fiction. The central character, Susan, has made a successful – if obscurely uneasy – second marriage. Her husband, Arnold, is a surgeon, away at a conference in New York. He too is on his second marriage. His first wife, Selena, went homicidally mad, and is incarcerated (Mrs Rochester-style) in an asylum. Susan receives a mysterious package out of the blue. It is a manuscript novel by her ex-husband (of fifteen years) Edward. His ambition to write was frustrated during the course of their marriage and he blamed Susan for having to do boring office work instead. The manuscript is entitled 'Nocturnal Animals'. As the story opens, a professor of mathematics, Tony Hastings, is driving by night (a daring departure from his normal practice) from Ohio to his holiday home in Maine. Travelling with him are his wife and teenage daughter. Their car is hijacked; Laura and Helen are raped and killed by three low-life drifters. Tony runs away – is he driven by self-preservation (they would surely kill him as well) or cowardice? A year later, the criminals are apprehended – but look as if they are going to get off on a legal technicality. With the aid of a local lawman, who is dying of terminal cancer and doesn't give a damn what he does, Tony embarks on a *Death Wish*-style vigilante campaign. He turns himself into an animal of the night.

So far, so conventional. What makes *Tony and Susan* unconventional is that the chapters are interspersed with Susan's chapter-by-chapter responses to the text she is reading. And as she reads, the gothic novel gradually permeates her cosy bourgeois home, and demons, long suppressed from her first marriage, are released. Obliquely, the novel is directed not to her, but at her. It works on her not as entertainment, but infection. *Tony and Susan* is a classic work of high-end crime fiction – and something more. It embodies decades of thinking about fiction. The novel was reprinted, seven years after Wright's death, in 2010. Its republication was accompanied by a round of belated applause. Saul Bellow, no less, praised it as 'marvellously written – the last thing you would expect in a story of blood and revenge. Beautiful.'

It calls out to be considered alongside *Recalcitrance, Faulkner, and the Professors*, which was written at the same period. Novels within novels are common enough (there are notable examples in *Don Quixote*, *Tom Jones* and *The Pickwick Papers*). Common too are 'framework narratives' – such as those in *The Turn of the Screw* or *Heart of Darkness*, in which the narrator tells his story to a listening audience. But that audience does not interrupt, interject, interpose or interact. They are literary décor and gradually fade into background invisibility. The double foreground of *Tony and Susan* is an unusual experiment in fiction, based on a classroom experiment described in *Recalcitrance, Faulkner, and the Professors*. That work recounts the diverse running response of a group of students to their first reading of William Faulkner's *As I Lay Dying*, giving equal attention to what was read and how it was received as it was read. Like the novel on its first appearance, the monograph (published by an obscure university press) made little impact.

For Wright's purpose, crime fiction was the ideal raw material. He explains why in chapter seven of *Tony and Susan*:

> Susan Morrow is running out of book ... Violence thrills her like brass in the symphony. Susan, who is well past forty, has never seen a killing. Last year in McDonald's she saw a policeman with a gun jump a guy eating a sandwich. That's the size of violence in her life ... In a book there is no future. In its place is violence ... Never forget what's possible, it says.

FN   Austin McGiffert Wright
MRT   *Tony and Susan*
Biog *Cincinnati Enquirer* obituary, 30 April 2003 (Rebecca Goodman)

232. V. C. Andrews 1923–1986

'V. C. Andrews' has become so much more than just a name, it has become a legacy.
V. C. Andrews official website

Cleo Virginia Andrews (she later transposed her first two names) was born in 1923 in Virginia – a region she loved and where, after an unsettled life, she chose to be buried (hence the transposition of first names; she may also have died virginal – or, at least, wanted it to be so thought). As a teenager, Virginia fell down the stairs at her school, incurring a horrific spinal injury. She would be handicapped for life – needing crutches and a wheelchair in her later years. After her father, a tool and die maker, died in 1957, she lived with her widowed mother (formerly a telephone operator), helping support the household as a commercial artist. There were three children. Virginia was a prize-winning schoolgirl but college was beyond her. None the less, she made heroic attempts to educate herself beyond twelfth grade by correspondence courses and self-improvement.

Allegedly, Andrews destroyed her first complete manuscript novel on the grounds that it was too 'personal'. According to devotional websites, 'in 1972, she completed her first published novel, *Gods of Green Mountain*, a science-fantasy story'. The work is currently available only as an e-text. At this point in her life, Andrews was in her fiftieth year and almost wholly disabled. But her writing hand wasn't. Between 1972 and 1979, she completed nine novels ('confession stories', she piquantly called them), and twenty short stories, of which only one would ever see the light of publication – 'I Slept with My Uncle on My Wedding Night.' Or was it in fact published? It has never been located and is hunted by fans as the Andrews Eldorado. The third most-asked question on www.completevca.com/faq.shtml is 'Where can I find a copy of "I Slept with My Uncle on My Wedding Night"?' Where indeed.

Incest would be a principal theme in her subsequent fiction – or, as Andrews herself quaintly put it, 'unspeakable things my mother didn't want me to write about'. Unspeakable, perhaps, but not unwritable – or, finally, unpublishable. Andrews at last broke into print with a paperback original, *Flowers in the Attic*, published in 1979 by Pocket Books. She was now fifty-six years old. Originally entitled 'The Obsessed', the manuscript was hugely overlong and had to be hacked into shape by the publishers. The 'uncut' version awaits publication. *Flowers in the Attic*, which attracted a measly advance of $7,500, tells the story of the four attic-incarcerated and sexually adventurous Dollanganger children. The novel ('a fictionalised version of a true story', the author tantalisingly calls it) derives, clearly enough, from *Jane*

Eyre – both the Red Room (in which young Jane is incarcerated) and the madwoman in the attic hover over the narrative. Anne Frank is also there somewhere – and, for more recent readers, Josef Fritzl. A sad brew.

In her 'pitch letter' in January 1978 to the agent who would eventually take her on, Andrews summarised the frame of her novel:

> Plot: A young wife is suddenly widowed. Left with four children. She is totally unskilled for the labor market, and deeply in debt. Her home and all she has is repossessed. However ... she has one solace. She is the sole heir to a fortune if she can deceive her dying father, and never let him know she is the mother of four children whom he would despise. Four children are imprisoned in an upstairs room of a huge mansion. Their playground is the attic.

Their 'play' becomes intense as they are 'tested' by adolescent hormone storms.

Andrews is credited with founding a distinct new line of gothic fiction – the 'children in jeopardy' genre. The term was taken over by the social service industries in the US and Britain and evolved, after a decade or two, into 'misery memoirs' of the *Child Called 'It'* and *Please, Daddy, No: A Boy Betrayed* kind. Harry Potter, as an abused waif in his cupboard under the stairs at Privet Drive, began his fictional life as a child in jeopardy – a Flower in the Closet. *Flowers in the Attic* went on to be a bestseller: the first of a whole string of sagas revolving around clusters of, typically, children in jeopardy. V. C. Andrews had begun late as a bestselling author and finished sadly early. Seven years after *Flowers in the Attic*, aged sixty-two, she died of breast cancer – a year before the release of the film of her novel in which she had a non-speaking cameo; she had always longed to be an actress. But her career as a novelist did not die with her. Works kept on pulsing out after her death under the auspices of the estate. An unceasing flow of *echt* Andrews was promised – and there could never be enough of it for her fans. Allegedly, Andrews had left some sixty scenarios at the time of her death. The family announced it was working 'closely with a carefully selected writer' to midwife the latent Andrews *oeuvre* into print. And they would, of course, be *her* novels – as much so as *Flowers*.

The identity of the 'carefully selected writer' was kept strenuously secret, so as not to contaminate the Andrews brand with another name. Many of the author's devoted readers, of course, had not apprehended she wasn't alive and writing the 'Andrews' novels which continued to pour out with her name only on the cover. By 2007, the count had reached something over seventy titles – two thirds of which have come out under the trademarked V. C. Andrews brand. The ghost in the Andrews machine was, after some years, discovered to be Andrew Neiderman: his name does not appear on the copyright pages. To this day the most asked question on the 'Complete V. C. Andrews website' is 'Where can I write to V. C. Andrews?'

FN Virginia Cleo Andrews (born Cleo Virginia Andrews)
MRT *Flowers in the Attic*
Biog E. D. Huntley, *V. C. Andrews: A Critical Companion* (1996)

233. Norman Mailer 1923–2007

Too much. Times Literary Supplement, 20 May 1949, in a dismissively brief notice of *The Naked and the Dead*

Adultery figures from time to time in the fiction of David Lodge. When asked whether he is thinking of himself, Lodge replies that he is a war reporter, not a warrior. It's a good answer – and very believable that those on the sidelines, with 'Press' on their flak jackets, see things more clearly than those blasting away with their firearms. War is proverbially foggy at the frontline.

Mailer's *The Naked and the Dead* (1948) was one of the last books George Orwell reviewed before dying, while writing his own, posthumous, bestseller, *Nineteen Eighty-four*. 'You will live with these men,' he wrote, of the fourteen-strong Intelligence & Reconnaissance platoon who supply the dramatis personae to Mailer's novel. Orwell's remark was splashed on the cover of the execrable, double columned, 6s, English paperback which was passed, hand to hand, among me and my schoolfriends in 1949. Sex, rather than the Second World War (in the 1940s we knew all about *that*) was what made it a book to devour out of sight of one's custodians. Particularly relished were passages such as the following, in a flashback to pre-war carnalities by the redneck 'Woodrow' Wilson:

> It is intensely hot in the cabin and he strains against her. Ah'm gonna tell ya somethin', they was a little old whore Ah had back a while ago that Ah took twelve times in a night, and the way Ah'm fixin' now, what with the honey in mah insides, Ah'm gonna beat that with you.

Twelve times!

Orwell's implication, assumed by the mass of early readers, was that *The Naked and the Dead* was a first-hand account: that Mailer, described, simply, by his American publisher in advertisements as a 'young rifleman', had been 'there'. The inference was both true and false and it raises some definitive issues about fiction, life and war – and about the author. Norman Mailer (Nachem Malek) was brought up in Brooklyn – the safest place in the world for a Jew to be between the wars, it was said. His father, Barney, was an immigrant from South Africa, recalled as charming but feckless (with a 'cockney accent' and an Irish nickname, oddly). Norman's life was dominated by his adoring mother (the co-dedicatee of *The Naked and the Dead*, tellingly), Fanny. Her only son was, as she liked to say, her 'king' and, when anglicising it, she gave him the discordant middle name, 'Kingsley'. A tigerish woman, Fanny made enough from a one-truck oil delivery business to push her beloved son through high school, where he excelled, and into Harvard in 1939, aged a precocious sixteen. To please his mother, Mailer enrolled to study aeronautical engineering, but he soon became infatuated with literature. The influences on Mailer at this formative period were Hemingway and Dos Passos.

Physically, Mailer was not warrior build. He was short (every one of his many wives would be taller than him, some toweringly so), underweight and myopic. None the less he had great presence and an ability, noted by all whose paths crossed with his, to melt into whatever society he found himself: he could be Irish, Southern, Brahmin-WASP – everything, he himself wryly noted, except 'a nice little Jewish boy from Brooklyn'. Mailer graduated from Harvard in June 1943 with a degree he would never use and, now twenty-one years old, impatiently awaited his draft letter. As one college friend recalled, 'Rather than thinking about the horror of war or the fact that he might get killed, he looked at it as an experience which would feed the novel he wanted to write afterward.' He had for some time been writing another massive novel – entitled, shamelessly, *Transit to Narcissus* – which was turned down by every publisher shown it. Too narcissistic.

Before being conscripted, he married his first of his many wives, Bea Silverman (the future co-dedicatee of *The Naked and the Dead* with the other Mrs Mailer). The marriage was kept secret from his mother, who, when she found out, vainly attempted to annul it. She was not disposed to share her 'king'. A few weeks later Mailer had been drafted and was on his way to Fort Bragg. He elected not to use his Harvard background to get into officer school. According to Bea, it was 'because he wanted to see combat'. After basic training he was posted to the 112th Armoured Cavalry Regiment, heading for the invasion of the Philippines. Combat didn't happen. Mailer was initially shuffled, to his chagrin, among various desk jobs – important to the war effort but not to him. He had brought with him a multi-volume set of Oswald Spengler's *Decline of the West* for cheerless reading in his bunk. It was mildewing in the tropical climate. After incessant pestering, he was finally transferred to frontline duty as a rifleman (lowest rank) in an I&R platoon.

Unlike the men in *The Naked and the Dead*, Mailer's platoon saw virtually no action. Probably a good thing. As one of his comrades recalled, 'He was a brave soldier but not a good one. He couldn't see worth a damn. Near sighted ... he couldn't hit anything with a rifle. It's a miracle Mailer lived through the war.' His wife Bea put it even more laconically: 'He took a few potshots, but I don't remember worrying every day that Norman would get killed. It wasn't that kind of fighting anymore.' What did happen – virtually every day – were long letters home from which would come the kernel of *The Naked and the Dead*. And Rifleman Mailer certainly picked up – at second-hand – what it was like to hear Jap bullets humming past your ears 'like a bee' as you strained to 'keep a tight ass-hole'.

For Mailer, as for Dos Passos before him, war was Sisyphean pointlessness. The central episode in *The Naked and the Dead* is the platoon's gruelling ascent of Mount Anaka. There is no military purpose: it merely expresses the fact that Sergeant Croft, the incarnation of Nietszchean will to power, wants the peak under his heel. The real foe is not Nippon, but the US Army, and the licence it gives to men like Croft, and the even more ruthless General Cummings, who relishes the prospect of the total militarisation of America. As in Orwell's *Nineteen Eighty-Four*, war is too useful to the men it empowers ever to have an end. As a soldier says in Dos Passos's *Three Soldiers*, 'I guess I wouldn't mind the war if it wasn't for the army.'

In mid-August 1945, the Japanese capitulated. Mailer stayed on for a while, as a sergeant-cook in Japan. Evidence is mixed as to how good he was in the kitchen. According to one jaundiced commentator he couldn't tell white from yellow in a hen's egg. On his return to civilian life in May 1946, Mailer had leisure, thanks to the GI Bill, to work full-time on *The Naked and the Dead*. He borrowed Dos Passos's 'objective' style for its word-sparing narration. The novel opens with the men preparing for their landing next morning on the beach of a (fictional) Philippine island, knowing that in twenty-four hours many of their number will die. But who? Nobody could sleep. When morning came, assault craft would be lowered and a first wave of troops would ride through the surf and charge ashore on the beach at Anopopei. All over the ship, all through the convoy, there was a knowledge that in a few hours some of them were going to be dead. A bunch of the I&R men are killing the night hours playing poker, wondering about the vagaries of luck (the winner of the poker pot will, as it happens, die horribly).

Mailer finished the 721-page manuscript in August 1947. It was accepted, eagerly, by the publisher Rinehart, who pushed it as a modern *War and Peace*. But Tolstoy's soldiers did not speak like soldiers. Mailer's did. The commissioning editor, Stanley Rinehart, was nervous about what his mother would think of the lavish F-wordage in the novel's dialogue. (Come to that, Mailer's mother wasn't that happy either with the 'language'.) It led to a compromise: the three-letter four-letter word 'fug'. When Dorothy Parker (some versions say Tallulah Bankhead) met Mailer a year or so later, she came out with the immortal wisecrack: 'So *you're* the young man who can't spell "fuck".' On publication in June 1948, *The Naked and the Dead* sold like hot cakes in high-priced hardback. At twenty-five, Norman Mailer was a king indeed. The novel's sales in the UK were boosted beyond a publicist's wildest dreams by a front-page editorial in the *Sunday Times* demanding the novel be withdrawn, on the grounds of its 'incredibly foul and beastly language ... no decent man could leave it lying about the house, or know without shame that his womenfolk were reading it'.

Could Mailer have written as good a war novel as *The Naked and the Dead* (assuming he survived the bloody Pacific campaign) had he been engaged more actively in its fighting? Typically the best war novels are written not by heroes, but by observers – such as Tolstoy, for example, who witnessed the carnage of Sebastopol but was not directly involved in the fight. Or Kurt Vonnegut, for whom the fighting-war was over almost as soon as he joined it, and was taken prisoner. One can add Rifleman Norman Mailer to that distinguished group of 'almost warriors, great war novelists'. He went on to write many more novels and pioneered the new genre of docufiction, notably in his bio-novelistic *The Executioner's Song* (1979), but the general verdict is that his best work is his first – however close or not he was to the action.

FN   Norman Kingsley Mailer (born Nachem Malek)
MRT   *The Naked and the Dead*
Biog H. Mills, *Mailer: A Biography* (1982)

234. Michael Avallone 1924–1999

I've been writing since I discovered pencils.

Avallone is a grand master of the trash detective story, arguably its grandest master – and if not the grandest, indisputably the most voluminous. His *oeuvre* is a bibliographer's circle of hell. Under a barrage of pen names (some, mischievously, incorporating other people's mistypings of his own tricky surname), he is reckoned to have turned out over 1,000 titles, along with a wealth of short stories, novelisations, radio scripts and screenplays. He also edited scores of magazines – many stuffed to bursting with *echt* Avallone. He is reputed to have written a *Man from U.N.C.L.E.* novelisation (one of his many profitable sidelines) in thirty-six hours and a 1,500-word short story in twenty minutes, to cover the bill for his dinner in a New York restaurant. He could, if pushed, have done it in a fast-food joint.

Prose artistry necessarily suffered under such pressures. One obituary opened: 'Few writers this century have committed more gross acts of grievous bodily harm upon the language of Milton, Shakespeare and the Authorised Version than Michael Angelo Avallone Jr.' But why restrict it to the twentieth century? John Gross, distinguished editor of the *New Oxford Book of English Prose*, cites, as the opposite of the excellence he anthologised, and possibly the worst simile in the annals of literature, Avallone's 'The whites of his eyes came up in their sockets like moons over an oasis lined with palm trees.' Parody wilts in the face of titles such as *Lust is No Lady*. Not that it bothered Avallone. He craved no praise from the critics – 'pinkos and perverts', all of them. As he often insisted, 'I never wrote a book I didn't like.' He also liked to say that he would rather write than eat or sleep. He loved writing and baseball and big breasts – the third of which feature pointedly in his fiction. Bill Crider, who knew Avallone, recalls: 'My own favorite Avo tale is that when he made a list of the Top Ten Private-Eye Novels of All Time, he put two of his own books on it. As I recall, however, he did modestly give Raymond Chandler the #1 position.'

Michael Avallone was born into a working-class Catholic home and brought up in New York. According to which version you go for, he was one of sixteen, or seven children of a stonemason. Numbers always get vague with Avallone. He was drafted into the army in the Second World War, saw action in Europe, won a medal, and made it to sergeant. On rejoining civilian life he worked for a short time in a stationery store, before turning full time to writing in the early 1950s. Thereafter he would need a store of his own to keep him in the paper and typewriter ribbons that he tore through daily. Unsurprisingly there is not much to record in his life thereafter, other than a growing mountain of pulp. But there was a hungry market for his wares. Story magazines for the masses were booming in the 1950s as were 'drugstore' paperback originals with lurid covers and selling for a quarter: wares which no self-respecting bookstore or library would give shelf space to. Publishers paid their hacks a routine penny-a-word, but if the hack turned out enough words (Avallone is supposed to have written twenty-seven novels in one year) he could keep ahead of the game.

Avallone's best-known, and bestselling, creation is the 'Private Eye', Ed Noon, introduced in *The Splitting Image* (1953) and *The Tall Dolores* (1953). Noon continued crime-busting and skull-busting through thirty or so titles until the late 1970s. The hallmark was the exotic female character. 'Tall Dolores', for example, is a six-foot two-inch moll (big breasts? don't ask). Noon was remodelled as a Bond-like secret agent in *The Living Bomb* (1963) – Ed is commissioned by the President to recover a key nuclear scientist for his country. Avallone's work includes novelisations ranging from the ultra-violent slasher-movie, *Friday the 13th, Part III*, to the all-American cosiness of *The Partridge Family*. He had a profitable sideline in pornography with his 'Coxeman' series, written under the pseudonym Troy Conway – detective thrillers with titles such as *The Cunning Linguist* (1970), *Eager Beaver* (1973), *A Stiff Proposition* (1971), *The Blow-your-Mind Job*, (1970), *The Best Laid Plans* (1969). These qualify him as the Russ Meyer of pulp. He occasionally touched the outside rim of class – as with his novelisation of Sam Fuller's cult classic film, *Shock Corridor* (1963). He was notorious for his literary feuds – notably against Stephen King, whom he considered a downright plagiarist. He married twice and died in Los Angeles, the city in which he spent most of his later life.

FN   Michael Angelo Avallone, Jr
MRT *The Tall Dolores*
Biog www.thrillingdetective.com/trivia/avallone.html

235. James Baldwin 1924–1987

I'm only black because you think you're white.

Baldwin was born in Harlem, New York. Illegitimate (his mother would never tell him who his father was) 'Jimmy' was brought up as the stepson of a 'storefront' Pentecostalist preacher, David Baldwin, whom he hated, in impoverished circumstances, among eight half-siblings. Both his parents had come north from the Deep South, looking for better times. His biological father, he was told, had been the son of former slaves and 'hated whites'. With nothing more than a high school education, in an area of New York 'geographically part of the United States but sociologically an island', as one biographer puts it, a member of a historically oppressed 'minority', convinced of his personal ugliness (particularly his 'frog eyes') and ashamed of his 'deviant' sexual longings, Baldwin was largely self-educated. He derived his powerful vision of the world, and his extraordinary eloquence, from the Baptist Church – the sole area of intellectual freedom, along with jazz, allowed blacks. He was, for three years in his adolescence, a 'young minister' and this carried over into his writing life. As Nelson Algren put it, 'Jimmy left the pulpit in order to preach.'

One could also argue that Baldwin left Harlem in order to write about it. Aged seventeen, he moved a couple of miles downtown to the Bohemian quarter of the metropolis, Greenwich Village, and began to write. Here it was he met Richard

Wright, the leading African American novelist of the time and – unlike Ralph Ellison, Wright's closest rival for that title – radically left-wing. Baldwin's Harlem background is reflected in the powerful *Bildungsroman* with which he made his name, *Go Tell It on the Mountain* (1953). Realistic in tone, it draws on Richard Wright's novel, *Native Son*, and was, for its time, shockingly 'frank' about race, sex and clashes of the two. In the light of his personal background, it is the ambivalent depiction of David Baldwin ('Gabriel Grimes') which is striking. His stepfather had died, mad and tubercular, in 1943. Baldwin was using fiction to understand, literally, where he came from.

Like other creative African-Americans (notably jazz musicians, such as Sidney Bechet, Don Byas and Dexter Gordon), Baldwin found a refuge from discrimination in Europe – particularly Paris, where he emigrated in 1948, with a borrowed $40 in his pocket. He may have been impelled by the growing interest in him and in Wright which was being taken by J. Edgar Hoover's men, suspicious as they were of undeferential blacks (notably Paul Robeson). Paris, on the other hand, was tolerant of gays. In Britain, or America, Baldwin's open affair with the first of his many lovers, seventeen-year-old painter, Lucien Happersberger, would have been an imprisonable crime – twice over, given Lucien's young age. His second novel, *Giovanni's Room* (1956), another work of self-exploration, dealt explicitly with homosexuality. A young, white American falls in love with a feckless Paris bartender, Giovanni. As in Baldwin's own life, permanent relationship was impossible – only transient moments of sexual connection. Sexual adventurers such as Henry Miller came to Paris for fulfilment and to get published. Baldwin came, as much as anything, for self-knowledge – to work things out.

The white hero in *Giovanni's Room* (much criticised during his lifetime) released Baldwin from the artistically hobbling 'protest novel' ghetto. He had been reading Joyce in Paris and there is a new level of art in his writing. *Giovanni's Room* enjoyed a *succès de scandale* in Anglo-Saxon markets less for the art than its taboo subject. It paved the way for Baldwin's apocalyptic tract about insurgent negritude in the US, *The Fire Next Time* (1963), and his more complicated treatment of the same themes (in the context of current Civil Rights agitation, urban riot, and reform) in *Another Country* (1962). Baldwin's position on race was hopelessly conflicted: as an exile himself (happiest in another country), an intellectual (in the French sense), and a sexual rebel, he could not easily take sides, even had he wanted to. Yet everyone wanted him to be a 'spokesman'. His biographer, James Campbell, describes him as a 'black James Dean'. He was 'mixed up', as the phrase of the day was. Radicals like Eldridge Cleaver thought him toothless. According to Cleaver, all James Baldwin wanted was to be a white man's bitch. He was a 'Negro' – afraid of being a 'Nigger' but too smart to be an Uncle Tom. Meanwhile, on the other side of the 'color line', the mass of middle-class whites found Baldwin too angry (did he not threaten them with 'fire'?) and, *au fond*, anti-American. French fragrance has never helped US writers with the home crowd.

Nor did it much help in Harlem – or Watts, or any other of the urban ghettoes which were on the point of explosion in the 1960s. African-Americans, particularly the church constituency in which Baldwin originated, were uneasy about his sexual orientation. His later novels dealing with African-Americanism, *Tell Me How Long the Train's Been Gone* (1968), *If Beale Street Could Talk* (1974), and *Just Above My Head* (1979) did not have the impact of their predecessors. He could not master the trick of turning 'the howl of the man who is being castrated' into art. But who could? His last years were spent as an eminent professor at Amherst, Massachusetts, and as an eminent expatriate in France – by now more of a home to him than the America he wrote about. Alcoholic, racked by multiple debilitating cancers, he died at his French country home in 1987: fifty years earlier, a doctor had informed his mother that her son would not live beyond the age of five.

FN   James Arthur Baldwin
MRT *Go Tell It on the Mountain*
Biog J. Campbell, *Talking at the Gates: A Life of James Baldwin* (1991)

236. Brian Aldiss 1925–

To contain the fuse of life, SF must be unsafe.

Aldiss's autobiography begins with an epiphanic experience – his arrival in India as an eighteen-year-old BOR ('British Other Rank'), in the 'forgotten' 14th Army, on its way to defeat the Japanese in the steaming jungles of Burma. The seething life of the Indian subcontinent as he and his fellow soldiers 'entrained' (the military loves such words) for their inland transit camp was a New World. 'Those days on the train', he recalls, 'were ones in which my determination to be a writer developed.' The clearest reflection of that experience is found in his finest SF novel, *Hothouse* (1962), and his most ambitious, the twin-sunned 'Helliconia' trilogy (1982–5).

Aldiss was brought up in the anything-but-hot Norfolk market town of East Dereham, the son of a gentleman's outfitter (whom, in his autobiography, he resolutely declines to call 'father'). At seven he was sent to a boarding school in Devon. In the dorm, 'new boys had to tell stories ... Soon I became champion story teller.'

But, if you were caught talking after lights out, teachers would swoop: 'The punishment was six strokes across the bum.' Inside every critic, thinks Aldiss, you can find 'a nasty little housemaster longing to get loose'. He saw active service in the Second World War and, more importantly, as the British Army routinely promised in its imperial heyday, he saw 'the world' – and its horrors. The war left a long wound. Aldiss loathed SF practitioners like Robert Heinlein, a novelist who glorified military combat (in works like *Starship Troopers*) but 'who had never been to war'. Back from war, Aldiss went to work in a second-hand bookshop in Oxford – an excrescence on the dreaming spires – and read voraciously. 'Bookshops', echoing Gorky, 'were his university'. His first published book was a Kippsian account of his life behind the counter.

In later years Aldiss reviewed his life in terms of four categories:

Bookshop = Commerce, Prison
Literature = University, Privilege
Far East = Poverty, Sun
SF = Freedom, Creativity.

He committed himself to SF and Freedom and Creativity, while serving gowned students (most, as he could not but observe, less well read than him). Aldiss made his Commerce + Prison-break when his first SF novel, *Non-Stop* (1958), was accepted by Faber, then headed by T. S. Eliot – an unlikely stroke of luck. Persuaded by the firm's editor Charles Monteith and Bruce Montgomery, friend of fellow SF-fan, Kingsley Amis, the most distinguished house in literary London was taking an interest in the genre. There were, Russell Square discovered (some fifty years after the fans had made the discovery), jewels in the pulp. It was Faber which took on *Lord of the Flies* after a dozen or more publishers had turned Golding down. As a practitioner of SF, Aldiss always embraced cultural risk, irrespective of how many strokes on the bum it might get him from life's boarding-house masters. He despised the 'safe' SF of John Wyndham, a writer he compared to a 'tea-cosy salesman for the Home Counties'. Not for Aldiss the 'cosy catastrophe' to be found in Wyndham's triffided England: Aldiss's visions were genuinely, not reassuringly, apocalyptic – and eerily prophetic as well. In *Earthworks* (1965), the 'Green', chemical-driven, agricultural revolution has produced a world in which cancer, and the death of wild flora and fauna, is universal. The novel is Rachel Carson's *Silent Spring* (1962) science-fictionalised. SF such as he, J. G. Ballard, John Brunner and William S. Burroughs practised was, Aldiss said, 'prodromic': it diagnosed the 'now' more accurately than realism ever could.

As the country's leading SF practitioner (contesting the title with Arthur C.

Clarke and J. G. Ballard), Aldiss resolutely expanded the frontiers of his genre, as well as its literary seriousness, creating a genuinely British style. Surfing the 'New Wave' of the 1960s, he wrote a Joycean experimental narrative – *Barefoot in the Head* (1969) – which infuriated the conservative fan-base – but then, so did Joyce. Aldiss, who had reviewed books for years for the *Oxford Times*, drew up the first comprehensive account of his genre in *Billion Year Spree* (1973), mapping its sprawling borders and raising its literary dignity by endowing it with a history. As a historian, he sees the origin of the genre – its 'big bang' – in Mary Shelley's *Frankenstein*. The concept is played with in his witty fantasia, *Frankenstein Unbound* (1973).

Aldiss's 'straight' fiction is as edgy as his SF. Martin Amis famously joked that in *Portnoy's Complaint* Philip Roth took the American novel all the way from the bedroom to the bathroom. In his Portnoyish 'Horatio Stubbs' trilogy (1970–78), Aldiss took the English novel from the Hampstead drawing room to the wanking exploits of the dorm and the barrack room. The Stubbsiad was accepted by Hutchinson but later rejected as 'filth' when the old-school proprietor of the firm happened to glance at the proofs of the first volume, *A Hand-Reared Boy* (1970). The book went on, inevitably, to be a bestseller under a more trendily sixtyish imprint.

In a striking parallelism with Ballard, Aldiss traces the origin of his creativity to childhood trauma. In late life, under therapy, as his second marriage was crumbling, he 'recovered' a primal memory, in which, aged three, his father – enraged by the baby's yowling – had held him out of a window. Infant Aldiss 'died' from shock and had to be resuscitated. 'That brutish act had its effect on my mental development ... [it] *caused* me.' More importantly, it caused the author in him: 'I wrote SF because I suspected the world was not as others saw it.' Aldiss was awarded an OBE in 2005 and deposited his literary remains at the Bodleian, the library of a university he never attended and which to this day regards SF as something sub-literary – unless, of course, written by C. S. Lewis.

FN   Brian Wilson Aldiss
MRT *Hothouse*
Biog B. Aldiss, *Bury my Heart at W. H. Smith's: A Writing Life* (1990)

237. Elmore Leonard 1925 –

I'm not gonna say anymore than I have to, if that. Chili Palmer

The greatest American novelist never to be mentioned in the same breath as 'Nobel Prize', Leonard was born into a Catholic household in New Orleans. His father was employed by General Motors (motto: 'What's good for GM is good for America') whose work eventually brought the family to the company's home town, Detroit, in the early 1930s. This was where Leonard stayed for most of his long life – although his speech, as interviewers noted, retained a southern lilt. When asked why, in old age, he had not moved to more clement climes – say Florida (where novels like *Stick* (1982) and *LaBrava* (1983) are set) or southern California (where *Get Shorty* (1990) and *Be Cool* (1999) are set) he says: 'Because I know all the streets now, and I'm too old to learn the streets anywhere else.' A more likely reason is his 'biblical' tribe of children (five), and (too many to count) grandchildren – and, as it happens, he just likes the grimy, run-down, once booming, city.

Leonard's lifelong love-affair with gunplay (or, more properly, the idea of it) was triggered shortly after his arrival in Detroit in the early 1930s. A journalist interviewing him in the 1990s noticed in his study a photograph of the young Elmore, 'dressed in a cap and suit, foot on the step of a curvy-bumpered car, brandishing a gun'. It's a child's re-enactment of the famous pose struck by Bonnie Parker, made famous the second time around in the 1960s movie, *Bonnie and Clyde*. Leonard confirmed the allusion, adding: 'There is something about that time which affected me. It was said that there were probably twenty bank robbers for every doctor in America then, and I was certainly aware of the desperadoes. I was aware of what was going on with Bonnie and Clyde, and Pretty Boy Floyd. It was in the papers all the time. They were all killed, but the important ones were killed in 1934.' In Leonard's latest phase, with novels such as *The Hot Kid* (2005) and *Up in Honey's Room* (2007), he returns to the Bonnie and Clyde era which so entranced him as a boy.

The Leonard household was wholly uncriminal, mildly bookish (his mother was a Book of the Month Club subscriber) and Leonard credits his sister with getting him to read avidly. At school he was nicknamed 'Dutch', after a now long-forgotten professional baseball pitcher. Leonard was obsessed with baseball, almost as much as with gangsters, and 'Dutch' stuck. He graduated from high school in 1943, and was recruited into the Navy 'Seabees' – construction battalions. He wanted to be a marine, but his eyes were too weak. In 1946, on the GI Bill, he studied English and Philosophy at the University of Detroit. By the time of his graduation in 1950, he was already married to his first wife, Beverly. He worked for a while as a copy writer for an advertising firm – which he hated. He was getting up at five to write fiction – which he liked. He had composed a couple of 'literary things' at university, but couldn't get them past quibbling editors. There was, he correctly anticipated, less quibble downmarket and he began writing Westerns on the Max Brand model. He had studied Hemingway's short story, 'The Killers', and absorbed its laconic style, letting the white space between words do the hard work, letting the dialogue do the talking and letting the narrative hang on the page.

His work sold. 'I've always been successful', he says. Two of his early stories were optioned (at $5,000 apiece) for what became very superior movies in the new 'psychological Western' mode: *The Tall T* (1957) – bungled stagecoach robbery, and *3:10 to Yuma* (1957) – honest guy has to take a criminal to justice in Yuma, with the criminal's gang likely to get to him before the train arrives. In both, Leonard builds up a complex interfusion of hero and villain. It is handled even more successfully in the finest film adapted from his Westerns, *Hombre* (1967), another bungled stagecoach robbery. The story for *Hombre* was published in 1961, when Leonard was moving away from the Western into crime-writing – his true *métier*, as admirers believe – although the motive was commercial. Boots and saddles had worn out their charm in Hollywood – smart thrillers were very much in. As a crime writer, Leonard mingled his existing style with that of George V. Higgins, the Boston-based author of *The Friends of Eddie Coyle*. Even more than Hemingway, Higgins's narrative pivoted on terse dialogue and ultra-tight plotting, making the reader work hard to fill the gaps. There was also a new street crudity of diction. Leonard's mother was appalled: 'Why don't you write those Westerns any more?' she asked, 'they were so *nice*.'

Leonard's early crime novels were set in Detroit – the 'city primeval' as he called it. The best is *52 Pick-Up* (1974) – businessman has fling, is blackmailed by sadist crook and goes vigilante, ingeniously. Leonard's later fiction roams far from Motown. *Glitz* (1985), the first of his novels to make the *New York Times* bestseller list, is set in Atlantic City and Puerto Rico; *Maximum Bob* (1991) in Palm Beach. *Pagan Babies* (2000) switches between Rwanda and Detroit. All, however, have Leonard's hallmark crispness and – the later works particularly – a play of enigmatic comedy over the action, however brutal. It creates a distinctive taste.

One work of Leonard's is different, though. *Touch* was written in 1977, but held back for ten years lest, as his publishers feared, it contaminate the tough-guy Elmore Leonard brand. He had been a heavy drinker for many years and was out of control by the early 1970s. He bobbed in and out of AA, and finally took his last drink at 9 o'clock, on 24 January 1977. His first marriage collapsed at the same time. *Touch* seems to return to the faith of the author's childhood. A young Michigan man, it seems, can make the blind see and perform miracles. He works with alcoholics: poor sods who need miracles, if anyone does. *Touch* can be glossed as a public vote of thanks to the 'fellowship' – AA. A 'recovering' Leonard remarried twice, the third time after his second wife died of cancer. He did not, as he says, like being single. Leave that to his heroes, like Stick.

Leonard's genius extends beyond what is found on the pages of his books. Uniquely, he inspires film directors and stars to their best work. Directors such as Budd Boetticher, Barry Sonnenfeld, John Frankenheimer, Martin Ritt and Steven Soderbergh make up a distinguished roll call, as do the Leonard movies they have done. Paul Newman and Richard Boone, playing against each other, have never given better performances than they did in *Hombre*. Leonard sharpens things. The director with whom Leonard has collaborated most fruitfully is Quentin Tarantino, in *Jackie Brown* (1997) – the novel was called *Rum Punch* (1992). Tarantino's masterwork, *Pulp Fiction*, can be read as an extended and subtle homage to Leonard. Among the most distinguished of his literary admirers is Martin Amis, who is on record as thinking that alongside Leonard, even Raymond Chandler looks clumsy – rather like saying Nureyev can't dance or Glenn Gould can't play. Leonard good-naturedly side-steps such encomiums: 'I don't have all the words like Martin Amis. He uses words I've never heard of; ones I've never seen on paper.'

FN   Elmore John Leonard, Jr
MRT *52 Pick-Up*
Biog P. Challen, *Get Dutch! A Biography of Elmore Leonard* (2000)

238. Flannery O'Connor 1925–1964

I live mainly in my work.

O'Connor's biographer, Brad Gooch, takes as his epigraph the author's wry put-down: 'There won't be any biographies of me because, for only one reason, lives spent between the house and the chicken yard do not make exciting copy.' Poultry were, in fact, a very big thing in O'Connor's life. Not least because, as she said (wry as ever) the birds did not know she was a writer. When O'Connor was just five years old, the Pathé News company dispatched a cameraman from its main offices in New York City to film a 'buff Cochin bantam' that she had, reportedly, taught to walk backwards. 'From that day,' she recalled, 'I began to collect chickens.' In later life her preference extended to the collection of more exotic fowl – particularly peacocks.

O'Connor was born, raised and lived her life Catholic in what she liked to call 'the Protestant South'. Throughout her life she attended mass daily. Her fiction is as Catholic – if differently so – as that of Graham Greene or François Mauriac, her most admired fellow novelist. In O'Connor's Deep South, Catholics, particularly Irish Catholics, were only a notch or two above Jews and Negroes in the social pecking order. Legislation such as the outrageous Convent Inspection Bill (designed to check that the Church was not into the kind of white slavery popularised by Maria Monk) was still on the books – if no longer in force – at the time of O'Connor's birth. She was born in Savannah, Georgia, a town for which she had no affection in later life – not that she did for any city. Of her state capital, she wisecracked: 'My idea about Atlanta is to get in, get it over, and get out before dark.' At least she never, like another Southern novelist, pictured it burned to the ground ('I sure am sick of the Civil War,' she once said – and sick of novels like Margaret Mitchell's as well). None the less, memorials of the 'war' were unforgettably all around her as she grew up. She was christened Mary Flannery O'Connor, her middle name that of a Civil War hero. Why were Southern novelists so good? she was once asked. 'Because we lost,' she briskly replied.

She was brought up under the protective wing of her redoubtable mother, the aptly named Regina. Her father, the royally henpecked Ed O'Connor, was a failed businessman, brought low by the Depression and chronic illness. Even so the family survived the awful decade of the 1930s more comfortably than some. 'There is,' Flannery's biographer records, 'no evidence that O'Connor's childhood was troubled'. In 1938, when she was twelve, the family moved to the family dairy farm, Andalusia, at Milledgeville, which Regina ran efficiently and profitably: there was still money in staples like milk and beef but not – with the boll weevil raging through the fields – cotton.

Incorrigibly self-deprecating, O'Connor records herself as having been 'a pidgeon-toed, only-child with a receding chin and a you-leave-me-alone-or-I'll-bite-you complex'. She attended convent school and recalled resolving 'to stay aged twelve for life'. She divulged virtually nothing of her adult inner life to posterity. She may have been sexually nervous, inclined to chastity on religious grounds, or bisexual (although she is recorded as thinking lesbianism 'unclean'). A college acquaintance observed that 'O'Connor never seemed interested in the opposite sex', or her own. Her biographer suggests that 'O'Connor expressed her inner life through her birds.' She was fascinated by the magnificent fan displays of the peacock and liked being pictured posed alongside her prize specimens.

She entered the Georgia State College for Women in 1942, aged seventeen. A high-performing student in the classroom, she wrote and drew cartoons for the college newspaper, graduated in 1945 and – considering a career in journalism

– went on to postgraduate study at Iowa. Momentously, she became involved in that university's creative writing programme – at the time the best in the country, under the charismatic Paul Engle. He encouraged her to write and her early exercises in short fiction were passed around by discriminating judges able to help her on her way. Embarking on a writing career, she adopted the androgynous pen name 'Flannery'. Of the alternative, 'Mary O'Connor', she inquired quizzically: 'Who's going to buy the stories of an Irish washerwoman?' Her narratives all revolve around male characters, and inevitably 'Flannery O'Connor' (like Harper Lee) was routinely mistaken for a man.

While at the Iowa Writers' Workshop, O'Connor was already immersing herself in religious commentary: Aquinas, Simone Weil, Teilhard de Chardin were of particular interest to her. 'I read a lot of theology,' she said, 'because it makes my writing bolder.' She read it typically at night, before going to bed. The next formative step in her career was a fellowship at the Yaddo writers' colony in New York State in 1948. She was there at the same time as Patricia Highsmith, currently working on her first novel, *Strangers on a Train*. O'Connor was meanwhile working on the short story, 'The Train', which would form the first chapter of her first novel, *Wise Blood*. She did not, like Highsmith, join in the high jinks and 'always left before they started to break things', but it was at Yaddo that she met Robert Lowell. A fellow Catholic, Lowell talked her work up (which was welcome) and went so far as to claim that personally she was a saint – a compliment which O'Connor found extremely distasteful. Acquaintances thought 'she fell' for Lowell. His wife, Elizabeth Hardwick, described O'Connor spitefully as 'plain' and 'whiney' – which adds to the suspicion that something may have been in the air.

In 1951, aged twenty-six, O'Connor was diagnosed with lupus erythematosus, the same disease – for which there was no cure – that had killed her father in 1941. It meant a life of progressive invalidism at Andalusia, in the care (devoted but overbearing) of her mother. After seven years perfecting her 'opus nauseous', O'Connor published *Wise Blood* in 1952. In a later preface (1962), she asserted it was 'a comic novel about a Christian *malgré lui*' – an interpretation which most readers may find a bit of a stretch. As the novel opens, it is 1947. Hazel Motes (the biblical allusion to eyes is meaningful) has come back from the war but we know nothing of his four years' service for his country other than that the army 'sent him half way round the world and forgot him'. He was wounded, and the shrapnel still in his body is poisoning him. Motes is first encountered on the train back to Taulkinham, Tennessee, wearing a suit of glaring blue, with the price tag attached ($11.98), and a 'fierce black hat'. He is resolved to be a preacher. Religion is buzzing around in his head 'like a wasp'. The problem is, he 'doesn't believe in anything'.

Hazel solves the problem by establishing the 'Church of Truth without Jesus Christ Crucified'. He preaches his Christless Christianity from the hood of his beat-up car, 'a rat-colored machine'.

He recruits two disciples: one is an idiot boy, Enoch Emery, who has 'wise blood' but an unwise head. A guard at the local zoo, Enoch is obliged (to promote a King-Kong style movie) to make himself even more ridiculous in a gorilla suit. As an act of devotion, he steals a holy relic for Hazel from the city museum – an Egyptian mummy ('a dead part-nigger shriveled up dwarf' is the recipient's blunt description). Hazel's other disciple is a pubescent, underage nymphomaniac, Sabbath Lily Hawks, who affords him cheaper relief than the local whorehouse (a setting which, as unkind male critics pointed out, did not show O'Connor at her most knowledgeable). In the climax of the story, Hazel blinds himself with quick lime, mortifies his body with barbed wire, and puts sharp stones in his shoes. Why? he is asked. 'To pay' is his reply. He finally dies of starvation in a ditch.

O'Connor called *Wise Blood* 'autobiographical'. It's a difficult comment to make sense of, but easier than the instruction mentioned earlier that the work should be read as comedy. The novel was published in 1952 to largely perplexed reviews ('Southern Gothic' was not yet an established genre) and a surge of scandalised protest in Milledgeville, where bookstores sold it in brown paper bags. A disapproving Regina stopped reading at page 9. The American publishers who, like other novelists, had great faith in O'Connor, sent a proof copy to Evelyn Waugh in the hope that, as a Catholic, he would recognise its genius. He replied, frigidly: 'If this is really the unaided work of a young lady, it is a remarkable product.' T. S. Eliot (Anglo-Catholic, and a Southerner by birth) was also shown the text, with a view to Faber publishing it, and returned it with the observation 'my nerves are just not strong enough'.

O'Connor had some unsatisfactory close relationships with men, one of whom reported that kissing her was like kissing a skeleton. She had a long, intimate correspondence with Betty Hester, who was alcoholic, lesbian and chronically suicidal. Hester went so far as to say she loved O'Connor but the relationship never went beyond the intimacy of letters. By 1954 O'Connor needed a cane to walk with and by the end of the decade crutches. A novel took her seven years of grinding work – but at least it could be said that this was three times the pace of her fellow Southern novelist, Katherine Anne Porter, who took twenty-four years over *Ship of Fools*. Short stories took O'Connor less time and she turned out a couple of volumes' worth from the mid-1940s on, with smart titles such as: 'You Can't Be Any Poorer than Dead', 'The Life You Save May Be Your Own', 'The Artificial Nigger' and, her most famous work in this area, 'A Good Man is Hard to Find'. By the time of her second, and last, novel in 1960, O'Connor was, with Eudora Welty, Carson McCullers and Porter, a dominant Southern fiction voice: the leader of a school where women, unusually, shared the lead.

Increasingly incapacitated, O'Connor was looked after by her mother and taken on a trip to Lourdes in 1958. It was her sole trip outside the US. Wry as ever, she commented that much as she loved the Catholic religion she was not sure that she was prepared 'to take a bath for it'. She declined to be dunked, but was profoundly moved by the experience, and by Rome. She was profoundly unmoved by the civil rights movement ('this race business') which was tearing the South apart in the early 1960s.

Her second novel, *The Violent Bear It Away*, was published in 1960. Like *Wise Blood*, it chronicles the 'hard facts of service for the Lord'. The narrative is more complex (she had been – tentatively – studying Faulkner). Death, redemption, temptation and salvation are again the themes. The novel opens:

> Francis Marion Tarwater's uncle had been dead for only half a day when the boy got too drunk to finish digging his grave and a Negro named Buford Munson, who had come to get a jug filled, had to finish it and drag the body from the breakfast table where it was still sitting and bury it in a decent and Christian way, with the sign of its Saviour at the head of the grave and enough dirt on top to keep the dogs from digging it up.

'Tarwater', readers of *Great Expectations* will recall, has overtones of 'snake oil' – false salvation of the body. The novel, one notes, is dedicated to the novelist's dead father whose inheritance – lupus – is killing her. Psychobiographers have had a fine time with Flannery O'Connor. Tarwater, it emerges, was kidnapped as a child (he does not know his age) by his uncle who believed he would grow up to have a mission. After a fraught passage with the devil, and an ugly rape, Francis's eyes are 'burned clean'. He hears the command of God to go out into the world and 'GO WARN THE CHILDREN OF GOD OF THE TERRIBLE SPEED OF MERCY'. Which he does.

The Violent Bear It Away, such being the fate of second novels, was less well received than its predecessor. But at the time of her death, O'Connor was becoming regarded as one of the very great American writers. The doomed John Kennedy Toole, author of the unpublishable *Confederacy of Dunces*, made a pilgrimage to Milledgeville just before connecting some garden hosepipe to the exhaust of his car and gassing himself outside Biloxi in Mississippi on 26 March 1969. He was just thirty-one years old, eight years younger than O'Connor at the time of her death.

FN   Mary Flannery O'Connor
MRT   *Wise Blood*
Biog   B. Gooch, *Flannery; A Life of Flannery O'Connor* (2009)

239. William Styron 1925–2006

Depression is a wimp of a word for a howling tempest in the brain.

William Styron was born in the literary decade defined as Gertrude Stein's 'lost generation'. '*They* weren't lost. What they were doing was losing *us*,' complains one of his characters. He hit his stride in the early 1950s as the 'Southern Novel', the literary school of which he was the last ornament (along with Faulkner, Katherine Anne Porter, Eudora Welty), was decaying, replaced by the smarter New York Jewish school (Roth, Malamud, Mailer). The 'Kingdom of the Jews,' he calls it, ironically, in the opening paragraph of *Sophie's Choice*. Jewish intellectuals and artists are typically alien elements in Styron's fiction.

It was Styron's fate in life always to arrive just after the great historical event. He was swept up in the patriotism of the Second World War and signed up as soon as he was age-eligible, but just on the brink of being shipped out they dropped the bomb. As a reservist officer recalled for Korea in 1951, he was invalided out with eye trouble – again on the eve of being posted into battle. But there was always money in Styron's life to cushion such frustrations. He was born into money, married more of it, and with two mid-career No.1 bestsellers, his situation was, as Victorians would have said, 'warm'. He could travel first class and choose where he lived – which was expensive places on the Eastern seaboard. Most significantly, he could take his time over his novels. He published only four major works in a sixty-year career. A forty-year 'abusive' drinking career was an added impediment – but money helped there as well.

William Clark Styron II was born in Newport News, Virginia. He offers a description in the opening pages of his debut novel, *Lie Down in Darkness* (1951), redolent with swamp smells, shoreline flotsam and the sprawling debris of a decaying Southern seaport which he left, but which never left him. Typically, the viewpoint is that of an arriving train, with the coffin of a returned suicide in its baggage car. Styron's grandfather had fought for the Confederates. It is him, one guesses, that Styron quotes in the person of the patriarchal Loftis, in his first novel: 'we stand at the back door of glory ... we are the driblet turds of angels'. The Styrons were a family historically engaged in coastal trade and (a mere sixty years earlier) plantations and slaves. His father, also William, with whom he had a difficult relationship, was a marine engineer working in the docks of 'Tidewater' – as Styron called the James River estuary. William's mother died lingeringly of cancer when he was fourteen. It was, he later recalled, traumatic.

His father remarried promptly and the Styron home was thereafter inhospitable for William Jr. After an undistinguished school career, where football mattered more to him than books, Styron ended up at Duke University. His undergraduate course was interrupted by his Marine service. After graduating, unbloodied, from Duke after the war, he gravitated – by literary magnetism – to New York, a city that was in creative ferment. Styron had, as he put it, 'the literary syrup inside him but it would not pour'. Like Saul Bellow's hero, he 'dangled' in a lodging house in Brooklyn. He had a day-job at the publisher McGraw-Hill. He wanted to be William Faulkner; they wanted someone to Roto-root through the slush pile. He walked out to become a full-time writer.

A former girlfriend's suicide was the 'germ' of his first novel *Lie Down in Darkness*, which he struggled with for three years. It is 1946 in the novel as it opens. Milton Loftis – well born, rich and cultivated – is terminally alcoholic, chronically adulterous and spiritually exhausted. His daughter Peyton, having fled the South to marry a Jewish artist in New York, has committed suicide. Her remains are returning 'home' to Tidewater, to lie down in final darkness. Milton's subsequent decline is accelerated by the pain of his incestuous lust for Peyton – the principal cause of his daughter's self-destruction (the novel veers very close to Faulkner's *The Sound and the Fury*, in this plot strand).

Lie Down was published in 1951, to superb reviews. Just twenty-six years old, Styron was suddenly at the top of the tree. His life thereafter was one of comfortable international 'wander' (his word). *Lie Down* earned him a Prix de Rome fellowship and he moved from the Italian capital to Paris, where he was instrumental in setting up the *Paris Review* in 1953. In one of its hallmark author interviews, Styron revealed that in his study he had posted over his desk a slogan from Flaubert: 'Be regular and orderly in your life, like a bourgeois, so that you may be violent and original in your work.' Drink, he found, was the catalyst for the necessary creative violence: 'I used alcohol', he later wrote, 'as the magical conduit to fantasy and euphoria.' It made the syrup pour. Around this period in Paris, Styron read Camus for the first time. It 'set the tone' for all his subsequent fiction. Put another way, it rinsed Faulkner out of his system and 'cleansed my intellect'. 'The Myth of Sisyphus' said it all for Styron: 'There is but one truly serious philosophical problem, and that is suicide.' As he later observed, in his introspective tract, *Darkness Visible*, suicide is the mainspring of all his plots – and he diced with it himself throughout his life.

Following the bourgeois injunction over his desk, in 1953 he had married Rose Burgunder, a department-store heiress from Baltimore. They returned to live in a converted farmhouse in Connecticut in the 1960s and remained happily married there for over half a century. Meanwhile, Styron's next work *The Long March* (1956) was inspired by his training for Korea. A reservist, Jack Culver, is called back to the service after six years in which he has grown flabby, thoughtful and wholly unbelligerent. The narrative opens with a Camusian 'absurdity'. A couple of duff mortar shells (held-over ordnance from the Second World War) have fallen short, killing eight of Culver's men, as they stood in a chow line. The story opens: 'One noon, in the blaze of a cloudless Carolina summer, what was left of eight dead boys lay strewn about the landscape, among the poison ivy and the pine needles and loblolly saplings.' Friendly fire, they call it. It is followed by another absurdity – a pointless, Sisyphean, 36-mile night march. Out of these absurdities, meaning is forged. Culver works out the peculiar compromise the civilian-warrior has to make.

Styron's pre-marital European years were the background to his second full-length novel, *Set This House on Fire* (1960). Set principally in Italy, it unravels, in cunning flashback, a rape, a murder and, inevitably, a suicide. The novel went down well in Europe, but left the Anglo-American reader cold. Styron would, however, generate heat in plenty with his next novel. In his Connecticut retirement he had made close friends with James Baldwin. As Styron recalled, 'Night after night Jimmy and I talked, drinking whisky through the hours until the chill dawn. He was spellbinding, and he told me more about the frustrations and anguish of being a black man in America than I had known until then.' These drink-sodden nocturnal conversations were the germ for *The Confessions of Nat Turner* (1967). Turner was, historically, the leader of 'the only effective revolt in the annals of American Negro Slavery', which had taken place not far from where Styron had been born, in 1831. The rebellion was put down without too much trouble and Turner was hanged. The novel opens with him in his cell, awaiting trial (the scenario, Styron admitted, was lifted from *L'Étranger*). Why did he do it? Nat – like Camus's Meursault – has no plausible answer.

The novel was published in 1967, just three years after the Civil Rights Act, two years after the Watts riots in Los Angeles, a year after the formation of the Black Panthers, and a few months before the assassination of Martin Luther King. It was OK for a white lady abolitionist to create 'Uncle Tom' in 1852 but it was not all right for a rich white Southerner (who didn't even live there, for God's sake) to think he could, because he was a 'liberal,' get inside a hero of the Black struggle a hundred years later. Nat Turner's 'Confessions' went straight to the top of the *New York Times* bestseller list and the top of the unofficial Index Librorum Prohibitorum for every right-thinking intellectual and black radical of the time. The novel won a Pulitzer, but that did not redeem it. Nor did the defence mounted by James Baldwin. All that Baldwin wanted, declared Eldridge Cleaver (with a sneer at the other writer's known homosexuality), was to be fucked by white men. The novel provoked hate mail and physical threats. 'The whole thing,' Styron told the British journalist James Campbell, 'soured me in being a friend of black people ... and I hate to say that.'

There followed years of silence before the publication of Styron's last major work, *Sophie's Choice* (1979). This novel intertwines yet another portrait of Styron ('Stingo') as a young man in post-war New York with the story of a mysterious Polish immigrant, Sophie Zawistowska, a fellow boarder at his lodging house. She is, it emerges, a non-Jewish survivor of Auschwitz. Her 'choice' was which child to sacrifice to the Dr Mengele figure and the SS executioners:

> 'So you believe in Christ the Redeemer?' the doctor said in a thick-tongued but oddly abstract voice, like that of a lecturer examining the delicately shaded facet of a proposition in logic. Then he said something which for an instant was totally mystifying: 'Did he not say, "Suffer the little children to come unto me"?' He turned back to her, moving with the twitchy methodicalness of a drunk.
>
> Sophie, with an inanity poised on her tongue and choked with fear, was about to attempt a reply when the doctor said, 'You may keep one of your children.'
>
> '*Bitte?*' said Sophie.
>
> 'You may keep one of your children,' he repeated. 'The other one will have to go. Which one will you keep?'
>
> 'You mean, I have to choose?'
>
> 'You're a Polack, not a Yid. That gives you a privilege – a choice.'

Stingo's consummating act of love with her, and Sophie's final, Styronian, act (the self-chosen death, inevitability) are the novel's climax. Styron received the record-breaking sum of $750,000 for the novel's film rights and the adaptation appeared in 1982. Meryl Streep won an Oscar for her portrayal of Sophie.

Over the remaining quarter of a century of his long life, Styron's only major publication (some short stories aside) was his confessional study of his lifelong depression, *Darkness Visible: A Memoir of Madness* (1990). He never completed his planned great work, *The Way of the Warrior*, a novel about the Korean conflict in which he had nearly been involved.

FN   William Clark Styron, Jr
MRT   *The Long March*
Biog   James L. West III, *William Styron: A Life* (1998)

240. John Berger 1926–

It's the struggle towards truthfulness which is the same whether one is writing a poem, a novel or an argument.

Perennial thorn in the thigh of authority, John Berger has been a political presence in British fiction since the publication of his first novel, *A Painter of Our Time*, in 1958. The painter of the title, a 'disappeared' Hungarian exile, is reconstructed through his diary – a document reflecting the oppressions on artistic expression of totalitarianism and the scarcely less sinister oppressions of the self-proclaimed 'free world'. The novel raised the ire of the CIA-funded Congress for Cultural Freedom (a body devised to roll back the tide of Marxist-intellectual orthodoxy infecting Europe) which attempted, unsuccessfully, to suppress *A Painter of Our Time* in the name of cultural freedom – neatly proving the novel's point.

Berger was born in Hackney, London, the son of a former army officer, Jewish by origin, who had converted to Christianity and had at one point aspirations to the priesthood. Berger's Englishness is, as he points out, only one generational layer deep. He may not, he sometimes feels, belong here: 'When I first went to Eastern Europe in the 50s, I had a very strange feeling. I had a feeling that there were little details of daily life which were incredibly familiar to me, although in fact I had never seen them before.' He had 'two educations', Berger claims, though school supplied neither of them. His first education began when he ran away, aged sixteen, to study at the Chelsea School of Art 'and see naked women'. It was the early 1940s. The war-time company he kept outside school 'was largely European refugees from fascism – political, mostly Jewish refugees'. Rootlessness would be his big theme.

Aged eighteen, he was conscripted into the armed forces, just as the war was coming to an end. On being demobbed he returned to the Chelsea School, studying, teaching and writing on art for the papers, notably those of a congenially left-wing persuasion, such as *Tribune* (where he was a colleague of George Orwell) and the *New Statesman*. This mingling of theory and practice, together with his fervid political radicalism, fed into his influential TV series, and accompanying monograph, *Ways of Seeing* (BBC, 1972), which introduced a generation of British viewers to the excitements of materialist aesthetics. The series was conceived as a counterblast to Kenneth Clark's high-connoisseurial series, *Civilisation*, three years earlier. Was 'art' something rich people hung on walls? Or the people's weapon against those rich people? Like other British intellectuals, Berger was bitterly disillusioned with international communism after the 1956 invasion of Hungary, although he has always maintained the intellectual rigour formed in his 'Permanent Red' (as he later called them) years. At the same period in the 1950s, he gave up painting for writing as his main vocation. Berger's writing since has ranged over higher journalism, film screenplays and – increasingly – fiction and social pamphleteering (sometimes the two mix with Berger). Early novels such as *The Foot of Clive* (1962) and *Corker's Freedom* (1964) are neo-realistic, reminiscent of David Storey, with whose work Berger's, at this period, has clear similarities. Both writers, interestingly, are trained pictorial artists.

Berger's great success in fiction came with the more overtly modernist *G.* (1972), a Kafkaesque study of alienated hyperconsciousness, set in the 1890s. *G.* – controversially – scooped both the Booker and James Tait Black prizes in 1972 and the author caused a huge stir when, on being presented the Booker award cheque, he disrupted the normally stultifyingly serene, black-tie ceremony by turning on the industrial combine which sponsored the event, accusing them of exploiting black labour in the West Indies. He would, he declared, give half the money to the Black Panthers. The movement, it subsequently emerged, no longer existed – but the gesture, politically empty and histrionic as it was, rocked the literary world. Perversely it was also rather good for the Booker Prize on the 'any publicity is good publicity' principle.

Since 1962 Berger has lived in a small village in the French Alps, a setting he has used in his fiction. He has over the years taken up the causes of both the European peasant and the European immigrant, the two great victim groups of the so-called European Union; see, for example, his polemic, *A Seventh Man: Migrant Workers in Europe* (1975). This, he says, has been 'My second education ... It began about 25 years ago [he is speaking in the late 1980s], when I moved to a village in the Alps. The people there, with whom I became quite close, were older peasants who had once been the children of subsistence farmers. From them I learned a lot about nature, the land, the seasons and a set of priorities by which they tried to live. I learned quite a lot of practical, physical tasks and a kind of ethical code.'

Detached from England, Berger's fictional settings have correspondingly internationalised. *To the Wedding* (1995), his most accomplished novel after *G.*, has a sero-positive heroine and examines the human repercussions of Aids, a subject from which – like immigration – modern fiction has largely averted its eyes. Berger has always made himself look at what others would not, or could not put themselves in a position to see. *King: A Street Story* (1999), for example, observes urban human suffering through the eyes of a homeless dog. In the twenty-first century, Berger has been increasingly preoccupied with the struggle of the Palestinians and their persecution by 'wall and bulldozer'. He calls for a 'cultural boycott' of Israel. Berger has never, it seems, seen a thigh in which he did not insert himself as a thorn.

FN   John Peter Berger
MRT G.
Biog G. Dyer, *Ways of Telling: The Work of John Berger* (1986)

241. John Fowles 1926–2005

The truth about any artist, however terrible, is better than the silence.

John Fowles was brought up in Leigh-on-Sea, a 'bloody town' which he grew up hating because 'it sapped all the beauty out of things' – specifically nature. If there was a British novelist Fowles felt an affinity to, it was Richard Jefferies, but who could imagine themselves Bevis in Leigh on bloody Sea? Fowles's father was in the tobacco import business. The family fortunes had sunk and Robert Fowles, a First World War survivor, was crippled for the rest of his days with lingering shell shock. He was, however, a keen amateur student of philosophy, forever pondering the big 'What does it all mean?' The philosopher Charles Sanders Peirce was a main interest; parenting interested him not at all. John was an only child until he was sixteen, at which point, he claimed, he metamorphosed overnight into a writer. He was brought up in a domestic environment of psychic loneliness and Peircian pragmatism. In later life he came to despise his father as 'a Victorian rabbit' and his mother as a 'Victorian vegetable': two great lumps of inertia who, as D. H. Lawrence once said about women, 'stopped men from reaching the stars'. He would get sweet revenge on Victorian England in *The French Lieutenant's Woman.*

Hitler, Fowles archly claimed, 'helped me greatly' because, aged thirteen when the war started, he was evacuated and spent five idyllic years in a remote and rural Devon village – Bevis at last. From adolescence onwards he kept voluminous diaries, journals and private writing. It was always more interesting to him than the stuff he later published; it was part of what he called his 'chauvinism of self', something, that is, more glorious than old-fashioned selfishness or egotism. In his teenage years Fowles was a boarder at a minor public school, Bedford School, which meant classics, cricket, painfully prolonged virginity, and chronic uncertainty about his heterosexuality. On leaving school in 1944, he was commissioned into the Royal Marines, an elite and highly selective arm of the service. Had Hitler been less friendly, and kept the war going a year or two longer, Lieutenant Fowles might have seen action as a commando. As it was he entered active service on the day, as he liked to recall, that the war ended.

Fowles became one of the demobilised military intake into Oxford University in 1947. He 'drifted', choosing, eventually, to do French – which meant existentialism and Brigitte Bardot. He was a virgin until he was twenty-two, when an experienced Frenchwoman, Micheline Gilbert, introduced him to sex and Camus. Both would be lifelong interests thereafter. Despite ill-health and a simmering nervous breakdown, he took a respectable degree and chose (declining his family 'trade') to teach abroad: first in France, then, in 1951, on the Peloponnesian island of Spetses, at what was grandly called 'the Eton of Greece'. He spent two life-changing years on the island, and enjoyed two tangled love affairs, before being dismissed for moral turpitude and general bolshiness. Out of the experience came a novel, *The Magus* (1965), which it would take him fifteen years to finish writing – one cannot say he ever completed it. It took him less time to relieve his best friend at the school (another hopeful novelist), Roy Christy, of his wife, Elizabeth. After much angst ('a slow moral crack-up,' he called it) and a messy divorce, Fowles and the former Mrs Christy married in 1957. At the same period, he gave up wildfowling – previously a main pleasure in his life and a connection with his idyllic years in Devon. The couple settled in Hampstead and he went through a succession of teaching jobs well below his abilities.

Fowles regarded himself as primarily a writer not a teacher, but he was constitutionally reluctant to publish. His first novel would not come out until he was thirty-seven, though it was worth waiting for. *The Collector* (1963) is a tour de force exercise in I-narration. The I-narrator is Frederick Clegg, an impotent young psychopath of the lower classes, who has two interests: catching, killing and mounting butterflies; and sexual voyeurism. Having won a lottery prize, Clegg (who prefers to be called 'Ferdinand') captures and imprisons in his cellar a young girl – Miranda (the Shakespearian allusions are pushed hard in the novel). Clegg's diary alternates with hers. It all ends bleakly, there being no Prospero in this Fowlesian world. The novel was an international bestseller and was adapted as a Hollywood film in 1965. Fowles scorned its happy ending. It was what the audience wanted, the director William Wyler patiently informed him. They were boss. Fowles took the hint and in his next two novels offered double endings. It was seen by his admirers as postmodernism, but it could also be seen as the Charles Peirce pragmatism his father had trained him in. At this period – around 1963 – Fowles came across *Le Grand Meaulnes*. Alain-Fournier's novel, first published fifty years earlier, and its celebration of the *domaine perdu* – the lost country – influenced him more than anything since Camus' *The Rebel*. Fiction itself was, he determined, that impossibly yearned-for other country.

Royalties from *The Collector* had now freed Fowles from the hated classroom and enabled him, finally, to wrap up work on *The Magus*. In the interim, however, he published (much against his publisher's advice) his philosophical manifesto, *The Aristos* (1964). It took the form of a majestic ('pompous,' as the universally hostile reviews thought) *non serviam*. 'My chief concern in *The Aristos*', declared Fowles loftily, 'is to preserve the freedom of the individual against all those pressures-to-conform that threaten our century.' What he advocated was a version of Carlyle's hero worship – individuals who could rise above the Heraclitean flux and the quotidian. 'I've never needed other human beings really,' he once said, and his misanthropy was enlarged on in a revenge-on-humanity fiction he never published called 'The Fucker'.

The Magus, earlier entitled 'The Godgame', is the acid test for Fowlesphiliacs. The novel-cum-fable was a decade and a half in the making – a quarter of a century if one includes the period between the first version (1966) and the second (1977). A fantasia woven out of his two, emotionally tempestuous, years on Spetses ('Phraxos' in the novel) it follows the perplexities of Nicholas Urfe, a young English teacher, the woman he loves, and the malignantly playful magician of the title, Maurice Conchis. The 1968 film of *The Magus* inspired Woody Allen's much-relished wisecrack, 'If I had to live my life again, I'd do everything the same, except that I wouldn't see *The Magus*.' Fowles thought the actors (principally Michael Caine, who played Urfe) did not understand the narrative – nor Woody Allen, evidently.

Fowles was now rich enough to take up residence in a fine house at Lyme Regis, the setting for his most successful novel, *The French Lieutenant's Woman* (1969). A neo-Victorian narrative of appropriately three-volume length, it celebrates – in the sexually rebellious heroine, and the reluctantly rebellious hero – profound anti-Victorianism. At this period of his writing career, Fowles felt close – spiritually and regionally – to Thomas Hardy. The 'woman' of the title and Eustacia Vye (*The Return of the Native*) clearly have much in common. The enigmatic triple-ending of the novel can be seen as English *roman nouveau*, or a wanton fracturing of the old (essentially Victorian) realisms of English fiction. By this stage of his career, Fowles was a darling of the American reading public and of American critics – who took to *The French Lieutenant's Woman* much more eagerly than their British counterparts, for many of whom Fowles's proper place was 'Pseud's Corner'. The novel was filmed, scripted by Harold Pinter and starred Meryl Streep, elegantly hooded, on the Cobb (sea wall) at Lyme Regis. Her image branded the paperback novel, and helped it to long-term bestseller status.

Fowles's last major effort in fiction is his most autobiographical and bitter. *Daniel Martin* (1977) opens in the Devon of the author's idyllic childhood before flashing forward (flashing everywhere, indeed) over the various locations of his later life with a particularly angry attention to 'Illusionville', as he sardonically called Los

Angeles – the epitome of the twentieth century's shallowness. The novel was poorly received ('gangbanged to death,' as Fowles's biographer put it), particularly in the UK, and confirmed the author's sense that he was an exile in his own country. He seems to have revelled in the feeling. When, the year before his death, he sanctioned the publication of his journals he insisted that passages (anti-Semitic, homophobic) reflecting badly on him *not* be removed: no whitewash for John Fowles.

He suffered a minor stroke in late 1988 and was widowed two years later. He had some absurd sexual infatuations in his later years (including one with a girl fifty years his junior) and remarried in 1998. Always parsimonious about publication, he put out nothing in his later years, working intensively, however, on his unpublished *Tesserae* – a title which, for most fans of *The French Lieutenant's Woman*, would need a footnote.

FN   John Robert Fowles
MRT   *The Collector*
Biog   E. Warburton, *John Fowles: A Life in Two Worlds* (2004)

242. Richard Yates 1926–1992

If there wasn't a Fitzgerald, I don't think I would have become a writer.

Richard Yates was of literature's nearly men. Born into an impoverished and dysfunctional family in Yonkers, New York (whose dysfunctions and monetary crises he reproduced, with Xerox fidelity, in his own roles of husband and father), he missed out on a university education. Throughout life he nursed a corrosive anger against novelists who had that advantage over him. 'I'd give anything to have gotten a college education,' he complained in later life. 'I feel the lack of it all the time.' He was, as photographs – and innumerable sexual partners – confirm, strikingly handsome, but in a style that he himself despised. Yates privately thought his looks feminine, and he had 'a lifelong horror of being perceived as homosexual'.

After leaving school, Yates served (just) in the Second World War and was measured a single IQ point short of qualifying for officer training. He was discharged 'with a Good Conduct medal and the rank of private first class', the lowest of the military low. He brought back no good war stories but, typically, made good fiction out of the lack of them. His early and finest short story, as he believed, 'A Really Good Jazz Piano', was turned down nine times, with gushing praise, by the best magazines in the United States. Only the devoted persistence of his agent got it into print. Yates's first published novel, *Revolutionary Road* (1961), had the misfortune to be a finalist for the National Book Award in 1962, an *annus mirabilis* for American fiction, coming up against Joseph Heller's *Catch-22*, J. D. Salinger's *Franny and Zooey*, Edward Lewis Wallant's *The Pawnbroker* and Walker Percy's *The Moviegoer*, which – amazingly – won. In later life, he taught creative writing (very well, apparently) at various universities but he failed to get tenure at his main base, the University of Iowa – something that embittered him inordinately.

Richard Yates was that most despised American thing, a loser. Bitterness stoically concealed – except when in drink or mania – was the presiding flavour of his career. Nothing ever went quite right for him. He arrived slightly too late on the literary scene and was overtaken by what he contemptuously called the 'post-Realistic School'. A cost was paid for all this disappointment. He was, as his biographer Blake Bailey portrays him, both a great writer and simultaneously 'a parody of the self-destructive personality'. He was a lifelong four-pack-a-day man. He chain-smoked in a tuberculosis sanatorium and puffed on even when chained to oxygen cylinders, his lungs rotten with terminal emphysema. On at least one occasion he burned down his apartment, toasting his work in progress which, prudently, he stored in his refrigerator. There was nothing else in it other than liquor. His workplace in such apartments, during his years of divorced solitude, was spartan in its simplicity and gothic in its squalor. 'Visitors were struck by certain awful details to which Yates himself seemed oblivious: the bloodstains on his desk-chair cushion (from piles), the calm roaches in plain sight, nothing but bourbon and instant coffee in the tiny kitchen.' His daily routine in later life was described by one of his daughters: 'He'd wake up tremendously hung over, and put himself together for about two hours. Then he wrote, and then he went out and got drunk for the rest of the day.'

Children of a failed artist mother, divorced from his father when Richard was three, Yates and his sister spent their infancy flitting from apartment to apartment. It was, as he described it, a domestic environment smelling of 'mildew and cat droppings and plasticine'. In later years his mother, always hysterical, descended into alcoholism and eventual dementia. Her image – ambivalently accented – haunts his fiction. The one aesthetic pleasure Yates records in his boyhood is the movie theatre. It was the hovel on his childhood heath. What saved him for literature was the good fortune of a few years at a private school, during one of the family's upswings. His experience at Avon Old Farms School in Connecticut is chronicled in his novel *A Good School* (1978). Here he learned to write for student magazines. Words, he discovered, came easily to him.

After being discharged from the army, Yates took on various jobs in which he could employ his verbal fluency. He was, variously, a copywriter and a malcontented journalist while, all the time, he laboured at his own writing. His best-paid work was with Remington Rand, merchandisers of the first commercially viable computer (something that interested Yates not at all). He was trapped, like other men in grey flannel suits, in a good job. He married, entrapping himself further. His wife Sheila, a gifted woman who could possibly have done well on the stage, had settled for the life of a 'no-nonsense New York secretary'. Their marriage produced two daughters before failing. It also produced a magnificent novel of suburban nightmare, *Revolutionary Road*.

Published in 1961, *Revolutionary Road* catches, almost before it had passed, the deep materialistic pointlessness of the Eisenhower-*Mad Men* 1950s (the 'you've never had it so good' era in Macmillan's UK). It was – there is no other word – boring:

> Then it was Sunday, with the living room deep in the rustling torpor of Sunday newspapers, and no words had passed between Frank Wheeler and his wife for what seemed a year. She had gone alone to the second and final performance of *The Petrified Forest*, and afterwards had slept on the sofa again.
>
> He was trying now to take his ease in an armchair, looking through the magazine section of the *Times*, while the children played quietly in the corner and April washed the dishes in the kitchen.

This is the 'good life'?

Yates entered into divorced middle age on his 'second bachelorhood'. It was followed by a second doomed marriage. During these years, and for the rest of his life, he freelanced. For a period in the 1960s he was a speechwriter for Attorney General Robert Kennedy. He hated being a hireling, and even if Dallas had never happened he would have drunk himself out of what, for less driven artists, would have been a dream job. That he was Lee Harvey Oswald was one of his delusions in late-life mental breakdowns. By mid-career, Yates was a full-blown alcoholic and regularly hospitalised. He obstinately drank through whatever drugs were prescribed, with disastrous physical effects – and, on the positive side, a powerful 'drinking novel', *Disturbing the Peace* (1975). His manias became increasingly florid. A display of self-crucifixion at the 1962 Bread Loaf conference has become, as Bailey drily records, 'part of the permanent lore of the place'. A man of limited cultural interests, Yates was a passionate lover of a few books – most passionately *The Great Gatsby*, which was for him 'holy writ'. One wonders whether a crack-up was, as for Fitzgerald, a creative necessity.

A decade and a half after his death, with an irony which would have amused him (what good was fame to him then?), Yates enjoyed huge posthumous celebrity with the publication of Bailey's bestselling biography and the success of the 2008

DiCaprio–Winslet, Oscar-nominated, text-faithful movie of *Revolutionary Road*. 'Nearly' no longer – but too late.

FN   Richard Yates
MRT   *Revolutionary Road*
Biog   B. Bailey, *A Tragic Honesty: The Life and Work of Richard Yates* (2003)

243. Jennifer Dawson 1929–2000

I shall never succeed in saying what I want to say.

Dawson has left little lasting mark on the annals of literary history. Although she worked for Oxford University Press, there is no entry on her in the *ODNB*, or in the *Oxford Companion to English Literature*. The facts of her life are readily summarised. She was born one of five children to a Fabian couple – veterans of the Left Book Club – and she was educated at the local girls' grammar school in Camberwell. There were slums all around this quarter of south London and the world, as she grew up, was in the grip of the Great Depression with another great war looming. That war brought rationing, austerity and universal 'shortages'. Depression, in one form or another, was the climate of the first forty years of Dawson's life.

A bright girl, Jennifer went on to read history at St Anne's College, Oxford. As Polly Pattullo recalls, Dawson 'had, she said, few clothes and little money and was suddenly confronted with upper-class students at ease in a rarified social milieu'. She was not cut out to be a class warrior. As one of her heroines quaintly puts it, 'in my adolescence and my school I had never really been *au fait*'. 'My greatest passion in life,' Dawson later wrote, 'has always been music. I regard writing as a last resort, a *faute de mieux* for me. In a world where language has been eroded, gutted ("pre-emptive strike", "take-out" for the murder of eight million civilians, etc.) all art "aspires to the condition of music", which cannot be exploited, interpreted, which explores the lost places of the heart, which makes all things new.' Music was, in other words, an 'asylum' – a place of peace and refuge.

One cannot, alas, live in music. In the third year of her studies, Dawson had a serious breakdown and spent six months at the Warneford Hospital on the outskirts of Oxford. Mental health was an area which the NHS, on its foundation in 1945, had resolutely ignored, and Dawson's treatment was little different from what a Victorian patient would have received – with such modern embellishments as 'maintenance ECT' and 'insulin shock treatment'. None the less she recovered sufficiently to return and take her degree in 1952. She went on to work for Oxford University Press as an indexer and researcher on the *Oxford English Dictionary* and – on a voluntary basis – undertook some work in mental hospitals. Elizabeth Mitchell, her friend at the Press (and later a collaborator on a book they wrote together), recalls Dawson in her mid-twenties: 'She ... was vivid and clear-cut, both in appearance, with her expressive dark eyes and short, shiny black hair; and in temperament, suffering disconcertingly abrupt shifts between exuberance and bleakest misery. For her, as for the young Wordsworth, the very shadow of the clouds had power to shake her as they passed.'

Mitchell guesses she was already laying foundations in her mind for *The Ha-Ha* (1961). The novel manifestly had its origin in Dawson's 1951 breakdown, hospitalisation and fragile recovery. The Warneford was a venerable lunatic asylum of early nineteenth-century foundation and in external appearance more resembling a country house than a 'loony bin' (as the institutions were commonly referred to in the unregenerate 1950s). It had, and still has, magnificent grounds – including, significantly, a ha-ha. The novel opens with Josephine on the path to 'recovery', as the institution defines it. She has been released from the locked ward, although she still suffers full-blown hallucinations, straight out of Mervyn Peake's *Gormenghast* (monstrous worms, insects and armadillos feature – 'things of the jungle'). She now has her own quarters, periods of free time, and a therapeutic 'job', arranging the library books of a nearby aged couple. She forms an emotionally sustaining relationship with one of the nurses, a German refugee.

Her breakthrough comes when she falls in love with a fellow patient, Alasdair Faber – a medical student who, influenced by the films of Ingmar Bergman, has discovered life wasn't worth it. She is not experienced in love. 'A man kissed me once,' she recalls, 'but it hurt. I think his teeth were too large.' They meet, clandestinely, by the ha-ha, a raised grassy bank which blots out dead ground, artfully creating an uninterruptedly beautiful long perspective for the viewer's eye. It is, of course, an illusion. Alasdair is in the business of destroying illusions: he sees 'treatment' as a sham and the asylum as a prison by a kinder name. It does not cure insanity: it creates insanity. He leaves without saying goodbye. Josephine relapses, runs away, and is brought back by the police. 'Recovery' will now be on her own defiant terms.

> If you could stay away for fourteen days, I remembered Alasdair had told me, they could not reclaim you, so I clambered over the pile of rubble [i.e. the ha-ha] that had been my wall and had enclosed my world, said good-bye to the hill, and ran until I knew for certain that I had not after all been extinguished and that my existence had been saved.

'The story', said Dawson with a nice turn of phrase, 'was really about a girl who did not have the knack of existing.' Or, as she put it with reference to herself, 'One feeling that has haunted me all my life is that life, social life as we know it, is a kind of game with correct moves, correct remarks and replies, correct procedures. I don't know the rules.' In which case, like Josephine, you must make your own if you wish to survive.

The Ha-Ha can be seen as a reticent Oxonian equivalent to Ken Kesey's *One Flew Over the Cuckoo's Nest*, which was published a year later, and vastly popularised by the subsequent Oscar-winning film. Dawson's novel was published in the wake of the radically reforming Mental Health Act of 1959 – a measure which gave the bulk of mental patients the same civil rights as patients in other hospitals with physical ailments. The aim was to destigmatise. Riding the wave of approval for this measure, *The Ha-Ha* won the UK's premier fiction prize, the James Tait Black, in 1961 (the Booker did not yet exist). It was dramatised in 1967 by Richard Eyre, ran as a radio play, and was a title promoted by Virago Press in the mid-1980s. Dawson doubtless got as much gratification from the fact that *The Ha-Ha* was widely prescribed as recommended reading for mental-health workers.

She met her future husband, the Oxford philosophy don Michael Hinton, on the 1963 Aldermaston march protesting the British nuclear deterrent. It was the period of the Cuban missile crisis when the world expected to be incinerated with four minutes' warning. On surviving this fate, the couple set up house in the village of Charlbury, on the outskirts of Oxford. Hinton's academic field – ambiguity and disjunctiveness – may well have chimed with Dawson's worldview, as expressed in her fiction. 'The thing that obsesses me most', she wrote, 'and which I feel I shall never put into language, is the strangeness of life, its accidentalness.' The Hintons had no children. Dawson wrote a handful of further novels, none of which enjoyed the success of her first. All have points of interest – *A Field of Scarlet Poppies* (1979), for example, ponders the failure of the Campaign for Nuclear Disarmament. Had it been worthwhile? Or was it as pointless as conscientious objection in the First World War? She never made her peace with Oxford, although she lived in its orbit for the rest of her life. Her last published book, *Judasland* (1989), is a satire on the unregenerate character of the university city and its insuperable patriarchy. It tells the story of a laundress in Sanctus Spiritus College who, like Josephine, isn't going to take it anymore. The allusion in the title is to Hardy's Jude Fawley – another of Oxford's excluded. *Judasland* won the Fawcett prize, awarded by the feminist society devoted to 'closing the gap between women and men'.

Dawson published no fiction in the last ten years of her life, although reportedly she was meditating a novel, revolving around her daily bus ride from Charlbury into the city and the characters she encountered on the journey. Her friend Elizabeth Mitchell recalls a poignant last encounter: 'She had been committed to the Campaign for Nuclear Disarmament from its early days. Two days before she died, one of her sisters found her old CND badge and brought it to her in the hospice. With it pinned to her night-dress, Jennifer Dawson said, "Now, I'm properly dressed."' Her husband died a few weeks later.

FN   Jennifer Dawson (later Hinton)
MRT *The Ha-Ha*
Biog *Guardian* obituary, 26 October 2000 (Polly Pattullo)

244. Marilyn French 1929–2009

A blowtorch aimed straight at the collective groin of Man the Master. Libby Purves

'This Novel Changes Lives' was the shoutline emblazoned across the front cover of the paperback edition of *The Women's Room* (1977). There is a story behind the slogan, as Fay Weldon records: 'One morning in 1977, the manuscript of *The Women's Room* came through my door, with a request for a quote from her publisher. I sat riveted while I read. The phone rang. It was a friend complaining of the way her husband misused her – and he had. "You must read this book," I said. "It will change your life."' The title was the best thing about the novel. The primary allusion was to Woolfian woman's room of her own – but French did not want the writer's solitude: leave that to Garbo. She wanted to be part of a movement, which is why 'women' was pluralised (and damn the problem with the possessive apostrophe) – and, of course, 'Woman's Room' is one of the many American euphemisms for lavatory. It is the one room which men cannot, under any circumstances, enter, and where a woman can be alone with her vagina.

The novel has sold, one is told with that PR airy indifference to statistical accuracy, some 20 million copies. It is one of the two major *romans à thèse* produced after Betty Friedan's excoriation of the feminine mystique in 1963, and the formation of the National Organization of Women. Erica Jong chose as her weapon in *Fear of Flying* (1973), the let-it-all-hang-out sexual explicitness of *Portnoy's Complaint*. French took the full-blooded melodrama of *Valley of the Dolls*. For a man reading *The Women's Room* at the time, it was like being whipped to death with discarded wire-framed brassières. French published this, her first novel, when she was closing on fifty. It tells the story of Mira Ward: an unhappy girl in the 1940s, a desperate housewife in the 1950s (her husband Norm does the dirty on her), and a divorced and liberated ex-wife in the 1960s – having put herself through Harvard and discovered 'the movement'. The novel's other most quoted line is uttered by one of Mira's friends after her daughter is gang-raped: 'all men are rapists, and that's all they are. They rape us with their eyes, their laws, and their codes.' It is not, it should be noted, uttered by the heroine and certainly not – as French pointed out time and again – necessarily endorsed by the author, but none the less it is uttered.

Marilyn Edwards was born in Brooklyn, New York, from a distantly Polish immigrant background. Her family was blue-collar, barely getting by in the Depression. Largely by her own efforts, Marilyn did a degree in English and Philosophy at Hofstra College, graduating in 1951. While still a student, she married Robert French Jr and there were two children born shortly thereafter. 'I saw my mother's life,' she said in a 2007 interview, adding ruefully, 'and I ended up in the same trap.' She drudged through a series of stultifying secretarial jobs to put her husband through law school and, part-time, did an MA herself at Hofstra. Her marriage was, she recalled, 'absolutely horrible', though it was the institution of marriage itself, as defined in the 1950s, which was principally to blame. It was not until 1967 that she escaped the marital trap, with divorce – nowadays, thanks to liberal pressure, easier than it had been for women like her mother. She won herself a place at Harvard to do a Ph.D. (on James Joyce – a version of her dissertation was published at the same time as *The Women's Room*). She was on her way – out and up.

French recalled being radicalised by Kate Millett's *Sexual Politics* (1970), a version of *her* Ph.D. literary thesis at Columbia. About the same period French's eighteen-year-old daughter Jamie was sexually assaulted. French did not rest until the rapist was imprisoned, where, behind bars, he might find out what rape felt like. It was a period of expansion in American higher education (a huge number of male students enrolled, to escape the Vietnam draft) and French, who got her doctorate in 1972, obtained a job teaching English at the College of the Holy Cross in Worcester, Massachusetts. Heterosexual, she had a number of 'romantic relationships' but never remarried. She had been writing fiction, unsuccessfully, for some time. But in the late 1970s – with feminism's 'second wave' – the time was right. *The Women's Room* served as a bawling recruiting sergeant for a movement on the march. The newly conscripted forgave the novel's dire literary quality, though critics were less forgiving – even women critics. In *The Times*, Libby Purves took exception to the partisan crudity. French's men, she said, 'are malevolent stick figures, at best appallingly dull and at worst monsters'. (On French's death, Purves wrote a more generous appreciation in the same paper – see the above epigraph.) The novel was compared, unfavourably, to Mary McCarthy's *The Group*. Such discrimination was irrelevant, however. You might as well say *Uncle Tom's Cabin* is less good a work of literature than *Middlemarch*.

It was the moment and the movement which made French a one-shot bestseller. None of her subsequent five novels had any success and, at the end of her life, no American publisher was interested in her fiction. Her scholarly works on Joyce and latterly on women's history did, however, earn her a respectable professional reputation and she was in demand as an academic lecturer and an essayist. She smoked heavily throughout her adult life (in the 1960s a woman smoking publicly was one of the smaller badges of independence). She contracted cancer of the oesophagus in her late sixties, beat it, and wrote a cancer memoir, *A Season in Hell* (1998), which posterity may well see as the most powerful of her publications. At the end of her life she conceded that 'most men are on our side', but insisted that she was still 'an angry person'.

FN   Marilyn French (née Edwards)
MRT   *The Women's Room*
Biog   *New York Times*, obituary, 3 May 2009 (H. Mitgang, A. G. Sulzberger)

245. Guillermo Cabrera Infante 1929–2005

I am the only British writer who writes in Spanish.

Cabrera Infante was born in the seaside town of Gibara, in Cuba, in 1929. It was where Columbus landed on the island – an event commemorated, often, in his later fiction. Guillermo was the eldest son of political activists who founded the Cuban Communist Party. Their politics led, inevitably, to friction with the authorities (Cuba was effectively a US possession following its colonial liberation from Spain) and his parents were imprisoned for disseminating propaganda in 1936. An acutely 'anxious' child, thereafter his personality was always fragile and prone to nervous breakdown. On their release – but now unemployable – the Cabrera Infantes went to live in Havana: the location which meant most to their son for the rest of his life. Six of the family were crammed into a tiny apartment in a region of the capital 'where the street lamps were so poor they couldn't even afford moths'. It is vividly evoked as something squalid yet romantic in his later book, *Infante's Inferno* (1984).

Cabrera Infante enrolled as a medical student at the University of Havana in 1949, but promptly switched to journalism. His father insisted he learn English, enrolling him in night school to do so. Films – especially Hollywood – were a passion with him. He claimed that he saw his first movie, aged twenty-nine days, when his mother took her newborn to see Ibáñez's *The Four Horsemen of the Apocalypse* (1921): it was a baptismal moment. He published on cinema enthusiastically and perceptively in the 1950s and loved movies all his life. He also imbibed dissidence in his mother's milk and, like his parents, spent time in prison. In his case, it was less politics than for a story the authorities found offensive (specifically the graphic description of an American tourist in Havana 'to have maaah balls sucked'). It was, the court decreed, 'offensive to national dignity'. Which nation was irrelevant since, under Batista, Cuba was the US's offshore brothel. Essentially it was an offence against tourism.

Prohibited from writing under his own name, he adopted a pseudonym 'G. Cain' (the biblical outcast, and CAbrera INfante) and continued annoying the Batista regime. When Fidel Castro ousted the American stooge and his corrupt regime in 1959, Cabrera Infante was, initially, a staunch supporter of the Revolution. He was installed in the newly set up state film institute and given free rein in the cultural supplement of the party's newspaper, *Lunes de Revolución*. For a year or two, he was able to brew his 'heady' mixture of Trotskyist politics and surrealist art. In his official capacity he met such international grandees as Pablo Neruda, Sartre and de Beauvoir. Cabrera Infante divorced his first wife and remarried at this period. In 1960 he published his first volume of fiction, *Así en la paz como en la guerra* ('As in Times of Peace, So in Times of War'). Written under the political influence of Sartre and the stylistic influence of Hemingway, he later 'disowned' it as too Castroist. He was already, at the time, chafing at the Party's institutional distaste for 'decadent' postmodernism and its censorship of artistic expression (particularly 'decadent' Hollywood films). The Party was also becoming impatient with him and closed down his literary supplement. In 1962, he accepted a diplomatic position in Belgium where he could feel himself unfettered (but not well off – Cubans were the paupers of the diplomatic world) and it was here that he wrote *Tres tristes tigres* (*Three Trapped Tigers*).

The novel came into his head, he said, as 'a narrative explosion'. It did not, exactly, explode on the publishing scene as the British edition's copyright page records:

> First published in Spain in 1965 as *Tres tristes tigres*
> First published in English in the USA in 1971
> First published in Great Britain in 1980

Over these fifteen years in fictional limbo, the novel – in Spanish and in English – won an impressive haul of prizes, but it did not sell well or make its author's name widely famous. 'My writing', Cabrera Infante once said, 'springs up not from life but from reading.' His library contained forty-six volumes by or on James Joyce (his other favourite text – strangely – was Raymond Chandler's *The Long Goodbye*). He loved and imitated Joyce's 'eye–ear polarities', i.e. 'Hold that Tyrant' – an acoustic pun in *Three Trapped Tigers* which partly explains the inscrutably enigmatic title. He also loved what Cubans call 'choteo' – cheek: for example his cheerful desecration of the most famous lyric of the country's most famous poet, José Martí:

> *Yo soy un hombre sincero*
> I'm a man without a zero
> *De donde crece la palma*
> From the land of the pawn-trees

The novel was everywhere praised – typically with the windy superlatives which signal that the person praising is bamboozled. The *New York Review of Books*, for example, devoted pages of lavish praise to *Three Trapped Tigers*, the luckless reviewer unaware that he had wholly jumbled up the principal characters – which is easily done. Essentially the narrative, loosely following the fate of a quartet of street-wise Habañeros, is a panorama of city low-life and café society in the years just before the Revolution: whether nostalgic or seditious is never quite clear. Music – the bolero – runs through the book thematically. The opening gives a flavour of the whole and the demands Cabrera Infante makes of the reader:

> Showtime! *Señoras y señores*. Ladies and Gentlemen. And a very good evening to you all, ladies and gentlemen. *Muy buenas noches, damas y caballeros*. Tropicana! The MOST fabulous night-club in the WORLD – *el cabaret MAS fabuloso del mundo* – presents – *presenta* – its latest show – *su nuevo espectáculo* – where performers of Continental fame will take you all to the wonderful world of supernatural beauty of the Tropics.

A little of this goes a very long way for most readers.

In 1965 his mother died and he returned from Europe for the funeral. But Havana now seemed to him 'like the wrong side of hell' and he finally resolved on exile from a country he loved, but could no longer live in. 'The truth,' he later wrote, 'is that Fidel Castro never cared about the theatre or literature, or even mural painting, for that matter. He only cares about power and its total tool, propaganda. He is known even to have used Beckett's plays, to have said that *Waiting for Godot* showed the kind of capitalist-induced misery you'll never find in Cuba now. Godot forbids.' After Franco's Spain denied him residency, Cabrera Infante moved, somewhat uneasily, to England, becoming a citizen in 1979 – the country's first Cuban novelist. In London he published novels, wrote screenplays and film reviews (his English was as proficient as any native speaker), and published a surrealist celebration of the cigar, *Holy Smoke* (1985).

Cuba had, by now, long disowned him as a traitor to the country and his books were banned on the island. Others saw him as Cuba's greatest living novelist. His last years in England were unhappy following a mental health breakdown in 1972. A long course of ECT may account for the recovery of mental stability and the decline of his creativity. He was, from childhood, morbidly sensitive to the pain of others: 'While working at his desk one day in his London apartment,' his biographer records, 'he had the misfortune to witness a jay killing and devouring a sparrow, a spectacle that caused him to faint.' But the greatest hurt was for his country. Castro, it seemed, would live for ever. Cabrera Infante himself died in the year that his fellow Cuban exile, the Hollywood star Andy García, contrived to get his screenplay for *The Lost City* (2006) – a lament for pre-Revolutionary Havana – on to the film screens of the world. The film bombed with the American critics and was banned in much of South America for what was seen as disrespect to the memory of Che Guevara (depicted as a thug).

Cabrera Infante died of an MRSA infection while being treated in a London hospital for a fractured hip. Ironically (a point Michael Moore would have made with relish), he would have done better under the Cuban Health Service than the NHS. He had requested, in the event of his death, that his ashes be kept, unburied, until – after Castro and his regime were gone – they could be interred in Cuba. They remain unburied.

FN   Guillermo Cabrera Infante
MRT   *Three Trapped Tigers*
Biog   R. D. Souza, *Guillermo Cabrera Infante: Two Islands, Many Worlds* (1996)

246. Dan Jacobson 1929–

It is not thy duty to complete the task; but neither art thou free to desist from it.
Epigraph to *The Beginners*

Dan Jacobson pluralised his past as 'autobiographies' – his was a life in many disparate parts. 'How to make sense of it all?' he mused in one of his later memoirs. One can begin with the bare facts. He was born in Johannesburg, in the ominous year 1929, of a Latvian-born father and a Lithuanian-born mother, both of whom had fled their birthplaces. Jacobson was brought up in Kimberley, a dull town (diamonds went down with everything else in the slump) – but one of the places on the globe where Jews were safe to enjoy a dull life like everybody else. His late-life memoir, *Heshel's Kingdom* (1998), was inspired by a visit to one of his parental homelands, Lithuania. Heshel Melamed, a stern rabbinical paterfamilias, was his maternal grandfather. On the old man's death in 1920, Dan's mother, Liebe, fled to South Africa. She was escaping her father as much as the Pale of Settlement. Had Heshel lived longer, Dan Jacobson would never have happened. The Nazi extermination of Jews in Lithuania (aided enthusiastically by local Lithuanians) was virtually total.

Dan's father, Hyman, ran Kimberley's butter factory. A vivid, child's eye view of the bustling place is given in *The Beginners* (1966), the assembly belts, the clanking churns and hissing pasteurising vats:

> It seemed impossible that in the tumult anyone could work or think. But, calmly, white men and Africans went about their duties, all of them clad alike in white overalls and gumboots.

The Jacobson home was well off, liberal in politics (the *New Statesman* was sub-scribed to) and non-coercive in matters of religion. Dan, one of four children, was brought up in an enclave within enclaves. There were around 100 Jewish families in Kimberley, none related to the Jacobsons. He went to a faux-English grammar school where, like the rest, he bellowed out his daily wish that God save his King. Meanwhile, outside, squads of barefoot blacks mowed the cricket grounds and whitewashed the boundary markers. It struck him, even as a boy, as somehow crazy.

After getting a top degree in English at Witwatersrand and suffering a few awkward months at a kibbutz in Israel, Jacobson spent a year in London. He worked there in a Jewish boys' school, pigged it in lodgings, and was very lonely. A 'demi-alien', he began, in his solitude, to write a novel: *The Wonder-Worker* (1973) recalls this period of London loneliness. It was, none the less, a happy time. He loved the way the English so expertly 'imitated' being English and it was on this trip, aged twenty-one, that he became committed to the place – though he would not settle there yet. He was dismissed from his teaching post for thoughtlessly informing his boys that the universe was (contra Genesis) millions of years old. He returned, wan-deringly, to South Africa, and did a number of desk jobs. More importantly, he was already publishing short fiction in American magazines such as *Commentary* and the *New Yorker*. In 1954 Jacobson married a Rhodesian teacher, Margaret Pye, and moved with her to London. He was by now highly regarded as a coming author in the US and in 1956 he spent a year as writer-in-residence at Stanford. The 1950s was a period when South Africa – and its Afrikaaner resistance to the winds of change – was front-page news across the world.

This phase of Jacobson's writing career climaxed with *The Beginners* in 1966. It was his *Buddenbrooks* and tells the story of a dynasty of Lithuanian Jews, the Glickmans, 'beginning' over again in South Africa. But it is their destiny to wander not settle: the Boers are settlers, the English are colonisers, the Jews are transients. The core issue in *The Beginners* is the same as in Mann's novel. What does the third generation – no longer faced with struggle or bound in by the disciplines of ideology – do? The question is resolved in the stories of Joel and David: one an 'engaged' man of action and Zionist, the other a student, observing life from its edge. The novel's ethical problems are articulated in a parable-like prelude in which Avrom, the patriarch of the Glickmans (a lovable man given to impulsive and foolish acts), returns to Lithuania with money, saved up by his hard-working sons, to bring the rest of the family to the safety of South Africa. On the way, at Bremen railway station, he sees a woman weeping, with three children around her. She is clearly Jewish. 'Is there anything a Jew can do?' asks Avrom. She has been robbed. He gives her the fifty sovereigns, intended for his own family – who must now wait years for their rescue. Has he done the right thing?

The Beginners was a valediction to South Africa. After a longish interval, Jacobson produced the biblical fantasia *The Rape of Tamar* (1970). As narrated in Leviticus and Samuel, there is an extraordinary – and spectacularly novelistic – episode. So much so that one wonders what it is doing in that particular book. Amnon, heir apparent to David, conceives an overwhelming desire for his half-sister, Tamar. Aided by his cousin, Jonadab, he feigns illness, lures her to her quarters and rapes her. Why? *The Rape of Tamar* is Jacobson's favourite novel. It would, he later surmised, have been in the running for the newly established Booker, except that glowing reviews were lost in the strife that was crippling Fleet Street at the time.

Karl Miller, who had materially furthered Jacobson's career as editor of *The Listener*, chided him for the shift away from South African subjects (a territory he would only return to, as a cold-eyed tourist, in his late-life travel writing). But Kafka, not Thomas Mann, was now the star Jacobson followed. Had he stayed in the groove of his first five novels he would have ended up, he felt, a superior Wilbur Smith. *The Confessions of Josef Baisz* (1977), a fable set in an imaginary country, is the most successfully experimental novel in this second phase of his career.

Cash prizes, Arts Council bursaries, royalties and journalism kept Jacobson going through the 1960s, but the life of a writer, with a growing family (there would be four children) was a tightrope walk. On his appointment to the Northcliffe chair at University College London, Karl Miller brought Jacobson into his entourage as a lecturer. It was a happy change of direction. There was an inner pedagogue in Jacobson, only too glad to be released. At UCL he was for some years a colleague of

A. S. Byatt. As she recalls, the two of them would discuss whether the academic life was good for their fiction. She eventually decided not, and left. He stayed until retirement in 1994. His later fiction was carefully wrought and continued the lines of narrative exploration he had opened in the 1970s. UCL, the godless place in Gower Street, which had been set up in large part as a home for the spiritually uncomfortable, fitted Jacobson like a glove. Its open-mindedness encouraged monographs such as *The Story of the Stories: The Chosen People and Its God* (1982) – the Bible was, he always thought, the best novel ever written. In his travel writing and memoirs, he settled his personal account with the country in which he was born (whose accent his speech never lost) and with Nazi-occupied Europe. 'They would have killed us, if they could have got to South Africa' he mused, contemplating the exterminations in Vilnius and Heshel's fortuitous death.

An image that recurs in Jacobson's writing is the pit, or abyss – sometimes materialising into the vast black holes left by the Kimberley diamond excavations of his childhood. At other more metaphorical moments, it takes shape as Conrad's heart of darkness. 'The pit of the future', he once wrote, 'is quite as deep as the pit of the past. Through it, too, all things fall endlessly.'

FN   Daniel Jacobson
MRT   *The Beginners*
Biog D. Jacobson, *Time and Again* (1985)

247. Chinua Achebe 1930–

The Western World must realise that Africa is made up of human beings.

Achebe is Nigeria's – or, more accurately, given the fissile nature of that country, the Igbo nation's – first great author: a title which, in later years, he contested with Wole Soyinka, the (Hausa nation) novelist who got the Nobel Prize Achebe didn't. By way of consolation, Achebe can claim authorship of the novel routinely described as 'the most read novel to have come out of Africa': *Things Fall Apart* (1958). Achebe was born in an 'impressive zinc house' and raised middle-class in a small town, Ogidi, in the east of Nigeria. His religious background was second-generation Protestant. He describes his father, Isaiah Okafor, as a 'missionary', a 'catechist' and an 'evangelist'. He was named after the Queen's consort, 'Albert', a colonial label he later shed.

'Albert Achebe' no longer exists – although he once did. Achebe's detachment from 'Victorian' (i.e. British nineteenth-century) hegemony has been lifelong, fraught, and as painful as removing a slaver's brand. 'Chinua', his chosen first name, is the abbreviation of an Igbo prayer.

The opening paragraph of his most famous novel, set in the period when the colonising missionaries arrived in Igbo territory, strikes a defiantly unBritish note, bleaching English of all its Englishness to do so:

> Okonkwo was well known throughout the nine villages and even beyond. His fame rested on solid personal achievements. As a young man of eighteen he had brought honour to his village by throwing Amalinze the Cat. Amalinze was the great wrestler who for seven years was unbeaten. He was called the Cat because his back would never touch the earth. It was this man that Okonkwo threw in a fight which the old men agreed was one of the fiercest since the founder of their town engaged a spirit of the wild for seven days and seven nights.

The syntax has the percussiveness of an African drum. Okonkwo is proudly heathen: his gods are Idemili, Ogwugwu, Agbala. But, one notes, the title of the novel comes from Yeats's chiliastic poem about 'The Second Coming'. The colonists' biblical book pursues Achebe like Francis Thompson's 'Hound of Heaven'.

In early reading of writers such as Rider Haggard, Achebe 'took sides with the whitemen against the "savages"'. He was brought up jointly steeped in Anglican theology (he recalls *The Pilgrim's Progress* as being the first novel he read) and the still vital folklore, and oral narratives, of his people. At the boarding schools he attended Achebe effortlessly passed exams and won scholarships. English was his daily, if never quite his mother, tongue. At the University of Ibadan (then an outpost of London University) he initially enrolled to study medicine, before switching to Humanities and Theology. Those subjects were taught exclusively by white academics. One course of lectures on Thomas Hardy made a particular impression on the young Achebe. The 'reality' of the sage of Wessex's world, he felt, 'was very close to mine.' He was already writing for publication and had adopted an increasingly articulate protest against the mind-forged shackles of colonialism – focused, specifically, on the Uncle-Tomist, paternalistic ('benign') racism of Joyce Cary's *Mister Johnson* (1939), and such observations as Hugh Trevor-Roper's that 'Africa has no history'. Achebe would mobilise a powerful counter-narrative.

But extra-curricular studies distracted him and he was awarded only a second-class degree. After a few months' back-country teaching, he took a job in the newly established Nigerian Broadcasting Service in Lagos, with a special responsibility for 'talks'. In 1956 he was seconded to London for a BBC course. Over this period he was writing *Things Fall Apart*. It is the story of a yam farmer, Okonkwo, who – like

Michael Henchard in Hardy's *Mayor of Casterbridge* – is a 'man of character' (a 'man of *strong* character', Achebe calls him), doomed by history. The harbingers of his downfall are the arriving missionaries to his village, Umuofia. The date of the action is, by Western reckoning, the early 1890s. Okonkwo is driven to justified murder and altruistic suicide, to spare his village punitive measures. The District Commissioner (later to reappear, named, as George Allen in *Arrow of God*) muses, apropos of a book he is thinking of writing on the colony:

> The story of this man who had killed a messenger and hanged himself would make interesting reading. One could almost write a whole chapter on him. Perhaps not a whole chapter but a reasonable paragraph, at any rate. There was so much else to include, and one must be firm in cutting out details. He had already chosen the title of the book, after much thought: *The Pacification of the Primitive Tribes of the Lower Niger.*

The novel was propelled into prominence by Macmillan's 'winds of change' – Nigeria was 'given' its independence in 1960. *Things Fall Apart* was first published in London by Heinemann, pioneers in making post-colonial literature known to Western readers. Released in a cautious run of 2,000 copies in June 1958, the novel got strong, if somewhat condescending, reviews and was on its way – via prescription in educational syllabuses – to sales of many millions over the succeeding years. Where the novel did not do well, paradoxically, was Nigeria. Localism (the patriotism of the village) was seen as divisive in the dubiously homogeneous new country. Achebe was out of step.

Meanwhile, he was rising to senior professional levels at the NBS. He married a colleague, Christie Okoli, in 1961, at a Christian ceremony at the (now independent) University of Ibadan. There would be four children – and, for the parents, continual problems as how indigenous/international their education should be. Fellowships, and his growing reputation, meant travel and public speaking. Achebe's second novel, *No Longer at Ease* (1960), was set in the modern period. Its hero, Obi (Okonkwo's grandson), is a civil servant in Lagos, caught up in the city's endemic corruption. By now Achebe's was no longer a voice in the wilderness. Other writers similarly published and pushed by Heinemann had appeared on the scene, notably Wole Soyinka and Ngugi wa Thiong'o. Post-colonial (earlier called 'Commonwealth') literature was a booming specialism in British and American universities and Achebe was a figurehead in the emergent field.

In what would become a famous proclamation, on his first visit to England in 1964, Achebe asserted that his fiction aimed not at protest, but at his nation recovering 'a belief in itself'. His third novel, *Arrow of God*, was published in 1964 (the year of civil rights riots across America). The action returns to the fraught collision of Europe and Nigeria at the start of the twentieth century and the imposition of colonial authority via obedient 'warrant chiefs'. A central role is assigned to the DC, George Allen, who had figured in the last paragraphs of *Things Fall Apart*. The ancient priest Ezeulu, worshipper of the god Ulu, is finally destroyed by the internal contradictions of colonised tribalism and dies 'like the lizard in the fable who ruined his mother's funeral by his own hand'. Christianity triumphs.

The tone of Achebe's fiction was now manifestly angrier. Anger intensified to razor sharpness in *A Man of the People* (1966), where it is principally directed against post-independence corruption. This phase of his career was, however, wholly overshadowed by the secession of the Igbo region of Nigeria and its declaration of independence as Biafra. A two-year civil war ensued, in which the UK staunchly backed Nigeria against the breakaway insurgents. Achebe, who narrowly escaped death before fleeing east, was denounced by Lagos. He threw in his lot with the new republic and served in the Ministry of Information under the Igbo leader, Emeka Ojukwu, in Enugu. He refused offers of safety abroad in the face of what he saw as genocide (engineered by the British). After Biafra was harshly subdued, Achebe retreated into academic life, taking up a succession of visiting posts in the US. Honorary fellowships and doctorates were showered on him, but he was anything but pacified by them. In a lecture at Amherst College, on 18 February 1975, Achebe delivered his canon-busting lecture, 'An Image of Africa: Racism in Conrad's *Heart of Darkness*', in which he denounced Conrad as 'a bloody racist'. Why, he asked, should his people, his continent, the plight of hundreds of millions of Africans be cast as the mere, anonymous, depersonalised 'backdrop' to one European's 'nervous breakdown'. His lecture was hugely influential in reassessing texts, such as Conrad's, complacently viewed in the West as being on the side of the angels and flattering to the white liberal conscience.

In 1987, Achebe published *Anthills of the Savannah*, a novel which reflected on the Biafran tragedy. Three years later, he was injured in a car accident, driving to Lagos, and would thereafter be wheelchair-bound for life. He moved, in what was now his retirement, to a series of honorific professorships in the US. In interviews, essays, poems and stories he continued to articulate the extraordinary pressures on African creativity in a post-colonial world. Achebe's huge reputation rests on a relatively small corpus of full-length novels and the distinction of his having led the way. Where that way led, not even he was sure.

FN   Chinua Achebe (born Albert Achebe)
MRT *Things Fall Apart*
Biog Ezenwa-Ohaeto, *Chinua Achebe: A Biography* (1997)

248. J. G. Ballard 1930–2009

America, I knew, was a future that had already arrived.

As he came to the end of his life, Ballard returned repeatedly to its beginnings, notably in *Empire of the Sun* (1984) and in his autobiography *Miracles of Life* (2008), on the last page of which he disclosed – in painful physiological detail – that he was dying of terminal prostate cancer. It is not an easy death, but neither was his life easy. Ballard was born in Shanghai, in the 'concession' enclave, where foreign businessmen like his father (a dealer in textiles) had permits to operate from the Chinese authorities. The Ballards' expatriate lifestyle was luxurious if 'very strange'. 'The honour guard of fifty Chinese hunchbacks outside the film première of *The Hunchback of Notre Dame*' stuck in the mind, Ballard recalls. 'Atrocity Exhibitions' would be a theme of his later work. The family were wholly insulated from the country around them: 'I had my first Chinese meal in England, after the war,' Ballard drily records.

Luxury ended in December 1941. In 1943 the Ballards, along with 2,000 other Europeans, were herded by the Japanese into Lunghua Civilian Assembly Centre – a genteel concentration camp. Perversely, the twelve-year-old Ballard found his years there 'happy and relaxed'. He made friends with Japanese guards, whose military code he admired as a young boy of his age might have admired Biggles in England. 'It was', he recalls, 'a prison where I found freedom.' The story of 'James' in *Empire of the Sun* explores the paradox. Lunghua, despite the forced intimacies of G-Block, estranged him from his parents. His father, on receiving a presentation copy of *The Drowned World* (1962), his son's early novel, merely pointed to 'one or two minor errors that I was careful not to correct. My mother never showed the slightest interest in my career until *Empire of the Sun*, which she thought was about her.'

On release from Lunghua, Ballard returned to England with his mother and his sister, finding the country 'derelict, dark and half ruined' – and, above all, 'cold' and class-ridden. It was a place, he discovered, 'where even hope was rationed'. The only brightness came from Hollywood films, paradoxically from film *noir*. Ballard hated 1950s England and was unsettled at his Cambridge boarding school: it was like Lunghua 'but the food was worse'. The more he found out about English life, 'the stranger it seemed'. If he had found freedom in prison, he found alienation in his home country.

Ballard studied anatomy at King's College, Cambridge, for two years – something that 'framed a large part of my imagination'. He had, of course, already seen more corpses than most doctors – dissection would be his principal artistic technique. A complex and oppositional world view was emerging out of the confusions of Ballard's personal history at this time: 'I sensed that a new kind of popular culture was emerging that played on the latent psychopathy of its audiences, and in fact needed to elicit that strain of psychopathy if it was to work.' He found starting points in Nietzschean philosophy, Freudian psychoanalysis, Buñuelian surrealism and – most powerfully – in James Joyce. Everywhere but in England. 'A jigsaw inside my head was trying to assemble itself,' he said, and in search of the missing piece, he transferred to London University in 1952 to read literature ('the worst possible preparation for a writer's career'), leaving after a year without any qualification.

After various false starts, he joined the RAF on a short-service commission. Posted to Canada for flight-training, he came across American science fiction. It was the missing piece of the jigsaw: 'Here was a form of fiction that was actually about the present day, and often as elliptical and ambiguous as Kafka ... Without thinking up a plan of action, I decided this was a field I should enter.' Enter and transform, a less modest writer than Ballard would have said. After resigning his RAF commission, he returned to London (renting, as it pleased him to note, lodgings adjoining John Christie's murder factory, 10 Rillington Place) and married, eventually settling with his family near 'slightly raffish' Shepperton, Middlesex, in south London, a setting which figures in much of his fiction. 'I enjoyed being married,' he testified.

He was currently developing what was to be a highly fruitful relationship with the SF magazine, *New Worlds*, devising sharp, dark scenarios in which traditional genre was mixed with modernist and Beat styles (William S. Burroughs was now an influence on his writing).

Ballard was as interested in what he called 'inner space' as the outer variety and he disdained the traditional genre props: space ships, little green men, time-travel and galactic warriors. He moved SF, it is said, from space opera to John Cage. Apocalypse would be his main theme – something keyed to the anxieties of a Cold War England, living under four minutes' warning of annihilation by nuclear bombardment. His distinctive style emerged in three early catastrophist masterpieces: *The Drowned World* (1962), *The Drought* (1965), *The Crystal World* (1966). There were personal catastrophes adding more darkness to the mix: in 1964 his wife Mary died of pneumonia, leaving him with three children to support by his pen.

He wrote what he called 'condensed novels' over this period, but in the 1970s he returned to uncondensed styles, breaking out of the SF 'ghetto' with postmodernist narratives such as *The Atrocity Exhibition* (1969), a work which flagrantly transgressed boundaries of permissibility for the period. Even more controversial was *Crash* (1973), an allegory of modern society's doomed, death-fuck love affair with the automobile: epitomised in the deaths of Kennedy and Dean. Ballard's cold gaze swept, apocalyptically, across the modern world with works such as *Concrete Island* (1974) and *High Rise* (1975) – expressions of his view that 'the future is going to be boring. The suburbanisation of the planet will continue, and the suburbanisation of the soul will follow soon after.' The infernal vision is not Dante but Sartre. His career took another – surprising – turn with his transparently autobiographical novel, *Empire of the Sun* (1984), a work which had risen from his Lunghua years like a slow bruise. Steven Spielberg filmed the book in 1987, propelling Ballard to new levels of fame in America. A second autobiographical work, *The Kindness of Women* (1991) followed in the early 1990s. J. G. Ballard was, momentarily in his career, James Ballard.

Ballard's latest phase was marked by a dystopian comedy, in which idealistic human communities collapse under the pressures of ineradicable human imperfection. *Cocaine Nights* (1996) and *Super-Cannes* (2000) chart the slide from architect's projection to apocalypse in a gated Spanish expat community and a French high-tech 'total' community. One of the very greatest writers of his time, Ballard has never quite shook off the SF albatross that critics have slung around his neck: 'If it's good, it can't be SF. If it's SF, it can't be good.' The prejudice haunted him even in this least science-fictional segment of his career. He declined a CBE in 2003 – disdaining to be associated with the 'Ruritanian charade' of the British honours system. The prostate cancer which he had calmly announced in 2008 finally caught up with him in April 2009. He was waiting. He had, his memoir records, seen worse.

FN   J. G. (James Graham) Ballard
MRT *Empire of the Sun*
Biog J. G. Ballard, *Miracles of Life* (2008)

249. John Barth 1930–

I think of myself as a romantic formalist.

A pioneer 'postmodernist', Barth was born, a twin, and brought up in Cambridge on the eastern shore of Maryland, the grandson of nineteenth-century German immigrants to the US. On leaving school, he attended the Juilliard School of Music in New York. His ambition was to be a jazz drummer, but music, he eventually discovered, was not for him and he moved on to Johns Hopkins University, where he majored in journalism. Hopkins was at the time the hotbed of what came to be called 'theory' – the high modes of critical thought imported from France via sages such as Roland

Barthes, Michel Foucault and Paul de Man. Theory was transforming the practice of literary criticism and seeping through into the practice of experimental fiction. Barth was open to both avenues. Unusually for the time, Hopkins also offered its students a creative writing option. Barth had an early appetite for genre fiction, but his literary taste was crucially formed by admiration for John Dos Passos and William Faulkner. Barth's own mature fiction would combine the strengths of both 'high' and 'low' – spiced by adventurous critico-philosophical speculations on the nature of fiction itself.

At university, while working on Boccaccio for his comp-lit class, he came across Ebenezer Cooke's 1707 doggerel poem 'The Sot-Weed Factor' (i.e. 'tobacco merchant'), a verse satire, set in seventeenth-century colonial Maryland. It was written by a luckless immigrant (the connection with Barth's origins was a further point of interest to him) and opens:

> *Condemn'd by Fate to way-ward Curse,*
> *Of Friends unkind, and empty Purse;*
> *Plagues worse than fill'd Pandora's Box,*
> *I took my leave of Albion's Rocks:*
> *With heavy Heart, concerned that I*
> *Was forc'd my Native Soil to fly.*
> *And the Old World must bid good-buy.*

This obscure, and comically inept, poem – with its clodhoppingly Hudibrastic sarcasms against New World barbarism – inspired the later novel which remained embryonic, but on Barth's mind, for a decade.

On graduating from Hopkins in 1953, Barth took up a post teaching English at Penn State University. Thereafter his career would follow two tracks: academic and creative. Over three violently inspired months in 1955, he wrote *The Floating Opera*. It is the story of Todd Andrews, a lawyer, who resolves to commit suicide on a specific day in June 1937. The novel was turned down by a succession of publishers, before being accepted, subject to major changes. Barth later, defiantly, published his original version.

In 1960 *The Sot-Weed Factor*, with Ebenezer Cooke as its hero, was published to immense success. A picaresque tale in high-pastiche mode, set in the seventeenth century, it mixes elements of Voltaire's *Candide*, Hervey Allen's *Anthony Adverse*, and what the 1960s revered as 'absurdism' – a literary style bolstered, theoretically, by French existentialism. More importantly, *The Sot-Weed Factor* laid the ground for the postmodernist 'Literature of Exhaustion'. The phrase is Barth's and the concept is his singular, and fruitful, bequest to modern fiction. Its basic tenet is that once all the stories are told, or no longer tellable, all the writer has left is 'narrative' – the empty, but still functioning, fictional machine. Barth's 'exhaustion' thesis helped the experimental novel onto its next stage of literary evolution, 'postmodernism'. Unlike the 'New Wave' fiction of Robbe-Grillet, or the convention-defying experiments of W. S. Burroughs, Barth's mock-epic connected with a large and appreciative readership from the start. It was 'advanced', but not offputtingly 'difficult', and daringly (for 1960) 'bawdy'. Jolly rape figures centrally, graphically and, for some later readers, disturbingly.

The influence of Borges's gamesomeness – and possibly that of Vonnegut – can be felt in Barth's third major work, a collection of short pieces, *Lost in the Funhouse* (1968). Fun is the theme – crossed with higher criticism which glosses 'fun' as 'aesthetic pleasure'. 'Night-Sea Journey', for example, is a travel story told from the point of view of a sperm. The idea was picked up by Woody Allen in *Everything You Always Wanted to Know About Sex (But were Afraid to Ask)* (1972). In 1972, Barth won an NBA for *Chimera* (three connected novellas). *LETTERS* (1979), as the title indicates, is an exercise in epistolary fiction. His fascination with the looping, interminable curves of the picaresque mode is further evident in *The Tidewater Tales* (1987). Unusually, his theoretical discourses on the nature of fiction (particularly his essay 'The Literature of Exhaustion', 1967) have been as influential as his fiction itself. It can be summed up in the cry 'fiction is dead: long live fiction'. As with Salman Rushdie and the '1001 Nights', the neverending sequence whose only function is simply to narrate is Barth's 'navigational star'. The novelist is not a story-teller, but a story-maker. Not all novelists approved: according to Gore Vidal, Barth's is a recipe for 'plastic fiction' – productive only of intolerable, self-satisfied dullness. Barth himself describes what he does as like knotting a tie while describing how to knot a tie, and offering a simultaneous digression on the history of tie-knotting.

In his later academic career he took up a post teaching creative writing at his alma mater, Johns Hopkins, retiring from the classroom in 1995. Over these years he divorced and remarried. His later career was crowned with honours. In 1974 he was elected to both the American Academy of Arts and Letters and the American Academy of Arts and Sciences, and in 1997 he was awarded the F. Scott Fitzgerald Award for Outstanding Achievement in American Fiction. He is routinely confused by the casual reader with his friend, Donald Barthelme – more happily than in most such cases, since their fiction has pleasing similarities. Not least the construction of verbal funhouses.

FN   John Simmons Barth
MRT   *The Sot-Weed Factor*
Biog Z. Bowen, *A Reader's Guide to John Barth* (1994)

250. Harold Brodkey 1930–1996

His reputation grew with each book he failed to publish. Jay McInerney

Harold Brodkey claimed to have been born 'Aaron Roy Weintraub' in Illinois. His father was a prize-fighter and junk-dealer. His birth mother died before he was able to know her. He was adopted ('sold', he claimed), aged two, by better-off distant relatives called Brodkey, comprehensively renamed and raised near St Louis, Missouri. These early years are the subject of his introspective novel, *The Runaway Soul* (1991). It continued to be a troubled childhood. Both his adoptive parents died before he was ten. As a child, he suffered nervous breakdowns and reportedly stopped talking for two whole years, retreating deep into himself. Not that he wasn't bright – prodigious, almost; he claimed to have learned to read 'in about thirty seconds'. If so, it was the quickest thing he ever did where the printed word is concerned. His most famous short story devotes thirty pages to describing a single act of sexual intercourse.

Aged seventeen, Brodkey gained entry to Harvard where he performed brilliantly, and married a Radcliffe student before graduation. They had one daughter in a ten-year marriage. In the early 1950s he was drawn, like a heliotrope to the sun, to New York. It was, as he always saw it, his destiny to live and die there: 'New York was the capital of American sexuality, the one place in America where you could get laid with some degree of sophistication ... I was always crazy about New York, dependent on it, scared of it – well, it is dangerous – but beyond that there was the pressure of being young and of not yet having done work you really liked, trademark work, breakthrough work.' Brodkey's breakthrough came early. He showed a story ('The State of Grace') to the editor of the *New Yorker* and – at only twenty-three – was taken on board. Harold Ross's magazine was the red carpet to literary fame. *First Love and Other Stories* was duly published in 1958 to great applause and a garland of prizes. Like all of Brodkey's fiction, he himself (his twentyish self that is, portrayed as 'Wiley Silenowicz') was the Narcissus-subject of his writing.

Now a fixture in the pages of the *New Yorker*, the world was at Harold Brodkey's feet. Many would have backed him against that other young literary meteor, John Updike, but the Brodkey feet never moved and thereafter his career was silence and rumour. Personal life may have been a factor. He and his first wife divorced in 1962 and he was for a while energetically bisexual. How long is unclear – he remarried in 1980. It was, over these years, put about that Brodkey had embarked on a gigantic work – possibly the greatest Great American Novel ever; a work which would make *Moby Dick* look like a newly spawned minnow. Six thousand pages were mentioned. He had, it was further intimated, been working on this novel since childhood: it would be called *A Party of Animals*, though the title gave nothing away. Meanwhile, Brodkey's silence was portentous. He had, it was said, a cork-lined room in his New York apartment, specially constructed on the Proustian model of interior decoration, in which he was forging his masterwork – it demanded no lesser an environment.

But did it exist? As his *New York Times* obituarist, Dinitia Smith, tartly records over the thirty-two years this GAN was in active composition, 'Mr. Brodkey received advances for it from at least five publishers, refinancing it much as some people do their homes with mortgages.' A provisional manuscript (some 5,000 pages, it was rumoured) had been lodged with one of Brodkey's publishers, Farrar, Straus & Giroux, 'in a form so that if something happens to me, someone can deal with it'. Indeed, something did happen to him. Brodkey contracted HIV from homosexual encounters 'largely in the 1960s', he claimed in an announcement 'To My Readers' in 1993 in the *New Yorker*. If so, the symptoms were, like his publishing output, abnormally slow to emerge. They did not appear for thirty years (and that without modern retroviral drugs). Brodkey insisted he wasn't gay but, like many writers, experimental by nature – and unluckier than most. His readers had endured a long, forty-year wait and an anti-climactic one. In 1991 there finally appeared the work which the world had been on tenterhooks to see. It was entitled *The Runaway Soul* and ran to a mere 853 printed pages. Brodkey announced that it was only the first instalment of *A Party of Animals*. But he was sixty-one and Methuselah couldn't have finished the work at this rate. He brought out another novel, *Profane Friendship*, in 1994, a rewrite of Thomas Mann's *Death in Venice*. He died in January 1996 of Aids – within the same 48 hours, curiously, as Joseph Brodsky, the Nobel Prize-winning novelist with whom, to Brodkey's irritation, he was perennially confused during life. Such things vexed him. He was famous for his feuds – accusing John Updike, for example, of depicting him as the Luciferian hero of *The Witches of Eastwick*.

In his last two years Brodkey penned a poignant account of his end, *This Wild Darkness: The Story of My Death* (1996). An *ars moriendi* (a venerable but obsolete genre), it traces his painful journey to the dying of the light. It reads more fluently, and with more narrative drive, than any fiction-proper he ever wrote. In it, he seems at times to mount a defence of the snail-like pace of his work. Published a few months after his death, he cannot quite be said to have to beaten the undertaker in the race to the finishing line, but he gallantly finished the course. His great novel didn't – if, indeed, it existed. In *This Wild Darkness*, Brodkey recalls that when he was six or seven years old, 'I asked everyone … I mean *everyone*, the children at school, the teachers, women in the caféteria, the parents of other children: How long do you want to live? I suppose the secret in the question was: What do you enjoy? Do you enjoy living? Would you try to go on living under any circumstances?' The question remained hanging.

FN   Harold Brodkey (born Aaron Roy Weintraub)
MRT   *This Wild Darkness*
Biog   *New York Times*, obituary, 27 January 1996 (Dinitia Smith).

251. Edna O'Brien 1930–

Any book that is any good must be, to some extent, autobiographical. Edna O'Brien

As O'Brien recalls, 'the first book I ever bought – I've still got it – was called *Introducing James Joyce*, by T. S. Eliot'. She proceeded to read *Portrait of the Artist as a Young Man* and 'reading that book made me realize that I wanted literature for the rest of my life'. As Joyce famously pronounced, the Irish author can only survive by 'silence, exile and cunning' and a willingness to offend Ireland. O'Brien passes the last in grand style: the first half-dozen of her novels were banned in Ireland. She also sails through on Joyce's exile criterion. She left Ireland in her early twenties and her career as an author – as flamboyantly Irish as her name – has been entirely passed in literary London. 'Silent' O'Brien has never been. Cunningly, however, she has kept hidden details of the many love affairs London literary gossip credits her with.

She was born in a village in County Clare in the west of Ireland in an atmosphere she describes as 'fervid, enclosed and catastrophic. The spiritual food consisted of the crucified Christ.' Since her family owned a run-down farm, the food on the table was that of the healthy peasant. Peasant-like, too, was the culture of her home. The opening chapters of her first novel, *The Country Girls* (1960), give a grim picture of that home. Her father was drunken and when in drink physically violent to his womenfolk. The novel opens with the fourteen-year-old heroine, Caithleen, waking with the petrified thought 'he had not come home' – which meant he had spent the night 'on the batter' and will perpetrate some domestic battery (which he duly does). The O'Briens had once been well off and there remained 'the relics of riches. It was a life full of contradictions. We had an avenue, but it was full of potholes; there was a gatehouse, but another couple lived there; we had lots of fields, but they weren't all stocked or tilled. I remember fields high with ragwort. I remember my father giving them to other people. There was a prodigality, which I regret to tell you I have inherited.' Her father would be the 'ogre figure' in much of her early fiction. Her mother, to whom *The Country Girls* was dedicated (she did not appreciate the gesture and went through her copy carefully obliterating all the dirty bits), had been to America and almost escaped her Irish destiny. Her daughter would succeed.

Aged eleven, Edna won a scholarship to a convent boarding school some forty miles away. The nuns, if her novel is to be believed, proved as tyrannical as her father – if more ingenious in their cruelties. 'Sins got committed by the hour, sins of thought, word and deed and omission.' In *The Country Girls* there are two girl-heroines who, as O'Brien records, reflect different aspects of her own personality. Caithleen (later Kate) is obedient, bookish, clever and shy. Baba, the daughter of a rather more decent veterinarian father, is rebellious, sluttish and dumb – but full of life. Caithleen's initial vocation is to take the veil, but, encouraged by her wayward alter ego, she too rebels. At the climactic moment, 'anger pervaded like a rash and then and there I knew that I would not be a nun rather I would be a film star and get a perm in my hair'. O'Brien left the Sisters of Mercy in 1946. Whether, like Caithleen (egged on by Baba), it was for writing blasphemous filth is not clear. If so, it would have been in character. *The Country Girls*, when it came out in 1960, offended the authorities on any number of scores but its most wounding charge against Irish society was that – while fanatically defending the traditional 'family' – it institution-alised sexual abuse of the young. The fourteen-year-old Caithleen is targeted, con-tinuously, by 'happily' married men. Ireland, we apprehend, is a cesspit of sexual hypocrisy and furtive male lust.

Aged eighteen, O'Brien went off to Dublin to qualify as a chemist's assistant. She worked in a shop by day, dispensing worm powders with gentian-stained hands. There was a glorious night at the 'pictures' once a week and evening classes. She pigged it in a bedsit, with few prospects other than the kind of marriage which had destroyed her mother. O'Brien has always been sensitive about the higher educa-tion she deserved and was denied. She takes malicious pleasure in relating the fact that a reviewer on the *New Statesman* was dismissed for calling her 'illiterate'. As she recalls in her semi-autobiographical book, *Mother Ireland* (1976), she lost her virtue in a field on the outskirts of Dublin. It was the 'ultimate crime' but she no longer felt it as such. She was eventually 'whisked away' from her dreary existence in the chemist shop by the Czech-Irish writer, Ernest Gébler. The complex nature of their relationship is reflected in the second volume of her 'girls trilogy' and only fully disclosed after his death in 1996.

Gébler earns a place in literary history as Ireland's first international bestsell-ing author. His novel, *The Plymouth Adventure* (1947), about the pioneer Ameri-can puritan voyage, was made into a film starring Spencer Tracy in 1952. Gébler was a Marxist, an intellectual fifteen years O'Brien's senior, and in the process of divorcing a rich American wife. On learning that his daughter was living in sin with a married man, Edna's father burst into the couple's house, as O'Brien recalled, decades later, in a radio interview: 'There was a fight so he [Gébler] was hit or kicked. That evening he had wounds and was livid. My father came with a priest. It was like something out of the Middle Ages.' The couple went on to marry after his divorce came through in 1954, 'in a very grim little wedding in the sacristy of a Catholic church in Blanchardstown and the witnesses were two builders'. They moved to London a few years later. According to O'Brien's memoir, *Mother Ireland*, 'I left Ireland without a wrench' – but, in every other than the geographical sense, the country would never leave her.

Gébler eventually became yet another tyrant in her life. Where men were concerned, O'Brien concluded, she was incorrigibly 'masochistic'. Gébler is portrayed as Eugene Gaillard (the initials are a giveaway) in the trilogy, thinly disguised as a middle-aged documentary film-maker with a previous wealthy American wife, '35 and going bald'. Gaillard is initially drawn to Caithleen by her innocence and docility. 'You're like Anna Karenina in that coat,' he compliments her, and she duly goes off to read the novel. As time passes and two children arrive, he comes to see her innocence as something to despise. 'He said I came from ignorance and peasants,' a pained Caithleen says.

It was now the turn of the decade. Through Gébler's connections, O'Brien (Mrs Gébler, as she was) had picked up part-time work as a reader for the publisher Hutchinson. Impressed by her fluent reports, they offered her £25 for a catalogue-filler. She dashed off *The Country Girls* in a few weeks, followed by *The Lonely Girl* in 1962 and *Girls in Their Married Bliss* in 1964. It was a decade of rebellion – whether James Dean's in southern California or Jimmy Porter's in London – and her novels about two Irish moral dissidents were hugely successful. It certified their success when the first volume was publicly burned by the parish priest in her home village.

Gébler was now in his mid-forties and had never been able to reproduce his early success. He found himself overshadowed by a woman whom he had always looked down on intellectually. In O'Brien's trilogy, Kate's infidelities, with distinguished lovers, did not help things along. The marriage was dissolved, angrily, in 1964. O'Brien suggests – something confirmed by her son Sasha's later memoir – that Gébler could not live with his wife's eclipsing him and convinced himself, in an extremity of paranoia, that he had actually written her bestselling trilogy. Those books forlornly express the view that 'there isn't a man alive who wouldn't kill any woman the minute she draws attention to his defects'. Kate and Baba, the trilogy concludes, will never find happiness. And O'Brien herself? In a late interview she confided that, 'now I am 78 years of age ... I haven't met the man with whom my whole being, heart, soul and body would be miraculously entwined. I didn't. My prayer has not been answered in that, nor is it likely to be.'

The trilogy ends on a note of terminal embitterment. O'Brien has given numerous hints that she has sought help along the way in psychotherapy. She records treatment by the trendy 1960s guru R. D. Laing whom she met socially 'with Sean Connery' (the true O'Brien touch). Laing gave her LSD, which was 'terrifying' – whether it helped or not she does not say. In the last volume of the trilogy, Kate attacks a railway station weighing machine for obscure reasons and is, for a while, hospitalised. Forcible hospitalisation in a mental institution is the harrowing subject matter of O'Brien's later novel, *In the Forest* (2002).

In the decades after the initial trilogy, now a successful woman of letters, O'Brien wrote fluently – novels, drama and non-fiction. Anger blazes, inextinguishably if sometimes smoulderingly, in virtually every word she put on paper. She revisits the woes of marriage, and pays out sadistic husbands, in *Time and Tide* (1992). She revisits the sexual nastiness of Ireland in *A Pagan Place* (1970), in which the girl heroine is seduced by a priest (this, O'Brien says, is her favourite among her own novels). Her campaign against the Irish Church has been unremitting. In one of the most strident of her novels, *Down by the River* (1996), an incestuously raped fourteen-year-old becomes the focus of a right-to-abortion battle. If they could, one suspects, the priesthood of her native land would make a bonfire of all her works – with Edna O'Brien on top. Her two-minded feelings about the IRA are laid out in *House of Splendid Isolation* (1994). She commemorated her eightieth year in 2011 with a string of lively interviews, the promise of a memoir (one which, it was hoped, would name names – who was that prominent politician 'Duncan' in *Girls in Their Married Bliss?*) and a collection of short stories, *Saints and Sinners* (2011). There was by now no question into which category the author placed herself. Reviews were indulgent, while noting that changes in post-Good Friday Agreement Ireland had rather passed her by. Exile was in danger of becoming dislocation and a relapse into savage nostalgia.

FN   Edna O'Brien (later Gébler)
MRT   *The Country Girls*
Biog   E. O'Brien, *Mother Ireland* (1976)

252. Donald Barthelme 1931–1989

It's entirely possible to fail to understand or actively misunderstand what an artist is doing.

A novelist and short-story writer whose work is jaggedly absurd, minimalist, wittily allusive, aggressively trivial, consciously postmodern – and above all funny (not a word which automatically collocates with 'postmodern') – Barthelme was born in Philadelphia, the child of two high-achieving, first-generation students at Ivy League Pennsylvania University. If a fairy godmother had hovered over infant Donald's cradle, she would doubtless have waved a Ph.D. scroll as well as the traditional wand. If any writer of the twentieth century is a child of the university ethos, it is Donald Barthelme. His whole life would intertwine with the academic world.

When he was two, the family removed to the University of Texas at Houston where his father eventually became a professor of architecture. Donald Barthelme Sr's tastes were advanced for the time and even more so for the place. He built himself a Mies van der Rohe house which his son recalls as seeming as exotic as a jewel in the head of a toad, in the featureless, windblown Texas plains. Another unimpressed son dismissed it as 'swoopy' and not at all homey.

Donald enrolled himself as a student at Houston – it was convenient, but a mistake. His relationship with his namesake father would be troubled throughout their lives. They fell out over issues ranging from his parents' (particularly his mother's) Catholicism to the kind of literature Donald eventually wrote (under his father's name, minus the easily overlooked 'Jr/Sr' suffix). He had decided, aged ten, that he would be a writer, although what kind was not immediately apparent. James Thurber and Edgar Allan Poe were early favourites – both pushing him towards brevity. In his teens he became a devotee of jazz, took up drums and had hopes of making it as a musician. Oddly, so did his friend, John Barth, in his youth. A doctoral thesis remains to be written on the coincidence (e.g. 'The Percussive Syntagm – Postmodernist Arrythmias'.) Barthelme majored in journalism, and was a powerhouse on the student newspaper while at university. He married in 1952. He left university as the Korean War broke out and, like other young men of his age group, was conscripted for a cause whose point was never entirely clear. It was all the less clear since peace broke out immediately after his infantry training. He persuaded the army 'his weapon was a typewriter' (they had intended assigning him to the bakery) and served his country for two years, editing an army newspaper.

On his discharge in 1955, Barthelme returned to Houston where he read and pondered philosophy under the guidance of Maurice Natanson – a thinker (only six years older than Barthelme) who is credited with introducing awareness of existentialism and phenomenology to the US. It was a partnership. A witty philosopher, Natanson was particularly interested in the connection of his subject with creative writing and explores the theme in his best-known book, *The Erotic Bird: Phenomenology in Literature* (1997). The foundation of Barthelme's later fiction would be Kierkegaard and Kafka rather than the post-romantic recklessness of the currently vogueish 'Beats'. For a few years Barthelme bounced around his home town, searching for his groove. He worked on local newspapers, edited little magazines, reviewed jazz, and for a short period was the director of an art museum. He supplemented his income by short-contract university teaching and helped set up a creative writing programme at his alma mater. Over these years he was dependent financially on his father, which rankled with both Barthelmes.

His career took a definite direction with his move to New York ('our Paris', as he called it), where he became a regular contributor of short fiction to the *New Yorker* under its editor, William Shawn, one of the great (if largely unrecognised) literary patrons of the time. Barthelme's first story in Shawn's pages, 'L'Lapse', a typically riddling title, was published in 1963. It nestled between pieces by John Cheever and Hannah Arendt. New York, with its lively modern jazz scene, avant-garde art and 'filth on the streets', was more of a home town to Barthelme than Houston ever was. Over the next few years he recruited a discriminating readership as the master of the bizarre scenario. What was grey 'theory' in other hands was as zany and comic as *Mad* magazine in his. In one of the more famous of his pieces, 'Mr. Edward LEAR, Nonsense Writer and Landscape Painter Requests the honor of Your Presence On the Occasion of his DEMISE. San Remo 2:20 a.m. The 29th of May' (the invitation is accompanied by an RSVP). In another, King Kong is appointed 'adjunct professor of art history at Rutgers'. In yet another, 'The King of Jazz', 'Hokie Mokie', with the death of 'Spicy MacLammermoor', a (trom)'bone man, finds himself 'king of jazz' – a verdict confirmed by white critics, who find in his 'few but perfectly selected notes the real epiphanic glow'. Along comes a Japanese trombonist who does to black music what the Lexus does to Chrysler, or the Fuji apple to the humble Granny Smith (Barthelme, while on R&R in the army, had been impressed how frighteningly good jazz was in Tokyo).

Best known among Barthelme's novels (or 'anti-novels') is *Snow White* (1967), a literary fantasy on Disney's cartoon fantasia of the original German fairy story. Barthelme's Snow White (the story begins with a corporeal inventory of her 'beauty spots' – including that on her buttock) misconducts herself disgracefully with her dwarfs in the shower. Like all his fiction, disconnectedness – a kind of asyntax – requires the reader to leap acrobatically from one sentence to another, often slipping.

Always he wrote 'against expectation', as he put it: dismantling the conventional. Barthelme, a modest writer, never saw himself as more than snot on the sleeve of high literature – appreciative admirers see him as a welcome antidote to pervasive high seriousness and the portentousness of critical 'theory'. He was both 'pomo' and 'accessible'. On the whole, Barthelme had little time for critics (most of whom he believed 'want me to stop what I'm doing'). He was of the firm belief that the only valid criticism of a work of art was another work of art. He was, above all else, a generous writer: Thomas Pynchon wrote *Gravity's Rainbow* (1973) while living rent-free in Barthelme's New York basement.

Barthelme's short-story collections include: *Unspeakable Practices, Unnatural Acts* (1968), *City Life* (1970), *Sadness* (1972) and *Great Days* (1979). 'Sadness' could well be the title for all of them, permeated as they are with a kind of exhausted, but none the less jaunty, world-weariness. New York was eventually too much, and his income too little – he needed a salary. Incredibly, as his biographer informs us, he never earned more than $1,000 a year from his books and depended almost entirely on his *New Yorker* stipend, a debt he never cleared. Barthelme returned to Houston to teach creative writing, quirkily, for the last years of his life. You could, despite what Thomas Wolfe said, go home again. Whether you would be happy there was something else. He had many lovers (some of them, like Grace Paley, fellow postmodernists), married four times (the last successfully) and died prematurely of throat cancer. Years of abusive drinking contributed to his death and, arguably, to the fractured syntax of his narratives. He had, one friend observed, 'an alcoholic's attention span'. And, alas, an alcoholic's abbreviated life-span. Did he know where he was, Barthelme was asked as he lay dying in hospital. Yes, he replied, 'in the antechamber to heaven'.

FN   Donald Barthelme
MRT *Snow White*
Biog T. Daugherty, *Hiding Man: A Biography of Donald Barthelme* (2009)

253. Toni Morrison 1931–

In 1992, there were four books by black women on the best-seller lists – at the same time. Terry McMillan's, Alice Walker's and two of mine. Now that's exhilarating!

Until the post-mortem exploiters get down to their work, Toni Morrison's life will be principally known from her own many accounts in interviews. She was born

Chloe Anthony Wofford in Lorain, Ohio, on the banks of Lake Erie. The state had been on the frontline of the abolition of slavery seventy years earlier, but where the Woffords lived was integrated. Chloe's mother, she recalled, was careful never to observe the informal segregation of cinema audiences, looking left and right of the aisle before she sat down. Chloe's father was a ship-welder and her grandparents had been sharecroppers. Her family, in terms of the restricted social scale accessible to blacks, was moving up but aspired to a yet higher place.

Chloe was encouraged to read widely in childhood (Jane Austen and Tolstoy are cited) while surrounded, conversationally, by oral narratives and blues lyrics brought from the South. Her mother belonged to a book club, parting with 'hard earned money' to do so. Chloe recalled being the only black child in her first grade class and the best reader. She was not, however, to forget her place in American life. In her early teens, she served as a housemaid for local white families: 'I started around 13. That was the work that was available: to go to a woman's house after school and clean for three or four hours. The normal teen-age jobs were not available. Housework always was. It wasn't uninteresting. You got to work these gadgets that I never had at home: vacuum cleaners. Some of the people were nice. Some were terrible. Years later, I used some of what I observed in my fiction.'

In 1949 she gained entrance to Howard University, an elite institution for black students. She took a BA in English and went on to Cornell University to pursue research on William Faulkner. He seemed to her 'the only writer who took black people seriously. Which is not to say he was, or was not, a bigot.' It was at university that she renamed herself 'Toni'. Her motive for doing so has been analysed in various ways – it being a name beloved by home permanent-wave merchandisers, targeted at young white women. On graduation, she was appointed an English instructor at Texas Southern University before returning as a junior professor at Howard – an academic career was in prospect.

That prospect was disrupted when, in 1958, she married a colleague, Harold Morrison, an architect. The marriage lasted six years and produced two children. It was, reportedly, difficult and is something which, otherwise forthcoming, she declines to be forthcoming about. Harold returned to his birthplace, Jamaica, leaving his former wife with sole responsibility for their children. After divorce, Morrison's career pattern altered. Her youngest son at the time of the separation was not a year old, so a doctorate was not an option. But it was not altogether a bad time: it was the mid-1960s and new opportunities were opening up for women and other 'minorities'. Morrison (she has kept her married surname – somewhat uneasily, one gathers) moved to New York where she worked for the publisher Random House. As she recalls from that period: 'whenever things got difficult I thought about my mother's mother, a sharecropper, who, with her husband, owed money to their landlord. In 1906, she escaped with her seven children to meet her husband in Birmingham, where he was working as a musician. It was a dangerous trip, but she wanted a better life. Whenever things seemed difficult for me in New York, I thought that what I was doing wasn't anything as hard as what she did.' As an editor she was instrumental in publishing African American writers such as Angela Davis and Gayl Jones. Black writing (as the favoured term then was) had begun to get traction in American culture and Morrison herself had been writing fiction as early as her time on the faculty at Howard.

One story in her mind from those years concerned a black girl who longed for blue eyes. This would be the basis of her first published novel *The Bluest Eye* (1970). It has never been regarded as her finest work (that accolade would probably go to *Beloved*) but *The Bluest Eye* has particular interest as Morrison's most autobiographical novel. The action is set in Lorain in 1940–41, the year in which America went to battle for the free world – rather ignoring the freedom of its black citizens who would have to wait a quarter of a century for their Civil Rights Act. The narrator of *The Bluest Eye*, Claudia MacTeer, is the same age as Chloe Wofford in that year. Hers is a solidly respectable family. They take in the child of an unrespectable family, Pecola Breedlove, who has been sexually abused and impregnated by her father. 'How do you get somebody to love you?' Pecola forlornly asks. She is fixated on Shirley Temple and convinced that blue eyes are the secret. They are not, she discovers. More abuse and premature death awaits. Claudia – the Morrison figure we apprehend – is made of stronger stuff. She dismembers her 'blue eyed, yellow-haired, pink-skinned' dolls to see what they are made of:

> But the dismembering of dolls was not the true horror. The truly horrifying thing was the transference of the same impulses to little white girls. The indifference with which I could have axed them was shaken only by my desire to do so.

The Bluest Eye did not make much impression at this stage of Morrison's career, although over the years – particularly after being selected by Oprah Winfrey for her Book Club – it has sold strongly. It was followed by *Sula* (1973) and *Song of Solomon* (1977) – which, unusually, has a black protagonist, Macon 'Milkman' Dead, searching out his roots in the old South.

By the end of the 1970s Morrison's fiction was gaining recognition – particularly among African American readers and opinion-formers. Her importance as an American writer, without qualifying epithet, was certified by *Beloved* in 1987. The story is based on the historical figure, Margaret Garner, a slave, who, when her escape was foiled, killed her children rather than have them taken back into captivity. She was prosecuted less for absconding than the destruction of property. By this stage of her career, Morrison's narrative technique had evolved into something akin to the fluidities of black musicians like Charlie Parker or Lester Young – an analogy confirmed by the title of her 1992 novel, *Jazz*.

Beloved triggered one of the most controversial events in her career when the novel failed to win an NBA award. A caucus of influential African American writers and critics bought advertising space to protest at what was seen by them as rank injustice. Justified as it was, one cannot imagine anything similar being done for Britain's 'Booker Bridesmaid', Beryl Bainbridge. Amends were made when *Beloved* won a Pulitzer Prize. Oprah Winfrey, whose book club had been consistently helpful in promoting Morrison's career, bought the rights and financed a later movie. The NBA protest, well intentioned as it was, had the perverse effect of suggesting that Morrison's success was the result of special interest lobbying and white cultural guilt. The allegation (typically voiced behind the scenes) would haunt her later career.

Beloved also provoked controversy for its cryptic epigraph: 'Sixty Million and more'. It is a tendentious statistic – and almost certainly inaccurate. The number of Africans estimated to have perished on the 'middle passage' to the New World, or in slavery there, has ranged as high as 120 million and as low (if that is the right word) as a tenth of that figure. No one – shamefully – will ever know precisely, because no one at the time bothered to count. Morrison quite clearly chose sixty million as a multiple of six million – that, notoriously, is the rounded estimate of the Jews who were murdered in the Holocaust. But as Morrison has elsewhere complained, 'There is no suitable memorial or plaque or wreath or wall or park or skyscraper lobby honoring the memory of the human beings forced into slavery and brought to the United States.' Not even, she noted, 'a small bench by the road'.

Morrison was angry in the 1980s, the Reagan years. The destiny of blacks in America, she believed, was to be forever degraded – it was the cement which held the country together: 'If there were no black people here in this country, it would have been Balkanized. The immigrants would have torn each other's throats out, as they have done everywhere else. But in becoming an American, from Europe, what one has in common with that other immigrant is contempt for me – it's nothing else but color. Wherever they were from, they would stand together. They could all say, "I am not that." ... When they got off the boat, the second word they learned was "nigger." Ask them – I grew up with them.' This phase of her career produced her most disaffected novel, *Tar Baby* (1981), in which a character concludes: 'White folks and black folks should not sit down and eat together or do any of those personal things in life.' At the same period, at a conference, she roundly declared: 'At no moment in my life have I ever felt as though I was an American. At no moment. The sole reason that I am invited here, and the whole reason that I am sitting here, is because some black children got their brains shot out in the streets all over the country. And had the good fortune to be televised … I am a read, as opposed to unread, writer because of those children.'

The next decade, crowned as it was by her Nobel Prize in 1993, found her mellower. The award gave her, she said, 'licence to strut'. Honours and doctorates followed in such profusion they must surely have impeded her creativity. She was now carrying the heavy load of spokeswoman – expected to negotiate 'major themes'. Controversially, she hailed Bill Clinton as America's 'first black president'. He displayed, she said, 'almost every trope of blackness: single-parent household, born poor, working-class, saxophone-playing, McDonald's-and-junk-food-loving boy from Arkansas'. Throughout her career, however, she has kept a wary distance from mainline feminism, offering such explanations as 'I don't subscribe to patriarchy, and I don't think it should be substituted with matriarchy' and 'I can't take positions that are closed'. Positions she was able to take were in America's Ivy League universities, culminating in an endowed chair in Creative Writing at Princeton.

Her later fiction has often encountered a stiffer reception. *Paradise* (1998), the story of a massacre of whites by blacks in 1970s Oklahoma, elicited a particularly sharp review from the influential *New York Times* critic, Michiko Kakutani: 'Unfortunately, *Paradise* is everything that *Beloved* was not: it's a heavy-handed, schematic piece of writing, thoroughly lacking in the novelistic magic Ms. Morrison has wielded so effortlessly in the past. It's a contrived, formulaic book that mechanically pits men against women, old against young, the past against the present.' By this stage in her career Morrison was sufficiently well grounded to withstand the occasional knock although, as Kakutani intimates, her major achievements in fiction, as opposed to life, will probably be located by posterity in the 1970s and 1980s.

FN   Toni Morrison (born Chloe Ardelia Wofford. The middle name 'Anthony' is also used by her instead of 'Ardelia')
MRT *The Bluest Eye*
Biog C. C. Denard, *Toni Morrison: Conversations* (2008)

254. Alice Munro 1931–

I think I knew that at heart I was an aging spinster.

There is keen contention as to who is the greatest Canadian writer of short fiction in the last half century. Top place would, quite likely, go to either Alistair MacLeod or Alice Munro (née Laidlaw), both of proudly Scottish extraction: one highland, the other lowland – very different extracts. Munro, the lowlander, can trace her ancestry back to the Ettrick shepherd (author of *The Private Memoirs and Confessions of a Justified Sinner*), James Hogg. Less regional than MacLeod (her Huron county Ontario does not have the rich Gaelic culture of St Edward's Island), she weaves an equally sensitive history of her country in her stories. Typically they pivot on enigmatic moments which resonate beyond the domestic background in which they occur.

'The Progress of Love', the title piece in her 1986 collection (first published in the *New Yorker*), illustrates the distinct Munro form, style and tone. There is, as usual, enough raw narrative matter for a whole novel, boiled down into a few pages. The story opens with the sentence, 'I got the call at work, and it was my father.' Her mother is dead ('gone,' as her father puts it). The story goes on to reconstruct a portrait of the dead mother, Marietta. Neurotically devout, she prays on her knees several times a day – forever 'saved', as she had been, at a camp meeting, aged fourteen. The narrator's father, less religious, is a farmer in a small way. The couple married late. Marietta would not consent to the wedding until she had paid back her own father every cent it had cost him to raise her. The story revolves around two discoveries made by the heroine, aged twelve in 1947, through her *louche* Californian aunt Beryl, who has come to visit and raise a little hell. Her mother, the narrator discovers, was traumatised as a little girl by seeing *her* mother in a barn with a rope around her neck, on a chair, evidently threatening to hang herself. Young Marietta runs off to town for help – without managing to get any – and is suffused with guilt. But it was Aunt Beryl who noticed that the rope was not fastened to the beam: the wife was merely intending to 'get a rise' out of her husband, with whom she was, for unspecified reasons, unhappy.

For Marietta, however, the event is lifelong traumatic – 'Her heart was broken.' She recoils into God. Later, after her father has died and the farm sold, Marietta inherits $3,000. She takes the money from the bank and – dirt-poor that she and her farmer husband are – burns the bills in a stove: 'She put in just a few bills at a time, so it wouldn't make too big a blaze. My father stood and watched her.' He did not protest. Or was he actually there? The narrative is uncertain on the point. Why did Marietta do it? Why did she, as few children do, repay her father?

Why did she not just refuse the money he left, or give it to charity rather than ritually destroy it? Why – most hurtfully – does she deny her children (the narrator, notably) the decent education that money would have bought? Was Marietta abused by her father? The story gives no answer other than, vaguely, that her daughter thinks the money-burn was 'right'. In fast-forward, the farm is taken over by a hippy commune, then becomes a small component in the agro-industry which is transforming the land. All is swallowed up, forgotten. Only the unanswered 'why?' remains.

Munro's best novels all have within them plots which, like Japanese water-flowers, could expand into full-size fiction. In her strongest collection, *Hateship, Friendship, Courtship, Loveship, Marriage* (2001), the title story centres on a plain, middle-aged servant (an orphan shipped in her childhood from Glasgow), Johanna. Two smart young teenagers maliciously send her letters leading her to believe that a man, hundreds of miles away, wants to marry her. She packs up and leaves. Indeed there is a man – he is dying and she saves his life. In gratitude, he marries her. The nasty young girls fare less well. Perhaps there is a God.

Alice Laidlaw was born in 1931, in the thin ribbon of Canada bordering the US, where 90 per cent of Canadians live – facing south, many of them, like heliotropes. Her father, Robert, was a mink and silver fox-farmer (for the manufacture of garments none of his own womenfolk would ever wear) in an unprosperous way, on the outskirts of the small town of Wingham, Ontario. He was prone to bouts of bad temper. Grumpy fathers – often seething impotently in retirement homes – recur frequently in Munro's fiction. Alice's mother was a former schoolteacher, credited as a principal influence on her daughter's literary career. But a heavy cost was paid. Mrs Laidlaw developed Parkinson's disease when Alice was nine and many of the household duties came Alice's way as she was growing up. The domestic atmosphere of her childhood was, she recalls, 'stifling'. She gives a close evocation of these early years in many of her stories – most closely 'Family Furnishings'. In this story she introduces a half-sister, a by-blow of the father's early years. Is it fiction? There is so much evident fact in 'Family Furnishings' that one is inclined to credit it as autobiographical.

At the University of Western Ontario, where she started a degree in English, Alice paid her way with a variety of meaningless jobs (waitressing mainly). On leaving UWO, after two years when her scholarship ran out, Alice Laidlaw married a fellow student, and fellow 'Scot', Jim Munro, in 1951. She was a mother at the age of twenty-one and would have four daughters. The Munros moved to Vancouver, where they opened a book store. Here it was, in the intervals between household chores (she hated, she says, being regarded as 'the little wife'), that she began tentatively putting out the short stories that she had been writing, practically from girlhood. Munro's first collection was published as she closed on forty, followed by the only novel she has published, *Lives of Girls and Women* (1971) – a title which describes much of her output. The novel is autobiographical and offers most of what the public knows of her early life and probably ever will until after her death when the 'post-mortem exploiters' do their grisly work.

On divorcing her first husband in 1972, Munro moved back to Huron, Ontario, and in 1976 she married an old friend from her early college days, Gerald Fremlin. They bought a house close to where Alice had been brought up. In this mature phase of her life, Munro pulsed out a steady stream of short stories. She was, by now, a fixture in the *New Yorker* and spent periods as writer-in-residence at various Ontario universities. The crowning honour was the UK's Man Booker International Prize, 2009. It was not otherwise an easy time: she had required a heart bypass and was also afflicted with cancer. In the same year that she won the Booker she diverted from her established pattern with the collection *The View From Castle Rock* (2006). In it she investigates her historical Scottish heritage. Karl Miller, a leading authority on James Hogg, recounts a disciple's visit (accompanied by the poet Seamus Heaney, and the novelist Andrew O'Hagan – Celts all) to the grave of the author, in the Ettrick Valley, in 2009. 'On returning to London', Miller recalls, 'I received a proof copy of the latest collection of Munro's stories, which begins in the Ettrick Valley with an attention to Will o' Phaup's tombstone and a role for Hogg's cousin James Laidlaw, who left Ettrick for North America at the age of 60 and settled in Ontario, where a descendant begat Alice Munro. The story describes how, on the top of Edinburgh Castle, Laidlaw, in his cups, had informed his children that to look over to Fife was to behold the shores of America.'

Munro's fiction, Miller argues, is 'true narrative' – true, that is, to the stern, ineradicable Presbyterianism of her Ettrick forebears. She has, in a sense, come home: back-migrated, as the demographers put it. Shrewdly Miller also discerns a Presbyterian inhibition in Munro's writing. That stern denomination has never much liked fiction, particularly its womenfolk: 'There was no interest in reading. It was almost considered disloyal to the idea of being a good housewife,' Munro recalls of her girlhood. In a 2005 interview, she further recalled that when her first collection was published, she hid her six copies in the downstairs cupboard where 'we put all the things we didn't use very often'. It wasn't shame, she explains, but a horror of exposure. A week later, when she was alone in the house, she forced herself to read one of the stories. 'I read the book cover to cover and, yes, it was OK.' The terse realism, and the brevity of her chosen form, can be connected with this ineradicable desire not to be caught writing a novel, perish the thought. But particles of fiction can slip past the internal, Presbyterian, censor. If, that is, you're quick and short about it.

FN   Alice Ann Munro (née Laidlaw)
MRT *The View From Castle Rock*
Biog R. Thacker, *Alice Munro: Writing her Lives: a Biography* (2005)

255. Trevanian 1931–2005

I read Proust, but not much else written in the 20th century.

No novelist of the late twentieth century put greater barriers between himself (in life) and his fiction than 'Trevanian' – the pen name of Rodney Whitaker. Whitaker was brought up, in impoverished circumstances, in Albany, New York. He gives a finely written description of his childhood in his last published work, *The Crazyladies of Pearl Street* (2005), and in the 'cybernotes' he offered on his official fansite to the 'novel'. (It was later reclassified by its publisher as a 'memoir', but in neither form did it sell beyond the diminishing circle of his fans.) Whitaker was brought up 'a believing Catholic', but in adolescence lapsed into 'mildly indifferent non-theism'. God, he said, was not on the first thirty pages of the important things in his life. Priests often come to gory ends in Trevanian's fiction – *Shibumi* (1979) ends with a particularly nasty wearer of the cloth impaled on the ice-pick of a man he betrayed. As a child Whitaker was lucky, as he saw it, to have benefited from 'the golden age of American elementary education'. A key text in the formation of his mind was Howard Fast's 'splendidly biased', *Citizen Tom Paine*. Whitaker himself was a fighter for civil rights in the 1950s, demonstrating at the docks for the right of negroes to work there. An early predisposition to alcoholism – a blood weakness on his mother's side, as he saw it – was nipped in the bud. He smoked heavily, however, a habit which eventually killed him somewhat before his time.

Whitaker was clever enough to win the fellowships and grants-in-aid which opened the way to an academic career. He graduated with a BA and MA from the University of Washington, did a stint in the US Navy during the Korean War, returning to complete his doctorate in communications and film at Northwestern University and, by mid-career, was chairman of the Department of Radio, TV and Film at the University of Texas, Austin. In his fortieth year, he published his major academic monograph, under his own name, on the language of film and, as 'Trevanian', his first novel. *The Eiger Sanction* (1972) introduced an unlikely Secret Service assassin,

Dr Jonathan Hemlock, an art historian who undertakes 'sanctions' (i.e. contract assassinations) in order to build a private art collection. No pointy-headed academic, Hemlock is also a world-class mountaineer and his current contract requires doing his deadly stuff on a fiendishly difficult climb up one of the most challenging cliff faces in the Alps. All nonsense.

With its sardonic take-off of Robert Ludlum's heavy-handed signature titles (e.g. *The Scarlatti Inheritance*, 1971), its preposterous hero, and his own pompous *nom de plume*, Whitaker intended satire. In a line of authors going back to Swift, he discovered that you should never underestimate the dumbness of the reading public. The novel was taken 'straight' and became a bestseller, boosted by excited speculation as to who the author was. (Ludlum on his day off? A consortium?) He had, Whitaker later said, created a 'monster'. A sequel was demanded and he went further over the top with *The Loo Sanction* (1973). 'Loo' –not the subtlest of jokes – is an ultra-secret department of the British intelligence services. They require Hemlock's services to track down a serial killer of the country's top people. (Whitaker had spent a year in England, on fellowship, as a young academic; he liked the place but – Tom Paine disciple that he was – hated its toffs.) The narrative opens with an anal impaling which, Whitaker later confided, was a satire on the gratuitous violence of the Kubrick–Burgess movie adaptation of *A Clockwork Orange*. Again the novel was gulped down, delightedly, by a readership which did not detect the slightest tang of satire in what they were gulping.

His fiction – and the Clint Eastwood-starring movie of the first novel – enabled the Whitakers (his wife and four children) to retire to the *pays Basque* in France, which became the setting for his most ambitious novel, *Shibumi* (1979). The hero, Nicholai Hel, has absorbed the wisdoms of East and West. His *Weltanschauung* is principally driven by a complex analysis of the Japanese game, Go. He is an expert speleologist – expert everything, in fact, including half a dozen languages and transcendental elevation – and he abuses Volvos (the 'Volvo-bashing' motif is a kick at the ever more ludicrous fleet of Bondmobiles). Hel is called upon to save the world, which he does. An authorial tongue is meanwhile deep in an authorial cheek. Reading *Shibumi* one feels that Whitaker could have gone on to become a giant in the genre, but he was not interested. 'I could have made more money if I'd stuck to one genre as most successful writers do,' he later said, but he had enough money for his needs. He wrote a medieval romance under another pseudonym, 'Nicholas Seare': *1339 or So ... Being an Apology for a Pedlar* (1975); a *roman policier* set in Montreal, *The Main* (1976); and a gothic romance, *The Summer of Katya* (1983), set in the Basque country in 1914. It begins idyllic and ends horrific.

Trevanian then went silent for fifteen years, cultivating his garden, and not even identifying himself when impostors (one of whom was taken seriously by the *New York Times*) identified themselves publicly as 'Trevanian'. 'I decided I would stop writing until I figured out what to do with this many-minded monster (Trevanian) I had been obliged to create,' he explained. The least predictable of novelists, he came back into print with a rollicking cowboy novel, *Incident at Twenty-Mile* (1998) and, in the year of his death, a sensitive recollection of his childhood, *The Crazyladies of Pearl Street*. Whitaker spent his last years as a family man, not an author – in the West Country of England, a semi-invalid with pulmonary problems. He made close friends in his new rural retreat, even the closest of whom did not know (and would not have cared) that he was 'Trevanian'. He seems never to have been proud of that part of his life and died never having given a live interview.

FN   'Trevanian' (Rodney William Whitaker)
MRT   *Shibumi*
Biog www.Trevanian.com

256. Beryl Bainbridge 1932–2010

I know Beryl. No doubt you know Beryl. Seemingly everyone in London knows Beryl.
Lynn Barber

Novelists are held in different degrees of affectionate regard by the reading public – none more affectionately than Beryl Bainbridge. Wails would go up whenever – shortlisted five times – she failed to win the Booker Prize. The 'Booker bridesmaid' they called her. Bainbridge was born in Liverpool. She claimed a birth date of 1934, but records indicate it was November 1932. Her persistent repetition of the false date may raise suspicions as to some gilding of the lily in her accounts of other areas of her life – particularly events connected with her sexually precocious girlhood. Her father is described as a travelling salesman and former bankrupt whom in later life she candidly admitted to wanting to kill. Her mother she adored. Given the cramped dimensions of their house, she grew up sharing a bedroom with her mother. Her brother Ian bunked with his dad. The Bainbridges were ill-assorted but, given the times and prejudices of their class, chained together like galley slaves. She wrote, she said, to drain the poison of her childhood out of her system.

Bainbridge claimed to have been traumatised at the age of eleven by seeing the post-war films of the Nazi death camps (it must, given her birth date, have been a little later). A bright girl, she attended the fee-paying Merchant Taylors' Girls School in Crosby only to be expelled as a 'corrupting moral influence'. According to one version of the event she gave, her mother discovered a filthy poem in her school uniform and shopped her to the headmistress. It must have made for a difficult night in the bedroom. This (dates are slippery) is reckoned to have happened when she was fourteen. She had already fallen in love with a German prisoner of war, Harry Franz, who was awaiting repatriation. There was furtive coupling in the bushes and heartbreak when, after he was sent home, re-entry to Britain was banned. The relationship was carried on by letter for a few years until the couple gave up trying and got on with their separate lives. Had he come back, Franz might have faced prosecution for carnal relations with a minor.

Her education cut woefully short, Bainbridge got a job, with her father's help, at the Liverpool Playhouse. Her experience there is recalled in *An Awfully Big Adventure* (1989). The stage-struck teenage heroine Stella finds herself in a sticky sexual relationship as the company rehearses the Christmas performance of *Peter Pan*. Doubtless Beryl, unlike Barrie's hero, grew up very fast. Doubtless, like Stella too, she was a very obstinate young woman. She was making a respectable start on a career in 'rep' – notoriously hard and unremunerative as the profession was – when in 1954 she married Austin Davies, an artist and scene painter at the Playhouse. The path of their marriage did not run smooth. Divorce from Davies followed two children later in 1959. Subsequently she became a Catholic, she later said, 'to get away from Aussie' and the whole sex thing. She remained a Catholic 'for about ten minutes', but recalled it as a delightful spiritual experience. While the couple divorced they cannot be said to have entirely separated. Austin bought her a house in Albert Street, Camden Town (an address which became smart over the forty years she lived there), and moved into the basement with his second wife and family. Sixties' moral cool sanctioned such things.

Later in life, Beryl would have a third child by the novelist Alan Sharp. That relationship broke down when she discovered his previous wives and a currently pregnant girlfriend. This life crisis furnishes the plot to *Sweet William* (1975). William (i.e. the love rat Sharp) 'doesn't believe in free fall ... he won't let go of the branch till he's sure of the next one'. As she related in later interviews, 'He showed up for Rudi's birth, but then went downstairs saying he was going to get a book out of the car and never came back.' Too cool even for the sixties. Her personal life was thereafter relatively untroubled and easy-going. She was happier with free fall. She gave up sex at sixty, she said, 'Because I was just getting too old – you'd have to do it in pitch blackness.'

Over the years she transformed the house in Camden into a *Wunderkammer* and it supplies the background to innumerable publicity pictures of her 'clever-monkey' face. Eric the stuffed water buffalo in the hall was as well known to her readers as London Zoo's Brumas the Polar Bear. Well known too, by report, was the bullet hole in the ceiling and the story behind it. Her mother-in-law had appeared at the front door, long after the marriage with Austin was over, enquiring as to some photographs. Bainbridge went to look for them and: 'When I came out of the room she was standing one flight down, a little matronly figure digging something out of her handbag. Just in time I realised she was taking out a gun and, used to playing soldiers when I was younger, I jumped forward, jerked her elbow and ducked as a shot was fired at the ceiling. A shower of newly applied plaster fell on us like snow. She then hurried out of the house. Not wanting to be late for work, I dusted myself down and ran towards the factory; there was no sign of my mother-in-law.' The factory in Camden resurfaces in the early work, *The Bottle Factory Outing* (1974), a novel which won the *Guardian* fiction prize. A. N. Wilson, a close friend of Bainbridge in her later years, reflects: 'Did the incident ever take place? I am not saying that Beryl was a liar, because I do not think she was. But she was a novelist, and the crafted versions of events always came to have more substance than mere facts.'

She completed her first novel in the late 1950s. It was based on the New Zealand Parker-Hulme murder case in which two young girls murdered one of their mothers. The same episode inspired a number of writers and film-makers – most famously Peter Jackson's *Heavenly Creatures* (1994). The British reading public was not, British publishers decreed, ready for Bainbridge's version in 1958. *Harriet Said* (1972) was not published until she hooked up with Duckworth, with whom, from the 1970s on, she published a novel a year or so. The relationship with the Haycrafts, man and wife, who ran the firm became the subject of angry disagreement after Bainbridge's death. A. N. Wilson, among others, went so far as to say that 'the Haycrafts, were both, in their different ways, monsters'. Wilson's less aggressive point was that Duckworth did not, as publishers, value fiction – even though Bainbridge became, over the years, a valuable property. The physical quality of the packaging they gave Bainbridge's books was abysmal. Michael Holroyd elsewhere pointed out the unusual contract arrangement by which the more she sold, the lower the royalty payment. This may partly account for the rapidity and brevity of her novels.

Bainbridge claimed not to have read anything from Graham Greene onwards. Strong storylines, tinged with black *coups de théâtre* were her way of doing fiction. Her career, she always said, took a leap forward when Karl Miller wrote a piece in the *New York Review of Books* in 1974, hailing her as 'possibly the least known of the contemporary English novelists who are worth knowing'. Miller dearly wanted *The Dressmaker* (1973), her Liverpool novel, to win the Booker, but was outvoted on the

1973 panel. He was still upset at the injustice a quarter of a century later. The novel stands out for at least a couple of reasons. It opens in a wartime Liverpool home, occupied entirely by women. 'Nellie had her hair net on and her teeth out,' opens an early scene and the novel recreates, with uncanny solidity, a house in which the inhabitants have their night-time 'cat's lick' in a washer-repaired tin bowl in the scullery before sharing beds 'for warmth'. The crux of the narrative concerns the young Rita's love for an American serviceman – suggestive of young Beryl's involvement with Franz.

Her fiction output falls into two distinct parts. The first half of her career was devoted to what A. N. Wilson calls 'deftly distorted autobiography' – narratives which drew on her own life, more or less closely. In the second half of her career she moved into historical fiction of a quirky and speculative kind. No historical novelist has less of what Scott called 'Dryasdust and Smellfungus' about her. She kicked off in this new style with *Young Adolf* (1978), which speculates a possible visit by Hitler to his Irish sister-in-law, Bridget Hitler, in Liverpool in 1912. It is a series of comical misadventures and ends with him returning to Austria, vowing revenge, and the resolve 'to grow a moustache'. Subsequent subjects included the sinking of the *Titanic*, *Every Man for Himself* (1996) which had the good luck to coincide with James Cameron's 1997 Oscar-winning movie; Dr Johnson as seen through the jaundiced eye of Mrs Thrale's daughter, *According to Queeney* (2001); *Master Georgie* (1998), a Crimean war novel; and *The Birthday Boys* (1991), about Scott of the Antarctic's failed last expedition. These novels scooped up prizes and brought in steady cash rewards for her and Duckworths. She was awarded a DBE in 2000 and a consolatory Booker (second-class) in 2011.

I can't – to pick up Lynn Barber's epigraph – say I knew her, but Bainbridge used to cut through the Camden lane where I live on her way back from Sainsbury's. A couple of times I helped her with her bags. Sometimes her lungs, weakened by sixty years of smoking, gave out and she would slump on a doorstep and exchange a few words with a local tramp, Tom. Apparently Yeats's poetry was a favourite topic of conversation.

FN   Beryl Margaret Bainbridge (Dame)
MRT *The Dressmaker*
Biog *Guardian*, obituary, 2 July 2010 (Janet Watts)

257. Malcolm Bradbury 1932–2000

The British provinces had been swallowing me like an eiderdown.

Bradbury was born in Sheffield, the son of an LNER railway executive. He was shunted around in his childhood, partly thanks to the Luftwaffe, partly to chronic ill-health, and partly to his father's cross-country job. He grew up in Nottingham, and was one of the very first grammar-school boys to benefit from the new Butler Education Act. Had he been born a year earlier, English literature might well have lost a distinguished novelist. He describes his adolescence with an irony just this side of self-contempt – a familiar flavour in his work: 'in addition to haunting the coffee bars of Nottingham, shouting about Sartre and nibbling the ears of leggy girls named Ernestine, I had spent three years being a student at a certain nameless English provincial university. A strange youth, who wore pink intellectual shirts and clip-on bow ties that kept falling off suddenly into cups of black coffee, and spent most of those three years writing a novel, about, of course, an English provincial university.' The nameless place of learning was the University College of Leicester. It was, as he says, horribly unfashionable: a dimness made no brighter by Kingsley Amis's using the College (a converted lunatic asylum, opposite the municipal grave-yard) as Jim Dixon's detested place of employment. Lucky for some.

It was, as it turned out, lucky for Bradbury. Leicester was where – across the way from the English department – British sociology was happening. The embryo of anti-heroic Howard Kirk, Bradbury's most famous character, was formed over his three years there. He was already, while still an undergraduate, having his comic papers published in *Punch*. Most importantly, Leicester bequeathed him the raw material for his first novel, *Eating People is Wrong* (1959). Unlike his comrade-in-fiction, David Lodge, Bradbury would go on to be the most wandering of scholars. Having picked up his first at Leicester, he did an MA at Queen Mary College, London. Then came a spell in America which, as he recalled, liberated him forever from the cultural fug of the British provinces. That 'forever' might, he knew, be quite short: from earliest childhood Bradbury had been sickly and it was expected that he would never live to any age. But an innovative heart operation in 1958 was deemed to be successful and promised a longer, if not a lengthy, span of life. One wonders whether the extraordinary hurry of his career originated with the sense of a ticking enemy in his breast – like Ransome in Conrad's story, *The Shadow-Line*.

Bradbury married in 1959, the year that *Eating People* was published. But the critical year in his view of the world was 1956 – the year of Suez and the Hungarian Uprising. It was in this year that 'barbarism' won. The old 'gentle' (as Orwell called it) English liberalism went under for ever. Forster's wych-elm was felled. Bradbury's title picks up a line in a Flanders and Swann song. After 1956, 'eating people' is OK (it's what Howard Kirk does). The hero of *Eating People*, Professor Treece (based on the academic who, as it happened, taught me as well as Bradbury) is a liberal who – young as he is by professorial standards – has outlived his moral age. He is historically irrelevant. The Professor Kirks will eat him alive – and do.

After a brief stopover at the University of Hull, Bradbury moved on to Birmingham as a lecturer in American literature (the Americans, with money distantly supplied by the United States Information Service, were encouraging the setting up of the subject in the UK. The CIA was behind it all with the worthy aim of wresting the intellectual high ground from the Communists). There he found himself the only lecturer under forty, alongside David Lodge. As Lodge recalls: 'Edith Wharton, writing in her memoirs of her friendship with Henry James, says, "the real marriage of true minds is for any two people to possess a sense of humour or irony pitched in exactly the same key, so that their joint glances at any subject cross like interarching searchlights". I often had that experience with Malcolm.'

In 1965 Bradbury went on to the gleamingly 'new' University of East Anglia, at Norwich, one of the campuses created by the Robbins expansion. Building new institutions of higher learning was gruelling work and his early novels came out at long intervals. *Stepping Westward* (1965) revolved around his life-expanding visit to America. His major novel was his third, *The History Man* (1975), set in the new university of 'Watermouth'. The 'man' of the title is Professor Howard Kirk, sociologist: amoral, brilliant, destructive, unstoppable, the man of the future – God help us all. Bradbury is fascinated, as a rabbit by a stoat, at what Kirk and his kind represent. He offers a Treecian vignette of himself in the novel:

> The door of a room adjoining opens a little; a dark, tousled-haired head, with a sad visage, peers through, looks at Howard for a little, and then retreats ... this depressed-looking figure is a lecturer in the English department, a man who, ten years earlier, had produced two tolerably well-known and acceptably reviewed novels, filled, as novels then were, with moral scruple and concern.
>
> Since then there has been silence.

Bradbury stayed on at Norwich, now writing more fluently, but never with quite the impact of his earlier campus fiction. With Angus Wilson he set up a pioneering creative writing course at UEA (Ian McEwan, Kazuo Ishiguro, Rose Tremain are distinguished alumni) and did effective, and lucrative, TV work. *The History Man*, starring Anthony Sher, was a high point in 1980s small-screen drama. He toured, indefatigably, for the British Council and produced a good novel on the subject, *Rates of Exchange* (1983). He was a loved teacher, a distinguished scholar, a valued mentor of young novelists and, one is told, a self-sacrificingly good parent. His weak heart finally caught up with him at the age of sixty-eight – years later than his doctors had earlier predicted. He was knighted in the year of his death: he would have made a good comic novel out of that.

FN   (Sir) Malcolm Stanley Bradbury
MRT   *The History Man*
Biog   *ODNB* (David Lodge)

258. V. S. Naipaul 1932–

Everything of value about me is in my books.

Considerable stir was caused in 2008 by Patrick French's *The World Is What It Is: The Authorized Biography of V. S. Naipaul*. That loaded word 'Authorized' usually translates in biographer-speak as 'flattering', but that was spectacularly not the case here: there were so many warts in Patrick French's portrait one could barely see the face. Why, people wondered, did Naipaul collaborate in a biography which he must have known would raise howls of execration against him? 'Frank' – that is, amazingly indiscreet – interviews were granted his Boswell and French enjoyed wholly unhindered access to the archive – some of which (his dead wife's diaries, for example) not even Naipaul had ever cared to look at. Moreover, no injunction was laid on the finished text. It is like Dorian Gray allowing his picture to go on display at the National Portrait Gallery – and then attending the private view. It's a relevant analogy. Like Oscar Wilde, Naipaul – for his own obscure motives – always sets out to scandalise, and he manoeuvred his biographer as, notoriously, he manoeuvred his would-be acolyte, Paul Theroux, author of the mortally wounded memoir, *Sir Vidia's Shadow* (1998). Naipaul loves to cast a dark shadow of himself over all who come into his orbit. Biographers, on their part, labour to cast light on their subject. Naipaul wins this particular battle. At the end of years' research French found himself, as the world has found itself, struggling, baffled, in the shadow of this majestic, but impenetrably enigmatic writer.

   Few writers have trudged a harder road to the Nobellist's podium. Born the descendant of 'indentured' (i.e. enslaved) workers, in an alien island in the Caribbean, Naipaul won a scholarship to Oxford, driven to excel by his journalist father. He encountered racism every inch of the way. 'Where are you from?' asked the don examining his thesis – before failing it. Vidia was only middlingly successful at university, and later at the BBC, but careers were irrelevant. He wrote all the time, so intensely that he would routinely wear out the nibs of his Parker 51 pens. Eventually the quality of that writing shone through. The breakthrough came with what is still his most-read work, *A House for Mr Biswas* (1961).

Literary achievement, and that biggest of prizes (the Nobel), warranted full biography, but what outraged readers were the moral monstrosities laid bare by the biography which ensued. Naipaul's unashamed depiction of himself, for example, as a 'prostitute man'. Why? Because, he confided, his wife Patricia, who had loyally supported him for four decades, 'did not attract me sexually at all'. She was, he coolly declared, 'the only woman I know who has no skill'. Readers of *Guerrillas* (1975) will recall Jane's description of her husband: 'He was excited only by prostitutes, swiftly bought and had; with Jane he was finished in a second, preferring more usually to be "tossed off".' If this is self-revelation, it is not something many novelists would divulge to a prurient world. Unless, that is, you despised the prurient hordes. Naipaul, we learn, knew many women. His long-serving mistress, Margaret Gooding, was both sexually attractive and – to employ his word – skilled. Her relationship with Vidia, however, ruined her life. He seems, if we credit his authorised biographer, not to have cared. Her utility for him was that he could 'mistreat' her. 'Many of the gruesome sexual depictions in the novels,' French records, 'were not the work of imagination, but drawn from his life with Margaret.' Field work. Pat, the wife, died lingeringly of cancer in 1996, aware she was unloved and betrayed. 'On the day after he cremated his wife,' French bleakly notes, 'V. S. Naipaul invited a new woman into her house.' It was a prospective second wife – but not Margaret, the long-serving mistress: she was, we are told, cast off.

If there were a Nobel Prize for rudeness, Naipaul would win outright. Indian by genetic origin, he sees the subcontinent as one great, uncleaned, lavatory ('Indians defecate everywhere'). Trinidadian by birthplace, he rarely mentions the West Indian island other than to insult it. Asked why he left, he says 'to join civilisation'. Africa? 'Black men assuming the lies of white men' (a disgusted authorial aside in *A Bend in the River*, 1979). Not that civilised England escapes his lash. Observing on a wall the graffiti 'Keep Britain White', he would, he blandly joked, insert a comma after 'Britain' and add an 's' to 'White'. The jest, bitter as it is, reminds one that Naipaul is a wit in the Oscar class, as well as the word which rhymes with 'wit' – king-sized. He is also, one concedes, a supremely great novelist.

But which, then, are Naipaul's great novels? The verdict among his admirers would probably be split between *A Bend in the River* (1979), *In a Free State* (1971) and *Guerrillas* (1975). The last is the most complex of the three and, following the rules of Naipaul's unusual literary game, the most successful. Like much of his fiction, it has a hard kernel of historical fact, laced with acidic contempt. The self-named 'Michael X' (in imitation of the American Malcolm X) was born Michael de Freitas, of mixed race, in Trinidad. Another of his self-awarded names was the Muslim 'Abdul Malik'. After fleecing various rich *bien pensant* dupes in the UK (John Lennon, famously), and falling foul of the law, Michael X fled back to Trinidad as a quasi-revolutionary leader. Among the 'commune' he set up there was an English convert, Gale Benson, the daughter of a Tory MP. She was murdered, hacked to death like a side of beef. De Freitas was convicted of the crime and hanged in 1975. By the contortions of West Indian jurisprudence, it was the British legal authorities that mandated the execution. A fascinated Naipaul wrote a long essay on the subject, 'Michael X and the Black Power Killings in Trinidad' (1980), and used him as a central character, Jimmy Ahmed, in *Guerrillas*.

The novel complicates things beyond the historical record, however. It is set on an unnamed West Indian Island, manifestly Trinidad, polluted – atmospherically and socially – by a multinational bauxite mining company. The three principals are a white South African intellectual, exiled for his black-liberation sympathies; his mistress, an upper-class white woman, Jane; and Jimmy Ahmed, on the run from the UK, where he is wanted for rape. The title – *Guerrillas* – is ironic: these are not freedom fighters – they are degenerates. The irony permeating the whole novel is implicit in the first sentence: 'After lunch Jane and Roche left their house on the Ridge to drive to Thrushcross Grange.' The allusion is mischievously obvious. Jane [Eyre] and Roche[ster] leave for the house which represents civilisation (as opposed to the savagery of Heathcliff's house in *Wuthering Heights*). The first Mrs Rochester, we recall, originated in the West Indies. Unlike Charlotte Brontë's Jane, Naipaul's Jane will end up anally raped and murdered by her super-potent lover. Everything, every value – moral, spiritual, ideological – is decayed. Naipaul contrives a landscape which breathes irremediable corruption:

> The cleared land had been ridged and furrowed from end to end. The furrows were full of shiny green weeds; and the ridges, one or two of which showed haphazard, failed planting, were light brown and looked as dry as bone.

Looking at it through the car window, Jane says: 'I used to think that England was in a state of decay.' Roche replies, 'Decayed from what?'

The rules of the Nobel Prize decree that the prize shall be given for literature of an 'idealistic' nature. Wherein lies the idealism in Naipaul? Not, clearly, in any political, religious or social system, but in the quality of his prose. In 'Literature' itself. It is both a noble, and a profoundly dispiriting, verdict on the human condition.

FN   (Sir) Vidiadhar Surajprasad Naipaul
MRT *Guerrillas*
Biog P. French, *The World Is What It Is: The Authorized Biography of V. S. Naipaul* (2008)

259. Sylvia Plath 1932–1963

Dying
Is an art, like everything else.
I do it exceptionally well.

Plath's short life has been subjected to more biography than any other Anglo-American writer of the period. Literary interest focuses principally on her poetry, but in the days before her suicide she published a novel, *The Bell Jar* (1963). Tepid reviews, it is suggested, may have been one factor in her decision to destroy herself. Plath was born in New England. Her father, Otto, was an immigrant to the US; her mother Aurelia's parents had emigrated from Austria. Germanic ancestry, and war guilt, would haunt their daughter. It is expressed most brutally in the poem 'Daddy' (1962), in which Otto is transmuted into an SS officer. The heroine of *The Bell Jar* also has a vaguely Jewish name, Esther Greenwood (an Anglicisation of 'Grünbaum').

Otto Plath did well in his new country. An entomologist, with a particular interest in the bee, he taught at Boston University. For wholly neurotic reasons – he was convinced he had lung cancer – he neglected to have his fatal diabetes treated and died when Sylvia was eight. It was a kind of suicide by self-neglect. He left two children and a wife poorly provided for. Her father's death devastated Sylvia. She would, she famously declared, 'never speak to God again'. About the same time she published her first poem. Outstandingly clever, she sailed through high school and won a full scholarship to Smith College in 1950 where she continued her prize-winning way. She was determined to write – whether poetry, fiction or journalism was, at this stage, immaterial.

While still an undergraduate, she had stories picked up by leading magazines and in her junior year (1953) she won the nationwide competition for an intern editorship with *Mademoiselle* magazine in New York. This would supply the kernel episode for *The Bell Jar*. She had, at this point, an eminently suitable boyfriend. During this summer, for reasons which have always been in dispute, things fell apart. She wrote in her journal 6 July 1953: 'Right now you are sick in your head ... Stop thinking selfishly of razors & self-wounds & going out and ending it all. Your room is not your prison. You are.' Plath took a hard knock when she was – uniquely for her – rejected by Harvard's creative writing programme: they may have been unimpressed by the *Mademoiselle* connection. She suffered a full-blown mental breakdown and, as was routine at that period, was subjected to electroconvulsive therapy. Suicidal episodes and intensive psychotherapy followed.

She was patched together sufficiently well (like a 'retread' car tyre, she said) to finish her studies at Smith, *summa cum laude*, dyed her hair ash blonde, and picked up a Fulbright scholarship to study for two years at Newnham College in Cambridge. Here she met Ted Hughes, a fellow student. Their violent first encounter, at a party, is chronicled in a later published short story:

> Leonard bent to his last supper. She waited. Waited, sighting the whiteness of his cheek with its verdigris stain, moving by her mouth.
> Teeth gouged. And held. Salt, warm salt, laving the tastebuds of her tongue.

The couple were married barely a year later, in June 1956, with only the revenue of a poet's garret to look forward to. Things looked up with the applauded publication of Ted's collection, *The Hawk in the Rain*, in 1957. She too was moving towards poetry as her principal outlet and, like him, picking up prestigious prizes. Both were evolving fast as writers – something that took a toll on their relationship.

Their life took a fresh turn with her getting a teaching post at Smith. Hughes got an adjunct position at a nearby Boston college. Robert Lowell's poems, later collected as *Life Studies*, had indicated ways in which psychic fracture could be fused into new forms. In 1959 she sat in on Lowell's classes at Boston University: it was, she later recorded, a breakthrough.

But Plath was again on the verge of breakdown. The return to Boston had awoken demons associated with the death of her father. By this point she was pregnant with Frieda, the first of the couple's two children, and well on the way to completing her first poetry collection, *The Colossus* (1960). In 1960 they moved back to London, where both their reputations were steadily growing. But just as steadily, they were growing apart. They moved to a spacious house in Devon for the birth of their second child. Like her father, Plath could now keep bees (the subject of some of her finest poems). She was, at this point, starting work on *The Bell Jar* – principally, she later said, to 'exorcise' her painful past. The theme, she wrote in her journal, was that the 'modern woman demands as much experience as the man'.

The marriage was being subjected to intolerable pressures as Hughes was involved in an intense affair. Sylvia and Ted separated in mid-1962 and the crisis of this period feeds into the remarkable poems written over the last few months of her life, later collected as *Ariel* (1965). She was at the same time completing *The Bell Jar*. In December 1962 she moved back to London with her children to endure what would be a historically bitter winter. *The Bell Jar* was published in the last week of January 1963. Two weeks later she committed suicide by gassing herself – making sure, before she did so, that her children were tucked up and safe.

The subsequent history of *The Bell Jar* was fraught. Published in Britain by Heinemann under the bland pseudonym 'Victoria Lucas', it would not appear in America until 1967, where it was suppressed on the grounds of its manifest libels and, nearer home, its cruel representation of Aurelia Plath and Sylvia's 1953 boyfriend. It was judged too close to the bone. In the intervening four years, the Woman's Movement took off with the formation of the National Organisation of Women and Betty Friedan's trail-blazing *The Feminine Mystique* (1963). *The Bell Jar* was custom-made for its moment. In a peculiarly misjudged review in the *TLS*, the anonymous reviewer had pronounced it 'promising', but instructed that the writer must learn to 'control' her material. As well say that 'Daddy' would be better written in heroic couplets. The novel opens with some of the most gripping prose Plath ever wrote:

> It was a queer, sultry summer, the summer they electrocuted the Rosenbergs, and I didn't know what I was doing in New York. I'm stupid about executions. The idea of being electrocuted makes me sick, and that's all there was to read about in the papers – goggle- eyed headlines staring up at me on every street corner and at the fusty, peanut-smelling mouth of every subway. It had nothing to do with me, but I couldn't help wondering what it would be like, being burned alive all along your nerves.

Apparently casual, it is prophetic: Esther too will be electrocuted. After her ECT she wonders, forlornly, 'what terrible thing it was that I had done'.

The novel opens with a public event. As the pages turn, what strikes one is the claustrophobic indifference to the outside world. Ethel Rosenberg, dubiously convicted with her husband Julius, should not have been executed: the injustice passes Greenwood/Plath totally by. America is at war: although Esther sleeps with a translator at the UN (under whose auspices America was fighting), Korea gets not a mention. Nothing is visible outside the glass walls of Esther's bell jar. The other striking feature is the downright spitefulness of the depictions in the novel, which is a close transcript of Plath's deadly summer, 1953, when she won her *Mademoiselle* internship and fell apart. To take one example, 'Philomena Guinea' is transparently based on Plath's well-meaning patron, Olive Higgins Prouty, who had funded the scholarship ('for promising young writers') which enabled her to study at Smith

College. Prouty's depiction in *The Bell Jar* is as malicious as the fictional name is absurd. To rub it in, the novel's opening paragraph is a mocking parody of Prouty's opening paragraph in her most famous novel, *Now, Voyager* (1941), nowadays more famous for the Bette Davis film, the story of a heroine 'reborn' to love and full womanhood by psychotherapy. Prouty lived to read *The Bell Jar*. It may not have persuaded her that her money had been well spent on this 'promising young writer'.

Feminists have debated the sexual politics of *The Bell Jar* without any consensus other than that the novel is important. Equally important is the point it makes about fiction – niceness must sometimes be abandoned in the interest of art. That realisation may perhaps be one of the many things that tore Plath apart.

FN   Sylvia Plath (later Hughes)
MRT   *The Bell Jar*
Biog   J. Rose, *The Haunting of Sylvia Plath* (1991)

260. John Updike 1932–2009

What a threadbare thing we make of life! Rabbit is Rich

Updike was born in semi-rural Pennsylvania, of deep-rooted Dutch-German stock, and grew up in Shillington – the kind of town his fiction would make, in its quiet way, familiar to a mass readership. He was the only child of a high-school maths teacher and a mother with a family background in farming and a fondness for writing, something, he claimed, that had a formative effect on him. His childhood after the age of thirteen was spent, much of it, on a farm ten miles out of town, recollected as the setting of his novella, *Of the Farm* (1965). Everything in his background, he once said, was 'middling'. In an age of celebrity novelists he was chronically self-deprecating: he never got into fights, like Mailer; never turned his back on the world, like Salinger; never cursed God, like (the later) Roth; never saw the horrors of war like Vonnegut.

A precociously clever boy, his first observed cleverness was with the artist's pencil. He might, he dreamed, become famous in that line. The dream lasted well into his twenties and it was a great moment in his later life when the *New Yorker* (with whom he would publish over a hundred short stories) took one of his cartoons. Working on a local paper over his summer holidays as a 'copyboy', he also cultivated a lifelong reverence for the printed word. He particularly admired the skills of the linotype operators (the Angstrom family trade in the 'Rabbit' tetralogy).

'The miracle of turning inklings into thoughts,' he said, 'and thoughts into words and words into metal and print and ink never palls for me.' A prize-winner at school, Updike won a full scholarship to Harvard where he continued to shine. He chose – as a devotional nod to his mother – to study English, although he retained a lingering affiliation towards his father's harder subject. Ostentatiously, knowledgeable riffs on science, technology and astronomy embellish his later fiction; one could learn all the average person needs to know about quantum mechanics from *Roger's Version* (1986) and more than one needs to know about computer assembly language from *Villages* (2004).

Harvard was formative on the young Updike – but unsettling: 'I felt toward those years, while they were happening, the resentment a caterpillar must feel while his somatic cells are shifting all around to make him a butterfly.' Oddly he never wrote anything that could be labelled a campus novel, though the refined aura of the Ivy League hangs over much of his work – notably *Couples* (1968), his only major work to be set near the city of Boston. He generally preferred what he called 'villages' – small, newly thrown together, exurban communities of the upwardly mobile. At Harvard he edited and was a star contributor to the college paper, the *Lampoon.* It was, he said, 'very kind to me. I was given, beside the snug pleasures of club solidarity, *carte blanche* as far as the magazine went – I began as a cartoonist, did a lot of light verse, and more and more prose. There was always lots of space to fill.' Such extracurricular activity usually means an undistinguished degree – but not for John Updike. He graduated in 1954 *summa cum laude.* The previous year he had married a Radcliffe student, Mary Pennington, and soon had a child on the way. A pipe-smoking, leather-elbowed academic career looked in prospect. Towards that end he took up a year's fellowship at Oxford and while in England placed a short story and poem in the *New Yorker.* It was, he said, 'the ecstatic breakthrough of my literary life' – an annunciation. Hereafter he would be a writer: the academy lost its Professor Updike.

The 'best of possible magazines' consolidated his early success by giving him a staff job. He gave it up after a couple of years not because he disliked the *New Yorker* but because he was uncomfortable in New York. He cited Hemingway's jaundiced crack that the city's literary world was 'a bottle full of tapeworms trying to feed on each other'. His natural habitat was the small towns of New England where he retired with his wife and growing family. It was also, he felt, the right locus for his writing. As he put it, 'once you have in your bones the fundamental feasibilities of a place, you can imagine there freely'.

At this period Updike is reported as having undergone a spiritual crisis and a religious conversion. Particularly influential were Kierkegaard and Karl Barth – thinkers frequently encountered in his fiction. The clearest exposition of his religious dilemmas and conclusions are found in *Roger's Version*. A work rarely ranked among his best, on account of its wordiness, the narrative centres on a long quarrel about God between a computer whizz, Dale Kohler, and Roger Lambert, a professor of divinity. The exchange is complicated by adultery between the whizz kid and the professor's wife. Both protagonists are 'believers', but the younger man, with all the resources of modern physics, astronomy and technology, believes he can prove the existence of a deity. Such a God, Roger believes, would not be worth believing in. He agrees with Barth on the subject: 'There is no way from us to God – not even a *via negativa* – not even a *via dialectica* or *paradoxica*. The god who stood at the end of some human way would not be God.' Omnipresent, too, in Updike's fiction (as in Kafka's later work) is the Kierkegaardian imperative to maintain faith in God, despite everything that most convincingly seems to deny his existence.

Not yet thirty, Updike, from his literary base on the *New Yorker*, had established a formidable reputation as a writer of short fiction and was tentatively moving into longer narratives. A notable moment in this shift was the first of the 'Angstrom agonistes' novels, *Rabbit, Run* (1960). All three successors would arrive calendrically at the end of a decade – as a kind of summing up of where America had just been and where it was heading. Initially Updike did not have a 'mega novel' in mind, but a 'biune' work partnering *The Centaur* (1963). The heroes of the twinned novels would, in Aesopian fashion, embody two complementary types in America, the rabbit and the horse. One plods dutifully through life, the other sprints away from responsibility. *Rabbit, Run* also began with a censorious impulse. Updike had been irritated by the 'irresponsibility' of Jack Kerouac's 'Beatnik Bible', *On the Road* (1957) and intended to offer, by way of moral contrast, 'a realistic demonstration of what happens when a young American family man goes on the road ... There [is] no painless dropping out.' The 'sloppiness' of Kerouac's writing also offended the stylist in him: the American novel deserved something better. By now Updike had settled down with his wife and children (there would be four, eventually) and had bought his first house in Ipswich, Massachusetts. Whatever else, he was not on the run.

Once given life on the page, Angstrom outgrew the original conception. Updike discovered he could be extraordinarily articulate through a character wholly unlike himself, even one who was, by his standards, inarticulate. Pentecostalism has its place in Updike's theology – the ability to speak in tongues not one's own. The most virtuosic of his ventriloquisms is the insertion of his writing self into the gloomy Jewish novelist, Henry Bech. An unhappy, unmarried, Nobel Prize-winner (which Updike never was) and New York man of letters who could not breathe the air outside Manhattan, Bech – in one hilarious episode – interviews John Updike for the *New York Times*. There would be three Bech books.

Rabbit Angstrom is very different. Blue-eyed, of Swedish stock, he is 'a high-school athletic hero in the wake of his glory days'. His home town, Shillington, Updike recalled, 'was littered with the wrecks of former basketball stars'. There is no more delectable fame in America than that of the sporting hero, but Rabbit's heroism has lasted a mere two seasons. He has some fifty unheroic leftover years to live in the shadow of his brief glory. 'After you're first-rate at something,' he discovers, 'no matter what, it kind of takes the kick out of being second-rate.' In fact, as we first encounter him, Rabbit is not even second-rate. A minimum wage sales-man selling a new-fangled (and useless) vegetable peeler on commission, Harry is a 'regular working guy', like most American males. This, as it emerged, was not a limitation, but the opposite for the kind of novel Updike had in mind. As he put it, 'Harry "Rabbit" Angstrom was for me a way in – a ticket to the America all around me'. Below him, he might more frankly have said.

As the saga opens, it is not yet the 1960s when the term 'dropping out' would become one of life's platitudes. Unhappily married, with a child and another on the way, Harry decides he can't take it any more and 'goes on the run'. He takes up with another woman, a part-time prostitute, whom he impregnates. His alcoholic wife, in her marital abandonment, accidentally drowns their daughter while hope-lessly drunk. It is 'the worst thing'. And he – not she – is the guiltier party. Harry remorsefully returns – abandoning his mistress and his child (a daughter, as it turns out). One of the technical innovations in *Rabbit, Run* was the use of the present rather than the past tense in the narrative. It added to the cursive feel. The novel's publication coincided with, and took advantage of, the new freedoms brought in with the 1959/1960 *Lady Chatterley* trials. Brilliant as Updike's narrative is, this liberation was not entirely beneficial. His extendedly detailed descriptions of sex can be wearing – and occasionally creepy (the description of flies hovering interestedly over the groin of the menstruating heroine in *Of the Farm* comes to mind). There are worthier *longueurs*. The Angstrom tetralogy, Updike notes, 'is deeply immersed in the Lutheran creed of my childhood'. It is, as he puts it in the novel, 'scratched into his heart like a weathered inscription'. The heart referred to is Angstrom's, but it could as well be Updike's, who often, as he records, plotted his novels sitting in church. *Rabbit, Run* spends many of its pages on long dialogues between the hero and the local minister, Jack Eccles (a closet gay, we apprehend, and spiritually unset-tled). Hovering over the whole book is the question: can a man be good and yet do bad things? It is a dilemma Harry will never solve but which his life, regarded in its entirety, poses.

The novel was well received but at this stage Updike did not contemplate going further with it. His breakthrough into the first rank of novelists came in 1968 with

Couples. Set in 'Tarbox' (identifiably the author's home town, Ipswich), the novel ponders the formation of American suburban, young, sexually adventurous communities. The two pillars of such communities are married couples and extramarital copulation. *Couples* shot to the top of the *New York Times* bestseller list and put its author's face ('snaggle-toothed', he complained) on the cover of *Time* magazine. Now rich and esteemed, Updike moved to England for a year in 1969, to read up in the British Museum on American history. It was not, as with many of his compatriots, to escape the Vietnam imbroglio. Surprisingly to some, he approved of that war.

Runaway rogue that he was, Rabbit endeared himself to readers. What, they asked, had happened to Updike's 'skittish pilgrim'? Does he die, does he disappear without trace, does he become a model husband and father? The last paragraph in the narrative, ending on the word 'run', is enigmatic on the point. Updike picked up the life-story again in the end-of-the-decade *Rabbit Redux* (1971) – the offputting title was a nod to Trollope's *Phineas Redux*, itself the second part of a series which ran to five titles. Rabbit is now in Dantean middle age, thirty-five years old, a linotype operator, alongside his similarly employed father, both of them imminently to be made redundant by the offset printing process. The US is in ferment. The *Apollo* moonshot is the novel's 'central metaphor' and the race riots rocking the country's cities are the big sub-lunar issue. The narrative gives a central role to a black dissident, Skeeter, from whom Harry learns the facts of American life and the hollowness of 'Civil Rights' legislation. This time round, his wife Janice has run away from him and he is shacked up with Skeeter, his pubescent son Nelson, and a drop-out hippy girl, Jill, whose death by arson (Rabbit having infuriated his neighbours to criminal revenge by lowering their property values) he causes. Yet again, 'he knows he is criminal, yet is never caught'. In the background, outside 'America's great glare', the towns like Harry's are dying. The whole country is moribund: 'so zonked out on its own acid', Harry observes, 'sunk so deep in its own fat and babble and laziness, it would take H-bombs on every city from Detroit to Atlanta to wake us up and even then, we'd probably think we'd just been kissed'.

The narrative of *Rabbit Redux* ends, enigmatically, with the question, 'OK?' The answer comes, after the statutory ten years, in *Rabbit is Rich* (1981). Over this decade, Updike's own life was in upheaval. In 1974 he separated from his wife and taught for a while in Boston University (the inspiration for Roger Lambert, in *Roger's Version*). In 1977 he remarried. His new wife brought three children into the marriage; he brought four. They settled not too far from Ipswich where he had owned his first house and where he had set *Couples*. In *Rabbit is Rich*, the hero is rich only by the standards of his 'modest working class background': he has grown fat on his relative prosperity. He is now a car salesman, thanks to his wife's family money and

Brewer's only Toyota franchise, and he makes a nice packet on the side, speculating in silver coins, and tries out some varieties of sex, outside marriage, which are new to him. There have been no more children and his relationship with his son Nelson is fraught. Life may be comfortable for Rabbit, but it continues to perplex him: 'In middle age', he discovers, 'you are carrying the world in a sense and yet it seems more out of control than ever.' And where is he going? 'Your life', he now realises, 'is over before you wake up.'

From his forecourt, Harry is helping flood US freeways and city centres with Japanese tin cans – cars which don't express anything, he thinks, unlike their noble Detroit predecessors. America, during the depressed Jimmy Carter years, is decaying, 'running out of gas ... the Great American Ride is ending'. Rabbit is now face to face with the Great American Paradox, that as we approach that happiness which is promised in the first line of the Declaration of Independence, 'we get emptier'. Back to Kierkegaard – except that Harry reads nothing but the latest issue of *Consumer Report*.

Rabbit is Rich won all three of America's major literary prizes 'as well as a place in the Washington critic Jonathan Yardley's list of the ten worst books of the year', the author sardonically recalls. The final instalment, *Rabbit at Rest* (1990) commemorates the Reagan decade. Rabbit likes the Great Communicator's 'foggy voice' and 'magic touch'. Harry himself had the magic touch once, on the basketball court. America is now in a condition of 'happy anaesthesia'. Harry and Janice spend the cold months in their Florida condo. 'Most of American life is driving somewhere and then driving back wondering why the hell you went,' Harry concludes. But there is no happy ending. Nelson, addicted to cocaine, ruins the car sales business. Harry, addicted to sex, makes love to Nelson's wife Pru, and goes on the run again. In a Florida ghetto he has one last pick-up ball game with some mystified black kids, suffers a heart attack and dies in hospital – lasting long enough to confide to Nelson, 'All I can tell is, it isn't so bad.' What is 'it'? Life? Death?

Updike produced a larger mass of fiction (too much, some think) than any other highly respected novelist of his time. His most popular work, thanks largely to its witty film adaptation, was his metaphysical comedy, *The Witches of Eastwick* (1984). The Devil still roamed New England, as he had 200 years earlier. But in an age of feminism, witches no longer needed to fear the fate of their Salem sisters. It is men who should fear – even Satan. Updike's last work was an Eastwick sequel and he may have foreseen a series. Among other interesting, but less memorable ventures were: *The Coup* (1978), the imaginary memoir of a corrupt, Islamic, African dictator; a quasi science fiction story, *Toward the End of Time* (1997), fantasising a future war between the US and China, which may yet prove prophetic; a reverse shot treatment of Hamlet, *Gertrude and Claudius* (2000); *Terrorist* (2006), a post 9/11 story of a convert to Islam who intends another spectacular outrage in Manhattan. Everything with Updike's name on the cover sold healthily but, as his achievement has been winnowed out, *Couples* and the Angstrom tetralogy are judged the novels that will last. He died, aged seventy-nine, of lung cancer, the great plague of his forever puffing generation, writing almost to the last and convinced, one is told, that he was about to meet his maker.

FN   John Hoyer Updike
MRT   *Rabbit, Run*
Biog http://www.theparisreview.org/interviews/4219/the-art-of-fiction-no-43-john-updike

261. B. S. Johnson 1933–1973

Oh, fuck all this lying!

B. S. Johnson was described, and loved to be described, as 'Britain's one-man avant-garde'. As in war, out in front is a dangerous place to be. His Quixotic quest to 'reinvent' the English novel was, at best, a gallant failure; at worst, a personal tragedy – but never less than interesting. Bryan Johnson was born, copper-bottomed working class, in Hammersmith. The working class was, in its millions, out of work at the time and his father held on desperately to his job as stock-keeper at the SPCK (Society for Promoting Christian Knowledge) bookshop. Their uplifting tracts were fiction of a kind. Mrs Johnson had, before marriage, been in service. His childhood was deformed (but, arguably, his skin saved) by wartime evacuation from the London Blitz: at the age of six he was uprooted to Surrey, then High Wycombe. Oddly, he was kept away from the London home for the duration – well after there was no danger from the Luftwaffe. His father served his country in the Catering Corps.

Once returned to the 'Smoke', Johnson formed an intense relationship with his mother – his umbilical cord was never severed. He lived at home until he was twenty-eight and was taking his washing home well into his thirties. His mother's sadly early death precipitated his own, which was tragically early. Johnson failed his eleven-plus in 1944 and was consigned to what was called a 'tech' – one notch above the sump-level 'Secondary Modern'. At school he made the first of his suicide attempts and cultivated adolescent passions for football, jazz and, oddly, Christopher Marlowe. Physically awkward and fat (like the hero of *The Third Man*), his schoolfellows wittily nicknamed him 'Orson Cart'. On leaving school at sixteen, Johnson took up various clerical and low-level accountancy jobs. Double-entry ledgers, with their eye-for-an-eye reckoning, would stick in his mind. Perforated eardrums (as a result of childhood illness) spared him national service. At night, and in his spare time, he taught himself Latin – with a view to getting into London University, one of the few institutions that encouraged late developers.

He was duly accepted at Birkbeck and in 1953 transferred up to King's College London to read English. As an undergraduate he worked harder on the student magazine, *Lucifer*, than on his classroom studies and left with a 2:2. It was in those days a creditable degree, but – with hindsight and all the evidence available – his was a finer mind than that result indicates. It added to his already sizeable inferiority complex: 'according to their rules,' he said, 'I was a lower-second-class of person.' He never accepted 'their' rules. All his life, he said, he was 'underestimated' – not least by literary critics. Johnson had some wretchedly unhappy love affairs at university and what satisfaction he had came from nightly masturbation, 'keeping', as he said, 'the appropriate muscles in fine fettle'. Armed with his mediocre degree, he took up the freebooting life of a London supply teacher in 1960, filling vacancies in mainly 'secondary-mods'. One of his pupils wrote of Johnson in an essay: 'he walks like a firy elephant'. Johnson took it (and repeated it in *Albert Angelo*) as the apocalyptic 'fiery elephant'. It was, his biographer Jonathan Coe surmises, more likely the schoolyard insult 'fairy elephant'.

At this period in his life, he was regularly spending his summers at the Lleyn peninsula in north Wales. He would hitch-hike west (Kerouac had made it sexy). *Travelling People* (1963), his first published novel, opens with the hero-narrator-observer thumbing it to Dublin (a Joycean pilgrimage), being offered a summer job by his 'lift' in a high-class country club, the Stromboli. Henry Henry is a version of B. S. Johnson (with the telling difference that he passed the eleven-plus, did his national service, got a good degree, and has less trouble pulling birds) and Henry accepts the offer. The club is owned by Maurie Bunde (not one of Johnson's happier jokes). The plot is minimal, involving the kinds of below-stairs friction which Arnold Wesker did better in *The Kitchen*, and a love story with a bitter aftertaste. Maurie has a fatal heart attack while having it off with his employee, Kim. She gratefully falls into the arms of Henry, who has covered for her leaving her dying lover's bed. The novel is written in Sterneian-jokey style. At times, as when Henry is on a London escalator and the advertisements slant across the page, the resemblance is to concrete poetry. Maurie's warning attack of angina is represented by a grey half-page; his final attack by a blocked-out black page. 'A page', proclaimed Johnson, 'is an area on which I may place any signs I consider to communicate most clearly what I have to convey.' Semiotics had come to English fiction. I read *Travelling People* when it first came out (indeed, it was the subject of the first review I ever published). It was an explosive arrival on the scene.

The flavour of Johnson's fiction is Russian formalism in a McAlpine donkey jacket. What comes through more entertainingly than the experimentalism is his comic gift – more Tony Hancock (whom he physically resembled) than Joyce; for example, this capsule reminiscence of Henry's boyhood:

> In return for Maurie's confidences and stories I told him about how they drummed me out of the Boy Scouts for playing a jukebox in a café when I was fourteen; a Fats Waller record it was, too; but this was only the culmination of a long campaign waged against me by the Scoutmaster from the day I proved that I could tie a knot so exactly like a bowline, but yet not, that he, disastrously, entrusted his weight to it.

Travelling People came out in 1963 to gratifying acclaim and a three-book contract from his new publisher, Secker and Warburg. In the same year he met his future wife, Virginia. She was a cut above him socially, unliterary, and brought domestic stability into his life. They married in 1964 and the first of their two children was born in 1965.

The year 1964 was his *annus mirabilis* with four books published, including the sensational *Albert Angelo* – a portrait of the artist as a supply teacher – with its famous hole in the page so you could see what happened next without turning it. Critics were taking notice of him, as, to his gratification, was Samuel Beckett. He won prizes, received writing awards, and got commissions for TV and radio work. What he did not get was sales. He continued doing new things. *Trawl* (1967) is a Proustian introspection, composed, unglamorously, not on the Loire or Spenser's 'sweet Thames' but on a twenty-three-day trip – voyage is the wrong word – on a fishing vessel in heavy seas. Proust meets 'Deadliest Catch'. *Dredger* might have been the more appropriate title. Johnson's most adventurous novel was a 'cut-up', *The Unfortunates* (1969), delivered to the reader in a box containing twenty-seven unbound sections. The mobile frame of the narrative centres on a trip to Nottingham, to report a football match for the *Observer* (one of Johnson's sideline activities). It was in that city, he recalls, that his friend (the dedicatee of *Travelling People*) died of cancer. In the last section Johnson offers one of his many explanations of the point of his experimentation:

> The difficulty is to understand without generalization, to see each piece of received truth, or generalization, as true only if it is true for me, solipsism again, I come back to it again, and for no other reason. In general, generalization is to lie, to tell lies.

Truth inheres in the particular. How better to catch it than with a novel in particles. That solves one problem, but leaves another unsolved: how to get people to read (or even assemble) the particles. The best of Johnson's six published novels is *Christie Malry's Own Double Entry* (1973). Less aggressively novel in its technique, it follows the career of an accounts clerk (such as Johnson himself had been in 1952) who balances moral offence with punishment among his friends and acquaintance. He dies, suddenly, of cancer.

Johnson's professional life was one of continuous rupture with agents and publishers, typically because they did not make him as successful as he ought to have been. He kept bread on the table with fellowships, Arts Council bursaries and British Council tours. His mother's death in 1971 affected him deeply. He was drinking heavily and his marriage was breaking down. Aged forty, he sliced his wrists in a warm bath, leaving a bottle of brandy for his friends to drink and a suicide note:

> *This is my last*
> *word*

FN   Bryan Stanley Johnson
MRT *Travelling People*
Biog J. Coe, *Like A Fiery Elephant: The Story of B. S. Johnson* (2004)

262. William L. Pierce 1933–2002

The most powerful and dangerous white supremacist in America.

It's rare to feel unalloyed pleasure at reading the obituary of a bestselling novelist. None the less, every novel-reader of goodwill would have rejoiced to read in July 2002 that 'Willy Pierce' ('Dr William Luther Pierce' to his co-fascists) had gone – somewhat prematurely, one further rejoiced to note – to his reward. Ding-dong, the witch was dead. Pierce was born in Atlanta, Georgia. His father was an insurance salesman; his mother a secretary and sometime journalist. In later life Pierce liked to claim descent from 'the aristocracy of the old South' and affected a 'Southern patrician' pose. His father was killed in a traffic accident when his son – one of two children – was eight. It being his line of work, he was well insured – not that Willy couldn't make his own way. He was very bright – with a noted scientific bent from his earliest days. He was educated at a Texas military academy (hoping at some point to go into the air force), and graduated from Rice University in 1955, supported on full academic scholarship all the way through. He spent a year or so at the elite California Institute of Technology as a postgraduate, studying physics and helping with NASA's embryonic space programme. At this point he made his first of five marriages, with a fellow student, and fell in with and then fell out with the rabid John Birch Society, whose HQ was just down the road from his lab. He evidently read with attention the Birchites' favourite novel-cum-tract, *The Franklin Papers*, but eventually found them not racist enough for his taste – too soft on Jews.

Caltech was too demanding – or his political activities too distracting – and Pierce moved on to Colorado, where he acquired his Ph.D. in physics. The subject was 'nuclear magnetic dipole and electric quadrupole interactions in a GaAs crystal'. Now a certified 'rocket scientist' (a breed few and far between among neo-Nazis), Pierce taught at college level for a while, before sacrificing his academic career 'to devote himself to the service of his people'. The turning point was disgust at a colleague in his department who had chosen to marry a 'mulatto woman' (Pierce's term). In a flash he saw the future – it was Brazil – mixed race hell. Not his people at all. To prevent that awful descent into miscegenation Pierce entered the service of the 'American Führer', George Lincoln Rockwell. When Rockwell was assassinated in 1967, Pierce went independent, with his 'National Alliance', later 'National Vanguard' movement, based in the mountainous back country of Pocahontas County, West Virginia. The population was 'sparse and all white'. In his neo-Nazi fastness Pierce ran a profitable publishing business, a radio station, and a clearing house for co-ideologues – spreading his word far and wide. It had the added advantage that the federal officials didn't come snooping around asking about the immigration status of his wives who, in his later years, were acquired over the internet from Eastern Europe. For tax purposes his HQ was registered as a church preaching what the Revd Pierce called 'Cosmotheism': its symbol was the 'life rune'. Pierce regarded Christianity as a hopelessly Jew-contaminated doctrine and 'the major spiritual illness of our people'. If you had to ask who 'our people' were, you weren't one of them.

Pierce spread his word most effectively as 'Andrew Macdonald', under which pen name he (self-) published the underground bestseller, *The Turner Diaries* (1978). The plot derives, transparently, from Jack London's 'Revolutionary Memoir', *The Iron Heel* (1907). (Pierce claimed that London was 'a National Socialist before his time'.) *The Turner Diaries* went on to become what the FBI called the 'Bible of the Racist Right', selling over half a million copies – and still selling. Pierce impudently used the FBI warning as a shoutline on his reprints. The 'diaries' are those of Earl Turner, the martyr who crowns a proud career of race vigilantism with a suicide bombing raid in an armed dust-crop plane on the 'Jewish capital', Washington DC.

(Tom Clancy wasn't the first to anticipate 9/11 in fiction, as Pierce and his followers indignantly claimed, after the outrage.) The heroic corps of American Nazis take over the USAF silos and nuke the other Jewish capital, Tel Aviv, and clean up the West Coast, their main base, with 'the Day of the Rope'. Hundreds of thousands of 'mestizos' (Hispanics) are marched into canyons to perish. Jews are shot out of hand – without even starving time allowed. At every intersection in Los Angeles, there dangles a corpse bearing one of two placards: 'I betrayed my race' (for traitors) or 'I defiled my race' (for women 'who were married to or living with blacks, with Jews, or other non-white males'). National Vanguard actually created a 'Day of the Rope' musical which outdoes Mel Brooks's 'Springtime for Hitler' in surrealist excess.

Many reprints of *The Turner Diaries* were called for. Skinheads pored laboriously over its pages, their lips moving as they struggled with the occasional polysyllable such as 'Hebrew' or 'miscegenation'. It sold, over the years, half a million copies, mainly through non-bookstore outlets. Famously, Timothy McVeigh – who sold the *Diaries*, cut-price, at gun shows, where military hardware could be bought, few questions asked – had seven, strategically highlighted, pages of the novel in his getaway car from the Alfred P. Murrah building bombing. One such passage instructed: 'The real value of our attacks today lies in the psychological impact, not in the immediate casualties.' The novel was plausibly linked to many other acts of domestic terrorism with huge psychological impact. Pierce blandly disowned them each and every one. It was 'only a novel', as Jane Austen would have said, but it sold particularly well among serving soldiers and vets, he was always pleased to note.

Even more poisonous than *The Turner Diaries* was the follow-up, *Hunter* (1984). Pierce-Macdonald's second novel is a neo-Nazi *hommage* to Brian Garfield's *Death Wish*, a pulp thriller about a citizen-vigilante in New York. In *Hunter*, the vigilante-hero is Oscar Yeager, a tall, blond Aryan. He's an ex-Vietnam fighter pilot (why, one wonders, didn't Chuck Yeager, he of Tom Wolfe's *The Right Stuff* (1979), sue Pierce?). Oscar has a Ph.D. in physics from the University of Colorado – like his creator, Dr William Pierce. Viscerally disgusted by 'race mixing' and the 'mud mongrels' it spawns, Yeager assassinates interracial couples: by rifle, knife, garrotte and bomb. Why? He just don't like 'em. Street-cleaning, you might call it – or mindless racist inhumanity.

Fiction, too, has its chamber of horrors and in it are works such as Jean Raspail's apocalyptic vision of Europe swamped by unrestricted immigration from the East, *The Camp of the Saints* (1973), much admired by Jean-Marie Le Pen; O. T. Gunnarsson's *Hear the Cradle Song* (1993) Nazi putsch takes over California; and Colin Jordan's *The Uprising* (2004) British heroes rise up against their ZOG – Zionist

Occupation Government. Top of the (dung) heap, however, will always be *The Turner Diaries*: a novel to make fiction ashamed of itself.

FN   Andrew Macdonald (William Luther Pierce)
MRT *The Turner Diaries*
Biog R. S. Griffin, *The Fame of a Dead Man's Deeds* (2001)

263. Reynolds Price 1933–2011

Mr Price hasn't exactly hidden the fact that he is gay; he is simply a private person who hasn't tattooed this information, in curly script, on one of his biceps. Dwight Garner

Reynolds Price was one of that golden generation of American novelists (Gore Vidal, William Styron and Truman Capote are others) who seemed to have been blessed in the cradle with genius, physical grace and – what writers need above all – good luck at the outset of their careers. Price was born, lower middle class, in Macon, North Carolina, a region devastated by the Depression. In his first volume of memoirs, *Clear Pictures* (1989), he recalls a family dominated by a loved, but alcoholic father and a loved, but fussily nervous mother.

The world he was brought up in was complacently racist and sternly Methodist. Price would lose the one, and cleave to the other. In a late-life interview he recalled: 'I think I had as miserable an adolescence as any human being can ever have had – at least outside the novels of Dickens ... My problems were simply the problems of being an unpopular kid in a small town who was always being beaten up – partly through my own fault but to a large extent through just the malice of my contemporaries.' It did not help that while at high school he realised that the 'magnetic core' of his personality was homosexual. It did help him escape – to more liberal places – and he won scholarships effortlessly. He took his first degree at Duke University, graduating in 1955, *summa cum laude* and Phi Beta Kappa. His notebooks indicate that he was determined from the first to write fiction, but he shrewdly qualified himself for an academic career as well: it would be his writer's crutch.

Price won a Rhodes Scholarship to Oxford in 1956. He was overcome with the beauty of the university town, but astonished at the filth of the Merton College 'bogs' (aptly so-called). He enrolled for a B.Litt. on *Samson Agonistes* with the congenial Lord David Cecil (Dame Helen Gardner proved less congenial). Most valuably, his time at Oxford coincided with W. H. Auden's as Professor of Poetry (Wystan's sanitary arrangements, he recalled, were as astonishing as Merton's). Auden made

himself accessible to students, every morning at coffee time; he took to the exquisitely well-mannered young American. Price had come to Oxford a virgin and while
there had a painfully inhibited relationship with a fellow student, Michael Jordan.
He lost his virginity to a young academic called, in his second volume of memoirs,
'Matyas'. That relationship, too, was unhappy. Less unhappily, Price sent a batch of
his unpublished stories to Stephen Spender, then literary editor of *Encounter*, on the
whimsical grounds that he thought the poet had 'the kindest face I have ever seen'.
Editorial kindness rarely extends to indulging the egos of hopeful postgraduates,
but Spender realised that an unusual talent had landed in his in-tray. He rushed
the stories into print and helped get Price's novel-in-progress placed. Half the first
sentence of *A Long and Happy Life* (1962) (Price loves long sentences) will convey
the quality Spender's editorial eye perceived –though quite how that eye pictured
'spraddle-legged' is uncertain:

> Just with his body and from inside like a snake, leaning that black motorcycle
> side to side, cutting in and out of the slow line of cars to get there first, staring
> due-north through goggles towards Mount Moriah and switching coon tails in
> everybody's face was Wesley Beavers, and laid against his back like sleep, spraddle-
> legged on the sheepskin seat behind him was Rosacoke Mustian who was maybe
> his girl and who had given up looking into the wind and trying to nod at every sad
> car in the line ...

Reynolds Price awoke and found himself famous. Within eighteen months, and
at the age of twenty-eight, *A Long and Happy Life* was hailed as a major literary event.
It won the William Faulkner Award for a best first novel and has never, since 1962,
been out of print. The story of Rosacoke Mustian's dreams, disillusionment and
eventual spiritual growth, the novel expanded into a trilogy and completed a quarter
of a century on with *Good Hearts* (1988). His early career went swimmingly and he
returned to take up a position teaching creative writing at Duke in 1958. By 1977,
he was James B. Duke Professor of English, a chair endowed in the name of the university's tobacco-enriched founder. He wrote a string of novels, winning prizes and
every fellowship he cared to apply for. He made money, built himself a fine house in the
woods and had, it seemed, a charmed life. Charm and a bubbling wit were what everyone noted about him. 'You make any house you are in golden,' Spender once told him.

Around him, the Duke English Department was rising to prominence under the
chairmanship of the charismatic Stanley Fish. At the same time the region was
developing into the North Carolina 'Research Triangle' – a magnet for scholars
worldwide. Among all this change, Price – North Carolinian, man and boy – embodied continuity. He knew everyone on and off the campus. Going into a Durham

restaurant with Reynolds was frustrating: so many people had to be conversed with before you reached the table.

But in 1984, Price's world disintegrated. It began when a friend noted something odd about his gait. He was diagnosed with cancer – a one-foot-long, slimy growth 'as thick as a pencil' had braided itself around his upper spinal cord: he called it 'the eel'. Duke's medical school led the world in the surgical treatment of cancer. Its expert scalpel and radiotherapy killed the eel – that was the good news. The bad news was that the 4,000 rads bombarded into Price's neck destroyed his nervous system. It was the cruellest of cures. At fifty-one, Price found himself cancer-free but paraplegic. Where other Americans might have enriched themselves with a vindictive malpractice suit, Reynolds confronted his condition not as an aggrieved patient, but as an author and a devout Christian. Although in constant pain, he refused painkillers, other than the evening martini, on the grounds that they dulled his mind. Out of the experience of losing his lower body, he wrote a book with the ironic title *A Whole New Life* (1994). As 'an American with disability' (as the 1976 federal statute defined it), Price preferred the honest Anglo-Saxon terms 'gimp' and 'cripple'. For the same reason, he always favoured the term 'queer' over 'gay.' He despised minced words.

Religion was, from the beginning, a central element in Price's fiction. *A Long and Happy Life* opens with an extended description of a 'Negro funeral service' and ends with an even more extended description of a Christmas service. In his later years, he became increasingly drawn to theology and the suffering of Christ – writing translations of the Gospels and the religious meditation, *A Serious Way of Wondering: The Ethics of Jesus Imagined* (2003). In the 1990s he also cultivated a nationwide presence as a radio-essayist on the National Public Radio broadcasting service – many of which were amiably secular sermons. As the decades after Stonewall rolled by, Price was criticised by more militantly gay writers such as David Leavitt for rarely dealing directly with queer themes in his fiction. Typically Price – as with the Rosacoke trilogy and his bestseller *Kate Vaiden* – employed female centres of consciousness. He shrugged off the objection with the excuse that the mass of ungay readers were not interested in gay fiction – and he liked having a lot of readers. Quietly, behind the scenes, he moved to get the traditionally conservative Duke to solemnise gay unions in its vast chapel.

Which of Price's forty-odd books will last? Certainly *A Whole New Life* and *A Long and Happy Life*. His own life was, as it happened, both long and – although less than whole for thirty years – not unhappy.

FN   Edward Reynolds Price
MRT *A Long and Happy Life*
Biog R. Price, *A Whole New Life* (1994)

264. Philip Roth 1933–

You know, even the best biographies are only two-thirds correct.
Philip Roth in conversation with Mark Lawson

Authors can be terrible liars and never more so than when they are in the autobiographical vein. Like salesmen, they are at their most dangerous when most sincere. Philip Roth has made a profession out of mischievous transgressions of fact and fiction. One of his titles, *Deception* (1990), could embellish the covers of all of his fiction as the name of the Rothian game. Roth's tell-it-all memoir, cheekily entitled *The Facts: A Novelist's Autobiography* (1988) – the title alludes to *Dragnet* hero Jack Webb's 'the facts, ma'am, nothing but the facts' – carries a subversive afterword, in the form of a letter from one of the platoon of Rothian alter egos, Nathan Zuckerman. 'You are far better off writing about me than "accurately" reporting your own life,' the figment sagely advises. But where's the dividing line? Disentangling Roth from his fictional characters is like trying to scrape the tomato sauce off spaghetti. He specialises in 'counterlives' – teasing reflections of himself, with heroes perversely named 'Philip Roth', but not Philip Roth. The funniest thing he has written by way of explication of his fiction is that 'the personal element is there' – an understatement that ranks with 'I may be gone for some time.'

When it was published, Roth's publishers trumpeted *The Facts* as just what its title said – 'Roth and his battles, defictionalised and unadorned'. It was suspicious since Roth's previous writings had played ducks and drakes with factuality and fictionality, and disentanglement is complicated by the fact that he manifestly does drop great authentic chunks of personal history into his fiction. He has used his childhood in Weequahic so often that even though I have never been to Newark, New Jersey, I feel I know its pre-war streets as well as I know the Bull at Ambridge. His 2010 novel, the last of the 'Nemesis' trilogy, opens:

> The first case of polio that summer [1944] came early in June, right after
> Memorial Day, in a poor Italian neighborhood crosstown from where we lived.
> Over in the city's southwestern corner, in the Jewish Weequahic section, we heard
> nothing about it, nor did we hear anything about the next dozen cases scattered
> singly throughout Newark in nearly every neighborhood but ours.

The seventy-five-year-old novelist – the 'dying animal', in his own phrase – writing this lives in a fine eighteenth-century farmhouse in isolated Connecticut (visitors are extremely unwelcome, but a pen-picture is given in *Exit Ghost*). The ten-year-old Philip Roth is somewhere on the sidewalk in New Jersey, 1944 – and will always be trapped there, unable to escape, like some sad ghost in an M. R. James tale.

Roth's titles routinely tease the reader with proffers of frank confession: e.g. *Reading Myself and Others* (1976), *The Ghost Writer* (1979), or the 1994 TV special, entitled, outrageously, *My True Story*. But 'confession' is false coinage with this writer. He doesn't hold with it. He has stated that a writer cannot *know* his past, he can only *recount* it. What then does it mean to 'come clean', or 'let go'? – *Letting Go* (1962), one recalls, is another of Roth's teasing titles. Probably *Portnoy's Complaint* (1969) offers his most persuasive answer. You come closest to telling the truth when you kvetch – when you whine – and when you are privately closeted with your analyst (hopefully the listener behind the sofa will not be as absurd as Dr Spielvogel, author of the treatise 'The Puzzled Penis').

The Facts is no kvetch, however. If anything, it's a surprisingly mellow evocation of the author's upbringing. Especially in the early sections, it recalls Woody Allen's over-tenderised *Radio Days*. Philip's was, we are to understand, a happy childhood. Nor is *The Facts* a transcript of what goes on between Roth and his therapist: it is the least offensively outspoken of any book he has written. No organisation of rabbis, league of Jewish mothers, or Southern Baptist preacher could have protested this publication. Anyone wanting to know if Roth himself actually did that awful thing described in the 'Salad Days' section of *My Life as a Man* (1974) to a young lady under the ping-pong table, yelping 'good shot' and 'nice return' to allay her parents next door, will be disappointed. *The Facts* contains not a single lavatorial or sex scene; no family liver is profaned; no anal sub-tabular tennis is played.

Roth, being Roth, will never keep the facts he does tell entirely straight. Framing the autobiography is an exchange with Nathan Zuckerman – the hero and sometimes the narrator of the 1980s tetralogy. Roth's letter requesting his alter ego's imprimatur forms a preface to *The Facts* and there he explains how he came to write it. Its quest for 'original pre-fictionalised factuality' grew out of certain 'necessities' and these were in turn the consequence of a 'crack-up' which the author suffered in the spring of 1987. Tantalisingly, Roth won't elaborate ('there's no need to delve into particulars here' – why not?). As part of a general nausea, he emerged sick of 'fictionalising' Roth. If this manuscript 'conveys anything, it's my exhaustion with masks, disguises, distortions and lies'. One knows what he is referring to. His immediately preceding novel, *The Counterlife* (1986), finished in a riot of fictional artifice with characters arbitrarily dying and coming to different ('counter') life and finally defecting from the novel in disgust at what their awful author was doing to them. 'I'm leaving you and I'm leaving the book,' the heroine tells the narrator in a farewell note. After *The Counterlife*'s excess of artifice, the author was evidently surfeited. 'Did literature do this to me?' David Kepesh asks when he wakes to find himself a gigantic breast. It did – and it has done awesome things to Roth.

As a postscript to his preface in *The Facts*, Roth touches on another 'necessity' – a settling of accounts with his mother's death in 1981 and his father's great age (eighty-six) and cancer-ridden fragility. The autobiography opens not with the hero's birth but with a vivid recollection of Herman Roth's near-fatal attack of peritonitis in late October 1944 when Philip was ten. He was saved by sulfa powder, newly developed during the early years of the war to treat battle-front wounds. But it was a very close thing and the revealed mortality of his father during the height of his Oedipal conflict affected Roth deeply. The narrative skips forty years to Herman at death's door – but this time there is no wonder drug to come to his rescue:

> now, when he is no longer the biggest man I have to contend with – and when I am not all that far from being an old man myself – I am able to laugh at his jokes and hold his hand and concern myself with his well-being, I'm able to love him the way I wanted to when I was sixteen, seventeen, and eighteen but when, what with dealing with him and feeling at odds with him, it was simply an impossibility.

Using a bleak and economical English, Roth goes back past those adolescent years to describe a Newark childhood in which the real enemies were not Germans or Japs but 'the Americans who opposed or resisted us – or condescended to us or rigorously excluded us – because we were Jews'. The theme is expanded in his 'alternative universe novel', *The Plot Against America* (2004), a sub-SF fantasy about 1930s anti-Semitism in a USA in which the national (but incorrigibly prejudiced) hero Charles Lindbergh comes to power, defeating Franklin Delano Roosevelt. It's fantasy on one level; on another, actual fears which the Roth family and Philip (all of whom are so-named characters in the novel) entertained in the 1930s. With the rise of the Bush dynasty in the 2000s he feared it again.

The tone of *The Facts* is dutiful and piously filial. Portraits are correspondingly respectful. For the record, his father – the insurance salesman – was never the constipated *nudnik* of *Portnoy*. Neither did his father disown Philip's writing and die in rage at its masturbatory offences to patriarchal Judaism. Herman Roth was the loyalest and proudest father an author could have. Further tribute was paid in *Patrimony* (1991). No father – as he went to his final rest – could want better tribute from a son. Although she figures only on the edge of *The Facts*, Roth's mother was, as he describes her, a quiet, intelligent woman – 'vigilant' perhaps, but nothing like the vampiric and castrating Sophie Portnoy: the kind of mother who would drive young Jewish boys to hang themselves in the cellar in a spirit of sheer filial dutifulness (leaving a note that the day's shopping would be found in the fridge). Roth's brother Sandy was and is nothing like Henry Zuckerman. And so on.

The narrative of *The Facts* touches briefly on Roth's beloved baseball – beloved because it was, in the 1940s, 'a great nationalistic church from which nobody had ever seemed to suggest that Jews should ever be excluded'. This great nationalistic sport, with Babe Ruth and Lou Gehrig as its heroes, inspired his one formal attempt at the great American novel (cheekily so entitled) and – paradoxically – his most innocently comic piece of writing ('Call me Smitty,' it begins). According to *The Facts*, the only true fellowship with his fellow Americans Roth has known in his life was playing ball at school. Put another way, baseball was his purest experience of being American, not Jewish-American. His 'baseball years', as he elsewhere calls them, extended until eighteen, when a new era opened with the reading of Conrad's *Lord Jim*. The bulk of *The Facts* is taken up with his formative college years, 1950–58, at Rutgers, Bucknell and Chicago (where he was taught by Saul Bellow). Among other revelations is a recollection – which future biographers will seize on – of his early storytelling activities at 95 per cent gentile Bucknell College. As an undergraduate, Roth would regale his goy friends with robust imitations and salty routines from his native Jewish Newark community, delivered in stand-up comedian manner. Meanwhile he was *writing* fey sub-Salingerian literary exercises in which 'the Jew was nowhere to be seen'.

The Facts skates over the educational aspects of his 'Joe College' years and ignores altogether his time in the Army – from which he was invalided out in 1955 after sustaining an injury during basic training. Those few months supplied the acrid short story, 'Defender of the Faith' with its whiff of self-despising Judaism. It was gathered into his first collection, *Goodbye, Columbus* (1959), the book which, with its 1959 NBA award, propelled him into fame, still in his twenties. The facts Roth principally engages with in *The Facts* are his three affairs with non-Jewish girls. The first was in 1954, when Roth fell in love with 'Polly Bates' (a pseudonym). Following various couplings in his lodgings, made acutely uncomfortable by the prying of his landlady – an episode recalled in the early sections of *When She Was Good* (1967) – Polly found herself pregnant, as she thought. Roth faced the prospect of buckling down to marriage and giving up the writing nonsense. To his relief (though perhaps not – desire for children that never came runs through *The Facts* as a pathetic refrain), Polly turned out not to be in the club, after all.

It was the end of the affair and Philip caddishly, as he later thought, left her to go off to Chicago, postgraduate study and his literary destiny. In that city in 1956 he met a divorcée with two children, 'Josie Jensen' (another pseudonym, taken to be Margaret Martinson). She was working as a waitress. Like Polly, Josie put the frighteners on Roth with an unplanned pregnancy and the child was aborted (semi-legally). By this time, however, he had seen 'the obvious strains' of marriage and children among his contemporary writer friends and resolved to avoid such enemies of promise. He messily separated from, and then allowed himself to be again entrapped by, his shiksa-witch Josie. Again she played the pregnancy card – this time dishonestly. Roth, if we believe him, was taken for a sucker. He married Martinson, although he claims he didn't have to. The marriage was short-lived. In 'My True Story', it is also rendered as hideously violent, with battery taking over from sex as the most gratifying form of marital intercourse. *The Facts* corrects the fictional version: the marriage certainly went badly wrong, but homicide was not on the cards. And there seems to have been a silver lining. Roth credits his wife's provocations with helping him make his all-important break from Henry James, noting, enigmatically, 'It took time and it took blood.' Hers.

After the inevitable divorce in 1963, Roth was skewered on ever-mounting alimony payments ($125 a week in 1967) and taunted (as recounted in *The Facts*) by Josie's promise never to remarry and release him. He killed her – as Lucy – in *When She Was Good*. Martinson went on to kill herself in a car accident in 1968. Roth felt less liberated than guilty. This personal crack-up coincided, ironically, with the publication of *Portnoy's Complaint* (1969), and bestsellerdom. The American public was ready for its jolly portrait of the artist as a young onanist. The last of Roth's great loves recalled in *The Facts* was 'May Aldridge'. He dwells on her money and good breeding, as if to make the point that the son of the insurance salesman from Newark has done well for himself. May was/is 'a gentile woman at the other end of the American spectrum from Josie', possessed of 'the civic distinction and social prominence that once came automatically to American clans of British stock'. Their affair lasted five years. *The Facts* ends – prematurely – in September 1968 with Roth vowing never to tie himself down to a woman again: 'I was determined to be an absolutely independent, self-sufficient man.' Roth Unbound.

But he wasn't. The publication of *The Facts*, with its declaration of independence, coincided with a mental and physical (triple bypass) breakdown. Illness – specifically prostate cancer (time's cruellest revenge on the puzzled penis) – increasingly preoccupies Roth's late fiction. One assumes – with the necessary tentativeness – that May Aldridge is a version of Claire Bloom, with whom he had, in the late 1980s, been involved for fifteen years. Despite the proclamation about never again tying himself down, Roth married Bloom in 1990. Anglo-American, a distinguished actress and renowned beauty, she matches in central ways the depiction of May Aldridge – 'classy', in a word. The marriage broke up four years later. Bloom published a marital-misery memoir, *Leaving a Doll's House* (she had played the part of Ibsen's Nora, and knew what she was talking about) in 1996 – before the ink on the divorce papers was scarcely dry. It was less the cruelty (although if Bloom's account is to be believed there was plenty of that) than the petty cruelty.

His charging her $150 an hour for reading her scripts, for example. Roth responded with the savage depiction of an ageing vindictive actress, Eve Frame, in *I Married a Communist* (1998).

It was a very public spat and the gossip – in print and more scurrilously in cocktail parties – buzzed on for years. The invasions into his private life infuriated Roth, particularly a piece by John Updike in the *New York Review of Books*, a journal which Roth felt should be above such malicious tittle-tattle. Anger has none the less always been powerful fuel for Roth. His resentment at the invaders of his privacy was distilled in the fiery prelude of his finest novel, *The Human Stain* (2000), which opens in the year of Monica Lewinsky, 1998. Roth, in the person of Zuckerman, launches a passionate defence of Clinton – the only president whose penis (could Lewinski identify it by its markings – or 'bent' following a dose of Peyronie's disease?) was solemnly discussed in the press. It was, in Roth's view, disgusting. The fury against intrusive 'reporters' and equally obnoxious intrusive biographers is continued, ragingly, in *Exit Ghost* (2007).

His later years have been vastly honoured with appointments at the best universities and every possible prize except – to Stockholm's shame – the Nobel. He writes, in these last years, not as the dying animal, but an ageing animal – and very grumpy with it. His novels excoriate political correctness, particularly on the campus, and the universal American timidity about racial matters. In his latest (not one hopes his last) novel, *Nemesis* (2010) he even takes on God, 'a sick fuck and an evil genius', whom he will never forgive for inflicting polio on New Jersey in 1944. Whether God will forgive Philip Roth we shall never know.

FN   Philip Milton Roth
MRT   *The Human Stain*
Biog R. Posnock, *Philip Roth's Rude Truth: The Art of Immaturity* (2006)

265. Wilbur Smith 1933–

History is a river that never ends.

Wilbur Smith came to fiction late in life. Like other male-action novelists – from Captain Marryat (bemedalled veteran of the Napoleonic Wars) to Chris Ryan (bemedalled SAS hero) – he saw action before he wrote it. He was born in 1933, in what was then Northern Rhodesia and is now one of those African countries with Zs in its name that most Britons have difficulty pinpointing on a map. Like his manly heroes, Smith was brought up a rifle-toting rancher, and educated very British. His grandfather Courtney James Smith inspired the series hero, Sean Courtney. Wilbur was an only son. He served in the Rhodesian armed forces in their most embattled years and saw, as he recalls, terrible things. 'When I was doing National Service in Rhodesia I saw little girls who had been held up by the legs and sliced down the middle. We had to fish them out of the pit lavatory ... witnessing such brutality affects my characters, just as it has affected me.' Just how it affected him we can only deduce from some of the more blood-chilling scenes in his fiction.

Smith's first published novel, *When the Lion Feeds* (1964), established the pattern of the thirty-odd yarns that follow. Typically the narrative opens with a big game hunt – big being the operative word. Nothing small for Wilbur Smith; he needed a continent-sized canvas for his vision of Africa and his stories clump, massively, into multi-volume sequences or 'sagas', in which characters and dynastic families separate and intertwine over hundreds of years. Call them mega-novels. The geo-politics are complex, but it is easy to see where Smith is coming from in literary-historical terms. He is the Rider Haggard of our time. More particularly, he writes in the tradition of the fifteen-volume-strong 'Hunter' Quatermain saga which began with *King Solomon's Mines* (1885) and ran, bestsellingly, for forty years under the series motto: *Ex Africa semper aliquid novi* (always something new out of Africa). All three of Smith's great fictional constellations are Afrocentric. The largest, comprising a dozen or so titles, is the 'Courtney' series, which follows the foundation, rise and, as Smith portrays it, the fall of modern South Africa from the seventeenth to the late twentieth century. The national narrative is set alongside the career of a family fabulously enriched from gold, diamonds and whatever other wealth is to be ripped from the country's soil during the colonist's brief tenure. The somewhat less voluminous Ballantyne sequence follows a Rhodesian colonial dynasty from slave-trading, through ranching, to post-Mugabe exile.

Smith's third fictional sequence, the 'Egyptian Novels', was begun in 1993, with *River God*. It was inspired by trips taken with his third wife, Danielle, along the Nile – 'a river which held us both in thrall'. Like Conrad's Congo, it takes Smith to the heart of the continent and its mystical Egyptian pre-history. After the death of Danielle, to whom seven of his novels are dedicated, Smith remarried. As he gleefully reported in an interview with the *Observer*: 'My new wife is thirty-two and I'm seventy. She's rejuvenated me totally ... My mother and sister are delighted with her. They say I seem twenty years younger, and my mates ask: "How did you get so lucky?"' Reincarnation and reinvigoration of the ancient hero, Taita's, 'manroot' is a principal theme in the Egyptian series. Smith's fiction rarely buries its meanings deep.

Smith's overarching motto is 'TIA' – 'This is Africa'. In point of fact, it should be 'This *was* Africa'. His long career as a bestselling author began, historically, with Macmillan's wind of change, whose decolonising gusts began to blow in the late 1950s. That 'wind' has done to Africa, in Smith's view, what Katrina did to New Orleans. His novels are permeated with a gloom which gathers force as the sagas unroll their interminable length. Craig Mellow's failure to recover the family farm in the later Ballantyne novels is symbolic. Now goats graze on its pastures, reducing what was once African Eden to desert. Twenty years ago, Smith believed Zimbabwe, Kenya and Malawi had 'a fighting chance'. No longer. 'Africa,' he has concluded, 'is going back to where it was before the white man intruded' – or, indeed, wrote novels about the doomed continent. He is now based in London.

FN   Wilbur Addison Smith
MRT *When the Lion Feeds*
Biog http://www.wilbursmithbooks.com

266. David Storey 1933–

I've never been an author in the way the middle class would understand, nor working class in the way a popular audience would listen to.

Say 'David Storey' and readers of my – and his – generation will recall the final shot of *This Sporting Life* (1963): Frank Machin (played by Richard Harris) mired, spavined, raising himself on the rugby field to lurch back into hopeless battle. His life as a professional player is over. Football chews up its workforce faster even than the pits he used to work in, but Machin doesn't take it lying down: he is no longer a sportsman but still a man. Storey adapted his original novel for Lindsay Anderson, who directed the film, but he curtailed the ending. On the printed page, after Machin's legs have 'betrayed' him on the pitch, there is a final scene in the changing-room. The players have had their communal bath. Someone, inevitably, has pissed in it. Machin looks around him, 'had my ankles strapped, got dressed and put my teeth in'. As in the film, the scene expresses a refusal to be ground down, but in a grittier, less self-glorifying way. Getting your teeth knocked out – something Anderson plays up – can be glamorous: wearing dentures for the next forty years less so.

The changing-room, with its naked truths about manliness, was to feature prominently in Storey's writing over the next three decades, notably in his play of that name. There are other elements which recur in Storey's work, most of which can be traced back to his own life: the miner father ambitious for his son to be something more (but not necessarily better); the free-booting marquee-erectors' world, in which for a few years Storey, a muscle-bound Defarge, earned his bread swinging a 14-pound hammer, pitching and striking tents for the champagne parties of his social superiors – it supplies the setting for his play *The Contractor* (1970); the Slade art school in Camden, which appears under various pseudonyms, as does his native Wakefield; the years of poverty before *This Sporting Life* (1960); the years of wealth after it; the prizes and glorious collaborations with Karel Reisz and Lindsay Anderson; the broken relationships and other breakdowns; the later years of prizeless oblivion and now the pathos of 'whatever happened to David Storey?'

The primal scene in Storey's fiction is to be found in the Booker-winning *Saville* (1976), in which Colin, the miner's son, takes his eleven-plus. Storey vividly evokes the huge, echoing, dusty examination rooms, the ink-stained desks, the shepherding, numbering and mysterious instructions, the nervy atmosphere of remembered threats and bribes, the sense of an inscrutable authority, the pointless Cyril Burtian questions designed to measure 'IQ' and the elusive 'G' ('How many words can you make from 'Conversation'?') A right or wrong answer to an enigmatic question might well determine the rest of your life.

Born in 1933, Storey took the exam in 1944, the year in which the Butler Education Act came into force. He was one of the saved (i.e. he 'passed') and made it to Queen Elizabeth's Grammar School in Wakefield. The problems of a grammar-school boy like Storey were authoritatively anatomised by Richard Hoggart in the last chapters of *The Uses of Literacy*. As it fed through to the creative writing of the 1960s, the grammar-school boy's educated self-alienation gave rise to a lexicon of fashionable literary terms – 'roots' (invariably cut off), 'outsiders', 'protest' and 'anger' (often in conjunction with 'young man'). 'Grammar school broke him in two,' Storey says of Leonard Radcliffe, in *Radcliffe* (1963) – upward mobility meant class exile. It is famous that Storey found himself in the Faustian situation of getting a scholarship to study at the Slade School just after signing a fifteen-year contract to play rugby league for Leeds. For four years in the early 1950s, artist Jekyll and athlete Hyde bounced between Camden (the Slade) and Yorkshire (the pitch). He finally bought himself out of the contract with three-quarters of the initial signing fee. Camden had won but the psychic divisions would rage on in his writing: he had unmanned himself to write.

The Storey hero invariably finds himself at bay. Physically, he is a wounded animal and the more dangerous for it. He has a 'craggy' face, with some prominently broken feature (a bent nose, missing teeth). Wherever he finds himself, he never belongs. One of the fathers in the novels tells his son: 'When I was younger, your age in fact, I suddenly made what I thought was a discovery: that you have only two choices, either to live in isolation or to be absorbed.' The fathers in Storey's fiction tend to choose absorption into pit, family and village. For their scholarship-liberated sons, the choice is less easy. The problem is that mobility can take you in any number of directions. Which is the right direction for a grammar-school boy – up, down or sideways? Storey's novels explore various possibilities and destinations. In *Pasmore* (1972), the art college teacher puts his family together again after it has broken up and slots back into his former middle-class professional groove:

> In the winter he returned to teaching. Outwardly, despite the events of the preceding year, little had changed. He still had a regular job, a home, a wife and children ... Yet something had changed. It was hard to describe. He had been on a journey. At times it seemed scarcely credible he had survived. He still survived. He still dreamed of the pit and the blackness. It existed all around him, an intensity, like a presentiment of love, or violence. He found it hard to tell.

The last phrase in *Pasmore* – 'He found it hard to tell' – is generally applicable to Storey's narration. He finds it hard to tell his stories; they come out knotted, tongue-tied, clumsy – but authentic.

The end of *Saville* is more uplifting than most, concluding as it does with the memorable Storeyism, 'The shell had cracked'. Colin Saville makes his break, turning like Paul Morel towards the light of the city on the hill. He's done with school-mastering. 'You haven't any lodgings or anything,' his lachrymose mother tells him as he prepares to catch the train to London. 'I don't need lodgings,' Saville replies, 'I can always sleep on the street.'

In *Present Times* (1984), Frank Attercliffe (a former footballer with a mad, institutionalised wife), after a dark night of the soul, breaks out of sports reporting for a Yorkshire newspaper to become world-famous with a play about a rugby league changing-room. It is, as one of his comrades grudgingly puts it, a 'bleak but promising' end to his struggles. The ending of *A Temporary Life* (1973) is bleak and unpromising. The hero Colin Freestone (former professional light-heavyweight, broken nose, explosive temper), having given up his marriage (his wife's mad), his affair with a toff's wife, and his job teaching at the local art college, takes on work as a dustman. 'This is the job I've chosen, of my own volition,' he defiantly declares. Scraping up dog turds with his council shovel parodies the mining which he has 'escaped'. The most curious of Storey's novels remains *Radcliffe* (1963), in which the sensitive, grammar-school-educated, artistic hero finally takes a marquee-erector's hammer to the head of his loutish working-class alter ego and, having exorcised his proletarian self, withers away in a prison for the criminally insane. There is no strength left in him. He has murdered his vital part – or perhaps England murdered it.

FN   David Rhames Storey
MRT *Saville*
Biog W. Hutchings (ed.), *David Storey: A Casebook* (1992).

267. Alasdair Gray 1934–

I know that Socialism can improve social life, that the work we like best is not done for money, and that books and art are liberating.

The English have always relished the story about the voice from the pit, after the first night of John Home's tragedy, *Douglas*: 'Whar's yur Wully Shakespeare noo?' Scots, we apprehend, revere Scottish literary genius. Despite his wishes in the matter it was Alasdair Gray who in 1981 (in the wake of his country's Devolution Referendum) was elevated to justify the cry 'Whar's yur Jimmy Joyce noo?' The loudest voice in the chorus was that of arch-Joycean Anthony Burgess, in his review of *Lanark*: 'The best Scottish novelist since Walter Scott.' (Wasn't there someone called Stevenson?)

Scottish fiction is not, as Burgess's bizarre literary history suggests, a centuries-long desert. Such comments also thrust a mantle on Gray which – the most engagingly self-deprecating of writers – he resolutely shrugs off. 'This is a man', his biographer reminds us, 'who insists on quoting negative reviews on the backs of his books and has invented a fictional critic to tear apart his own work.' As an artist (a field in which he has also been hosannaed), Gray groups himself with 'those interesting second-raters'. Genuflection is, as he reminds us, a bad posture from which to read his novels or look at his pictures. He was born in east Glasgow, the son of a folding-box machine-cutting operative. His mother was a former shop assistant. The couple met on a works outing. Gray's father, Alexander, had served in the ranks in the First World War, surviving to bring back a shrapnel wound in his belly, a small pension and lifelong radicalism. There was a bookshelf full of the English translations of Lenin's works in the house Alasdair grew up in.

He was the first of three children and the only son. The family had settled in one of the new post-war housing schemes in Riddrie. It was not, Gray stresses, a slum but a working-class community – even if that meant 'communal lavatories on the communal stair' and municipal bath-houses. Alexander is recorded as 'skelping' (bashing) his son, which Alasdair connected with his later writing blocks. He was, from childhood, always readier with the crayon than the pencil. It was also in childhood that his lifelong afflictions of eczema, asthma and susceptibility to tormenting nightmares became apparent. This, like the skelping, affected his later work. 'Healthy children', he writes in *Lanark*, 'exercise their imagination by playing games together. I was not healthy. My imagination was mainly exercised in solitary fantasies fed by films and pictures and books.' And, one could add (thinking of *1982, Janine* (1984) and *Something Leather* (1990)), violent sexual fantasies.

Gray was five years old when war broke out. Alexander's factory skills were suddenly at a premium and he was transferred, with the family, to northern England where, for the duration, he wore a suit and tie and was a temporary member of the middle class. 'We even had a cleaner,' Gray's sister wistfully recalled. It was, Alasdair said, 'the happiest time of my life'. After the war it was back to the working class, the communal bog, and Riddrie – where people like them belonged. An escape route opened up for Alasdair with the 1944 Butler Education Act which enabled him to win a 'scholarship' to the local 'grammar'. It was this enlightened political measure, he said, 'that finally made me an author and an artist' and spared him the kind of impoverished lives bleakly chronicled in *Lean Tales* (1985).

Gray's mother died of cancer when he was eighteen. At the same period there were the first stirrings of what would, after thirty years of slow cooking, become *Lanark*. The conception of its depressive-asthmatic-wholly unlovable alter ego hero, Duncan Thaw, was the initial building block; another block was E. M. W. Tillyard's book on the epic. Ironically, given his Virgilian aspiration, it was Gray's failure to get a sufficiently good grade in Latin which prevented him from going to university. But already large ambitions as a poet, novelist and mural artist (the most socialist variety of painting) had been formed. The last of those ambitions was fostered by his being admitted to Glasgow School of Art. Despite illness, he won prizes and travelling scholarships – although he was never happy away from home. Like other art-school graduates, he fell back on short-term teaching contracts as his standby source of income. He was, a friend observed, 'pathologically careless with money'. His vision as an artist was grand in scale but he was already fascinated by typography and book design – functions which, as an author, he would wrest from the publisher with the result that one *sees*, as much as *reads*, a Gray novel (oddly, given the narratives embedded in his murals, one can read those works as stories).

At the 1961 Edinburgh Festival, Gray met the woman who would become his first wife, the Danish nurse, Inge Sorensen. He was twenty-six and inhibited sexually – and drunk when he proposed (it always worked for him, he later said). The couple married in post haste and honeymooned on Arran where, it is reported, sex did not occur. They would later have a child, born in 1964, before the marriage broke down. Gray married again, happily, in 1991, and has one son, Andrew.

Over the 1960s and 1970s he picked up work scene-painting in Glasgow theatres. There were commissions for murals, occasional falling back on the dole, and – most significantly – a string of dramatic works for BBC radio and TV. His attempts to place early drafts of *Lanark* were wholly unsuccessful, but he had better luck with some shorter pieces. And readings from his great work in progress had already brought him to the attention of literary and university circles in Glasgow. *Lanark: A Life in Four Books* was finally published by the Edinburgh firm, Canongate, in 1981 and showered with prizes. For the common reader, however, it was – and still is – a tough nut to crack. Following the epic's *in medias res* rule, it begins with Book Three, with the Prologue and Epilogue similarly perversely located. The narrative adopts three distinctly different stylistic modes. Most striking to the eye are the exuberant and erotic cover illustrations Gray designed (a feature which made the production unusually expensive). In the primary storyline, a character who cannot remember his name, and adopts that of a region, 'Lanark', finds himself in a mysterious world which has the characteristics of Glasgow. It is identified as 'Unthank' (ungrateful place). The hero, searching for sun and his own identity, develops a scaly skin condition, 'dragonhide' (a transparent allegory of Gray's eczema) which will eventually metamorphose him into the thing traditionally slain in literature. W. S. Burroughs's 'mugwumps' in *Naked Lunch* may also come to mind.

The second stream in *Lanark* – the story of Duncan Thaw – is realistic, a recognisable transcript of Gray's own life, in conventional narrative style. It is a grimly unvarnished tale. 'Let Glasgow flourish by telling the truth' is the motto on Gray's frontispiece. Duncan, believing himself a sex murderer, commits suicide. The book is embellished with a number of flamboyantly eccentric features: a meeting between Thaw and his creator, Gray; an owlishly elaborate 'Index of Plagiarisms' covering everyone from Kafka to Walt Disney who may be thought to have been an influence. Ralph Waldo Emerson, it is sagely recorded, is *not* plagiarised. Looming over the whole is a sense of vast historical, social, personal deprivation. 'Why are you content with so little?' Lanark is asked. He replies: 'What else can I have.'

The book makes a physical impact on its reader. Gray the novelist does to the traditional book form what Gray the mural artist did to the traditional wall, often by deft touches – the 'GOODBYE' on the last page of *1982, Janine*, for example. Culturally the impact of *Lanark* was momentous. James Campbell's verdict, 'probably the greatest Scottish novel of the century', attracted little contradiction. It was, as Joyce said of *Finnegans Wake*, a book to keep the professors busy and a Gray industry subsequently cranked up in the Scottish universities. Gray was appointed a writer-in-residence at Glasgow University and would over time get the degrees *honoris causa* that his poor Latin had earlier denied him. Wry as ever, he claimed *Lanark* was 'overrated'.

After 1981 he was a literary lion – although never flush with money. Sexual attention he did get and, as his biographer records, he enjoyed it. Sex would, in fact, be the preoccupation of his next major work, *1982, Janine* (1984). The novel began as a short story and was conceived in a seething mood of anti-Thatcherism. The hero, Jock McLeish, is the Glasgow equivalent of that era's 'Mondeo Man'. A middle-class conservative salesman, 'happily' married, he has an involved, fetishised, sado-masochistic relationship in his head with a cerebral sex-toy, Janine, or 'Superb' (Superbitch):

> Superb is a greedy sexy bitch who knows how to get what she likes. Helen [his wife] was a gentle woman I want not to remember, shy of sex and with no greedy appetites (could I be wrong about that?).

The novel came to him, he said, looking around and trying to imagine what was going on behind the inscrutable faces he observed in places like railway stations. The novel's stream of consciousness ends: 'I will stand on the platform an hour from now, briefcase in hand, a neater figure than most but not remarkable.' Will McLeish kill himself? 'I will not do nothing,' he promises himself. But perhaps he will. The misogyny disturbed many of Gray's admirers – particularly women. Was Scotland's greatest novelist a pornographer? By way of defence, he contends that 'life for most women is a performance in a male sex fantasy' and for men, sexual torment. Why do women's clothes say such different things from women's mouths, McLeish wonders? He tells it as he sees it.

Gray continued writing and painting in conditions of less financial and physical discomfort, but writing remained hard work. His experimental *Book of Prefaces* (2000) was thirteen years in preparation and his visual-textual *A Life in Pictures* (2010) almost as long. His socialist principles softened somewhat, although his 1992 polemic *Why Scots Should Rule Scotland* confirmed his lifelong dislike of the Union with England and his distaste for those gifted Scottish people who, unlike himself, 'fucked off down to London'.

FN   Alasdair Gray
MRT   *Lanark: A Life in Four Books*
Biog   R. Glass, *Alasdair Gray: A Secretary's Biography* (2008)

268. J. G. Farrell 1935–1979

We look on past ages with condescension, as a mere preparation for us ... but what if we're only an after-glow of them? The Siege of Krishnapur

What was it that 'made' J. G. Farrell a writer? An impossible but oddly tantalising question. What one can say is that if Jonas Salk had been a year earlier with his vaccine, we would not have had the so-called Empire Trilogy: *Troubles*, *The Siege of Krishnapur* and *The Singapore Grip*. And, had the novelist who wrote them not died in 1979 (mysteriously, as his biographer Lavinia Greacen is at pains to stress), he might well, by now, have joined Salk on the Nobel winner's platform at Stockholm.

When he went up to Oxford in October 1956, after two gap years, 'Jim' Farrell had it all. Head boy at his public school, 'rugger was pretty well my life', he later recalled. He was clever and had got a place at Brasenose to read law. It was not his choice: his parents wanted their son (the second of three) to become 'an eminent Dublin solicitor or barrister'. Jim was handsome, shy with girls, and tipped the scales at just under 14 stone. He was what in earlier times was called a 'hearty' and now a 'jock'. A 'full blue' was in prospect, a respectable degree – and a lot of post-game piss-ups in the Turf Tavern along the way. This was the era of Oxbridge immortalised by Frederic Raphael's *Glittering Prizes* TV mini-series. The university's cream of the crop were not, like their predecessors, merely 'brilliant' – they were 'celebrities'. Greacen gives a roll call of Jim Farrell's starry contemporaries: Brian Walden, Alan Coren, Dudley Moore, Paul Johnson, Grey Gowrie, Ferdinand Mount, Paul Foot, Richard Ingrams, Ved Mehta, Auberon Waugh and Dennis Potter – to name, as they say, a few.

As Potter later observed, on reading *Krishnapur*, none of this golden crew knew the burly young undergraduate at Brasenose. Why should they? Oiks like Farrell came in bunches of fifteen. One only took notice of them when they came back sloshed on Saturday nights and honked on the stairs. On 28 November 1956, the height of the season, Jim Farrell had a bad game. He didn't feel right in the changing room afterwards, 'cut the usual drinking session', took a bus back to college and crawled fully clothed into bed. He had polio. Six days later he was in an 'iron lung', that life-saving apparatus which was half Edgar Allan Poe's *Buried Alive* and half medieval torture-rack. Salk's vaccine became widely available six months later, and the iron lung would join the hook-hand in the medical museum. In his 1965 novel, *The Lung*, he gives a graphic description of the virus's early flu symptoms, suicidal disarrangement of the mind, physical collapse and the ultimate horror: 'a white metal box on wheels. Any similarity between this box and a coffin was purely coincidental.' But, as the novel graphically relates, it isn't. When he was recovered sufficiently for 'physio', he was three stone lighter and had shoulders that, to his mortification, he heard one girl call 'flabby'. It was like the Charles Atlas strip-advertisement in reverse: the husky young athlete had become a 90-pound weakling. 'Jim Farrell' became 'J. G. Farrell': an 'outsider', in the term popularised by Colin Wilson that same year. No longer a player, he became a spectator. The novelist happened.

Farrell was advised that law would be too demanding for him and, having transferred to Modern Languages, scraped a third in 1960. The setback did not upset him as he had already resolved to write. That was what outsiders did best. Over the next few years, he scraped by on various teaching jobs abroad and travelling fellowships, compensating for his disability by sexual athleticism, running three or four girlfriends at the same time (one of the side-show attractions of Greacen's biography is reading between the lines for the well-known literary ladies who at various times warmed Farrell's bed). Women fell for the slim, nerve-wracked, good looks. He was, says Robert Harris, 'the Great Shagger of English Literary Fiction, 1960–79'. For his part, he would never commit to any one woman. Unfaithful in love, Farrell was steadfast to the muse. As Wordsworth put it, what the writer needs above all is 'independence and resolution'. In one of his letters to a girlfriend, Farrell wrote, 'One has to be lonely in order to get up the steam to write fiction.' Nowhere had he been lonelier than in the white box.

Farrell's first ventures in fiction did nothing to separate him from the thousands of would-be novelists every year who try their luck and get nowhere. *A Man from Elsewhere* (1963), *The Lung* (1965) and *A Girl in the Head* (1967) were all apprentice works. Reviewers were variously cool, snide or wholly unnoticing. He kept body and soul together with support from his publisher, Jonathan Cape, and a fellowship to study in America. He was never, as Greacen testifies, a well-read novelist (he did not discover Dickens until a few years before his death, for example). But over these formative years two writers were particularly influential on him: Richard Hughes and Malcolm Lowry. In honour of the second he made a visit to Mexico.

Farrell, meanwhile, was mining his own family background – the Anglo-Irish ascendancy, the Anglo-Indian professional classes, the army officer caste. He was a pioneer in what is now called 'post-colonial fiction', that genre born out of the exhaustions and guilt of Empire. Sprightlier than Paul Scott, his fiction was less consciously 'post-modern' than that of Salman Rushdie, an admirer. He offered 'a good read', while taking the novel into interesting new fields. Late in his career, in conversation with his friend Paul Barker, he said the biggest thing to have happened in his life was the decline of the British Empire – but he did not lament that decline.

Novelists, like generals, need luck. Farrell's story of the aftermath of the Irish uprising, and the battles between the IRA and the Black and Tans, *Troubles*, came out in 1970, a few months after Ulster exploded into flames. Few novels have been more timely. Despite some sniffy reviews, the novel was generally applauded, but his oddly comic tone (a cross between Evelyn Waugh and P. G. Wodehouse, as one critic neatly put it) is very much an acquired taste. At the centre of *Troubles'* narrative is the statutory big house – in this case the Majestic Hotel. Its decay, under its fanatically pro-Union owner, Edward Spencer, is a metaphor for the decay of the Ascendancy. A moment in its final crumbling gives the distinctive tang of Farrell's narrative:

> One unseasonably warm day the giant M of Majestic detached itself from the façade of the building and fell four storeys to demolish a small table at which a very old and very deaf lady, an early arrival for Christmas, had decided to take tea in the mild sunshine that was almost like summer. She had looked away for a moment, she explained to Edward in a very loud voice (almost shouting, in fact), trying to remember where the floral clock had been in the old days. She had maybe closed her eyes for a moment or two. When she had turned back to her tea, it had gone! Smashed to pieces by this strange, seagull-shaped piece of cast iron (she luckily had not recognised it or divined where it had come from).

If ever there were an argument for supporting the Arts Council, it is found in the next phase of Farrell's career. He was, at this period, chronically broke. On the strength of *Troubles* he was given an Arts Council fellowship of £750, which he used to follow up research he had done in the British Museum to travel (third-class all the way) across India. The novel which ensued, *The Siege of Krishnapur*, went on to win the Booker Prize in 1973. This middle section of what came to be known as the 'Empire Trilogy' (not Farrell's description and 'anti-Empire' would be more apt) is based on an actual siege in northern India. It describes the uphold-ers of the Raj – principally the Collector, the Magistrate, the Soldier, the Poet, the Padre – going patriotically lunatic as they fight off the sepoy hordes. After months of holding out, the relieving force discovers survivors indistinguishable, as one of the officers observes, from 'untouchables'. As in most of Farrell's fiction, there is no overwhelmingly sympathetic character and a bitter comedy which perplexes as much as it amuses. In the last desperate stages of the siege, for example, the British defenders have run out of cannonballs and use the heads from busts of literary figures in the Residency:

> And of the heads, perhaps not surprisingly, the most effective of all had been Shakespeare's; it had scythed its way through a whole astonished platoon of sepoys advancing in single file through the jungle. The Collector suspected that

the Bard's success in this respect might have a great deal to do with the ballistic advantages stemming from his baldness.

The Empire can still strike back.

Like John Berger the year before, Farrell used his prizewinner's speech to attack the 'unacceptable face of capitalism', incarnated in the donor firm which had made its millions out of sweated labour in the West Indies. Every year, he jested, Booker should expect an ever more horrible monster washed up on its prize shores. Novelists were not company men. None the less the bad manners and bad headlines were, as always with Booker, good publicity.

Farrell, only thirty-eight, was suddenly – as authors go – rich and famous. He sold the film rights to his novel, fired his agent and went into tax exile in Kilcrohane, county Cork, in 1979. Here, living close to the land and the sea, and beyond the call of the telephone, he found, for the first time, *douceur de vivre*. He managed one more great novel before going into tax exile, *The Singapore Grip* (1978), about the ignominious surrender in 1942 which marked the end for the British Empire. As Robert Harris observes, 'his theme is chaos, and the ceaseless attempts of a hypocritical society to keep it at bay'. At the time the novel received disappointing reviews, but has lasted and been revalued more generously. Farrell was at work on a sequel to *The Siege of Krishnapur* at the time of his death. It was tidied up and published, posthumously, as *The Hill Station* in 1981.

There was enough juice in the death-throes of the British Empire to have kept Farrell going for many more decades – but it was not to be. Having, belatedly, developed a taste for his fiction, the world would be denied more of it. Lavinia Greacen's biography makes much of the strange episode of Farrell's death, aged only forty-four, on 11 August 1979. He was fishing in high seas near his home in southwest Ireland and was knocked off the rock on which he was standing by a wave, falling into the water. It was stormy (the same storm which would later drown fifteen contestants in the Fastnet yacht race). What was odd, according to witnesses, was that Farrell made no effort to save himself. He did not shout for help and his body was only recovered six weeks later. In 2010, the year in which he won the so-called 'Lost Man Booker Prize' (for the missing year, 1970) with *Troubles*, a belated witness report only added to the mystery of his end. Was it suicide? An IRA hit? Is J. G. Farrell, like Elvis, still alive? In all probability, what killed him was the long-term debility of his polio: he was too weak to save himself. What made him a writer killed him.

FN   James Gordon Farrell
MRT   *The Siege of Krishnapur*
Biog L. Greacen, *J. G. Farrell, the Making of a Writer* (1999)

269. George MacDonald Fraser 1925–2008

It was a common custom at that time, in the more romantic females, to see their soldier husbands and sweethearts as Greek heroes, instead of the whore-mongering, drunken clowns most of them were. However, the Greek heroes were probably no better, so it was not so far off the mark. Harry Flashman's view of his trade

There is a moment – hilarious and darkly symbolic – in *The Siege of Krishnapur* (1973) where the central character, the Collector (i.e. the officer charged with extorting revenue from the colony for the East India Company) stands under the cantonment's flagpole as it is hit by a rebel cannonball. The Union Jack falls on him and he finds himself 'struggling on his back with the stifling presence of the flag wrapped round him like a shroud'. It has the typical Farrell tang – high comedy and savage anti-imperialism. The flag is not lowered, ceremonially; it falls down ignominiously.

It was common, after the success of *The Siege of Krishnapur*, to compare Farrell with John Fowles, whose *The French Lieutenant's Woman* came out three years earlier. In fact there is a closer analogy to be found in George MacDonald Fraser's comic fiction. Fraser's first novel, *Flashman*, was published in 1969. Oddly, in view of his later success, Fraser had huge difficulty finding a publisher for his manuscript and the book finally came out under the imprint of one of the more obscure, but more perceptive, London firms, Barrie and Jenkins.

Fraser's basic idea was beguilingly simple. Flashman is the utter cad in *Tom Brown's Schooldays* (1857). Thomas Hughes's novel begins with a long prelude praising the 'Browns of England' who – to continue the chromatic theme – had covered a third of the globe imperial red. If Waterloo was won on the playing fields of Eton, as the proverb put it, the British Empire was built in classrooms of Rugby, as reformed under the formidable hand and cane of Dr Thomas Arnold in the late 1830s. In Hughes's novel, Harry Flashman is the degenerate school bully. In one central scene he roasts Brown, his junior, over a fire. He finally meets his condign fate when, having drunk himself stupid, he is brought back to school insensible on a hurdle. The Doctor expels him. We know what happens to Tom Brown after this: he becomes cock of the school, goes on to Oxford, and does great things for Queen and country. But what happens to Flashman? This is Fraser's starting point in what would, over the next thirty years, become a twelve-volume series. Allegedly, the answer is to be found in the 'Flashman Papers ... discovered during a sale of household furniture at Ashby, Leicestershire, in 1965'. Mr Fraser, we apprehend, has been given the honour of 'editing' them.

Yellow to the core – but damnably lucky – Flashy is discovered to have ended up, in the opening volume, a hero of the first Afghan War. 'Possibly there has been a greater shambles in the history of warfare,' he observes, 'probably there has not.' In a final siege of an outpost in Jellalabad, his unconscious body is found by the relieving force wrapped in the regimental flag, dead bodies all around. It is assumed that this is an act of conspicuous gallantry. In fact he was intending to give it to the Afghans in the hope that they would spare him. He returns to England a national hero and is honoured with one of his monarch's first Victoria Crosses. As he confesses, VD is more Flashy's style.

His charmed, wholly disreputable career, has him riding into the Valley of Death, fighting at Little Big Horn (the only survivor), and – inevitably – saving his skin in the Indian Mutiny. He emerges from all such crises. As Fraser put it, 'I led him on his disgraceful way, toadying, lying, cheating, running away, treating women as chattels, abusing inferiors of all colours, with only one redeeming virtue – the unsparing honesty with which he admitted to his faults.' Fraser's models in his hugely entertaining saga were Rafael Sabatini (a 'God', whose *Captain Blood* Fraser read, aged ten) and Anthony Hope, the author of *The Prisoner of Zenda*, on which the successor to Flashman, *Royal Flash* (1970), is based.

Flashman was the book of the day and the business with the flag has striking similarities with Farrell's episode in *The Siege of Krishnapur*. More interesting are the two authors' similar views about Empire. Like Farrell, Fraser was clearly inspired by the wholly amazing collapse of the British Empire, which had been a supposedly permanent thing, between Harold Macmillan's 'Wind of Change' speech in 1960 and Denis Healey's pull back from 'East of Suez' in 1967. In what was, historically, the blinking of an eye, it was gone. As Fraser observed:

> No generation has seen their country so altered, so turned upside down, as children like me born in the 20 years between the two world wars ... Other lands have known what seem to be greater upheavals, the result of wars and revolutions, but these do not compare with the experience of a country which passed in less than a lifetime from being the mightiest empire in history, governing a quarter of mankind, to being a feeble little offshore island whose so-called leaders have lost the will and the courage, indeed the ability, to govern at all.

Not even Gibbon could have made it a dramatic story. It was not epic, nor tragic – only comedy would serve. The end of Empire was a peculiarly British, more specifically an English, event. It was something that the Irish and Scottish novelist, connected but not central, might be expected to see more clearly – and, to add to the comedy, that Americans had difficulty seeing at all. They never quite got the point.

As Fraser recalled, 'when *Flashman* appeared in the US in 1969, one-third of forty-odd critics accepted it as a genuine historical memoir. "The most important discovery since the Boswell papers" is the one that haunts me still … I'd never supposed that it would fool anybody … And fifty British critics had recognised it as a conceit.'

Fraser had come to such conceits late in life. He was born the son of a doctor and a nurse, in the historically uneasy borderlands between Scotland and England. His novels *The Steel Bonnets* (1971) and *The Candlemass Road* (1993) are set there. Genetically, he was from North of the Border and proud of it: 'My forebears from the Highlands of Scotland were a fairly primitive, treacherous, blood-thirsty bunch and, as Robert Louis Stevenson once wrote, would have been none the worse for washing. Fine, let them be so depicted, if any film maker feels like it; better that than insulting, inaccurate drivel like *Braveheart*.' He was educated at grammar school and had hopes of a medical career, but couldn't pass his Latin exams. Aged eighteen, he volunteered for the Border Regiment in 1943 and fought with the 'forgotten' 14th army (as did fellow novelist Brian Aldiss) in Burma. He rose – somewhat inconsistently – through the ranks and was commissioned after the war into the Gordon Highlanders. He saw active service in such post-war hotspots as the Middle East and North Africa as the British Empire creaked on its way to dissolution. His military service is commemorated in the wry memoir *Quartered Safe Out Here* (1992) and his 'McAuslan' stories, which follow the career of the incorrigibly wayward Private John McAuslan, 'the dirtiest soldier in the world'.

Fraser left the army in 1947 (the year that India left the Empire) to work as a journalist. He married a fellow journalist, Kathleen Hetherington, in 1949, and had three children. They emigrated to Canada in the early 1950s but returned after a year to Glasgow where Fraser embarked on a fifteen-year stint on the *Glasgow Herald*. He rose steadily from sub-editor to deputy editor but, failing to get the top job on the paper, he resolved, aged forty-four and encouraged by his wife, 'to write his way out' with a novel – *Flashman* as it would be. Drawing on his journalist's fluency, 'it took 90 hours, no advance plotting, no revisions, just tea and toast and cigarettes at the kitchen table'. After its insulting round of rejection by London's major publishers, *Flashman* took off like a rocket. Fraser was, within a year, rich enough to take tax exile on the Isle of Man. *Flashman* volumes pulsed regularly from his typewriter as did even more lucrative film screenplays and other books – such as a homage to Sabatini, *The Pyrates* (1983) – which he had always wanted to write. One of the more interesting of his non-fiction works is *The Hollywood History of the World* (1988), in which he argued for popular film as a great educator as to the nature of the past. The argument applies to his own popular romance, founded as it is on impressive research, buttressed with owlishly pedantic footnotes to get up the nose of the academics.

Fraser had rather more mixed views about Empire than Farrell. He saw it as a gigantic fake, but admired the 'standards and values' which it generated – even Flashy behaves with decency, when the chips are down. He was, Fraser liked to say, a believer in – not an enemy of – the Empire and, with unusual appropriateness, was awarded an OBE in 1999. By this period he had become thoroughly brassed off with post-imperial Britain and, in 2008 (the Flashman saga having concluded in 2005), he loosed a final salvo:

> The United Kingdom has begun to look more like a Third World country, shabby, littered, ugly, run down, without purpose or direction, misruled by a typical Third World government, corrupt, incompetent and undemocratic ... I feel I speak not just for myself but for the huge majority of my generation who think as I do but whose voices are so often lost in the clamour. We are yesterday's people, the over-the-hill gang. (Yes, the old people – not the senior citizens or the time-challenged, but the old people.) Those of ultra-liberal views may take consolation from this – that my kind won't be around much longer, and then they can get on with wrecking civilisation in peace.

He wouldn't be around much longer, dying a few months later of cancer through whose long affliction he had written a number of his later works.

FN   George MacDonald Fraser
MRT *Flashman*
Biog G. M. Fraser, *The Light's on at Signpost* (2002)

270. David Lodge 1935–

I had been aware for some time (and you, gentle reader, have no doubt made the same observation) that I had not only strayed into a zone of Jamesian ironies as a result of writing Author, Author, *but I was in some measure re-enacting the story of my own novel.*

Those who have kept David Lodge company over the nearly fifty years of his novel-writing career will be able to construct a CV from the words on the fictional page, supplemented by throwaway comments in interviews and essays. Born in London, an only child, David was evacuated during the Blitz with his mother to the safety of the rural southwest. This figures in the opening, 1940s section of *Out of the Shelter* (1970). In *The Year of Henry James* (2006), Lodge discloses, in passing, that he is 'a quarter Irish'. His publisher, Tom Rosenthal, liked to disclose that Lodge is 'part Jewish'. His upbringing, however, was wholly Catholic: 'My mother,' he has written 'was a dutiful but undemonstrative daughter of the Church.' His father was 'a jobbing musician' who served in an RAF dance-band during the war, in a succession of remote but safe postings. The father of the hero in *Deaf Sentence* (2008), Lodge informs us, is as close a representation as is the hero himself (retired university professor of English with hearing problems) of Lodge Jr. In the novel, aged a frail ninety, Desmond's dad lives in the same house that the Lodge family did, in Brockley, southeast London ('Brickley' in the novels). Desmond's mother has been dead for a long while: she was 'twenty-five years as an underpaid clerk in the office of a local builders' merchant' (if we follow the novel).

Young Lodge sailed through the eleven-plus and went to a Catholic grammar school in Blackheath. Like other lonely children of the 1940s, he loved the velvety comforts of the cinema – *The Picturegoers* (1960). His 'Saturday Night and Sunday Morning' were 'Flicks and Mass'. He was clever, but the school had no easily opened doors to Oxbridge and he was put off 'because he'd read enough Waugh to know that it was all getting debagged in the quad by raving drunken aristocrats'. He got a first in English at UCL, the godless (and wholly aristocratless) place in Gower Street, then did his two years' national service. The experience angered him: not just the army, but the class system which underpinned it – 'All those upper-class chinless wonders.' As an 'angry young man' (he recalls the impact of Osborne's *Look Back in Anger* on him), he got an AYM novel, *Ginger You're Barmy* (1962), out of his two years in the Royal Armoured Corps. The hero, as did Lodge, presumably, refuses to let himself be put forward for officer training: 'I felt that if I became an officer I'd be participating in that injustice.' Like Bartleby, he'd rather not.

On demob, he returned to do an MA at UCL on Graham Greene. This supplied the raw material for *The British Museum is Falling Down* (1965). The novel portrays the UCL English Department, then in a sad state of post-war decay, with as savage a comedy as publisher Secker & Warburg's libel lawyers would allow. The copyright lawyers forbade him his first choice of title, 'The British Museum has Lost its Charm'. Lodge takes a rueful delight in how 'the first batch of review copies was mysteriously lost, and never reached a single newspaper or magazine'. The novel was met with thundering critical silence. None the less he remained loyal to the publisher (and to UCL). On graduation in 1959 Lodge married Mary Frances Jacob, a fellow student and fellow Catholic whom he had known for six years. He worked briefly for the British Council (who, he later discovered, thought little of him). The early years of marriage were 'very precarious financially … We were attempting to use the permitted form of Catholic birth control that didn't work very well. We had two children within four years, and then another one, and then we made a rational decision to use birth control.'

Unfunny in life, the birth control problem supplies the extremely funny first scene in *The British Museum is Falling Down*, where Adam's wife – attempting to work out the 'rhythm' method – lies in bed with so many thermometers sticking out of her that she resembles a hedgehog in heat, while he prepares to go out and slave under Panizzi's dome. Lodge went further into the issues of New Catholicism in *How Far Can You Go?* (1980), a novel which brought him, as he says, to the 'edge of belief'. The question in the title, in those pre-pill days, normally referred to 'heavy petting', as it was called. Sexual temptation crops up frequently in his fiction. *Changing Places* (1975), for example, could as readily be called 'Changing Spouses'. Lodge wittily describes himself as a war reporter – not a combatant – in the battle of the sexes.

Lodge's career was set with his appointment to a tenured position in the English Department at Birmingham ('Rummidge' in the Philip Sparrow novels). Here it was his path crossed with that of Malcolm Bradbury, the novelist with whom his name is routinely associated, and sometimes facetiously merged ('Bradlodge', or 'Blodge'). As the dedication to *The British Museum is Falling Down* testifies, it was Bradbury who shrewdly persuaded Lodge to forego realism for ironic comedy as his dominant narrative mode. In his campus novels, Lodge offers a more subtle critique of higher education than anything that has ever come out of Whitehall. What, for example, is the balance, or useful friction, between Oxbridge, metropolitan, provincial and 'new' universities? The implied answer, in *Thinks* ... (2001), is that new universities are, as their name implies, the most open conduits to new thinking. What, *Changing Places* makes the reader wonder, can the American and British systems learn from each other? Does the pressure-cooking of scholarship in off-campus 'conferences' raise its quality, or does this 'Small World' privilege an elite of in-group hierophants, speaking a dialect the outside world (including the undergraduate community) cannot understand?

When asked how he came across the idea for *Deaf Sentence* (2008), a rueful cogitation on his late-life loss of hearing, and the loss of his father, he recalled: 'Well, it came to me as a comic novel, as I was shaving and thinking about some recent humiliation'. The H-word is resonant. In *Changing Places*, the hero Philip Sparrow introduces his American hosts to a parlour game called Humiliation. The winner is the academic who can honestly reveal the most famous work of literature he *hasn't* read. The game is won by an over-achieving American who trumps all other shameful omissions by confessing never to have read *Hamlet*. His tenure prospects are blown. To win is to lose: to lose is to win.

Humiliation is the climate of Lodge's fiction, and flavours the image of himself which he has cultivated for his readers (no more genuine, one suspects, than Charlie Chaplin's tramp outfit). The major novel of his late period, *Author, Author* (2004), is a veritable stew in which every ingredient is a variety of humiliation. The author is Henry James. His friend George du Maurier offers him the idea for a novel – a Jewish hypnotist who can 'create' a great opera singer out of a street girl. Henry turns it down: 'not my line'. Du Maurier goes on to write the superseller, *Trilby*. Mrs Humphry Ward, whom James has encouraged to write fiction, sells a million or more with the clodhopping *Robert Elsmere*. He, meanwhile, can't clear a thousand of *The Aspern Papers*. What, he asks his friend H. G. Wells, is he up to? Something called *The Time Machine*, he is told. Everyone's stuff sells like hot cakes except 'the master's' stuff. And then, the crowning humiliation: at the end of the first night of his play, *Guy Domville*, that he expects to make his fortune, he is mischievously called on to the stage – 'Author! Author!' – only to be hooted off it. Loser.

It's wonderfully done, and pure Lodge. But, as is now famous, Domvilleian disaster struck as he was preparing *Author, Author* for press. Colm Toíbín, a novelist whose career was meteorically in the ascendant, was bringing out his Jamesian novel on exactly the same subject. *The Master* would beat *Author, Author* to the post. And, as the first book does, it got the longer reviews. Lodge created a self-lacerating book out of his humiliation, *The Year of Henry James: The Story of a Novel* (2006). But time has its own ironies. A hundred years on and who has lasted? Mrs Humphry Ward? Be serious. 'Henry, wherever you are, take a bow' is Lodge's ironic reply. It is amazing – and wrong – that Lodge, the greatest comic novelist of our time, has never won Britain's premier literary prize, the Booker, nor been shortlisted other than once for it. But, one suspects, his time will come. If the judges wait too long, humiliatingly, he will not be around to make his bow, wherever he then is.

FN   David John Lodge
MRT   *The British Museum is Falling Down*
Biog B. K. Martin, *David Lodge* (1999)

271. Alistair MacLeod 1936–

We all come from some place, and if you are in your place for some time, your place intensifies you.

Alistair MacLeod was born in North Battleford, Saskatchewan, Canada. In his childhood the family moved to a farm in Dunvegan, on Nova Scotia's Cape Breton Island. He attended various universities, full and part time (teaching in the intervals), from 1957 to 1968, graduating with a doctorate in Victorian Literature from Notre Dame, in 1968. He taught for three years at Indiana University before taking up a post as professor of Creative Writing at the University of Windsor in Ontario. MacLeod, over the course of his professional life, kept a foothold in his native region, writing (during the long summer vacations his profession afforded) in a clifftop cabin 'looking west toward Prince Edward Island'.

MacLeod's is the most compact of literary careers. Over the four decades of his writing, he has published fewer than a score of short stories, initially in literary journals and subsequently gathered in two modest collections, *The Lost Salt Gift of Blood* (1976) and *As Birds Bring Forth the Sun* (1986). In 1999, he published his first novel, *No Great Mischief*. All of MacLeod's fiction, short and long, deals with life in Nova Scotia – New Scotland – on the eastern Canadian seaboard. The people in his stories are miners, fishermen, loggers, crofters, their wives and offspring. Historically, these people are poised on a cusp. Their ancestors as far back as the seventh generation followed the same hard path: they hauled nets, quarried the earth, felled trees, ploughed and grazed the ungrateful, winter-blasted soil. They also spoke Gaelic – a language that is, as the author puts it, a 'beautiful prison', a dialect that unites the clan and cuts it off from the outside world. As one of MacLeod's wise old women observes: 'No one has ever said that life is to be easy. Only that it is to be lived.' Despite its hardships, it is a rich and authentic life – stocked with the wisdom, hard-won skills and cultural possessions of a people. What does the future hold? One of MacLeod's spokesman heroes, a miner whose children will have a 'better' life, offers a bitter prophecy:

> Our sons will go to the universities to study dentistry or law and to become fatly affluent before they are 30. Men who will stand over six feet tall and who will move their fat, pudgy fingers over the limited possibilities to be found in other people's mouths. Or men who sit behind desks shuffling papers relating to divorce or theft or assault or the taking of life. To grow prosperous from pain and sorrow and the desolation of human failure. They will be far removed from the physical life and will seek it out only through jogging or golf or games of handball with friendly colleagues.

These wayward sons of Nova Scotia will have 'gentler deaths'. In return for what? Emptier lives. The Gaelic songs will be sung for only one generation more – to an audience of anthropologists and folklorists with their recording machines, in performances that are less preservation than cultural taxidermy.

As his clan name indicates, MacLeod derives from that wave of Highlanders driven into exile by the Clearances – ethnic cleansing, early-nineteenth-century style. Ancient anger smoulders, like the glow of a peat fire, at the heart of these stories. A more complex anger, one senses, is directed inward. The author is himself one of those sons who deserted the 'physical life' of his people. In one of his stories, sardonically entitled 'Clearances', a Cape Breton sheep farmer is urged by his restless son to sell the family property. Its 'ocean frontage' has taken the idle fancy of some rich Germans who want a second home. It must have crossed MacLeod's mind, as he sat gazing through the window of his second home, maintained with the earnings of distant classrooms, that he has something in common with those foreigners.

In his mid-sixties, MacLeod was suddenly famous. He was 'discovered' and now ranks as a great Canadian author (a conjunction that would once have raised a patronising sneer in New York and London). Literary history will situate him among the 'post-colonial' writers, connoisseurs of ancient oppression, and he deserves to rank high in that company. Chauvinistically (my name, after all, is as clannish as his), I would also like to reclaim a part of MacLeod for Scottish literature – alongside Lewis Grassic Gibbon, a writer with whom he has affinities. There is something immensely reassuring about MacLeod's late-career success. Good writing, it seems, will out. Talent like his needs no hype. Nor need it deal with metropolitan or modishly high-concept themes. His narrative technique is deceptively simple. Judging by the texture of his prose and the sparseness of his output, he is a craftsman who patiently whittles and winnows until he has the perfectly shaped literary object. The bare-bones style of MacLeod's writing (which has not significantly changed over the course of thirty years) and his habit of heaping detail upon detail like stones on a cairn are best shown by quotation. Here, in the title story from his first collection, 'The Lost Salt Gift of Blood', he describes the most important room in an old woman's home:

> The kitchen is small. It has an iron cookstove, a table against one wall and three or four handmade chairs of wood. There is also a wooden rocking chair covered by a cushion. The rockers are so thin from years of use that it is hard to believe they still function. Close by the table there is a washstand with two pails of water upon it. A washbasin hangs from a driven nail in its side and above it is an old-fashioned mirrored medicine cabinet. There is also a large cupboard, a low-lying couch and a window facing upon the sea.

As he lay in the hospital dying of tuberculosis, George Orwell found that he could calm his panic by writing down, as a reporter might, the exact contents of the room around him. There was comfort in inventory. One feels the same painful pressure – and artistic relief – in MacLeod's writing.

In the largest sense, MacLeod's fiction articulates the pathos of social progress. His is the generation of Nova Scotians that broke away from an essentially peasant existence – anachronistically preserved by a wilderness and its natural resources (mature forests, coal, cod) that no longer exist. His is the last generation that, from indelible childhood memory, knows the past. But he knows much else. He went to the university, cultivated his mind, bettered himself. He is none the less haunted by a sense of lost authenticity, by the life not lived.

FN   Alistair MacLeod
MRT *No Great Mischief*
Biog *The Canadian Encyclopedia* (Colin Boyd)

272. John Kennedy Toole 1937–1969

It isn't really about anything.
Simon and Schuster's explanation for rejecting an early draft of *A Confederacy of Dunces*

The circumstances surrounding John Kennedy Toole's fictions are as American gothic as anything even Flannery O'Connor could devise. Without any of his friends suspecting he had authorial ambitions, Toole wrote *A Confederacy of Dunces* (1980) in the early 1960s, while doing his national service in Puerto Rico. Eerily apt, in the light of later events, the title is taken from Jonathan Swift's jaundiced rule of literary life: 'When a true genius appears in the world, you may know him by this sign, that the dunces are all in confederacy against him.' The manuscript was submitted to Simon and Schuster, where Robert Gottlieb, after dickering about for two years, eventually turned it down in 1966. By 1969 Toole had been for some years an English instructor at Dominican College, working in his spare time on his Ph.D. A modestly fulfilling academic career was in prospect. But in the late 1960s Toole began to behave in a paranoid way, as his friends and colleagues recall, and he suddenly disappeared. It later emerged that he had taken off on a three-month automobile odyssey to California. On his way back, he called by Flannery O'Connor's house in Georgia. Then, outside Biloxi in Mississippi, on 26 March 1969, he connected some garden hosepipe to the exhaust of his car and gassed himself. He was just thirty-one years old.

Toole left no will. An only child, he did leave a suicide note for his parents, which his mother read and destroyed without divulging its contents. Among her son's effects she found the manuscript of his rejected novel, which she had never read, and his correspondence with Simon and Schuster. Thelma Toole thereafter always maintained that the New York publishers (more particularly, that 'Jewish creature', Gottlieb) had effectively murdered her son by first raising, then dashing, his hopes. More than one commentator has hinted that John's relationship with his overwhelming mother may have had something to do with his suicide; it certainly conditions much of his fiction.

Although she was seventy and had an invalid husband (a car salesman in his earlier years), Thelma Toole devoted the rest of her life to getting John's novel published and his genius vindicated. *A Confederacy of Dunces* was eight times rejected. But after eleven years, Mrs Toole, with the help of writer Walker Percy, induced Louisiana State University Press to accept it. Percy wryly recalls: 'While I was teaching at Loyola in 1976 I began to get telephone calls from a lady unknown to me. What she proposed was preposterous ... her son, who was dead, had written an entire novel during the early sixties, a big novel, and she wanted me to read it. Why would I want to do that? I asked her. Because it is a great novel, she said ... if ever there was something I didn't want to do, this was surely it: to deal with the mother of a dead novelist ... I read on. And on. First with the sinking feeling that it was not bad enough to quit, then with a prickle of interest, then a growing excitement, and finally an incredulity: surely it was not possible that it was so good.' The narrative – unsurprisingly perhaps – centred on a gloopy young man's relationship with his domineering mother in steamy New Orleans. *A Confederacy of Dunces* was duly published, won a posthumous Pulitzer Prize in 1981, became an instant bestseller and a work of cult fiction to rival *Catcher in the Rye*.

Reportedly, Toole's literary remains comprised a carbon of the rejected *A Confederacy of Dunces* and the finished manuscript of another novella called *The Neon Bible* (1989). He had allegedly written it for a literary competition when he was sixteen, just after going up to Tulane University. Apparently Mrs Toole knew nothing about this other work until well after her son's death. It would have seemed logical to publish *The Neon Bible* in the immediate uprush of Toole's posthumous fame, in the early 1980s. But there were difficulties, most of them originating with the author's mother. Since he had died intestate, Louisiana law made all Toole's relatives on his father's side co-owners of his estate. Thelma Toole – who evidently despised her dead husband's family as 'shanty Irish' – had persuaded them to waive their rights in *A Confederacy of Dunces*, but they were not inclined to part with their shares of *The Neon Bible*.

There was also the complication that Mrs Toole had early on given the manuscript to another publisher, Rhoda Faust, with verbal permission (as Ms Faust claimed) to publish the work – and Faust was disinclined to surrender the property. There followed a complicated series of lawsuits during the course of which – in 1984 – Mrs Toole died. In her will, she nominated Kenneth Holditch as trustee for *The Neon Bible* and left instructions that he was to prevent publication in perpetuity. Mrs Toole's resentment at her relatives and Ms Faust now exceeded her desire to get her son's work in print. Having fought like a lioness to have him published, she now fought even from beyond the grave to have him suppressed. A reluctant Holditch followed her instructions until the courts finally overruled him in 1987. Thus it is that – literally over Mrs Toole's dead body – posterity had *The Neon Bible*. It is certainly worth having – not least for the biographical light it throws on this strangest of novelists.

The story covers a period from around 1937 to 1953 and is set in rural Mississippi, a landscape of baked clay and shacks with cinder yards. David, the hero-narrator, grows up an only child in redneck poverty. His shiftless father drifts from job to job, beats his wife and lets David get beaten up by young thugs his own age. The family are ostracised by respectable townspeople, because they cannot afford to pay church dues. Eventually the father dies, a GI in Italy. His survivors do not much care. David gets love only from his eccentric Aunt Mae, a sixty-year-old floozy, but she resurrects her show-business career for the duration and goes off to Nashville, leaving the boy wholly friendless. David's world is one of mysterious violence, utter solitude and a rock-hard Southern Baptist Church, whose neon sign on Main Street (a garishly coloured page of the Bible) threatens his eventual damnation.

The personality that comes through the story is repulsive. At sixteen, David proposes marriage to the only girl he has ever dated. By way of reply she screams, claws his face and runs away, her hair flying. The novel ends with much blood and some spectacular violence against mothers, all of it filtered through David's anaesthetised gaze and precocious schoolboy prose. The power of *The Neon Bible* resides in its descriptions of the small town where David's childhood is unspent. But, as the reader admires Toole's writing, questions form. Was he really only sixteen when he wrote it? Did he perhaps revise or wholly rewrite the text at a later time? There are tantalising gaps in the record – about, for example, the mysterious writing competition in 1953.

The Neon Bible begins and ends with a train journey which strongly recalls Chapter Eight of *The Catcher in the Rye*. Salinger's novel came out in 1951. Was the fourteen-year-old Toole one of the original readers of the hardback or did he – like most of his generation – encounter Holden Caulfield in paperback later in the decade? Thelma Toole was fanatical on the subject of her son's genius. As the work of a young man, *The Neon Bible* is interesting but nothing very wonderful. As the work of a boy, it is prodigious. One would, however, like clinching proof that it is a boy's novel. No one is now going to forget John Kennedy Toole; his mother can rest in peace on that score. He is a legendary figure – a Louisiana Rimbaud.

FN   John Kennedy Toole
MRT   *A Confederacy of Dunces*
Biog   R. P. Nevils, D. G. Hardy, *Ignatius Rising* (2001)

273. Margaret Atwood 1939–

They [Americans] had a vague idea that such a place existed – it was that blank area north of the map where the bad weather came from.

Atwood was born in Ottawa, the middle child of three. Her father, Carl, was a forest entomologist and his field work meant a nomadic childhood for Margaret, much of it spent 'roughing it' in the Canadian wilderness. She was largely (and efficiently) home-schooled by her mother, a former dietician. Both parents came from Nova Scotia, 'a province from which they felt themselves in exile all their lives'. Atwood's life settled somewhat when her father took a university job in Toronto – but not happily. 'I was now faced with real life,' she recalled, 'in the form of other little girls – their prudery and snobbery, their Byzantine social life based on whispering and vicious gossip.' As novelists do, she took her revenge cold – but razor-sharp – in her seventh novel, *Cat's Eye* (1988). The most autobiographical of her works, the novel ponders girl-on-girl sadism. The mid-career painter, Elaine, returns to Toronto and finds herself in 'two places at once': her schooldays and her current artistic success. How are they connected?

A remarkably clever pupil (something that may have made her even less loved by schoolmates), Atwood went on to read English at Toronto University – then, under the domination of proto-theorist Northrop Frye, one of the most distinguished departments in North America. Throughout her growing up, there was 'the sub-layer of fear'. Canada, being where it was on the USSR doorstep, would be the first to go in the coming Armageddon. She graduated in 1961 and progressed, via Radcliffe College, to Harvard. An academic career was in prospect, but Atwood decided to discontinue her research. She felt, she later said, like 'a little wart or wen on the great academic skin', and she wanted more than wartiness. Writing about writing was futile.' Writing itself wasn't futile – she was already a prize-winning poet. None the less, for the next few years she supported herself by teaching jobs. Lacking the necessary Ph.D., they were necessarily 'low on the totem pole'. Women had more difficulty scaling that pole even with a doctorate. In her own time she was writing – principally poetry, although some of her later fiction was drafted in this turbulent decade.

Her first novel, *The Edible Woman*, was published in 1969. It partook of the sixties' turbulence. Its connection with the emergent woman's movement, and the doctrinal text, Betty Friedan's *The Feminine Mystique*, is readily observed. In the UK, she was taken up by Carmen Callil for her combative Virago imprint. *The Edible Woman* pivots on a symbolic moment – the serving and consumption of a wife-baked cake, in the shape of the baking wife. Atwood's own marital life was in transitional change at the time. In 1968 she had married Jim Polk, a fellow postgraduate at Harvard. They drifted apart after a year (1970) in Europe and divorced in 1973. Atwood had for some time been associated with the Anansi Press in Toronto, set up in 1967 on a policy of 'Canada First'. After her divorce she set up home with fellow Anansi novelist Graeme Gibson, whom she has not married. The couple farmed for a few years and had a daughter in 1976. In 1980, partly for the sake of her daughter's education, partly for a career which was taking off, Atwood and Gibson returned to Toronto.

Now a committed writer of fiction, Atwood was feeling her way through a variety of genres. *Lady Oracle* (1976) explored high Gothic, which Atwood sees as 'very much a woman's form', adding the savage parenthesis: 'Why is there such a wide readership for books that essentially say "your husband is trying to kill you"?' Gothic was not, however, the genre in which she would find international celebrity. That, paradoxically, was the traditionally masculinist preserve of science fiction (which, like Robert Heinlein, Atwood prefers to call 'speculative fiction'). *The Handmaid's Tale* (1985) swept the board of science fiction prizes. More significantly, it became a hugely prescribed text (replacing Huxley's *Brave New World*) in schools across the English-speaking world, which wanted to sugar-coat class discussions of feminism.

She had been inspired to write *The Handmaid's Tale* by a newspaper story that pollution in drinking water was radically diminishing male sperm count and by the rise of evangelism in the US. The novel fantasises a male-totalitarian tyranny in which the US, now the Republic of Gilead, has reverted to neo-Puritan oppression of women (and, to a lesser extent, Blacks and Jews). In the face of calamitously declining fertility, those few women who can reproduce ('Handmaids') are kept like brood mares, for the use of powerful men and their infertile mates. The story, framed in a historically distant academic conference on Gilead, follows the fortunes of Offred (i.e. 'property of Fred'), a rebellious Handmaid. In the novel, her final fate is uncertain. In the film made of the novel, scripted by Harold Pinter, she finds refuge in the North American wilderness. For all its narrative brilliance, *The Handmaid's Tale* faces the inevitable criticism of such apocalyptic prophecy – it didn't happen, and probably won't. Put another way, 1984 wasn't, as it turned out, at all like *Nineteen Eighty-four*. A quarter of a century on, under-population and Christian radicalism are not our direst threats, although they may have been so conceived when she wrote the novel. In her dystopian follow-up, *Oryx and Crake* (2003), Atwood switched her Cassandraism to genetic engineering and the scientific violation of nature.

Living up to a work as successful as *The Handmaid's Tale* was tricky, but the artistically restless Atwood declined to stay in any one groove, finding multiple generic outlets for her underlying ideological commitments. Her Canadian historical novel, *Alias Grace* (1996) – see the entry on Moodie below – won the Booker, for which she has had a record number of nominations. In *The Penelopiad* (2005) she rewrites the Odyssey from the point of view of Penelope and the handmaidens that Ulysses and Telemachus slaughter as part of the cleaning up of the court at Ithaca. Atwood has said on many occasions that fiction must matter. She is that nineteenth-century thing, a 'novelist with a purpose'. Her great achievement is to have balanced what would seem irreconcilable purposes. In her early fiction it was the nationalism of 'Canadian Writing' against the supranational woman's movement (put as a conundrum, does Atwood have more in common with her fellow Canadian novelist, Graeme Gibson, than with Homer's Penelope?). In her manifesto non-fiction work, *Survival: A Thematic Guide to Canadian Literature* (1972), she identifies the prime ingredient of Canadianness to be 'wilderness' – a property of the world as much as of a country.

In her later career, a third, essentially international, commitment became prominent: namely environmentalism. Both Gibson and Atwood are active 'greens'. It is easy to see how this connects with wilderness, and with Atwood's own childhood when, as she says, the northern forests 'were my hometown'. It is less easy to find the connection with third-age feminism. Atwood's 2009 novel, produced after a tantalisingly long interval, *The Year of the Flood*, engages head-on with what she prophesies as planet-wide ecological catastrophe. A mysterious epidemic has wiped out most of the human race and multinational companies are destroying what is left. Hope resides in an Edenic sect, 'God's Gardeners', and their messiah, Adam One. The novel is said to have so infuriated the chair of the Man Booker judges that year that he threw it across his bedroom, denting the wall. It is, probably, a response that Atwood would have relished almost as much as the prize itself.

FN Margaret Eleanor Atwood (later Polk)

MRT *The Handmaid's Tale*

Biog N. Cooke, *Margaret Atwood: A Critical Companion* (2004)

POSTSCRIPT

274. Susanna Moodie 1803–1885

Your place is empty.

Margaret Atwood's *Alias Grace* (shortlisted for the 1996 Booker Prize) fictionalised an actual murder case she read about in Susanna Moodie's memoir, *Life in the Clearings versus the Bush* (1853). In it, Moodie records encountering the murderess, judged insane by the court, in her asylum:

> Among these raving maniacs I recognised the singular face of Grace Marks – no longer sad and despairing, but lighted up with the fire of insanity, and glowing with a hideous and fiend-like merriment. On perceiving that strangers were observing her, she fled shrieking away like a phantom into one of the side rooms. It appears that even in the wildest bursts of her terrible malady, she is continually haunted by a memory of the past. Unhappy girl! when will the long horror of her punishment and remorse be over? When will she sit at the feet of Jesus, clothed with the unsullied garments of his righteousness, the stain of blood washed from her hand, and her soul redeemed, and pardoned, and in her right mind?

It is hard to think that echoes of Bertha Mason, in *Jane Eyre*, are not reverberating in Moodie's mind. In line with the revisionary readings of Brontë's novel, following Susan Gubar and Sandra Gilbert's 1979 polemic, *The Madwoman in the Attic*, Atwood probes Marks's 'guilt' sceptically. Her more general interest in Moodie had been longstanding: one of her earliest published works was *The Journals of Susanna Moodie* (1970), poems written in the assumed voice and character of the Canadian pioneer. The poems follow the process by which Moodie became 'the spirit of the land she once hated'.

Susanna Strickland was not born Canadian. She was brought up in Suffolk, England, one of the five genteel daughters of a famous writing family – her sister, Agnes, published the bestselling *Lives of the Queens of England* (1840–48). The Stricklands suffered serious economic setbacks when Susanna was fifteen. She published her first novel, *Spartacus* (1822), before she was twenty (and wrote it, she claimed, aged thirteen). In 1831 she married Lieutenant John Wedderburn Dunbar Moodie (1797–1869), the traveller and adventurer. In a spirit of adventure, the newly married couple voyaged to Canada in 1832. Like others, they were seduced by immigrant pamphlets published by interested parties, which prominently set forth all the good to be derived from a settlement in the backwoods of Canada, 'while they carefully concealed the toil and hardship to be endured in order to secure these advantages … They talked of log houses to be raised in a single day, by the generous exertions of friends and neighbours, but they never ventured upon a picture of the disgusting scenes of riot and low debauchery exhibited during the raising, or upon a description of the dwellings when raised – dens of dirt and misery, which would, in many instances, be shamed by an English pig-sty.'

For a while the Moodies farmed. John later served in the Niagara militia and eventually became a sheriff in Ontario. But in 1852 the family fell on hard times, and to earn money, Susanna began publishing books, the most interesting of which recall her bleak pioneer experiences. The first of these, *Roughing it in the Bush* (1852), is now regarded as an early classic of Canadian literature. She also wrote some fifteen novels, of which the most interesting, *Mark Hurdlestone* (1853), is the story of a Jewish 'gold-worshipper' or miser, in which Moodie seems to be paying back the moneylenders who ruined her husband a few months earlier:

> There was not a drop of the milk of human kindness in his composition. Regardless of his own physical wants, he despised the same wants in others. Charity sued to him in vain, and the tear of sorrow made no impression on his stony heart. Passion he had felt – cruel, ungovernable passion. Tenderness was foreign to his nature – the sweet influences of the social virtues he had never known.

It would be interesting to know if George Eliot, the author of *Silas Marner*, had read *Mark Hurdlestone*.

Mysteriously, Moodie stopped writing fiction on her husband's death in 1869 and it is suggested he may have been the author, or co-author, of some of the works that bear her name.

FN   Susanna Moodie (née Strickland)
MRT *Mark Hurdlestone*
Biog C. Gray, *Sisters in the Wilderness: The Lives of Susanna Moodie and Catharine Parr Traill* (1999)

275. Jeffrey Archer 1940–

When I was three, I wanted to be four. When I was four, I wanted to be prime minister.

The details of Archer's early life have always been somewhat fuzzy. He was born in London on 15 April 1940, his father's occupation on the birth certificate being entered as 'journalist' (some accounts add 'bigamist'). Archer and his family moved from their North London boarding house to Weston-super-Mare in Somerset later in 1940, presumably to escape the Blitz. At this point, his father was known as 'Captain Archer', although not apparently a serving officer. He was considerably older than his wife and is recorded as dying in 1956. In 1951, young Archer went as a boarder to Wellington School, Somerset – not to be confused, although Archer is sometimes accused of making few attempts to prevent any confusion, with the more famous Wellington College. At school, he shone as a sportsman rather than a scholar and left without 'A' levels. In 1958 he enlisted as a regular soldier in the Duke of Wellington's Regiment but promptly bought himself out. In 1960, he joined the Metropolitan Police in London, but again resigned after a few weeks. The following year, Jeffrey Archer was appointed sports master and geography teacher at Dover College, the public school in Kent. According to some accounts, he may also at some time have been enrolled at the Royal Military Academy, Sandhurst, and at the University of California at Berkeley.

Archer was accepted, aged twenty-three, to study for a Postgraduate Diploma of Education (a one-year course) at Oxford University's Education department. At Oxford, he distinguished himself as an athlete, establishing a record for the 100-yard sprint. He was also active in charity work and recruited the Beatles to attend a banquet. Ringo Starr made the much-quoted comment, 'He's the kind of bloke who would bottle your piss and sell it for five pounds.' The amount, given Archer's selling skills, was an underestimate.

In 1966 he married Mary Weeden, a scientist (she it was, he once quipped, who helped translate his fiction into English; the same assistance has often been credited to Archer's editor, Richard Cohen), and the couple had two sons. Later, in the 1980s, the family took up residence at the Rectory, Grantchester, immortalised by the poet Rupert Brooke. Archer's interests had meanwhile taken a political turn. In 1969, after success as a GLC councillor, he won a by-election as Conservative Member for Louth in Lincolnshire by a large majority. At twenty-nine he was the youngest member of the House of Commons, as he has frequently reminded the world. In 1974, however, his apparently meteoric rise suffered a setback. A Canadian firm, Aquablast, in which he had invested £272,000 of borrowed money, collapsed. He was financially ruined and did not seek re-election at the next general election. Ever resilient (rubber is rock compared to Jeffrey Archer), he resolved to write a novel based on his downfall in the world of high finance. *Not a Penny More, Not a Penny Less* (1976) was a bestseller in Britain and did well in America too. He followed it, a year later, with *Shall We Tell the President?*, a political thriller set in the very near future, which fantasises an assassination attempt on 'President' Edward Kennedy. Viking Press (one of whose senior employees, Jacqueline Kennedy Onassis, was connected with the deal) paid £250,000 for the rights, but sales in America were anaemic. Kennedy Onassis resigned from Viking shortly after.

Archer's next novel, *Kane and Abel* (1980), was a more ambitious work, chronicling the feuds of two future magnates born on the same day in 1906: William Kane, a blue-blooded Boston banker, and Abel Rosnovski, a self-made Polish immigrant to America. It spawned an equally successful sequel, *The Prodigal Daughter* (1982), in which Rosnovksi's daughter becomes America's first woman President. *First Among Equals* (1984) returned to the English political scene and chronicles the story of four politicians competing to become Prime Minister. Like other of his novels, the work was adapted as a mini-series for British television. By now, Archer was, along with Len Deighton, Frederick Forsyth and Jack Higgins, one of the elite of Anglo-American bestselling novelists. His other career interests had equally prospered. He had paid off his debts by his pen and was once again a prosperous businessman.

Archer rose in the Conservative Party (although he never stood again as an MP) and in 1985 was appointed Deputy Chairman by Margaret Thatcher. In 1986, however, his career took another apparently catastrophic knock. Using a proxy, he arranged to pay a prostitute £2,000 to leave the country. The woman, Monica Coghlan, was in the pay of the *News of the World*. Archer resigned his political post but sued the *Daily Star* for libel, denying everything other than being harassed by Coghlan. In a sensational trial in 1987 – in which Mary Archer gave key evidence, and was famously complimented in his summing up by the judge on her 'fragrance' – he was awarded £500,000 in damages by the jury for the libel on his character. In 1990 the vindicated Archer signed a three-book contract with HarperCollins which – at a reported $20 million – made him the highest paid novelist in the world (though the scale of the publisher's payment has never been confirmed, and may have been exaggerated). *As the Crow Flies* (1991) is another rags-to-riches fable, telling the story of Charlie Trumper's rise from the East End of London and a costermonger background to immense wealth as the owner of London's greatest department store – an establishment rather like Harrods.

In 1992, after having been previously rejected, he was made a life peer as Baron

Archer of Weston-super-Mare, of Mark in the County of Somerset, by the Queen on the advice of the Prime Minister, John Major. Two years later, Archer was again touched by scandal, with (unproven) allegations of insider dealings through his wife's position on the board of Anglia TV. His much-hyped 1996 novel, *The Fourth Estate*, in many judgements his best, was based on the rise and fall of newspaper tycoon Robert Maxwell. Thirteen years after the first Coghlan trial, in October 1999, Ted Francis contacted the publicist Max Clifford to reveal that the alibi he had then provided for Archer was false. The *News of the World*, still stinging, set up a telephone conversation between the men which confirmed Francis's revised version. At the time, Archer was a front-runner for the Mayor of London election (subsequently won by Ken Livingstone) and had published a novel – *The Eleventh Commandment* (1998) – cheekily predicting his success.

On 20 November 1999 he withdrew from the mayoral race, and was expelled, prejudicially, from the Conservative Party in February 2000. After a second sensational trial in 2001, he was sentenced to four years' imprisonment for perjury, on 19 July. He wrote a Dantean trilogy recounting his time inside: *A Prison Diary, Vol. I: Hell – Belmarsh* (2002), *Vol. II: Purgatory – Wayland* (2003), *Vol. III: Heaven – North Sea Camp* (2004). They are regarded by discerning critics as perhaps his finest work of fiction.

FN   Jeffrey Howard Archer (Baron Archer of Weston-super-Mare)
MRT   *The Fourth Estate*
Biog   M. Crick, *Jeffrey Archer: Stranger than Fiction* (1995)

276. J. M. Coetzee 1940–

Autre-biography

I was a judge in 1999 when J. M. Coetzee won his second Booker prize, for *Disgrace*. He didn't turn up to collect his prize, any more than he had when he won his first in 1983 for the *Life & Times of Michael K*. The photographers were obliged, yet again, to take a picture of a copy of the novel in an empty chair. The gesture spoke volumes. Keep your distance, it said. You may read my novels but don't think you have any right to *judge* them. More importantly, don't think you have any right to *know* me. It's odd, then, that this excessively private man should be so forthcoming in the 'fictionalised memoir' sequence, *Scenes from Provincial Life*, of which the third part, *Summertime*, was published in summer 2009 (it was shortlisted, inevitably, but there was not a hope in hell that the Booker people were going to allow a third empty chair). The trilogy began with *Boyhood* (1997), covering the then unnamed protagonist's upbringing in South Africa. It continued with *Youth* (2002), which followed the still unnamed character in his years of exile in London. Both books conformed exactly to the known facts of Coetzee's own career.

Born English-speaking Afrikaaner, with a dash of Slav, in Cape Town, Coetzee had an unsettled childhood in an unsettled country. Apartheid separated the races and, globally, South Africa itself from the 'family of nations'. John Coetzee graduated from university with honours in English and Maths – a typical disjunction, in a life disjoined to the point of continuous fracture. In the 1960s, with national service in prospect, he left for England, where he was one of the first generation of computer programmers with IBM. London did not swing for J. M. Coetzee. He married in 1963, separated, and divorced in 1980. He did a second degree with a thesis on Ford Madox Ford.

Following this second career line, he went to the University of Texas at Austin on a Fulbright scholarship. Combining algorithms and minimalism, he did a Ph.D. on computer analysis of the style of Samuel Beckett (is silence digitisable?). It was pioneer scholarship. Coetzee went on to teach in the American university system and a promising academic career was in prospect. It was at this period, and in America, that Coetzee began writing fiction. He applied to naturalise in the US, but was turned down on the grounds that he had taken part in anti-Vietnam protests – notably an occupation of his university administrative offices, for which he was arrested and charged with criminal trespass. Nomadic again, Coetzee returned to South Africa where he taught at the University of Cape Town. He rose through the academic ranks, writing, on the side, increasingly admired fiction until his retirement in 2002. In the same year he emigrated to Australia, where he took up a senior position in the University of Adelaide, and in 2003 he was awarded the Nobel Prize in Literature, which he did collect in person. But he insists that for him all such laurels are withered garlands: 'In its conception the literature prize belongs to days when a writer could still be thought of as, by virtue of his or her occupation, a sage, someone with no institutional affiliations who could offer an authoritative word on our times as well as on our moral life.' He became an Australian citizen in 2006.

With the third volume of Coetzee's fictional memoir, the narrative became overtly autobiographical. The protagonist was finally given a name 'John Coetzee' – alias Yours Truly. *Summertime*'s narrative leap-frogs over what was the most dramatic period of Coetzee's life – his years in America. As it opens, the hero has recently returned – deported and in disgrace (the perennial Coetzee theme) – to live, grumpily, with his father in a South Africa which is falling apart; it is not a happy domestic arrangement. 'Fathers and sons', John says, 'should never live in the same house.' Nor, one apprehends, should different races live in the same country. John Coetzee does manual work – something whites in the early 1970s would never deign to do. Why else had God invented blacks? He picks up an extra pittance tutoring – wasting his scholarly abilities (no honourable senior position in the ivory tower for this Coetzee), but in this trough of his life 'John' – as did 'J.M.' – publishes his first novel, *Dusklands* (1974). Literature doesn't always come from happy places.

So far so parallel, with the odd fictional swerve. But at this point autobiography melts – perplexingly – into fiction. 'John Coetzee', we gather, later emigrated to Australia (as did 'J.M.' in 2002), but died there in 2006 (when, in point of biographical fact, 'J.M.' became an Australian citizen). His posthumous biography is now being written by a shadowy Boswell called 'Vincent'. Vincent, an extremely dull fellow, we gather, is interested solely in the years in Coetzee's life in the early 1970s. He has some uninformative notebooks and the testimony of former lovers, colleagues and a cousin – they give very little away. So is the dead 'John Coetzee' to be taken as the live 'J. M. Coetzee'? Experienced novel-readers will be wary of this 'catch me if you can' trick. Young James Ballard, for example, in J. G. Ballard's novel (so categorised) *Empire of the Sun*, has experiences strikingly similar to those of the young James Ballard, when his family was interned in the war by the Japanese. But the hero 'James Ballard' in J. G. Ballard's novel (so categorised) *Crash* is nothing like J. G. Ballard. He wasn't meant to be. Ballard explained what he was doing in *Crash* in a 1995 preface to the novel: 'I feel that the balance between fiction and reality has changed significantly in the past decades. Increasingly their roles are reversed. We live in a world ruled by fictions of every kind – mass merchandising, advertising ... the pre-empting of any original response to experience by the television screen. We live inside an enormous novel.'

The author obtruding 'himself' into the fictional action, like Alfred Hitchcock's hallmark cameos in his movies, is no new device. If you go back to one of the fathers of the English novel, Tobias Smollett, one discovers him doing it. Christopher Isherwood ('Herr Issyvoo') also did it in *Goodbye to Berlin*. Philip Roth began introducing a whole regiment of para-Philip Roths into his fiction with *Deception* (aptly named). Is 'Jeanette' in *Oranges Are Not the Only Fruit* Jeanette Winterson? Is 'W.G. Sebald' (the inverted commas are meaningful), the narrator-wanderer in *The Rings of Saturn*, ruminating about life as he ambles around East Anglia, Max Sebald? You shouldn't do this kind of thing, protested Kingsley Amis, when young Martin went ahead and did it by introducing 'Martin Amis' into *Self*, 'it's breaking the rules', 'buggering about with the reader'. But who says novels have rules? It's not association football.

Assuming that *Summertime* is a bona fide self-portrait, it's the least flattering since Dorian Gray's. 'John Coetzee', his near and dear ones grimly recall after his 'death', was 'scrawny', 'seedy' and exuded 'an air of failure'. He 'had no sexual presence whatsoever, as though he had been sprayed from head to toe with a neutralising spray'. His 'teeth are in bad shape'. He is 'sexless'. Intercourse with him, reports one disgusted lover, 'lacked all thrill'. His cousin (with whom he has an arid fling in a broken-down pick-up truck) calls him 'slap gat' – an Afrikaans word for a loose anus (Americans have a homelier phrase). Another lover comes as near as dammit to accusing him of an unhealthily paedophiliac interest in young girls. Above all, John Coetzee has no faith in his art. 'Why', he asks himself, 'does he persist in inscribing marks on paper, in the faint hope that people not yet born will take the trouble to decipher them?' No answer is given.

But, to return to the question, is this sad apology for a man and a novelist 'J. M. Coetzee'? Reviewing Philip Roth's novel, *Operation Shylock: A Confession* (1993) – in which the principal character is 'Philip Roth' – Coetzee observed, in the course of an extremely subtle analysis, 'We are in the sphere of the Cretan Liar' (i.e. 'everything I say is a lie, including this'). *Summertime*, one suspects, is in the same riddlingly Cretan sphere.

'Autre-biography', as what Coetzee does has been called, is a bent genre in which, like alloy, the elements of personal biography and impersonal fiction are so artfully intermingled that they defy disentangling. Is it a dead end, or one of the new mansions in James's House of Fiction? An interesting dead end, in my view, but one should never underestimate novelists' ingenuity in escaping the traps they set themselves. Like the magician, their next trick is always impossible.

FN   J. M. Coetzee (John Maxwell Coetzee)
MRT   *Summertime*
Biog   D. Attwell, *J. M. Coetzee: South Africa and the Politics of Writing* (1993)

POSTSCRIPT

277. Bret Easton Ellis 1964–

I could never be as honest about myself in a piece of non-fiction as I could in any of my novels.

As novelists insert versions of themselves and the events of their lives more and more into the pages of their fiction, the boundaries between truth and make-believe, fiction and biography, blur. No writer has taken the blur of autre-biography to a blurrier extreme than Bret Easton Ellis in *Lunar Park* (2005) and its successor, *Imperial Bedrooms* (2010). *Lunar Park* is supposedly named after the place where the main action happens. There is – I've checked – no town of that name in New York State, any more than there is a Stepford in Connecticut, or an Ambridge in Borsetshire. The hero-narrator of *Lunar Park* is 'Bret Easton Ellis': a real person of that same name wrote the novel set in the fictional place. In a long authorial preface to *Lunar Park*, Bret (let's say 'Bret') confesses to gargantuan excess after the runaway success of his precociously early super-sellers, *Less than Zero* and *American Psycho*, had shot him to bestsellerdom, millionairedom and the ranks of front-page celebrity as the brattiest leader of fiction's brat-pack.

So far, so true. The young 'Bret' embarks on a bender of conspicuous consumption, fashion trashing, and self-indulgence:

> I was doing Ray-Ban ads at twenty-two. I was posing for the covers of English magazines on a tennis court, on a throne, on the deck of my condo in a purple robe. I threw lavish catered parties – sometimes complete with strippers – in my condo on a whim ('Because it's Thursday!' one invitation read). I crashed a borrowed Ferrari in Southampton and its owner just smiled (for some reason I was naked). I attended three fairly exclusive orgies ... I dined at the White House in the summer of 1986, the guest of Jeb and George W. Bush, both of whom were fans.

The Bushes are real (too real for some) but I doubt that they were ever fans of *Less than Zero* – even in the hot days of their youth. And if the Bush boys were fans of Ellis's 'black candy', it was very wise to keep it secret from the religious right, which voted one brother into presidency and the other into governorship of the conservative state of Florida.

Briefly for 'Bret', as chronicled in *Lunar Park*, it was 'top of the world, ma!' But, inevitably, under the glare and temptations of celebrity, he took to heroin, cocaine and vile sexual practices and ended up lying in a squalid hotel bedroom for seven days 'watching porn DVDs with the sound off and snorting maybe 40 bags of heroin, a blue plastic bucket that I vomited in continually by my bed'. His descent to the blue bucket was, 'Bret' divulges, fuelled by the death in August 1992 of his father, Robert Martin Ellis, a couple of months after the publication of *American Psycho*. The portrait of Ellis Sr offered in *Lunar Park* is one that most sons would keep in the attic. He was a real-estate crook, and 'careless, abusive, alcoholic, vain, angry, paranoid'. Chapter and verse is supplied for these paternal shortcomings. Bret's dad was, apparently, the inspiration for Patrick Bateman, the sociopath hero of *American Psycho*. In *Lunar Park*, Mr Ellis Sr's dead body 'was found naked by the

22-year-old girlfriend on the bathroom floor of his empty house in Newport Beach'. He left, among many squandered millions, a wardrobe of over-sized Armani suits. When 'Bret' (who, like Bateman, is partial to Armani) took the clothes to the tailor to be altered, he recounts: 'I was revolted to discover that most of the inseams in the crotch were stained with blood, which we later found out was the result of a botched penile implant he underwent in Minneapolis.'

Robert Martin Ellis was, so to speak, real. He was, I have read, a realtor. He did indeed die in August 1992 and *Lunar Park* is dedicated to his memory. Whether it was with a surgically enhanced penis that he went to the crematorium fire, or the unsullied member with which he engendered young Bret, literary history may never know. 'Bret Easton Ellis' – he of the novel – suspects that Robby, his love child by the woman who later became his wife, Jayne Dennis, was engendered by Keanu Reeves, 'who had been a friend of mine when he was initially cast in *Less than Zero*, [before being] replaced by Andrew McCarthy'. So suspicious was 'Bret' of the actor that he launched a paternity case in which his lawyer asserted in court that Dennis's child 'bears a striking resemblance to a certain Mr Keanu Reeves'. Litigation was subsequently dropped, 'Bret' and Dennis were reconciled, married, and went to live in Lunar Park with Robby and a daughter born in wedlock. Reeves is, so to speak, real – although, as one reads *Lunar Park*, the idea of what is or isn't real gets as hard to hold as a wet bar of soap. The real Reeves enjoys, one understands, cordial relations with the real Ellis. Before becoming a superstar Reeves was, initially, cast as the lead in *Less than Zero* and replaced by the equally real Andrew McCarthy. Jayne Dennis (although she had a website around the time of *Lunar Park*'s publication) is not real; nor is the dubiously sired Robby Ellis. They are figments of the fictional *Lunar Park*. Ellis is not married and has no child. In August 2009 he told the *New York Times* that he was bisexual, and that his best friend and lover for six years, Michael Wade Kaplan, had died in January 2004, aged thirty. That is not the history of 'Bret' in *Lunar Park*.

The main narrative of *Lunar Park* chronicles the disintegration of the Ellis–Dennis marriage. Patrick Bateman, the murderous, paternally inspired, serial killer of *American Psycho*, comes to life off the page and haunts his creator – a lunatic. Bateman is not real, while his author is – but perhaps not entirely, in *Lunar Park*. Ellis's epigraph to *Lunar Park* explains what he is doing. Celebrity – such as he has been exposed to – means that the traditional aesthetic categories of subject and object dissolve into one thing: 'image'. Images can be real, as in a mirror, or chimerical, as in a drug-induced hallucination. But images are all that there is. 'The occupational hazard of making a spectacle of yourself, over the long haul,' Ellis says, 'is that at some point you buy a ticket too.' If, that is, you live inside enormous celebrity, you become the spectator of your own spectacle and indivisible from it. Or, as the pungent idiom puts it, you start believing your own shit, and living it.

Ellis goes further into the autre-biographical maze in his 2010 novel, *Imperial Bedrooms*. The narrative picks up from Ellis's first published novel, the hugely successful *Less than Zero* (that novel and *Imperial Bedrooms* both take their titles from Elvis Costello songs – trendier, perhaps, in 1985 than 2010). The sequel opens, twenty-five years later, with the hero, Clay, ruminating about what the 'author' (i.e. Bret Easton Ellis) did to 'us' in the earlier novel and what the movie industry (*Less than Zero* was filmed in 1987) had done to 'us' in its adaptation of Ellis's novel:

> They had made a movie about us. The movie was based on a book written by someone we knew. The book was a simple thing about four weeks in the city we grew up in and for the most part was an accurate portrayal. It was labeled fiction but only a few details had been altered and our names weren't changed and there was nothing in it that hadn't happened. For example, there actually had been a screening of a snuff film in that bedroom in Malibu on a January afternoon, and yes, I had walked out onto the deck overlooking the Pacific where the author tried to console me, assuring me that the screams of the children being tortured were faked, but he was smiling as he said this and I had to turn away.

As it goes on, *Imperial Bedrooms* emerges as what, in the 'decadent' 1890s, would have been called an *étude* – a study of prodigiously moneyed, modish and privileged *ennui*. It is not, one may be confident, a factually reliable portrait of the author as a no longer young man.

Despite the ostentatious self-display and plays with his name in his fiction Ellis is a secretive man. One's expectation is that posterity will – once Henry James's posthumous exploiters get to work – have a more trustworthy sense of who Bret Easton Ellis actually is than his current readers do. Until then we must be content to be merely dazzled at the self-images he throws up.

FN   Bret Easton Ellis

MRT *Lunar Park*

Biog not an exit. A 'celebrity website', notanexit.net, has up-to-date gossip on Ellis.

278. Michael Crichton 1942–2008

It would be a refreshing change to write something where I'm not attacked.
Michael Crichton, 1994, after the furore about the 'anti-scientific' bias of *Jurassic Park*

All that California has given the world, Woody Allen bitterly jested, is right on red. For a generation of thoughtful popular novelists and film-makers, it has in fact given the world something else – the theme park. It was the annual trip to Disneyland and 'Autopolis' that inspired young George Lucas – *Star Wars* was born on that excited little boy's ride. Ira Levin's *The Stepford Wives* is a riff on the 'animatronics' of the 'Pirates of the Caribbean' ride at Anaheim. As, of course, is *Pirates of the Caribbean*, the movie. Michael Crichton saw the Californian theme park as the material embodiment of the Great American Dream – cross-hatched with nightmare. His miniature masterpiece, *Westworld* (1973), a film over which he had total artistic control, fantasises a theme park which takes over the world that made the theme park: which (in the brooding inhumanity of Yul Brynner – inspiration for James Cameron's *Terminator*) unleashes not merely the joy, but the ineradicable violence in the American soul. The film *Jurassic Park* (1993) is bigger, but suffers from the statutory five lumps of Spielberg sugar added to its mordant, Crichtonian, mix. He was not, given his artistic freedom, a cheerful sage.

Crichton was – in intellectual pedigree if not artistic practice – one of the more academically distinguished novelists of the twentieth century. The son of a Chicago journalist (sometimes described as a 'corporate president'), whom he later called in print, somewhat paradoxically, 'a first-rate son of a bitch' and child-beater, Michael seems to have had an unhappy but materially comfortable childhood. Whatever the misery he endured, young Michael was precociously clever: he had a column published in the travel section of the *New York Times* at the age of fourteen. Other glittering prizes followed. He graduated from Harvard *summa cum laude*, Phi Beta Kappa, with a degree in natural sciences. He went on to do research at Cambridge University in anthropology. He eventually took an MD from his alma mater and did post-doctoral work at the Jonas Salk Institute in California. He could have spent the rest of his life publishing in learned journals like *Materia Medica*.

As resourceful young Americans of that time did, Crichton had worked his way through college but, unlike other young Americans, he did so by writing half a dozen works of popular fiction under the pen names 'John Lange' and 'Jeffrey Hudson'. They were slyly chosen. Jeffrey Hudson is history's most famous dwarf and '*lange*' is German for 'long'. Crichton stood 6 feet 9 inches in his socks. One of these 'tuition fee' novels, *A Case of Need* (1968), won the 1969 Edgar Allan Poe award and convinced Crichton that there were richer pickings at the typewriter than in the laboratory – particularly for a man who knew something about labs. A year later, in 1970, Crichton was the first SF novelist to make the *NYT* bestseller list with *The Andromeda Strain*. It centres on invasion, not by aliens (Crichton is on record as disbelieving in the existence of intelligent life elsewhere in the universe) but by a lethal micro-organism. The text is speckled with computer printouts, graphs, tables and pseudo-scientific bulletins. What *The Andromeda Strain* did, with its hi-sci-fi lingo, was to give the Great American Public a handle on the moonshots.

Crichton candidly admitted he had taken the idea of *The Andromeda Strain* from Arthur Conan Doyle's 'The Poison Belt' and the ultra-documentary style (including computer printouts and graphs) from Len Deighton's similarly encrusted *Ipcress File*. It was *Scientific American* made palatable for those who never made Engineering 101 and didn't know a neutrino from a neutered cat. Crichton was a great science teacher. You want to know what nanotechnology is? Forget Wikipedia; read *Prey* (2002). Ditto the Human Genome Map and *Next* (2006). Ditto *Timeline* (1999) and the 'worm holes' that physicists like Stephen Hawking theorise about. Ditto behavioural psychology and *The Terminal Man* (1972).

Posterity will inscribe various critical verdicts on Michael Crichton's tombstone. He was a Great Educator, via the sugar-coating of fiction. He was also a pig-headed contrarian: *Disclosure* (1994), based on the 'fact' that men are the luckless victims of sexual harassment, making up at least 25 per cent of such offences, is calculated to infuriate women. The dense accompanying information about the tricky manufacture of out-sourced computer hard disks does not mollify. His justification for writing *Disclosure* was that novels like his were the only place where the subject of reverse sexism could be ventilated. Fiction was outside 'the protected area … where things aren't debated or fully discussed'. It may also be that he was sore about alimony. One of his four divorces had recently cost him $20 million, almost a third of his annual income at that time. None the less he survived such dents to his ballooning fortune in good shape. The Jasper Johns he kept in his bedroom went for $29 million in May 2010, and his whole art collection for little under $100 million.

The least palatable of Crichton's works is *Rising Sun* (1992), a 'yellow peril' novel, permeated with racist stereotypes which fantasised a sneaky Japanese corporate takeover of America – Pearl Harbor via the country's boardrooms. It coincided with the collapse of the Japanese economy and Tokyo's postponement of world domination for at least a few more years. Crichton's touch failed even more spectacularly in 1980 with *Congo* (super-gorillas), the film of which regularly does well in polls of all-time turkeys. Most cross-grained of the Crichton oeuvre was *State of Fear* (2004) with its thesis that global warming is nothing but a big scam by scientists hungry for research grants and that 'environmentalism' is a religion – unworthy of scientific respect. It became a favourite novel of George W. Bush, and Crichton was called to give evidence on climate change to Congress. That a mere novelist should be so listened to infuriated the senior environmentalist in the US, Al Gore, who, when his turn came, told Congress: 'If your baby has a fever, you go to the doctor. If the doctor says, "You have to intervene here," you don't say, "Well, I read a science fiction novel that says this isn't important."' When he wrote *State of Fear*, Crichton (always very secretive about his personal life) may well have been in the early throes of the throat cancer which would prematurely kill him. Ironically, he believed, despite his impressive medical qualifications, that such ailments were typically psychosomatic in origin – the body's fictions.

FN   John Michael Crichton
MRT   *The Andromeda Strain*
Biog   www.michaelcrichton.net

279. Peter Carey 1943–

Well, we're the only country on earth, as far as I know, that has its beginnings in a concentration camp, a penal colony. And a genocide, too. That affected us forever.

Peter Carey was born in the delightfully named township of Bacchus Marsh in Victoria, Australia. He offers a thumbnail description of the place in one of the more perversely autobiographical of his novels, *Theft: A Love Story* (2006): 'We were born and bred in Bacchus Marsh, thirty-three miles west of Melbourne, down Anthony's Cutting. If you are expecting a bog or marsh, there is none, it is just a way of speaking.' Distinctive 'ways of speaking' are a central element in Carey's fictional method – as is the misleadingness of words, particularly Australian words. His father was in the motor trade and had the prosperous General Motors franchise. At eleven Peter was packed off to board at Geelong Grammar School (annual fee, £600), an institution which claims among its alumni Rupert Murdoch and Prince Charles. Neither of them coincided with young Carey's six years there. Those school chums would have been the making of an interesting novel.

The route to the worldwide fame Carey now enjoys was indirect. He attended Monash University in Melbourne and did a year's science before dropping out in 1962. The given reasons are vague. A car crash is mentioned, as is disaffection with chemistry. And, in that hectic decade, dropping out was a rite of passage. Australia's business world was meanwhile booming and Carey found remunerative freelance employment in advertising agencies in Melbourne and Sydney, reading modern fiction all the while. Pioneer fabulists such as Borges and Kafka were of particular interest to him, although he records that it was reading Faulkner's *As I Lay Dying* which was primal. In his spare time he wrote himself and had the odd piece picked up by little magazines. His day job took him across the country and abroad and, although as yet unpublished (his first four submitted novels were either rejected by publishers or withdrawn), his abilities were noted by fellow writers. He was 'driven' by the desire for literary success. One of his three wives accuses him of being willing to sacrifice everything for it – including wives. This latency period of his creative life lasted for thirteen years.

Carey married his first wife, Leigh Weetman, in 1964. Breaking with his habitual pattern of personal reticence in 1995, he published a piece in the *New Yorker* describing a premarital abortion procured with a borrowed £50 (the operation was criminal in 1961). At the age of thirty-one, he finally made it into hard covers with *The Fat Man in History* (1974). This first collection of stories has two singular features: most striking is political indignation. There was, as it happens, rage among Carey's age group at this period when, as a signatory to the SEATO agreement, Australia had been dragged as a combatant into Vietnam. In one of the stories in *The Fat Man in History*, 'A Windmill in the West', Australia is allegorically pictured as split down the middle by an electric fence. On one side of the fence is US territory; on the other side is a vast theme-park-cum-concentration-camp for the delectation of dumb American tourists. As a character says, 'The Americans pay one dollar for the right to take our photographs. Having paid the money they are worried about being cheated.' Radical protest of the late 1960s to early 1970s remained a topic of interest to Carey. In one of his later novels, *His Illegal Self* (2008), he would revisit it at mature length.

The Fat Man in History enjoyed critical and sales success and this relates to its other salient feature. It was not published by any of the commercial Australian, or international, houses, but by the University of Queensland Press. Even after he became a highly profitable author, Carey remained loyal to the small academic outfit which had taken a chance with him. *Oscar and Lucinda*, winner of the 1988 Booker Prize, is to date the only winner with a university imprint. Carey's loyalty enabled UQP to expand its scholarly publications significantly. However, *The Fat Man in History* and its following collection did not immediately liberate Carey into full-time authorship. He continued to work part-time in advertising, in which he now enjoyed executive positions. He was good at it. During increasingly lengthy breaks, he worked furiously on his writing – always more important to him. His first full-length fiction, *Bliss* (1981), is the story of an advertising man, Harry Joy. Extravagantly fabulist in technique, it follows Harry's death and unjoyous resurrection from hell to a more hellish earth than the one he left. *Bliss* won the Miles Franklin Award and virtually every other prize for which Australian novelists are eligible, including one for science fiction. The film rights sold and a film was made, but it was not everywhere successful. A child incest episode, central to the narrative, raised hackles.

The Careys divorced in 1974. For a few years after, he lived with the painter Margot Hutcheson – and took from the relationship an expertise on pictorial art which enriches his later fiction, notably *Theft*. In the mid1970s he was commuting to his advertising work from a bohemian commune base in Queensland. Writing was now preoccupying him more than copy-writing. The decade 1981 to 1991 saw an explosive burst of creativity. After *Bliss* came *Illywhacker* (1985). A version of Thomas Mann's Felix Krull, the 'Confidence Man', the 139-year-old hero is the incarnation of Australia. The novel aligns itself with other powerfully introspective books on the topic of the country's 1988 bicentenary celebrations – Thomas Keneally's *The Playmaker* (1987) and Robert Hughes's (non-fiction) *The Fatal Shore* (1988). Like those books, *Illywhacker* asked perplexing questions rather than firing off metaphorical rockets outside the Sydney Opera House.

Illywhacker was followed by the Booker-winning *Oscar and Lucinda* (1988), a work distantly allusive to Edmund Gosse's memoir *Father and Son* (1907) and more closely allusive to Werner Herzog's 1972 film, *Aguirre, the Wrath of God* (Carey admires German film-makers and later collaborated with Wim Wenders). This reputation-building phase culminated with *The Tax Inspector* (1991) – interesting biographically for its recollection of the car-dealership world in which the author passed his early childhood. This corpus established Carey as one of Australia's elite novelists – along with the venerable Patrick White, the infuriatingly slow-producing Murray Bail, and Thomas Keneally (a writer, like Carey, taken with the 'concentration camp' origins of his country and even more fiercely republican). What was singular about Carey was how different each of his novels was from all the others in subject matter and preoccupation. He is, in a word, restless.

Restless in every sense. In 1990 his career took a violent swerve. He sold off the advertising firm he part-owned and moved to New York. Here he could write full-time – interspersed with creative writing posts in top-ranked universities. He had by this point (1985) married his second wife, the theatre director Alison Summers, and now had a family. Resident in the US (something which caused occasional chauvinistic grumbles in the home country press), his fictional territory remained Australian and it was in his early New York period that he produced *Jack Maggs* (1997), the most inter-textually subtle of his works. A fantasia based on Dickens's *Great Expectations*, it reconstructs the unwritten novel around Magwitch, the transported criminal who, a convict in Australia, supplies Pip's gentlemanly expectations. *Jack Maggs* is resonant, but not congruent with, *Great Expectations*. It is an unsettling effect frequently encountered in Carey's narratives – not that he doesn't write with crystalline simplicity, as in the vivid opening sentences. All those years of copywriting had convinced Carey you need to hook the reader from the first syllable:

> It was a Saturday night when the man with the red waistcoat arrived in London. It was, to be precise, six of the clock on the fifteenth of April in the year of 1837 that those hooded eyes looked out the window of the Dover coach and beheld, in the bright aura of gas light, a golden bull and an overgrown mouth opening to devour him – the sign of his inn, the Golden Ox.

Hemingway could not do more with fewer words.

The basic idea in *Jack Maggs* is that once transported to Australia criminals could never – under pain of execution – return to Britain: unless, that is, they acquired a 'ticket of leave'. By this period of his career, Carey would have needed a mantelpiece as long as a Wild West saloon bar to accommodate all his literary trophies. *Jack Maggs* picked up his third Miles Franklin and his first Commonwealth Writers' Award. Mischievously he found it 'inconvenient' to come to Buckingham Palace to receive the CWA from the English monarch – the implied reason being he had no 'ticket' and feared for his neck.

'Carey' is an Irish surname. There is no mystery as to why so many Irish ended up in colonial Australia. 'Kelly' is another Irish surname and one which is immortalised in the annals of national criminal heroism. Ned Kelly's 'rebellion' is the theme of the country's most distinguished artist's best-known sequence. Sidney Nolan is also, of course, possessed of an Irish surname. Peter Carey ventured into the same subject matter with *True History of the Kelly Gang* (2000), the novel for which he won his second Booker Prize, in the millennial year 2001. The novel is an exercise in indigenous vernacular, using as its source the one, self-exculpating, letter of Kelly's which has survived. Carey picks out from that testament Kelly's lament for the 'unfairness' at the heart of the Australia national existence. The Booker Prize release describes it as less a novel than a national anthem in fictional form: '*True History of the Kelly Gang* is the song of Australia, and it sings its protest in Ned Kelly's voice ... By the time of his hanging in 1880 a whole country would seem to agree that he was "the best bloody man that has ever been in Benalla". Carey skilfully makes art from his country's great story and helps us all to understand the measure of that "best bloody man".'

But was Carey – 'a man with two passports', as he described himself – still Australian? He moved to American subject matter with *His Illegal Self* (2008), the story of 1960s domestic terrorists. The novel was perplexing to many reviewers, particularly its second half in which the location changes abruptly, and for obscure narrative reasons, to the site of Carey's own hippy-commune days of the mid 1970s in up-country Queensland.

No year went by, it seemed, without Carey scooping up prizes and headlines. In 2003 he underwent a publicly acrimonious divorce from Summers and formed a relationship with the publisher, Frances Coady. His 2006 novel, *Theft*, opens with bitter complaint that the hero has been 'eviscerated by divorce lawyers', working for his 'alimony whore' of a separated wife. Summers took it personally, noting in a combative website, the string of dedications and 'without whom' acknowledgements Carey had made her. The novel was, she said, 'emotional terrorism'. The allegation, Carey retorted, was 'bullshit'. The newspapers had the kind of field day which fiction rarely supplies. One of Summers's accusations was that Carey was prepared to sacrifice anyone and anything in his 'ruthless drive to the top'. If so, he succeeded. He was hugely remunerated for his novels (a $2 million contract with Random House was gossiped about in the book trade). He continued turning out novels, each one as unpredictable as the last had been. No one, in 2010, for example, anticipated an elegant historical novel, *Parrot and Olivier in America*, based on Alexis de Tocqueville's 1830s tour. What next? is always the question with Carey.

FN   Peter Philip Carey

MRT   *Jack Maggs*

Biog   www.theparisreview.org/interviews/5641/the-art-of-fiction-no-188-peter-carey

280. W. G. Sebald 1944–2001

I am a periscope.

Does Sebald qualify for inclusion in this book? Was he a novelist? Was he an English-language novelist? He offers his own enigmatic answers. In the description he filed on his University of East Anglia home-page ('home', one notes, is never quite the right word for Sebald), he listed the four masterworks he composed in middle age as 'prose fiction', distinguishing them from his earlier works of scholarship. But he listed that 'fiction' under its German titles. Why, Sebald was once asked, did he

– having lived in England for thirty years, with a perfect command of English – write in what was, by the 1990s, his second language? Because, he replied, separation from his country meant that the 'antique' German he used was clinically pure – uncontaminated by the country's 'recent' (i.e. post-1933) past. And so close was Sebald's relation with one of his translators, Michael Hulse, that it could, more properly, be called collaboration. Germenglish.

Little of Sebald's personal history is yet known. The vacuum around him was self-created and a main component of his art. The facts, as stark as the information on an *Ausweis* (it amuses him to reproduce his radically uninformative ID 'papers' in his fiction) are as follows. He was born in a small village in southern Bavaria, in the Alps, near the Swiss border, at that strategic historical moment when the war was lost but could no more be stopped from its final destructiveness than an avalanche. His family, long resident in the region, had once been glass-makers. Sebald saw the past, he once said, through 'a glass mountain' – an immovable, but transparent, obstacle. In his only extended description of Wertach im Allgäu, he calls it 'W' (to signal it is no longer what it was, denuded of its history). It was, when he grew up there, 'a village of about a thousand inhabitants, in a valley covered in snow for five months of the year', a place 'where Jews didn't exist'. *Judenfrei* by history, not ethnic cleansing.

His full name was Winfried Georg Maximilian Sebald. As an author he stringently avoided full first names, using the initials 'W. G.' The 'M' was suppressed, although to those who knew him, he was 'Max'. Why this little nominal shuffle? On the literary level, it is *hommage* to 'K' (Kafka) and 'VN' (Nabokov), but there is a more intimate reason for alphabetisation. Sebald was born when the Nazi Party ordained, by state catalogue, 'acceptable' German names. Hence the universality in Sebald's generation of Teutonic-heroic Helmuts, Siegfrieds and Ulrichs. He chose 'Max' because it's a name associated with Jews as much as Gentiles. When, in 1933 (ominous year), Max Baer did heavyweight battle with Max Schmeling (Aryan versus Hitler's favourite pugilist) the Jewish American wore a Star of David on his shorts and, ring history records, beat the crap out of the Führer's Max.

Sebald was brought up Catholic in a Catholic village. He was one of four children – effectively a half-orphan. His father had joined the Wehrmacht in 1929 and rose, by 1945, to the rank of captain in a transport unit. The family, Sebald sardonically recalls, 'made the grade during the fascist years'. His father was a rare visitor home. After the war he was a POW until 1947 and thereafter worked in a distant town, but he was a good provider and the family 'rose again' to middle-class respectability. During the war, as Max discovered from a photo album, his father had served in the 'Polish Campaign'. One of the photographs he sent home to his family was of a laughing Polish gypsy mother and child – behind barbed wire, one notices on closer inspection. Can one inherit complicity? As he was growing up, Max's closest attachment was to his maternal grandfather, with whom he attended church. He died when Max was twelve, a blow from which he 'never recovered'. The death severed all living connection he had with Germany before 1933.

Sebald sailed through the post-war school system. While still a pupil he saw the Belsen concentration camp films, which the whole German population was made to view, as if to rub their nose in their own filth. He played football afterwards. The films made no immediate impression on him. The effect hit later. As a student at the University of Freiburg, he was nauseated by the 'deNazified' professoriate's 'conspiracy of silence'. It was universal. 'I doubt my mother and father,' he speculated, 'even among themselves, ever broached any of these subjects.' Those 'subjects' were not merely the Nazi crimes, but the German people's suffering during the war and post-war periods.

Sebald then emigrated (or went into exile) to England – where there was 'memory' – the 'backbone of literature', as he called it. He was particularly drawn to provincial England and finally established his career at the 'new' University of East Anglia, lecturing in German. He married in 1967 and had a daughter. He loved Norfolk's flatness (his own style was often described with the same adjective). But rooted as he became there, it was never his home. The last pages of *Vertigo* (1990) describe a journey, often taken, from London to Norwich:

> The train rolled slowly out of Liverpool Street station, past the soot-stained brick walls the recesses of which have always seemed to me like parts of a vast system of catacombs that comes to the surface there. In the course of time a multitude of buddleias, which thrive in the most inauspicious conditions, had taken root in the gaps and cracks of the nineteenth-century brickwork. The last time I went past those black walls, on my way to Italy in the summer, the sparse shrubs were just flowering. And I could hardly believe my eyes, as the train was waiting at a signal, to see a yellow brimstone butterfly flitting about from one purple flower to the other.

Sebald, too, had found his cranny at UEA.

Liverpool Street Station, a place which fascinated him, inspired his last novel, *Austerlitz* (2001):

> When I was in London this summer, I found myself with some time to spare waiting for a train at Liverpool Street Station. I made a point of going out to the small open space on the south side of the station, known as Hope Square. Here you will find a plaque and a monument to remember the children of the *Kindertransports*.

Some 10,000, mainly Jewish, children found sanctuary in pre-war England. Most came through the grimy station. *Austerlitz* follows the life of one such fictionalised child (compressed, Sebald recalls, from four he knew), who finds himself in a wholly uncongenial Welsh foster home. Spiritual isolation within physical alienation is the human condition in Sebald's universe.

Sebald's creative phase of writing began in his mid-forties, with four novels produced in rapid succession: *Vertigo* (1990), *The Emigrants* (1992), *The Rings of Saturn* (1995) and *Austerlitz* (2001). This astonishing creative flow was stopped by his death, aged fifty-seven. Driving in East Anglia, he is thought to have suffered a heart attack. He crashed and died. Had his daughter Anna not been travelling with him – given the pervasive morbidity of Sebald's mind – one could have suspected suicide. No one thinks it was. He was already being talked of as a Nobel laureate and his reputation had been boosted by laudatory commentary in London and New York's opinion-forming journals. 'Where', asked Susan Sontag, 'has one heard in English a voice of such confidence and precision, so direct in its expression of feeling, yet so respectfully devoted to "the real"?' Answers were not invited. Assisted by such golden verdicts, Sebald's sales were elevated to bestseller levels by his agent, the famously aggressive Andrew Wylie (nicknamed 'the jackal'). W. G. Sebald at the time of his death was on the verge of becoming a cult.

The most revealing of Sebald's novels is *The Rings of Saturn*. It is the saturnine planet, the astrological realm of the melancholy. The world, he suggests, can only be known by circling around it. The novel opens:

> In August 1992, when the dog days were drawing to an end, I set off to walk the county of Suffolk, in the hope of dispelling the emptiness that takes hold of me whenever I have completed a long stint of work.

There was also, the early pages inform us, a recent breakdown requiring hospitalisation. Sebald, in his usual circumambient way, talks about the hospital window, his only link to the outside world, but gives no details about the breakdown. In fact, as we follow it, his wander is not 'into' but along the edge of Suffolk – the coastal rim (bleak shingle all the way) from Lowestoft to Felixstowe. What, one asks, makes *The Rings of Saturn* different from, say, Cobbett's *Rural Rides* or J. B. Priestley's *English Journey*? The difference is that these other writers look at what is before their eyes, in their 'pilgrimages'. Sebald's eye ricochets back into his mind.

By the second page, *The Rings of Saturn* moves from observation to a quirky meditation on the skull of the famous Suffolk doctor (author of *Religio Medici*), Sir Thomas Browne. Browne's writing (notably *Pseudodoxia Epidemica*, his encyclopaedia of 'vulgar errors') is a literary *Wunderkammer*, a hall of curiosities. But Sebald's contemplation of the skull recalls, inescapably, the Ignatian exercise of meditation. Like Prospero in Shakespeare's *The Tempest*, his every third thought is of death. Cobbett and Priestley, by contrast, see English life on their travels: he sees human mortality. *The Rings of Saturn* indulges that national German pastime, 'wandering'. The solitary wanderer's thoughts ramble in aimless rhythm (there is, incidentally, a dearth of dialogue in Sebald's fiction: it is virtually soundless). He labelled his narrative technique 'tangential', 'hypotactic', 'periscopic'. Thoughts, he said, 'disintegrate before I can fully grasp them'. Among the many oddities of British public life that fascinated him was the London Tube injunction, 'Mind the gap!' Sebald minds little else.

On a stylistic level, the effect is one of unechoing 'emptiness'. There is little or no antecedent information offered. Why is he always walking alone? In *Vertigo* there is a vaguely indicated 'personal crisis' (but what?). The prose, while formal at the level of the sentence (one of which goes on for nine pages), lacks paragraph breaks. One whole novel lacks any white space whatsoever. Sebald's prose drones, monotonously. But if he is talking to himself ('mining the salt mines of the soul,' as he puts it) why shouldn't his discourse be toneless? The stream is only broken by captionless photographs. Does one think in words, or pictures? If the latter, the pictures need no labels.

In *Vertigo* the first of the novel's four sections chronicles the post-war life of a Napoleonic soldier 'Marie Henri Beyle' – his fraught love affairs, syphilis and wretched end. Nowhere does Sebald trouble to tell the reader that Beyle is the novelist Stendhal. In the last of the novel's sections, '*Il ritorno in patria*', a similarly nameless Sebald goes back to a similarly nameless home town. He traces its history as a book of the dead: in 1511, the Black Death claims 511; in 1569, a fire destroys 100 houses; 700 die of the plague in 1635. The casualty list goes on through war after war until reaching 125 in the Second World War. It is a catalogue of death, but not quite (even in a village of 1,000 souls) a neverending holocaust. Such death rates can be lived with. The total destruction of the European Jewish population is, by contrast, the pervasive fact in his fiction. He despised both the shroud of silence in Germany after the war and the exploitative 'Holocaust Industry', which he dates as cranking up in the mid-1960s. 'He claimed no false intimacy with the dead,' his friend Michael Hamburger said. In Sebald's view of things, the Holocaust could not be forgotten out of existence, but neither could it be directly confronted, at least not by a writer who had never been directly there – any more than a hairdresser could 'do' Medusa's hair.

But the Holocaust is always somewhere around in Sebald's writing. Describing the intricate business of the silk industry in East Anglia, he notes, for example, that every year the luckless worms, having woven their cocoons, are exterminated 'to pre-empt racial degeneration' (the phrase 'racial degeneration,' rather than 'species deterioration' is loaded with historical reference). Had he not swerved into the path of an oncoming truck on that Norfolk road on 14 December 2001, what would Sebald have gone on to write? He would not, one may be sure, have maintained a Germanic silence.

FN   W. G. Sebald (Winfried Georg Maximilian ('Max') Sebald)
MRT   *The Rings of Saturn*
Biog   *Guardian* obituary, 17 December 2001 (Eric Homberger)

281. Vernor Vinge 1944–

Skynet begins to learn at a geometric rate. It becomes self-aware at 2:14 a.m. Eastern time, August 29th [1997]. The character John Connor in the 1991 film, *Terminator 2: Judgment Day*

As the date of *Terminator 2* suggests, fiction – even science fiction – has a poor track record in scientific prophecy. Its long suit has always been paranoia. Recently, paranoia has switched from the traditionally big-brained master criminal – Professor Moriarty, Ernst Blofeld or Dr Evil – to the all-powerful computer. If you canvas student scientists in the US (as my teaching commitments have allowed me to do) as to who their favourite SF writers are, two names come up, time and again: one is the graphic novelist, Neil Gaiman; the other, more cerebral and textual, is Vernor Vinge (pronounced 'Vin-jay', a shibboleth for the knowing, like 'Anthony Powell', pronounced 'Pole'). Vinge is the young scientists' SF writer of choice, the caviar of the genre. He's both techno-savvy and technophobic, especially where powerful computers are concerned.

Vinge is not himself young – a retired San Diego maths professor, he began writing SF with his left hand, in his late twenties. He was born in the Midwest, took a doctorate at Michigan, landed a job at the San Diego campus of the University of California in La Jolla (Raymond Chandler's 'Poodle Springs') in 1972 and stayed there after his retirement from nearby San Diego State University in 2000. Little is publicly known of Vinge's personal life and what little is known is very SF. On arrival at SDSU, he married Joan Carol Dennison, a student recently graduated, 'with highest honors', from the anthropology department. The marriage broke up seven years later. She promptly married one of Vinge's friends, and his editor, James

Frenkel. SF people tend to hang out with each other. By the time of her divorce, in 1979, as 'Joan D. Vinge', she had already established herself as a 'salvage archaeologist' and one of the few women writers in the SF genre. Her *Eyes of Amber* won the 1977 Hugo Award for Best Science Fiction Novella and *The Snow Queen* (a variation on Hans Christian Andersen's fairy story) won the 1981 Hugo Award for Best SF Novel of the year. In recent years, until a crippling car accident in 2002, Joan D. Vinge cultivated a lucrative line in 'novelisations' of big box-office SF and fantasy films, such as *Star Wars*, *Willow* and *Lost in Space*.

Mathematicians have a small, but distinguished corpus of fiction (e.g. Edward Abbott's *Flatland*, J. B. S. Haldane's *Daedalus*, Lewis Carroll's 'Alice' books), none more so, or more substantial, than Vernor Vinge's. He wrote his first published short story in 1966 for the 'hard SF' magazine, *Analog*. 'Bookworm, Run!' has a plot similar to that of Daniel Keyes's better known *Flowers for Algernon* (1959). But whereas in Keyes's short story it is surgery which enhances the mouse Algernon's mental powers to super-rodent levels, in Vinge's story it is computer-database linkage which makes the chimp Norman a super-simian, or 'simborg'. Like everything Vinge writes, the theme of the story is both witty and scientifically timely. Chimps were, in the late 1960s, being shot into space in rockets – going boldly where no chimp had gone before. Vinge's subsequent work coincided with such communication-science developments (which he was lecturing on) as the formation of ARPANET (the military precursor of the internet), the World Wide Web and, in the 1990s, its universal domestic connectivity.

His SF revolves around two major paradoxes. One is that as the machines become smarter, the human beings that operate them necessarily become dumber. A broadly educated person could, for example, change a typewriter ribbon, but might well be at a loss as how to replace a motherboard in their desktop – which they were using for the same purposes as their old manual typewriter. The second paradox is that cyber-connection is both a weapon of liberation and equally a tool of state oppression. Does the rapidly evolving computer portend the end of tyranny, or its future perfection? Will it create McLuhan's harmonious 'global village' or Jeremy Bentham's 'Panopticon' (the basis of the nineteenth-century British jail system, in which the prisoner is under constant, all-seeing, surveillance). Who knows? We are, in Vinge's pungent metaphor, speeding far ahead of our headlights. All we have as a map is SF – speculative fiction.

Vinge established himself as a genre leader with his novella, *True Names* (1981). It was, he recalls, 'the first story I ever wrote with a word processor – a Heathkit LSI 11/03'. The story is set in 2014 and takes as its premise Arthur C. Clarke's paradox that, at its most extreme development, technology is indistinguishable from magic.

It opens:

> In the once upon a time days of the First Age of Magic, the prudent sorcerer
> regarded his own true name as his most valued possession but also the greatest
> threat to his continued good health, for – the stories go – once an enemy, even
> a weak unskilled enemy, learned the sorcerer's true name, then routine and
> widely known spells could destroy or enslave even the most powerful. As times
> passed, and we graduated to the Age of Reason and thence to the first and second
> industrial revolutions, such notions were discredited. Now it seems that the Wheel
> has turned full circle (even if there never really was a First Age) and we are back to
> worrying about true names again.

As the narrative continues, a 'coven' of 'warlocks' – effectively anarchist hackers
– are at war with the 'Great Adversary', the American government. Their protection
(their magic cloak, in Hogwartian terms) is their pseudonymity. The state cannot
find out who they are. Enter a third player in the cybergame, 'the Mailman'. He, it
emerges, is an AI construct. Once he has, vampire-like, sucked in every computer
avatar on the web, he – the machine – will rule. Exit humanity.

Vinge achieved fame, outside the SF village, with his Hugo-winning 1992 novel,
A Fire Upon the Deep. (If you don't know who the 'Hugo' is named after, incidentally,
SF is not for you). He won the award again for *A Deepness in the Sky* (1999), for the
novella *Fast Times at Fairmont High* (2001), and for *Rainbows End* (2007).

His later work is more cosmic in its scenarios. He creates a new cyber-universe,
defined by the architectures of information. *A Fire Upon the Deep* is, for example, set
in the frictional areas between the 'Zones of Thought' and chronicles a battle over a
data archive. The tenor of Vinge's vision, as it has been expressed over the decades,
is pessimistic. He foresees thought-capable technologies which are no more compre-
hensible to the human (or SF-writing) mind than Jehovah – they move in mysterious ways. Human consciousness, whose offspring they are, can react to them, but
will never understand them any more than a Pekinese can understand quantum
mechanics.

This future catastrophe (for us, not for the thoughtful machines) Vinge terms
the 'Singularity'. He outlined it in detail in a much-cited article in 1993. 'Within
thirty years,' Vinge predicted, 'we will have the technological means to create superhuman intelligence. Shortly after, the human era will be ended. Is such progress
avoidable? If not to be avoided, can events be guided so that we may survive? These
questions must be investigated.' They are investigated in his dozen or so novels.
His vision of digito-apocalypse was popularised in *The Terminator*'s 'Skynet'. What
happens when machines 'wake up'? Very bad things for their inventors – and no
Arnie to help us.

FN   Vernor Steffen Vinge
MRT   *True Names*
Biog Interview with Vinge (Mike Godwin, interviewer), reason.com/
archives/2007/05/04/superhuman-imagination

282. Julian Barnes 1946 –

Why does the writing make us chase the writer? Why can't we leave well alone?

It's easier to know a dead novelist than a living novelist. Fences fall on death – the libel lawyer's sabre turns to putty, trespassers will no longer be prosecuted. But with all this access there is a loss of living contact. One's in communication with a naked corpse. Of all the living novelists of his generation, Julian Barnes has privileged his readers with the kind of insight that usually only the Jamesian post-mortem exploiter can turn up. It is to be found in his book-length meditation on death, *Nothing to be Frightened of* (2008). The tone is Schopenhauerian. Why live, asked that philosopher – answering himself with the observation that the will would not concur with what the mind rationally resolved on the matter. Schopenhauer, however, is the wrong reference here. Since his university years Barnes has been a disciple of the French sceptic Montaigne. He could take as his motto the title of the Frenchman's essay, 'That to philosophize is to learn to die', with the slight change: 'to write novels is to learn how to die'. Let us get used to it, says Montaigne. Or, as the other Frenchman Gustave Flaubert puts it, 'People like us should have the religion of despair ... gazing down into the black pit at one's feet, one remains calm.'

The outline of Barnes's life (but very little of his private life) is on record. He was born the son, and grandson, of school teachers – which meant, as he drily puts it, books, chalk and bourgeois decencies in the house. That his father taught French was manifestly influential. He was born in Leicester – lifelong support of whose football team is the only legacy (it is, he likes to point out, a very middling Midland club – no metropolitan flash). Until his father's retirement, Barnes's upbringing was London inner suburban: thereafter London outer suburban. He grew up under the shadow of an elder brother, Jonathan, justly regarded as brilliant, whereas he, Julian, was credited with being a good all-rounder. His sense of fraternal inferiority is a main element in *Nothing to be Frightened of*, and is given wry expression in the book's opening sentences:

I don't believe in God, but I miss Him. That's what I say when the question is put. I asked my brother, who has taught philosophy at Oxford, Geneva and the Sorbonne, what he thought of such a statement, without revealing that it was my own. He replied with a single word: 'Soppy.'

Some philosophers, one recalls, say the same thing about novels. Are his dozen volumes of fiction merely a 'trivial response to mortality'? Barnes asks himself.

At school he was not outstanding in the classroom, but stood out on the sports field. His lifelong love of sport keeps him, he says, in touch with his inner athlete, his 'macho' self. The word is ironically inflected. He confesses to having masturbated heroically in adolescence. The absence of any divine mark of disapproval pushed him towards his lifelong agnosticism. He offers a snapshot of his early literary leanings at the same time of life:

> When I was fourteen or fifteen I was just beginning to read in French, but the first time I read *Madame Bovary* it was certainly in English ... At the time we were obliged once a week to put on army uniform and play at soldiers in something called the Combined Cadet Force. I have a vivid memory of pulling out *Crime and Punishment* along with my sandwiches on a field day; it felt properly subversive.

The City of London School does well by even its less than highest flying pupils and Barnes was accepted to read modern languages at Oxford. Modern French, he found, was taught there as a 'dead language': unmodern French. He changed course, briefly, in his second year to philosophy but discovered all those genes had gone to his brother, Jonathan. If he wanted answers, he would have to find them in literature. He ruefully recalls Oxford's judgement on him:

> When I had a viva for my finals one of the examiners ... said to me – looking at my papers – What do you want to do after you've got your degree? and I said, Well, I thought I might become one of you. I said that partly because my brother had got a first and had gone on to become a philosophy don ... [The examiner] toyed with my papers again and said, Have you thought about journalism?

Oxford was the loser and English fiction (not to mention higher journalism) the gainer. Eventually, one must add, he did not fly from the starting blocks. On graduating, Barnes worked as a lexicographer on the *Oxford English Dictionary*, researching etymologies in the C–G letter range. 'I doubt it shows through in my fiction,' he says, but his Flaubertian addiction to lists and categories suggests otherwise. He left OUP to read for the bar, which brought him to London where he began, as the dons had advised, to drift into journalism. His TV reviews were particularly brilliant.

He did not venture on writing fiction until his mid-twenties. After encouragement by the publisher Jonathan Cape, and delays induced by his own 'doubt and demoralisation', Julian Barnes finally published his first work, *Metroland* (1980), at the age of thirty-four. Few career-making novels can have been nursed in a spirit of such carefully fermented inadequacy: 'I didn't see that I had any right to be a novelist', he recalls. *Metroland*, he later pronounced 'was about defeat' and he wrote it in a defeated spirit. It remains, none the less, the only autobiographical novel Julian Barnes can be said to have written and even if it weren't a strikingly good piece of work, it would be readable for that reason alone. The narrative is divided into three sections: One, Metroland (1963); Two, Paris (1968); Three, Metroland II (1977). The narrative circuit is familiar from Orwell's *Keep the Aspidistra Flying*: both novels record a young Englishman's failure to escape the gravitational pull of bourgeois mores; his 'past' denies any future. Barnes's hero vainly attempts to come up for air, but his handicaps are too great. He is suburban, English and non-Jewish – and anyway his heart isn't in it. Finally, mellowed, he accepts his destiny: *j'habite Metroland*.

Metroland is itself a symbol of England's failed leap into Europe. An old stager whiles away the commuter's tedium by instructing Barnes's hero on the Metropolitan line's grand design:

> Fifty miles from Verney Junction to Baker Street; what a line. Can you imagine – they were planning to join up with Northampton and Birmingham. Have a great link through from Yorkshire and Lancashire, through Quainton Road, through London, joining up with the old South Eastern, then through a Channel Tunnel to the Continent. What a line.

Metroland never made it. It became a dormitory: 'you lived there because it was an area easy to get out of.' Neither does young Christopher make it. He goes to Paris in 1968, but he misses the events; he and they didn't seem made for each other. Christopher also fails in his liaison with his exciting French partner, Annick, and lapses into marriage with the sensible English girl, Marion. And, in the last significant episode of the novel, a Metrolander once more, he doesn't commit adultery. At the end, he has become what he once tried to escape: stuffy, English and indomitably decent. Defeated. It is one of the ironies of Barnes's later career that he, the author, did make it. He is England's most honoured novelist in France.

Metroland and its successor, *Before She Met Me*, two years later, a study of retroactive jealousy (can one feel cuckolded by one's partner's former lovers?) enjoyed critical success but barely break-even hardback sales. Barnes's subdued voice was drowned out by louder practitioners of the day: he was out-Martined, out Salmaned, out-Ianed (all of whom would become companions in fiction). His career took on new force with his marriage to the gifted literary agent Pat Kavanagh in 1979 and it was with his third novel, *Flaubert's Parrot* (1984) – and with Kavanagh's assistance, one suspects – that he made his breakthrough. As the title proclaims, it is ostensibly homage to the French novelist through incidentals: a stuffed parrot (a flock of dubious contenders survive to stimulate the idle mind), a recycled public statue (the Nazis dismantled the original for war scrap), the books Flaubert never got round to writing. The narrator, Geoffrey Braithwaite, is a late-middle-aged Normandy landing veteran, a widowed doctor with an unhappy marriage behind him, only fragments of which surface in chinks between his obsessive, bordering on manic, cogitations on his beloved Gustave. Although the ostensible subject is the most constructive novelist of the nineteenth century, the form is that of the Montaigne essay – 'loose sallies of the mind'. Lists, catalogues and reverse shots abound. There are expostulations against Oxford dons, critics, the bourgeois reader, life, death, everything. The one constant feature is that the author is not writing 'the kind of book I knew I did not want to write'. It is a novel constantly in denial about itself.

Barnes had low expectations for this resolutely eccentric work (one should, however, beware the traps in his chronic self-deprecations): 'I suspected that *Flaubert's Parrot* might interest a few Flaubertians, and perhaps a smaller number of psittacophiles.' The novel in fact did very well – although arguably not as supremely well as it should have done. As is often the case with Barnes's fiction, it was, in a sense, too good for its own good. Time will confirm it as a high point in twentieth-century literature.

No novelist – whilst politely communicative in interview – maintains a more dignified silence than Julian Barnes about private things. He declines to comment on his (childless) marriage, for example, and a mid-1980s breakdown in his relationship with Kavanagh. The third party, a woman novelist as famous as Barnes, went public. The furious quarrel with Martin Amis ten years later, on his leaving Kavanagh's firm for a sexier American agent, is known entirely from Amis's engagingly indiscreet account in his memoir, *Experience* (2000). In Barnes's memoir (dedicated to 'P'), the uninformed reader would not know that Barnes is married. Success, on the scale of *Flaubert's Parrot*, might have been expected to lay down future patterns. But if there is one thing Barnes dislikes as a novelist it is the rut, or furrow. He declined to follow up with 'Tolstoy's Gerbil', or 'Turgenev's Tortoise.' He did, however, write a novel called *The Porcupine* (1992), which came out in the euphoric aftermath of the fall of the Evil Empire when all the talk was of the end of history and peace dividends. *The Porcupine* surveys this supposed turning point in world history with styptic Montaignean scepticism. A thinly veiled *roman-à-clef* (his first in that genre), based on the trial of the Bulgarian leader, Todor Zhivkov, it is a subtler version of Arthur Koestler's *Darkness at Noon* (Barnes and Kavanagh were both admirers of Koestler). Neither sympathetic nor hostile, the novel expresses Barnes's belief that fiction is elegant lies with a 'hard core of truth at its centre'. In this case, the hard truth is that there is nothing clean-cut about the fall of empires. *The Porcupine* carries the most unusual dust-jacket recommendation in the annals of English literature from Zhivkov's actual prosecutor (a principal character, under thin disguise, in the narrative).

Barnes did not get any similar endorsement from Rupert Murdoch for his satire on Robert Maxwell in his 'condition of England novel', *England, England* (1998). His country's condition, he sternly implies, is not healthy – reduced as it is to a theme-park husk of what it once was. The most simply entertaining of Barnes's works from this productive, and profoundly sceptical, phase of his career is *The History of the World in 10½ Chapters* (1989). It opens with a jaundiced history of Noah, the flood, the ark and the new covenant from the revisionist point of view of a stowaway woodworm. The next chapter leaps forward to a modern cruise liner, hijacked on the seas. The TV celebrity lecturer on history, recruited to entertain the passengers, finds himself – as do the passengers – *in* history as the hijackers throw passengers overboard, 'two by two'. It is a painful experience. So the chapters go on, subverting received ideas on every page. The novel (if that is what it can be called) was reprinted eight times in hardback in its first year.

Flaubert is Barnes's God – no question about that. But one can detect another less expected link with Kingsley Amis, the modern avatar of John Bullism. 'One evening in 1983', Barnes recalls, 'I was having a drink with Kingsley Amis. He made the mistake of asking me what I was working on. I made the mistake of telling him … My account would have involved words such as 'Flaubert and 'parrot' … As I was nearing the end of my preliminary outline – still with some way to go – I glanced up, and was confronted with an expression poised between belligerent outrage and apoplectic boredom.' Barnes duly sent a complimentary copy of the book to Amis who informed him, without compliment, that he gave up at Chapter 3, 'though he might have considered plodding on a bit further if only one of the two chaps there had pulled out a gun and shot the other chap'. The amusingly recounted episode suggests a gulf as wide as the English Channel between England's arch-Tory and its most 'Europeanised' novelist. In fact, entirely the opposite may be argued. Kingsley Amis loved trying his hand at genre literature: whether James Bond (*Colonel Sun*), the cosy 1930s crime novel (*The Riverside Villas Murder*), the ghost story (*The Green Man*), or science fiction (*The Alteration*). Barnes is as fascinated by the possibilities of genre, if less skittish. In 1980 he began putting out a series of Soho based crime novels under the pseudonym 'Dan Kavanagh', featuring a series hero, 'Duffy', a bisexual, sleazy, soccer-loving, private eye. Duffy came, said Barnes, 'from a different part of my brain.' No mystery as to where 'Kavanagh' came from.

Barnes's big novel in the early twentieth century, *Arthur & George* (2005), came, indubitably, from the Francophile part of that organ, but it too was based on crime and detection. Not Duffy, but the creator of literature's most famous sleuth, was the detective in question. *Arthur & George* re-examines Arthur Conan Doyle's investigation of the falsely convicted victim of a bizarre horse-mutilation case, George Edalji. It is a kind of English Dreyfus, complete with racial discrimination, and one which subtly defines national differences within the overarching dimension of human prejudice.

In *Nothing to be Frightened of*, Barnes records that he thinks of death every day – his novelist's orison. The problem is, think of it as you will, death's awful ingenuities can never be anticipated – in Emily Dickinson's bitter phrase, he kindly stops for us. But where and when he makes that stop is, unless we forestall him with suicide, entirely up to him. Very suddenly, in 2008, the dedicatee of every one of Barnes's books since they married was diagnosed with a brain tumour and, within weeks, died. Barnes, following his inflexible code of privacy about personal matters, made no public comment. His 2011 novel involved Camus' assertion that the one serious issue in life is whether to end it. Its title, *The Sense of an Ending*, echoes that of Frank Kermode's critical meditation on teleology in literature (1967). Particularly relevant is Kermode on 'peripety' – the surprisingness of bad things. Kermode would have been the ideal reviewer. Alas, his own life ended in August 2010.

In *Nothing to be Frightened of*, the novelist fantasises about 'the last reader of Julian Barnes's fiction' – that as yet unborn antiquarian who shakes the dust off the volumes in the vaults of the far distant Bodleian or British Library (or, happy thought, the *Bibliothèque Nationale*). The image he evokes is that of the Duracell TV adverts in which battery-powered marching dolls stop, one by one, as they run out of juice, but the advertised brand marches on. It too will, of course, stop eventually. Barnes's fiction, particularly *Flaubert's Parrot*, will, one expects, be the Duracell doll among his gifted fiction-writing cohort. But, as Barnes foresees, a time will come when even Flaubert will be unread. Nothing to be frightened of. Probably.

FN   Julian Patrick Barnes
MRT   *Flaubert's Parrot*
Biog   J. Barnes, *Nothing to be Frightened of* (2008)

283. Sue Townsend 1946–

I am from the working class. I am now what I was then. No amount of balsamic vinegar and Prada handbags could make me forget what it was like to be poor.

George and Weedon Grossmith's *Diary of a Nobody* was first published serially in *Punch* in 1891. The authors were London cockneys, sons of a *Times* court reporter and occasional music-hall entertainer. In their youth the brothers trod on the boards themselves, specialising in 'patter songs' and humorous recitative. They graduated in later life to comic journalism – writing their patter. The 'nobody' of the title is Charles Pooter, who works in a city office as a clerk under Mr Perkupp. He lives in a rented villa, The Laurels, Brickfield Terrace, Holloway, with his wife Carrie, and it is on taking possession of his Englishman's Castle that he resolves to keep a diary to immortalise Pooteresque daily adventures.

The Grossmiths' bestseller spawned a whole progeny of Pooters. H. G. Wells's 'little men' (Kipps, Mr Polly) are in the line direct, as is Charlie Chaplin's indomitable tramp. The latest, and most successful, late fruit of the Pooter tree is Sue Townsend's Adrian Mole saga. Townsend was born in 1946, one of the post-war demographic 'bulge', engendered by the false optimism of victory and a people's government. The eldest of three sisters ('Very Chekhovian,' she drily comments), Sue was brought up in Leicester, a city enriched by the hosiery industry and forever weighed down with a huge urban inferiority complex. Her father was a postman, and she records her childhood as 'happy'. The family lived in a succession of council-owned 'prefabs'. Ugly, hutch-like things, they none the less had the mod cons (hot water, refrigerators) lacking in the slum artisans' cottages they replaced. Prefabs did not, however, elevate the occupant's spirit. I lived in one for a while.

Townsend failed the eleven-plus; clinching proof, if one needed it, of the unintelligence of that misconceived intelligence test. She attended a 'secondary modern' (i.e. school for the second rate), a stone's throw away from the grammar school she did not attend. She left school at the earliest possible moment, at fifteen. After three years' unskilled work, she married a semi-skilled sheet-metal worker and, by the age of twenty-two, had three children under school-age. She credits her impressive education to Penguin Classics, the series launched by Allen Lane in the same year that she was born.

In her early marriage she embarked on what she calls 'secret writing'. An insomniac ('like Margaret Thatcher' – the only similarity, she is at pains to stress), Townsend wrote after midnight and stored her writing in a hidden box. She attended a writers' group until she was in her late thirties. It was sponsored by Leicester's progressive Phoenix Theatre and she won a major prize for a play set in a gynaeco-logist's waiting room – *Womberang* (1979). One of the judges, John Mortimer, took a particular interest in her and his Rumpolisms, proletarianised, would be an inspiration. It was a dramatic monologue, broadcast in 1982 on BBC radio (featuring 'Nigel' Mole) which was the forerunner of the first instalment of her great work of fiction, *The Secret Diary of Adrian Mole, Aged 13¾*. The name was changed to 'Adrian' to avoid too obvious a lifting from the 1950s 'skuleboy' hero, Nigel Molesworth, the creation of Geoffrey Willans and Ronald Searle. The difference was, 'as any fule kno', that Nigel was minor public school ('St Custards').

Adrian's secret diary went on to be the bestselling fiction title of 1982, inspiring TV and film adaptations and a cult following. It was, Townsend claimed, the whining of one of her brood which inspired her. Like Joe Orton (brought up in a neighbour-ing house in Leicester), she had an unerring ear for the dialect of her uneasy class and place. She also had an acute insight into the trials of early adolescence. One of the early covers of her books portrayed a bathroom cup with a Noddy-toothbrush and a dispos-able razor. Adrian (Albert) Mole is trapped between the two. A child of the 1960s, life never swings for Adrian. The diary begins in the high point of the Thatcher years, an administration Townsend loathes. (She has, however, a certain fondness for the Iron Lady's successor: 'I didn't see Adrian's face,' she once mused, 'well – not until I saw John Major on the telly.') It is unlikely that Townsend began with the intention of writing a saga of *Coronation Street* unendingness. But the triumph of her first volume launched 'Moleiad': a nobody's progress. There followed eight further instalments of Adrian's career, chronicling his rueful misfortunes, and becoming progressively darker in tone. The darkness spilled over from Townsend's own life. She was diagnosed with diabetes in her thirties, registered blind in 2001. In 2005 her kidneys failed, and in 2009 she had a transplant (the organ was donated by her son). In the latter volumes she was wheelchair-bound and obliged to dictate her books to her husband.

The Mole diaries are increasingly bitter at New Labour, reaching a climax in *Adrian Mole and the Weapons of Mass Destruction* (2004). 'God, I can't stand them now,' Townsend says: 'I support the memory and the history of the party and I consider that these lot are interlopers.' Pandora – Adrian's Helen of Troy (she has launched a thousand masturbation fantasies) – is, in the later instalments, a Blair Babe and the focus of Townsend's unreconstructed Old Labour satirical venom. She announced an intention to do away with Adrian in 2007, but in *Adrian Mole: The Prostrate Years* (2009), he was given a stay of execution. The diarist-hero is aged thirty-nine and a quarter and it is 2007. He is living (if you can call it that) in a con-verted pigsty – semi-attached to his dysfunctional parents' house, on the outskirts of Leicester. He works in a second-hand bookshop which is going bust. His illegitimate son, Glenn, is serving in Afghanistan. Thank heavens, his parents savings are in Northern Rock and Adrian's own meagre hoard in an Icelandic bank. He is up all night with a worrisome bladder (more worrying, it transpires, than he suspects) and has not had sex with his wife Daisy for six months.

It's odd that the first novel in our literature with 'Prostate' in the title (disfigured by its inevitable malapropism) is by a woman with incurable eye disease. Sue Townsend did her research for *Adrian Mole: The Prostrate* [sic] *Years*. At 39¼ Adrian is not, technically, in that red zone of life: commonly assumed to be a man's late sixties onwards. But it can strike young – if you're unlucky. No one is unluckier than Mr Mole. Like others diagnosed with PCa, Adrian has treatment options (surgery, radiotherapy, hormone therapy, high-intensity focused ultrasound) thrown back in his lap – literally. Why? Because the medical profession itself isn't sure. 'I only got a C– in biology,' Adrian complains, vainly. He chooses radiotherapy, on hearing another patient in the waiting room say: 'I wouldn't have a prostrate operation again for all the tea in China.' Has Adrian Mole chosen right? Will he live to die, as they like to say, with PCa, rather than of it? Ominously, Townsend has said again she wants him to 'face death'.

Townsend declares herself 'a passionate socialist', with broad streaks of fondness for *ancien régime* England: notably the royal family. One of her more charming productions is *The Queen and I* (1992), which fantasises Red Revolution. The House of Windsor is rehoused in a Leicester Council House, in Hellebore Close. The royals, except for the incorrigible Philip, adapt splendidly. The queen (and her 'dorgis') ingeniously makes do on her OAP pension; Charles talks all day to his garden plants; Diana misconducts herself with fellows up the street. When the Queen Mum dies, the street comes together to give her a mini-state funeral.

Townsend is as secretive as Adrian about her private life. Her first marriage broke up after seven years. She later married Colin Broadway ('a canoe maker and expedition leader') and had a fourth child. It was at this point, in early middle age, her career took off. She still lives in Leicester and is dedicated to the city – although she has risen well past the prefab level and now lives in a converted vicarage. The local university gave her an honorary doctorate and she has given the city two pubs, admirably run by her husband. They keep her, she claims, 'working class'. Her papers (but not her private papers) are stored, alongside Joe Orton's unbuttoned confessions, in the University archives. Only her own journals, one suspects, could enlighten us as to why it was not the 'Secret Diary of Adriana Albertina Mole'. But, she declares, 'I prefer to keep my secrets to myself, to the grave ... and beyond!'

FN   Susan Lillian Townsend (later Broadway)
MRT   *The Queen and I*
Biog   S. Townsend, *Public Confessions of a Middle-aged Woman* (2001)

284. Paul Auster 1947–

When we're in dark circumstances we survive them by cracking jokes.

Auster was conceived on his Jewish parents' honeymoon at Niagara Falls, and born in Newark, New Jersey. 'I think of it sometimes', he later wrote, 'how I was conceived in that Niagara Falls resort for honeymooners. Not that it matters where it happened. But the thought of what must have been a passionless embrace, a blind, dutiful groping between chilly hotel sheets, has never failed to humble me into an awareness of my own contingency. Niagara Falls. Or the hazard of two bodies joining. And then me, a random homunculus, like some dare-devil in a barrel, shooting over the falls.' God protect parents from their children's 'imagination'.

Auster Sr was a well-off property owner – on the respectable side of slumlordism, Paul insists. His mother, at twenty-one, was thirteen years younger and, even on the honeymoon, was unhappy in the marriage. His father, Auster later deduced, was not a bad man – nor, technically, a bad family man, but he needed nothing the world had to offer a man like him. Like other New York kids, Auster spent the roasting summer months in up-state camps. In 1961 he was standing next to a fellow camper who was struck by lightning. The event, he claimed, worked radioactively in his imagination. 'I think that was one of the most important experiences I ever had. I think it really shaped my thinking about the world in ways that I was never even consciously aware of. But as I look back I understand how important it was to me. How fragile and fluky the world is. One minute you're standing next to someone, the next he's dead.' 'Chance', he came to believe, 'is the only certain thing in life.' In his senior year at high school, Auster's parents divorced. He lived, thereafter, with his mother, who remarried a labour lawyer. Neither of Auster's parents were college-educated.

He enrolled at Columbia where, in 1966, he fell in love with Lydia Davis, the daughter of one of his professors and it was through the Davises that Auster was introduced to modern French literature – which he consolidated with a year abroad in Paris in 1967 (an exciting year in the French capital, with student rebellion threatening a second revolution). On his return to Columbia, Auster graduated well and stayed on to do research; he was already publishing in campus journals. He escaped the draft (which could have meant Vietnam) and embarked on a doctorate in French Renaissance literature, which he never completed. In a later interview he recalled: 'I didn't want to be an academic, which is probably what I was best suited for, but I just didn't want to be in school anymore, and the idea of spending my life in a university was just awesomely terrible.' What, then, did he want to be?

There followed many unsettled years before he found out. In the grand tradition of American literature, he 'hoboed'. His stepfather landed him a berth on an oil tanker and, for a few months, he was a merchant seaman. For another few months he worked with the US Census Bureau. The episode (and his mischievous habit of inventing non-existent Americans) crops up in *The Locked Room* (1986). America was increasingly uncongenial and in 1971 he returned to Paris for four years. It was, 'a fundamental time' for him. He supported himself by a series of menial jobs; by now he was steeped in the *roman nouveau* and the New Wave film movement (notably Jean-Luc Godard, whose *Alphaville* was clearly inspirational). On his return to New York in 1974, Auster and Davis married. They had one child, Daniel, in 1977. But Paul did not settle down – he was still at a loose end. Fluent, clever and well read he picked up journalistic, translating and ghost-writing assignments, while creatively he believed himself to be a playwright or poet. 'The only thing I actually did during that period [i.e. the mid-1970s]', he recalled, 'was write a detective novel under another name [*Squeeze Play*, by 'Paul Benjamin'], in about six weeks, just to make money, I was so desperately poor, so that was actually the first novel I wrote. This period went on for about a year and a half and I produced absolutely nothing.'

Then his vocation came suddenly and unexpectedly: 'By 1978 I felt I had been running into a brick wall with my work and a moment came when I just stopped altogether. I thought I wouldn't write anymore. At the beginning of 1979 I had a kind of breakthrough and started writing again. The first piece I wrote was prose and not poetry. Strangely enough, the night I finished that prose piece, about 10 or 15 pages, my father died. I found that out the next morning. I began in a few weeks writing a book about him and that led to all the work I've been doing since.' He inherited money from his father, which eased his circumstances. He was, however, breaking up with Davis, which complicated his life, as did the chronic ill-health of Daniel. What mattered most in his father's death was its bringing home to him the realisation of the '*modern nothingness*', which was to become his theme.

By now he had completed 'Portrait of an Invisible Man', an extended meditation on his father's death that makes up the first half of *The Invention of Solitude* (1982). The second half deals with his own solitude and failed fatherhood. These were starting points for him, although it took three years to work through them. In 1981, at a poetry reading, he met the woman (another professor's daughter), Siri Hustvedt, who would become his second wife. They married on Bloomsday. Now closing in on forty, Auster was still not a novelist. He embarked on that career with *City of Glass* (1985), the first of the 'New York Trilogy'. However, the book world was not ready for Auster and the manuscript received seventeen rejections, until being accepted by the small, extravagantly hippyish, Sun & Moon Press in Los Angeles. *City of Glass* is a 'metaphysical detective story'. Its famous narrative 'hook' is a midnight phone call: 'It was a wrong number that started it, the telephone ringing three times in the dead of night, and the voice on the other end asking for someone he was not.' The not-someone is 'Paul Auster, of the Paul Auster Detective Agency'. The recipient of the call is Daniel Quinn who writes detective fiction (under the pseudonym William Wilson) who, none the less, pretends, for reasons he himself cannot explain, to be Paul Auster and takes on the case for 'Peter Stillman'. In following it up, Quinn-Auster draws on the expertise of 'Max Work' (Quinn's series hero PI). Genres bend.

Stillman, he discovers, was kept in solitary confinement for nine years by his father, when growing up, so that he might develop the primeval language of Adam. His father has been released from prison, and will now, it is feared, kill his son. *City of Glass* was, bizarrely, nominated for an Edgar Award by the Mystery Writers of America. Poe himself might have approved. For Auster, the mystery was not the crime, but hermeneutics – the act of interpretation. The 'trilogy' completed with *Ghosts* (1986) and *The Locked Room* (1986).

Fiction was now streaming fast from Auster's pen – something he attributed to the inspirational assistance of Hustvedt. And with the publication of the trilogy, he became commercially marketable and intellectually respectable. In 1986, he was appointed to a writing position at Princeton, which he held four years.

In his fiction he moved through genres and styles like a hermit crab: the dystopian *In the Country of Last Things* (1987) the bulky family saga, *Moon Palace* (1989), the story of 'Marco Stanley Fogg' – the name is an amalgam of three explorers and *The Music of Chance* (1990), a fable about men building a wall as the most notorious wall in history was coming down in Berlin. Auster was currently developing a secondary career in film and would collaborate with director Wayne Wang, most successfully with *Smoke* (1995), which enjoyed general release and good reviews. Auster's other film projects have failed to break out of the art-house, festival circuit. His fiction of the early 1990s had become markedly more fanciful. *Leviathan* (1992) opens: 'Six days ago, a man blew himself up by the side of a road in northern Wisconsin.' There are evocations of Timothy McVeigh and the Unabomber – except that Ben Sachs's mission is blowing up replicas of the Statue of Liberty. *Mr. Vertigo* (1994) opens more cheerfully:

> I was twelve years old the first time I walked on water. The man in the black clothes taught me how to do it, and I'm not going to pretend I learned that trick overnight. Master Yehudi found me when I was nine, an orphan boy begging nickels on the streets of Saint Louis, and he worked with me steadily for three years before he let me show my stuff in public.

The speaker is Walt Rawley (echoes of Walter Raleigh who, although he didn't walk on it, sailed on water virtuosically) and the year is 1927, when Lindbergh flew the Atlantic in the *Spirit of St Louis* (flying is another trick Yehudi teaches Walt).

In *Timbuktu* (1999) the narrator is a dog, Mr Bones, companion to a homeless Brooklyn man on a quest south. It is designed as homage to *Don Quixote*, the one book, Auster says, that he keeps going back to: 'It seems to present every problem every novelist has ever had to face, and to do it in the most brilliant and human way imaginable.' His stories, Auster has said, 'come to me out of my unconscious. I never look for them. They find me.' One, more topical, story that found him was *Man in the Dark* (2008), a novel which intertwines the American Civil War with the war in Iraq – another divisive conflict. Auster has, God willing, many more novels inside him. Of all writers, it is hard to predict what they will be.

FN   Paul Benjamin Auster
MRT   *City of Glass*
Biog www.stuartpilkington.co.uk/paulauster/biography.htm (Kenneth Kreutzer)

POSTSCRIPT

285. Lydia Davis 1947– ; Siri Hustvedt 1955–

I remember I wrote something that I worked on for three months and I showed it to Paul and he said, 'you know what, you should just dump it.' The thing was that it was awful and I knew there was something wrong with it which was why I showed it to him. I was so relieved to put that stuff in the garbage I can't tell you. Siri Hustvedt

Two lines of intertwined fiction and family extend out from Paul Auster. Both share his concerns about narrative, but work those concerns out in strikingly divergent ways. Lydia Davis, Auster's first wife, was born in Northampton, Massachusetts. Her parents were both writers – her mother, Hope Hale Davis, being the more distinguished. Lydia arrived late in her mother's eventful career. Hope (well named) was married four times. Her first husband, a 'vaudeville scenery painter', did not last long. In 1932 she moved on to an even shorter-lasting union with the gadfly British Marxist, Claud Cockburn (at the time a *Times* correspondent in America, soon to join the *Daily Worker*). Hope's third marriage was to the German economist Hermann Brunck. By now she was writing short stories and was, with her husband, a clandestine member of the Communist party. Brunck killed himself in

1937, under the intolerable pressure, it is recorded, of having to pretend to be a Nazi sympathiser while spying for Moscow. In 1939, Hope made her fourth match with Robert Gorham Davis, a professor of English at Columbia University. This marriage endured until his death, in 1998. Hope Davis herself lived to be a hundred. To the end she wrote well-received short fiction and memoirs.

Lydia Davis was born in 1947. In interviews she lays stress on the simplicities of the 'Dick and Jane' books, which introduced her to the world of reading, during one of her father's years' teaching abroad, in Austria, in the early 1950s. The tightness of those infant fables formed her literary reflexes, she suggests. She earned her first degree from Barnard College in 1970 and took up work as a literary translator from French – a line of work which would, eventually, earn her high honours. In 1971 she went to Paris with Paul Auster – to prosecute her career as much as his, which was, currently, seriously adrift as he tried, single-handedly, to refashion the American novel. They moved back to New York in 1974 and married.

The Austers divorced some years later. There was one child, Daniel, who grew up living principally with his father and stepmother – Auster's second wife, Siri Hustvedt. Davis went on to marry the painter, Alan Cote, by whom she had a second son. It was in this phase of her career that Davis began publishing the minimalist fiction which has earned such extravagant plaudits as Rick Moody's: 'The best prose stylist in America.' Publicists never have to hunt far for a strapline to Davis's paperbacks. Her first collection was entitled *Break It Down* (1986). The phrase is apposite. No writer has broken down fiction more dramatically into icy, glittering splinters. She has said that the epigrammatic brevity of her own narratives is a polar reaction to the sweeping prose of Proust, of whom she is her country's leading translator.

She taught creative writing at Bard University and was awarded a five-year MacArthur 'Genius' Award in 2003. Her reputation has grown to rival, even outshine, that of her ex. It's a thought-provoking rivalry. She wrestles with the same intractable generic problems: how, that is, to bend (or buckle, in her case) fiction to the needs of the 'real thing'. His solution has been artful genre fusions, in which Paul Auster is both fictional protagonist, subject matter and author. Her solution is compression to a diamond-like narrative crystal.

Like the diamond, her stories, so to call them, glint with faceted meanings. The following, for example:

Collaboration With Fly
I put that word on the page,
but he added the apostrophe.

A fly, we gather, has landed on the page as she writes, creating an unwanted effect of punctuation – an inverted comma. But is it misleading? 'Apostrophe', as a figure of speech, not punctuation, means something along the lines of 'breaking off' (flying off?) to directly address the reader. And why is the interfering fly 'he'? The well-read reader will recall William Blake's song of innocence on the fly – also a 'Man':

> Little Fly,
> Thy summer's play
> My thoughtless hand
> Has brushed away.
> Am not I
> A fly like thee?
> Or art not thou
> A man like me?

Davis's narrative miniatures use resonance rather than depiction. They do not yield their meanings – they suggest them. In the Lilliput dimensions she works in, Davis's fiction can be extraordinarily rich. The following 'story', for example, of marital ennui (another favourite subject, particularly, one may note, in the period after her separation from Auster):

> Childcare
> It's his turn to take care of the baby. He is cross.
> He says, 'I never get enough done.'
> The baby is in a bad mood, too.
> He gives the baby a bottle of juice and sits him well back in a big armchair.
> He sits himself down in another chair and turns on the television.
> Together they watch The Odd Couple.

The TV series, one notes, ran in the US from 1970 to 1975, with re-runs for a few years thereafter. Roughly coincidental, that is, with the Austers' marriage. It is tempting to 'read into' the broken-down relationship chronicled in so extraordinarily few words.

*

Auster married his second wife, Siri Hustvedt, in 1981. She was born, of Scandinavian-American descent (something carried over into the dramatis personae of all her fiction), in Northfield, Minnesota. Her father, Lloyd, taught Scandinavian literature at the local college, which Siri herself duly went on to attend. Her mother had immigrated from Scandinavia at the age of thirty. Norwegian was the primary language spoken at home during what seems to have been a happy upbringing, tempered by inherent Scandinavian gloom.

After graduating with her first degree, Siri moved to New York to work on a doctorate from Columbia. Her thesis on Dickens's *Our Mutual Friend* was accepted in 1986. Columbia was, over these years, a hotbed of 'literary theory' and – as well as an affection for Dickens's traditional realisms – Hustvedt cultivated a career-long interest in contemporary debate on the poetics of fiction. She decided against an academic career. Had she chosen that route she might well have moved, she says, across into art history. None the less there remained something donnish in her creative personality. Characters writing dissertations, along with dour Norwegian-Americans, crop up in all her novels. Hustvedt and Auster met at a poetry reading. At the time they were both 'completely unknowns'. She was beginning her thesis: he was suffering his seventeen rejections for the manuscript of *City of Glass*. 'We've shared his whole prose career', Hustvedt insists, with a backward glance at her predecessor, who, we apprehend, preceded that prose career – or, at least, its published manifestation.

There were two children in the second Auster marriage: Daniel (the son by Lydia Davis) and a daughter, Sophie. Hustvedt, like her husband, followed a traditional route into fiction, publishing first poetry then short stories. Her earliest work displays her fascination with perception-altering brain malfunction – principally migraine. She herself is a 'migraineur' and, for some time, ran a blog on the ailment in the *New York Times*. The truths of fiction and the fictionality of truth are nagged-at Hustvedt themes. We use narrative, her narratives suggest, to shape experience. Without that narrative reshaping (and falsification) we see nothing. The idea is prominent in her first novel, *The Blindfold* (1992). Hustvedt's second published novel, *The Enchantment of Lily Dahl* (1996), is set in the nowhere of her native Minnesota. The heroine, a short-order waitress, has her banal existence disturbed by a visiting Jewish artist. Love and violence ensue. Distant allegories of her marriage to Auster (small-town Norwegian American girl/New York Jewish novelist) may be detected. Hustvedt consistently teases the reader with glimpsed elements of her own life. Her early stories, for example, centred on a character called Iris – 'Siri' spelled backwards.

Hustvedt's emergence as something other than the novel-writing wife of novelist Paul Auster was established with her third effort, *What I Loved* (2003). If the preceding novel had teased with its suggestions of autobiography, this novel did so sensationally. In 1998 Hustvedt's twenty-year-old stepson, Daniel Auster, was arrested for involvement in a horrific murder. The victim was a drug dealer, Angel Melendez, who supplied the Manhattan club world with its necessaries. After a quarrel about money, Melendez was murdered by a New York 'party promoter', Michael Alig, who forced Drano down the luckless pusher's throat, strangling him with a rope before finishing him off with a hammer. He and an accomplice then chopped the body into pieces, stuffed the dismembered flesh and bone into a cardboard box and threw it into the Hudson River. Melendez was identified, months later, by dental records.

Alig meanwhile had partied on. The trial was sensational and further sensation-alised by the movie *Party Monster* (2003), with Macaulay Culkin in the Alig role. Hustvedt's novel was released two months before the film. The connection between them was transparent – at least to anyone who read New York newspapers. Daniel Auster (reportedly) admitted being actually present at the murder, but passed out on heroin. He pleaded guilty to stealing $3,000 from Melendez and was sentenced to five years' probation. Alig and his accomplice got twenty years in prison for pleading down, on their side, to manslaughter.

Paul Auster has never spoken publicly about his son's crime or written about it. Hustvedt has. *What I Loved* is narrated by an aged Jewish art history professor at Colum-bia, Leo Hertzberg, who is slowly going blind as his past life becomes clearer to him. The most important person in that life is not his wife, Erica, from whom Leo is separated, but his friend, the concept artist Bill Wechsler. Wechsler's art is marked by 'a brutal desire for purity and resistance to compromise'. He believes that 'seeing is flux' – and only art can 'fix' the flux. His works of art are contained in transparent boxes. Hustvedt admits to Wechsler being inspired by Auster. After the death of his own son, Matt, in a freak accident at summer camp (one recalls the boyhood friend of Auster's, struck dead by lightning at a summer camp), Leo's 'story' has stopped. In his loneliness, he assumes the role of favourite uncle to Bill's son, Mark. Mark (an exact contemporary of Leo's lost son, Matt) is, it gradually emerges, an incorrigible psychopath. Obliquely it is sug-gested that this may be the fault of his mother, Bill's first wife, the minimalist poet Lucille Alcott. The daughter of a professor of law, Alcott is cold and ruthlessly self-contained. The gossip circuit in New York has implied that Hustvedt had Davis in her sights.

Bill, having broken up with Lucille, makes a second marriage with a young woman of Scandinavian descent and Minnesota background, Violet Blom. Warm to Lucille's cold, she is 'more beautiful' even than her husband's portraits of her. Violet is engaged on writing a dissertation at Columbia when they meet. The subject of the dissertation is women's hysteria and their spectacular nervous ailments, as something culturally conditioned. (Why, for example, did Victorian women faint so epidemically? Why did Salem girls actually 'see' the Devil? Hustvedt eventu-ally published a book along these lines, *The Shaking Woman, or a History of My Nerves*, in 2009.) Mark falls in with the demonic Teddy Giles, a transvestite 'she monster', whose preferred art form is homicidal sadism. The action climaxes with the torture, murder and dismemberment of a Spanish kid, Rafael Hernandez, whose remains are stuffed into a suitcase and deposited in the river. He is identified by his dental records. Mark is present and implicated in the murder but finally exoner-ated, although his stepmother Violet continues to have 'doubts' and, as her final comment on the matter, says 'I hate Mark'. The title, *What I Loved*, echoes ironically.

The novel's correspondence with the crime and the movie triggered consternation. As the journalist Joe Hagan put it, what Daniel Auster had gone through, was 'not the sort of event any father would want his son to be involved in, and not the sort of story a father would want the world to spend too much time pondering. But now the world – or at least the New York literary community – can do just that, thanks to Ms Hustvedt's new novel.' On the face of it, *What I Loved* is less a *roman-à-clef* than a bunch of keys hurled in the face of the reader. Hustvedt, without conceding transcription, has confessed to the work being 'emotionally autobiographical'. Auster, to whom the work is dedicated, denies all connection.

Hustvedt followed up with a more ambitiously designed work, *The Sorrows of an American* (2008). Allusions to Theodore Dreiser's *An American Tragedy* (1925) are invoked. In this novel about America, she investigates what she sees as an active ingredient in the national character – Scandinavian gloom. The narrator-hero, Erik Davidsen, is a recently divorced New York psychotherapist. He has also recently lost his father, Lars, a professor resident in what is recognisably Hustvedt's home town (her own father died in 2003). In his loneliness Erik sets himself the task of putting his father's papers in order. Of particular interest is his Second World War journal (Hustvedt used her own father's journal, verbatim, for this inset portion of the novel). Among the meticulously ordered documentary remains, is a mysterious letter, which suggests a pre-marital sexual entanglement – and, possibly, an illegitimate relative. Uncovering this mystery forms a principal narrative strand.

Erik's sister, Inga, is also in mourning – not merely for her father, but for her Jewish-novelist husband, Max. Max is pursued, after death, by carrion-feeding 'biographers' – a breed Hustvedt clearly loathes. Inga is writing a dissertation on the theme that reality can only be made sense of by stories – fiction. It is something Erik has perceived in his dealings with his patients, who can also only come to terms with their psychological problems by transforming them into narrative. Gloom is the climate of Hustvedt's fiction: it hangs over her novels like a Scandinavian February in a particularly overcast fjord. Arguably, it eclipses the reader's interest. Too much sorrow.

FN   Lydia Davis (later Auster)
MRT *Samuel Johnson is Indignant*
Biog National Book Award with Lydia Davis, 2007, www.nationalbook.org/ nba2007_f_davis_interv.html (interviewer, B. A. Johnston)

FN   Siri Hustvedt (later Auster)
MRT *The Sorrows of an American*
Biog http://sirihustvedt.net/

286. Paul Auster 1947–; and Siri Hustvedt 1955–

Hustvedt claims that her, and her husband's work, have 'drawn into' each other. One could, tentatively, draw that conclusion from Auster's 2010 novel, *Sunset Park*, a work which is – set against the background of his earlier fiction – strikingly un-Austerian and as strikingly Hustvedtian. The novel's title throws back the ironic echo of the more famous 'Sunset Boulevard' – the Los Angeles address which (as in Billy Wilder's sardonic movie *Sunset Boulevard*) incarnates the Hollywood Dream, which, Auster's novel suggests, with dense reference to movies, has become the American Dream.

Sunset Park, an actual place, is a run-down area of Brooklyn alongside a huge cemetery. Here it is that dreams die and American idols are buried alongside the nobodies who never made it. The story centres on a lost son/stepson. It is 2008. Miles Heller, who may or may not have murdered his stepbrother (even he is not sure), has drifted away from his publisher father, a character who has resemblances to Auster. His parents have broken up. His mother is a film and stage actress currently playing Winnie in Beckett's *Happy Days* (Beckett, one recalls, is the author whom Lydia Davis cites as her principal influence). Miles's stepmother is an academic, specialising (as did Hustvedt) on mid-Victorian fiction.

As the novel opens, Miles Heller is employed as part of a four-man 'trashing out' team in Florida. Their job is to gut foreclosed-on properties, so they can be sold at auction. The wave of foreclosures, following the 2008 Wall Street crisis has done to whole swathes of suburban America what the tornado did to Dorothy's farm shack in *The Wizard of Oz*. 'Each house is a story of failure – of bankruptcy and default, of debt and foreclosure.' Miles, to the irritation of his workmates, photographs the sites which the 'Dunbar Realty Corporation' strips of all human identity:

> he has taken it upon himself to document the last, lingering traces of those scattered lives in order to prove that the vanished families were once here, that the ghosts of people he will never see and never know are still present in the discarded things strewn about their empty houses.

One thinks of the 'dust heaps' (i.e. mountains of human rubbish) in Dickens's *Our Mutual Friend*, the text on which Hustvedt wrote her doctoral dissertation.

After complications with his underage Cuban-American girlfriend, Pilar, Miles drifts back to New York where he joins a squat, until the heat cools, in a foreclosed-on, but as yet untrashed, property, with three fellow drifters. Over the years of wandering he has become a connoisseur of the random vanities of human existence.

The novel contains long musings on star baseball players, and movie stars, whose careers were cut short by freak accidents. There is an extended central meditation on the 1946 William Wyler-directed, Oscar-winning movie, *The Best Years of Our Lives* (Miles's fellow squatter, Alice Bergstrom, a body-obsessed Scandinavian-American is writing a Columbia dissertation on the subject). Wyler's film, in the glow of victory in the Second World War, expresses jubilant optimisms about America and its post-war future. Where, *Sunset Park* enquires, did all that hope go? Trashed, is the answer, like all those Florida family houses.

Revolving ironically around happiness (whose 'pursuit', the Declaration of Independence promises, every American is entitled to), *Sunset Park* recalls the Beckett play in which Miles's mother is starring. There are no happy days in America any more ('happy days are here again' was, of course, the campaign song of FDR, who dragged his country out of depression). Gloom everywhere. What strikes the reader of Auster's other work is how different *Sunset Park* is from, say, *The New York Trilogy*. There remains the author's irrepressible mischievousness (a character named Hertzberg, for example, walks across from *What I Loved*). The novel is different – looser, simpler, more story-driven – from anything the novelist has previously offered his readers.

A similar loosening is evident in Hustvedt's *The Summer Without Men*, published in 2011, a month or two after *Sunset Park*. The narrative bursts on to the page:

> Sometime after he said the word *pause*, I went mad and landed in the hospital. He did not say *I don't ever want to see you again* or *It's over*, but after thirty years of marriage *pause* was enough to turn me into a lunatic whose thoughts burst, ricocheted, and careened into one another like popcorn kernels in a microwave bag.

It is 2008 – around thirty years after Hustvedt married Auster, one may pruriently calculate. Mia Fredricksen is a poet-professor of creative writing at Columbia, of Minnesota-Scandinavian origins. Her husband is a world-famous scientist. Unusually, the narrative of *The Summer Without Men* is interspersed with cartoons of Mia. As the novel's jacket photo confirms, they are witty representations of the author herself. There are, as usual, coy allusions to Auster's fiction embedded in the story. And, of course, there is the author's love of nominal anagram – as in Iris/Siri. Mia anagrammatises as Mia/I am [Fredricksen] or, more fancifully 'am I Fredricksen?'

Mia resolves, during the marital pause, to return to her home town. Here she involves herself in two practical exercises in literary appreciation. She takes over a reading group for the ancient ladies of the town, among whom is her widowed mother. And she runs a creative writing class for a class of pubescent schoolgirls. Literature, she discovers, can do more for her than any prescription drug. She recovers her sanity – and, it is intimated, her husband. The story is told with an economy and spareness which is something new in her work. It will be interesting to see how it further evolves.

Fancifully one can perceive a kind of marital duet. Or, if one stands a little further back – to take in the first Mrs Auster – a trio, all playing ensemble. It is a unique concatenation of novelists' lives.

287. Salman Rushdie 1947–

He could start a brawl in a Trappist monastery.

The date of birth is significant. If not, like his most famous character, Saleem Sinai, born on the stroke of midnight, 14 August 1947, Salman came into the world in the period when India again became India: simultaneously a very old and a very new country. Rushdie was born Muslim in Bombay (when Bombay was Bombay – he still prefers that name over Mumbai), a city in which 'the West was *totally* mixed up with the East'. He was brought up in a home where English and 'Hindustani' – a 'colloquial mixture of Hindi and Urdu' – were spoken indiscriminately. Hindustani, he helpfully adds, is 'the language of Bollywood movies', that sublimely jumbled film genre. His grandfather had a reputation as an Urdu poet and imbued his grandson with a lifelong love of P. G. Wodehouse, a writer, as Rushdie mischievously claims, peculiarly congenial to the Indian mind.

His father was a briefcase-carrying, Cambridge University-educated (Literature), businessman. Theirs was a vexed relationship. Rushdie Sr took offence at the satirical depiction of himself in *Midnight's Children* (1981). Salman 'pissed him off' further by observing he had tactfully left most of the paternal satire out. Their reconciliation is recorded in the touching last sections of *The Satanic Verses* (1988), a novel which Anis Ahmed Rushdie did not live to read. Salman, the only son, was, as he records, pampered by the women in the family. He recalls as a primal literary experience seeing the film of *The Wizard of Oz*. 'After I saw the film, I went home and wrote a short story called "Over the Rainbow." I was probably nine or ten.'

When asked what his great theme is, Rushdie answers 'worlds in collision'. His upbringing is a bewildering series of post-colonial frictions. He, a child of the mosque, had his first formal education at Bombay's Cathedral School. At thirteen-and-a-half he was sent halfway around the world to finish his school education at Rugby, Tom Brown's school. Hughes's novel starts with an extended tribute to England's 'Browns', who have been instrumental in covering the globe imperial red. It was not an entirely congenial institution for someone literally brown. Dr Arnold's school still had its Flashmans, one gathers. Rushdie says he knew 'everything about racism' by the time he left Rugby; he found escapist relief in *The Lord of the Rings*.

Meanwhile, back in the subcontinent, his family was the victim of ethnic cleansing, forcing them to relocate to Karachi. Salman Rushdie was now a Pakistani. But if he felt he had roots anywhere it was two generations back in Kashmir. This is the region which supplies the beautifully composed prelude to *Midnight's Children*. A continuously contested region, Rushdie 'took it on' at full-length in *Shalimar the Clown* (2005). Kashmir, he believes, is where the Third World War will start, kicked off by confrontation between the planet's two most volatile nuclear powers. Those who question the prophetic powers of Salman Rushdie should be wary. His New York novel *Fury* (2001), with a dustjacket, chosen by the author, depicting the Empire State Building struck by lightning, came out five days before 9/11. *Shalimar* is a novel which the Western reader should ponder.

Rushdie went on to King's College, Cambridge, where he was, he recalled, happy. It was E. M. Forster's college. His views on *Passage to India* have never, as far as I know, been recorded. He read history – against his father's wishes, who demanded something more practical – economics, for example. Rushdie Sr was appalled at the thought that his son and heir should be a writer: 'A cry burst out of him: What will I tell my friends? What he really meant was that all his friends' less intelligent sons were pulling down big bucks in serious jobs and what – I was going to be a penniless novelist?' Whatever else, the author of *Midnight's Children* was not destined to be penniless.

The subcontinent was currently wracked by war in which Rushdie was, by background, on both sides. He could have stayed on at the university – his third background – but, as the hero decides in *Fury*, the narrowness, infighting and 'ultimate provincialism' of Cambridge was intolerable. He went to London where he 'futzed around': it was an exciting decade, commemorated in the middle sections of *The Ground Beneath Her Feet* (1999). Everyone of his age cohort was futzing. His first idea was to go on the stage – something, one fancies, which would have elicited an even louder wail from his father. His talent, he realised after a few performances, was inadequate (though the thrill is still there: he is always willing to do cameos for any film director who asks). He was broke, alienated from his father, living in a garret when – through one of his theatrical pals – he landed a job in advertising: the novelist's equivalent to street-walking. All through the 1970s he would keep body and soul together coming up with tags and jingles for the commercial world. Meanwhile, he was writing fiction in his spare time – 'flailing about', as he later put it.

His first published novel was *Grimus* (1975). The title of the novel, we are told (few occidental readers would have guessed) 'is an anagram of the name "Simurg", the immense, all-wise, fabled bird of pre-Islamic Persian mythology'. Rushdie's later verdict on the novel is an uncompromising 'garbage' and there was nothing in the reviews to correct that opinion. 'After the critical beating *Grimus* took,' he records, 'I completely rethought everything. I thought, OK, I have to write about something that I care about much more.' He was also 'scared' at this period in the late 1970s; he felt he was losing the race. Amis and Ian McEwan and many other young stars were 'zooming' past him.

The problem was, he recognised, 'to find himself', not to find a subject. He did so with Saleem Sinai and *Midnight's Children*. Once created, it was Saleem, he felt, who was battering away at his typewriter keys. It was Saleem who mastered the trick of 'dragging in everything'. The narrator-hero of the novel is conceived as one of the 1,000 children born at the precise chime of the moment of Indian Independence. They are blessed, or cursed, with 'powers' (Saleem's is located in his majestic conk) and are inter-clairvoyant. Science fiction readers will recognise them as a version of the aliens in John Wyndham's *The Midwich Cuckoos* – there is usually a broad strand of science fiction in Rushdie's fictional tapestry. Saleem's lifelong foe, and twin, will be Shiva, named after the Hindu god of destruction. Mythology – Hindu, Greek, Iranian and Roman – is another broad strand. Saleem and Shiva's interwoven narratives comprise a history of the new, but primevally old, country. There are no English characters, although a strain of colonial blood, we learn, may course through Saleem's veins thanks to some hanky-panky by the family's now departed occidental landlord and some mischief in the hospital where he was born.

The novel won the 1981 Booker Prize – and then kept on winning (as the Booker of Bookers). It was Salman Rushdie who was now zooming. He followed up with *Shame* (1983), which dumped – as controversially as its predecessor – on Pakistan and its ruling Bhutto dynasty. His novels were gaining him fame and making him dangerous enemies in equal measure. The Gandhi dynasty were mightily displeased by elements in *Midnight's Children* and reached for their lawyers, but Rushdie had realised that the novel was one of the few free-fire zones left in modern life and rejoiced in the fact. Nothing was to be sacred. Sacrilege is a risky profession. The momentous date in his CV is (he loves the irony) St Valentine's Day 1989 when he received, from the paramount leader of Iran, Ayatollah Khomeini, a 'love letter' in the form of a fatwa. The word was not one familiar in the West although, thanks to Salman Rushdie, it now forever will be. The offence was, of course, *The Satanic*

Verses, published a few months earlier. The novel opens with a powerfully symbolic episode. An Air India jumbo jet explodes. Two Indians fall 30,000 feet on to Hastings – that symbolic beach, where William the Conqueror ate his symbolic mouthful of sand. Gibreel Farishta and Saladin Chamcha are, like William, illegal immigrants. Or angel and devil. Or Hindu and Muslim anti-types.

Mid-air explosions which slaughter hundreds of infidels were not something to distress the Ayatollah Khomeini. What drew down his theocratic wrath was (1) an impudent depiction of his fundamentalist self in *The Satanic Verses*; (2) an even more satirical depiction of the Prophet, under the insulting Western name 'Mahound'; and (3) the allegation that the Qur'an had been strategically altered ('Satanically') and rephrased by a Persian scribe called 'Salman'. Rushdie's aim was less heresy than to suggest the same kind of imagination at work in the Muslim holy text that German New Criticism had found, a hundred years earlier, in the Bible. Put another way, the holy book was not Revelation but the almighty's novel. The fatwa laid on every devout Muslim the obligation to kill the apostate. Rushdie was bundled into protective custody by Britain's Special Branch, under instructions from Mrs Thatcher – 'Mrs Torture' in the novel. It was wormwood for the ruling Tory party. Geoffrey Howe, Foreign Secretary in 1989, observed that 'The British government, the British people, do not have any affection for the book ... It compares Britain with Hitler's Germany.'

Diplomatic relations with Iran broke down and Rushdie would spend years in the ground beneath the world's feet. As his friend Martin Amis wittily put it: 'He vanished into the front page.' His own view was that it was like 'a bad Salman Rushdie novel'. Whatever else, it disrupted his personal life and, as doubtless biographies will one day reveal, may at least partly explain a series of broken marriages and short-term relationships with beautiful women (something else that kept him on the front pages). He produced in this jail-time children's books and major works, notably *The Moor's Last Sigh* (1995), depicting an India where he was no longer able to go, on peril of his life, but which he still cared about. The most ambitious work of this period is *The Ground Beneath Her Feet* (1999), a novel which, among much else, examines the new supranational culture of pop music. Rushdie later ventured on concert appearances with U2, for whose congenial leader, Bono, he wrote lyrics. Hard to imagine Kingsley Amis doing anything of that kind.

By the turn of the century Rushdie, with necessary precautions, was free to emerge from underground. He moved to America, citing as one reason the bitchiness of literary London. He has no explanation for the personal animosity he evokes. 'It was a strange feeling', he says, 'to be characterised by some in the British press as an unlikable person. I'm not quite sure what I did to deserve it.' He was also recoiling from the breakdown of his latest marriage. The fictional outcome was *Fury* (2001).

In it Malik Solanka, a former Cambridge professor, similarly recovering from a broken marriage and broken career, sets out to find a new life in New York City. It can be seen as what alcoholics call a 'geographical cure'. But simply because history deposited him in Manhattan didn't mean Rushdie liked his new home any more than he liked 'Mrs Torture's' Britain, Bhutto's Pakistan or the Gandhi's India. As he pictures New York, it's a circle of hell, metropolitan fury, wide-bore, full-volume: 'Garbage trucks like giant cockroaches moved through the city, roaring. He was never out of earshot of a siren, an alarm, a large vehicle's reverse-gear bleeps, the beat of some unbearable music.'

Disowned as it might be, England still felt it had a stake in him and in 2007 Salman Rushdie was knighted. Predictably it provoked riots across the Islamic world and threats of retaliatory suicide bombing. *The Enchantress of Florence* (2008) was written in the throes of yet another divorce and doubly centred on Renaissance Italy and the Mughal Empire. In a hostile review Nirpal Dhaliwal made the case that the novel is Hinduphobic. The art of making friends constantly eludes Rushdie. He continues to write and stir up hornets. His depictions of what that writing amounts to are self-deprecating and ironic. One depiction, in *Midnight's Children*, is the dying man's pickle factory – a place where dead fruit preserves a misleadingly tangy artificial afterlife. Another ironic portrayal is that in *Fury*, where the hero Malik goes from academia into show-business, doing 'philosophical dolls' for TV: half Wittgenstein, half *Thunderbirds*.

Overarching all Rushdie's works are two grand symbolisms: one – most fully developed in *The Ground Beneath her Feet* – is that of Orpheus, the postmodernist icon. Torn apart, his dismembered head continues to sing, unstoppably. The other grand symbol is that of Scheherazade and the 1001 nights – the story which must go on, if life is to go on. Rushdie is rarely one for short narratives. His oeuvre has been lumbered with the label 'magic realism'. What is more significant is how that fiction divides commentators into ferociously opposed camps. He refuses to recant, pull in his horns, or recycle – 'Midnight's Grandchildren' will never happen. And, with every change of step, Rushdie irritates. But, as Cocteau said, savage reviews are love letters, of a kind. Like fatwas.

FN   Salman Ahmed Rushdie
MRT   *Midnight's Children*
Biog www.theparisreview.org/interviews/5531/the-art-of-fiction-no-186-salman-rushdie

288. Stephen King 1947–

I am the literary equivalent of a Big Mac and Fries.

Like others of my generation (and his), I have grown old with Stephen King. I first encountered his work, some thirty-five years ago, with the primal 'Gunslinger' episodes in the magazine *Fantasy & Science Fiction*. The mixture of Mallory and Sergio Leone was not to my taste – although sufficient numbers of fans liked it well enough to encourage King to continue it as his seven-part *Dark Tower* saga. His first-published 'Our-World' novel, *Carrie* (1974), was indeed to my taste. Carrie White is an unhappy little girl in a crummy little town who discovers she has 'powers'. It's payback time for all those school mates who have picked on her. She goes on a telekinetic shooting, slaughter and urban demolition spree. It's justified Columbine.

Carrie bears the hallmarks of King's later fiction. He had a deprived childhood himself and – a sickly, geeky kid – was bullied. He found comfort in comic books. The picked-on child, from Carrie, through Arnie Cunningham (*Christine*, 1983) to Duddits (*Dreamcatcher*, 2001), is a fixture in King's fictional universe. So, too, is the gory nemesis for whole communities – whether by vampiric infestation (*Salem's Lot*, 1975), diabolic takeover (*Needful Things*, 1991), telekinetic flame-throwing (*Firestarter*, 1980), alien invasion (*The Tommyknockers*, 1987), nasty things seeping out of the sewers (*It*, 1986), or – most preposterously – a demonically possessed saloon car (*Christine*, 1983). There are many energies at work in King's fiction, but fantasised revenge on his long-ago tormentors is clearly among the more powerful. 'Lost childhoods', as Graham Greene observed, make interesting novelists. Authors, like generals, need luck and King has had a lot of it. *Carrie* was Class-A pulp, but what gave it the edge over, say, John Farris's *The Fury* (1976), or David Seltzer's *The Omen* (1976)? King's first stroke of luck was his publisher, Doubleday, landing a $400,000 deal for the paperback rights. He was, at one leap, in the big time. The second stroke of luck was the film rights being optioned for a movie directed by Brian De Palma.

Like John Grisham, Mario Puzo and Peter Benchley, King has been blessed with film tie-ins frankly better than the novels they adapt. Stanley Kubrick (*The Shining*, 1980), John Carpenter (*Christine*, 1983), David Cronenberg (*The Dead Zone*, 1983), Rob Reiner (*Stand by Me*, 1986), George Romero (*The Dark Half*, 1993), have added collateral lustre to King's reputation. And it's not just directors – King's narratives elicit terrific performances. One thinks of Jack Nicholson's 'Here's Johnnie!' (which, incidentally, King hated), but even more unexpected is James Mason doing a prince of darkness in a TV *Salem's Lot* (1979) – the role the velvet-voiced one was born to play. *The Dead Zone* (1979) is not one of King's great works, yet Christopher Walken

– maimed and bent on presidential assassination – gives the performance of a life-time. Even actors whose facial expression is as constipated as James Caan's (*Misery*, 1990) or as inscrutable as Tim Robbins's (*The Shawshank Redemption*, 1994) relax in the narrative environment King creates. And, without King, Kathy Bates (*Misery*, *Dolores Claiborne*, 1995) would still be a supporting actress. If, as the Hollywood proverb goes, there are actors whom the camera 'likes', there are also writers too. There have, of course, been clunkers – *The Lawnmower Man* (1992) which King disowns; and *The Running Man* (1987) which he ought to disown, come to mind, though even they have a kind of horrible watchability. Who would miss the spec-tacle of the future Governor of California in skin-tight spandex, doing battle with the future Governor of Minnesota dressed up as a tin can?

The other thing that King had going for him was energy of composition. The 'firestorm', as fans called the spate of writing in his early career, was fuelled, as a cleaned-up King later confessed, by cocaine and booze (he cannot, he claims, remember writing *Cujo* (1981), his shaggy-dog horror tale). In the ten years fol-lowing *Carrie*, King turned out eighteen full-length novels and four volumes of col-lected stories. When his publisher felt he might be glutting the market, he invented an alter ego, Richard Bachman, to share the burden. Bachman, alas, has since died of 'cancer of the pseudonym'. It remains a supreme feat of authorial athleticism.

And it paid off. In 2003, Stephen King made number 14 on the *Forbes* wealthiest celebrity list, with an estimated income of $50 million-plus. Only novelist Michael Crichton ranked higher, and Crichton was, by contrast with King, a child of privilege. He was writing bestselling novels while a Dean's List medical student at Harvard. Stevie King had no such advantages and believes that he is denied respect. Unlike Crichton, he pulled himself up by his bootstraps, from mobile home to mansion. In his acceptance speech for the lifetime award given him in 2003 by the National Book Foundation, he recalled how he, and his wife Tabitha, 'lived in a trailer and she made a writing space for me in the tiny laundry room with a desk and her Olivetti portable between the washer and dryer … When I gave up on *Carrie*, it was Tabby who rescued the first few pages of single spaced manuscript from the wastebasket, told me it was good, said I ought to go on.'

Big as his sales are, King's inferiority complex is bigger. He has a burning sense of 'injustice' – against himself. He despises 'smarmy' literary critics but yearns for their attention. The main thrust of his NBA speech was *Carrie*-style payback. They hadn't emptied a bucket of pig's blood over his head, but the literary establishment was guilty of 'tokenism' – treating him like a house Negro with their confounded 'lifetime award'. What did they know of his life? The literary establishment declined to be cowed by some hack, who had struck it rich with a reading public even less cultivated than himself. Harold Bloom, who is to literary criticism what Einstein was to physics, declared that the NBA's decision to give an award to King was 'another low in the shocking process of dumbing down our cultural life. I've described King in the past as a writer of penny dreadfuls, but perhaps even that is too kind. He shares nothing with Edgar Allan Poe. What he is is an immensely inadequate writer on a sentence-by-sentence, paragraph-by-paragraph, book-by-book basis.'

He deserves better than Harold Bloom. What sets King apart from other super-selling authors is his constant straining against the limitations of genre. Works like *Gerald's Game* (1992; a wife is victimised by an S&M loving husband), *Rose Madder* (1995; a wife goes on the run from a sadistic husband), and *Dolores Claiborne* (1992; a battered wife is driven to homicide) are, probably, husbandly homage to the admirable Tabitha. But they also indicate King's willingness to write against the grain of his branded product. Ever restless, King revived the Dickensian novel in numbers, issuing *The Green Mile* (1996) in serial instalments. Less successfully, he had a stab at the e-novel, with *Riding the Bullet* and *The Plant*. Together with Peter Straub, King has pulled off, with *The Talisman* (1984) and *Black House* (1989), that rarest of literary achievements, the tandem-authored novel that is, at least, half decent.

Few novelists have been as graphic about the trials of authorship. *The Shining* (1977) is, on one level, about the problem of writing with a wife and child distracting you (why not chop them up?). In *Misery*, the writer is – as King must often feel – in bondage to his number one fan. King's fear of unconsciously plagiarising is dramatised in *Secret Window, Secret Garden* (1990). In *The Dark Half* (1989), the novelist hero is bifurcated into a 'class' novelist and a 'hack' – King's own agonising dualism. *Bag of Bones* (1998) is a fantasy about writer's block: few writers have allegorised their professional plight as imaginatively as King. As the many websites testify, Stephen King stimulates what can only be called cultism among his more devoted followers – those who could earnestly discuss for hours whether 'Ka' turns clockwise or anti-clockwise. Running through his work is the vision of a Manichaean struggle between the powers of light (almost always represented by a child) and the powers of darkness – variously incarnated as Randall Flagg, Walter o'Dim, the Fisherman, the Man in Black or – latterly – the Crimson King. King's dualistic cosmos is most starkly portrayed in *The Stand* (1978). After a global epidemic, the world is stripped down to two camps; Armageddon and apocalypse ensue. Who wins the day is enigmatic.

King's philosophy of bestsellerdom, ruefully expressed over the years, is that the money is nice, the adulation is nice, but he yearns for an ordinary man's privacy – the privilege, for example, of going to a Red Sox game and not being recognised. Ever since his horrific accident, when he was run down walking along the high road in Maine in June 1999, there was something missing from King's fiction. He noted it himself, in typically wry fashion: 'I watched *Titanic* when I got back home from the hospital, and cried. I knew that my IQ had been damaged.'

FN Stephen Edwin King
MRT *The Stand*
Biog S. Spignesi, *The Essential Stephen King* (2001)

289. Robert Jordan 1948–2007

I'm not a guru or a sage. I'm a storyteller. The only times I get disturbed is when I find people who seem to be taking this too seriously.

When it came out in mid-October 2009, Robert Jordan's posthumous *A Memory of Light* (completed by another hand) shot to the top of the hardback American best-seller list. Jordan's publishers, Tor Books, were unsurprised. They had authorised a first print run of a million copies on the basis of the novel's thirteen predecessors in *The Wheel of Time* cycle. *A Memory of Light* caters to hard-core initiates of fantasy fiction. If you have to ask who Robert Jordan is, you'll probably never know or care to find out. According to Amazon, those who like this book also go for the sword, sorcery and pseudo-religious sagas of George R. R. Martin, Terry Goodkind, Raymond E. Feist, Robin Hobb and Fritz Leiber – names which will ring few bells with the general reader, but all of whom have their faithful bands of devotees.

Jordan (real name James Oliver Rigney Jr) was born in Charleston, South Carolina, and was proudly Southern his whole life. An older brother introduced him to the works of Jules Verne (at four years old, Jordan claimed), which left an indelible impression. It was not, in his early manhood, destined to be a literary life. He served two tours in Vietnam as a helicopter gunner, winning a chest full of medals (most honourably the Distinguished Flying Cross, for gallantry under fire). On being discharged he took a degree in physics at the Citadel, the military academy in South Carolina, and then he was assigned to the US Navy, as a nuclear engineer. Jordan did not begin writing seriously until 1977. 'From the age of five I intended to write, one day. When I had established myself in a more stable profession. Then I had an accident that resulted in a month's stay in the hospital, during which I almost died, and I decided life was too short to wait on "one day". So I started writing.'

It came easily to him. Under the pseudonym 'Reagan O'Neal', he turned out a series of pirate romances set in mid-eighteenth-century Charleston. His career as an author was assisted by his wife, Harriet McDougal, his editor at Tor Books. The couple lived in a 1797 Charleston mansion, of which Jordan was inordinately proud. As his skills developed he moved on from swashbuckling to Westerns, then – most successfully – to sword and sorcery. He did not, he later attested, ever want to write about Vietnam – or anything even allegorically connected with that horror. Fiction was escape; it may even have been therapy.

Jordan is credited with seven Conan novels between 1982 and 1984, beginning with *Conan the Invincible* and ending with *Conan the Victorious* (see Robert E. Howard for the origin of the Barbarian hero). On the American version of *Desert Island Discs*, Jordan chose his trusty M16 rifle as one of the three objects he would take with him. Like dog-owners, authors, it seems, come to resemble their heroes.

The first in the 'WoT' series, *The Eye of the World*, came out in 1990. Like Tim LaHaye's and Jerry Jenkins's bestselling *Left Behind* series – a fictionalised Book of Revelation – Jordan aimed to complete his series in twelve volumes (in the writing, it extended to fourteen). Both series concluded with versions of Armageddon, the final battle.

Despite the parallels, it is doubtful that their readerships overlap. Jordan casts his net beyond the evangelical belief system of LaHaye and Jenkins deep into heathen-ish hinterlands. It's easy to read his fantasy as an allegory of current, real-world American anxieties. It was observed that sales of Jordan's series jumped after 9/11.

It is impossible to summarise, with any lucidity, the swirling plots of the 'WoT' saga. One of Jordan's devotional websites makes a gallant stab at doing so for the first in the series:

> A crazed Lews Therin Telamon wanders through the wreckage of his palace, not seeing the corpses of his wife and children. A man named Elan Morin Tedronai appears to kill him, but is angered to realize that Lews Therin is too insane to recognize him, and heals him (painfully) using the Dark One's power. Returned to sanity, Lews Therin sees the dead body of his wife Ilyena and begins sobbing uncontrollably. Tedronai offers to bring her back from the dead if Lews Therin will serve the Dark One.

It gets more complicated over the next fourteen volumes – and cosmic in its time and space frames:

> 'Ten years! You pitiful fool! This war has not lasted ten years, but since the beginning of time. You and I have fought a thousand battles with the turning of the Wheel, a thousand times a thousand, and we will fight until time dies and the Shadow is triumphant!'

In book-trade terms, 'WoT' (as 'WoT maniacs' like to call it) is a prime example of 'franchise fiction' – spinning off, profitably, into computer games, comics and sponsored competitions. Later titles were promoted by 'Internet Hunts', in which experts could navigate twelve riddling websites to win their prize. There is also a 'theoryland' website devoted to exegesis of the finer points of Jordanology.

In early 2006, Jordan announced on his Dragonmount blog that he was suffering from cardiac amyloidosis, that it was fatal, and that he would not live more than four years – if that. He stated, gallantly, that he would keep writing to the end and that he would fight the disease. New treatments for Jordan's rare ailment proved unavailing and he died a few months later. His huge collection of knives and swords was sold on eBay, including such favourites as the Nepalese Kukuri, the Japanese Katana, the Cold Steel Magnum Tanto and an Applegate-Fairbairn fighter. His cycle was completed by a disciple.

FN   Robert Jordan (born James Oliver Rigney, Jr)
MRT *A Memory of Light*
Biog www.imdb.com/title/tt1298655/ (documentary film by Hunter Wentworth)

290. Ian McEwan 1948–

Sometimes I think I'll never quite escape my early reputation.

Ian McEwan was born in 1948, a dreary year, in that dreariest of garrison towns, Aldershot. His father, David, was a senior NCO, later an officer, in the British Army. A pen portrait of him is given as a motorbike dispatch rider in *Atonement*, in the Dunkirk section. He was, his son recalls, 'very handsome, erect, with a dangerous look about him. A hard-drinking man, quite terrifying. He was a great stickler for all the spit and polish of traditional army life, and at the same time he adored me as I grew older.' A Glaswegian, David McEwan lied about his age to sign up in 1933 (an even drearier year than 1948) to escape the dole and see the world. Both he and his mother, McEwan recalls, 'were rather frightened of him'. She was a fourteen-year-old school leaver who had gone into service; he was a child of the post-war 'bulge' – as significant, demographically, as being an Indian midnight's child. It meant, after some time in postings abroad, a good boarding school education, while his parents continued to follow the pipe and drum across the shrinking Empire.

Vivid flashes of McEwan's childhood found in the fourth chapter of *The Child in Time* (1987) – his father, for example, slathering Brylcreem on his son's pomaded, then short back and sides, sticks in the mind. As an adult, while he still had it, McEwan's hair would run very wild. At school he read widely, was 'rather lonely', and toyed with science A-levels before being redirected to literature by a charismatic teacher. L. P. Hartley's *The Go-Between* is cited as lastingly influential and could, one suspects, furnish an interesting Ph.D. on the topic of juvenile treachery – a favourite theme of both novelists. On leaving school, McEwan went to Sussex, one of the 'new' 1960s universities built to accommodate the 'bulge' and the previously excluded cohort liberated into higher education by the 1944 Education Act. The syllabus was flexible and cross-disciplinary. It suited him well. The boundary between science and humanities has never been an insurmountable obstacle for Ian McEwan.

He marks out 1970 as a turning point. He had heard something about a new MA course at another new university, East Anglia. It was the first creative writing course in the country, founded by the novelists Malcolm Bradbury and Angus Wilson. As McEwan recalls, 'I phoned the university and amazingly got straight through to Malcolm Bradbury. He said, Oh, the fiction part has been dropped because nobody has applied. This was the first year of the program. And I said, Well, what if I apply? He said, Come up and talk to us.' It was an ideal nursery for the young would-be writer. His first instinct, under Bradbury's cosmopolitan influence, was to move away from the pervasive 'greyness' of English fiction towards what was being done in America. In this frame of mind he composed ultra-gothic short stories which, while he was still a student, were picked up by little magazines in the US and the UK. Connection with Ian Hamilton's *New Review* brought him into social contact with other young writers in Hamilton's merry Soho stable: Julian Barnes, Martin Amis, Clive James. He saw himself as Aesop's country mouse come up to town. He was still in his early twenties and very much on his way.

After UEA, McEwan dropped out to do the hippy thing, wandering as far afield as Afghanistan. He was not, one suspects, smoking Woodbines (his early characters, such as the couple in *The Comfort of Strangers* (1981), enjoy a relaxing joint after the day's business. Thirty years later, in *Saturday* (2005), it's fine wine for the McEwan hero – precisely vintage-checked). He had inherited his father's work ethic and after six month's hippydom he dropped back into a full-time career in writing. Jonathan Cape, under Tom Maschler, the dominant patron of up-and-coming novelists, took on his first two collections of short stories, *First Love, Last Rites* (1975) and *In Between the Sheets* (1978). Abused children feature centrally in these collections. The opening story of the first volume, 'Homemade', for example, climaxes on an elder sibling complacently raping his young sister. It ends:

'You've wet inside me,' and she began to cry. Hardly noticing, I got up and started to get dressed. This may have been one of the most desolate couplings known to copulating mankind, involving lies, deceit, humiliation, incest, my partner falling asleep, my gnat's orgasm and the sobbing which now filled the bedroom, but I was pleased with it.

McEwan is at pains (and one believes him) to record that his own childhood, though at times straitened, was straight. His fiction signally wasn't. These early stories revel in rape, paedophilia, castration, bestiality and perversion – the sheets were very twisted. But all the reviewers lined up to agree, that whatever their disgust, a major new talent had arrived. He was, in literary terms, a made man. He followed up with two short novels (he habitually writes shorter than his peers), *The Cement Garden* (1978) and *The Comfort of Strangers*. The first is routinely compared to *Lord of the Flies*. Four suddenly orphaned children decide to live in a juvenile commune, without informing the adult world of their parents' death. Bad things ensue (McEwan, following his own 1960s brush with it, has little time for the hippy life: it comes under his satirical lash again in *Enduring Love*). *The Comfort of Strangers*, set in an unnamed Venice (to avoid evocation of Thomas Mann, one suspects) is a study in decadent sexual sadism. An initially rather boring, and terminally bored, English tourist couple discover, to their alarm, the masochist within themselves.

Looking back, McEwan sees a break at the mid-1980s point in his career, away from 'formally simple and linear short fiction, claustrophobic, desocialised, sexually strange, dark'. There followed a string of substantial and more ambitious works. *The Child in Time* (1987) opens with one of McEwan's 'powerful moments'. A man is walking through rush-hour London, by Millbank. He sees everything around him with crystal clarity – not because he is an artist but because he is looking for his (now) five-year-old daughter, abducted from a supermarket, two years previously. *The Innocent* (1990) contains another hammeringly powerful set-piece, the description of the dismemberment of the corpse of the hero's lover's earlier lover for packing up in a suitcase and clandestine disposal. *Black Dogs* (1992) offers elegant play with time schemes – the hounds of the title, as the last section of the narrative reveals – are emblematic of a Nazi evil that will never die. *Enduring Love* (1997) opens with a delicately poised mind-game: a helium balloon flies off its anchorage in the Chilterns; a child is marooned in its basket. A miscellaneous crew of men, who happen to be near by, grab the tie ropes. But their attempt to help sets up an ethical dilemma. If they hang on, they discover, they will all be pulled away to their death or injury. But who will break ranks and let go first, who will hold on, whatever the consequence? What binds us together in society, the novel implies, is love. But love, like everything else, has its breaking strain. It endures only so long.

The fine 'set-pieces' highlight one of the cruxes of McEwan's fictional method. Is his long fiction merely the setting for inset short stories? Any such suspicion was put to rest by *Amsterdam*, the novel which won the 1998 Booker Prize. The plot centres on a suicide compact between two friends – one of whose mutual friends has died prematurely and degradingly. They agree to take the other to the Dutch city, where euthanasia is legal, should the trip prove necessary. They 'fall out and lure each other to Amsterdam simultaneously for mutual murder', as McEwan summarises the plot. He describes the novel as 'comedy'. In fact, *Amsterdam* takes in large questions – about art (should one sacrifice everything for it) and about modern journalism (one of the pact-makers is the editor of a newspaper very like the *Guardian*). The shortest novel ever to win Britain's premier fiction prize, *Amsterdam* is constructed with a watchmaker's art.

His reputation went 'nova' – another way of saying he became very big in America – with *Atonement* (2001). The plot pivots on a wickedly perceptive child who grows up and becomes a prize-winning novelist – this McEwan sees the destiny of James's Maisie had the other novelist followed it through. McEwan's own father was recently dead and *Atonement* reconstructs the Dunkirk evacuation in which David McEwan was swept up. As Ian recalls:

> Many ex-servicemen have found it difficult or impossible to talk about their experiences of war. My father never had any such problems. He never tired of telling me, a bored adolescent, and later, an attentive middle-aged son, how his legs were shot up by a machine gun mounted on a German tank; how he teamed up with a fellow who had been wounded in both arms, and how between them they had managed the controls of a motorbike to drive to the beaches of Dunkirk and eventual evacuation.

The story was profoundly uninteresting to the young McEwan, but fascinating as he himself entered late middle age.

Age is relevant elsewhere. One of the questions frequently posed by those who have followed his fiction is 'Do you prefer the early or the late?' His later work has evolved in various ways. It has become less jaggedly disturbing, whilst dealing with the same central issues. In *On Chesil Beach* (2007), the lives of a honeymooning couple are deformed by their 1960s unfamiliarity with the mechanics of sex. 'Do not begin your marriage with a rape,' warned Balzac. Don't begin it with a sperm-showering fumble, advises McEwan. Along with the softening of edge is an enlargement of scope: in *Saturday* (2005) he takes on the Iraq War; in *Solar* (2010), global warming.

Reviewing McEwan's life so far, a number of distinctive features emerge. One is the fluidity with which his fiction slips into celluloid. His hit rate, in big-screen adaptation, is rivalled only by Stephen King's. In a 1999 lawsuit brought by his former wife, an estimate of annual earnings of £500,000 were alleged. If true (it seems, on the face of it, untrue), much of that income must have come from film rights. He has turned his own hand to screenplays – notably, with Richard Eyre and *The Ploughman's Lunch* (1985), a scathingly satirical 'Condition of England' film.

Another salient feature in his career is the way in which, despite what looks like a constitutional desire for privacy, headlines seem to seek him out. In the late 1990s, the press made much of a dispute between him and his divorced wife, Penny Allen (the dedicatee of his early work) over the custody of their now teenage children. The couple had married in 1982 and separated in 1995. She had carried their children off to France, in defiance of an English court order. The row gave rise to surreal ruses, which would have seemed far-fetched in a novel (Ms Allen's new partner renaming himself, for example, 'Ian Russell McEwan'). McEwan maintained silence, other than to express grateful acknowledgement that his legal rights were finally observed. It must, one assumes, have been distraction verging, at its worst, on downright torment. In 1997 he married again, to Annalena McAfee, then literary editor of the *Guardian*, and the couple had moved from Oxford to Fitzrovia, North Soho, the closely charted setting of *Saturday*. Location has always been worth noting in McEwan's fiction. One of his sons studying science at nearby UCL seems, plausibly, to have revived the novelist's own fascination with the discipline in his later career – making him a favourite guest lecturer at such front-line institutions as MIT and Caltech.

In 2007 McEwan was less painfully in the headlines when the existence of a hitherto unknown brother was revealed. This elder son of his mother, then Rose Wort, had been 'given away as an illegitimate child at a railway station in 1942'. She had become adulterously pregnant by another soldier (Ian's father David, it transpired) while her first husband was serving abroad. He was subsequently killed in the Normandy landings, and Rose married Ian's father, David, in 1947. It was wartime and such things happened. The child was adopted by a childless couple and Ian was kept in the dark for sixty years, as was his brother. It all came to light as Rose McEwan was dying of vascular dementia. The two brothers – one a bricklayer, the other Britain's most applauded novelist – hit it off, McEwan records. Another headline squall was whipped up in 2006 when Julia Langdon, in the *Daily Mail*, pointed out resemblances between passages in *Atonement* and Lucilla Andrews's memoir, *No Time For Romance* (a work cited by McEwan in his acknowledgements). He felt obliged to take over the front page of the *Guardian* to proclaim 'I am not a Plagiarist', which served to make it gossip for the whole world. A band of distinguished fellow novelists, including the notoriously secretive Thomas Pynchon, sprang to his defence. Not that he is incapable of defending himself.

What is interesting are the reverberations from these public squalls, which over-ingenuity can pick up in the fiction. Abduction in *The Child in Time*, for example, at a period when McEwan was exercised about the custody of his children. *Atonement*'s focus on Dunkirk, wartime love affairs, and the vascular dementia which finally kills Briony can be connected with the life. Intellectual theft is a main plank in *Solar*'s narrative and reviewers pounced on the 'alleged plagiarism' brouhaha of a few years earlier. One should not push such things too far, or any distance at all, but keyholes onto the lives of novelists are, sometimes, irresistible, however one hates oneself for peeking through them.

FN   Ian Russell McEwan
MRT *Enduring Love*
Biog www.theparisreview.org/interviews/393/the-art-of-fiction-no-173-ian-mcewan

291. Martin Amis 1949– ; and Richard Hughes 1900–1976

Our only way of experiencing the identity of others. Richard Hughes on fiction
Osric. Martin Amis's nickname for himself

Even as he closed in on his bus-pass years – a date British newspapers gleefully commemorated – Martin Amis ('young Marty', in laddish journo-speak) was lumbered, like some wartime evacuee, with a worn-out French label for which, *hélas*, there is no sufficiently classy English equivalent: *enfant terrible* ('Bad Boy', as popularised by the German band Cascada, has a very different lexical tang). Precocious (never infantile) is the appropriate term. Everything came early: brilliant first at Oxford; assistant literary editor at the *Times Literary Supplement* at twenty-three; acclaimed first novel at twenty-four; the Somerset Maugham Prize, designated for the young novelist, was his by right at twenty-five. (The Booker, by contrast, has always been beyond his reach: probably he will be too young if he lives to a hundred.)

The *New Statesman*, where he was assistant literary editor, aged twenty-six, ran a competition, inviting readers to come up with something to rival in owlishness the recently published *Jane Austen and the French Revolution* (1979). '*Mein Kampf*, by Martin Amis' won, sardonically. Amis's first volume of autobiography came out in 2000. It was hard not to recall B. S. Johnson's ironic: 'Aren't you Rather Young to be Writing Your Memoirs?' At the launch party for *Experience*, Amis's editor predicted the book would still be read in 200 years' time. He may be right: it's very good. But anyone reading *Experience* would be justified in assuming that the most important fact in Martin Amis's life is Kingsley Amis. Picking up this cue, the first biography of Martin, in 2003 (again rather premature an event) is entitled: *Father and Son*.

There is, however, another novelist who briefly crosses the young meteor's path in *Experience* – unmeteorically, it must be said. In 1963, as Martin's parents' marriage was breaking up – with traumatic impact, it seems clear, on their fourteen-year-old son – his mother had a nervous breakdown. During this difficult time, Elizabeth Jane Howard (with whom Kingsley was now living), intending kindness, introduced Martin to Alexander Mackendrick, a film director, with titles such as *The Ladykillers* and *Whisky Galore* to his credit. His current project was not an Ealing comedy, but a film version of Richard Hughes's *A High Wind in Jamaica* (1965). Hughes's novel had enjoyed a huge success on its publication in 1929 and interest in its adaptation had been reignited by the current success enjoyed by the 1963 film of *Lord of the Flies*, directed by Peter Brook. Both novels are about the monstrosity of children. They were routinely compared by reviewers with long memories when Golding's novel was published in 1959.

Hughes's narrative is set in the Victorian era. A violent storm, graphically described, induces a colonial settler, Bas-Thornton, to send his children, three girls and two boys, off to safety in England. En route, their vessel is taken by pirates and they find themselves stowaways. The eerily precocious Emily wins over the pirate captain – seduction of a kind is involved. The children are the ultimate pirates. It is the quality of the writing, Hughes's supporters argue, which raises his novel notches above Golding's – that and the strangely powerful detail (the amputation in the early pages of a monkey's cancerous tail, for example). Above all, Hughes's revisionary idea of childhood is more powerful. Young humans are, above all, strange. This is how Hughes describes the youngest of the children, Laura:

> Being nearly four years old, she was certainly a child: and children are human (if one allows the term 'human' a wide sense): but she had not altogether ceased to be a baby: and babies of course are not human – they are animals, and have a very ancient and ramified culture, as cats have, and fishes, and even snakes: the same in kind as these, but much more complicated and vivid, since babies are, after all, one of the most developed species of the lower vertebrates.

Not easy to graft this into a movie. None the less Mackendrick would try, and invited Martin to play the Bas-Thornton son, John. As Amis recalls, 'a few weeks later I was taking my mother – first-class BOAC – on a highly paid as well as complimentary two-month holiday in the West Indies.' It may, one suspects, have been set up by the well-disposed Howard as therapy.

On location, the newly created young star 'played chess with my co-star, the consistently avuncular Anthony Quinn' (the film's Long John Silver). Amis was later to describe film-making as waiting around until you do the same thing over and over again and, luxurious as the experience was, he did not like it. 'My acting duties were light,' he recalls, 'because I died just over halfway through: blood-thirstily watching a cockfight in the square below, I fell from a window of [a] bordello.' The scene is different in the novel. But in both versions, the sudden death of John Thornton jolts. One does not expect it.

Amis is dismissive of his 'talentless' performance. It was years before he 'steeled' himself to watch the film, which got mixed reviews. He thought his bum looked big. Much later even than that, Amis read *A High Wind in Jamaica* and found it 'a thrillingly good book ... more continuously sinuous and inward (and enjoyable) than Golding'. Hughes, he recalls, visited the set, 'Otiosely tall ... he was pleased, impressed, tickled ... I keep meaning to read more of him *but something prevents me*.' I fancy that what prevents him is the fact that Hughes, in a sense, 'killed' him. Fictional victims rarely meet their authorial murderers, and it is fascinating when they do.

The film and renewed interest in the source novel made Hughes an in-demand public speaker. He was invited to speak at the University Teachers of English conference at the University of Sussex (spit-new in those days) in 1965. It was the first such conference that I (spit-new lecturer myself) attended. Hughes gave the expected readings from his work in progress but then diverged to muse at inordinate length on the mysteries of inspiration, particularly the death of John Thornton in *High Wind*. Why, Hughes asked himself – somewhat to the bemusement of his audience – had he killed the boy? It was never in his plan for the novel. The need for this act of authorial homicide had come to him suddenly, from nowhere, and irresistibly. Although Martin Amis wasn't (as I recall) mentioned, the boy actor, physically there in the flesh, had obviously 'tickled' his curiosity, and perhaps even his guilt. Why had he done it?

In Hughes's own background, one can find speculative answers. He was born one of three children of a civil servant. By the time Richard was two, the other elder children in the family had died, and his father died three years later. He recalled the event all his life: 'I wanted to ask Father something [and] scampered up to his bedroom, burst open the door ... Under the stiff folds of the sheet lay what looked like a not very skilful wax copy of him.' The family was a hecatomb of sudden, untimely, death. Hughes was educated at Charterhouse and Oxford. He narrowly missed being called up for the war (another hecatomb). By the time he graduated, he had gained some reputation as a poet. The fourth-class degree mattered little to him. As the

ODNB entry, written by a close friend, records: 'While still at Oxford ('that intense white incandescence of young minds', he calls it in *The Fox in the Attic*), he began travelling as a way of countering the strain of creative writing, and, within a week of graduating, he was sailing a boat down the Danube and dabbling dangerously in Balkan politics; thus began a wanderlust and taste for adventure which he was to indulge for the rest of his active life.'

The 'strain' of creative writing proved paralysing, despite all the travelling. After *A High Wind in Jamaica* (begun on the shores of the Adriatic, finished in Connecticut, on the blustery Atlantic), he found the fame intolerable and exiled himself to Morocco ('his favourite country after Wales'), where 'he bought a house in the Kasbah of old Tangier for two donkey-loads of silver'. He returned to Britain in 1932 and married a wealthy wife. They had five children. The family lived the life of country gentry in rural Wales. Although a novelist by vocation, Hughes would produce no second novel until *In Hazard* (1938), a tale of storm in the Caribbean, prophetic of war. During the stormy years of the war, Hughes worked in a civilian capacity in the Admiralty. In the post-war years he jobbed around, never desperate for money, but always glad to have it – reviewing, lecturing, and doing screenplays for Ealing Studios (hence the connection with Mackendrick).

Meanwhile he embarked on his life's work, a multi-volume sequence called *The Human Predicament*, a conspectus of the history and origins of the Second World War from the Nazi takeover in 1923 to VE day. Two volumes saw the light of print before his death in 1976: *The Fox in the Attic* (1961) and *The Wooden Shepherdess* (1973). *The Fox in the Attic* has a forlorn Foreword indicating that this is the first particle of a work 'conceived as a long historical novel of my own times culminating in the Second World War'. The reader, Hughes says, may wonder why 'a novel designed as a continuous whole rather than as trilogy or quarter should appear volume by volume'. The plain truth, he confesses, 'is I am such a slow writer that I have been urged not to wait'.

The advice was sound. The trilogy, after its somewhat less good second part, delivered to the world twelve years later, would never reach completion. Whoever urged Hughes to publish *The Fox in the Attic* prematurely deserves the thanks of posterity. It ranks as arguably one of the finest works of the post-war period – if one of the least conventional. It can itself be considered as tripartite. The narrative opens with a passage of breathtaking beauty:

> Only the steady creaking of a flight of swans disturbed the silence, labouring low overhead with outstretched necks towards the sea.
>
> It was a warm, wet, windless afternoon with a soft feathery feeling in the air: rain, yet so fine it could scarcely fall but rather floated. It clung to everything it

touched; the rushes in the deep choked ditches of the sea-marsh were bowed down with it, the small black cattle looked cobwebbed with it, their horns were jewelled with it.

Two men appear in this damp Welsh landscape – back from shooting birds in the coastal marshes. One is carrying something over his shoulders. It is not the usual brace of duck, but a dead child.

The first section of Hughes's novel is, despite the little corpse, country-house comedy – P. G. Wodehouse crossed with *Cold Comfort Farm*. The hero Augustine just escapes the First World War: he was about to be called to the Front when the Amnesty came. His cousin Henry was killed in the trenches. Augustine becomes heir to the family's decaying mansion: it is 1922. His world – what is left of it – is similarly decayed. He flagrantly neglects the traditions and duties of his class and is falsely suspected at the inquest of killing the dead girl. In fact he removed the body merely to protect it from water rats. He decides to go to Germany, where he has distant relatives and where he hopes to find signs of life. The middle section of *The Fox in the Attic* is a prose essay on the death of liberal England and the scar of the war, which will never heal. It is a lump of historical discourse framed in fiction. The third section is set in Munich, in the days surrounding the failed 1923 Nazi *Putsch*. The young Adolf Hitler flares, darkly, across the narrative, 'an ego without a penumbra'. Augustine falls in love with a cousin, Mitzi, who is going blind and has symbolic visions of imminent catastrophe. If England's inter-war plight is symbolised in the dead child, Germany's is in the stinking fox in the castle attic. Mitzi joins a convent while Augustine drifts on, aimlessly, as history prepares for something worse even than the First World War.

There are those who consider Hughes's fiction as among the best that never quite got round to happening; others who think him, apart from the best two novels, negligible. There is occasional curiosity as to the origin of his monumental writing block. D. J. Taylor wonders if Hughes's interest in 'little girls' merits closer attention than it has received. We shall never know. If Amis is the hare on steroids, Hughes is the tortoise with arthritis. With the difference that the tortoise, in this instance, lost the race.

FN   Martin Louis Amis; Richard Arthur Warren Hughes
MRT   *London Fields; A High Wind in Jamaica*
Biog   G. Keulks, *Father and Son: Kingsley Amis, Martin Amis and the British Novel since 1950* (2003); R. P. Graves: *Richard Hughes: A Biography* (1994)

292. Patricia Cornwell 1956–

It's important for me to live in the world I want to write about.

Cornwell claims to be descended from Harriet Beecher Stowe, the author of *Uncle Tom's Cabin* (1852). Calculator-bustingly large sales figures would seem to be one of the things the two have in common. 'Patsy' Daniels was born the daughter of a Miami lawyer. Her parents divorced when she was five. 'It killed me,' she recalls. A couple of years later, what was left of the family moved to North Carolina. A couple of years after that, broke and broken down, her mother deposited Patsy and her two brothers with neighbours – the evangelist Billy Graham and his wife Ruth, who passed them on to be fostered by missionary friends (whom the young Patsy loathed – she kills her foster-mother, she says, in every novel).

Aged eighteen, Patsy was treated for anorexia in the hospital where her mother had earlier been a mental patient ('like *One Flew Over the Cuckoo's Nest'*, the novelist jauntily recalls). She made it to college, got a degree in English and capped that achievement by bagging her professor, Charles Cornwell, as her husband. In 1979, the new Mrs Cornwell got a job as a reporter on the *Charlotte Observer* and was contracted as Ruth Bell Graham's authorised biographer. The book came out in 1983. When she got a post at the office of the Chief Medical Examiner in Richmond, Virginia, her husband moved with her, giving up his academic career to take up a position in the church. The marriage was a 'disaster' from the start and collapsed soon after.

Patricia, meanwhile, had become fascinated by her paper's 'crime beat' – particularly the 'bone farm' – and had formed a friendship with the Chief Medical Examiner for Virginia, Dr Marcella Fierro (the original of Kay Scarpetta). Fierro is the dedicatee of Cornwell's fourth book, *Cruel and Unusual* (1993), with the coy comment 'You taught Scarpetta well.' What Cornwell apprehended, very early in the game, was that new forensic techniques, particularly DNA analysis, gave the detective an entirely new instrument – a magnifying glass more revealing than anything Sherlock wielded. More importantly, the forensic lab – unlike the mean streets – was an arena where women were entirely equal with male police officers.

Cornwell had the unpublished author's traditional difficulty getting her first Scarpetta novel accepted. After being turned down by seven publishers, *Postmortem* was finally taken by Scribner's, who gave her a tentative $6,000 advance, but only after the author had taken the advice to change the sex of the narrator-hero(ine) from 'Joe Constable'. Largely written in the mid-1980s, it was eventually published in 1991.

Scarpetta, a tough-talking, gun-toting, chain-smoking (up to *Cruel and Unusual*), whisky-drinking, detective, is clearly cut from the same genre cloth as Sara Paretsky's V. I. Warshawski, introduced in *Indemnity Only* (1982); and Sue Grafton's Kinsey Millhone, introduced in *A is for Alibi* (1982). *Postmortem* won five major genre prizes and golden opinions from connoisseurs of crime fiction. It made the *New York Times* bestseller list. By the end of the 1990s, with a novel a year pulsing out, Cornwell could plausibly claim –and did, insistently – to be the bestselling woman novelist in the world. Only Grisham's legal thrillers outsold her.

Ms Scarpetta is Chief Medical Examiner in Richmond, Virginia. Her duties go well beyond the routines of autopsy, written report and expert courtroom witness. She solves crimes and invariably blows the bad guys away with her own formidable fire power. The formula is repetitive. A serial killer is on the loose and is terrorising the law-abiding citizenry of the American South. His (always his) victims are post-mortemed by the heroine. Inexorably the killer's sights turn on Scarpetta herself. In her fight against crime, she is assisted by her lesbian niece, FBI field agent Lucy, and her faithful police buddy, Pete Marino.

By the turn of the century, 'Cornwell Enterprises' was very big business. The author herself travelled with an entourage of twelve people, including bodyguards. Her houses are reported to be bristling with motion detectors, CCTV cameras and 'stockpiles of guns'. In 1993, Cornwell, after an evening discussing film projects with Demi Moore, drunkenly crashed her Mercedes in Malibu – Jaws of Life were required to extract her from the wreckage. She was sentenced to the first offender's twenty-eight days rehab, and was diagnosed bipolar. At first she thought it was a reference to her sexuality. Lithium stabilised her, allegedly. There were, however, further scandals. In June 1996 a maddened former FBI agent went on a gun-wielding, hostage-taking rampage, claiming that Cornwell had alienated the affections of his wife. In 2007, Cornwell let it be known that she had contracted a marriage a couple of years before with Dr Staci Ann Gruber.

Cornwell also attracted notoriety with her much-publicised theory that Jack the Ripper was the Camden artist, Walter Sickert. She demolished one of the artist's canvases to discover the DNA which would clinch her case. Art historians are as unimpressed by her art history as criminologists by her criminology, but readers continue to devour Scarpettas (nineteen of them by 2011).

FN   Patricia Carroll Cornwell (née Daniels)
MRT   *From Potter's Field*
Biog   G. Fabrikant, *New York Times*, 23 March 1997; www.patriciacornwell.com

293. Alice Sebold 1963–

My life was over; my life had just begun. From *Lucky*

There's no scale by which to measure the distance between lived life and written fiction. According to Charles Bukowksi, 93 per cent of his fiction is fact. The pseudo-precision is, of course, a joke. Sometimes, however, fiction and life are so inter-meshed, that they collapse on each other, creating a genre for which we have, as yet, no handy term.

Alice Sebold was born in Wisconsin in 1963, and brought up in Philadelphia, where her father, Russell P. Sebold, was a distinguished professor of Romance languages at 'Penn', one of the Ivy League colleges. Her mother, a journalist, was, as her daughter recalls, an unhappy, eventually alcoholic woman. Sebold later suspected her mother was a frustrated writer. The marriage was solid, but emotionally frigid. By her own account, Alice was a difficult child. She was precocious, fat and 'too loud'. Nor was she – unlike her elder sister – dutifully academic. 'I wanted,' she said, 'to be the moron of the family.' She 'ended up going to Syracuse because I didn't get into the University of Pennsylvania, which is where my father taught. It looked like I was a shoo-in, a faculty kid – and I got rejected.'

She went to less demanding Syracuse University, in New York State. It was in her first semester, walking through the tunnel of the campus amphitheatre on the way back to her dorm, that Sebold was raped. It was a defining event: one which she would describe (reliving it? exorcising it?) in memoir, fiction and interviews. She was beaten up. Her plaintive protests that she was a virgin were ignored, she was multiply penetrated, and – final indignity – urinated on. Her attacker was black – a source of some embarrassment with interlocutors in later publicity interviews. In the same tunnel, the police later informed her, another girl had been raped, killed, and dismembered. She was 'lucky'. She was taken home where her father asked her if she needed food. She had spirit enough to reply, 'that would be nice, considering the only thing I've had in my mouth in the last 24 hours is a cracker and a cock'. She went on to reassure him, 'I'm still me, Dad' – but what kind of me? She would not know until she had written it up. As she tells it in her memoir, a few months later she met her rapist ('Gregory Madison') in the street. He greeted her with a cheery but puzzled, 'Hey, girl, don't I know you from somewhere?' She certainly knew him, picked him out from a line-up, gave evidence at two trials – batting off hostile cross-examination, and saw him given a maximum sentence. It was the early 1980s.

On graduation from Syracuse she went far away to Houston, Texas, to do an MA in writing, but dropped out. She returned to New York, working part-time as an instructor at Hunter College, but effectively 'drifting'. Everyone in New York, she later said, 'thinks they're a literary genius'. She wrote poetry – much of it about her traumatic experience in the tunnel. By her own account Sebold went off the rails in her twenties; doing drugs and living a promiscuous life. It was two decades too late for dropping out to be glamorous.

In her early thirties she moved to Southern California (where, as she completes her wisecrack, 'everyone thinks they're famous'). She was, by now, writing more seriously and had drafted parts of a novel provisionally called 'Monsters' about a fourteen-year-old rape victim. She enrolled in a writing course at the University of California, Irvine, in 1995. On her first day of class she met the man she would later marry, Glen David Gold. They were both, Gold later said, 'weirdos' – made for each other. It must have been a strong intake that year at Irvine. Gold too would produce a bestselling novel, *Carter Beats the Devil* (2001), a few months before his wife's bestselling *The Lovely Bones*.

Her first published work had been, in point of fact, not the novel, but a memoir (later seen as a pioneer of the so-called 'misery memoir'), *Lucky*, an ironic echo of the cop's sublimely tactless consolatory remark all those years ago. *Lucky* was published in 1999 and generally ignored. It, and what she learned at UCI, helped her pull 'Monsters' into shape and a friend, the writer Wilton Barnhardt, forwarded it to his agent.

After much editing, 'Monsters' was published in 2002 as *The Lovely Bones*. The publisher, Little Brown, expected no great things from a first novel, on an extremely uncomfortable subject, by an unknown novelist but – as was later surmised – 9/11 had shaken things up and fiction about coping with gross trauma was in demand. The book generated powerful word of mouth and sold in the millions. Over the years Sebold had worked out an ingenious scenario. The narrative opens:

> My name was Salmon, like the fish; first name, Susie. I was fourteen when I was murdered on December 6, 1973. In newspaper photos of missing girls from the seventies, most looked like me: white girls with mousy brown hair. This was before kids of all races and genders started appearing on milk cartons or in the daily mail. It was still back when people believed things like that didn't happen.

Over the subsequent years, from a strangely drab heaven (a bit like a never-ending junior high school), Susie observes her family fall apart and studies, with minute attention, her rapist-killer, the banal bachelor neighbour, Mr Harvey. Things eventually work out more or less well for the Salmons – less well for the rat next door.

In the novel's wake, *Lucky* was brought back from oblivion. The two narratives of rape were read side by side, along with interviews which stressed the inspirational trauma which inspired the works. Fictional and factual merged: both books became prescribed reading on 'Victimology' in American colleges. Now rich (Gold's novel, a fantasy about magicians and pacts with the devil, had also done well), the married authors retired to San Francisco. No more eating chickpeas straight out of the can, as Sebold wryly observed.

Never one to rush into print, it was five years until she produced her second novel, *The Almost Moon* (2007). It, like its two predecessors, had the now trademark wham-bang Sebold opening: 'When all is said and done, killing my mother came easily.' The middle-aged heroine, Helen, murders her demented eighty-eight-year-old mother – the novel reconstructs the lives that led up to the act. *The Almost Moon* fell very flat. Reviewers were universally critical. Was Sebold a one-novel novelist? If so, that one novel had life left in it. The film of *The Lovely Bones*, which came out in 2010, was a huge success and jumped the book back into the bestseller lists.

FN   Alice Sebold (later Gold)
MRT   *The Lovely Bones*
Biog   A. Sebold, *Lucky* (1999)

294. Rana Dasgupta 1971–

Paradoxically, the more the world becomes interwoven the less it seems possible to tell a single, representative story of it … yet the connections are real and lived. So how do you narrate this?

I have chosen to end this very selective biographical run through the novel in English with Dasgupta – though not with any sense that I am anointing him as anything other than an interesting variety of the novelist of the future. 'Symptomatic', in a word and, it can be claimed, potentially distinguished. Rana Dasgupta is described as a 'British-Indian novelist'. The term does him ethnic injustice. He was born in Canterbury, grew up in Cambridge, took his first degree at Balliol College, Oxford, did postgraduate work at the Conservatoire Darius Milhaud in Aix-en-Provence, and the University of Wisconsin-Madison. He worked for some years in New York, in marketing, before moving to Delhi – his current (if that word means anything in the Dasgupta progress) residence. His first novel was published when he was thirty-four. His second novel was published first in Australia, then in India, finally in the UK and US.

Does travel broaden the mind? J. R. R. Tolkien never left England (rarely Oxford and rarely even his own college) other than for a brief excursion, on Norse-scholar business, to Scandinavia. But, as other 'two-inches of ivory' novelists attest, novelists that do not go far can, none the less, mine very deep. Dasgupta's first novel, *Tokyo Cancelled* (2005), was an updated *Canterbury Tales* (homage to his birthplace) in which stranded airline travellers swapped stories about different cities of the world. Thirteen passengers (fateful number) on route to Tokyo find themselves stranded – 'socked in' by snow – at a nameless nowhere airport. They tell each other tales to pass the time in that most vacant of places, the terminal concourse. There is no termination, no concurrence in that misnamed location. The stories are surreal – one, for example, features Robert De Niro's misbegotten, half-Chinese son, who has mastered the transubstantiation of matter. A Japanese businessman becomes infatuated, to the point of self-destruction, with a sex-doll. In another, human minds are evacuated of memory, which is stored safely on CDs. The world becomes historyless, as – with jet travel – it has become placeless. What is the difference between an international airport in Los Angeles (LAX) or Heathrow (LHR)?

Walter Benjamin famously declared that the novel was the end of story-telling and a symptom of the end of community. In a fragile, accidental, way Dasgupta fantasises its being momentarily restored:

> The book is not *only* the stories; the book is a reflection on story telling. Now I think that story telling is rather rare in our culture – it's disappearing. We don't meet people who tell stories anymore. We feel a lot of that. We feel that there is something good when we sit around our grandmothers and listen to their stories, because there is wisdom in them. So I wanted to say, okay, here are 13 middle class modern travelers, who decide to tell stories, and they can.

If there is one word that attaches itself to Dasgupta's fiction, it is 'global'. But *Solo* (2009), his second novel, is, on the face of it, more local than its predecessor – at least, for its first 168 pages. The novel is set in Bulgaria, a country which, to paraphrase Neville Chamberlain, is far away and of which we know little, and care even less. The hero is Ulrich, whom we first meet aged 100 years, in 2005. Bulgaria itself is scarcely older. It was invented, as a European constitutional monarchy, out of the Balkan cauldron in 1878. Ulrich is blind. Like Sophocles's Tiresias, this means he can see his country's history, and destiny, more clearly than those of his compatriots with eyes.

Ulrich's father was a visionary railway engineer, who dreamed of shining steel rails which would connect Baghdad, Sofia and Paris, and drag Bulgaria 'out of Asia'. When young Ulrich shows early stirrings of musical talent, he is encouraged by his mother but savagely suppressed by his father, who smashes his son's violin and throws it in the fire, with the words:

> 'You won't do this, my son! I won't have you waste your life. Musicians, artists, criminals, opium addicts ... You'll end up poor and disgraced. I won't have it.'

Ulrich is sent to Berlin where his study of chemistry is cut short by European hyperinflation. He returns to his native country to work in a shoe factory, then as a lowly lab-rat in a chemical products firm. He marries but the marriage fails. His father is mutilated, and his dreams shattered, in the First World War. Bulgaria fights on the German side, as it does in the Second World War. Big mistakes. Thereafter, the country came under the Kremlin's heel and Moscow's dullest stooge, Todor Zhivkov. Uncorking a vial of sulphuric acid, Ulrich accidentally blinds himself. Like everything in the novel it is described unexcitedly. These things happen. Ulrich's mother is hauled off, for no reason, to a Bulgarian gulag and returns a madwoman. Rich in natural resources Bulgaria, Ulrich's mother-country, is plundered and polluted by its Communist masters so that women's nylons dissolve at the first touch of Sofia's polluted air. Ulrich spends his last days, alone, in a shabby room by the bus-station, going nowhere.

Why did he choose Bulgaria? Dasgupta is asked – as God might be asked why he chose the Jews, or Mallory why he climbed Everest. 'I refuse to be categorised,' he blandly replies. But he does concede that *Solo*'s theme is music – the ways in which, out of group harmony, single voices can emerge. If there is hope in the world, it lies not in the European Union, but in that shattered violin, and the dream it represented for Ulrich. We recognise the theme. It is that of Salman Rushdie's *The Ground Beneath her Feet*. In that novel, set in Bombay, London and New York, it is the Orphic lyre alone – art – which can bring the world together. Like Rushdie, Dasgupta is a fragmented man whose fiction seeks, desperately and ingeniously, for cohesion. A man, one might say, without biographical base. These, one fears, are the novelists of the twenty-first century, as the author of *The Waste Land* was the poet of the twentieth. But where does Dasgupta go from here? Lots of places, one expects – resting nowhere.

FN   Rana Dasgupta
MRT *Tokyo Cancelled*
Biog www.ranadasgupta.com

Epilogue

The Preface claims this book to be an idiosyncratic history of fiction in English. What, having come some four hundred years, is its future history? We have not always had the novel, said the critic Walter Benjamin, and there will come a time, he bleakly foresaw, when we shall no longer have it. I should not like to live in it. But that fictionless time seems, at the present moment, thankfully distant. There are today more novels, and more kinds of novel, than ever before in literary history – too many for most readers. Trying to make sense of the novel in English, as we come into the second decade of the twenty-first century, is like sculpting with sand or paddling in a tsunami.

Some handholds can be found. The six great nineteenth-century genres – Romance, Male Action ('Adventure'), Crime, Science Fiction, Horror, Fantasy – march on. They still map out the topography of the typical bookstore. Nowadays they are supplemented by what one can call 'constituency' literature: gay fiction, chicklit, ladlit, teen fiction. Constituency fiction is defined by customer affinity, not style. It thrives vigorously as new social constituencies pop up. The old vertical architecture remains obstinately in place: the literary novel, experimental fiction, middlebrow- blockbuster, pulp fiction. As to how these will be rearranged, dissolved, or redefined in the future is unknowable. The factors and pressures which will carry future changes through can, however, be defined as a set of binarisms.

Globalism and atomism

Viewed through trade papers (*Publishers Weekly*, the *Bookseller*), the trend over the last fifty years would seem to be one of inexorable agglomeration. The fusion of producers (literary agents, publishers, retailers – electronic and walk-in, transnational reading publics) into ever larger structures has been remarkable and seems unstoppable. In the nineteenth century, when both firms came into being, the notion of HarperCollins, yoking Glasgow and New York, would have seemed something from the pen of Mr H. G. Wells. It has happened. Fiction is, in the twenty-first century, a global operation. Leading practitioners conform to that globalism – see, for example, Rana Dasgupta above, or Salman Rushdie's bold proclamation:

> I suppose if you were asking me formally, I would still think of myself as a British citizen of Indian origin. But I think of myself as a New Yorker and as a Londoner. I probably think of those as being more exact definitions than the passport or the place of birth.

A main instrument of the agglomerated apparatus is the bestseller list. There will be close congruence – irrespective of the national origins of the authors – between what appears weekly in the *New York Times* and what appears in the *Sunday Times*. Is Rushdie, when he appears on those lists, a British or an American property? One thing is certain, he is not an Indian or Pakistani property, and will never be until the subcontinent develops a publishing and distributive machinery to rival that of London and New York. Novelists, like everyone else, follow the money. And the money, currently, is in two big cities.

Alongside all this skyscraper publishing, there has been a downscaling unprecedented in literary history. It originated in the mid-1990s, with nationwide internet connectivity. Most fiction which is produced nowadays will never see a printed page, but will none the less be widely read. It remains in the domain of so-called 'fanfic'. The most read of the fanfictioneers, Cassandra Claire – famous for her *Lord of the Rings* extension, *The Very Secret Diaries* – is, effectively, self-published and expects no revenue. All that is required for Claire's kind of novel is a keyboard, an internet connection, and accessible companions in her chosen 'fandom'. Atomistic publishing will surely advance over the foreseeable future – already it is vast.

Scriptive and pictorial

The novel is, conventionally, a textual form: words on the page. It is one of the things which, sadly, renders it unattractive to many young readers whose culture (via iPod, screen, Facebook, and TV game console) is audio-visual and increasingly 'virtual'. Translating black marks on a white surface into narrative is not sexy. There has, however, been some symptomatic hybridisation. One is the growing popularity of the graphic novel, and of practitioners such as Alan Moore (*Watchmen*, *V for Vendetta*) and Neil Gaiman (*The Sandman*). Graphic fiction eases itself into film readily, creating a large knock-on readership. The economic rise of Japan and China, whose writing systems are substantially pictographic, will add force to this mutation, one can surmise. Put grandly, I have seen the future of the novel – and it's something you see, not read. At the very least a revival of the illustrated novel, so popular in the nineteenth century, may be confidently anticipated.

New novels/old novels

The name of the form suggests newness, or 'novelty'. But unlike other new lines of product – the latest models of car, TV or computer, for example – fiction does not disappear once consumed and is no longer used. Fiction keeps piling up, like cultural plaque. How many novels in English are there in the dusty vaults of the British and North American copyright libraries? Probably, using Dewey Decimal calculation, around two million. While they are lying in the dust they do not much trouble the novel of the day in its appeal to the customer. But when the Google Library Project makes all those millions of novels, in highly readable form, cheap or free of charge, instantly available on one's electronic reader (iPad, Sony, Kindle), how will that affect reading practices?

Within the short historical space of half a century, British and American literary culture has moved from managed shortage (symbolised in the public library waiting list) to unmanageable surplus. Whatever else, one can foresee a Darwinist struggle for space ('exposure') and the disposable time of the reading public. Shall I read the latest Julian Barnes or go back and read Laurence Sterne? – a couple of brushes of the finger on the keyboard will decide the matter. Ideally what will happen will be a better sense and utilisation of the whole territory of fiction. The worst that will happen is that readers, as a whole, will feel utterly swamped and surrender to whatever ephemeral pressures come their way – word of mouth, importunate advertising, celebrity endorsement (of the kind pioneered by Oprah Winfrey).

For the moment we can, and should, revel in the plenty which we, unlike all previous generations, enjoy. Long live the novel, and Walter Benjamin be damned.

Index